Exam AZ-300 & AZ-301 Study & Lab Guide Part 2
Microsoft Certified Azure Solutions Architect Expert

Harinder Kohli

kindle direct publishing

Exam AZ-300 & AZ-301 Study & Lab Guide Part 2
Harinder Kohli

This edition has been published by arrangement with **Kindle Direct Publishing**.

ISBN
ISBN: 9781692841409

Edition: 1st Edition, September 2019

Contact Author

Email: harinder-kohli@outlook.com
Linkedin: www.linkedin.com/in/harinderkohli
Azure Blog @ https://mykloud.wordpress.com

Downloads

Download TOC and Sample Chapter from Box.com
https://app.box.com/s/15do0d3vdyowpo61llxvxcpug4b5gr35

Errata & Updates
Information about Book Errata & Updates will be published at following link @ Box.com.
https://app.box.com/s/f0hw0x038bnh52fya5x2brk5z17bq3xr

Contents at a Glance

Contents at a Glance (Contd)

Contents

Lab Exercises

Lab Exercises (Contd)

Lab Exercises (Contd)

Lab Exercises (Contd)

Lab Exercises (Contd)

Case Studies

- Azure Web App High Availability
- Design a Business Continuity Solution for Web/App tier and Database Tier
- Choosing a Database tier
- Oauth2 Authentication
- Integrating Structured and Unstructured Data into Azure SQL DW using Azure Data Factory
- Integrating & Processing Non- Structured Data with Azure Data lake Analytics

Introduction

Azure Solutions Architect Expert Certification (AZ-300 & AZ-301) is targeted towards Azure Architects who can Implement & Design Azure Cloud Solutions.

Exam AZ-300: Microsoft Azure Architect Technologies focuses on **Implementation** of Azure Cloud Solutions. Exam AZ-300 focuses both on **Infrastructure Topics** such as Virtual Servers, Networks, Storage, Azure Active Directory, Azure CDN, Azure Key Vault, Monitoring Solutions and **Database & PaaS Topics** such as SQL Database, Web Apps, Containers, NoSQL, Batch Computing & Service Bus. One of the key success points to pass the exam is to work with Azure portal and practice configuring various Azure services.

Exam AZ-301: Microsoft Azure Architect Design focuses on **Design** of Azure Cloud Solutions. Exam AZ-301 focuses on design of Virtual Networks, Compute, Storage, Azure AD, Azure Backup & DR, Security with Azure Key Vault, Azure SQL Database, Web Apps, Containers, Cosmos DB, Messaging Services, Batch Computing, Monitoring with Log Analytics & Azure Automation etc.

Architecting Microsoft Azure Solution Lab & Study Guide helps you prepare for AZ-300 & AZ-301 Exam. It contains Topic lessons, Lab Exercises & Design Case Studies. It is being published in 2 separate Books.
Part 2 (Which is this book) Focuses on Implementation and Design of Database, PaaS, Security, Monitoring and Automation Solutions.
Part 1 focuses on Implementation and Design of Infrastructure Topics. It is being published separately but simultaneously with Part 2.

The twin focus of this book is to get your fundamental on Azure Services on strong footing and to prepare you to Implement & design cloud solutions. Topic lessons, Design case studies and lab exercises are all geared towards making you understand Azure fundamentals.

Best of Luck for AZ-300 & AZ-301Exam.

I would be pleased to hear your feedback and thoughts on the book. Please comment on Amazon or mail to: harinder-kohli@outlook.com.

Harinder Kohli

Topics to read for AZ-300 and AZ-301

Topic to read for AZ-300 Exam

For AZ-300 Exam read all Topics except for following:

1. Topics which are Italicized.
2. AZ-301 specific Chapters. In this book you have Ten AZ-301 specific Chapters – Chapter 13, Chapter 14, Chapter 15, Chapter 16, Chapter 17, Chapter 18, Chapter 19, Chapter 20, Chapter 21 & Chapter 22.

Topic to read for AZ-301 Exam

For AZ-301 Exam, read all topics. AZ-301 exam builds on the theory and Labs covered in Exam AZ-300. For AZ-301 Exam we have also included case studies.

You have common topics between these exams such as Virtual Network Peering, UDR, S2S VPN, Express Route, Service Endpoints, VM high Availability, VMSS, Load Balancing Solutions, Azure AD, Subscription and cost management etc.

In theory we discuss Architecture, components and uses cases. These are all foundation topics for designing.

I am once again stressing that for AZ-301 Exam go through all topics. For example topic VM high Availability is a common topic in both AZ-300 & AZ-301. VM high Availability (Availability Set & AZ) is a good topic for designing highly available VM solutions.

Please note that Common topics for Exam AZ-300 & AZ-301 are not marked with Italics. So for Exam AZ-301 you must go through all topics.

Lab Requirements & Tricks

Resource Naming

In Exercises I keep referring to resources created in previous exercises. My suggestion would be that you name your resources by adding some letter or number to my resource names.
The above suggestion is just for lab exercises in this book and not for your production use case.

Browser Requirements for Lab Exercises

You will require 3 Browsers for completing Lab Activities. I used following Browser options for completing lab activities.

1. **Chrome Browser** was my main Browser. I used it with Subscription User. This was the user with which I signed for Azure Subscription.
2. **Firefox Browser** was used with users created in Azure AD.
3. **Tor browser** was used to simulate suspicious locations.

Custom Domain & Public Certificate Requirement for Lab Exercises

In Part 1 book (This Book) i used domain **mykloud.in**. This was used in 2 Exercises – Azure DNS and Add Custom Domain in Azure AD. I purchased it for around USD 9.

In Part 2 Book i used domain **hksystems.in**. This was used in 2 Exercises – Azure Web App Custom Domain and HTTPS. I purchased it for around USD 7.
For Part 2 Book I also purchased **Public Certificate** from Azure Portal. This was used for enabling HTTPS connection on Web App. I purchased it for around USD 66 with a validity of one year.

How to Save Azure Credits

1. Stop the Virtual Machine in Azure Portal if you are not using it. This will save you lot of money.
2. Delete the resources which you longer require.

How to go to Resource Dashboard

In lab Exercises I will just tell you to go resource dashboard but will not explain how to go. Read below on how to go to Resource Dashboard.

How to go to Resource Dashboard: Preferred Approach

In Azure Portal click the resource type in left pane. For Example if you have to go Virtual Machine or Storage Account or Resource Group Dashboard click the Virtual Machines or Storage Account or Resource Group in left pane and select your Resource in Right pane.

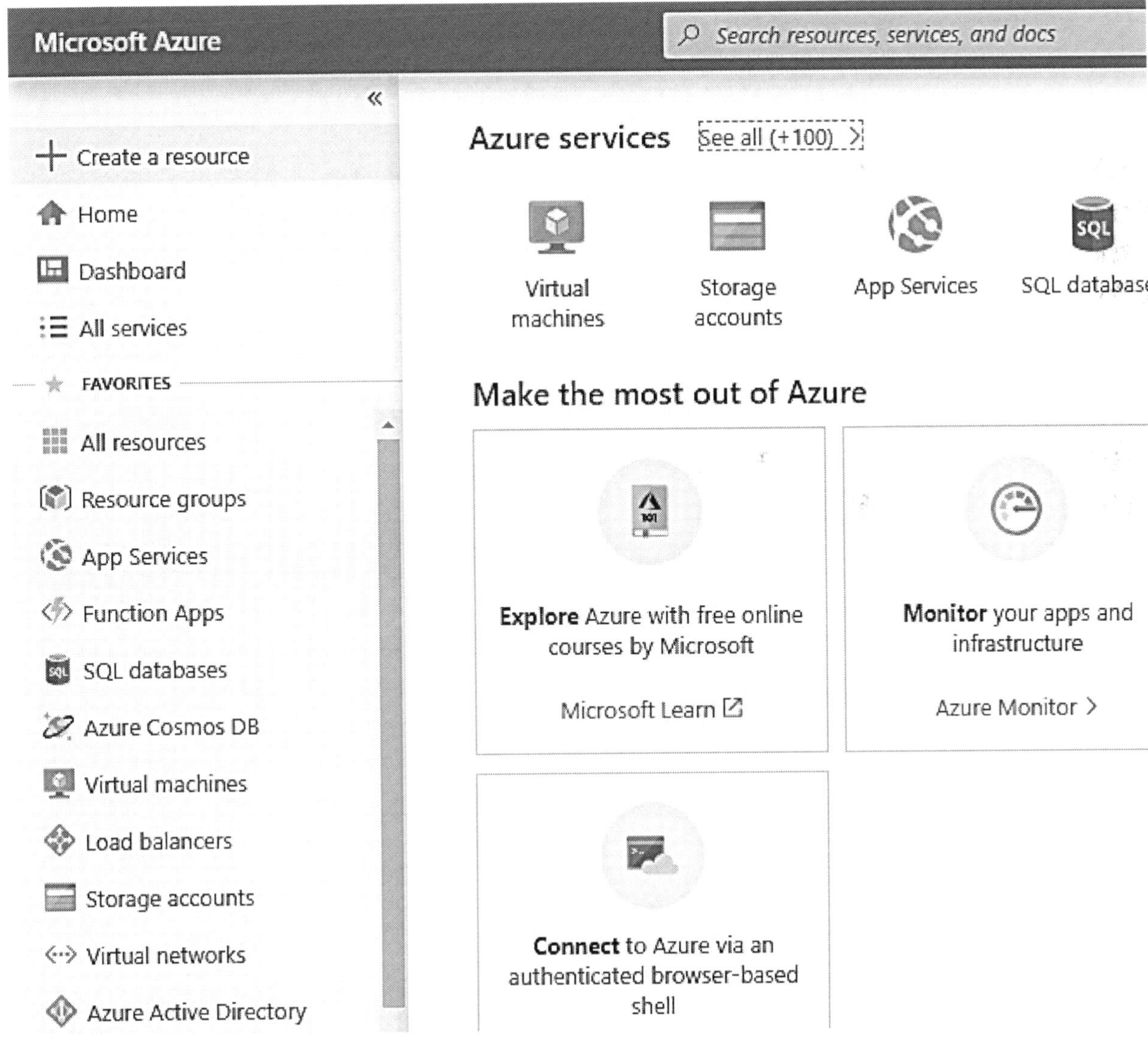

How to go to Resource Dashboard: Option 2

You will not find certain Resources like Azure Automation or Azure DNS etc in left pane in Azure Portal. Click All Resources in left pane. This will show all Resources which you have created till now. Click your resource to go to dashboard.

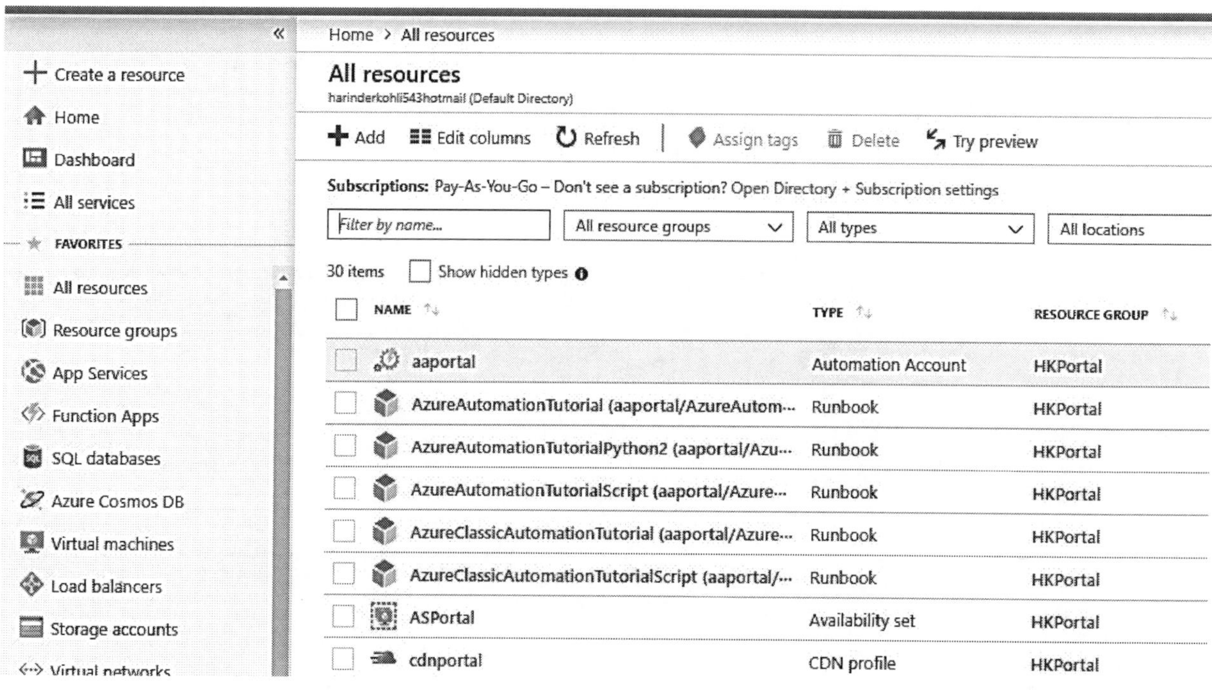

How to go to Resource Dashboard: Option 3

In Azure Portal Click All Services in left pane> In right pane select your resource type. This will open pane for that Resource type. Select your resource to go to its dashboard.

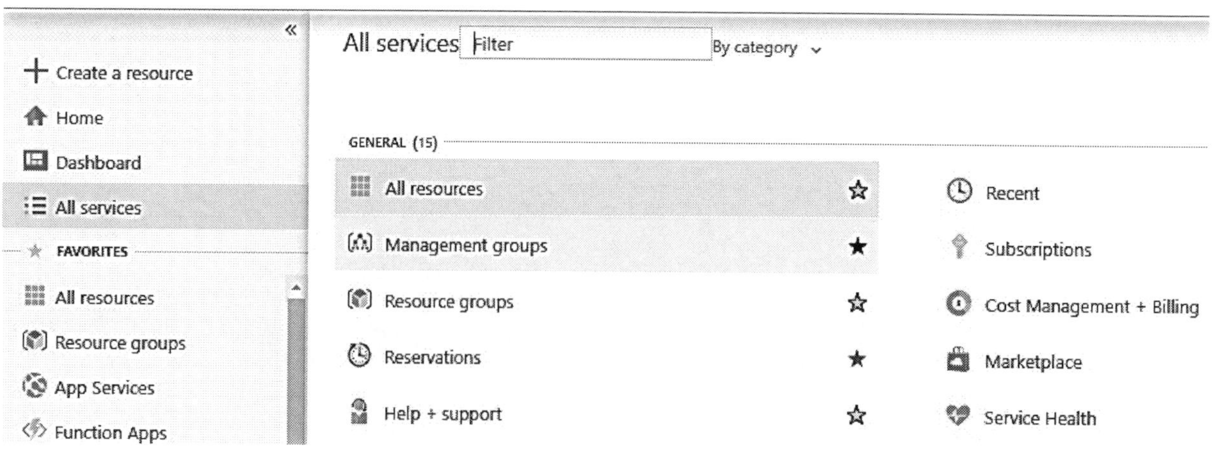

How to Create Azure Resource

How to Create Resource: Preferred Approach

In Azure Portal Click + **Create a resource** in top left pane> Select category of your resource and then the resource itself.

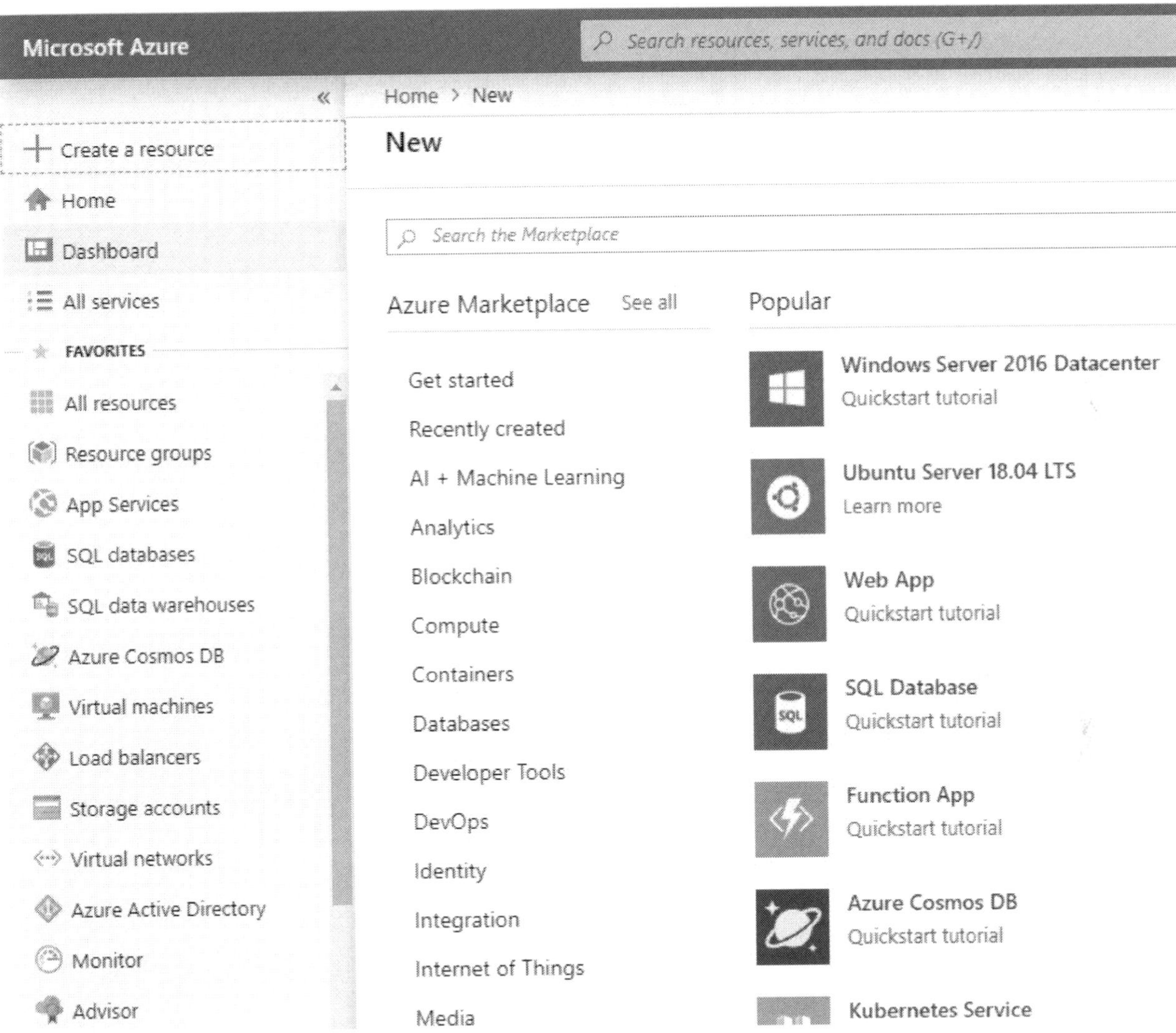

How to Create Resource: Option 2

Many times you will not find your required resource using option 1 (+ **Create a resource**). In this case you need to use option 2.

In Azure Portal Click **All Services** in left pane>All Service pane opens> Select category of your resource and then the resource itself.

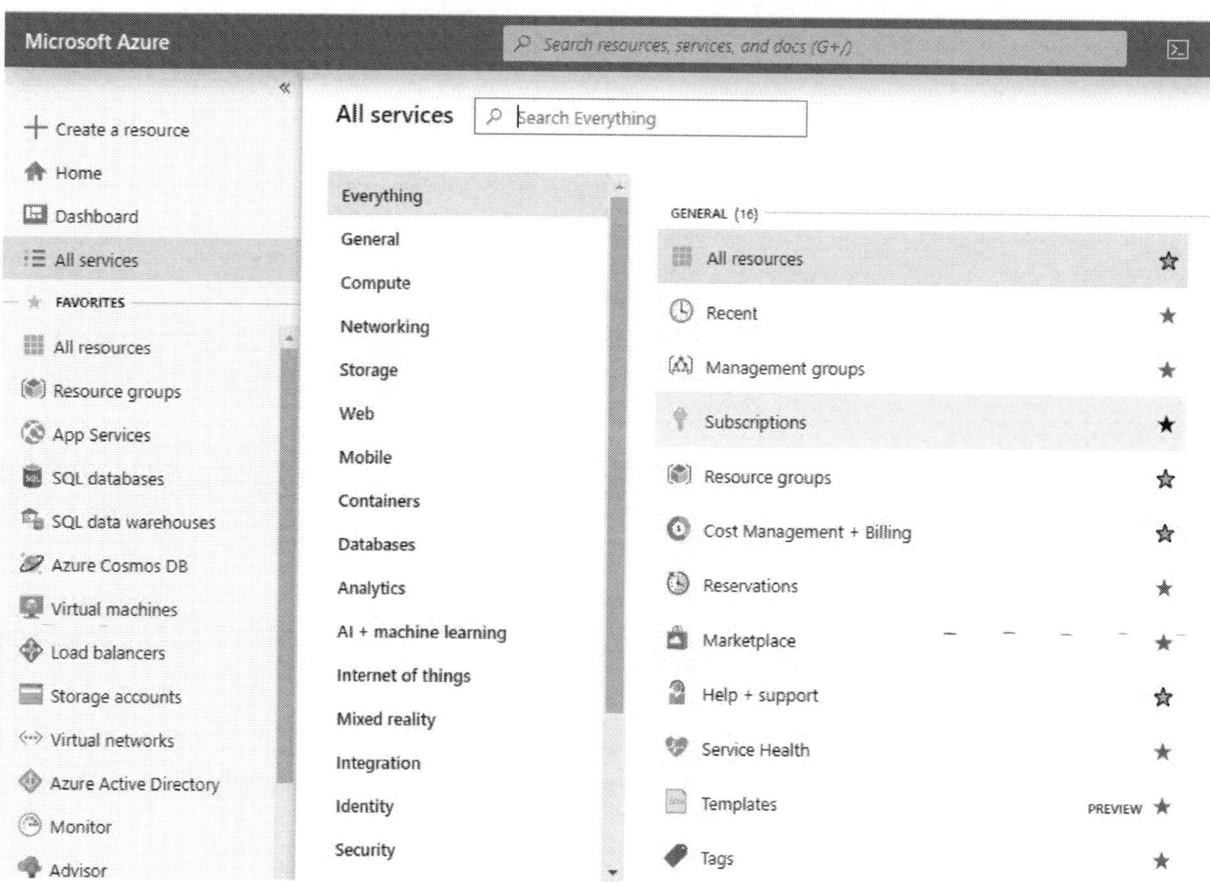

Note: I might have used option 1 to create a resource. There is a possibility that you may not find the resource with option 1. In that case you can use option 2 to create the resource.

Topologies

Students will create below topology as they progress through Chapter Labs.

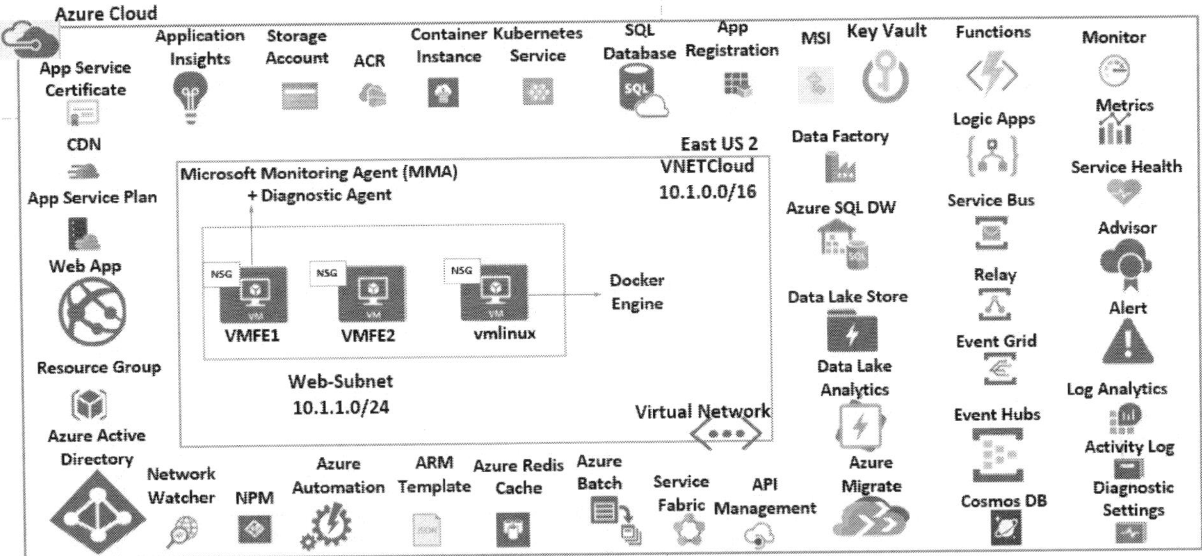

Note: Virtual Network VNETCloud was created In Part 1 Book.

Chapter 1 Azure App Services or Web Apps

This Chapter covers following Topic lessons

- Azure App Services or Web Apps
- Comparing Windows VM and Web Apps
- Web App Features
- App Service Plan
- Deployment Slot
- Application Platform
- Continuous Integration and Deployment (CI/CD)
- Custom Domain Name
- App Service Certificate
- Assign SSL certificate to Web App
- Website Authentication with identity providers
- Web App Scale Up
- Web App Scale out (Manual or AutoScaling)
- Website Performance Test
- Diagnostics logging for Apps in Azure App Service
- Application Insights
- Web App Backup
- WebJobs
- MySQL in Web App
- Web App Networking Options
- Web App VNET Integration
- Web App Hybrid Connection
- Azure CDN with Web Apps
- Web App Access Restriction
- App Service Environment (ASE)
- Web App Extensions
- Web App SCM Site
- Web App for Containers
- App Services Pricing

This Chapter Covers following Lab Exercises

- Create Empty App Service Plan (Standard S1 Plan)
- Create Web App
- Add FTP Credentials
- Create Custom Website Code
- Upload index.html to Web App HKWA1 using FileZilla
- Create Deployment Slot
- Swap the Production Web App with Deployment Slot
- Swap Back the HKWA1 and delete the deployment Slot HKWA2
- Exploring CI/CD options
- Adding Custom Domain Name
- Purchase and Configure App Service Certificate
- Upload & Bind SSL Certificate
- Enabling Authentication/Authorization
- Web App Scale Up
- Web App Manual scale out
- Web App Autoscaling
- Configuring Performance Test
- Enabling and downloading Web App Diagnostic Logs
- Exploring Application Insight dashboard
- Manual Backup
- Restoring Backup
- Configuring Hybrid Connection
- Adding CDN to Web App HKWA1
- Web App Access Restrictions
- Adding Extensions
- Accessing & Exploring Kudu Dashboard

This Chapter covers following Case Studies

- Azure Web App High Availability

Chapter Topology

In this chapter we will add App Service Plan, Web App HKWA1, Resource Group RGWA, App Service Certificate, Azure CDN, Application Insights & Storage Account to the topology. Default Azure AD is created when you sign for Azure subscription.

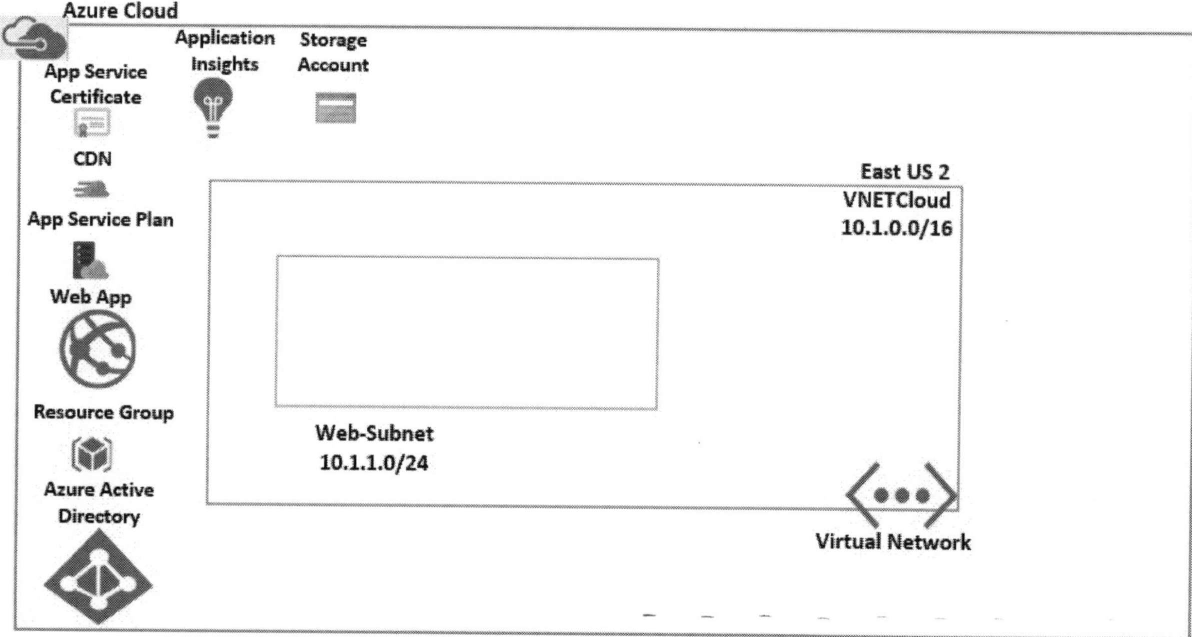

Note: Virtual Network VNETCloud and Web-Subnet were created In part 1 Book. The Labs in this Chapter do not use Virtual Network. 1-2 labs in subsequent chapters will use Virtual Network.

Azure App Services or Web Apps

Azure App Services or Web Apps is a fully managed compute platform that is optimized for hosting websites and web applications.

Web Apps is a managed Windows VM with pre-installed IIS web server with a option to choose application framework (You can choose from Dot Net, PHP, Node.js, Python & Java) at Web App creation time.

(Note: In this chapter we will discuss web app for windows only and not WebApp for linux).

The Diagram below shows the difference between Azure IaaS VM and Azure Web App. **The boxes with Dark grey color are managed by Azure Cloud (Imp Points).**

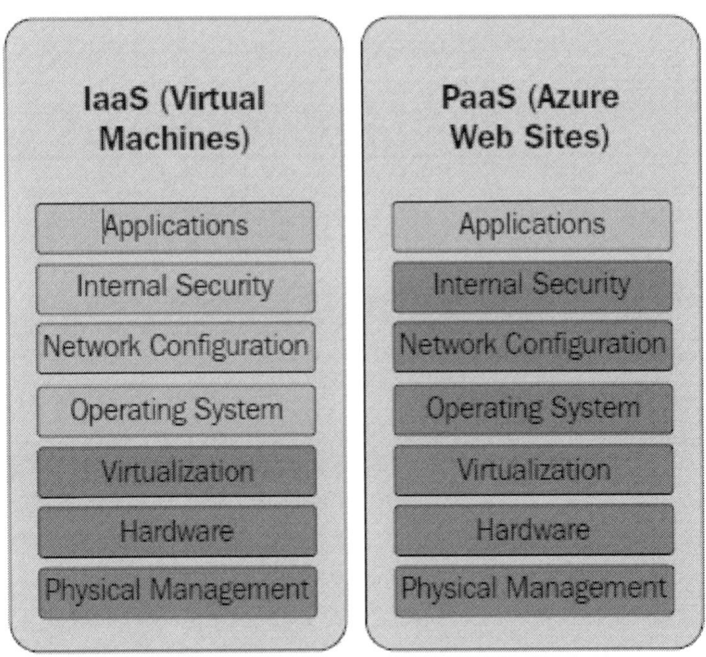

Using Web App you can develop in your favorite language, be it .NET, .NET Core, Java, Ruby, Node.js, PHP, or Python. Web Apps adds the power of Microsoft Azure services to your application, such as security, load balancing, autoscaling, and automated management. You can also take advantage of its DevOps capabilities, such as continuous deployment from VSTS, GitHub & Docker Hub.

Comparing Windows VM and Web Apps

Feature	Windows Azure VM	Web Apps
Deployment time	10-15 minutes	Within a minute
Pre-installed IIS Web Server and Application Framework	No	Yes
Available Option to choose for Application Framework	None	Dot Net, PHP, Node.js, Python & Java
Automatic OS updates, patches and security update by Azure team	No	Yes
Scale out without configuring any load balancer	No	Yes
Built in additional Features available with Web App only.		continuous integration and deployment, User authentication with Multiple identity providers, Deployment slot, Built in Website Performance Test, Built in Load Balancer

Web App Features

1. **Multiple languages and frameworks** - Support for ASP.NET, Node.js, Java, PHP, and Python.
2. **DevOps optimization** - Set up continuous integration and deployment with Visual Studio Team Services, GitHub, or BitBucket. Promote updates through test and staging environments.
3. **Global scale with high availability** - Scale-out manually or automatically.
4. **Connections to SaaS platforms and on-premises data** - Choose from more than 50 connectors for enterprise systems (such as SAP, Siebel, and Oracle), SaaS services (such as Salesforce and Office 365), and internet services (such as Facebook and Twitter). Access on-premises data using Hybrid Connections and Azure Virtual Networks.
5. **Security and compliance** - App Service is ISO, SOC, and PCI compliant.
6. **Visual Studio integration** - Dedicated tools in Visual Studio streamline the work of creating, deploying, and debugging.

App Service Plan

Each Web App is associated with App Service Plan. An App Service plan defines a features and set of compute resources available for a Web App to run.

To host Web Apps, Six Pricing tiers are available in App Service Plan: **Free, Shared, Basic, Standard, Premium and Isolated.**

Apps in the same subscription, region, and resource group can share an App Service plan. But individual Web App can be part of only one service plan.

All applications assigned to an **App Service plan** share the resources defined by it. This sharing saves money when hosting multiple apps in a single App Service plan.

	Free	**Shared**	**Basic**	**Standard**	**Premium**	**Isolated**
Web, mobile, or API apps	10	100	Unlimited	Unlimited	Unlimited	Unlimited
Disk space	1 GB	1 GB	10 GB	50 GB	250 GB	1 TB
Maximum instances	NA	NA	3	10	20	100
Deployment Slots	NA	NA	NA	Supported	Supported	Supported
Custom domain	NA	Supported	Supported	Supported	Supported	Supported
SSL			Supported	Supported	Supported	Supported
Hybrid Connections			Supported	Supported	Supported	Supported
Auto Scale	NA	NA	NA	Supported	Supported	Supported
VPN Hybrid Connectivity	NA	NA	NA	Supported	Supported	Supported
Virtual Network	NA	NA	NA	NA	NA	Supported
Use Cases	Trying out or Dev/Test	Dev/Test	Dedicated Test/Dev and low volume traffic	Production Workloads	Enhanced Performance for workloads	Scale, Security and Isolation

App Service Plan creation options

1. Create an empty App Service plan.
2. Create App Service Plan as part of Web App creation.
3. Use system created S1 App Service Plan as part of Web App creation. This option is only available if there is no App Service Plan exists.

Exercise 1: Create Empty App Service Plan (Standard S1 Plan)

In this exercise we will create App Service Plan Standard S1. **We will also create Resource Group RGWA.**

1. In Azure Portal click Create a Resource>Web>App Service Plan> create App Service Plan Blade opens> For resource Group click link create new. A box pops up. Enter name of Resource Group **RGWA** and click ok> Enter a name for App Service Plan> Under OS Select windows> Location East US 2>By default Standard S1 Plan is selected. If S1 is not selected then Click change size. Click Production and select S1 and then click apply> Click Review + Create.

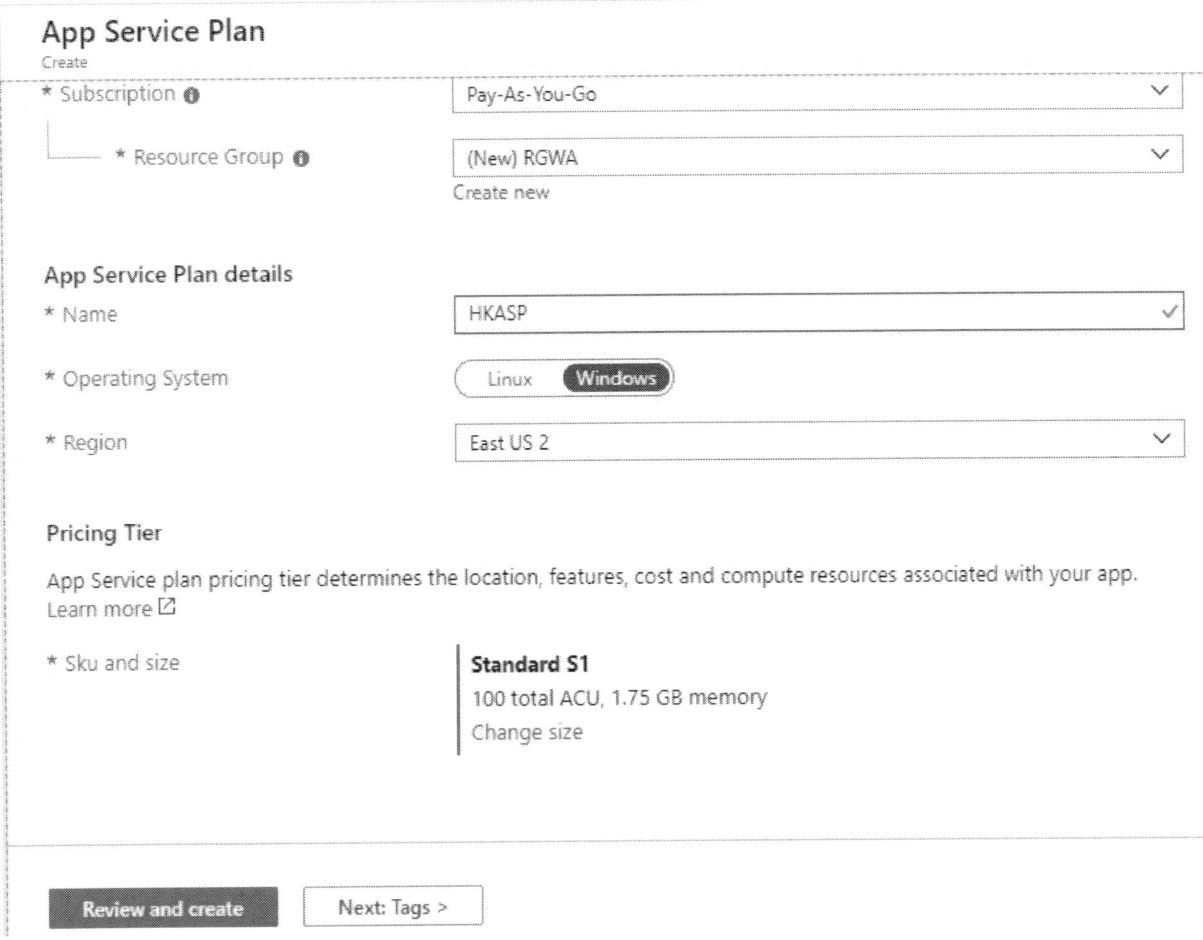

2. After Validation is passed click create (Not Shown).

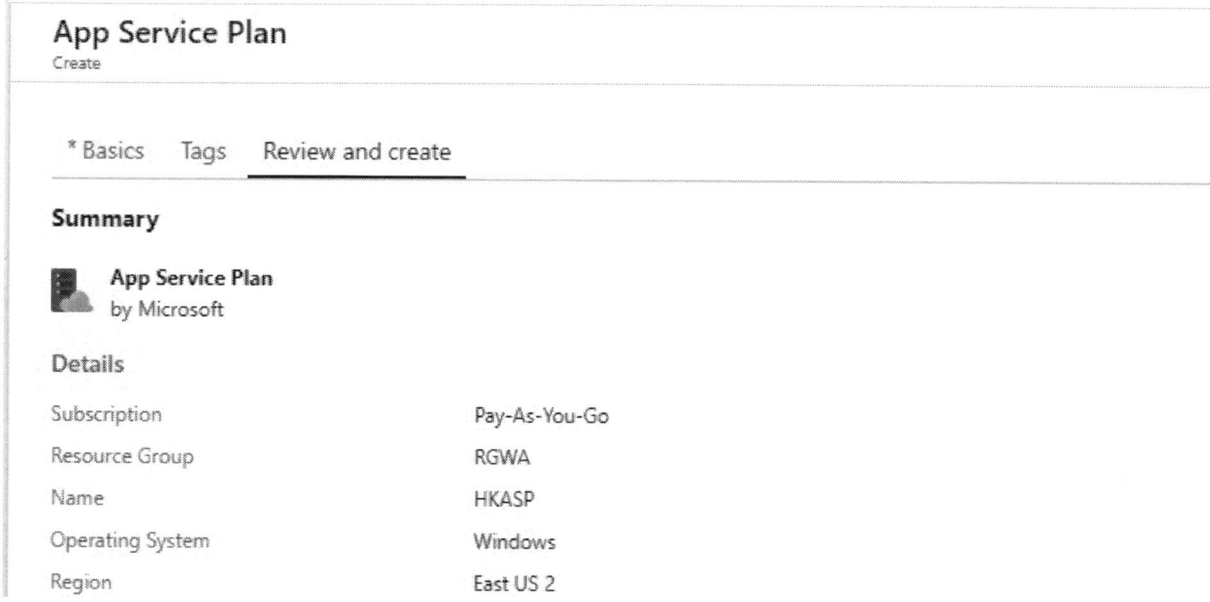

3. Figure below shows Dashboard of App Service Plan HKASP.

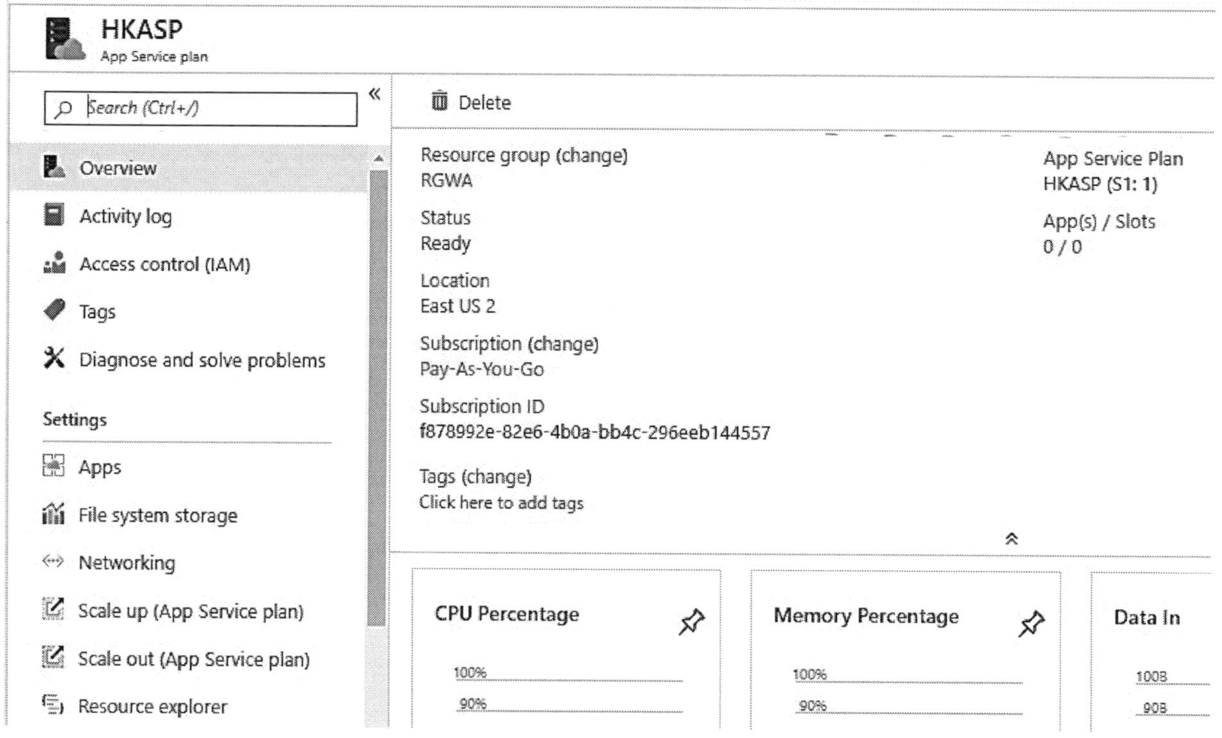

Note: Readers are requested to explore options in left pane of App Service Plan Dashboard.

Exercise 2: Create Web App

1. Click +Create a New Resource>Web>Web App>Create Web App blade opens> Select Resource Group RGWA created in Exercise 1> Enter name for Web App>Select Runtime Stack as per your requirement. I selected ASP.NET V4.7> For OS select Windows>System Automatically selects App Service Plan created in Exercise 1. If not then select the App Service Plan created in Exercise 1> Click Next:Monitoring.

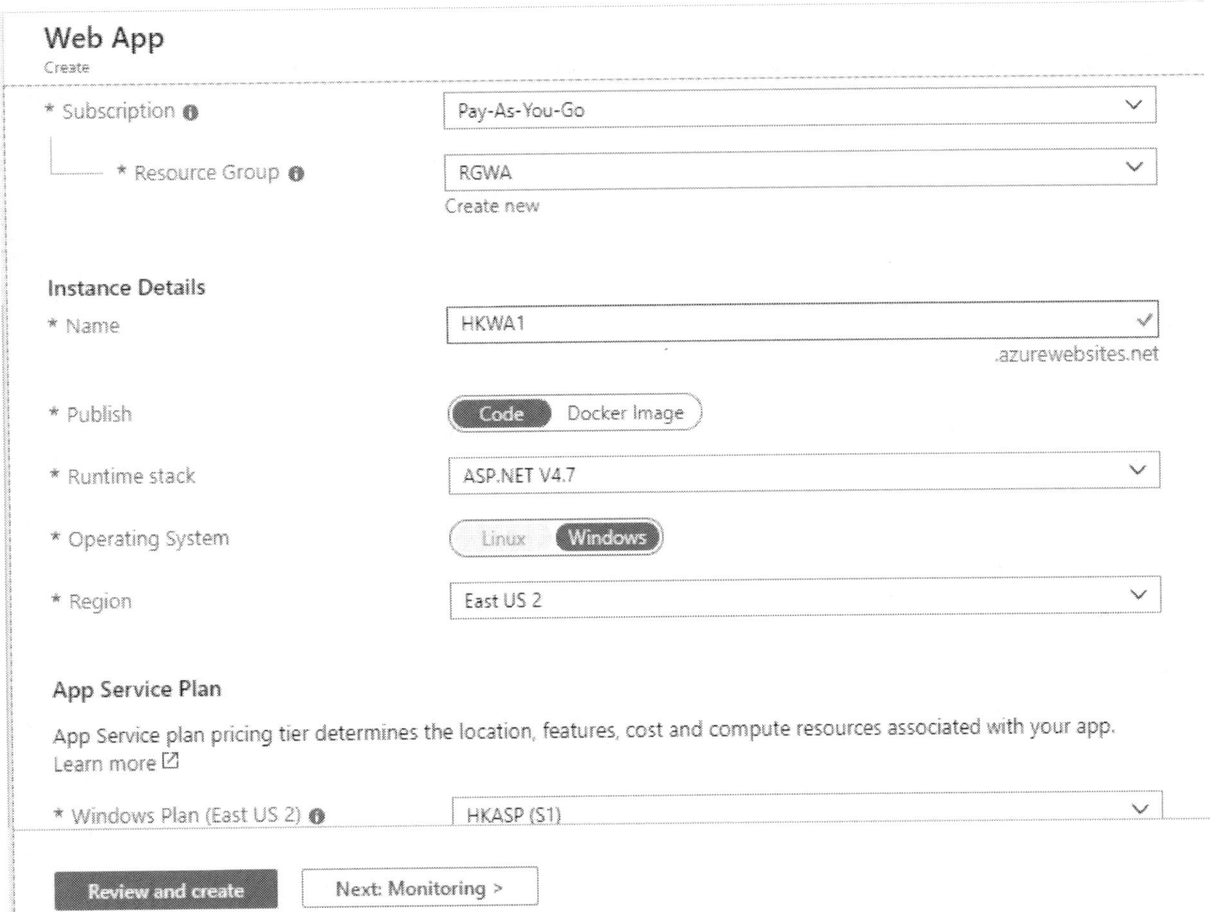

Note: Readers are requested to see other options for Runtime stack in dropdown box. Options available are as follows: Dot Net Core, ASP.Net, Java, Node.js, PHP, Python and Ruby.

2. In Monitoring pane make sure that Application Insight is enabled. Click Review + Create (Not Shown)

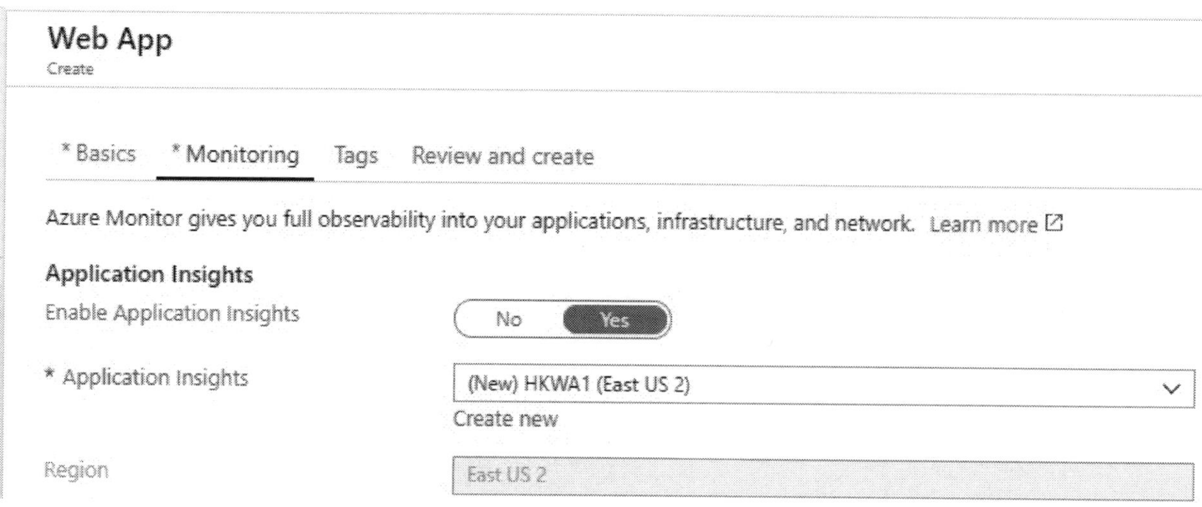

3. After validation is passed click create.

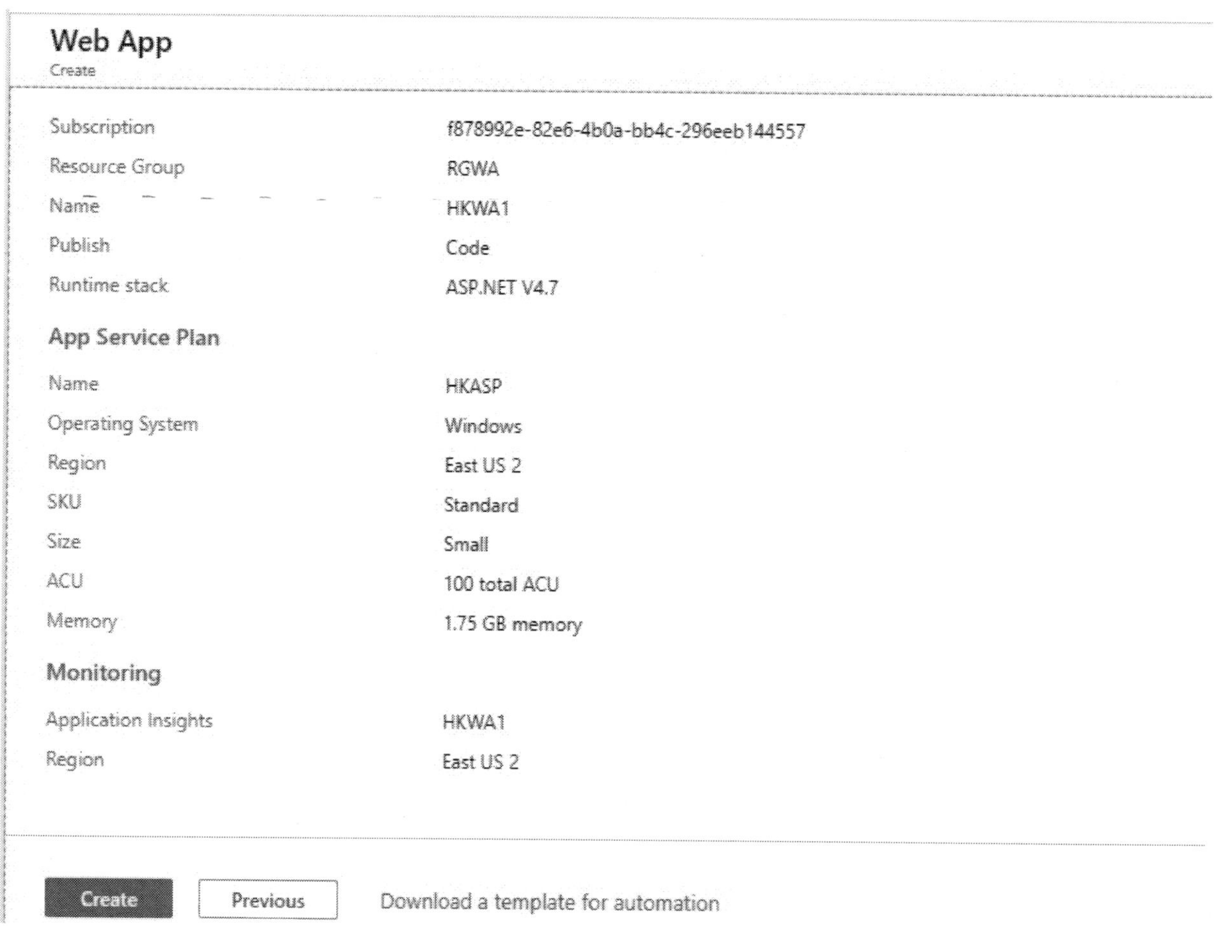

4. Figure below shows the dashboard of Web App HKWA1. Note DNS of the Web App in right pane. Note FTP deployment username Kdeploy1 in right pane. In next lab we will create password for Kdeploy1. Readers are requested to explore options in left pane.

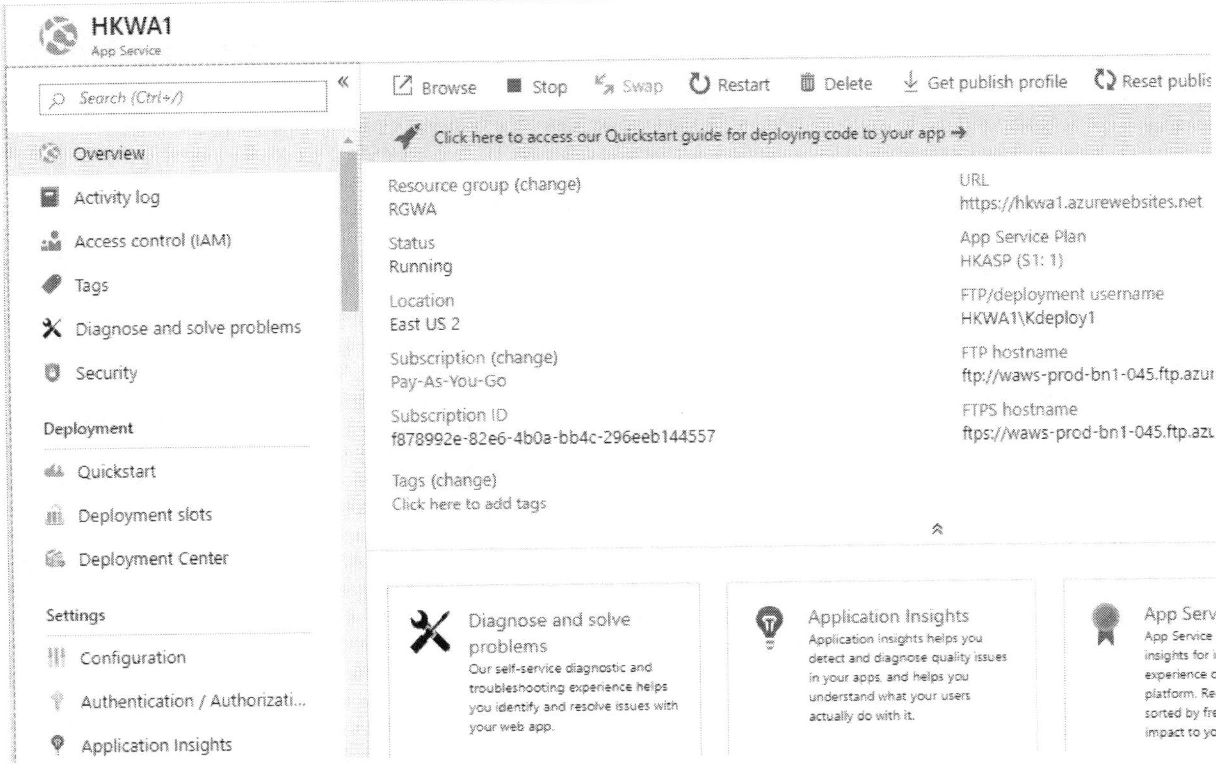

5. Copy DNS name of Web App (URL) from Right pane and open it in a Browser. Default Website opens.

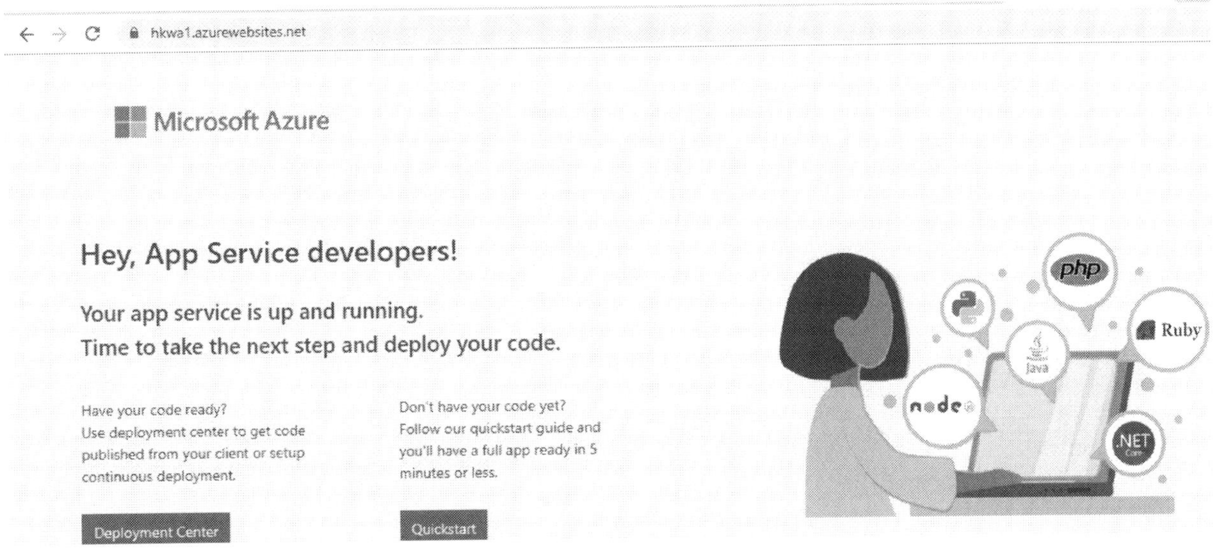

Exercise 3: Add FTP Credentials

FTP can't authenticate using the account you're signed in with, so we need to create a new FTP user and password. We will use FTP user to deploy Custom Website code to Web App HKWA1. In this lab we will create password for FTP username Kdeploy1.

1. Go to Web App HKWA1 Dashboard> Click Deployment Center in left pane> In Right pane scroll down and select FTP>Dashboard Tab will appear.

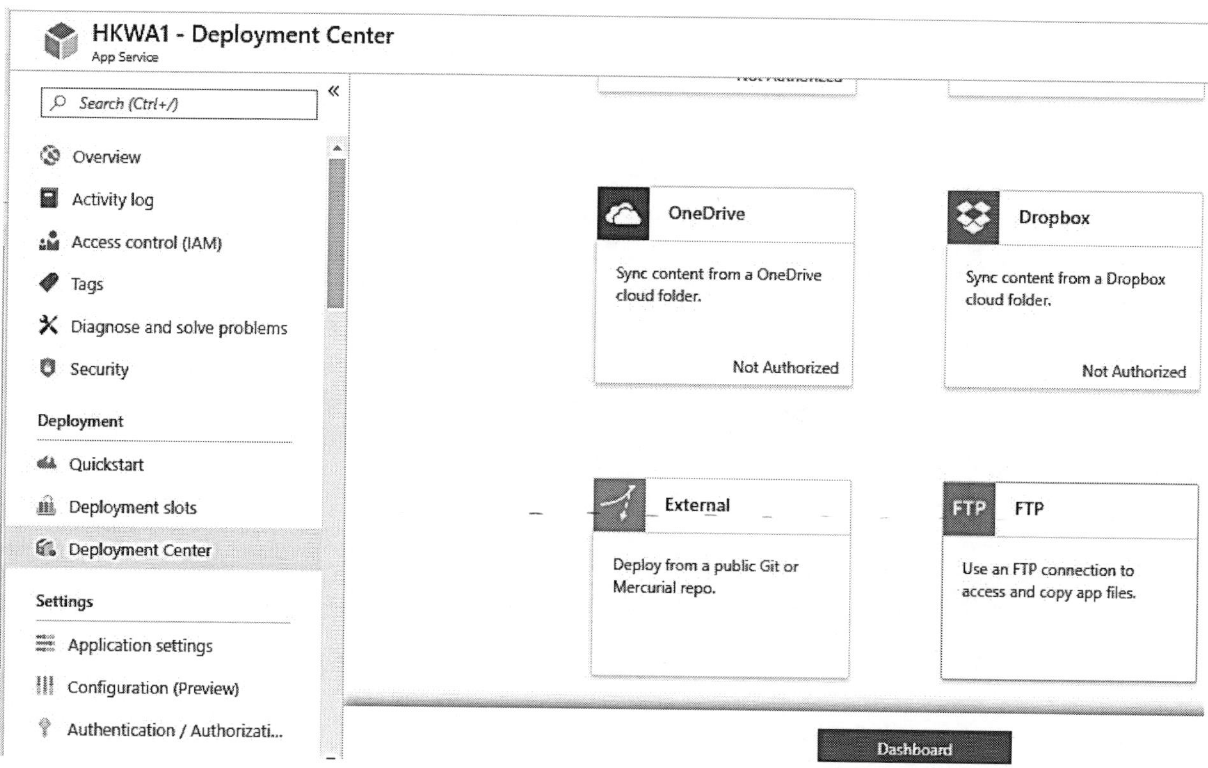

2. Click Dashboard>FTP Blade pops up>Click User Credentials> FTP User name kdeploy1 is already entered> Enter password>Click Save Credentials> After you get notification of saving credentials close the FTP Blade.

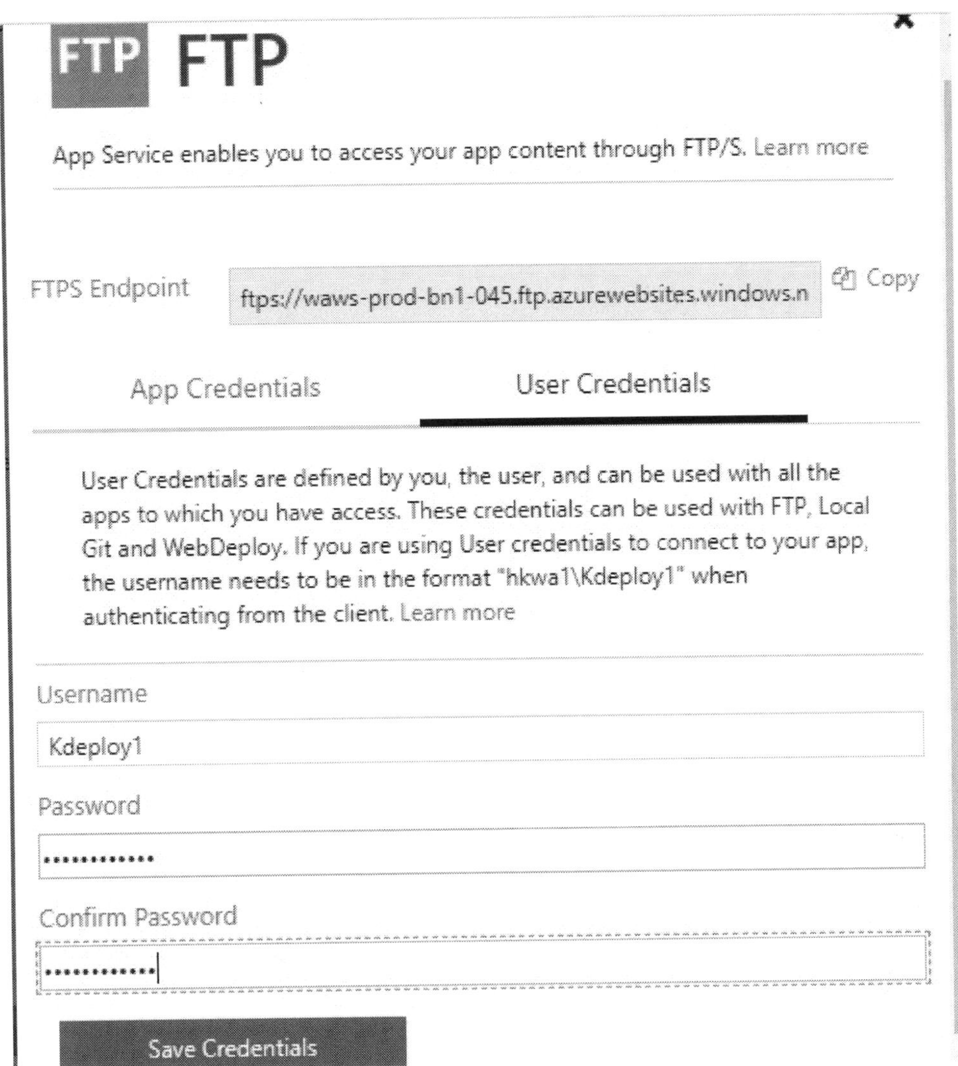

Note: If FTP Username was not generated when you created Web App then you can enter Username in above figure.

Exercise 4: Create Custom Website Code

1. On your desktop/laptop open notepad and enter following:

```
<!DOCTYPE html>
<html>
<head>
<title>AZ-300 & AZ-301 Study & Lab Guide</title>
<meta charset="utf-8">
</head>
<body>
<h1>Exam AZ-300 & AZ-301 Study & Lab Guide</h1>
<p> Exam AZ-300 & AZ-301 Study & Lab Guide prepares you for Azure Solutions Architect Expert Certification.</p>
<p> Author: Harinder Kohli </p>
</body>
</html>
```

2. Save the file as **Index.html** on your desktop.

Note: You can download code entered in index.html file from from Box.com link @ https://app.box.com/s/uyyt3zvgi1cv2mbpy16hzgpr4o280qtw

Exercise 5: Upload index.html to Web App HKWA1 using FileZilla

1. Download & Install FileZilla client from https://filezilla-project.org/download.php?platform=win64

2. From Web App dashboard copy FTP Username and FTP hostname.

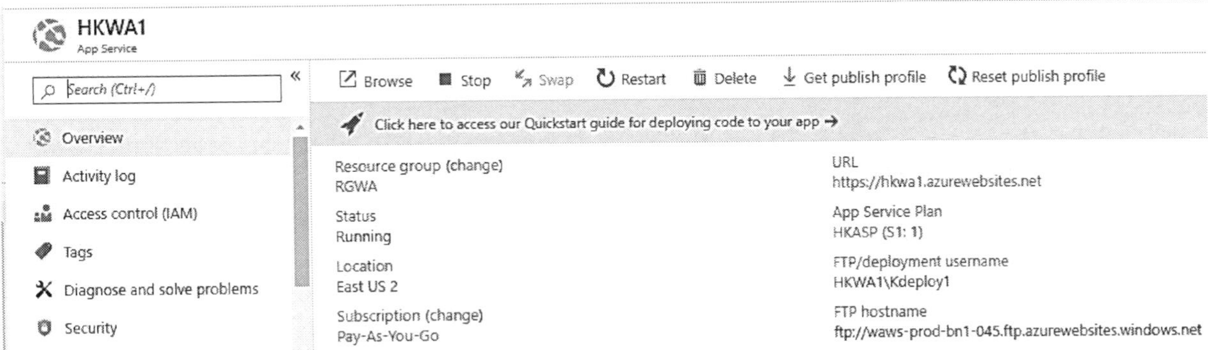

3. Open FileZilla Client>Click File>Click Site Manager>Site Manager Box pops up as shown below.

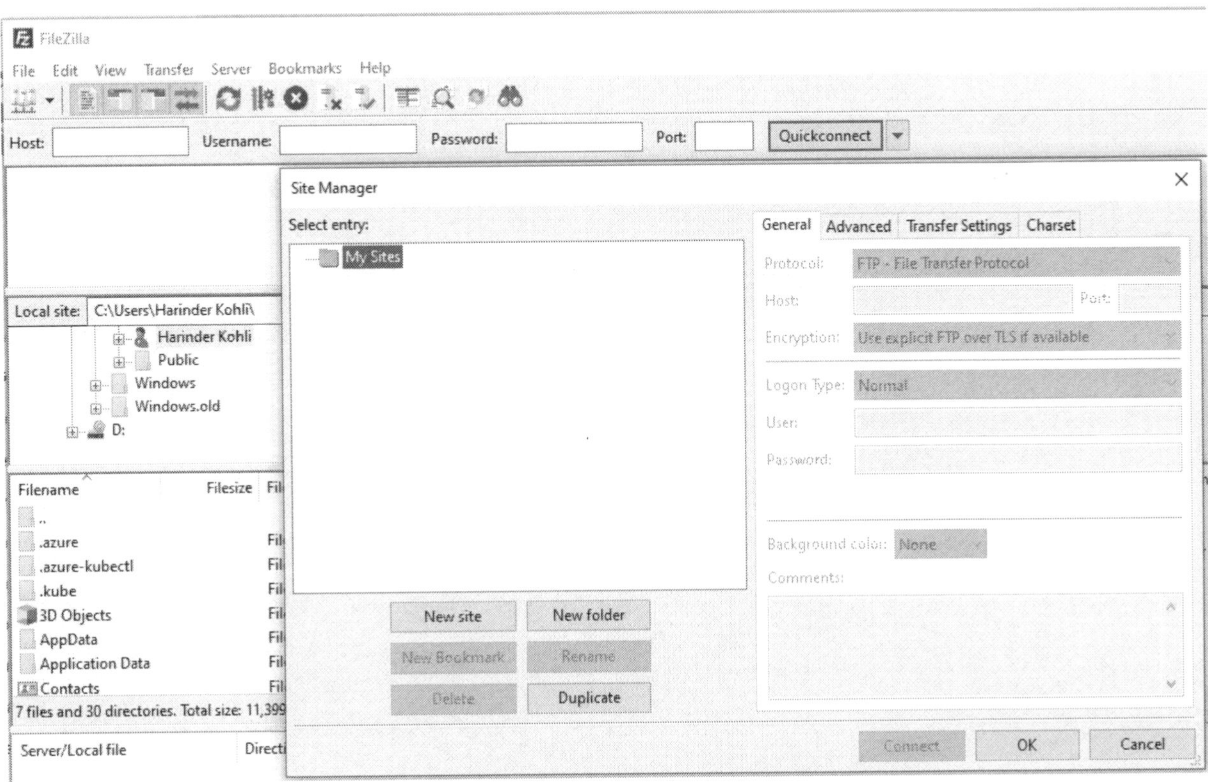

4. Click New Site in left pane> In Right pane in Host enter ftp hostname as seen Azure Web App Dashboard> In Logon type Select Normal>In User enter FTP/Deployment username as seen in HKWA1 Dashboard> Enter Password you created in Exercise 3>Click Connect>

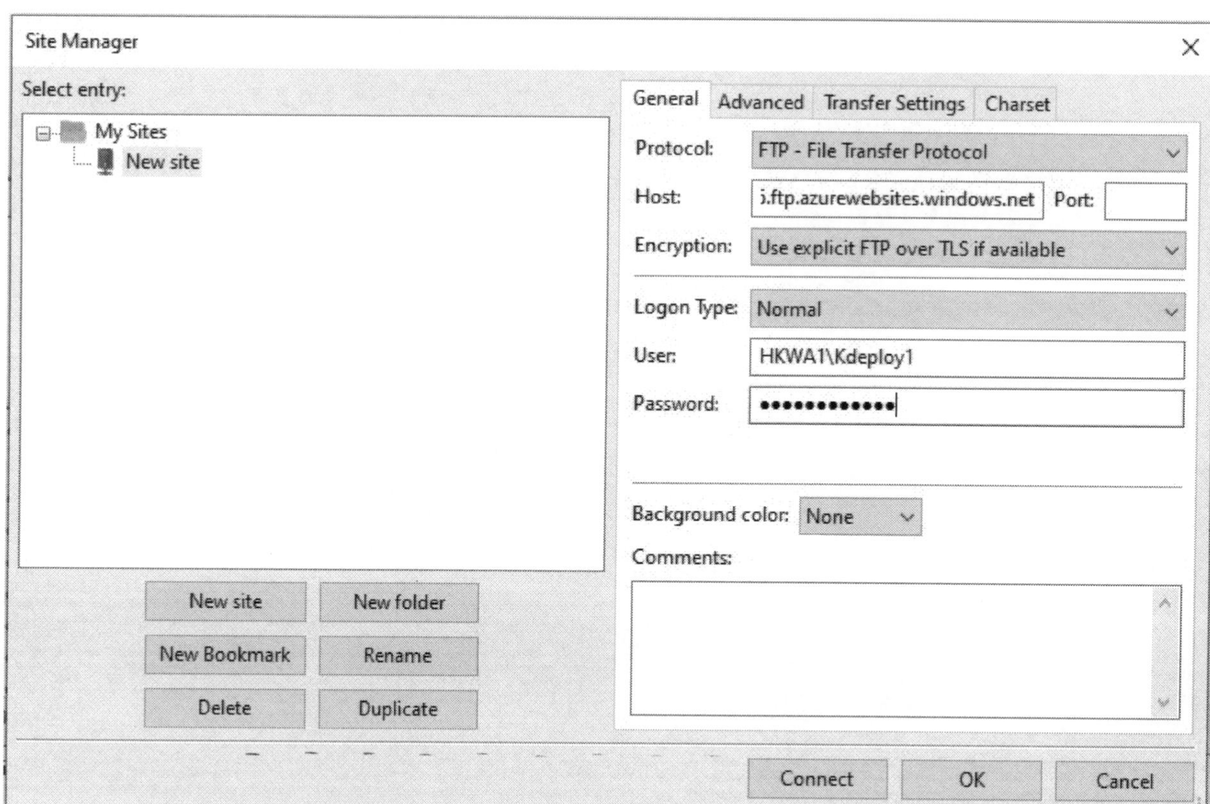

5. After connection is established click **+Site in right pane to expand it** >Click wwwroot>You can see the default website html file hostingstart.html in bottom pane.

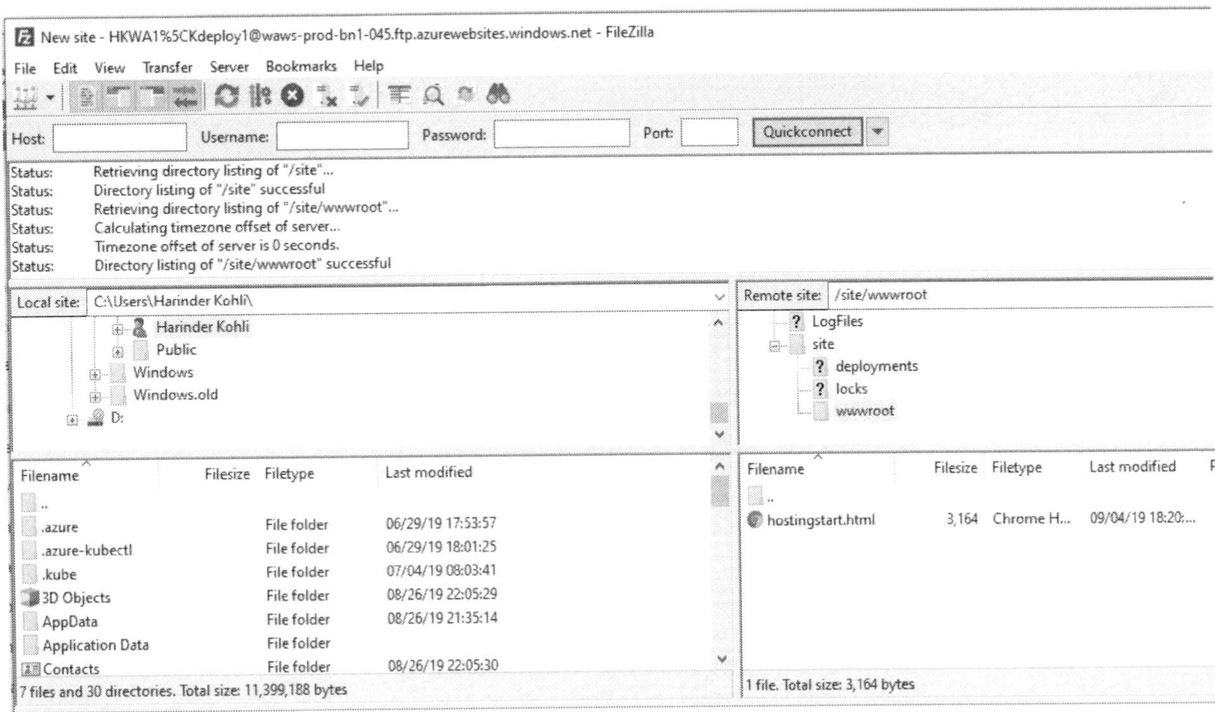

6. We will drag index.html file (Created in Exercise 4) from our desktop to wwwroot folder. You can now see index.html file in bottom pane.

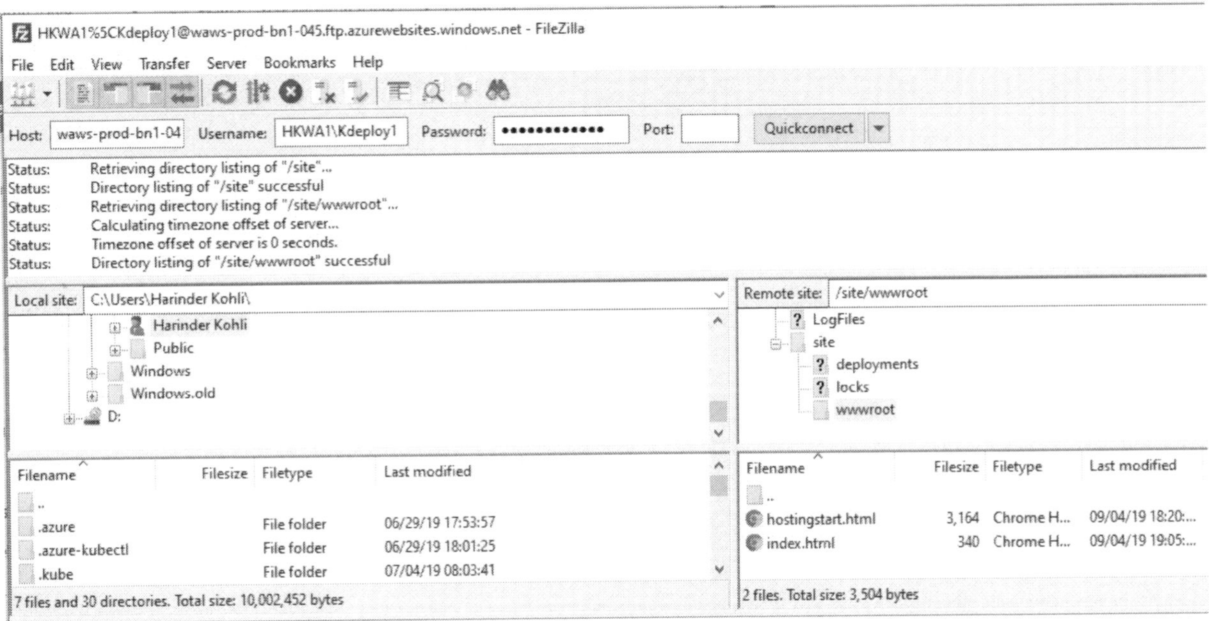

7. Open Browser and enter DNS name of Web App HKWA1. You can now see the Custom Website. If required press f5.

Exam AZ-300 & AZ-301 Study & Lab Guide

Exam AZ-300 & AZ-301 Study & Lab Guide prepares you for Azure Solutions Architect Expert Certification.

Author: Harinder Kohli

8. Instead of Default web site hostingstart.html we now have index.html.

Deployment Slot (Important Concept)

Web Apps have a deployment slot where you can also deploy websites for testing website features. You can validate websites changes in a deployment slot before swapping it with the production slot without any downtime.

Deployment slots are live apps with their own DNS hostnames.

Deployment Slot feature is only available with Standard or Premium app Plans. **You need to add deployment slot from Web App dashboard before you can use it.**

Benefits of Deployment Slot

1. Validate app changes in a staging deployment slot before swapping it with the production slot.
2. If the changes swapped into the production slot are not as expected, you can perform the same swap immediately to get your "last known good site" back.
3. Deploying app to Deployment slot first and swapping it into production ensures that all instances of the slot are warmed up before being swapped into production. This eliminates downtime when you deploy your app. The traffic redirection is seamless, and no requests are dropped as a result of swap ops.

Figure below shows the Dashboard Web App deployed in the deployment Slot.

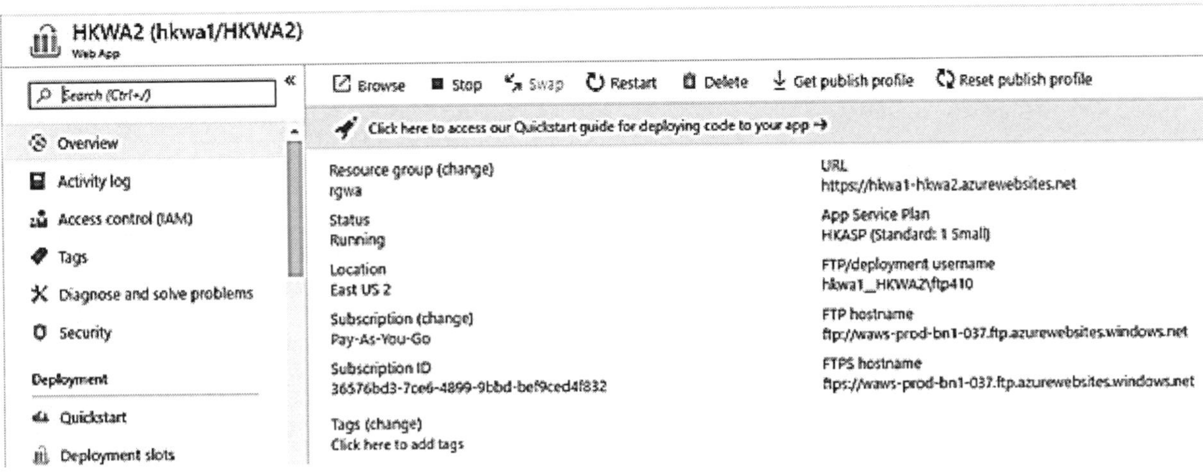

Exercise 6: Create Deployment Slot

Note: Deployment slots are live apps with their own DNS hostnames.

1. In HKWA1 dashboard click Deployment Slots in left pane>In right pane click +Add Slot>Add Slot Blade opens>Enter a name. I entered HKWA2> Click Add (Not shown)> Click Close after slot is created.

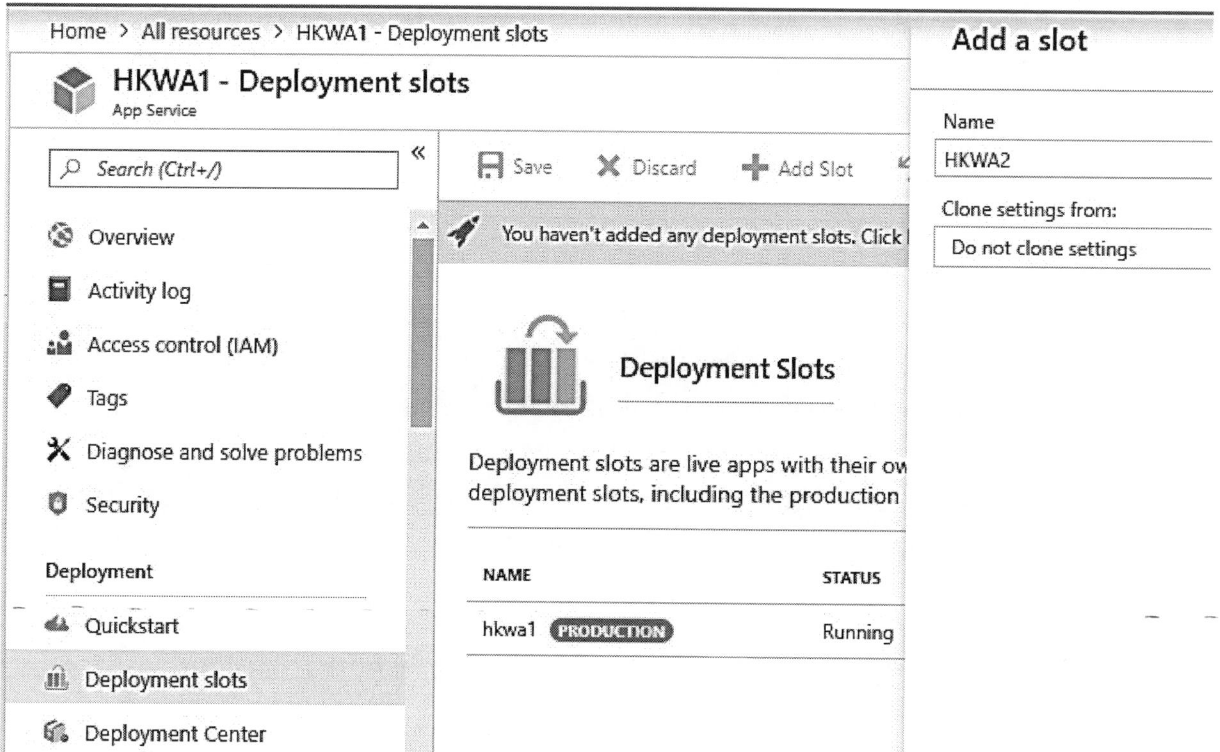

Figure below shows both Production slot and deployment slot hkwa1-HKWA2.

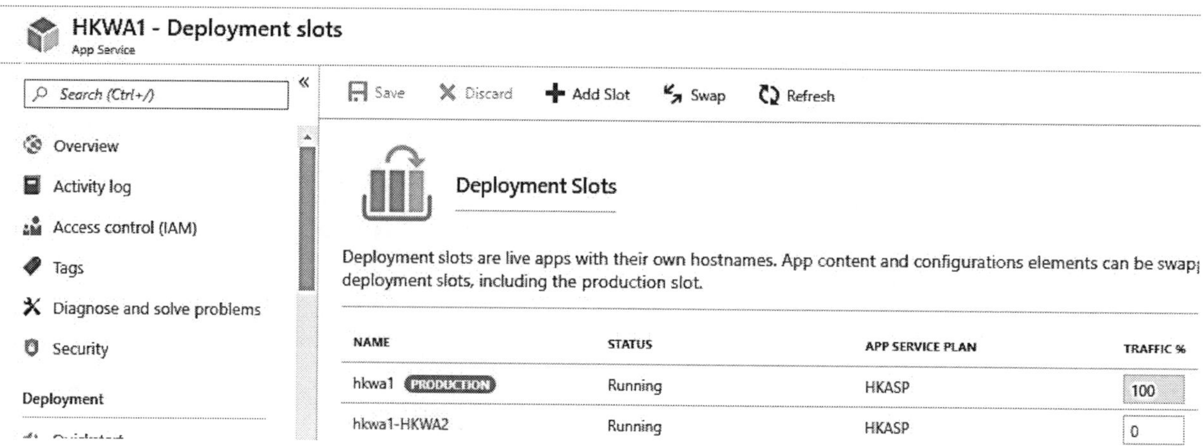

2. Click the Deployment slot hkwa1-HKWA2 in previous screen>Deployment Slot HKWA2 dashboard opens as shown below.

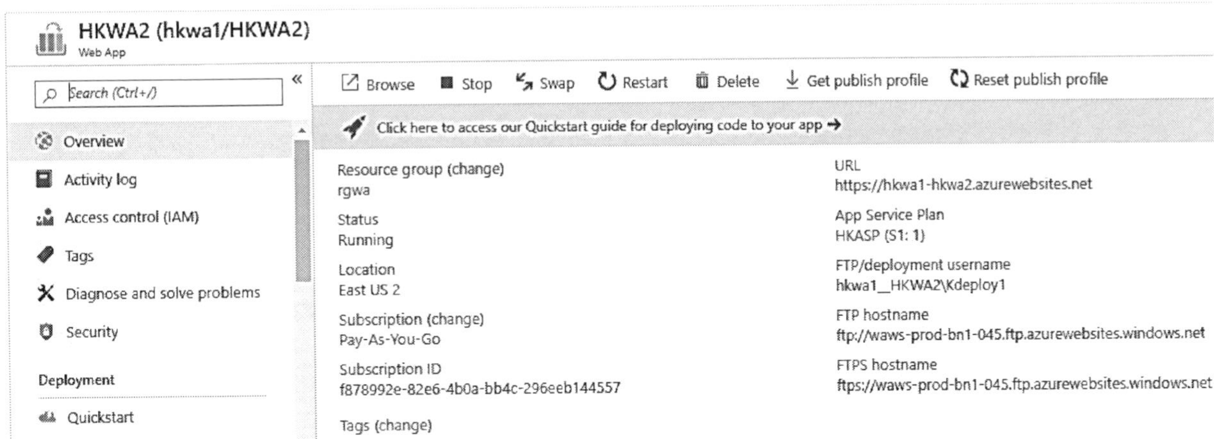

3. Copy the DNS name of the Deployment slot and enter it in a browser> You can see the default website opens.

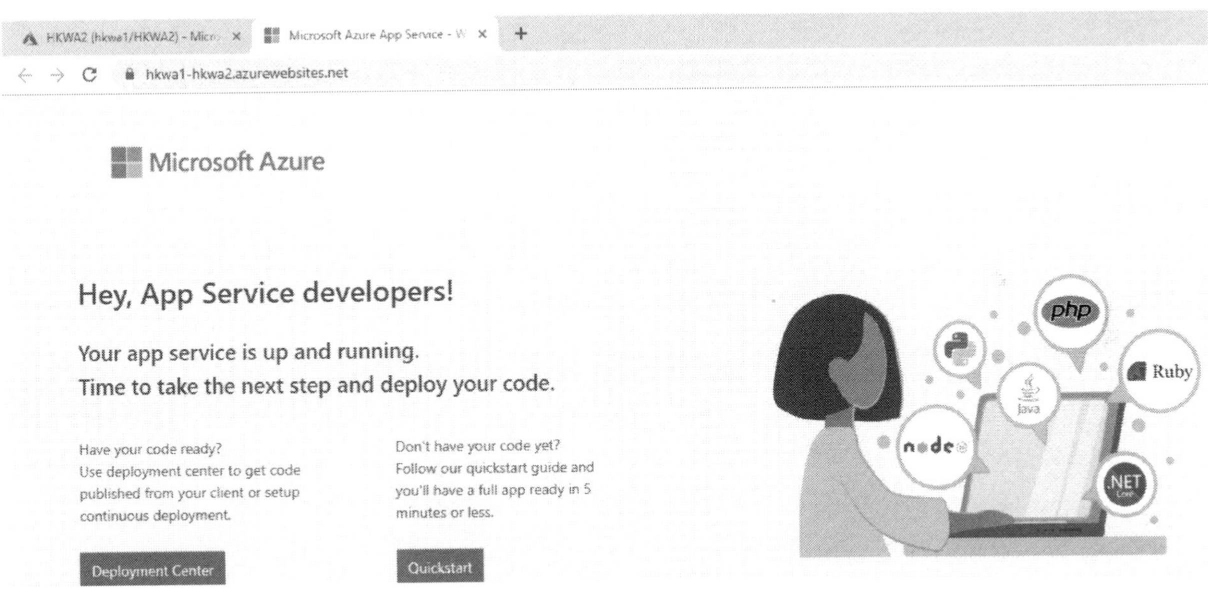

Exercise 7: Swap the Production Web App with Deployment Slot

1. Go to Production Web App HKWA1 dashboard>Click Swap in top right pane>Swap Blade opens>Click Swap (Not Shown)>Click close after swapping is completed.

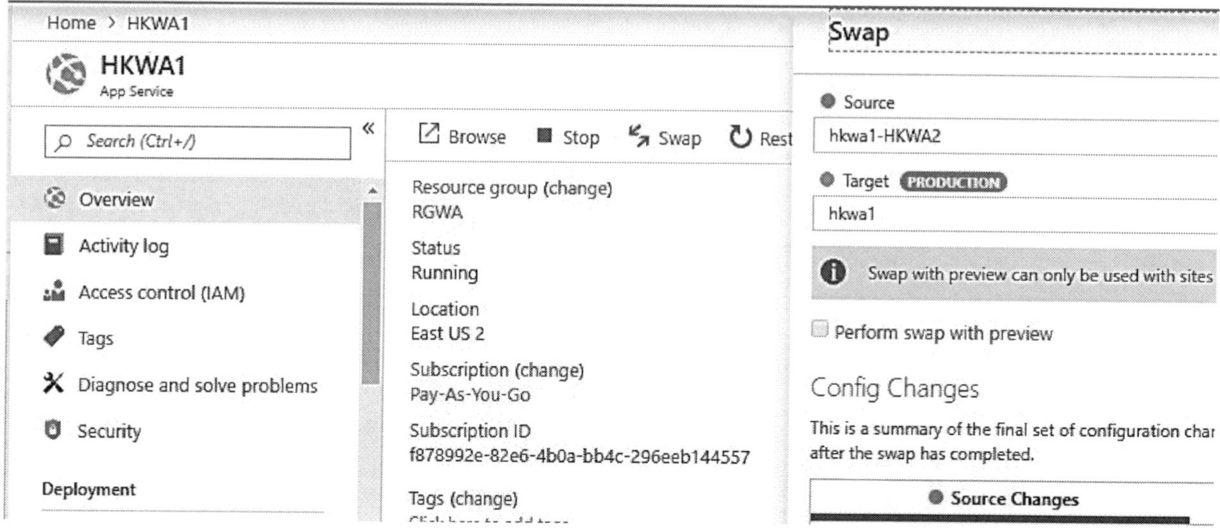

2. From HKWA1 dashboard Copy the DNS name and open it in browser. https://hkwa1.azurewebsites.net

Note: It is no longer showing the custom website we created in earlier Exercise. It is showing the default website of Deployment slot web app.

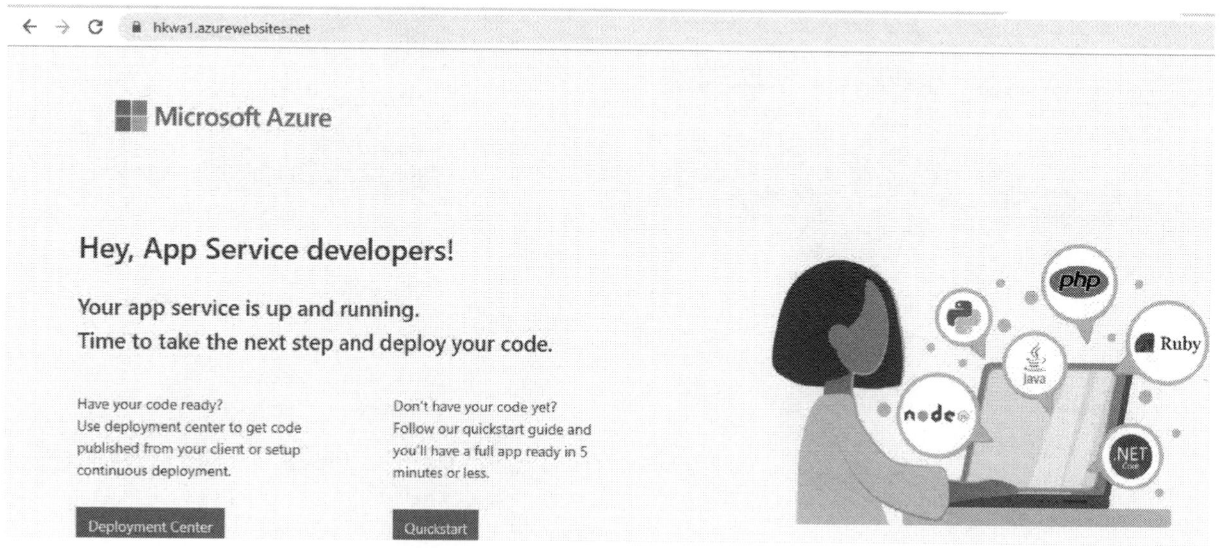

Exercise 8: Swap Back the HKWA1 and delete the deployment Slot HKWA2

1. Go to Web App HKWA1 dashboard>Click Swap in top right pane>Swap Blade opens>Click Swap (Not Shown)>Click close after swapping is completed.
2. From HKWA1 dashboard Copy the DNS name and open it in browser. https://hkwa1.azurewebsites.net
   It is now showing back the custom website.

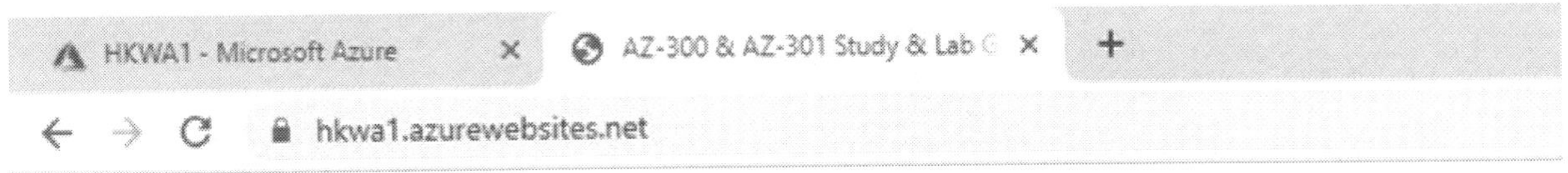

Exam AZ-300 & AZ-301 Study & Lab Guide

Exam AZ-300 & AZ-301 Study & Lab Guide prepares you for Azure Solutions Architect Expert Certification.

Author: Harinder Kohli

3. In Web App HKWA1 dashboard Click deployment slot> Click the Deployment slot hkwa1-HKWA2> hkwa1-HKWA2 Dashboard opens>Click Delete in right pane>Delete blade opens>Enter name of deployment Slot> Click Delete (Not Shown).

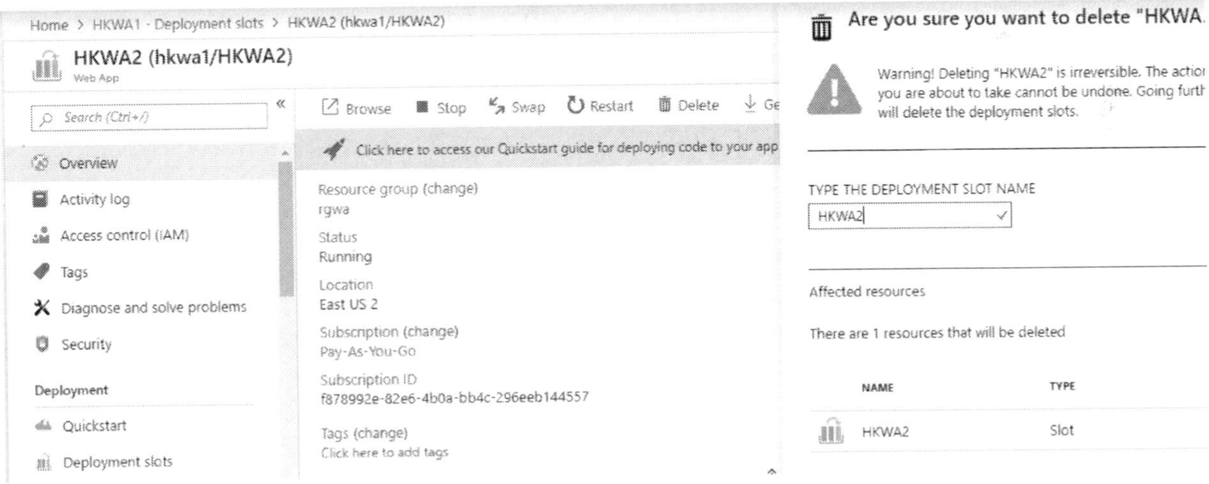

Continuous Integration and Deployment

Continuous integration and deployment is available out of the box for Azure Repos (Formerly Visual Studio Team Services (VSTS)), Local Git Repository, GitHub, One Drive, Dropbox or BitBucket.

With CI/CD any change in website code in VSTS, GitHub, One Drive or Dropbox etc is immediately propogated to the live website.

Exercise 9: Exploring CI/CD options

In Web App Dashboard Click Deployment Center in left Pane> In Right pane select your option as per your requirement. Scroll down to see more options including One Drive and Dropbox.

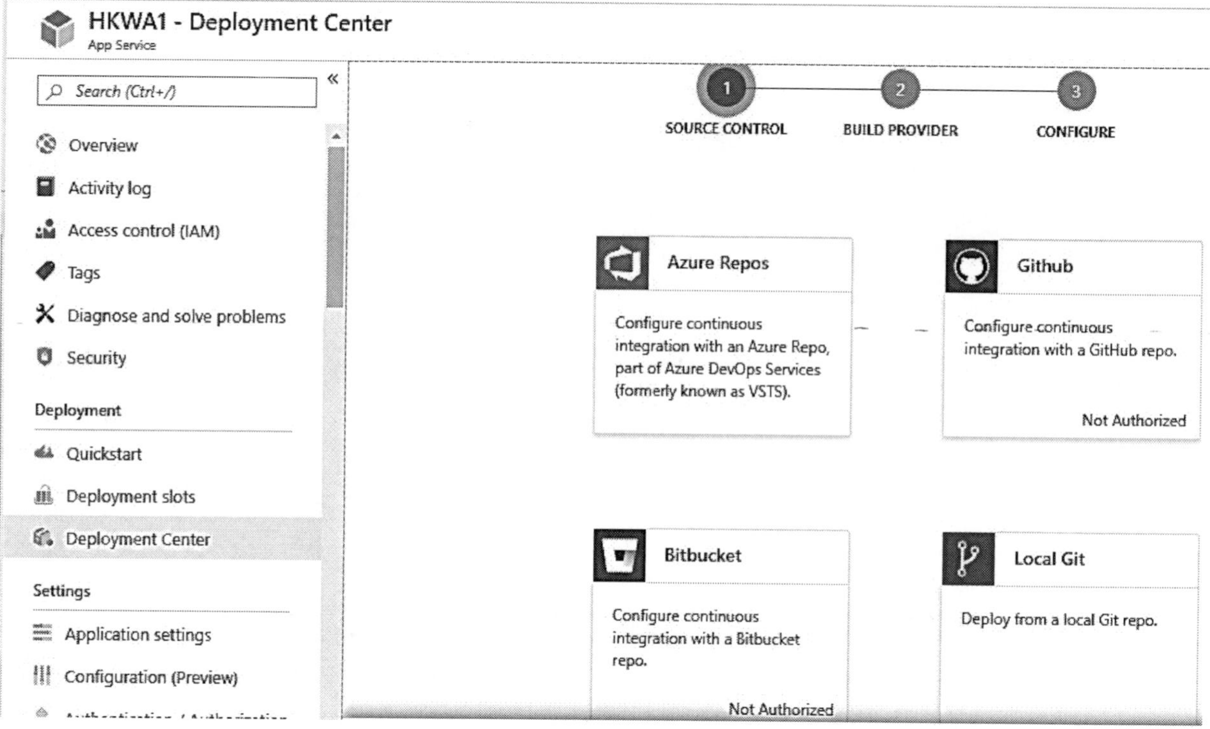

Best practice is to test CI/CD using deployment slot.
You can validate websites changes in a deployment slot before swapping it with the production slot without any downtime.

Custom Domain Name

Azure Web App comes with an initial domain name in the form of http://<app_name>.azurewebsites.net.

It would be difficult for users to remember the format of Default Web App domain name. Adding custom domain names such as **test.com** allows user to access the website easily without the need to remember complex default domain name.

Pre-Requisite for Adding Custom domain

You own a domain name and have sign-in rights to update DNS records with the Domain Name Registrar.

Exercise 10: Adding Custom Domain Name

In this Exercise we will map Domain www.hksystems.in to Web App HKWA1 DNS address using **CNAME Record**. Domain hksystems.in is registered with GoDaddy.

1. Go to Go Daddy DNS Management Console for Domain hksystems.in.

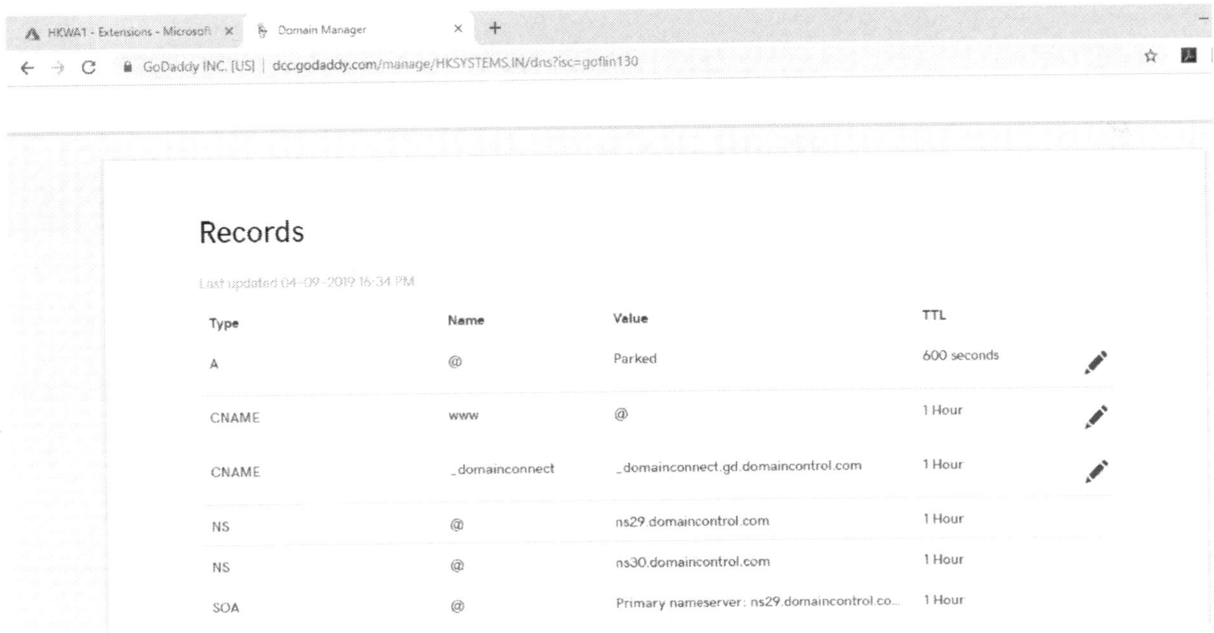

2. In second row (Type CNAME) Click Pencil type edit button>Make sure Host entry is **www**> In points to enter DNS name of HKWA1- **hkwa1.azurewebsites.net** > Click save.

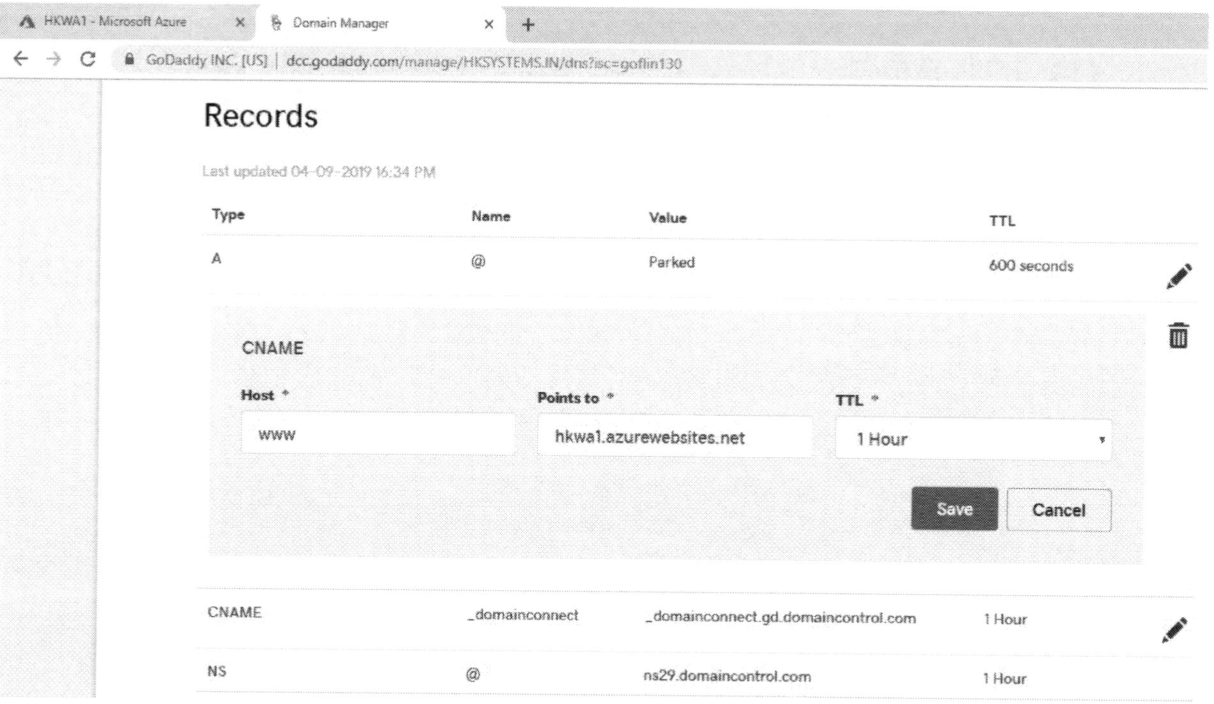

3. Figure below shows the updated CNAME record (Second Row).

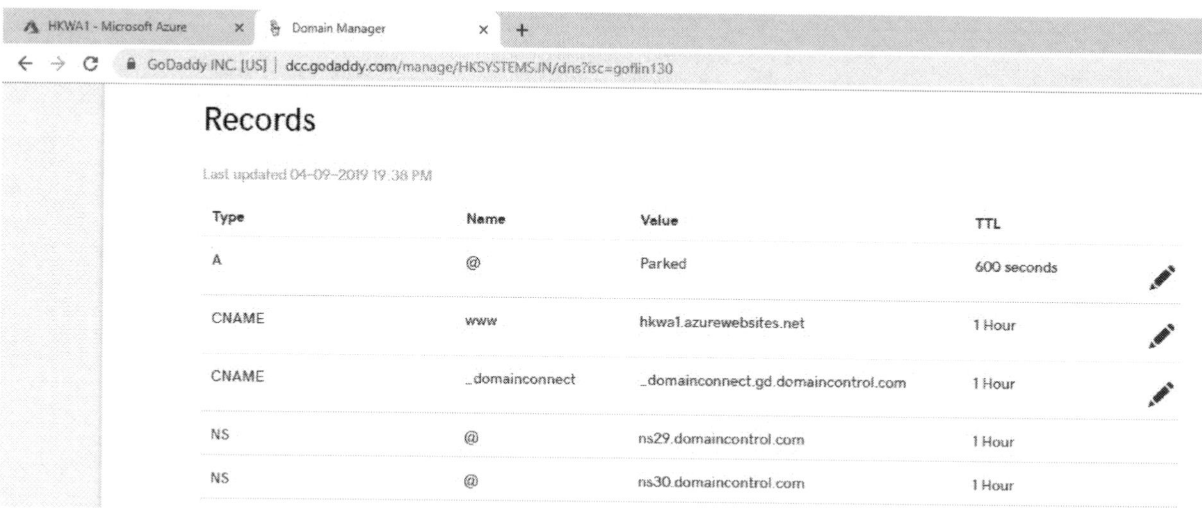

4. In Web App HKWA1 Dashboard click Custom Domains in left pane> In right pane Make sure HTTPS only is off> Click + **Add hostname**>Add hostname blade opens>Enter www.hksystems.in and click validate>CNAME configuration pops up below>Click Add hostname

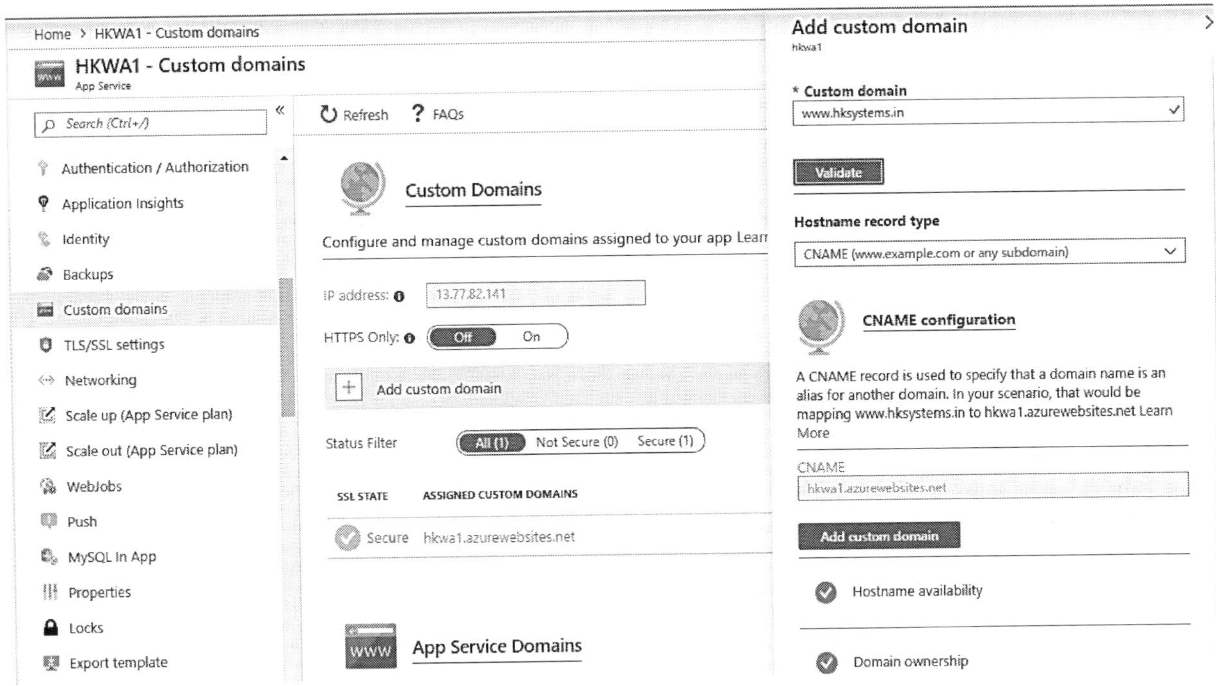

5. Figure below shows www.hksystems.in is assigned to Web App HKWA1.

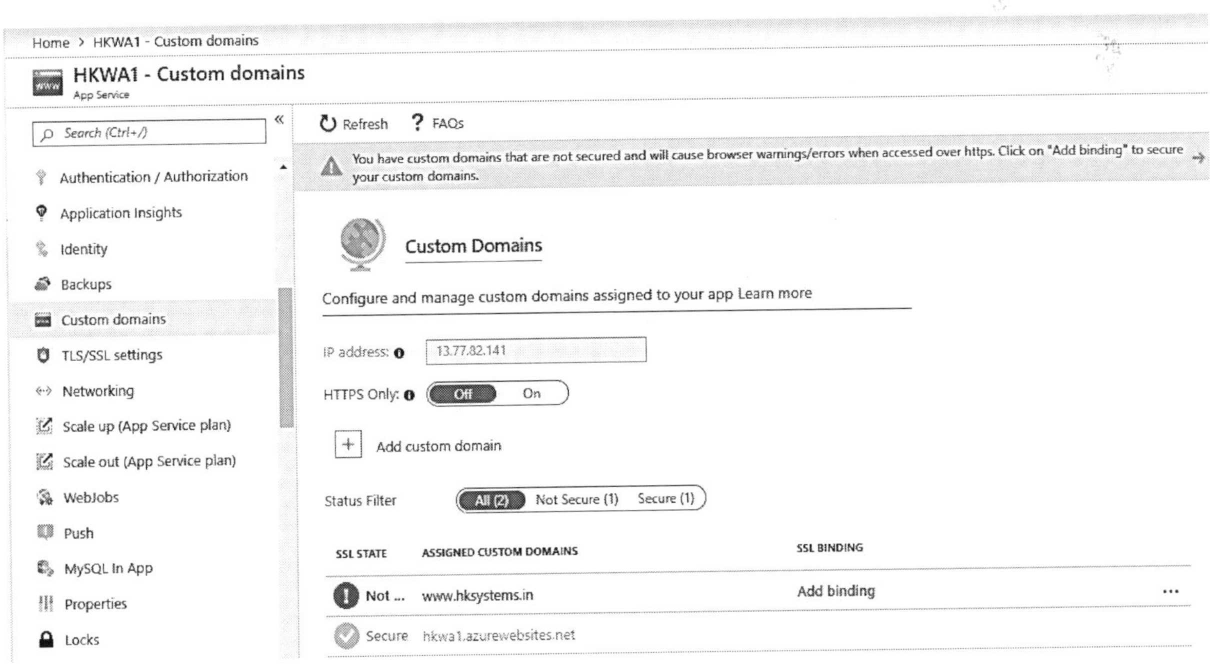

6. Open browser and enter www.hksystems.in> Custom website on Web App HKWA1 opens. It says not secure as it has no lock button in the browser bar.

Exam AZ-300 & AZ-301 Study & Lab Guide

Exam AZ-300 & AZ-301 Study & Lab Guide prepares you for Azure Solutions Architect Expert Certification.

Author: Harinder Kohli

Click on the i in the browser bar and you can see connection is not secure.

In next exercise we will enable secure https access for hksystems.in.

App Service Certificate

App Service Certificate option allows you to purchase SSL Certificates from Azure Portal. You can then assign SSL Certificate to your Web App for enabling HTTPS secure connections.

Features of App Service Certificate

- Secure one Web App (root domain and WWW).
- Secure one Web App and all its sub-domains (Wildcard SSL).
- 1 year validity with auto renewal.
- A Domain Validated Certificates (DV) with easy and intuitive validation process.
- By default, Certificates secrets are stored in Azure Key Vault.
- SHA-2 and 2048-bit encryption – the strongest on the market.
- Compatible with all major browsers.

Steps for enabling HTTPS on Web App with App Service Certificate

- Create App Service Certificate.
- Store it in Azure Key Vault.
- Verify the Domain ownership.
- Import the Certificate in Web App.
- Bind the Certificate.

Exercise 11: Purchase and Configure App Service Certificate (Optional Exercise)

Note 1: Do this Exercise after you have done Exercise 64 in Chapter 5 where we created Key Vault kvcloud.
Note 2: App service Certificate Cost is around 66 USD. In case you don't want to spend USD 66 then you can avoid this and next lab exercise.

App Service Certificate will be used to enable HTTPS access on Web App HKWA1. In this Exercise we will Purchase and create App Service Certificate specifying the Domain name hksystems.in. We will then import the App Service Certificate to Key Vault kvcloud. We will use Manual method to verify domain ownership. Domain name hksystems.in is registered with GoDaddy.

1. In Azure Portal Click All services in Left Pane> Click Web. Note the App Service Certificates option (4th from Bottom).

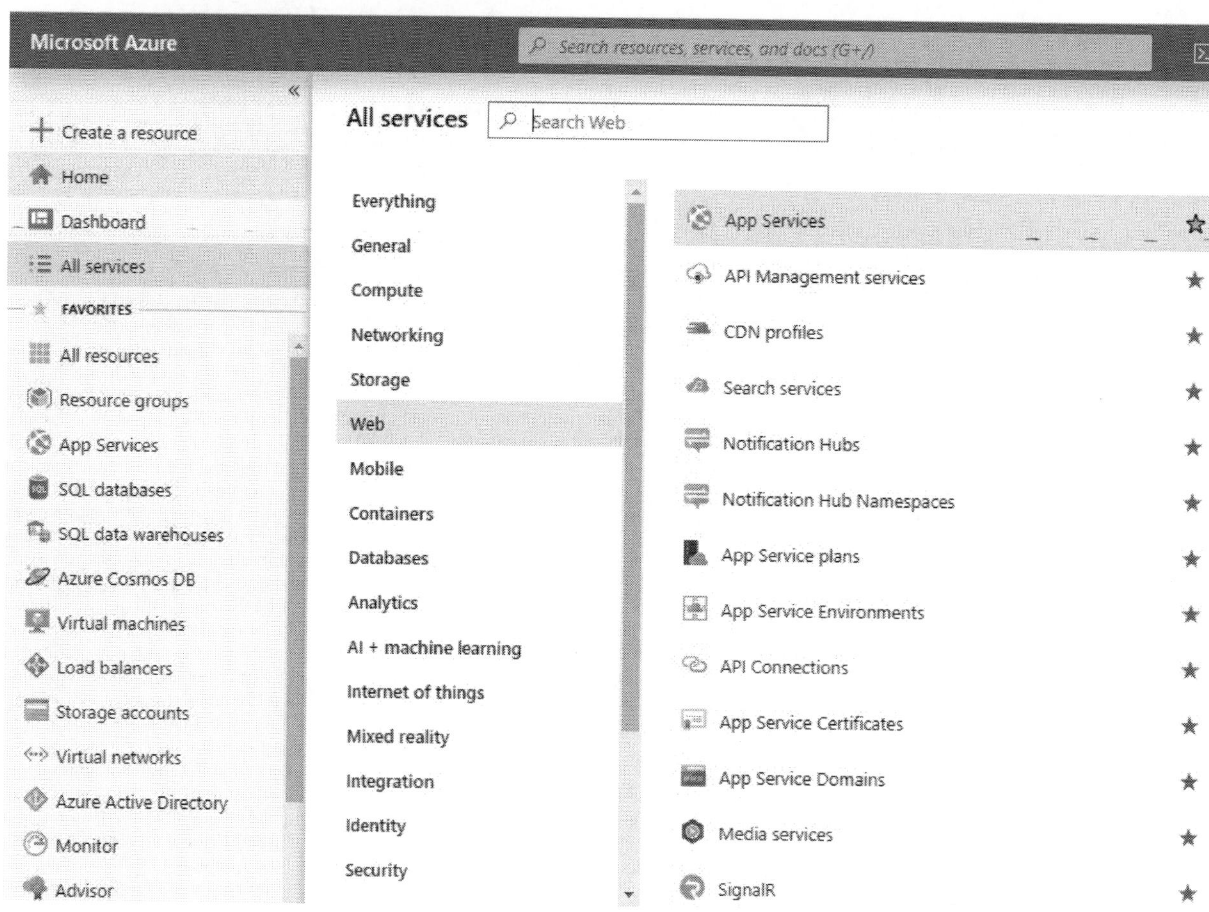

2. Click App Service Certificates in right pane>All App Service Certificate Blade opens>Click + Add> Create App Service Certificate blade opens>Enter name>Enter Domain hksystems.in>In resource group select RGWA created in exercise 1>Click Certificate SKU and select S1 Standard Certificate>Click Select > Click legal terms and accept terms and conditions by clicking OK> Click create.

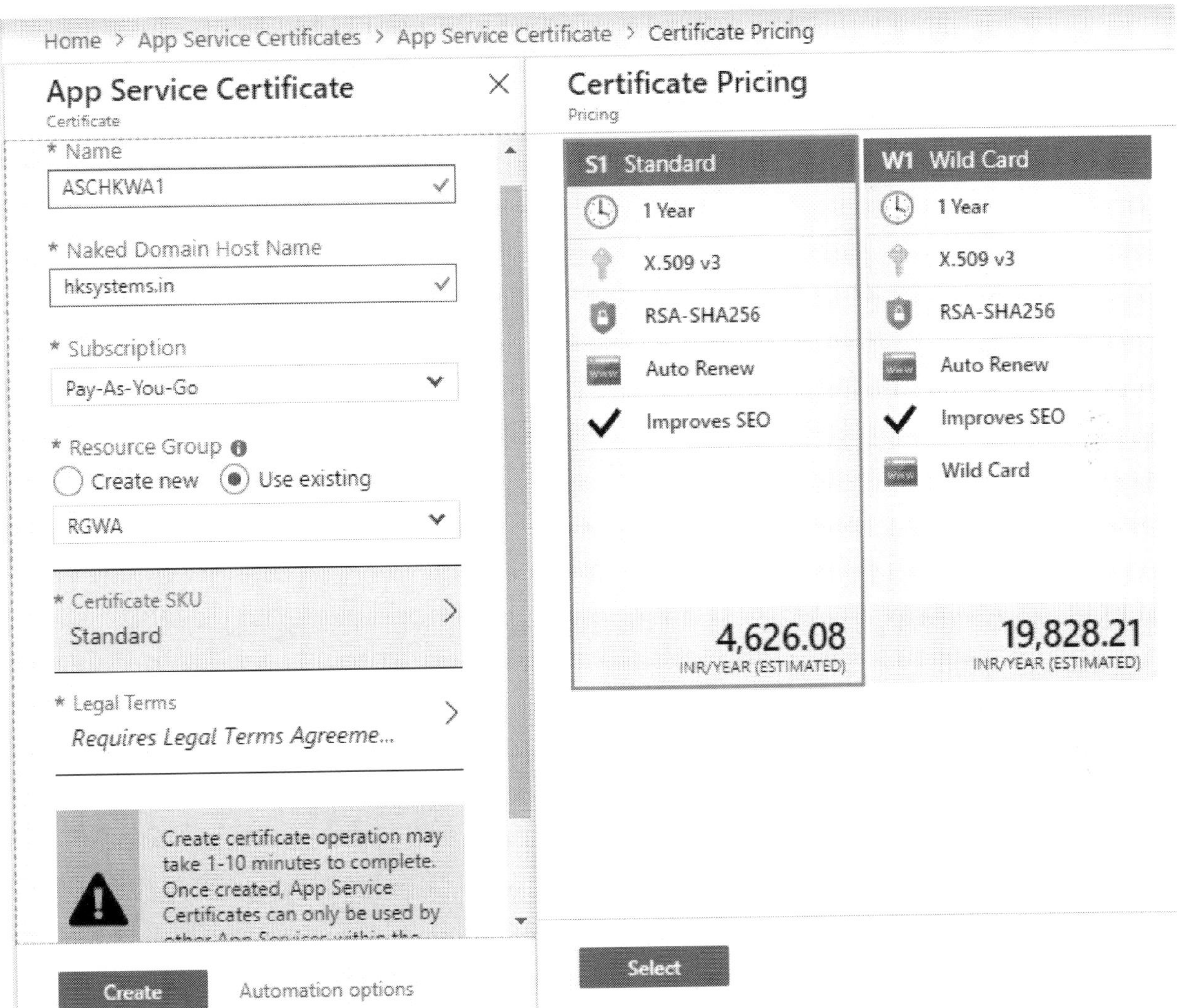

Figure below shows dashboard of App Service Certificate.

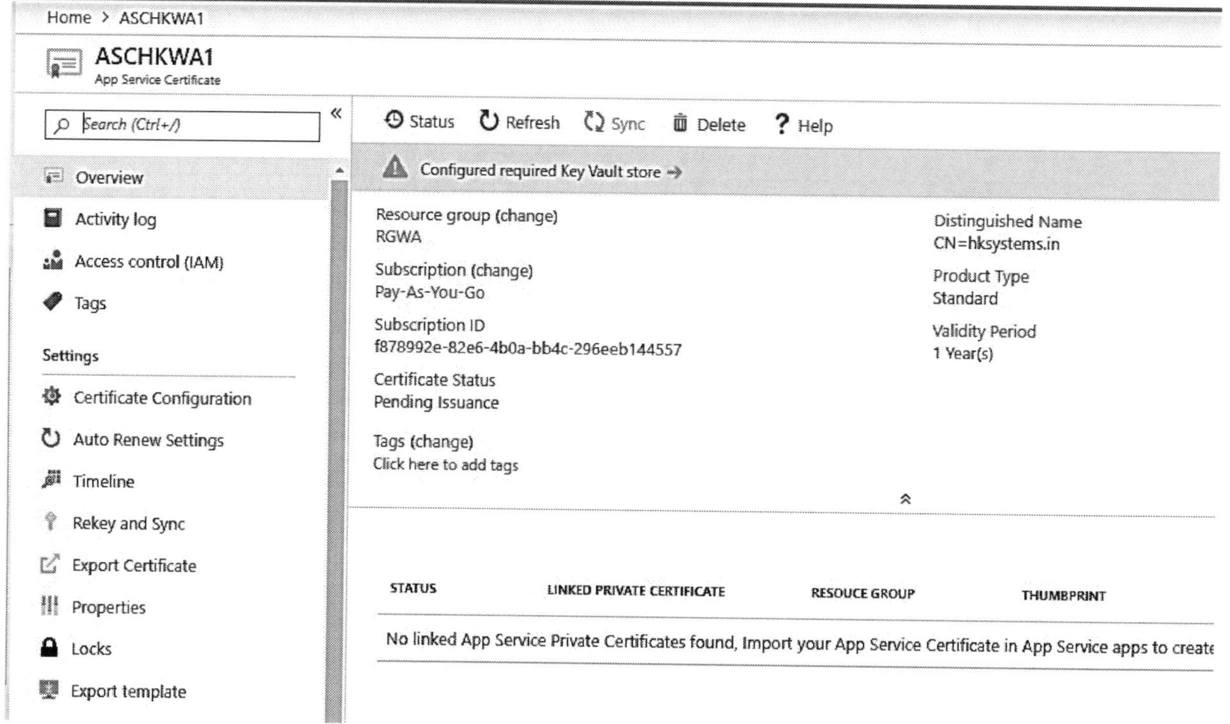

3. **Import Certificate into Key Vault kvcloud**. Key Vault kvcloud was created in Exercise 64, chapter 5. In App Service Certificate dashboard Click Certificate Configuration in left pane.

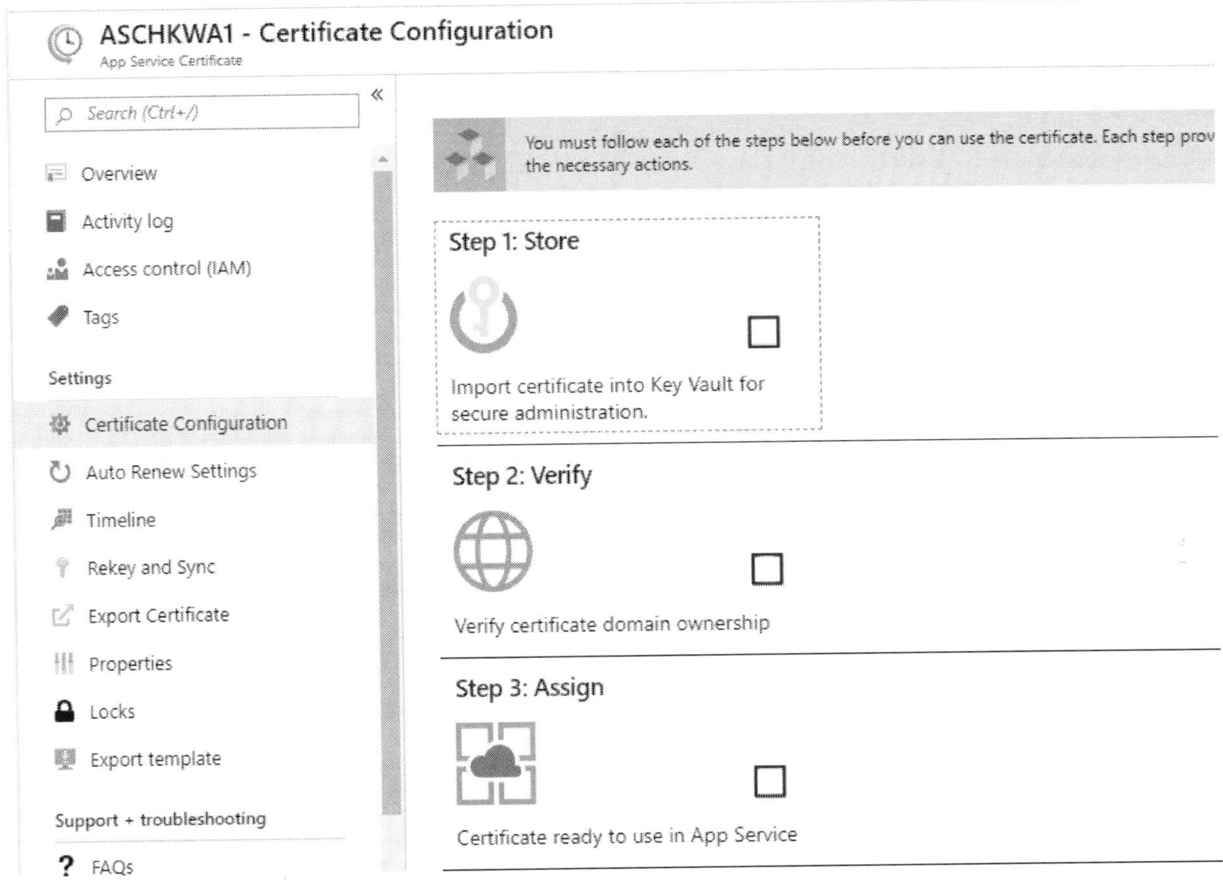

Click **Step 1: Store** Box in Right pane>Key vault Configuration pane opens>Select Key Vault kvcloud>After you get notification of successful setting close the Pane.

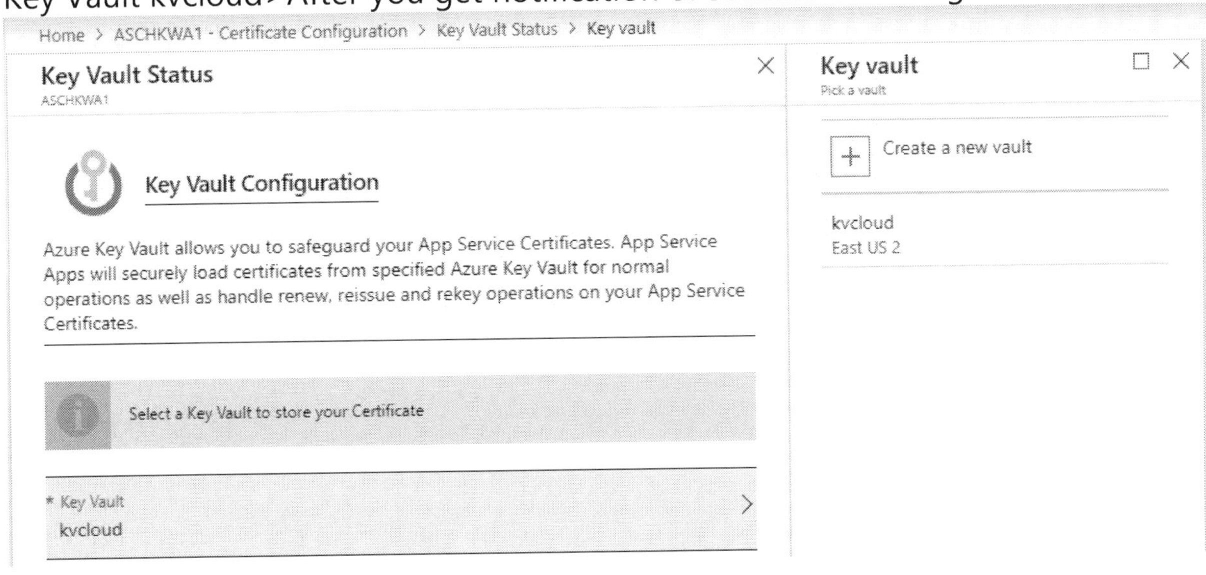

4. **Verify Domain ownership of hksystems.in**. We will use Manual verification method. We will add TXT record in GoDaddy with name @ and value will be Domain verification Token.
   In App Service Dashboard with Certificate Configuration selected Click **Step 2: verify** Box in Right pane>Domain verification pane opens. Copy down the Domain verification Token.

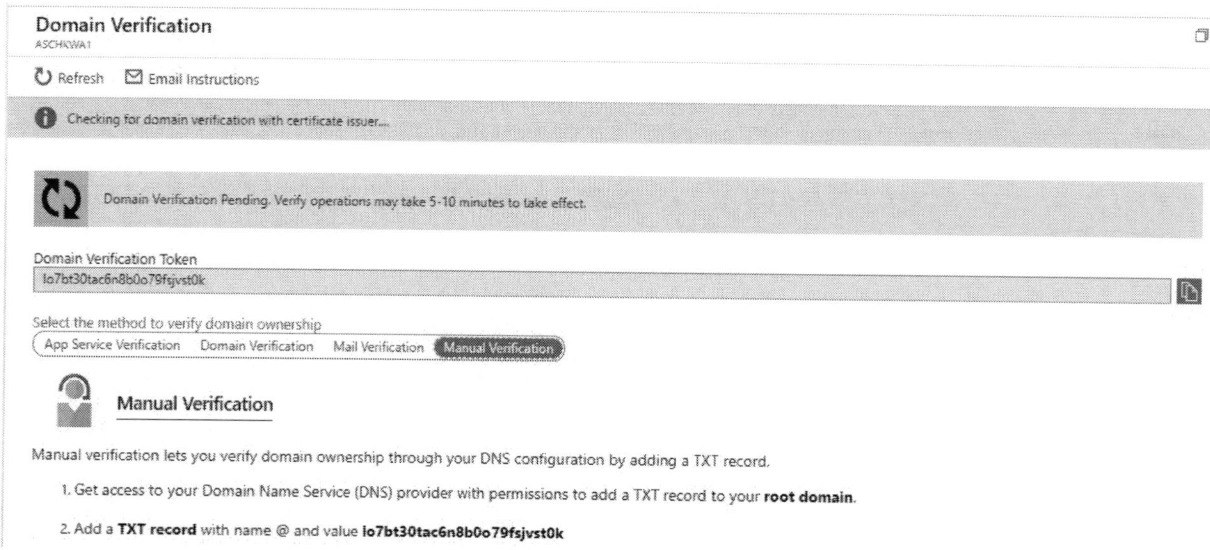

Go to GoDaddy DNS management pane for Domain hksystems.in>Click Add in bottom right>Record Type box pops up>Select TXT record>In Host enter @>In Value enter Domain Verification Token>Click save (Not Shown).

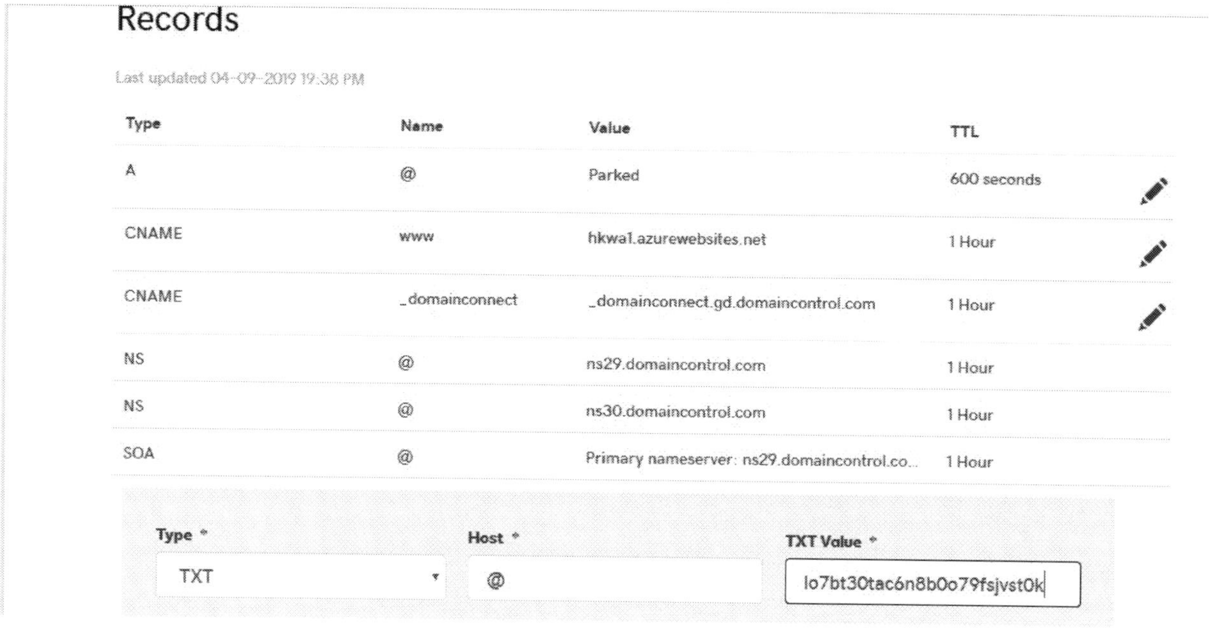

Wait a few minutes for DNS propagation to take place. After 2-5 minutes I got notification in the pane that Domain verification is successful.

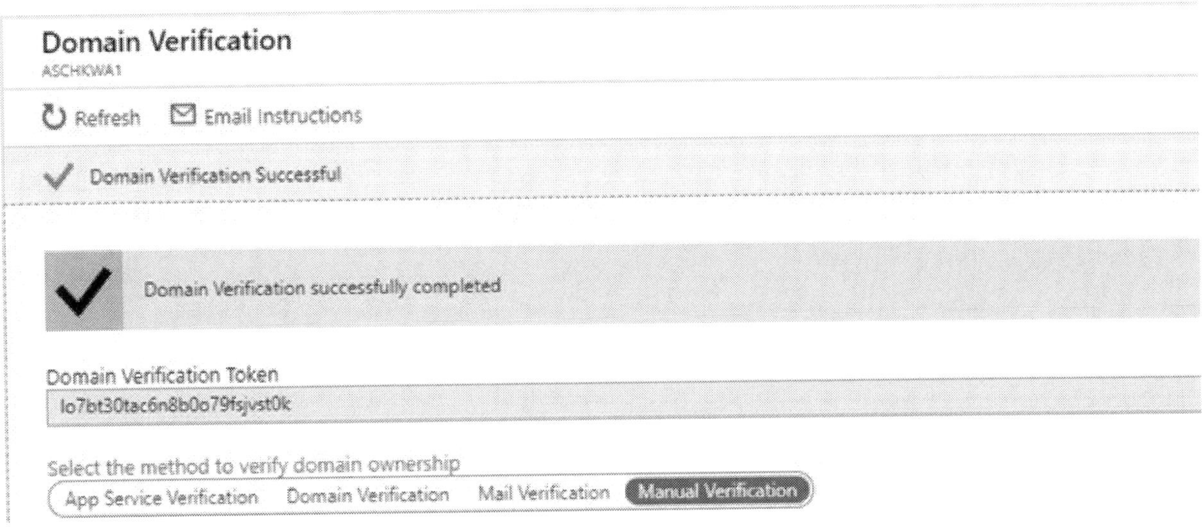

In App Service Certificate Dashboard you can see that Step 1 & 2 are completed. In next exercise we will bind/Assign Certificate to Web App HKWA1.

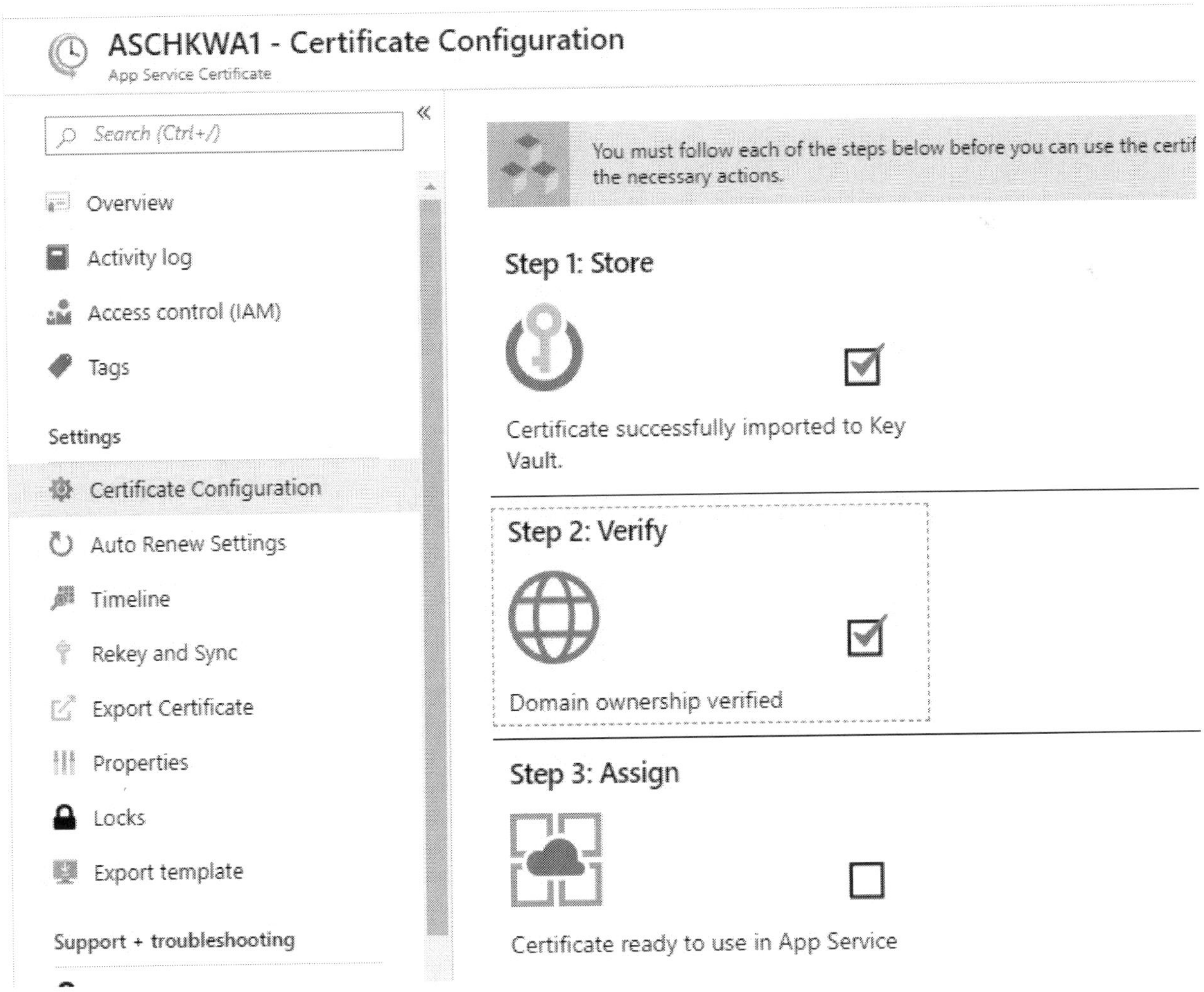

ASCHKWA1 - Certificate Configuration
App Service Certificate

Search (Ctrl+/)

Overview
Activity log
Access control (IAM)
Tags
Settings
Certificate Configuration
Auto Renew Settings
Timeline
Rekey and Sync
Export Certificate
Properties
Locks
Export template
Support + troubleshooting

You must follow each of the steps below before you can use the certif
the necessary actions.

Step 1: Store
Certificate successfully imported to Key Vault.

Step 2: Verify
Domain ownership verified

Step 3: Assign
Certificate ready to use in App Service

Assign SSL certificate to Web App

SSL Certificate allows secure connections from a web server to a browser. Once a secure connection is established, all web traffic between the web server and the web browser will be secure HTTPS.

Assigning SSL certificate to Web App is a 2 step process:

1. Upload SSL Certificate.
2. Bind your SSL Certificate.

To bind a custom SSL certificate to your web app, your App Service plan must be in the Basic, Standard, Premium or Isolated Tier.

Bindings let you specify which certificate to use when responding to requests to a specific hostname over HTTPS. SSL Binding requires valid private certificate (.pfx) issued for the specific hostname.

SSL Type Options

SNI SSL - Multiple SNI-based SSL bindings may be added. This option allows multiple SSL certificates to secure multiple domains on the same IP address. Most modern browsers (including Internet Explorer, Chrome, Firefox, and Opera) support SNI (find more comprehensive browser support information at Server Name Indication).
IP-based SSL - Only one IP-based SSL binding may be added. This option allows only one SSL certificate to secure a dedicated public IP address.

Note: In next Exercise we will upload App Service Certificate ASCHKWA1 to Web App HKWA1. App Service Certificate ASCHKWA1 was created in previous Exercise.

Exercise 12: Upload & Bind SSL Certificate

1. Go to Web App HKWA1 dashboard and Click TLS/SSL Settings in left pane>In right pane click Private Key Certificates>Click + Import App Service Certificate > Import App Service Certificate blade opens> Select App Service Certificate ASCHKWA1 and click ok.

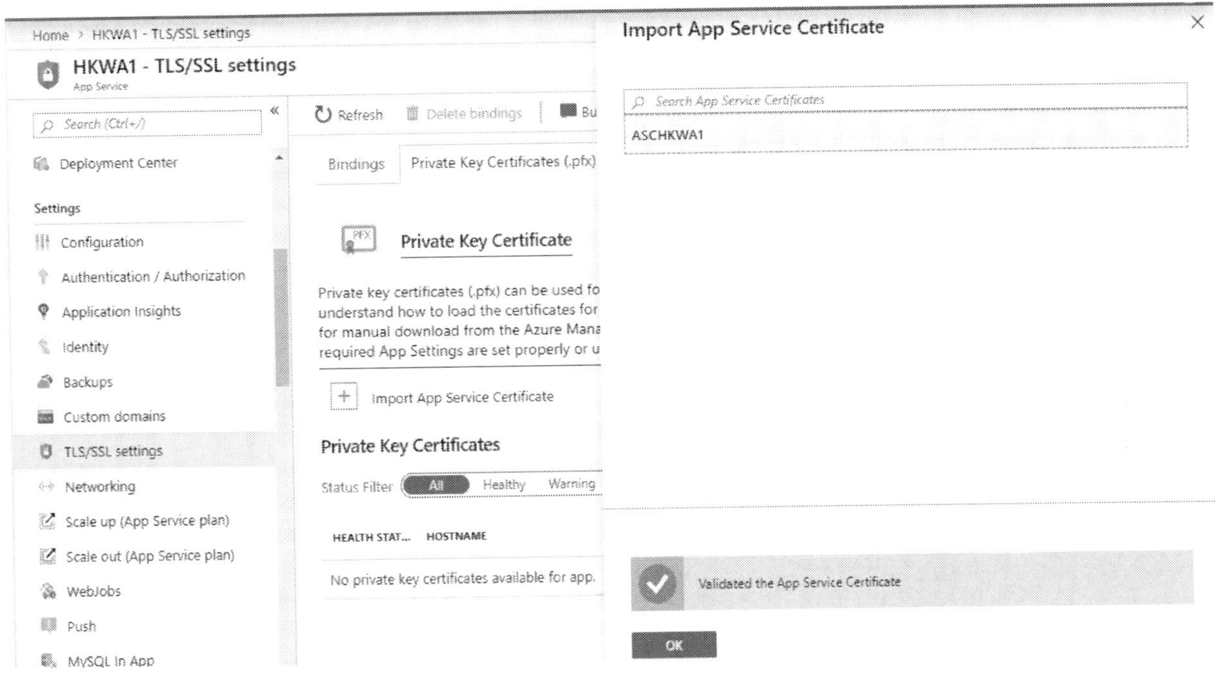

You can see the certificate is uploaded to Web App.

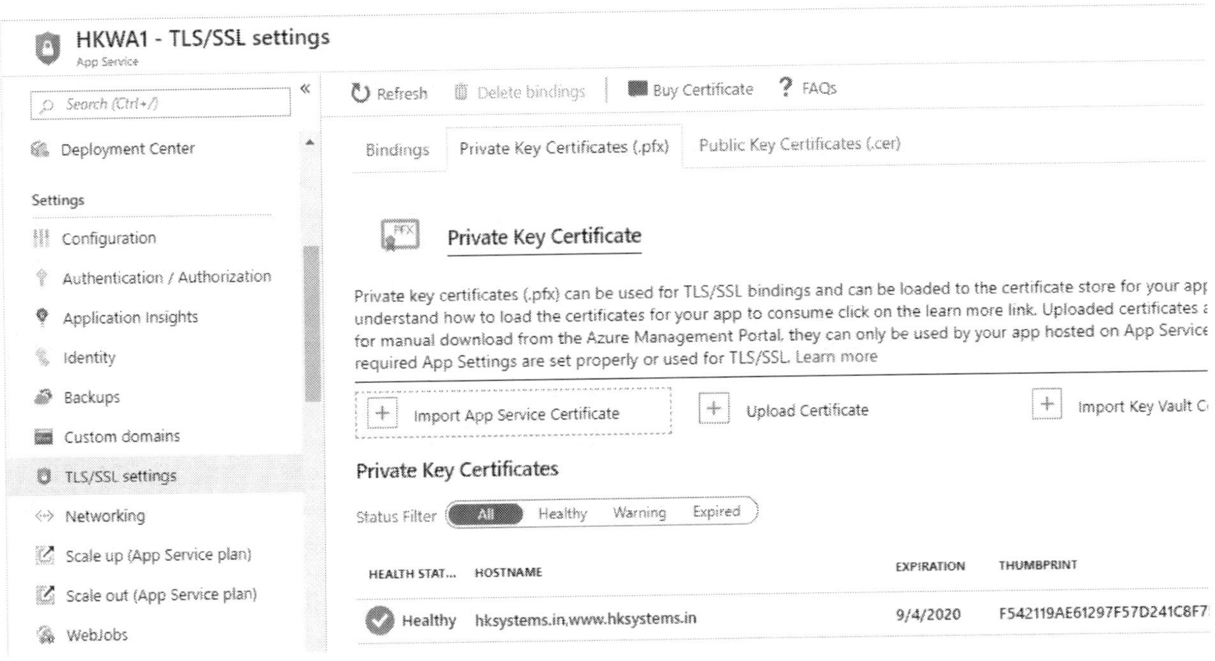

2. **Binding:** In TLS/SSL Setting pane Click Bindings in Right pane>Under TLS/SSL Binding Click +Add TLS/SSL Binding>TLS/SSL Binding Blade opens>In Custom Domain select www.hksystems.in>Select your Private Certificate Thumbprint from dropdown box> In TLS/SSL select SNI SSL>Click Add Binding (Not Shown).

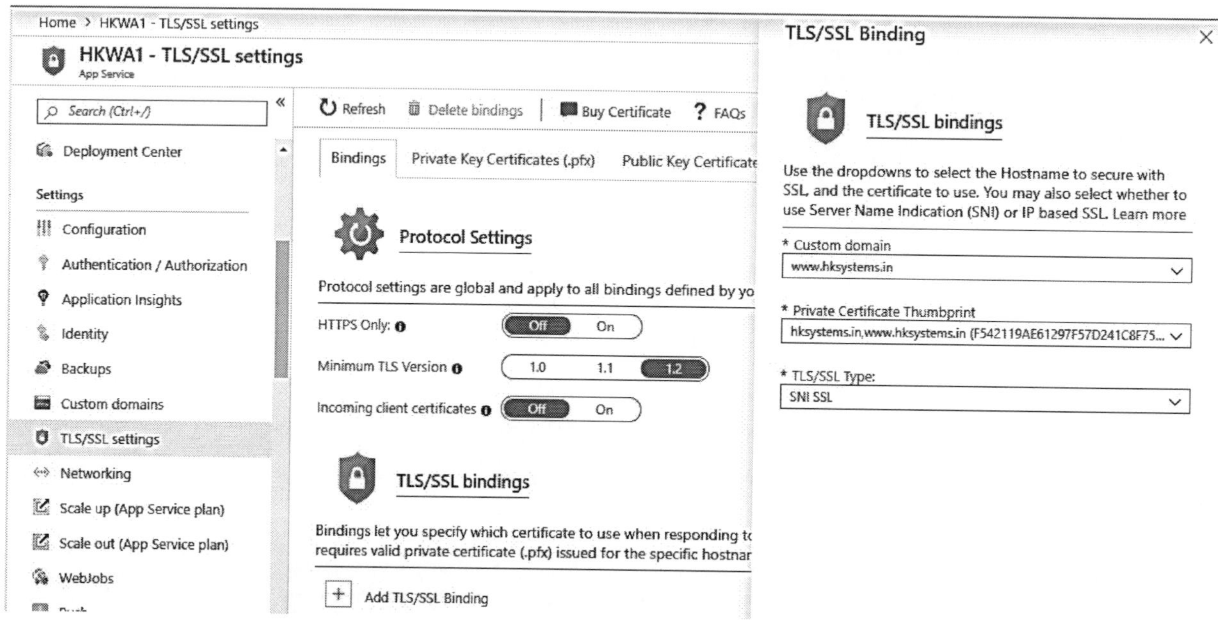

3. **Verify HTTPS Access.** Open browser and enter https://www.hksystems.in. You can see the lock button in browser bar which verifies that it is a secure https access.

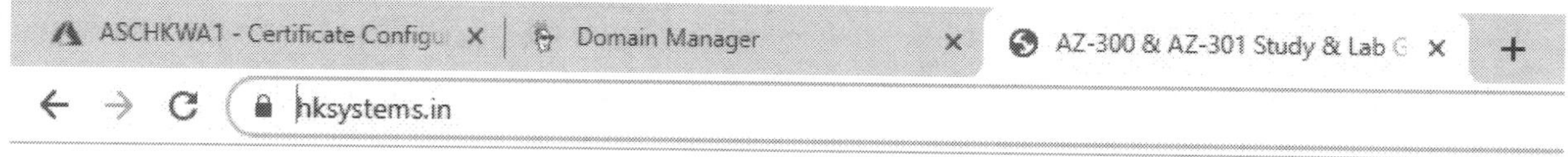

Exam AZ-300 & AZ-301 Study & Lab Guide

Exam AZ-300 & AZ-301 Study & Lab Guide prepares you for Azure Solutions Architect Expert Certification.

Author: Harinder Kohli

Click on the lock button in browser bar and then click on certificate.

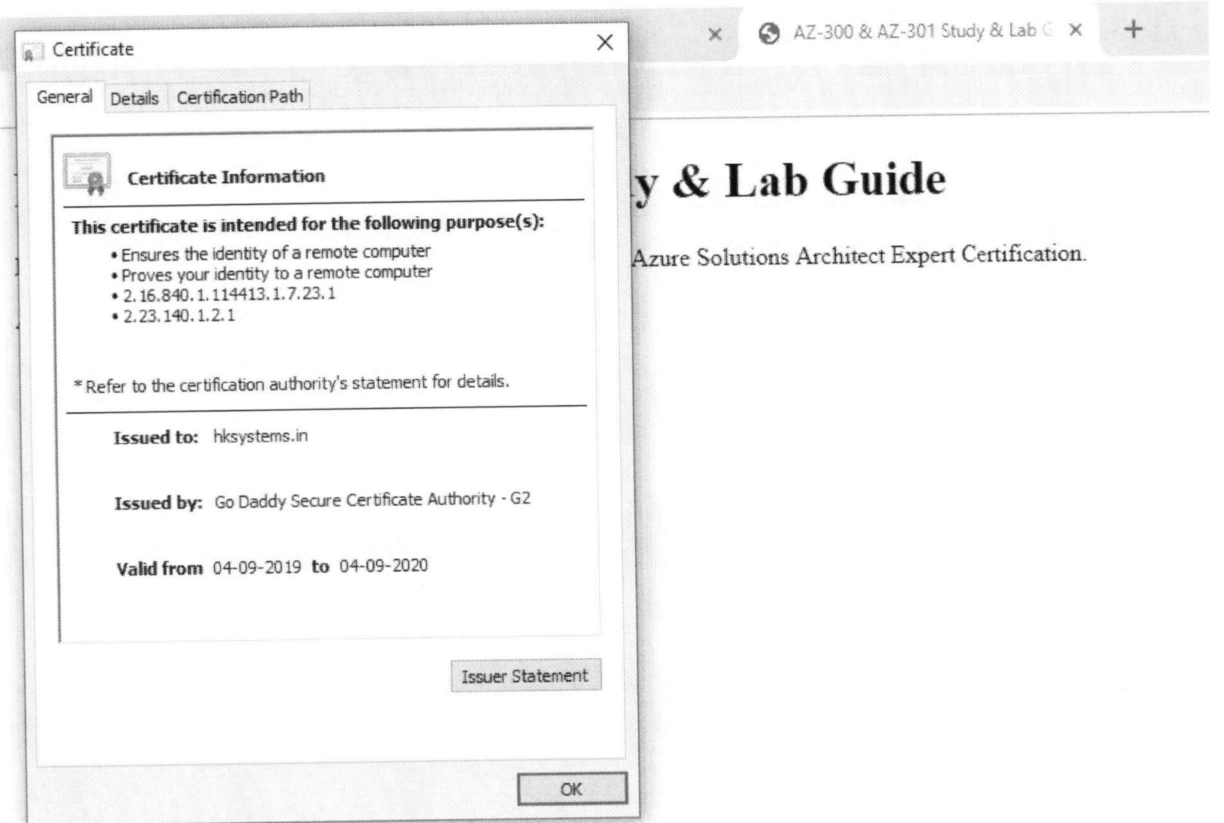

Website Authentication with identity providers

You can add authentication to your website. Web App supports multiple authentication providers. App Service supports five identity providers out of the box: Azure Active Directory, Facebook, Google, Microsoft Account, and Twitter.

The biggest benefit of Web App authentication feature is that you don't have to add any code in the application to enable Web App Authentication.

Exercise 13: Enabling Authentication/Authorization

In this exercise we will enable Authentication on Web App HKWA1 using Azure AD Option.

In Web App HKWA1 Dashboard Click Authentication/Authorization in left Pane> In Right pane Under App Service Authentication select On> Under **Action to take** select Log in with Azure Active Directory.

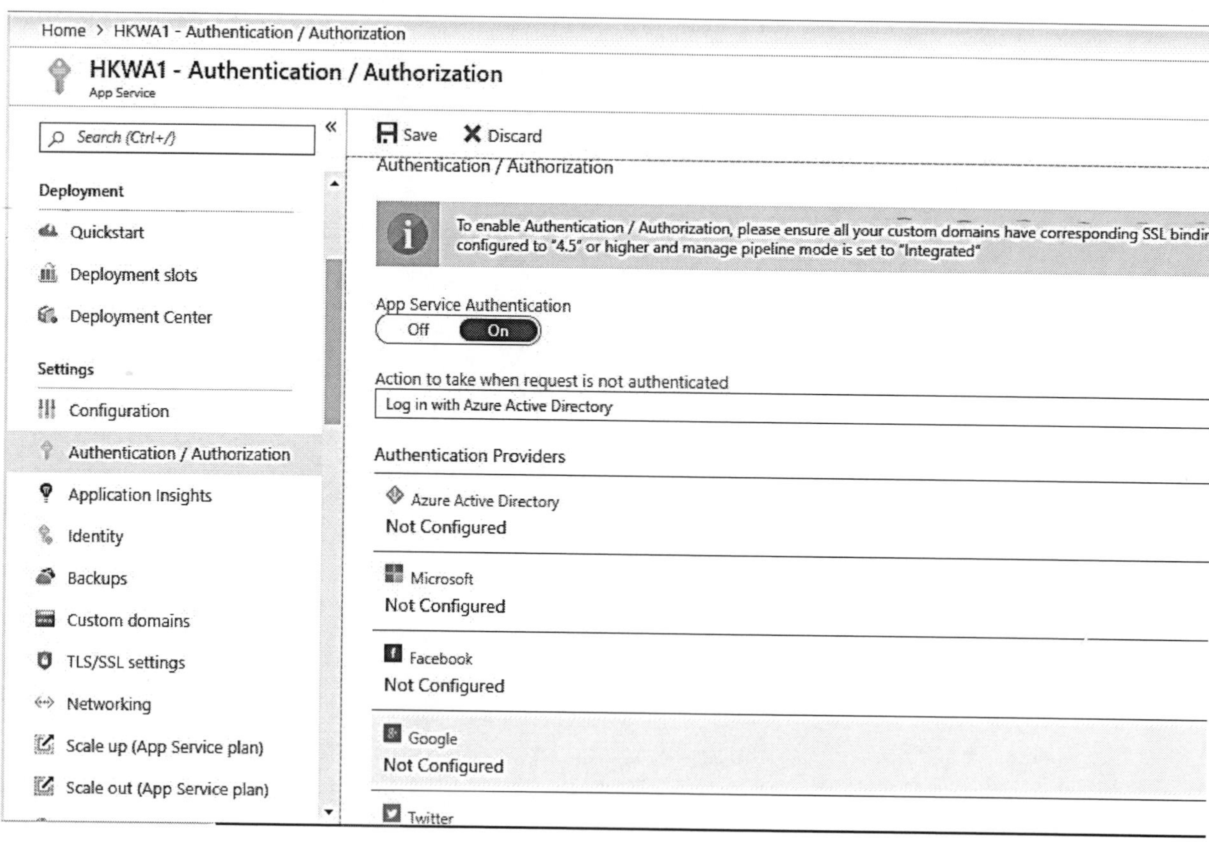

Under Authentication Providers Click Azure Active Directory and Azure Active Directory Settings Blade opens>In Management mode select Express> Rest Select Default Values>Click OK>Click **Save**.

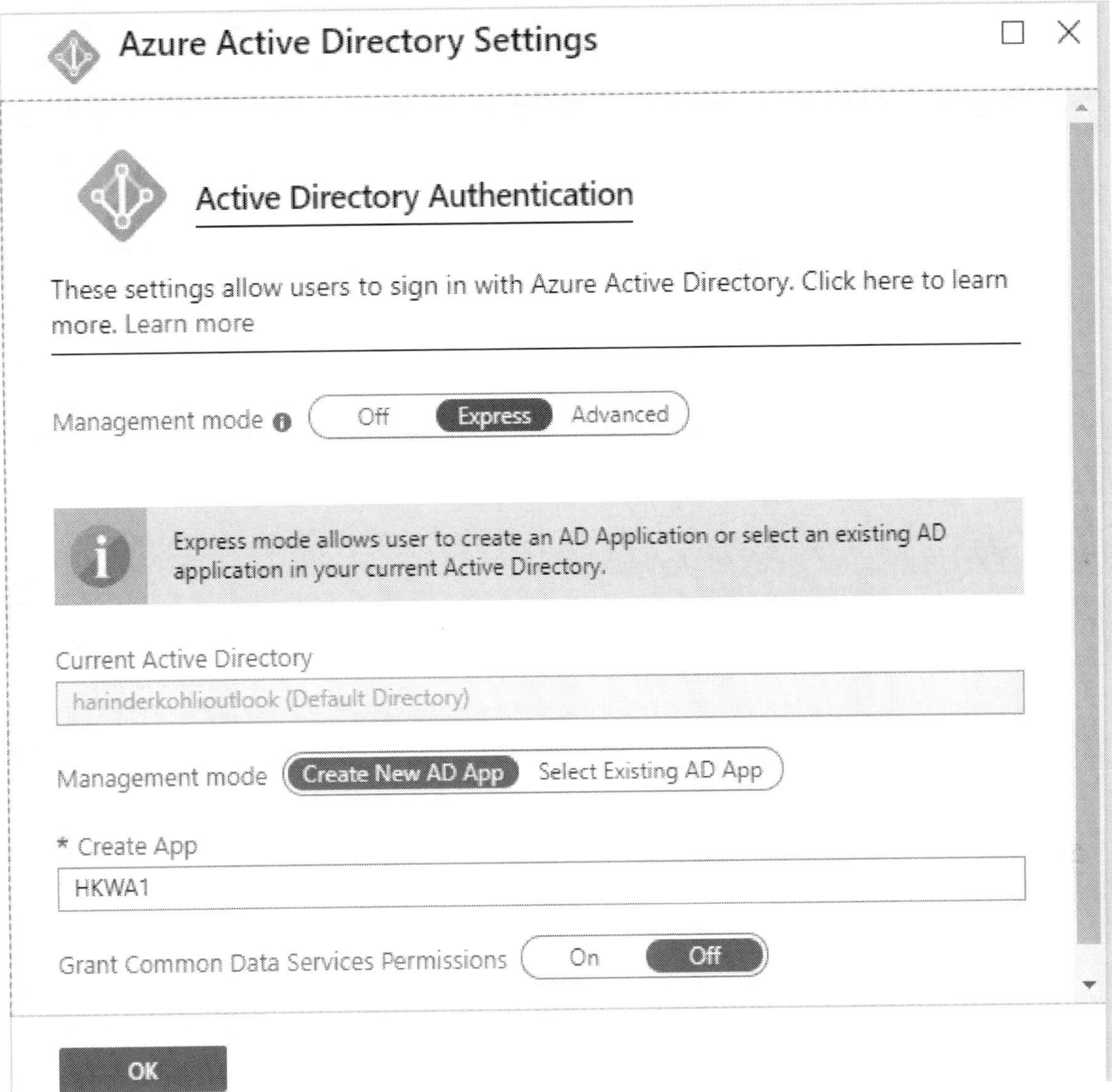

3. Open Firebox browser and https:// www.hksystems.in. Website is asking for authentication. I entered User1 credentials (user1@harinderkohlioutlook.onmicrosoft.com) and password. Azure AD user User1 was created in Exercise 101, Chapter 12 in Part 1 of the book.

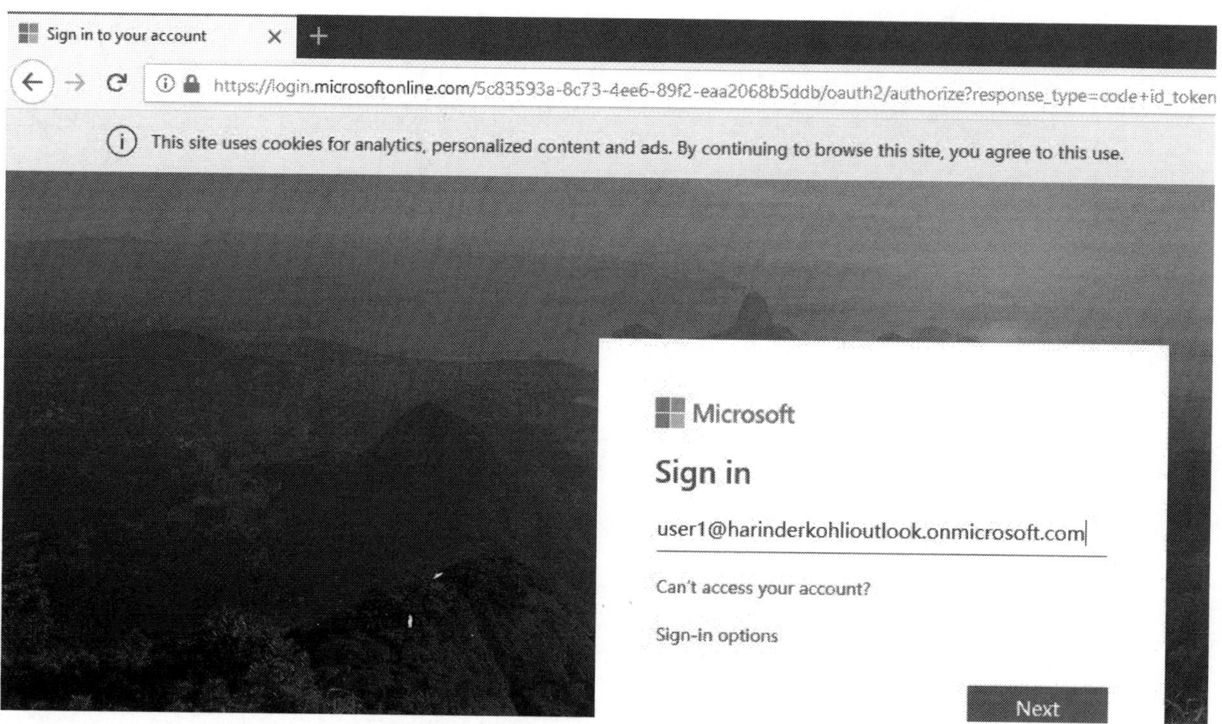

After Authentication Web App HKWA1 custom website opens as shown below.

Exam AZ-300 & AZ-301 Study & Lab Guide

Exam AZ-300 & AZ-301 Study & Lab Guide prepares you for Azure Solutions Architect Expert Certification.

Author: Harinder Kohli

From above you can see that you can enable authentication on Web App without adding any code in the application.

4. Disable App Service Authentication as we no longer require it.

Web App Scale Up

With Scale Up option you can add more CPU, Memory, Disk Space and other features to your Web App.

You can scale up by changing the pricing tier of the App Service plan that your app belongs to.

Exercise 14: Web App Scale Up

1. In Web App HKWA1 Dashboard Click Scale Up in left pane>In Right pane you can choose App Service Plan as per your requirement. Currently our App Service Plan is S1. You can Scale up to P1V2 or P2V2 etc. Click link see additional options to see more pricing tiers.

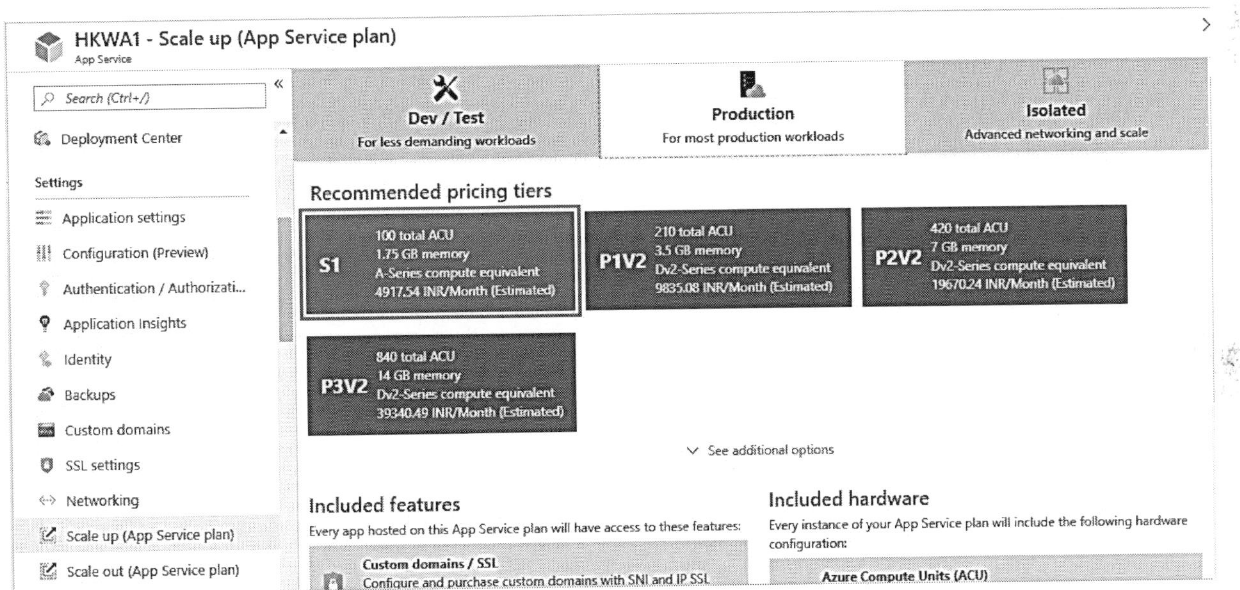

Note: We are not changing any settings here.

Web App Scale out (Manual or Autoscaling)

Web App Scale out option increases the number of Web App instances that run your app. You can scale out to as many as 20 instances, depending on your pricing tier. App Service Environments in **Isolated tier** further increases your scale-out count to 100 instances.

Web Apps can be **scaled out manually** by setting the instance count or can **automatically scale out (Autoscaling)** based on pre-set metrics. Pre-set metrics can be based on Web App CPU or Memory % or External Metrics such as Azure Storage Queue length etc.

With Autoscaling, Web App instances can be added (scale-out) or removed (scale-in) automatically based on rules configured for metrics (CPU utilization, Memory utilization, Storage Queue etc.).

The important point here is load balancing between Web app instances is automatic and you don't have to set any load balancer.

Exercise 15: Web App Manual scale out

In Web App Dashboard click Scale Out in left Pane> In Right pane make sure Manual Scale box is selected> Under Manual Scale enter the number of instances as per your requirement.

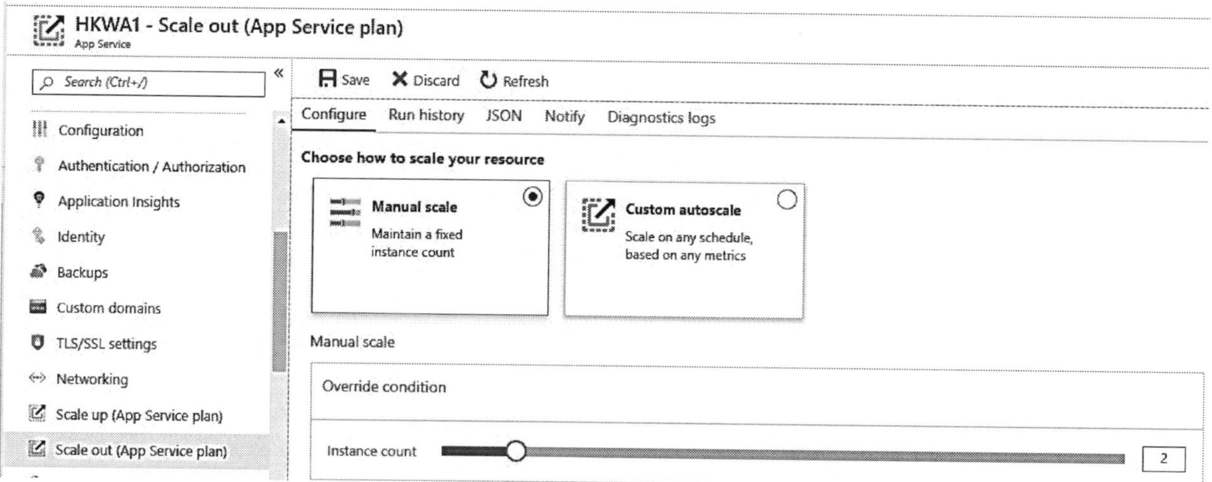

Note: We are not changing any settings here so don't click save.

Exercise 16 Web App Autoscaling

In this Exercise we will enable Autoscaling and create Scale-out rule based on CPU Percentage utilization. If Percentage CPU utilization is greater than 70% for a period of 10 minutes than 1 instance of Web App will be added. We will not create Scale-in rule as we are keeping both default and minimum instances at 1 only.

Scale-out rule increases the Instance count. **Scale-in rule** decreases the instance count. To create Scale-out rule you need to select **increase count by** from dropdown box under operation. To create Scale-in rule you need to select **decrease count by** from dropdown box under operation.

1. In Web App Dashboard click Scale Out in left Pane> In Right pane select Custom autoscale box>Configure Custom Autoscale Blade opens below>Enter name and Select Resource Group RGWA>Select Scale based on Metric> In instances limit keep the default values of 1,2 & 1.

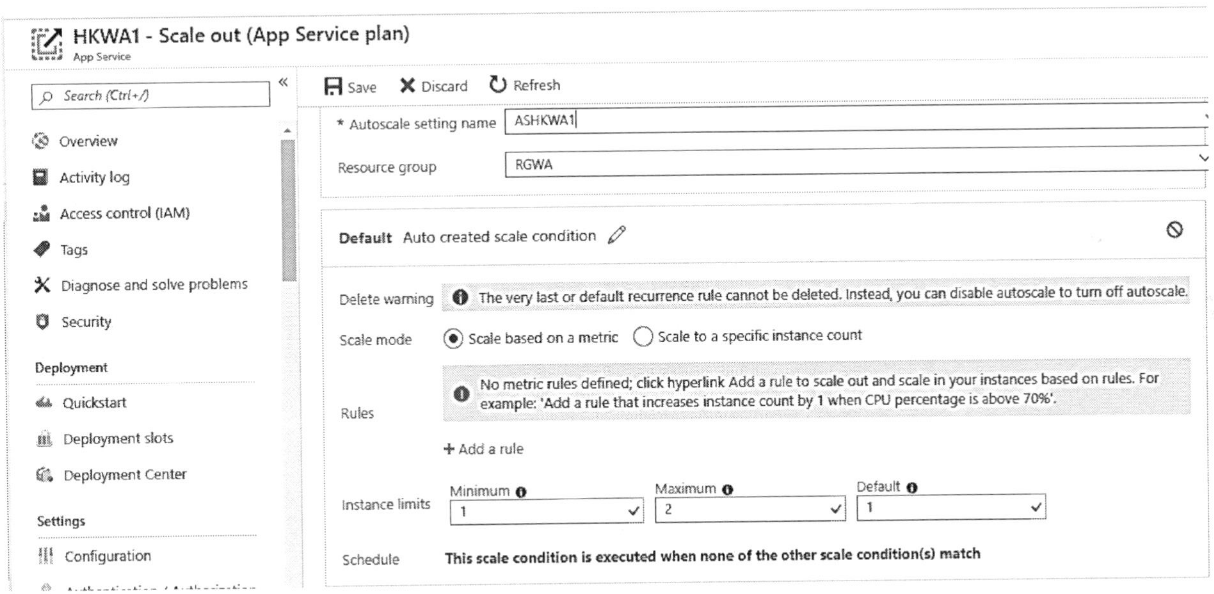

Note +**Add a rule** option in right pane. We will use this to create Scale-out rule.

2. **Add Scale-Out Rule**: Click + **Add a Rule** link>Scale Rule blade opens> Select CPU % in Metric Name Box> In operation Box Under Action select **increase count by**> **Leave other values as default**>Click Add.

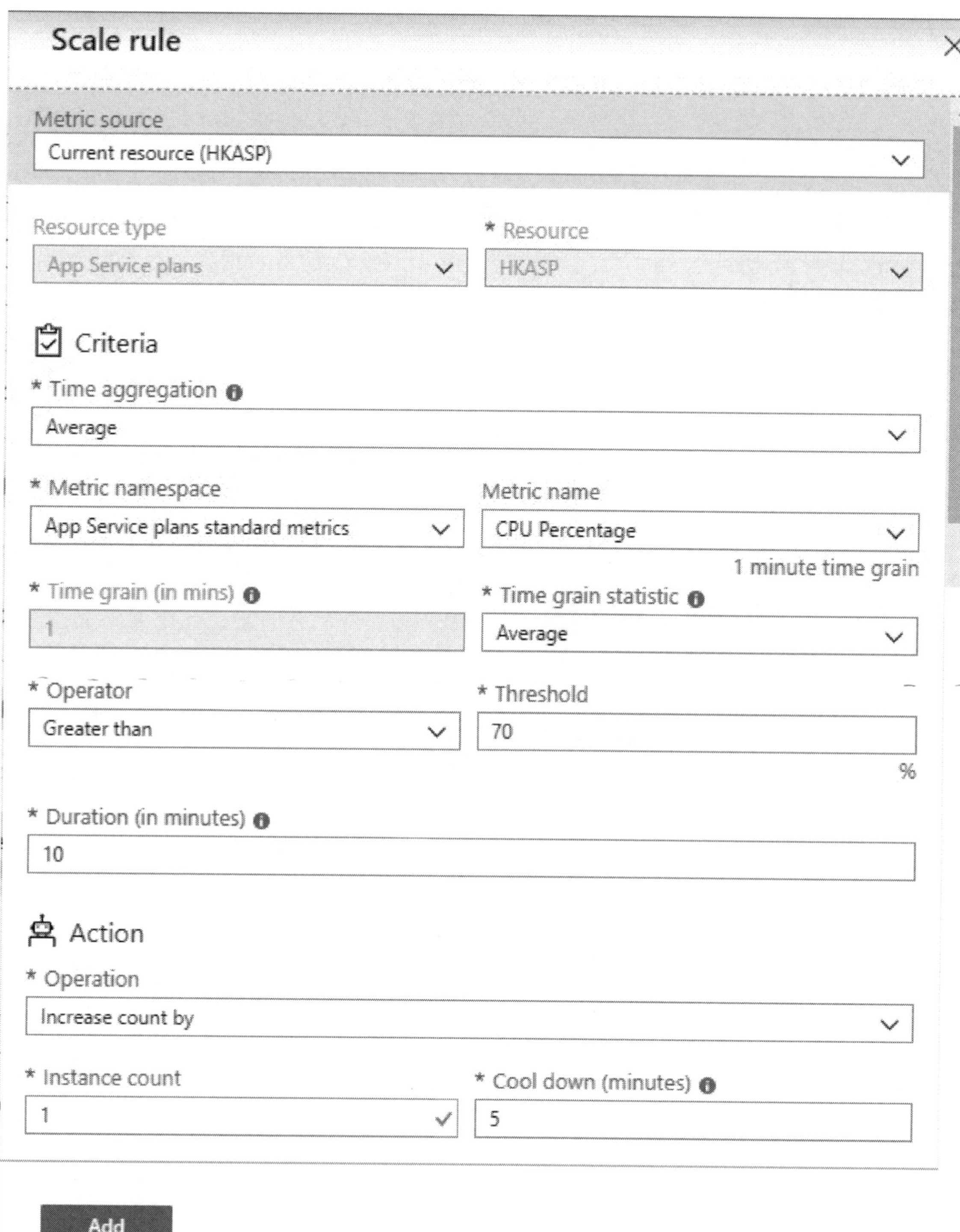

3. In scaling pane you can see the Scale-out rule created> **Click Save.**

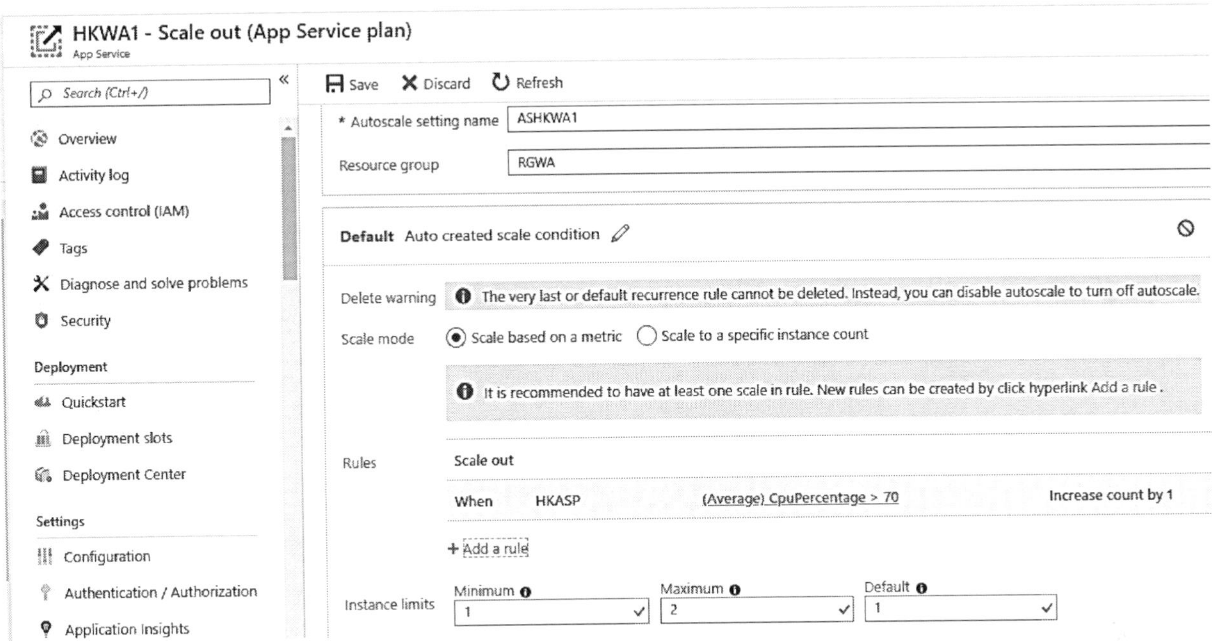

Note: Autoscaling was discussed in detail in Part 1 Book.

Website Performance Test

You can test your website response time, CPU and memory usage against varying user load **without creating elaborate testing infrastructure.** This can help you choose the right web app edition and to choose the right number of instances to deploy.

Exercise 17: Configuring Performance Test

In this exercise we will create performance test with 250 user load.

1. In Web App HKWA1 Dashboard Click Performance Test under Development tools in left pane.

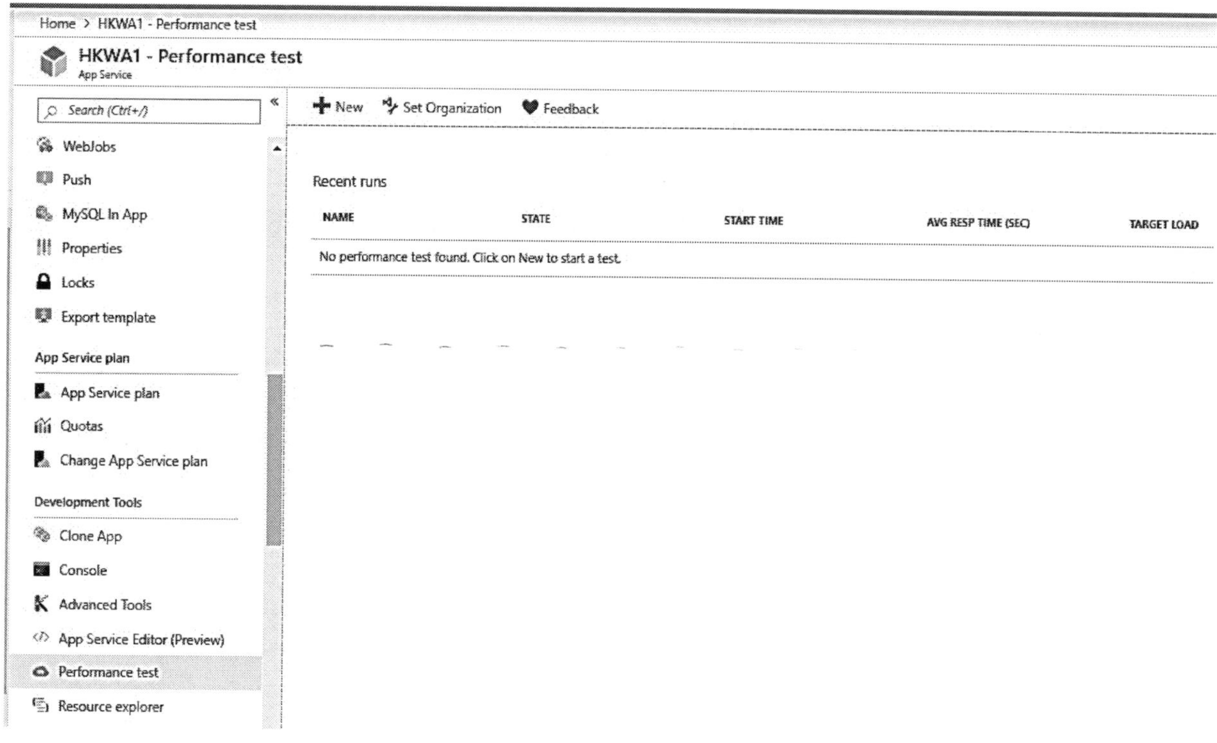

2. Click +New in right pane> New Performance Test Blade opens>Keep all values at default>Click Run Test (Not Shown).

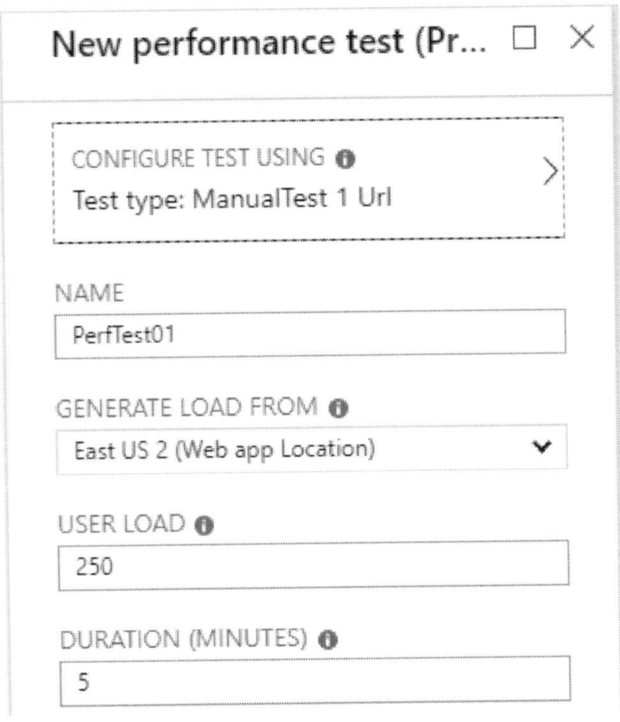

3. **Monitor test**: In HKWA1 Dashboard you can see the newly created test with name PerfTest01. It is showing in Progress.

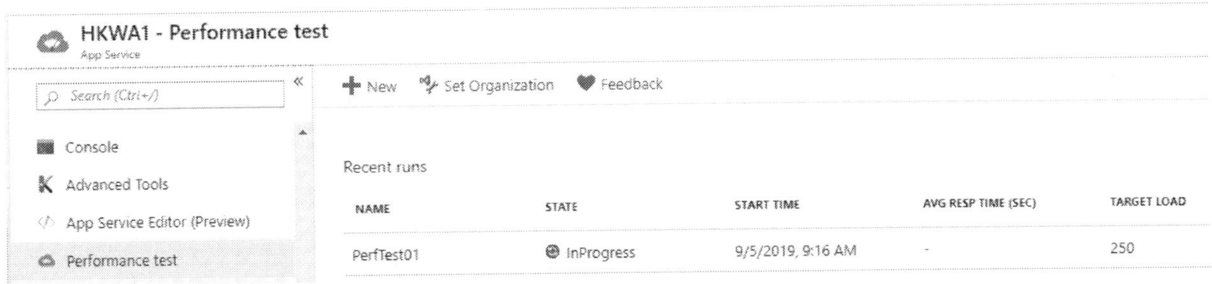

4. After 5-6 minutes click the PerfTest01>PerfTest01 Blade opens> You can see all requests to Web App were successful.

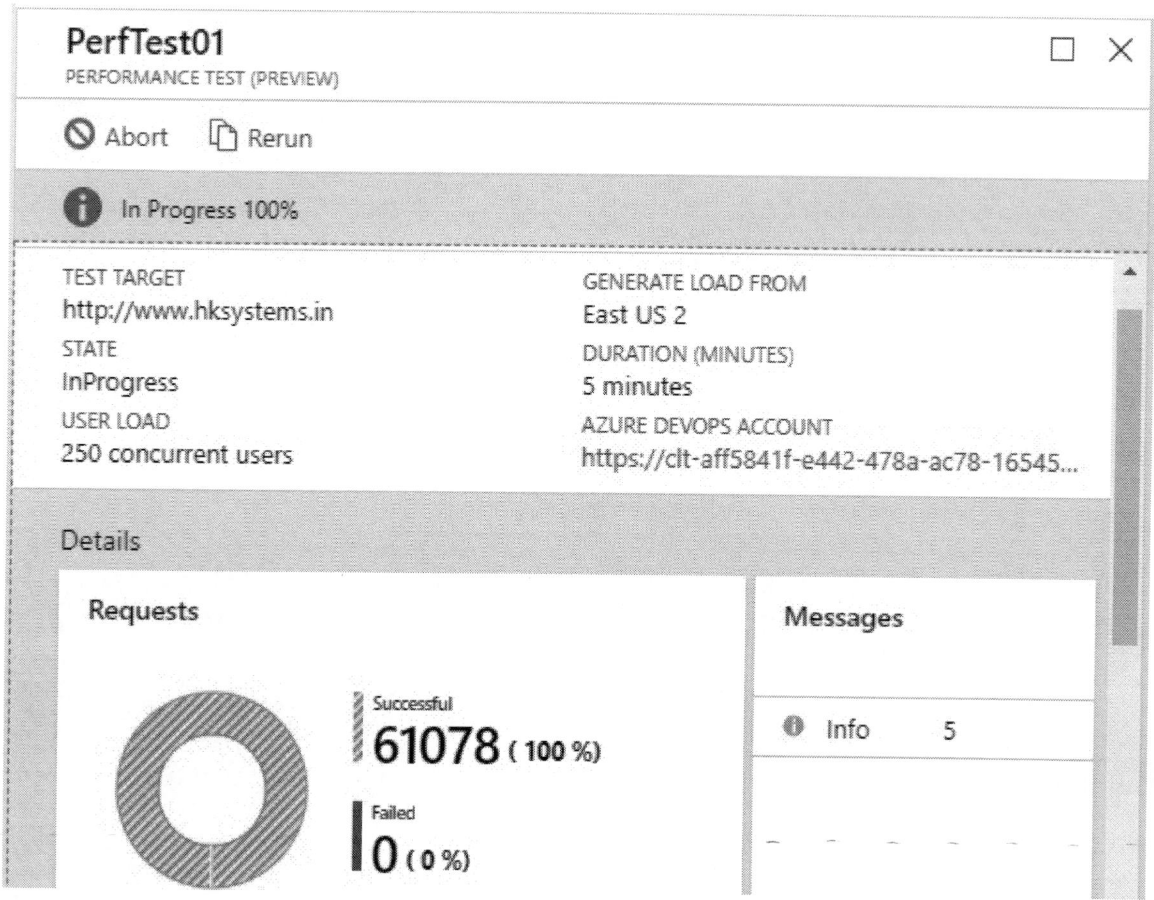

5. Scroll down and you will see performance graph under full load and CPU & Memory graph.

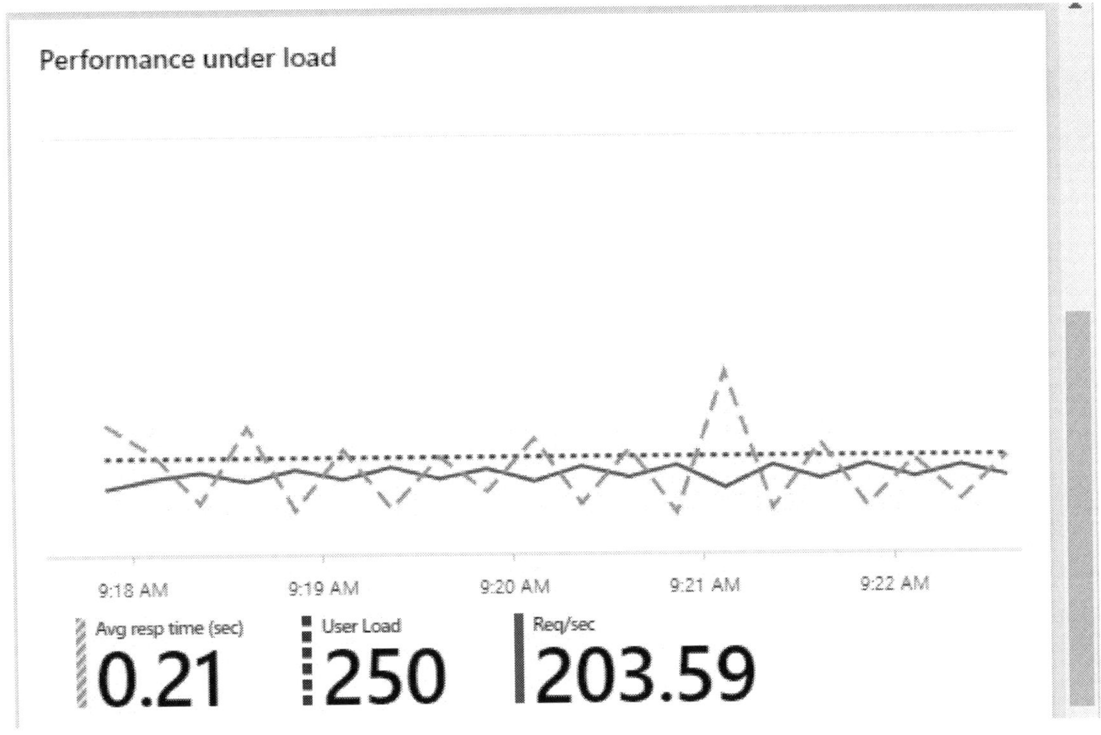

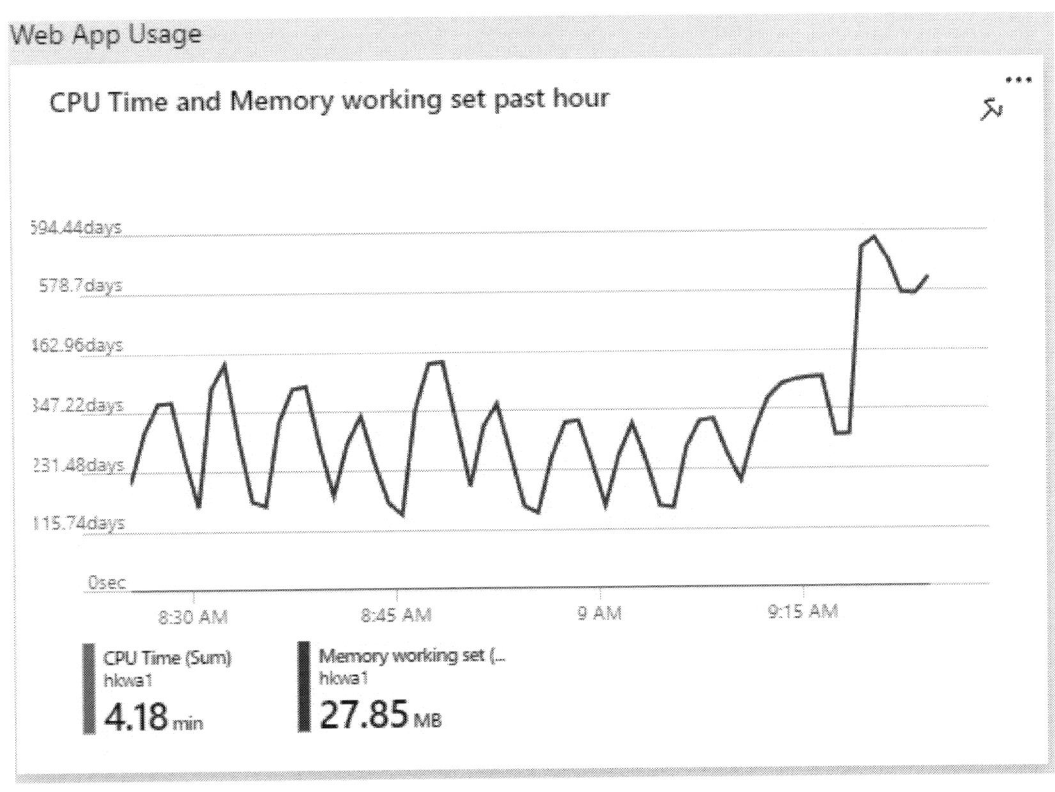

Diagnostics logging for Apps in Azure App Service

App Service provides diagnostic functionality for logging information from both the web server and the web application. These are logically separated into **web server diagnostics** and **application diagnostics**.

Web Server diagnostics

You can enable or disable the following kinds of logs for Web Server.

Detailed Error Logging - Detailed information for any request that results in HTTP status code 400 or greater.
Failed Request Tracing - Detailed information on failed requests, including a trace of the IIS components used to process the request and the time taken in each component. It's useful if you want to improve site performance or isolate a specific HTTP error.
Web Server Logging - Information about HTTP transactions using the W3C extended log file format. It's useful when determining overall site metrics such as the number of requests handled or how many requests are from a specific IP address.

Application Diagnostics

Application diagnostics allows you to capture information produced by a web application. When you enable **application diagnostics**, you also choose the **Level**. The following table shows the categories of logs each level includes:

Level	Included log categories
Error	Error, Critical
Warning	Warning, Error, Critical
Information	Info, Warning, Error, Critical
Verbose	Trace, Debug, Info, Warning, Error, Critical

For **Web server logging**, you can select **storage** or **file system**.
Selecting **storage** allows you to select a storage account, and then a blob container that the logs are written to.
If you store logs on the **file system**, the files can be accessed by FTP or downloaded as a Zip archive by using Azure CLI.

How to Download logs

Logs are stored in Logfiles folder.
Connect to Web App using FTP and go to LogFiles folder to download the logs.

Exercise 18: Enabling and downloading Web App Diagnostic Logs

1. In Web App dashboard click App Service logs under monitoring>In right pane enables log as per your requirement and click save. I enabled Application logging, Web Server logging and failed request tracking.

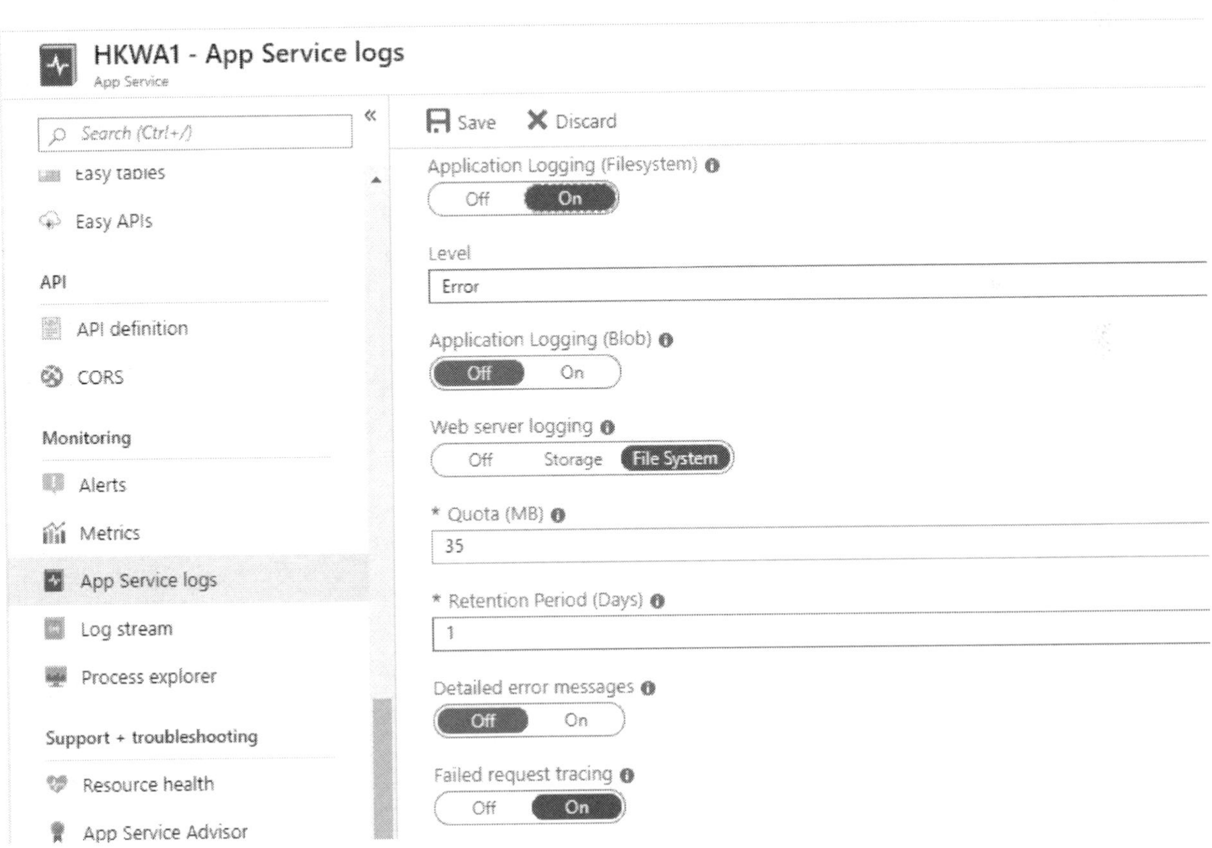

2. FTP to web App using Filezilla Client and Navigate to LogFiles Folder as shown below. Scroll down to see more folders under LogFiles. Click RawLogs Folder and you can see a text file in Filename pane. You can right click the text document to download it.
   Note: How to log on to Web App using FTP was shown in Exercise 5.

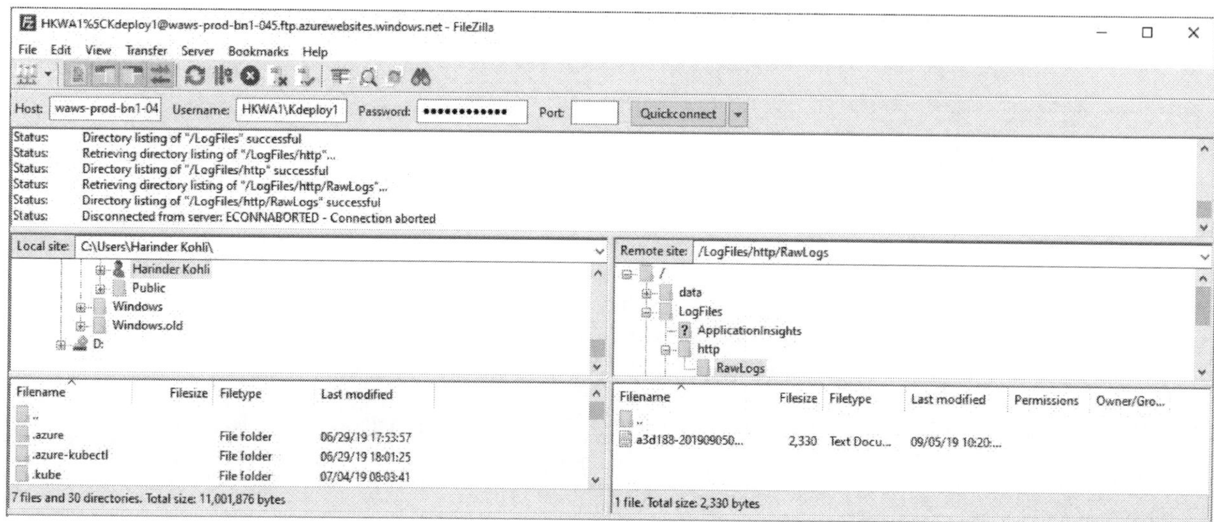

Application Insights

Application Insights is a Managed Application Performance Management (APM) service for web applications running on **Web Apps**, Virtual Machines or Physical Servers in the cloud or on-premises.

Azure Application Insight monitor's live Web Application for **availability, performance, and usage.** You can also identify and diagnose errors in your application without waiting for a user to report them.

It works for apps on a wide variety of platforms including .NET, Node.js and J2EE, hosted on-premises or in the cloud. It integrates with DevOps process, and has connection points to a variety of development tools. It can monitor and analyze telemetry from mobile apps by integrating with Visual Studio App Center.

Parameters Monitored by Application Insights

Request rates, response times, and failure rates - Find out which pages are most popular, at what times of day, and where your users are. See which pages perform best. If your response times and failure rates go high when there are more requests, then perhaps you have a resourcing problem.
Dependency rates, response times, and failure rates - Find out whether external services are slowing you down.
Exceptions - Analyse the aggregated statistics, or pick specific instances and drill into the stack trace and related requests. Both server and browser exceptions are reported.
Page views and load performance - reported by your users' browsers.
AJAX calls from web pages - rates, response times, and failure rates.
User and session counts.
Performance counters from your Windows or Linux server machines, such as CPU, memory, and network usage.
Host diagnostics from Docker or Azure.
Diagnostic trace logs from your app - so that you can correlate trace events with requests.
Custom events and metrics that you write yourself in the client or server code, to track business events such as items sold or games won.

Architecture, Components and Working of Application Insight

The Figure below shows the Architect & Components of Application Insight (Shown in Purple Color) for Monitoring and Availability of Web Applications.

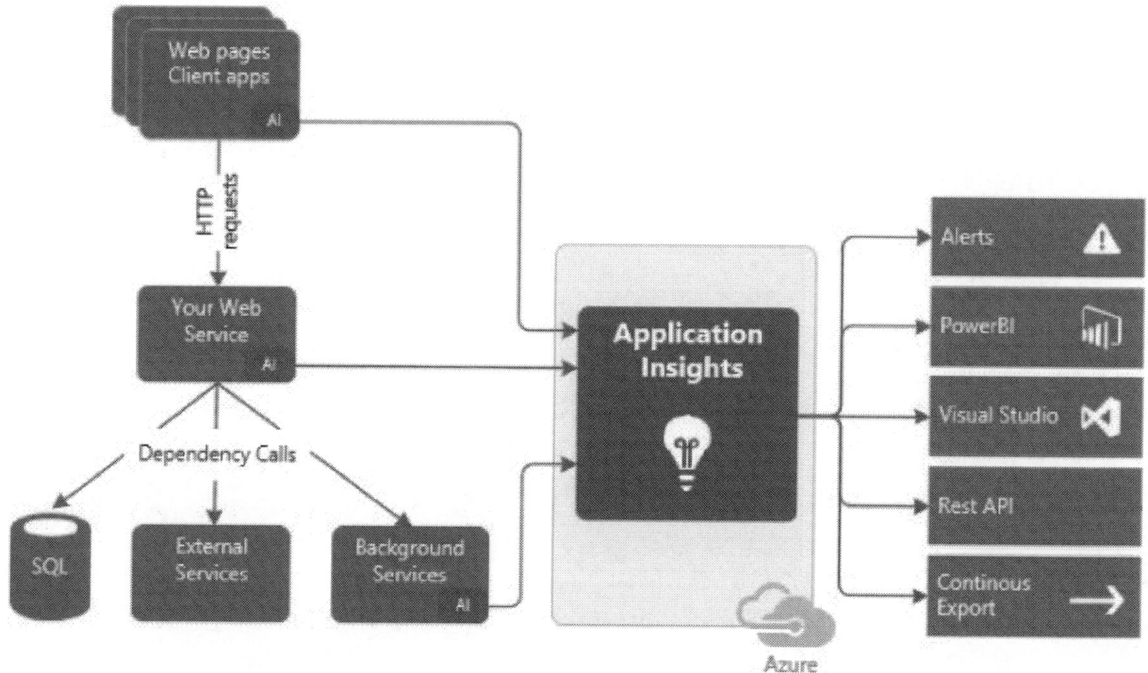

Components of Application Insight

Application Insight Managed Service in Azure.
Application Insight Agent in your application code.

Brief Working

1. Setup Application Insight Service in Azure.
2. Install Application Insight Agents in Applications running in Cloud or on-premises.
3. The Application Insight Agent monitors application and sends telemetry data to the portal.
4. You can Graphically view Application performance data in real time .
5. You can apply analytic and search tools to the raw data in Application Insight service in Azure.
6. You can setup alerts on the metrics which can trigger a response when threshold is breached.
7. You can export your data to Business Intelligence tools like Power BI.

Application Insight & Web App

During Installation of Web App in Exercise 2 we enabled Application Insight. Enabling Application Insight resulted in following:

Application Insight Managed Service was created in Azure.
Application Insight Agent was installed in Web App.

Exercise 19: Exploring Application Insight dashboard

1. In Web App Dashboard click Application Insight under settings>In Right pane click View Application Insights Data>Application Insight Dashboard opens as shown below..

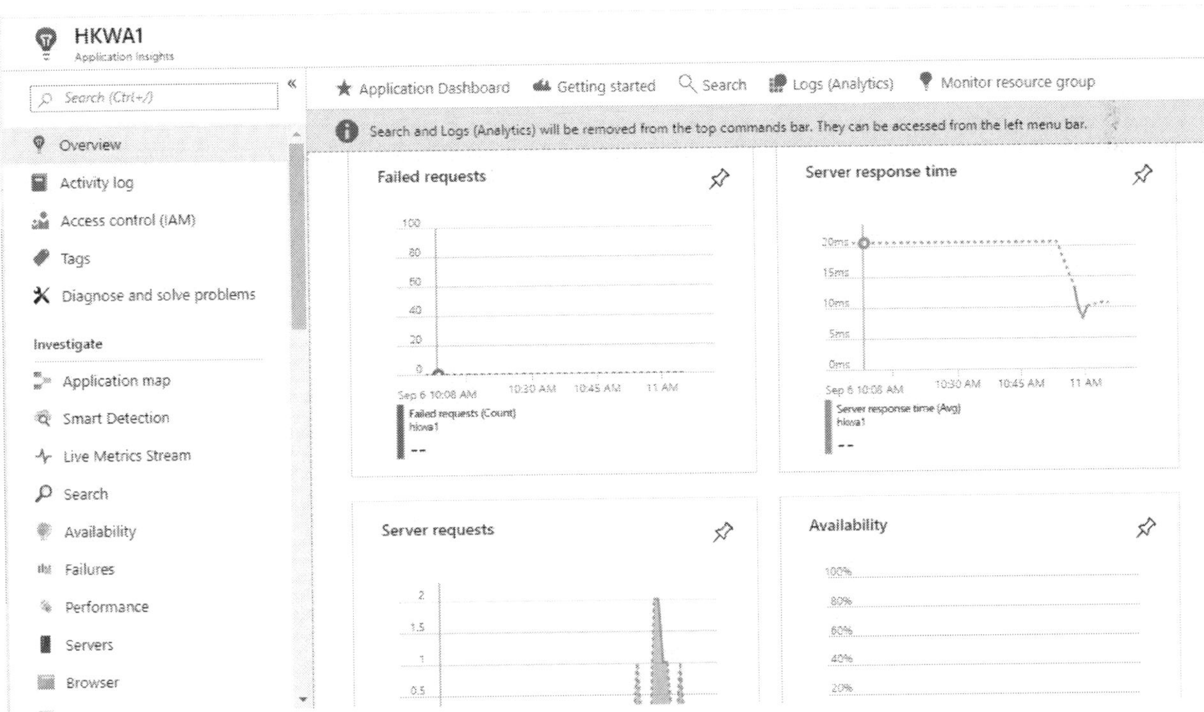

2. Click on Application Maps and you can see response time and number of calls made to Web App.

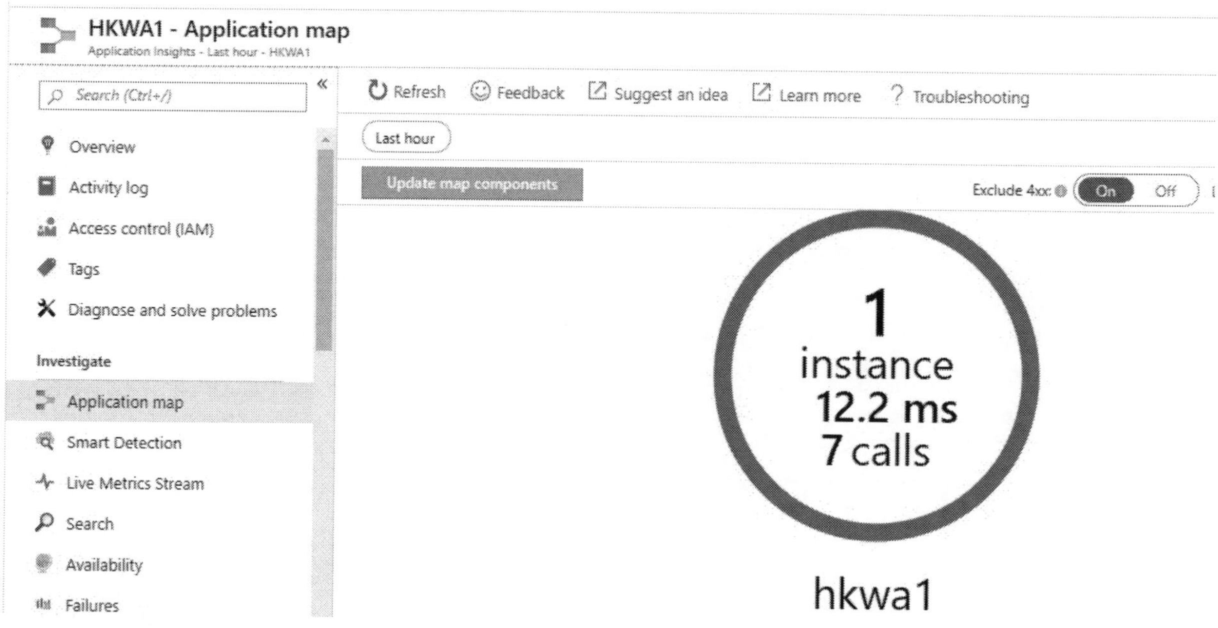

Application Insight Smart Detection

Smart Detection automatically warns you of potential performance problems in your web application. It performs proactive analysis of the telemetry that your app sends to Application Insights. If there is a sudden rise in failure rates, or abnormal patterns in client or server performance, you get an alert. This feature needs no configuration. It operates if your application sends enough telemetry.

You can access Smart Detection alerts both from the emails you receive, and from the Smart Detection blade.

Accessing Smart Dashboard: In Application Insight Dashboard click Smart detection in left pane> In Right pane click the link Click here to view detections from the last seven days> You can see that there are currently no detections.

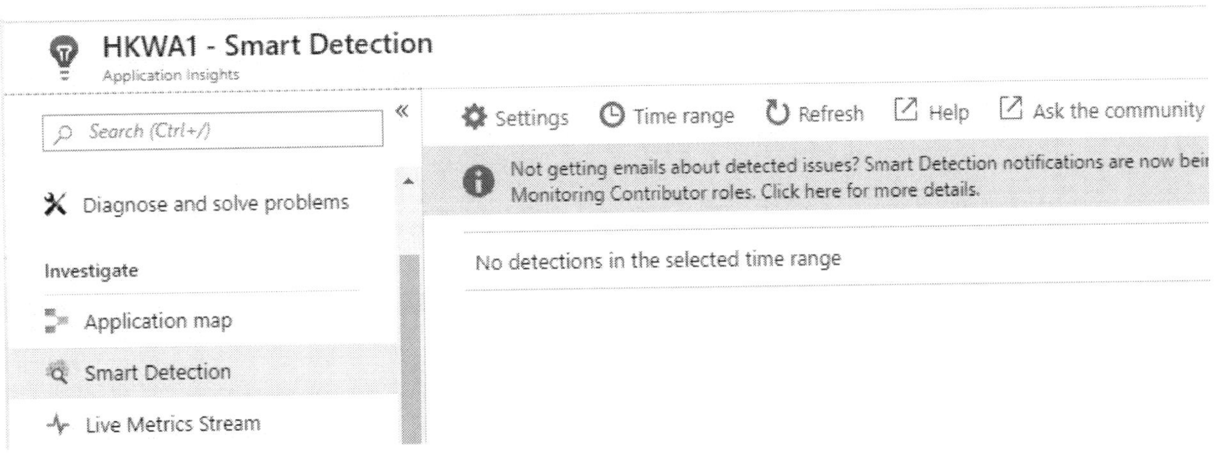

Web App Backup

By using Backup feature in Azure App Service you can create Web App backups manually or on a schedule. You can restore the app to a snapshot of a previous state by overwriting the existing app or restoring to another app.

Requirements for Backup Feature

1. The Backup and Restore feature requires the App Service plan to be in the **Standard** tier or **Premium** tier. **Premium** tier allows a greater number of daily backups than **Standard** tier.
2. Azure storage account and container are required in the same subscription as the app that you want to backup.
3. Using a firewall enabled storage account as the destination for your backups is not supported.
4. Backups can be up to 10 GB of app and database content. If the backup size exceeds this limit, you get an error.

What gets backed up

App configuration
File content

You have the option to include backup of Database connected to your app. The following database solutions are supported with backup feature:
SQL Database
Azure Database for MySQL
Azure Database for PostgreSQL
MySQL in-app

Backup Types

Manual Backup
Automated Backup by configuring Backup Schedule

Exercise 20: Manual Backup

For this Exercise we will use Storage Account sastdcloud and container hk410. sastdcloud & container hk410 were created in Chapter 8 in Azure Study & Lab Guide Part 1.

1. In Web App Dashboard Click Backup in left pane> Backup pane opens.

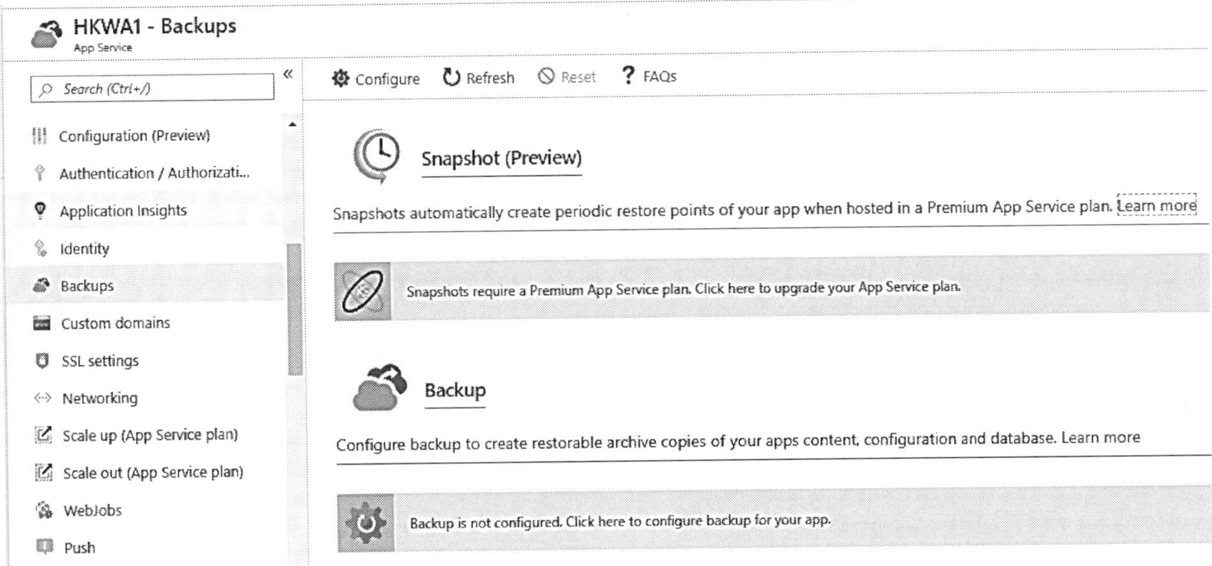

2. In right pane Under Backup click link Click here to configure backup for your App>Backup Configuration pane opens as shown below.

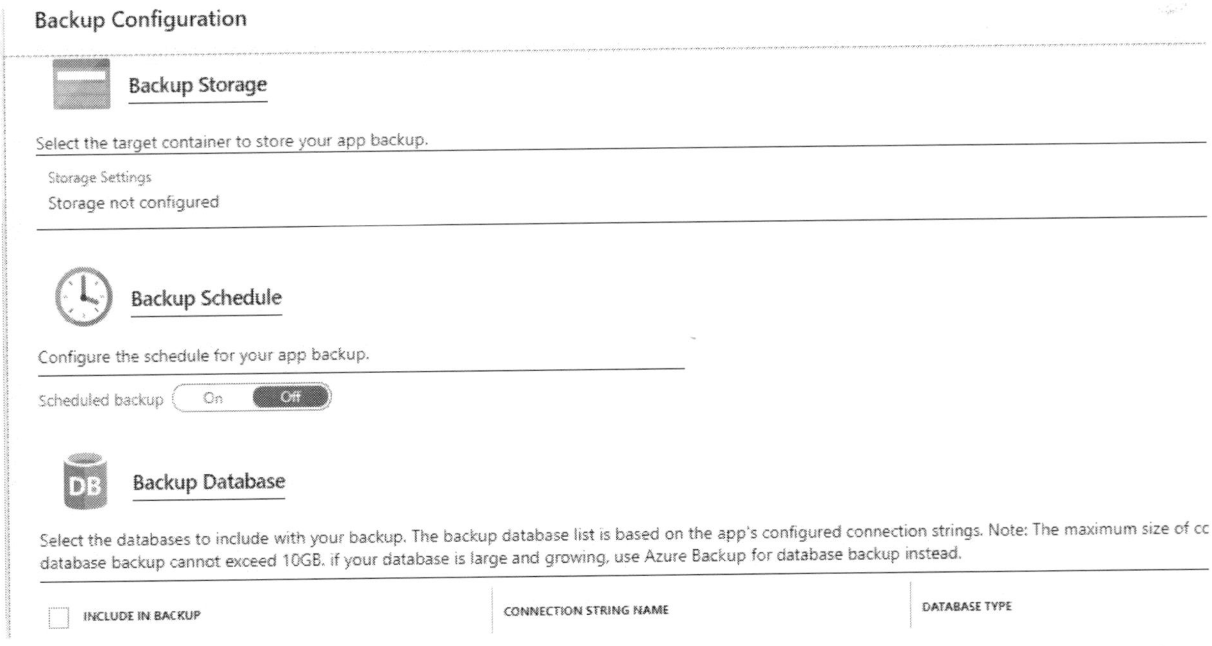

3. Under Backup Storage click Storage Settings> Click Storage Account sastdcloud> click Container hk410 and click select> Back in Backup Configuration pane you can see Container hk410 added under storage settings. Note the option to include database for Backup.

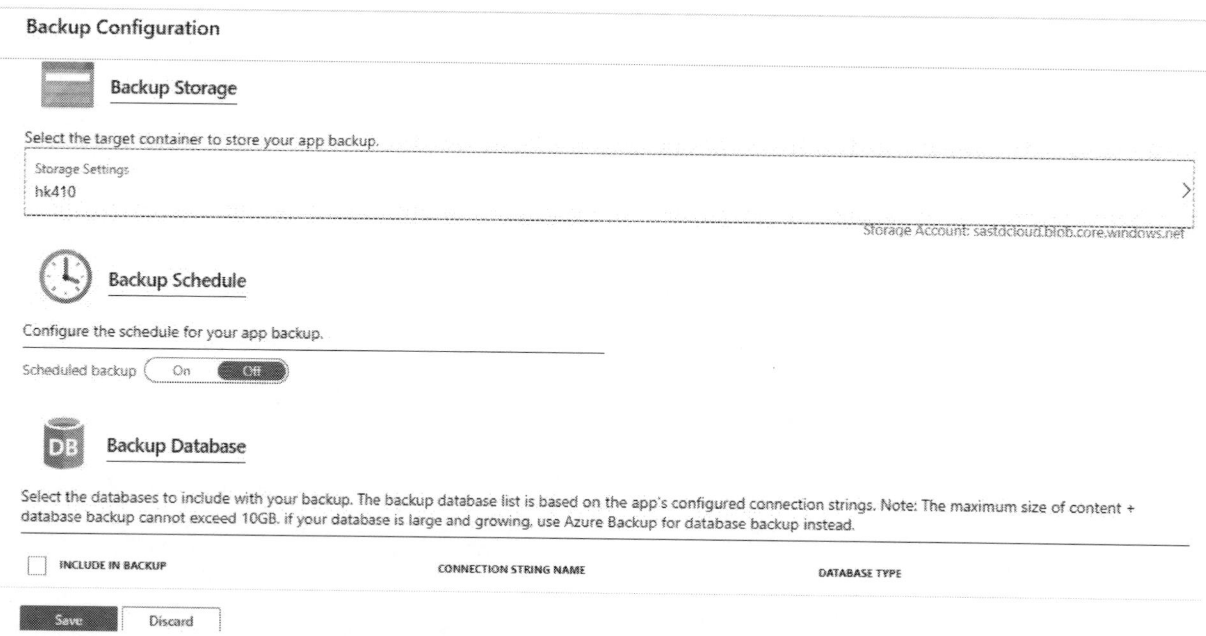

4. Click save. You are returned back to Backup pane which says backup configured.

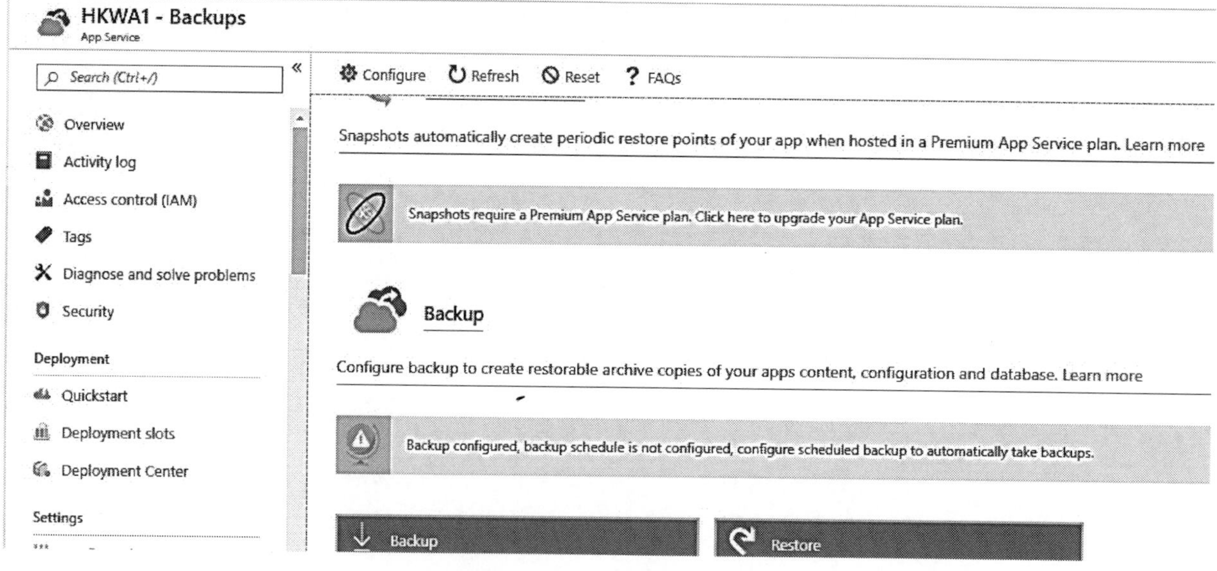

5. In backup page click Backup to start the backup. You can see the progress in the Back up pane. After Backup is complete you can see the Succeeded Status.
   Note: Once the storage account and container are configured, you can initiate a manual backup at any time.

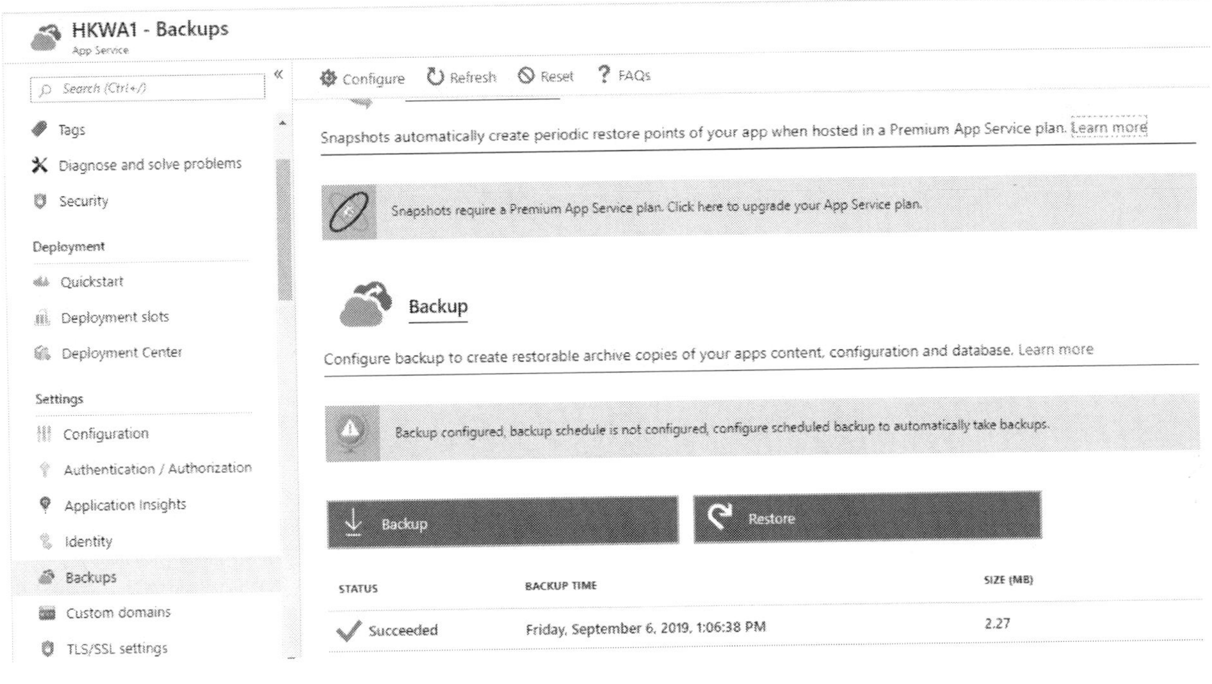

Exercise 21: Restoring Backup

In this lab we will just demonstrate how to restore Web App Backup but will not do any restore. You can restore the app to a previous state by overwriting the existing app or Create a new Web App.

In Backup pane as shown in previous figure click Restore> Restore Backup pane opens as shown below. Note the Restore destination options: Overwrite and New or Existing App.

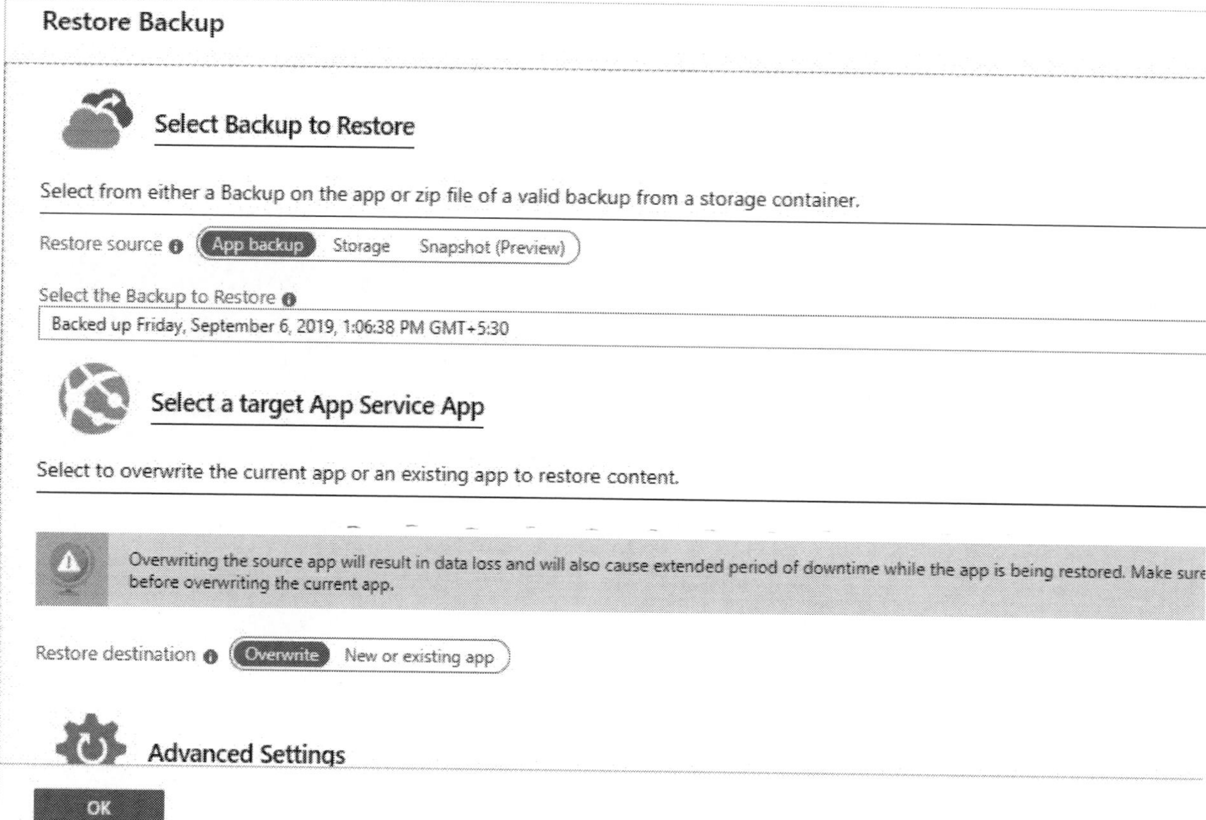

WebJobs

WebJobs enables you to run scripts or programs as background processes in the context of your app. WebJobs type can be Continuous or Triggered.

Continuous	Triggered
Starts immediately when the WebJob is created.	Starts only when triggered manually or on a schedule.
Runs on all instances that the web app runs on. You can optionally restrict the WebJob to a single instance.	Runs on a single instance that Azure selects for load balancing.

To add WebJobs: Click WebJobs in Left Pane> Click +Add> Add WebJob blade opens> Upload a file to run a script or program and choose other options as per your requirement and click ok.

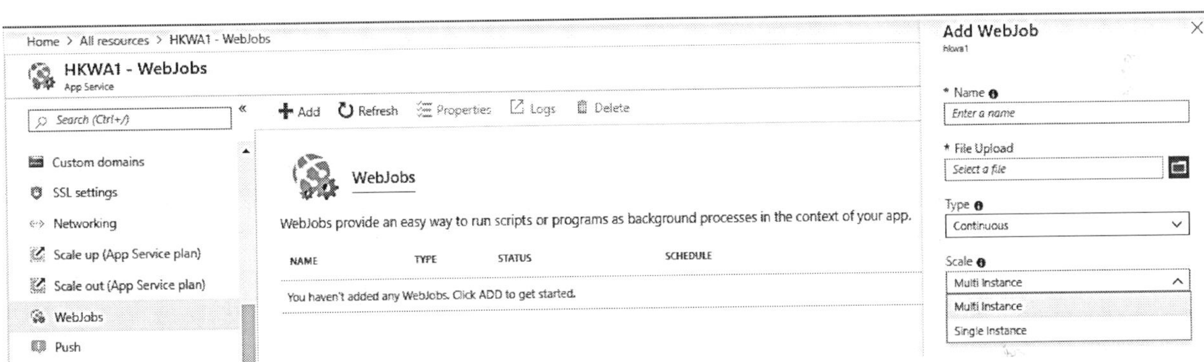

Supported file types for scripts or programs: The following file types are supported:

.cmd, .bat, .exe (using Windows cmd)
.ps1 (using PowerShell)
.sh (using Bash)
.php (using PHP)
.py (using Python)
.js (using Node.js)
.jar (using Java)

MySQL in Web App

MySQL In App runs a local MySQL instance with your app and shares resources from the App Service plan.

Note that apps using MySQL In App are not intended for production environments, and they will not scale beyond a single instance.

Add MySQL in the Instance: In Web App Dashboard Click MySQL in App> In Right Pane select on>Click Save.
Note: No need to save as we don't intent to run MYSQL.

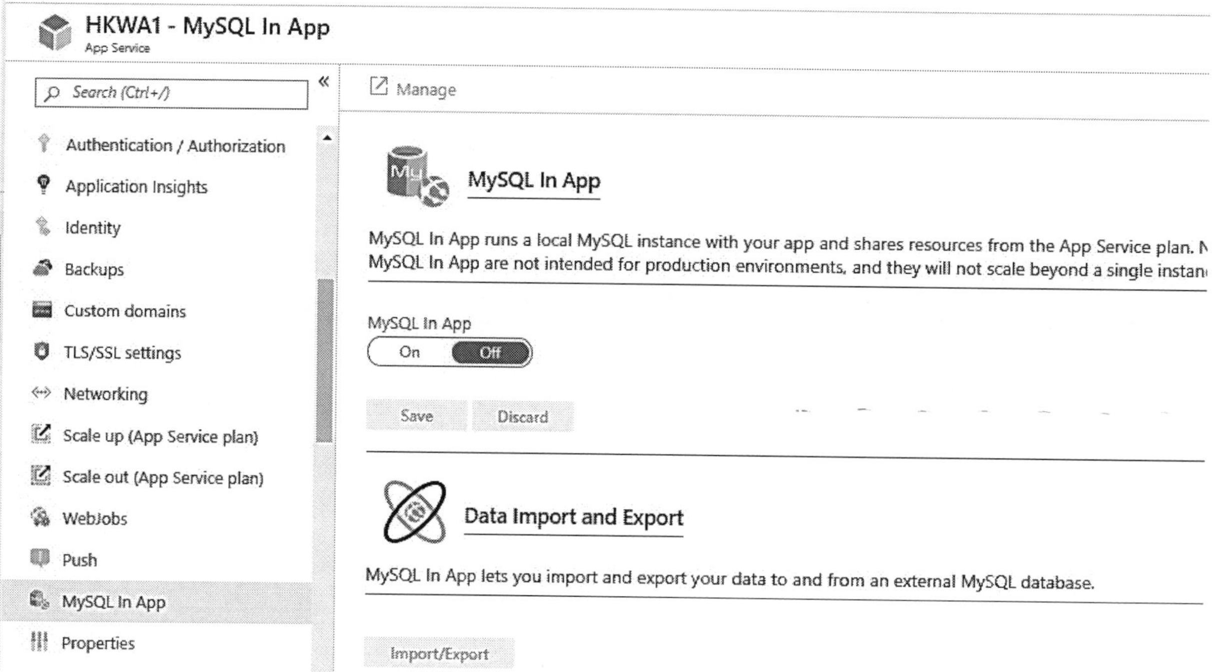

MySQL In App lets you import and export your data to and from an external MySQL database.

Web App Networking Options

In Web App Dashboard Click Networking in left pane and you can see following 4 options in Web App Networking.

VNET Integration
Hybrid Connections
Azure CDN
Access Restrictions

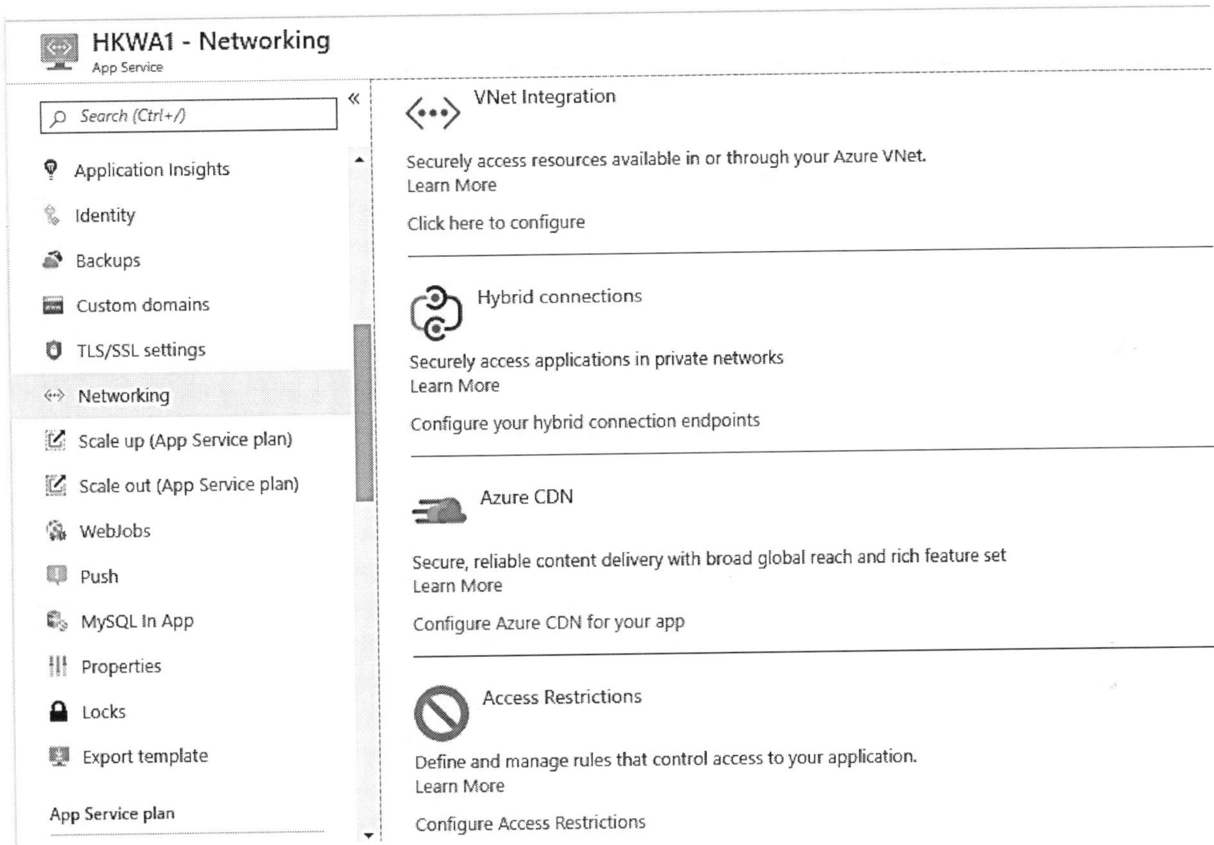

Web App VNET Integration

VNET Integration gives your web app access to resources in your Virtual Network. VNET Integration does not grant private inbound access to Web App from Virtual Network. VNET Integration is only for making outbound calls from your Web App into your VNET.

VNET Integration only works with apps in a Standard & Premium pricing plans.

VNET Integration Versions: Gateway VNET & Regional VNET Integration

Gateway VNET Integration: Gateway VNET Integration enables Web App integration with VNET in same or different regions. Target Virtual Network must have point-to-site VPN enabled with a Dynamic routing VPN gateway before it can be connected to an app. If your gateway is configured with Static routing, you cannot enable point-to-site Virtual Private Network (VPN).

Figure below shows how the system works. A VPN Gateway is created and attached to VNET. Azure Web App connects to VNET using Point to Site VPN. VPN client software gets installed in Web App during VNET Integration.

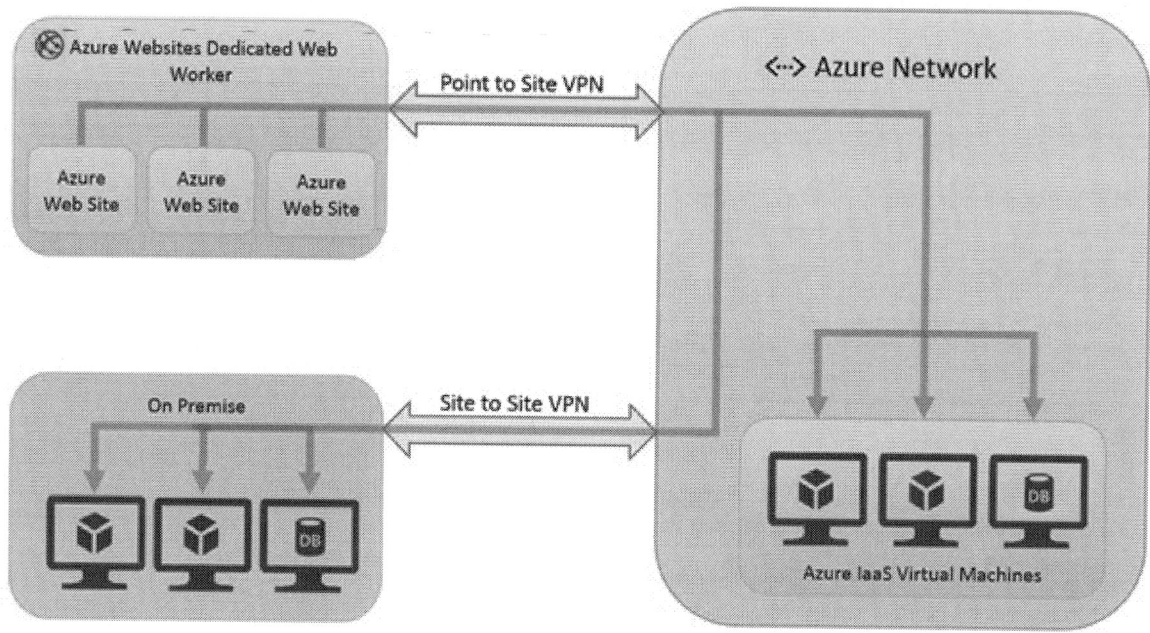

Features of Gateway VNET Integration

1. Requires a Virtual Network Gateway that is configured with Point to Site VPN.
2. Can be used to connect to VNETs in any region.
3. Enables an app to connect to only 1 VNET at a time
4. Enables up to five VNETs to be integrated with in an App Service Plan
5. Allows the same VNet to be used by multiple apps in an App Service Plan without impacting the total number that can be used by an App Service plan. If you have 6 apps using the same VNet in the same App Service plan, that counts as 1 VNet being used.

Regional VNET Integration (Preview)

Regional VNET Integration enables Web App integration with VNET in same region only. Target Virtual Network must have a dedicated subnet with at least 32 addresses. The subnet cannot be used for anything else. You can have only one regional VNet Integration per App Service plan.

The figure below shows the working of Regional VNET Integration. VNet Integration works by mounting virtual interfaces of Web Apps with addresses in the delegated subnet. By using addresses in your VNet, your Web App is enabled to do following.

- Access resources in the VNet you are connected to.
- Make calls to service endpoint secured services like Azure Storage.
- Access resources across ExpressRoute connections.
- Access resources across peered connections including ExpressRoute connections.

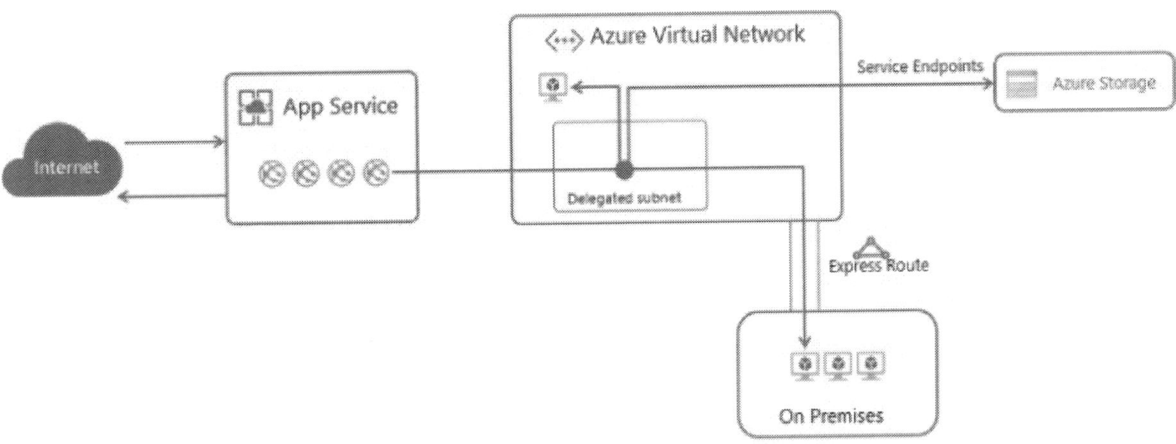

Configuring VNET Integration: In Web App Dashboard Click Networking in left pane>Note the link in Right Pane Under VNET Integration **Click here to configure**.

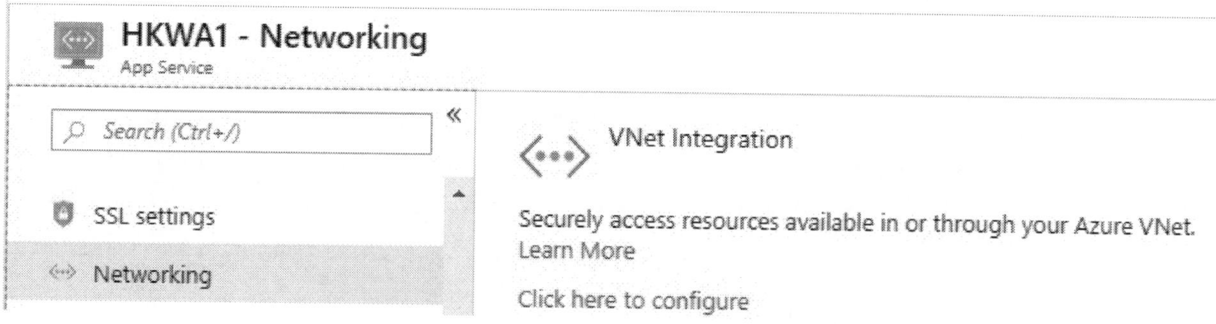

When you click link Click here to configure> VNET Integration Blade opens> under VNet Configuration you have 2 options: +Add VNet and + Add VNet (Preview).

+ Add VNet is used for Gateway VNET Integration.
+ Add VNet (Preview) is used for Regional VNET Integration.

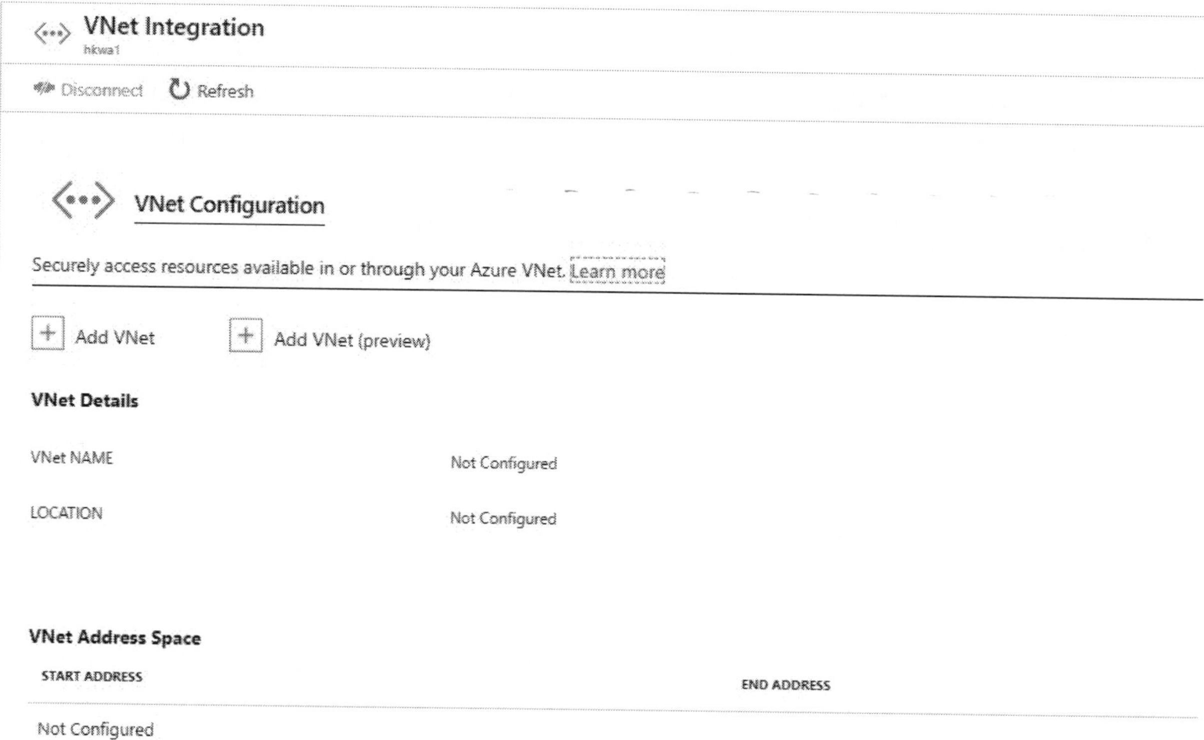

Web App Hybrid Connection

Using Hybrid Connections Web App can securely access application resources in other networks including on-premises network.

The Hybrid Connections feature is available in Basic, Standard, Premium & Isolated plans.

Web App Hybrid connection requires Azure Relay Service & Hybrid Connection Manager (HCM). HCM is installed on a windows server. The HCM is a relay agent that you deploy within the network hosting the resource your Web App is trying to access. Azure Service Bus Relay is Azure managed Service which provides Synchronous bi-directional communication between applications (In this case Web App & application resource which your Web App will access) .

Web App Hybrid connection Working

Figure below shows how the Web App Hybrid connection works. HCM Is installed on-premises on a windows server. Azure Relay service is created in Azure Cloud. For Conecting Web App and Application in another network through Azure Relay service we will use Hybrid Connection feature of Azure Relay. Hybrid Connection feature consists of two outbound calls to Azure Service Bus Relay. One from Web App and other from Hybrid Connection Manager.

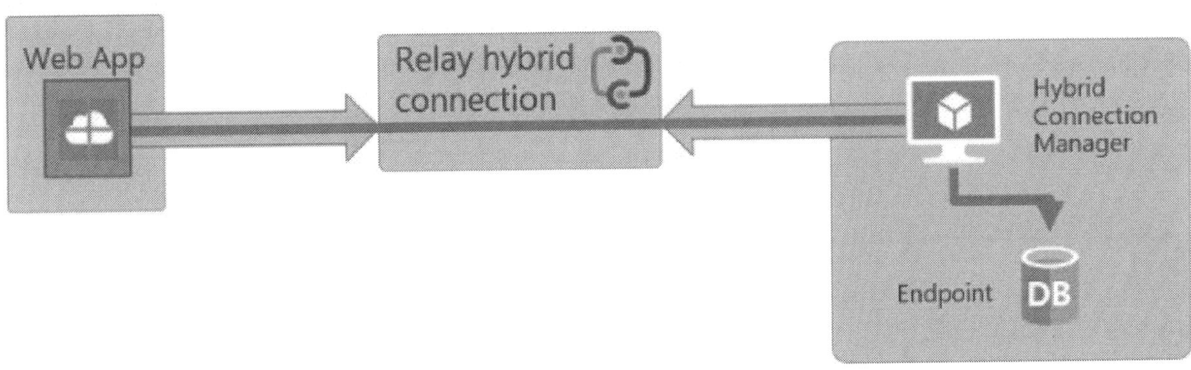

Note: Azure Relay is discussed in detail in Chapter 7 including Lab exercise.

Pre Req for Configuring Hybrid Connection

- Hybrid Connection Manager (HCM) installed on Windows server.
- Azure Relay service configured in Azure. You also have the option to create Azure Relay service when creating Hybrid Connection.

Exercise 22: Configuring Hybrid Connection

This is a Demonstration Exercise. I will just show show you the steps for Configuring Hybrid Connection.

In Web App Dashboard Click Networking in left pane>In Right Pane Under Hybrid Connections click the link Configure your hybrid connection endpoints >Hybrid Connection Blade opens as shown below.

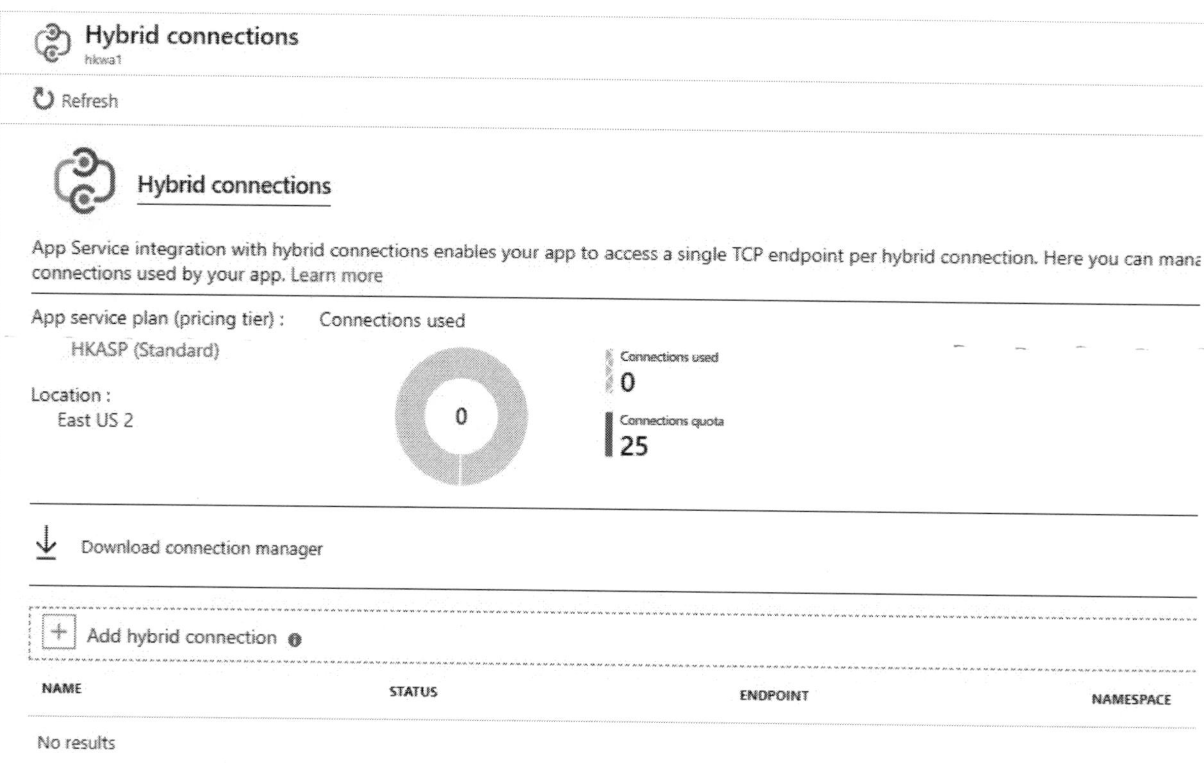

From here you can Download Hybrid Connection Manager (HCM).

Click + Add Hybrid Connection> Add Hybrid Connection Blade opens>click create new Hybrid connection> create new Hybrid connection blade opens> Enter as per your requirement and click Ok.

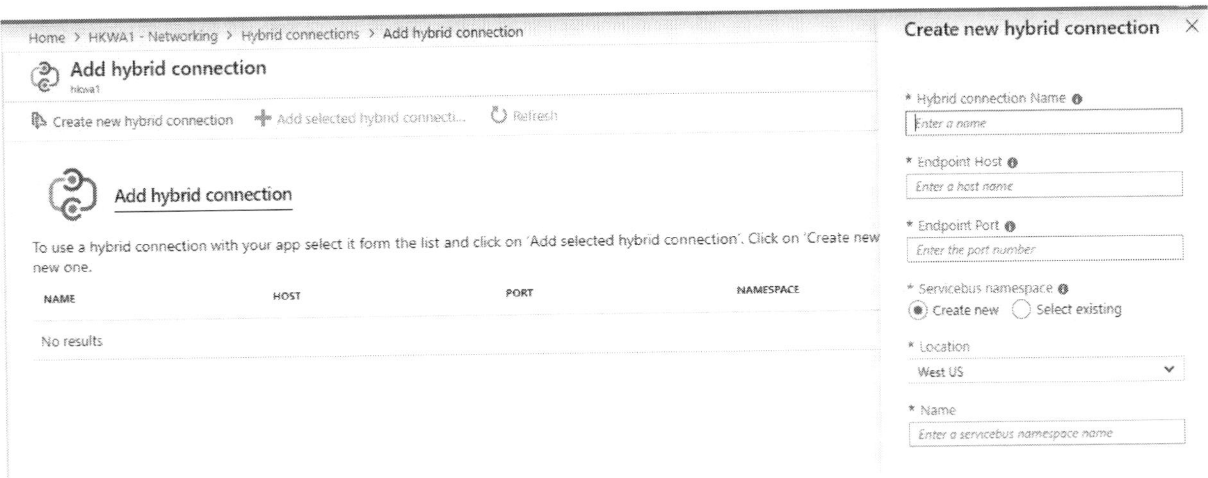

Here Endpoint Host is the Hostname for the endpoint which must resolve on the host where the hybrid connection manager is installed.

In Servicebus Namespace you can enter your existing Servicebus Namespace or create a new Servicebus Namespace.

Note: Chapter 7 has a lab exercise on Azure Relay Hybrid connection.

Azure CDN with Web Apps

A content delivery network (CDN) is a distributed network of servers that deliver web content to users faster than the origin server. The Azure Content Delivery Network (CDN) caches web content from origin server at strategically placed locations near to users to provide maximum throughput for delivering content.

Figure below shows Cached image being delivered to users by CDN server which is faster than the origin server.

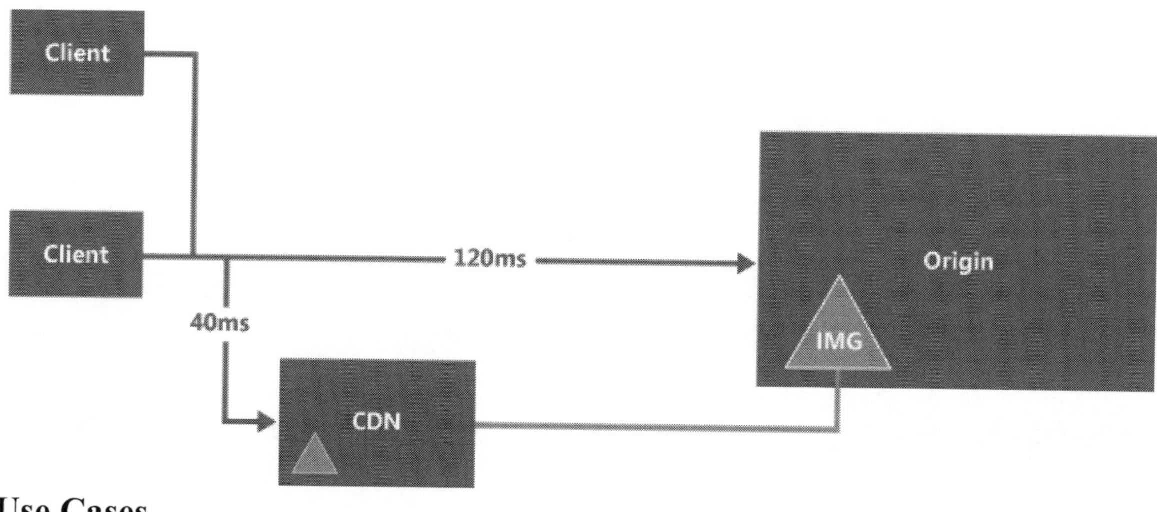

Use Cases

1. Azure CDNs are typically used to deliver static content such as images, style sheets, documents, client-side scripts, and HTML pages.
2. Streaming Video benefits from the low latency offered by CDN servers. Additionally Microsoft Azure Media Services (AMS) integrates with Azure CDN to deliver content directly to the CDN for further distribution.

Benefits of Azure CDN

1. CDN provides lower latency and faster delivery of content to users.
2. CDNs help to reduce load on a web application, because the application does not have to service requests for the content that is hosted in the CDN.
3. CDN helps to cope with peaks and surges in demand without requiring the application to scale, avoiding the consequent increased running costs.
4. Improved experience for users, especially those located far from the datacentre hosting the application.

Azure CDN Architecture

Azure CDN Architecture consists of Origin Server, CDN Profile and CDN endpoints.

Origin Server

Origin server holds the web content which is cached by CDN Endpoints geographically closest to the user based on caching policy configured in CDN endpoint.

Origin Server type can be one of the following:

Storage
Web App
Cloud Service
Publically Accessible Web Server

CDN Profile

A CDN profile is a collection of CDN endpoints with the same pricing tier. CDN pricing is applied at the CDN profile level. Therefore, to use a mix of Azure CDN pricing tiers, you must create multiple CDN profiles.

CDN Endpoints

CDN Endpoint caches the web content from the origin server. It delivers cached content to end users faster than the origin server and is located geographically closest to the user. CDN Endpoints are distributed across the world.

The CDN Endpoint is exposed using the URL format ***<endpoint name>*.azureedge.net** by default, but custom domains can also be used.

A CDN Endpoint is an entity within a CDN Profile containing configuration information regarding caching behaviour and origin Server. Every CDN endpoint represents a specific configuration of content deliver behaviour and access.

Note: Refer to Exam AZ-300 Study & Lab Guide Part 1 for a detailed discussion on Azure CDN including various CDN tiers and Features.

Azure CDN Working

Figure below shows the working of Content Delivery Networks.

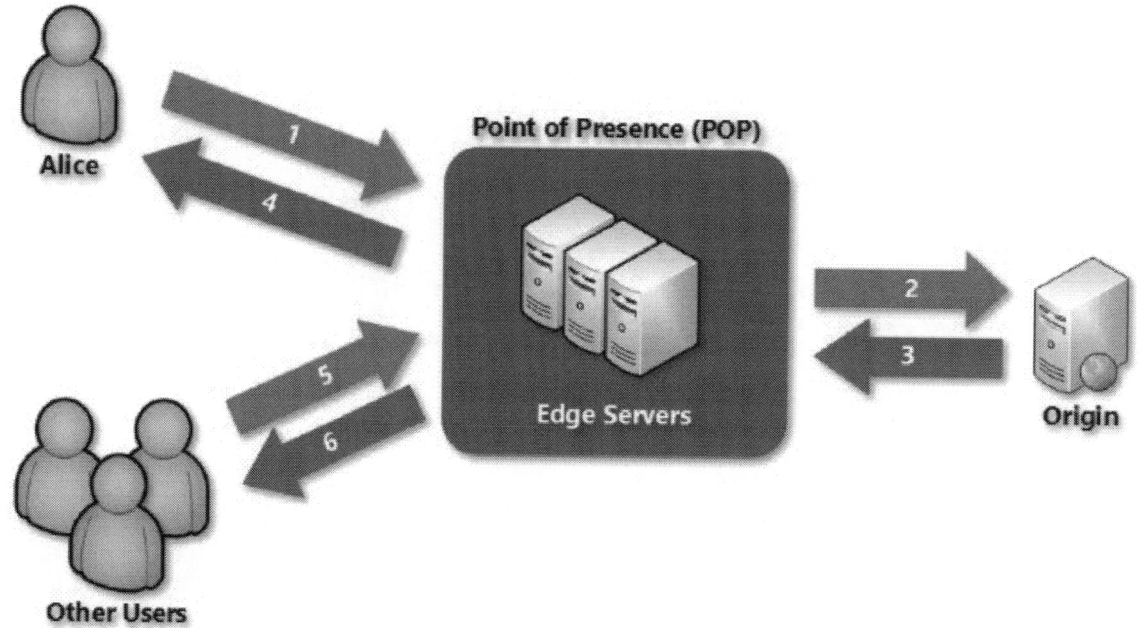

1. User Alice requests a file using URL **(<*endpoint name*>.azureedge.net**) in a browser. DNS routes the request to the CDN edge server Point-of-Presence (POP) location that is geographically closest to the user.

2. If the edge servers in the POP has file in their cache, it returns the file to the user Alice.
3. If the edge servers in the POP do not have the file in their cache, the edge server requests the file from the origin server. The origin server returns the file to the edge server, including optional HTTP headers describing the file's Time-to-Live (TTL). The edge server caches the file and returns the file to the user Alice. The file remains cached on the edge server until the TTL expires. If the origin didn't specify a TTL, the default TTL is seven days.

4. Additional users who request same file as user Alice and are geographically closest to the same POP will be get the file from Cache of the edge server instead of the origin server.

5. The above process results in a faster, more responsive user experience.

Exercise 23: Adding CDN to Web App HKWA1

In this exercise we will create CDN Profile in Resource Group RGWA. We will add CDN endpoint to the CDN Profile. CDN endpoint will contain information about origin server which in this case is Web App HKWA1. CDN endpoint will cache website on Web App HKWA1. **Web App HKWA1 was created in Exercise 2.** Resource Group RGWA was created in Exercise 1.

Create CDN Profile: In Azure portal click create a resource>Web > CDN> Create CDN profile blade opens>Enter name, select resource group as RGWA, select pricing tier. We have the option to add CDN endpoint but we will add later>Click Create (Not shown).

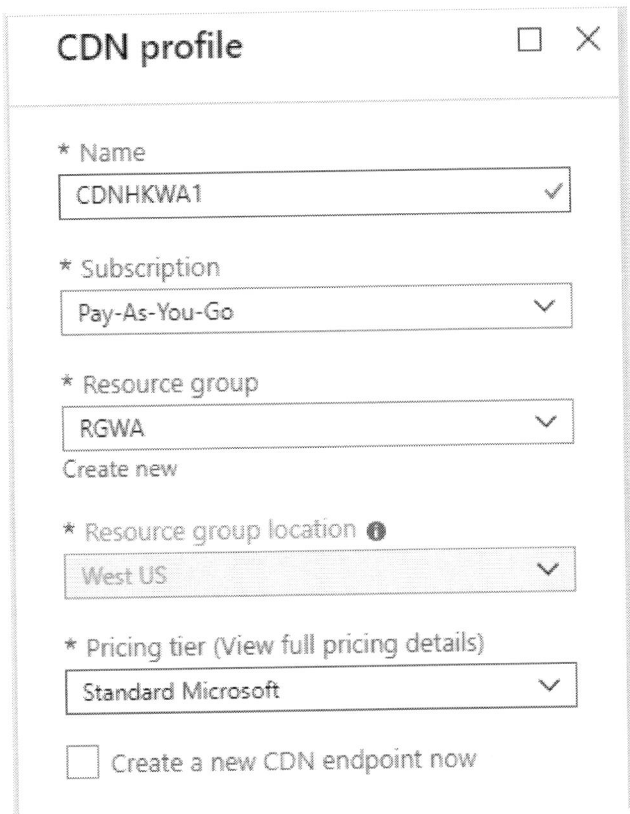

Note: You have the option of creating CDN from Web App Dashboard by clicking Networking in left pane.

Fig below shows CDN Profile Dashboard.

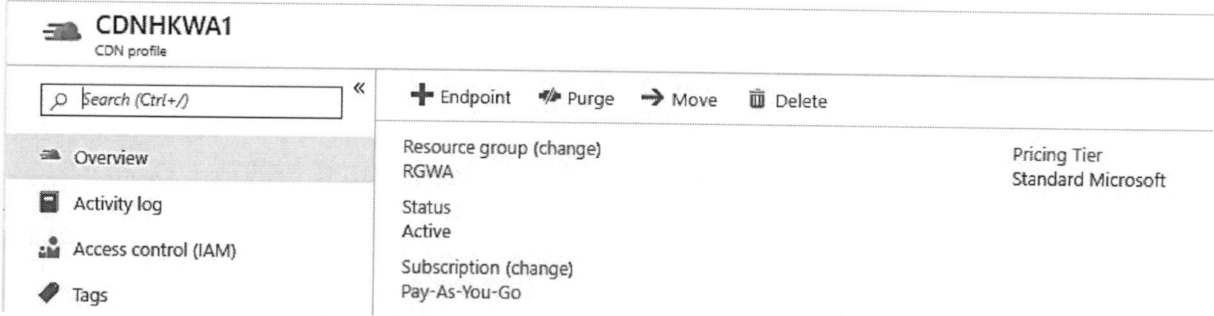

ADD CDN Endpoint: In CDN Profile dashboard click +Endpoint>Add an Endpoint Blade opens>Enter a name>In Origin type select Web App>select HKWA1 DNS address (www.hksystems.in) in origin hostname> Rest select all default values>Click Add (Not Shown).

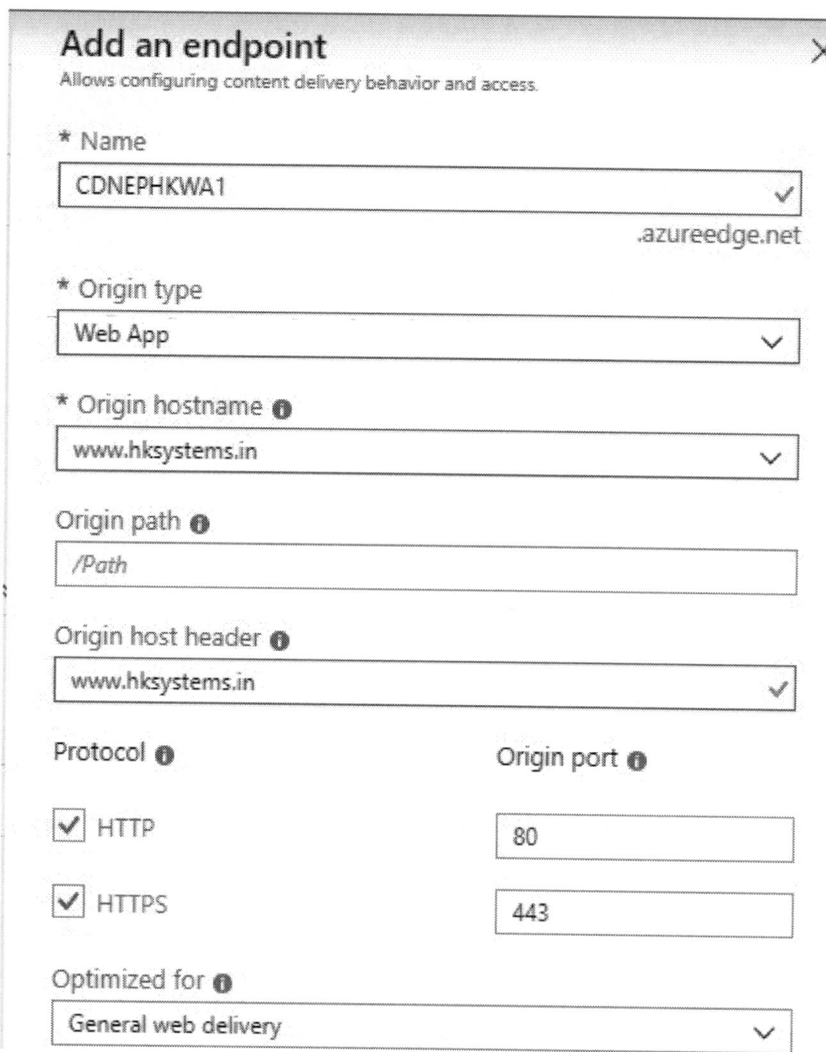

Click newly created CDN Endpoint in CDN Profile dashboard. Figure below dashboard of CDN Endpoint.

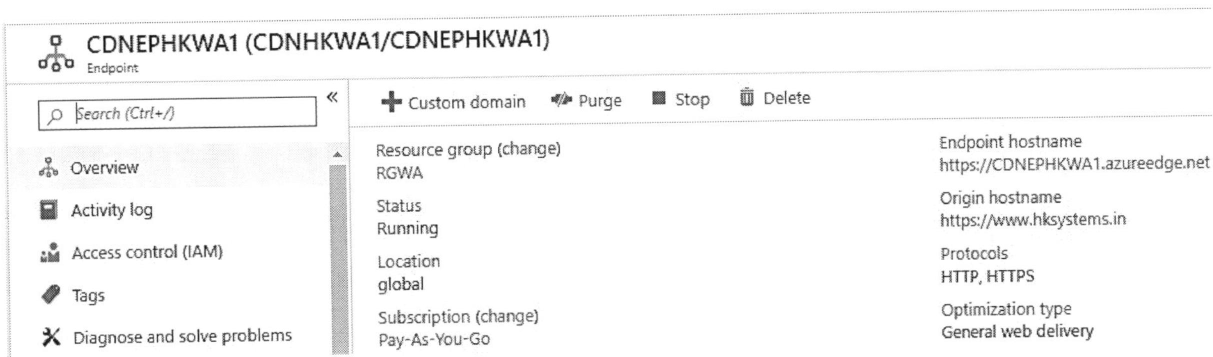

Access custom website on HKWA1 using CDN endpoint address: From CDN Endpoint Dashboard copy the Endpoint address- **https://CDNEPHKWA1.azureedge.net**. Open a browser and paste the CDN Endpoint address. The custom website on HKWA1 opens.

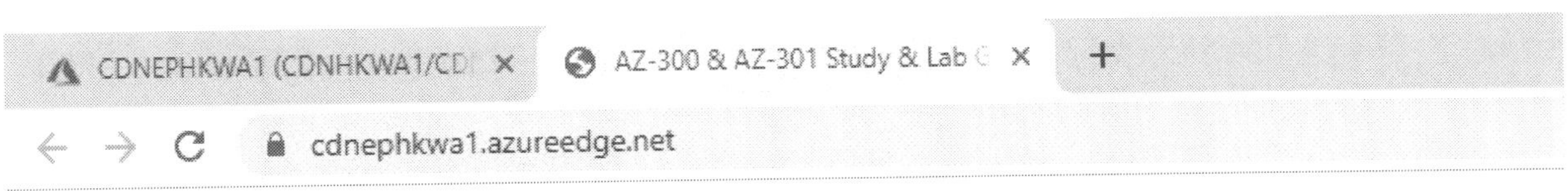

Exam AZ-300 & AZ-301 Study & Lab Guide

Exam AZ-300 & AZ-301 Study & Lab Guide prepares you for Azure Solutions Architect Expert Certification.

Author: Harinder Kohli

CDN endpoint will cache the website on Web App HKWA1 which is closest to user. This means when a user is accessing HKWA1 website from India then CDN endpoint in India will cache the website. All users from India subsequently will access the website from CDN endpoint located in India resulting in faster access.

Note: Delete the CDN Endpoint and CDN Profile as we no longer need it.
Note 2: First access of Web App through CDN endpoint address required couple of reloading of webpage using f5.

Web App Access Restriction

Web App Access restrictions allows you to add list of IP addresses and Virtual Network Subnets that are allowed or Denied access to your Web App. Access restrictions using Virtual Network subnet uses Service Endpoints. Service Endpoints was disussed in Chapter 1 in Study & Lab Guide Part 1.

Exercise 24: Web App Access Restrictions

In Web App Dashboard Click Networking in left pane>In Right Pane Under Access Restrictions click the link Configure Access Restrictions> Access Restrictions pane opens as shown below.

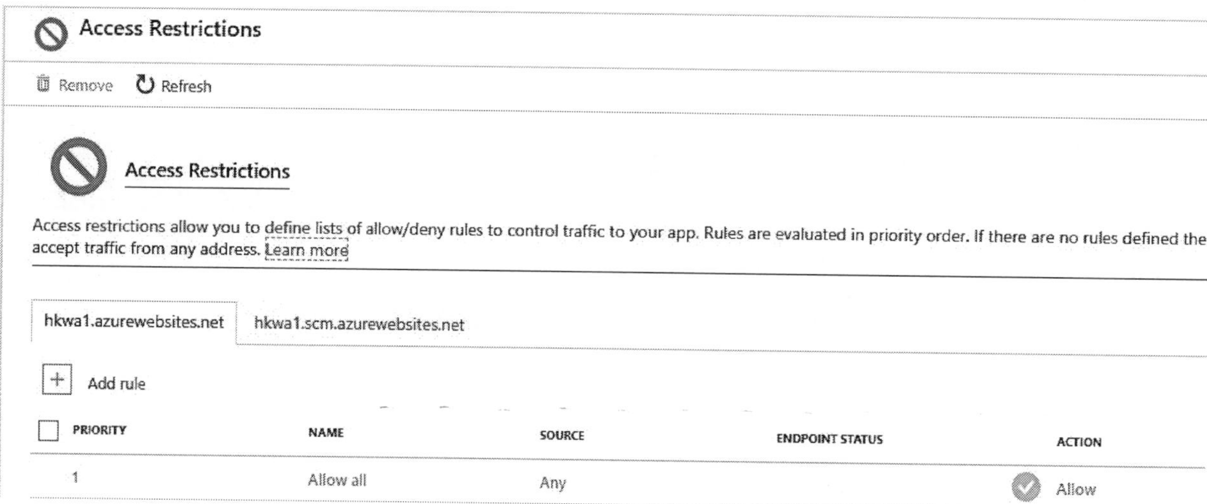

Click + Add Rule> Add Access Restriction blade opens> Here you can add restrictions based on IP Address and Virtual Network subnet> You can select Allow or Deny Action.

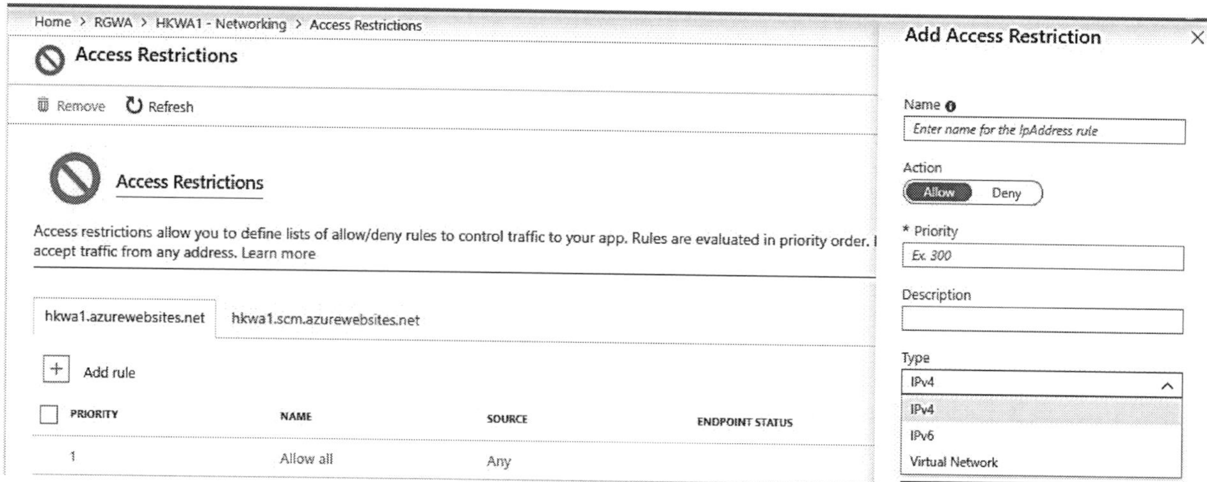

App Service Environment (ASE)

The Azure App Service Environment (ASE) is an Azure App Service feature that provides a fully isolated and dedicated environment for securely running App Service apps at high scale. Azure App Service Environment (ASE) is a deployment of Azure App Service into a subnet in an Azure virtual network. ASE can host following types of Apps:

Windows web apps | Linux web apps | Docker containers | Mobile apps | Functions

You can use NSG features of virtual networks to control inbound and outbound network communications for your apps.

An ASE can be either internet-facing **(External ASE)** with a public IP address (VIP) or internal-facing **(Internal ASE)** with Azure internal load balancer (ILB) address.

ASE requires App Service Isolated Tier Service Plan.

Architecture

An ASE is composed of front ends and workers. Front ends are responsible for HTTP/HTTPS termination and automatic load balancing of app requests within an ASE. Workers are roles that host customer apps. Workers are available in three fixed sizes: One vCPU/3.5 GB RAM, Two vCPU/7 GB RAM, Four vCPU/14 GB RAM.

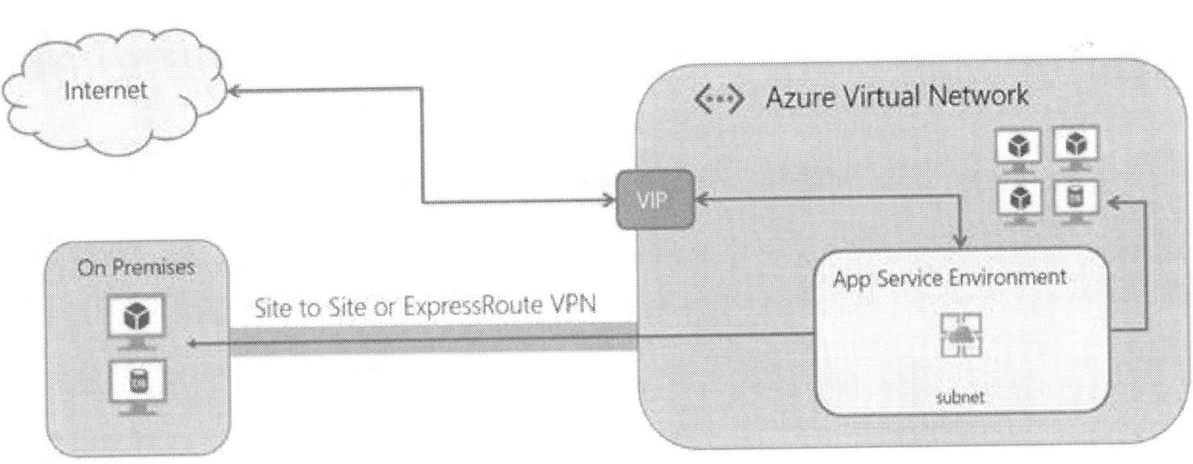

Note: Customers do not need to manage front ends and workers.

ASE Use Cases

1. Applications requiring large compute capacity. ASE supports upto 100 Instances. To add compute capacity beyond 100 instances you can scale horizontally by adding multiple ASE.
2. Isolation and secure network access.
3. High memory utilization.

Note 2: ASE can be ASEv1 or ASEv2. This chapter focuses only on ASEv2.

ASE Horizontal Scaling

Application like Voting applications, sporting events and televised entertainment events require extremely large compute capacity.

High scale compute requirements can be met by horizontally scaling with **multiple ASE deployments**.

Figure below shows **Multiple ASE deployments** load balanced with Azure Traffic Manager.

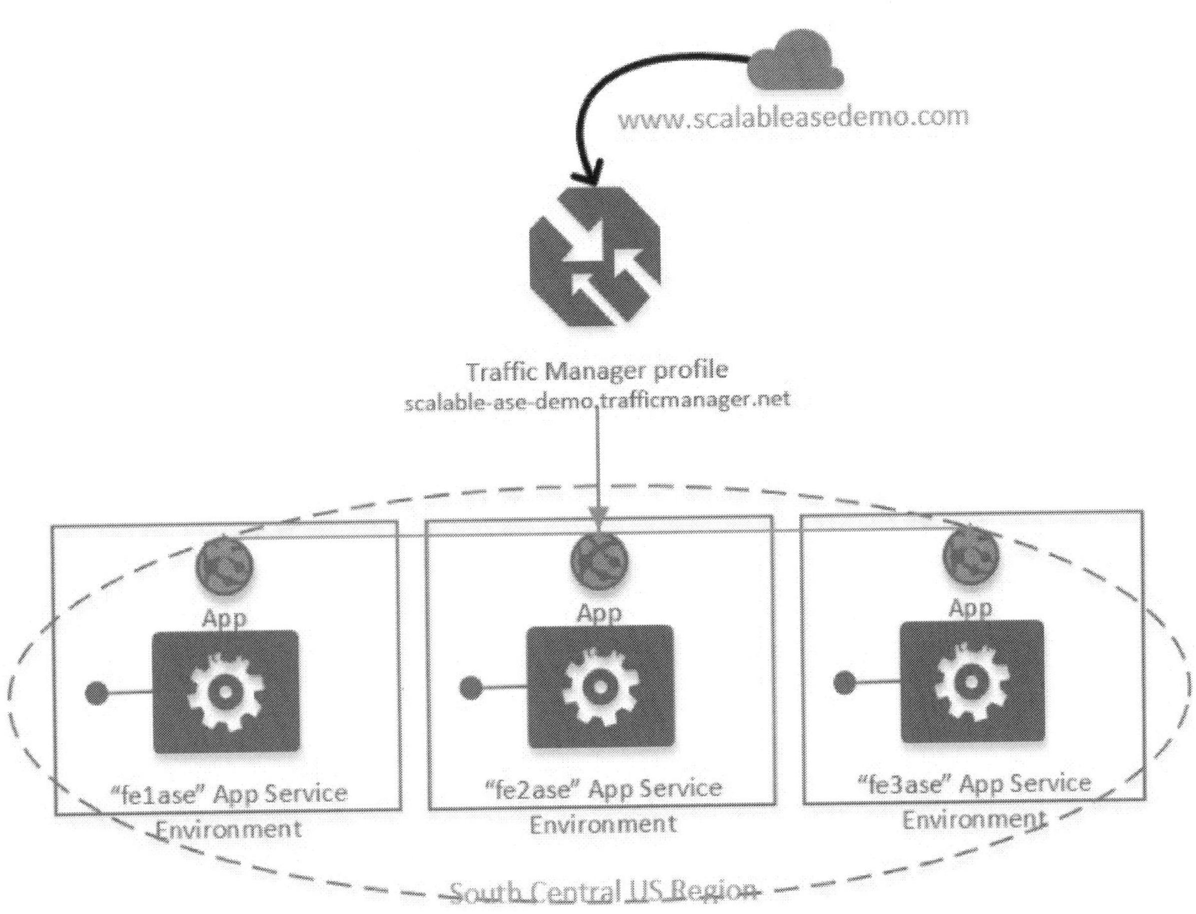

Web App Extensions

Extensions add functionality to your App Service. These extension provide tools which helps you manage Azure Web Apps.

Exercise 25: Adding Extensions

In Web App HKWA1 dashboard click Extensions under Development tools>In right pane click +Add> Add Extension blade opens>Choose Extension as per your requirement>Accept Legal terms>Click Ok.

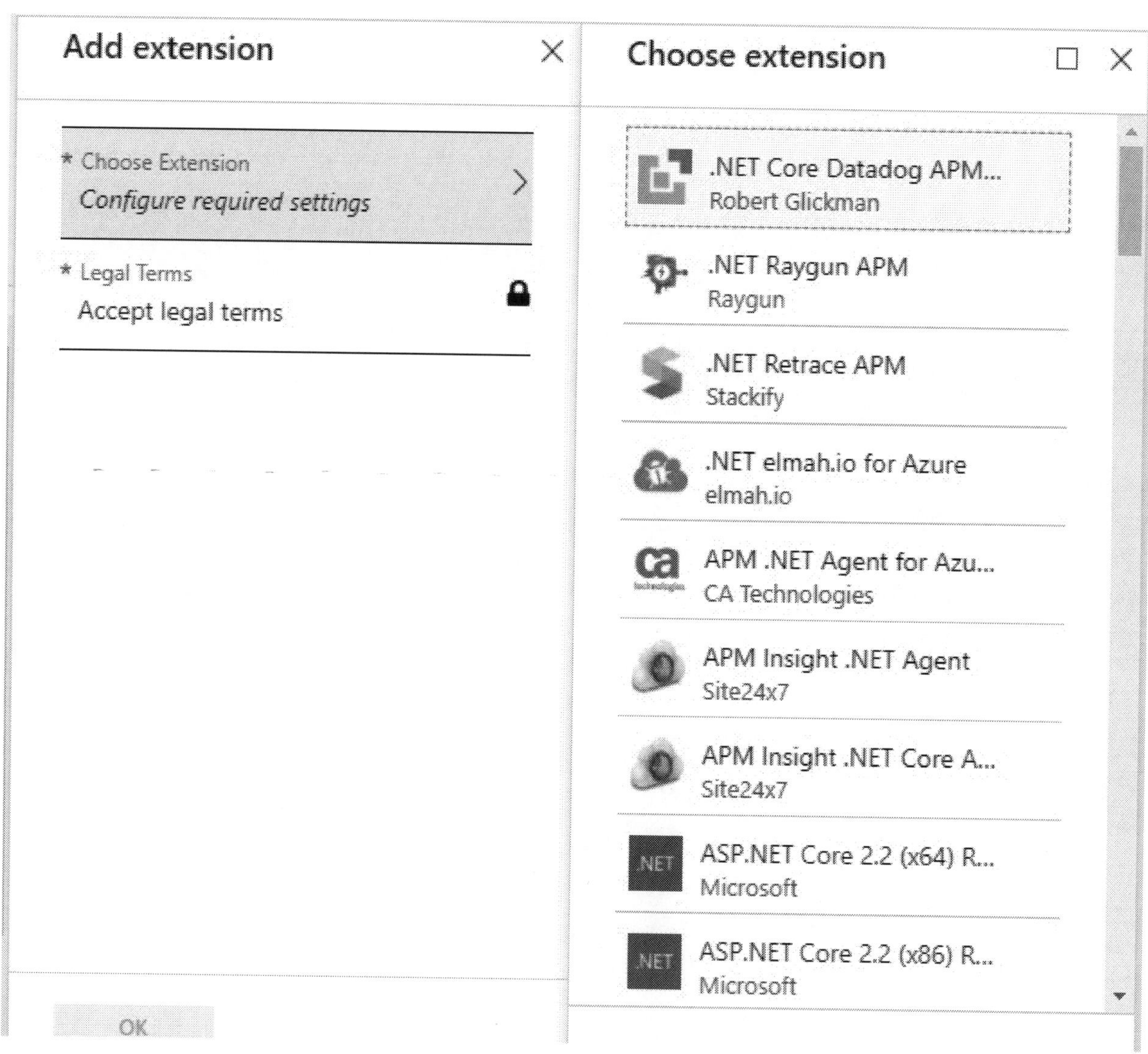

Web App SCM Site

Every Azure web site has an associated scm service site which runs both Kudu console and other Site Extensions. Kudu itself is a Site Extension which is provided with every Web App.

Kudu Dashboard provides a collection of developer oriented tools for your App Service.

Kudu handles the Git integration to a Web Site. It provides an API endpoint for programmatic access to app settings, deployment information, files, active processes, runtime versions, source control information, web hooks and web jobs.

If your web site has URL https://hkwa1.azurewebsites.net then the URL of the Kudu service is https://hkwa1.scm.azurewebsites.net

Exercise 26: Accessing & Exploring Kudu Dashboard

Open browser and enter https://hkwa1.scm.azurewebsites.net> Kudu Dashboard opens as shown below.

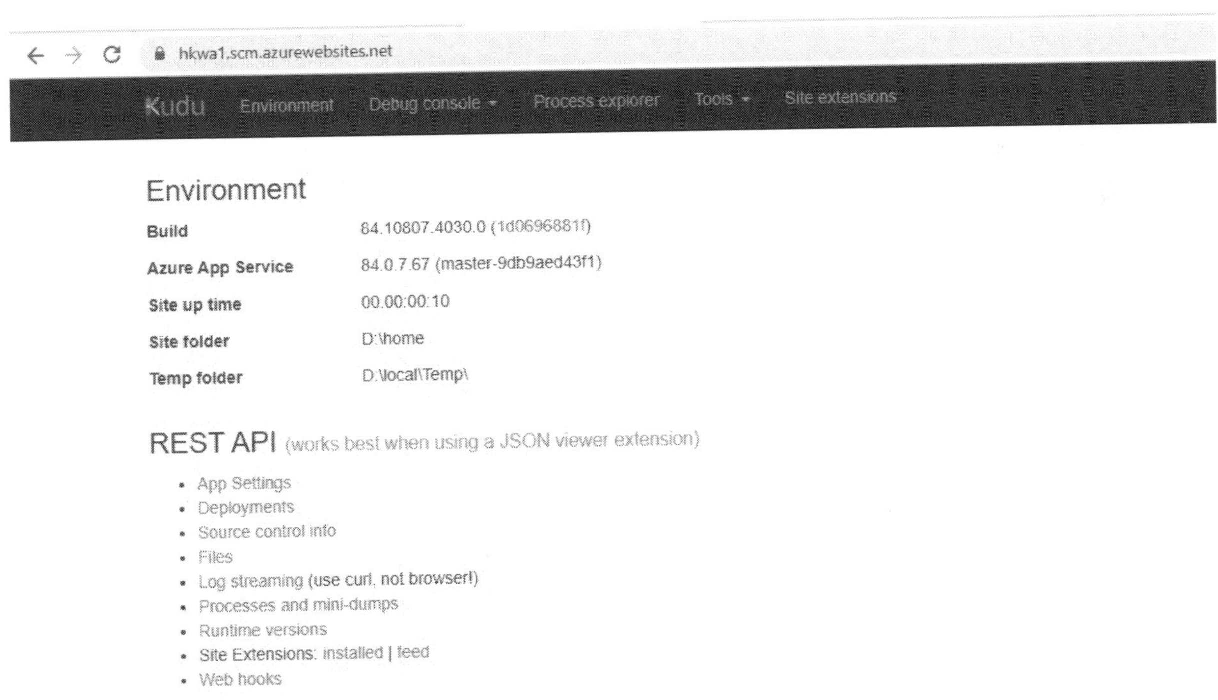

Environment Tab: The Environment tab in Kudu Dashboard shows information on System Information, App Settings, Connection Strings, Environment Variables, PATH, HTTP Headers and Server Variables. Click Environment Tab in Kudu Dashboard.

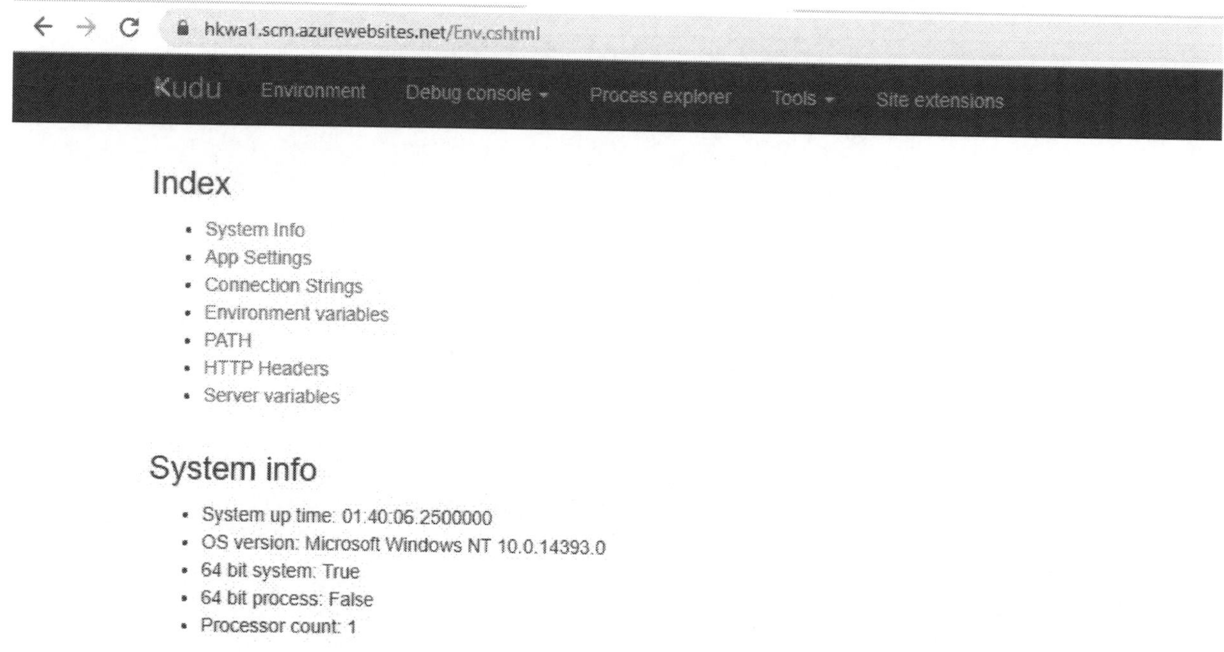

Debug Console: The Debug Console enables you to run command line tools against the Web Site. Click Debug console and select CMD>Command line console opens> I entered **dir** to see the files unde D:\home

```
Microsoft Windows [Version 10.0.14393]
(c) 2016 Microsoft Corporation. All rights reserved.

D:\home>dir
 Volume in drive D is Windows
 Volume Serial Number is 0211-4CB9

 Directory of D:\home

09/04/2019  01:01 PM    <DIR>          .
09/04/2019  01:01 PM    <DIR>          ..
09/05/2019  02:32 AM    <DIR>          data
09/05/2019  04:50 AM    <DIR>          LogFiles
09/06/2019  03:04 AM    <DIR>          site
```

Lets create a Directory **test** under D:\home

1. Enter command **mkdir test**.

2. Enter **dir** under D:\home to check the test directory. test directory is created and is last in the below screen.

```
D:\home>mkdir test

D:\home>dir
 Volume in drive D is Windows
 Volume Serial Number is 0211-4CB9

 Directory of D:\home

09/07/2019  05:13 AM    <DIR>          .
09/07/2019  05:13 AM    <DIR>          ..
09/05/2019  02:32 AM    <DIR>          data
09/05/2019  04:50 AM    <DIR>          LogFiles
09/06/2019  03:04 AM    <DIR>          site
09/07/2019  05:13 AM    <DIR>          test
               0 File(s)              0 bytes
               6 Dir(s)  53,683,122,176 bytes free

D:\home>
```

Change to test directory by entering command **cd test** and then **dir** command.

```
D:\home>cd test

D:\home\test>dir
 Volume in drive D is Windows
 Volume Serial Number is 0211-4CB9

 Directory of D:\home\test

09/07/2019  05:13 AM    <DIR>          .
09/07/2019  05:13 AM    <DIR>          ..
               0 File(s)              0 bytes
               2 Dir(s)  53,683,122,176 bytes free
```

Lets check the index.html file we uploaded in Exercise 5.

Go to D:\home\site\wwwroot Directory and enter **dir** command. You can see index.html file.

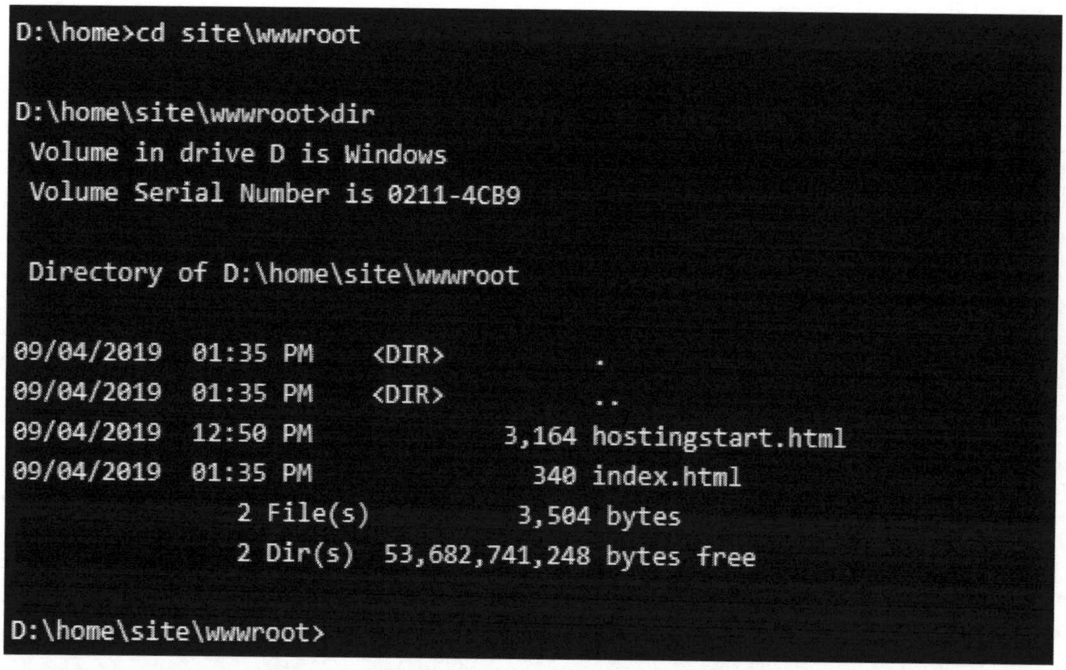

```
D:\home>cd site\wwwroot

D:\home\site\wwwroot>dir
 Volume in drive D is Windows
 Volume Serial Number is 0211-4CB9

 Directory of D:\home\site\wwwroot

09/04/2019  01:35 PM    <DIR>          .
09/04/2019  01:35 PM    <DIR>          ..
09/04/2019  12:50 PM             3,164 hostingstart.html
09/04/2019  01:35 PM               340 index.html
               2 File(s)          3,504 bytes
               2 Dir(s)  53,682,741,248 bytes free

D:\home\site\wwwroot>
```

Readers are requested to further explore Kudu Dashboard.

Web App for Containers

Web App for Containers is covered in Chapter 2.

App Services Pricing

App Service plans are billed on a per second basis.

Free & Shared Tier Service Plan: The Free and Shared service plans run on the same Azure VMs as other apps. Some apps may belong to other customers. These tiers are intended to be used only for development and testing purposes. Free and Shared plans are metered on a per App basis.

Instance	Cores	RAM	Storage	Prices
F1 (Free)	Shared (60 CPU minutes / day)	1 GB	1 GB	Free
D1 (Shared)	Shared (240 CPU minutes / day)	1 GB	1 GB	$0.013/hour/Site

Basic Tier Service Plan

Instance	Cores	RAM	Storage	Prices
B1	1	1.75 GB	10 GB	$0.075/hour
B2	2	3.5 GB	10 GB	$0.15/hour
B3	4	7 GB	10 GB	$0.30/hour

Standard Tier Service Plan

Instance	Cores	RAM	Storage	Prices
S1	1	1.75 GB	50 GB	$0.10/hour
S2	2	3.5 GB	50 GB	$0.20/hour
S3	4	7 GB	50 GB	$0.40/hour

Premium Tier Service Plan

Instance	Cores	RAM	Storage	Prices
P1v2	1	1.75 GB	250 GB	$0.10/hour
P2v2	2	3.5 GB	250 GB	$0.20/hour
P3v3	4	7 GB	250 GB	$0.40/hour

Isolated Tier Service Plan

Instance	Cores	RAM	Storage	Prices
I1	1	1.75 GB	1 TB	$0.30/hour
I2	2	3.5 GB	1 TB	$0.60/hour
I3	4	7 GB	1 TB	$1.20/hour

Case Study 1: Azure Web App High Availability

A Global Multinational company is running dealer management application in Azure Web App. Azure Web App uses Azure SQL Database as backend.

They want to have a High Availability and DR solution in a different region. All traffic would be served from primary region. In case of outage in Primary region, Application traffic will be re-directed to Secondary region.

They want to minimize the cost of the HA & DR Setup. They have given a RTO of 30 minutes -60 minutes. There should be no data loss in Azure SQL Database. They want secondary region to be activated without any complicated procedures or operational & administrative overheads. Suggest a solution which satisfies the above requirement.

Solution

Options for High Availability across Primary and Secondary Regions

Active/passive with hot standby: Traffic goes to one region, while the other waits on hot standby. Hot standby means the Web App in the secondary region are running at all times.
Active/passive with cold standby: Traffic goes to one region, while the other waits on cold standby. Cold standby means the Web App in the secondary region are not running until needed for failover. This approach costs less to run, but will generally take longer to come online during a failure.
Active/active: Both regions are active, and requests are load balanced between them. If one region becomes unavailable, it is taken out of rotation.

We will choose **Active/passive with cold standby option** as cost of HA& DR setup is one of the main requirements given by the company.

Web App Setup: One Web App will be setup in each region. Primary Region Web App will be active and will serve all traffic. Secondary region Web App will be in **powered off mode** to save cost. In case of outage Web App in Secondary will be activated and will serve the application traffic. Each Web App will be connected to Azure SQL Database in their region only.
Azure SQL Database: Azure SQL Database in Primary region will be primary database and will be Geo-Replicated to Secondary region in read only mode. Each Azure SQL Database will be connected to Azure Web App in their region

only. In case of outage in primary region, Azure SQL Database in Secondary region will be promoted as Primary Database.

Azure Traffic Manager: Traffic Manager will route incoming requests to the primary region. For the above scenario we will use *Priority* routing. With this setting, Traffic Manager sends all requests to the primary region unless the endpoint for that region becomes unreachable.

Steps to be taken for activating secondary region

1. Power-on Azure Web App in Secondary Region.
2. Promote Secondary region SQL Database as primary database.

Figure below shows the Architecture of the solution.

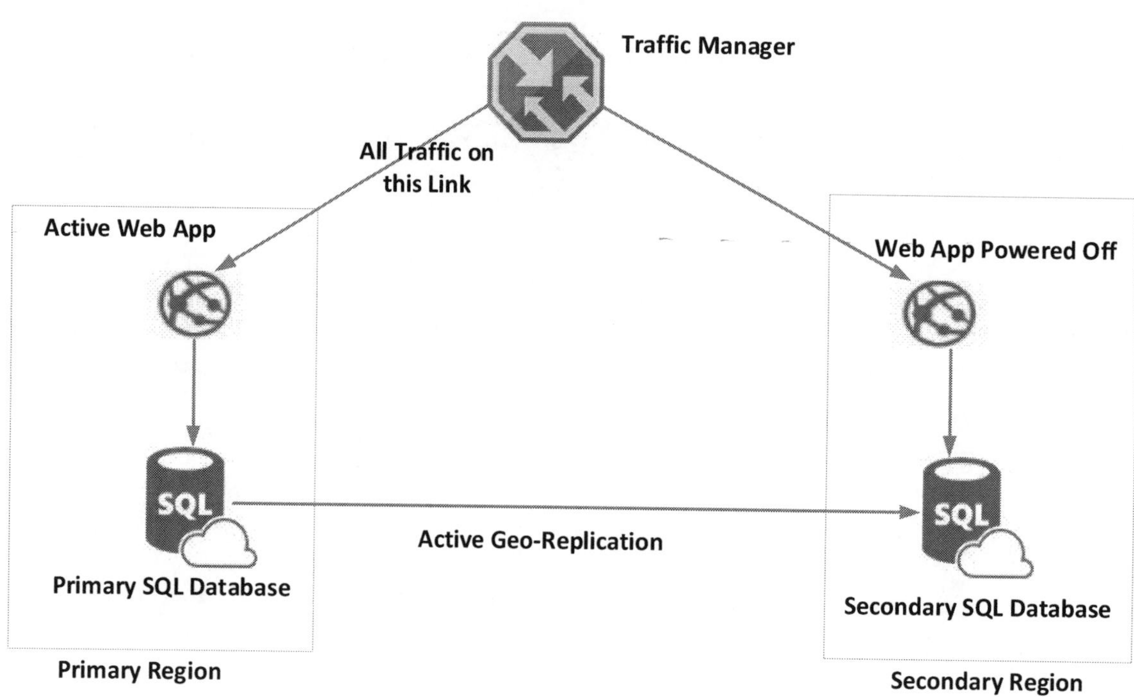

Chapter 2 Containers

This Chapter covers following

Containers
Virtual Machines V/S Containers
What is required to run Containers
Benefits of Container Technology
Drawbacks of Container Technology
Container Deployment Options in Azure
Common Docker commands for running containers
Dockerfile
Container Registry
Azure Container Registry (ACR)
Architecture of Azure Container Registry
Azure Container Registry Tiers
Access to Azure Container Registry
Content formats supported in Azure Container Registry
Azure Container Registry Geo Replication
Content trust in Azure Container Registry
Azure Container Instances (ACI)
Container Groups in ACI
Azure Container Instance use case scenarios
Azure Web App for Containers
Web App for Containers Pricing Tier (Premium Container Plan)
Image Sources in Web App for Containers
Azure Kubernetes Service (AKS)
Azure Kubernetes Service (AKS) Architecture
Kubernetes Cluster Architecture
AKS Networking Options
HTTP Application Routing
Container Monitoring
Authenticate to Azure Container Registry from AKS

This Chapter Covers following Lab Exercises

Create Azure Ubuntu VM
Connect to Ubuntu VM and update the VM
Install Docker Engine and Deploy Container on Ubuntu VM
Deploy NGINX Container on Azure Ubuntu Linux VM
Browse Public Container Registry Docker Hub
Create Azure Container Registry (ACR)
Install Azure CLI on Ubuntu VM vmlinux
Login to ACR and push image hello-world to ACR
Run hello-world:v1 image from Registry ACRCloud
Login to Azure Container Registry using Docker Login Command
Exploring Replication feature
Exploring Content Trust feature
Deploy Azure Container Instance (ACI) using Public Image
Deploy Web App for Containers
Create AKS Cluster with Basic Networking
Install Kubectl
Connect to AKS Cluster using kubectl
Access Kubernetes Web UI Dashboard
Deploy NGINX Container to AKS Cluster
Edit the NGINX Application
Deploy Second NGINX Container to AKS Cluster

Chapter Topology

In this chapter we will add Ubuntu Linux VM, Azure Container Registry (ACR), Azure Container instance, Azure Web App for Containers and Azure Kubernetes Service (AKS) to the topology. We will also install Docker Engine on the Ubuntu VM and then deploy Hello World & NGINX container on the VM.

In this chapter Azure Kubernetes Service (AKS) Cluster will be deployed in System Generated Virtual Network using basic networking option.

Note: Labs in Azure Kubernetes Service topic require that Azure CLI is installed on your Laptop/Desktop from where you are accessing Azure Portal. Installation of Azure CLI is shown in Chapter 21, Part 1 Book.

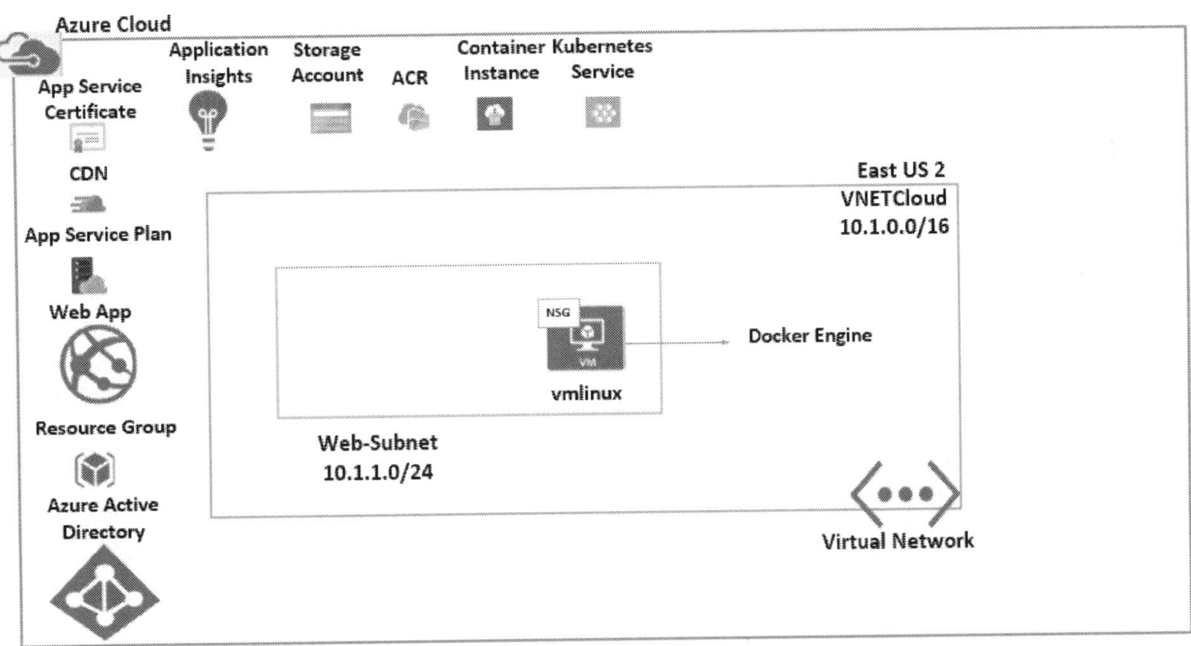

Containers

Containers provide alternate method of running applications.

Before going into containers let's discuss currently how applications are deployed. Application runs on top of Operating system. Operating System can be running on Bare Metal host or in a Virtual Machine known as Server Virtualization.

Containers provide operating system virtualization on Windows and Linux. Multiple Independent containers can run within a single Linux or Windows instance avoiding the overhead of starting and maintaining virtual machines.

Containers allow you to package application with their entire runtime environment—all of the files necessary to run. Container image contains all application's dependencies, it is portable and consistent as it moves from development, to testing, and finally to production.

Figure below shows the **Architecture of Containers.**

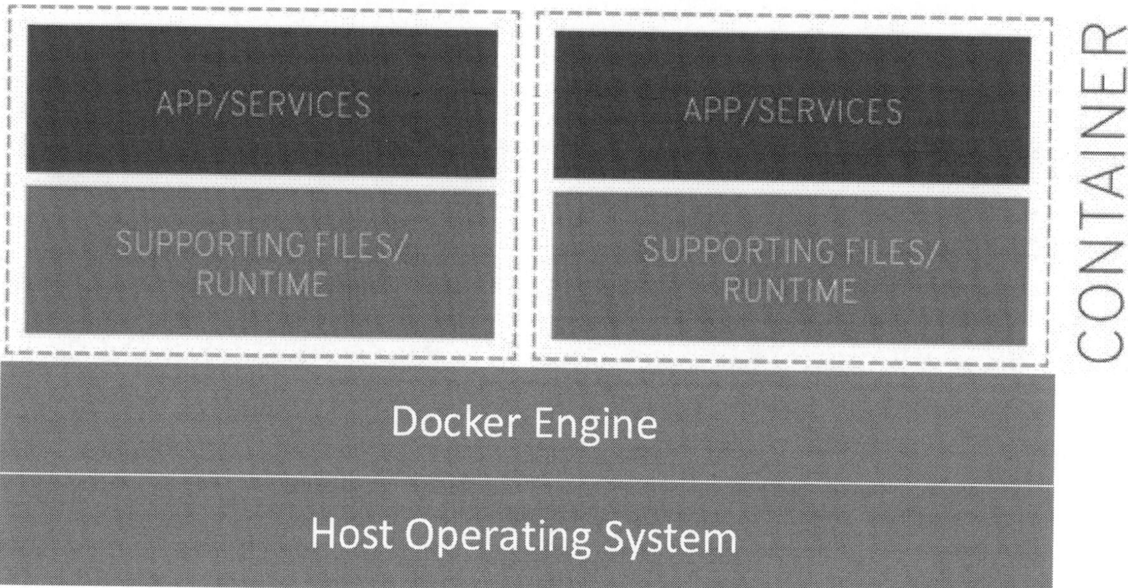

Docker uses the resource isolation features of the Linux kernel such as cgroups and kernel namespaces, and a union-capable file system such as OverlayFS. The Linux kernel's namespaces isolates an application's view of the operating environment, including process trees, network, user IDs and mounted file systems, while the kernel's cgroups provide resource limiting, including the CPU, memory, block I/O, and network.

Virtual Machines V/S Containers

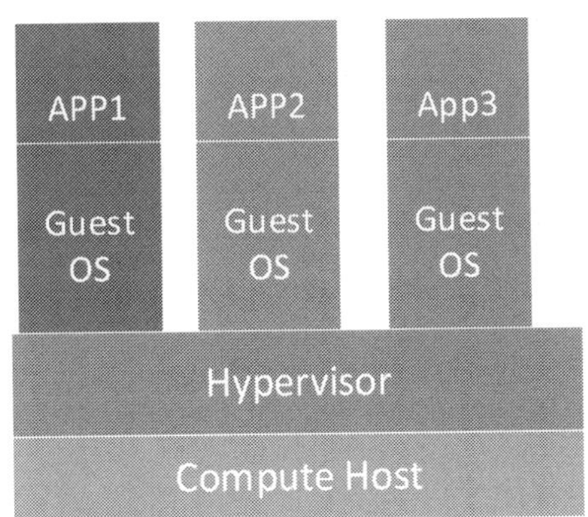

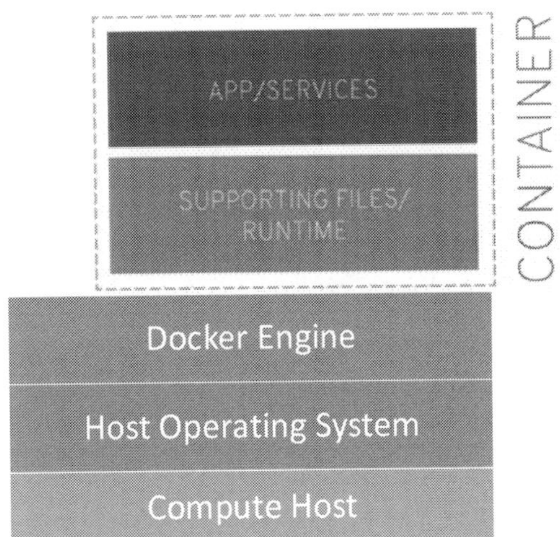

Virtual Machines: A hypervisor installed on compute host creates and runs Virtual Machines. Each virtual machine runs a unique guest operating system. VMs with different operating systems can run on the same physical server—a Windows VM can sit alongside a Linux VM.

Containers: Containers provide operating system virtualization. Multiple Independent containers can run within a single Linux or Windows OS instance. Containers allow you to package application with their entire runtime environment—all of the files necessary to run.

Feature	Container	VM
Defination	OS virtualization.	Server Virtualization.
Operating System	Containers shares Host OS	Each VM has its own OS
Size	Megabytes	Gigabytes
Time to start	Seconds	Minutes
Kernel	Shared with host	Each VM has its own Kernel
Density of Application workloads	Containers can run 2-3 times more applications.	
Benefits	Containers share a common OS which reduces mgmt. overhead. Containers are light weight and are more portable than VMs and can be deployed across public- private cloud and Traditional Data Centres.	Consolidates Multiple applications on a single system reducing server footprint.
Drawbacks	Higher Fault Domain and are less secure than VMs.	VMs are not portable across Public-Private Clouds.

What is required to run Containers

You require 2 components to run Docker Containers – Docker Engine and Docker image.

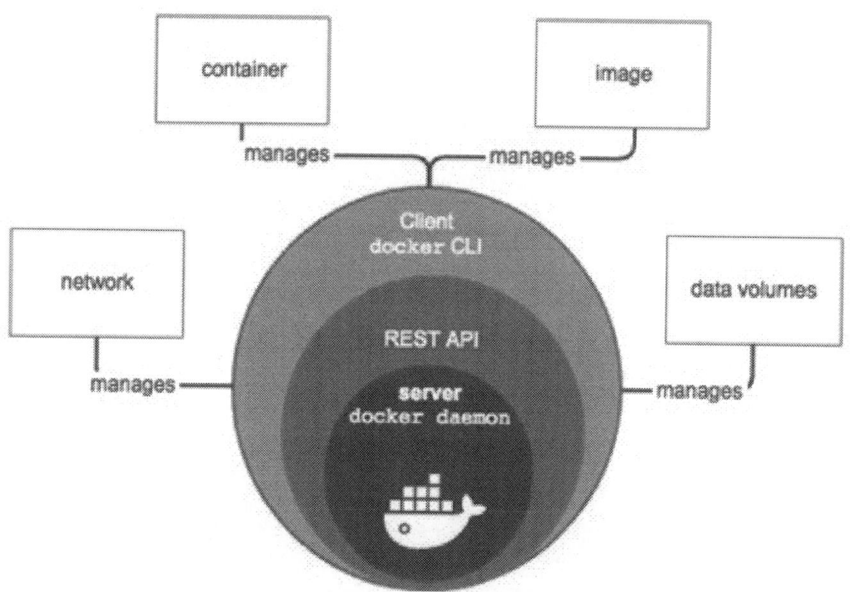

A **Docker Engine** need to be installed on a Linux or a Windows host or VM. The engine creates a server-side docker daemon process that hosts images, containers, networks and storage volumes.
The engine also provides a client-side command-line interface (CLI) that enables users to interact with the daemon through the Docker Engine API.
Docker Engine provides 3 Network Models including Bridge Network and Overlay Networks.

Docker Image is used to create containers. It can be downloaded from Azure Container registry or Docker Hub or from any accessible container registry.

Containers are built from images that are stored in one or more repositories. These repositories can belong to public or private container registries. An example of a public registry is **Docker Hub**. An example of a private registry is the **Docker Trusted Registry**, which can be installed on-premises or in a virtual private cloud. There are also cloud-based private container registry services including **Azure Container Registry**.

Benefits of Container Technology

1. Containers are more portable than VMs and can be deployed across Public Clouds, Private Cloud and Traditional Data Centers without any conversion.

2. Container Streamline software development lifecycle across development, test and production systems as you don't need to have similar hardware and software environment across development and production systems. The container application has the necessary configurations (and files) so that you can move it from development, to test, to production without any side effects.
3. Testing and bug tracking also become less complicated since there is no difference between running your application locally, on a test server, or in production.

4. Containers are light weight and can start in seconds. If there is spike in traffic you can Provision additional containers in few seconds.

5. Containers share a common OS which reduces management overhead as you need to Patch or bug fix a single Operating System.

6. Containers are a very cost effective solution. They help decrease operating cost (less servers, less staff) and development cost (develop for one consistent runtime environment).
7. Running containers is less resource intensive then running VMs so you can add more computing workload onto the same server.
8. Containers are a great option for DevOps and continuous deployment.

Drawbacks of Container Technology

1. Containers have higher fault domain as containers share host OS.
2. Containers are less secure than VMs. Containers share the kernel and other components of the host OS and have root access. If there is vulnerability in the kernel it can jeopardize the security of the containers.
3. Less flexibility in operating systems. You need to start a new server to be able to run containers with different operating systems.
4. Implementing container networking and Storage is still a challenge as compared to virtual machines.

Container Deployment Options in Azure

Container can be deployed in Azure in following ways:

1. Azure Linux or Windows VM with Docker engine installed.
2. Azure Container Instances.
3. Azure Web App for Containers.
4. Container Orchestration Platform. Orchestration platform provide a cluster of container ready virtual machines. Azure offers following Container Orchestration platforms:
   Azure Kubernetes Service (AKS)
   Azure Service Fabric Cluster
   Azure Container Service (ACS) (DC/OS, Swarm & Kubernetes) - Deprecated

Note: Azure Container Service (ACS) is deprecated.

Common Docker commands for running containers

Download Container image from Registry to Local Registry
Docker pull <image id>

View the images in your local registry
docker image list

Start a Docker container
docker run <image id>

View active containers
docker ps

Stop Container
Docker stop <Container id>

Restart Stopped Container
Docker start <Container id>

Remove a stopped Container
Docker rm <Container id>

Remove Docker Image
Docker image rm <image id>

Exercise 27: Create Azure Ubuntu VM

In this exercise we will create Ubuntu Server VM in **Web-Subnet** of Virtual Network **VNETCloud**, in Resource Group **RGCloud** and in location **East US 2**. **Note:** Virtual Network **VNETCloud, Web-Subnet** and Resource Group **RGCloud** were created in Chapter 1, AZ-300 & AZ-301 Study & Lab Guide Part 1.

1. In Azure Portal Click Create a Resource> Compute> Ubuntu server 18.04 LTS> Create Virtual Machine Blade opens>Select Resource Group RGCloud, Region East US 2, Enter Username and Password and select none for inbound ports.

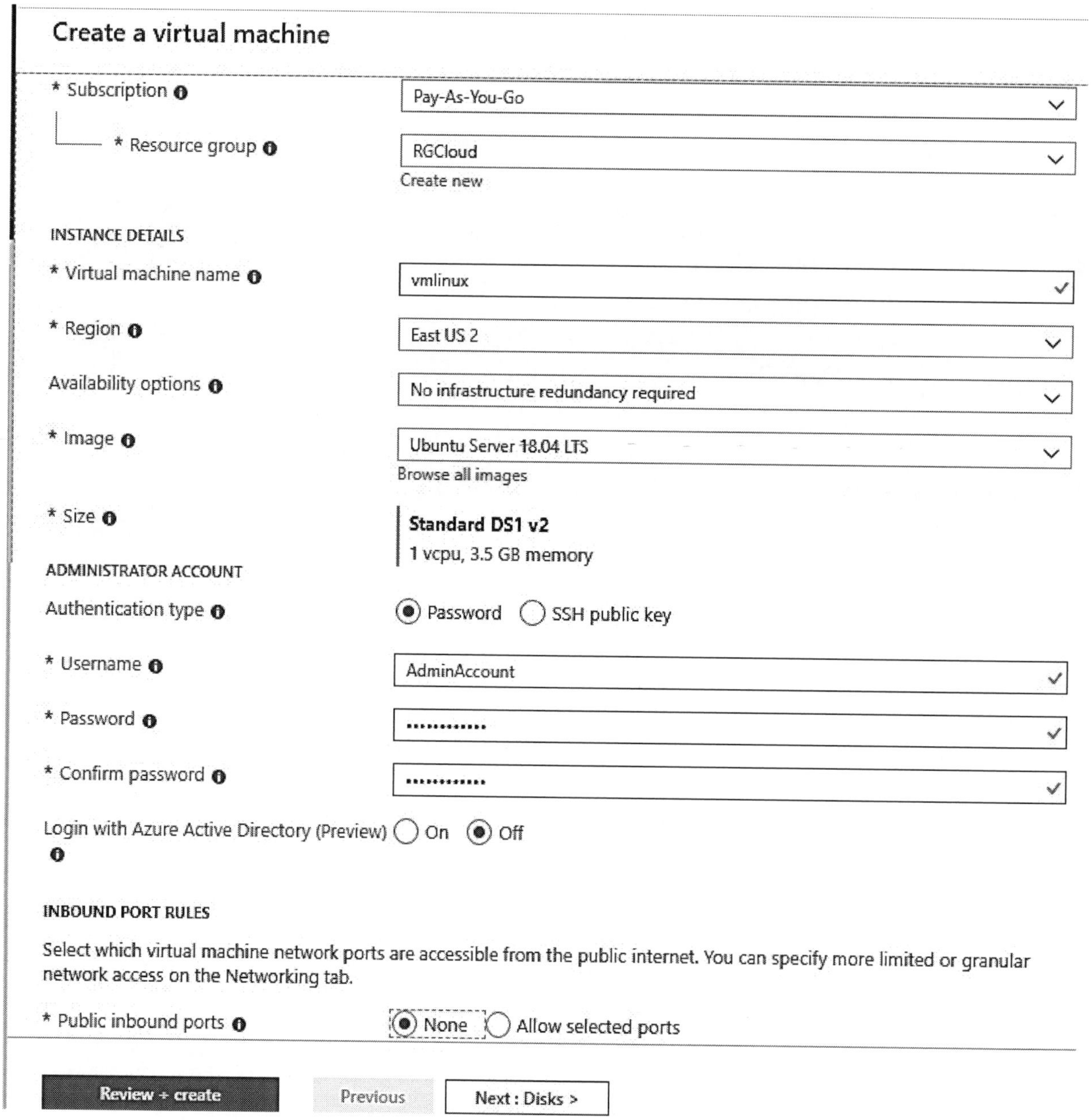

Create a virtual machine

* Subscription: Pay-As-You-Go
* Resource group: RGCloud
Create new

INSTANCE DETAILS
* Virtual machine name: vmlinux
* Region: East US 2
Availability options: No infrastructure redundancy required
* Image: Ubuntu Server 18.04 LTS
Browse all images
* Size: **Standard DS1 v2**
1 vcpu, 3.5 GB memory

ADMINISTRATOR ACCOUNT
Authentication type: Password / SSH public key
* Username: AdminAccount
* Password: ••••••••••••
* Confirm password: ••••••••••••
Login with Azure Active Directory (Preview): On / Off

INBOUND PORT RULES
Select which virtual machine network ports are accessible from the public internet. You can specify more limited or granular network access on the Networking tab.
* Public inbound ports: None / Allow selected ports

Review + create | Previous | Next : Disks >

2. Click Next:Disks in bottom pane or Disks in Top pane> Disk pane opens>Select Standard HDD. We are using Managed Disk option.

Create a virtual machine

Basics Disks Networking Management Advanced Tags Review + create

Azure VMs have one operating system disk and a temporary disk for short-term storage. You can attach additional data disks. The size of the VM determines the type of storage you can use and the number of data disks allowed. Learn more

DISK OPTIONS

* OS disk type: Standard HDD

The selected VM size supports premium disks. We recommend Premium SSD for high IOPS workloads. Virtual machines with Premium SSD disks qualify for the 99.9% connectivity

3. Click Next:Networking>Networking pane opens> Select **VNETCloud** and **Web-Subnet** from drop down box>Dynamic Public is automatically created>Select **Basic** for NSG>Select **Allow Selected Ports** and select **HTTP** and **SSH**.

Create a virtual machine

* Virtual network: VNETCloud
Create new

* Subnet: Web-Subnet (10.1.1.0/24)
Manage subnet configuration

Public IP: (new) vmlinux-ip
Create new

NIC network security group: None / Basic (selected) / Advanced

* Public inbound ports: None / Allow selected ports (selected)

* Select inbound ports: HTTP, SSH
- [x] HTTP (80)
- [ ] HTTPS (443)
- [x] SSH (22)
- [ ] RDP (3389)

Accelerated networking: On / Off (selected)
The selected VM size does not support accelerated networking.

LOAD BALANCING

Review + create | < Previous | Next : Management >

4. Click Review + Create> After Validation is passed Click create.

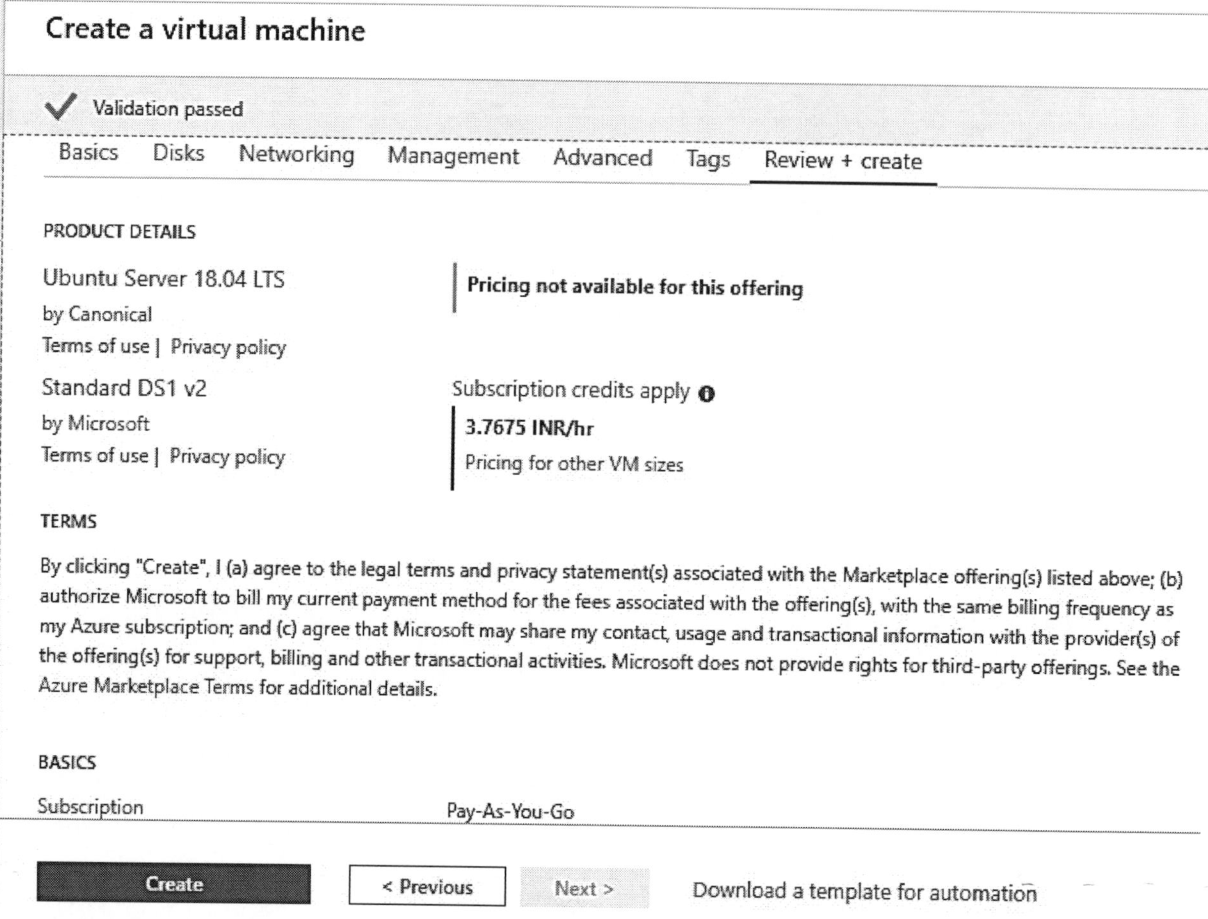

5. Figure below shows dashboard of vmlinux. In right pane note the Link under DNS name. We will use it in next step to configure DNS name for vmlinux.

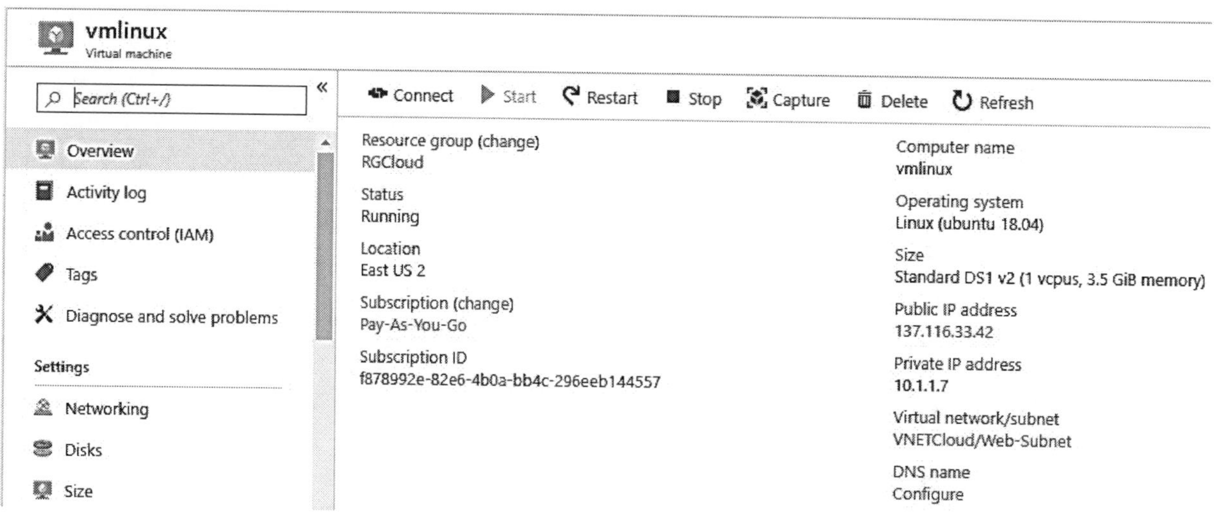

6. **Configure DNS name.** Click Configure in Right pane under DNS>Public IP Address pane opens> Enter a name. In this case I entered **vmlinuxu**>click save. Close the Public IP Pane. In VM dashboard click refresh and you can see DNS name of VM.

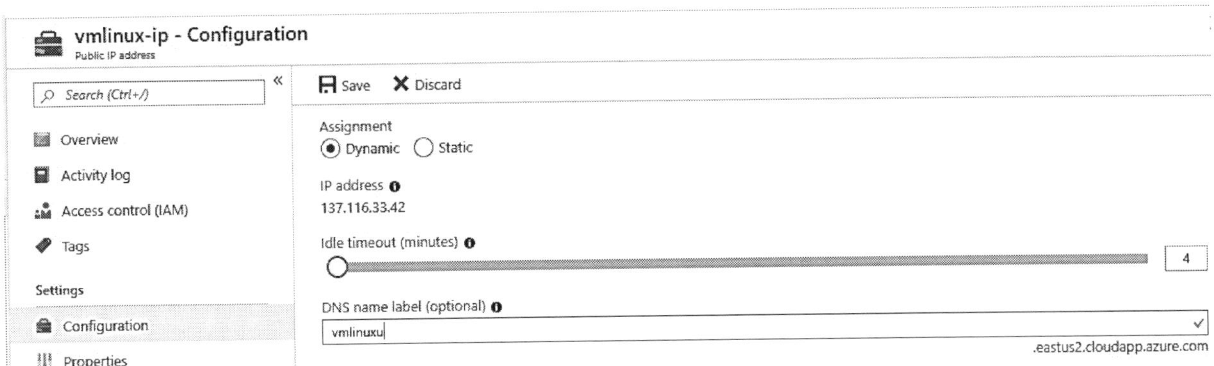

7. In VM click refresh and you can see DNS name of VM.

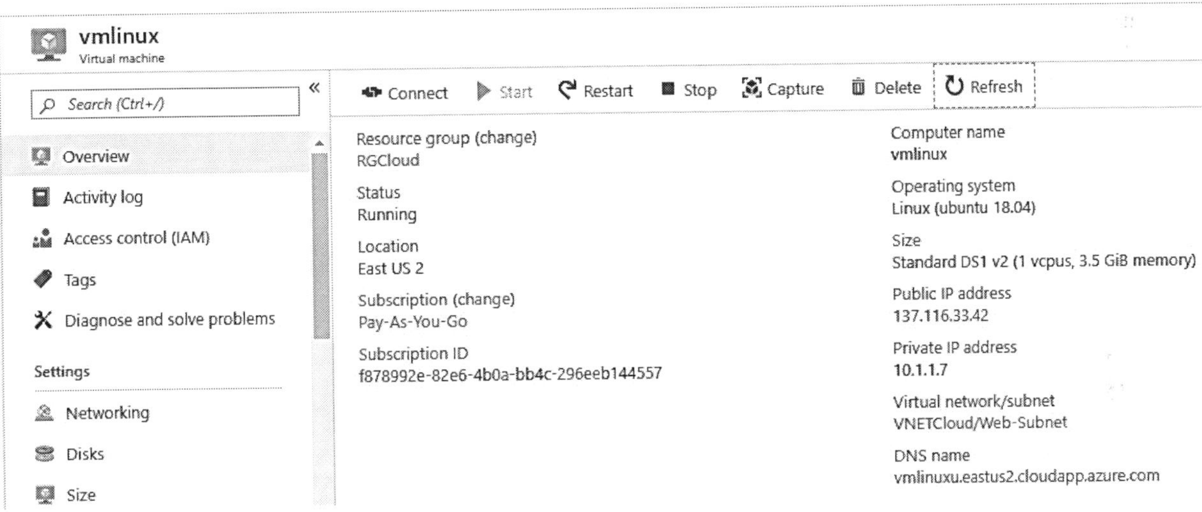

Exercise 28: Connect to Ubuntu VM and update the VM

For this exercise I downloaded and installed Putty client.

1. Open putty Client and enter Linux VM DNS name and select SSH.

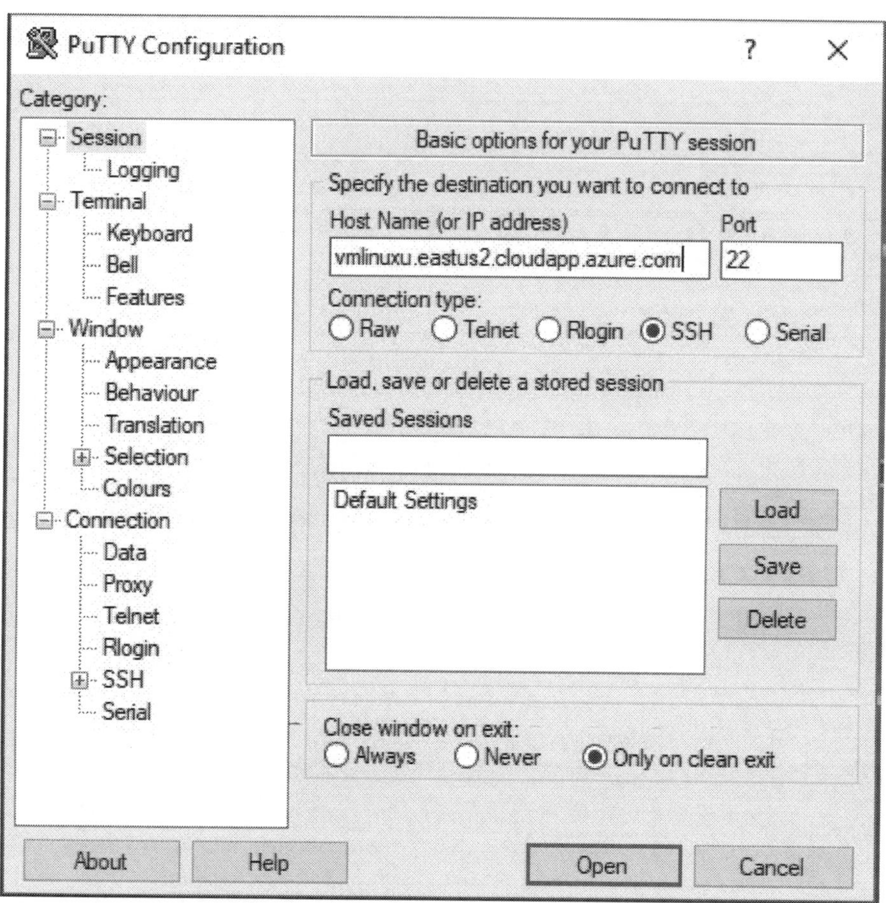

2. Click open and Putty client connects to Linux VM> Enter Username and password you entered during VM creation>Press Enter> You are now connected to Linux VM.

AdminAccount@vmlinux: ~

```
login as: AdminAccount
AdminAccount@vmlinuxu.eastus2.cloudapp.azure.com's password:
Welcome to Ubuntu 18.04.2 LTS (GNU/Linux 4.18.0-1023-azure x86_64)

 * Documentation:  https://help.ubuntu.com
 * Management:     https://landscape.canonical.com
 * Support:        https://ubuntu.com/advantage

  System information as of Fri Jun 28 01:15:18 UTC 2019
```

3. **Update the Ubuntu VM:** sudo apt-get –y update

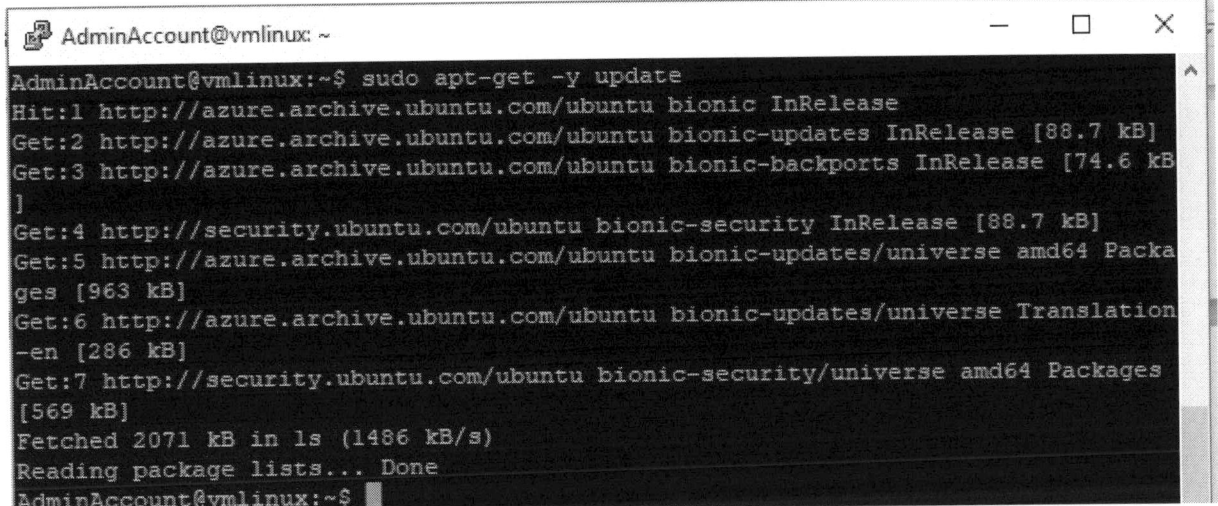

Exercise 29: Install Docker Engine and Deploy Container on Ubuntu VM

In this Exercise we will install Docker Engine on Ubuntu VM vmlinux. We will then download **hello-world** image from **Docker Hub** and then run it. Ubuntu VM vmlinux was created in Exercise 27.

1. Login to vmlinux using putty client.
2. To Install Docker engine, enter command **sudo apt install docker.io.** Click y if prompted.

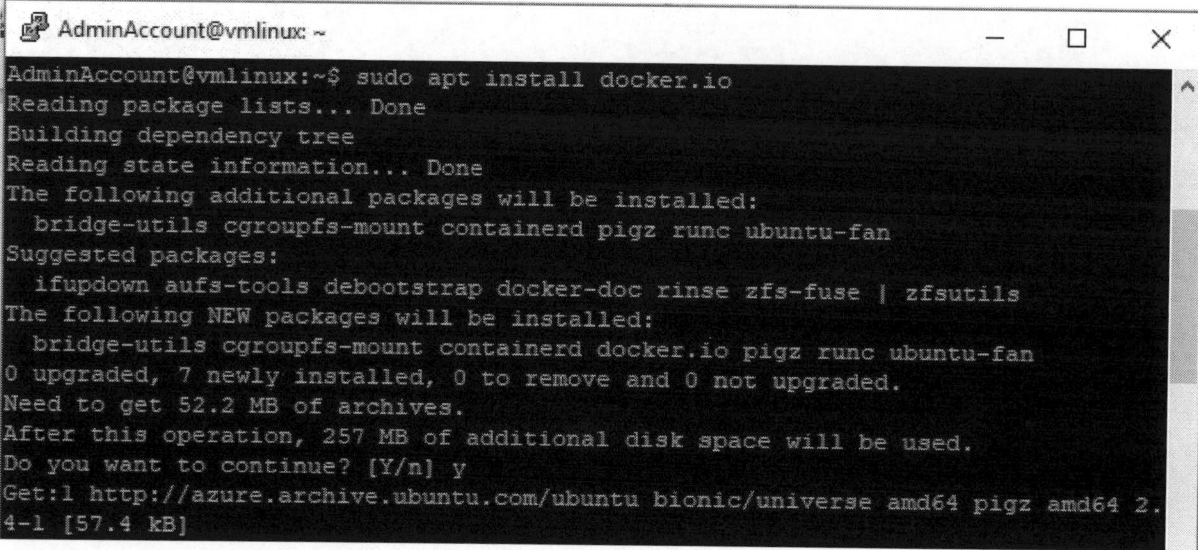

3. To check Docker version enter command **sudo docker version.**

```
AdminAccount@vmlinux: ~
AdminAccount@vmlinux:~$ sudo docker version
Client:
 Version:           18.09.5
 API version:       1.39
 Go version:        go1.10.4
 Git commit:        e8ff056
 Built:             Thu May  9 23:11:19 2019
 OS/Arch:           linux/amd64
 Experimental:      false

Server:
 Engine:
  Version:          18.09.5
  API version:      1.39 (minimum version 1.12)
  Go version:       go1.10.4
  Git commit:       e8ff056
  Built:            Thu May  9 22:59:19 2019
  OS/Arch:          linux/amd64
  Experimental:     false
AdminAccount@vmlinux:~$
```

4. Pull hello-world server image from Docker Hub: **sudo docker pull hello-world.**

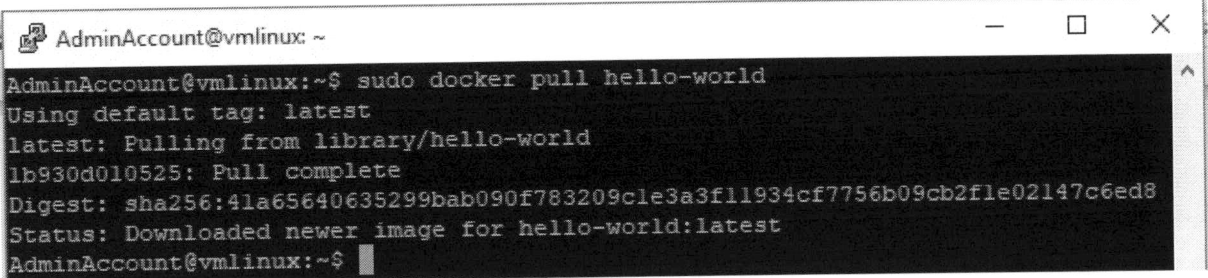

AdminAccount@vmlinux: ~
AdminAccount@vmlinux:~$ sudo docker pull hello-world
Using default tag: latest
latest: Pulling from library/hello-world
1b930d010525: Pull complete
Digest: sha256:41a65640635299bab090f783209c1e3a3f11934cf7756b09cb2f1e02147c6ed8
Status: Downloaded newer image for hello-world:latest
AdminAccount@vmlinux:~$

5. Check the downloaded image: **sudo docker images**

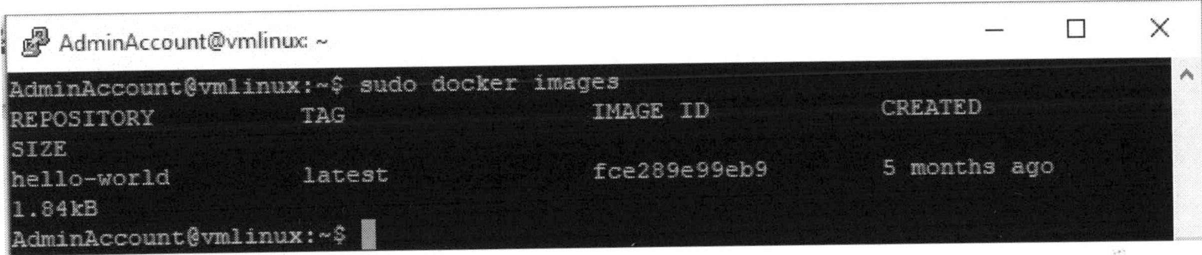

6. Run the hello-world image to create container: **sudo docker run hello-world**

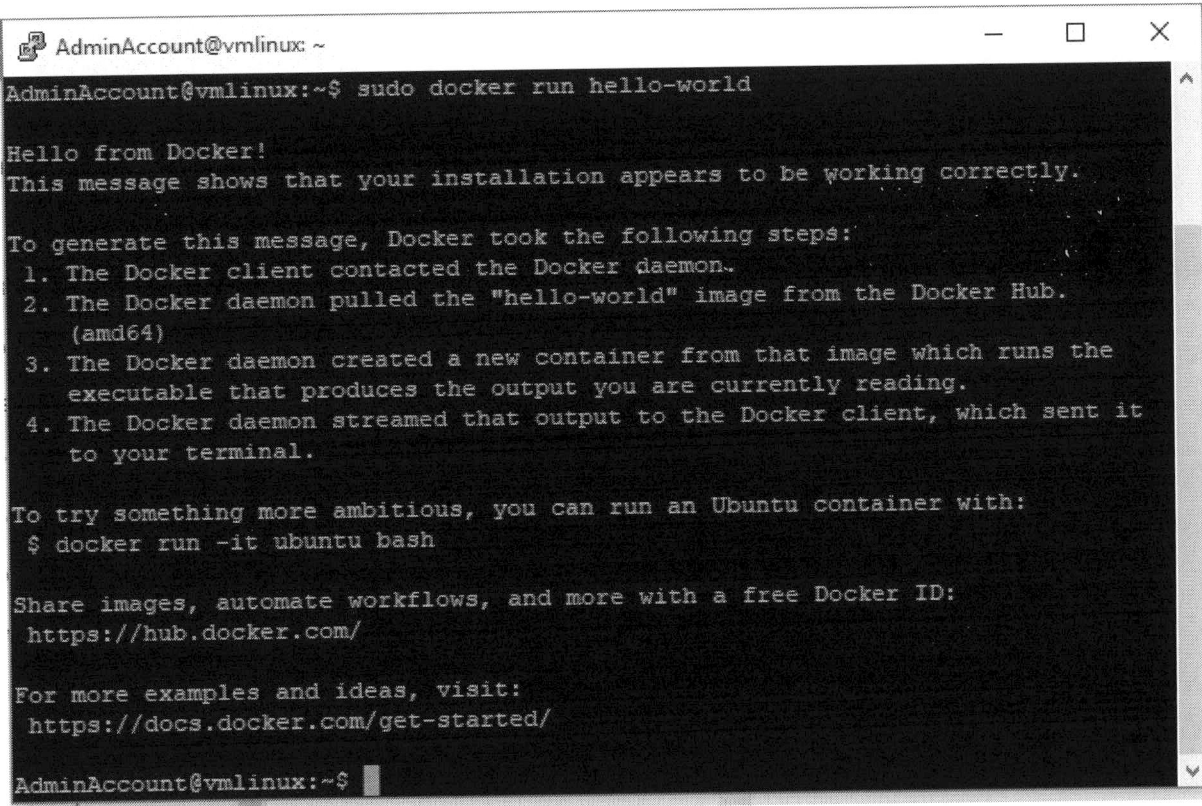

Exercise 30: Deploy NGINX Container on Azure Ubuntu Linux VM

In this Exercise we will download NGINX image from Docker Hub to Ubuntu VM vmlinux. We will then deploy the NGINX container image using docker run command.

1. Pull nginx image from Docker Hub to Ubuntu VM: **sudo docker pull nginx.**

2. Check the downloaded image: **sudo docker images.**

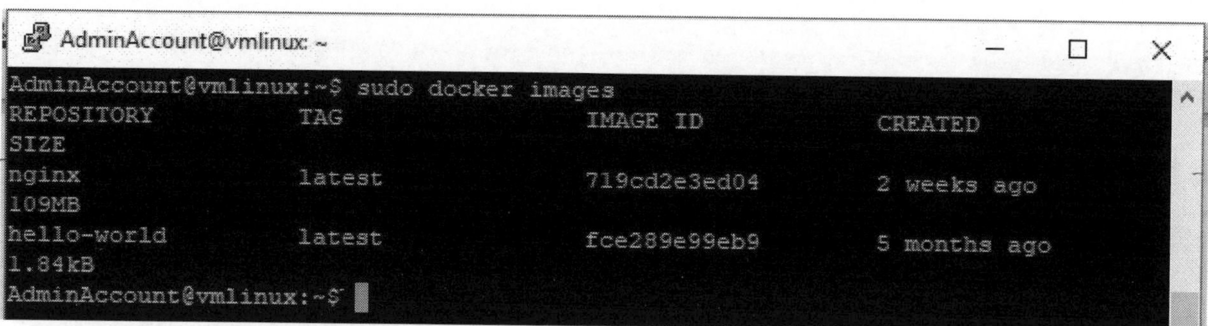

3. Run the nginx image: **sudo docker run --name mynginx1 –p 80:80 –d nginx**.

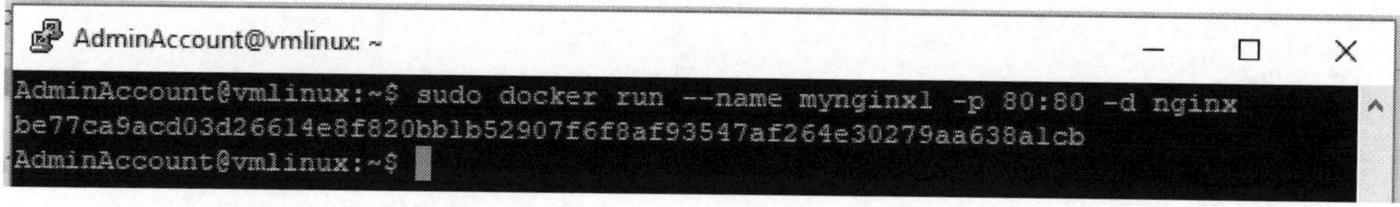

4. Check the Status of active containers: **docker ps**
   You can see from below figure that nginx container mynginx1 status is up.

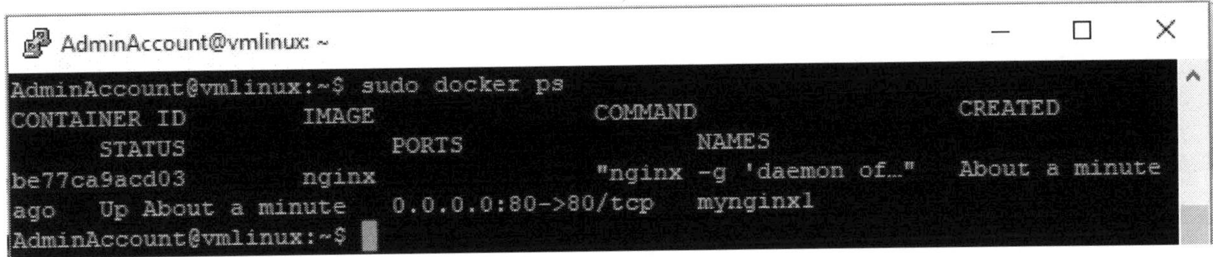

5. From vmlinux dashboard note down DNS name and in your browser enter **vmlinuxu.eastus2.cloudapp.azure.com.** Default NGINX website opens.

Welcome to nginx!

If you see this page, the nginx web server is successfully installed and working. Further configuration is required.

For online documentation and support please refer to nginx.org.
Commercial support is available at nginx.com.

Thank you for using nginx.

Dockerfile

Dockerfile is used to build custom container image containing your application. A **Dockerfile is a plain text file** containing all the commands needed to build an image.

Docker build command is then used to build image from Dockerfile.

Following docker build command builds an image from Dockerfile.

$ docker build -f /path/to/a/Dockerfile

Following command will save the image into repository (shykes) with a tag.

$ docker build -t shykes/myap

Container Registry

Containers are built from images that are stored in one or more repositories. These repositories can belong to public or private container registries. A registry is a web service to which Docker can connect to upload and download container images.

An example of a public registry is **Docker Hub**. Examples of private registries are **Docker Trusted Registry** and Cloud based **Azure Container Registry**. Private repositories do not support unauthenticated access.

You can also upload your custom image to Container Registry and make it available as public or private.

Exercise 31: Browse Public Container Registry Docker Hub

1. Open Browser and https://hub.docker.com>Click Browse Popular images> Scroll down and you can see millions of images listed.

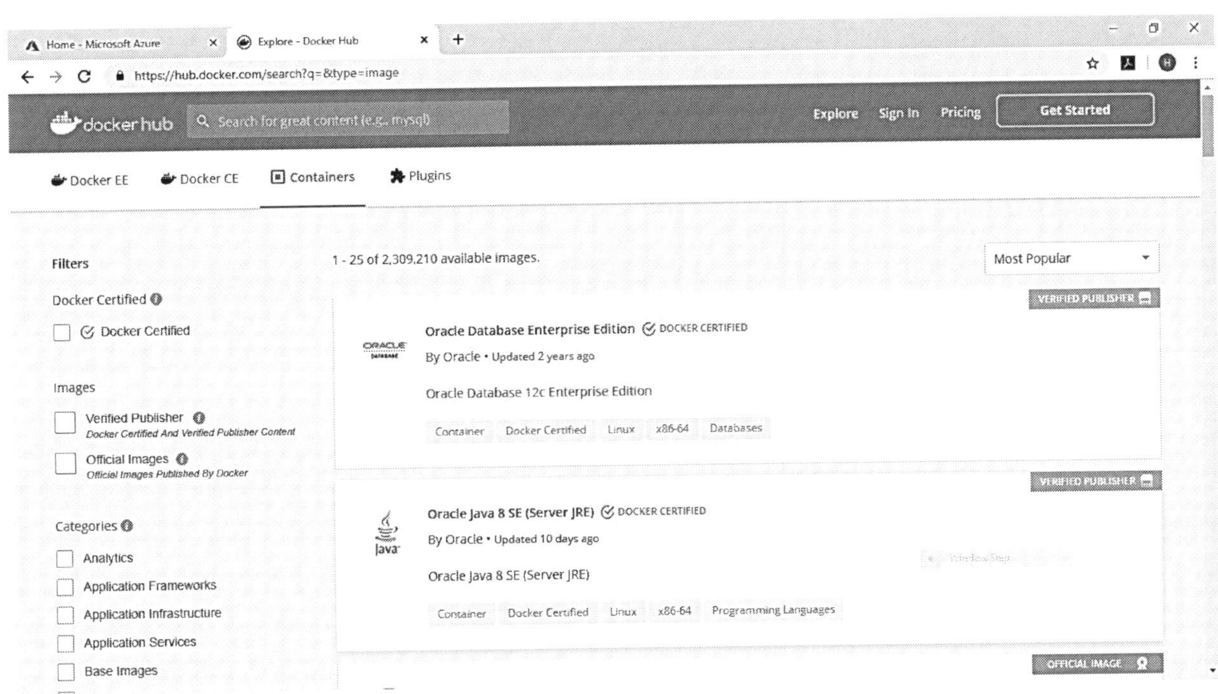

You can retrieve container image from Container Registry using **Docker Pull** command.

Azure Container Registry (ACR)

Azure Container Registry stores private container images and is based on open-source Docker Registry 2.0.

Additional capabilities include geo-replication, image signing with Docker Content Trust, Helm Chart Repositories and Task base compute for building, testing, patching container workloads.

Apart from storing Container images, **Azure Container Registry Tasks** can build container images. ACR Tasks uses a standard Dockerfile to create and store a container image in Azure Container Registry without the need for local Docker tooling. With Azure Container Registry Tasks, you can build on demand or fully automate container image builds.

Architecture of Azure Container Registry

Registry: Registries are available in three SKUs: Basic, Standard, and Premium, each of which supports webhook integration, registry authentication with Azure Active Directory, and delete functionality.
Repository: A registry contains one or more repositories, which are virtual groups of container images with the same name but different tags or digests. Azure Container Registry supports multilevel repository namespaces. With multilevel namespaces, you can group collections of images related to a specific app.
Image: Stored in a repository, each image is a read-only snapshot of a Docker-compatible container. Azure container registries can include both Windows and Linux images.

Azure Container Registry Tiers

Basic tier is a cost-optimized SKU and is targeted towards developers.
Standard tier is targeted towards Production scenarios. Standard tier offer the same capabilities as Basic with increased storage and image throughput.
Premier tier is targeted towards high-volume scenarios. Premium tier has highest amount of included storage and concurrent operations, enabling high-volume scenarios. Premium tier has additional features including geo-replication for managing a single registry across multiple regions, content trust for image tag signing and firewalls and virtual networks to restrict access to the registry.

Table below shows Comparison between different tiers.

	Basic	**Standard**	**Premier**
Storage (GB)	10	100	500
ReadOps/minute	1000	3000	10000
WriteOps/minute	100	500	2000
Download bandwidth MBps	30	60	100
Upload bandwidth MBps	10	20	50
Web hooks	2	10	100
Geo-Replication	Not Supported	Not Supported	Supported
Content trust	Not Supported	Not Supported	Supported
Price per day	$0.167	$0.667	$1.667

Access to Azure Container Registry

Azure Container Registry repositories are private — they do not support unauthenticated access. To authenticate to Azure Container Registry repository you can use following option:

1. Use the docker login command.
   docker login <*registry_name*>.azurecr.io

2. Use Azure CLI command.
   az acr login --name <*registry_name*>

3. Use Azure AD backed Service Principal option. Service principals allow role-based access to a registry.

Content formats supported in Azure Container Registry

Docker-compatible container images.
Open Container Initiative (OCI) Images.
Helm charts: Azure Container Registry supports repositories for Helm charts. Helm charts is a packaging format used to quickly manage and deploy applications for Kubernetes.

Exercise 32: Create Azure Container Registry (ACR)

In Azure Portal Click Create a Resource> Containers> Container Registry>Create Container Registry pane opens> Enter a name. I entered **ACRCloud**>Select Resource Group RGCloud> Location East US 2> select Enable for Admin User> Select SKU and click create.

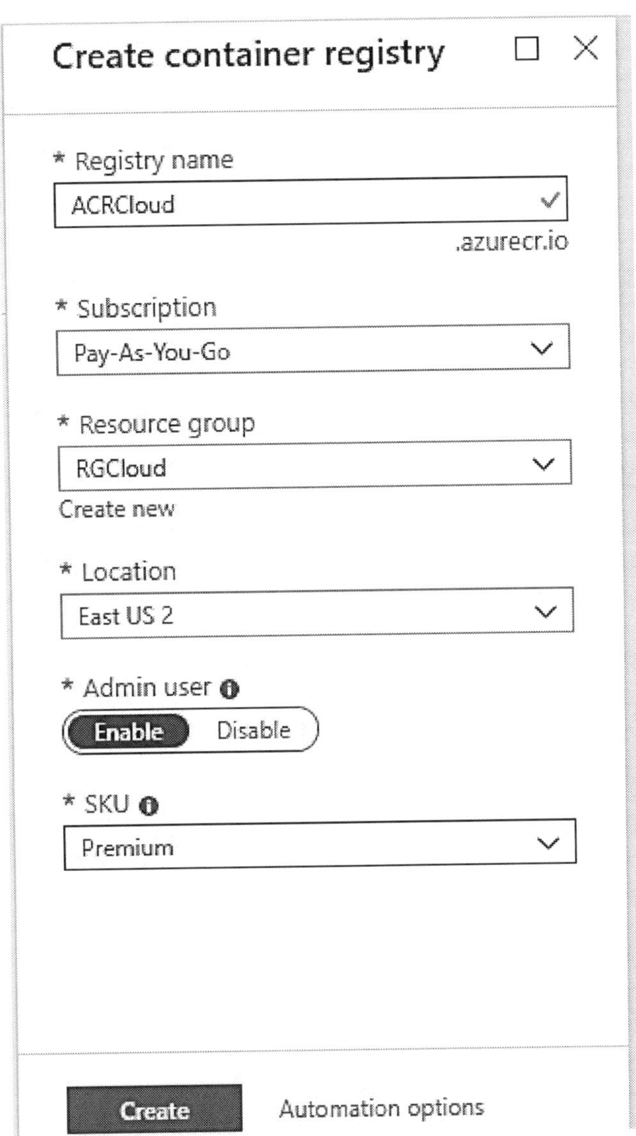

Note 1: Name of the Registry will be **acrCloud.azurecr.io**
Note 2: By enabling Admin User you can use registry name as user name and user access keys as password to login to Azure Container Registry.

2. Figure below shows dashboard of Azure Container Registry ACRCloud.

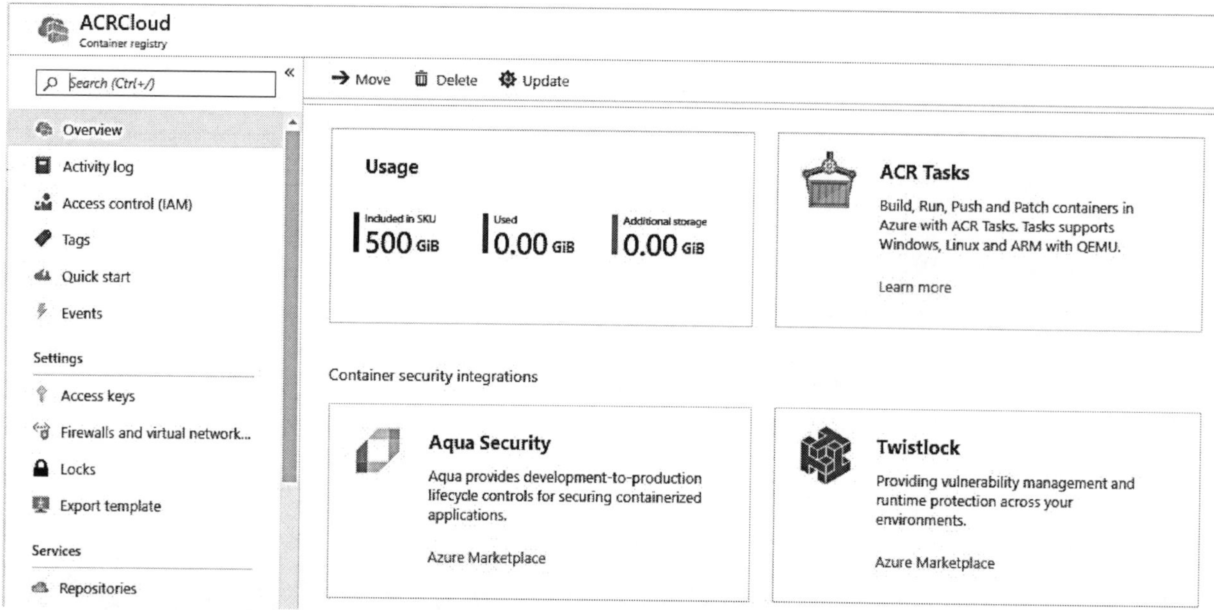

3. Click repositories in left pane> You can see that there are no images. In next exercise we will push hello-world image in linuxvm to Azure Container registry.

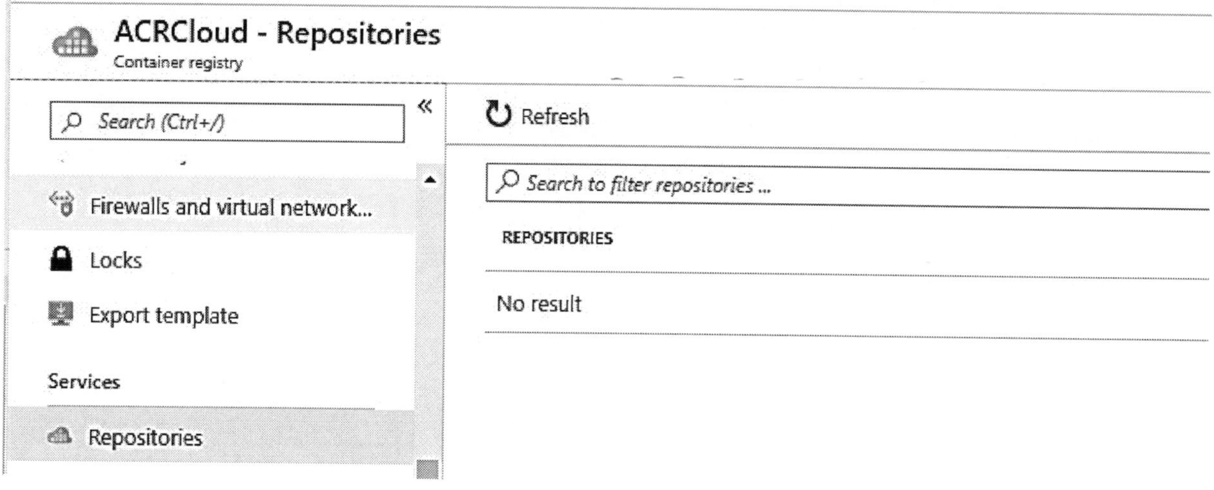

4. Click Access keys in left pane. You can see the password to login to Azure Container Registry.

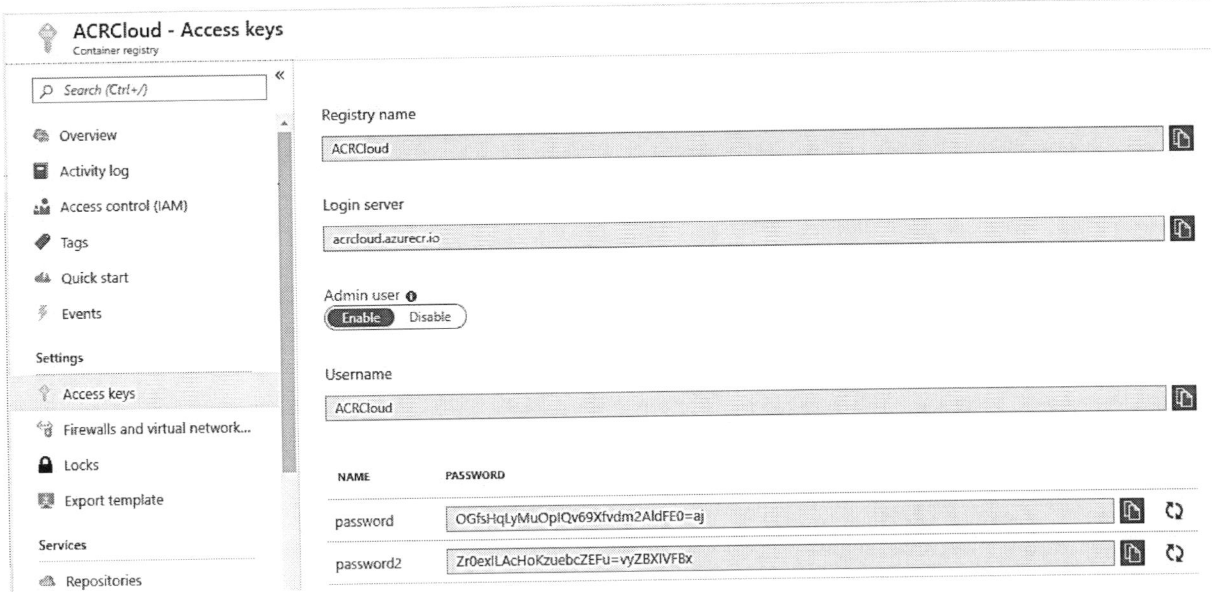

Exercise 33: Install Azure CLI on Ubuntu VM vmlinux

Ubuntu VM vmlinux was created in Exercise 27.

1. Login to vmlinux using putty client.
2. To Install Azure CLI, enter below command:
   curl -sL https://aka.ms/InstallAzureCLIDeb | sudo bash

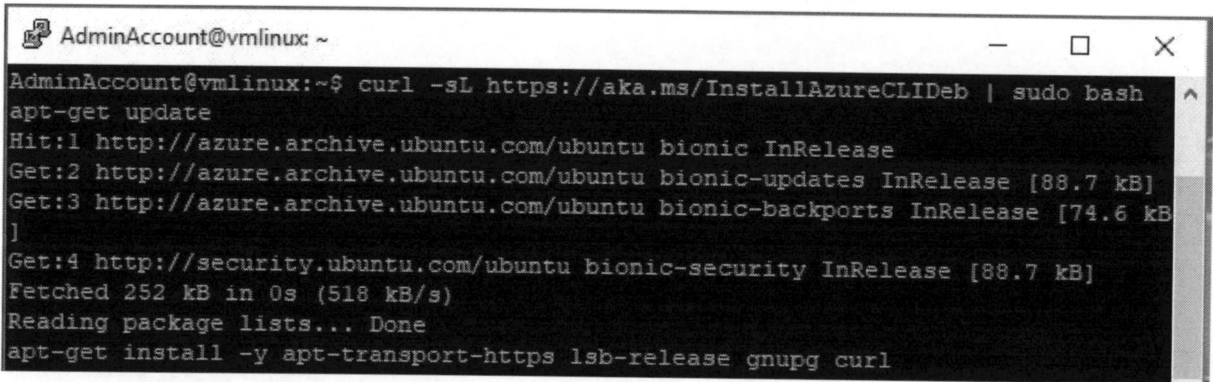

Exercise 34: Login to ACR and push image hello-world to ACR

In this exercise we will login to Azure Container Registry ACRCloud from Ubuntu VM vmlinux. We will then push hello-world image located in local registry in vmlinux to Azure Container Registry ACRCloud. Recall that hello-world image was downloaded from Docker Hub to vmlinux in Exercise 29.

1. **From Ubuntu VM vmlinux Login to Azure**: az login.
   From your Laptop/Desktop Open a browser to https://microsoft.com/devicelogin and enter the code mentioned in the putty client.

```
AdminAccount@vmlinux: ~
AdminAccount@vmlinux:~$ az login
To sign in, use a web browser to open the page https://microsoft.com/devicelogin
 and enter the code A6TG3R8CF to authenticate.
```

2. After you have successfully authenticated to Azure through Browser, The Putty Client will now show Azure information as shown below.

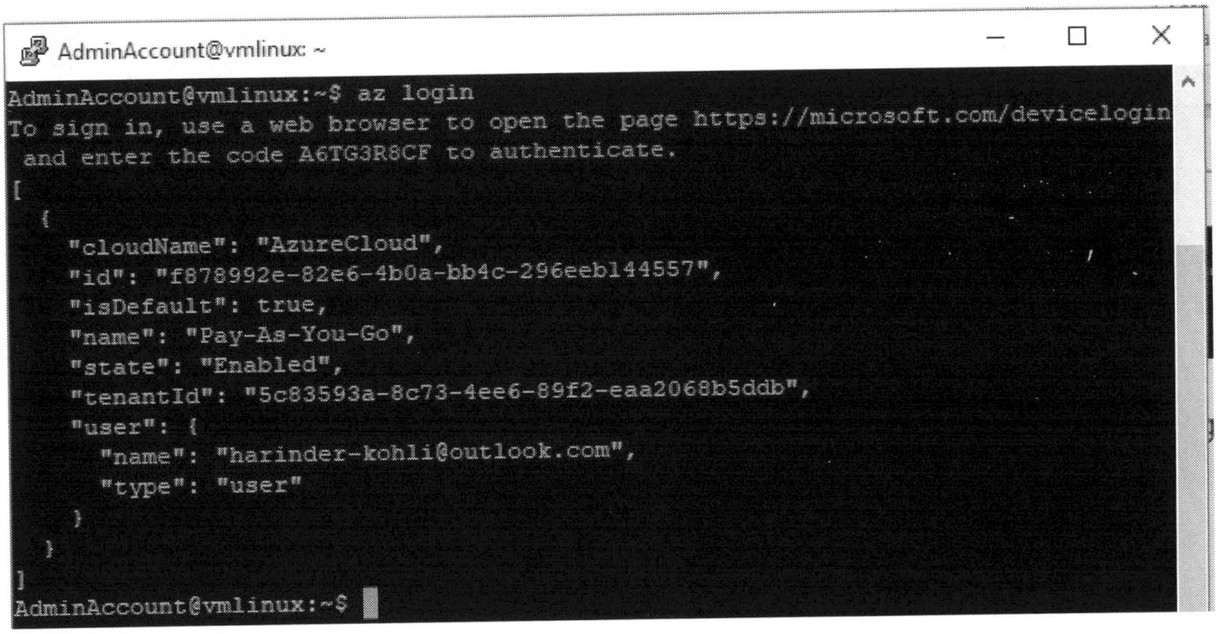

```
AdminAccount@vmlinux: ~
AdminAccount@vmlinux:~$ az login
To sign in, use a web browser to open the page https://microsoft.com/devicelogin
 and enter the code A6TG3R8CF to authenticate.
[
  {
    "cloudName": "AzureCloud",
    "id": "f878992e-82e6-4b0a-bb4c-296eeb144557",
    "isDefault": true,
    "name": "Pay-As-You-Go",
    "state": "Enabled",
    "tenantId": "5c83593a-8c73-4ee6-89f2-eaa2068b5ddb",
    "user": {
      "name": "harinder-kohli@outlook.com",
      "type": "user"
    }
  }
]
AdminAccount@vmlinux:~$
```

3. **Login to ACR:** sudo az acr login --name acrcloud

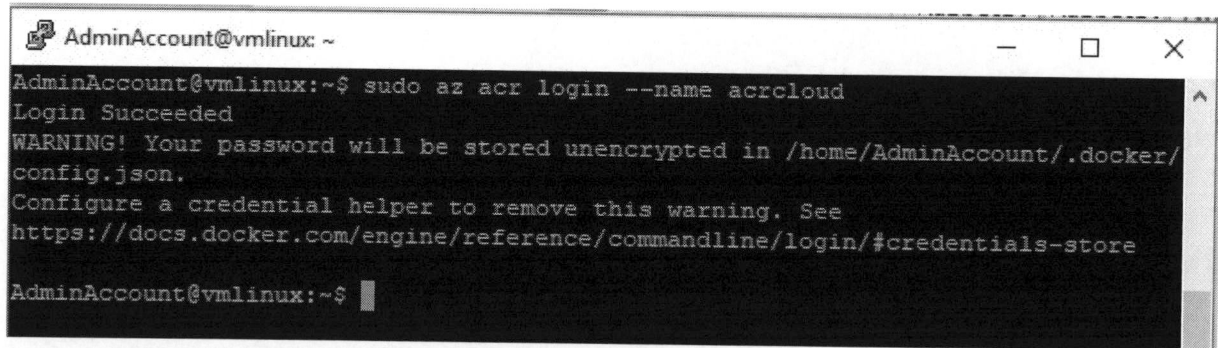

4. **Tag hello-world image located in vmlinux**. Make sure to use FQDN of ACR. **sudo docker tag hello-world acrcloud.azurecr.io/hello-world:v1**

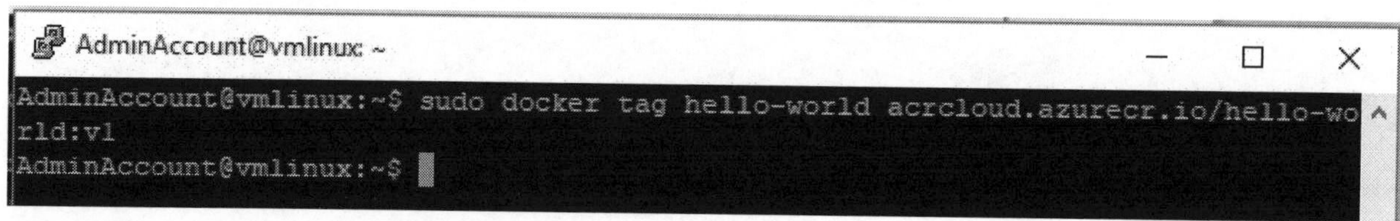

5. Check the image created

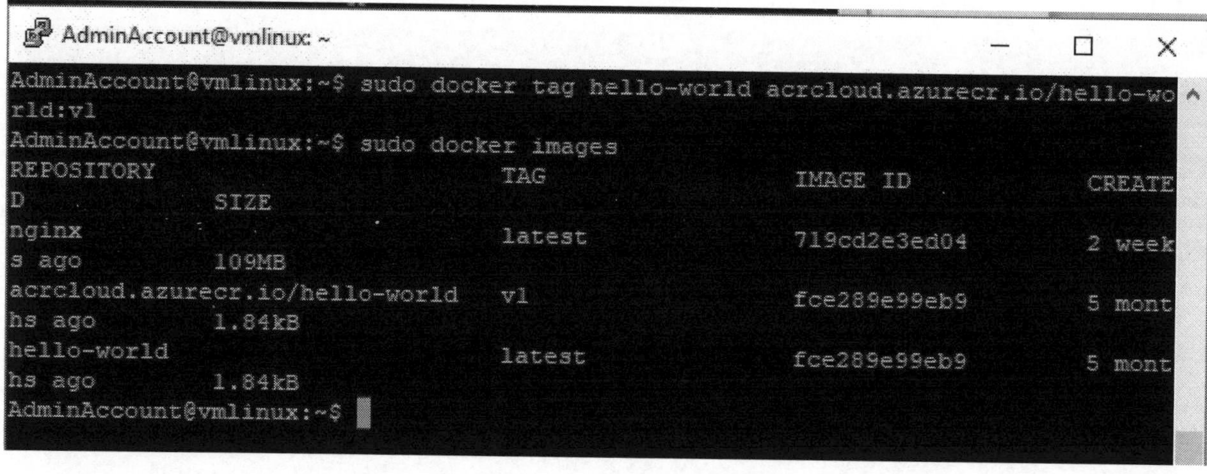

6. Push the image to ACR: **sudo docker push acrcloud.azurecr.io/hello-world:v1**. Make sure to use FQDN of ACR. This will create the **hello-world** repository, containing the hello-world:v1 image.

```
AdminAccount@vmlinux:~$ sudo docker push acrcloud.azurecr.io/hello-world:v1
The push refers to repository [acrcloud.azurecr.io/hello-world]
af0b15c8625b: Pushed
v1: digest: sha256:92c7f9c92844bbbb5d0a101b22f7c2a7949e40f8ea90c8b3bc396879d95e8
99a size: 524
AdminAccount@vmlinux:~$
```

7. **Check the image in ACR ACRCloud:** In ACR Dashboard click Repositories in left pane>You can see the repository hello-world>Click Repository hello-world and you can see the image.

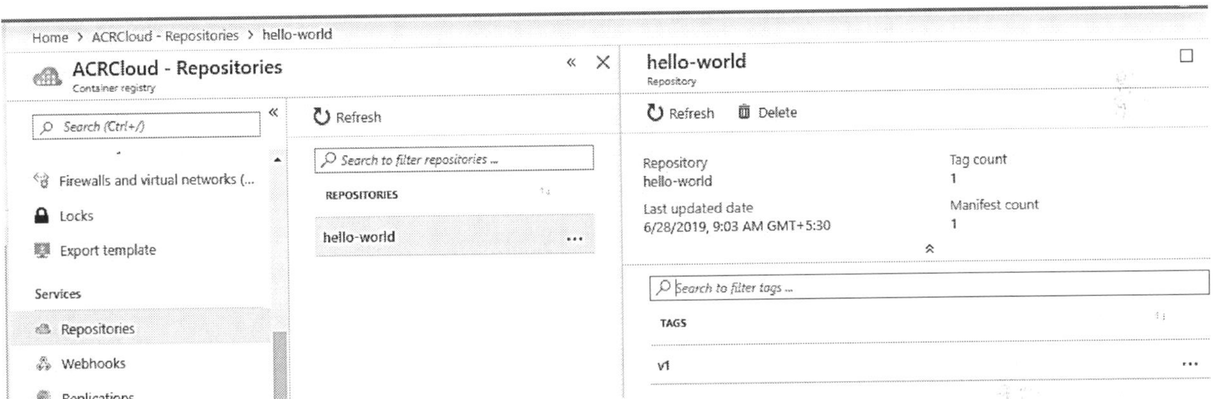

8. **Remove both hello-world images from vmlinux local repository:** sudo docker image rm <image id of hello-world:v1 or hello-world> -f

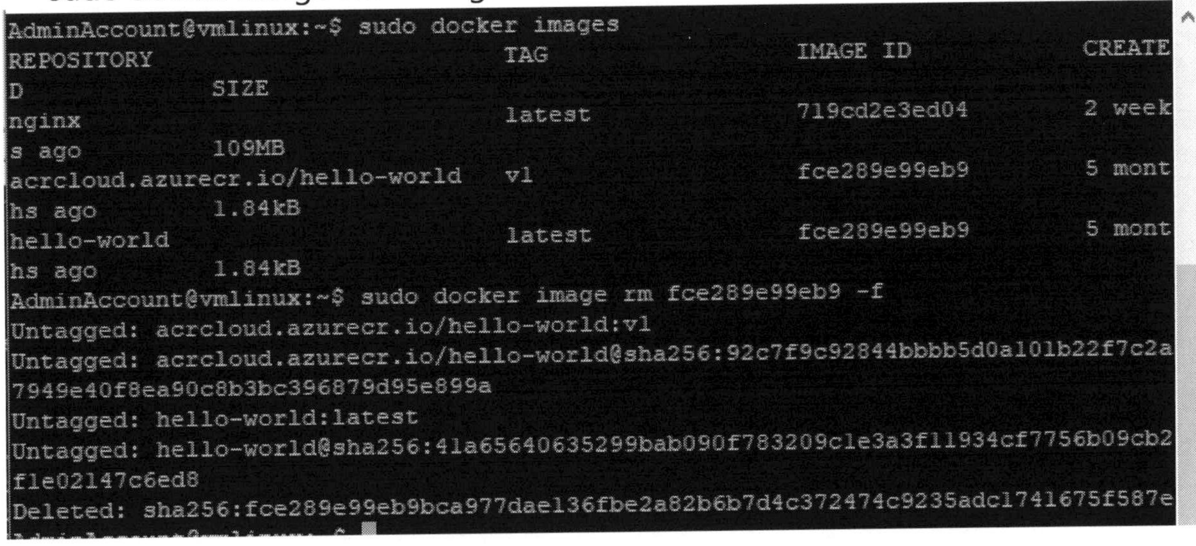

```
AdminAccount@vmlinux:~$ sudo docker images
REPOSITORY                          TAG                 IMAGE ID            CREATE
D                   SIZE
nginx                               latest              719cd2e3ed04        2 week
s ago               109MB
acrcloud.azurecr.io/hello-world     v1                  fce289e99eb9        5 mont
hs ago              1.84kB
hello-world                         latest              fce289e99eb9        5 mont
hs ago              1.84kB
AdminAccount@vmlinux:~$ sudo docker image rm fce289e99eb9 -f
Untagged: acrcloud.azurecr.io/hello-world:v1
Untagged: acrcloud.azurecr.io/hello-world@sha256:92c7f9c92844bbbb5d0a101b22f7c2a
7949e40f8ea90c8b3bc396879d95e899a
Untagged: hello-world:latest
Untagged: hello-world@sha256:41a65640635299bab090f783209c1e3a3f11934cf7756b09cb2
f1e02147c6ed8
Deleted: sha256:fce289e99eb9bca977dae136fbe2a82b6b7d4c372474c9235adc1741675f587e
```

Exercise 35: Run hello-world:v1 image from Registry ACRCloud

1. Login to vmlinux using Putty client.
2. Sudo docker run acrcloud.azurecr.io/hello-world:v1

AdminAccount@vmlinux: ~

```
AdminAccount@vmlinux:~$ sudo docker run acrcloud.azurecr.io/hello-world:v1
Unable to find image 'acrcloud.azurecr.io/hello-world:v1' locally
v1: Pulling from hello-world
1b930d010525: Already exists
Digest: sha256:92c7f9c92844bbbb5d0a101b22f7c2a7949e40f8ea90c8b3bc396879d95e899a
Status: Downloaded newer image for acrcloud.azurecr.io/hello-world:v1

Hello from Docker!
This message shows that your installation appears to be working correctly.

To generate this message, Docker took the following steps:
 1. The Docker client contacted the Docker daemon.
 2. The Docker daemon pulled the "hello-world" image from the Docker Hub.
    (amd64)
 3. The Docker daemon created a new container from that image which runs the
    executable that produces the output you are currently reading.
 4. The Docker daemon streamed that output to the Docker client, which sent it
    to your terminal.

To try something more ambitious, you can run an Ubuntu container with:
 $ docker run -it ubuntu bash

Share images, automate workflows, and more with a free Docker ID:
 https://hub.docker.com/

For more examples and ideas, visit:
 https://docs.docker.com/get-started/

AdminAccount@vmlinux:~$
```

Exercise 36: Login to Azure Container Registry using Docker Login Command

In this exercise we will use docker login command to login to Azure Container registry acrcloud. We will login using Admin username and password. Admin user name is name of the Azure Container Registry and password can be found in Access keys option in Azure Container Register.

1. Go to acrcloud dashboard and click Access key in left pane>note down the password.

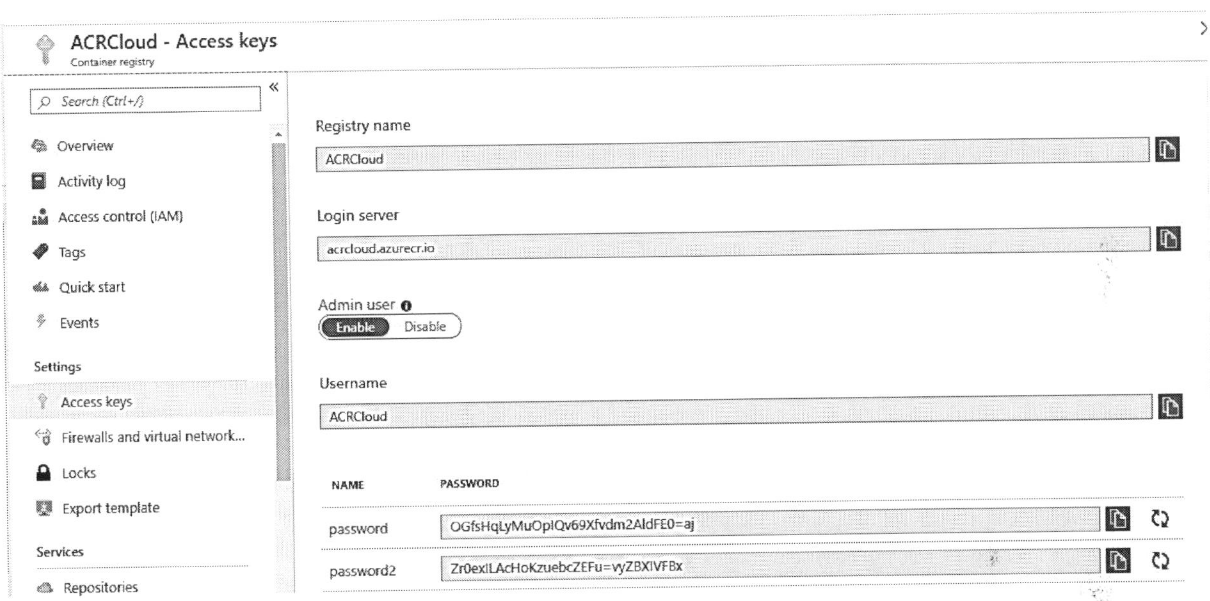

2. Using Putty client login to vmlinux.
3. Enter Command: Sudo docker login acrcloud.azurecr.io.
4. For username enter acrcloud> enter password copied in step 1.

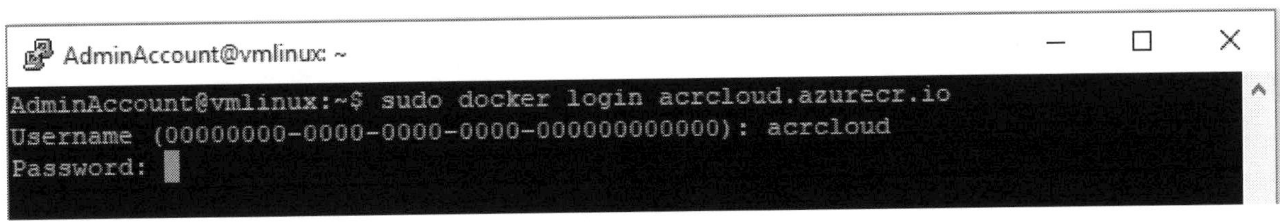

Azure Container Registry Geo Replication

With Geo Replication feature you can create replica of Azure Container Registry to supported region/regions of your choice.

Geo Replication is a feature of ACR Premier SKU.

Exercise 37: Exploring Replication feature

In this exercise we will explore Replication feature but will not implement it.

1. In ACRCloud dashboard click Replication> click + Add> Create Replication blade opens> Select Location from dropdown box.

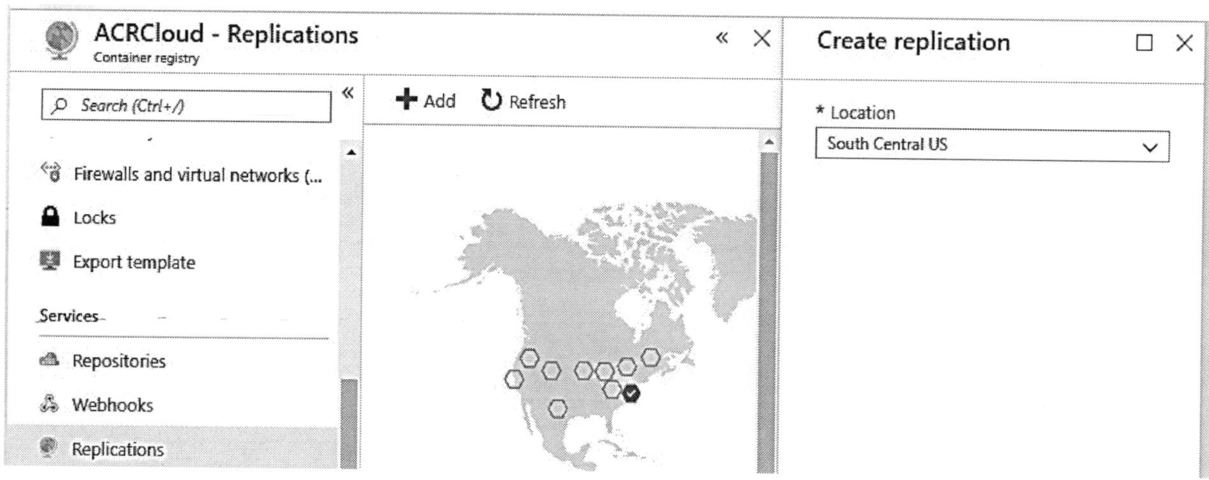

Content trust in Azure Container Registry

Content trust feature in Azure Container Registry enables pushing and pulling of signed images.

As an image publisher, content trust allows you to **sign** the images you push to your registry. Consumers of your images (people or systems pulling images from your registry) can configure their clients to pull *only* signed images. When an image consumer pulls a signed image, their Docker client verifies the integrity of the image. In this model, consumers are assured that the signed images in your registry were indeed published by you, and that they've not been modified since being published.

Content trust is a feature of ACR Premier SKU.

You can enable Content trust using Azure Portal or Azure CLI. Figure below shows enabling content trust from ACR dashboard.

Exercise 38: Exploring Content Trust feature

In this exercise we will explore Content Trust feature but will not implement it.

1. In ACRCloud dashboard click Content Trust in left pane> Content Trust blade opens in right pane> From here you can click enable the feature.

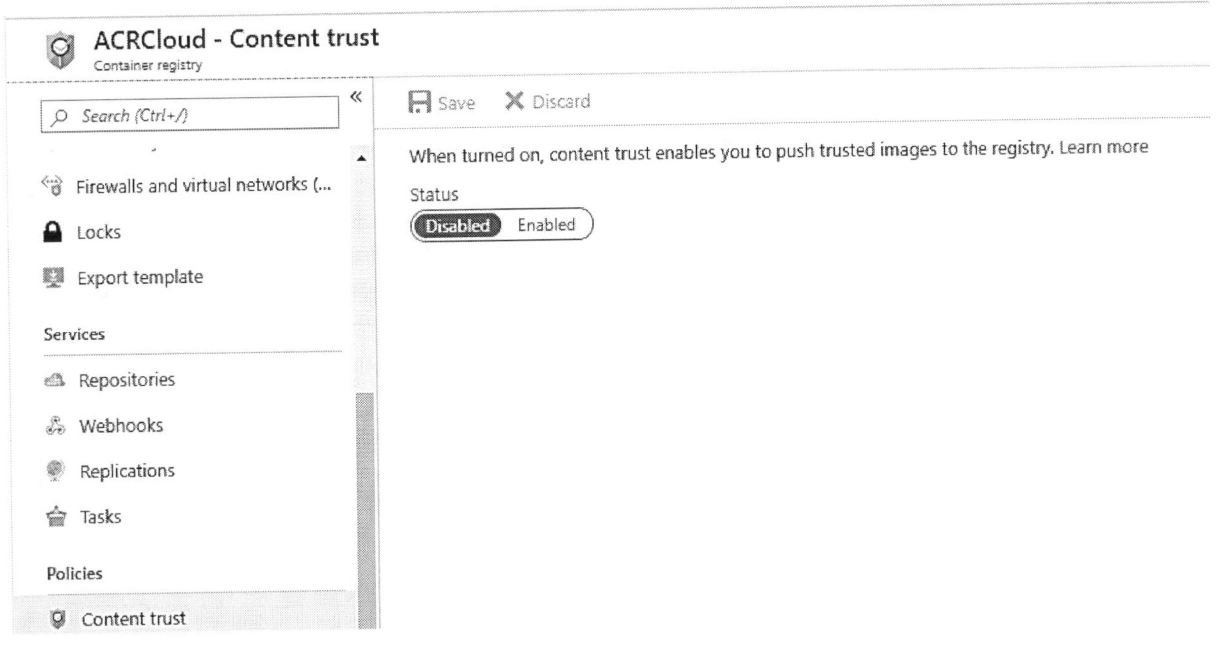

Azure Container Instances (ACI)

Azure Container Instances offers simple way to run a container in Azure, without having to provision any virtual machines and without having to adopt a higher-level service.

The benefit of using Azure Container Instances is that you don't need to provision or manager underlying Virtual Machines.

Features of Azure Container Instances (ACI)

Fast startup times: Azure Container Instances can start containers in Azure in seconds, without the need to provision and manage VMs.

Public IP connectivity and DNS name: Azure Container Instances enables exposing your containers directly to the internet with an IP address and a fully qualified domain name (FQDN).

Hypervisor-level security: With Azure Container Instances application is as isolated in a container as it would be in a VM.

Custom sizes: With Azure Container Instances you can specify CPU cores and memory for your container instance.

Persistent storage: By default, Azure Container Instances are stateless. To persist state with Azure Container Instances, you have the option to mount container instances on Azure Files shares.

Linux and Windows containers: Azure Container Instances can schedule both Windows and Linux containers with the same API. Simply specify the OS type when you create your container groups.

Container Groups: A container group is a collection of containers that get scheduled on the same host machine. The containers in a container group share a lifecycle, local network, and storage volumes. It's similar in concept to a *pod* in Kubernetes.

Exercise 39: Deploy Azure Container Instance (ACI) using Public Image

In this exercise we will deploy Azure Container Instance (ACI) using Public Image from Microsoft Container Registry (MCR).

1. In Azure Portal click create a resource> Containers>Container Instances> Container Instances blade opens>Select Resource Group RGCloud> Enter container name>Location East US 2>In Image name enter mcr.microsoft.com/azuredocs/aci-helloworld>For OS type select Linux.

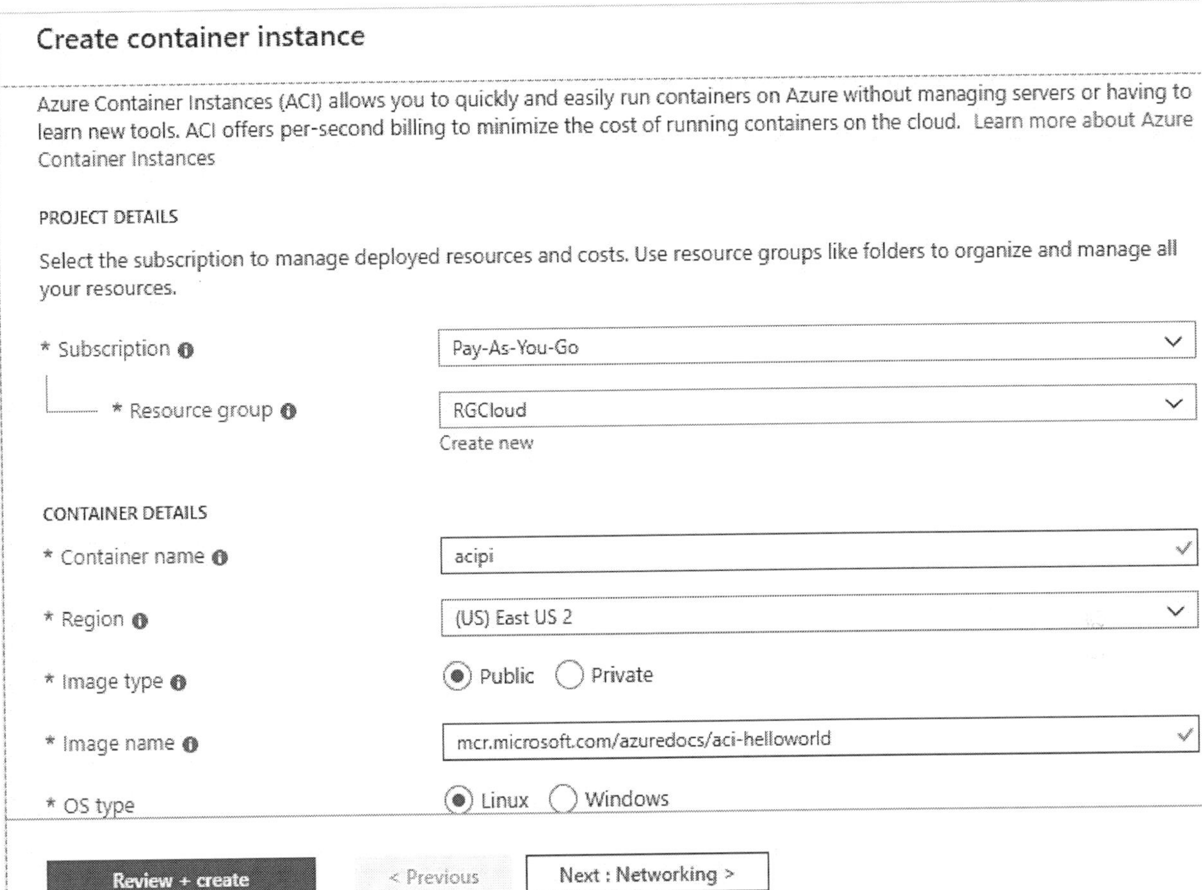

2. Click Next:Networking>Networking Pane opens>In DNS name enter **acipi**.

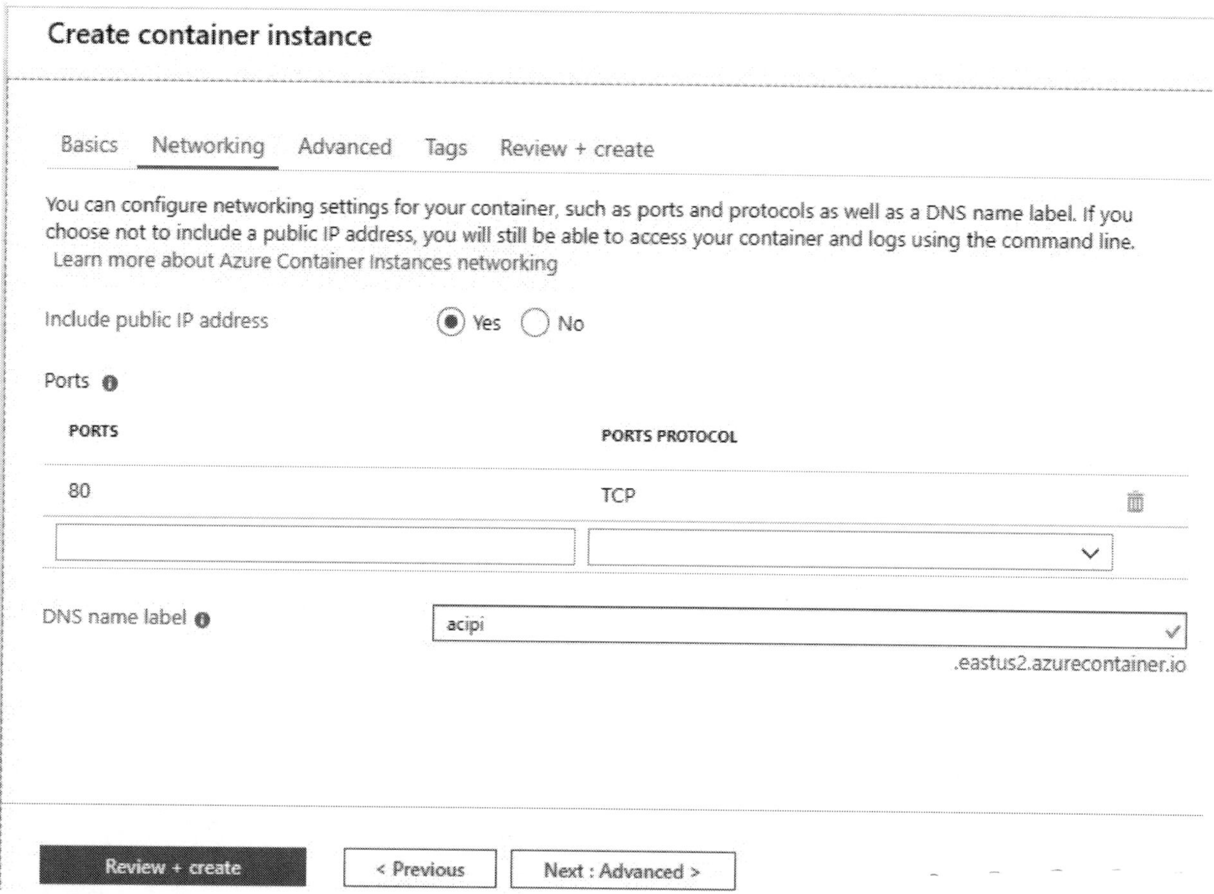

3. Click Review+ Create>After Validation is passed click create (Not Shown).

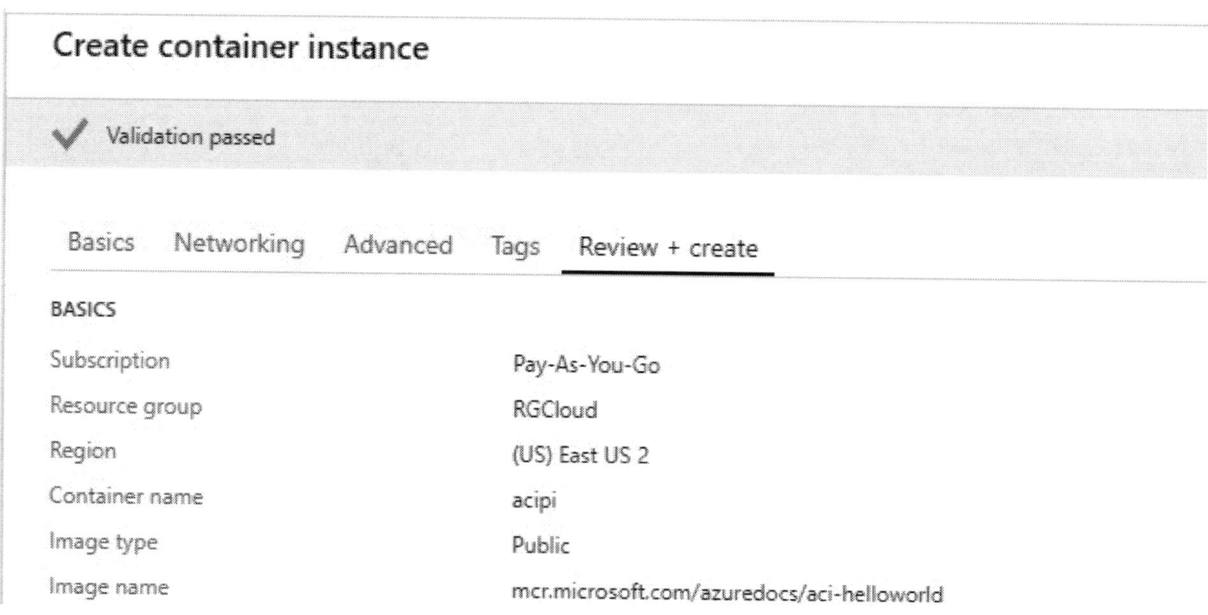

4. Figure below shows the Dashboard of acipi container instance.

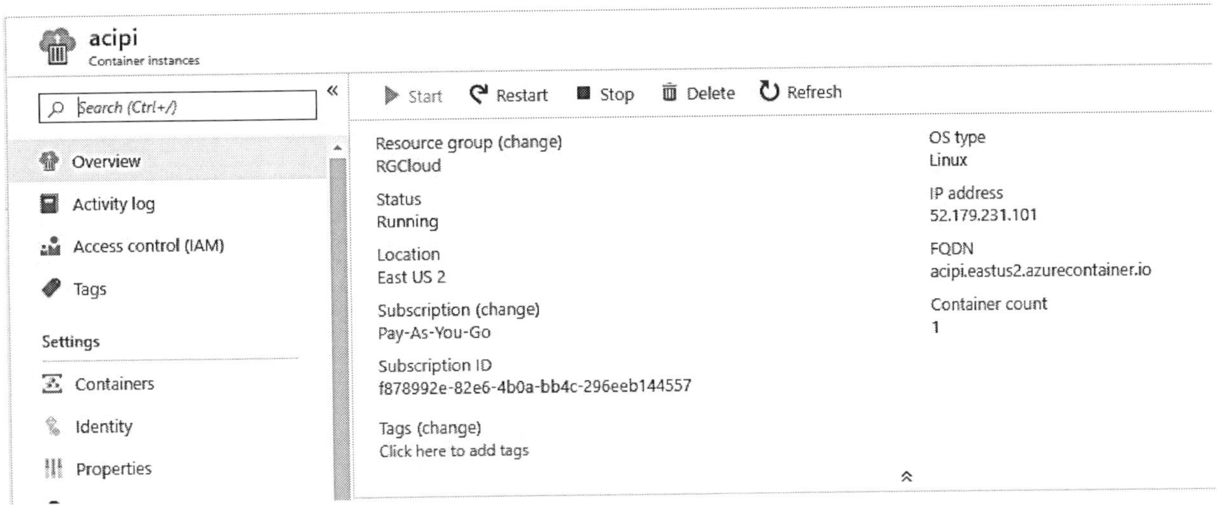

5. From Dashboard copy the FQDN of the acipi container instance and open it in a browser. FQDN is acipi.eastus2.azurecontainer.io.

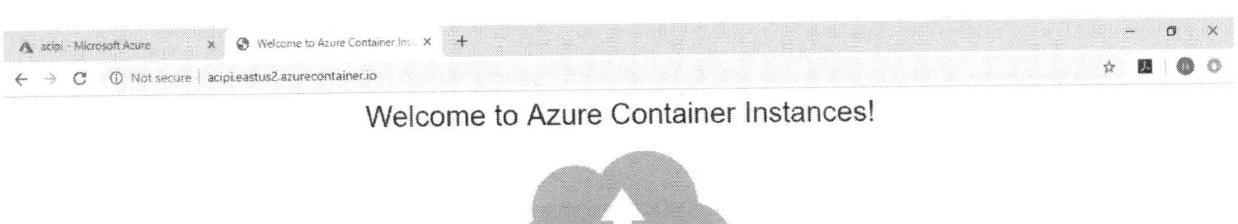

6. In Container instance dashboard click containers in left pane> In right pane you can see Events, Properties, Logs and Connect tab.

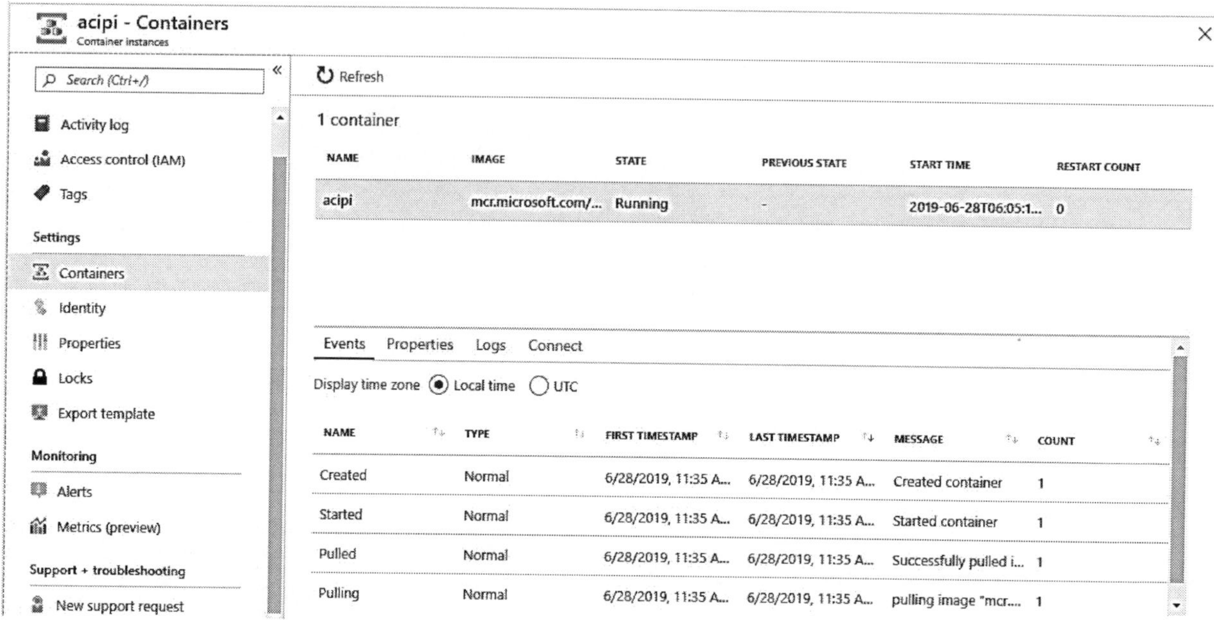

Users are requested to explore the tabs.

Container Groups in ACI

A container group is a collection of containers that get scheduled on the same host machine. Azure Container Instances supports the deployment of multiple containers onto a single host using a container group.

A container group is useful when building an application sidecar for logging, monitoring, or any other configuration where a service needs a second attached process.

The containers in a container group share a lifecycle, local network, and storage volumes. It's similar in concept to a pod in Kubernetes.

The following diagram shows an example of a container group that includes multiple containers:

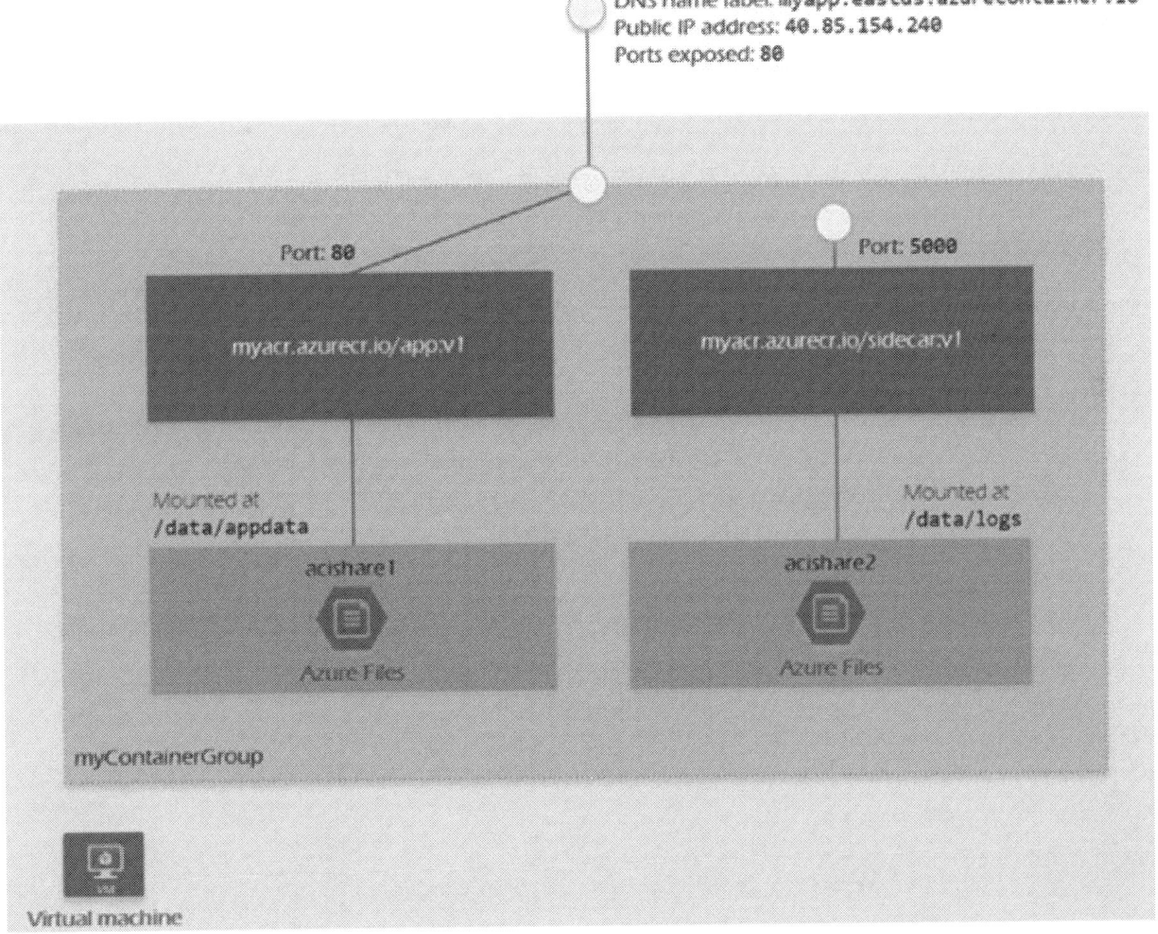

From the above Container Group Example we can infer following:

- Is scheduled on a single host machine.
- Is assigned a DNS name label.
- Exposes a single public IP address, with one exposed port.
- Consists of two containers. One container listens on port 80, while the other listens on port 5000.
- Includes two Azure file shares as volume mounts, and each container mounts one of the shares locally.

Azure Container Instance use case scenarios

Azure Container Instances is a great solution for any scenario that can operate in isolated containers, including simple applications, task automation, and build jobs. Use Container Orchestration Platform such as AKS or ACS for scenarios where you need full container orchestration, including service discovery across multiple containers, automatic scaling, and coordinated application upgrades.

Elastic bursting with AKS: When you run out of capacity in your AKS cluster, scale out additional pods in ACI without any additional servers to manage.

Event-driven applications with Azure Logic Apps: Combine ACI with the ACI Logic Apps connector, Azure queues and Azure Functions to build robust infrastructure which can elastically scale out containers on demand.

Cost Savings: Use Azure Container Instances for data processing where source data is ingested, processed and placed in a durable store such as Azure Blob storage. By processing the data with ACI rather than statically-provisioned virtual machines, you can achieve significant cost savings through per-second billing.

Azure Web App for Containers

Web App for containers is a fully managed compute platform (PaaS) that is optimized for running container applications.

Web Apps for container is a managed Linux or Windows VM with **pre-installed Docker Engine.** Figure below shows difference between IaaS and PaaS Platform.

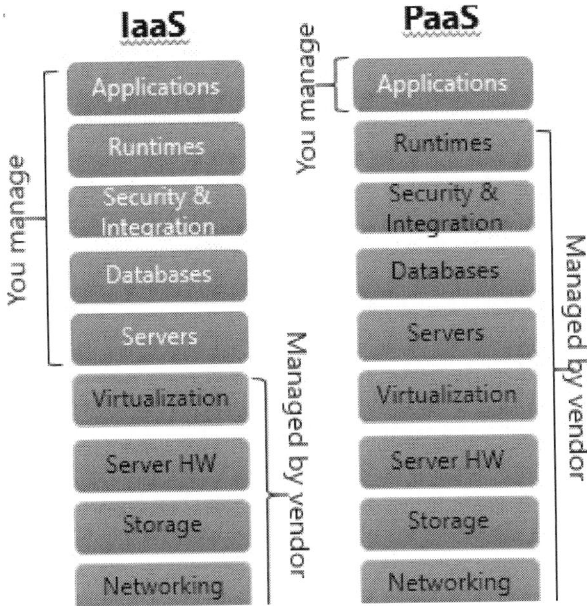

Features and Benefits of Web App for Containers

1. Web App for containers comes with Pre-Installed Docker Engine.
2. It is a managed platform (PaaS) which means Azure automatically takes care of OS and Docker engine patching and updates.
3. Deploy containers in seconds by pulling images from Docker Hub and Azure Container Register.
4. Supports Continuous Integration and Deployment (CI/CD) for custom container image from Docker Hub and Azure Container Registry. CI/CD will automatically deploy your container image hosted in Docker Hub or Azure Container Registry if you push changes to your image.
5. Built in Auto Scaling and Load Balancing for automatically scaling up and scaling out container applications.
6. Web apps have a deployment slot where you can deploy containers for testing. You can validate changes in a staging deployment slot before swapping it with the production slot without any downtime.

Web App for Containers Pricing Tier (Premium Container Plan)

The Premium Container plan features Dv3-series VMs with faster processors, SSD storage and higher memory-to-core ratio compared to Standard.

Table below shows Premium Plan for Windows. Windows Plans are in preview and are billed at 50% discount during preview period.

Instance	Cores	RAM	Prices
PC2	2	8	$0.182/hour
PC3	4	16	$0.363/hour
PC4	8	32	$0.725/hour

Table below shows Premium Plan for Linux.

Instance	Cores	RAM	Prices
P1V2	1	3.5 GB	$0.20/hour
P2V2	2	7 GB	$0.40/hour
P3V2	4	14 GB	$0.80/hour

Figure below shows features included with Premium Plan for Windows -Custom Domain/SSL, Autoscale, Staging Slots and Traffic Manager.

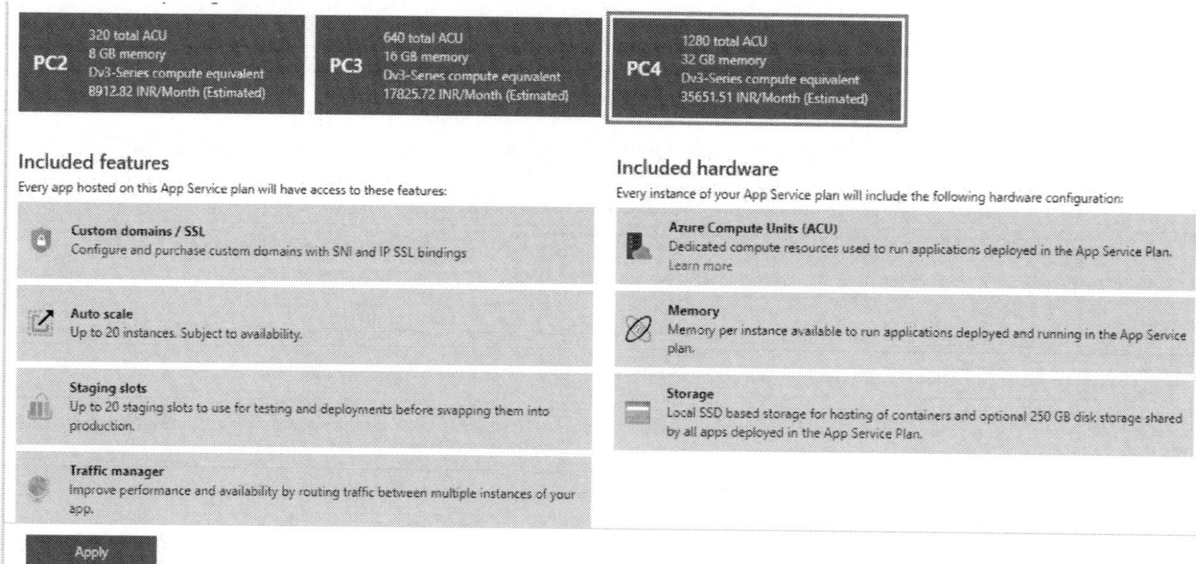

Figure below shows features included with Premium Plan for Linux -Custom Domain/SSL, Autoscale, Staging Slots, Daily backups and Traffic Manager.

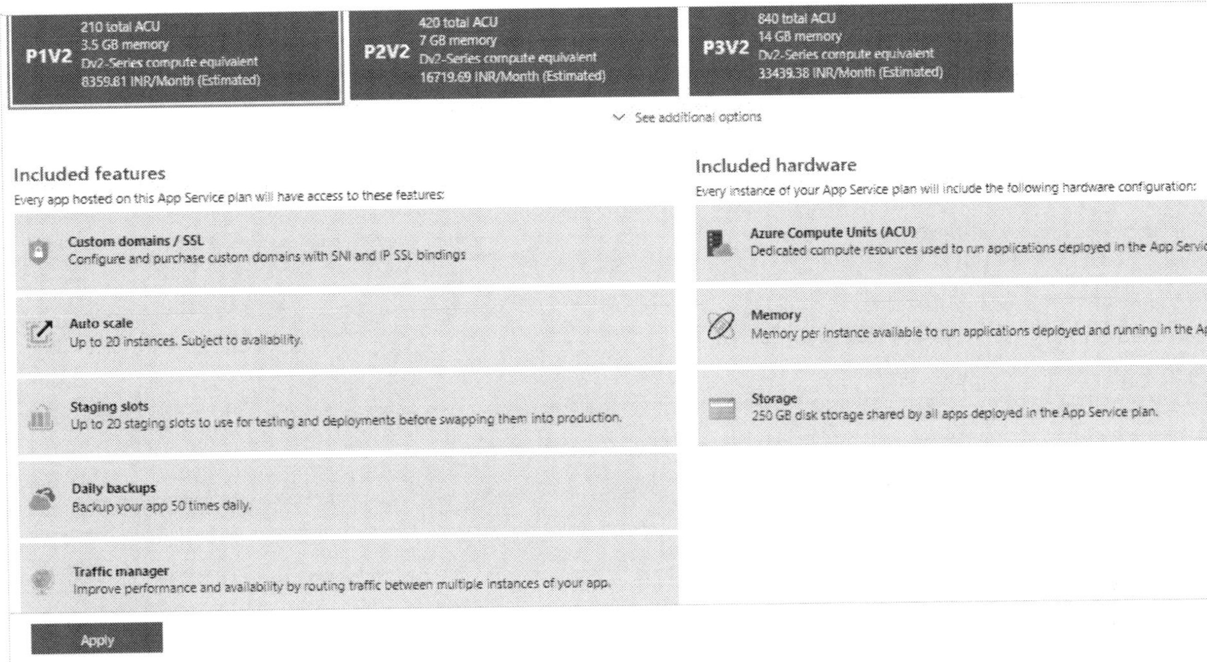

Image Sources in Web App for Containers

Azure Container Registry
Docker Hub
Private Registry

Exercise 40: Deploy Web App for Containers

1. In Azure Portal click create a resource> Compute >Scroll down and click Web App for containers > create web App for containers blade opens>Enter name>In Resource Group select RGCloud>For OS select Linux>Select Default Plan only>In Configure Container select NGINX image in Quickstart Tab and Click apply>Click Create.

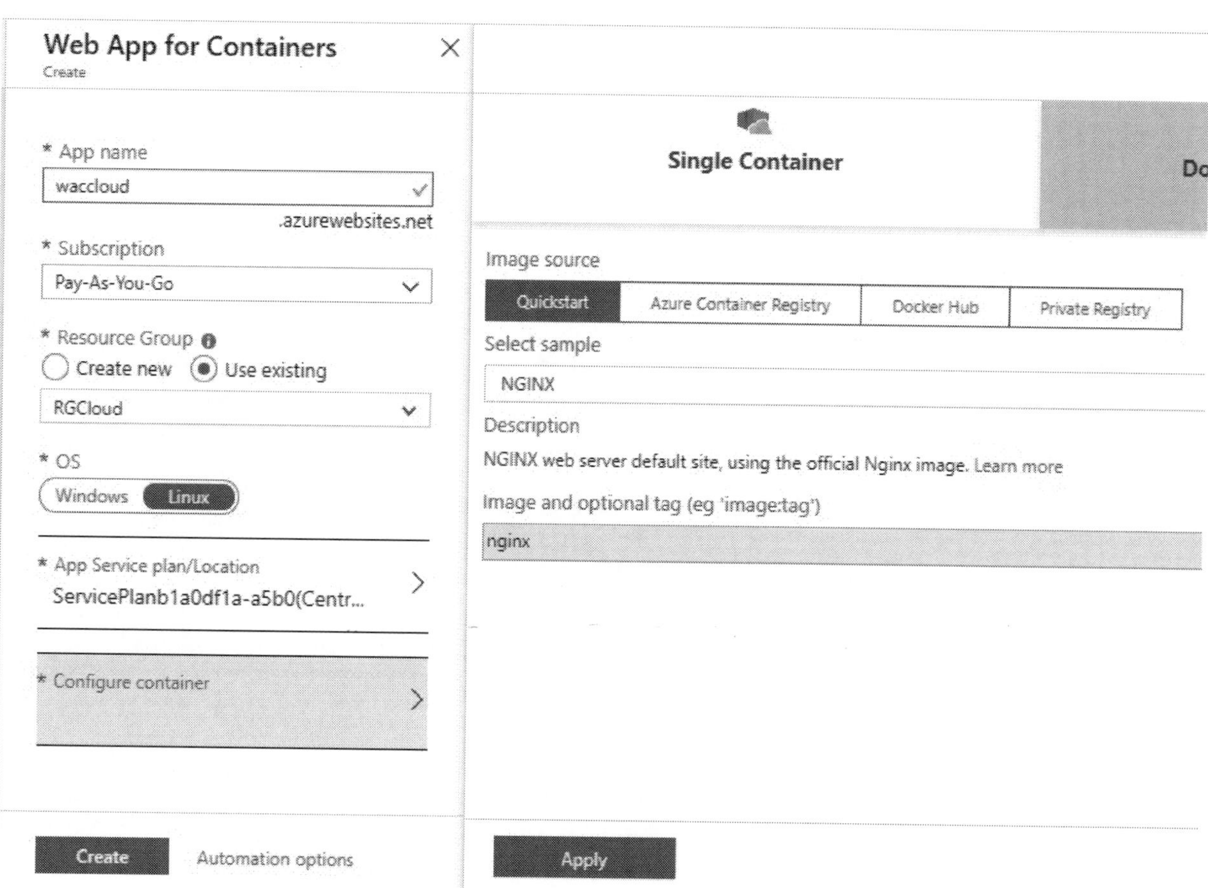

2. Figure below shows the Dashboard of Web App for containers.

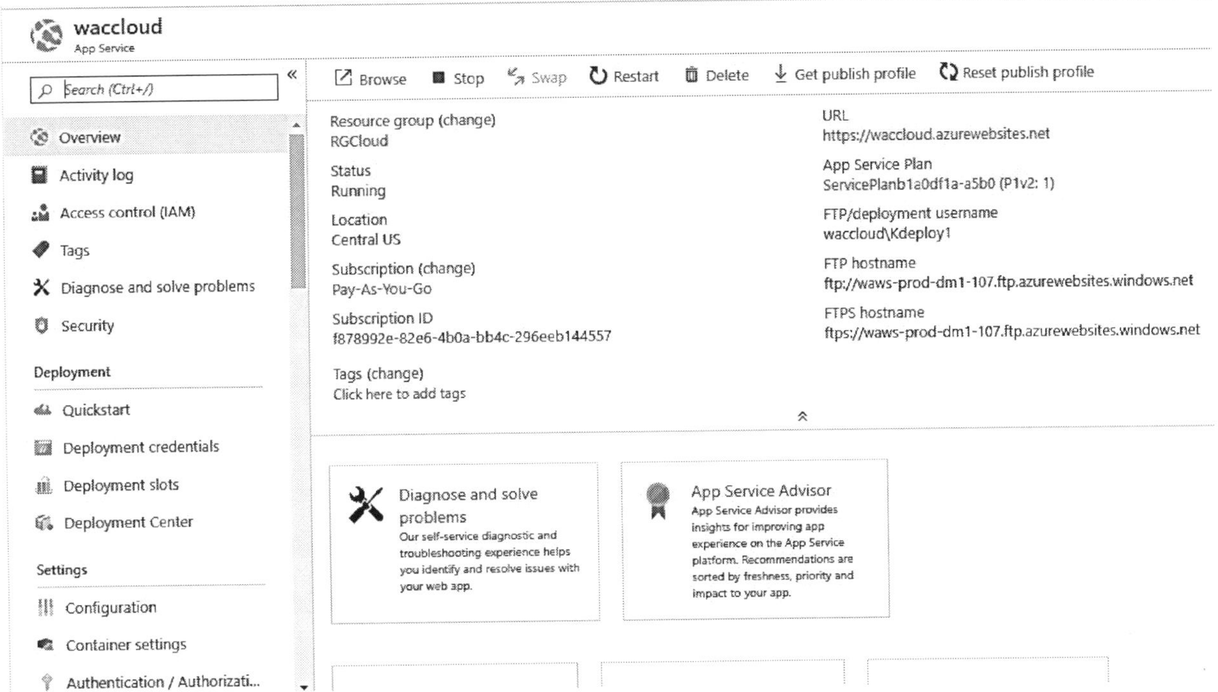

3. From Dashboard copy DNS name and open it in browser. DNS name is **https://waccloud.azurewebsites.net/**

Welcome to nginx!

If you see this page, the nginx web server is successfully installed and working. Further configuration is required.

For online documentation and support please refer to nginx.org. Commercial support is available at nginx.com.

Thank you for using nginx.

Readers are advised to through options in left pane of the Web App for Containers dashboard.

4. Delete the Web App and App Service Plan. Click Delete in Web App dashboard>Delete pane opens>Enter web App name and click delete.

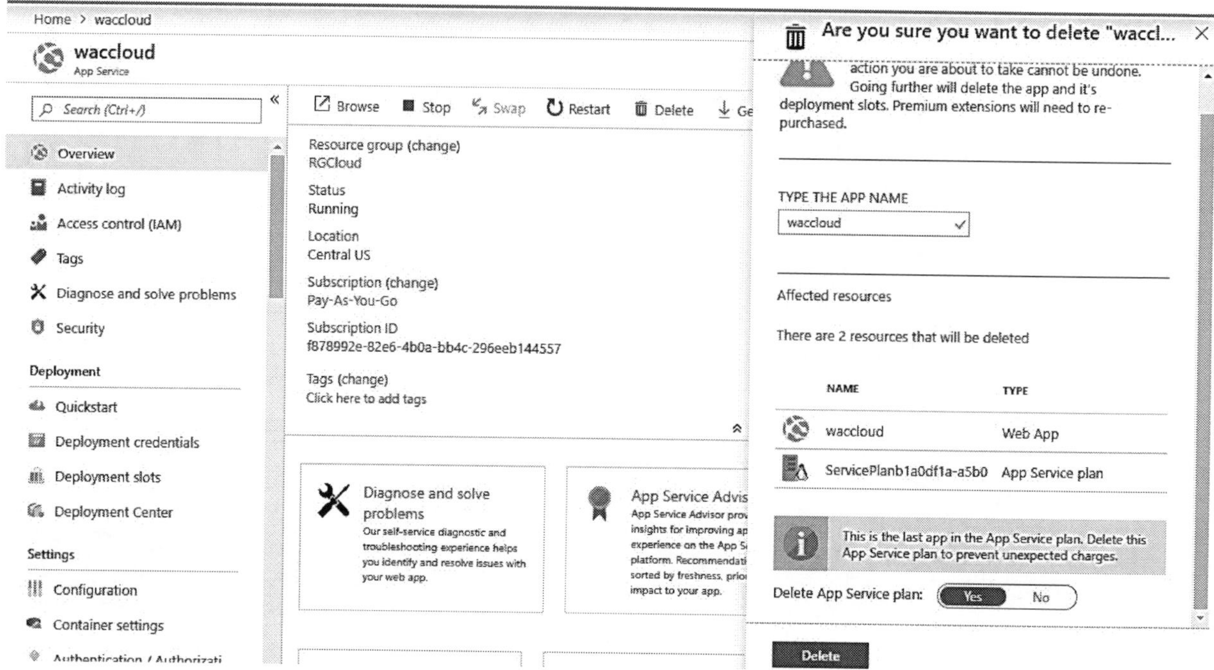

Azure Kubernetes Service (AKS)

Azure Kubernetes Service (AKS) is a container orchestration platform to deploy containers on a cluster of virtual machines (Agent Nodes) that are preconfigured (Docker Engine Pre-Installed) to run containerized applications.

Azure Kubernetes Service (AKS) consists of Cluster of Master Nodes and Agent Nodes deployed in Virtual Network.

By using AKS, you can take advantage of the enterprise-grade features of Azure, while still maintaining application portability through Kubernetes and the Docker image format.

Azure Kubernetes Service (AKS) is a managed service and is based on Google's open source Kubernetes Orchestration Platform.

Features of AKS

Kubernetes automates deployment, scaling, and management of containerized applications. It has a rich set of features including:

- Self-healing hosted/managed control plane (masters nodes).
- Automated Kubernetes version upgrades and patching.
- Easy cluster scaling of agent nodes with a single click.
- Cost savings - pay only for running agent pool nodes.
- Service discovery and load balancing.
- Secret and configuration management.
- Storage orchestration.

Pre-Installed Kubernetes Components on Agent Nodes

- **Kubelet**: An agent that runs on each node in the cluster. It makes sure that containers are running in a pod.
- **Proxy**: Maintains network rules on the host and performing connection forwarding.
- **Container Runtime Engine**: Responsible for running containers.

Azure Kubernetes Service (AKS) Architecture

Kubernetes consists of Cluster of Master Nodes and Agent Nodes deployed in Virtual Network. Following are deployed as part of AKS deployment.

Master nodes are Azure Managed and are highly available. Configuration and number of master nodes is known to Microsoft only. Master Node runs the Kubernetes Orchestration Platform which manages, monitors and schedules workloads on Agent Nodes.
Agent Nodes is a Cluster of Container ready Virtual Machines deployed in Virtual Network in an Availability Set. Agent Nodes run your application workloads.
Virtual Network: A Pre-configured VNET or a custom VNET is deployed with AKS Cluster depending upon networking option chosen.
Load Balancer is also deployed with Kubernetes Cluster.
DNS Zone (If Application Routing is enabled)

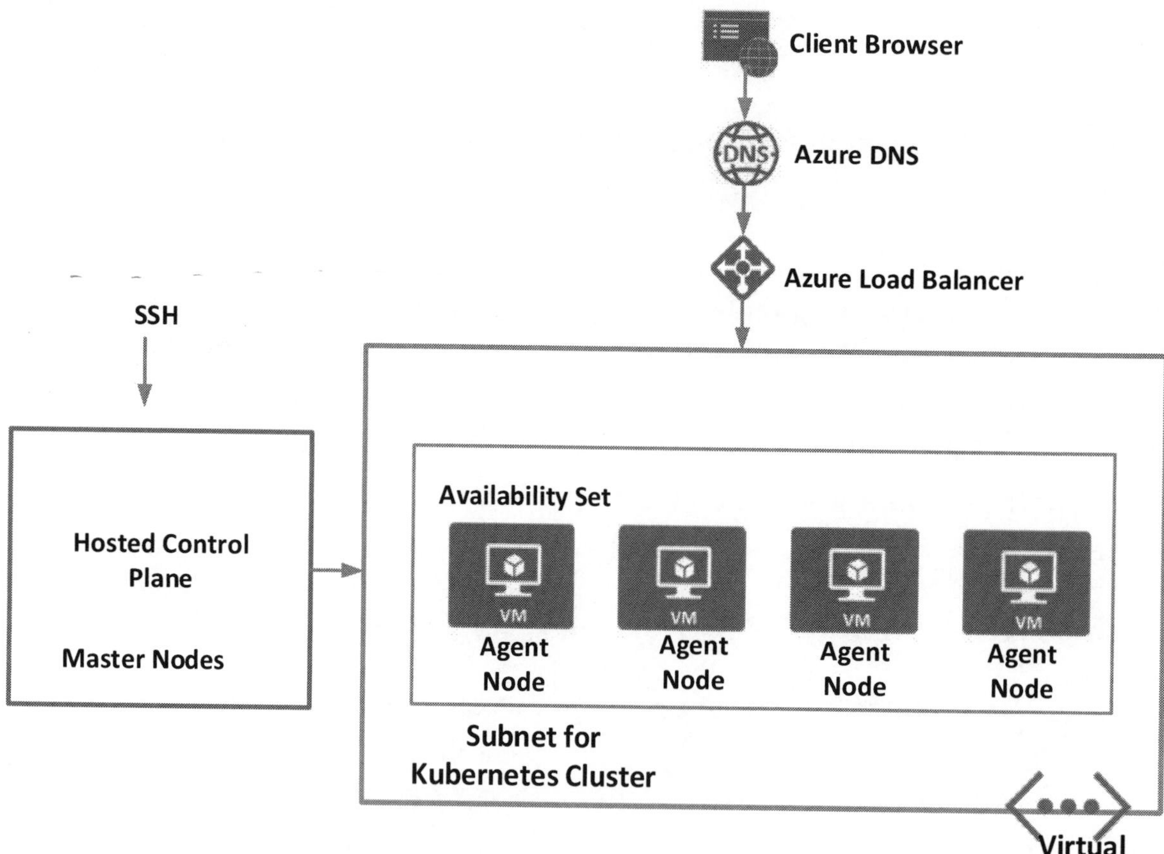

PODs in Kubernetes: A POD is a collection of containers that get scheduled on the same host or Virtual Machine.

Kubernetes Cluster Architecture

Kubernetes consists of Cluster of Master Nodes and Agent Nodes deployed in Virtual Network as shown in figure below.
Cluster master nodes provide the core Kubernetes services and orchestrates application workloads on Agent Nodes.
Nodes run your application workloads.

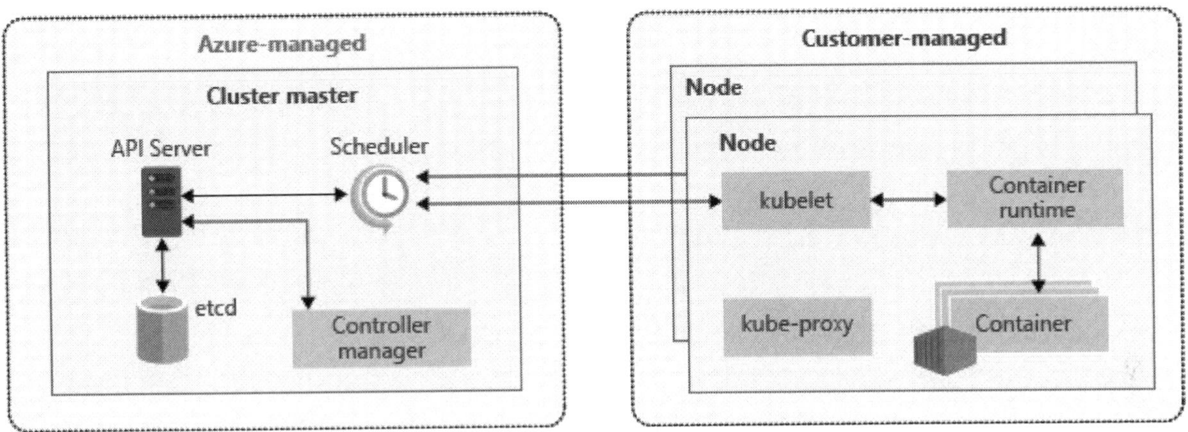

Cluster Master Node

When you create an AKS cluster, a cluster master is automatically created and configured. Cluster master nodes provide the core Kubernetes services and orchestration of application workloads. There's no cost for the cluster master node.

The cluster master includes the following core Kubernetes components:

kube-apiserver - The API server is how the underlying Kubernetes APIs are exposed. This component provides the interaction for management tools, such as kubectl or the Kubernetes dashboard.
etcd - etcd is a key value store within Kubernetes to maintain the state of Kubernetes cluster and configuration.
kube-scheduler - When you create or scale applications, the Scheduler determines what nodes can run the workload and starts them.
kube-controller-manager - The Controller Manager oversees a number of smaller Controllers that perform actions such as replicating pods and handling node operations.

Cluster Master Nodes are Azure Managed which means that you don't need to configure components like a highly available *etcd* store. Since Master Nodes are managed you can't access the cluster master directly.

If you need to configure the cluster master in a particular way or need direct access to them, you can deploy your own Kubernetes cluster using aks-engine.

Agent Nodes

Nodes run your application workloads. An AKS cluster has one or more agent nodes, which is an Azure virtual machine (VM). Agent Nodes are deployed in Virtual Network. Agent Nodes include following Kubernetes components:

- The **kubelet** is the Kubernetes agent that processes the orchestration requests from the cluster master and scheduling of running the requested containers.
- Virtual networking is handled by the **kube-proxy** on each node. The **kube-proxy** routes network traffic and manages IP addressing for services and pods.
- The **container runtime** is the component that allows containerized applications to run and interact with additional resources such as the virtual network and storage. In AKS, Moby is used as the container runtime.

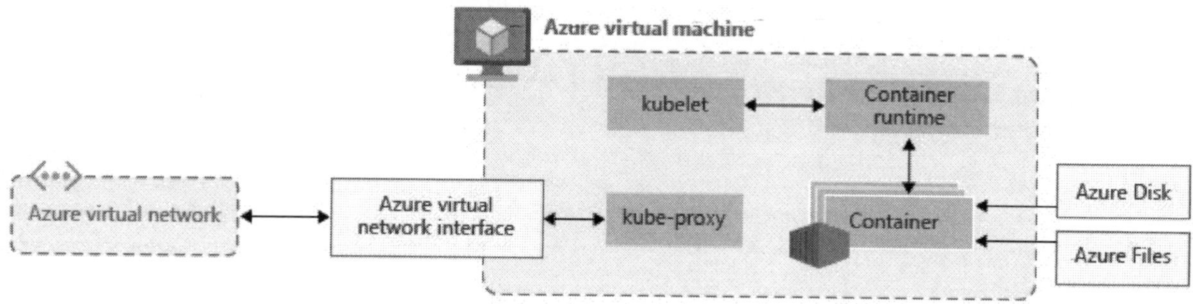

AKS Networking Options

Basic networking creates a new VNET for your cluster using Azure provided default values. You do not have control over network configuration such as subnets or the IP address ranges assigned to the cluster.
Advanced networking allows clusters to use a new or existing VNET with customizable addresses. Application pods are connected directly to the VNET which allows for native integration with VNET features.
Nodes in an AKS cluster configured for advanced networking use the Azure Container Networking Interface (CNI) Kubernetes plugin.

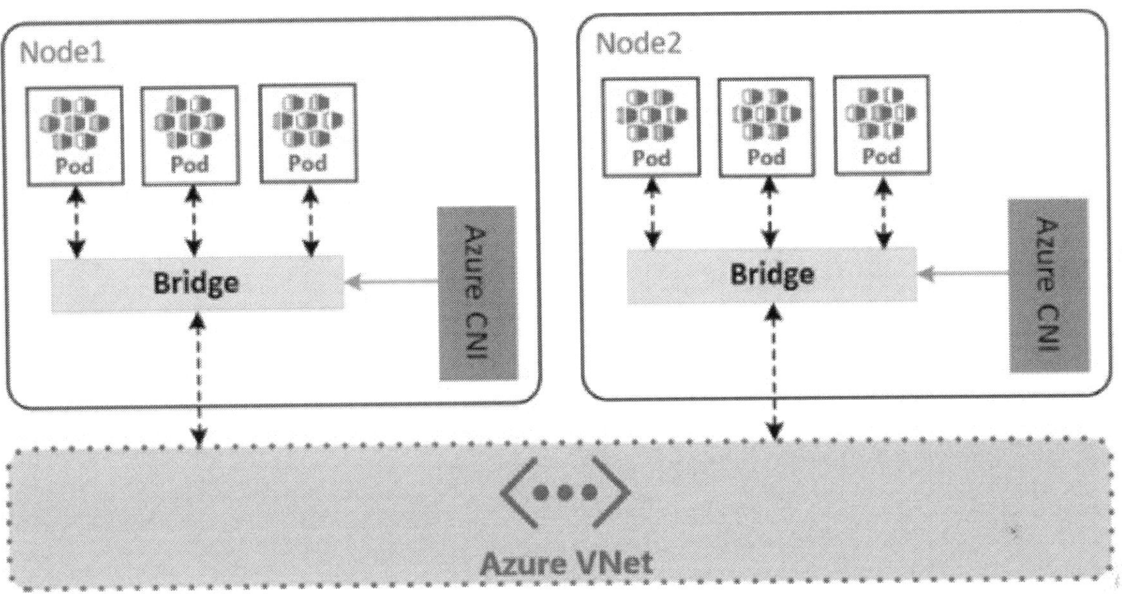

Features of Advanced Networking

1. Pod in the cluster is assigned an IP address in the VNET and can directly communicate with other pods in the cluster and other VMs in the VNET.
2. A pod can connect to other services in a peered VNET and to on-premises networks over ExpressRoute and site-to-site (S2S) VPN connections. Pods are also reachable from on-premises.
3. Expose a Kubernetes service externally or internally through the Azure Load Balancer. Also a feature of Basic networking.
4. Pods in a subnet that have service endpoints enabled can securely connect to Azure services, for example Azure Storage and SQL DB.
5. Use user-defined routes (UDR) to route traffic from pods to a Network Virtual Appliance.

HTTP Application Routing

The HTTP application routing solution makes it easy to access applications that are deployed to your Azure Kubernetes Service (AKS) cluster by creating publicly accessible DNS names for application endpoints.

When the solution is enabled, it configures an Ingress controller in your AKS cluster. It also creates a DNS Zone in your subscription. As applications are deployed, the solution creates publicly accessible DNS names for application endpoints.

As shown in figure below, HTTP application routing add-on can be enabled through the Azure portal when deploying an AKS cluster. You can also enable HTTP application routing post installation through AKS Dashboard.

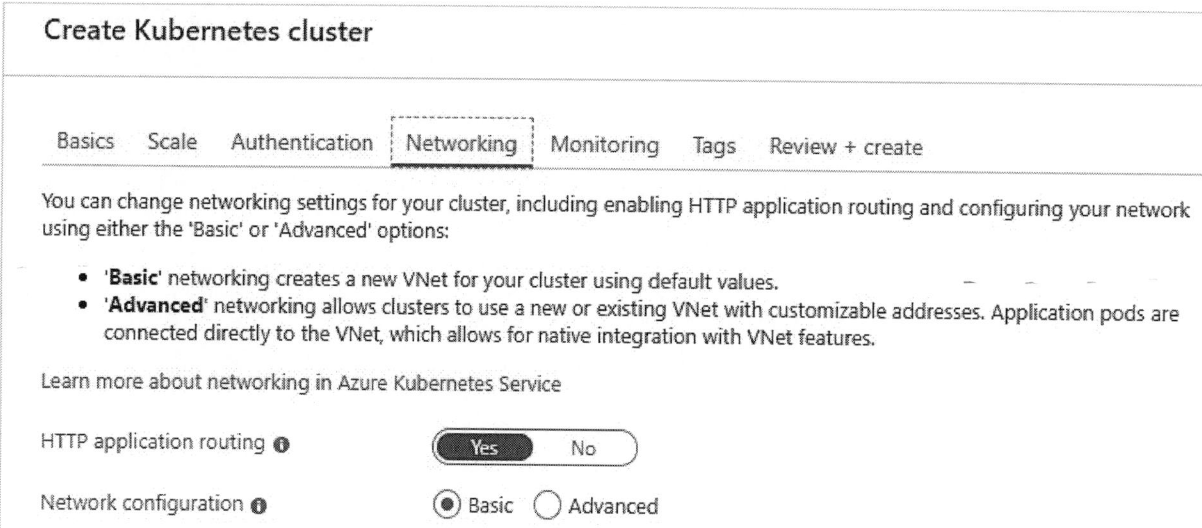

Note: This add-on is not recommended for production use. The HTTP application routing add-on is designed to let you quickly create an ingress controller and access your applications.

Container Monitoring

Container monitoring solution provides insight into performance and health of your entire Kubernetes Cluster.
Container Monitoring Solution requires Log Analytics Workspace.

As shown in figure below, Container Monitoring can be enabled through the Azure portal when deploying an AKS cluster. You also need Log Analytics Workspace. Log Analytics Workspace will be discussed in Chapter 9.

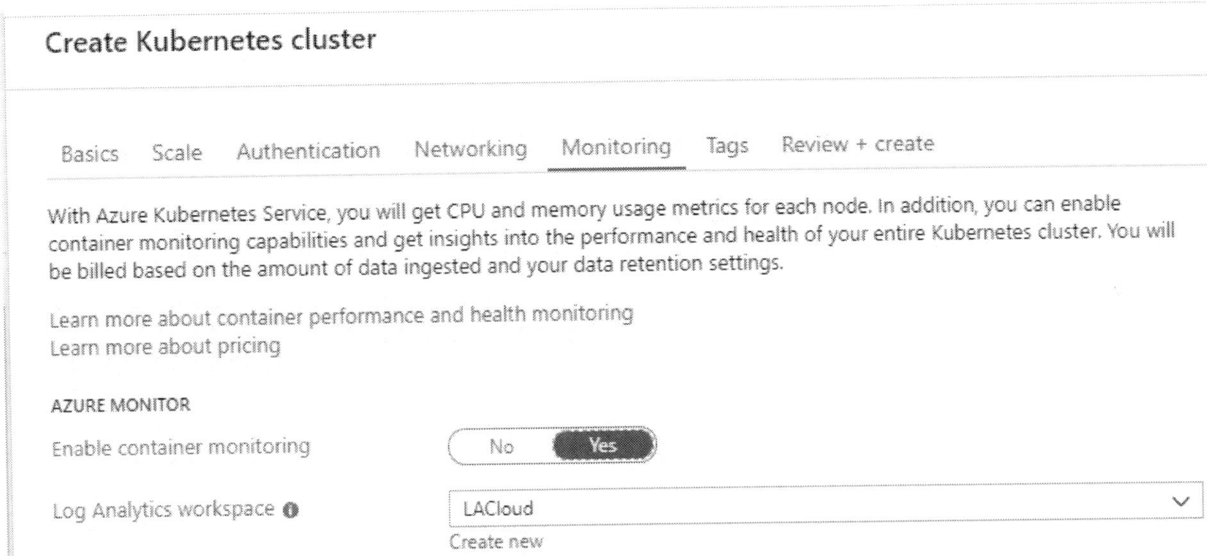

Accessing Container Monitoring

Azure Monitor
AKS Dashboard

Features of Container Monitoring

1. Identify AKS containers that are running on the node and their average processor and memory utilization.
2. Identify where the container resides in a controller or a pod.
3. Review the resource utilization of workloads running on the host that are unrelated to the standard processes that support the pod.
4. Understand the behavior of the cluster under average and heaviest loads.
5. Configure alerts to proactively notify you or record it when CPU and memory utilization on nodes or containers exceed your thresholds.

Authenticate to Azure Container Registry from AKS

When using Azure Container Registry (ACR) with Azure Kubernetes Service (AKS), an authentication mechanism needs to be established to Grant AKS access to ACR.

Following are 2 Authentication which you can use to grant AKS access to ACR. You only need to configure one of the authentication methods.

1. Grant access using the AKS service principal.
2. Grant access using Kubernetes secrets.

Grant access to ACR using the AKS service principal

When you create an AKS cluster, Azure also creates a service principal to support cluster operability with other Azure resources. You can use this auto-generated service principal for authentication with an ACR registry. To do so, you need to create an Azure AD role assignment that grants the cluster's service principal access to the container registry.

Figure below shows **Auto Generated Service Principal** being created through the Azure portal when deploying an AKS cluster.

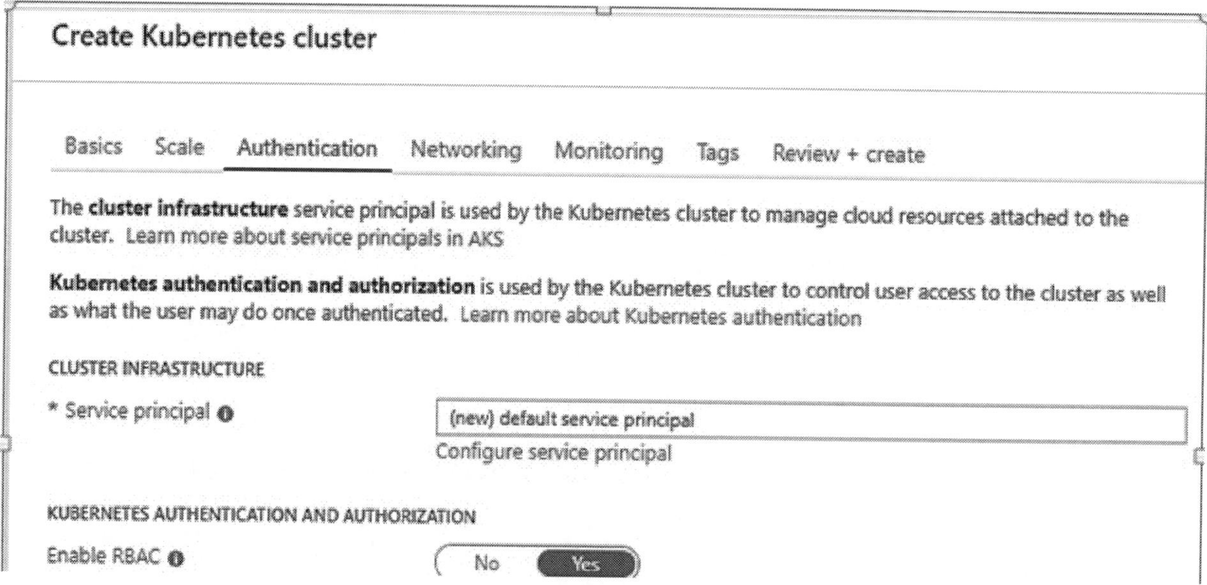

Grant access to ACR using Kubernetes secrets

In some instances, you might not be able to assign the required role to the auto-generated AKS service principal granting it access to ACR.

In this case you first create a new service principal. You then use Kubectl command to create the Kubernetes secret.

Note: Service Principal will be discussed in the Chapter 4.

Exercise 41: Create AKS Cluster with Basic Networking

1. In Azure Portal click create a resource> Containers>Kubernetes Service> Create Kubernetes Cluster blade opens>In Resource Group select RGCloud>Enter a name. I entered akscloud>In Region select West US 2 >Select Default value for Kubernetes version>In DNS name I entered akscloud.

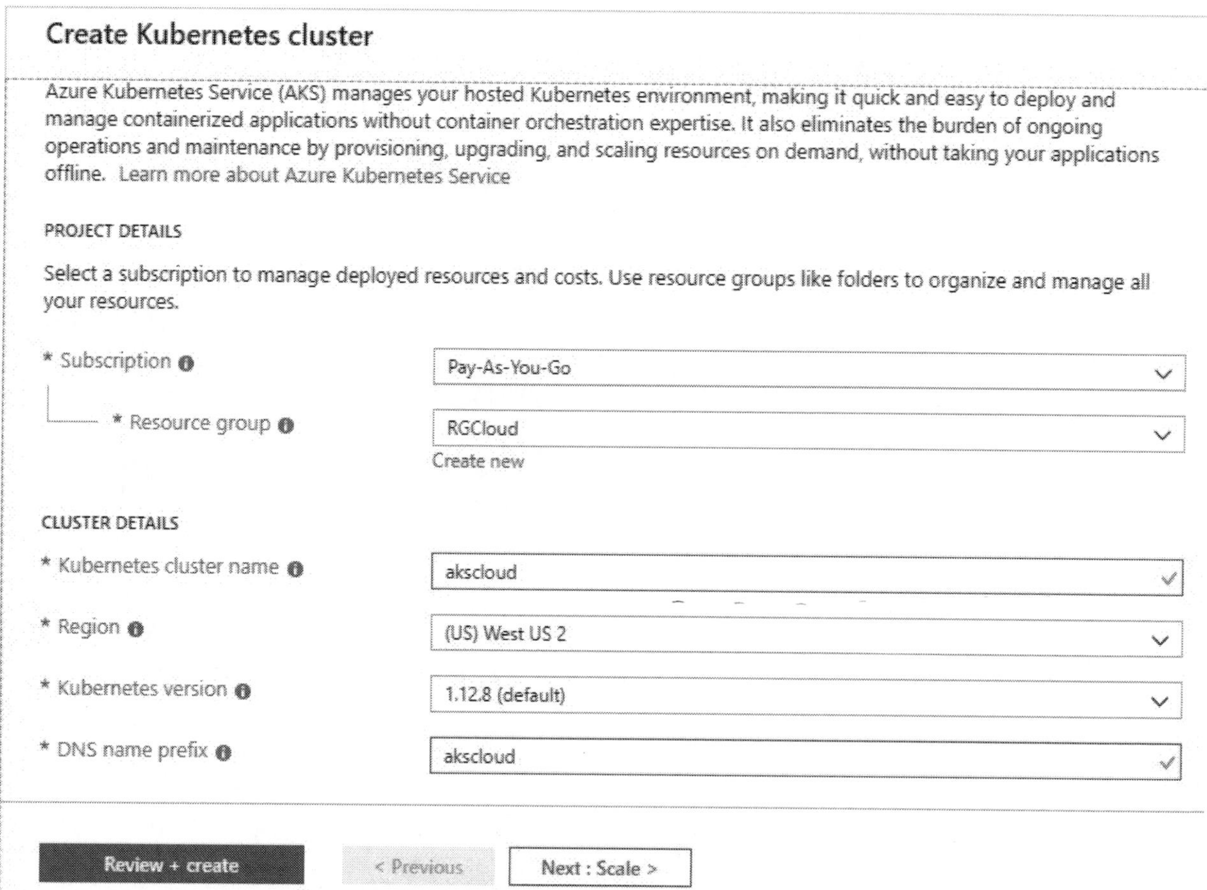

Note: I have changed the node count from 3 to 2. Node count is not shown in above figure. You need to scroll down.

Note 2: I used location West US 2 instead of East US 2 as I was getting error during validation. This might have happened because I might I have run out of quota for CPU cores.

2. Click Next: Scale. Scale Pane opens> Keep all values at default. Note the VM Scale Set option which is in preview.

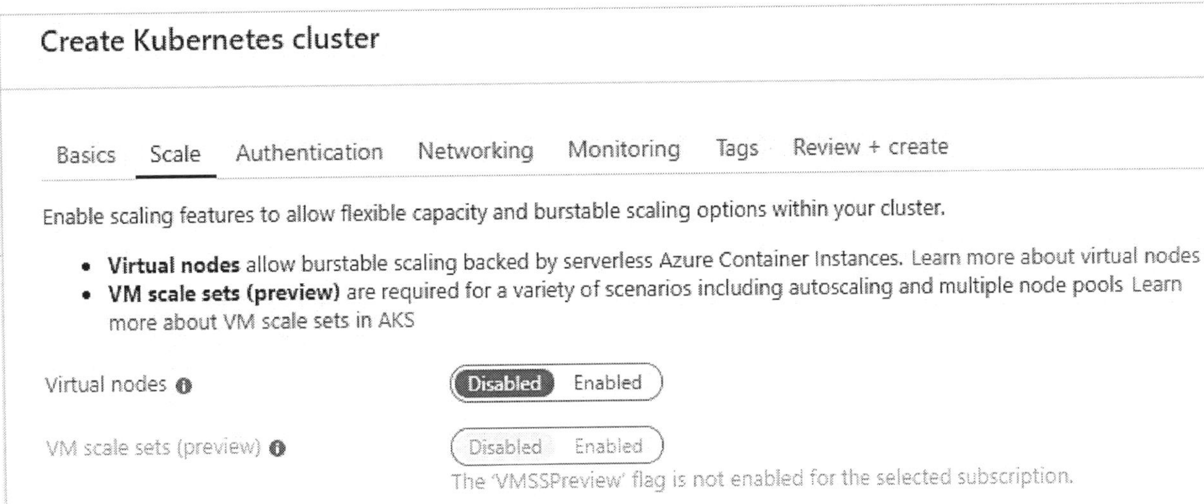

3. Click Next: Authentication> For Service Principal keep value at default> Select **No** for RBAC.

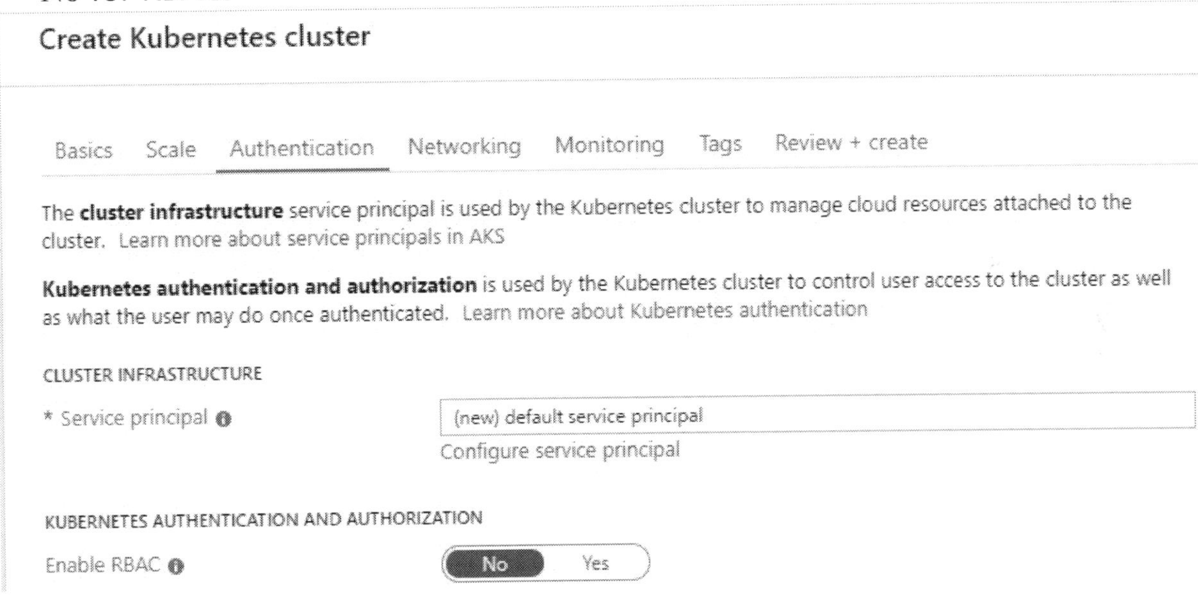

Note 1: In Production Scenario we will not be selecting No for RBAC.
Note 2: We are selecting No so that we can access Kubernetes Web UI without creating *ClusterRoleBinding*.
Note 3: *In case you are selecting YES for RBAC. Then you need to run following kubectl command to enable access to Kubernetes Web UI Dashboard.*
kubectl create clusterrolebinding kubernetes-dashboard --clusterrole=cluster-admin --serviceaccount=kube-system:kubernetes-dashboard

4. Click Next: Networking> Networking Pane opens> Select No for HTTP application Routing>Select Basic for Network configuration.

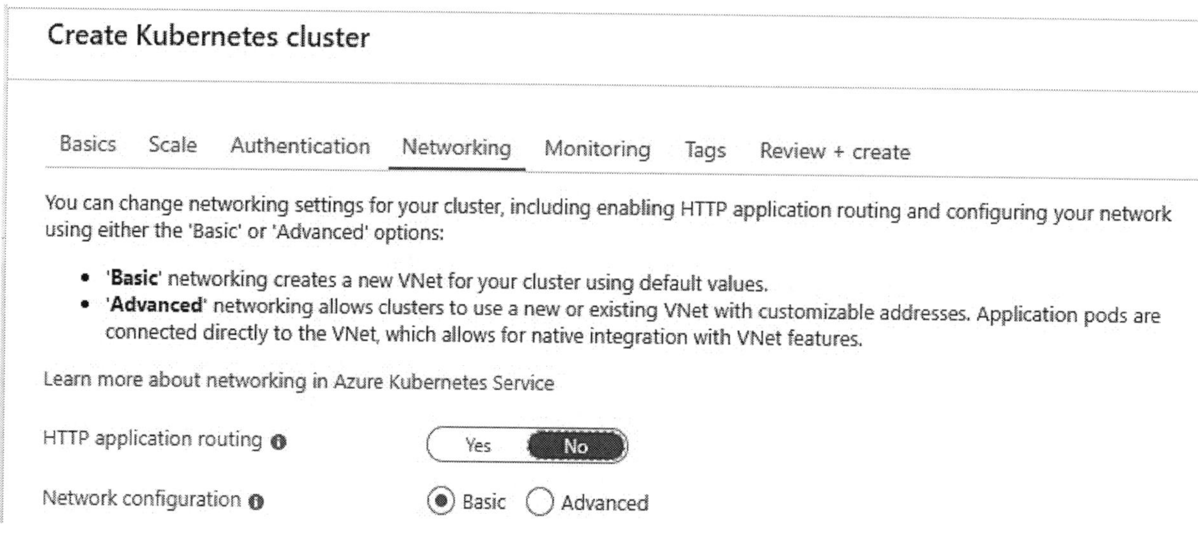

5. Click Next: Monitoring> Monitoring Pane opens> Select No for Container monitoring.

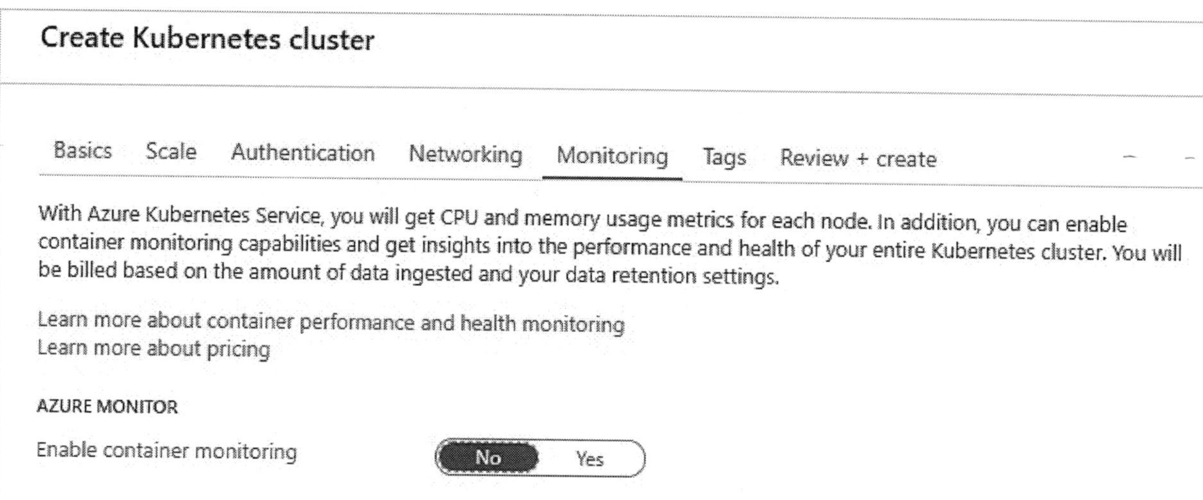

Note: If you select yes then you need to select Log Analytics workspace.

6. Click Review+ Create>After Validation is passed click create.

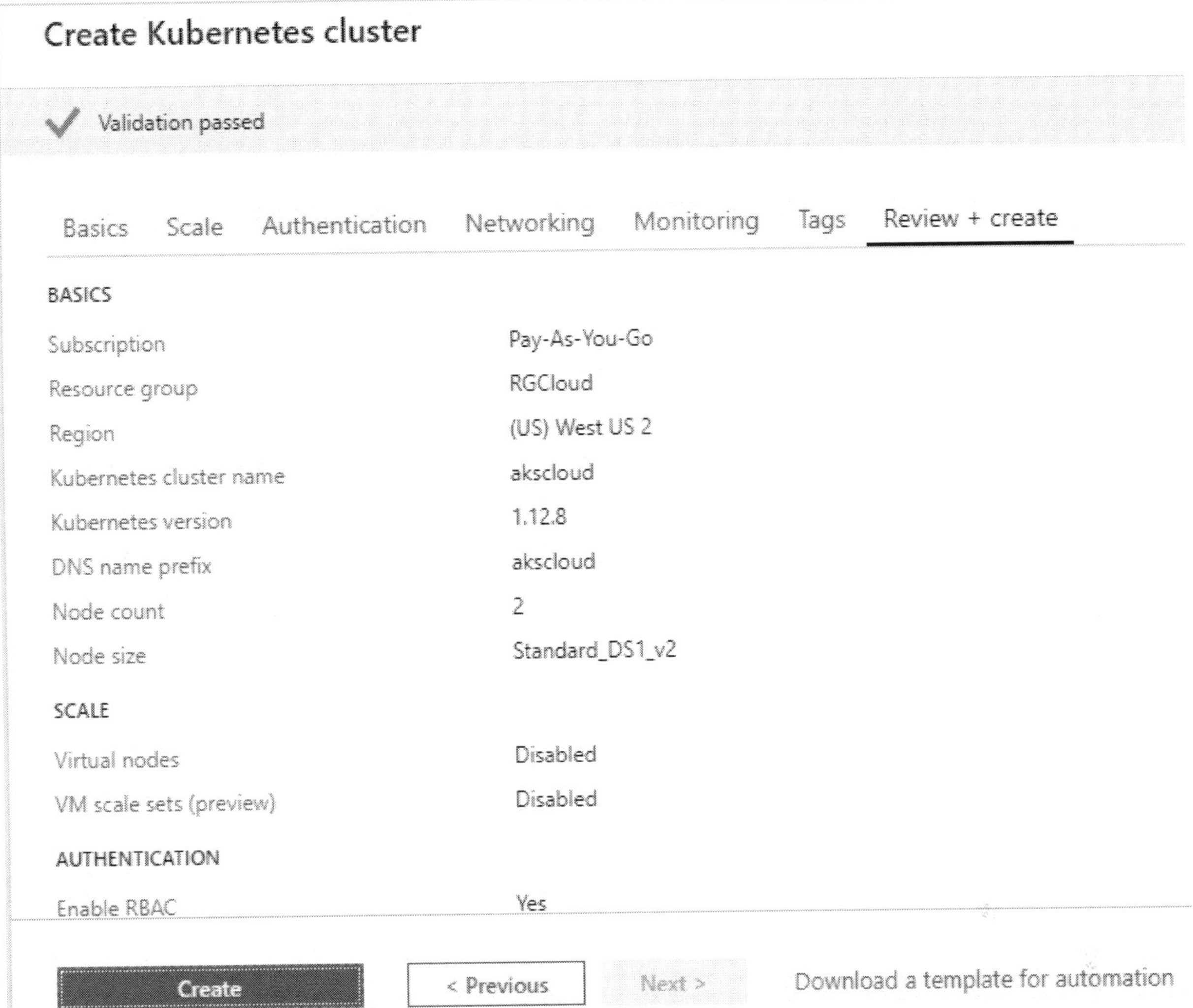

7. Figure below shows the Dashboard of AKS Cluster.

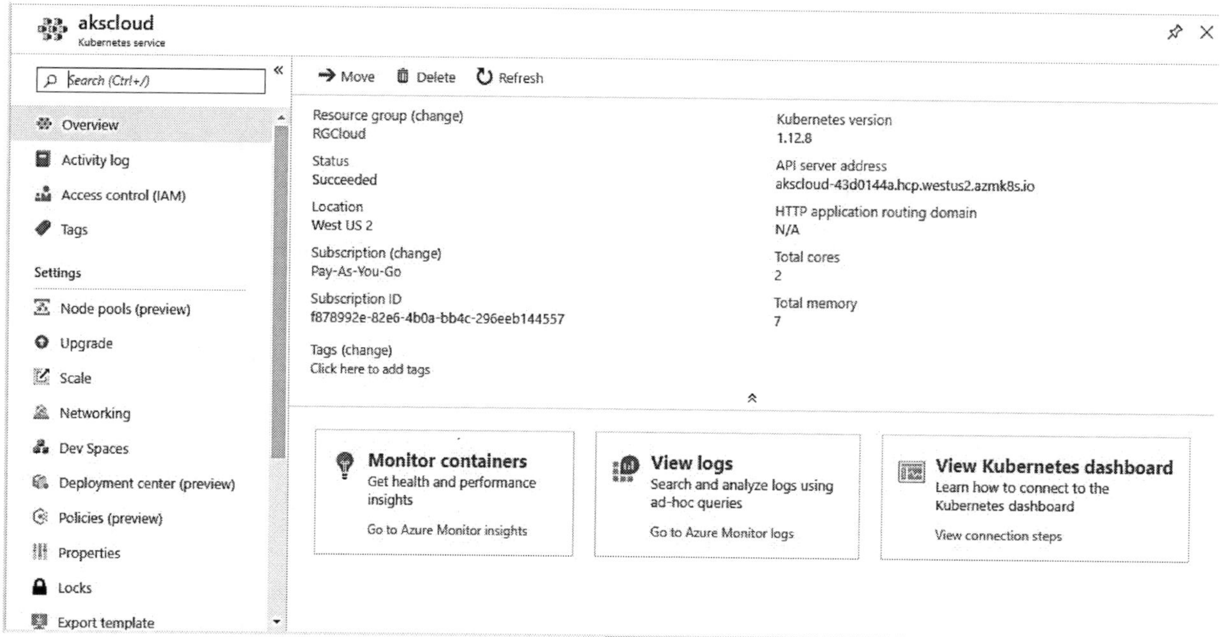

Exercise 42: Install Kubectl

Kubectl is Kubernetes command-line client to manage Kubernetes cluster.

In this Exercise we will install kubectl on our laptop using Azure CLI command **az aks install-cli.** Make sure you have installed Azure CLI on your system. Azure CLI installation is shown in Chapter 21, AZ-300 & AZ-301 Study & Lab Guide Part 1.

1. Open Windows Command Prompt (CMD)> az login. This will open a browser. Enter your azure subscription Username and password credentials.

2. After you have successfully authenticated to Azure through Browser, The CMD window will now show Azure information as shown below.

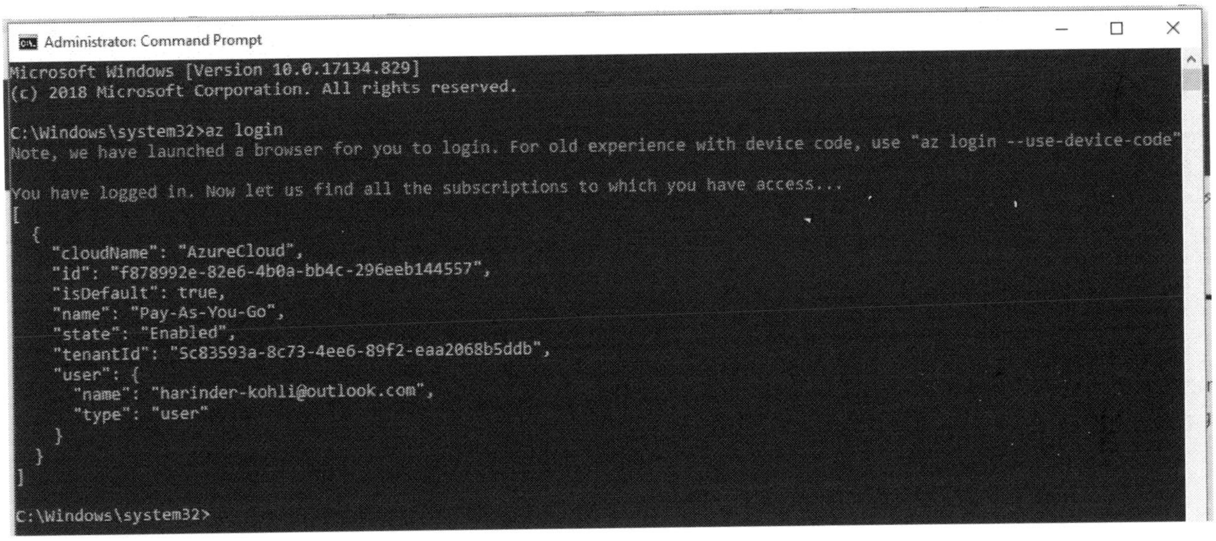

```
Administrator: Command Prompt
Microsoft Windows [Version 10.0.17134.829]
(c) 2018 Microsoft Corporation. All rights reserved.

C:\Windows\system32>az login
Note, we have launched a browser for you to login. For old experience with device code, use "az login --use-device-code"

You have logged in. Now let us find all the subscriptions to which you have access...
[
  {
    "cloudName": "AzureCloud",
    "id": "f878992e-82e6-4b0a-bb4c-296eeb144557",
    "isDefault": true,
    "name": "Pay-As-You-Go",
    "state": "Enabled",
    "tenantId": "5c83593a-8c73-4ee6-89f2-eaa2068b5ddb",
    "user": {
      "name": "harinder-kohli@outlook.com",
      "type": "user"
    }
  }
]

C:\Windows\system32>
```

3. **Install kubectl>** az aks install-cli

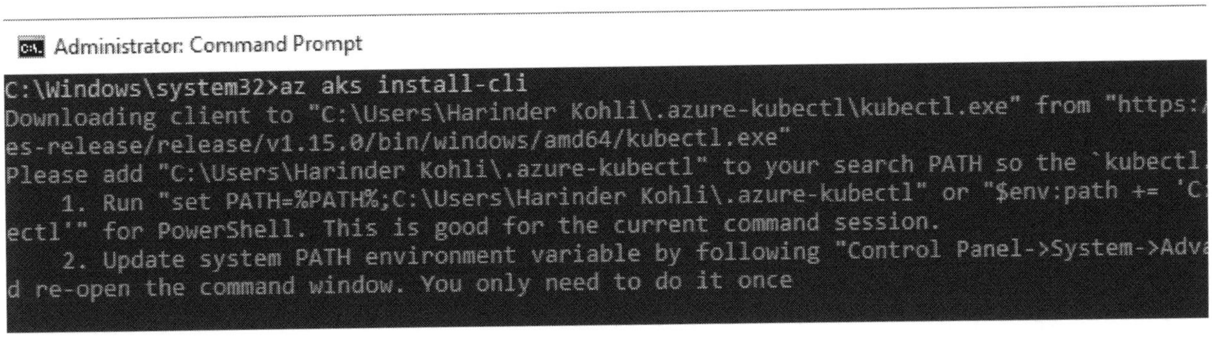

```
Administrator: Command Prompt
C:\Windows\system32>az aks install-cli
Downloading client to "C:\Users\Harinder Kohli\.azure-kubectl\kubectl.exe" from "https:/
es-release/release/v1.15.0/bin/windows/amd64/kubectl.exe"
Please add "C:\Users\Harinder Kohli\.azure-kubectl" to your search PATH so the `kubectl
    1. Run "set PATH=%PATH%;C:\Users\Harinder Kohli\.azure-kubectl" or "$env:path += 'C
ectl'" for PowerShell. This is good for the current command session.
    2. Update system PATH environment variable by following "Control Panel->System->Adv
d re-open the command window. You only need to do it once
```

4. Kubectl.exe was saved **C:\Users\Harinder Kohli\.azure-kubectl** folder as shown in previous figure.

5. On your Laptop right click This PC> Properties> Advanced System Settings>Environment Variables> Under User Variables select Path and click Edit>Click New> Add the kubectl.exe folder path as shown in step 4 above>Click ok>Click ok.

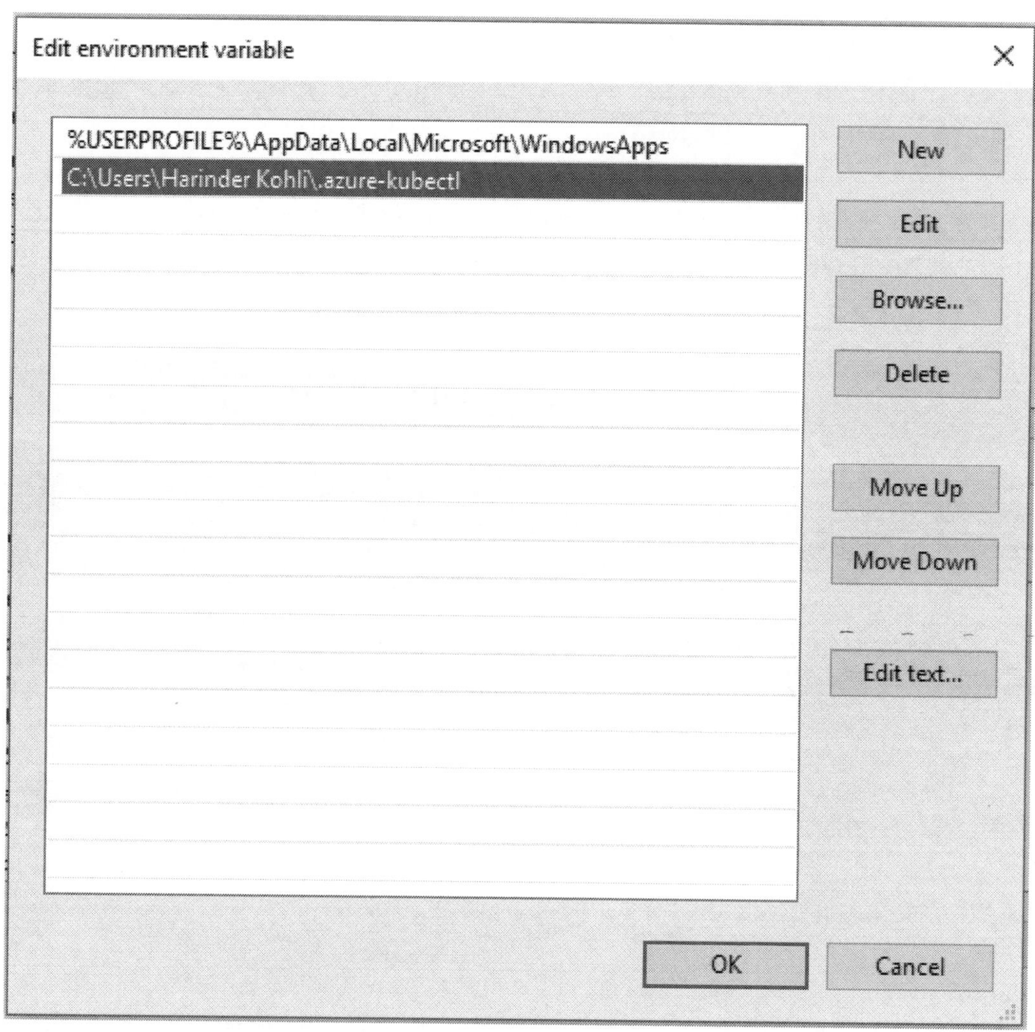

Exercise 43: Connect to AKS Cluster using kubectl

To configure kubectl to connect to your Kubernetes cluster, use the **az aks get-credentials command**. This command downloads credentials and configures the Kubernetes CLI to use them.

1. az aks get-credentials --resource-group RGCloud --name akscloud
2. kubectl get nodes

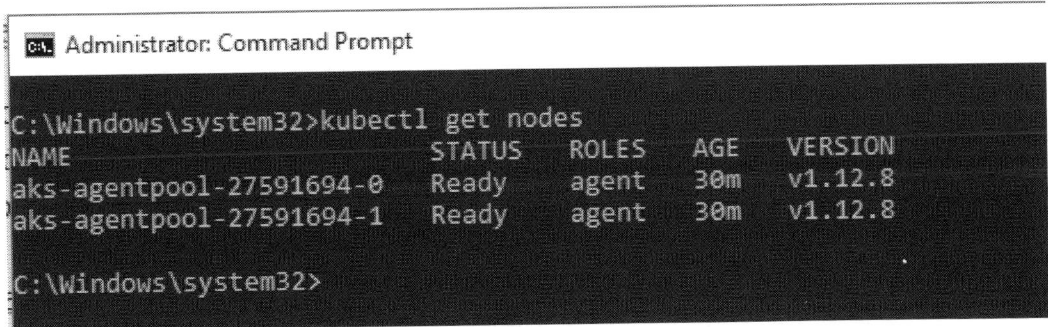

Kubectl Command to deploy Application
kubectl apply –f <Path to *.yaml file)

Kubectl Commands to know the external IP of Application Deployed
Kubectl get service <name of the front end service)

Exercise 44: Access Kubernetes Web UI Dashboard

Kubernetes includes a web dashboard that can be used for basic management operations. This dashboard lets you view basic health status and metrics for your applications, create and deploy services, and edit existing applications.

1. To start the Kubernetes dashboard, use the **az aks browse command**. This command creates a proxy between your development system and the Kubernetes API, and opens a web browser to the Kubernetes dashboard.
   az aks browse --resource-group RGCloud --name akscloud

Administrator: Command Prompt - az aks browse --resource-group RGCloud --name akscloud

```
C:\Windows\system32>kubectl get nodes
NAME                        STATUS   ROLES   AGE   VERSION
aks-agentpool-27591694-0    Ready    agent   30m   v1.12.8
aks-agentpool-27591694-1    Ready    agent   30m   v1.12.8

C:\Windows\system32>az aks browse --resource-group RGCloud --name akscloud
Merged "akscloud" as current context in C:\Users\HARIND~1\AppData\Local\Temp\tmpsu20y1k2
Proxy running on http://127.0.0.1:8001/
Press CTRL+C to close the tunnel...
```

2. This automatically opened a browser with Kubernetes dashboard. Note the **+ CREATE** link in top right.

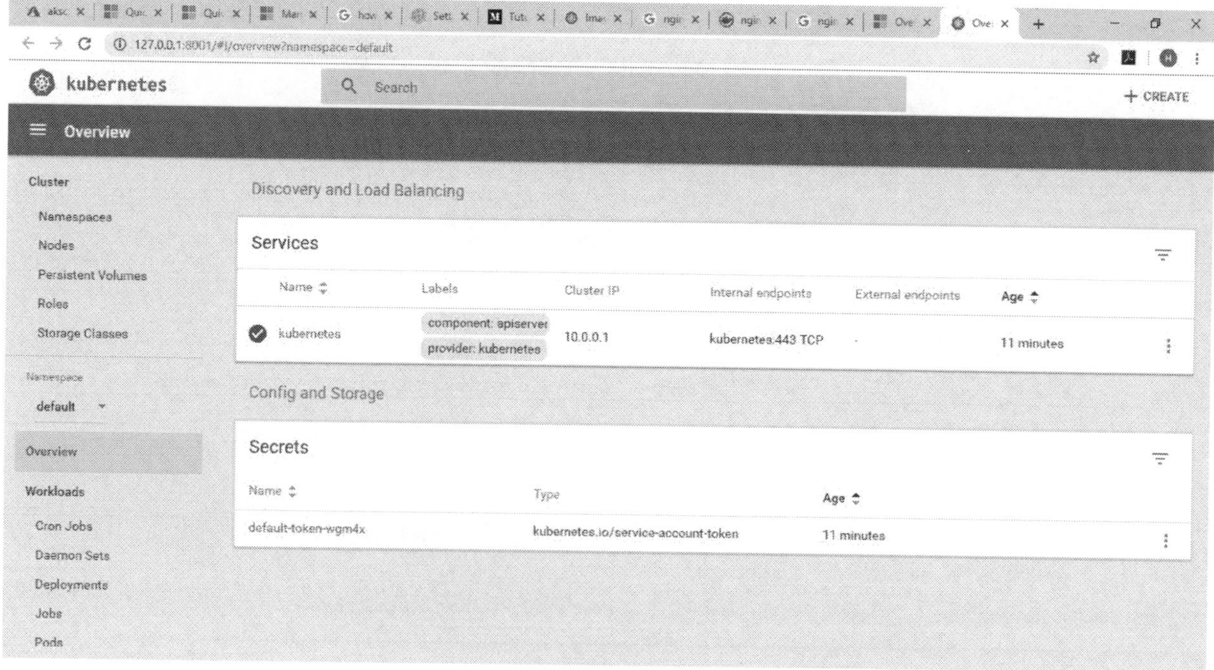

Exercise 45: Deploy NGINX Container to AKS Cluster

1. In Kubernetes Web UI Click +create link in top right>Click Create AN APP. Create AN App blade opens>Enter a name> For container image enter nginx:1.17.0> Under Service click External and enter 80 for both the port and target port>Click Deploy (Not shown)

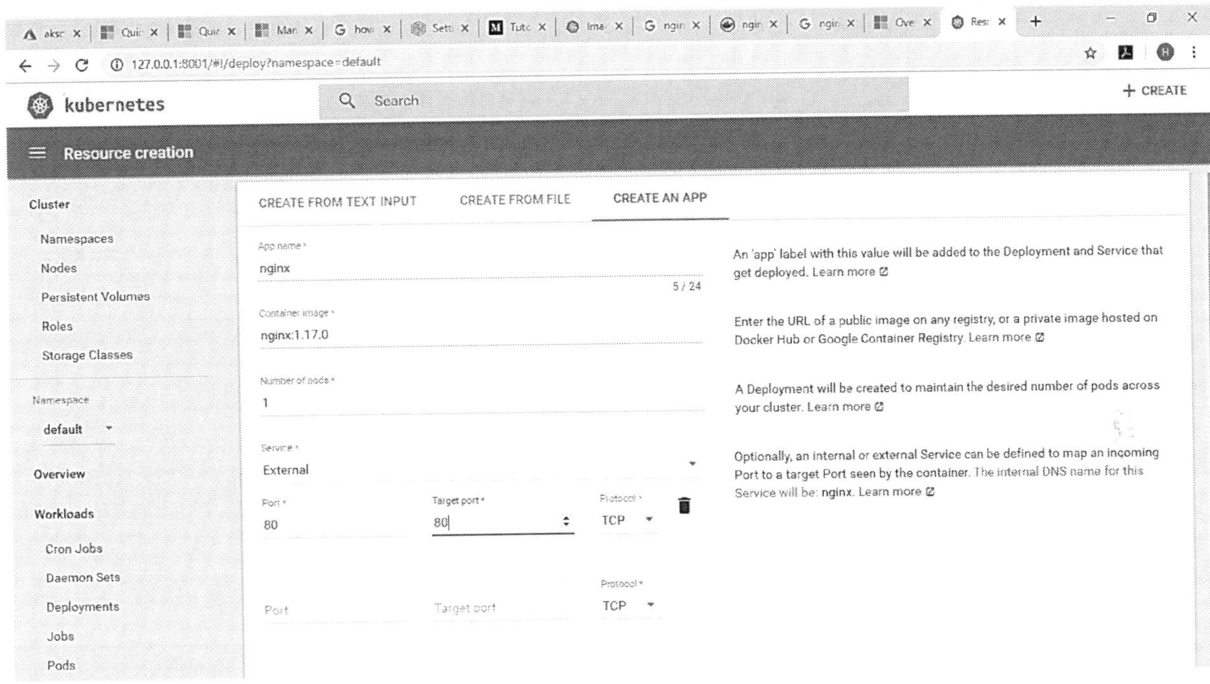

2. It will take 1-2 minutes for public external IP address to be assigned to the Kubernetes service. In left pane in Kubernetes Web UI under **Discovery and Load Balancing** Click **Services**. Your application's service is listed, including the nginx application *External endpoint (IP Address)*.

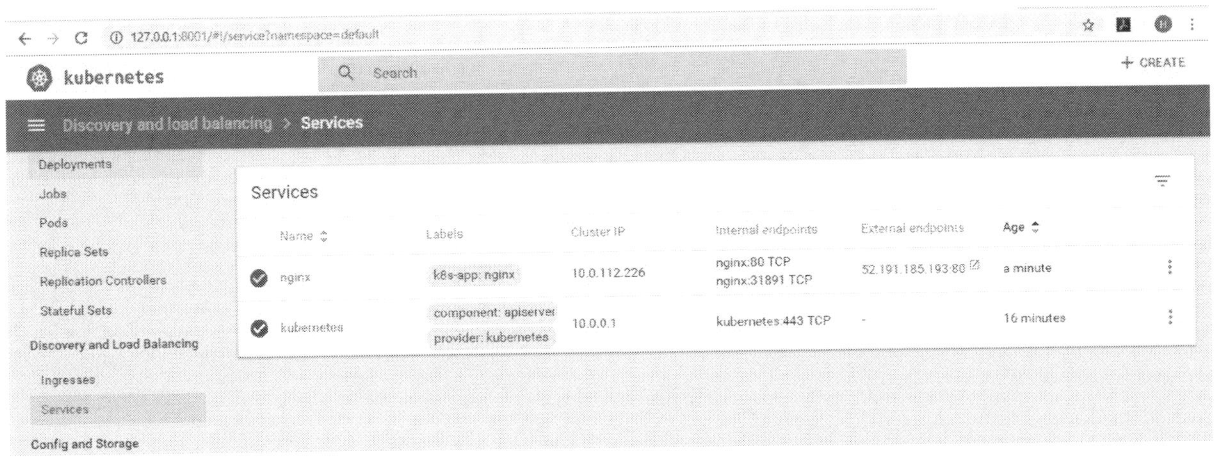

3. Open a browser and enter endpoint address shown in previous figure. NGINX default website opens.

Welcome to nginx!

If you see this page, the nginx web server is successfully installed and working. Further configuration is required.

For online documentation and support please refer to nginx.org.
Commercial support is available at nginx.com.

Thank you for using nginx.

Important Note: Connection from your desktop to Kubernetes Web UI can get disconnected. In this Case you need to enter following command again.
az aks browse --resource-group RGCloud --name akscloud

4. Click Overview Web UI and you can see the Pods and replica set of NGINX Application. You can see Pod is running on agent pool 1.

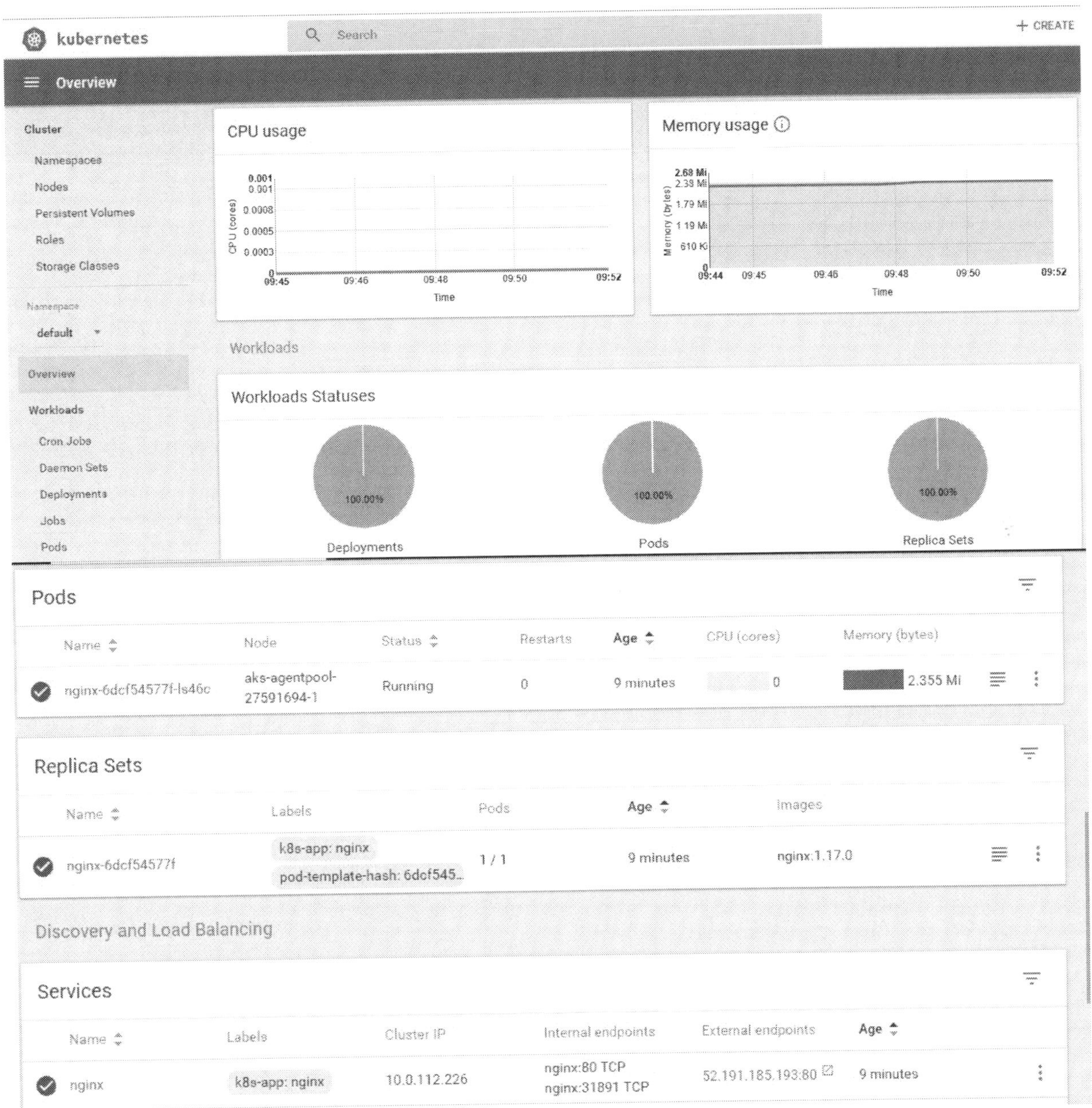

Exercise 46: Edit the NGINX Application

1. In Kubernetes Web UI Dashboard click **Deployments** in left pane> Click your nginx deployment.
2. Select **Edit** in the Top Right> Edit a deployment pane opens.
3. In Edit a deployment pane Locate replica value on line 20. Increase number of replicas for the application from 1 to 2>Update.

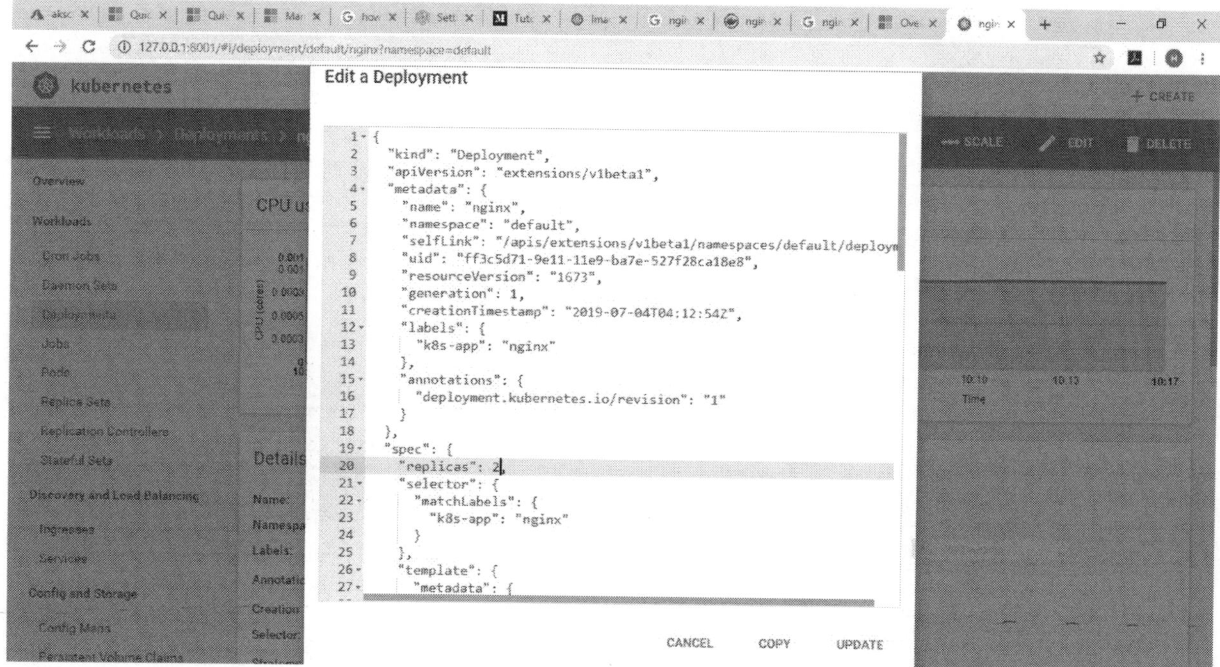

3. Click replica sets in left pane>Click the Replica Set> You can see a **new POD** is running on agent pool 0.

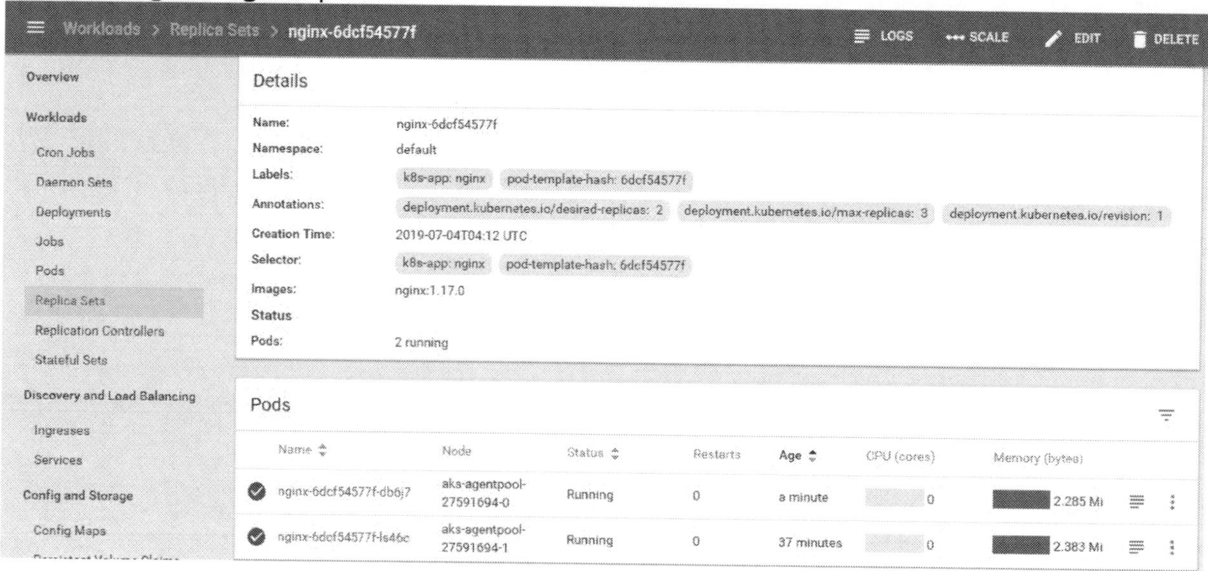

Exercise 47: Deploy Second NGINX Container to AKS Cluster

1. In Kubernetes Web UI Click +create link in top right>Click Create AN APP. Create AN App blade opens>Enter a name> For container image enter nginx:1.17.0> Under Service click External and enter 80 for both the port and target port>Click Deploy (Not shown)

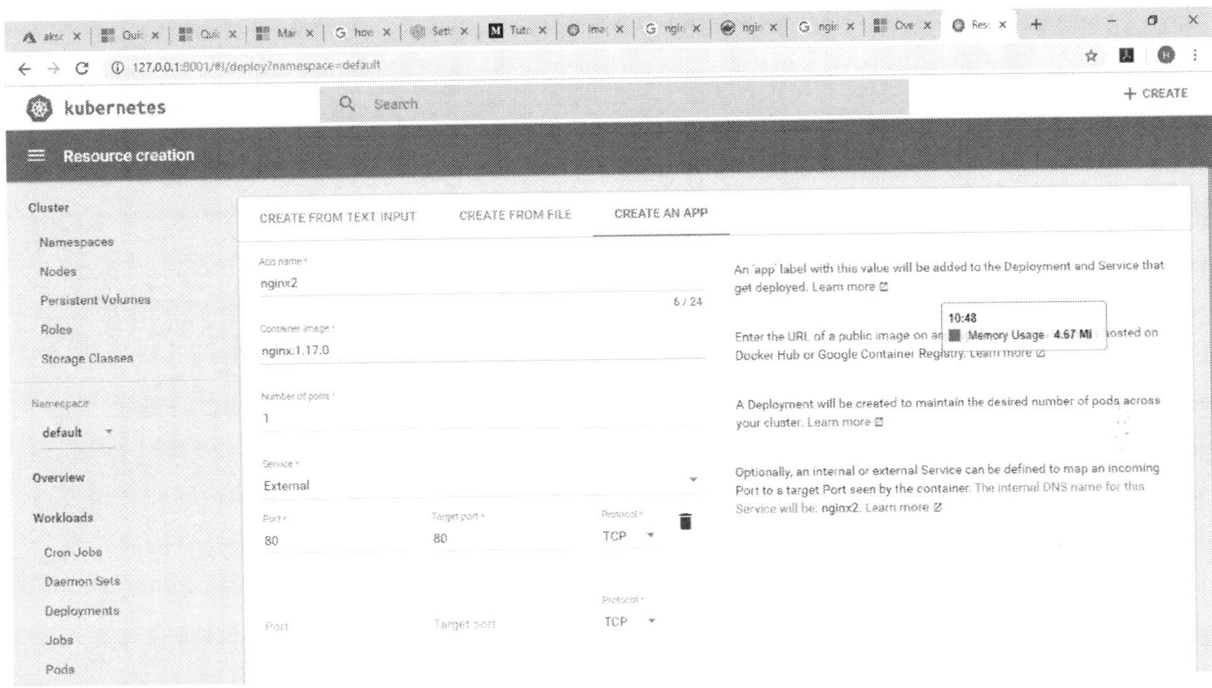

6. It will take 1-2 minutes for public external IP address to be assigned to the Kubernetes service. In left pane in Kubernetes Web UI under **Discovery and Load Balancing** Click **Services**. Your application service nginx2 is listed and *External endpoint* address (52.229.21.218) is shown below. You can see that for both nginx and nginx2 internal port numbers are different.

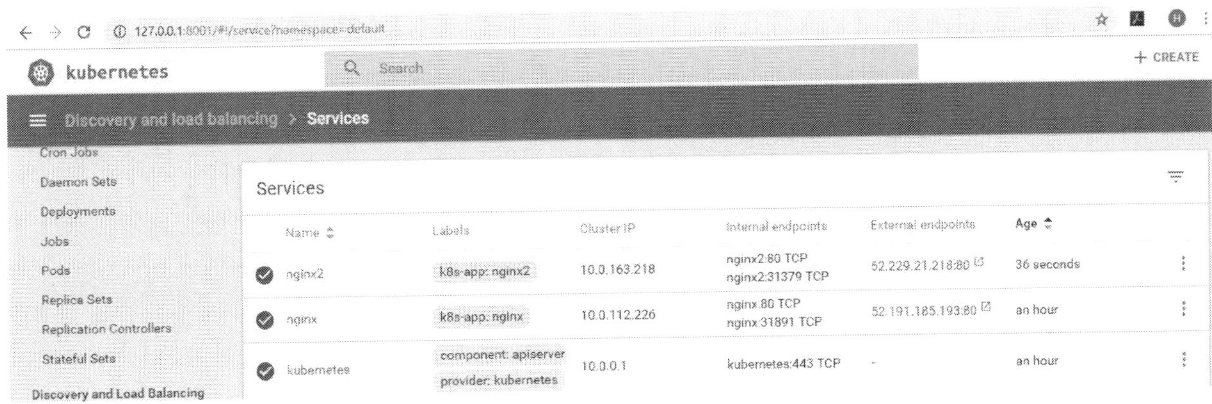

2. Open a browser and enter endpoint address shown in previous figure. NGINX default website opens.

Not secure | 52.229.21.218
Welcome to nginx!
If you see this page, the nginx web server is successfully installed and working. Further configuration is required.
For online documentation and support please refer to nginx.org.
Commercial support is available at nginx.com.
Thank you for using nginx.

Chapter 3 Azure SQL Database

This Chapter covers following

- Azure SQL Database
- Azure SQL Database v/s SQL Server
- Comparing Azure SQL Database (PaaS) to SQL Server running on Azure VM (IaaS)
- Azure SQL Database Deployment Options
- Azure SQL Database - Single Database Model
- Azure SQL Database – Elastic Pool Model
- Azure SQL Database – Managed Instance
- Azure SQL Database service tiers (DTU Model)
- Azure SQL Database service tiers (vCore Model)
- vCore Model – Hyperscale Service Tier
- Azure Hybrid Benefits in vCore Model
- Choosing between vCore and DTU Purchasing Model
- Data Migration Assistant (DMA)
- Business continuity options with Azure SQL Database
- Azure SQL Database Backup and Restore
- Azure SQL Database High Availability Using Active Geo-Replication
- High availability using Active Geo-Replication and Failover groups
- Long Term Backup Retention
- Scaling up or scaling down a single database
- In-Memory technologies in SQL Database
- Azure SQL Database Access Control
- Protecting SQL Data
- Transparent Data Encryption (For Data at Rest)
- Always Encrypted (For Data in Use)
- Advanced Data Security
- Azure SQL Database Auditing
- Azure SQL Database Threat Detection & Auditing
- SQL Database Dynamic Data Masking
- SQL Server Stretch Database
- Azure SQL Pricing DTU Model (Standard Tier)
- SQL Pricing vCore (General Purpose) – Single Database/Elastic Pool

This Chapter Covers following Lab Exercises

- Create and Connect to Azure SQL Single Database (DTU Model)
- Enabling Azure AD Authentication for User1

- Create Azure SQL Single Database (vCore Model)
- Point in Time Restore
- Active Geo-Replication. Creating Replica of Primary Database
- Configuring Long Term Backup Retention
- Transparent Data Encryption at database level
- Transparent Data Encryption at Server level
- Enabling Advanced Data Security
- Enabling Database Auditing at Server Level
- Adding Dynamic Data Masking Rule

This Chapter Covers following Case Studies

- Design a Business Continuity Solution for Web/App tier and Database Tier
- Choosing a Database tier

Chapter Topology

In this chapter we will add Azure SQL Database to the topology.

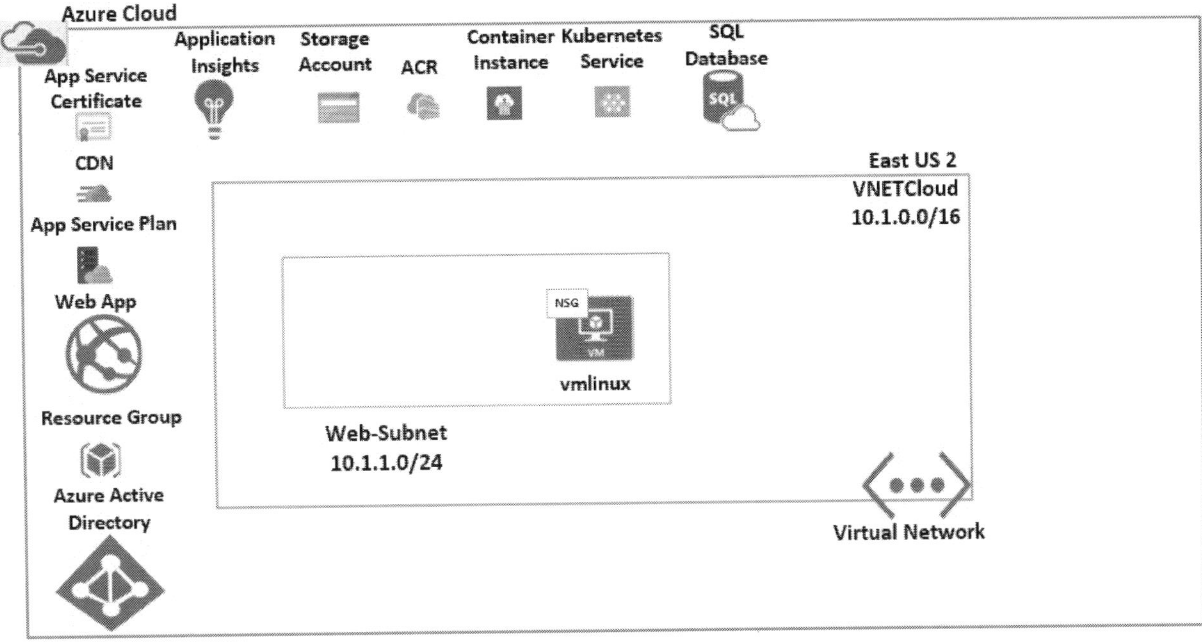

Following Topology will be used in Geo-Replication Exercise lab to replicate Primary Database in West US 2 Region to East US 2 Region. West US 2 Region and East US 2 Region are paired regions.

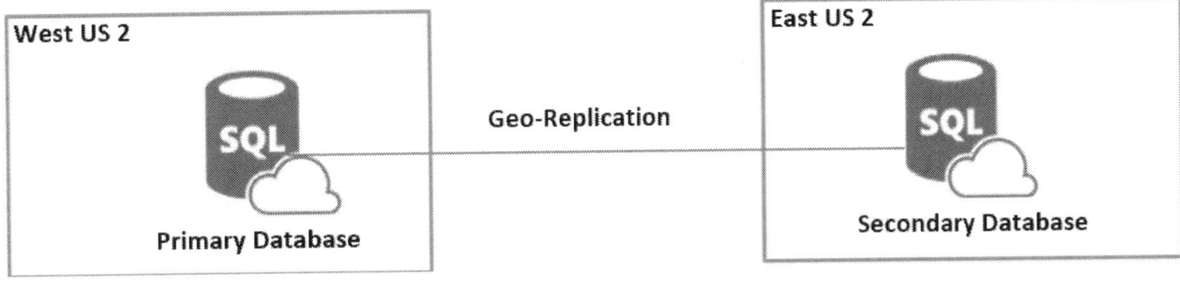

Azure SQL Database

Azure SQL Database is a relational database-as-a-service (DBaaS) in the cloud built on the Microsoft SQL Server platform. Azure SQL Database is a managed resource which means we don't have to install, upgrade or patch the database. You also don't have to manage the underlying infrastructure – Hardware and Operating System.

Benefits of Azure SQL Database

1. The benefit of using the Azure SQL Database service is the ability to spin up and consume a relational database in minutes; it can then easily be replicated for geo redundancy without all the infrastructure deployment and management normally required.
2. SQL Database supports existing SQL Server tools, libraries, and APIs. As a result, it is easy to develop new solutions, to move your existing SQL Server solutions, and to extend your existing SQL Server solutions to the Microsoft cloud without having to learn new skills.
3. Third we don't have to manage any upgrade or patching or underlying hardware and operating system.
4. You can Scale up or scale down a database at any time without downtime.

Azure SQL Database v/s SQL Server

SQL Database can be used in two ways- Azure SQL Database or SQL Server as a VM.

Azure SQL Database is a managed resource. We don't have to install the database or patch it. Scale out requires no downtime. Geo Replication can be configured in just 3-4 steps.

In case of SQL Server we need to install SQL server on a windows VM. This option requires more operational overhead and skilled resources are required for administration, installation and deployment. Replication configuration is complex and requires skilled resources for deployment.

Comparing Azure SQL Database to SQL Server running on Azure VM

Feature	Azure SQL	SQL Server on Azure VM
Feature	Not all features are supported.	Supports all SQL Server Features.
PaaS vs IaaS	This is a PaaS (Platform as a service) also referred to as DBaaS.	This is IaaS. SQL Server Installed on a Windows Server VM.
Administrative Overhead	There are very less Admin overhead required to maintain the database.	This requires specialized IT resources to Install and maintain the database and underline OS.
High Availability and Business Continuity	Built in High Availability and DR features. Features include Geo-Replication and Automated Backups.	You need to plan for all HA & DR. This requires very specialized IT resources for implementation.
Scalability	Very easy to scale up and down. You can add or remove resources when required without anytime.	You have to Plan for scalability and will require downtime.
Upgrades	You get all new features free of cost. They are implemented without any admin overhead.	You need to Plan for upgrades/patches which requires downtime. For next Major version of the database you need to pay the upgrade cost. Minor upgrades are free.
Max Database Size	**4 TB. Increased to 100 TB with Hyperscale Tier in vCore Model.**	**64 TB**
License	License is included in PaaS. On-premise license can be ported with vCore Purchasing model.	License is included as part of IaaS Marketplace. On-premise license can be ported
Use Case	New cloud-designed applications that have time constraints in development and marketing.	Existing applications that require fast migration to the cloud with minimal changes.
Use Case	Building Software-as-a-Service (SaaS) applications.	Migrating and building enterprise and hybrid applications.

Azure SQL Database Deployment Options

You can Deploy Azure SQL Database in 3 ways as shown in figure below.

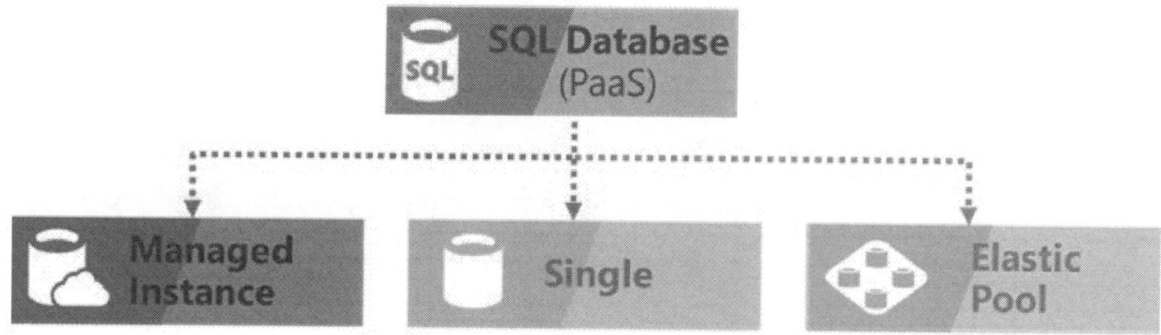

Single Database has its own set of resources managed via a SQL Database server. A single database is similar to a contained database in SQL Server.

An **elastic pool** is a collection of databases with a shared set of resources managed via a SQL Database server. Single databases can be moved into and out of an elastic pool.

Managed instance is a collection of system and user databases with a shared set of resources. A managed instance is similar to an instance of the Microsoft SQL Server database engine and is deployed in Virtual Network.

Note:
SQL Database shares its code base with the Microsoft SQL Server database engine. With Microsoft's cloud-first strategy, the newest capabilities of SQL Server are released first to SQL Database, and then to SQL Server itself. This approach provides you with the newest SQL Server capabilities with no overhead for patching or upgrading

Azure SQL Database - Single Database Model

Single database are individual and fully isolated database optimized for workloads when performance demands are somewhat predictable. **Single Database** has its own set of resources managed via a SQL Database server. Single Database can be created with **DTU-based** or **vCore-based** purchasing model.

DTU Based

Database transaction unit (DTU) based purchasing model provides bundled compute and storage packages balanced for common workloads.

Database Transaction/Throughput Units (DTUs) is a blended measure of CPU, memory, and data I/O and transaction log I/O that are guaranteed to be available to a standalone Azure SQL database at a specific performance level.

Azure SQL Database offers three tiers in Single Database DTU Model – **Basic, Standard, Premium**. There are Multiple Performance levels within a tier to handle different workloads. Each database tier is distinguished primarily by performance, which is measured in **Database Transaction/Throughput Units (DTUs).**

The figure below shows various service Tiers and performance level within each tier and their associated DTUs.

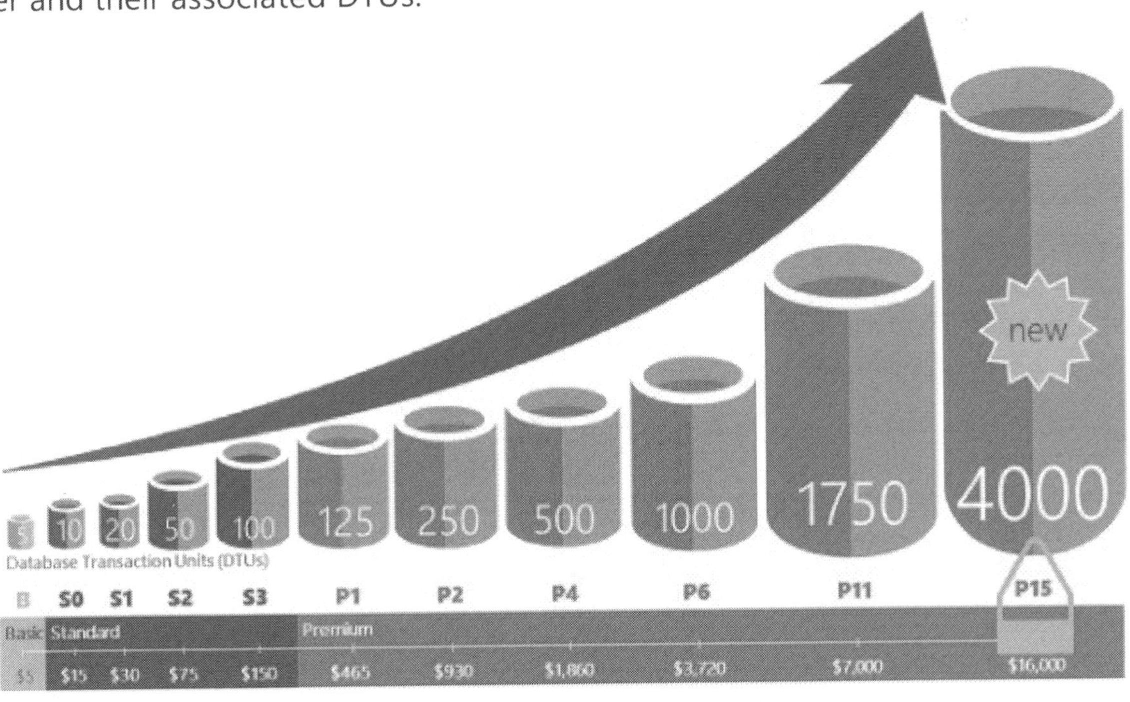

vCore Based

vCore model allows you to independently scale compute and storage resources based upon your workload needs.

The vCore-based purchasing model lets you choose the number of vCores, the amount or memory, and the amount and speed of storage.

The vCore based purchasing model also allows you to use Azure Hybrid Benefit for SQL Server to gain cost savings.

Azure SQL Database offers three tiers in Single Database vCore Model – **General Purpose, Business Critical & Hyperscale.**

Note 1: Hyperscale Tier is not offered with Elastic Pool Model and Managed Instance.
Note 2: You can change service tiers at any time with minimal downtime to your application.

Azure SQL Database – Elastic Pool Model

SQL Database elastic pools are used for managing and scaling **multiple databases that have varying and unpredictable usage demands**. The databases in an elastic pool are on a single Azure SQL Database server and share a set number of resources at a set price.

Elastic pools solve the problem of unpredictable usage patterns by allocating performance resources to a pool rather than an individual database, and pay for the collective performance resources of the pool rather than for single database performance.

Databases best suited for pools

Databases with varying activity over time are great candidates for elastic pools because they are not active at maximum level at the same time and can share eDTUs.

Advantage of Elastic Pool Model

One of the advantage of Pools is that you can reduce the cost of Databases as the pool eDTUs are shared by many databases.

For the same value, eDTU is priced 1.5 Times that of DTU.

Elastic Pool Purchasing Model options

Elastic Pool Database can be created with **eDTU-based** or **vCore-based** purchasing model.

Database transaction unit (DTU) based purchasing model provides bundled compute and storage packages balanced for common workloads.

vCore model allows you to independently scale compute and storage resources based upon your workload needs.

eDTU Based

A eDTU is a blended measure of CPU, memory, and data I/O and transaction log I/O that are guaranteed to be available to a Azure SQL database Elastic pool.

Individual Databases in the elastic pool can consume varying level of eDTU but Pooled databases consumption don't exceed the limits of the pool, so your **cost remains predictable even if individual database usage doesn't.**

An elastic pool is given a set number of eDTUs, for a set price. Within the pool, individual databases are given the flexibility to auto-scale within set parameters. Under heavy load, a database can consume more eDTUs to meet demand. Databases under light loads consume less, and databases under no load consume no eDTUs.

Azure SQL Database offers three tiers in Elastic Pool eDTU Model – **Basic, Standard, Premium**. There are Multiple Performance levels within a tier to handle different workloads. Each database tier is distinguished primarily by performance, which is measured in elastic Database Transaction/Throughput Units (DTUs). **Elastic Database Transaction Units (eDTUs)** determine the performance tier of the databases in an elastic pool.

The figure below shows various service Tiers and performance level within each tier and their associated DTUs.

Elastic Database Pool
Shares 100-1200 eDTUs

Auto-scale up to 5 eDTUs per DB
Basic

Auto-scale up to 100 eDTUs per DB
Standard

Auto-scale up to 1000 eDTUs per DB
Premium

vCore Based

vCore model allows you to independently scale compute and storage resources based upon your workload needs.

The vCore-based purchasing model lets you choose the number of vCores, the amount or memory, and the amount and speed of storage.

The vCore based purchasing model also allows you to use Azure Hybrid Benefit for SQL Server to gain cost savings.

Azure SQL Database offers Two tiers in Elastic Pool vCore Model – **General Purpose & Business Critical.**

Azure SQL Database – Managed Instance

A managed instance is similar to an instance of the Microsoft SQL Server database engine.

Managed instance deployment option of Azure SQL Database, provides near 100% compatibility with the latest SQL Server on-premises (Enterprise Edition) Database Engine.

Managed Instance is deployed in Virtual Network (VNET). Deployment in Virtual Network addresses common security concerns and provides a business model favorable for on-premises SQL Server customers.

Managed Instance is offered with **vCore-based** purchasing model only. Azure SQL Database offers Two tiers in Managed Instance vCore Model – **General Purpose & Business Critical.**

The vCore based purchasing model also allows you to use Azure Hybrid Benefit to gain cost savings.

Advantages of Managed Instance

1. The managed instance deployment model allows existing SQL Server customers to lift and shift their on-premises applications to the cloud with minimal application and database changes.

2. Managed instance deployment option preserves all PaaS capabilities including automatic patching and version updates, automated backups, high-availability that drastically reduces management overhead and TCO.

Key Features of Managed Instance

Figure below shows features of Azure SQL Database – Managed Instance.

What is SQL Database Managed Instance?

New deployment option that enables frictionless migration for SQL apps and modernization in a fully managed service

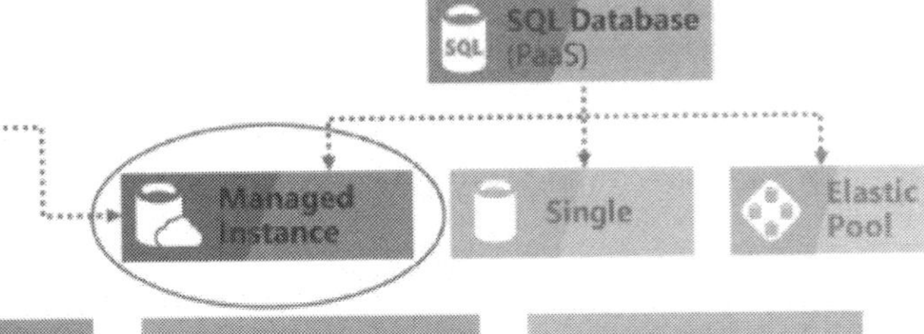

Easy lift and shift	Fully managed PaaS	Full isolation and security	New business model
• Fully-fledged SQL instance with nearly 100% compat with on-prem	• Built on the same PaaS service infrastructure • All PaaS features	• Native VNET implementation • Private IP addresses	• Competitive • Transparent • Frictionless

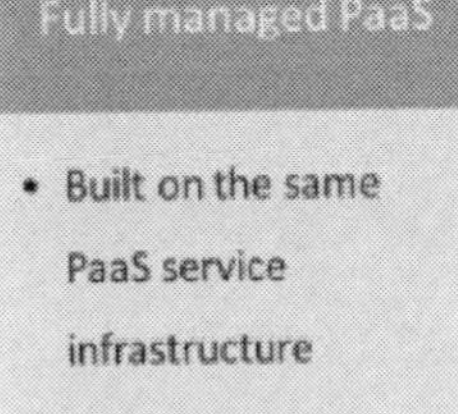

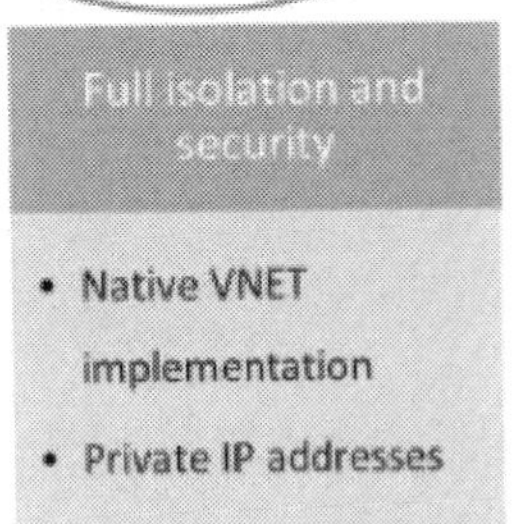

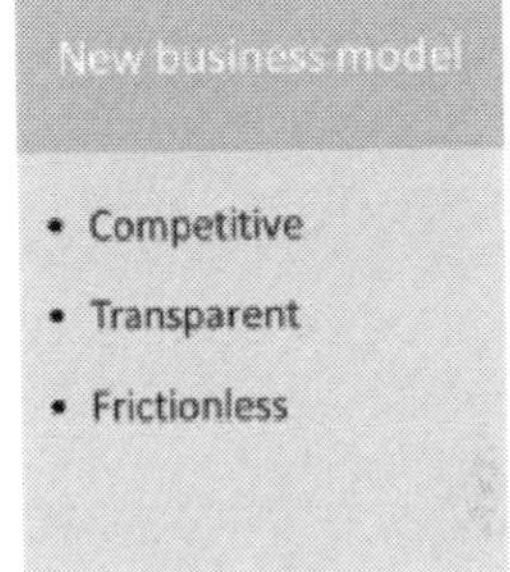

PaaS benefits	Business continuity
No hardware purchasing and management No management overhead for managing underlying infrastructure Quick provisioning and service scaling Automated patching and version upgrade Integration with other PaaS data services	99.99% uptime SLA Built in high-availability Data protected with automated backups Customer configurable backup retention period User-initiated backups Point in time database restore capability

Security and compliance	Management
Isolated environment (VNet integration, single tenant service, dedicated compute and storage) Transparent data encryption (TDE) Azure AD authentication, single sign-on support Azure AD server principals (logins) (**public preview**) Adheres to compliance standards same as Azure SQL database SQL auditing threat detection	Azure Resource Manager API for automating service provisioning and scaling Azure portal functionality for manual service provisioning and scaling Data Migration Service

Azure SQL Database service tiers (DTU Model)

Azure SQL Database offers **Basic**, **Standard**, and **Premium** service tiers in DTU Model. Service tiers are primarily differentiated by a range of performance level (DTUs), storage size & I/O Performance

Basic Tier: Basic Tier is best suited for a Test/Dev or low end application environment, supporting typically one single active operation at a given time.
Standard Tier: Best suited for cloud applications with low to medium IO performance requirements, supporting multiple concurrent queries.
Premier Tier: Designed for IO-intensive production workloads with high-availability and zero downtime, supporting many concurrent users. Examples are databases supporting mission critical applications.

Single Database Model

	Basic Tier	Standard	Premium
Maximum DTUs	5	3000	4000
Max Database size	2 GB	1 TB	4 TB
Backup retention	7 days	35 days	35 days
IO throughput	2.5 IOPS/DTU	2.5 IOPS/DTU	48 IOPS/DTU
IO latency	5ms (read), 10ms (write)	5ms (read), 10ms (write)	2ms (read/write)
Performance Levels within tiers	1	S0, S1, S2, S3, S4, S6, S7, S9 & S12	P1, P2, P4, P6, P11 & P15
In-memory OLTP	NA	NA	Supported

Elastic Pool Model

	Basic Tier	Standard	Premium
Maximum eDTUs per database	5	3000	4000
Maximum eDTUs per pool	1600	3000	4000
Maximum storage size per database	2 GB	1 TB	1 TB
Maximum storage size per pool	156 GB	4 TB	4 TB
Max Number of Databases/pool	500	500	100
Backup retention	7 days	35 days	35 days
IO throughput	Low	Medium	Higher
IO latency	> Premium	> Premium	< Basic & Std
Performance Levels within tiers	Multiple	Multiple	Multiple
Max in-memory OLTP storage (GB)	NA	NA	Supported

Azure SQL Database service tiers (vCore Model)

In vCore model Azure SQL Database offers General Purpose and Business Critical Service tiers for Single Database Model, Elastic Pool Model and Managed Instance. A Hyperscale tier is also offered with Single Database Model only.

vCore model allows you to independently scale compute and storage resources based upon your workload needs. The vCore-based purchasing model lets you choose the number of vCores, the amount of memory and the amount and speed of storage.

The vCore based purchasing model also allows you to use Azure Hybrid Benefit for SQL Server to gain cost savings.

In vCore Model, Compute is based on Gen 5 logical CPUs (Intel E5-2673 v4 (Broadwell) 2.3 GHz processors.) In Gen 5, 1 vCore = 1 hyper thread. There is option for Gen 4 CPUs also.

	General Purpose	**Business Critical**
Compute	2 to 80 vCore	2 to 80 vCore
Memory	5.1 GB Per vCore	5.1 GB Per vCore
Storage	**Premium remote storage, 5 GB – 4 TB**	**Local SSD storage, 5 GB – 4 TB**
I/O	500 IOPS per vCore with 7500 maximum IOPS	5000 IOPS per core with 200,000 maximum IOPS
Availability	1 replica, no read-scale	3 replicas, 1 read-scale, zone redundant HA
Backups	RA-GRS, 7-35 days (7 days by default)	RA-GRS, 7-35 days (7 days by default)
In-Memory	NA	Supported
Use Case	Most business workloads. Offers budget oriented balanced and scalable compute and storage options.	Business applications with high IO requirements. Offers highest resilience to failures using several isolated replicas.

vCore Model – Hyperscale Service Tier

A Hyperscale tier in vCore Model is offered with Single Database Model only.

A Hyperscale tier in vCore Model offers scale out storage and compute resources for an Azure SQL Database substantially beyond the limits available for the General Purpose and Business Critical service tiers.

Hyperscale Service Tier Additional Capabilities

1. Support for up to **100 TB of database size.**
2. Nearly instantaneous database backups (based on file snapshots stored in Azure Blob storage) regardless of size with no IO impact on compute resources
3. Fast database restores (based on file snapshots) in minutes rather than hours or days (not a size of data operation)
4. Higher overall performance due to higher log throughput and faster transaction commit times regardless of data volumes
5. Rapid scale out - you can provision one or more read-only nodes for offloading your read workload and for use as hot-standbys
6. Rapid Scale up - you can, in constant time, scale up your compute resources to accommodate heavy workloads as and when needed, and then scale the compute resources back down when not needed.

Hyperscale Service Tier Use Cases

1. The Hyperscale service tier is primarily intended for customers who have large databases either on-premises and want to modernize their applications by moving to the cloud or for customers who are already in the cloud and are limited by the maximum database size restrictions (1-4 TB).

2. It is intended for customers who seek high performance and high scalability for storage and compute.

3. The Hyperscale service tier supports all SQL Server workloads, but it is primarily optimized for OLTP. The Hyperscale service tier also supports hybrid and analytical (data mart) workloads.

Hyperscale Service Tier Specifications

In vCore Model Hyperscale tier, Compute is based on Gen 5 logical CPUs (Intel E5-2673 v4 (Broadwell) 2.3 GHz processors.)
In Gen 5, 1 vCore = 1 hyper thread.
There is an option for Gen 4 CPUs also.

	Hyperscale
Compute	2 to 80 vCore
Memory	5.1 GB Per vCore
Storage	**Supports up to 100 TB of storage.** Uses local SSD storage for local buffer-pool cache and local data storage. Uses Azure remote storage as final long-term data store.
I/O	Hyperscale is a multi-tiered architecture with caching at multiple levels. Effective IOPs will depend on the workload.
Availability	1 read-write replica, plus 0-4 read-scale replicas.
Backups	Snapshot-based backups in Azure remote storage. Restores use these snapshots for fast recovery.
In-Memory	Not Supported
Use Case	Most business workloads with highly scalable storage and read-scale requirements.

Azure Hybrid Benefits in vCore Model

In vCore-based purchasing model, you can exchange your existing licenses of on-premises SQL Server with Software Assurance for discounted rates on SQL Database by using Azure Hybrid Benefit for SQL Server. **This allows you to save up to 30 percent** on Azure SQL Database by using your on-premises SQL Server licenses with Software Assurance.

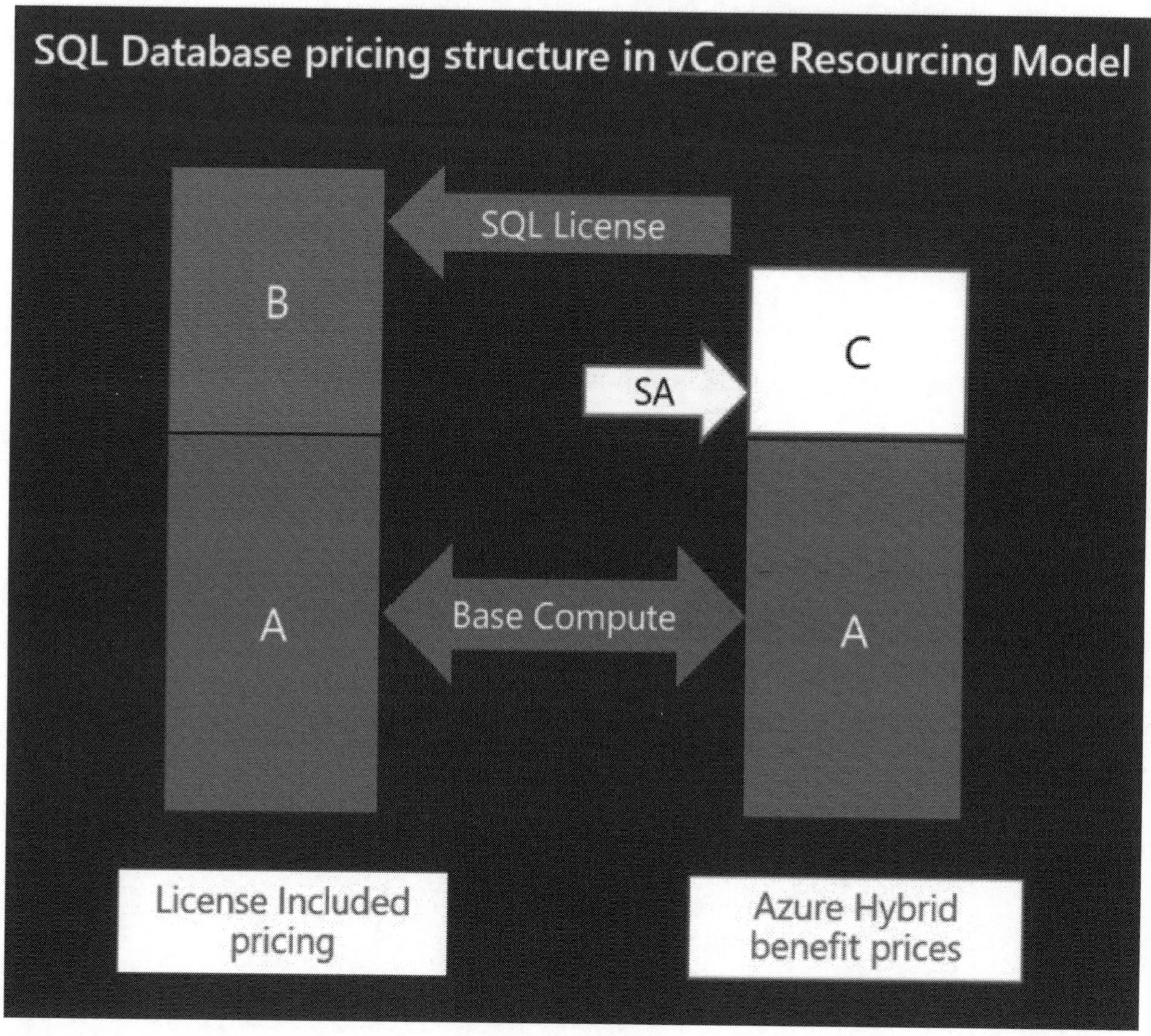

With Azure Hybrid Benefit, you pay only for the underlying Azure infrastructure (Base Compute pricing) as shown in above figure (Right Side).

Without Azure Hybrid Benefit you pay for both the underlying infrastructure and the SQL Server license as shown in above figure (Left Side).

Choosing between vCore and DTU Purchasing Model

Purchasing Model	Description	Best For
DTU-based model	This model is based on a bundled measure of compute, storage, and I/O resources. Compute sizes are expressed in DTUs for single databases Model and in elastic database transaction units (eDTUs) for elastic pool Model.	Best for customers who want simple, preconfigured resource options.
vCore-based model	This model allows you to independently choose compute and storage resources. The vCore-based purchasing model also allows you to use Azure Hybrid Benefit for SQL Server to gain cost savings.	Best for customers who value flexibility, control, and transparency.

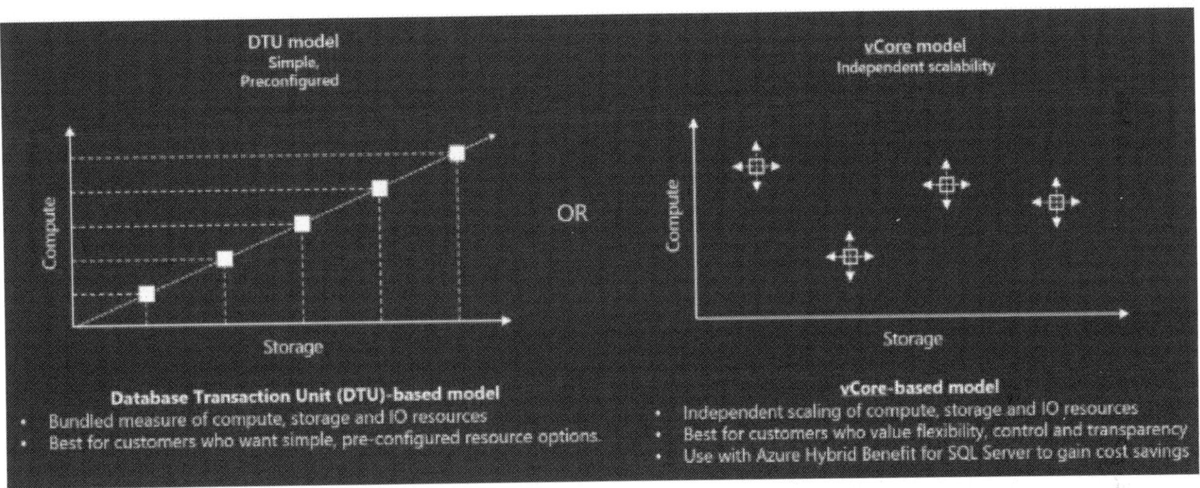

Data Migration Assistant (DMA)

If you have an existing database on SQL Server that you want to migrate to Azure, you can install **Data Migration Assistant (DMA)** that will analyze your databases on SQL Server and find any issue that could block migration to the single database deployment option. If you don't find any issue, **you can export your database as .bacpac file** and **import it using the Azure portal or SqlPackage.**

Data Migration Assistant (DMA) enables you to detect compatibility issues that can impact database functionality on your new version of SQL Server. It recommends performance and reliability improvements for your target environment. It allows you to not only move your schema and data, but also uncontained objects from your source server to your target server.

You can download Data Migration Assistant (DMA) from below link.
https://www.microsoft.com/en-us/download/details.aspx?id=53595

Bacpac File

You can export existing Database Instance of SQL Server to Bacapac file.

Using SQL Server Mnagement Studio export Database instance to Bacpac file and then save the Bacpac file locally or in Azure Storage. You can then import Bacpac to Azure SQL database.

Note: DMA is also available as part of Azure Migrate. Refer to Azure Migrate Chapter 22.

Exercise 48: Create and Connect to Azure SQL Single Database (DTU Model)

In this exercise we will create **Azure SQL Database** in **West US 2 Location**. We will also **create resource Group SDDTU**.

There are 3 steps involved in this: Create SQL Database (Single Database Model), Create server level firewall rule and Connect to SQL Database using SQL Server Management Studio (SSMS) from a client machine.

Step 1 Create Azure SQL Database

1. In Azure Portal Click +create a resource>Databases>SQL Database>Create SQL Database Blade opens with Basic Tab (Not Shown).
2. For Resource Group click Create new under Resource Group box and enter SDDTU.
3. Enter a database name. I entered samplesql.
4. In Server click create new> New Server blade opens>Enter a name>Enter name of user and password>Location Select West US 2>Select Allow Azure Services>Click OK.

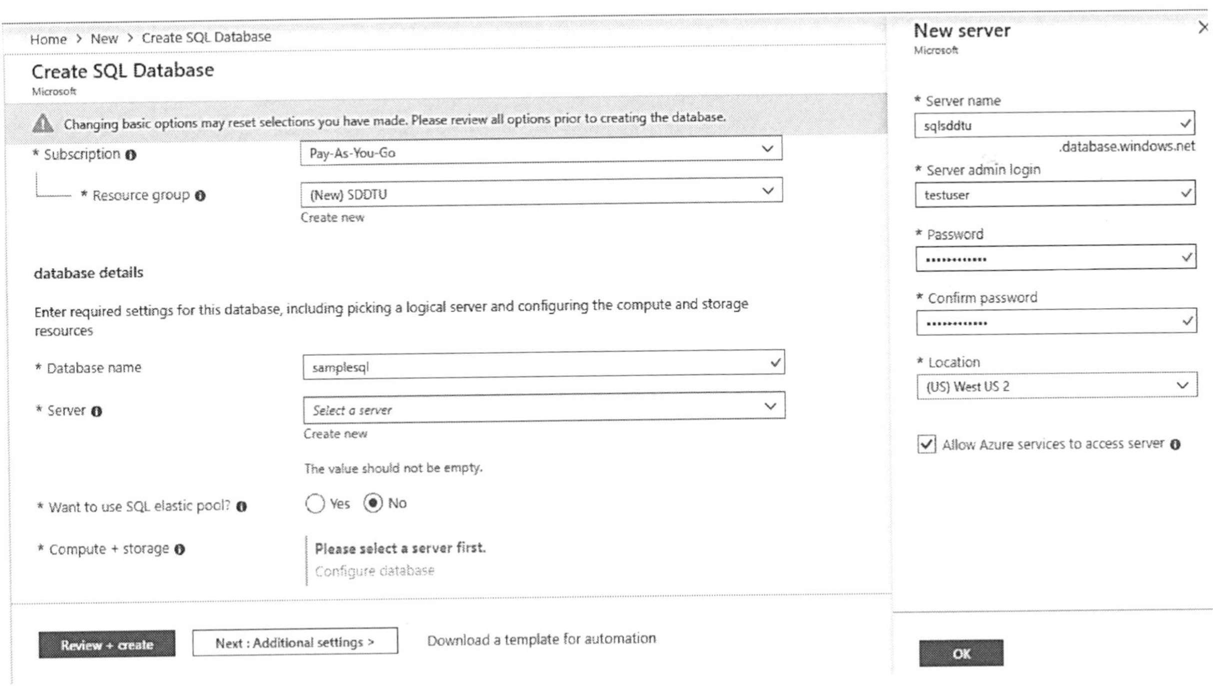

5. In Elastic Pool option select No.

6. In Compute + Storage click configure Database> Configure Database opens> Click Looking for Basic, Standard, Premium Box in Top Row left side>Select Standard Tier> Select Default options for DTU & Storage>Click Apply.

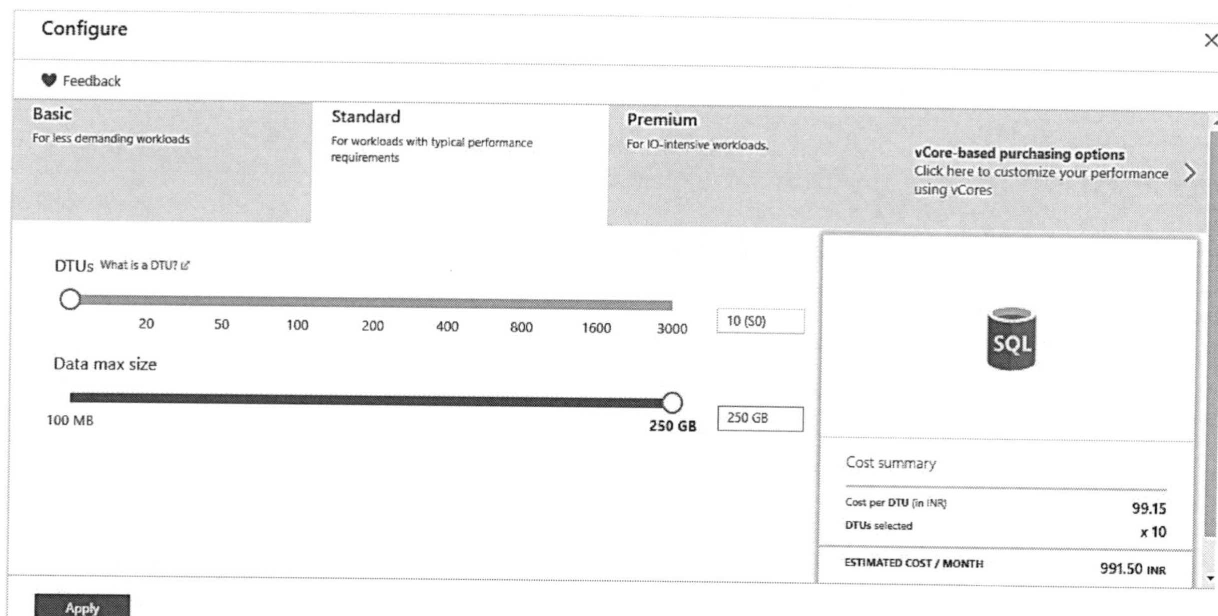

7. Figure below shows Basic Tab (Not Shown) with all options entered.

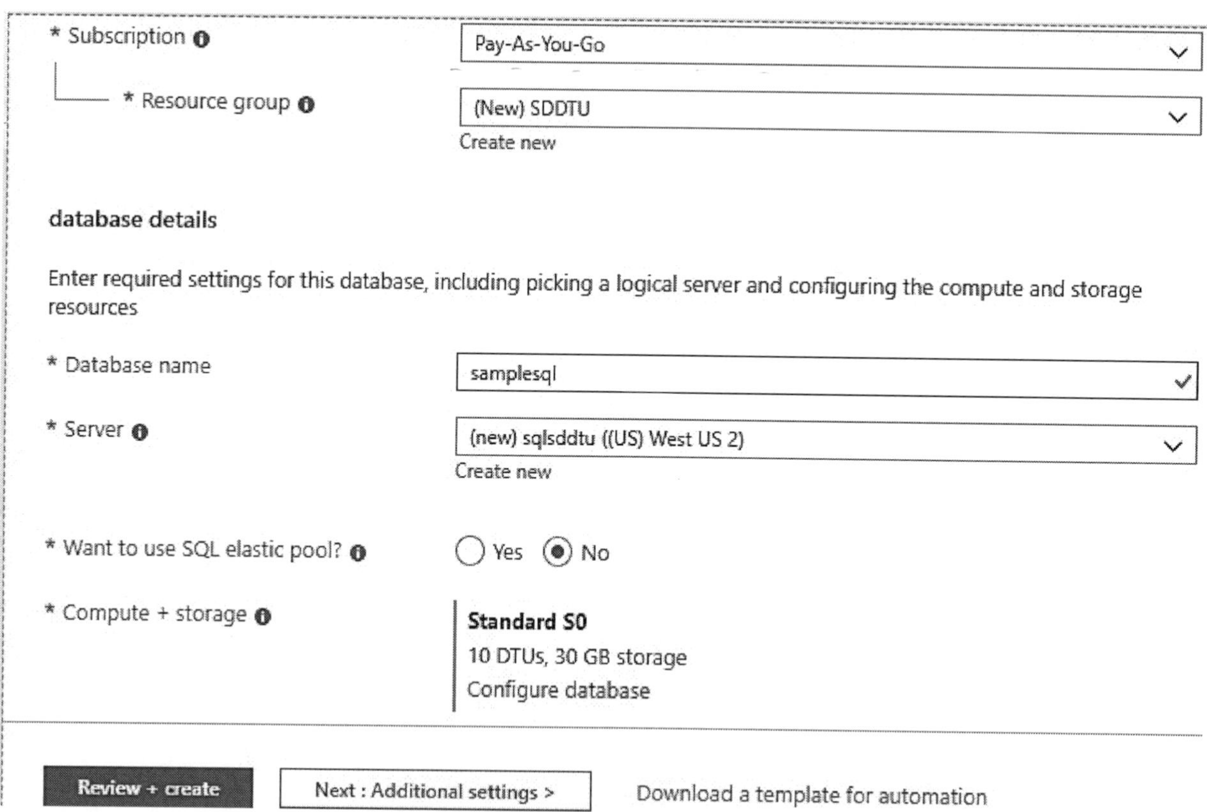

8. Click Next: Additional Settings>Select Sample Tab. This will populate AdventureWorksLT sample Data in the sample database samplesql.

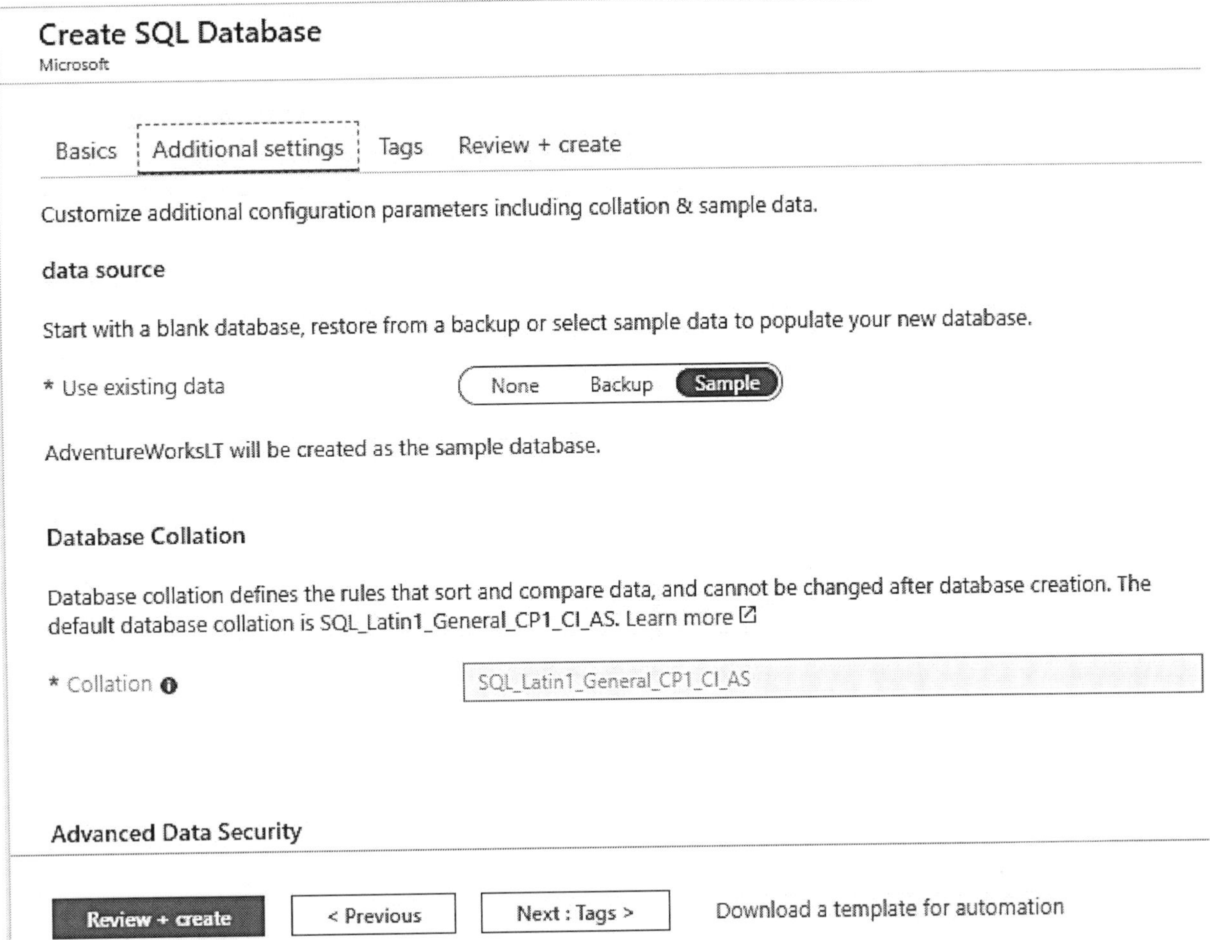

9. Click Review + Create> Click Create.

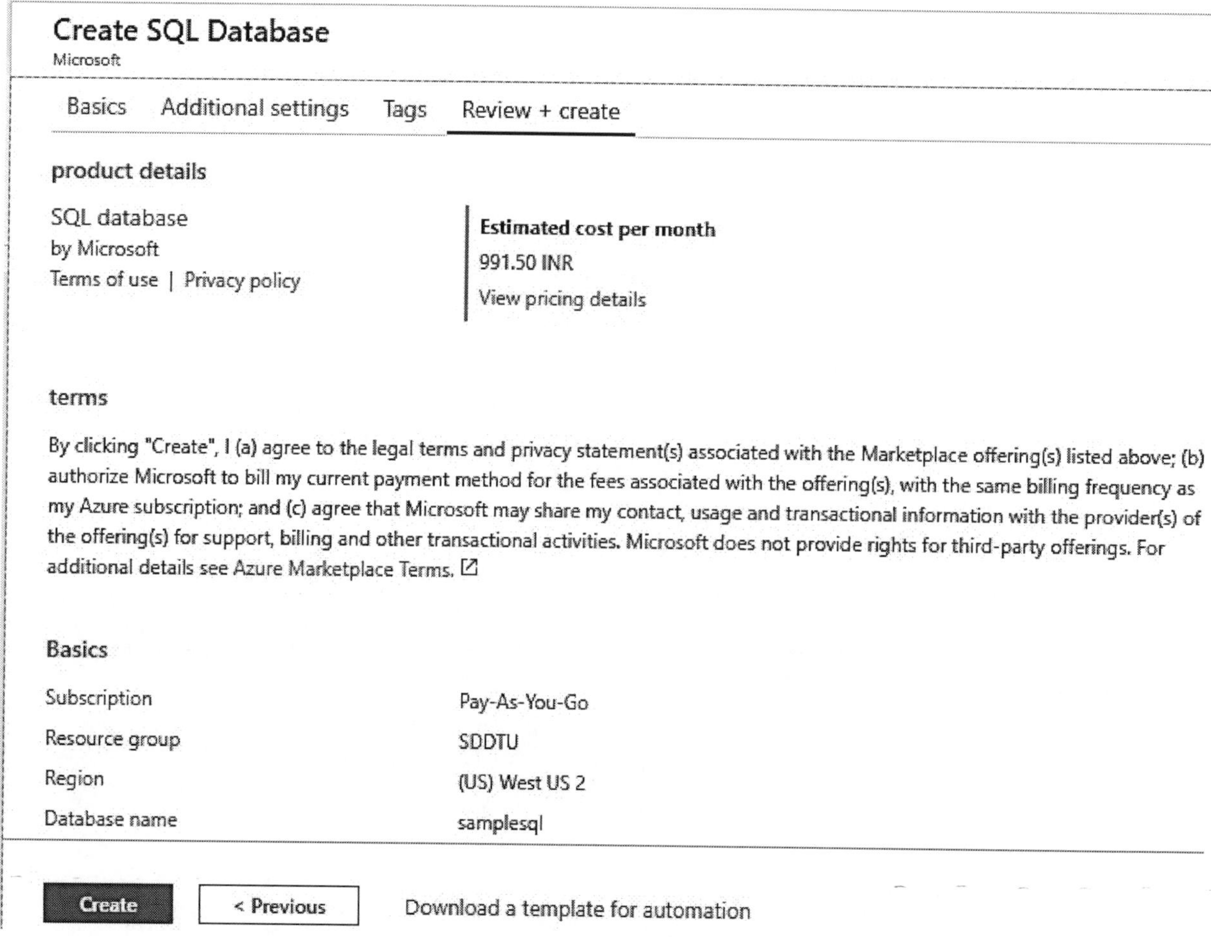

10. Figure below shows dashboard of Azure SQL Database. Note the Server name in right pane. We will use this in SQL Server Management Studio to connect to the Database.

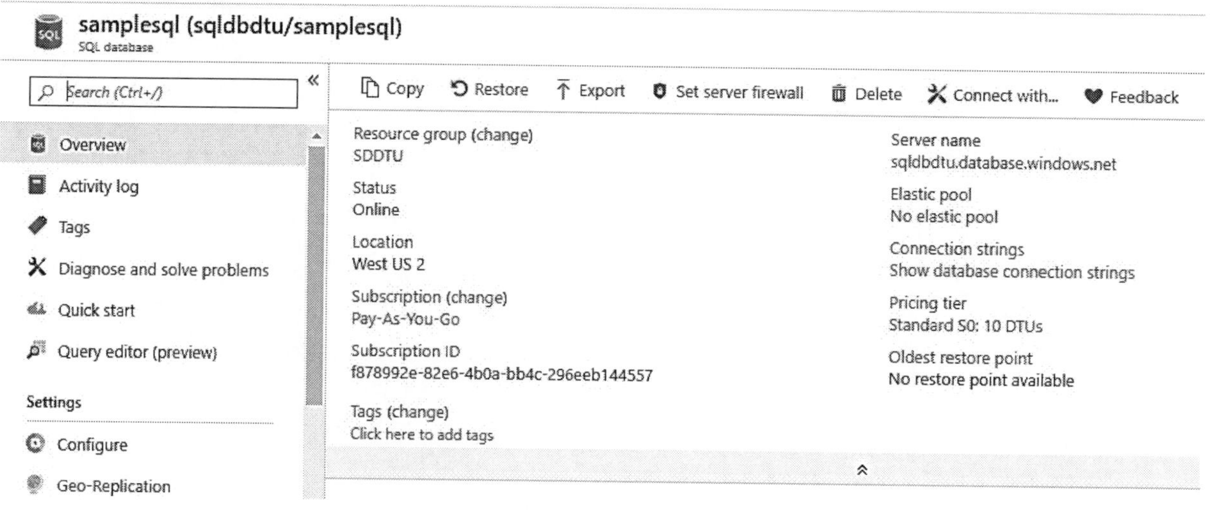

11. In SQL Database samplesql Dashboard Click Link under Server name in right pane>SQL database Server sqldbdtu dashboard opens.

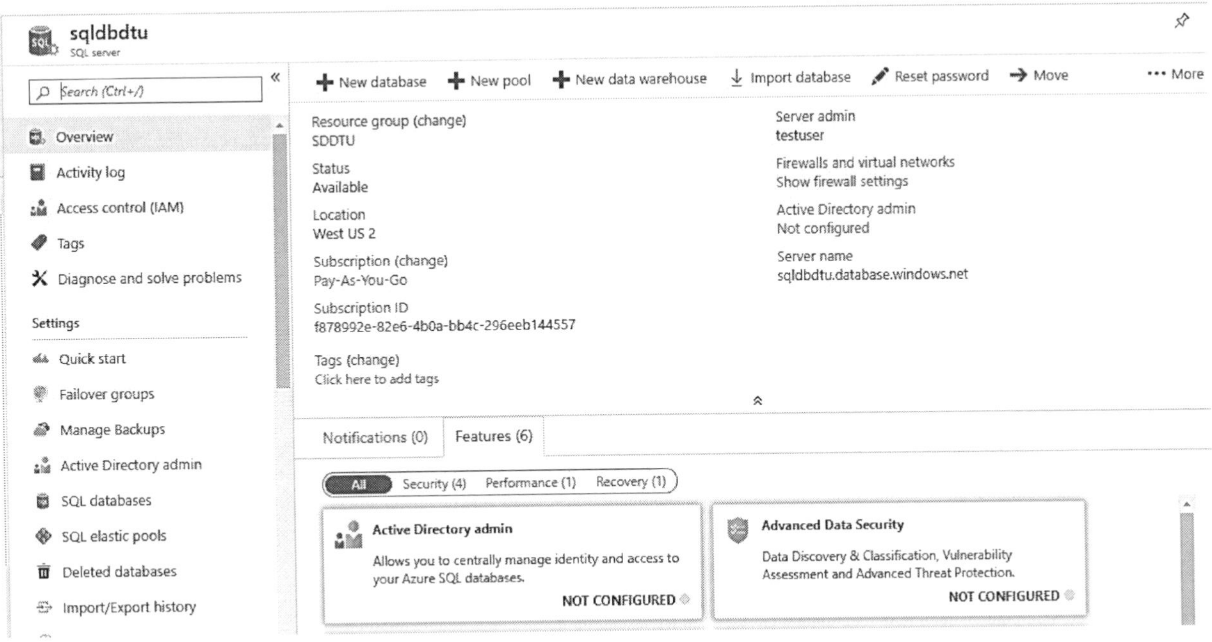

12. To go back to Azure SQL Database dashboard click SQL databases in left pane> In Right pane click Azure SQL Database samplesql>Sql Database dashboard opens.

Important Note: In Azure SQL Database labs we have to work with 2 Dashboards. One for SQL Database Dashboard and one for SQL Database Server Dashboard.

Step 2: Create SQL Database server level firewall rule

Firewall service on newly created Azure SQL Database server prevents external applications and tools from connecting to the server unless a firewall rule is created to open the firewall for specific client IP addresses. **In this Exercise we will enter IP address of laptop/Desktop connecting to Azure SQL Database.**

1. Go the newly created SQL Database Dashboard.

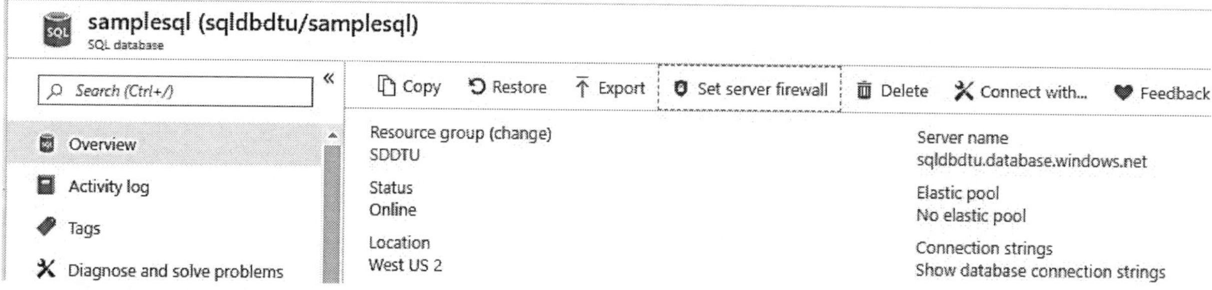

2. Click Set Server Firewall in top pane>Firewall Setting Blade opens>Here enter the client IP address which will connect to Azure SQL Database and click enter>Click **Save**> Close the Firewall pane.

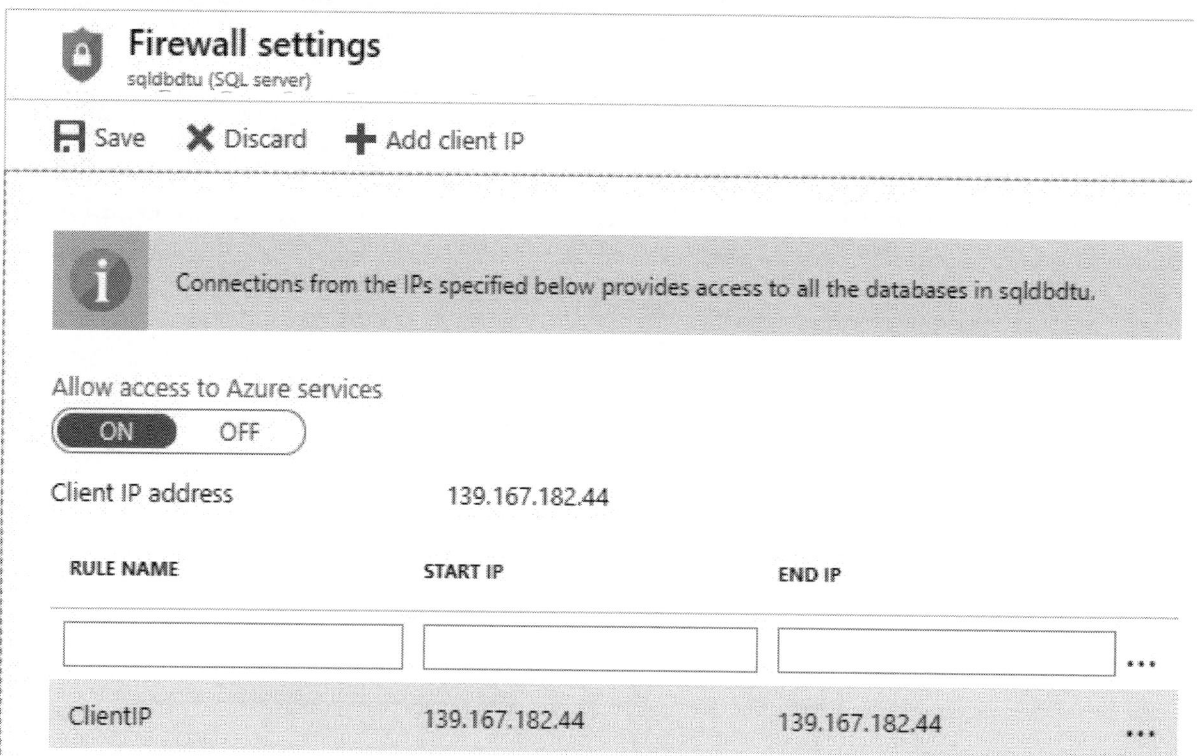

Step 3 Connect to SQL Database using SQL Server Management Studio (SSMS)

1. On the client machine whose IP was entered in step 2, open SSMS and enter Azure SQL database server name, Select SQL Server Authentication and enter username and password you entered during Azure SQL Database creation time> Click Connect.

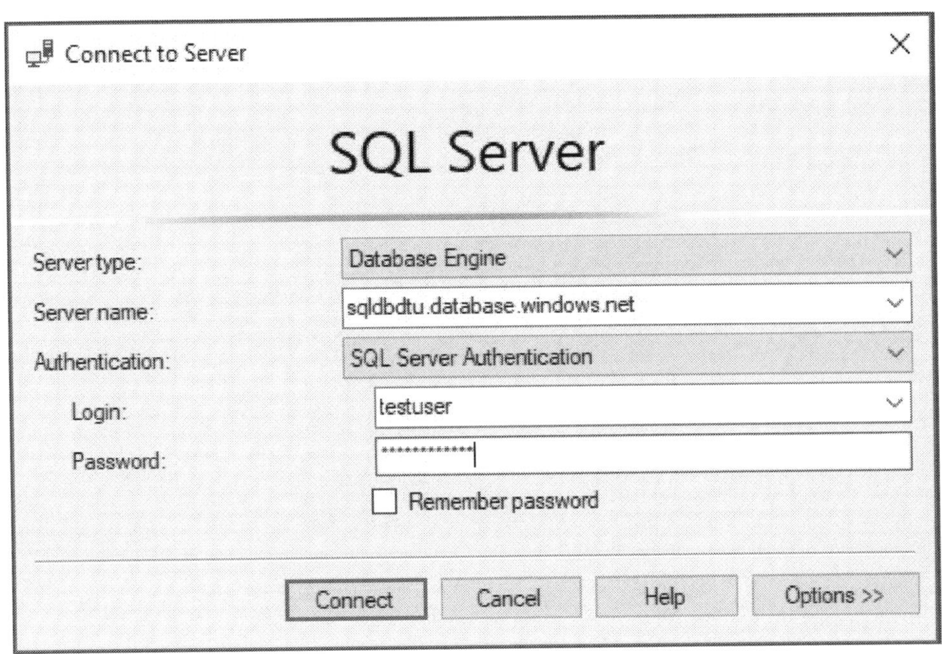

2. SSMS opens. You can see samplesql database created in step 1.

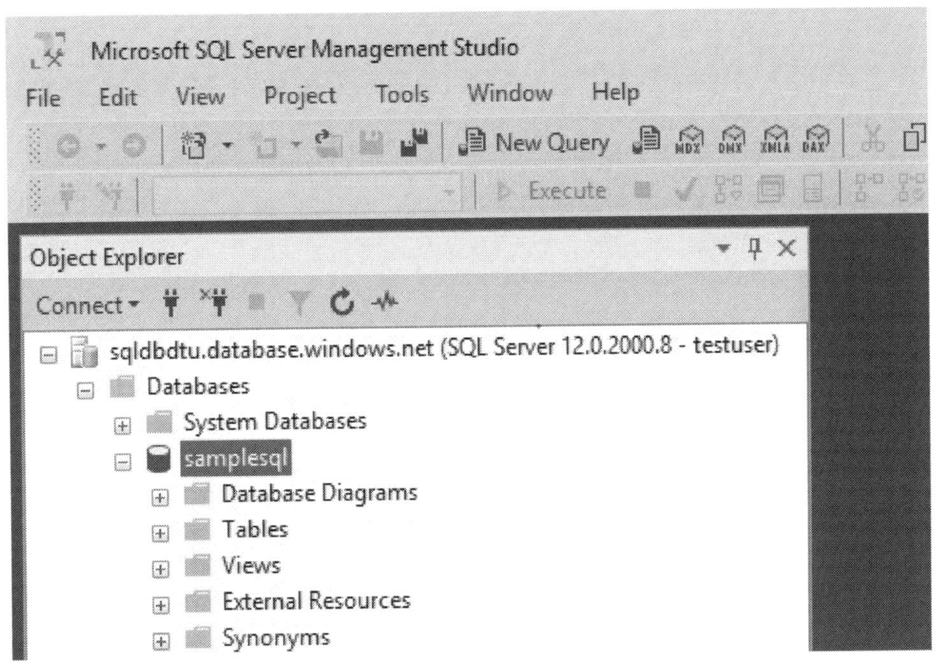

Step 4: Connection Strings

For your application to access SQL database you need to add connection strings in the application code. In SQL Database dashboard click connection string in left pane>In Right pane you can see connection strings for your application type.

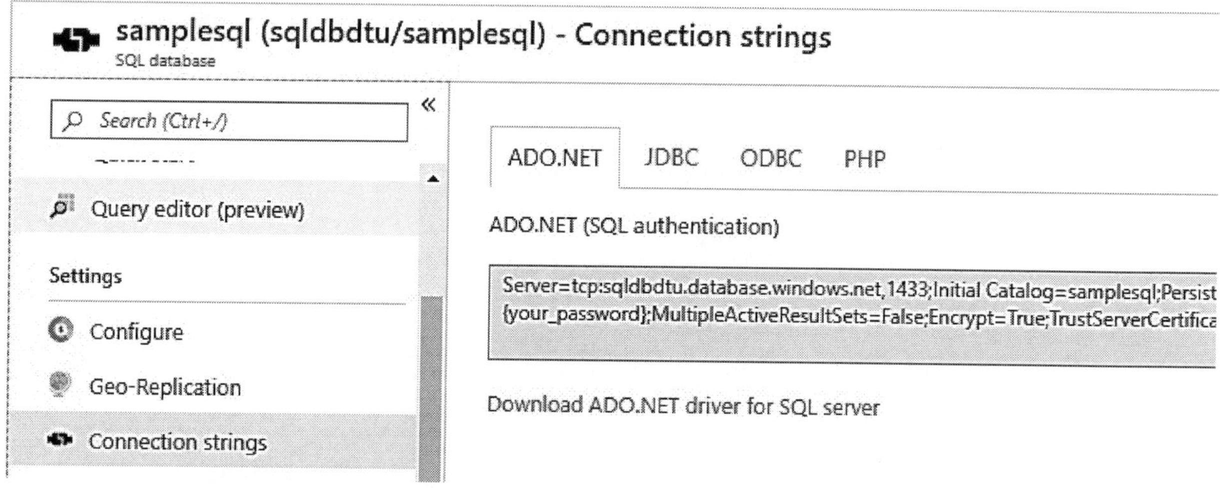

Exercise 49: Enabling Azure AD Authentication for User1

In this exercise we will enable Azure Active Directory Authentication to SQL Database for User1. User1 was created in Exercise 101, Chapter 12 of AZ-300 & AZ-301 Study & Lab Guide Part 1.

1. Go to Azure SQL database Server dashboard sqldbdtu and click Active Directory Admin in left pane.

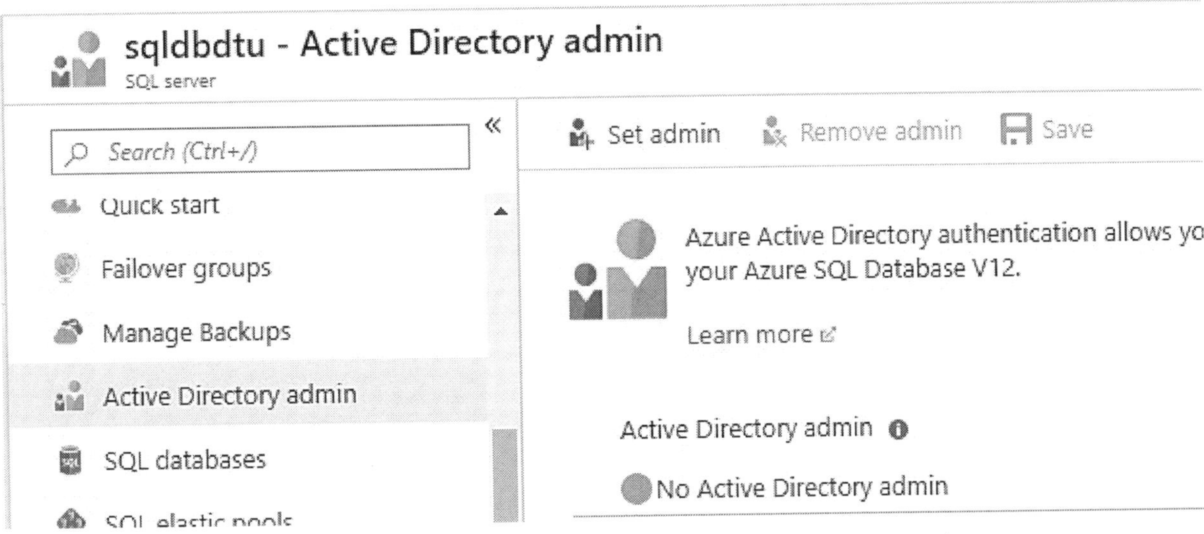

2. Click Set admin in Right pane>Add Admin Blade opens>In search Box type User1>In Result Select User1>Click Select.

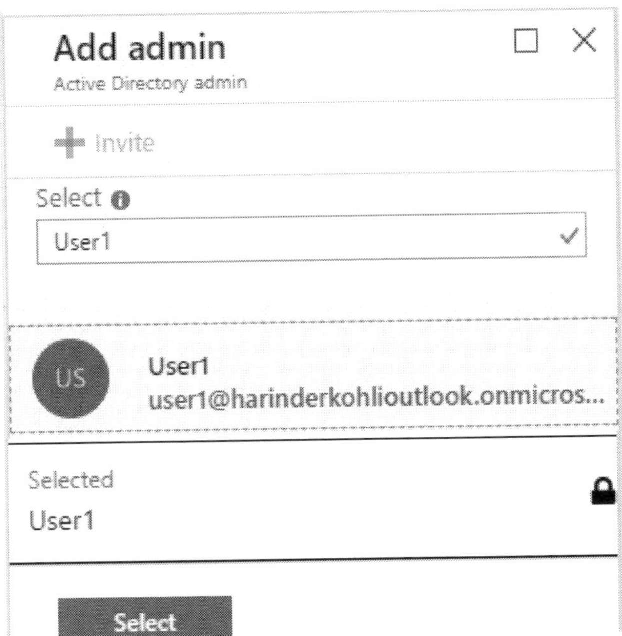

3. User1 is added as Azure Active Directory Admin>Click Save.

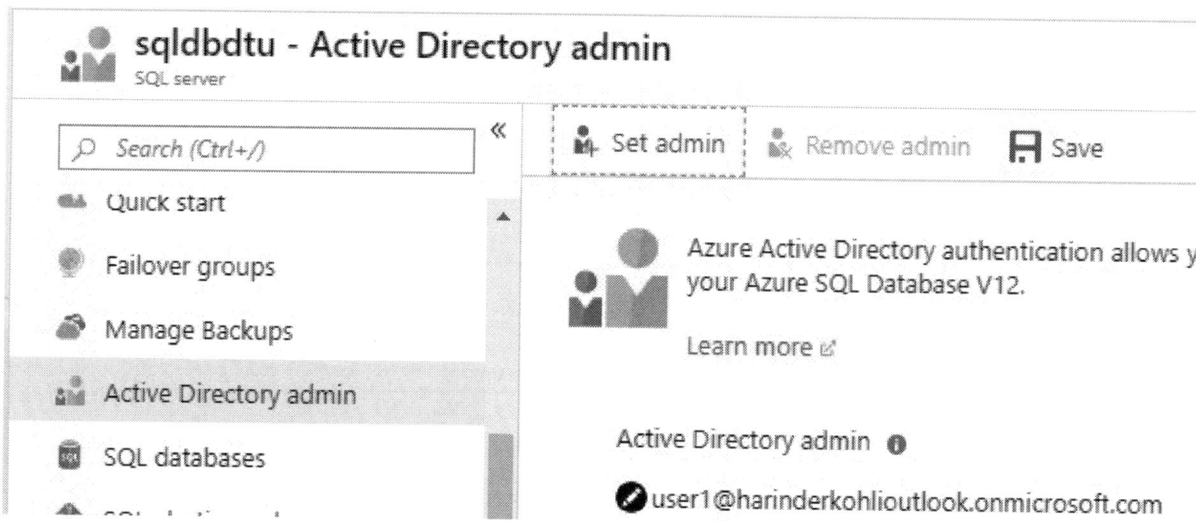

4. Open SSMS>Click File and click Connect Object Explorer>In Server name enter sqldbdtu.database.windows.net> In Authentication Select Active Directory Password.
5. In Username enter user1@harinderkohlioutlook.onmicrosoft.com> Enter password of User1 and click Connect.

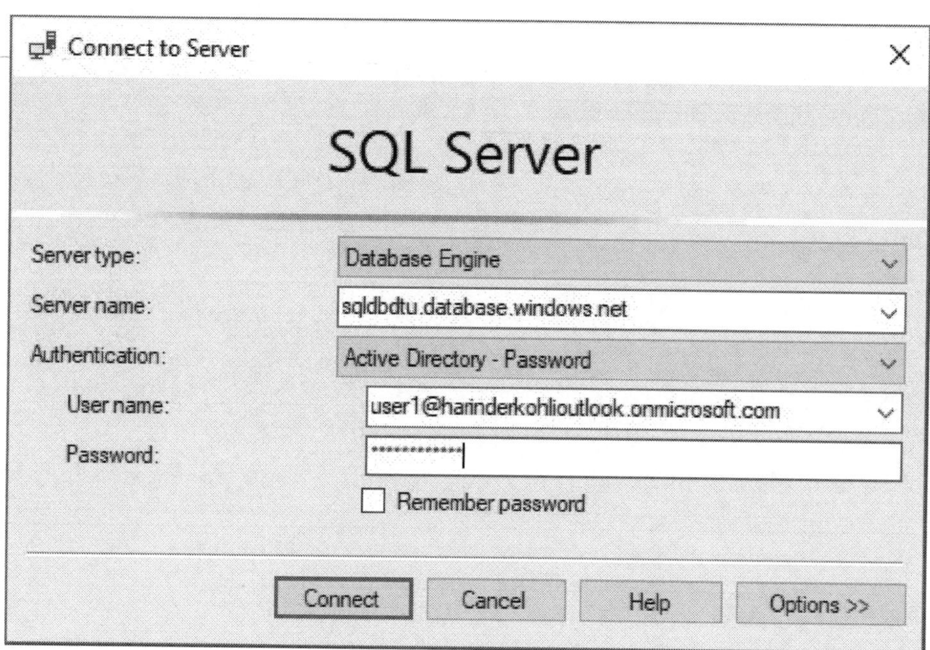

6. Figure below shows User1 successfully logs on and connects to Azure SQL Database Server.

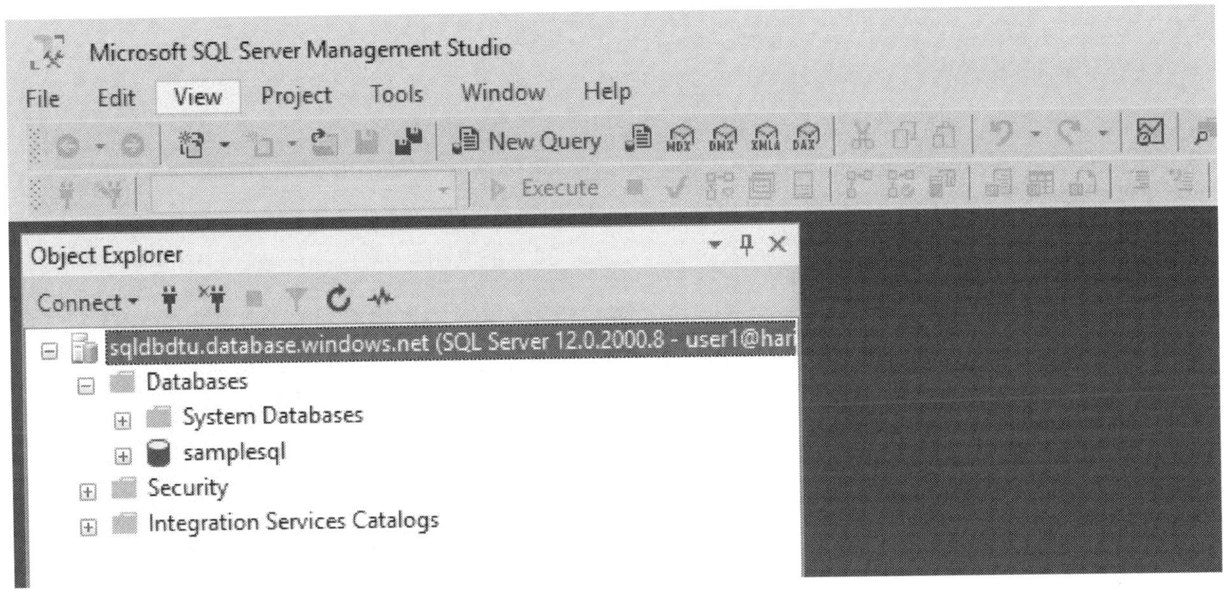

Exercise 50: Create Azure SQL Single Database (vCore Model)

This is Demonstration Exercise and we will not create Azure SQL Database. I just want to show you option for **Azure Hybrid Benefits** in vCore Model and option to **select number of CPU cores.**

1. In Azure Portal Click +create a resource>Databases>SQL Database>Create SQL Database Blade opens with Basic Tab (Not Shown).
2. For Resource Group click Create new under Resource Group box and enter SDDTU.
3. Enter a database name. I entered samplesql.
4. In Server click create new> New Server blade opens>Enter a name>Enter name of user and password>Location Select West US 2>Select Allow Azure Services>Click OK.

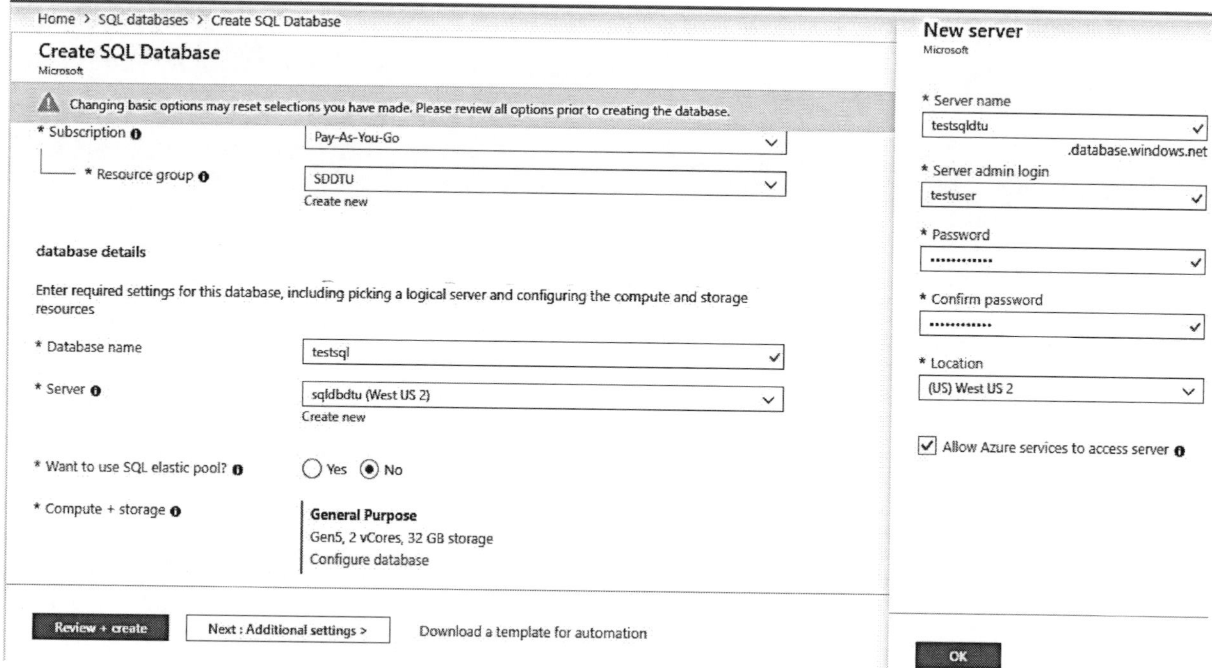

5. In Elastic Pool option select No.

6. In Compute + Storage click configure Database> Configure Database opens >Select General Purpose Tier> Scroll Down and you can see option for Azure Hybrid Benefit for saving Money. You can also select CPU cores and Storage as per your requirement.

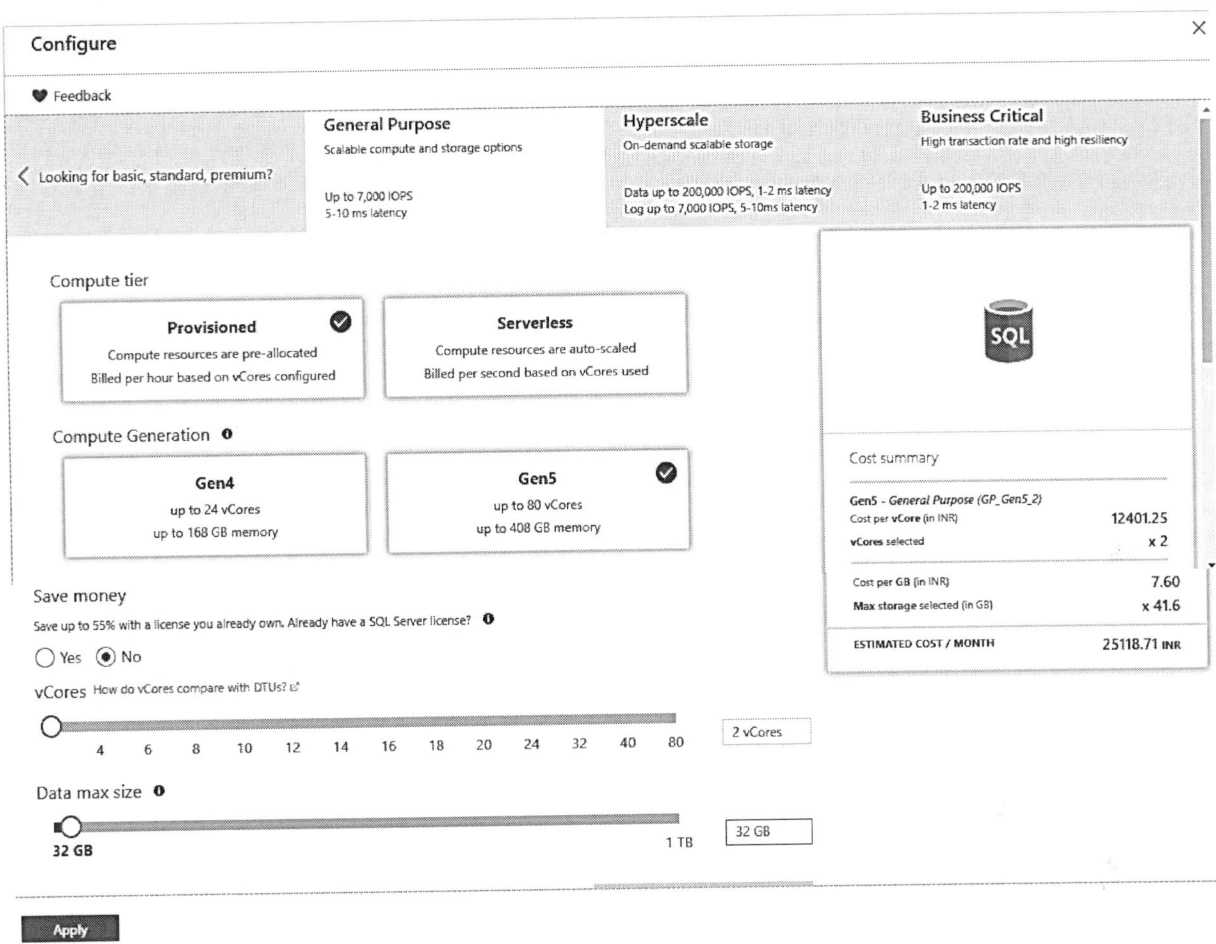

Note: In Top Row left Box gives you the option to create SQL Database with DTU Model. We used this option to create Azure SQL Database in Exercise 43.

3. Close the configure pane>Close Create SQL Database pane.

Business continuity options with Azure SQL Database

SQL Database provides several business continuity features including automated backups, Long- term backup retention and database replication.

Point-in Time Restore from Automated Database Backups: SQL Database automatically performs a combination of full database backups weekly, differential database backups hourly, and transaction log backups every five minutes to protect your business from data loss. These backups are stored in geo-redundant storage for 35 days for databases in the Standard and Premium service tiers and seven days for databases in the Basic service tier.

Geo-Restore: With Geo-Restore you restore database to a new server in any Azure region from the most recent geo-replicated full and differential backups. Recovery usually takes place within 12 hours - with data loss of up to one hour determined by when the last hourly differential backup with taken and replicated.

Long-Term Backup Retention: The **Long-Term Backup Retention** feature enables you to store your Azure SQL Database backups in an Azure Recovery Services vault for up to 10 years. **Long-Term Backup Retention** is used for applications that have regulatory, compliance, or other business purposes that require you to retain the automatic full database backups beyond the 7-35 days provided by SQL Database automatic backups.

Active Geo-Replication: Geo-Replication replicates a database to same or another region. You can configure an automatic failover policy or use manual failover to promote the secondary to become the new primary.

Comparing RTO and RPO of various backup and replication options

Capability	RPO/RTO
Point in Time Restore from backup	Any restore point within 7 days for Basic and 35 days for Standard and Premier tiers
Restore from Azure Backup Vault	RTO < 12h, RPO < 1 week
Geo-Restore from geo-replicated backups	RTO < 12h, RPO < 1h
Geo-Replication	RTO < 30s, RPO < 5s

RTO is the time required to bring database back online.
RPO is the Data loss within the defined period.

Azure SQL Database Backup and Restore

Azure SQL Database has built-in provision to take Automatic backups for up to 35 days. These backups are created automatically and at no additional charge. Backups are stored Geo-Redundant storage (RA-GRS). If you want to keep backups in your own storage container you can configure a long-term backup retention policy.

Backups are used to restore your server to a **Point-in-time Restore.** You can also use **Geo-Restore** to restore your server to a different region or same region.

Backup Retention

Automated Backups retention in the Geo-Redundant Storage is based on Service Tier of the database. All backups are encrypted using AES 256-bit encryption.

Basic service tier is 7 days.
Standard service tier is 35 days.
Premium service tier is 35 days.

Backup Frequency: Azure SQL Database takes full, differential and transaction log backups. Full backups occur weekly, differential backup happens every few hours and transaction log backup occur every 5-10 minutes.

Point in Time Restore

Point-in-time restores an existing database to a specified point in time within the retention period as a new database on the same logical server.

Geo-Restore

Geo-restore recovery option is used when your database is unavailable because of an incident in the region where the database is hosted.

You can restore a SQL database to a new server in any Azure region from the most recent geo-replicated full and differential backups. Geo-restore uses a geo-redundant backup as its source and can be used to recover a database even if the database or datacenter is inaccessible due to an outage.

Exercise 51: Point in Time Restore

In this Exercise we will just demonstrate how to create Point in Restore but will not save it.

Go to Azure SQL database samplesql dashboard>Click Restore in right pane>Restore pane opens>under source Select Point-in-time>Choose a restore point>**Don't Click ok as this is just a demonstration exercise.**

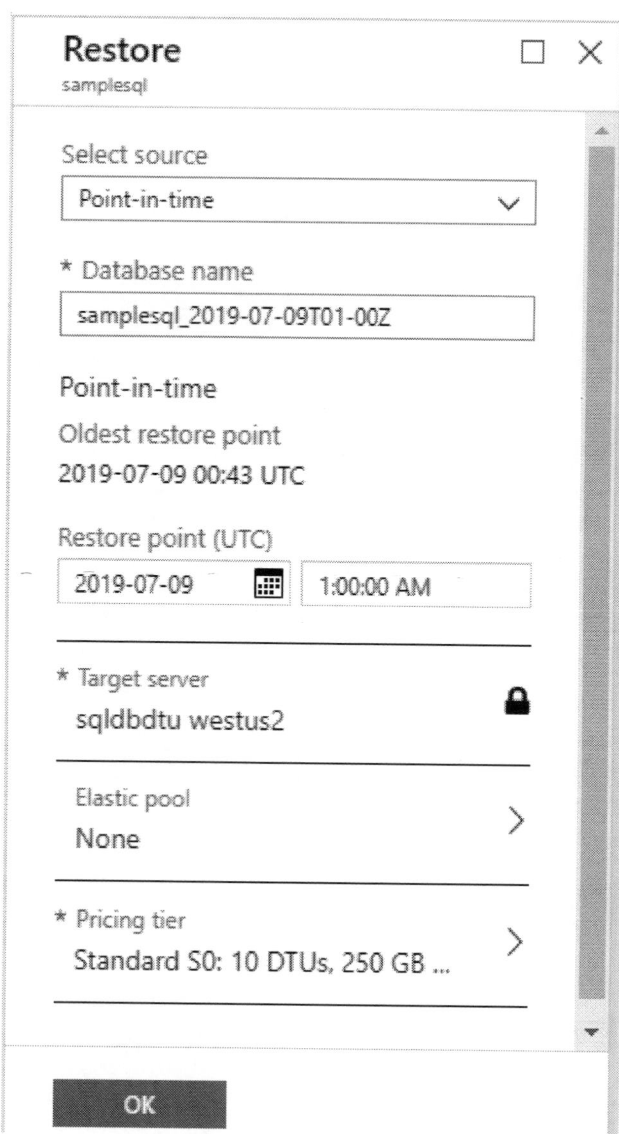

Azure SQL Database High Availability Using Active Geo-Replication

Geo-Replication replicates a database to have up to four readable secondary databases in the same or different regions of your choice.

These secondary databases are kept synchronized with the primary database using an asynchronous replication mechanism. Active geo-replication leverages the Always On technology of SQL Server to asynchronously replicate committed transactions on the primary database to a secondary database using read committed snapshot isolation (RCSI). At any given point, the secondary database might be slightly behind the primary database, the secondary data is guaranteed to never have partial transactions.

Secondary databases are available for querying and for failover in the case of a data center outage or the inability to connect to the primary database. The failover must be initiated manually by the application of the user.

Figure below shows Primary SQL database being replicated to secondary regions using Active Geo-Replication.

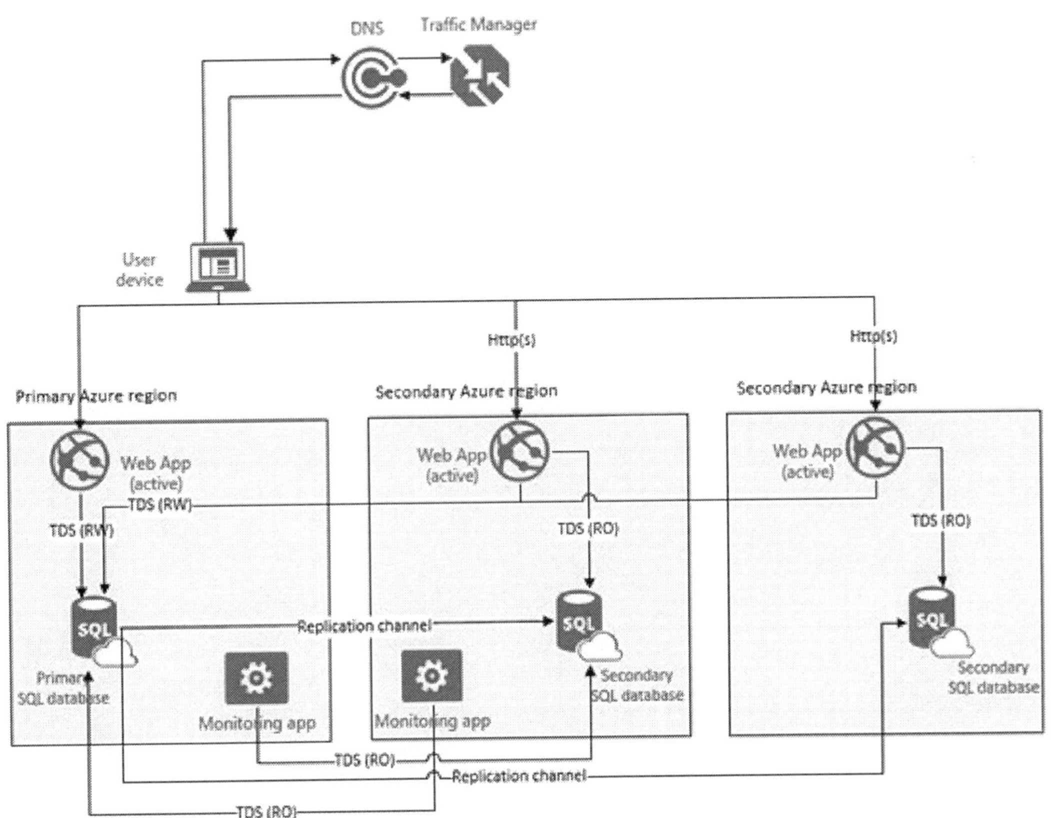

High availability using Active Geo-Replication and Failover groups

With Geo-Replication failover to secondary is manual operation. Geo-Replication with auto-failover groups results in automatic failover.

Auto-failover groups works on top of active geo-replication but the same asynchronous replication mechanism is used.

Auto-failover groups support replication of all databases in the group to only one secondary server in a different region. Active geo-replication, without auto-failover groups, allows up to four secondaries in any region.

Auto-failover groups provide read-write and read-only listener end-points that remain unchanged during failovers. Additionally, they can use the readable secondary databases to offload read-only workloads.

Figure below shows Traffic Manager using Priority Routing is sending all Traffic to Primary Region. If Primary Region fails TM will direct all traffic to Secondary Region. Database failover will be automatic because of failover groups.

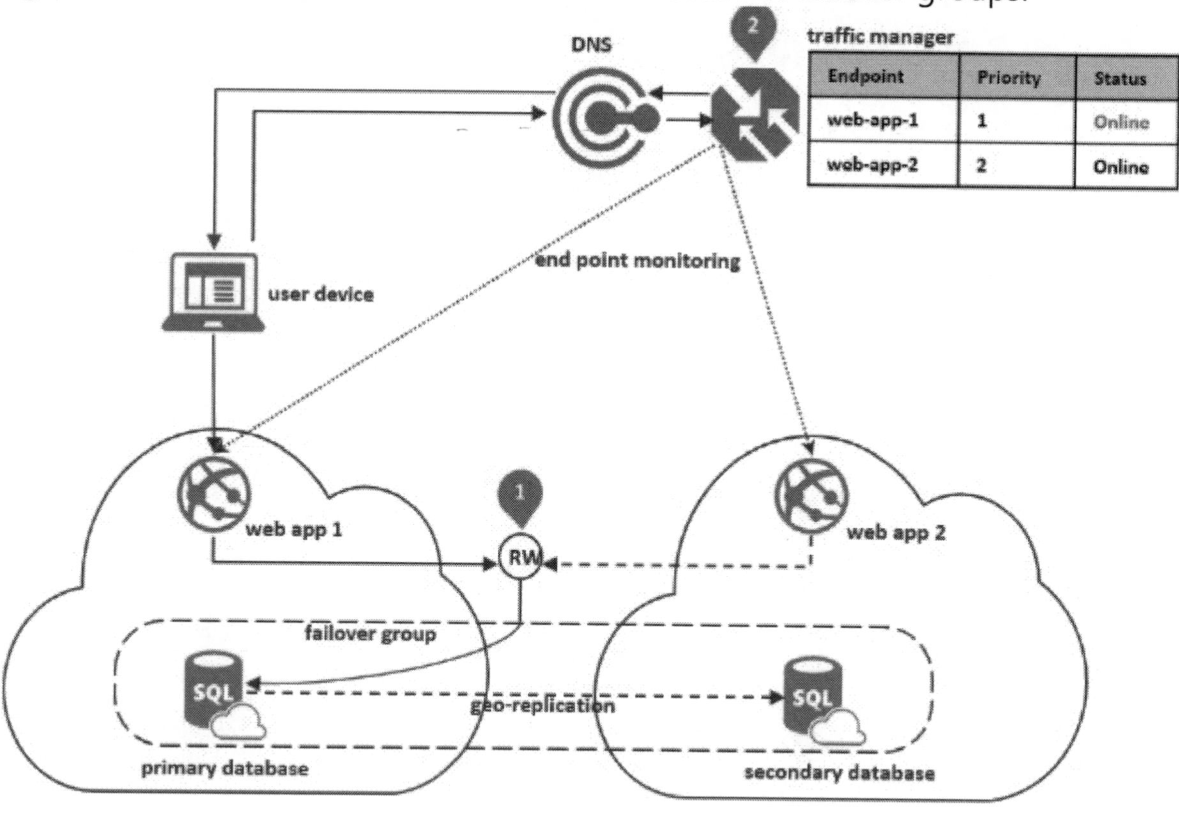

Exercise 52: Active Geo-Replication. Creating Replica of Primary Database

In this exercise we will replicate SQL Database samplesql from West US 2 Location to East US Location using Active Geo-Replication.

1. In Azure Portal go to SQL Database samplesql Dashboard created in Exercise 48 > Click Geo-Replication in left Pane> In Right pane you can see target regions for replication in a Map. Scroll down and you can see target regions are listed. Here we will select East US 2 Region.

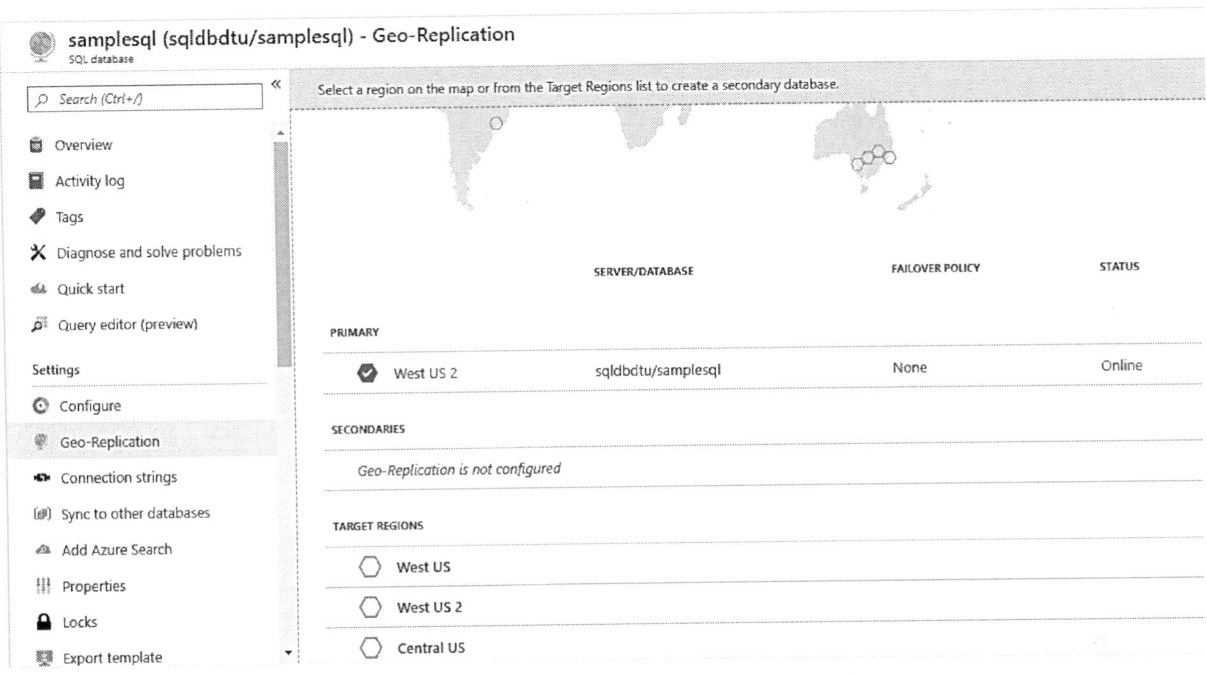

2. Select East US 2 Region>Create a Secondary Database Blade opens>Click Target Server>New Server Blade opens> Enter a name. I entered rsqldbdtu>Enter Username and Password>Check Allow Azure services>Click select>Click OK> Deployment begins.

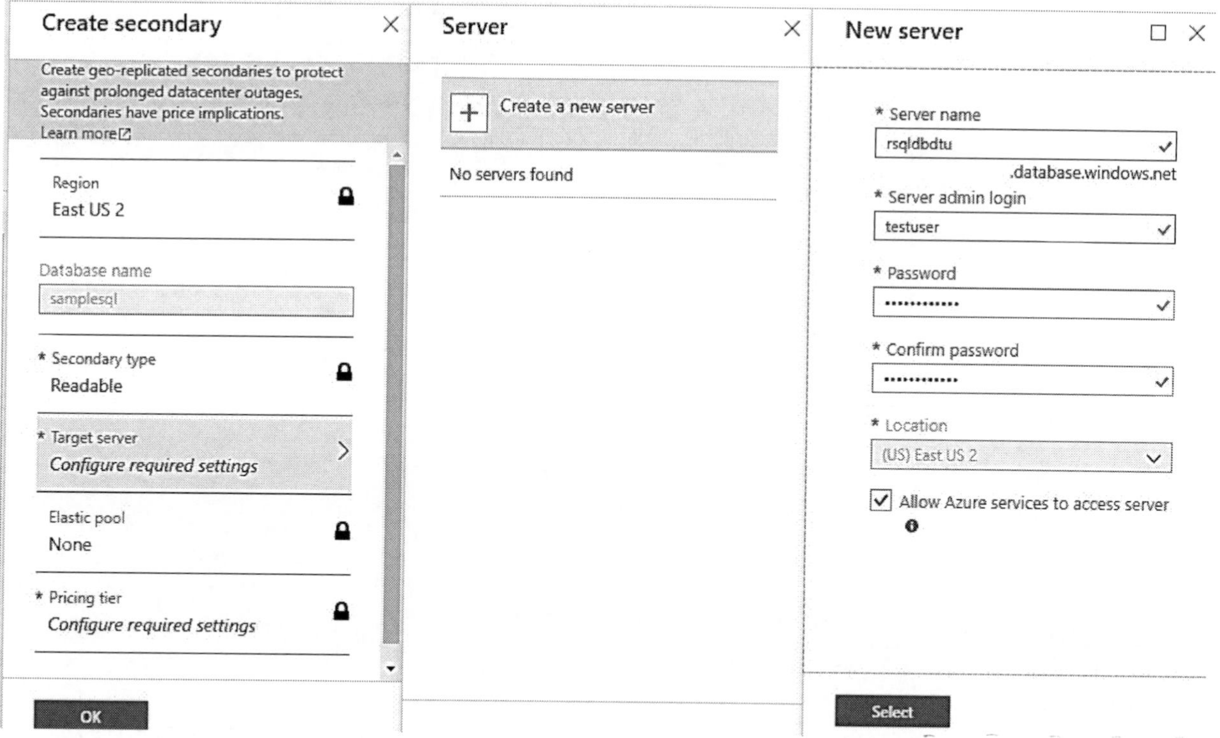

3. After Deployment finishes Click Geo-Replication in dashboard again> you can see both primary and secondary Database which is readable only.

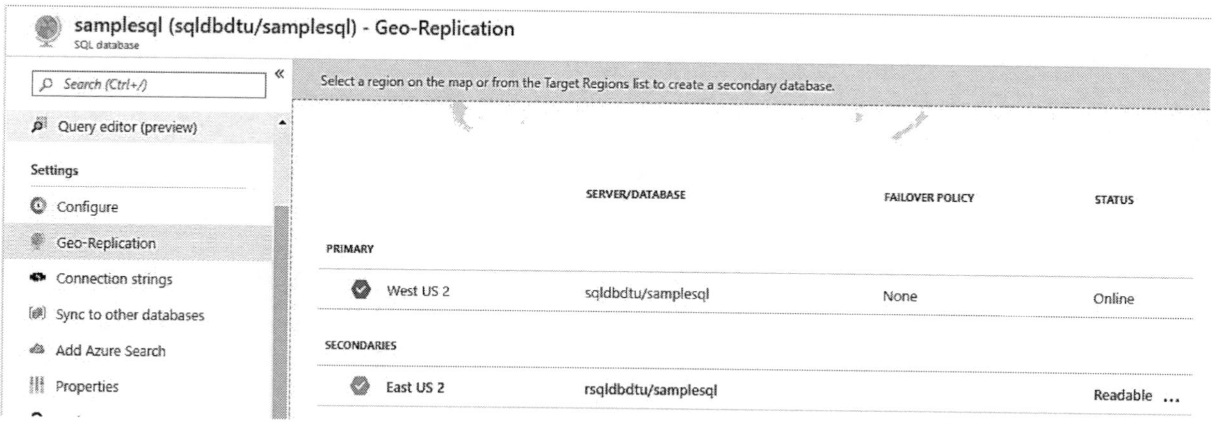

4. Click on the Secondary Database and you can see the options for Forced Failover and Stop Replication.

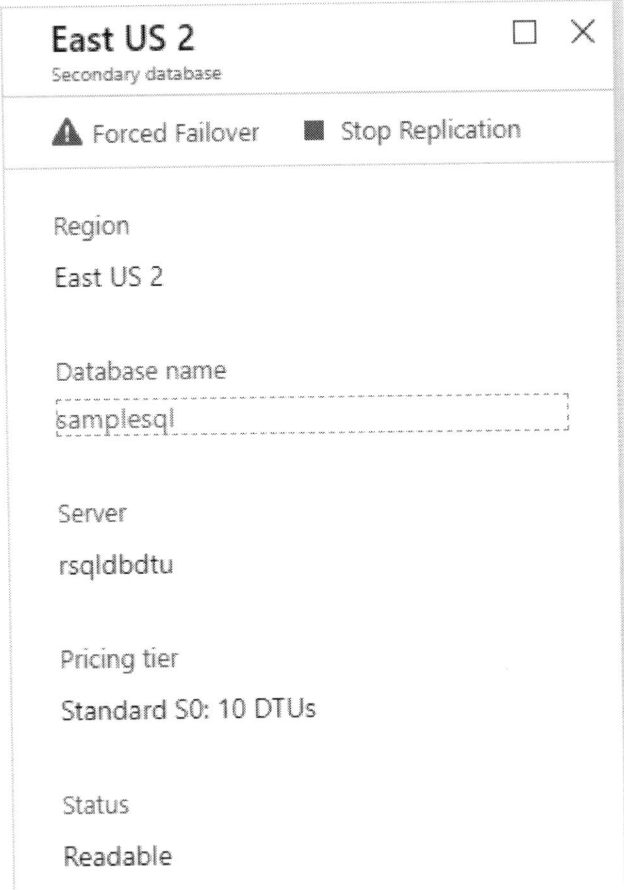

5. Figure below shows the dashboard of SQL Database samplesql server rsqldbdtu. Note Failover Group options in left pane.

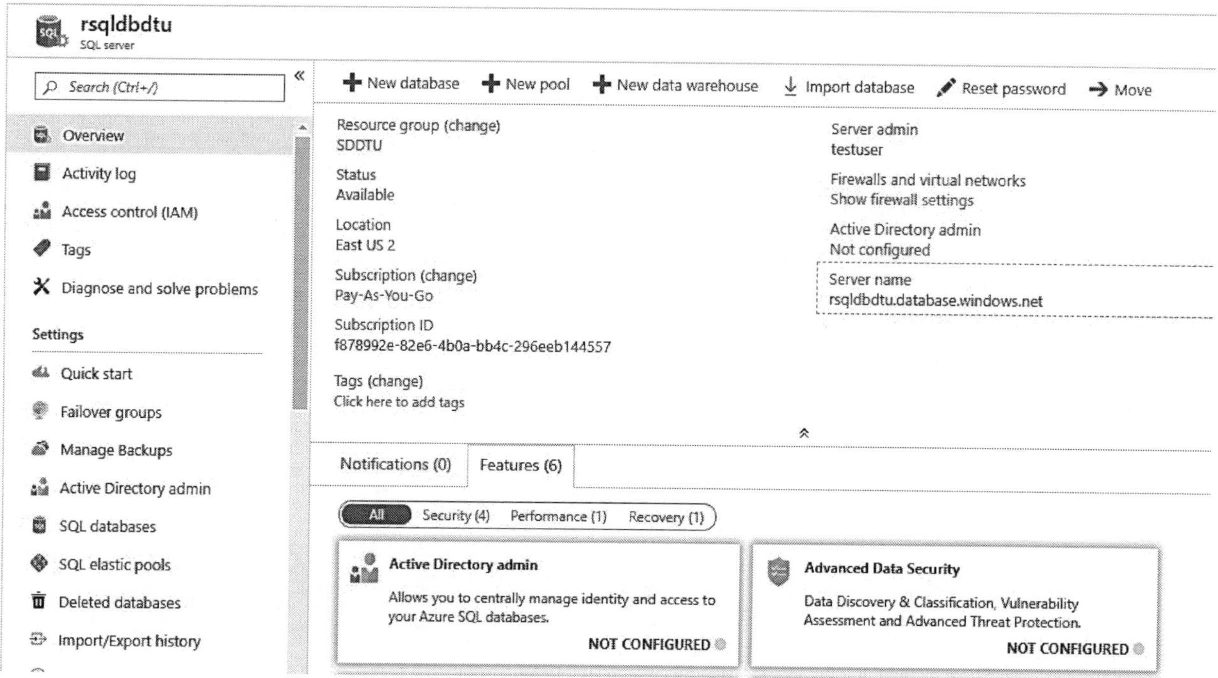

6. Delete the Geo Replicated Database. Click More in Top Right>Delete>Enter name of the server and click delete (Not Shown).

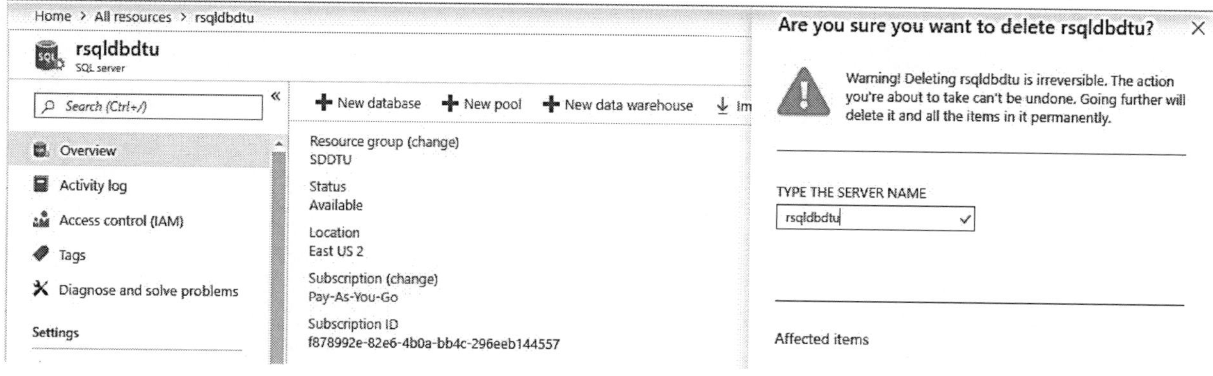

Long Term Backup Retention

In Azure SQL Database, you can configure a single or a pooled database model with a long-term backup retention policy (LTR) to automatically retain backups in Azure Blob storage for up to 10 years.

Note: Azure SQL Database Managed Instance does not currently support long-term backup retention.

Exercise 53: Configuring Long Term Backup Retention

Go to Azure SQL database Server sqldbdtu dashboard>Click Manage Backups in left pane>In Right pane select samplesql database>Click Configure retention> configure Polices pane opens>Select your options and click apply.

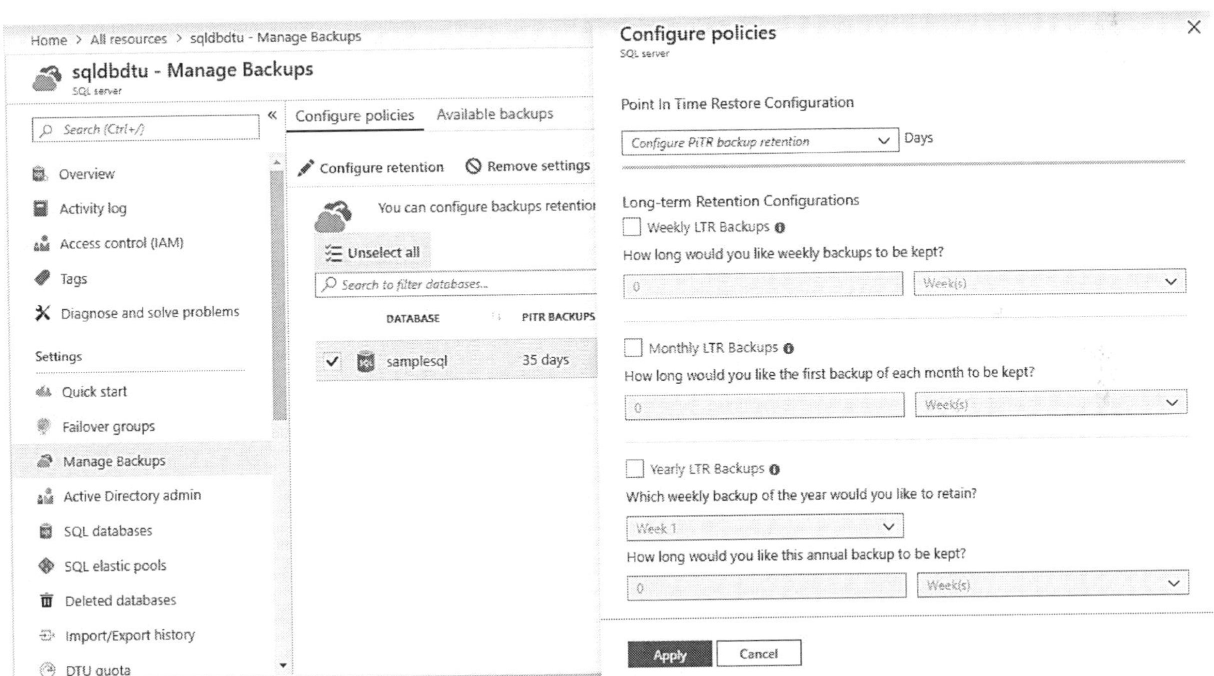

Scaling up or scaling down a single database

You can change the service tier manually or programmatically at any time without downtime to your app.
Changing the service tier and/or performance level of a database creates a replica of the original database at the new performance level, and then switches connections over to the replica. No data is lost during this process but during the brief moment when we switch over to the replica, connections to the database are disabled, so some transactions in flight may be rolled back.

In-Memory technologies in SQL Database

In-memory Database relies on computer memory (RAM) instead of slower hard disks for storage.

In-Memory technologies in Azure SQL Database, improve performance of various workloads: transactional (online transactional processing (OLTP)), analytics (online analytical processing (OLAP)), and mixed (hybrid transaction/analytical processing (HTAP)) by processing Data in memory instead of Slower hard Disk.
In-Memory technologies reduces cost by eliminating the need to upgrade the pricing tier of the database to achieve performance gains.

In-Memory technologies are available in the Premium tier only.

In-Memory technologies available with Azure SQL Database are as follows:

1. ***In-Memory OLTP*** increases throughput and reduces latency for transaction processing.
2. ***Clustered columnstore indexes*** reduce your storage footprint (up to 10 times) and improve performance for reporting and analytics queries.
3. **Non-clustered columnstore indexes** allow very fast execution of analytics queries on the OLTP database, while reducing the impact on the operational workload.

You can also combine In-Memory OLTP and columnstore indexes. This allows you to both perform very fast transaction processing and run analytics queries very quickly on the same data.

Azure SQL Database Access Control

Database access control is done both at server level and at database level.
Database access control at server level is done with Firewall.
Database access control at database level is done with Authentication.

Firewall

Firewalls prevent all access to your database server until IP address of the connecting computer is specified in Azure SQL Database Server.
The firewall grants access to databases based on the originating IP address of each request.
Note: Firewall feature was shown in step 2 of exercise 48.

Authentication

SQL Database supports two types of authentication – SQL Authentication and Azure Active Directory Authentication.

SQL Authentication uses a username and password which were specified during database creation.

Azure Active Directory Authentication uses identities managed by Azure Active Directory.

Note 1: SQL Authentication features was shown in step 3 of exercise 48.
Note 2: Azure Active Directory Authentication was shown in Exercise 49.

Authorization

Authorization refers to what a user can do within an Azure SQL Database, and this is controlled by your user account's database role memberships and object-level permissions.

Protecting SQL Data

SQL Database secures you data by providing encryption for data in motion using **Transport Layer Security**, for data at rest using **Transparent Data Encryption**, and for data in use using **Always Encrypted**.

Transparent Data Encryption (For Data at Rest)

Azure SQL Database transparent data encryption performs real-time encryption and decryption of the database, associated backups, and transaction log files at rest without requiring changes to the application.

Transparent data encryption encrypts the storage of an entire database by using a symmetric key called the database encryption key. This database encryption key is protected by the transparent data encryption protector. The protector is either a service-managed certificate (service-managed transparent data encryption) or an asymmetric key stored in Azure Key Vault (Bring Your Own Key).

By Default TDE is enabled at database & Server level using Azure service Managed Keys. **TDE at Server level gives you the option to use your own keys.**

Exercise 54: Transparent Data Encryption at database level

Go to SQL Database samplesql dashboard>Click Transparent Data encryption in left pane> You can see TDE is enabled using Azure Service Managed Keys.

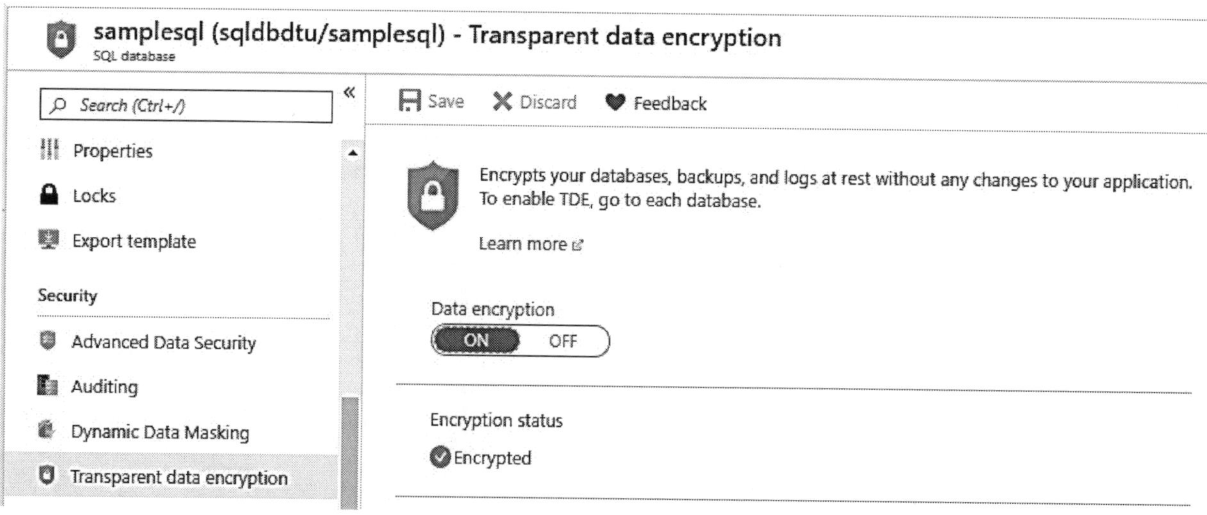

Exercise 55: Transparent Data Encryption at Server level

By Default TDE is enabled at Server level using Azure service Managed Keys. **TDE at Server level gives you the option to use your own keys.**

Go to SQL Database server sqldbdtu dashboard>Click Transparent Data encryption in left pane>By Default TDE is enabled using Azure Managed Keys>Click Yes under use your own key> Now you can select your Key from your key vault.

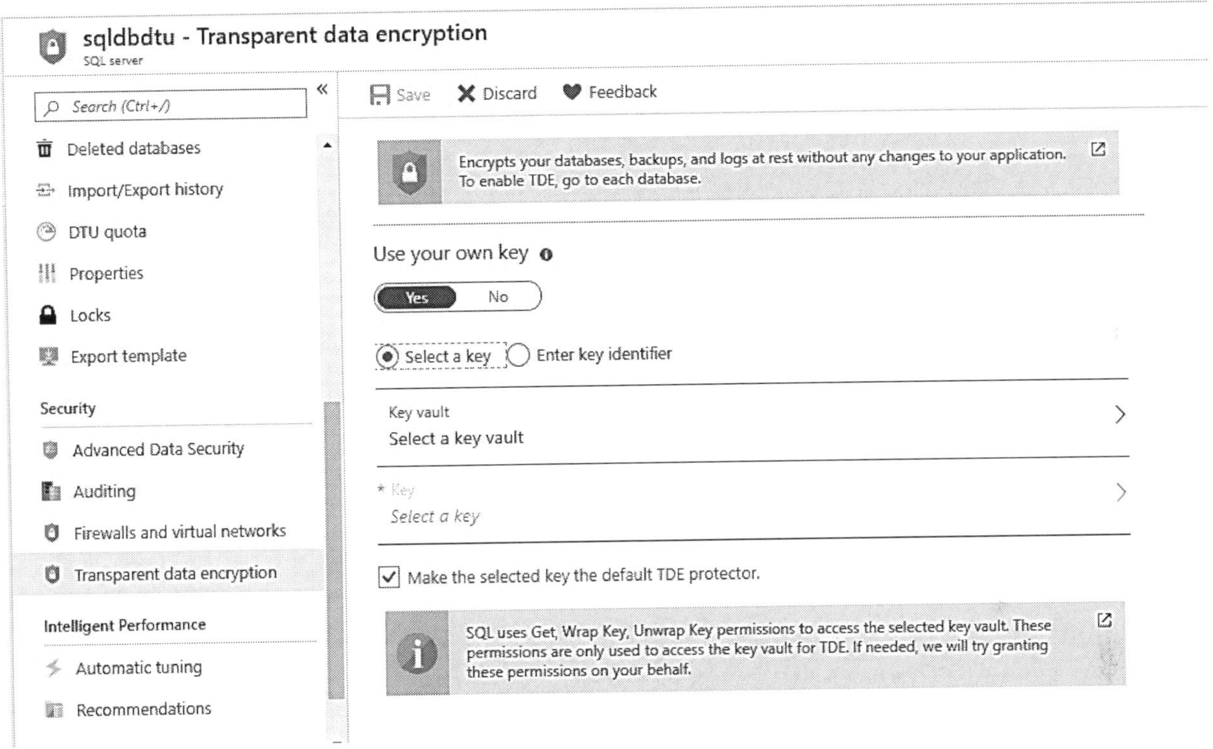

Note: Key Vault was discussed in Chapter 5.

Always Encrypted (For Data in Use)

Always Encrypted protect data by allowing clients to encrypt sensitive data inside client applications and never reveal the encryption keys to the Database Engine (SQL Database or SQL Server).

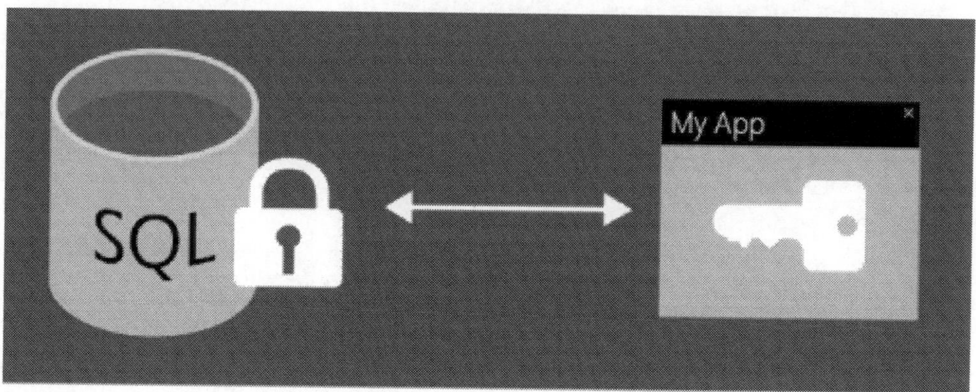

Always Encrypted is a feature designed to protect sensitive data stored in Azure SQL Database from access by Azure SQL Database (cloud) administrators. Data stored in the database is protected even if the entire machine is compromised, for example by malware.

Always Encrypted provides a separation between those who own the data (and can view it) and those who manage the data (but should have no access). Always Encrypted ensures that on-premises database administrators, cloud database operators, or other high-privileged cannot access the encrypted data. Always Encrypted enables customers to confidently store sensitive data outside of their direct control.

Always Encrypted makes encryption transparent to applications. An Always Encrypted-enabled driver installed on the client computer achieves this by automatically encrypting and decrypting sensitive data in the client application. The driver encrypts the data in sensitive columns before passing the data to the Database Engine, and automatically rewrites queries so that the semantics to the application are preserved. Similarly, the driver transparently decrypts data, stored in encrypted database columns, contained in query results.

Working

Always Encrypted leverages client-side encryption: Uses a **database driver inside an application** to transparently encrypts data, before sending the data to the database. Similarly the driver decrypts encrypted data retrieved in query results.

With Always Encrypted, cryptographic operations on the client-side use keys that are never revealed to the Database Engine (SQL Database or SQL Server). There are two types of keys in Always Encrypted:

Column encryption keys are used to encrypt data in the database. These keys are stored in the database in the encrypted form (never in plaintext).

Column master keys are used to encrypt column encryption keys. These keys are stored in an external key store, such as Windows Certificate Store, Azure Key Vault or hardware security modules. For keys stored in Azure Key Vault, only the client application has access to the keys, but not the database, unlike TDE.

Always Encrypted is available in SQL Server 2016 and SQL Database.

TDE v/s Always Encrypted

	Always Encrypted	TDE
Supports	Azure SQL Database; SQL Server 2016 and above	Azure SQL Database; SQL Server 2008 and above
Free in Azure SQL Database	Yes	Yes
Driver required in Client Application	Yes	No
Protects data at rest	Yes	Yes
Protects data in use	Yes	No
Protects data from SQL administrators and admins	Yes	No
Data is encrypted/ decrypted on the client side	Yes	No
Data is encrypted/ decrypted on the server side	No	Yes
Encrypt at column level	Yes	No
Transparent to application	No	Yes
Encryption key management	Customer Managed Keys	Service or Customer Managed Keys
Protects keys in use	Yes	No

Advanced Data Security

Advanced data security is a unified package for advanced SQL security capabilities. It includes functionality for discovering and classifying sensitive data **(Data Classification)**, surfacing and mitigating potential database vulnerabilities **(Vulnerability Assessment)** and detecting anomalous activities that could indicate a threat to your database **(Advanced Threat Protection)**.

- **Data Classification** provides capabilities built into Azure SQL Database for **discovering**, **classifying**, **labeling** & **protecting** the sensitive data in your databases. It can be used to provide visibility into your database classification state, and to track the access to sensitive data within the database and beyond its borders.

- **Vulnerability assessment** service can **discover**, **track**, and **remediate** potential database vulnerabilities. It provides visibility into your security state, and includes actionable steps to resolve security issues, and enhance your database fortifications.

- **Advanced Threat Protection** detects anomalous activities indicating unusual and potentially harmful attempts to access or exploit your database. It continuously monitors your database for suspicious activities, and provides immediate security alerts on potential vulnerabilities, SQL injection attacks, and anomalous database access patterns. It provides details of the suspicious activity and recommends action on how to investigate and mitigate the threat. You can enable following in Advanced Threat Detection:

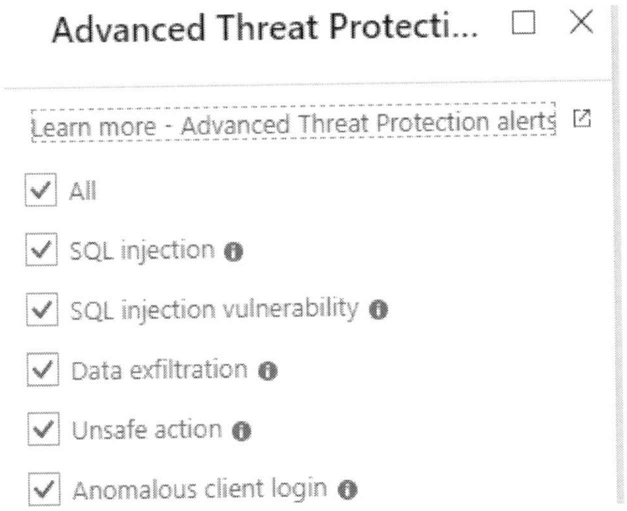

Advanced Threat Protecti...

Learn more - Advanced Threat Protection alerts

- [x] All
- [x] SQL injection
- [x] SQL injection vulnerability
- [x] Data exfiltration
- [x] Unsafe action
- [x] Anomalous client login

Exercise 56: Enabling Advanced Data Security

1. Go to Azure SQL database samplesql dashboard>Click Advanced Data Security in left pane> In Right Pane click enable Advanced Data Security on the server.

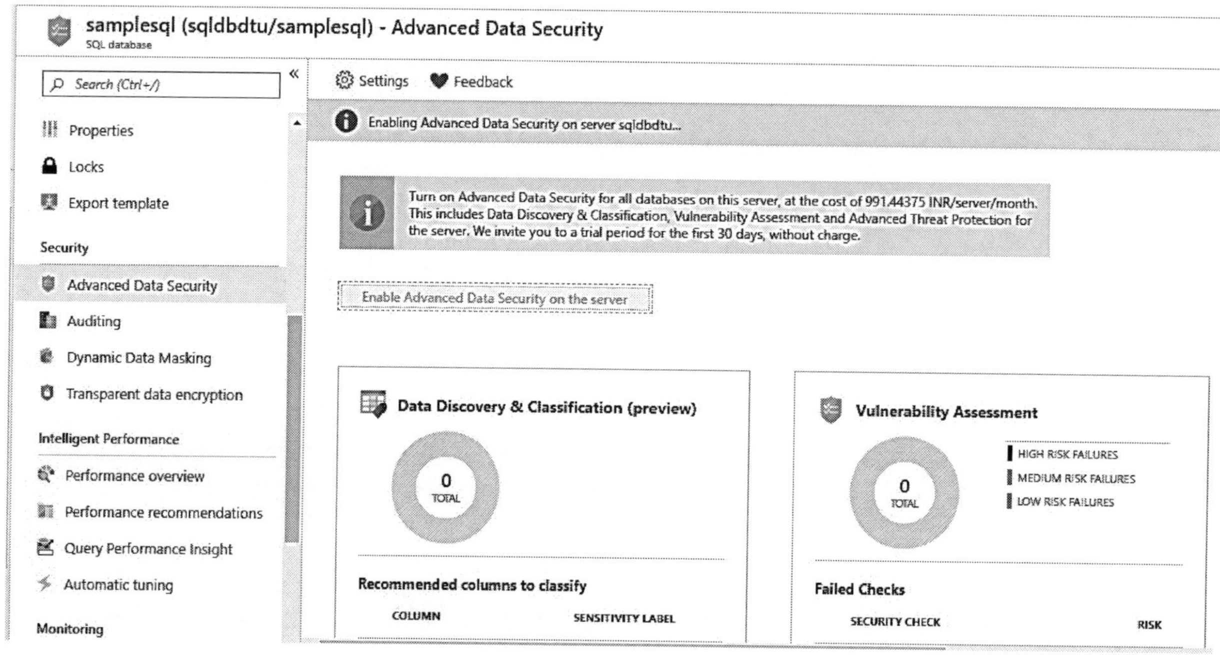

2. After Advanced Data Security is enabled you get the result for Data Discovery, Vulnerability Assessment & Advanced Threat Detection.

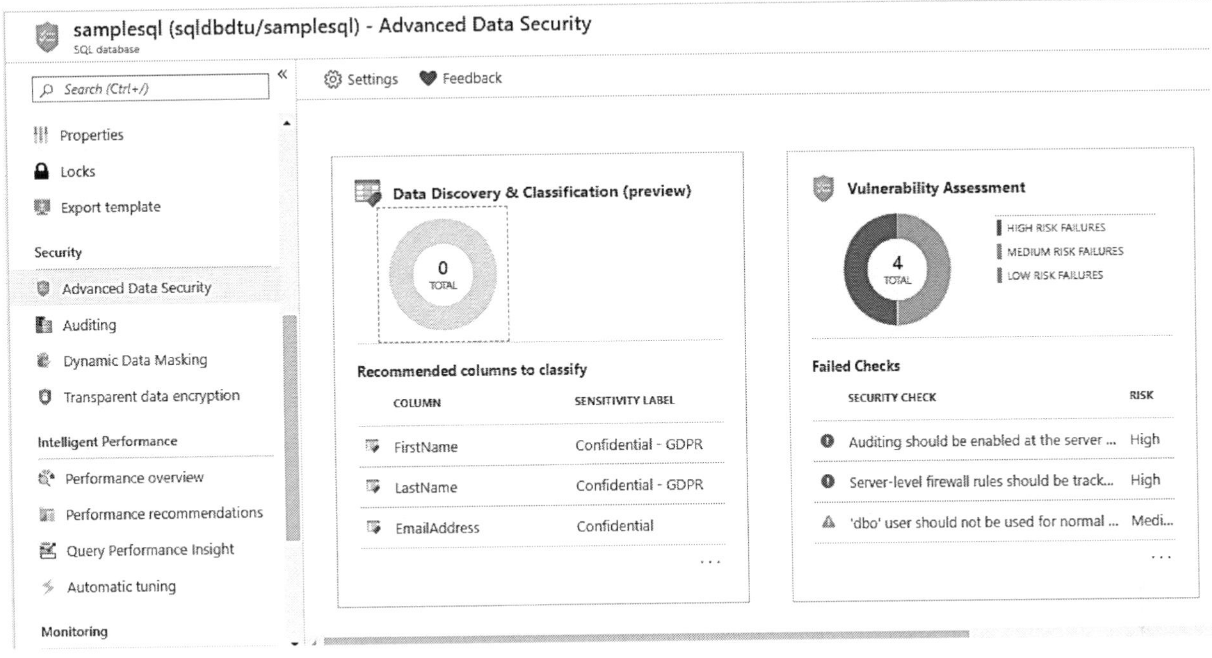

3. Scroll down to right and you can see result for Advanced Threat Detection. It is asking you to turn on Auditing for Full Investigation experience.

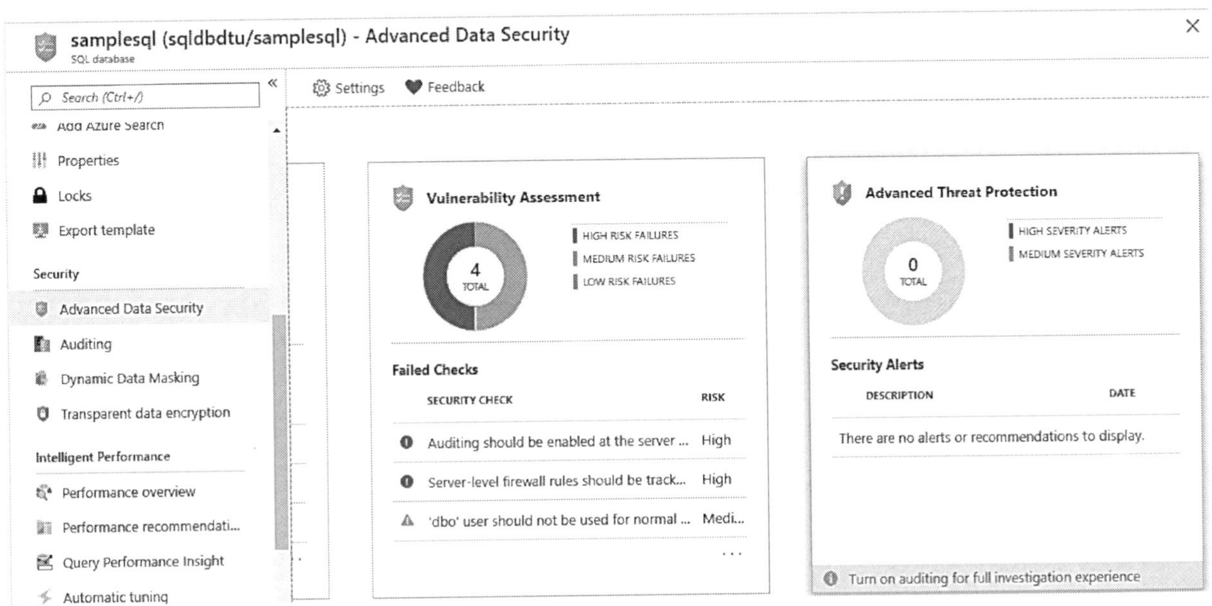

4. Click on the Vulnerability Assessment pane to see the results.

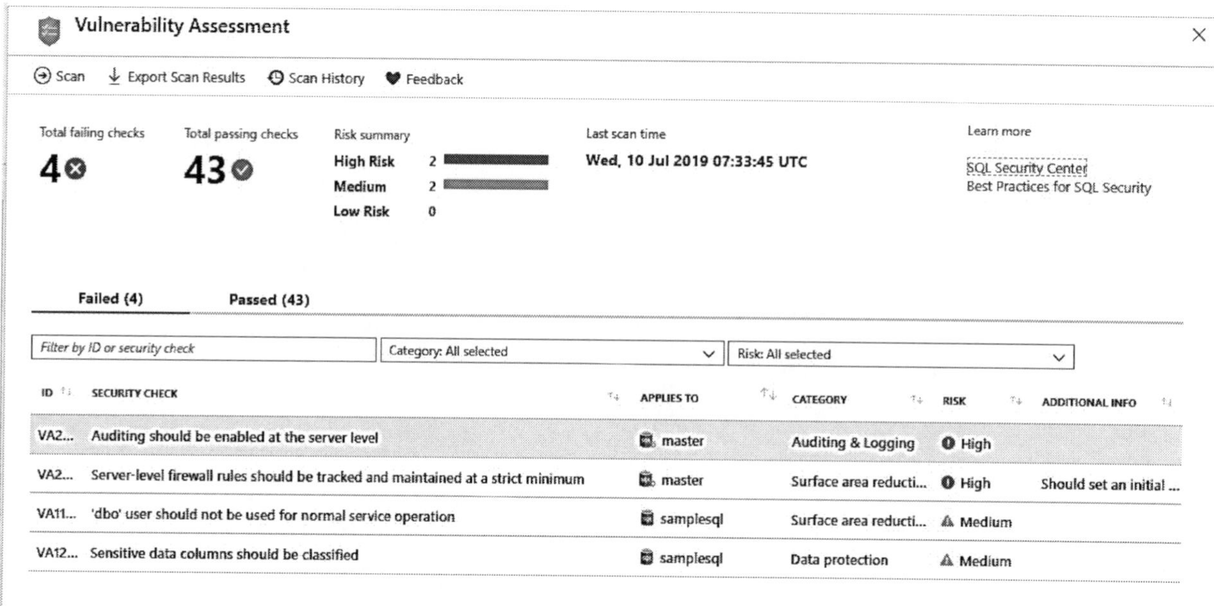

Azure SQL Database Auditing

Azure SQL Database Auditing tracks database events and writes them to an audit log in your Azure Storage account, Log Analytics workspace or Event Hubs.

What can you do with Azure SQL database auditing

- **Retain** an audit trail of selected events. You can define categories of database actions to be audited.
- **Report** on database activity. You can use pre-configured reports and a dashboard to get started quickly with activity and event reporting.
- **Analyze** reports. You can find suspicious events, unusual activity, and trends.

Azure SQL Database Auditing Use cases

Auditing can help you maintain regulatory compliance, understand database activity, and gain insight into discrepancies and anomalies that could indicate business concerns or suspected security violations.

Exercise 57: Enabling Database Auditing at Server Level

1. Go to Azure SQL database samplesql server sqldbdtu dashboard>Click Auditing in left pane> In Right Pane click ON to enable Auditing>Select Log Analytics Box.

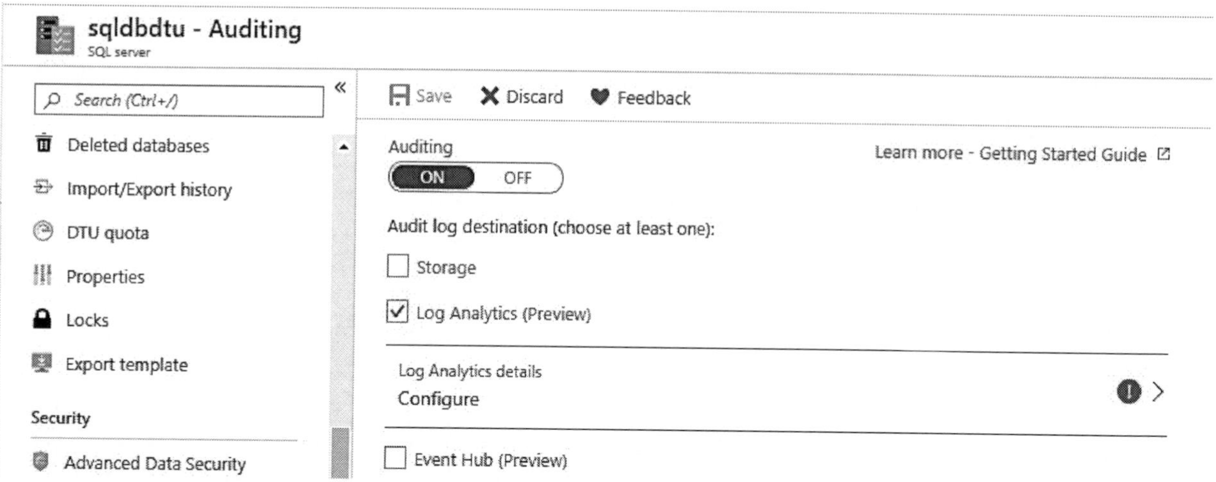

2. Click Configure in Log Analytics Details> Log Analytics Workspaces Blade opens> Click +Create New>Create New Log Analytics Workspaces Blade opens>Enter a name>For Resource Group select SDDTU. SDDTU was created in Exercise 48>Location West US 2>Click Ok.

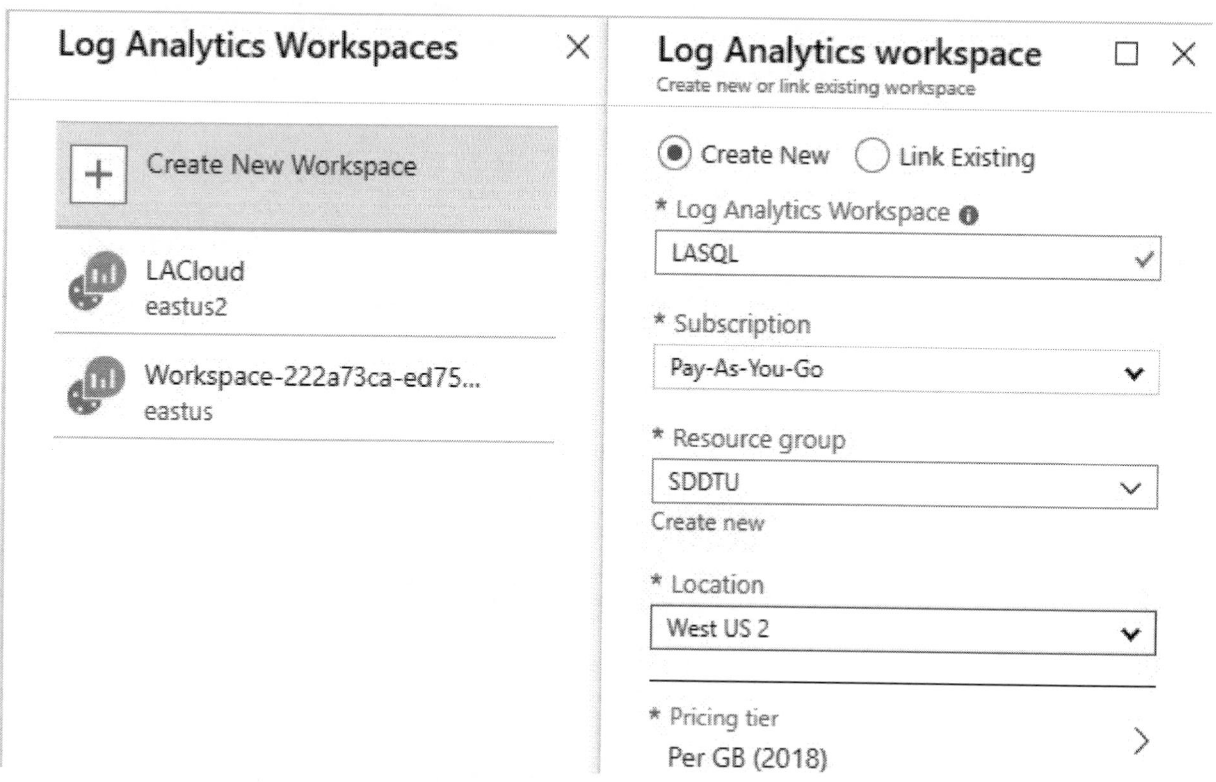

3. After Validation click save.

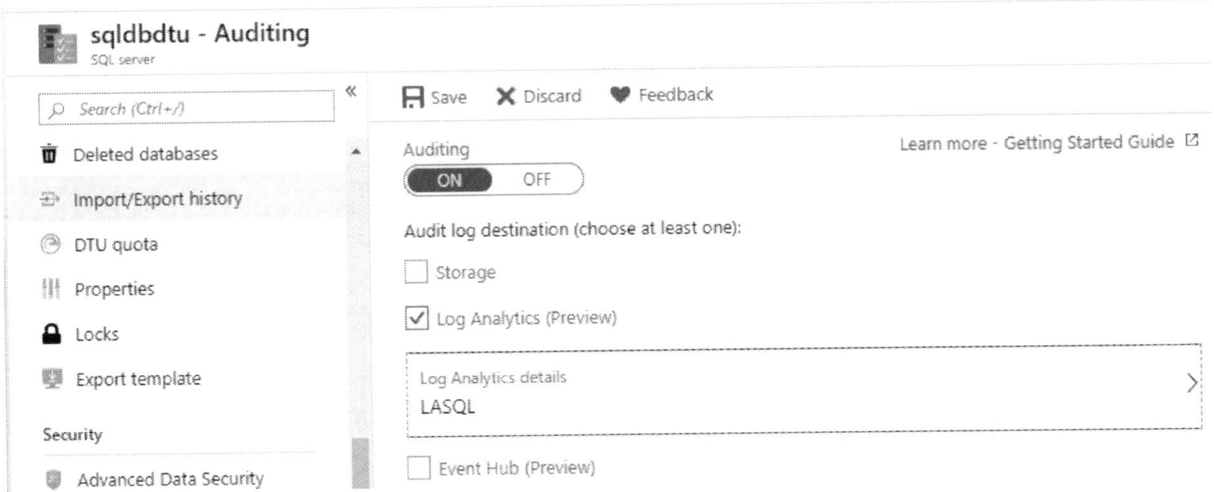

4. Go Azure SQL Database samplesql dashboard>Click Auditing in left pane>In right pane click View Audit Logs>Currently there are no records.

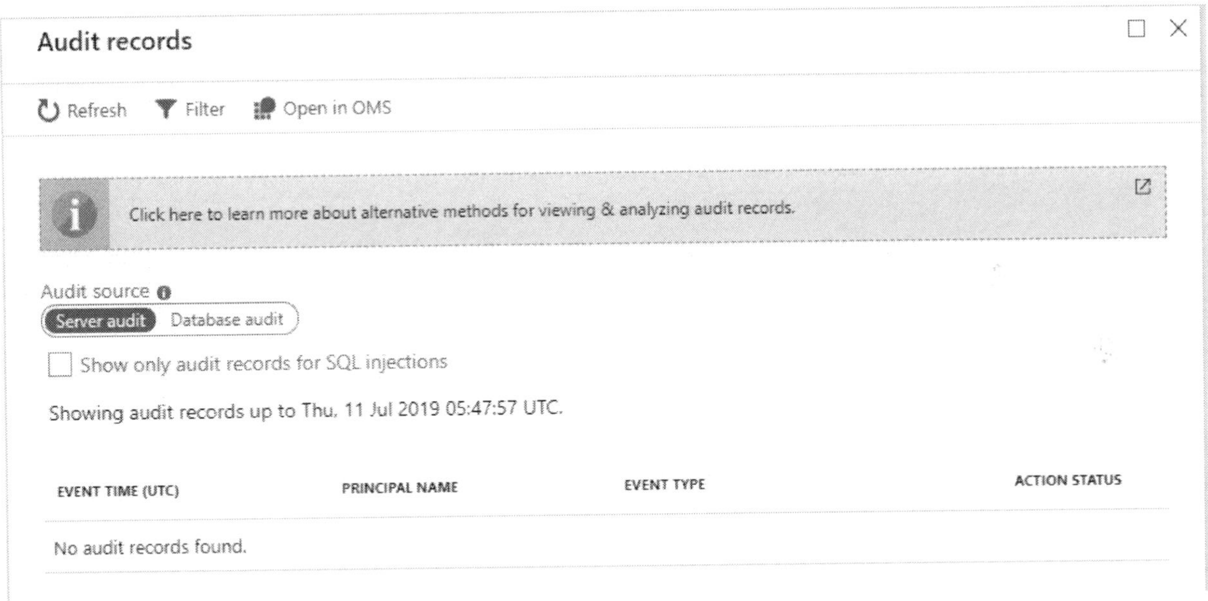

Note: If Blob Auditing is enabled on the server, it will always apply to the database, regardless of the database settings.

SQL Database Dynamic Data Masking

SQL Database dynamic data masking limits sensitive data exposure by masking it to non-privileged users.

It's a policy-based security feature that hides the sensitive data in the result set of a query over designated database fields, while the data in the database is not changed.

Dynamic Data Masking Example

Call center agent of a Bank are provided access to customer credit card details to resolve customer queries when they call. A masking rule can be defined that masks all but the last four digits of any credit card number in the result set of any query.

Exercise 58: Adding Dynamic Data Masking Rule

In this exercise we will mask email address in samplesql database.

1. Go to SQL Database samplesql dashboard>Click Dynamic Data Masking in left pane in left pane> Note the row containing EmailAddress (6th from top) as shown in figure below.

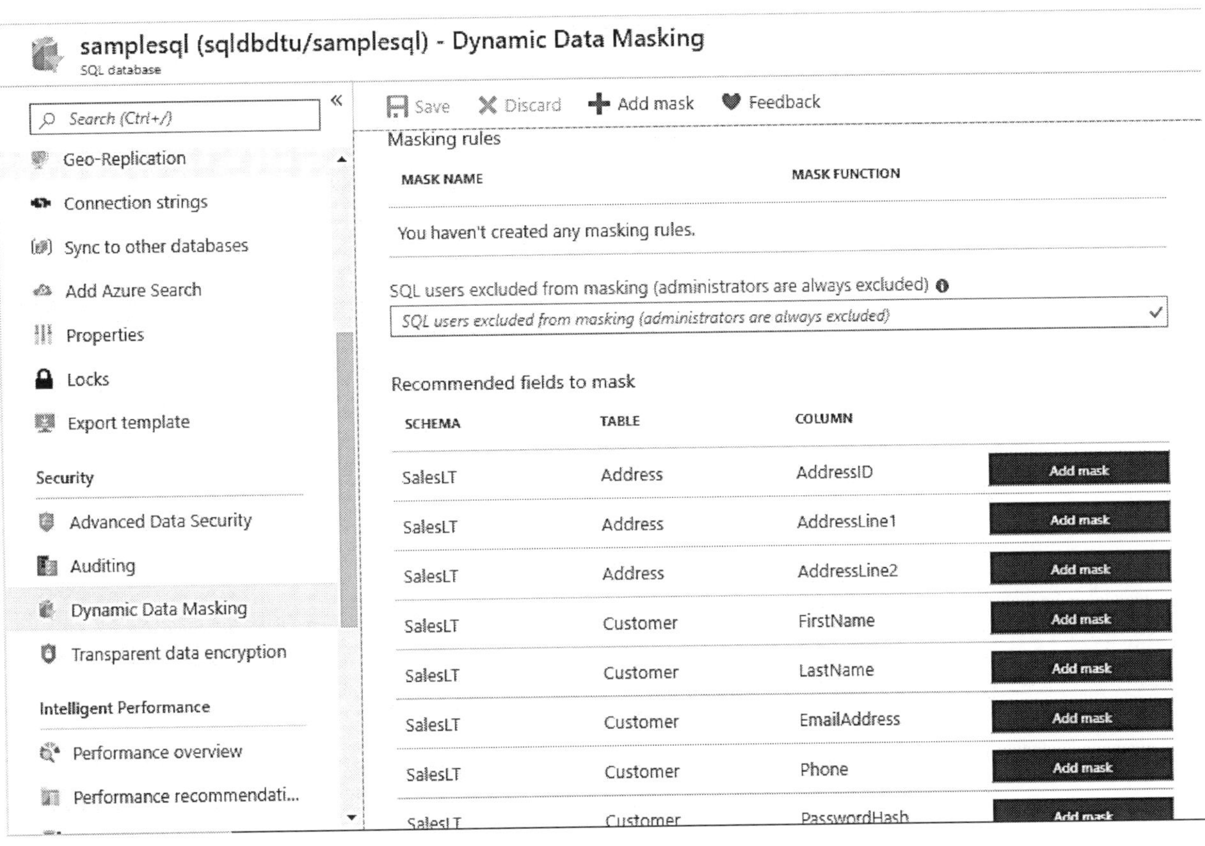

2. Click **Add mask** on the 6th row containing EmailAddress>A masking rule is now showing in top which masks email address from SQL Users>Click save.

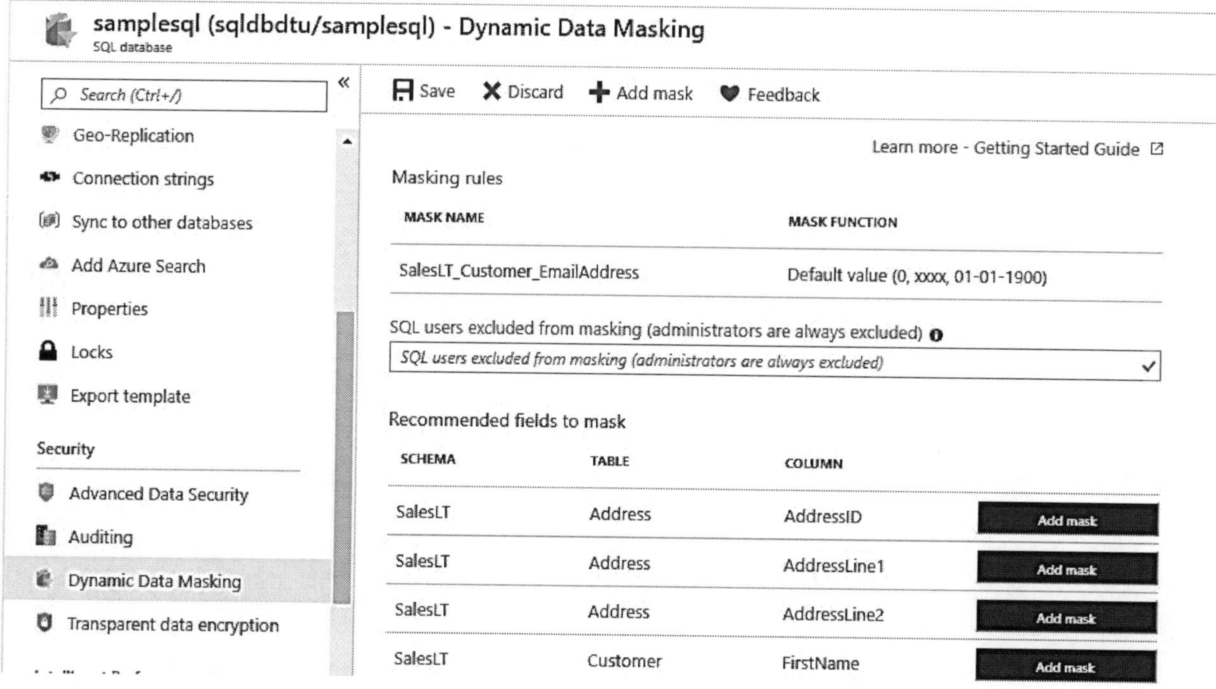

SQL Server Stretch Database

SQL Server Stretch Database feature migrates warm & cold data from on-premises SQL Server transparently and securely to the Microsoft Azure cloud.

Stretch Database is a feature of SQL Server 2016.

Figure below shows the architecture of SQL Server Stretch Database.

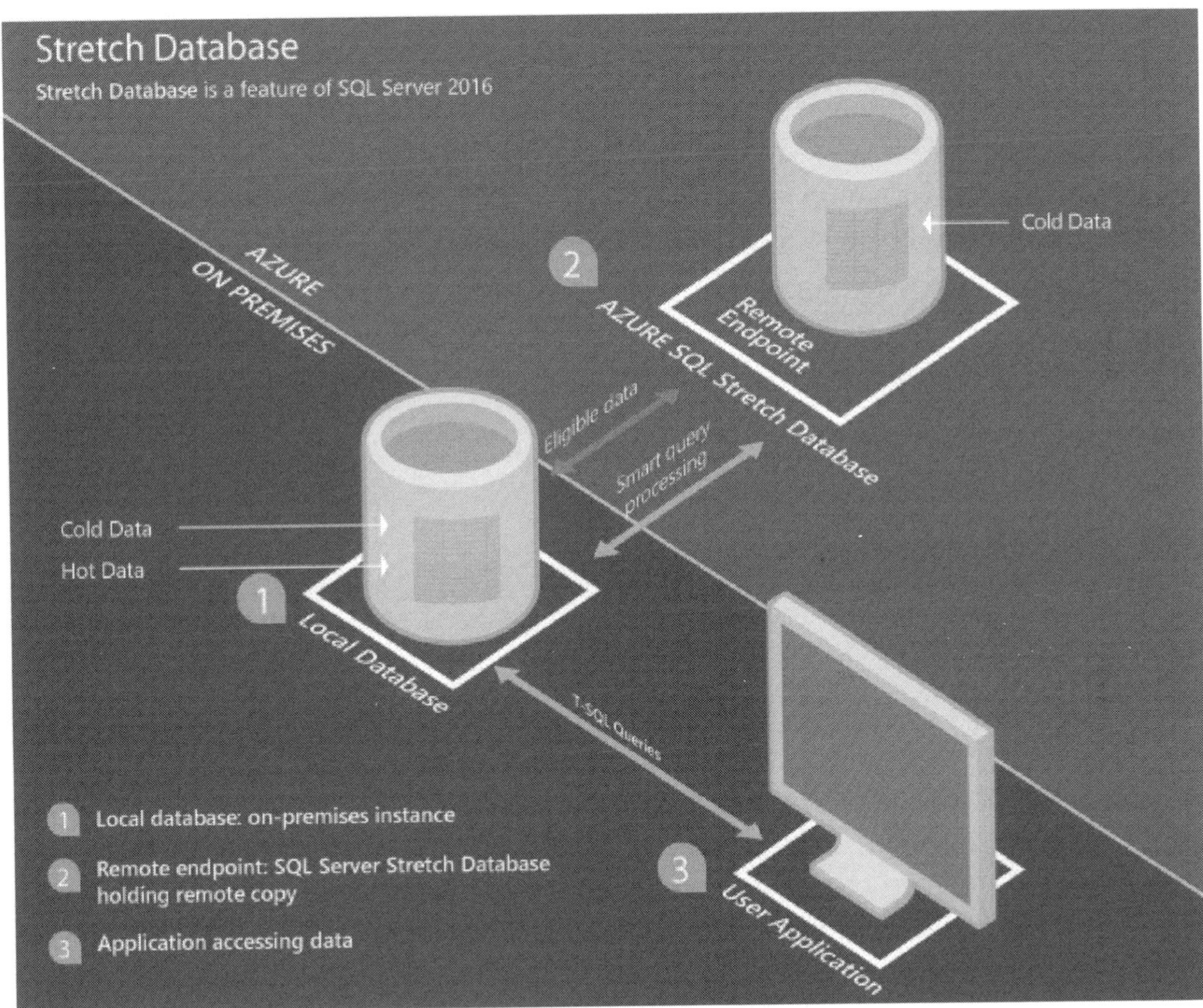

When you enable Stretch Database feature on your on-premises SQL Server, then an Azure SQL instance is created in Azure cloud. Secondly cold data is migrated to Azure cloud and is always available for querying.

Stretch Database lets you provide longer retention times for large amounts of data without scaling up enterprise storage.

Benefits of Stretch Database

1. Cold data migrated to Azure is always online and available to query.
2. Benefit from the low cost of Azure rather than scaling expensive on-premises storage. Azure storage can be 80% less expensive than adding to on-premises SSD.
3. Stretch Database doesn't require any changes to existing queries or applications – the location of the data is completely transparent to the application. SQL Server handles the data movement in the background.
4. Reduction in on-premises maintenance and storage for your data. Backups for your on-premises data run faster and finish within the maintenance window. Backups for the cloud portion of your data run automatically.
5. SQL Server's Always Encrypted provides encryption for your data in motion. Row Level Security (RLS) and other advanced SQL Server security features also work with Stretch Database to protect your data.

Enabling SQL Server Stretch Database

1. In SQL Server Management Studio, in Object Explorer, select the database on which you want to enable Stretch> Right-click and select **Tasks**, and then select **Stretch**, and then select **Enable** to launch the wizard.

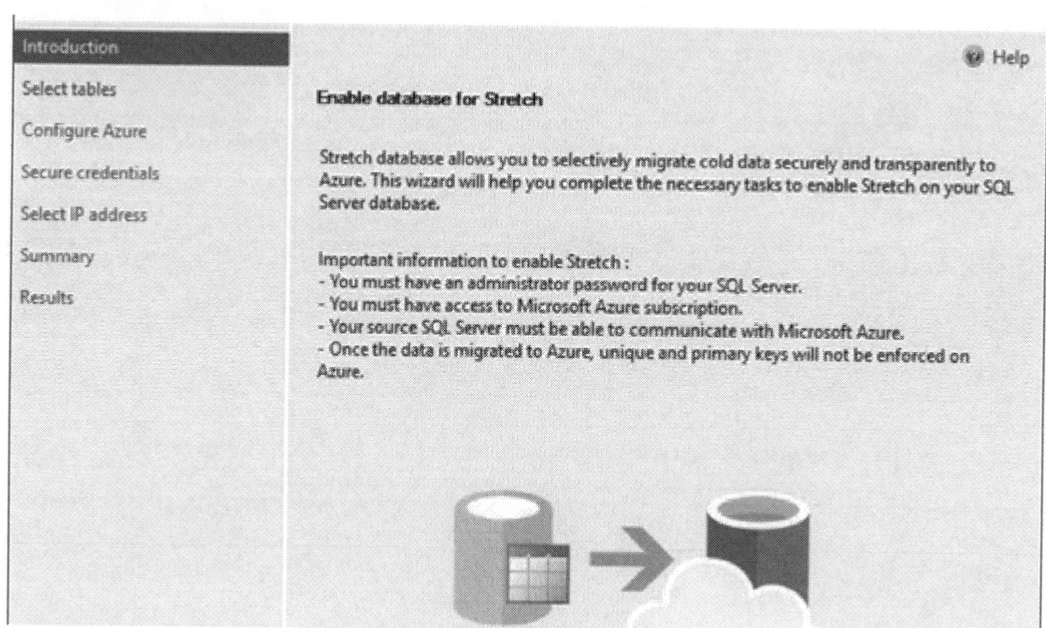

SQL Server Stretch Database Pricing

SQL Server Stretch Database has following pricing components:

Compute

Compute usage is represented with Database Stretch Unit (DSU) and customers can scale up and down the level of performance/DSUs they need at any time.

PERFORMANCE LEVEL (DSU)	PRICE
100	$1,825/month
200	$3,650/month
300	$5,475/month
400	$7,300/month
500	$9,125/month
600	$10,950/month
1000	$18,250/month
1200	$21,900/month
1500	$27,375/month
2000	$36,500/month

Storage

Data storage is charged based at $0.16/GB/month. Data storage includes the size of your Stretch DB and backup snapshots. All Stretch databases have 7 days of incremental backup snapshots.

Note: Storage transactions are not billed. You only pay for stored data and not storage transactions.

Geo-Backup (Optional): Storage for geo-redundant copies is billed at $0.12/GB/Month.

Outbound Data Transfer

Outbound data transfers are charged at regular data transfer rates.

Azure SQL Pricing DTU Model (Standard Tier)

I will just put Pricing for Standard Tier for both Single Database and Elastic Pool so that you can compare the prices of both models.

Single Database Model: Standard Tier Pricing

Tier	DTUs	Max Storage Per DB	Price
S0	10	250	$0.0202/hr
S1	20	250	$0.0404/hr
S2	50	250	$0.1009/hr
S3	100	250	$0.2017/hr

Elastic Pool Model: Standard Tier Pricing

eDTU per Pool	Max storage Per Pool	Max DBs per pool	Max eDTUs per Database	Price
50	50 GB	100	50	$0.1511/hr
100	100 GB	200	100	$0.3021/hr
200	200 GB	500	200	$0.6042/hr
300	300 GB	500	300	$0.9063/hr
400	400 GB	500	400	$1.2084/hr
800	800 GB	500	800	$2.4167/hr
1200	1.2 TB	500	1200	$3.625/hr
1600	1.6 TB	500	1600	$4.8334/hr
2000	2 TB	500	2000	$6.0417/hr
2500	2.4 TB	500	2500	$7.5521/hr
3000	2.9 TB	500	3000	$9.0625/hr

Note: For the same value, eDTU is priced 1.5 Times that of DTU. But with eDTU you can put multiple Databases in the pool which then reduces the price.

Active Geo-Replication Pricing: Secondary active geo-replication databases are priced at 1x of primary database prices. The cost of geo-replication traffic between the primary and the online secondary is included in the cost of the online secondary.

SQL Pricing vCore (General Purpose) – Single Database/Elastic Pool

I will show prices upto 6 vCores. Prices are same for Single Database and Elastic Pool Model.

Compute Prices

vCore	Memory (GB)	Max Num of Databases/Pool	License Included Price	Azure Hybrid Benefit Price
2	10.2	100	$0.5044/hour	$0.3045/hour
4	20.4	200	$1.0088/hour	$0.6089/hour
6	30.6	500	$1.5131/hour	$0.9134/hour

Storage Prices

In the General Purpose tier, you are charged for **Premium blob storage** that you provision for your database or elastic pool. **Storage can be configured between 5 GB and 4 TB with 1 GB increments**.

	Price
GB/Month	$0.115

SQL Pricing vCore (Business Critical) – Single Database/Elastic Pool

Compute Prices

vCore	Memory (GB)	Max Num of Databases/Pool	License Included Price	Azure Hybrid Benefit Price
2	10.2		$1.3589/hour	$0.6089/hour
4	20.4	50	$2.7178/hour	$1.2178/hour
6	30.6	100	$1.8267/hour	$3.4370/hour

Storage Prices

In the Business Critical tier, you are charged **for local SSD storage** that you provision for your database or elastic pool.

	Price
GB/Month	$0.25

Note 1: In Business critical Tier Elastic Pool starts from 4 Cores.
Note 2: Max Num of Databases/Pool column is applicable for Elastic Pool only.

Design Case study 2: Design a Business Continuity Solution for Web/App tier and Database Tier

An Automobile giant is running a 2-tier Dealer application – web/app tier running on Azure Web App and Database Tier running on Azure SQL Database. Recently they had a regional outage and had to face a downtime of 3 hours. They want to have a Disaster recovery solutions hosted in different region which can be activated in case of an outage or a regional disaster. They want DR site should be up and running within 30 minutes of outage or disaster at primary site.

They have constraint that Cross-region connectivity between the application and the Primary database is not acceptable due to latency. This was confirmed during a pilot test.

Design a solution which satisfies the above requirement.

Solution

Designing Web/App Tier

For web/app tier we will have active-passive deployment of Azure Web App as cross region connectivity between the application and the Primary database is not acceptable due to latency. Web App in Primary Region will be active and Web App in secondary will be passive.

Azure Traffic Manager (TM) will be used to Load balance traffic between web apps in Primary and secondary regions. As it is Active-Passive deployment, Traffic Manager should be set up to use failover routing.

Web App in each region will be connected to Azure SQL Database in there region only.

Designing Database Tier

Primary Region already has Azure SQL Database running. Using Active Geo-Replication a secondary Database will be created in secondary Region. Database in each region will be paired to the Web App in there region only.
Azure SQL Database in Primary Region is active and is Primary Database.

Active Traffic and Disaster Recovery to Secondary Site

All Traffic will be served through primary region. In case of outage Traffic will be shifted to Secondary Region. Secondary Database will be promoted to Primary Database manually or automatically using a monitoring app.

Figure below shows the Business Continuity solution for 2-tier Dealer Application.

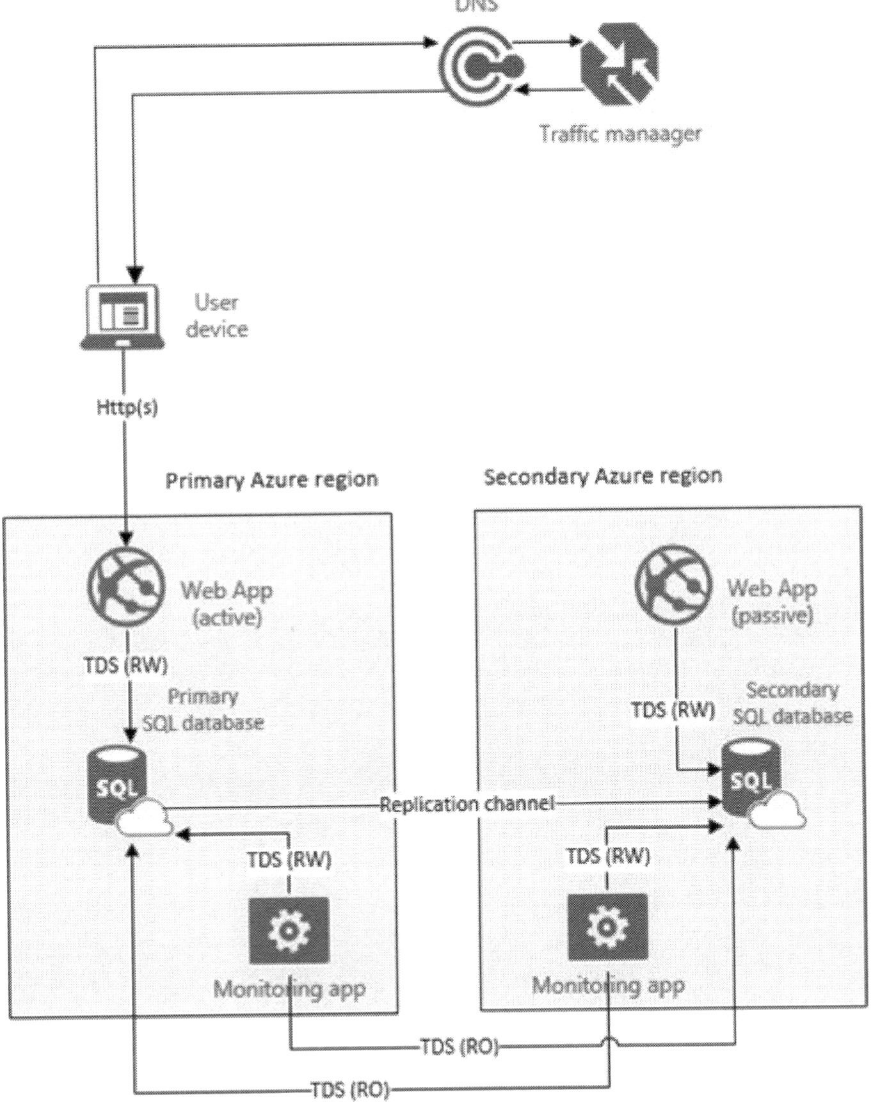

Note: MS is now recommending failover groups to be used with Geo-Replication. With Geo-Replication, failover to secondary is manual operation. Geo-Replication with auto-failover groups results in automatic failover.

Design Case study 3: Choosing a Database tier

A corporate company is deploying a 2 tier application - Web/App tier and Database tier in Azure. They have chosen Azure SQL Database as there backend.

The application team has given there requirement for Database tier. Database size will be 400 GB and they want Database performance DTU of upto 50.

Based on above Requirement choose the appropriate Database tier.

Solution

Standard S2 Tier gives a DTU of 50. Maximum Database size in S2 is 250 GB.
Premium P1 Tier gives a DTU of 125. Maximum Database size in P1 is 500 GB.

Premium P1 Tier will be chosen as it satisfies both DTU and Size requirements. Whereas Standard S2 Tier satisfies only DTU Requirement.

Chapter 4 Implement Authentication

This Chapter covers following Topic Lessons

- Windows Integrated Authentication
- Form based Authentication
- Implement authentication using Certificates
- Certificate-based authentication in Azure Active Directory
- oauth2 Authentication
- Managed Service Identity (MSI)

This Chapter Covers following Lab Exercises

- Windows Integrated Authentication
- Implementing Point to Site (P2S) VPN using Certificates

Chapter Topology

In this chapter we will add Managed Service Identity (MSI) & App Registration to the topology.

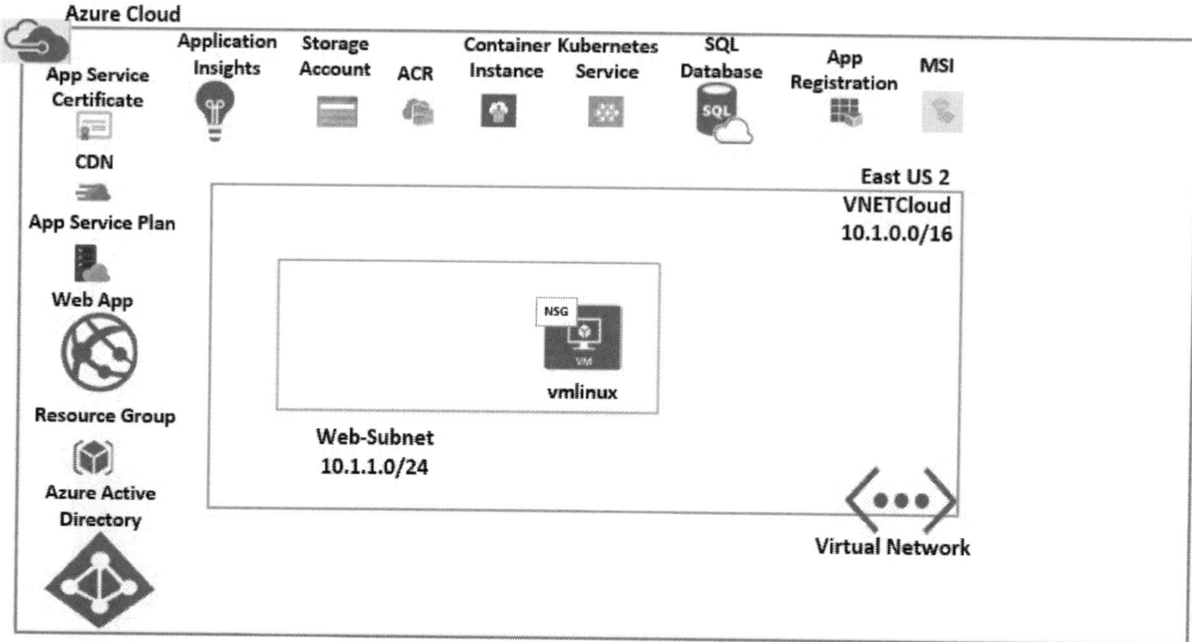

Certificate Authentication Lab Exercise

We will also create a new Virtual Network vnp2s in a new Resource Group p2s. GatewaySubnet will be created in Virtual Network vnp2s. Virtual Network Gateway (VNG) will be created in GatewaySubnet. Virtual Network Gateway wil be configured with P2S VPN. We will then generate Self Signed Certificate on our Windows 10 Laptop. We will export Public Key of certificate to Virtual Network Gateway. Using P2S VPN Client software Windows 10 will connect to Virtual Network through Virtual Network Gateway and will use Self-signed Certificate for Authentication.

Windows Integrated Authentication

Windows Integrated Authentication is used in Intranet/Internal Web Application where users are part of a Windows based Domain Network have Active Directory as Directory Server.

Integrated Windows authentication enables users to log in with their Windows credentials using Kerberos or NTLM. The client sends credentials in the Authorization header.

To enable Windows Integrated Authentication in your Web Application you need to add authentication mode as windows in the Web.config file as shown below.

```
<system.web>
<authentication mode=Windows />
</system.web>
```

If you are using Visual Studio to create your web application then select the "Intranet Application" template in the MVC 4 project wizard. This template will automatically put the above code in Web.config file.

Advantages of Windows Integrated Authentication

One of the advantages of Windows Integrated Authentication is that it is built into Internet Information Server (IIS). You need to just enable it in IIS management console without adding any code as shown above.

Form based Authentication

Forms based authentication is used with internet web applications. Internet web applications like Hotmail, Yahoo mail and Gmail use form based authentications wherein users need not be members of their domain network.

Forms authentication uses an HTML form to send the user's credentials to the server. Forms authentication is only appropriate for web APIs that are called from a web application so that the user can interact with the HTML form. Forms-authentication uses a session cookie to authenticate requests. Browsers automatically send all relevant cookies to the destination web site.

To enable Form based Authentication in your Internet Web Application you need to add HTML code (Which generates form consisting of username and password) to your application.

If you are using Visual Studio to create your Internet web application then select the "Internet Application" template in the MVC 4 project wizard.

Figure below shows form based authentication for yahoo mail.

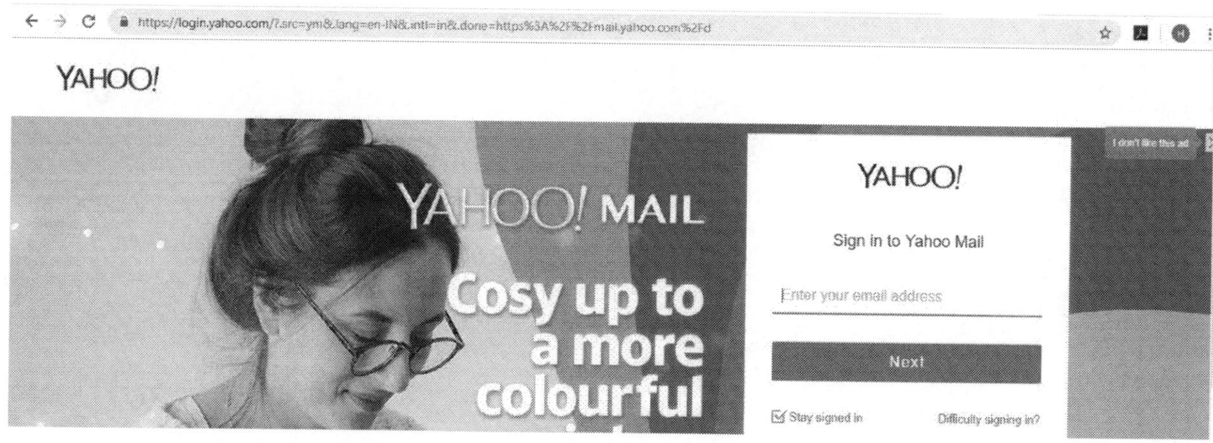

Implement authentication using Certificates

Certificate-based authentication use Digital Certificate to identify a user, machine, or device before granting access.

One differentiator of certificate-based authentication is that unlike some solutions that only work for users, such as biometrics and one time passwords (OTP), the same solution can be used for all endpoints – users, machine, devices and even the growing Internet of Things (IoT).

Certificates are stored locally on the machine or device. This not only saves on costs, but can also alleviate management pains around distributing, replacing and revoking tokens.

Digital Certificate Issuing Authority

Digital certificates are issued by Certificate Authorities (CAs). Certificate Authorities (CAs) can be internal or external.

Internal Certificate Authority is managed and operated by end user organizations. For Example organizations can create Active Directory Certificate Services to issue Certificates.

External Certificate Authorities are third part entities such as GlobalSign, Verizon and Symantec etc which issue Digital Certificates to organizations.

Digital Certificates Working

Digital Certificate use Public-key cryptography. Public-key cryptography is an encryption scheme that uses 2 different keys - a public key and a private key. The public key is used to encrypt and the private key is used to decrypt.

Public key is freely shared allowing users to encrypt content easily. Private Key is kept secret ensuring that only the owners of the private keys can decrypt content.

Digital Certificates Authentication Working for Machine Authentication

From the Root Certificate **Public Key** is uploaded to the Server. **Client certificates (Private Key)** is generated from root certificate and is installed on client computer. The client certificate is then used to authenticate the client computer when it initiates a connection to the Server.

Exercise 59: Implementing Point to Site (P2S) VPN using Certificates

In this Exercise we will Connect Windows 10 Client machine to Azure Virtual Network over Point-to-Site (P2S) VPN connection. We will Generate Self Signed Root Certificate for this Exercise. From Self Signed root certificate we will upload **Public Key (.cer file)to Azure.** From Self Signed Root Certificate we will generate **client certificates (Private Key)** to be installed on our Windows 10 Machine.

The client certificate is used to authenticate the client (Windows 10 Machine) when it initiates a connection to the VNET over P2S VPN Connection.
For this exercise we will create a new Virtual Network in a new Resource Group.

Step 1: Create Virtual Network
In Azure Portal click create a Resource>Networking>Virtual Network>Create Virtual Network Blade opens>Enter a name>Enter Address space 172.16.0.0/16> In Resource Group click create new. A Box pops up. Enter a name and click ok>Location East US 2>In Subnet Address range enter 172.16.0.1/24>Create.

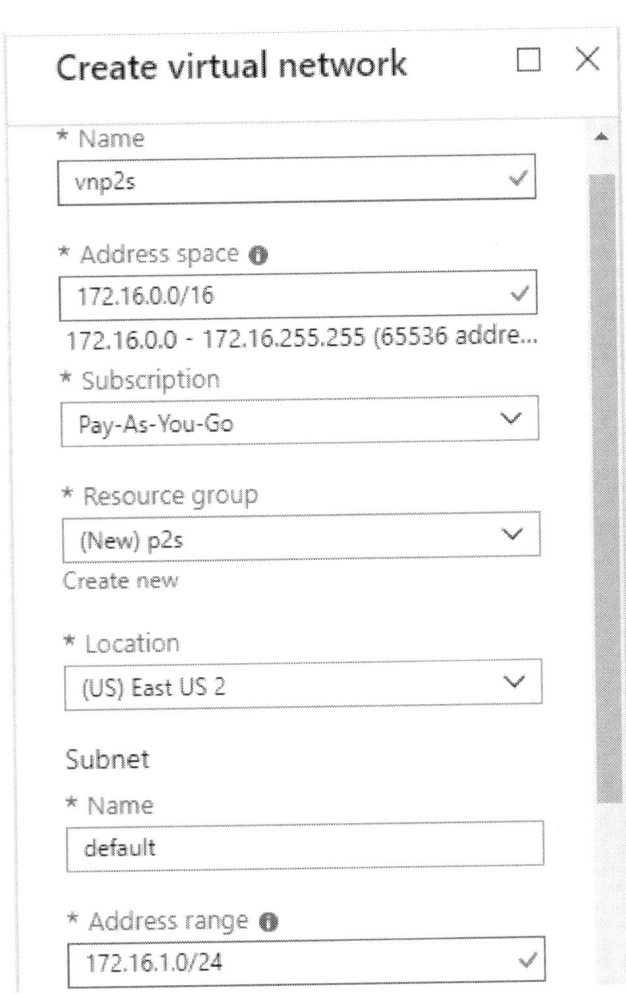

Figure below shows the dashboard of Virtual Network vnp2s.

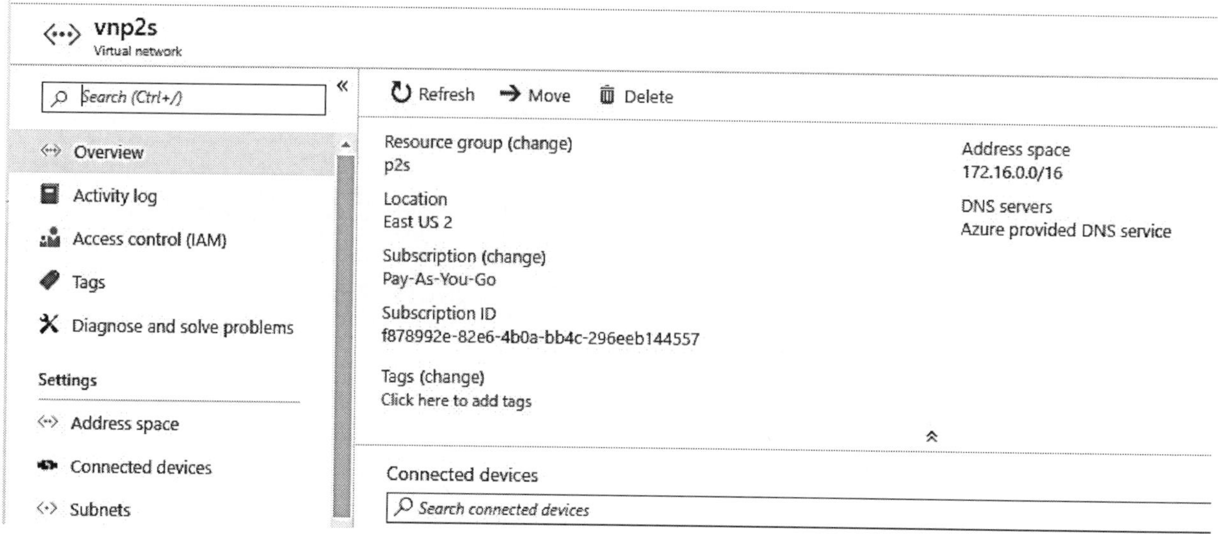

Step 2: Create Gateway Subnet

In Virtual Network dashboard click Subnets in left pane>In Right pane click + Gateway Subnet>Add Subnet Blade opens>In Address range enter 172.16.3.0/24 > Rest select all default values and click ok (Not Shown).

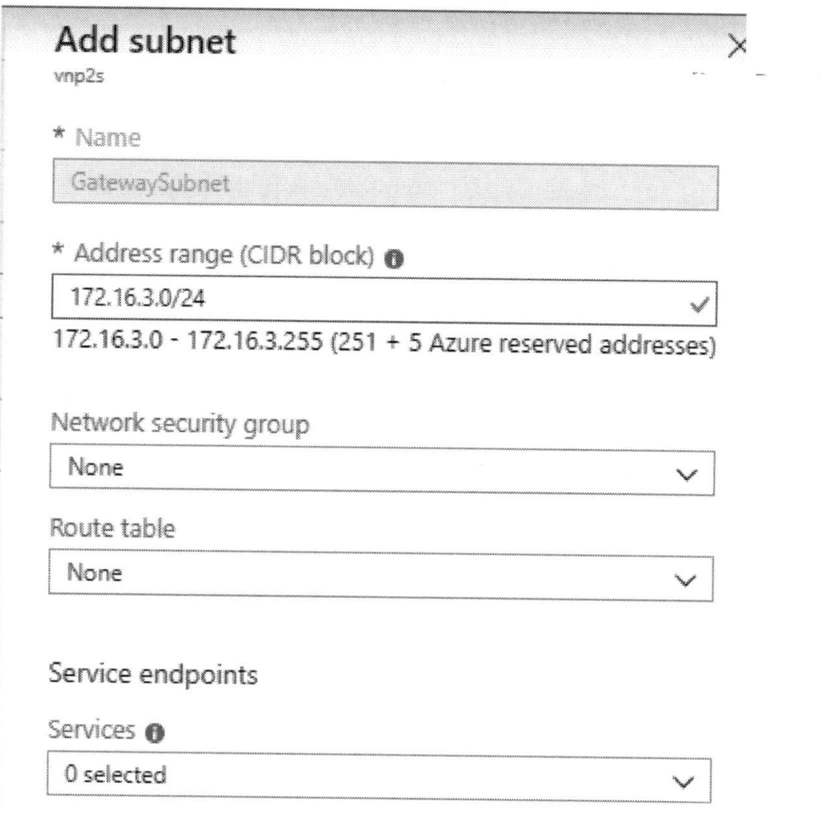

Step 3: Create Virtual Network Gateway

In Azure Portal click All Services in left pane> Networking> Virtual Network Gateways> +Add> Create Virtual Network Gateway blade open>Enter a name>Select default values for Gateway type, VPN Type and SKU> Select Virtual Network vnp2s created in Step 1> In Public IP address select create new and enter a name> Rest select all default Values>Click Review + Create> After Validation click create

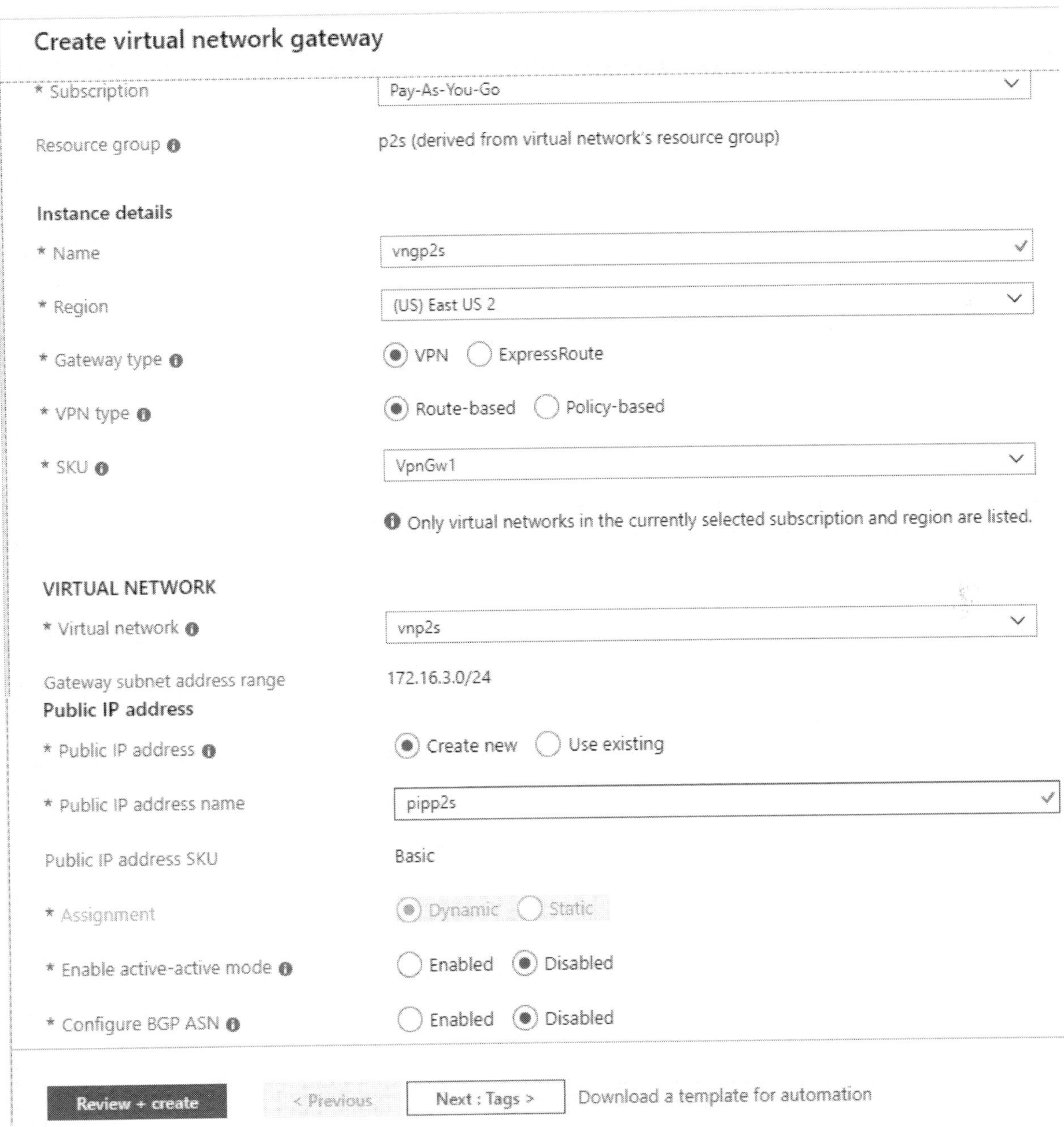

Figure Below shows the dashboard of Virtual Network gateway. It took around 20-25 minutes for Virtual Network Gateway Deployment.

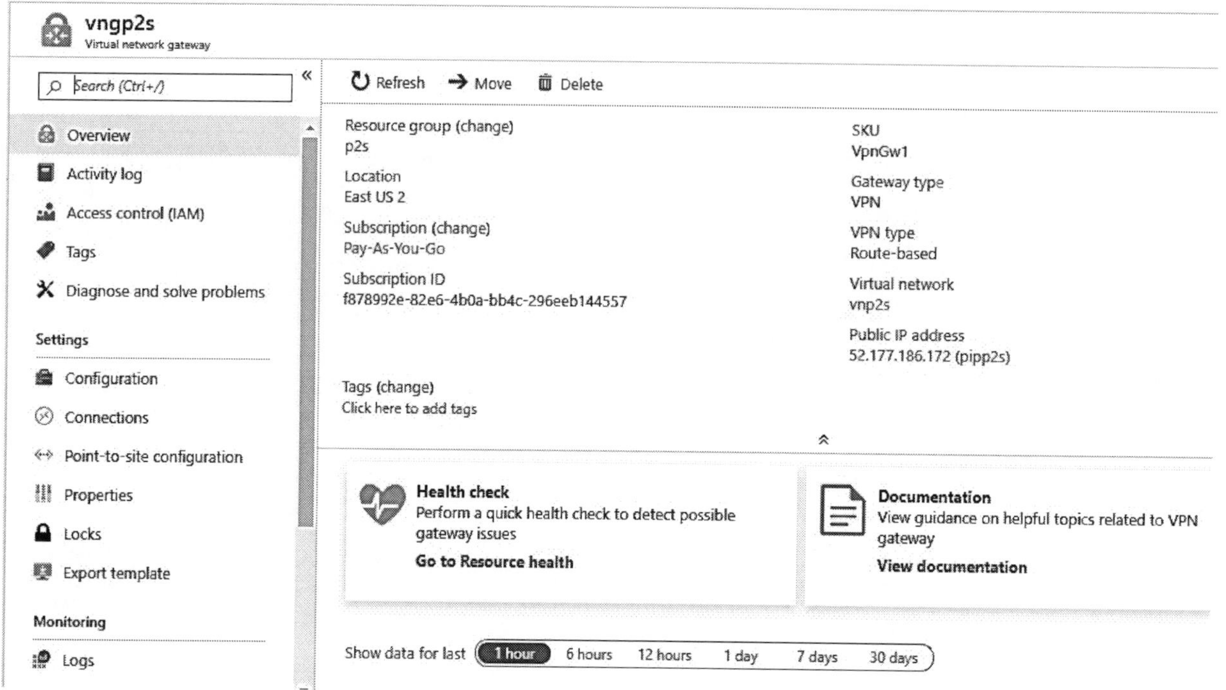

Step 4: Create Self Signed Root Certificate on your Windows 10 Laptop

On Your Windows 10 Machine open Powershell and enter following command.

```
New-SelfSignedCertificate -Type Custom –KeySpec Signature -Subject "CN=P2SRootCert"
 -KeyExportPolicy Exportable -HashAlgorithm sha256 -KeyLength 2048 -CertStoreLocation
"Cert:\CurrentUser\My" -KeyUsageProperty Sign -KeyUsage CertSign
```

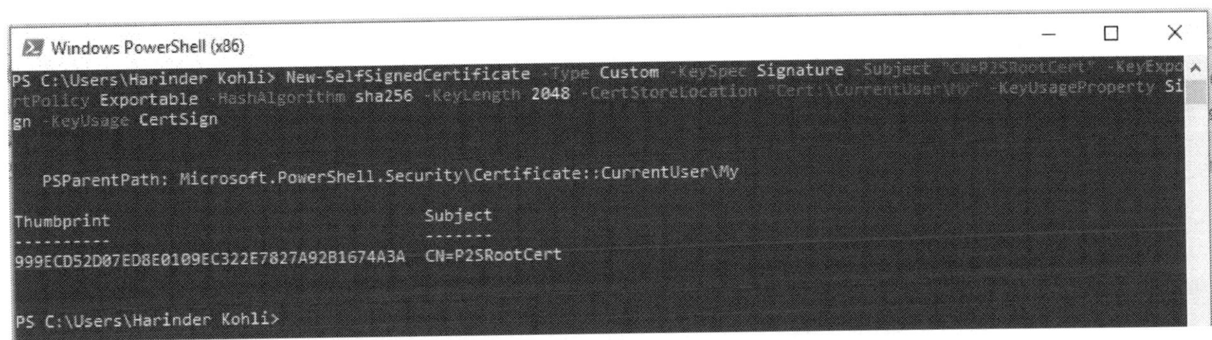

Note: Copy Down the Thumbprint. We will use this in next Step.

Step 5: Generate a client certificate

Declare a variable for the root certificate using the thumbprint from the previous step.

```
$cert = Get-ChildItem -Path "Cert:\CurrentUser\My\999ECD52D07ED8E0109EC322E7827A92B1674A3A"
```

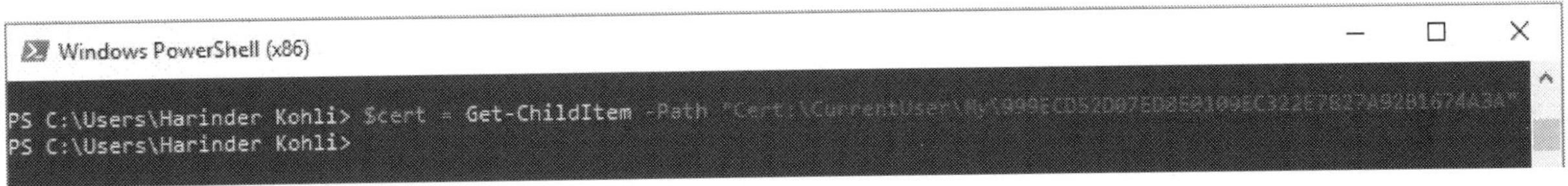

Generate the client Certificate with following command

```
New-SelfSignedCertificate -Type Custom -DnsName P2SChildCert -KeySpec Signature
-Subject "CN=P2SChildCert" -KeyExportPolicy Exportable -HashAlgorithm sha256
-KeyLength 2048 -CertStoreLocation "Cert:\CurrentUser\My" -Signer $cert
-TextExtension @("2.5.29.37={text}1.3.6.1.5.5.7.3.2")
```

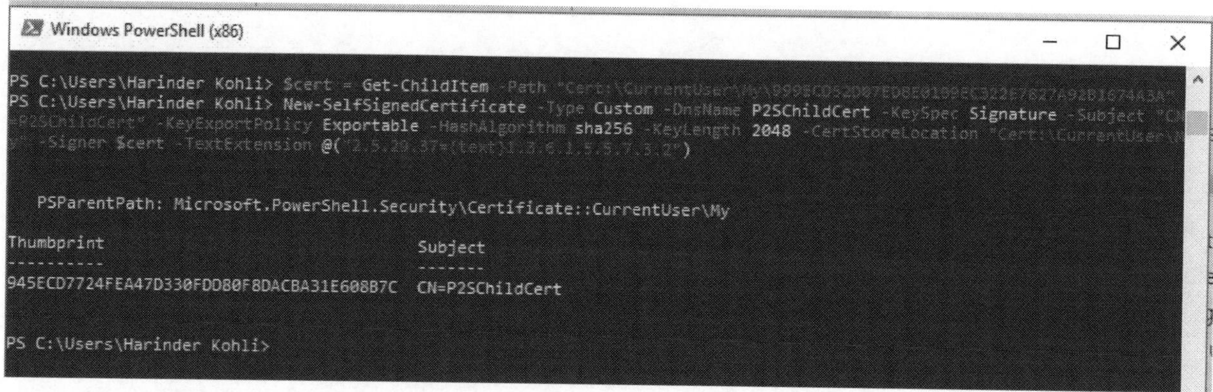

<u>**The above command also installs the Client Certificate on the Windows 10 Machine.**</u>
When you generate a client certificate, it's automatically installed on the computer that you used to generate it.

Step 6: Check the Certificates Generated

On your Windows 10 Machine in search box type Run>Click Run App>Run App opens>Enter certmgr.msc>Cert Manger opens>Under Certificates – Current User click personal and then click Certificates> In Right pane you can see both Root Certificate and Client Certificate.

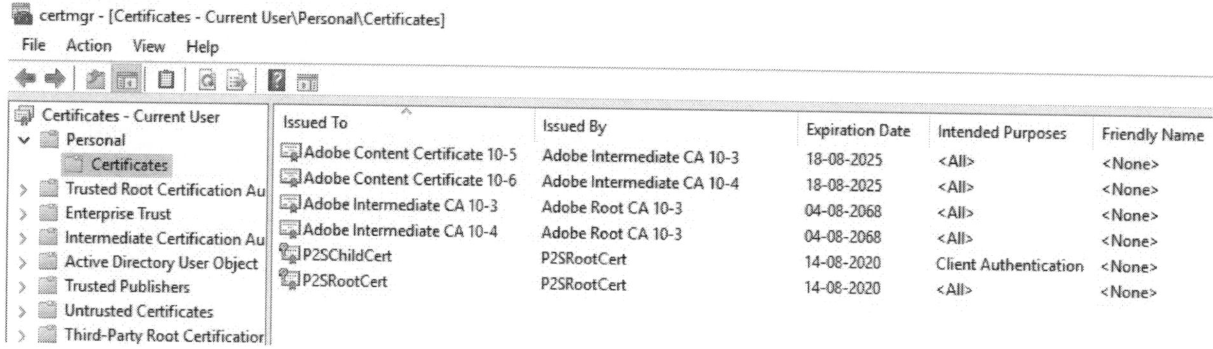

Step 7: Export the root certificate public key (.cer)

1. In Windows 10 Cert Manager Right click P2SRootCert>All Tasks>Export> Certificate Export Wizard opens.

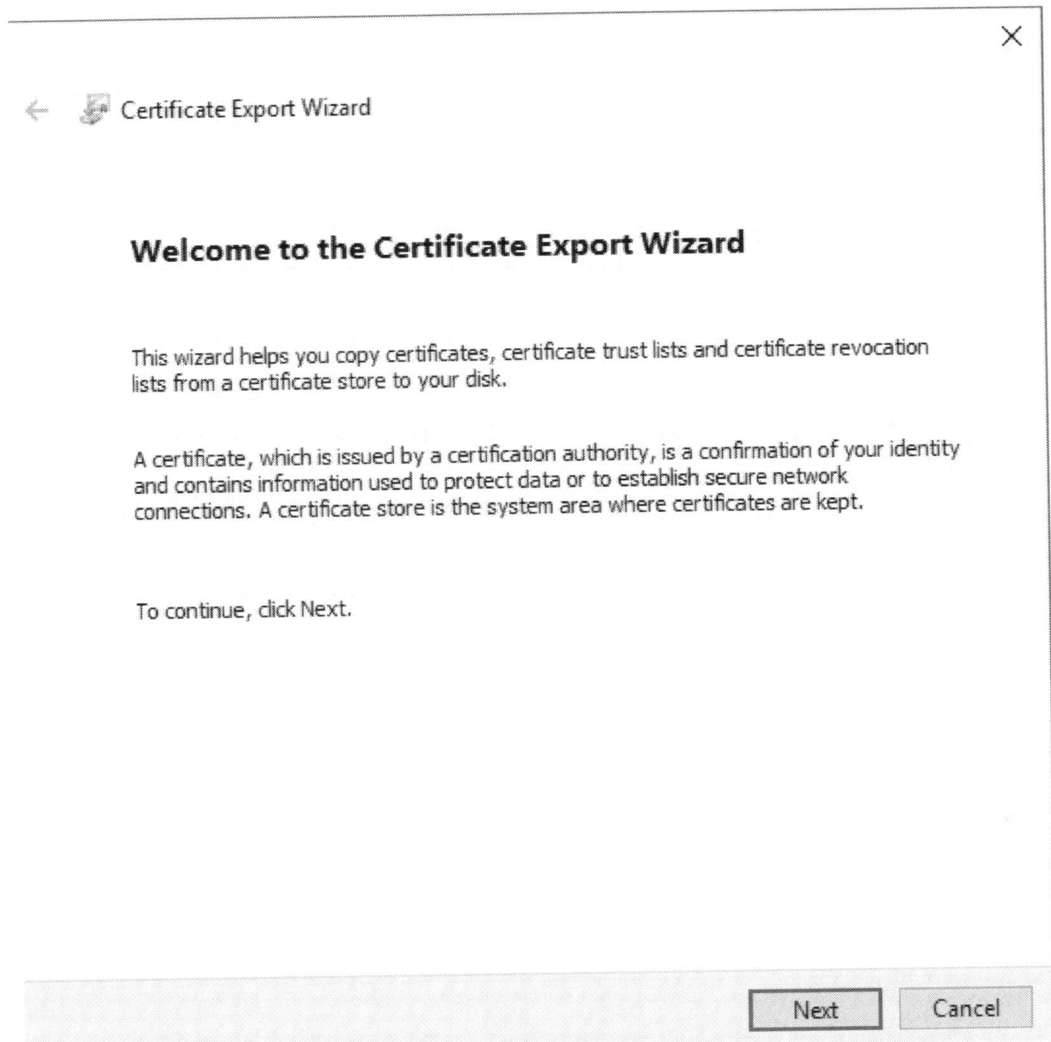

2. Click Next> Select **No, do not export the private key,** and then click **Next**> On the **Export File Format** page, select **Base-64 encoded X.509 (.CER).**, and then click **Next**>Click Browse to and choose a location and enter filename and click **Next**>Click **Finish.**

3. Open the Certificate File in Notepad>Copy the value. We will use it step 7.

PublicKey - Notepad

File Edit Format View Help

-----BEGIN CERTIFICATE-----
MIIC5zCCAc+gAwIBAgIQfDvztdEmQ5BCcRRmIEjm1TANBgkqhkiG9w0BAQsFADAW
MRQwEgYDVQQDDAtQM1NSb290Q2VydDAeFw0xOTA4MTQwMjIxNTNaFw0yMDA4MTQw
MjQxNTNaMBYxFDASBgNVBAMMC1AyU1Jvb3RDZXJ0MIIBIjANBgkqhkiG9w0BAQEF
AAOCAQ8AMIIBCgKCAQEAqmW1CUOAfB3UVO9nLGg4VNYccBWHxK4nhEXPVArdyp5s
Q2qRAyhIcmPjtJYv9uGhpX8v/MyPiYkszlqbWfgK9MMOv6uKZe9ngy5c5i57EwbX
BwIZ84XKWChFGg/i2fZDoTjbsHWTIdXKVmH+gs6fueLfOE/x10CcKdDYDtnnkWYG
XAN5fYo4bNFHKVI4wwGVSo14phglUAOkxOUavBRfbHmK/S3sUHeqW2WjyYRGs7YV
dsslIgoIuy2STz/rhfsekj8CO7Kyq0B5vyDFF67j6WNH6vEunbofgtwLIrPFp2g9
Gk8f/shRMX3mccJwlHT+8OdXP/DvrmsFKUXEFBQxEQIDAQABozEwLzAOBgNVHQ8B
Af8EBAMCAgQwHQYDVR0OBBYEFECuuos1PtT+NizeMdikl2Rbc8ZuMA0GCSqGSIb3
DQEBCwUAA4IBAQA7vgbRQc+7esXnYpk04cXk8DBd+TckAhRHz4twfNsuf3EYZt5N
8Phk2ysdT+K8JqSui1c4SpDShKWdaWpm/H37XCmXspYswqerXuhzRQOTTUv8y3T8
ZO0vrF2KDxpyGfl2ws+NsW0jGwFz+qttgKK8IhOYl+JKuhXcCtM111fSm3Kc2jRf
pYyGClRNH1XZVD9TPL1wU/f5sUsZH6bpy69heBjzjtyd2nWnlAnbla0Bwk2pKcWi
Lo8z0fx/nWnAl3K7F9hUrlIqj/Z47CCQxrEiqBwKOoZtZuR/VSNAwfVPsDzbnXNR
FxEMAtaqN/0NG9ubih/N8U/XaoDAtqVn7/ev
-----END CERTIFICATE-----

Step 8: Create client address pool, Tunnel type & Authentication type

In Virtual Network gateway dashboard click Point-to-site configuration in left pane>In right pane click configure now>Configuration Blade opens in Right pane>For Client Address pool enter 10.0.0.0/24>For Tunnel type select IKEv2 and SSTP>For Authentication type select Azure certificate> Under Root Certificate for Name enter P2SRootCert and For Public Certificate Data Paste the value copied in Step 7>Click save at the top.

Note 1: From Address Pool, address will be assigned to Windows 10 Machine when they connect over P2S VPN Connection.

Note 2: Proceed to next step only after you get notification saved Virtual network gateway.

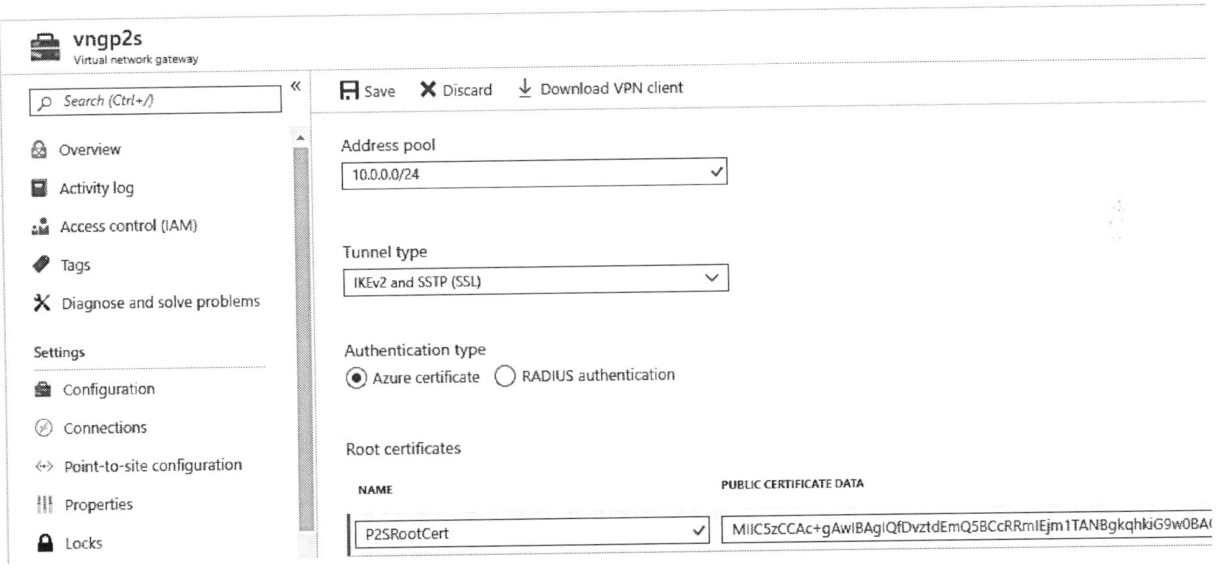

Step 9: Download VPN Client on Windows 10 Machine

In Virtual Network gateway dashboard click Point-to-site configuration in left pane>In right pane click Download VPN Client and select a location on your windows 10 machine to save it. Client is in winzip format>Unzip it> Browse the Folder and click WindowsAMD64>You can see the VPNClientSetupAmd64.

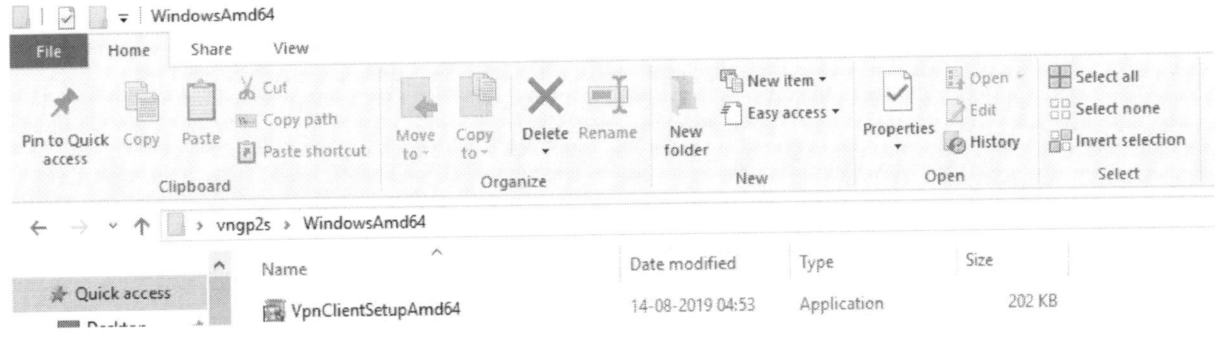

Step 10: Install VPN Client on your Windows 10 Machine

On your Windows 10 Machine double Click the VPNClientSetupAmd64 downloaded in previous step for Installation.

Step 11: Connect to Virtual Netwirk using VPN Client

On your windows 10 Machine go to Controp Panel>Click Network & Internet>Under Network & Sharing Center Click Connect to a network>A screen pops up. Click vnp2s>Click vnp2s again>Click Connect.
Note: vnp2s is the name of the Virtual Network created in Step 1.

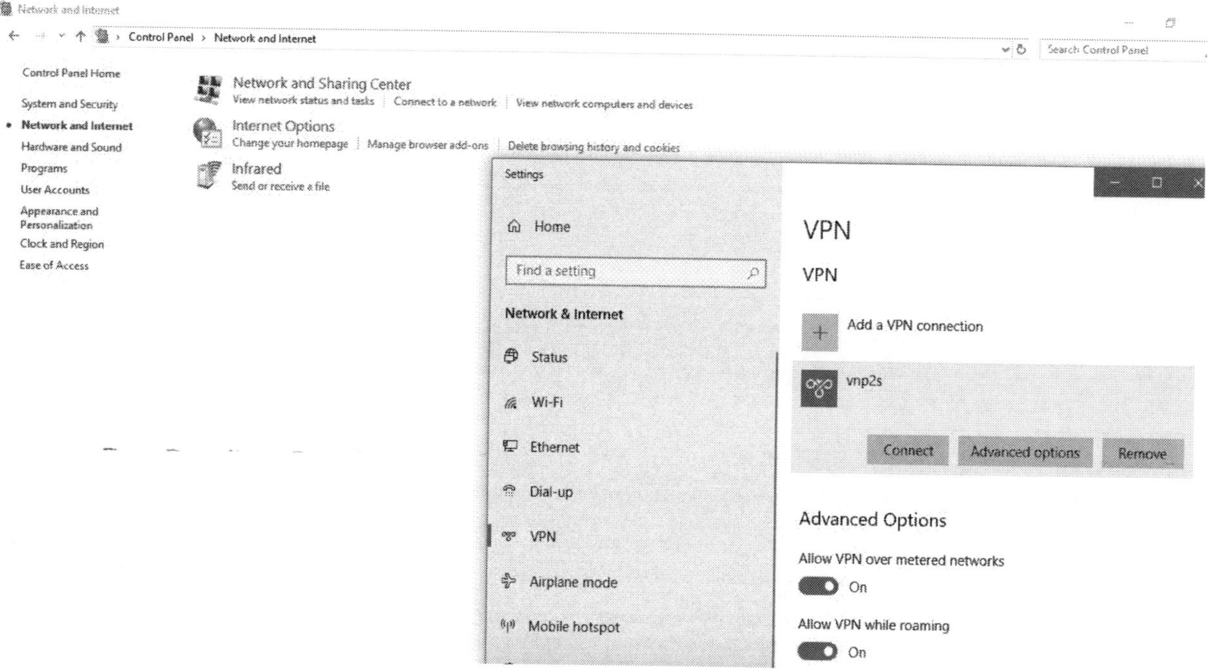

Note: VPNClientSetupAmd64 is for 64 Bit System.
Note 2: VPNClientSetupX86 is for 32 Bit System.

A new screen pops>click Conect

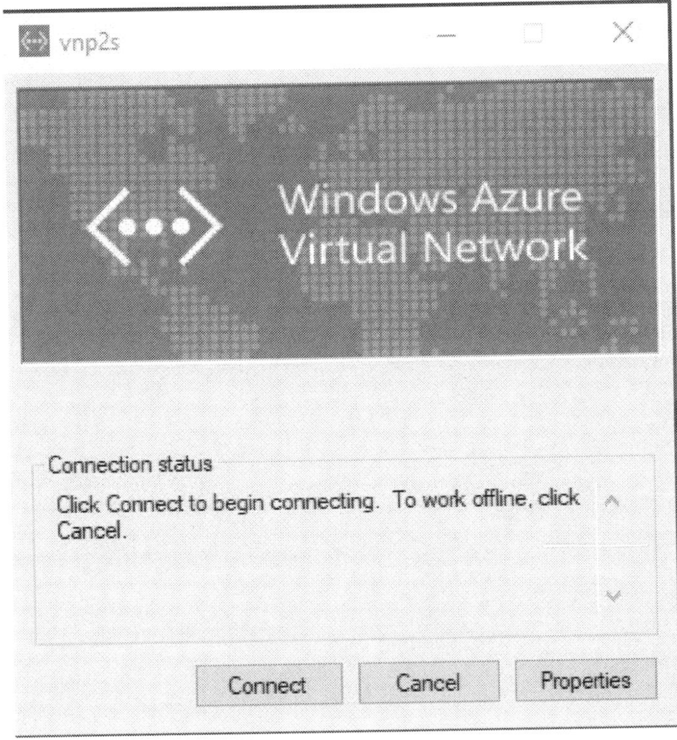

Your Control pane setting screen will now show connected.

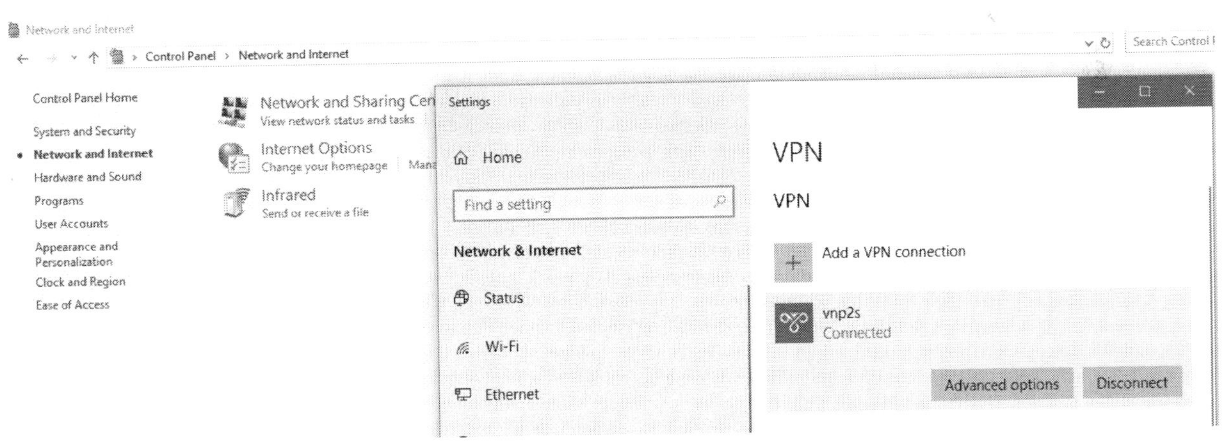

Step 12: Verifying the connection

On your Windows 10 Machine open Command prompt and enter command **ipconfig/all** (Not Shown). Scroll down to adaptor vnp2s. In the results you can see the IP address you received is one of the addresses within the Point-to-Site VPN Client Address Pool that you specified in your configuration in Step 8.

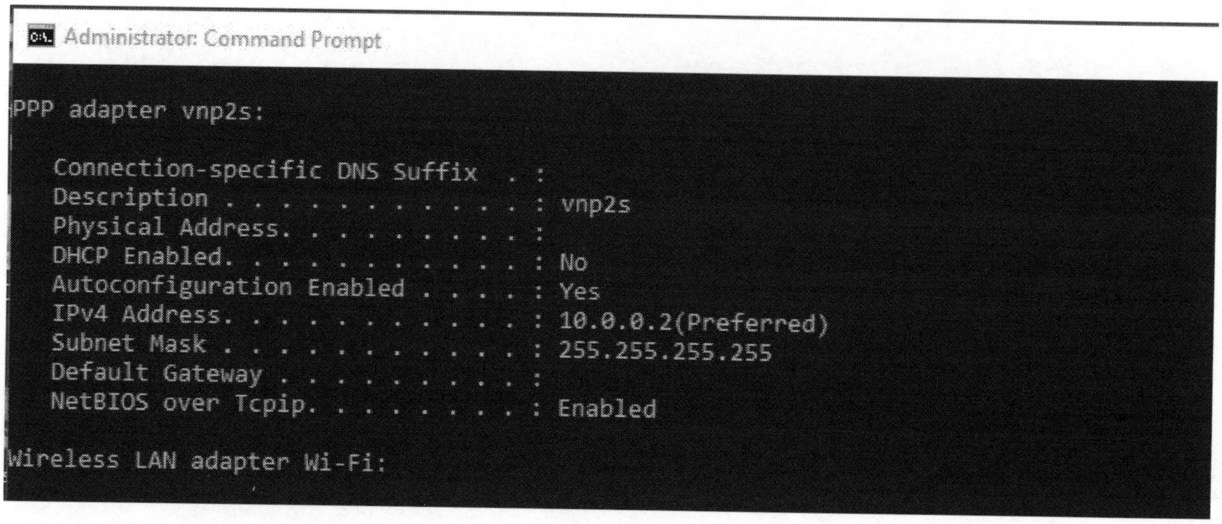

```
Administrator: Command Prompt

PPP adapter vnp2s:

   Connection-specific DNS Suffix  . :
   Description . . . . . . . . . . . : vnp2s
   Physical Address. . . . . . . . . :
   DHCP Enabled. . . . . . . . . . . : No
   Autoconfiguration Enabled . . . . : Yes
   IPv4 Address. . . . . . . . . . . : 10.0.0.2(Preferred)
   Subnet Mask . . . . . . . . . . . : 255.255.255.255
   Default Gateway . . . . . . . . . :
   NetBIOS over Tcpip. . . . . . . . : Enabled

Wireless LAN adapter Wi-Fi:
```

Oauth2 Authentication

Oauth2 is an identity or sign in protocol.

Oauth2 Authentication framework separates Resource Provider or Service Provider (For Example Website) from Identity Provider. Using Oauth2 authentication the resource provider need not maintain its own identity infrastructure, it can use external identity providers for authentication.

This decoupling allows applications to use a identity provider with a predefined protocol, and not care about the implementation details of identity provider.

This allows a system to provide controlled Access to its resources to a user that belongs to another security realm without requiring the user to authenticate directly to the system and without the two systems sharing a database of user identities or passwords.

Oauth2 Architecture

Oauth2 Authorization framework enables the applications to obtain limited access to User accounts on an HTTP service such as Facebook, linkedin, Twitter, ADFS and OKTA etc. Figure below show the Oauth2 Architecture. Oauth2 working is discussed in next section.

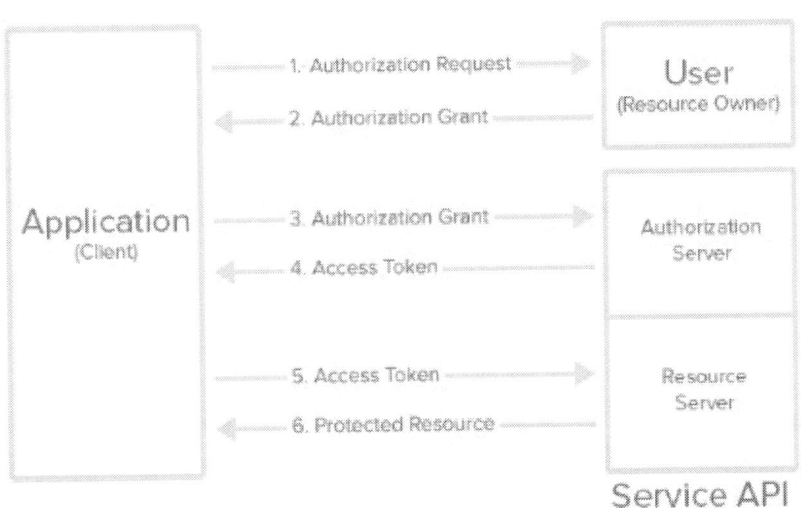

Note: Here Application (Client) is the user accessing the Resource Server. Authorization Server is from Facebook, Linkedin, ADFS etc.

Oauth2 Working

An end user is accessing a Secure Website (Resource Provider). The website does not have its own identity Infrastructure. It depends upon external identity providers like Facebook, linkedin, Hotmail, Active Directory Federation Server (ADFS) & Okta etc for authentication.

Following 3 components are involved when a user accesses secured Website or Application which is configured with Oauth2 Protocol to allow controlled access after authenticating users against External Identity Providers.

1. Sign-in Protocol
2. Authentication Protocol
3. Token Type

Oauth 2.0 is sign-in or identity protocol. When a user accesses secured website which is configured with Oauth 2.0 protocol, they are redirected to external Identity Providers using Oauth 2.0 **sign-in** or **identity Protocol.**

External Identity Providers prompts you for Authentication using Authentication protocol. This **Authentication protocol** will be form based for OAuth 2.0.

After authentication external identity provider **will issue token containing a series of claims about user.** User will be provided required access based on claims.

Case Study 4: Oauth2 Authentication

Inidan Railways (IR) has fourth largest railway network in the world by size, with a route length of 67,368 kilometre and total track length of 121,407 kilometre. Indian Railway (IR) runs more than 20,000 passenger trains and 9,200 freight trains daily.

Despite the best effort by IR more than 50% of Passenger trains have delayed arrival and departure time.

A private company in association with Indian Railways has started a free web site where passengers can input train number and arrival or destination City name. The result will give the arrival and destination time for the train at that particular station.

To monetize the Web Site they show relevant ads when the results are displayed for arrival and destination time.

They want Passengers to log on to website before the results can be shown. They don't want to maintain identity infrastructure for authentication. They want Passengers to log on to website with their social Accounts like Facebook, linkedin and Twitter etc before the results can be shown.

For website to authenticate Passengers using using social accounts they want to use modern and a light weight protocol.

Suggest a solution which satisfies above requirement

Solution

Oauth2 is a modern and lightweight identity or sign-in protocol.

We will use Oauth2 Authorization framework that will enable the application to obtain limited access to Passenger accounts on an HTTP service such as Facebook, linkedin & Twitter etc.

Using Oauth2 identity or sign-in protocol website need not maintain identity infrastructure for passenger authentication.

Managed Service Identity (MSI)

Before going into Managed Service Identity (MSI) let's discuss why we need it in first place. A common challenge when building cloud applications is how to securely manage the credentials that needs to be in your code for authenticating to cloud services. Adding security credentials in application code or applying to Azure VM is not only a security problem but also an operational & Administrative Overhead.

Let's take an Example. Dot NET application installed on Azure Windows VM wants to Access Azure Blob Storage. For Dot NET application to access Azure Blob Storage you need to enter Storage Account key in your application code. Entering Storage Account key in Azure Windows VM Dot NET application is a security loophole.

Managed Service Identity (MSI) solves this problem by giving Azure Resource (For example Azure VM) an automatically managed identity in Azure Active Directory (Azure AD). You can use this identity to authenticate to any Azure service that supports Azure AD authentication including Azure Storage without having any authorization credentials in your application code.

Defining Managed Service Identiy (MSI) in Simple term

When you enable Managed Service Identity (MSI) on an Azure Resource then an identity of that Resource is created in Azure AD. You can then use this identity to authenticate to any Azure service that supports Azure AD authentication without needing any authorization credentials in your application code.

When to use Managed Service Identity (MSI)

If your application running on Azure Resource (such as Virtual Machine) supports Managed Service Identity and it accesses resources that support Azure AD Authentication then Managed Service identity is a better option.

Azure Resources on which MSI can be enabled

Azure Virtual Machines | Virtual Machine Scale Set (VMSS) | Azure App Services
Azure Blueprints | Azure Functions | Azure Logic Apps
Azure Data Factory v2 | Azure API Management | Azure Container Instances

Azure Resources that support Azure AD authentication

The following services support Azure AD authentication request from Azure Resources that use Managed Service Identity.

Azure Resource Manager
Azure Key Vault
Azure Data Lake | Azure SQL | Azure Storage Blobs and Queues
Azure Event Hubs | Azure Service Bus | Azure Analysis Services

Example of MSI eliminating Administrative Overhead

Let's take an example of an application running in Azure VM that needs to retrieve some secrets from a Key Vault.

Without MSI you would need to create an identity for the application in Azure AD, set up credentials for that application (also known as creating a *service principal*), configure the application to know these credentials, and then communicate with Azure AD to exchange the credentials for a token that Key Vault will accept. This requires lot of Administrative overhead to configure the solutions.

Using MSI Azure VM automatically gets its own identity in Azure AD and the app can use its identity to retrieve a token from Azure AD that Key Vault will accept.

Exercise 60: Enabling MSI on Azure VMs

In this Exercise we will just demonstrate on how enable MSI on VM VMFE1. In Next Chapter we will actually enable MSI on VMFE1.

1. Go to Virtual Machine VMFE1 dashboard and click identity in left pane> In Right pane you can see that current the status is off.

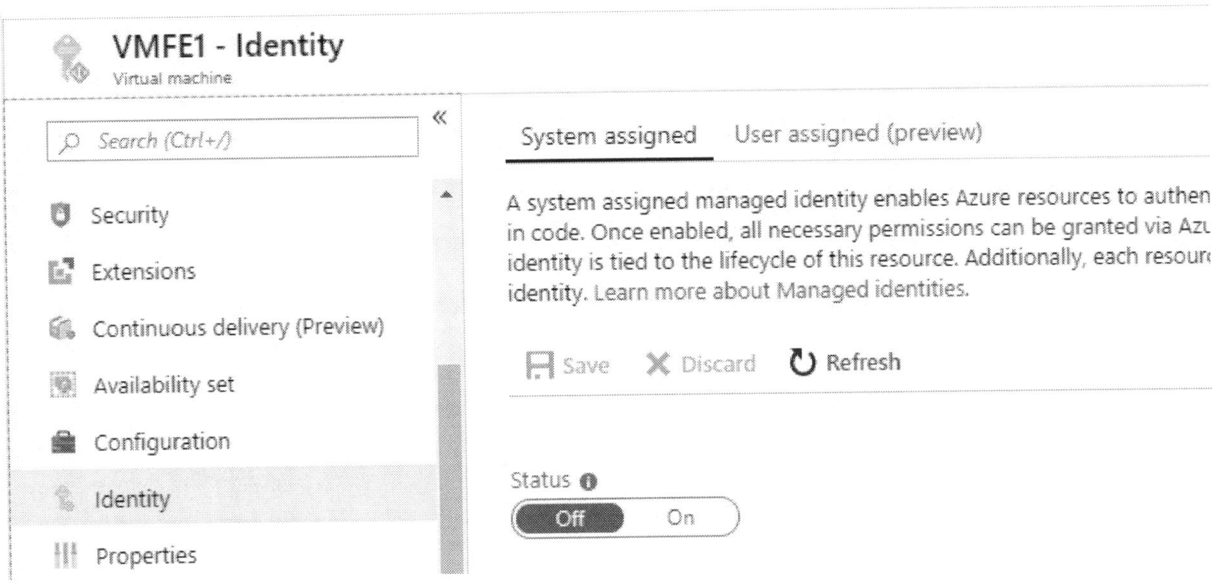

Click on>Click save>Click Yes. **Don't click Yes here. We will do this in next Chapter.**

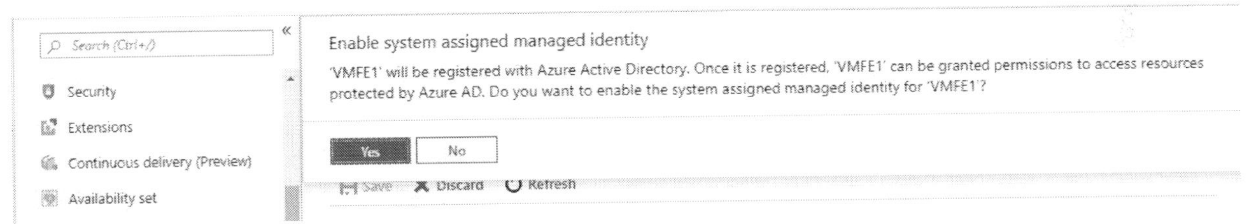

Result of Enabling MSI on Azure VM (Very Important)

<u>When MSI is enabled on Azure VM, Azure Resource Manager creates identity of the VM in Azure AD.</u>

After the identity is created in Azure AD, the credentials are provisioned onto the instance. Azure Resource Manager configures the Service Principal details of the MSI VM Extension in the VM by configuring **client ID** and **certificate** used by the extension to get access tokens from Azure AD.

Step By Step Azure AD MSI Working after MSI is enabled on Azure Resource

Figure below shows working of MSI when MSI is enabled on Azure VM.

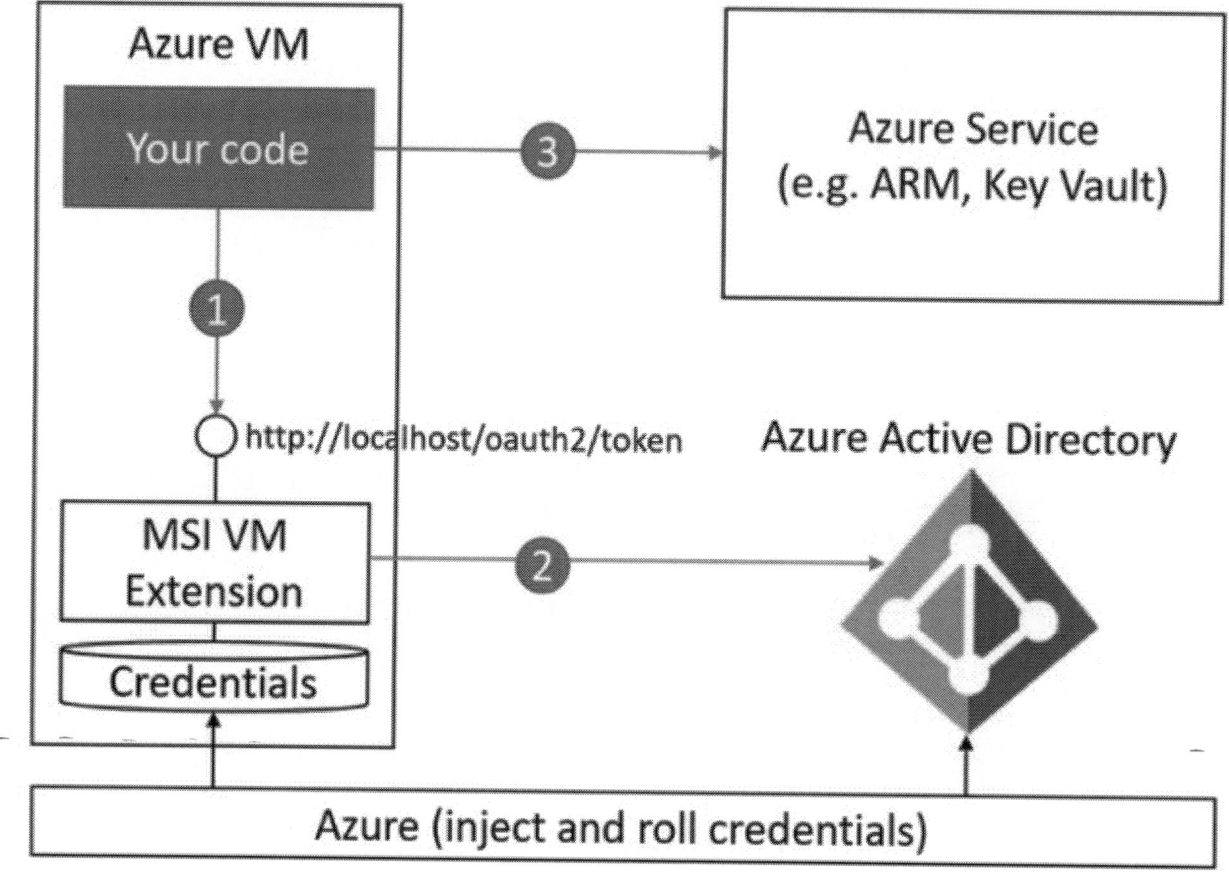

1. When The Azure VM needs to authenticate to Azure Resource, Your code running on the VM requests a token from a local endpoint that is hosted by the MSI VM extension by sending request @ http://localhost/oauth2/token
2. The MSI VM Extension uses its configured client ID and certificate to request an access token from Azure AD. Azure AD returns a JSON Web Token (JWT) access token.
3. Your code sends the access token on a call to a service that supports Azure AD authentication. **You also need to grant access right in target resource for Azure VM.**

Managed Service Identity Pricing

MSI is part of Azure AD. There is no additional cost for Managed Service Identity.

Note: MSI VM Extension is getting deprecated. It is being replaced by Azure Instance Metadata Service (IMDS) as shown below.

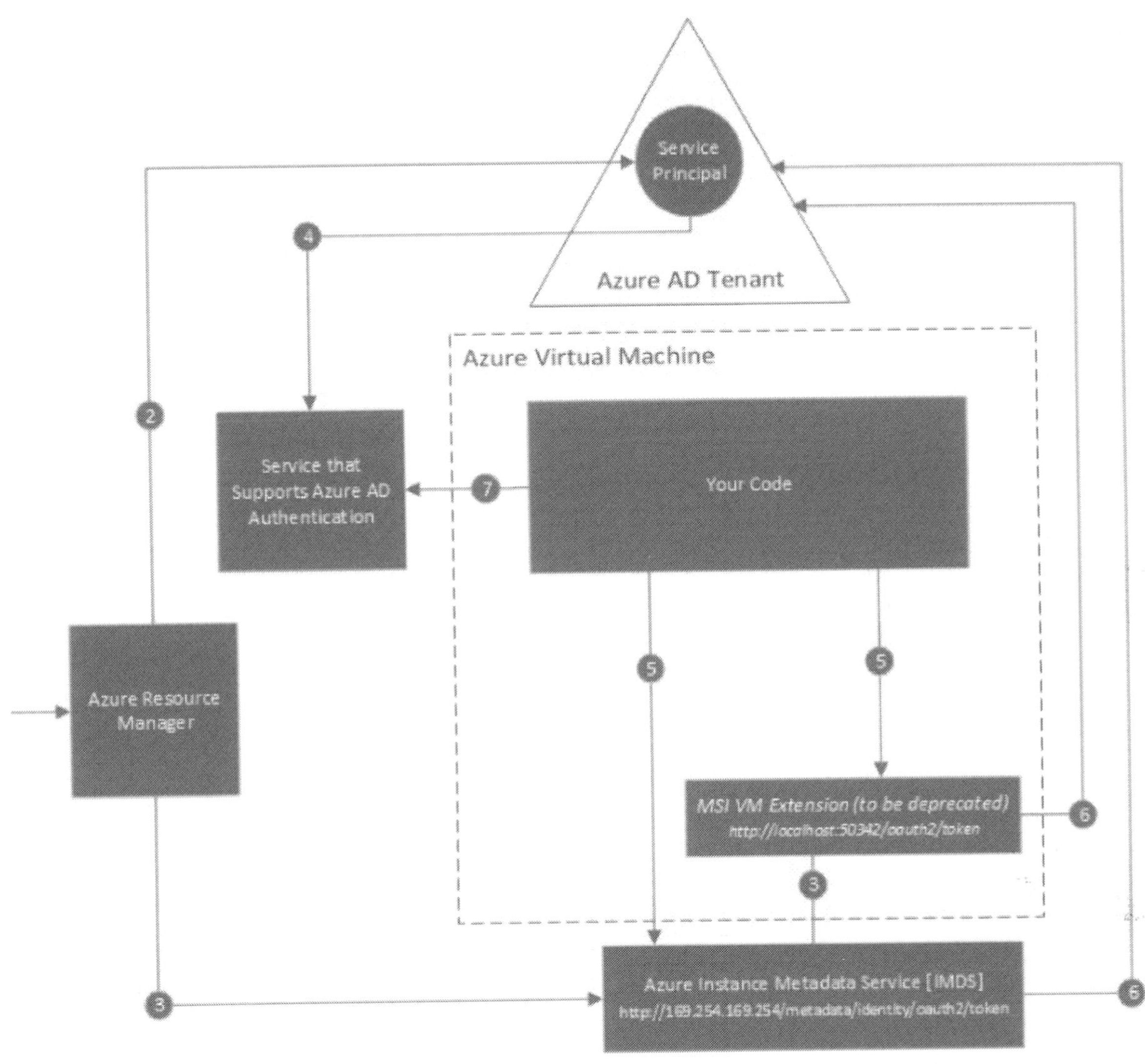

Note: In next Chapter we have a Key Vault Exercise using MSI. This will clear your doubts about MSI.

Service Principal

An Azure Service Principal is a security identity used by user-created apps & services to access specific Azure resources. **This Identity is created in Azure AD.** You can then assign required permissions to Service Principal at Resource or Resource Group or Subscription level using Azure AD Role based Access control feature.

A Service Principal is a type of security principal that represents an application. The service principal provides an identity for your application in Azure AD, allowing you to delegate only the necessary permissions to that service principal using Azure AD Role based Access control feature.

In Short you can define Service Principal as follows:
Identity for an Application in Azure AD is known as Service Principal. You can then assign the required permissions to the service principal.

Service Principal Values to be Added in the Application Code

You need to add following Service Princial Values, Tenant & Subscription ID in your application code to Access Azure Resources.

- Application ID
- Client Secret
- Tenant ID
- Subscription ID

Exercise 61: Generating Service Principal Values

Step 1: Register an App in Azure AD to Generate Application ID and Client Secret

1. In Azure AD dashboard Click App Registrations in left pane> In Right pane Click +New Registration>Register an Application Blade opens>enter a name and rest select all default Values>Click Register.

Register an application

* Name

The user-facing display name for this application (this can be changed later).

AR410

Supported account types

Who can use this application or access this API?

(•) Accounts in this organizational directory only (harinderkohlioutlook (Default Directory) only - Single tenant)

( ) Accounts in any organizational directory (Any Azure AD directory - Multitenant)

( ) Accounts in any organizational directory (Any Azure AD directory - Multitenant) and personal Microsoft accounts (e.g. Skype, Xbox)

Help me choose...

Redirect URI (optional)

We'll return the authentication response to this URI after successfully authenticating the user. Providing this now is optional and it can be

By proceeding, you agree to the Microsoft Platform Policies

Register

Note: This step will generate identity for an Application in Azure AD.

2. Figure below shows the dashboard of App Registered with Azure AD. **Note down the Application Id.**

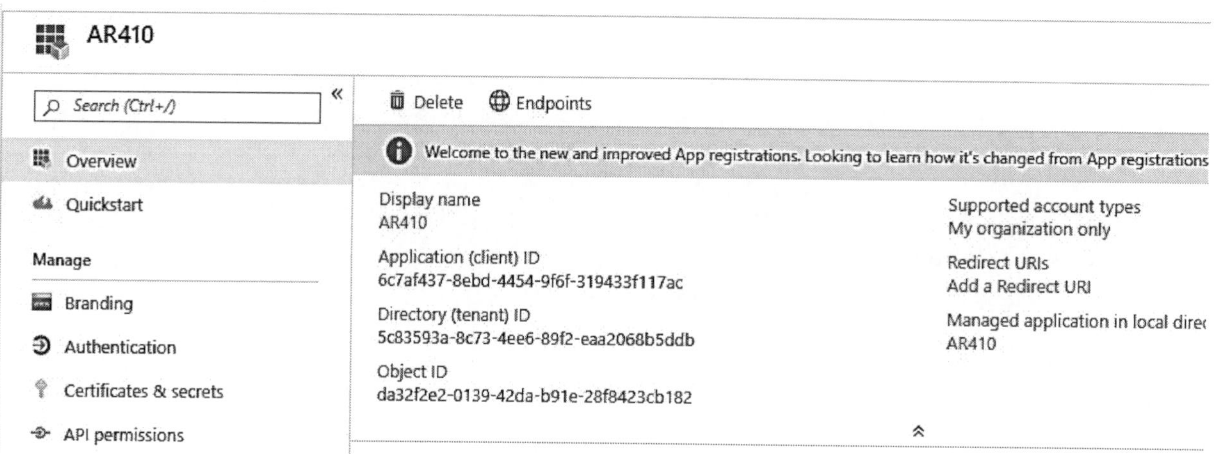

3. In your registered app dashboard click Certificates & Secrets in left pane> Under Client Secrets Click New client secret> Add a client secret blade opens>enter a Description and select duration

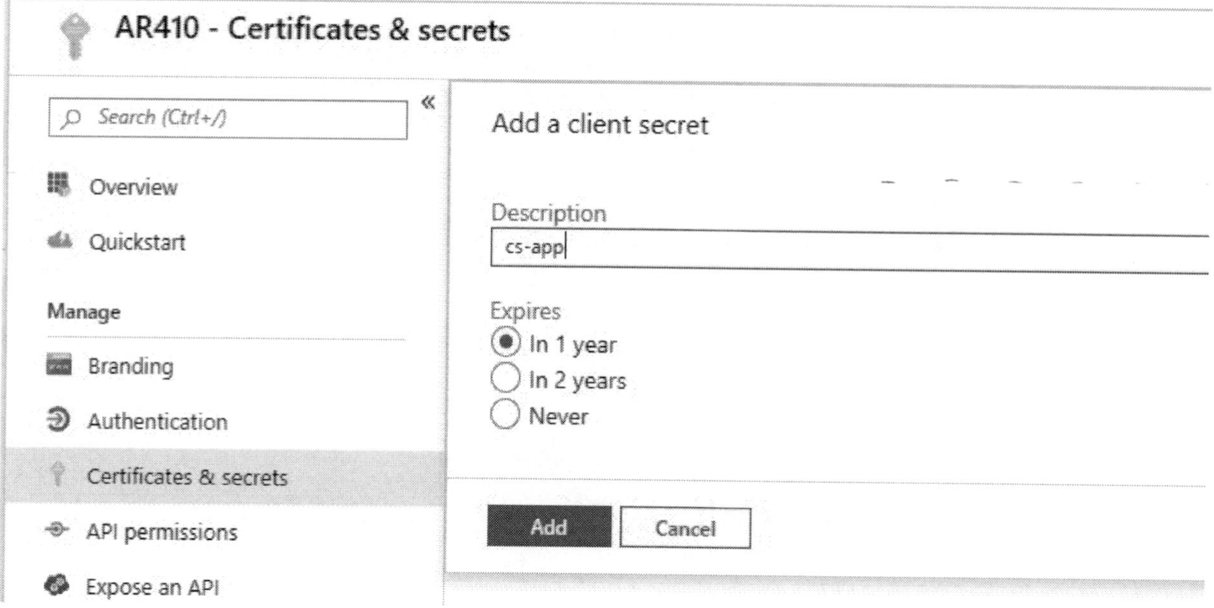

4. Click Add and a value generated. Note down the value. This will be your **client secret.**

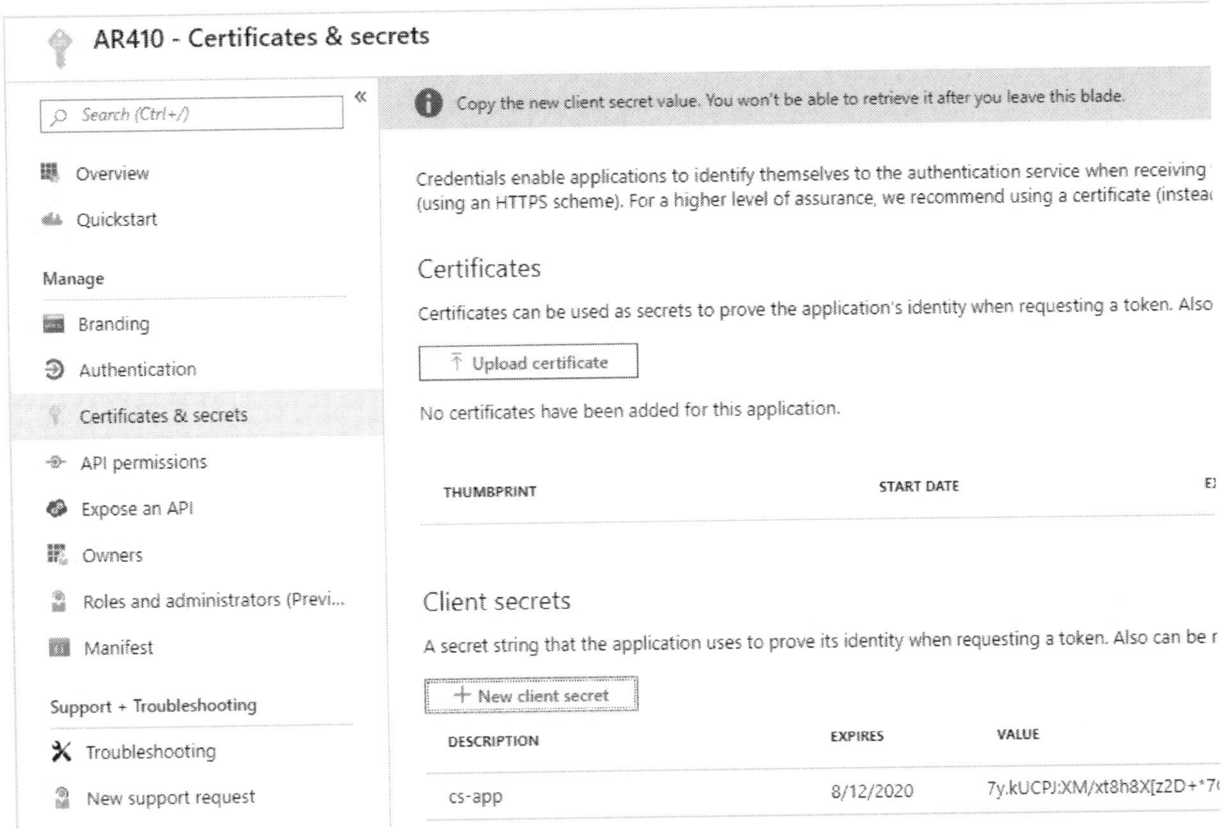

Note: Copy the new client secret value. You won't be able to retrieve it after you leave this blade.

Step 2: Note Down Tenant ID

In Azure AD Dashboard Scroll down and click properties in left pane> In Right pane note down the Directory ID. Directory ID is Tenant ID.

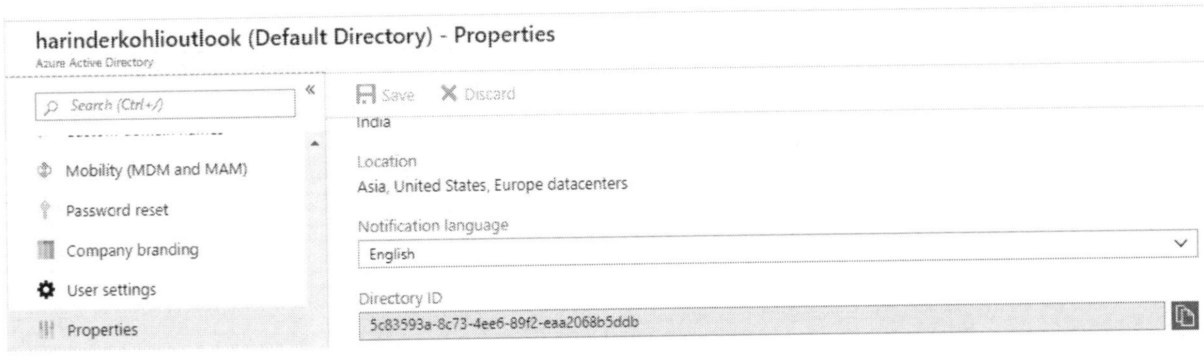

Step 3: Note Down Subscription ID

In Azure Portal Click Cost Management + Billing in left pane> Cost Management + Billing Dashboard opens> In Right pane click your subscription>Subscription Dashboard opens>In Right pane nore down the Subscription ID.

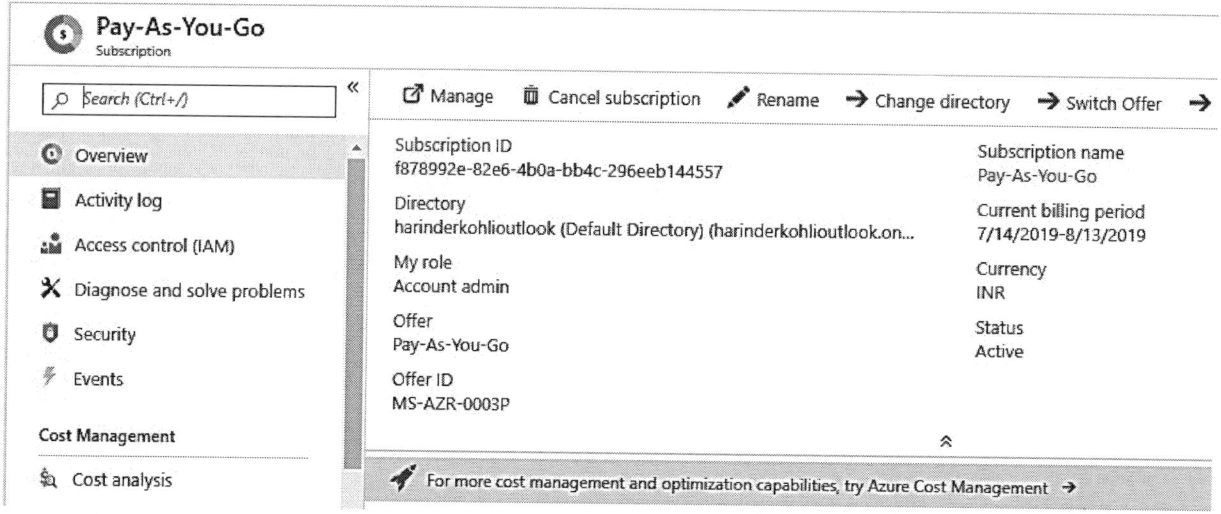

Step 4: Assign the Application AR410 to a Role

Access to Azure resources by users and applications is authorized through Role-Based Access Control (RBAC). To allow an application to access resources in your subscription using its service principal, you must assign the service principal to a role for a specific resource. Specific Resource can be Subscription or Resource Group or an Azure Resource.

You can assign the application to a role at subscription or Resource Group or at Resource level. In this Exercise we will Assign **Application AR410 to a Role at Subscription level.** Application AR410 was registered with Azure AD in step 1.

1. Navigate to the resource you wish to allow the service principal to access. In this example we are assigning the service principal to a role at the subscription level. We will go to the Subscription Dashboard. Step 3 showed how to go to subscription dashboard.

2. Go to Subscription Dashboard and Click **Access control (IAM)** in left pane>In right pane click Add a Role Assignment>Add a Role Assignment blade opens>Select a role from Dropdown box>In Assign Access select Azure AD user, group or Service Principal> In Select box enter AR410 and in result click AR410>Click save.

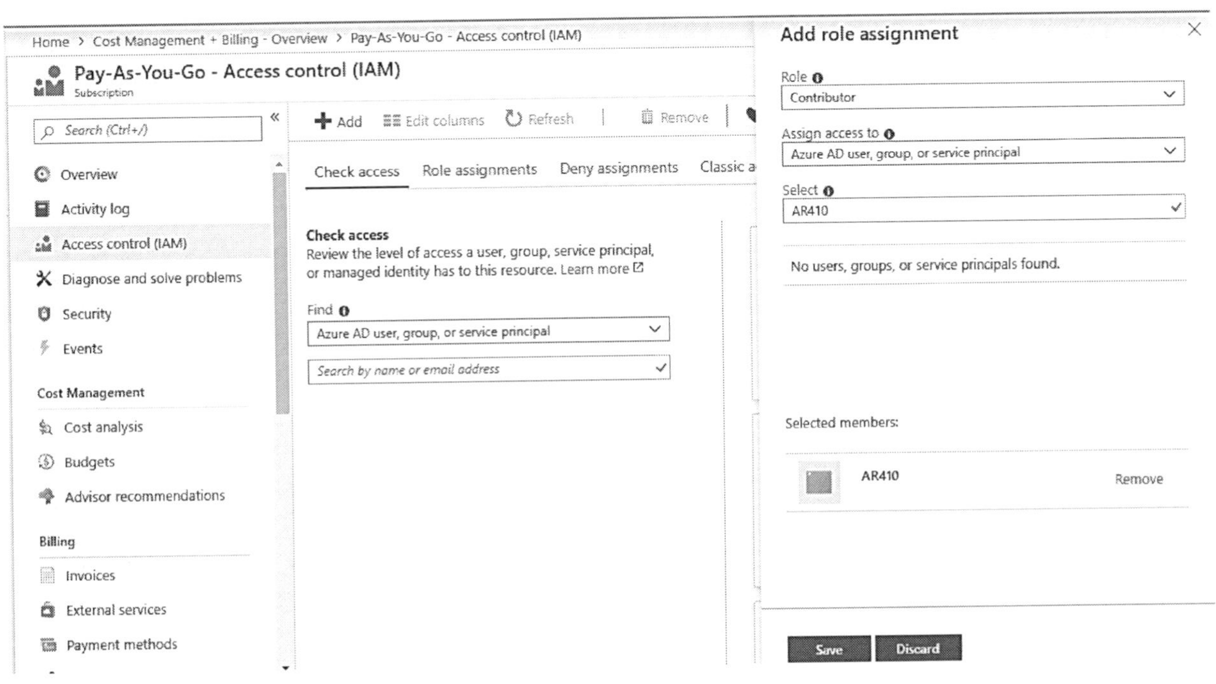

Step 5: In your Application code Add Service Principal Values

In your Application code Add following Service Principal Values:

- Application ID (Generated in Step 1)
- Client Secret (Generated in Step 1)
- Tenant ID (Generated in Step 2)
- Subscription ID (Generated in Step 3)

Note 1: You can see from the above exercise that you need Multiple steps if we use Service Principal option. This increases the Administrative overhead.

Note 2: MS recommends to use MSI option instead of Service Principal option.

Note 3: In next Chapter we have a Key Vault Exercise using MSI & Service Principal. This will clear your doubts about MSI & Service Principal.

Managed Service Identity or Service Principal

Microsoft Recommends enabling and using Managed Service Identity for Azure Resources to represent Application identity instead of creating Service Principal for your application identity.

When to use Managed Service Identity (MSI)

If your application running on Azure Resource (such as Virtual Machine) supports Managed Service Identity and it accesses resources that support Azure AD Authentication then Managed Service identity is a better option.

Chapter 5 Implement Secure Data Solutions

This Chapter covers following

- Containers
- Virtual Machines V/S Containers
- What is required to run Containers
- Benefits of Container Technology
- Drawbacks of Container Technology
- Container Deployment Options in Azure
- Deploying Containers on Azure Ubuntu Linux VM
- Azure Container Instances
- Azure Web App for Containers
- Azure Container Service (ACS)
- Azure Kubernetes Service (AKS)

This Chapter Covers following Lab Exercises to build below topology

- Deploying Containers on Azure Ubuntu Linux VM
- Deploying Container Instances
- Deploying Web App for Containers
- Deploying Azure Kubernetes Services

Chapter Topology

In this chapter we will add Key Vault to the topology.

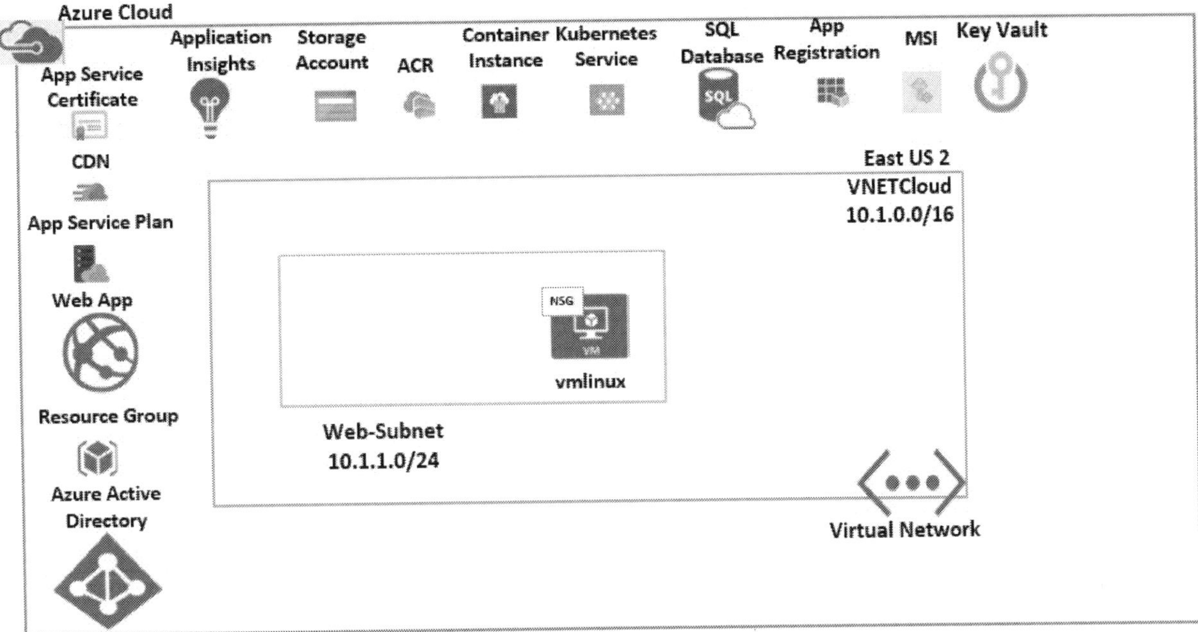

Encryption at Rest

Encryption at rest provides data protection for stored data (at rest). Encryption at rest is designed to prevent the attacker from accessing the unencrypted data by ensuring the data is encrypted when on disk.

The Encryption at Rest design in Azure uses symmetric encryption to encrypt and decrypt data. With Symmetric Encryption same key is used for encryption and decryption. Symmetric encryption keys are often encrypted with asymmetric encryption to further limit access.

Note 1: Asymmetric Encryption uses Public Key to encrypt and Private Key to Decrypt.
Note 2: Symmetric Encryption uses same key for encryption and decryption.

Encryption at rest options for Azure Storage

Storage Service Encryption is always enabled and automatically encrypts storage service data when writing it to Azure Storage.
Client-side encryption encrypts the data before it's transferred into Storage and decrypts the data after it is transferred out of Storage.
Azure Disk Encryption enables you to encrypt the OS disks and data disks of Azure VMs.

Encryption at rest options for Azure SQL Database

Refer to Chapter 3 Azure SQL Database.

Data Encryption Models in Azure

- Server-side encryption using Microsoft Managed keys.
- Server-side encryption using customer-managed keys in Azure Key Vault.
- Server-side encryption using customer-managed keys on customer-controlled hardware.
- Client-side encryption.

Client side Encryption Model

Client Encryption refers to encryption that is performed outside of Azure by the application. The encryption can be performed by the service application in Azure or by an application running in the customer data center.

Client-side encryption encrypts the data before it's transferred into Storage and decrypts the data after it is transferred out of Storage.

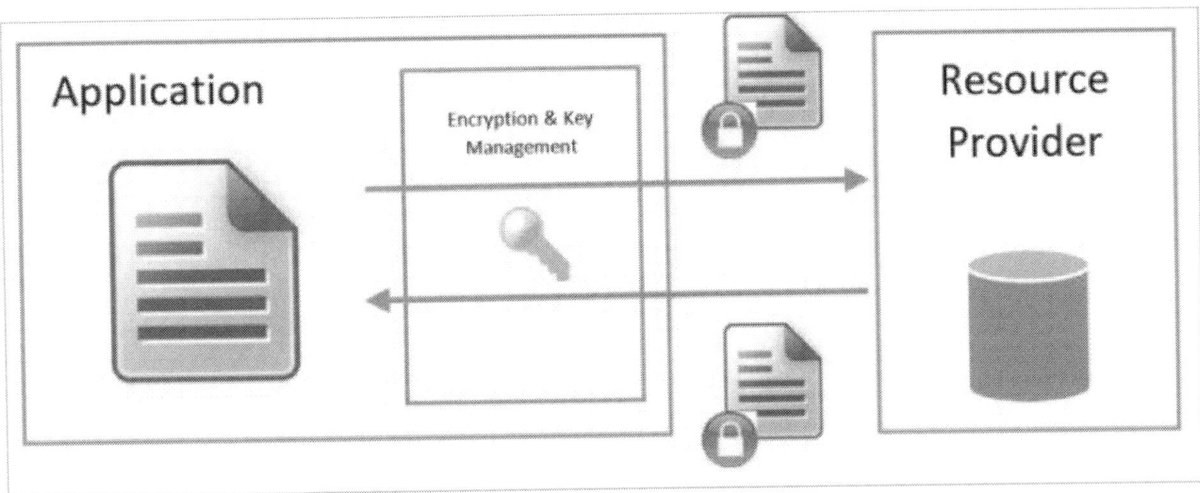

Server-side encryption model

Server-side Encryption models refer to encryption that is performed by the Azure service. In this model the Resource Provider performs encrypt and decrypt operations. The Resource Provider might use encryption keys that are managed by Microsoft or by the customer depending on the provided configuration.

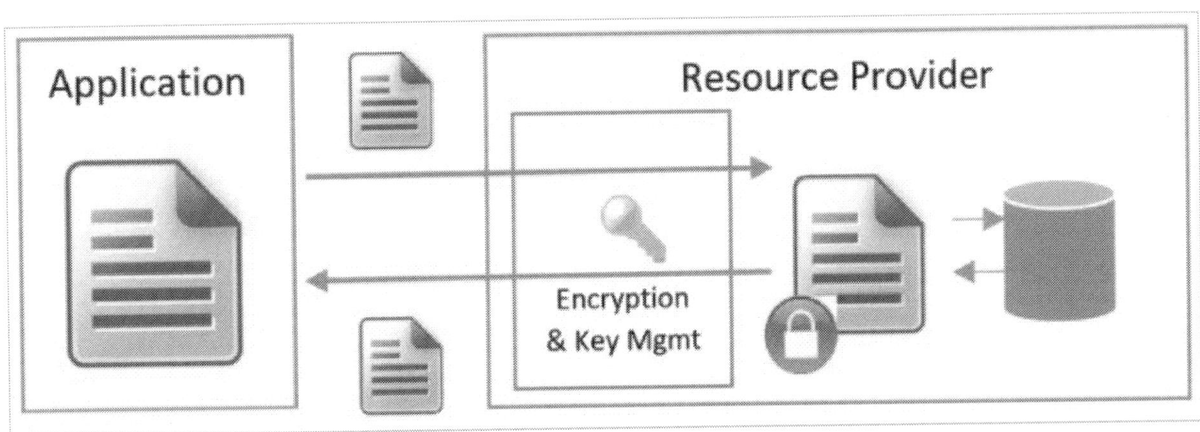

Azure Storage Service encryption (Server-side encryption)

Azure Storage Account automatically encrypts your data in the cloud. Data in Azure Storage Account is encrypted and decrypted transparently using 256-bit AES encryption.
You can either use Microsoft-managed keys for the encryption of your storage account or you can manage encryption with your own keys using Azure Key Vault.

By default, your storage account uses Microsoft-managed encryption keys for encrypting data at rest for Blobs, Files, Tables and Queues. For Blobs and Files you have the option to bring your own key for encryption. Tables and Queues will always use Microsoft Managed Keys.

Azure Storage encryption is enabled for all new and existing storage accounts and cannot be disabled. Because your data is secured by default, you don't need to modify your code or applications to take advantage of Azure Storage encryption.

With Azure Storage encryption all Azure Storage accounts and the resources they contain are encrypted including the page blobs that back Azure virtual machine disks.

Exercise 62: Checking Storage Service Encryption (MS Managed Keys)

In this exercise we will use Storage Account sastdcloud. sastdcloud was created in Exercise 69, chapter 8 in Exam AZ-300 & AZ-301 Study & Lab Guide Part 1.

Go to Storage Account sastdcloud dashboard> Click Encryption in left pane>In Right pane you can see it is written **"By default, data is encrypted using Microsoft Managed Keys for Azure Blobs, Tables, Files and Queues."**

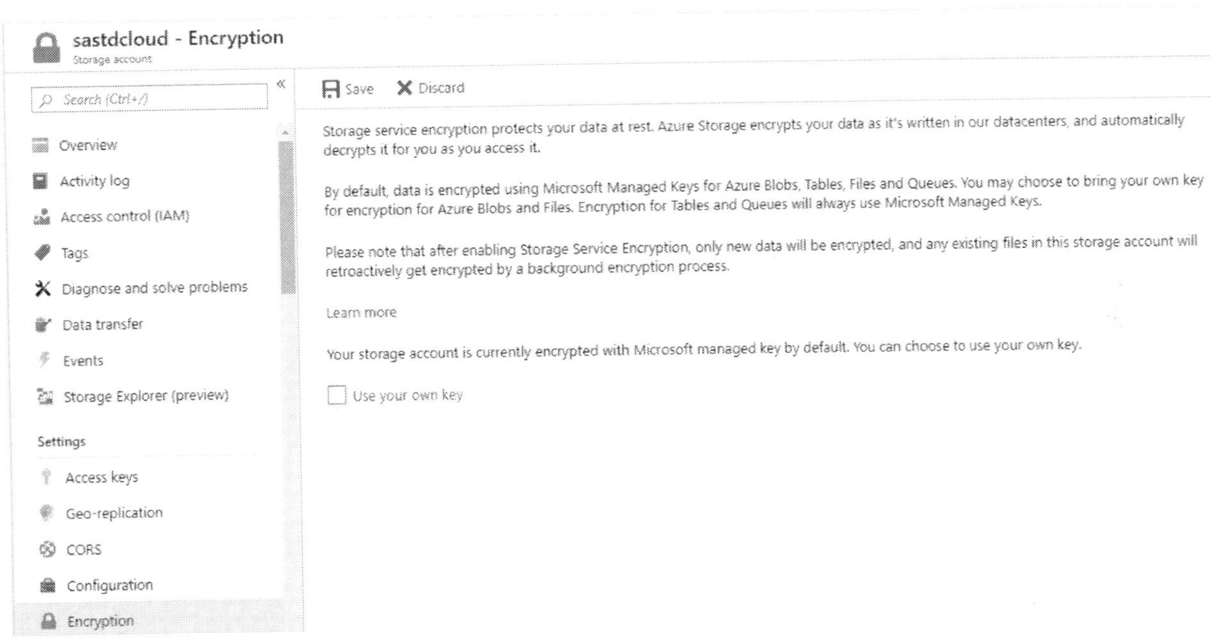

Note the Option **Use your own key**. We will use this option in Exercise 64 (in this chapter) to encrypt the Storage Account using Key Vault.

Azure Disk Encryption

Azure Disk Encryption encrypts your Azure Windows VM and Azure Linux VM disks. Disk Encryption leverages **BitLocker** feature of Windows and the **DM-Crypt** feature of Linux to provide volume encryption for the OS and data disks.

BitLocker is an industry-recognized Windows volume encryption technology that is used to enable disk encryption on Windows IaaS VMs.

DM-Crypt is the Linux-based, transparent disk-encryption subsystem that is used to enable disk encryption on Linux IaaS VMs.

The solution is integrated with Azure Key Vault to help you Protect and manage the disk encryption keys (windows VM) and secrets (Linux VM) in your key vault subscription.

You can use Azure Command Line interface (CLI), Azure PowerShell or Azure Resource Manager templates to encrypt an Azure VM Disks.

Figure below shows step by step configuration of Disk Encryption.

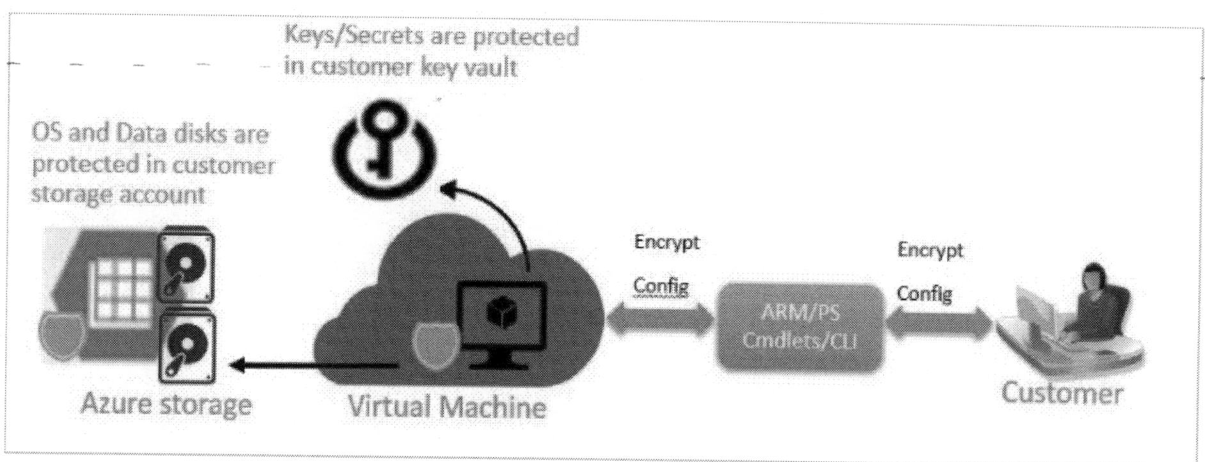

Design Nugget: VM Disk encryption feature encrypts VM disks using Customer managed keys.

Design Nugget: By default Storage Service encryption (SSE) feature encrypts data at rest for all VM disks stored in Storage Account using Azure Managed keys. You have the option of using your own keys.

If you use Azure Security Center, you're alerted if you have VMs that aren't encrypted.

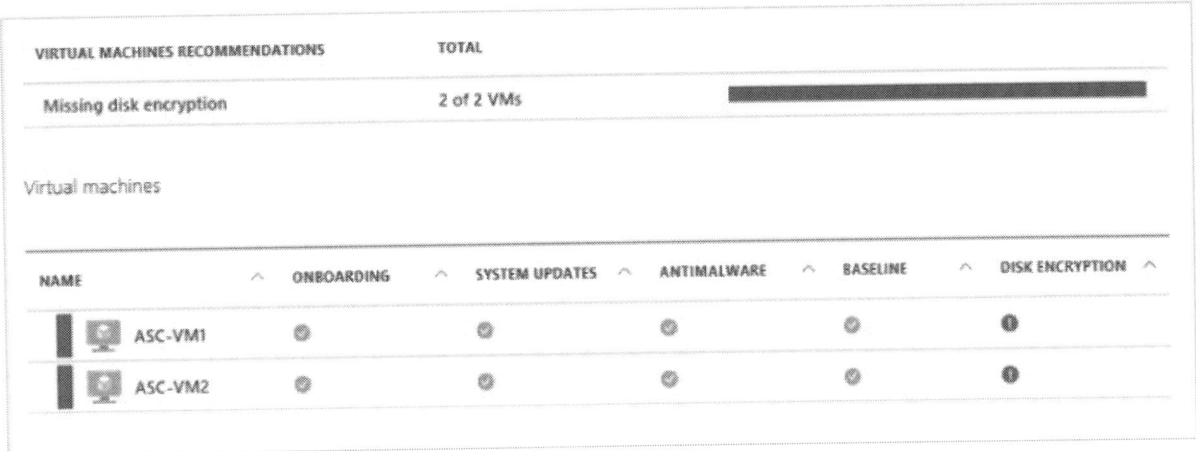

Difference between Storage Service Encryption and Disk encryption

SSE happens at Storage Account level and Disk Encryption happens at VM Disk Level.

With Azure Storage encryption, all Azure Storage accounts and the resources they contain are encrypted, including the page blobs that back Azure virtual machine disks.

Additionally, Azure virtual machine disks may be encrypted with Azure Disk Encryption. Azure Disk Encryption uses industry-standard BitLocker on Windows and DM-Crypt on Linux to provide operating system-based encryption solutions that are integrated with Azure Key Vault.

Encryption in transit for Azure Storage

Encryption in transit is a mechanism of protecting data when it's transmitted across networks.

You have following 3 options to secure Data going in and out of Azure Storage:

- **Transport-level encryption** uses HTTPS for secure transfer of data into or out of Azure Storage.
- **Client-side encryption** encrypts the data before it's transferred into Storage and decrypts the data after it is transferred out of Storage.
- **Wire encryption** such as SMB 3.0 encryption of Azure file shares. This feature is required when Mounting Azure File shares on Servers located in another Azure region or on-premises. Note that mounting Azure File shares in another region and on-premises happens over internet.

Transport Level Encryption using HTTPS

HTTPS protocol ensures secure and encrypted communication over the public Internet.

You can enforce the use of HTTPS when calling objects in storage accounts by enabling **Secure transfer required** for the storage account. Connections using HTTP will be refused once this is enabled.

The "Secure transfer required" option enhances the security of your storage account by only allowing requests to the account from secure connections. For example, when you're calling REST APIs to access your storage account, you must connect by using HTTPS. "Secure transfer required" rejects requests that use HTTP.

Note 1: By default, the "Secure transfer required" option is enabled when you create a storage account in Azure Portal.
Note 2: By default, the "Secure transfer required" option is disabled when you create a storage account with SDK.

Exercise 63: Checking Status of Secure Transfer Required

In this exercise we will use Storage Account sastdcloud. sastdcloud was created in Exercise 69, chapter 8 in Exam AZ-300 & AZ-301 Study & Lab Guide Part 1.

Go to Storage Account sastdcloud dashboard> Click Configuration in left pane >In Right pane you can see Secure Transfer required is enabled by default.

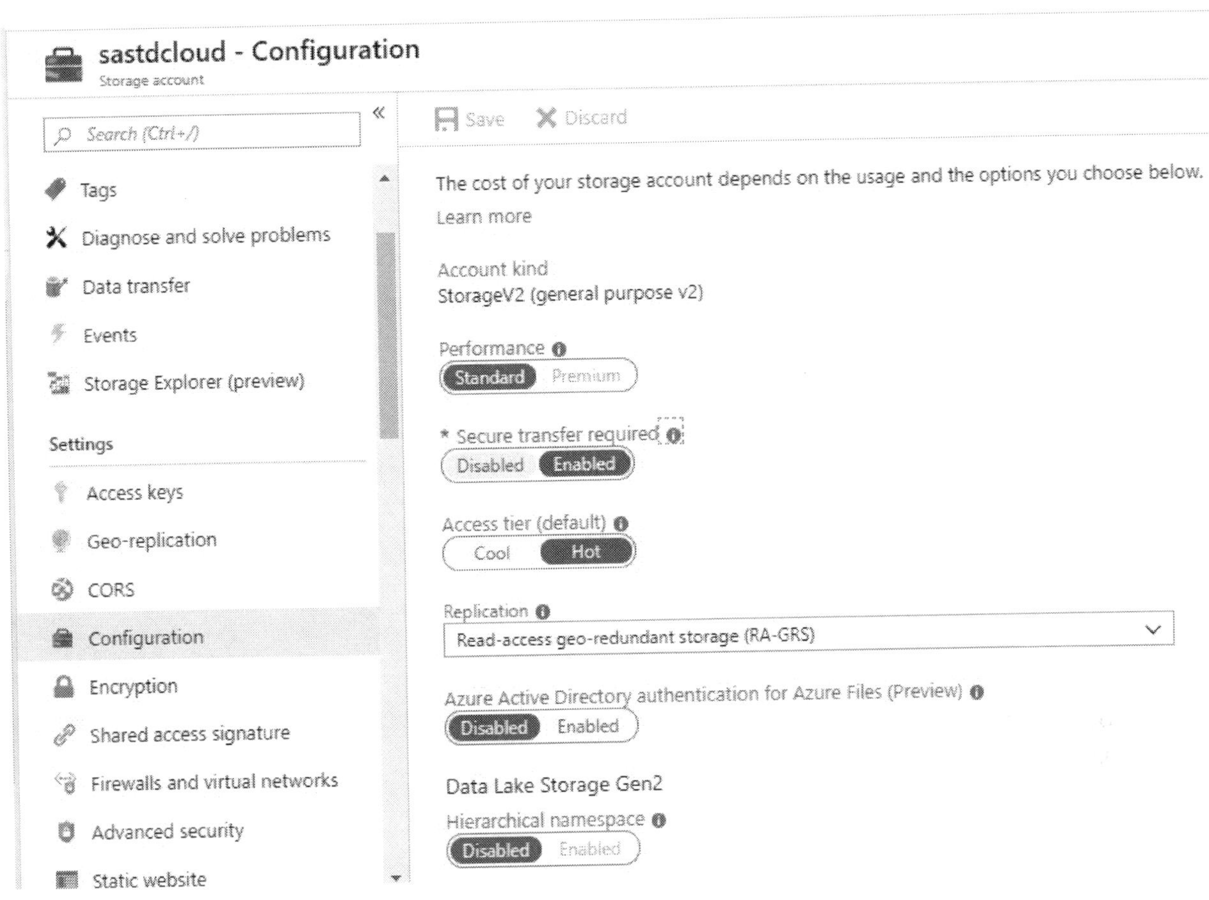

Note: Enable Secure Transfer Required also enables SMB 3.0 encryption for Azure file shares.

TLS/SSL Communication

Transport Layer Security (TLS)/**Secure Sockets Layer** (SSL) are cryptographic protocols designed to provide **communications security** over a computer network. They are widely used in applications such as web browsing, email, instant messaging, and voice over IP (VoIP). It is widely used in internet where Websites use TLS to encrypt all communications between servers and web browsers.

Note: SSL is now deprecated but is interchangeably used for TLS.

TLS & HTTPS

HTTPS is HTTP protocol with a layer of TLS on top of it. HTTPS is used by websites for secure communication between websites and browsers.

TLS Working

The TLS protocol aims to provide **data privacy**, **data integrity & mutual authentication** between two or more communicating computer applications.

Data Privacy: Data remains private or secure because symmetric cryptography is used to encrypt the data transmitted. The keys for this symmetric encryption are generated uniquely for each connection and are based on a shared secret that was negotiated at the start of the session (TLS handshake).

Mutual Authentication: TLS handshake also handles authentication, which consists of the server proving its identity to the client. This is done using public key cryptography.

Data Integrity: Once data is encrypted and authenticated, it is then signed with a message authentication code (MAC). MAC ensures that no alteration of the data has happened during transmission.

Note: Enabling HTTPS on Website for Secure communication between Website and Client Browser is an example of TLS/SSL Communication. Refer to exercise 10, 11 & 12 in Chapter 1 where we enabled HTTPS on Web App HKWA1 using App Service Certificate.

Azure confidential Computing

Azure Confidential Computing is aimed at protecting data while it's processed in the cloud.

Azure Confidential Computing is bringing Trusted Execution Environments (TEEs) such as Intel SGX and Virtualization Based Security (VBS - previously known as Virtual Secure mode) to the cloud. TEEs protect data being processed from access outside the TEE.

To know more about Azure Confidential Computing read the Azure blog post available at following link.
https://azure.microsoft.com/en-us/blog/azure-confidential-computing/

Azure Key Vault

Before going into Key Vault, let's discuss why we need it in first place. A common challenge when building cloud applications is how to securely manage the Security Keys or secret that needs to be in your code for authenticating to another application or service. Adding security credentials in application code is not only a security problem but also an operational & Administrative Overhead.

Azure Key Vault provides key management as a service.

Azure Key Vault stores and safeguard cryptographic keys, secrets and certificates used by cloud applications and services for authentication and encryption of data.

Keys are stored in a Key vault and invoked by URL when needed by applications. Keys are safeguarded by Azure, using industry-standard algorithms, key lengths, and hardware security modules (HSMs).

Key Vaults provides following 3 options to protect your sensitive data:

Keys: Key Vault supports RSA (2048, 3072 & 4096 bit) and Elliptic Curve keys only. Keys can be generated by the Key Vault or can be imported. Keys can be software-protected or HSM- Protected. **Keys are used for encryption and decryption.**

Secrets: Key Vault accepts any value as a secret, and these are stored in binary. **Example of Secret can be Database Connection Identifier which you want to protect.**

Certificates: Using key Vauly you can create self-signed or signed by a supported certificate authority or you can import a certificate. **Certificates are commonly used for enabling HTTPS secure access and for Authentication.**

Design Nugget

Azure key vault works on a per region basis. What this means is that an Azure key vault resource should be provisioned at the same region where the application and service is deployed. If a deployment consists of more than one region and needs services from Azure key vault, multiple Azure key vault instances should be provisioned.

Key Vault Advantages

1. When you change the security key or secret you not need redeploy application as application get the updated key or secret from the Azure Key Vault automatically.

2. You can separate the application administration function and security administration function. Security can now be centrally managed by the Security operations team.

3. Azure Key vault provides additional security ability by granting access to keys only to application which are registered with Azure AD.

Key Vault Features

1. **Encrypt keys and small secrets** like passwords using keys in Hardware Security Modules (HSMs).
2. **Import or generate your keys in HSMs certified to FIPS 140-2 level 2 standards** for added assurance, so that your keys stay within the HSM boundary.
3. **Simplify and automate tasks** for SSL/TLS certificates, enroll and automatically renew certificates from supported public certification authorities(CA).
4. **Manage and automatically rotate** Azure Storage account keys, and use shared access signatures to avoid direct contact with the keys.
5. **Provision and deploy new vaults and keys in minutes** without waiting for procurement, hardware, or IT, and centrally manage keys, secrets, and policies.
6. **Maintain control over encrypted data**—grant and revoke key use by both your own and third-party applications as needed.
7. **Segregate key management** duties to enable developers to easily manage keys used for dev/test, and migrate seamlessly to production keys managed by security operations.
8. **Rapidly scale** to meet the cryptographic needs of your cloud applications and match peak demand.
9. **Achieve global redundancy** by provisioning vaults in Azure datacenters worldwide, and keep a copy in your own HSM for added durability.

Software-Protected and HSM-Protected Keys

Key Vault stores Secrets, Keys and Certificated in Hardware Security Module (HSM).

With **Software-Protected keys**, Secrets, Keys and Certificates are stored in Hardware Security Module (HSM) but cryptographic operations (encryption and decryption) are performed in software.

With **HSM-Protected Keys** not only Secrets, Keys and Certificates are stored in Hardware Security Module (HSM) but cryptographic operations (encryption and decryption) are also performed directly on Hardware Security Module (HSM). Using Azure Key Vault, you can import or generate keys in hardware security modules (HSMs) that never leave the HSM boundary.

Use case for Software-Protected keys: Software-protected keys are used for test & development workloads.

Use case for HSM-Protected keys: HSM-Protected keys are preferred for production workloads.

Design Nugget 1: Azure Key Vault uses Thales nShield family of HSMs to protect your keys.
Design Nugget 2: To generate HSM-Protected keys you need Azure Key Vault Premium Tier.
Design Nugget 3: Software keys can be exported from key Vault whereas HSM keys can never be exported.

Hardware Security Module (HSM)

A **hardware security module (HSM)** is a physical computing device that safeguards and manages digital keys for strong authentication and provides cryptoprocessing.
HSMs possess controls that provide tamper evidence such as logging and alerting and tamper resistance such as deleting keys upon tamper detection. Each module contains one or more secure cryptoprocessor chips to prevent tampering and bus probing.

Using Keys with Key Vault

Keys are used for encryption and decryption.

Azure Key vault supports RSA and Elliptic Curve keys.

Azure Key Vault Supports RSA key size of 2048 bit, 3072 bit and to 4096 bit.

Exercise 64: Azure Storage Service Encryption (customer-managed keys)

In This Exercise we will encrypt storage account sastdcloud. sastdcloud was created in Exercise 69, chapter 8 in Exam AZ-300 & AZ-301 Study & Lab Guide Part 1.

We will first create Azure Key Vault. We will then create RSA key. The same key RSA key will be used for encryption and decryption of Storage Account.

1. **Create Key Vault:** In Azure Portal Click **All Services**>Security>Key Vaults> All Key Vaults pane opens > click + Add> Create Key Vault blade opens> Enter a name>In Resource Group Select RGCloud> In Location select East US 2>Rest select all default values>Click create.

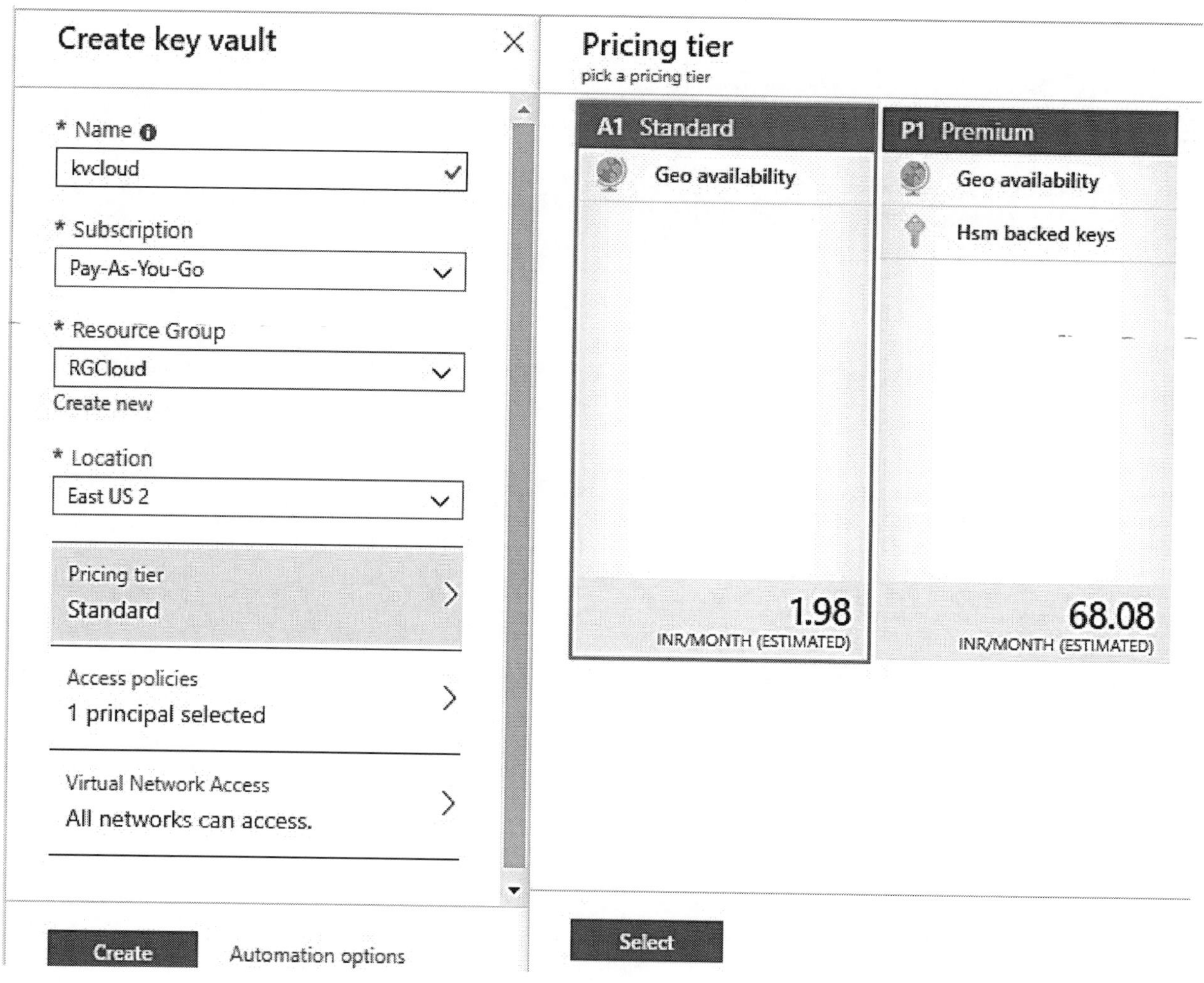

2. Figure below shows dashboard of Key Vault kvcloud.

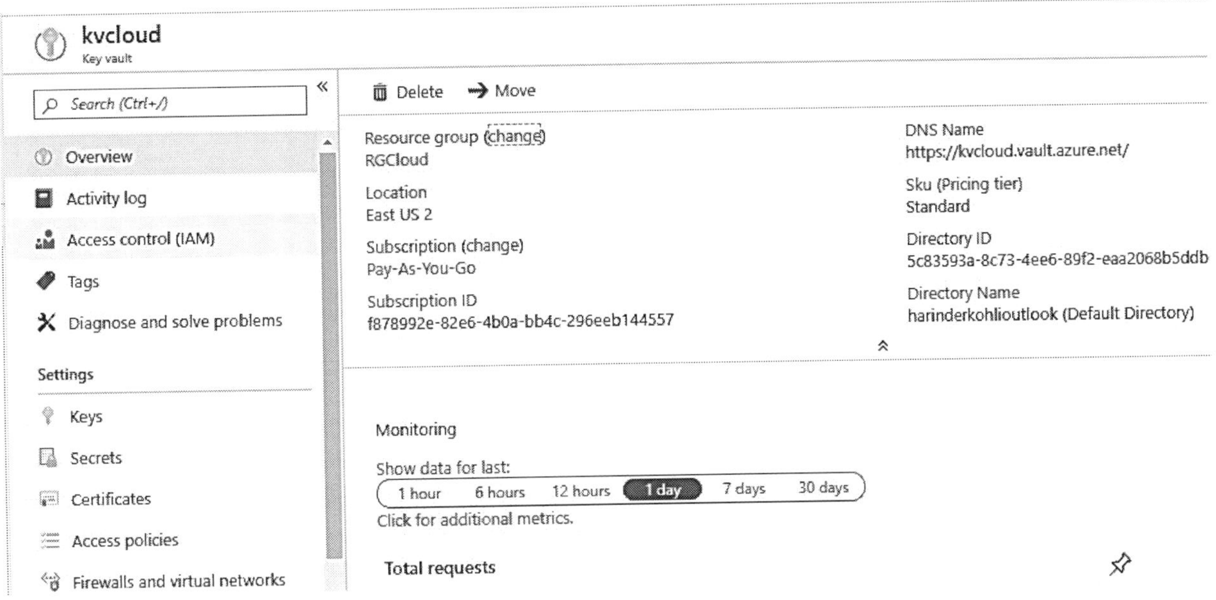

3. **Create RSA Keys:** In Key Vaults dashboard click Keys in left pane>In Right pane click + Generate/Import>Create a key blade opens>Enter a name>Key type select RSA>Key Size 2048>Click Yes for enabled>Click create (Not shown).

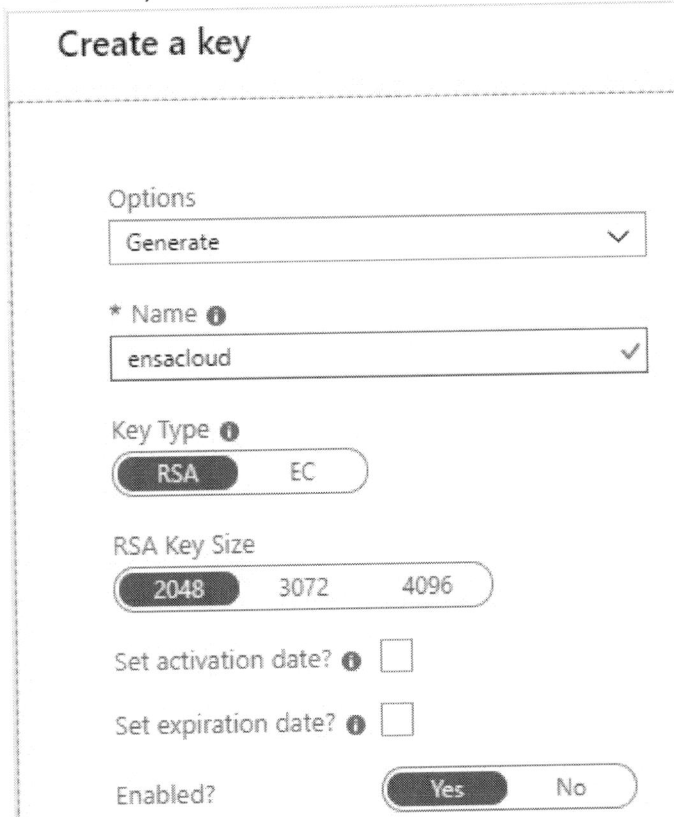

4. Figure below shows the key created in step 3.

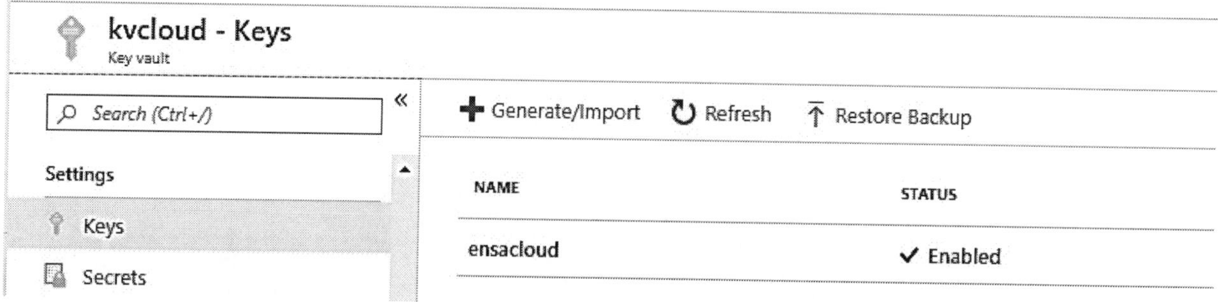

5. Click on the Key ensacloud>Click on the Key Version> Key version Dashboard opens>**Copy the Key Identifier URL.**

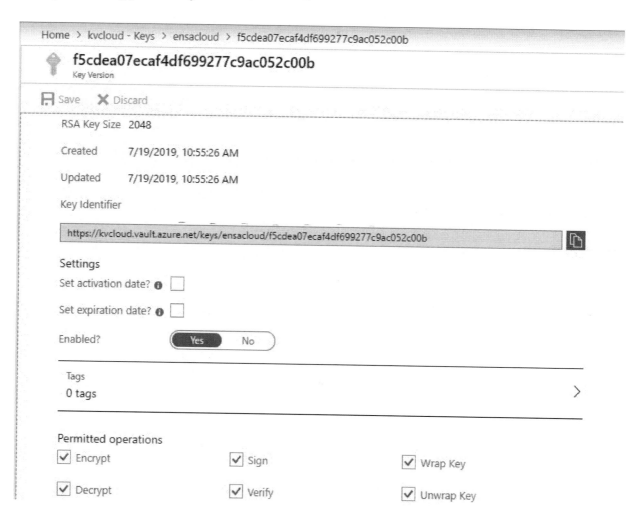

Home > kvcloud - Keys > ensacloud > f5cdea07ecaf4df699277c9ac052c00b

f5cdea07ecaf4df699277c9ac052c00b

Key Version

Save Discard

RSA Key Size 2048

Created 7/19/2019, 10:55:26 AM

Updated 7/19/2019, 10:55:26 AM

Key Identifier

https://kvcloud.vault.azure.net/keys/ensacloud/f5cdea07ecaf4df699277c9ac052c00b

Settings

Set activation date?

Set expiration date?

Enabled? Yes No

Tags

0 tags

Permitted operations

Encrypt Sign Wrap Key

Decrypt Verify Unwrap Key

6. **Enable Encryption on Storage Account:** Go to Storage Account sastdcloud dashboard> Click Encryption in left pane>In Right pane select **Use your own key**>select radio button **Enter key URI**> In Key URI Box enter the Key URI copied in step 5>Click Save.

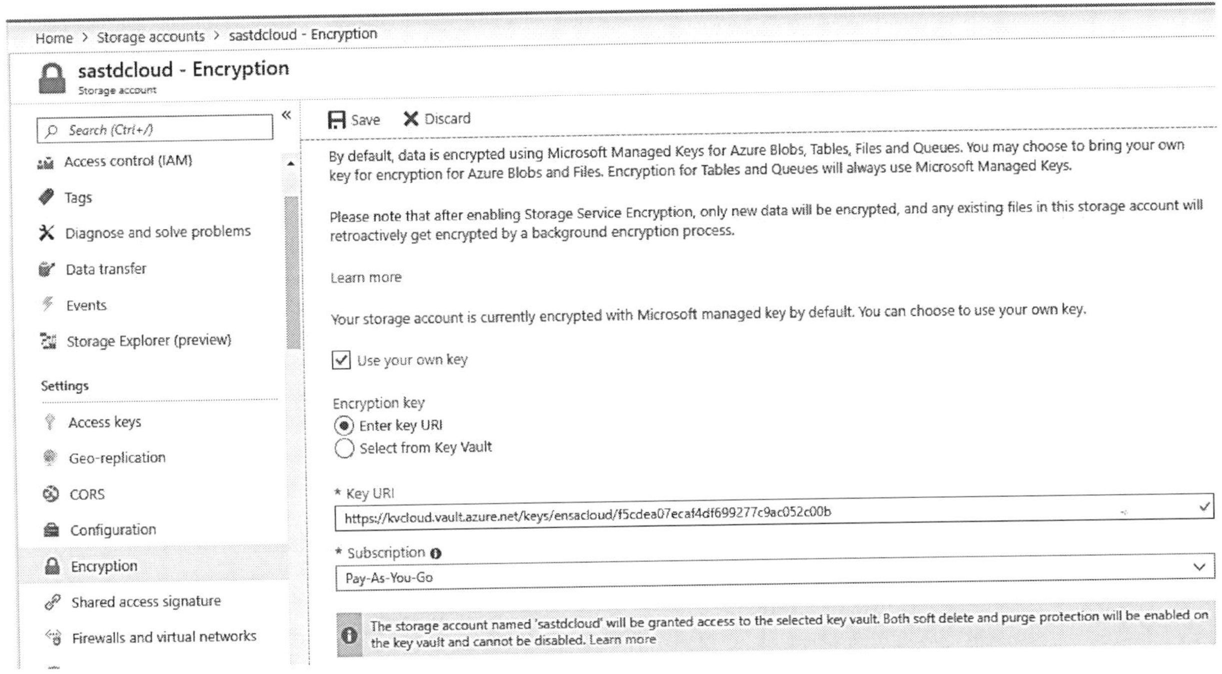

7. After it is saved you get notification: **Successfully updated server side encryption for 'sastdcloud'.**

Important Note

Using customer-managed keys with Azure Storage encryption requires that the key vault have two required properties configured, **Soft Delete** and **Do Not Purge**. These properties are enabled by default when you create a new key vault in the Azure portal. However, if you need to enable these properties on an existing key vault, you must use either PowerShell or Azure CLI.

Using Secrets with Key Vault

Azure Key vault Secrets store application secrets that you don't want to expose in Application Configuration files or code. Examples of secrets include database connection strings. You can protect Database Connection Identifier using Azure Key Vault Secret. Application can fetch Database Connection Identifier using URL of Key Vault secret Identifier.

Exercise 65: Protecting Database Connection Identifier with Key Vault Secret

In this Exercise we will protect Database Connection Identifier of Azure SQL Database sqlcloud using Azure Key Vault Secret. For this Exercise we will use Key Vault kvcloud created in Exercise 64.

In exercise 48, Chapter 3 we created Azure SQL Database **samplesql**. In step 4 of the Exercise we copied the Database Connection identifier for ADO.net In this Exercise we will create secret for Database Connection Identifier in Key Vault.

In our Application code we will add URL of the key vault Secret Identifier which will fetch the Database Identifier from Azure Key Vault. Database Connection identifier will not be added in the application code.

Database Connection Identifier copied from Exercise 48, Step 4

```
Server=tcp:sqldbdtu.database.windows.net,1433;Initial Catalog=samplesql;Persist
Security Info=False;User
ID={your_username};Password={your_password};MultipleActiveResultSets=False;Encrypt=Tr
ue;TrustServerCertificate=False;Connection Timeout=30;
```

In this exercise we will show the solution using both MSI and Service Principal option.

Steps for implementing the Solution

Step 1: Create a secret for Database Connection identifier using key vault.
Step 2 (Option 1): Create Managed Service Identity (MSI) of the VM VMFE1 where your application is running.
Step 2 (Option 2): Register the application with Azure AD to generate Application ID and Client secret.
Step 3 (For Option 1 in Step 2): Assign permissions to the VM VMFE1 identity to access Key Vault.
Step 3 (For Option 2 in Step 2): Authorize the Registered Application to access Key Vault Data Plane.
Step 4: In your application code add URL of the key vault Secret Identifier, Application Id & Client Secret. Application Id & Client Secret will be added only if you are using option 2.

Important Note

In Step 2 I am showing you 2 options.

First option is Managed Service Identity (MSI). This will create identity of the VMFE1 in Azure AD.

Second option is register an App with Azure AD to generate Service Principoal Values (Application-id and Client Secret). This step creates identity of the Application in Azure AD also known as Service Principal.

Preferred is to go with Option 1 which is MSI option. MSI option is easy to implement. If you see Azure Docs then most examples are using MSI option only.

Step 1 - Create a secret for Database Connection Identifier using key Vault Dashboard

1. Go to Key Vault kvcloud dashboard>Click Secrets in left pane.

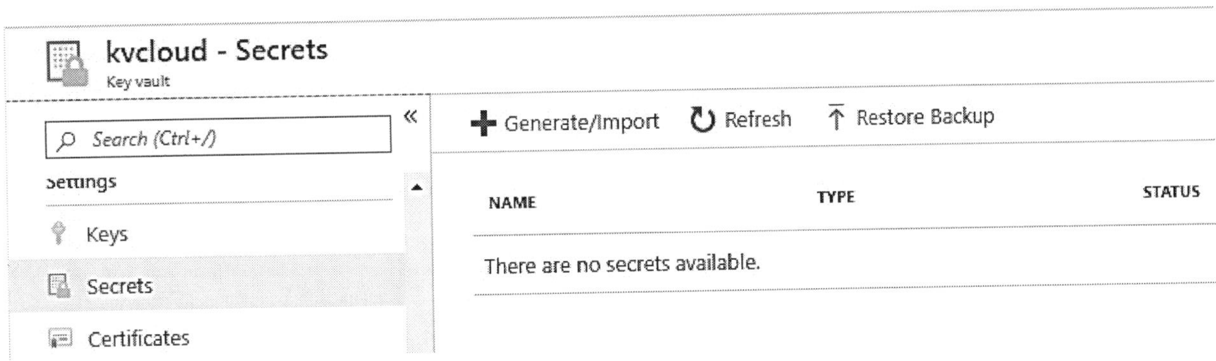

2. In Right pane click + Generate/Import> Create a secret dashboard opens> select manual from drop down box> Enter a name> In Value paste the **Database Connection identifier of Azure SQL Database samplesql**> Make sure Enabled is set to Yes>Click create (Not Shown).

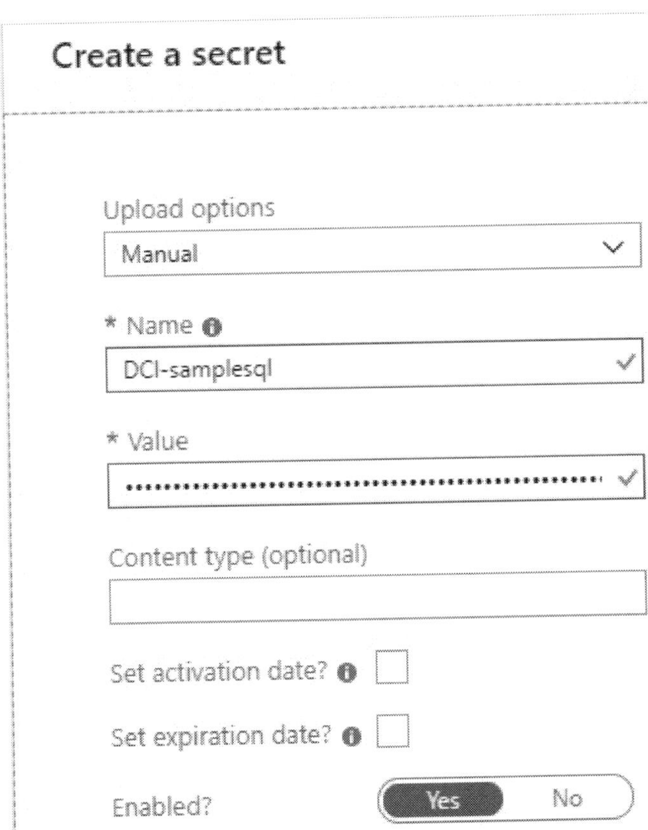

3. Figure below shows the secret which was generated.

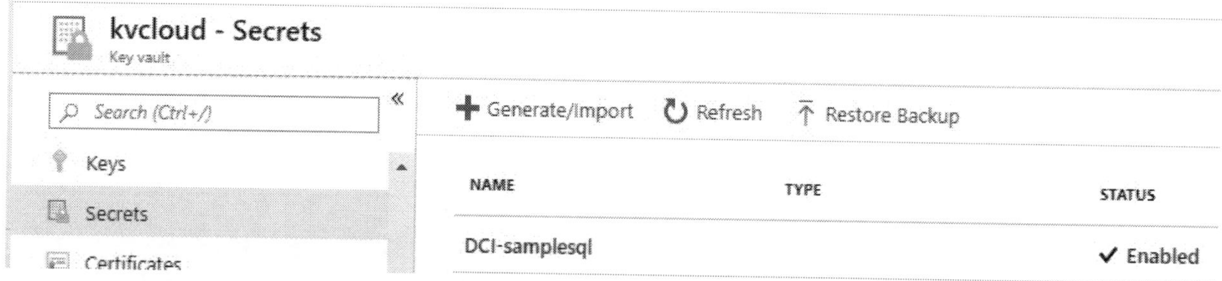

4. Click the secret DCI-samplesql in right pane>Click the current version> Dashboard for Secret opens.

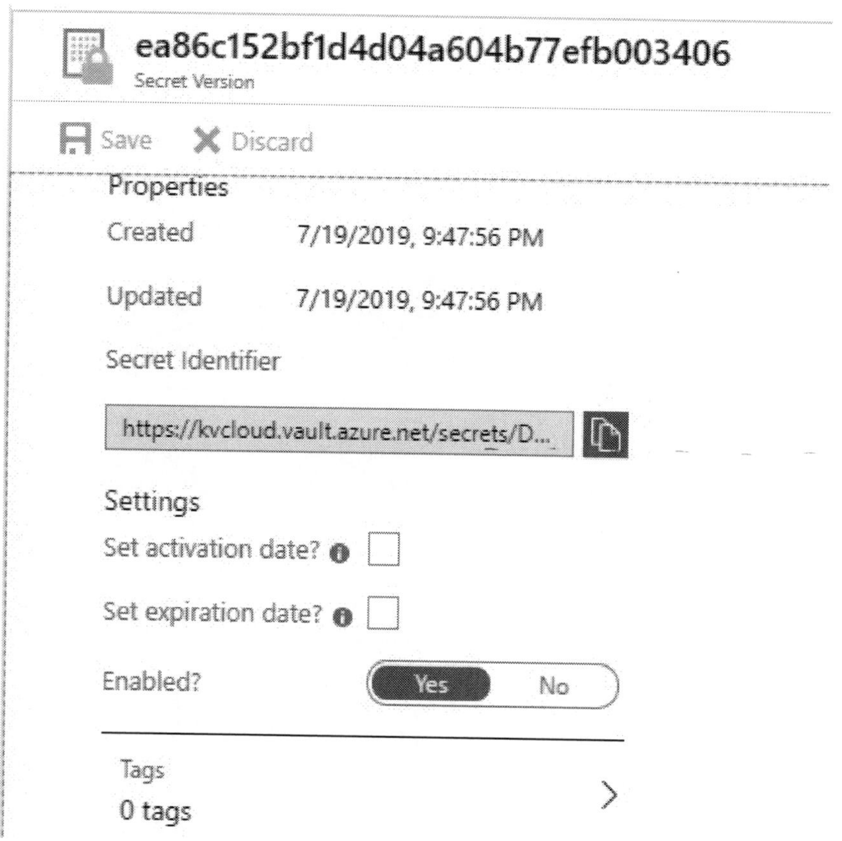

Copy the Secret Identifier URL: https://kvcloud.vault.azure.net/secrets/DCI-samplesql/ea86c152b...............

Step 2 (Option 1) – Enable Managed Service Identity on Azure VM VMFE1
Note: You can use either option 1 or Option 2 for Step 2.

We will use Virtual Machine VMFE1 for this Step. **We will assume that Application is installed on VMFE1.** VMFE1 was created in Exercise 24, Chapter 4 in Exam AZ-300 & AZ-301 Study & Lab Guide Part 1.

1. Go to Virtual Machine VMFE1 dashboard and click identity in left pane> In Right pane you can see that current the status is off.

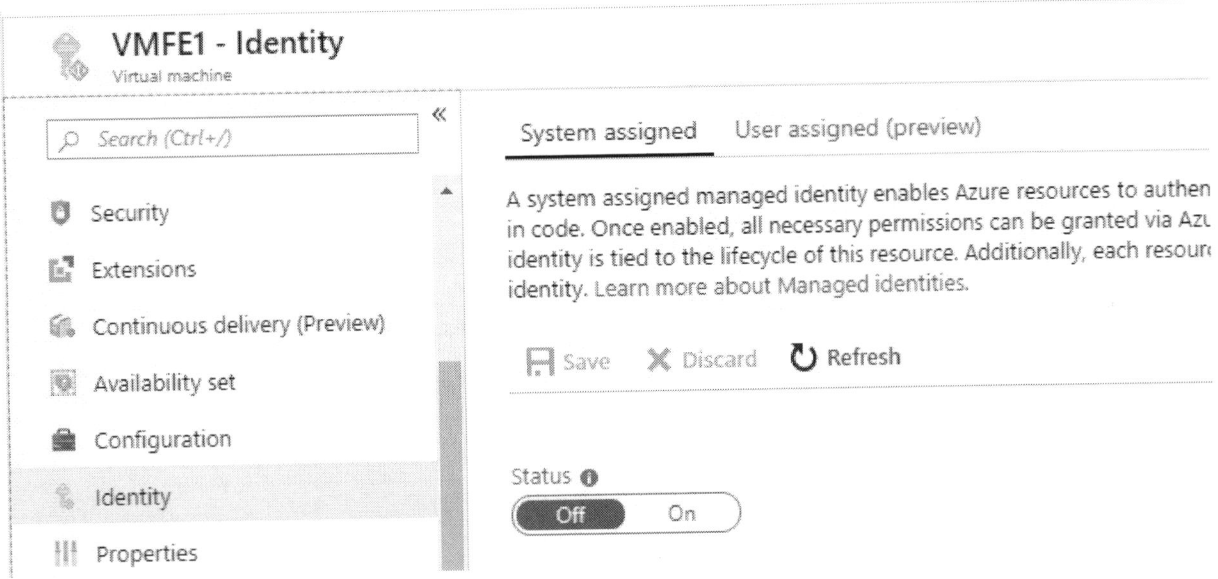

2. Click on>Click save>Click Yes.

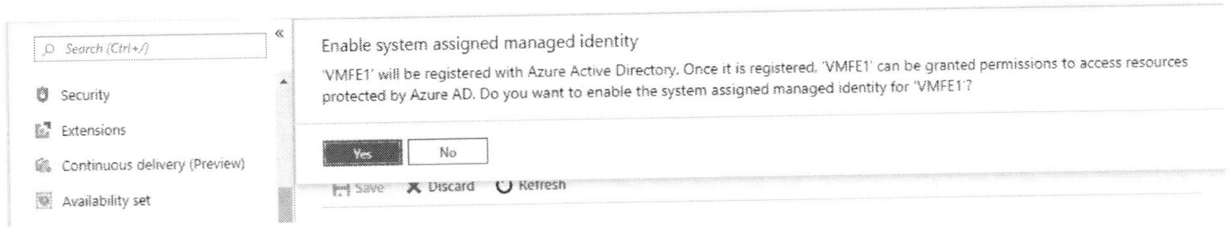

3. A Unique identifier (Object-id) is generated.

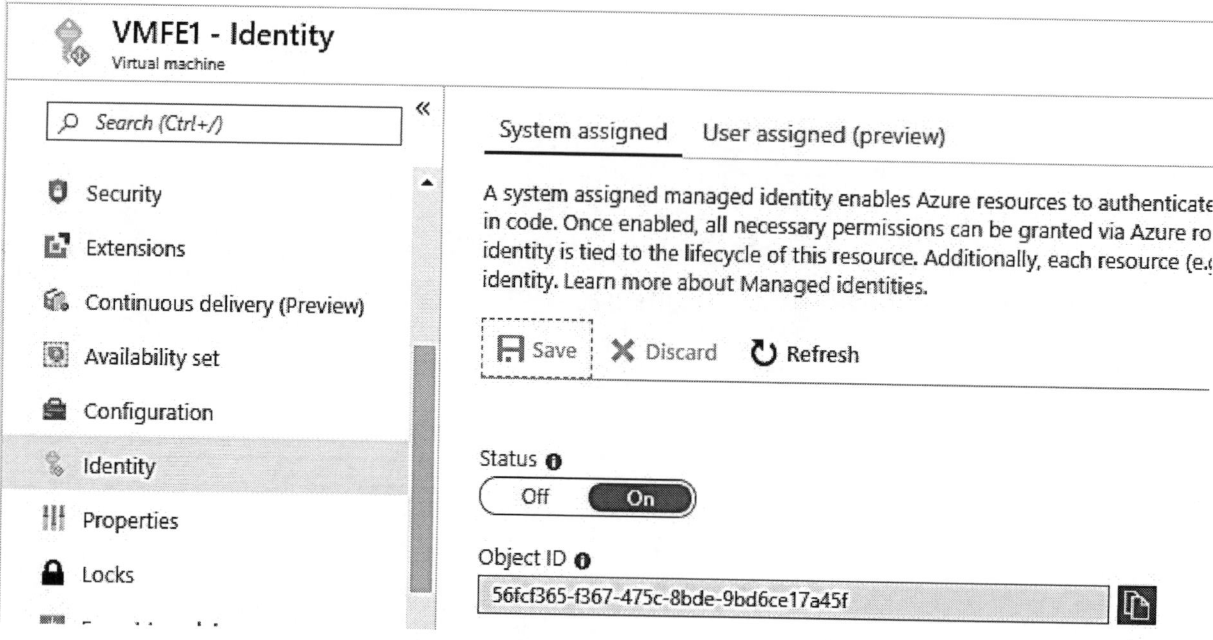

Copy the Object ID: 56fcf365-f367-475c-8bde-9bd6ce17a45f
We will use it in step 3 option 1.

When you enabled MSI on Azure VM VMFE1, Azure created a service principal. Services Principal creates identity of the VM in Azure AD. It also injects the service principal credentials into VM instance.

Application code running on VM does following:

1. Fetch a token from the local MSI endpoint on the VM. Doing so also fetches a token from Azure AD.
2. Pass the token to your key vault, and then fetch your secret.

Step 2 (Option 2) - Register your application with Azure AD to generate Application ID and Client secret (Service Principal Option).

This Step creates identity of the application in Azure AD also known as Service Principal.

Applications that use a key vault must authenticate to Key Vault by using a token from Azure Active Directory. To do this, application must first register the application in their Azure Active Directory. At the end of registration, the application owner gets the following values:
Application ID
Client Secret
The application must present both these values to Azure AD to get a token.

1. In Azure AD dashboard Click App Registrations in left pane> Click +New Registration>Register an Application Blade opens>enter a name and rest select all default Values>Click Register.

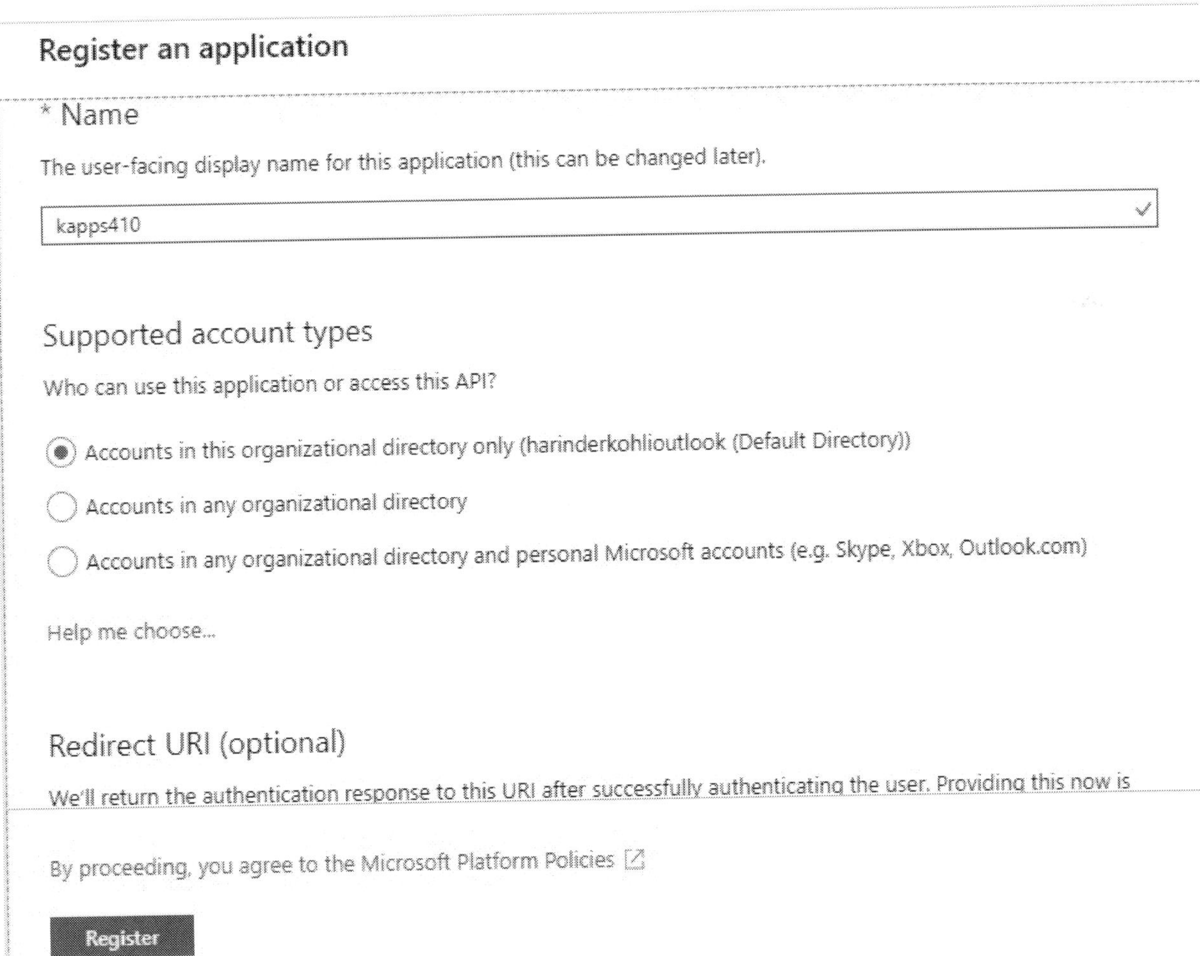

5. Figure below shows the dashboard of App Registered with Azure AD. Note down the Application Id.

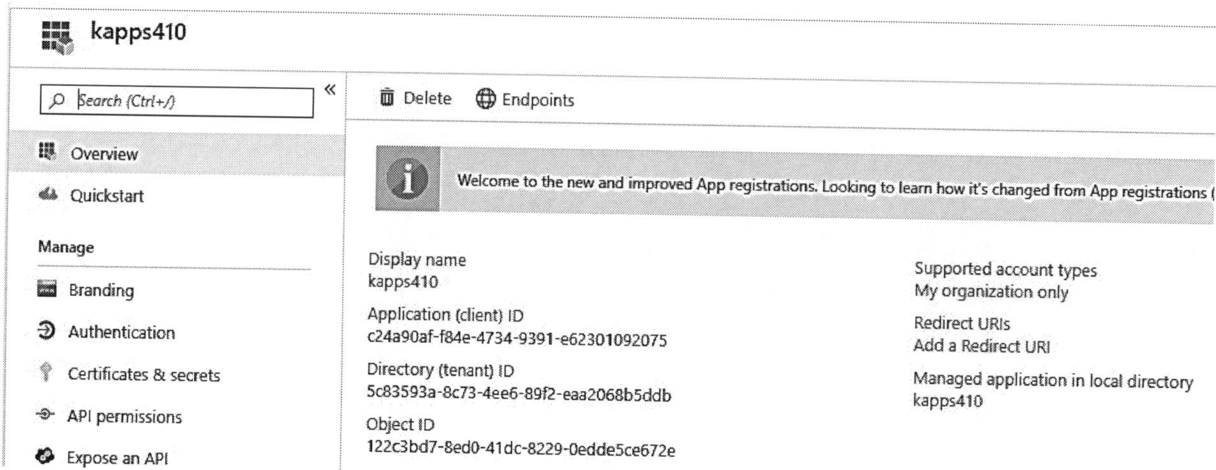

6. In your registered app dashboard click Certificates & Secrets in left pane> Under Client Secrets Click New client secret> Add a client secret blade opens>enter a Description and select duration

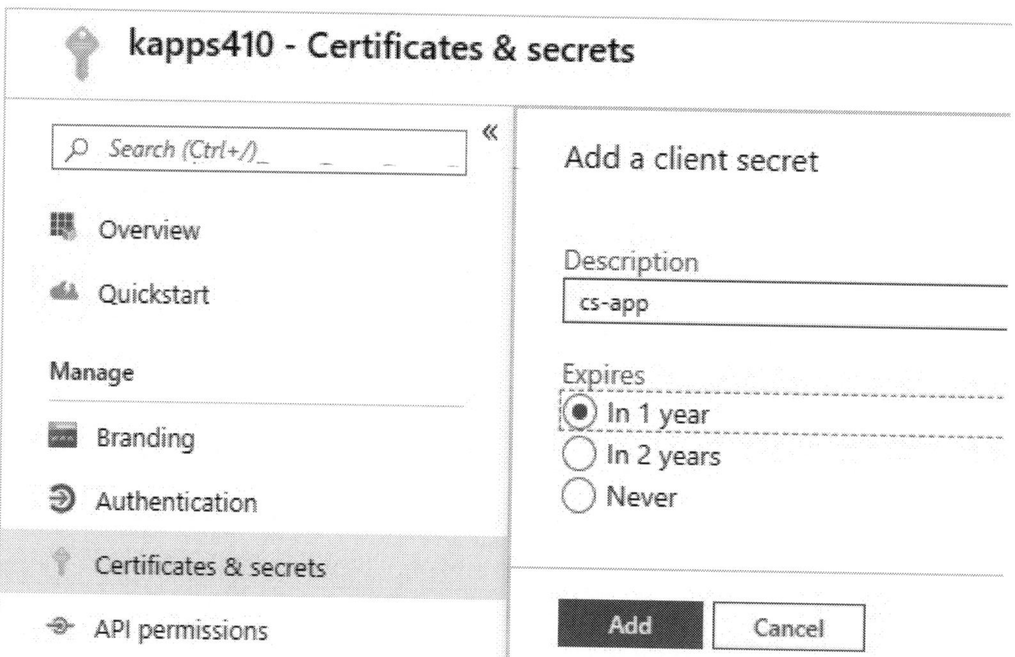

7. Click Add and a value generated. Note down the value. This will be your **client secret.**

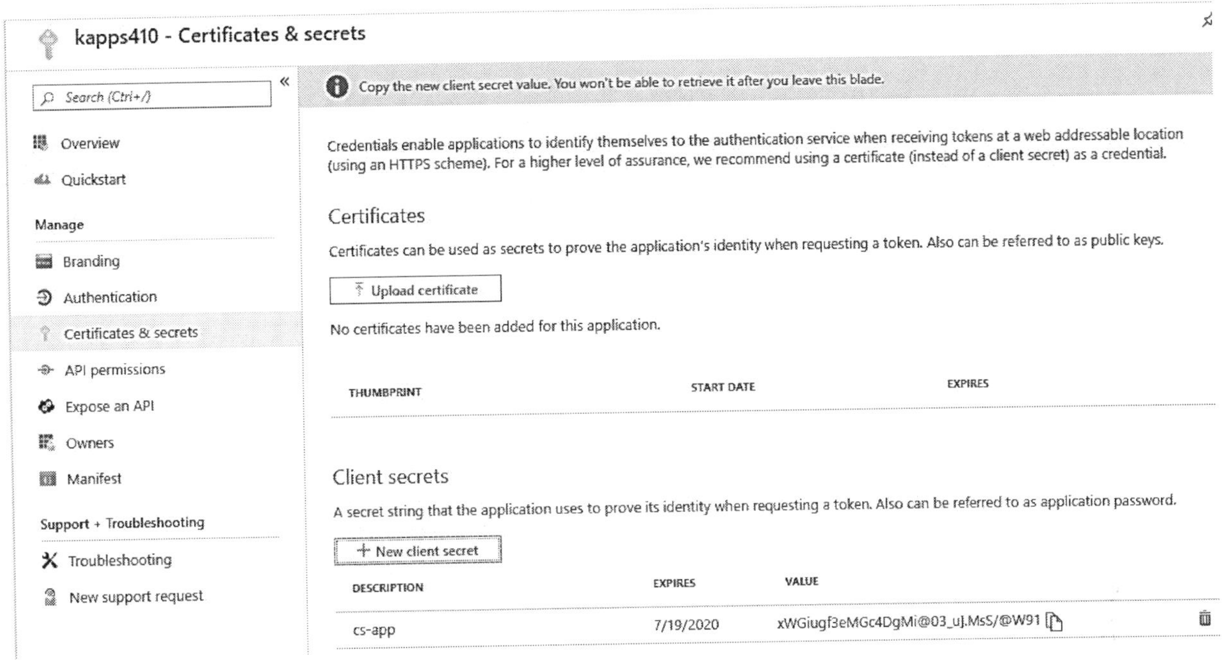

Step 3 (If you have used option 1 (MSI) in Step 2) - Assign permissions to the VM identity to access Key Vault kvcloud.

az keyvault set-policy --name <YourKeyVaultName> --object-id <VMSystemAssignedIdentity> --secret-permissions get list

az keyvault set-policy --name kvcloud –object-id 56fcf365-f367-475c-8bde-9bd6ce17a45f --secret-permission get list

This above command gives the identity (MSI) of VM permission to do **get** and **list** operations on Key Vault kvcloud.

Step 3 (If you have used option 2 in Step 2) - Authorize the Registered Application kapps410 to access Key Vault Data Plane

1. In Azure Key Vault Dashboard click **Access Policies**> Click +New> Add Access Policy Blade opens>In search Box enter kapps410> In the result select kapps410 and click Select.

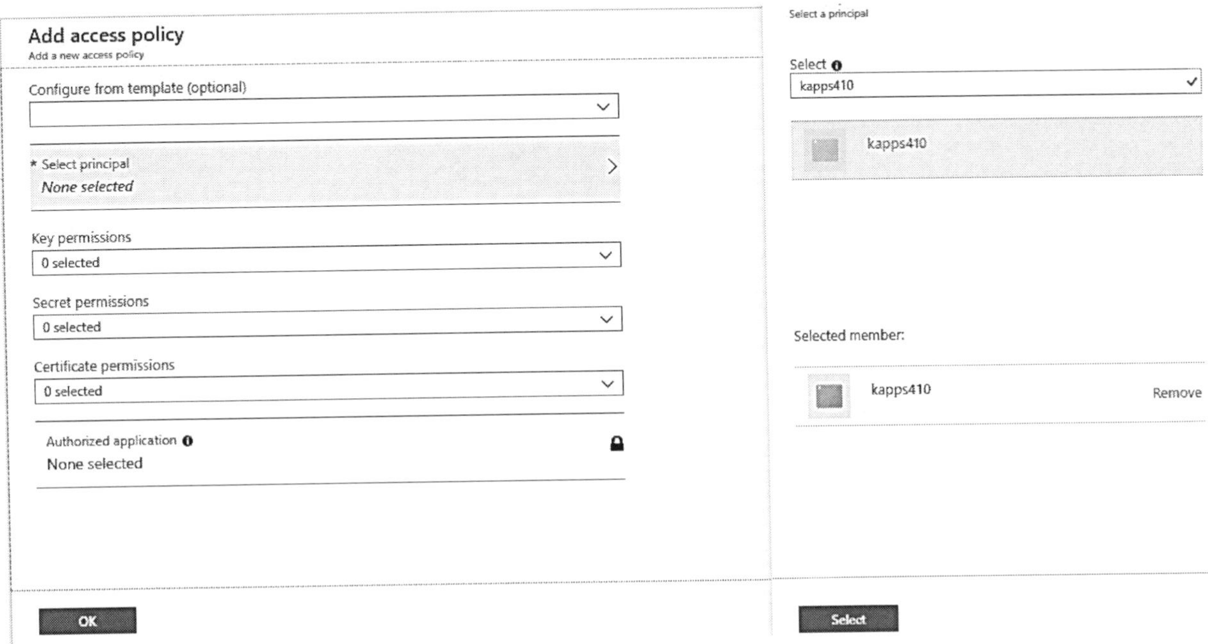

2. Under Secret Permission select Get & List options>Click OK (Not Shown)>Click save.

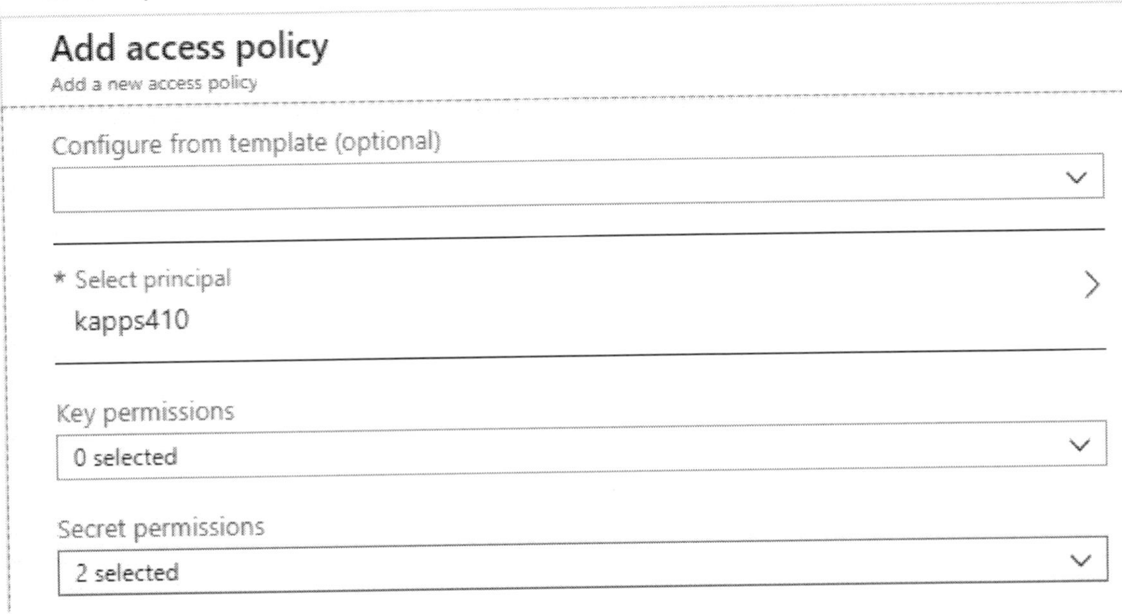

Step 4 - In your application add URL of the key vault Secret identifier (Database Connection String)

If you are using option 1 (Managed Service Identity) in Step 2

In your application code add **URL of the Key Vault Secret Identifier**(See Step 1)
https://kvcloud.vault.azure.net/secrets/DCI-samplesql/ea86c152bf1d4d04a604b77efb003406

If you are using option 2 (Service Principal) in Step 2 then add following in your Application code

URL of the Key Vault Secret Identifier (See Step 1)
https://kvcloud.vault.azure.net/secrets/DCI-samplesql/ea86c152bf1d4d04a604b77efb003406
client id/application id (generated in Step 2, option2.)
client secret (generated in Step 2, option2.)

Note: You need to also add Tenant id and Subscription id in your application code.

Using Certificates with Key Vault

Certificates are commonly used with web servers and application for **secure communication (Enabling HTTPS)** and **authentication**.

For example a website with address https://www.test.com indicates that traffic is encrypted with certificate. This is an example of Secure Communication.

For Example you want to Authenticate a Device (laptop) to a Server before granting it access to resources on the Server. You can use Certificate here. Private Key will be installed on the Device and Public Key will be uploaded to Server. This is an example of authentication using Certificates.

You Store Certificates in Key Vault.

Certificate can be a self-signed certificate or issued by a Certificate Authority (CA).

Using Azure key vault you can generate or import certificates. Key vault can generate a self-signed certificate. Self-signed certificate is not recommended for production workloads. For Production workload it is recommended to import certificate from trusted Certificate Authority (CA) and then issue it.

Using Key vault you can inject stored certificate in Azure Virtual Machine. Applications running on Virtual Machine can access and use the certificate.

Note: See Exercise 11 & 12 in chapter 1 for using Certificate with Azure Key Vault. Certificate was used for enabling HTTPS on Web App HKWA1.
Note 2: See Exercise 59 in Chapter 4 for using Certificates for authentication.

Exercise 66: Generating Self-Signed Certificate

In this Exercise we will create self-signed certificate. For this Exercise we will use Key Vault kvcloud created in Exercise 64. We will use this certificate in Service Fabric Chapter 16.

1. Go to Key Vault kvcloud dashboard>Click Certificates in left pane.

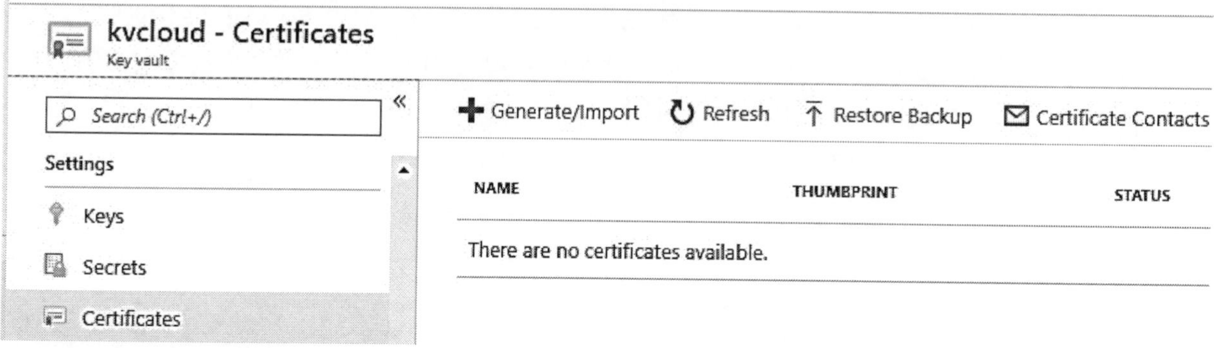

2. In Right pane click + Generate/Import> Create a certificate blade opens> select Generate from drop down box> Enter a name> In CA select Self-signed certificate>In Subject enter **CN=www.mykloud410.com**>In DNS enter **www.mykloud410.com**> Rest select all default values>Click Create.

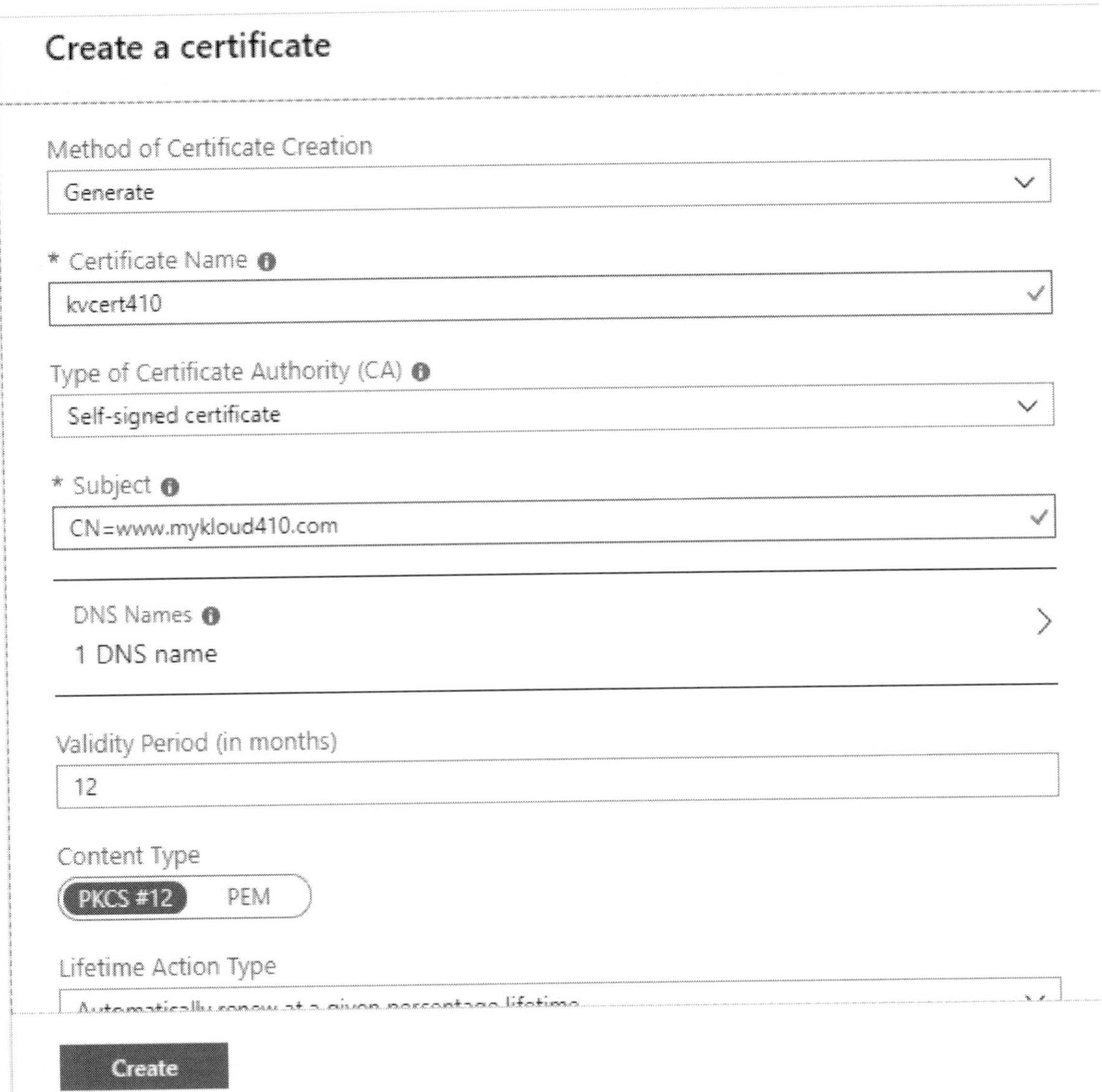

Note: It will take 1 minutes for Certificate creation process to complete.

3. Figure below shows newly created certificate.

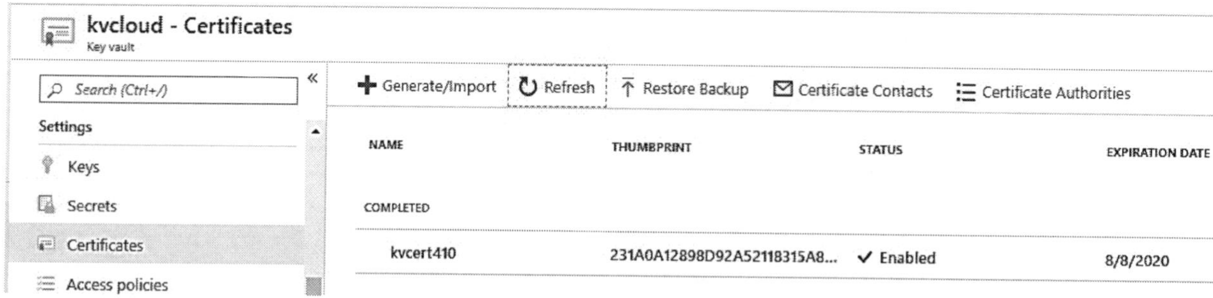

Note: We will use this Certificate in Service Fabric Chapter Lab Exercise.

4. Copy Values for Secret Identifier and Thumbprint.
   Click the certificate created> Click Current Version>Certificate Version pane opens>Sroll down and copy Thumbprint & Secret Identifier.

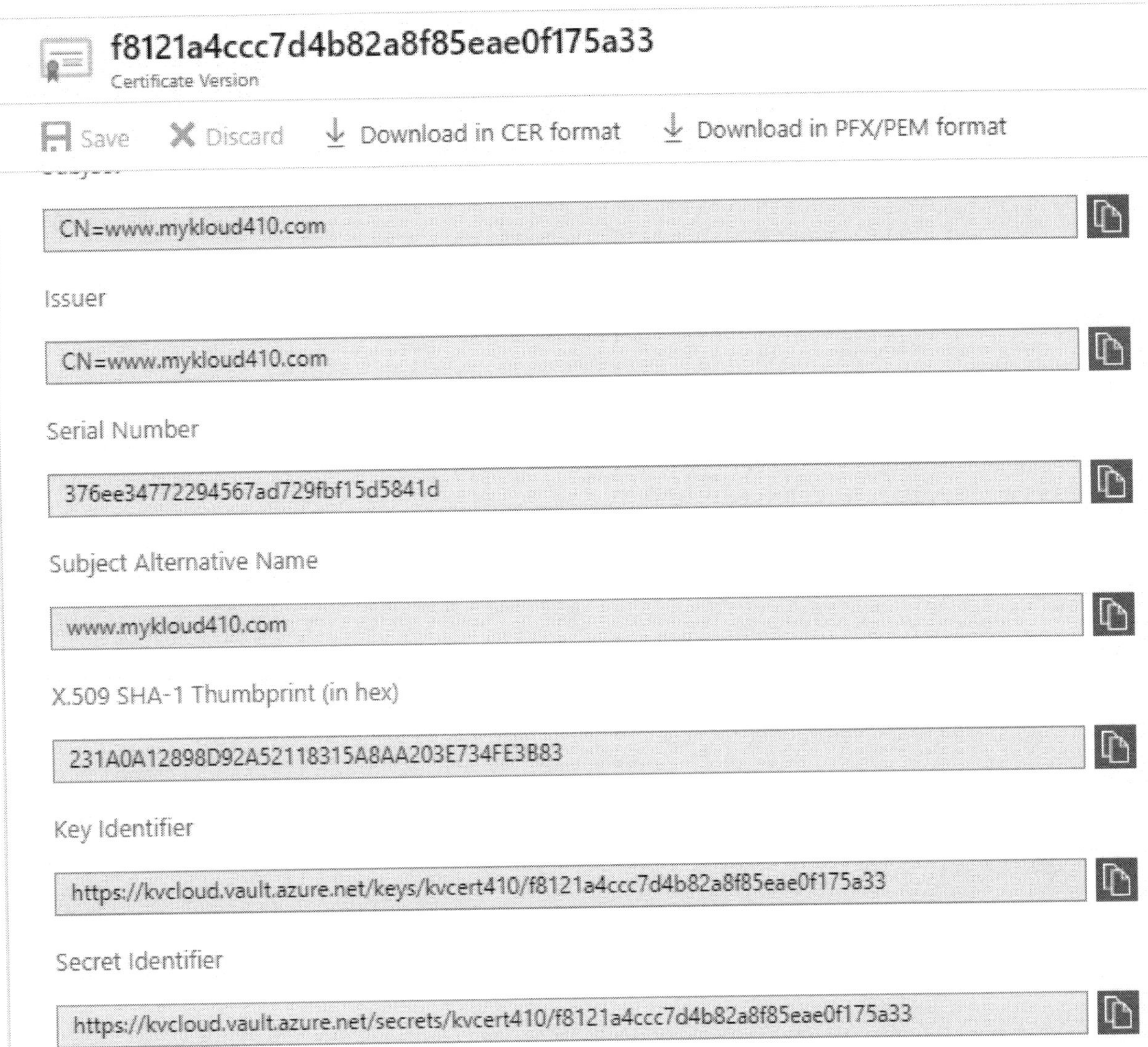

5. **Copy Key Vault Resource ID**. In Key Vault kvcloud Dashboard Click Properties in left pane> In Right pane copy Resource ID value.

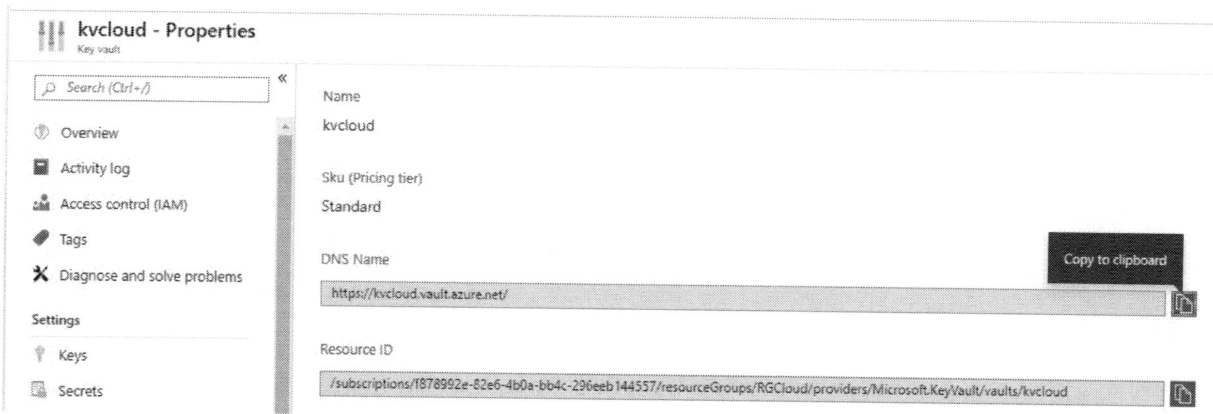

Note: We will use Resource ID, Secret Identifier and Thumbprint in Service Fabric Cluster Lab.

Using Key Vault Secret with ARM Templates

ARM Templates are infrastructure as code which can deploy multiple Azure resources. For example with ARM template you can deploy Azure Virtual Network, Storage Account and Virtual Machine simultaneously.

Same Azure ARM template can be used multiple times by different departments or organizations. This means we cannot reference the key vault secret in the template itself. Azure template will refer to a parameter file. Parameter file will have reference to Key Vault.

Figure below shows how the parameter file references the secret and passes that value to the template.

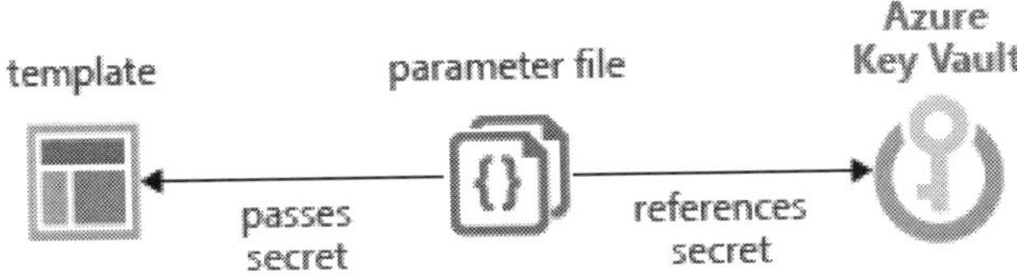

Step By step adding Support for Azure Key Vault secret in ARM Templates

1. Create a Key Vault for the secrets you want to use with Template deployment.
2. Put secrets into the vault.
3. Set advanced Access Policies on the Key Vault to allow Azure Resource Manager to retrieve secrets during deployment.
4. Edit or Author an ARM template with reference to the parameter file for login and Password.
5. Create a parameter file for the preceding template. In the parameter file, specify Key Vault Subscription ID and Secret Name.
6. Deploy the template with the Parameter file specified in step 5.

Note: Same template can be used by different organisation. You need to create separate parameter file. ARM template remains the same.

Securing Azure Key Vault Management and Data Plane

Access to a key vault is controlled through two separate interfaces: Management Plane and Data Plane.

The management plane and data plane access controls work independently. For example, if you want to grant an application access to use keys in a key vault, you only need to grant data plane access permissions using key vault access policies and no management plane access is needed for this application. Whereas Management plane interface is used to manage key vault.

For authentication both management plane and data plane use Azure Active Directory. For authorization, management plane uses role-based access control (RBAC) while data plane uses key vault access policies.

Granting Access to Key Vault Data Plane using Access Policies

Key Vault Data plane access is granted by access policies. **Using Access Policies a user, group, application or Azure services is authorized to access Key Vault.**

1. In key vault dashboard click access Policies in left pane>

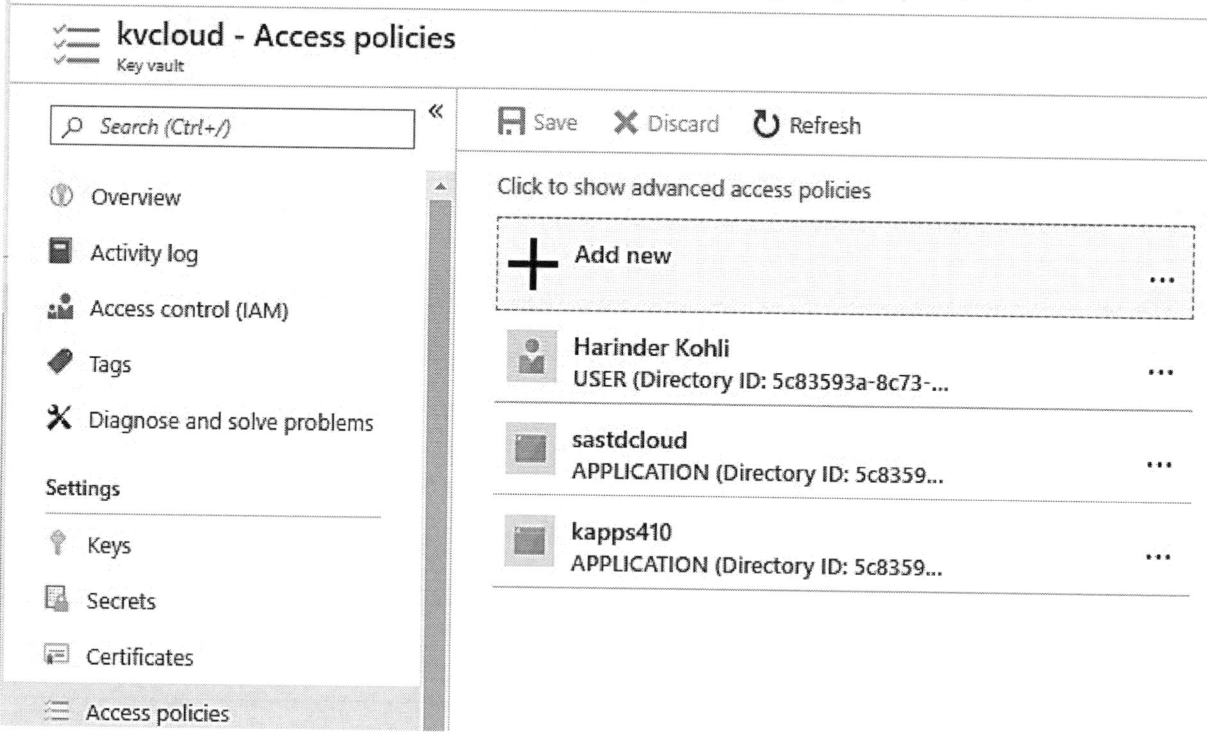

2. **Granting Key Vault Access to Custom Applications, Azure AD users or Azure Services.** Click +**Add new** in Access Policies>Add Access Policy blade opens> Here we can add Application registered with Azure AD, Azure AD users or Azure Services.

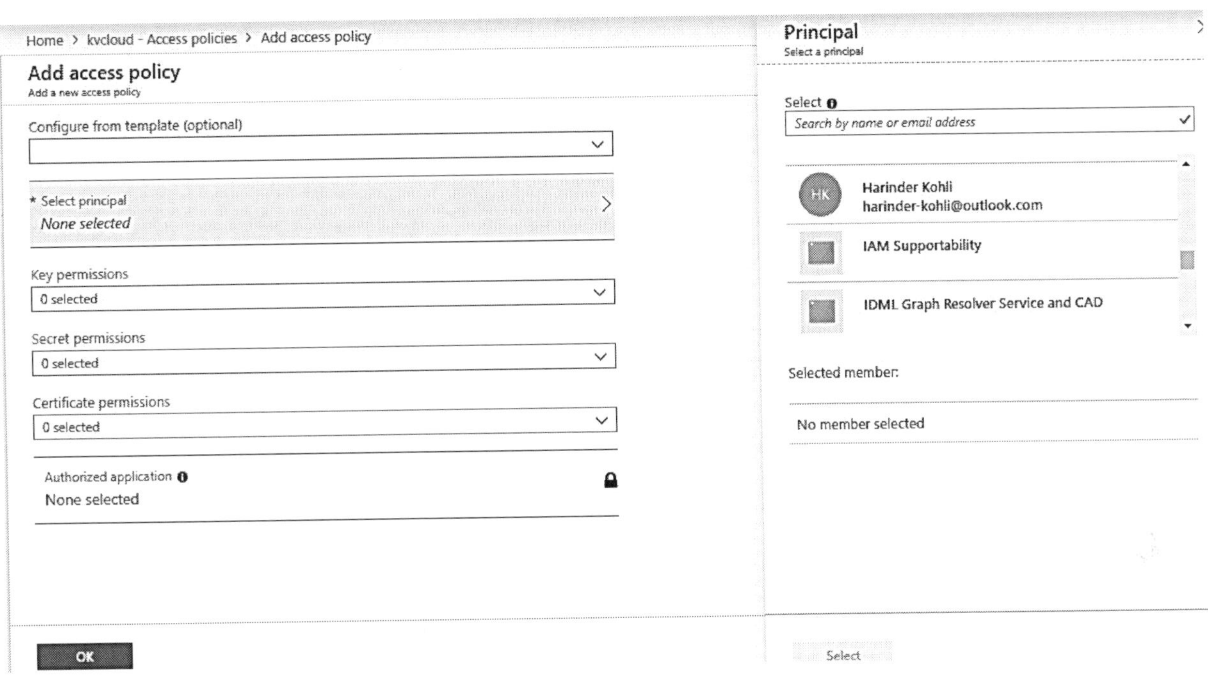

Key Vault Advance Access Policies

Following 3 advance access Policies can be enabled from Key Vault Dashboard.

1. **Enable access to Azure Virtual Machines for deployments:** Specifies whether Azure Virtual Machines are permitted to retrieve certificate stored as secrets from the Key Vault.

2. **Enable access to Azure Resource Manager for template deployments:** Specifies whether Azure Resource Manager is permitted to retrieve secrets from the Key Vault.

3. **Enable access to Azure Disk Encryption for volume encryption**: Specifies whether Azure Disk Encryption is permitted to retrieve from the Key Vault and unwrap keys.

Exercise 67: Enabling Key Vault Advanced Accees Policies

In this exercise we will enable Advanced Accees Policies. We require this for Service Fabric Chapter where we will deploy certificate to Service Fabric Cluster. You must do this exercise.

1. In Key Vault Dashboard Click Access Policies in left pane> In right pane Click to show advanced access policies> Select all 3 Advance access policies>**Click save.**

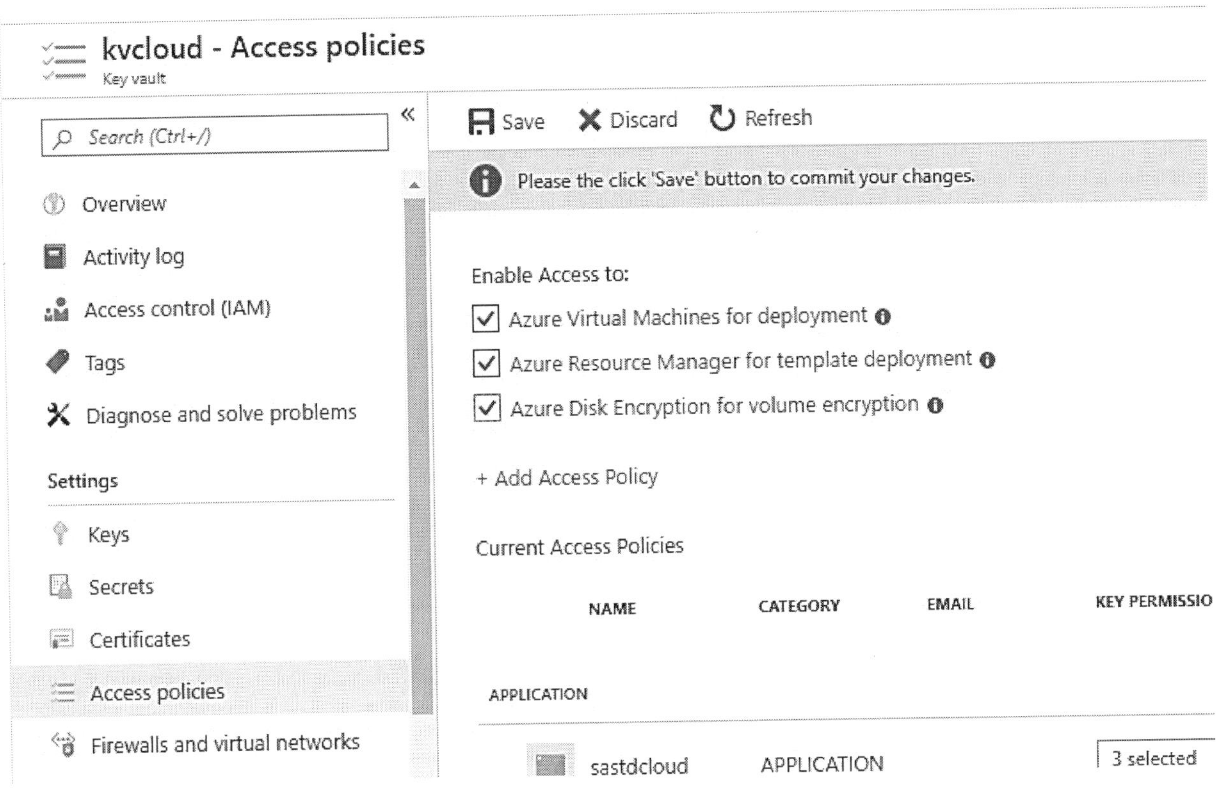

Key Rotation

There is a possibility that your key might compromised. One of the advantages of using Key Vault is the ability to change keys without affecting the application.

Each key or secret can have one or more versions associated with it.

Exercise 68: Key Rotation

In this Exercise we will create new version of RSA key ensacloud. RSA key ensacloud was created in step 3 of Exercise 64.

1. In the Key vault kvcloud Dashboard click keys in left pane>In the right pane select your key ensacloud>ensacloud Key versions pane opens. You can see your current version of the key as shown in the figure below.

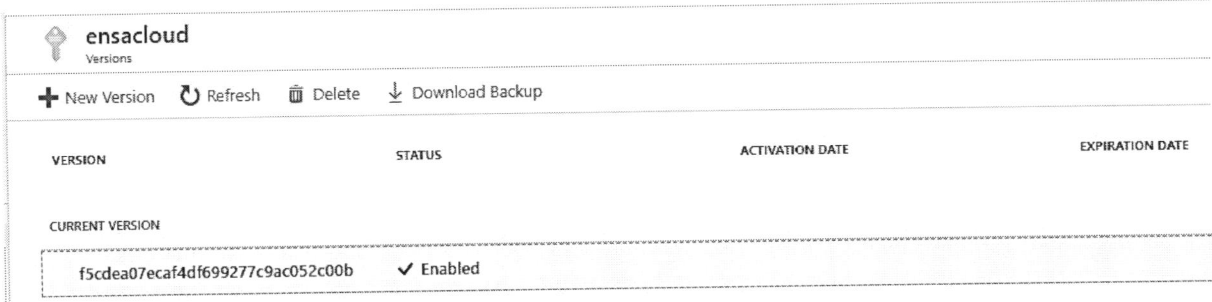

2. Click + New Version>Create a key Blade opens> Select all default values>Click create.

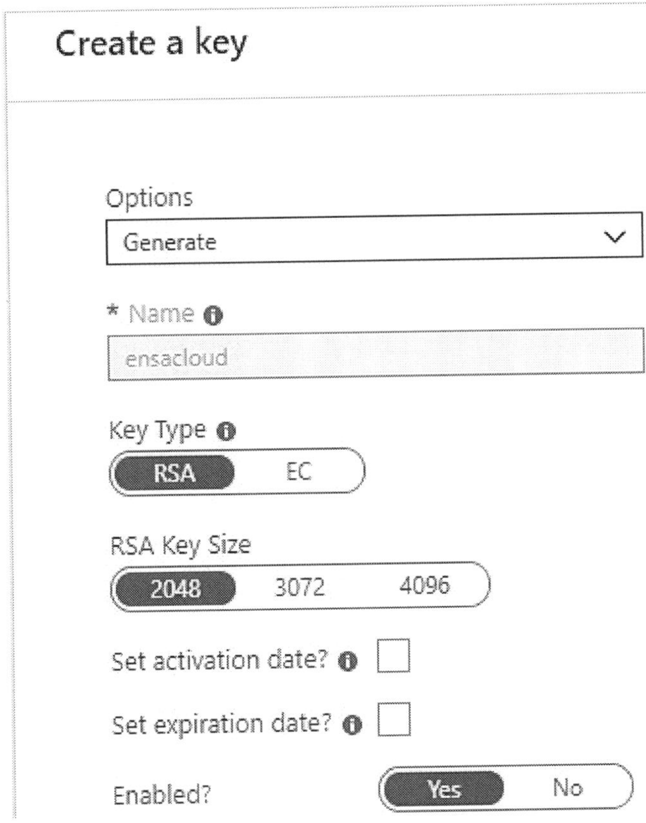

3. A new version is of the key is created as shown below. New key becomes current version. New key has a different Key URI. You can now update your application with Key URI of the new key.

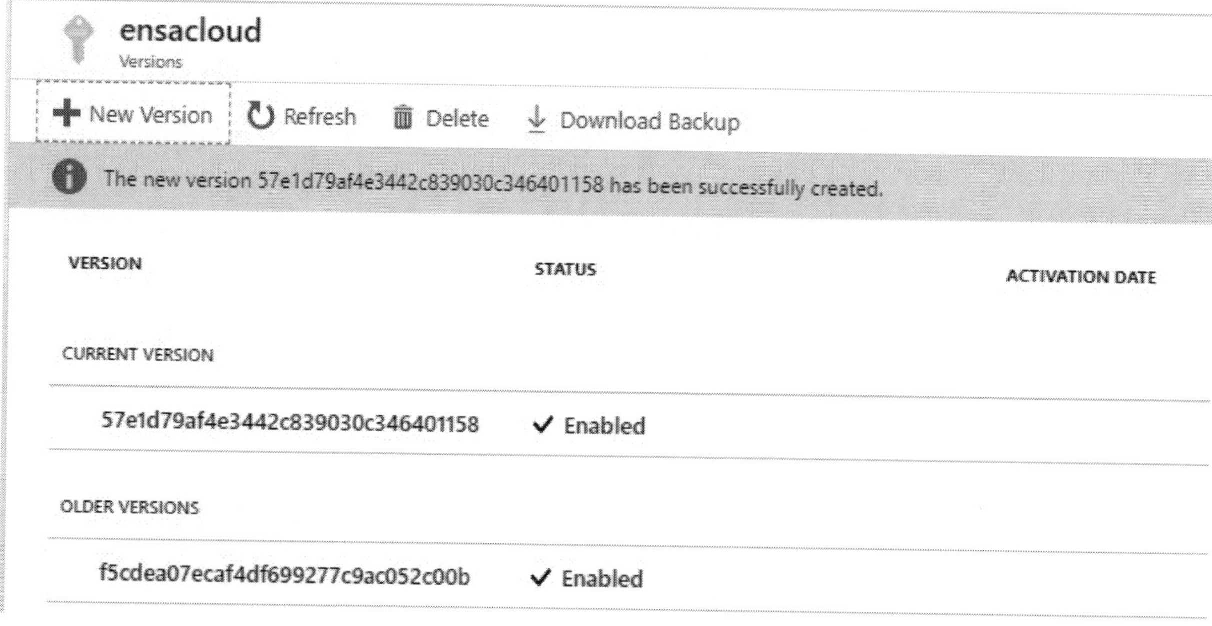

Soft Delete

Key Vault's soft delete feature allows recovery of the deleted vaults and vault objects.

Why do we need Soft Delete Feature

Accidental or intentional delete of Key Vault or Key Vault objects can cause Business disruptions.

Scenario 1: A user may have inadvertently deleted a key vault or a key vault object.
Scenario 2: A rogue user may attempt to delete a key vault or a key vault object.

By enabling Soft Delete feature you can separate the deletion of the key vault or key vault object from the actual deletion of the underlying data. Soft Delete feature allows recovery of deleted vaults and vault objects. Soft Delete feature can be used as a safety measure.

Enabling Soft Delete Feature

You can enable Soft Delete feature through Powershell or CLI.

Key Logging

Access to Key Vault can be monitored by enabling logging. Following types of logs are generated:

1. Key Vault operation to create delete or change settings.
2. Key Vault operations that involve Keys, Secrets and Certificates.
3. Rest API requests.

Azure Key Vault Tiers

Azure Key Vault is offered in two service tiers—standard and premium. Table below shows comparison between the tiers.

Features	Standard	Premium
Secrets operations	Yes	Yes
Certificate operations	Yes	Yes
Software-protected keys	Yes	Yes
HSM-protected keys	No	Yes

Azure Key Vault Pricing

Table shows the pricing of Azure key vault standard and Premier Tiers.

	Standard	Premium
Secrets operations	$0.03/10,000 request	$0.03/10,000 request
Certificate operations	$3 per renewal request	$3 per renewal request
Software-protected keys (RSA 2048-bit keys)	$0.03/10,000 Transactions	$0.03/10,000 Transactions
Software-protected keys (RSA 3072-bit, RSA 4096-bit and Elliptic-Curve Cryptography (ECC) keys)	$0.15/10,000 Transactions	$0.15/10,000 Transactions
HSM-protected keys (RSA 2048-bit keys)	NA	$1 per key per month +$0.03/10,000 transactions

Chapter 6 Azure Serverless Computing

This Chapter covers following

- Azure Functions
- Common scenarios for Azure Functions
- Triggers and Bindings
- Azure Functions pricing
- Azure Functions scale and hosting
- Azure Logic Apps
- Connectors
- Types of Triggers
- Examples of Logic Apps workflow Automation

This Chapter Covers following Lab Exercises

- Publishing Hello World using http triggered Functions
- Check Trigger Option Templates to create a Function
- Use Blob Storage Trigger Template to create a Function
- Exploring Function App HWCloud Settings, Config & Platform Features
- Exploring Function (MyBlob) Settings
- Delete Function MyBlob
- Create Logic App workflow (Check RSS Feed)

Chapter Topology

In this chapter we will add Azure Functions and Logic Apps to the topology.

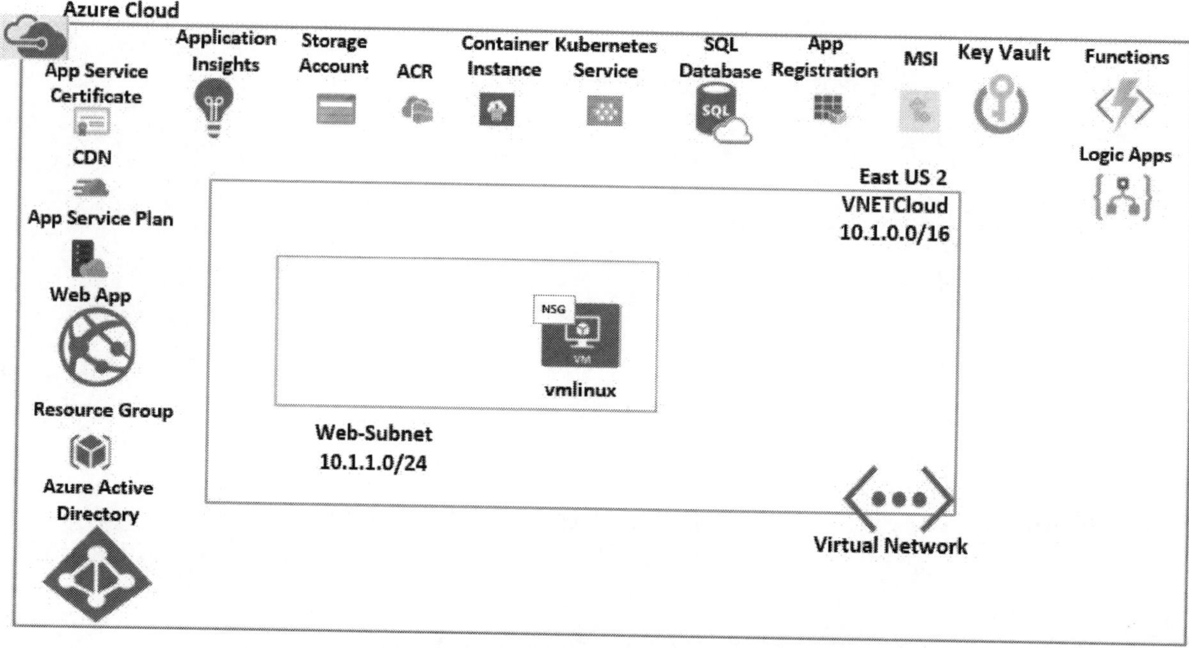

Azure Functions

Azure Functions is a serverless compute service that enables you to run compute code on-demand in response to a variety of events, without having to explicitly provision compute infrastructure.

Events can be occurring in Azure or 3rd party service as well as on-premises systems. Azure Functions makes it easy to connect to data sources for generating, processing and reacting to events.

Azure Function Features

Serverless: No worry about the infrastructure and provisioning of servers.
Choice of language: Write functions using C#, F#, Node.js, Python, PHP, batch, bash, or any executable using easy-to-use web-based interface.
Pay-per-use pricing model: Pay only for the time spent running your code.
Accelerate development: Write your code in the Functions editor in the portal or set up continuous integration and deploy your code through GitHub, Visual Studio Team Services etc.
Simplified integration: Easily leverage Azure services and external services such as Box, Dropbox, Microsoft OneDrive, SendGrid etc to get input into or output from Functions without writing any code.
Integrated security: Protect HTTP-triggered functions with OAuth providers such as Azure Active Directory, Facebook, Google, Twitter and Microsoft Account.

Common scenarios for Azure Functions

Real-time stream processing: Internet of Things (IoT) devices send messages to Azure Stream Analytics, which then calls an Azure Function to transform the message. This function processes the data and creates a new record in an Azure SQL database.

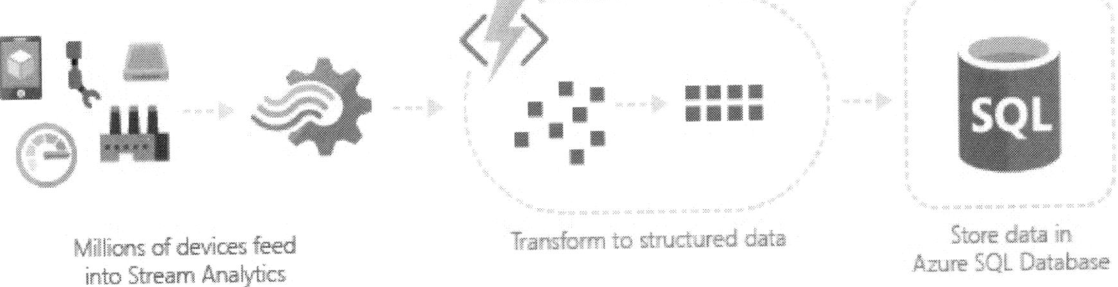

Azure service event processing: Azure Functions supports triggering an event based on an activity in an Azure service. For example, execute serverless code that reads newly discovered test log files in an Azure Blob storage container, and transform this into a row in an Azure SQL Database table.

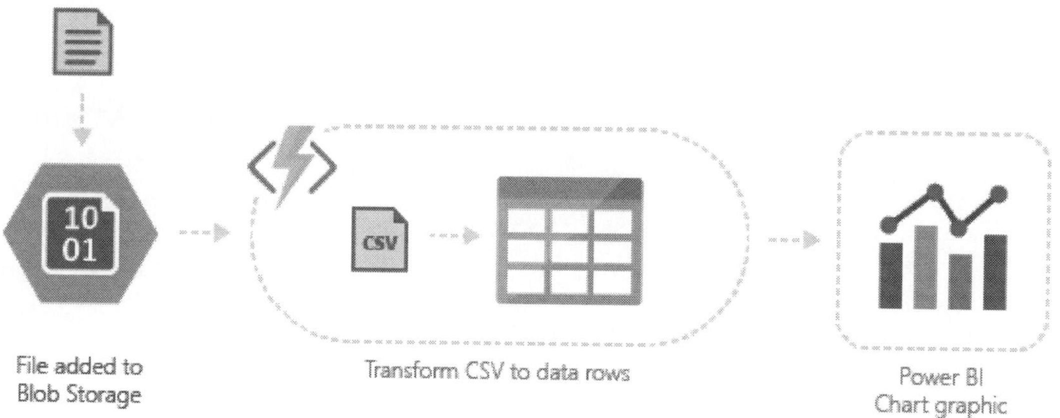

SaaS event processing: Azure Functions supports triggers based on activity in a SaaS service. For example, a file saved in OneDrive, triggers a function that uses the Microsoft Graph API to modify the spreadsheet, and creates additional charts and calculated data.

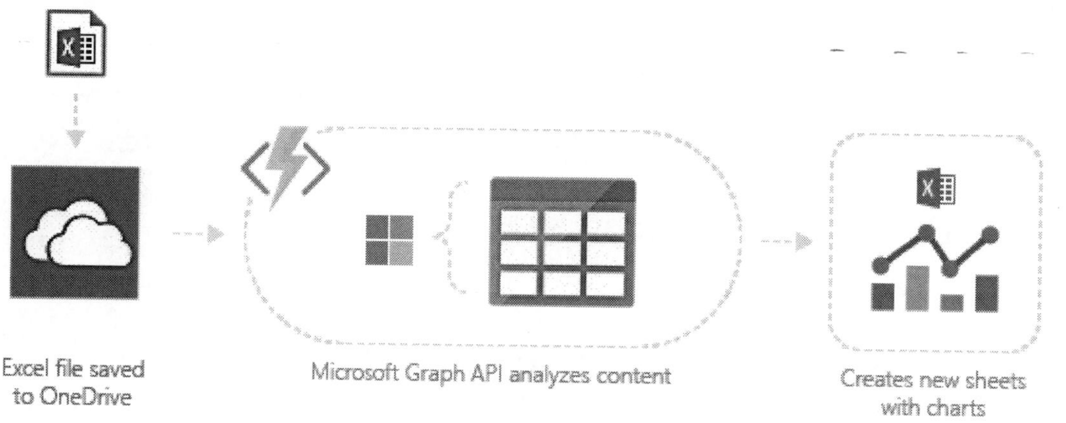

Serverless mobile back ends: A mobile back end can be a set of HTTP APIs that are called from a mobile client using the WebHook URL. For example, a mobile application can capture an image, and then call an Azure Function to get an access token for uploading to blob storage. A second Azure Function is triggered by the blob upload and resizes the image to be mobile-friendly.

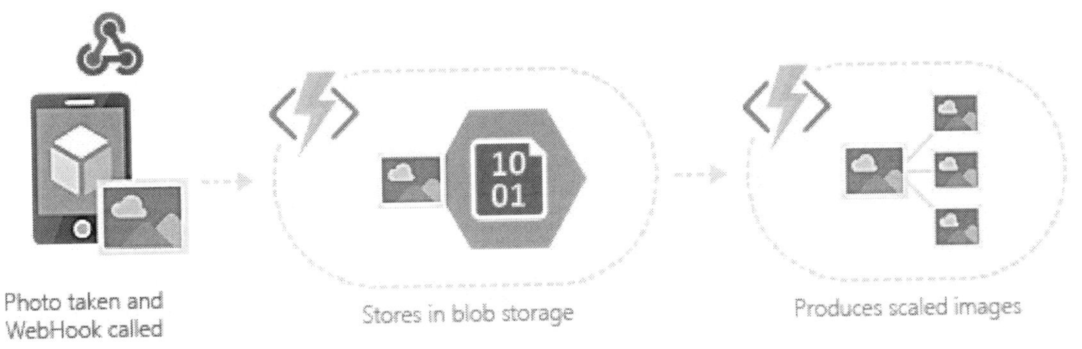

Triggers and Bindings (Important Concept)

Triggers are what cause a function to run. A trigger defines how a function is invoked. **A function must have exactly one trigger**. Triggers have associated data which is often provided as the payload of the function.

Binding to a function is a way of connecting another resource to the function. Bindings may be connected as ***input bindings***, ***output bindings*** or **both**. Data from bindings is provided to the function as parameters.

Triggers and bindings let you avoid hardcoding access (You won't have to write code) to other services.

The table below shows various examples of how we can implement Functions using Triggers and Bindings.

	Trigger	**Input Binding**	**Output Binding**
A new queue message arrives which runs a function to write to another queue.	Queue	None	Queue
A scheduled job reads Blob Storage contents and creates a new Cosmos DB document.	Timer	Blob Storage	Cosmos DB
The Event Grid is used to read an image from Blob Storage and a document from Cosmos DB to send an email.	Event Grid	Blob Storage and Cosmos DB	SendGrid
A webhook that uses Microsoft Graph to update an Excel sheet.	HTTP	None	Microsoft Graph

Azure Functions integrates with various Azure and 3rd-party services. These services can trigger your function and start execution, or they can serve as input and output for your code. Some of the service integrations supported by Azure Functions are as follows:

Azure Cosmos DB | Azure Event Hubs | Azure Event Grid
Azure Notification Hubs | Azure Service Bus (queues and topics)
Azure Storage (blob, queues, and tables) | GitHub (webhooks)
On-premises (using Service Bus) | Twilio (SMS messages)
Timer

Figure below shows relationship between Function code, Trigger, Input Binding and Output Binding.

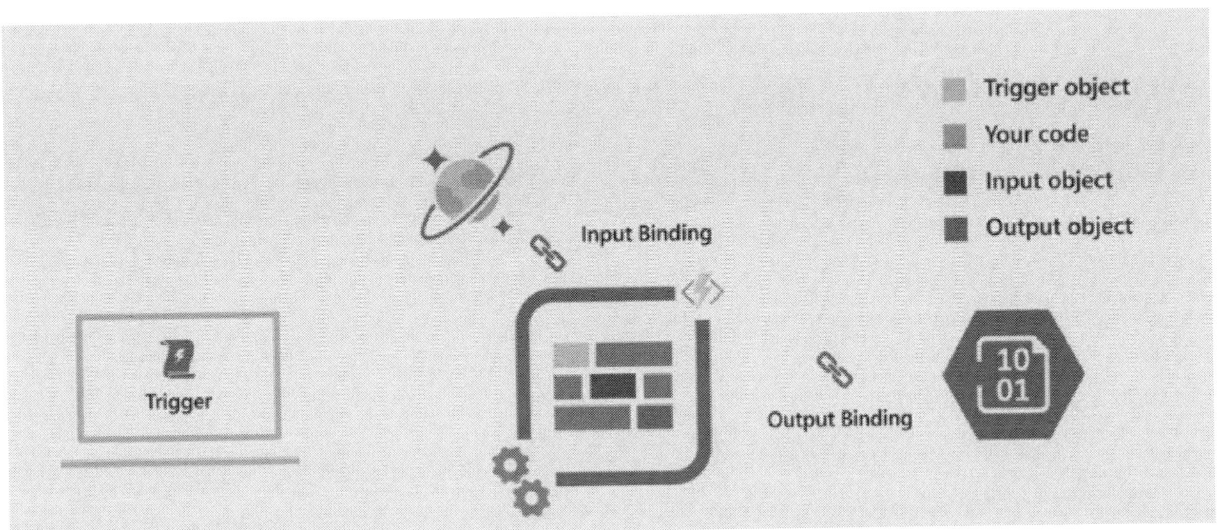

Exercise 69: Publishing Hello World using http triggered Functions

In this Exercise we will create http triggered function. We will also create **Resource Group HWCloud**. We will also create **Storage Account**. System will pick Storage Account Name based on App Name. In this case it picked **hwcloud8456**.

1. **Create Function App:** In Azure Portal Click the + Create a resource>Compute > **Function App**> Create Function App Blade opens> Enter a name>In Resource Group select create new and enter a name. I entered HWCloud>In Storage make sure Create new is selected. A name is entered automatically based on App Name. In this case it was **hwcloud8456**. Rest select all default values> Click create.

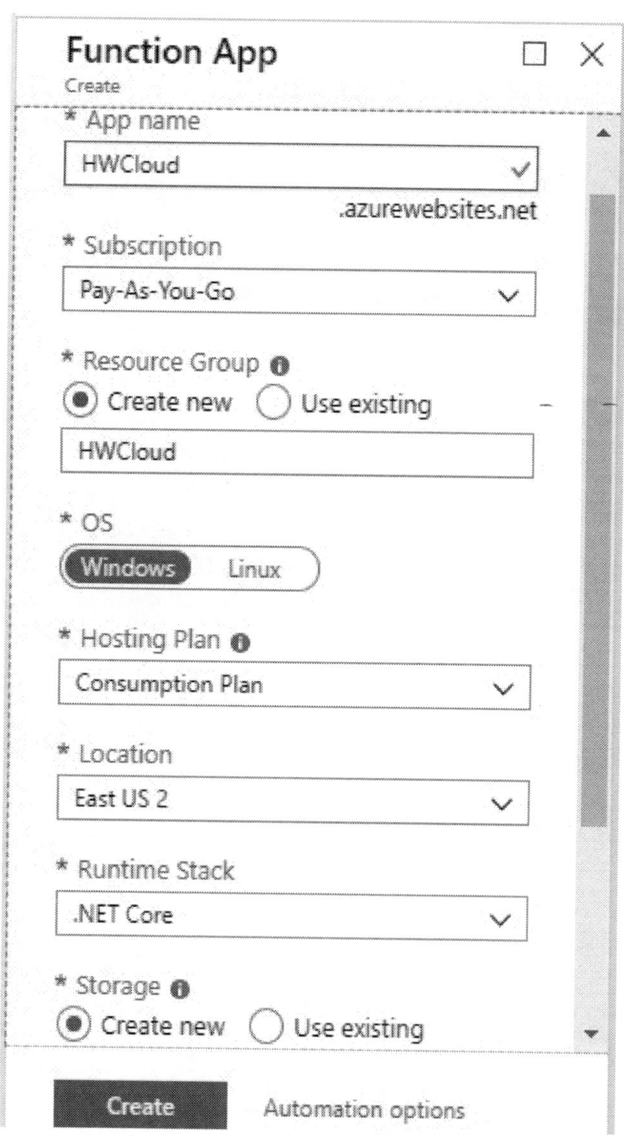

2. Figure below shows Function App HWCloud Dashboard. Make sure you have select HWCloud in left pane.

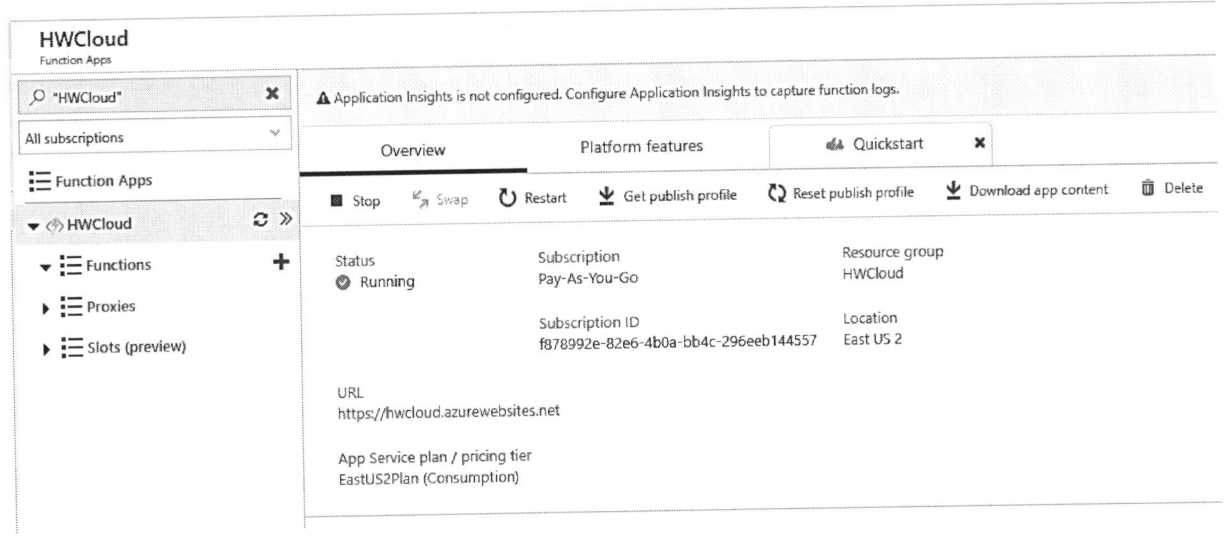

3. Copy Function App URL from the dashboard as shown above and open it in browser.

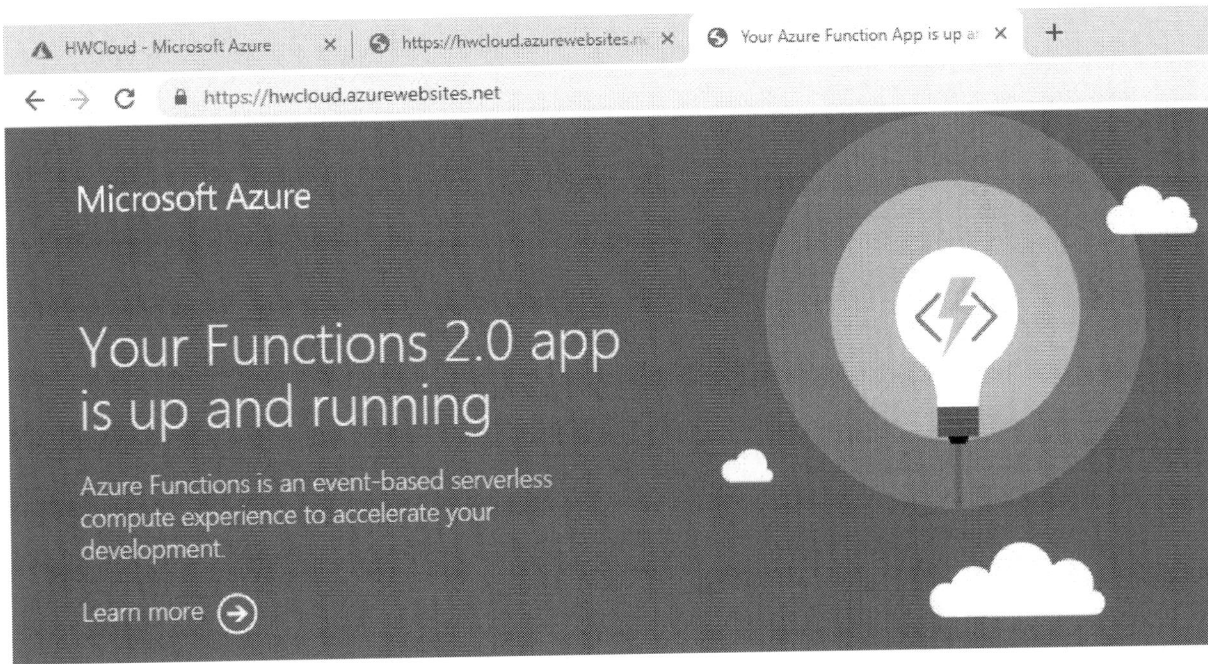

4. **Create HTTP Triggered Function:** In the Function App HWCloud Dashboard> Click + next to Function> Scroll down and select In-portal and click Continue.

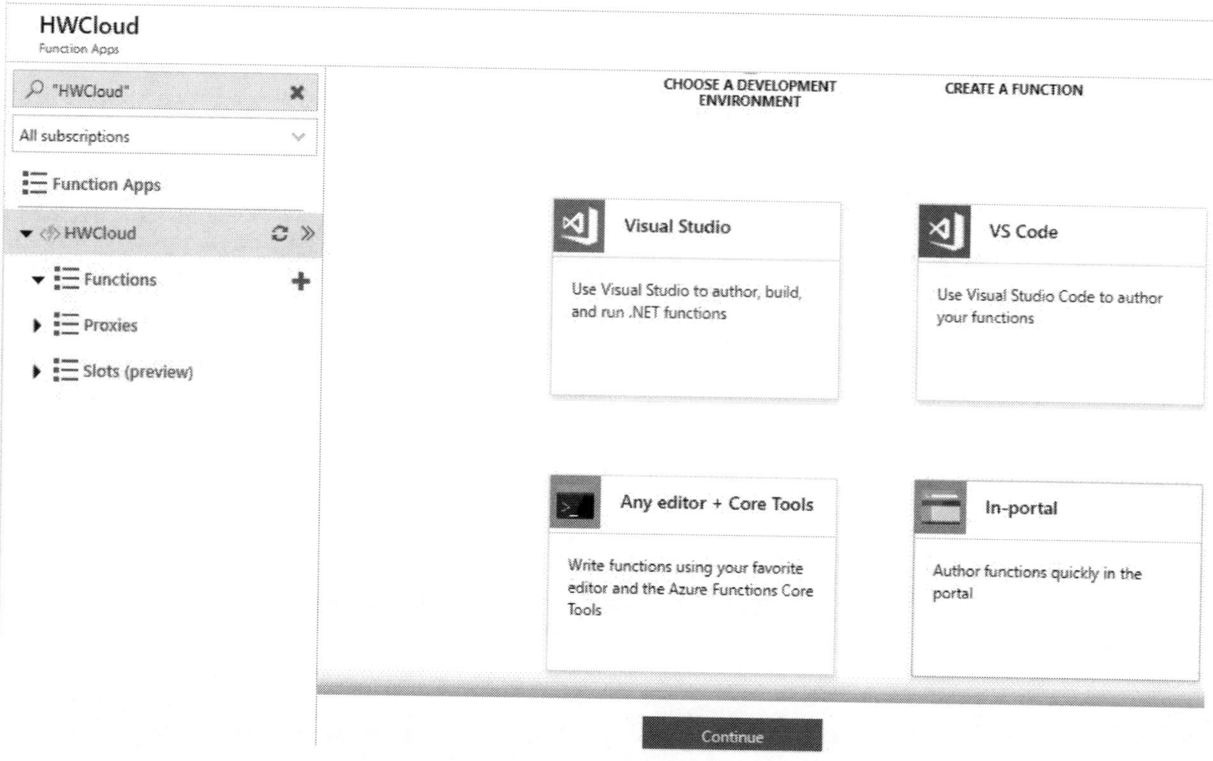

5. Select Webhook + API>Click Create.

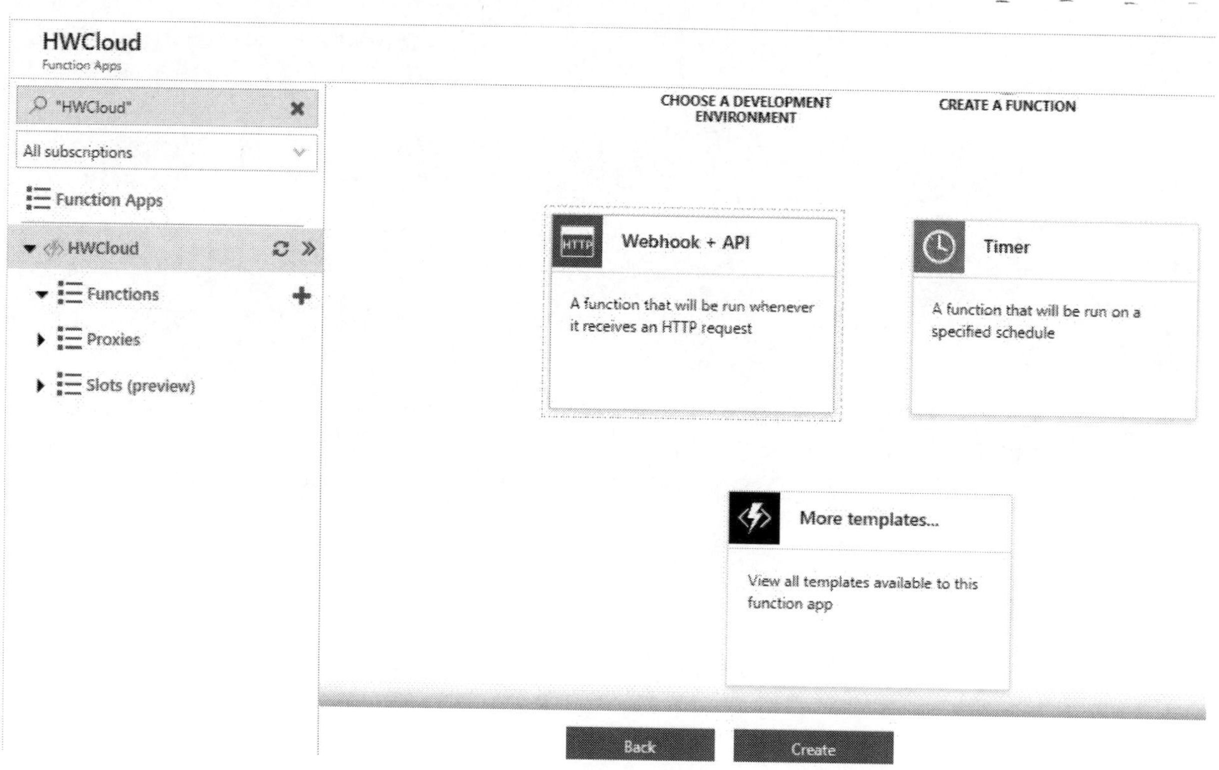

6. A function is created using the template for an HTTP triggered function.

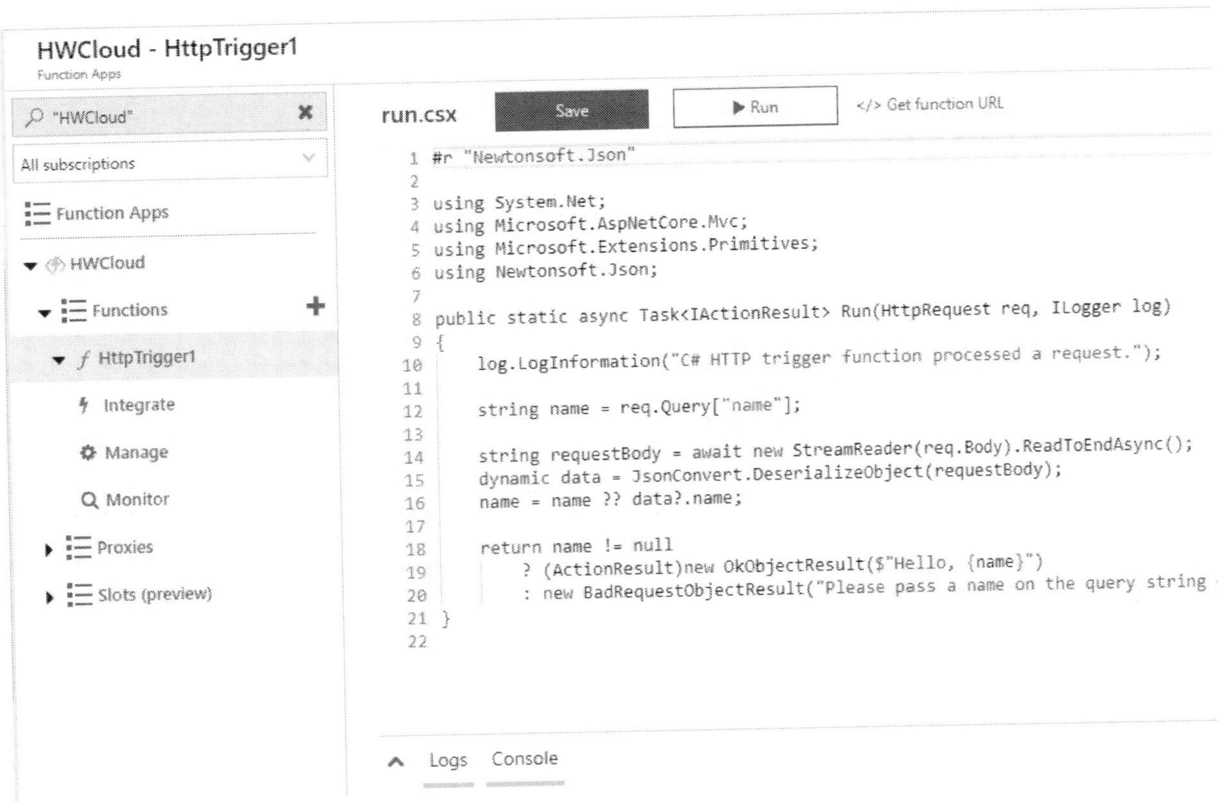

7. In your new function, click </> **Get function URL** at the top right, select default (Function Key) and then click **Copy**.

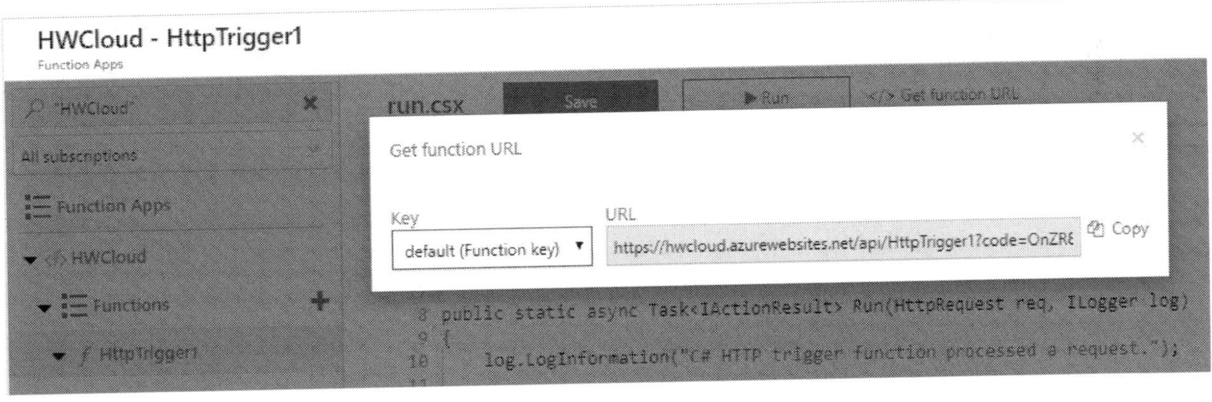

Here is the copied URL.
https://hwcloud.azurewebsites.net/api/HttpTrigger1?code=OnZR8CXmQjnX8SUcaNOCa6loXAa/JJk/PaaLLEAULj7qAugO8NEaHQ==

8. **Test the Function by sending an http request.** Open a Browser and paste the copied function URL. Add to the URL **&name=world.**

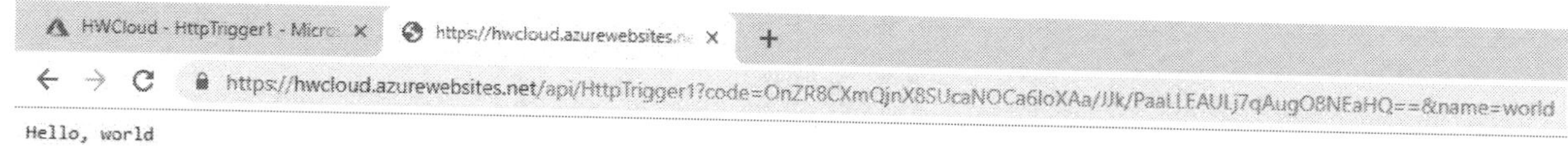

You can see from above how Hello World was executed without creating Virtual Machine Infrastructure in Azure Cloud.

9. When your function runs, information is written to the logs. To see the trace output from the previous execution, return to your function in the portal and click the arrow at the bottom of the screen to expand the **Logs**.

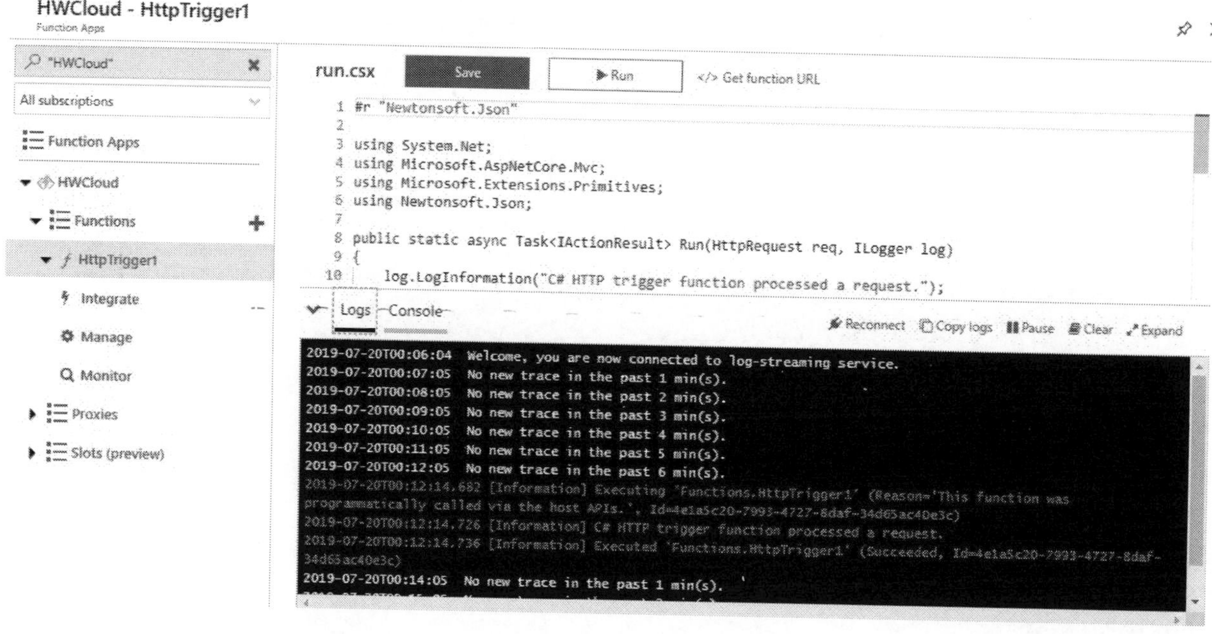

Exercise 70: Check Trigger Option Templates to create a Function

1. In the Function App HWCloud Dashboard> Click + next to Function. If required Click New Function> You can see various Trigger options templates to create function. Scroll down and you can see more template options.

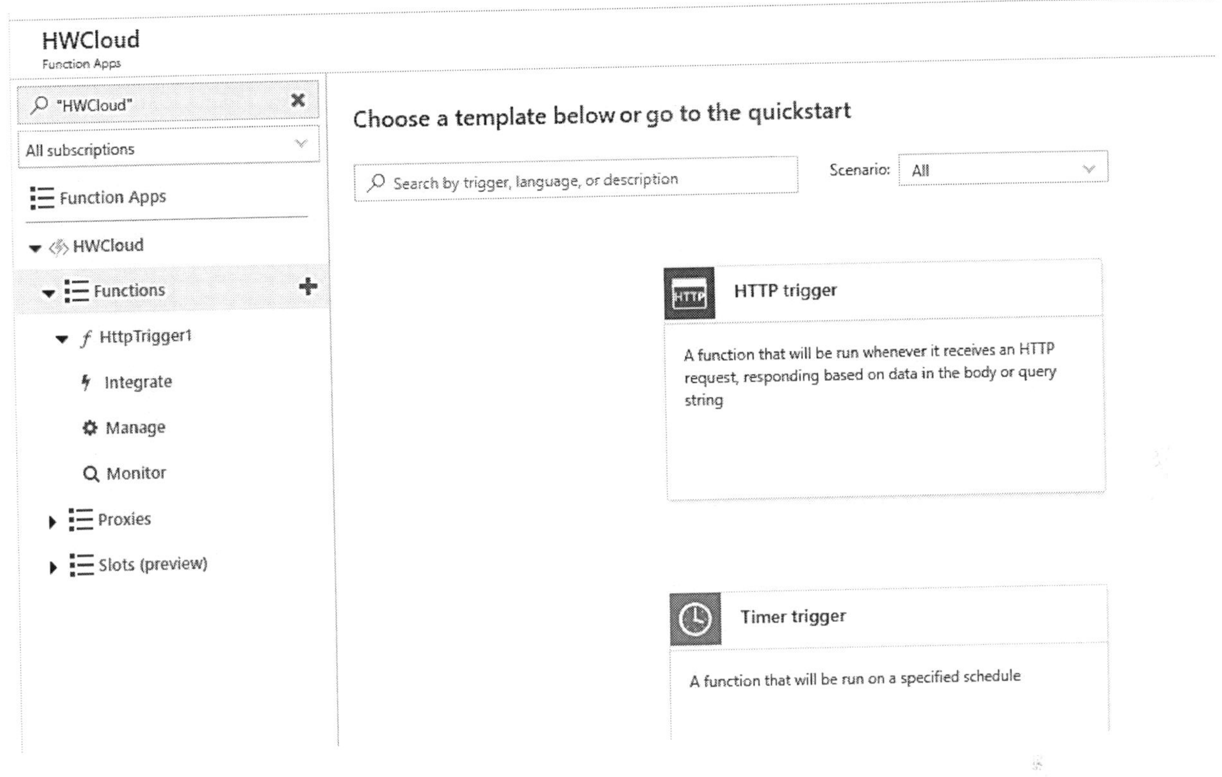

Exercise 71: Use Blob Storage Trigger Template to create a Function

Blob Storage Trigger Template option creates a function whenever a Blob file is added to a specified container. This function processes the Blob File.

In this Exercise we will use **Function App HWCloud & Storage Account hwcloud8456**. **HWCloud** & **hwcloud8456 were** created in Ex 69.

1. In the Function App HWCloud Dashboard> Click + next to Function. If required click + New Function> You can see various Trigger options templates to create function. Scroll down and you can see Azure Blob Storage Trigger Template option.

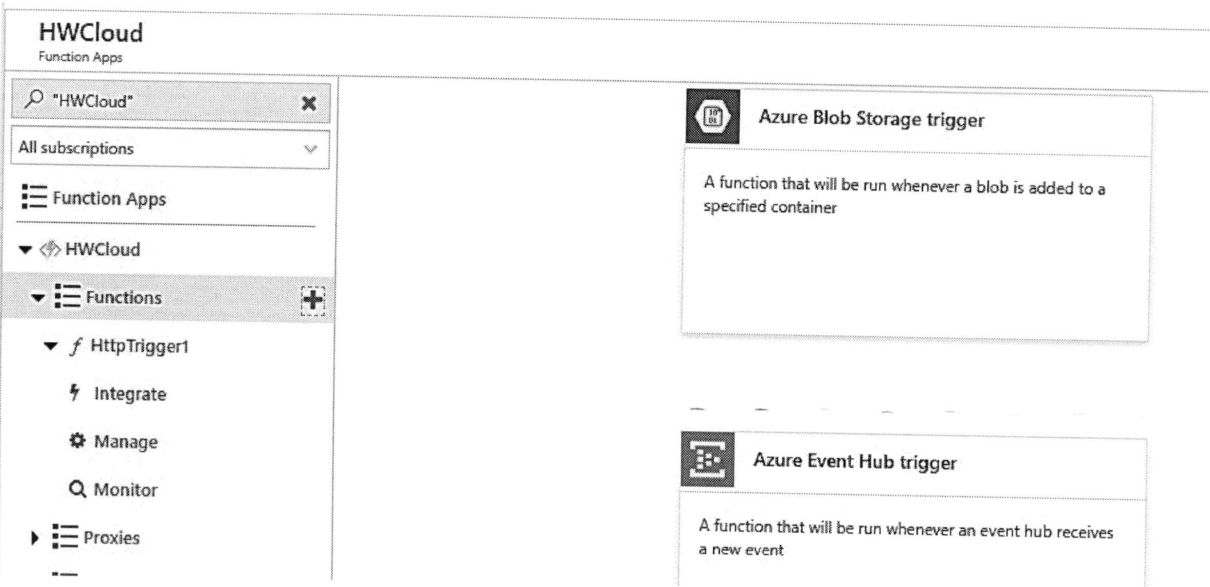

2. Select Blob Storage Trigger Template> System asks to Install an Extension> Click Install.

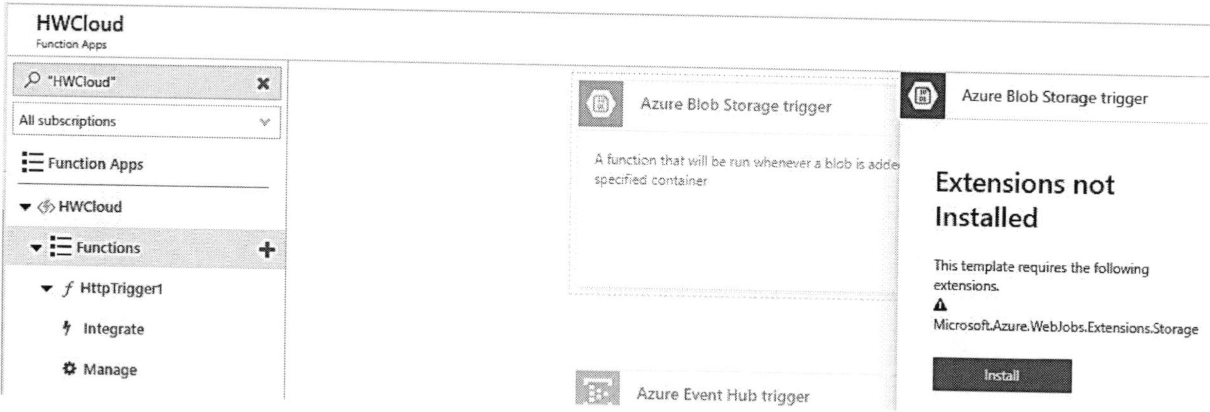

3. After Installation succeeds click continue

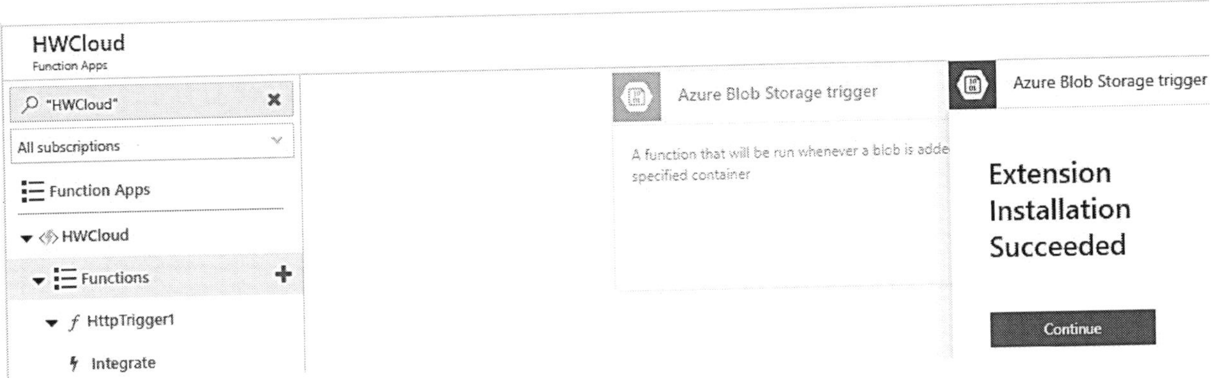

4. New Function Blade opens> Enter a name. I entered **MyBlob**>Rest Select all default values>Click create.
   Note: In Path Box note the **samples-workitems.** You need to create the Blob Container with this name or you can change the name here and then create Blob Container with changed name.

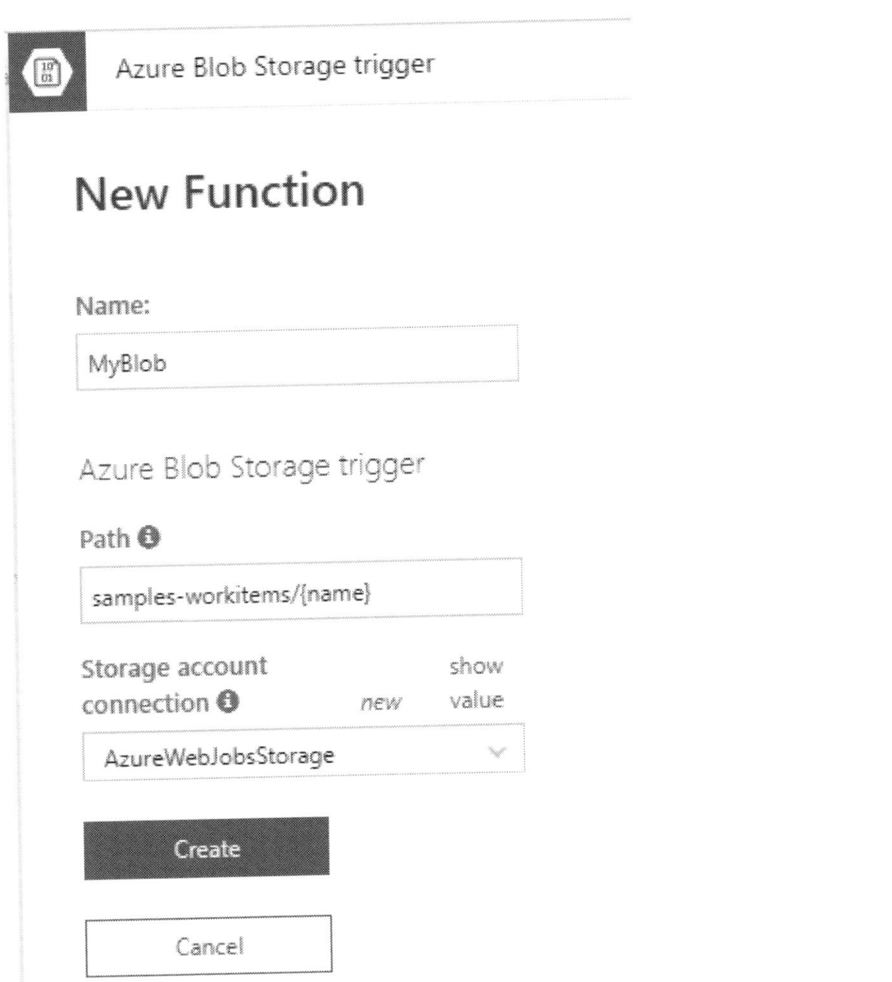

5. In Function App HWCloud dashboard Click MyBlob>You can see function is created.

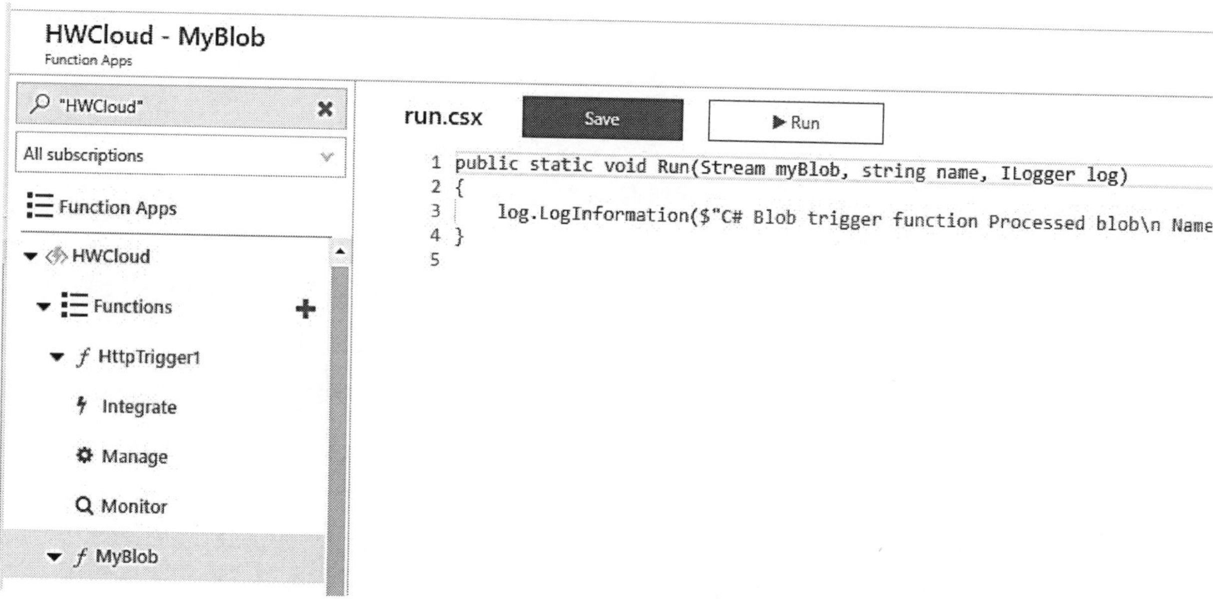

6. In Function App HWCloud dashboard select and Expand MyBlob>Click Integrate>In Right pane expand Documentation> Copy the Storage Account Name and Account Key. We will use Storage Account Name and Account Key to connect to Storage Account using Storage Explorer.

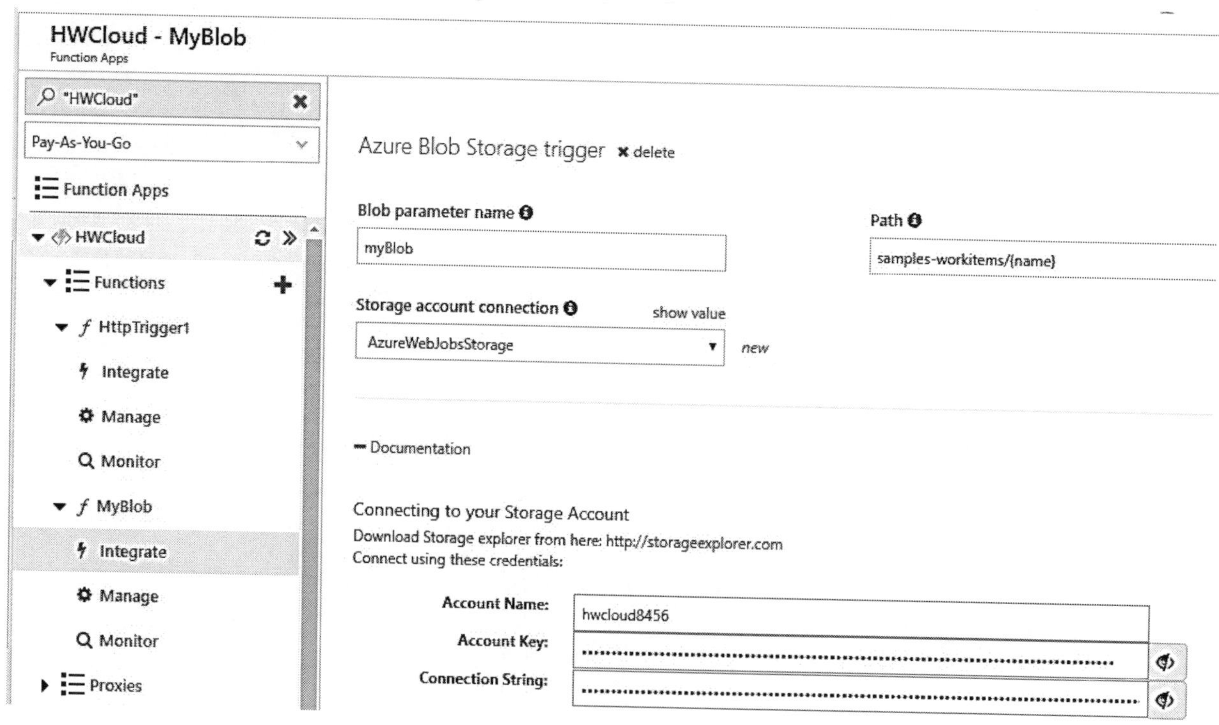

7. In your laptop open Storage Explorer>Right Click Storage Account and select Connect to Azure Storage>Connect to Storage Box opens>Select use a storage account name and key Radio Button.

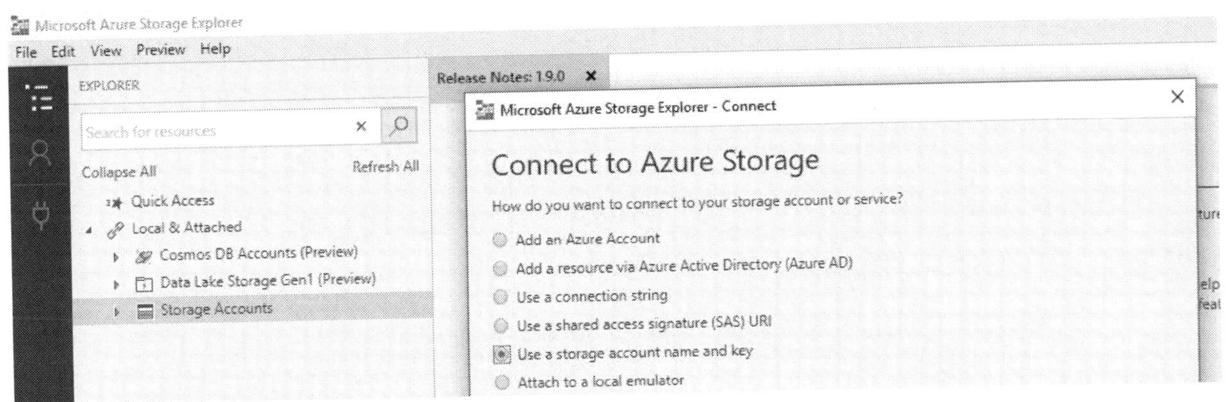

8. Click Next> Connect with Name and Key Blade opens> Enter Dispaly name. I entered FCC>Enter Storage Account Name>Enter Storage Account Key>Click Next (Not Shown).

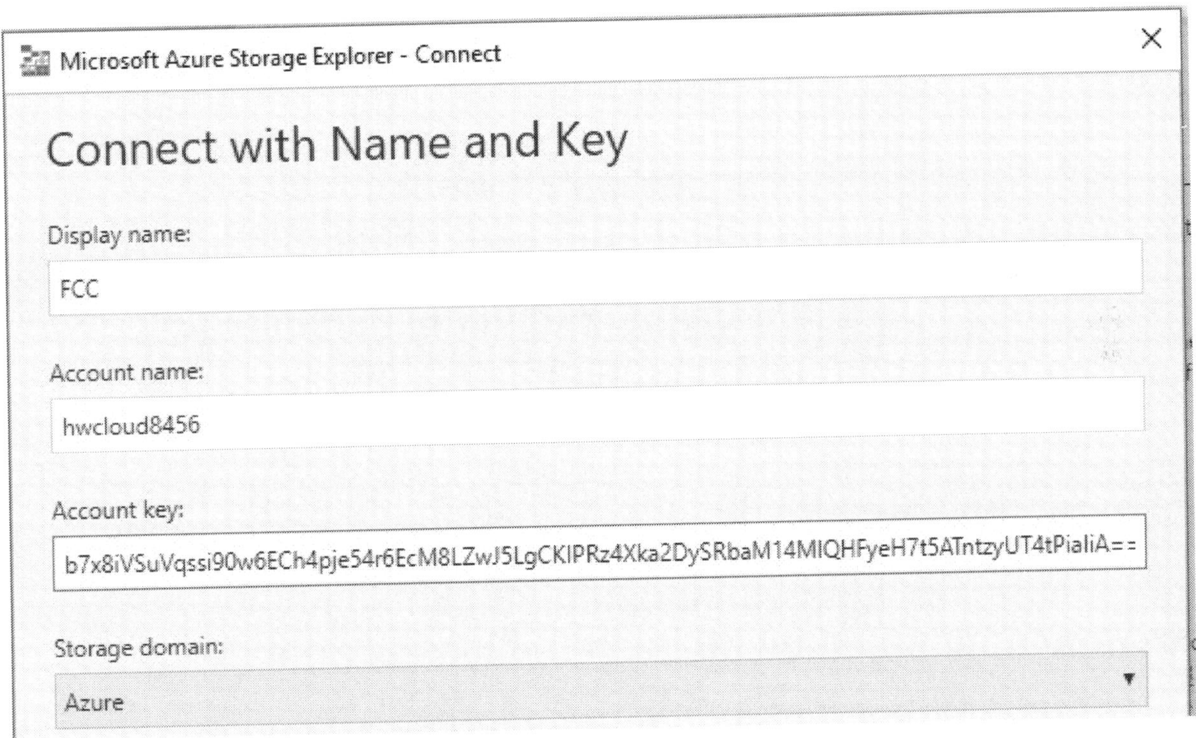

9. Click Connect>You get connected to Storage Account. Expand FCC. **FCC was display name given to Storage Account hwcloud8456 in step 8.**

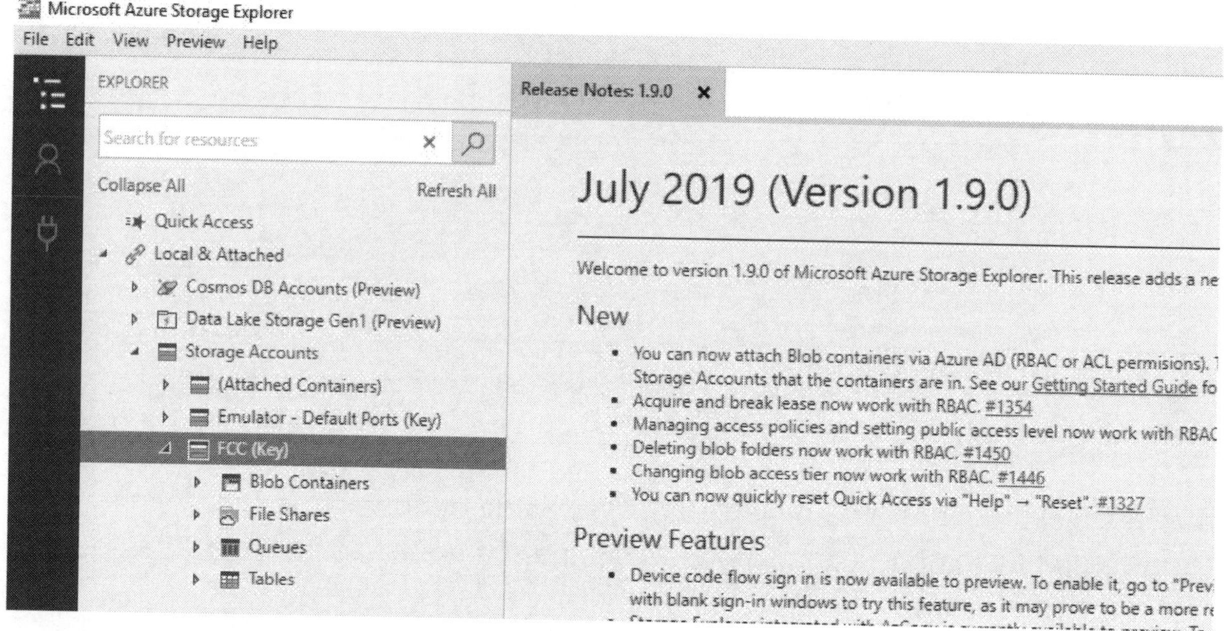

10. Under FCC Right Click Blob Container> Click Create Blob container>A Box opens. In Box enter **samples-workitems** and click Enter. You can see Blob Container **samples-workitems** is created. We discussed in Step 4 that we need to create container with name **samples-workitems**

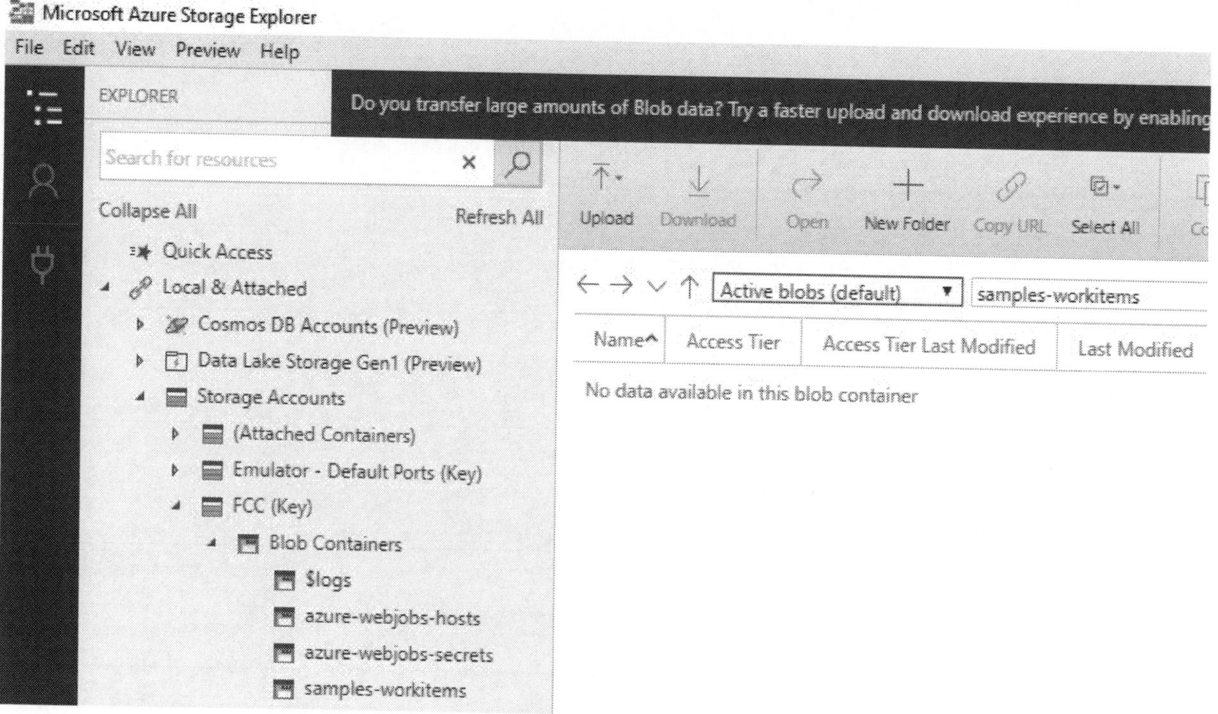

11. with **samples-workitems** selected in left> In Right Pane click upload>Click Upload Files>Upload Files Box opens>Under Files Click box with ellipsis ...> Select an image file from you laptop. I select CP.jpg file>Click upload.

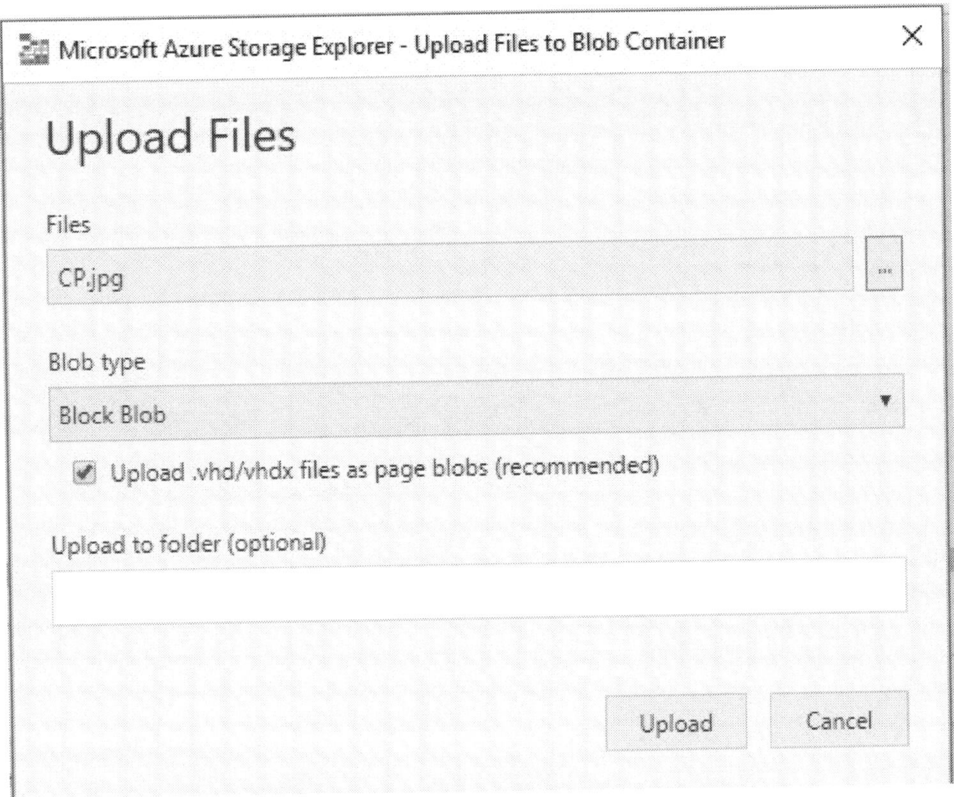

12. Go Back to Function App Dashboard>Click Function MyBlob>In the right pane Expand Logs>You can see Blob Trigger Function processed Blob file CP.jpg.

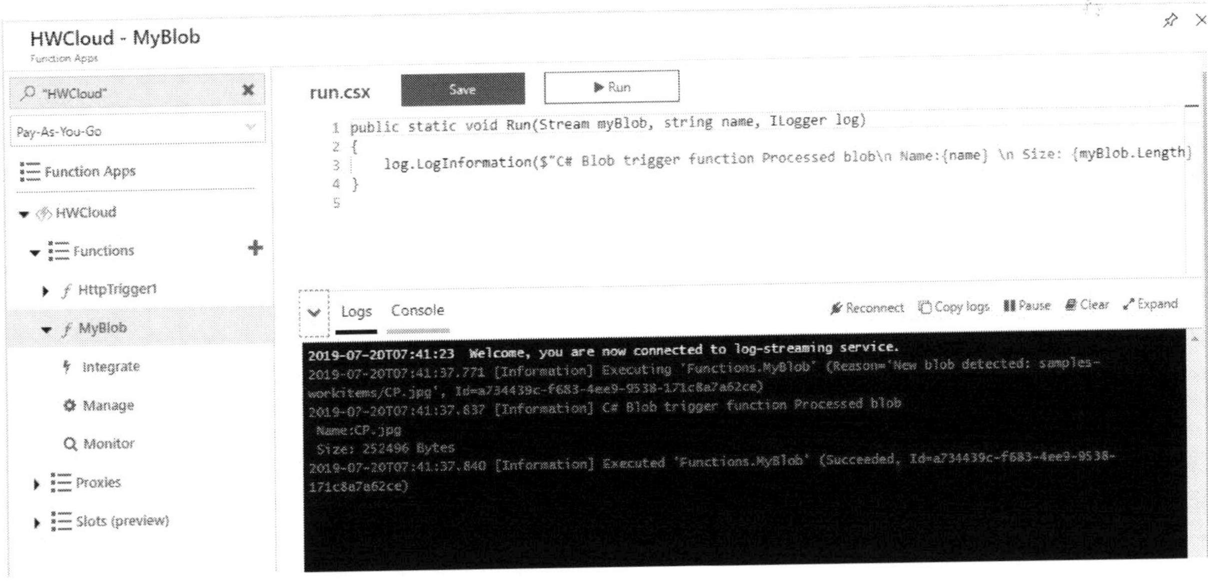

Exercise 72: Exploring Function App HWCloud Settings, Config & Platform Features

1. Go to Function App HWCloud Dashboard> Make sure HWCloud is selected in left pane> In Right pane you can see the option for Platform features, Function app settings and Configuration.

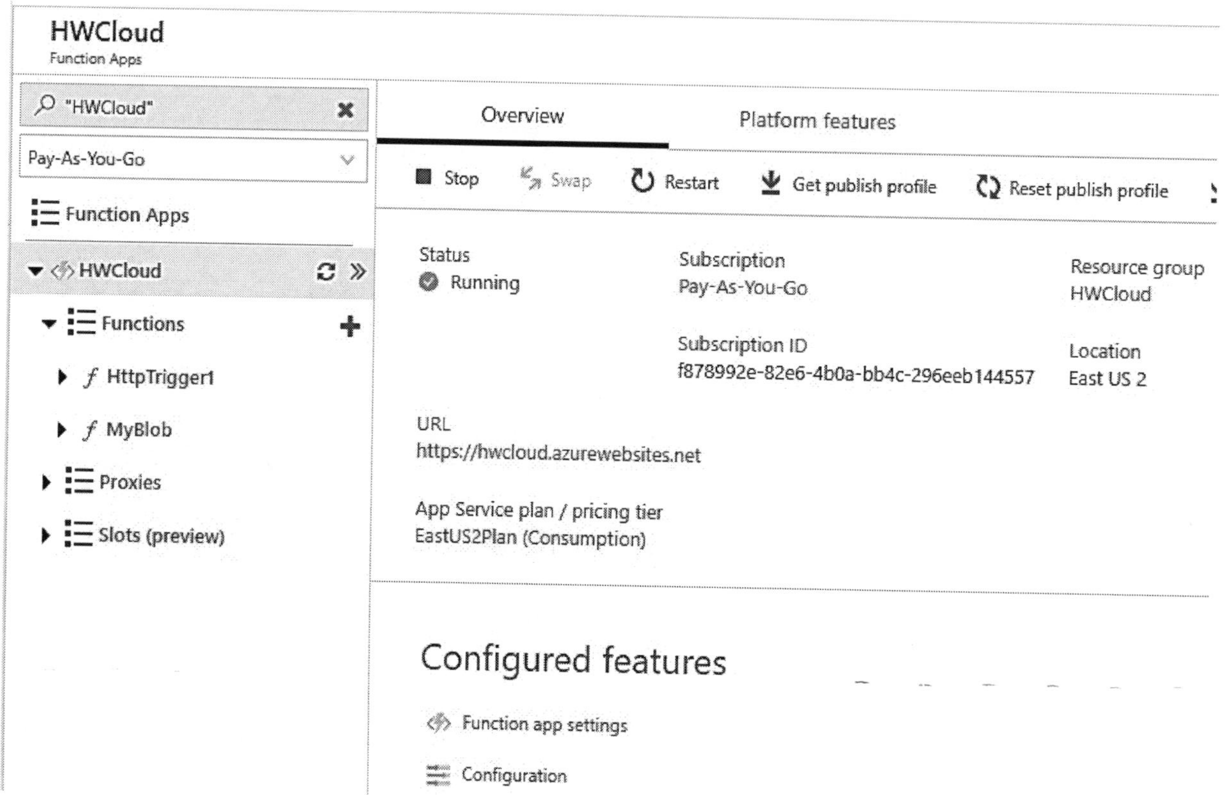

2. **Explore Function app settings**: Under Configured features Click Function app settings in right pane> Function app settings pane opens.

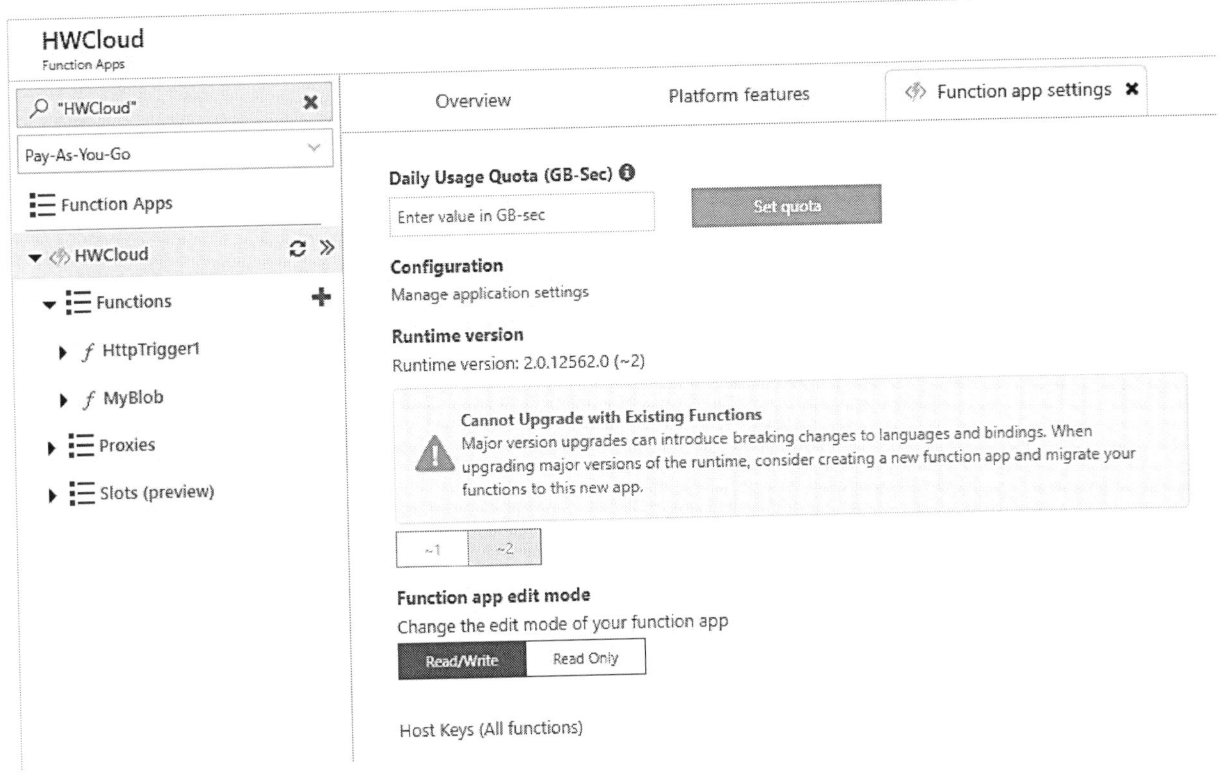

3. Click Manage Applications settings>Click General settings.

Save Discard

Application settings General settings

Platform settings

Platform 32 Bit

Managed pipeline version Integrated

FTP state All allowed — FTP based deployment can be (secure) connections. Learn mo

HTTP version 1.1

Web sockets On Off

Debugging

4. **Explore Platform Features**: In Function App HWCloud Dashboard close the Function app setting pane>Click Platform feature>Platform feature pane opens. Readers are requested to explore the features here.

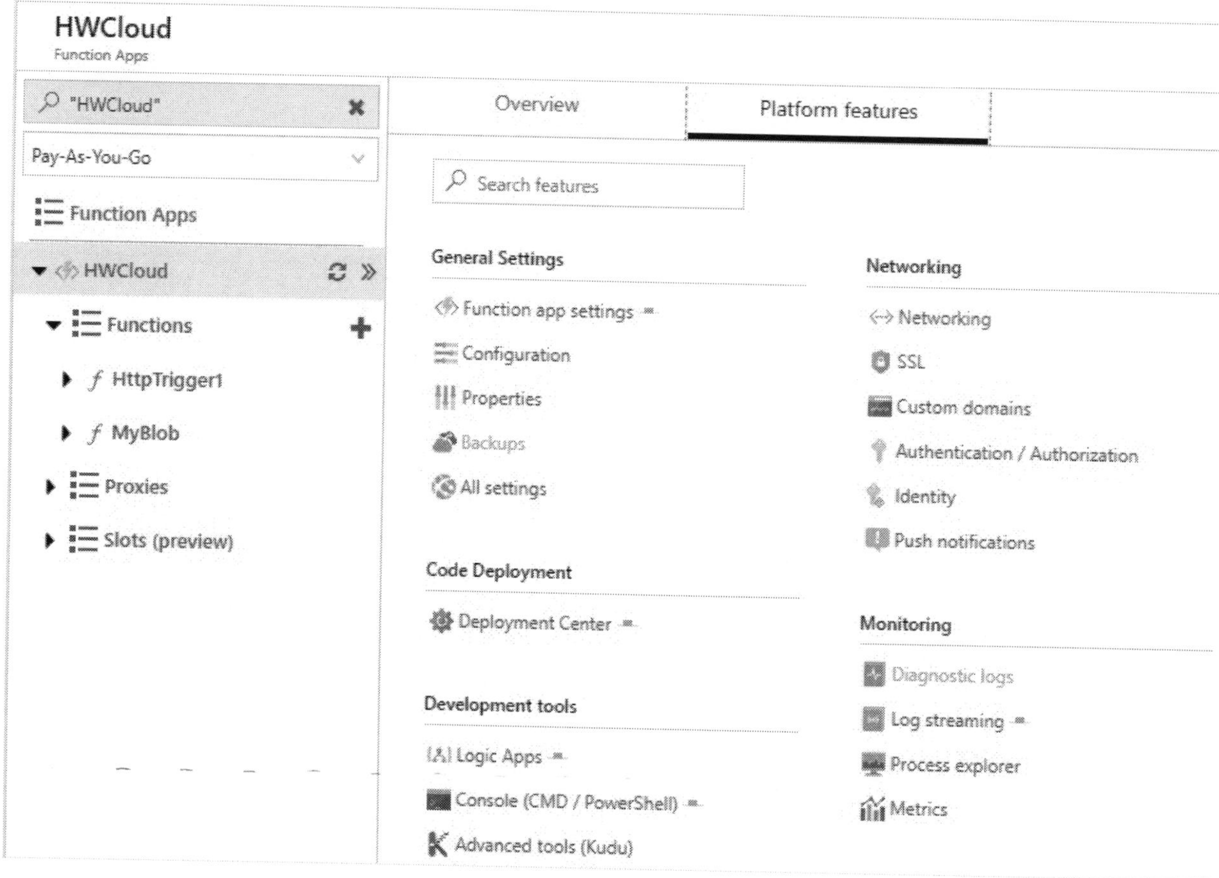

Exercise 73: Exploring Function (MyBlob) Settings

For this Exercise we will use Function MyBlob. MyBlob was created in Step 4, Exercise 71.

1. Go to Function App HWCloud Dashboard>Select and Expand Function MyBlob> Click Integrate>Here you can add input and output Bindings to the Function.

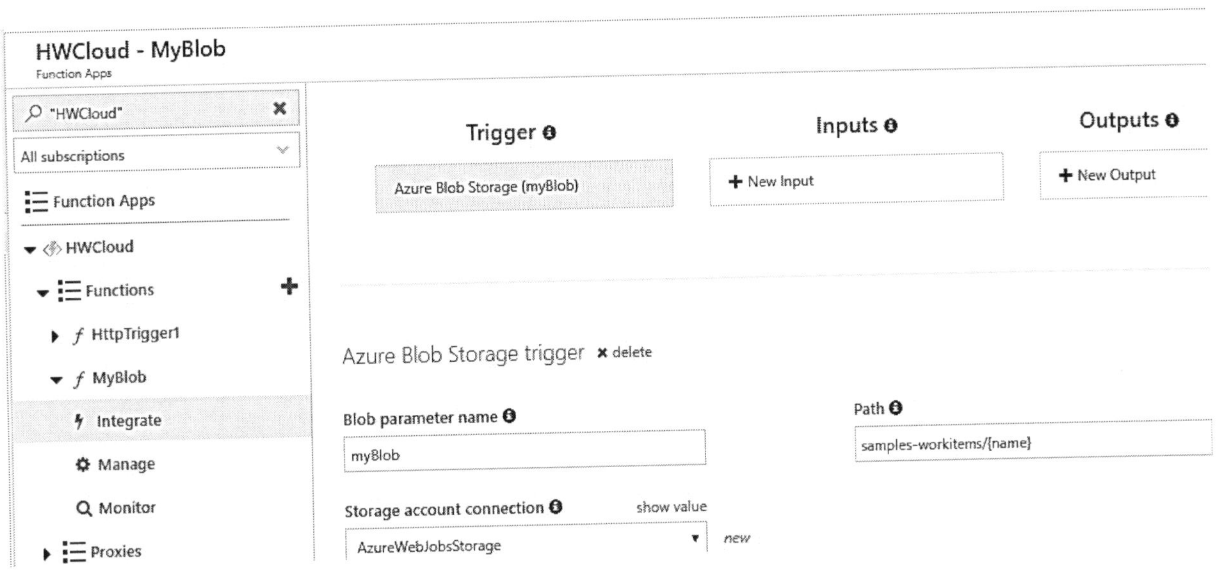

2. Click Manage>Here you can enable or disable the function. You can also delete the function.

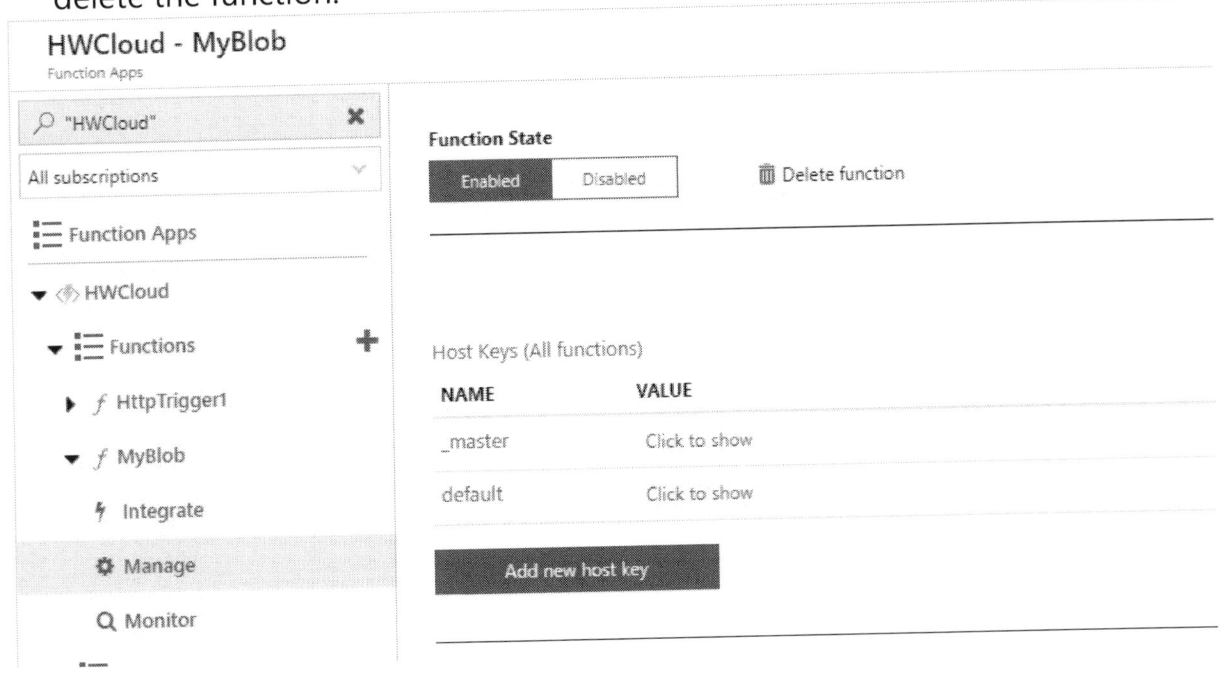

3. Click Monitor> You can monitor Function using Application insights.

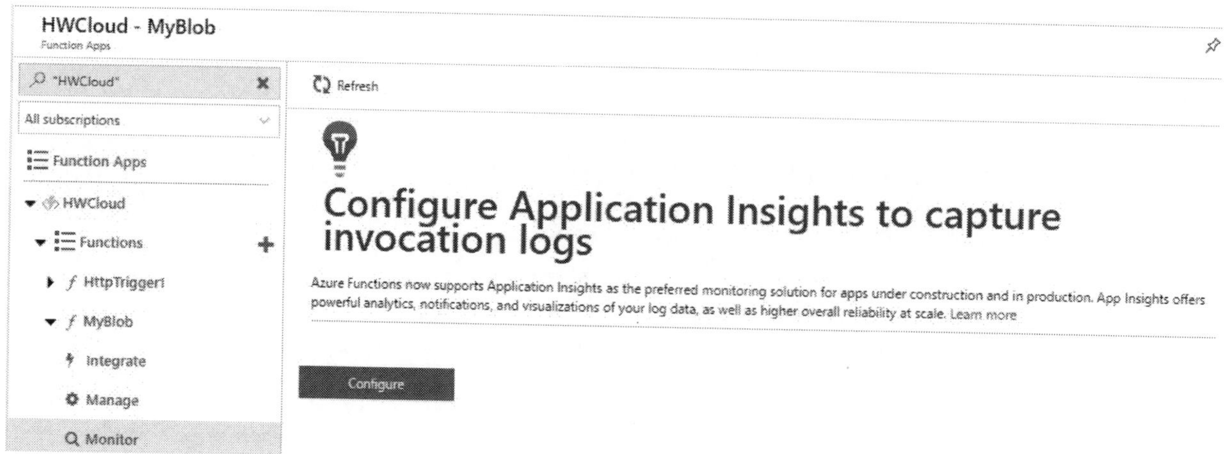

Exercise 74: Delete Function MyBlob

1. Go to Function App HWCloud Dashboard>Select and Expand Function MyBlob> Click Manage

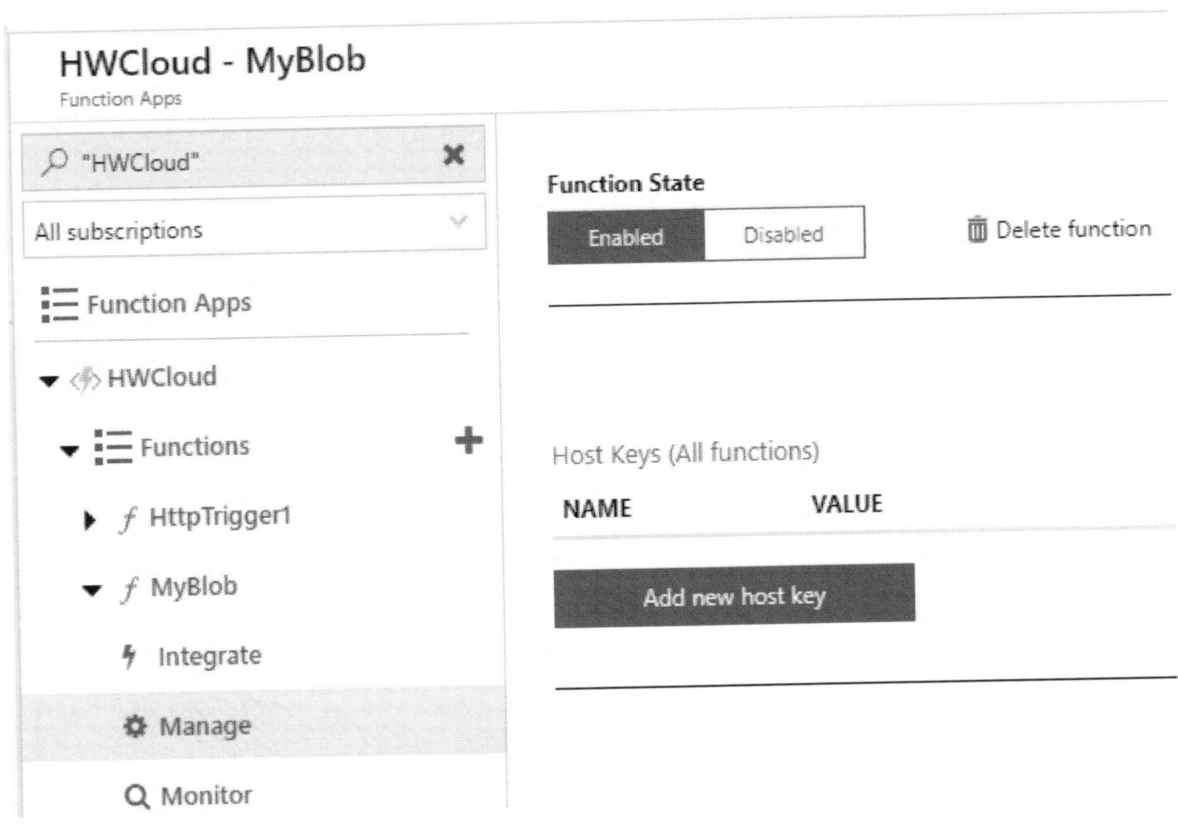

2. Click Delete Function in Right pane>A Popup Box opens>Click Ok.

Azure Functions pricing

Azure Functions has two kinds of pricing plans.

Consumption Plan

Azure Functions consumption is billed monthly and is sum of **resource consumption per second** and **executions**. Consumption plan pricing includes a monthly free grant of 1 million requests and 400,000 GB-s of resource consumption per month.

Resource consumption in gigabyte-seconds (GB-s): Computed as a combination of memory size and execution time for all functions within a function app.
Executions: Counted each time a function is executed in response to an event trigger.

	Price	**Free Grant Per Month**
Resource Consumption	$0.000016/GB-s	400,000 GB-s
Executions	$0.20 per million executions	1 million executions

You only pay for the resources and execution when the code runs. You don't pay for the idle time.

Note – Cost of Storage is separate. A storage account is created by default with each Functions app. The storage account is not included in the free grant. Standard **storage rates** charged separately as applicable.

App Service plan

Run your functions just like your web, mobile, and API apps. If you are already using App Service for your other applications, you can run your functions on the same plan at no additional cost. Refer to Web App Chapter for App Service Plan.

Azure Functions scale and hosting

When you're using a Consumption plan, instances of the Azure Functions host are dynamically added and removed based on the number of incoming events. This plan scales automatically, and you are charged for compute resources only when your functions are running. On a Consumption plan, a function can run for a maximum of 10 minutes.

The default timeout for functions on a Consumption plan is 5 minutes. The value can be increased to 10 minutes for the Function App by changing the property functionTimeout in the host.json project file.

When you use the Consumption hosting plan, function code files are stored on Azure Files shares on the function's main storage account. When you delete the main storage account of the function app, the function code files are deleted and cannot be recovered.

In the Consumption plan, the scale controller automatically scales CPU and memory resources by adding additional instances of the Functions host, based on the number of events that its functions are triggered on. Each instance of the Functions host is limited to 1.5 GB of memory. An instance of the host is the Function App, meaning all functions within a funciton app share resources within an instance and scale at the same time.

Azure Functions uses scale controller to monitor the rate of events and determine whether to scale out or scale in. The scale controller uses heuristics for each trigger type. For example, when you're using an Azure Queue storage trigger, it scales based on the queue length and the age of the oldest queue message.

The unit of scale is the function app. When the function app is scaled out, additional resources are allocated to run multiple instances of the Azure Functions host. Conversely, as compute demand is reduced, the scale controller removes function host instances. The number of instances is eventually scaled down to zero when no functions are running within a function app.

Figure below shows Function scalability based on incoming events.

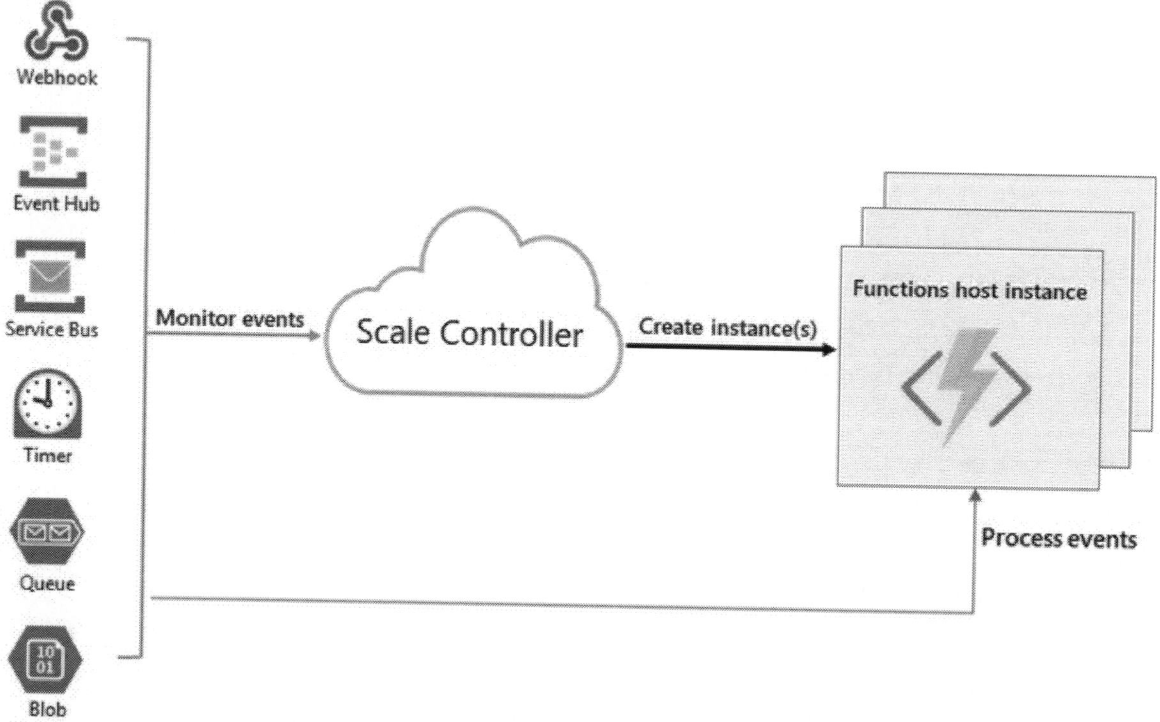

Understanding scaling behaviors

Scaling can vary on a number of factors, and scale differently based on the trigger and language selected. However there are a few aspects of scaling that exist in the system today:

- A single function app will only scale to a maximum of 200 instances. A single instance may process more than one message or request at a time though, so there isn't a set limit on number of concurrent executions.
- New instances will only be allocated at most once every 10 seconds.

Logic Apps

Azure Logic Apps automates business process execution and workflow using an easy-to-use visual designer without writing a single line of code.

Using Logic Apps you can connect your business-critical apps and services and automate your workflows without writing a single line of code.

Logic Apps Working

Every logic app workflow starts with a trigger which fires when a specific event happens or when new available data meets specific criteria. Each time that the trigger fires the Logic Apps engine creates a logic app instance that runs the actions in the workflow.

For example following logic app starts with a Dynamics 365 trigger with the built-in criteria "When a record is updated". If the trigger detects an event that matches this criteria the trigger fires and runs the workflow's actions. Here, these actions include XML transformation, data updates, decision branching and email notifications.

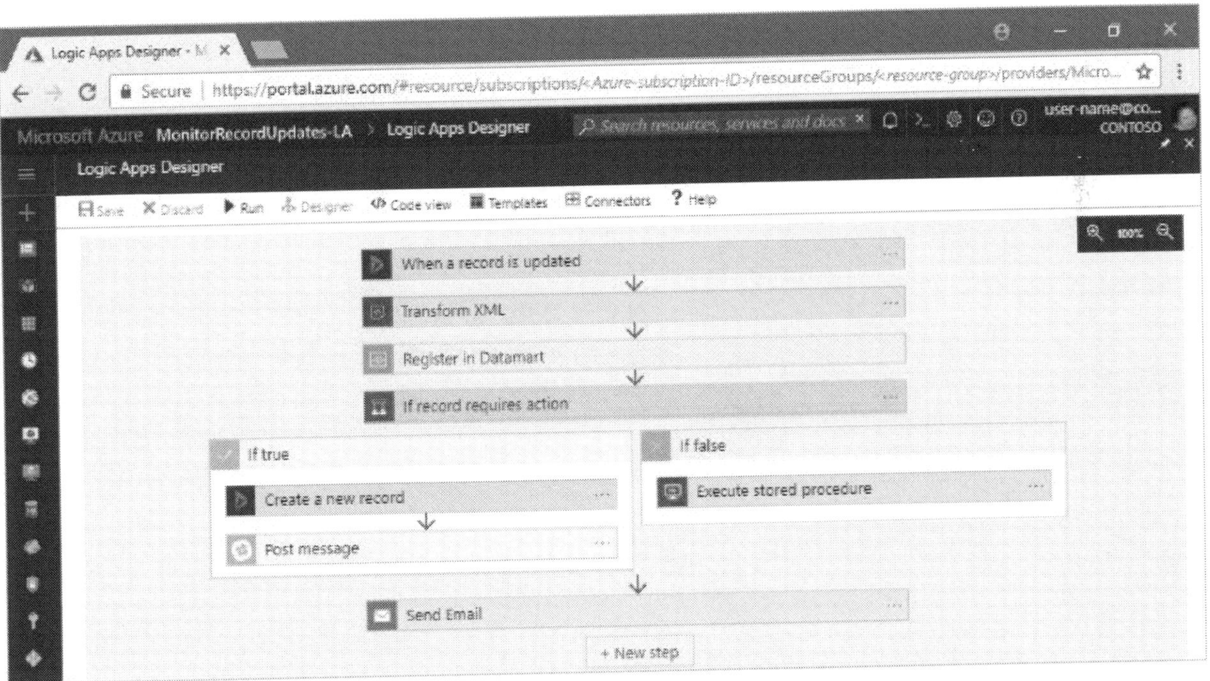

Connectors

Logic Apps connectors are used to connect Logic App instance to Applications and Data sources in Azure, on-premises and other clouds.

Connectors can provide ***triggers***, ***actions***, or **both**. A *trigger* is the first step in any logic app execution process. After a trigger fires, Azure Logic Apps creates an instance of your logic app and starts running the *actions* in your logic app's workflow. Actions are the steps that follow the trigger and perform tasks in your logic app's workflow.

The connectors are available as either as **built-in triggers and actions** or **managed connectors**.

Built-in triggers and actions are "native" to Azure Logic Apps and help you create logic apps that run on custom schedules, communicate with other endpoints, receive and respond to requests and call Azure functions, Azure API Apps (Web Apps) and nested logic apps that can receive requests. You can also use built-in actions that help you organize and control your logic app's workflow, and also work with data. Figure below shows some of the Built-in triggers and actions:

Schedule

- Run your logic app on a specified schedule, ranging from basic to complex recurrences, with the **Recurrence** trigger.

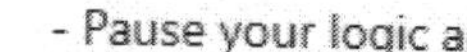

- Pause your logic app for a specified duration

HTTP

Communicate with any endpoint over HTTP with both triggers and actions for HTTP, HTTP +

Azure Functions

Call Azure functions that run custom code snippets (C# or Node.js) from your logic apps.

Azure API Management

Call triggers and actions defined by your own APIs that you manage and publish with Azure

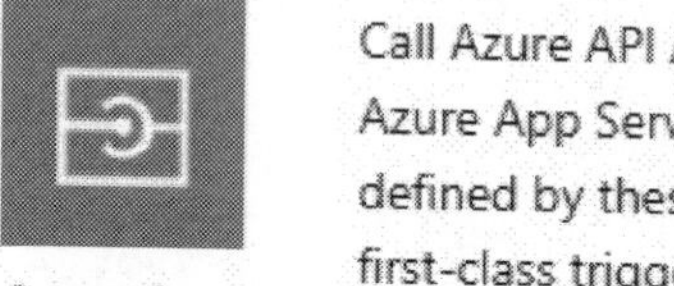

Azure App Services

Call Azure API Apps, or Web Apps, hosted on Azure App Service. The triggers and actions defined by these apps appear like any other first-class triggers and actions when Swagger is included.

Azure Logic Apps

Call other logic apps that start with a Request trigger.

Managed Connectors: Provide access to APIs for various services by creating API connections that the Logic Apps service hosts and manages. **There are 4 types of Managed Connectors.**

Standard Connector: Standard Connectors provide access to cloud based Applications. Example of Standard connectors include, Power BI, OneDrive, Event Hubs, Azure Blob Storage, Twitter, Sharepoint online etc.

Azure Blob Storage

If you want to automate any tasks with your storage account, then you should look at this connector. Supports CRUD (create, read, update, delete) operations.

Dynamics 365 CRM Online

One of the most-asked for connectors. It has triggers and actions to help automate workflows with leads, and more.

Event Hubs

Consume and publish events on an Event Hub. For example, you can get output from your logic app using Event Hubs, and then send the output to a real-time analytics provider.

FTP

If your FTP server is accessible from the internet, then you can automate workflows to work with files and folders.

SFTP is also available with the SFTP connector.

Office 365 Outlook

Lots of triggers, and a lot more actions to use Office 365 email and events within your workflows.

This connector includes an *approval email* action to approve vacation requests, expense reports, and so on.

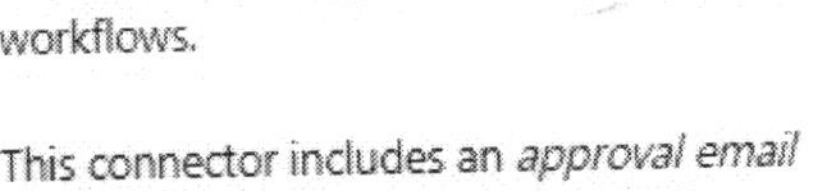

Office 365 users are also available with the Office 365 Users connector.

Salesforce

Easily sign in with your Salesforce account to get access to objects, such as Leads, and more.

Service Bus

The most popular connector within logic apps, it includes triggers and actions to do asynchronous messaging and publish/subscribe with queues, subscriptions, and topics.

SharePoint Online

If you do anything with SharePoint, and could benefit from automation, we recommend looking at this connector. Can be used with an on-premises SharePoint, and SharePoint Online.

On-premises connectors: Connect to server applications on-premises using the on-premises data gateway. On-premises connectors include SharePoint Server, SQL Server, Oracle DB, file shares etc.

DB2

Oracle DB

SharePoint Server

File System

SQL Server

BizTalk Server

Integration account connectors: These connectors process business-to-business messages with AS2 / X12 / EDIFACT, and encode and decode flat files.
If you work with BizTalk Server, then these connectors are a good fit to expand your BizTalk workflows into Azure. BizTalk Server also has a Logic Apps adapter that includes receiving from a logic app, and sending to a logic app.

AS2 decoding

AS2 encoding

EDIFACT decoding

EDIFACT encoding

Enterprise connectors: Includes MQ and SAP for accessing enterprise systems, such as SAP and IBM MQ.

MQ

SAP

SAP

Types of Triggers

Recurrence trigger: This trigger runs on a specified schedule and isn't tightly associated with a particular service or system.

Polling trigger: This trigger regularly polls a specific service or system based on the specified schedule, checking for new data or whether a specific event happened. If new data is available or the specific event happened, the trigger creates and runs a new instance of your logic app, which can now use the data that's passed as input.

Push trigger: This trigger waits and listens for new data or for an event to happen. When new data is available or when the event happens, the trigger creates and runs new instance of your logic app, which can now use the data that's passed as input.

Examples of Logic Apps workflow Automation

- Send email notifications with Office 365 when events happen in various systems, apps, and services.
- Move uploaded files from an SFTP or FTP server to Azure Storage.
- Monitor tweets for a specific subject, analyze the sentiment, and create alerts or tasks for items that need review.

Exercise 75: Create Logic App workflow (Check RSS Feed)

In this exercise we will create a logic app that regularly checks a website's RSS feed for new items. If new items exist, the logic app sends an email for each item.

When a RSS feed item is published – Trigger.
Send an email when a new item appears in the RSS feed **– Action.**

As shown below is Logic App workflow at high level for this exercise.

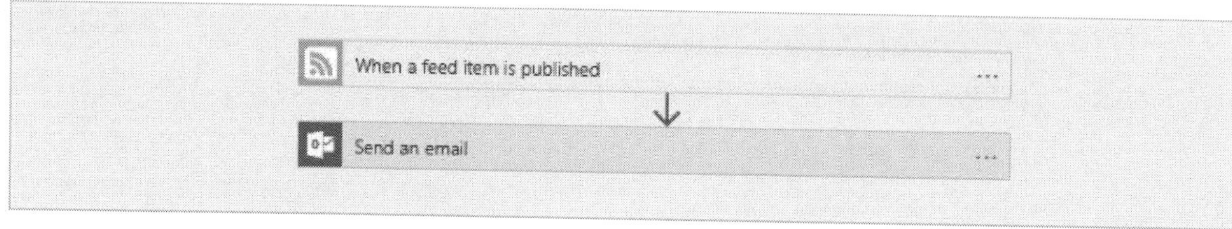

Step 1: Create Logic App Instance

1. In Azure portal Click +Create a resource>Enterprise Integration>Logic App> Create logic app blade opens> Enter a name> In Resource Group select RGCloud. **RGCloud was created** Ex 1, Chapter 1 in Exam AZ-300 & AZ-301 Study & Lab Guide Part 1>Location East US 2> Click Create (Not Shown).

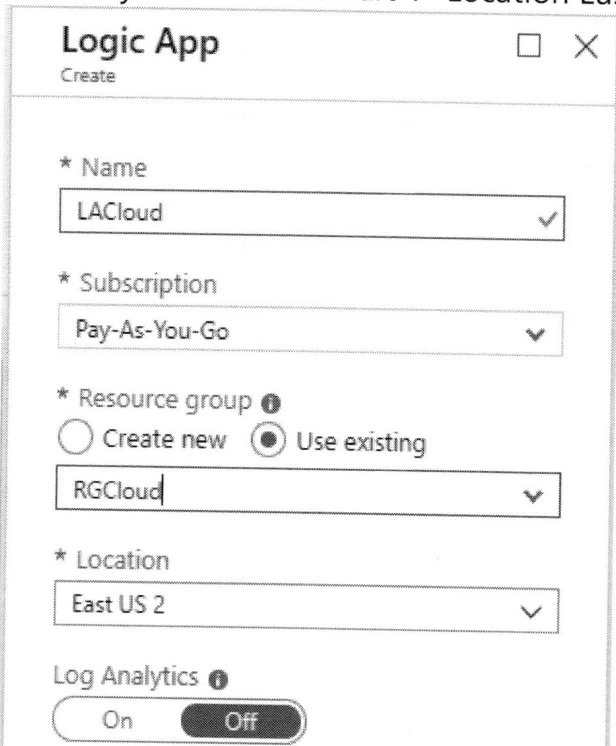

2. Figure below shows dashboard of Logic App Instance LACloud.

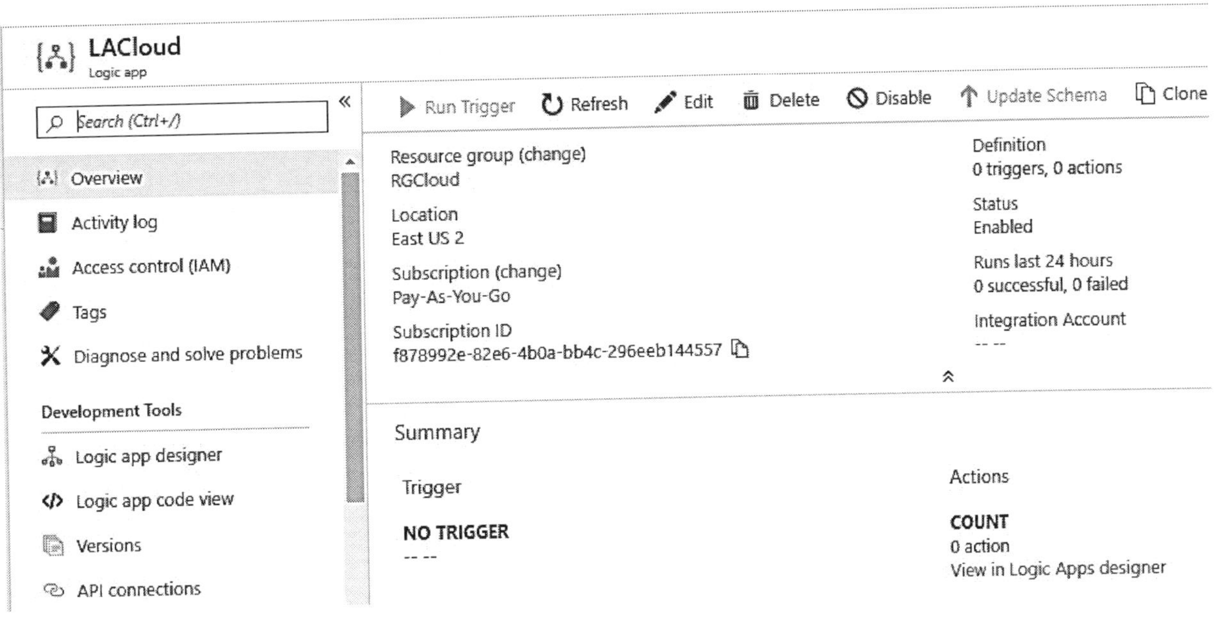

Step 2: Add an Action

1. In Logic App dashboard Click Logic app designer in left pane> Logic app designer pane opens>Scroll down and you can see Blank Logic App Template.

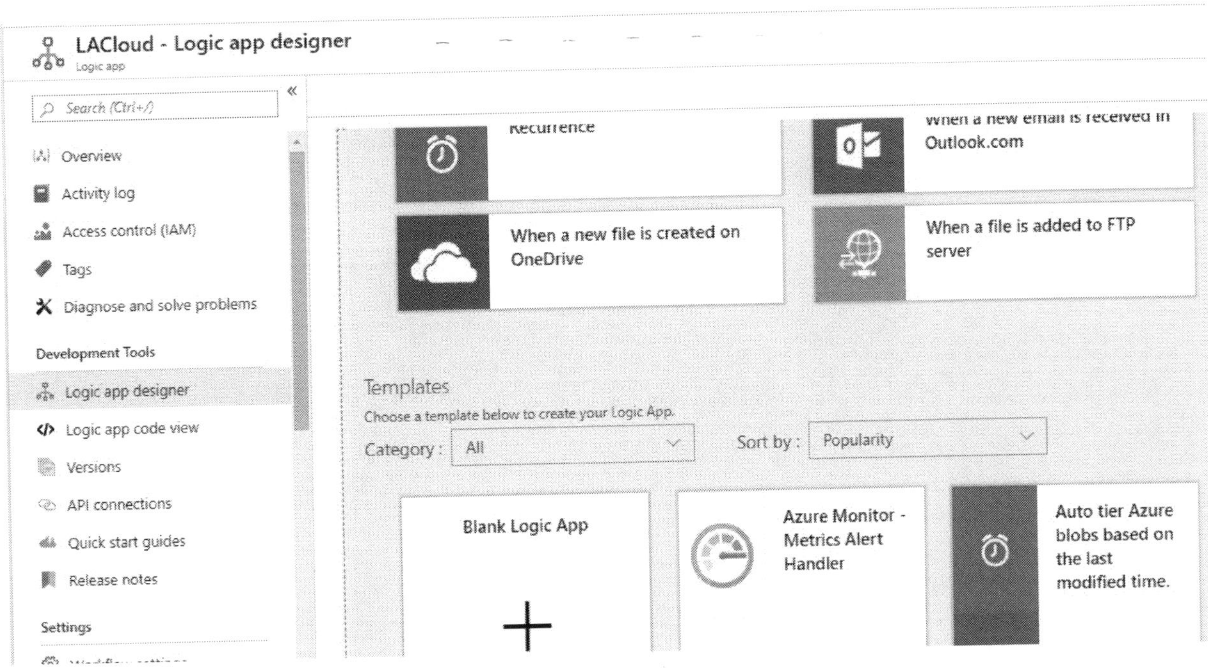

2. In Logic app designer pane Click Blank Logic App Template>A new pane opens>Just below search Click **All**> In search Box enter RSS> From the triggers list, select the trigger: **When a feed item is published – RSS**

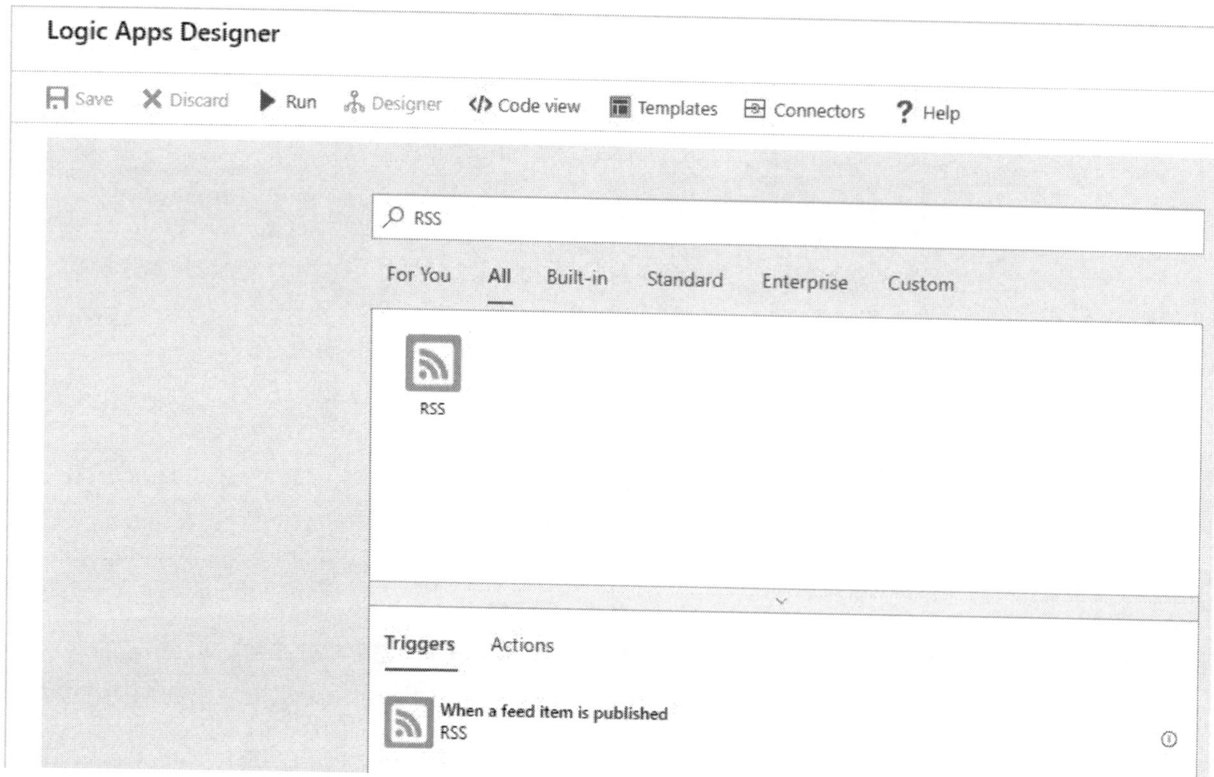

3. A new pane opens for when a feed is published> In RSS Feed URL box enter http://feeds.reuters.com/reuters/topNews> In Interval enter **1**> In Frequency select **Minutes**> Click Save.

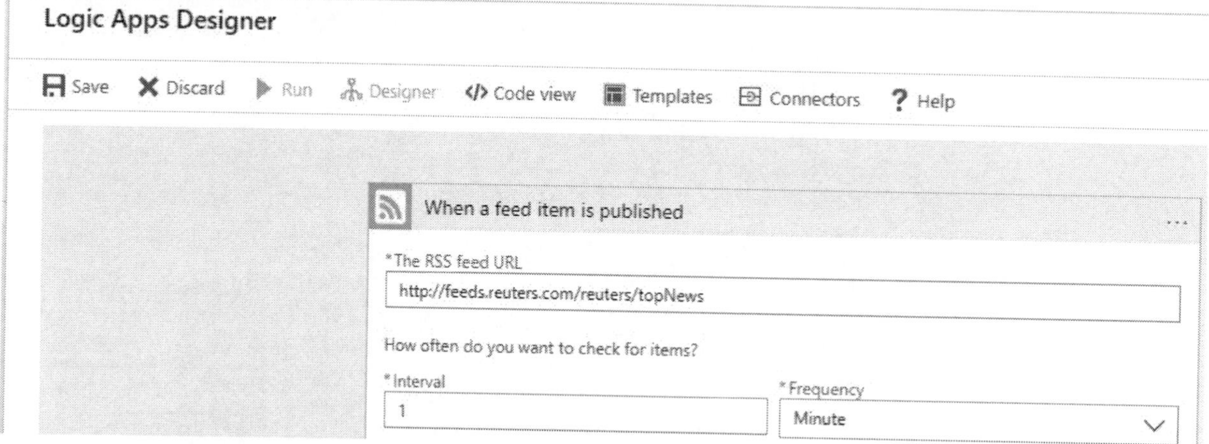

Interval and frequency define the schedule for your logic app's trigger. This logic app checks the feed every minute.

Step 3: Add an action –Send email

In this step we will add an action that sends email when a new item appears in the RSS feed.

1. Under the **When a feed item is published** pane Note the + **New step** Link

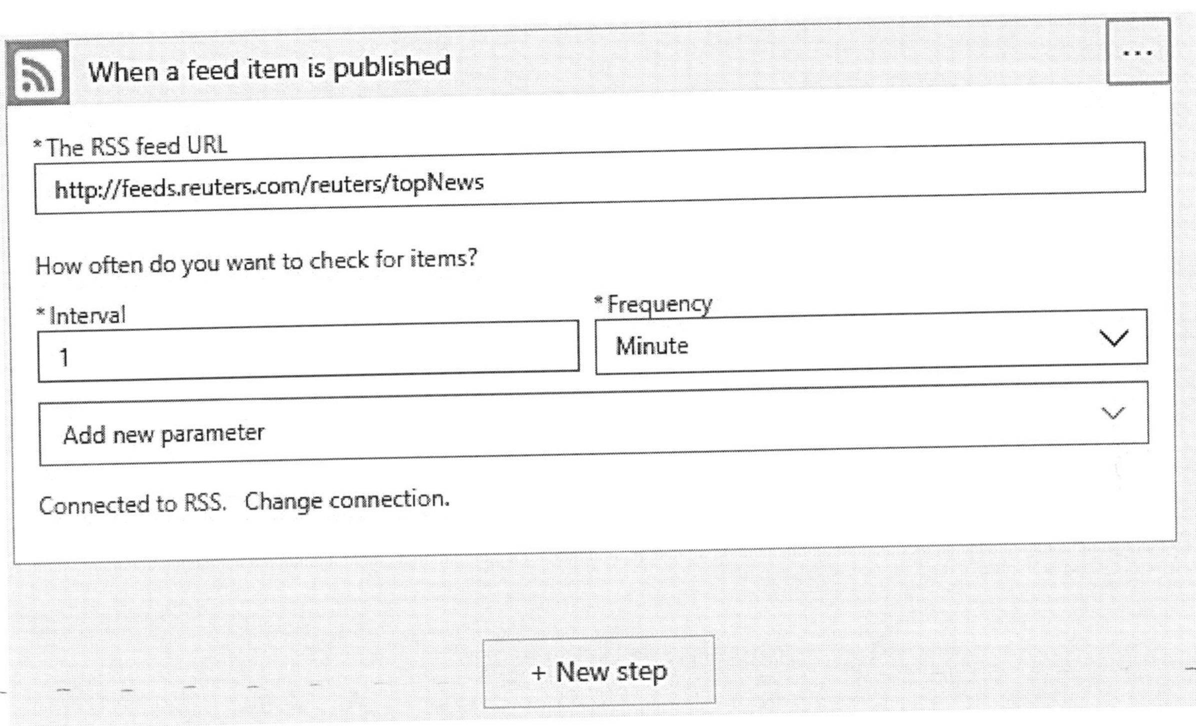

2. Click + New Step>Choose an Action pane opens> In search box type **send an email**> Under Action select **send email (Gmail)**.

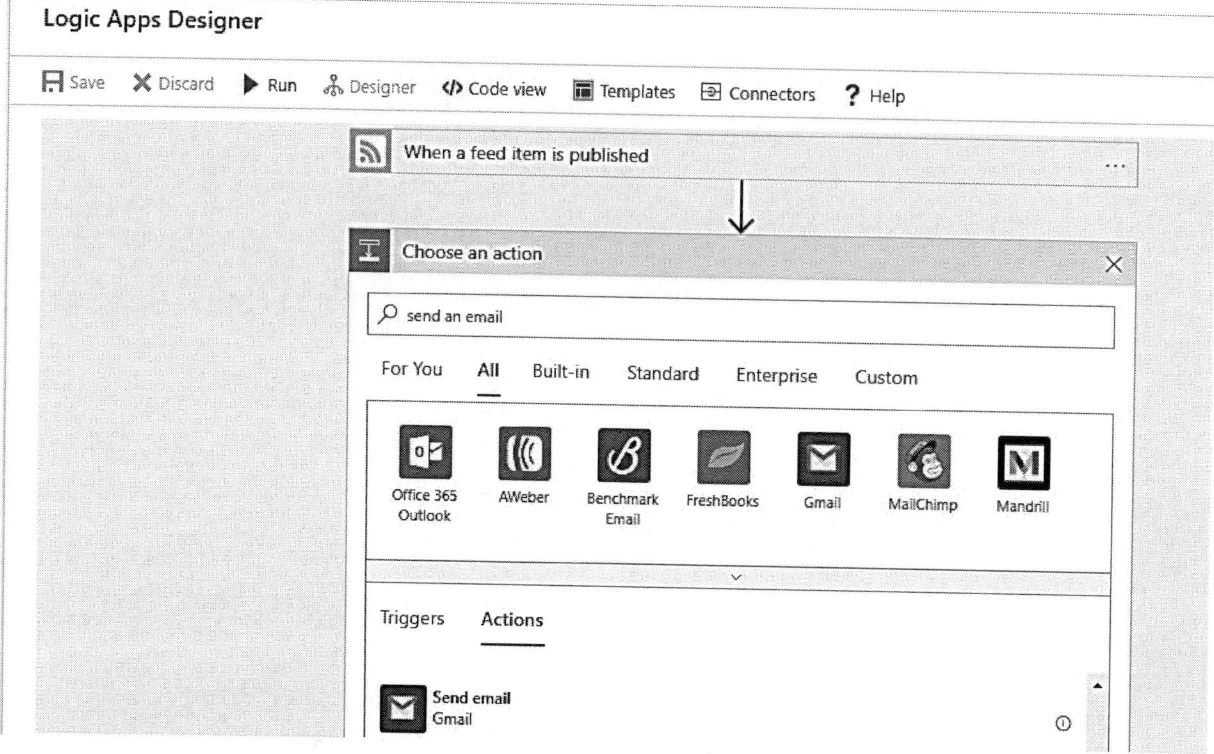

3. A new pane asking for Gmail credentials opens>Click Sign in> A new Gmail pane opens asking for credentials. Enter the credentials> Click allow.

4. Send email pane opens>Enter your **Gmail email id.**

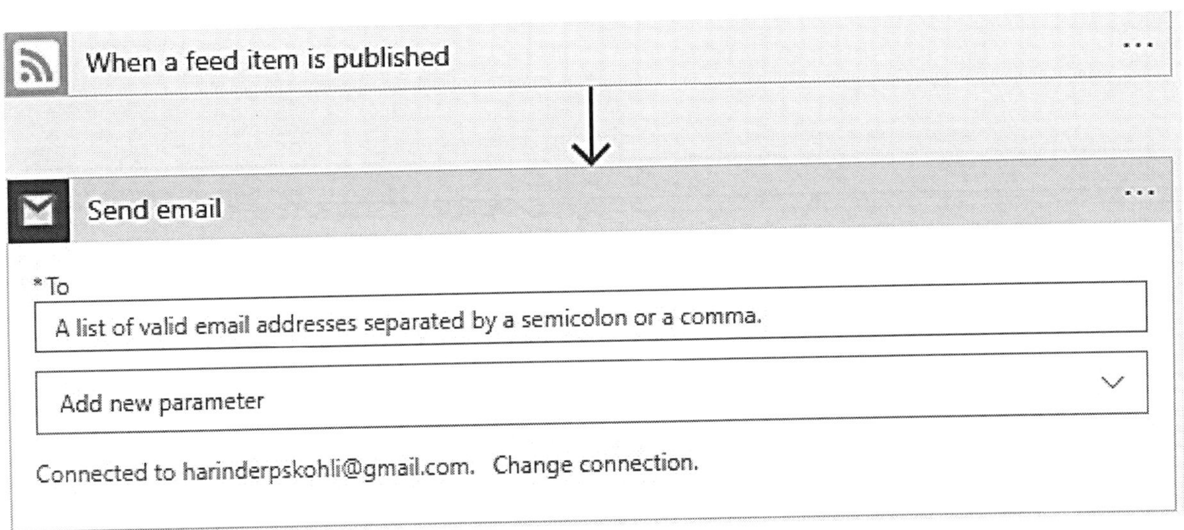

5. In **Add New parameter dropdown Box (As shown above)** select Subject>Subject Box opens> In the subject Box enter **New RSS item:**

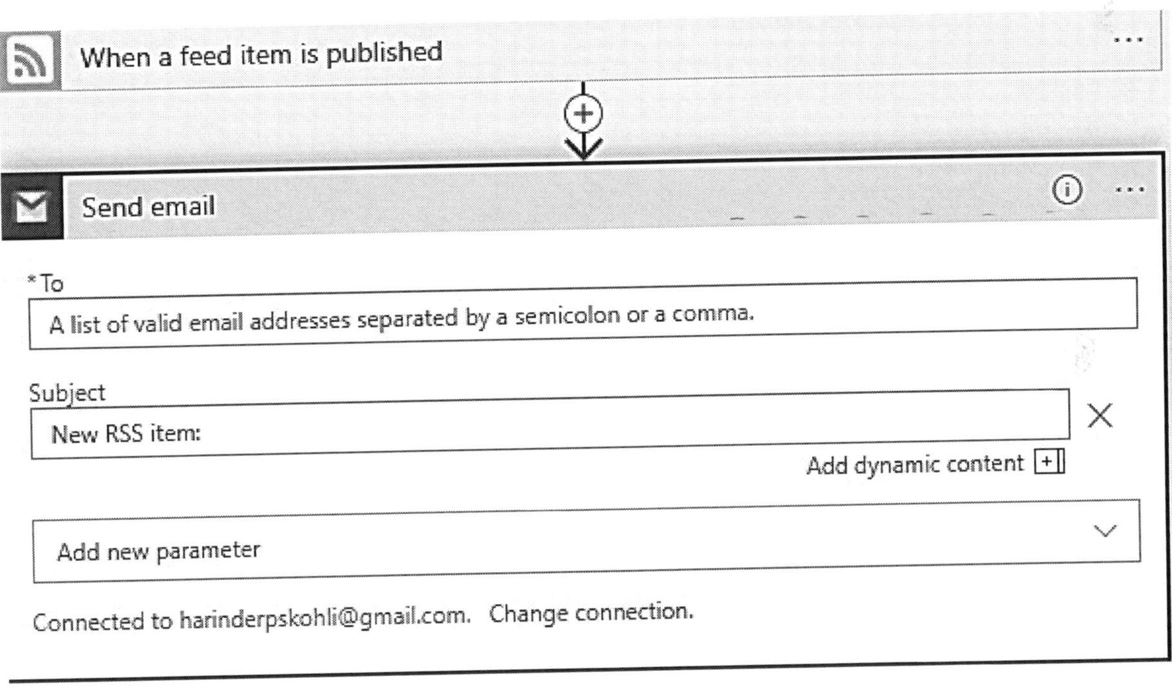

6. Click Add dynamic content below subject box>Dynamic content pane opens in right side>Select Feed title.

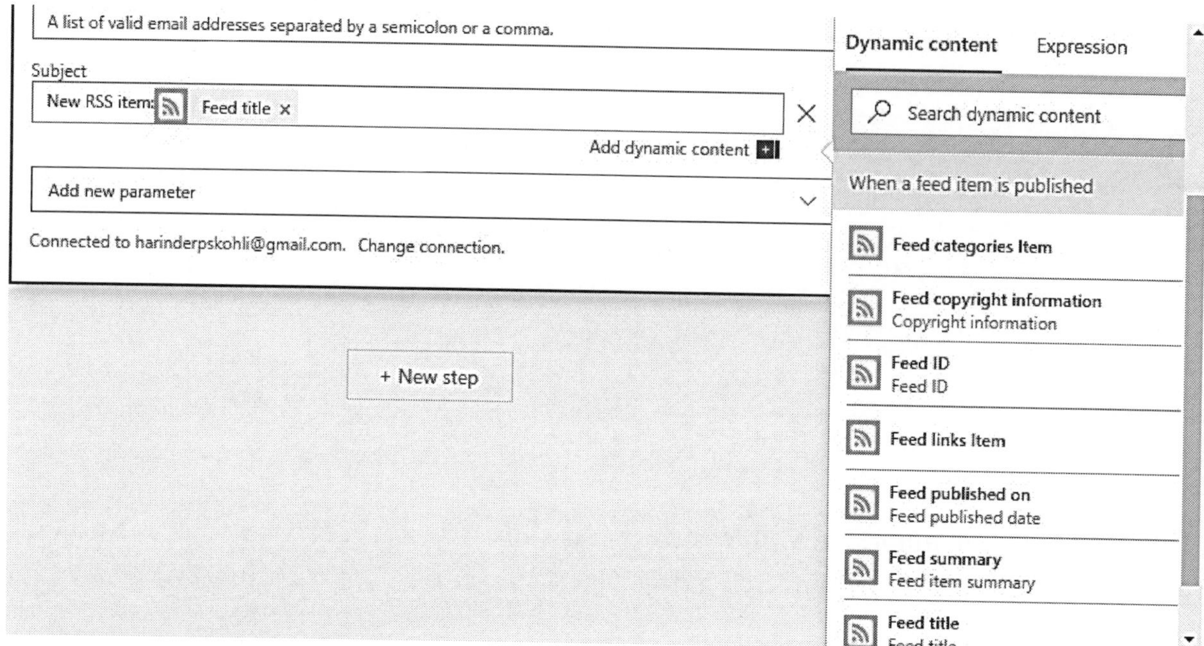

7. Click save.

Step 4: Test Your logic App

To manually start your logic app, on the designer toolbar bar, choose **Run** or wait for your logic app to check the RSS feed based on your specified schedule (every minute).
After 5-7 minutes I got 2 mails. Figure below shows one of the Email.

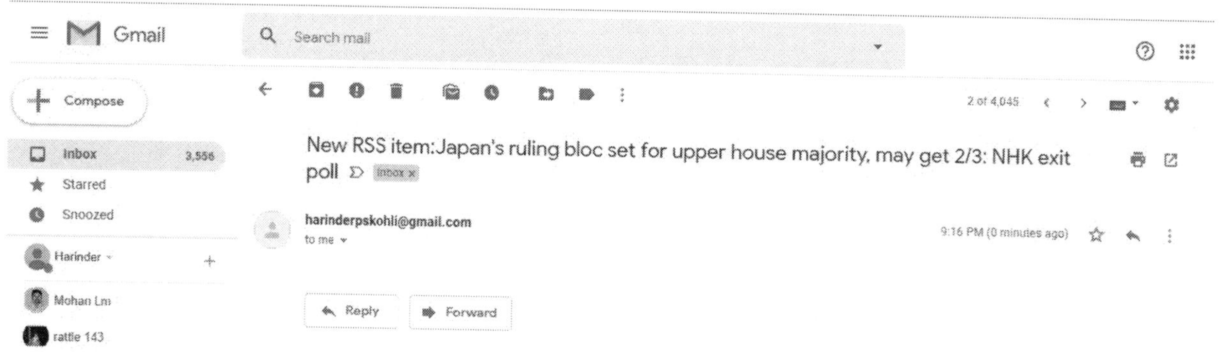

Note: Delete the Logic App after you are done.

Logic Apps pricing

Every time a Logic App definition runs the triggers, actions and connector executions are metered.

	PRICE PER EXECUTION
Actions	$0.000025
Standard Connector	$0.000125
Enterprise Connector	$0.001

Chapter 7 Azure Messaging Solutions

This Chapter covers following

- Azure Service Bus
- Azure Service Bus Queues
- Azure Service Bus Topics
- Service Bus Architecture (Queues and Topics)
- Service Bus Tiers
- Azure Relay
- Comparing Queues, Topics and Relays
- Azure Notification Hubs
- Azure Notification Hubs Tiers & Pricing
- Azure Event Grid
- Event Grid use cases
- Event Grid Pricing
- Azure Event Hub
- Event Hub Use Cases
- Event Hub Anti Use Cases
- Azure IoT Hub and Azure Event Hubs Comparison
- Azure Event Hub Tiers & Pricing
- SendGrid Email Service

This Chapter Covers following Lab Exercises

- Implementing Service Bus Name Space
- Create Service Bus Queues
- Implementing Topics & Subscriptions
- Implementing Relay Namespace & Connections

Chapter Topology

In this chapter we will add Service Bus, Azure Relay, Event Grid and event Hubs to the topology.

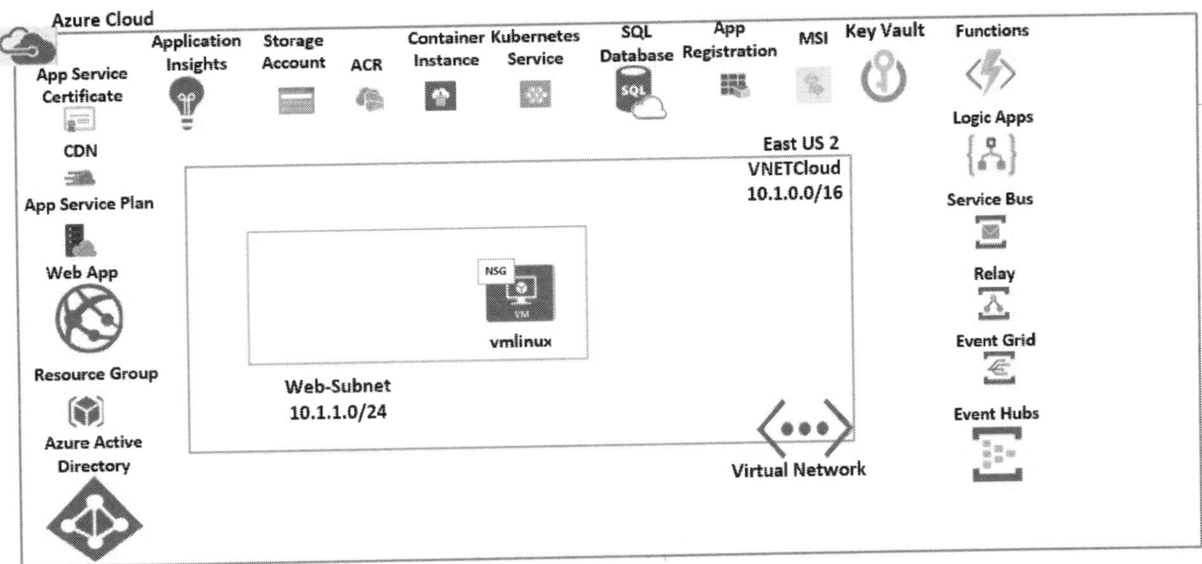

Azure Service Bus

Service Bus provides Messaging as a Service (MaaS). Azure Service Bus is a messaging infrastructure that sits between applications allowing them to exchange messages.

Service Bus Messaging entities provide temporary decoupling between applications by storing or passing message generated by one application for another application.

Service Bus Messaging Entities

Service Bus supports two distinct messaging patterns: *Service Bus Messaging and Azure Relay.*

The messaging entities that form the core of the brokered messaging capabilities in Service Bus are **Queues, Topics/Subscriptions & Relays**. Queues and Topics use Service Bus Messaging Pattern. All three entities store and forward messages in different ways.

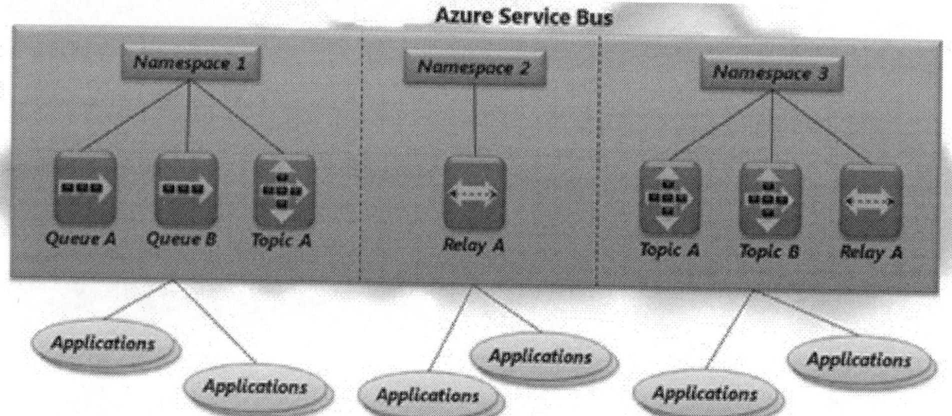

Queues: *Queues* allow one-directional asynchronous communication. Queues stores sent messages until they are received. Each message is received by a single recipient.
Topics: *Topics* provide one-directional asynchronous communication using *subscriptions. A* single topic can have multiple Receivers.
Relays: *Relays* provide Synchronous bi-directional communication between applications. Relay does not store messages. Azure Relay service connects application within corporate network to application outside the corporate network without having to open a firewall connection or configure VPN.

Azure Service Bus Queues

Service Bus Queues acts as an intermediary that stores sent messages until they are received. Each message is received by a single recipient.

Service Bus Queues, allow one-directional asynchronous communication.

Service Bus Queues entities provide temporary decoupling between applications. Service Bus Queues store sent messages until they are received or deleted.

Service Bus queues are similar to Queue Storage but offer additional capabilities such as **advanced middleware capabilities (dead lettering, auto-forwarding, sessions, duplicate detection, etc.).**

The figure below shows Service bus queue storing the message by the sender. The queue then passes the message to the receiver when it is ready to receive it.

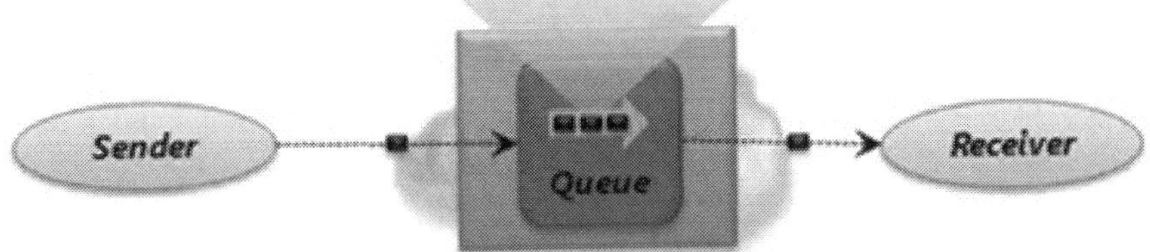

A key benefit of using queues is to achieve "temporal decoupling" of application components. In other words, the producers (senders) and consumers (receivers) do not have to be sending and receiving messages at the same time, because messages are stored durably in the queue. Furthermore, the producer does not have to wait for a reply from the consumer in order to continue to process and send messages.

A related benefit is load leveling. Load leveling enables producers and consumers to send and receive messages at different rates. In many applications, the system load varies over time; however, the processing time required for each unit of work is typically constant. Intermediating between message producers and consumers with a queue means that the **consuming application only has to be provisioned to be able to handle average load instead of peak load.**

Service Bus Queues offer First In, First Out (FIFO) message delivery to one or more competing consumers. Each message is received and processed by only one message consumer.

Service Bus queues Capabilities

Following capabilities can be enabled during Service Bus Queue creation.

Duplicate Detection: Duplicate Detection configures queue to keep a history of all messages sent to the queue for a configurable amount of time. During that interval queue will not accept any duplicate messages.

Dead Lettering: Dead Lettering involves holding messages that cannot be successfully delivered to any receiver in a separate Queue after they have expired. Messages do not expire in Dead Letter Queue.

Sessions: Sessions guarantee first-in first-out delivery of messages.

Partitioning: With partitioning queue is partitioned across multiple message brokers and message stores. This increases the throughput of the queue.

Azure Service Bus Topics

Topics provide one-directional communication between sender and multiple receivers using *subscriptions*. **Topic Store messages from producer similar to queues.** A single topic can have multiple subscriptions.

The difference between Topic and queues is that topics enable each receiving application to create its own *subscription* by defining a *filter*. A subscriber will then see only the messages that match that filter.

The figure below shows message from sender going to multiple receivers through Service Bus topics. The sender Message is stored in topics. The Figure below shows sender, topic messaging broker and three subscribers.

- Subscriber 1 receives only messages that contain the property *Seller="Ava"*.
- Subscriber 2 receives messages that contain the property *Seller="Ruby"* and/or contain an *Amount* property whose value is greater than 100,000. Perhaps Ruby is the sales manager, so she wants to see both her own sales and all big sales regardless of who makes them.
- Subscriber 3 has set its filter to *True*, which means that it receives all messages. For example, this application might be responsible for maintaining an audit trail and therefore it needs to see all the messages.

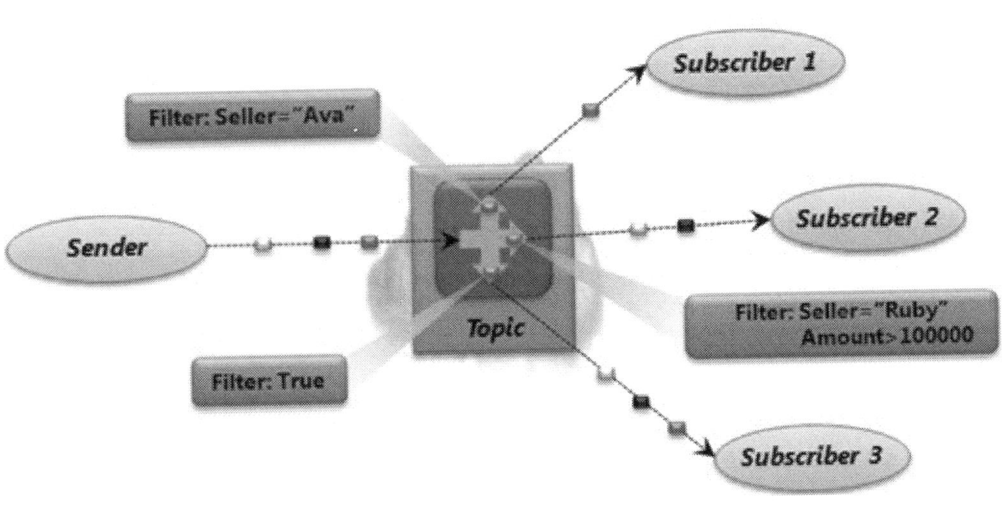

Service Bus Architecture (Queues and Topics)

Service Bus is organized by *scale units*. A scale unit is a unit of deployment and contains all components required run the service. A Service Bus namespace is mapped to a scale unit. The scale unit handles all types of Service Bus entities (queues, topics, subscriptions).

Figure below shows Service Bus Architecture.

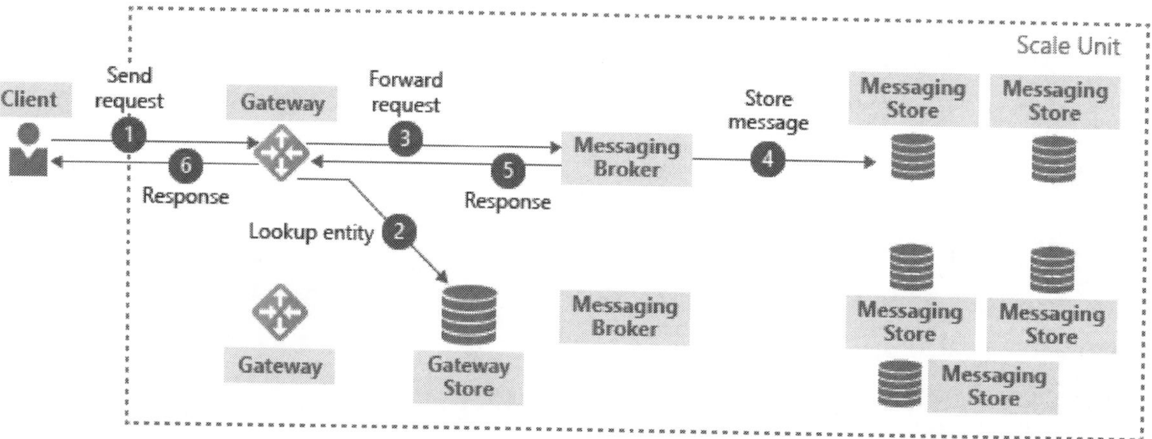

Service Bus scale unit components

A set of gateway nodes. Gateway nodes authenticate incoming requests. Each gateway node has a public IP address.

A set of messaging broker nodes. Messaging broker nodes process requests concerning messaging entities.

One gateway store. The gateway store holds the data for every entity that is defined in this scale unit. The gateway store is implemented on top of a SQL Database instance.

Multiple messaging stores. Messaging stores hold the messages of all queues, topics and subscriptions that are defined in this scale unit. It also contains all subscription data. Unless partitioning messaging entities is enabled, a queue or topic is mapped to one messaging store. Subscriptions are stored in the same messaging store as their parent topic. Except for Service Bus Premium Messaging, the messaging stores are implemented on top of SQL Database instances.

Exercise 76: Implementing Service Bus Namespace

A namespace is a scoping container for all messaging components. Multiple queues and topics can reside within a single namespace, and namespaces often serve as application containers.

1. In Azure Portal click + Create a resource> Integration> Service Bus> create namespace blade opens>Enter a name>Select Standard in Pricing Tier>In Resource Group select RGCloud. Resource Group **RGCloud was created** Exercise 1, Chapter 1 in Exam AZ-300 & AZ-301 Study & Lab Guide Part 1> In Location select East US 2>Click Create.

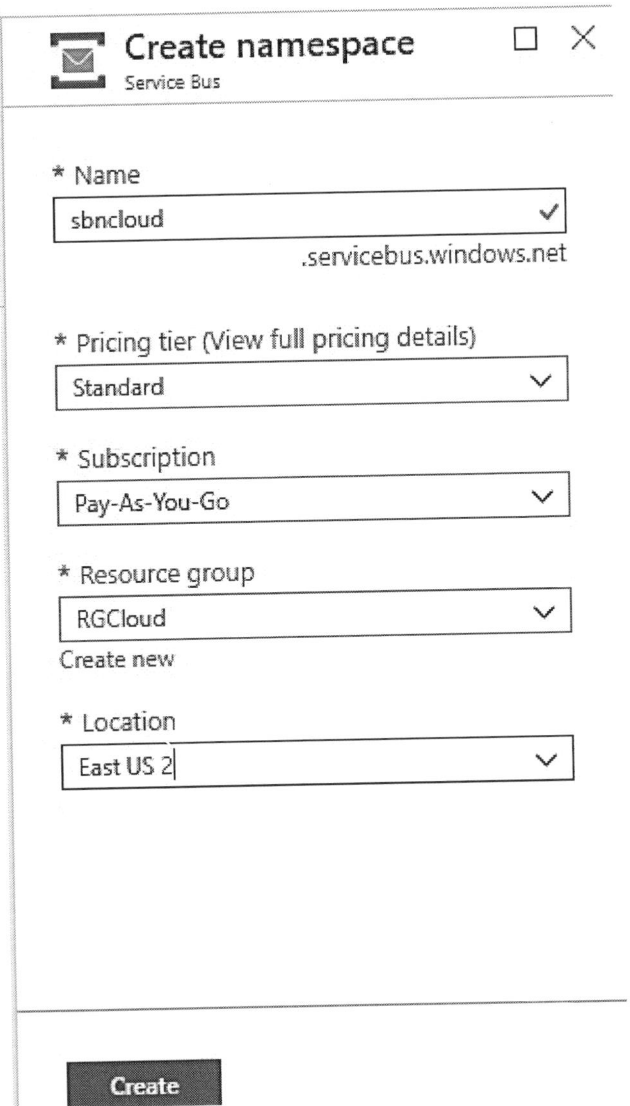

2. Figure below shows the Dashboard of Service Bus Namespace.

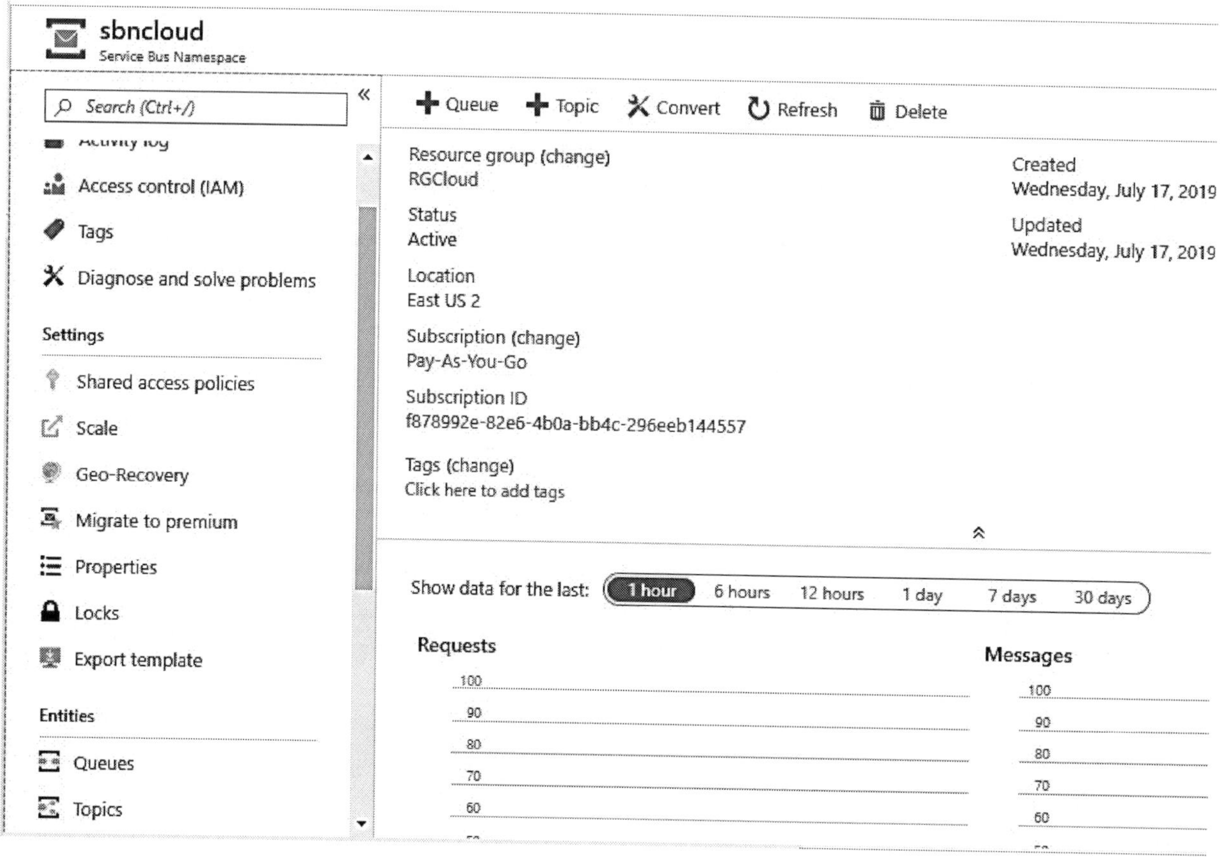

3. **Copy Primary Key:** Primary Key will be used by applications to authenticate to Service Bus.
   Click Shared Access Policies in left pane>Click Root Policy>Copy Primary Key in Extreme right pane.

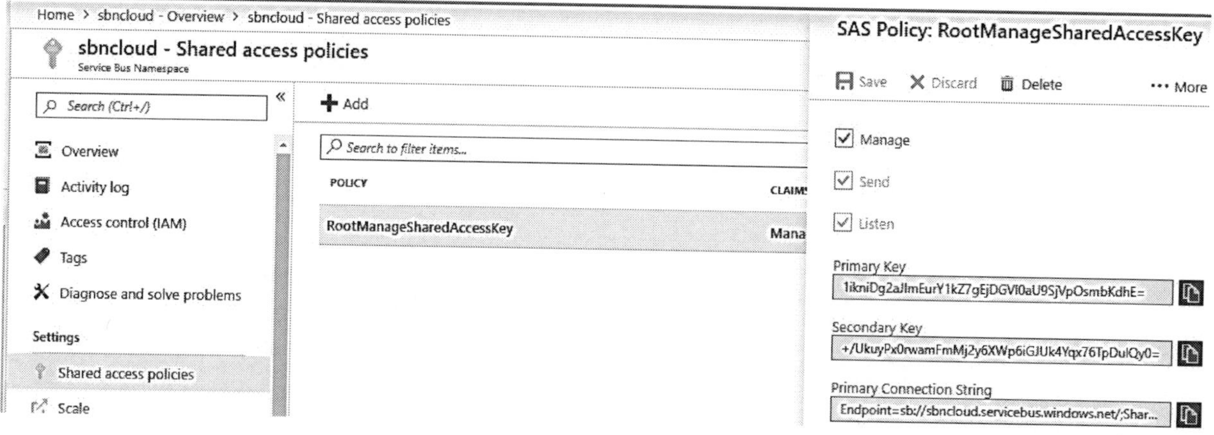

Exercise 77: Create Service Bus Queues

In Service Bus namespace dashboard Click Queues in left pane>+Queue >create queue blade opens> Enter a name and select all default values>click create.

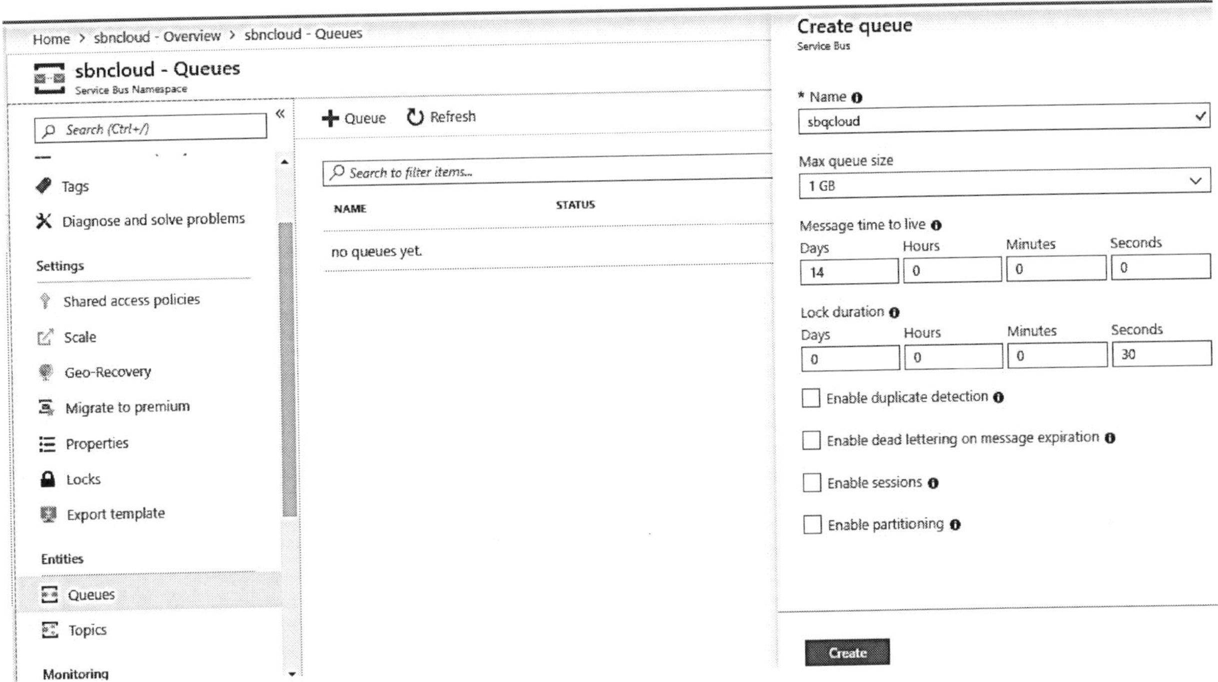

2. Click on the newly created Queue> Queue sbqcloud dashboard opens. **Note down the Queue URL in right pane.**

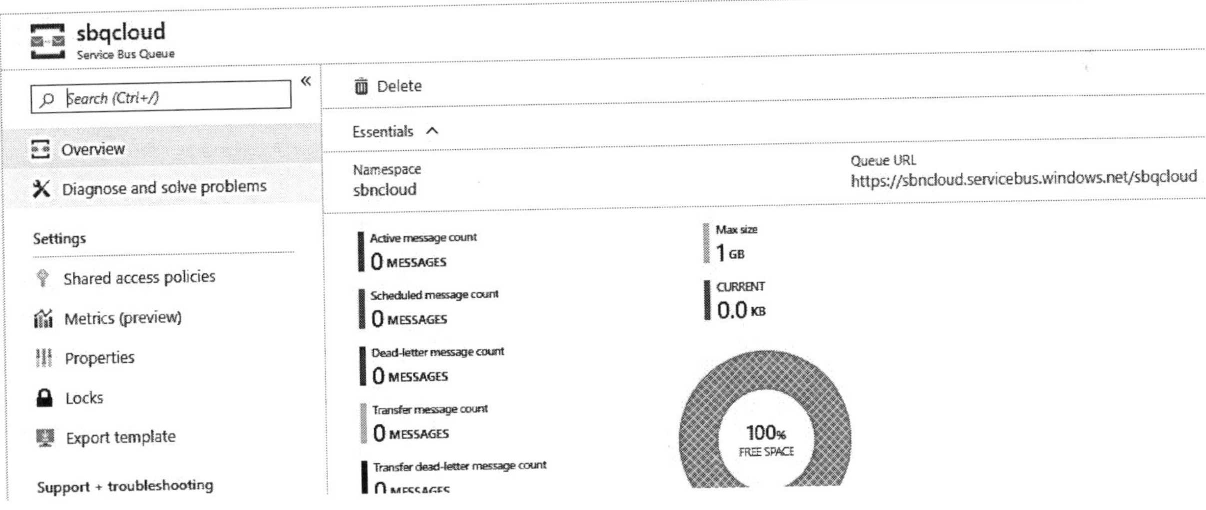

3. In both sender application and Receiver application add the Primary Key of the Service Bus Namespace and URL of the Queue. Configure your application to use Service Bus.

Exercise 78: Implementing Topics & Subscriptions

1. **Create Topics**: In Service Bus namespace dashboard Click Topics in left pane>+Topic> create Topic blade opens> Enter a name and select all default values>Click Create (Not Shown).

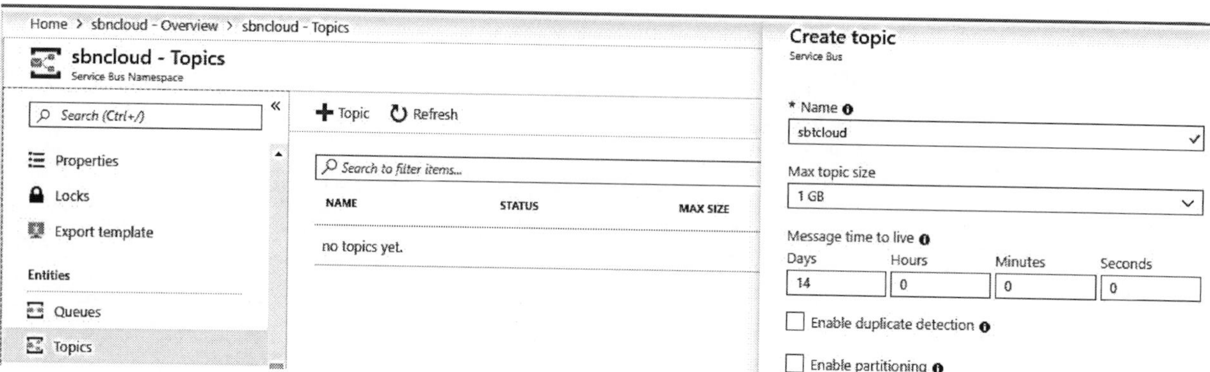

2. Click the newly created Topic > Topic dashboard opens as shown below. **Note down the Topic URL.**

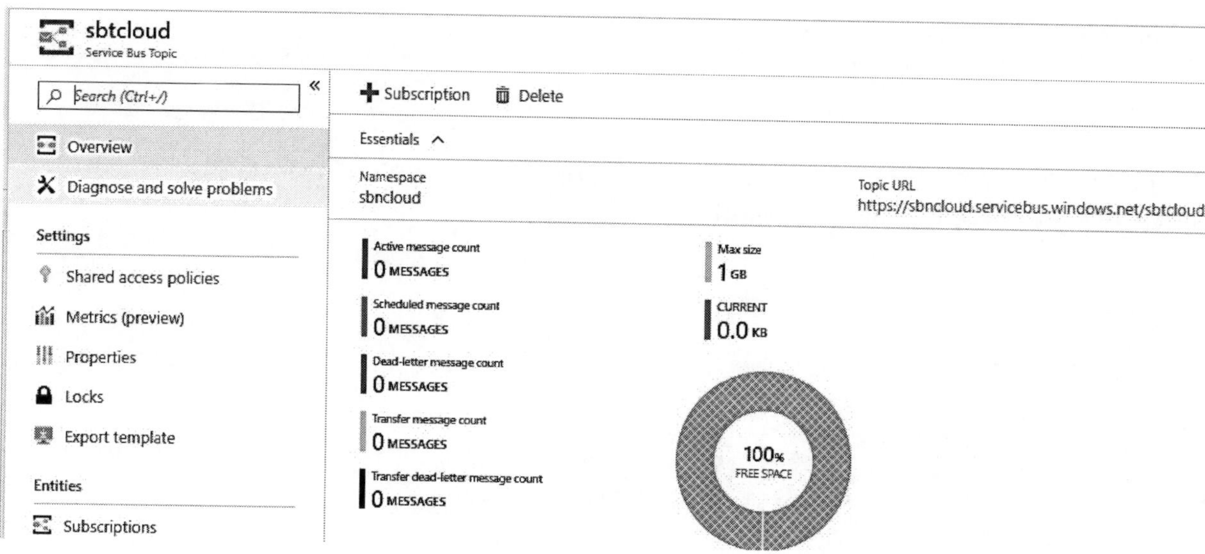

3. **Create Subscription**: In Topics dashboard click Subscriptions in left pane>Enter a name and Rest all default values>Click Create.

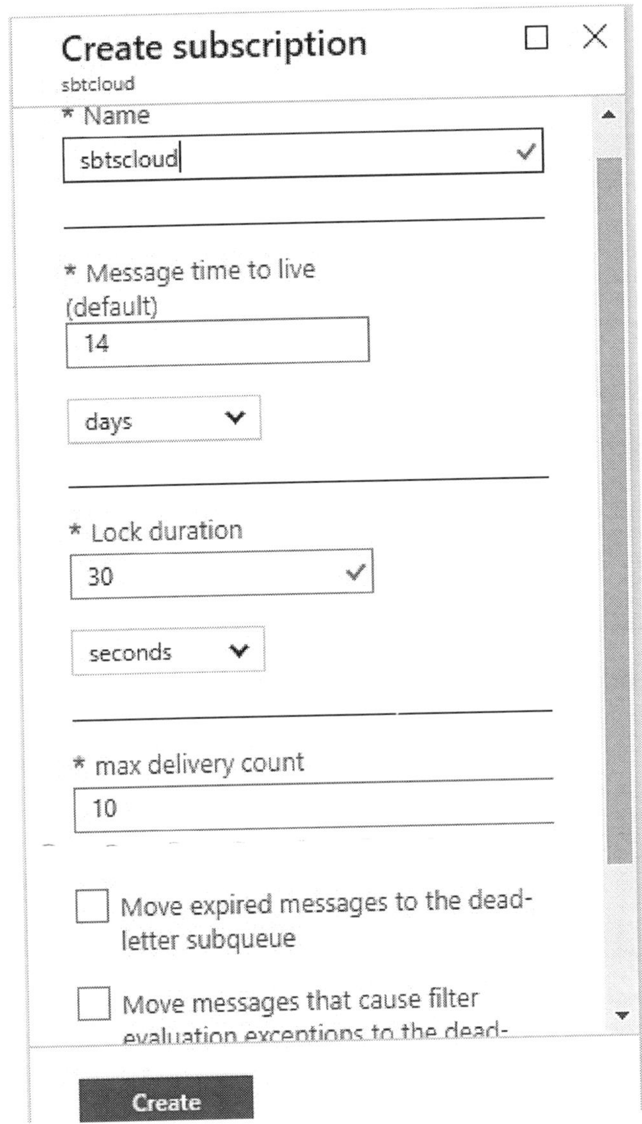

4. In sender application add the Primary Key of the Service Bus Namespace and the Topic URL. Configure your application to use Service Bus.

5. In Receiver application add the Primary Key of the Service Bus Namespace, Topic URL and the name of Subscription. You also specify a filter to receive events from Topics as per your requirements. Configure your application to use Service Bus.

Service Bus Tiers

Service Bus comes in Basic, standard, and premium tiers. Service Bus premium runs in dedicated resources to provide higher throughput and more consistent performance.

	Basic	Standard	Premium
Queues	✓	✓	✓
Scheduled messages	✓	✓	✓
Topics	X	✓	✓
Transactions	X	✓	✓
De-duplication	X	✓	✓
Sessions	X	✓	✓
ForwardTo/SendVia	X	✓	✓
Message Size	256 KB	256 KB	1 MB
Brokered connections included	100	1000	1000 per MU
Brokered connections (overage allowed)	X	Billable	1000 per MU
Resource isolation	X	X	✓
Geo-Disaster Recovery (Geo-DR)	X	X	✓
Messaging Operation Charges	$0.05 per million operations	$0.0135/hour + Operation Charges	$0.928/hour

Azure Relay

Azure Service Bus Relay managed cloud service connects application within corporate network to application or clients outside the corporate network without having to open a firewall connection or configure VPN on corporate network.

Azure Relay provides Synchronous bi-directional communication between applications. <u>Azure Relay does not store messages.</u>

The figure below shows Azure Relay Service providing Synchronous bi-directional communication between applications.

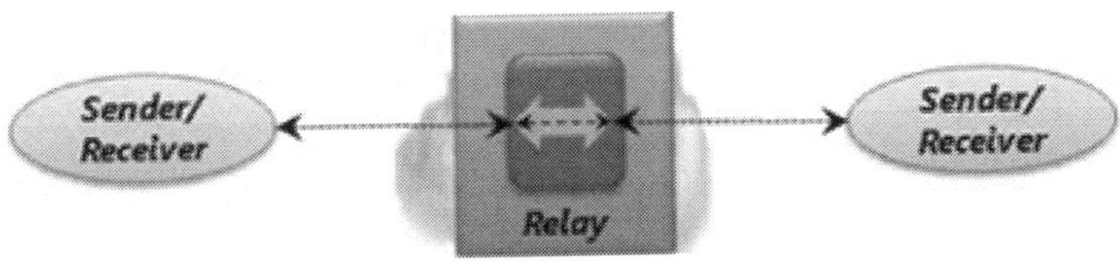

Relay supports a variety of different transport protocols and web services standards.

Service Bus Relay Working

In the relayed data transfer pattern, an on-premises service connects to the relay service through an outbound port and creates a bi-directional socket for communication tied to a particular rendezvous address. The client can then communicate with the on-premises service by sending traffic to the relay service targeting the rendezvous address. The relay service will then "relay" data to the on-premises service through a bi-directional socket dedicated to each client. The client does not need a direct connection to the on-premises service, and the on-premises service does not need any inbound ports open on the firewall.

The client that waits for and accepts connections is the listener. The client that initiates a new connection towards a listener via the Relay service is called the sender.

Service Bus Relay Example

An airline reservation system running in on-premises datacenter is to be be accessed from check-in kiosks, mobile devices, and other computers. Using Azure Relay, clients can connect to Corporate Application without configuring any VPN or configuring Firewall rules.

Azure Relay Connection Types

Azure Relay provides following 2 option for connecting Application and client through Azure Relay Service.

Hybrid Connection: Hybrid Connections uses standard based HTTP and WebSockets Protocols. The Azure Relay Hybrid Connections can be implemented on any platform and in any language that has a basic WebSocket capability, which explicitly includes the WebSocket API in common web browsers.

WCF Relays: WCF Relay is the legacy relay offering based on Windows Communication Foundation (WCF). WCF Relay works for the full .NET Framework (NETFX) and for WCF. You initiate the connection between your on-premises service and the relay service using a suite of WCF relay bindings.

Table below shows difference between WCF and Hybrid Connections.

	WCF Relay	**Hybrid Connections**
WCF	✓	
.NET Framework	✓	✓
.NET Core		✓
JavaScript/NodeJS		✓
Standards-Based Open Protocol		✓
Multiple RPC Programming Models		✓

Exercise 79: Implementing Relay Namespace & Connections

1. In Azure Portal click **All services**> Integration> Relays> All Relay Blade opens >click +Add> create Relay namespace blade opens>Enter name>In Resource Group select RGCloud>In Location select East US 2>Click create.

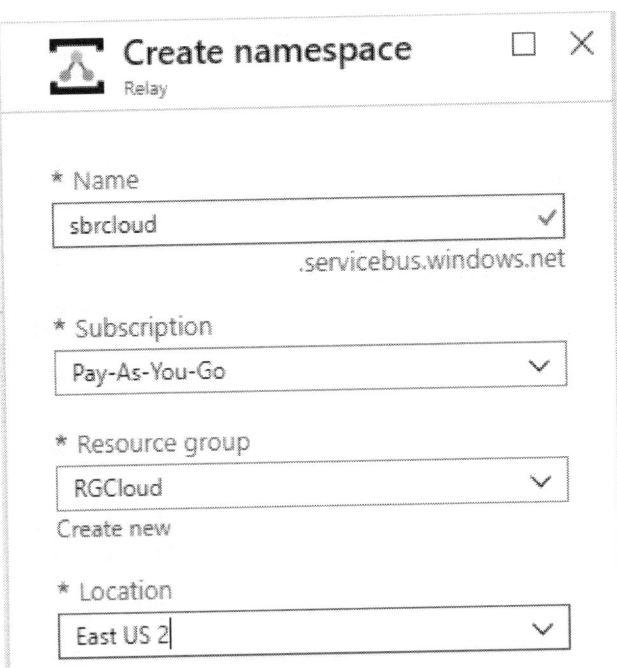

2. Figure below shows dashboard Relay Namespace.

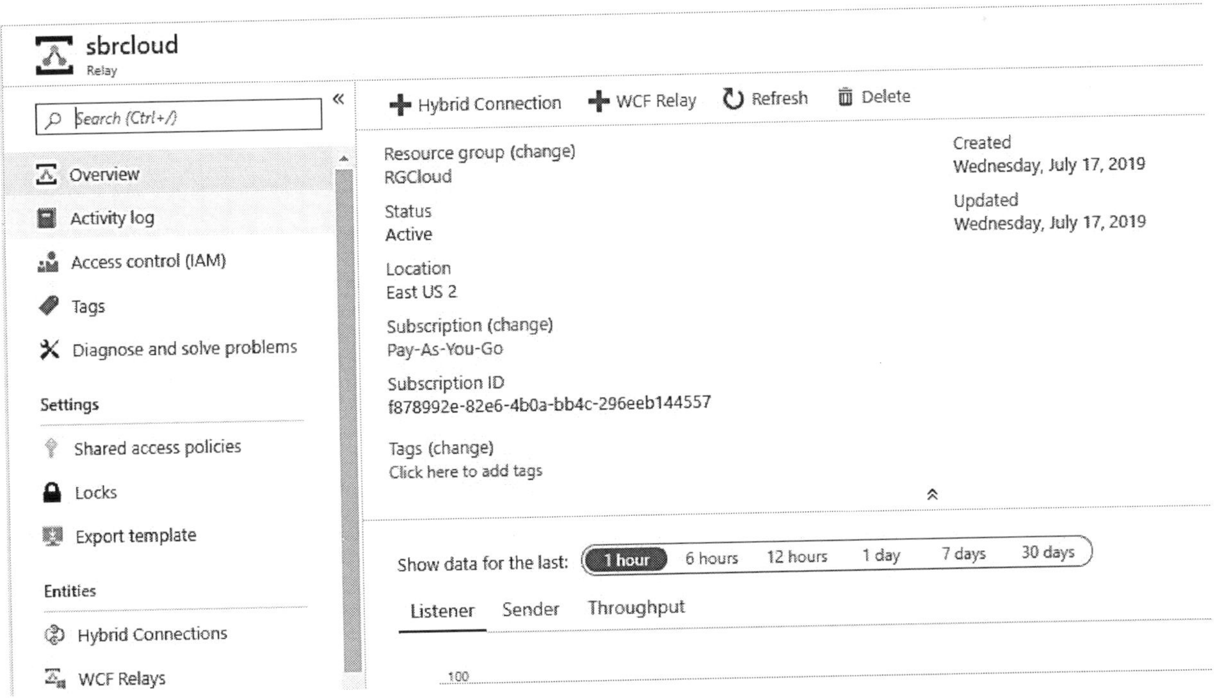

3. **Copy Primary Key**: Primary Key will be used by applications to connect and authenticate to Relay Service.
   Click Shared Access Policies in left pane>Click Root Policy>Copy Primary key in Extreme right pane.

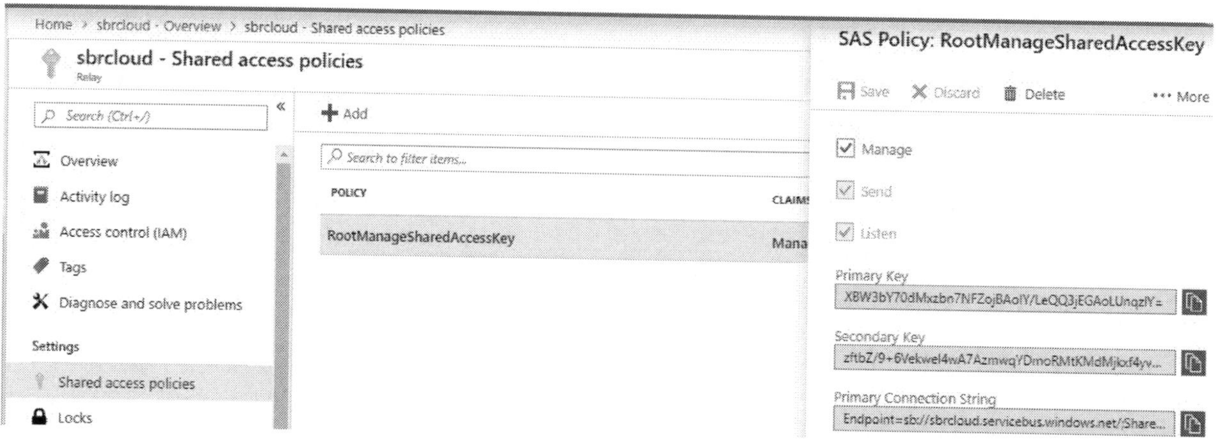

4. **Create Hybrid Connection**: Click Hybrid Connection in left pane> + Hybrid Connection> Create Hybrid Connection Blade opens> Enter name and rest select all default values>Click Create.

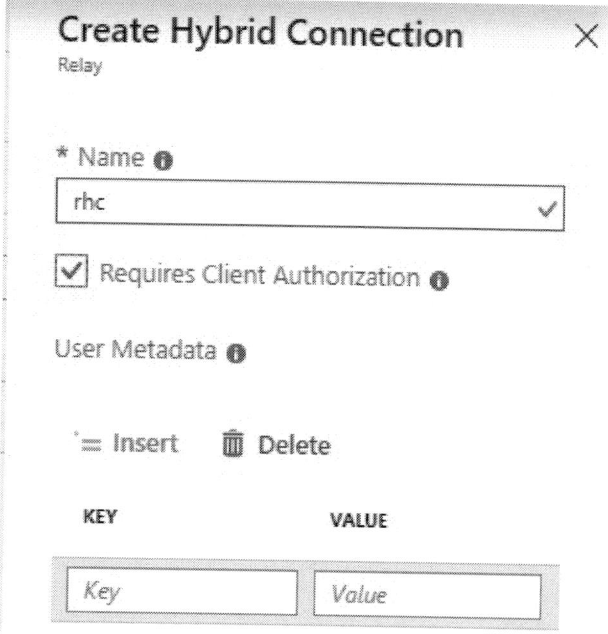

5. **Copy URL of Hybrid Connection**: Click newly created Hybrid connection in Relay Namespace>Hybrid connection dashboard opens> Copy the URL from right pane.

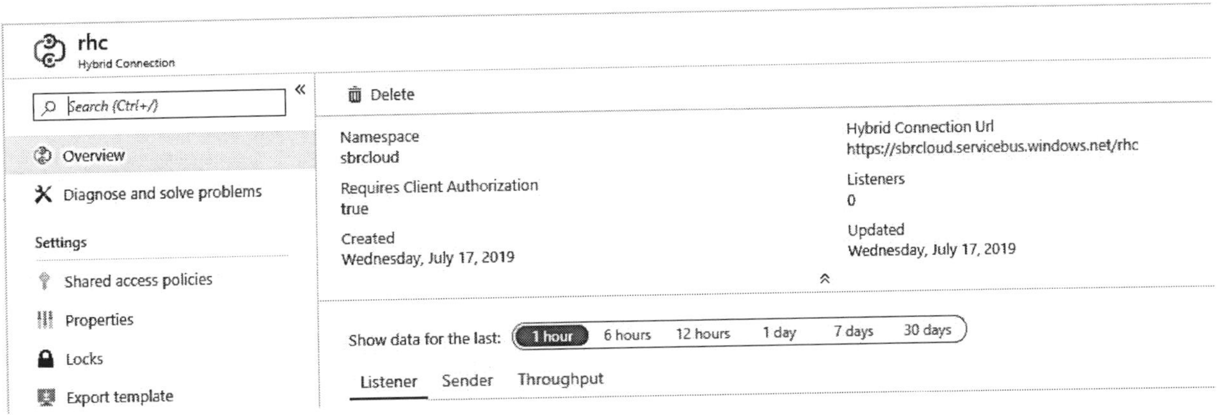

6. In both sender application and Receiver application or client add the Primary Key copied in step 2, Hybrid Connection URL and each other endpoint address. Configure your application to use Azure Relay.

Comparing Queues, Topics and Relays

Features	Queues	Topics	Relays
Communication	Asynchronous	Asynchronous	Synchronous
Message Storing	Yes	Yes	No
Receivers	Single	Multiple	Single

Azure Notification Hubs

Azure Notification Hubs provides a scalable, cross-platform push notification infrastructure that enables you to either broadcast push notifications to millions of users at once, or tailor notifications to individual users.

Azure Notification Hubs provides push notification to iOS, Android, Windows, or Kindle devices, working with APNs (Apple Push Notification service), GCM (Google Cloud Messaging), WNS (Windows Push Notification Service), MPNS (Microsoft Push Notification Service), and more.

Azure Notification Hubs plugs into any back end—Microsoft .NET, PHP, Java, Node.js—whether it's located on-premises or in the cloud.

Challenges with Push Notification without using Notification Hub

Push notifications is a form of app-to-user communication where users of mobile apps are notified of desired information in a pop-up or dialog box.
Push notifications are delivered through platform-specific infrastructures called *Platform Notification Systems* (PNSes).

To send a notification to all customers across the iOS, Android, and Windows versions of an app, the developer must work with Multiple Platform Notification Services such as APNS (Apple Push Notification Service), FCM (Firebase Cloud Messaging), and WNS (Windows Notification Service) etc.
Setting up and working with Multiple Platform-specific infrastructures is one of biggest operational and Administrative overhead.

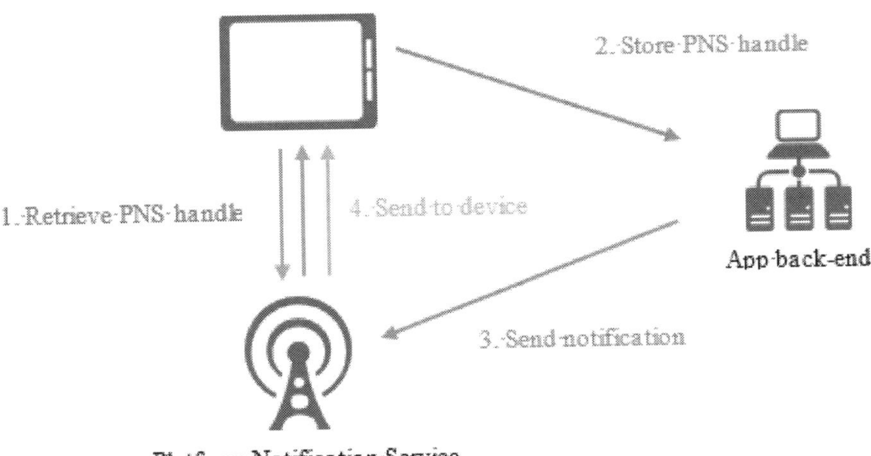

How Notification Hubs overcome conventional Push Notification Challenges

Notification Hubs multi-platform notification infrastructure reduces push-related codes and simplifies your backend.

With Notification Hubs, devices are merely responsible for registering their PNS handles with a hub, while the backend sends messages to users or interest groups, as shown in the following figure:

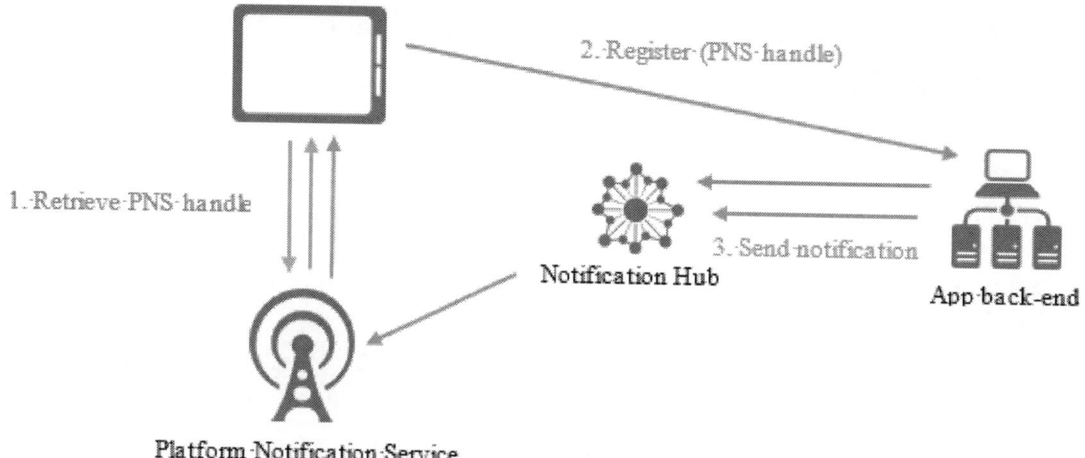

Advantages of Notification Hubs

Cross platforms: Support for all major push platforms including iOS, Android, Windows, and Kindle and Baidu. Provides common interface to push to all platforms in platform-specific or platform-independent formats with no platform-specific work.

Cross backends: Cloud or on-premises using .NET, Node.js, Java, etc.

Rich set of delivery patterns: *Broadcast to one or multiple platforms, Push to device, Push to user, Push to segment with dynamic tags, Localized push, Silent push, Scheduled push, Direct Push and Personalized push.*

Rich telemetry: General push, device, error, and operation telemetry is available in the Azure portal and Per Message Telemetry tracks each push.

Scalability: Send messages to millions of devices.

Azure Notification Hubs Tiers & Pricing

Notification Hubs is offered in three tiers—free, basic, and standard. Base charge and quotas are applied at the namespace level. Pushes exceeding included amounts are aggregated at the subscription level for each tier.

	Free	Basic	Standard
Base charge per namespace	Free	$10/month	$200/month
Included pushes per subscription per tier	1 million	10 million	10 million
Additional pushes 10– 100 million	NA	$10	$10
Additional pushes over 100 million	NA	$1	$2.50
Namespaces per tier	100	100	Unlimited
Hubs per namespace	100	100	100
Active devices per namespace	500	200,000	10,000,000
X-plat push to individual devices	✓	✓	✓
Push variables	✓	✓	✓
Telemetry	Limited	Limited	Rich
Queryable audience (registration queries)	✓	✓	✓
Scheduled push			✓
Bulk import			✓
Multi-tenancy			✓
SLA	None	Covered	Covered

Azure Event Grid

Event Grid is a fully managed event routing service that provides reliable message delivery at massive scale. Event Grid is broker between Event Publishers and Event Subscribers. Event Grid will store events for a maximum of 24 hours. At the end of this time, events will be deleted.

Event Grid uses a publish-subscribe model. Publishers emit events. Event Grid stores event. Subscribers decide which events they want to handle.

Event Grid enables you to create subscriptions to events raised by Azure services or third-party resources.

Event Grid has built-in support for events coming from Azure services, like storage blobs and resource groups. Event Grid also has custom support for application and third-party events, using custom topics and custom webhooks.

Architecture

The figure below shows events produced by event publishers being delivered to Event handlers through Event Grid.

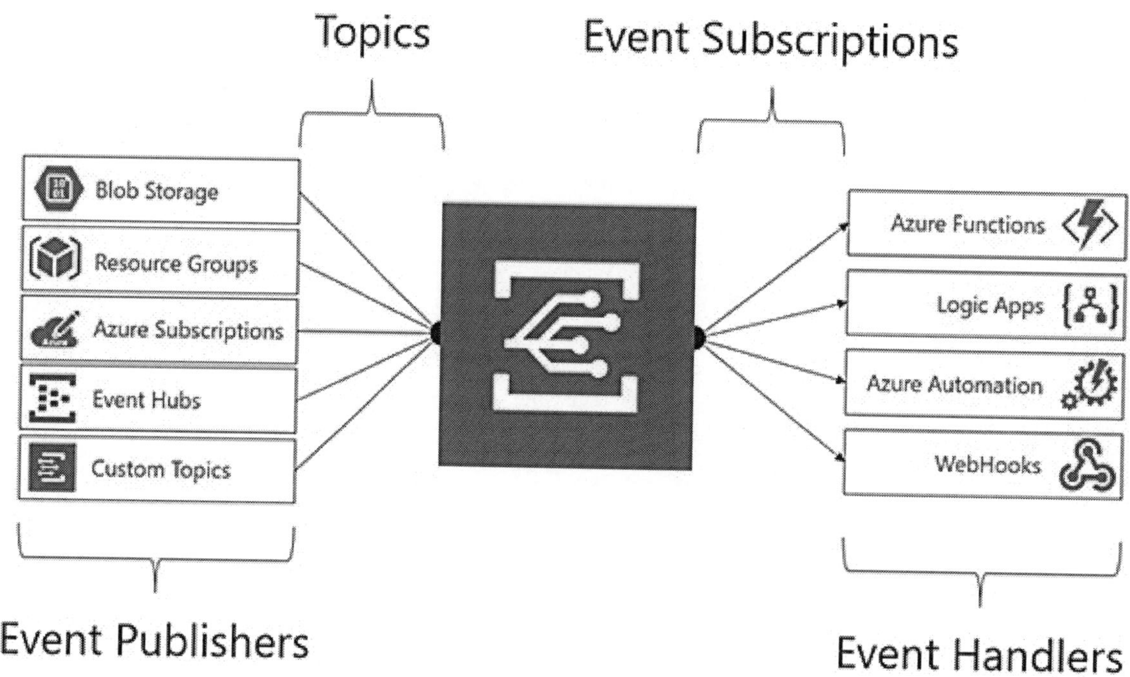

Components involved in Event Grid working

Event Grid connects data sources and event handlers. Event grid Solution has following five components:

Events: What happened. Generated by Event Publishers.

Event publishers: Event publishers generate events to Event Grid. Event publishers can be Azure service or custom services which generate events. Currently, the following Azure services have built-in publisher support for event grid:

Resource Groups (management operations)
Azure Subscriptions (management operations)
Event Hubs
IoT Hub
Storage Blob
Storage General-purpose v2 (GPv2)
Custom Topics
Additional Azure Event Publishers will be added by MS on Regular basis.

Topics: The endpoint where publishers send events.

Event subscriptions: The endpoint to route events to Event Handler or to multiple handlers. Subscriptions are also used by handlers to intelligently filter incoming events.

Event handlers: Azure app or service reacting to the event. Currently, the following Azure services have built-in handler support for Event Grid:

Azure Functions
Logic Apps
Azure Automation
WebHooks
Microsoft Flow

Event Grid Working

Event Grid is an event routing service.

Event Grid Subscribes to events generated by Event Publishers. We then configure Event Grid by adding a endpoint where the Event will be routed.

Example of Event Grid Working

For Example we want any file uploaded to Blob Storage container to be processed by Azure Web App.

1. Event Grid will Subscribe to Events generated by Blob Storage. This is done in Blob Storage Dashboard by clicking **Event** Tab in left pane.

2. In Event pane we add Webhook and configure the webhook with DNS address of Azure Webapp (Event Handler).
   Note: Using Webhook you can send events as http pushes to the webhook endpoint.

3. An Event is triggered whenever a file is uploaded to Blob Container. File is then routed to Azure Web App through Event Grid.

Features of Event Grid

Simple to setup: Aim events from your Azure resource to any event handler or endpoint without adding any code.

Built-in Events: Get up and running quickly with resource-defined built-in events.

Custom Events: Event Grid route, filter, and reliably deliver custom events in your app.

Advanced filtering: Filter on event type or event publish path to ensure event handlers only receive relevant events.

Fan-out - Subscribe multiple endpoints to the same event to send copies of the event to as many places as needed.

High throughput - Build high-volume workloads on Event Grid with support for millions of events per second.

Advantages of Event Grid

1. The biggest adavnatge of using Event Grid is that no custom code is written to integrate Event Publishers and Event Handlers through Event Grid. You don't have to write code to subscribe to events. Many Event Handlers such as Azure Functions, Logic Apps, Webhooks & Azure Automation have built in support for Event Grid.

2. Eliminate polling—and the associated cost and latency. With Event Grid, apps can listen for and react to events from virtually all Azure services, as well as custom sources. These events are delivered through push semantics, simplifying your code and reducing your resource consumption.

3. Many Azure services such as Blob Storage, Event Hub etc can generate events to Event Grid without writing any code.

Event Grid use cases

Serverless Architectures

Event Grid can automatically trigger a serverless function whenever Event handler generates a specific Event to Event Grid.

For example, use Event Grid to instantly trigger a serverless function to run image analysis each time a new photo is added to a blob storage container.

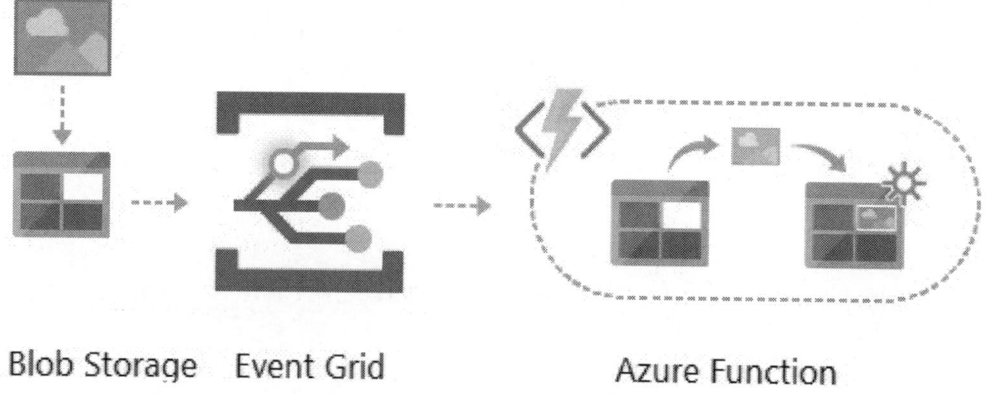

Automatic Policy Enforcement on Azure Resources

With Event Grid you can automatically enforce required compliance on specific Azure resources using Azure Automation.

For example, Event Grid can notify Azure Automation when a virtual machine is created, or a SQL Database is spun up. These events can be used to automatically check that service configurations are compliant according to organization policies and tag the non-compliant Azure Resources.

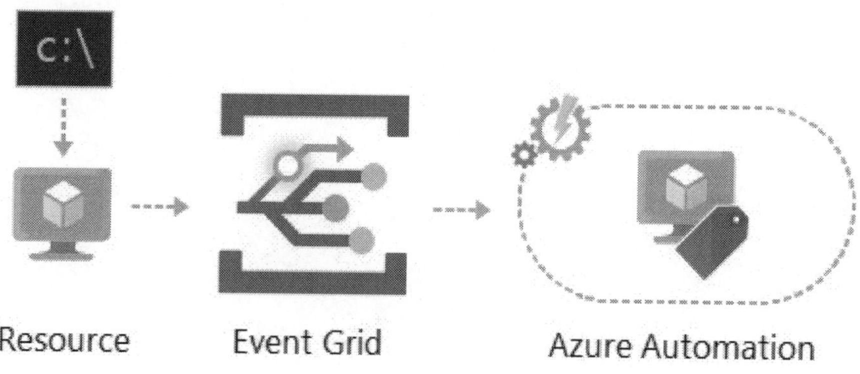

Exercise 80: Create Storage Account and Add a Blob Container

1. In Azure Portal click Create a resource>Storage>Storage Account>Create Stoarge Account Dashboard opens>In Resource Group click **create new** link. A box pops. Enter Resource group name as **eg410** and click ok>Enter name of Storage Account>Location select East US 2> Rest select all default values>Click Review +Create>After Validation is passed Click create.

Create storage account

* Subscription	Pay-As-You-Go
* Resource group	(New) eg410 Create new

Instance details

The default deployment model is Resource Manager, which supports the latest Azure features. You may choose to deploy using the classic deployment model instead. Choose classic deployment model

* Storage account name	eg410
* Location	(US) East US 2
Performance	(•) Standard ( ) Premium
Account kind	StorageV2 (general purpose v2)
Replication	Read-access geo-redundant storage (RA-GRS)
Access tier (default)	( ) Cool (•) Hot

Review + create   < Previous   Next : Advanced >

2. Figure below shows dashboard of Storage Account. Note the Events Tab in left pane.

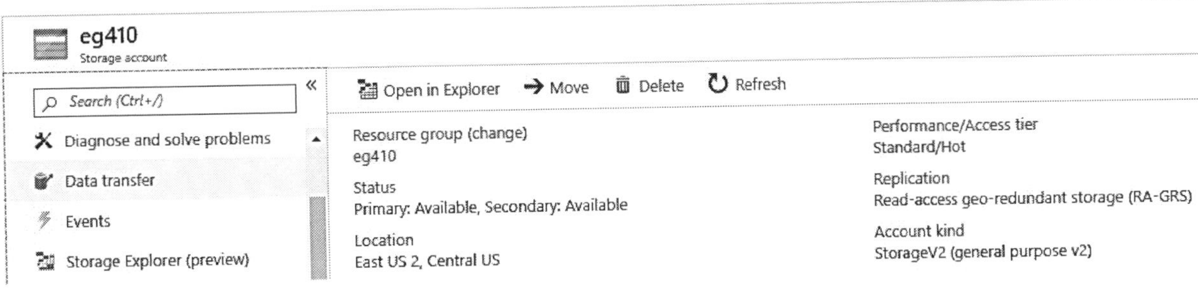

3. In Storage Account Dashboard click Blobs in right pane>Click +Container> New Container Blade opens>Enter a name and click ok.

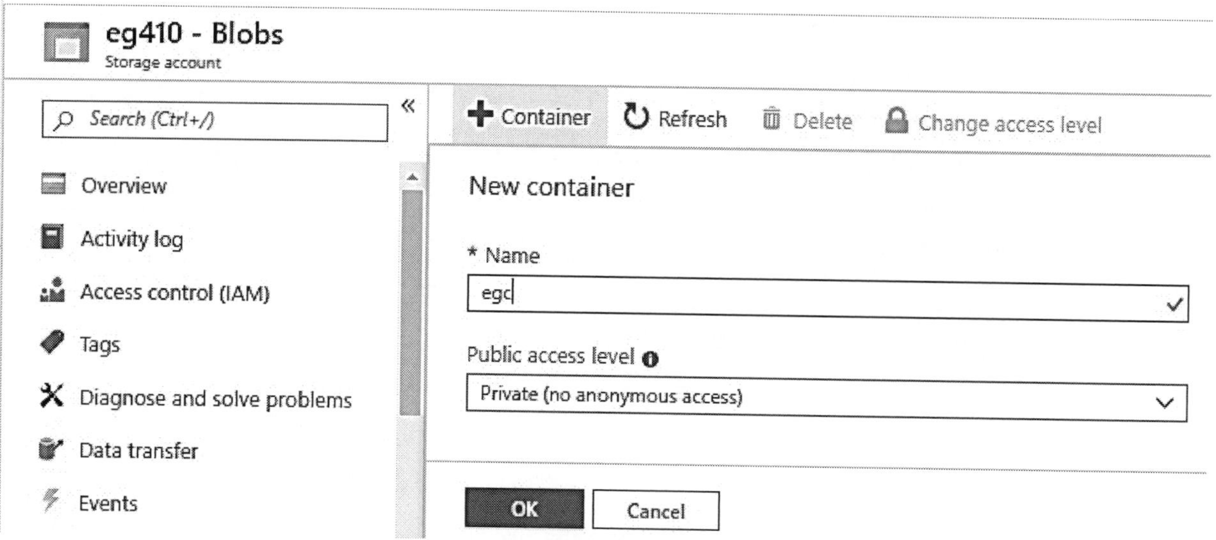

Note: In this exercise we also created resource group eg410 in step 1.

Exercise 81: Routing Blob Storage Events toWeb Endpoint (Azure Web App)

Using Event Grid, Blob Storage Events will be sent to Web Endpoint (Azure Web App). Event will be triggerd in Blob Storage whenever a file is uploaded to Blob Container.

In this case Event Grid will subscribe to Events in Blob Storage. We will then configure Event Grid to route events to Web Endpoint (Azure Web App) using Webhooks.

Web Endpoint will be a Pre-built Azure Web App.

Step 1: Create a message endpoint (Azure Web App)

In this Step we will deploy Azure Web App with a source code from GitHub that displays events from Azure Event Grid in near-real time. We will use the link in GitHub to deploy the Web App.
We will deploy the Web App in Resource Group eg410 which was created in previous exercise.

1. Go to GitHub @ https://github.com/Azure-Samples/azure-event-grid-viewer> GitHub Page opens>Scroll down and you can see **Deploy to Azure** Link.

Azure Event Grid Viewer

This repository contains the source code for a site that displays events from Azure Event Grid in near-real time. It is built on ASP.NET Core 2.1 and leverages SignalR to display incoming messages.

For details about how it was put together, please refer to the accompanying blog post.

Deploy the solution

1. Select Deploy to Azure

This will launch a custom template for the Azure portal instance that you are logged into.

2. Fill out the required fields

This will take about 2-5 minutes to provision.

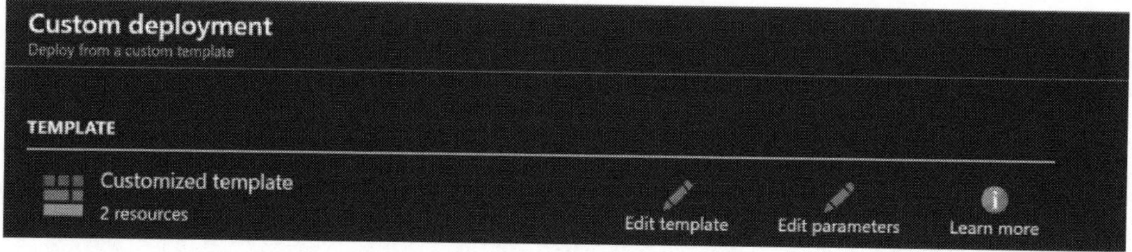

2. Click on Deploy to Azure Link> Azure Portal opens with Deploy from a Custom Template option> In Resource Group select eg410 created in previous exercise>Enter Site name>Enter Hosting Plan name>SKU Select F1>Agree to Terms and Conditions>Click Purchase.
   Note: SKU F1 is free plan.

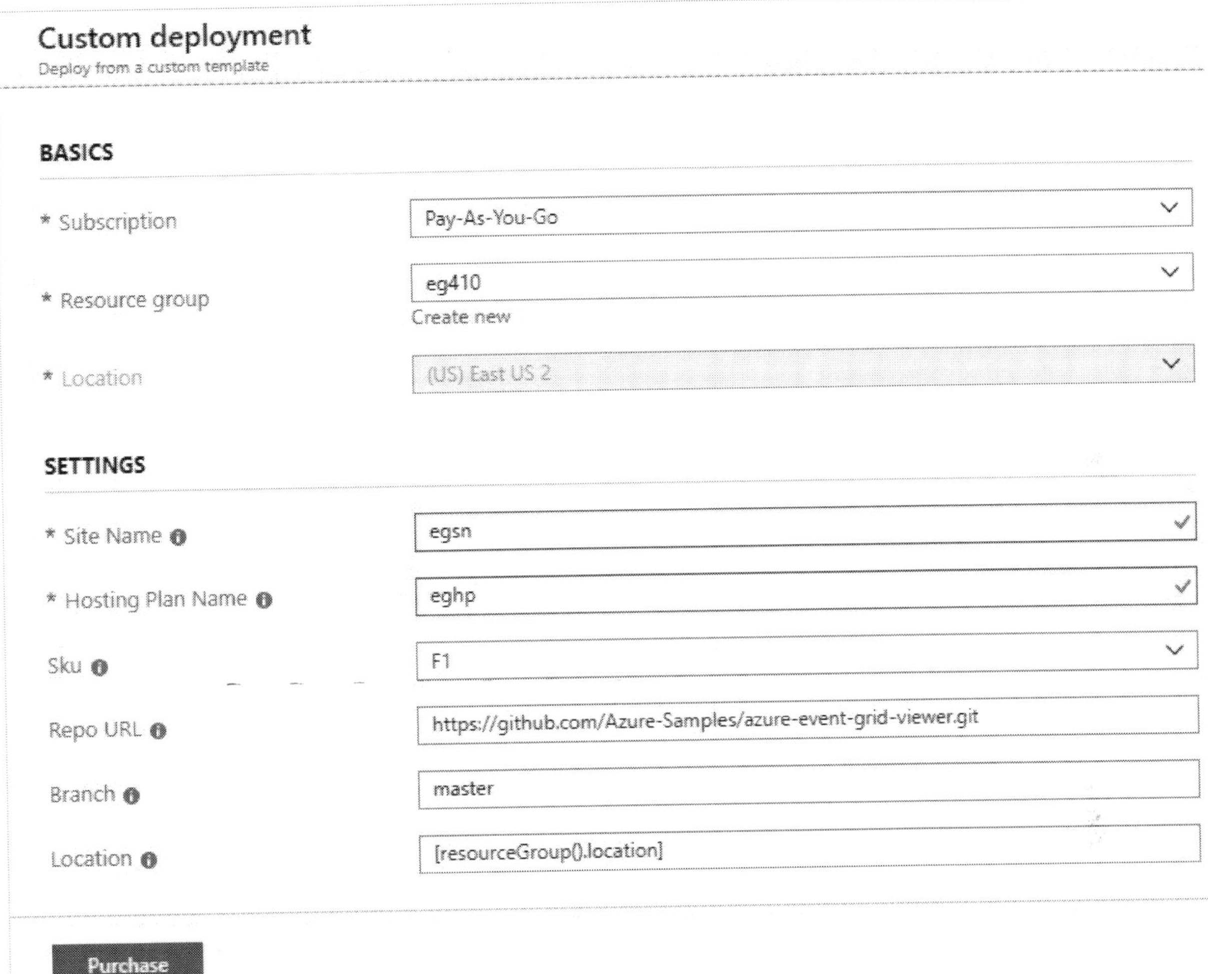

3. Figure below shows the dashboard of Web App egsn.

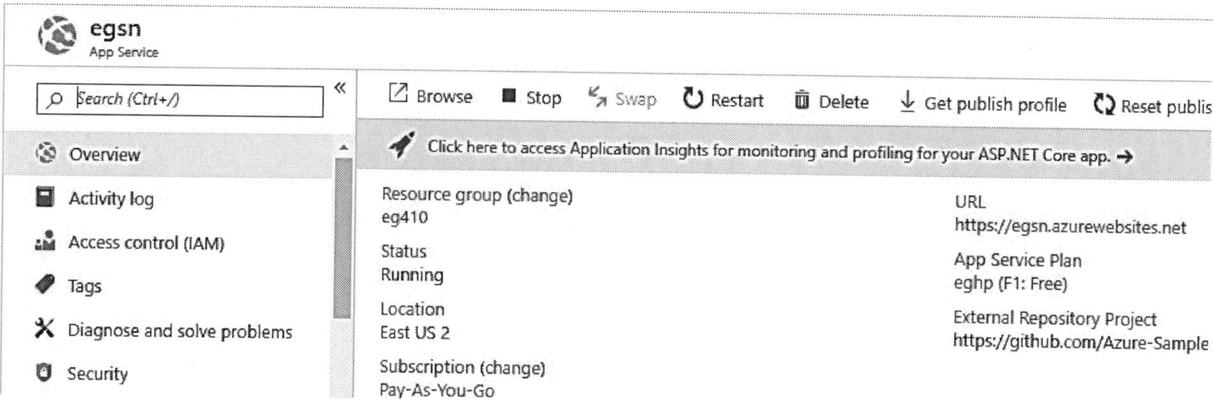

4. Copy the DNS name of Web App from right pane and open it in browser. You can see the Web App site but with no events posted.

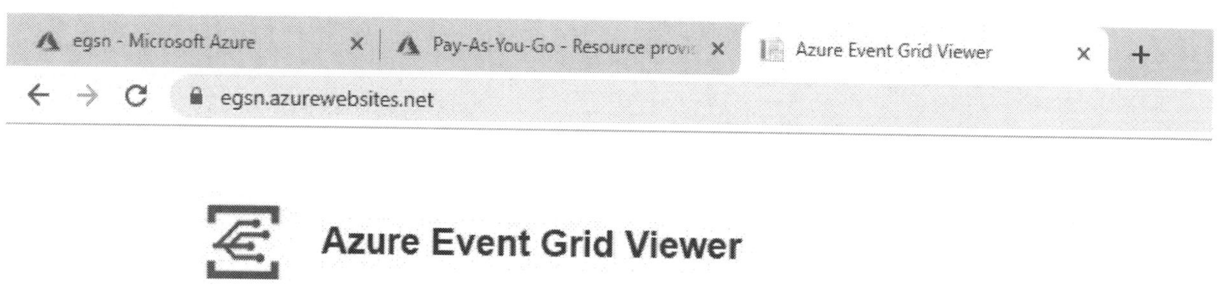

In Step 4 we will upload file to Azure Storage which will trigger the event.

Step 2: Enable Event Grid resource provider

This Step is only required if you have not previously used Event Grid in Your subscription. You need to register the Event Grid resource provider.

1. In Azure Portal Click Cost Management + Billing in left pane> Cost Management + Billing Dashboard opens>In Right pane click your subscription>Subscription Dashboard opens> In left pane under settings click Resource Providers>In Right pane scroll down and select Microsoft.EventGrid.

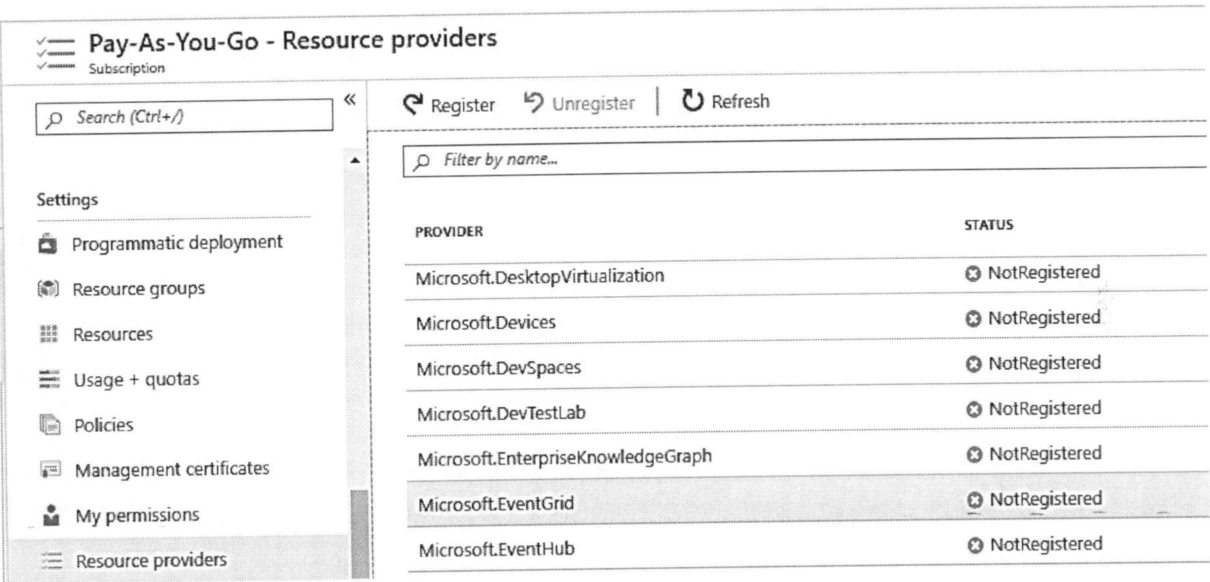

2. After you select Microsoft.EventGrid Click Register in Top> Click Refresh>It will show registering>After some time it will show Registered. You need to continuously Press Register to see the status change.

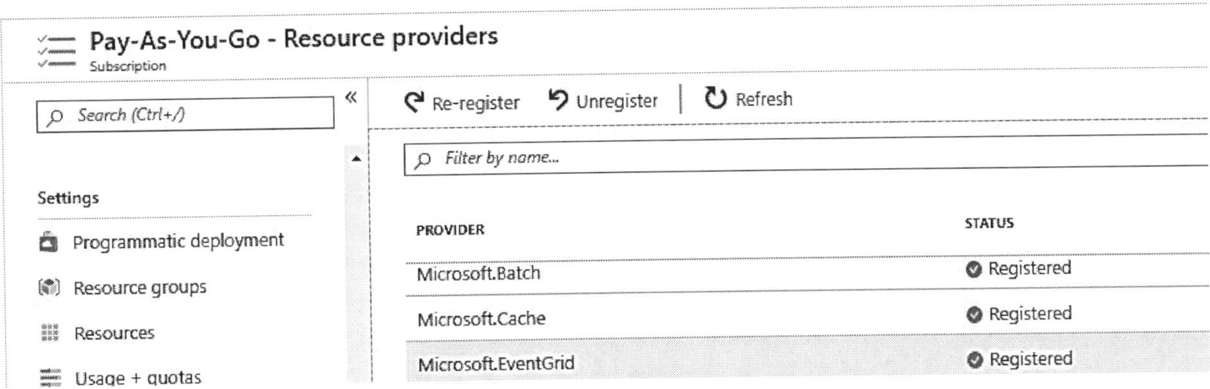

Step 3: Subscribe to Blob Storage Events

In this Step You subscribe to a topic to tell Event Grid which events you want to track and where to send the events.
We will subscribe to events in Storage Account eg410. Storage Account eg410 was created in previous exercise.

1. Go to Storage Account eg410 Dashboard>Click Blobs in Right pane> Storage Account Blob Dashboard opens> Note the Event Tab in left pane.

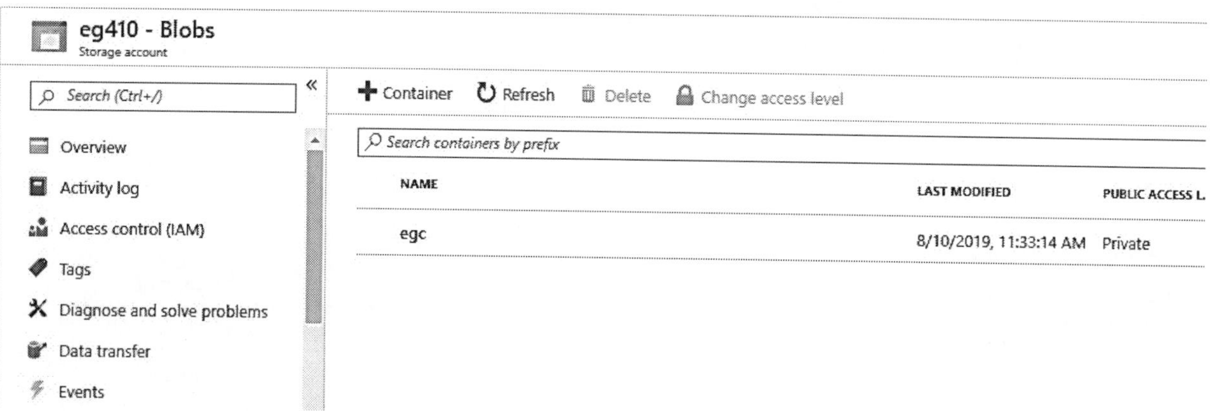

2. Click Events in left pane>In Right pane click More options>Scroll down and you can see Web Hook option.

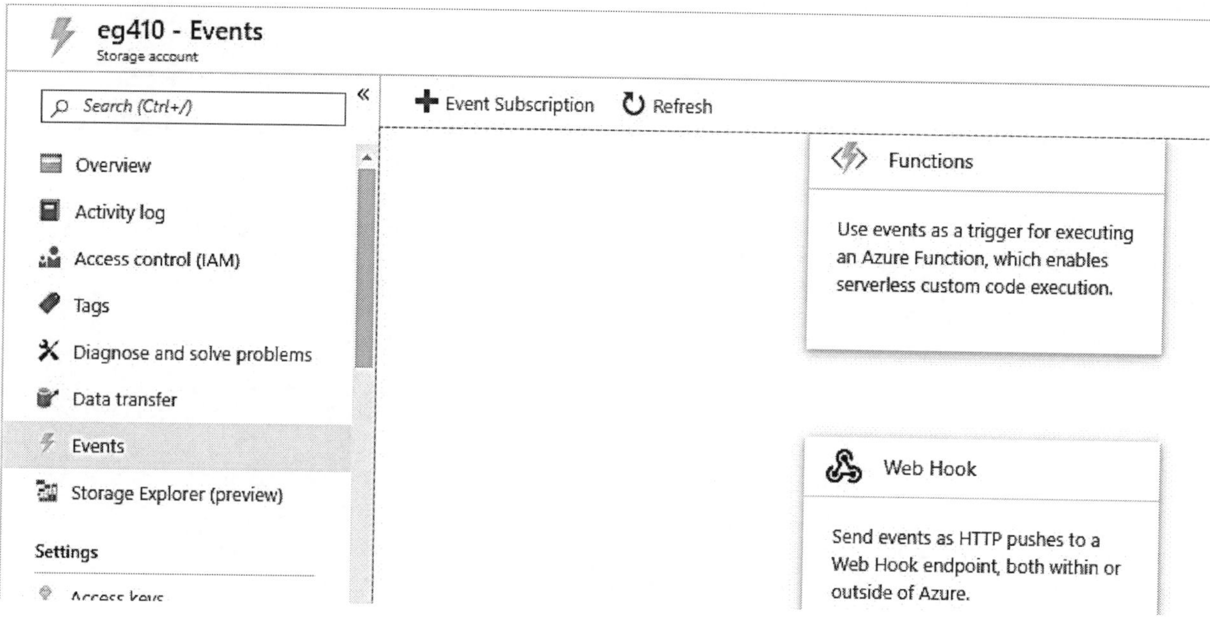

3. Click on Web Hook>Create Event Subscription blade opens>Enter a name>In endpoint type Select Web Hook>**Select an Endpoint** Link generated below endpoint type. Click Select an Endpoint>Select Web Hook Pane opens> In Subscriber Endpoint enter https link of Web App created in Step 1 appended with api/updates. The complete link will be as follows:
https://egsn.azurewebsites.net/api/updates
Click Confirm Selection>Click create.

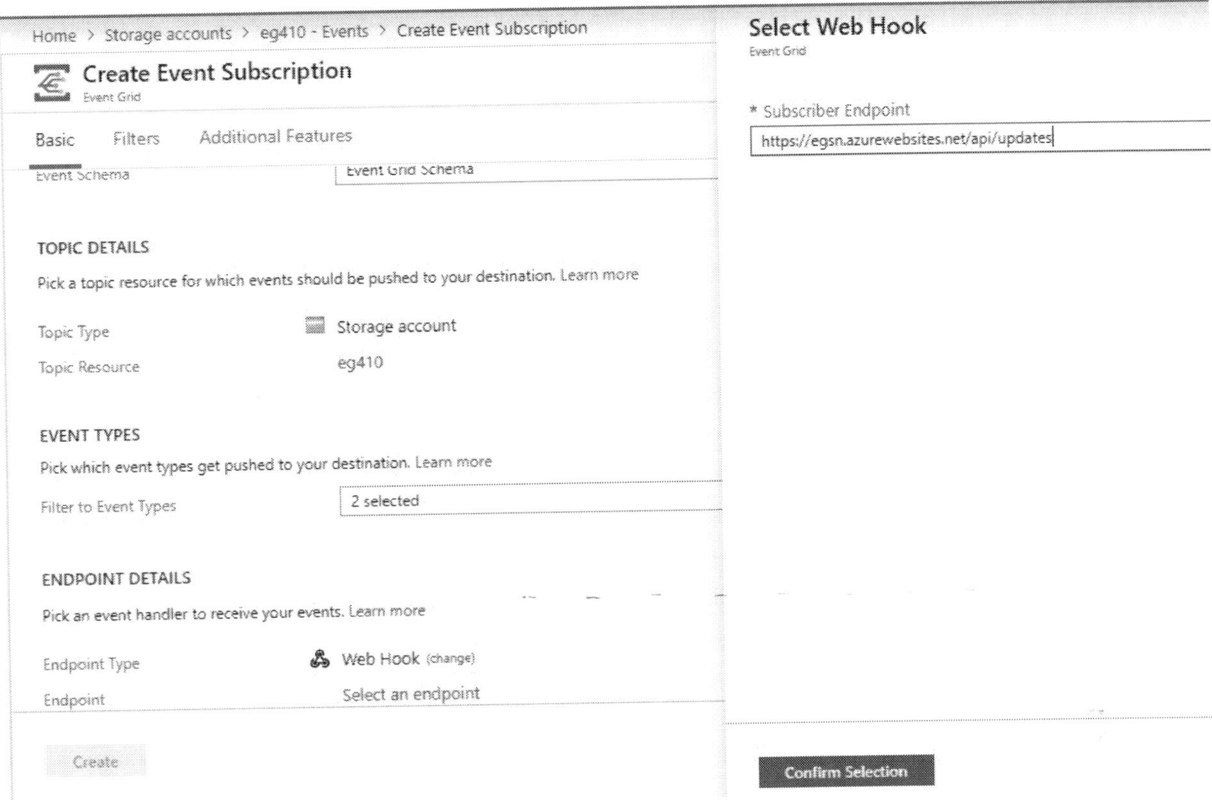

4. View your web app again, and notice that a subscription validation event has been sent to it.

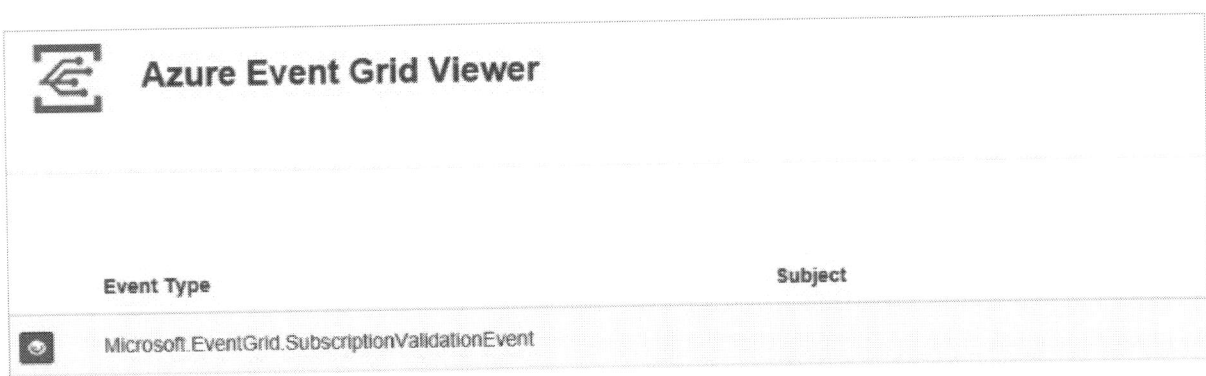

Step 4: Trigger an event in Blob Storage

You trigger an event for the Blob storage by uploading a file. In this step we will upload a file from our desktop to **Blob Container egc** which was created in previous exercise.

1. Go to Storage Account eg410 Dashboard>Click Blobs in Right pane> Blob storage Dashboard opens> In Right pane click container egc>Container dashboard opens>Click upload in right pane>Upload Blob blade opens>Click the folder icon and upload a file>Click upload.

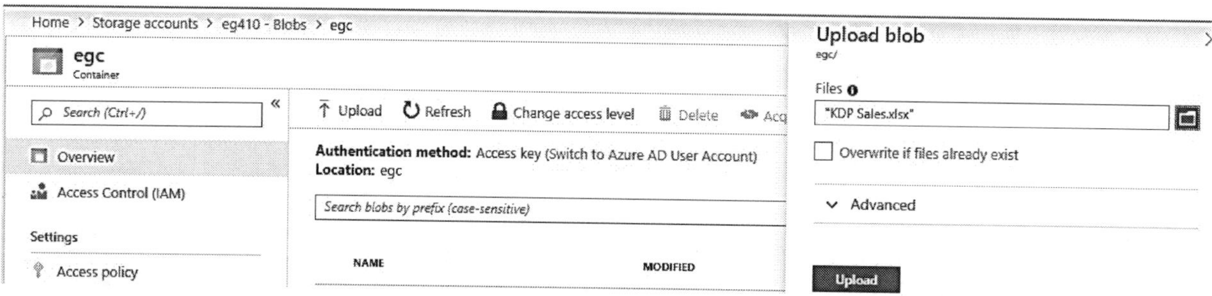

2. View your web app again, and notice that a Event was logged in the Web App>Click on the eye icon to expand the event data.

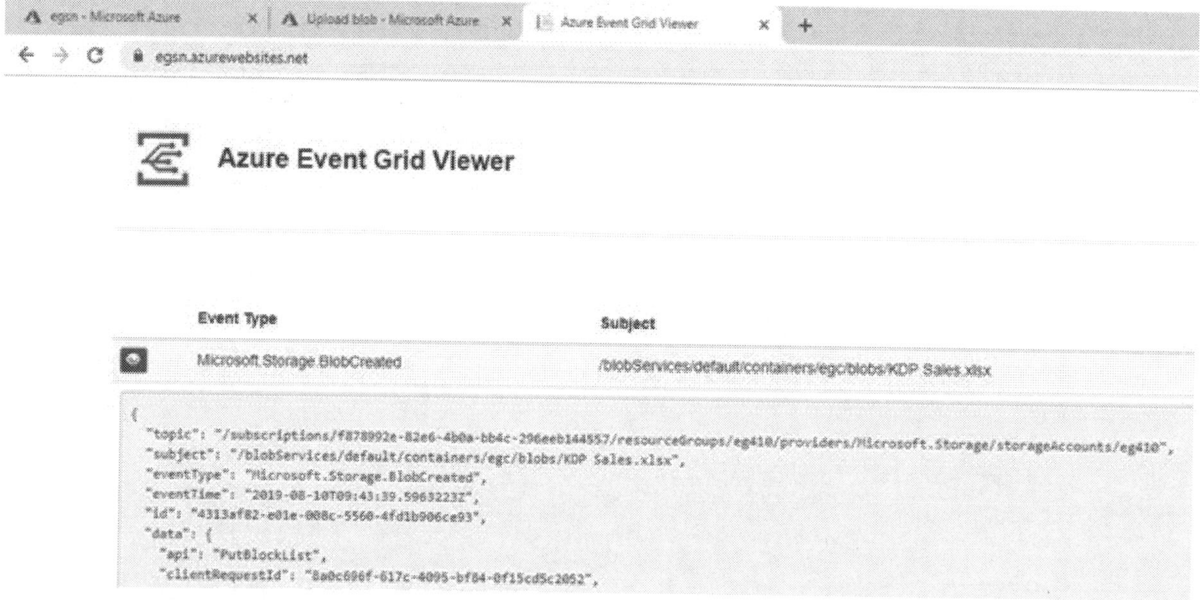

3. Delete the Resource Group eg410.

Event Grid Pricing

Event Grid pricing is based on operations performed. Operations include all ingress events, advanced match, delivery attempt, and management calls. Pricing includes a monthly free grant of 100,000 operations.

Price per million operations	$0.30
Free usage per month	100,000 operations

Azure Event Hubs

Azure Event Hubs is a managed service capable of ingesting millions of events per second from connected devices, Applications, Websites & Real Time Streaming Events.

Event Hubs is the intermediate ingestion point of events between the data sources and the event processing engine. Data is collected into an Event Hub and then transformed using Services such as Stream Analytics or Machine Learning. Figure below shows placement of Event Hub in Real Time Analytic Solutions.

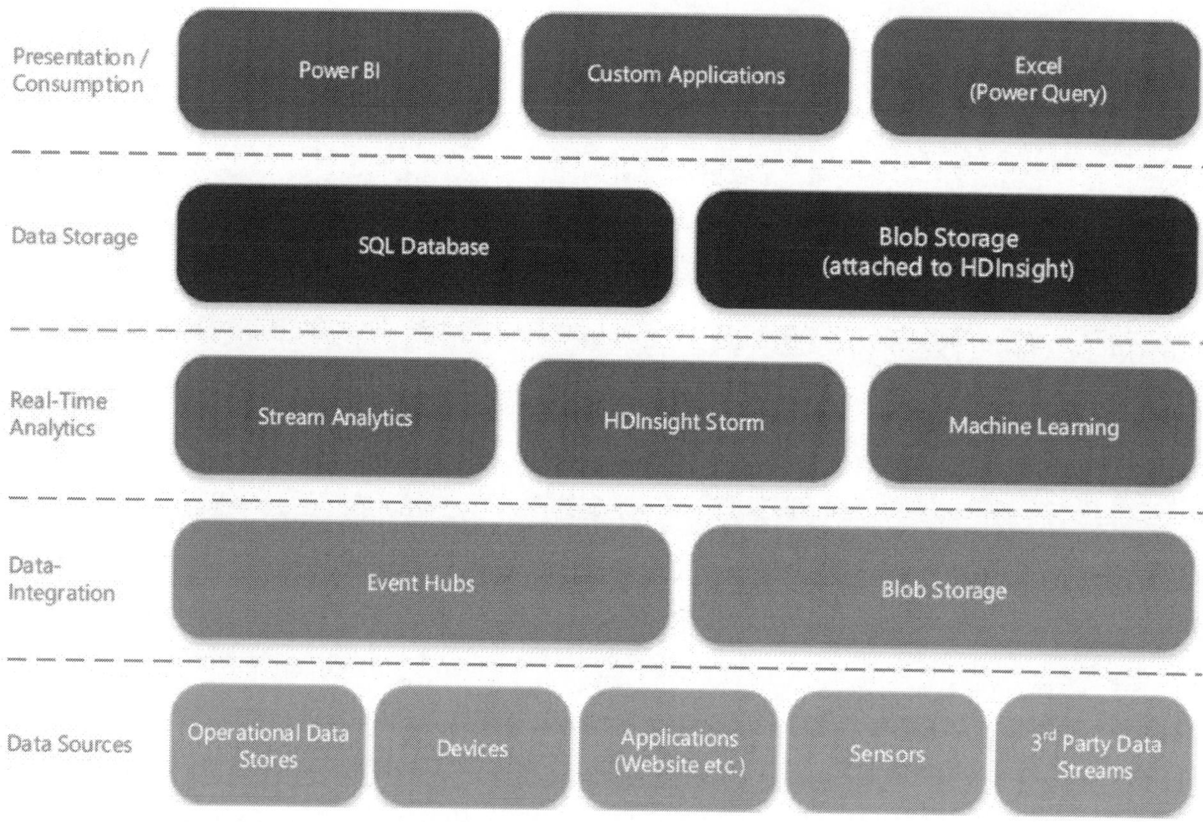

Input to Event Hub: In Event Hub, Event producers send Event Data after authenticating to Event Hub using Shared Access Signatures.
Input sources can be IOT Devices, Sensors, Applications, Websites, Real time Twitter Streams or 3rd Party Streams (Streams are sent to a Web Application. In Web Application, Connection string and authentication of Event Hub is specified. Web Application then sends real-time stream to Event Hub).

Output of Event Hub can be sent to Azure Stream Analytics for Analytics in Real time, Azure Storage for Archiving, Data lake store for Batch Analytics or to the Supported Application. The figure below shows output of Event Hub being ingested into Stream Analytics Service. Azure Services like Stream Analytics have built in adaptor to connect to Event Hub.

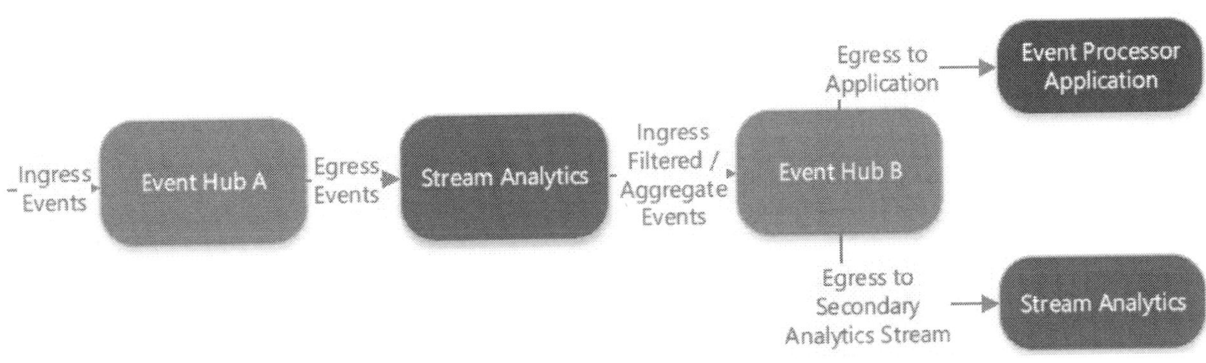

As shown in the figure above Event Hub also supports Stream Analytics as input Data source.

Events are persisted in Event Hub for a period of time which can be configured through Event Hub dashboard.

Event Hub Use Cases

1. Telemetry data collected from industrial machines, connected vehicles, or other devices.
2. Traffic information from web farms.
3. In-game event capture in console games.
4. Behavior tracking in mobile apps.

Event Hub Anti Use Cases

1. Does not support Bi-Directional Communication with devices. You cannot send messages back to devices to update properties or invoke an action.
2. Cannot implement Device-level identity helps to secure your system.
3. No support for Edge computing as in the case of IOT Hub using IoT edge.

Event Hub Architecture

Event Hubs is a managed service that sits between event publishers and event consumers to decouple the production of an event stream from the consumption of those events.

Event Hub uses Publish/Subscribe model. Event Producers publish event to event Hubs. Events are stored in Event Hub. Subscribers can register for specific events.

Figure below shows the Architecture of Event Hub Solution.

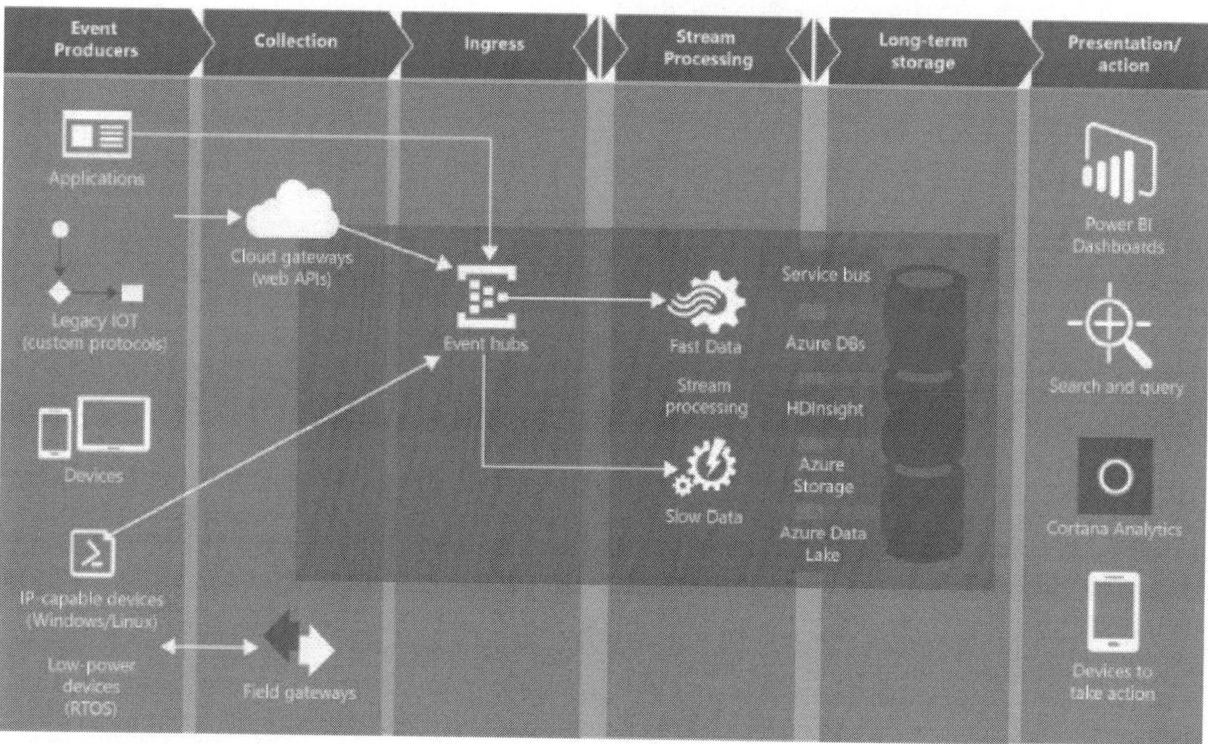

Event Hub Solution components and features

Event producers/publishers is an entity that sends data to an event hub. Event producers can be IOT devices, IOT Gateways and Applications. Event publishers publish events using HTTPS or AMQP 1.0.

SAS tokens: Event producers use a Shared Access Signature (SAS) token to identify themselves to an event hub.

Event Hubs is a managed service that sits between event publishers and event consumers. Event Producers publish event to event Hubs. Events are stored in Event Hub. Subscribers can register for specific events.

Event Hub Partition: A partition is an ordered sequence of events that is held in an event hub. The number of partitions is specified at creation of Event Hub and must be between 2 and 32. You cannot change this afterwards.
Partition enables each consumer to only read a specific subset or partition of the event stream

Partitions help in scaling Event hub Processing, Availability and Parallelization. The number of partitions in an event hub directly relates to the number of concurrent readers you expect to have. There can be at most 5 concurrent readers on a partition per consumer group; however **it is recommended that there is only one active receiver on a partition per consumer group**.

A single partition has a maximum scale of one throughput unit.

Figure below shows Event Hub configured with 4 Partitions. Partitions are independent and contain their own sequence of data, they often grow at different rates.

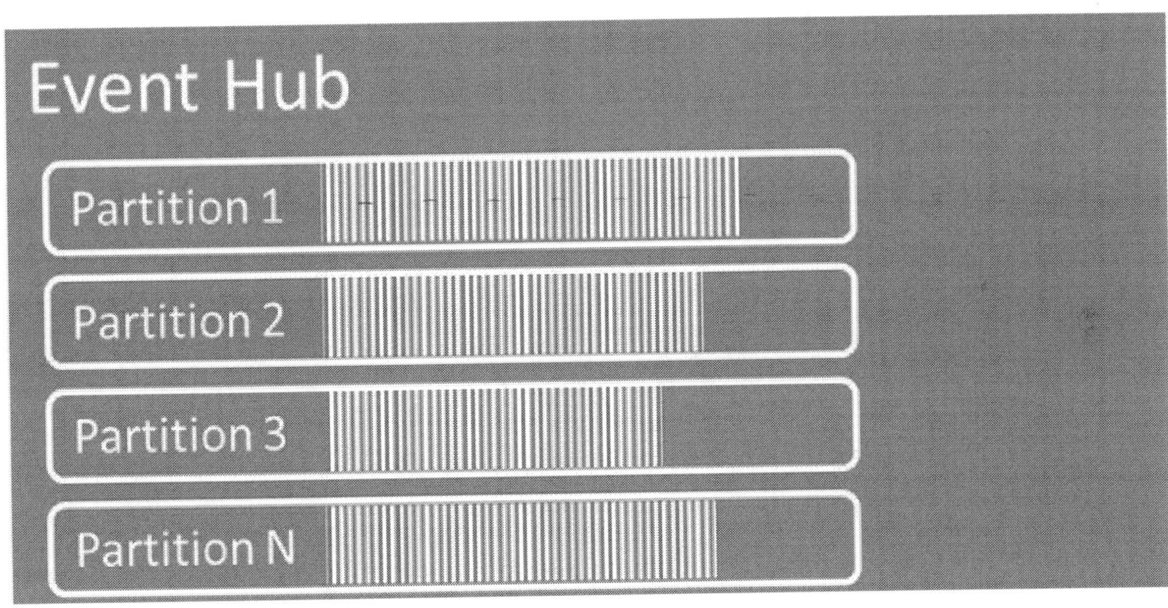

Partition Key maps incoming event data into specific partitions. The partition key is a sender-supplied value passed into an event hub. If you don't specify a partition key when publishing an event, a round-robin assignment is used. The event publisher is only aware of its partition key, not the partition to which the events are published. This decoupling of key and partition insulates the sender from needing to know too much about the downstream processing.

Event consumers is an entity that reads event data from an event hub. Event Consumers can be Azure Stream Analytics, Azure Machine learning service, Blob storage & Data lake store etc. Event consumers must subscribe for specific events they want to use. Event consumers connect via AMQP 1.0. Many of the Event consumers like Azure Stream Analytics have built in adaptor to connect to Azure Event Hubs.

Consumer groups: The publish/subscribe mechanism of Event Hubs is enabled through *consumer groups*. Consumer groups enable multiple consuming applications to each have a separate view of the event stream, and to read the stream independently at their own pace and with their own offsets.
You can only access partitions through a consumer group. There can be at most 5 concurrent readers on a partition per consumer group; however **it is recommended that there is only one active receiver on a partition per consumer group.** You can create up to 20 consumer groups for a Standard tier event hub.

In a stream processing architecture, each downstream application equates to a consumer group. If you want to write event data to long-term storage, then that storage writer application is a consumer group.

The figure below shows the Event Hubs stream processing architecture.

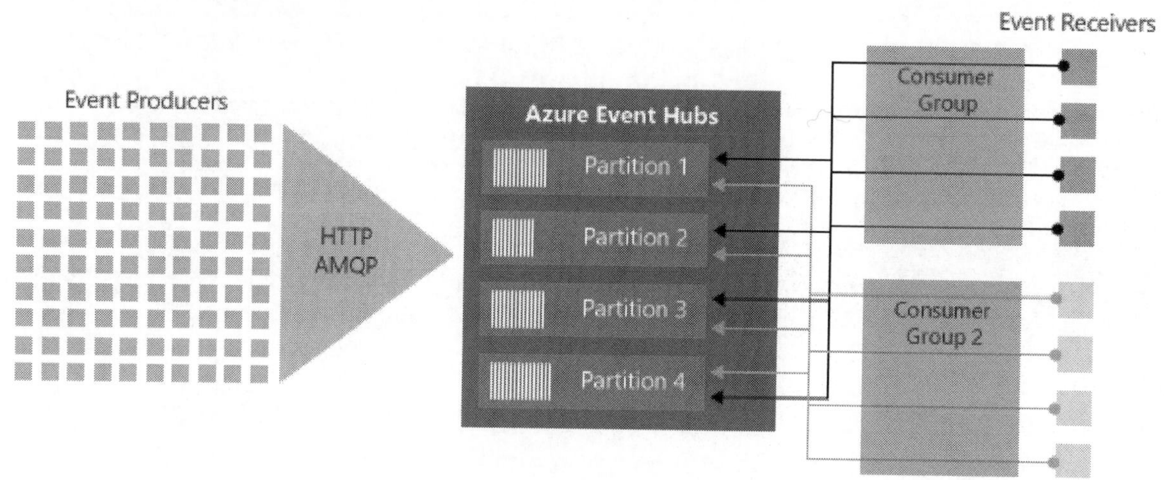

Azure IoT Hub and Azure Event Hubs Comparison

Both Azure IoT Hub and Azure Event Hubs are cloud services that can ingest large amounts of data and process or store that data for business insights.

IoT Hub was developed with the specific capabilities needed to support at-scale internet of things (IOT) scenarios.

Event Hubs is designed for event ingestion at a massive scale, both in the context of inter-datacenter and intra-datacenter scenarios (Ingestion from Azure Services) but doesn't provide the rich IoT-specific capabilities that are available with IoT Hub.

Some of the important differentiator's between IoT Hub and Event ingestion services are as follows:

1. IoT Hub includes features that enrich the relationship between your devices and your backend systems.
2. IoT Hub Bi-directional communication capabilities mean that while you receive data from devices you can also send messages back to devices to update properties or invoke an action.
3. IoT Hub Device-level identity helps secure your system.

Table below shows comparison between IOT Hub and Event Hubs.

	IoT Hub Standard tier	IoT Hub Basic tier	Event Hubs
Device-to-cloud messaging	✓	✓	✓
Protocols: HTTPS, AMQP, AMQP over websockets	✓	✓	✓
Protocols: MQTT, MQTT over websockets	✓	✓	
Per-device identity	✓	✓	
File upload from devices	✓	✓	
Device Provisioning Service	✓	✓	
Cloud-to-device messaging	✓		
Device twin and device management	✓		
IoT Edge	✓		

Azure Event Hub Capacity

The capacity of Event Hubs is controlled by ***throughput units***. A single throughput unit includes the following capacity:

Ingress Events (events sent into an event hub): Up to 1 MB per second or 1000 events per second (whichever comes first).
Egress Events (events consumed from an event hub): Up to 2 MB per second.
Storage: Up to 84 GB of event storage.

Number of throughput units is selected during Event Namespace creation. By enabling **Auto-inflate feature**, you can automatically increase the number throughput units as your usage increases.

Figure below shows throughput unit options that can be selected during Event Namespace creation.

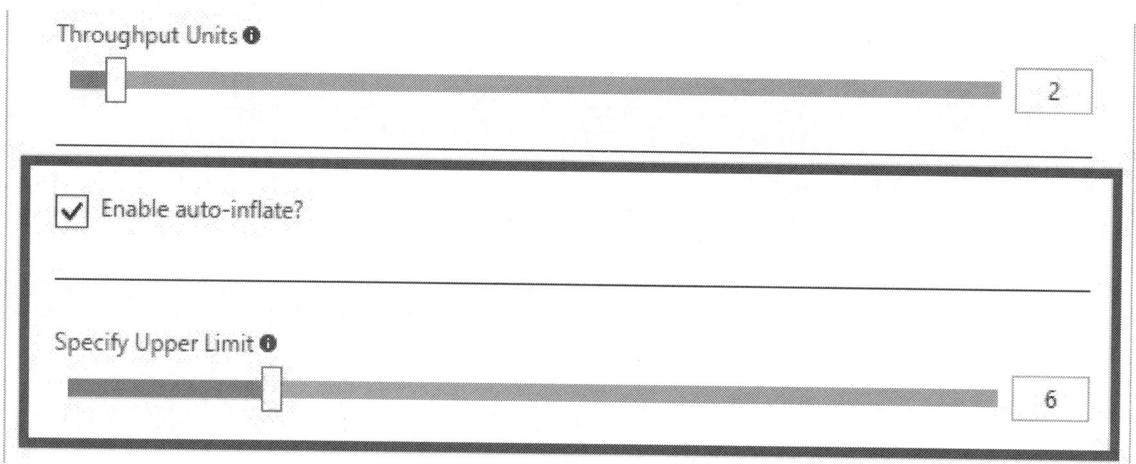

Throughput units are billed per hour and are pre-purchased. Up to 20 throughput units can be purchased for an Event Hubs namespace and are shared across all Event Hubs in the namespace.

Design Nugget: A single partition has a maximum scale of one throughput unit. The number of throughput units should be less than or equal to the number of partitions in an event hub.
Design Nugget: As you increase the number of throughput units in your namespace, you may want additional partitions to allow concurrent readers to achieve their own maximum throughput.

Azure Event Hub Tiers & Pricing

Azure Event Hub comes in 3 tiers: Basic, Standard & Dedicated. The Dedicated tier is not available to deploy from Azure Portal. Customers need to contact billing support to get Dedicated Cluster.

The Standard tier of Azure Event Hubs provides features beyond what is available in the Basic tier. The following features are available only in Standard & Dedicated Tier:

1. Longer event retention
2. Additional brokered connections, with an overage charge for more than the number included
3. More than a single Consumer Group
4. Capture

	Basic	**Standard**	**Dedicated**
Ingress events	$0.028 per million events	$0.028 per million events	Included
Throughput unit (1 MB/s ingress, 2 MB/s egress)	$0.015/hour	$0.03/hour	Included
Message size	256 KB	256 KB	1 MB
Publisher policies		Yes	Yes
Consumer groups	1 Default Group	20	20
Message replay	Yes	Yes	Yes
Maximum throughput units	20	20	
Brokered connections	100 Included	1000 Included	25K Included
Additional brokered connections		Yes	Yes
Message retention	1 day included	1 day included (See Note 1)	Up to 7 days included
Capture		$0.10/hour	Included

Note 1: In the standard tier, Messages can be retained up to seven days, but message retention over one day will result in overage charges.

Exercise 82: Create Event Hub Namespace

1. In Azure Portal click All Services in left pane> Internet of Things>Event Hubs>+ Add>Create Event Hubs Namespace blade opens> Enter Name>Select Pricing as per your Requirement>Select Resource Group RGCloud>Location East US 2> Select Auto-Inflate and enter 5 in maximum units>click create.

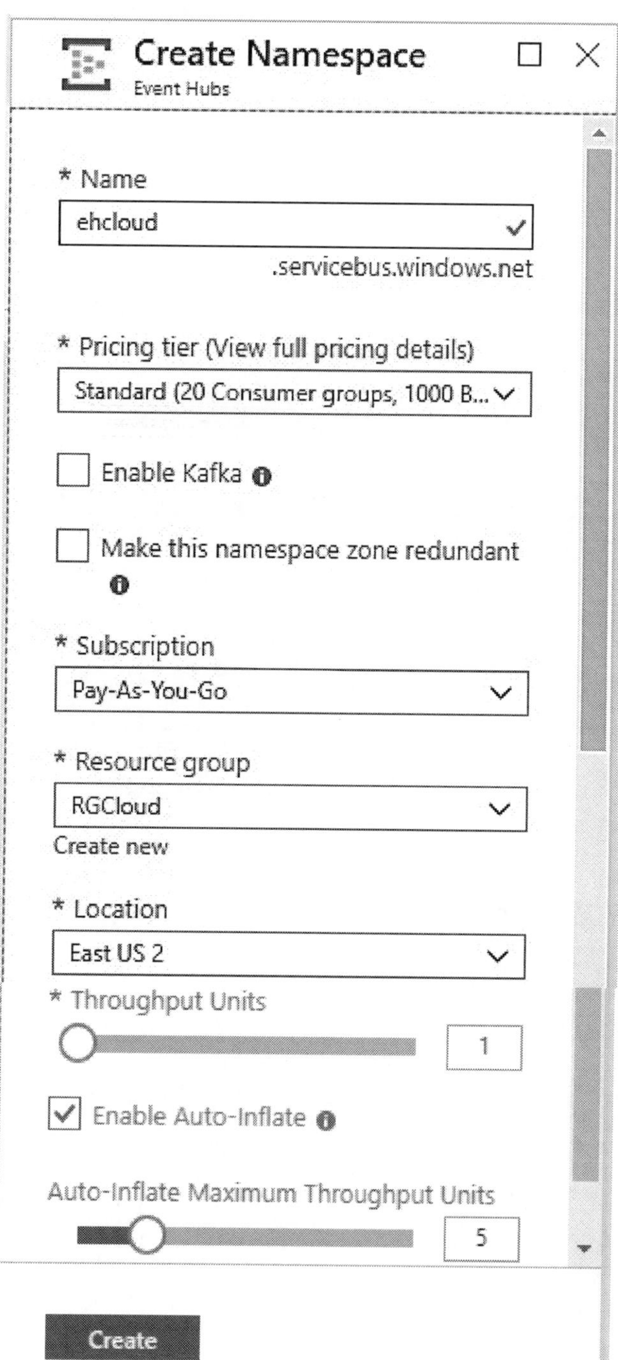

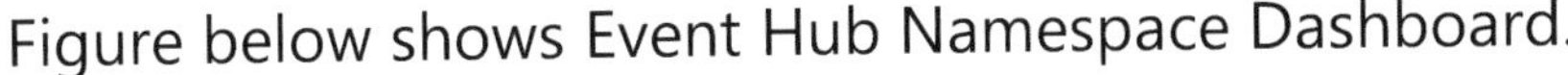

Figure below shows Event Hub Namespace Dashboard.

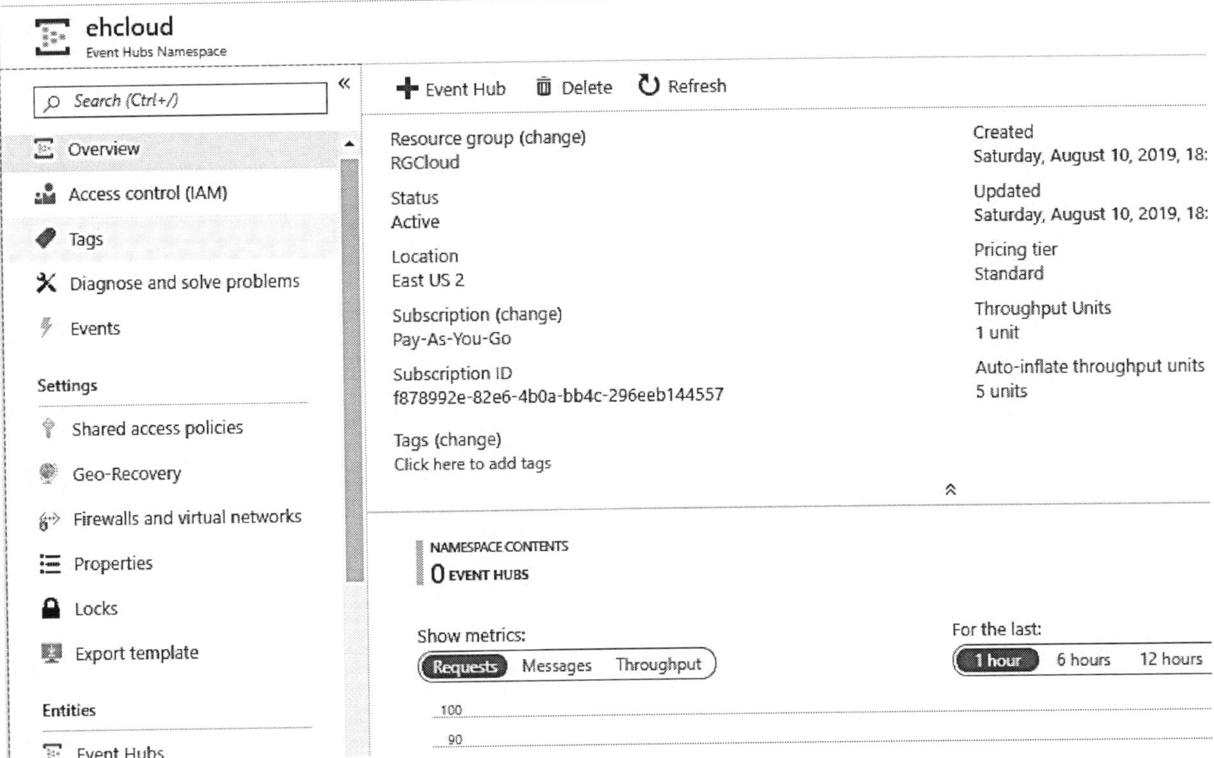

Note: By enabling Auto-Inflate feature, throughput-units will automatically increase based on usage to a specified upper limit.

Note: In this Exercise we used Resource Group **RGCloud.** Resource Group **RGCloud was created** Exercise 1, Chapter 1 in Exam AZ-300 & AZ-301 Study & Lab Guide Part 1

Exercise 83: Create Event Hub

1. In Event Namespace Dashboard Click Event Hubs in left pane>In Right pane Click +Event Hub>Create Event Hub Blade open> Enter a name>Rest Select all default values>Click create (Not Shown).

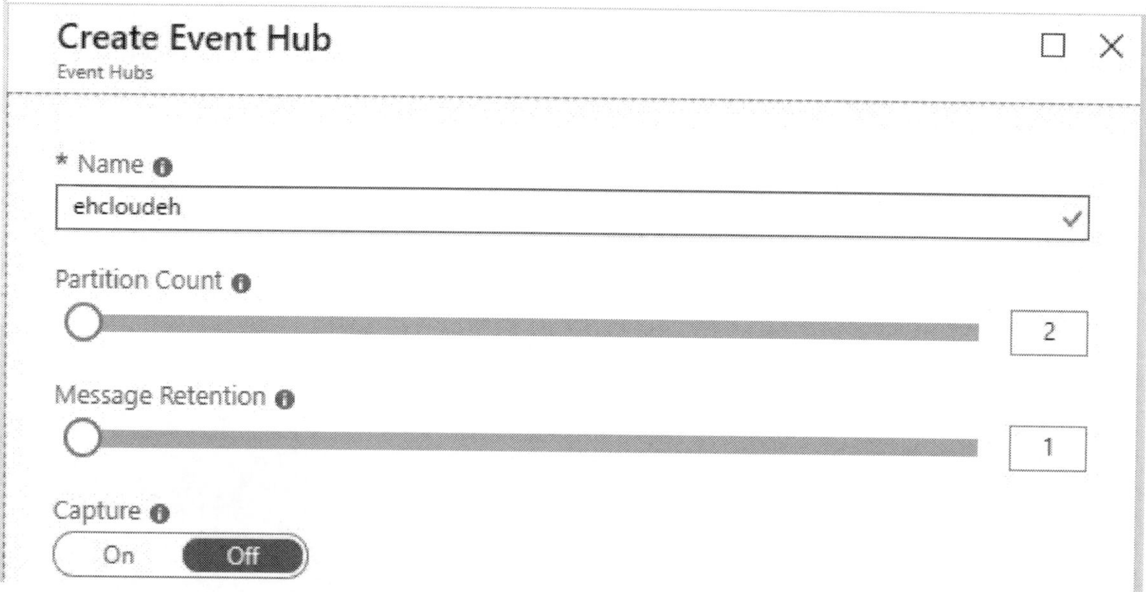

2. Figure below shows Dashboard of Event Hub. From here we can create consumer groups. Through consumer groups Event consumers will read event data from event Hubs. A default consumer group is created with Event Hub.

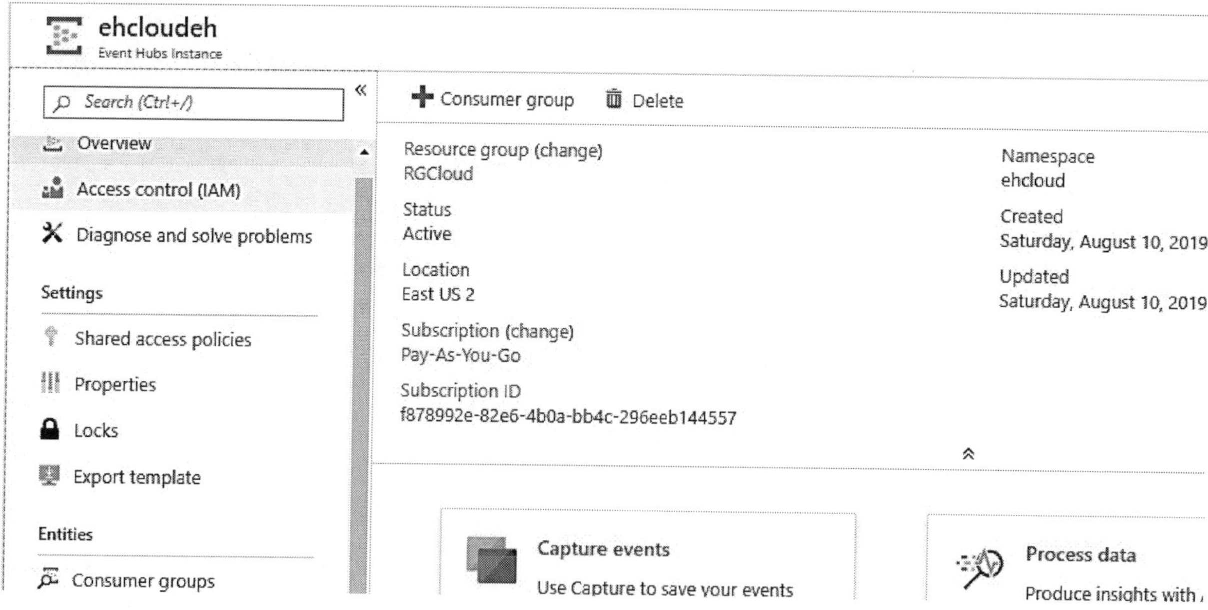

Exercise 84: Configure Event Producers to Send Events to Event Hub

Create and Copy Connection string-Primary Key from Event Hub Dashboard. Connection string will be used by Event Producers to connect and authenticate to Event Hub and sending events to Event Hub.

1. In Event Hub Dashboard>Click shared Access Policies in left pane>In right pane Click + Add>Add SAS Policy Blade opens>Enter a name> Select Manage>Click create (Not Shown).

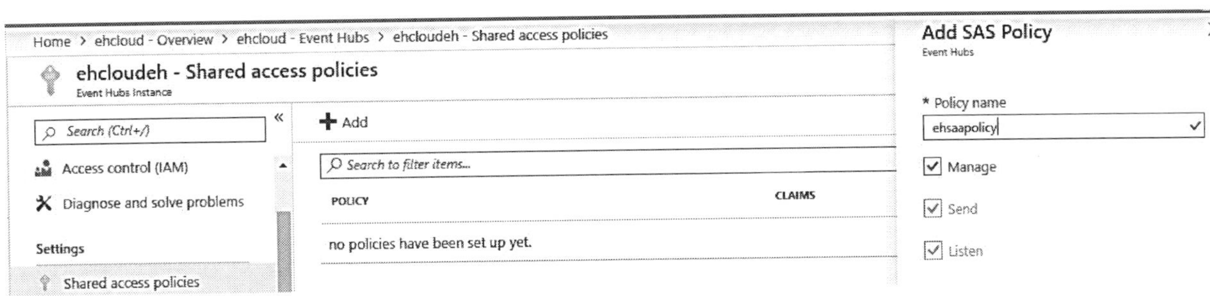

2. Click the newly created Policy>SAS Policy Blade opens>Copy the Connection string-Primary Key.

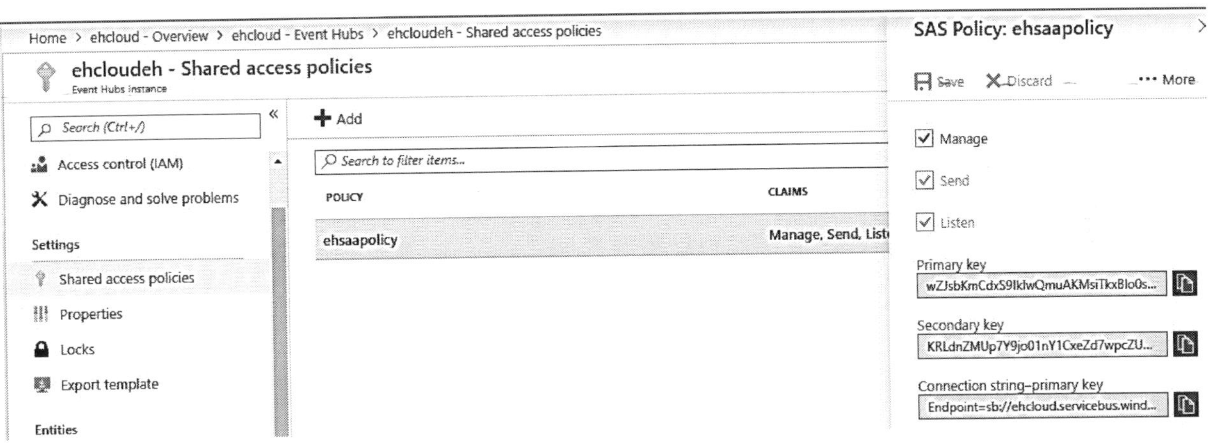

3. In Event Producers add Connection string-Primary Key from Event Hub.

Exercise 85: Send Output of Event Hub to Stream Analytics

Stream Analytics will be used to Query the Event Hub Data in Real Time.

Create Stream Analytics Job

In Azure Portal click Create a resource>Analytics>Stream Analytics Job>Create Stream Analytics Job blade opens>Enter a name>In Resource Group select RGCloud>Location East US 2> Rest Select all default Values>Click create.

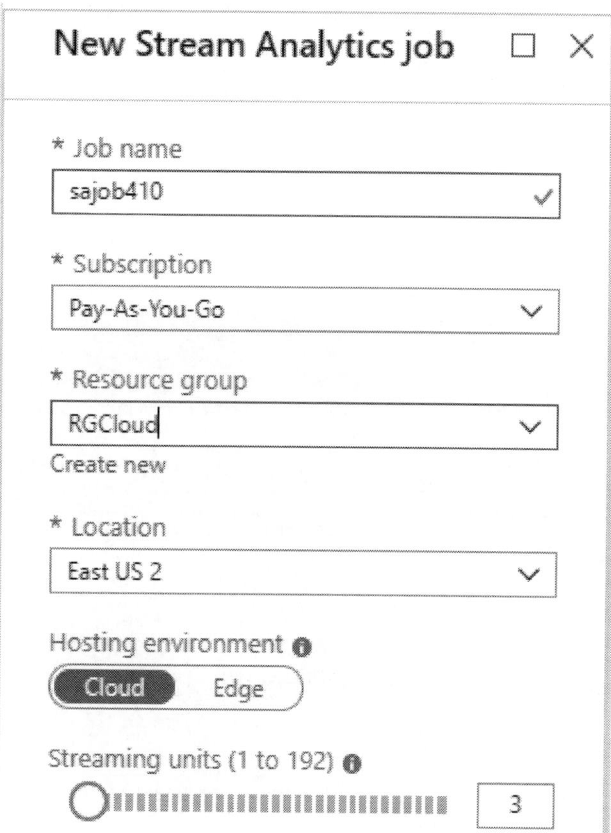

Figure shows Stream Analytics Dashboard. Note the inputs option in left pane.

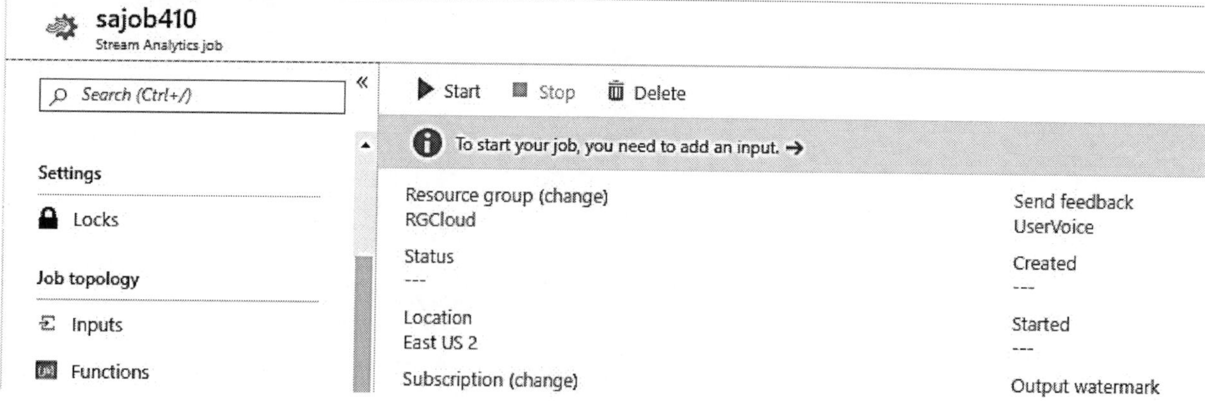

In Stream Analytics Job Dashboard Click input in left pane> In Right Pane click +Add Stream Input> A Box Pops up. select Event Hub> New input blade opens>Enter input Alias>Select Event Hub Namespace created in Exercise 82>Select Event Hub created in Exercise 83>Rest Select all default values>click save.

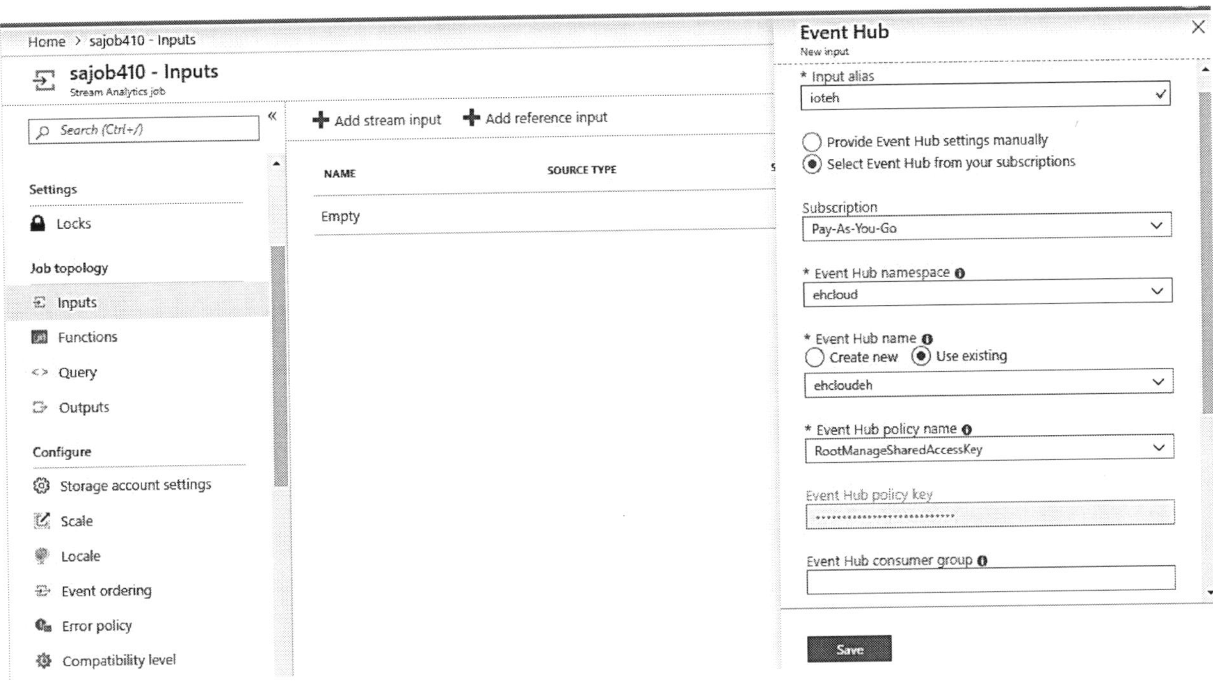

Query the Event Hub data: Click Query in left pane> In Middle pane select the Event Hub Input Alias ioteh>In right pane you can enter your query to do real time analytics on data ingested from Event Hub.

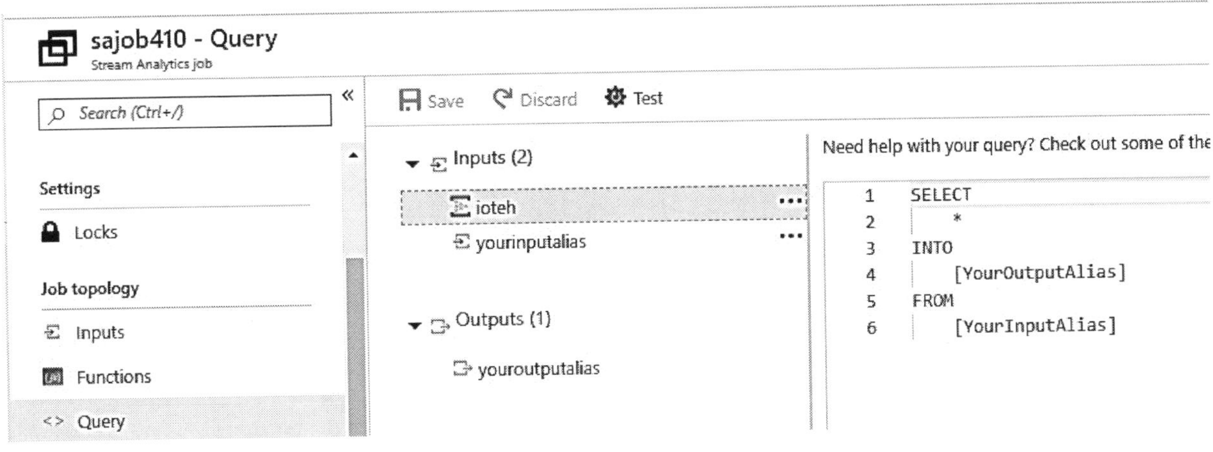

You can send output of Stream Analytics to Power BI.
Click Output in Stream Analytics Job Dashboard>In Right pane Click +Add> Box pops and you can select your options for Output.

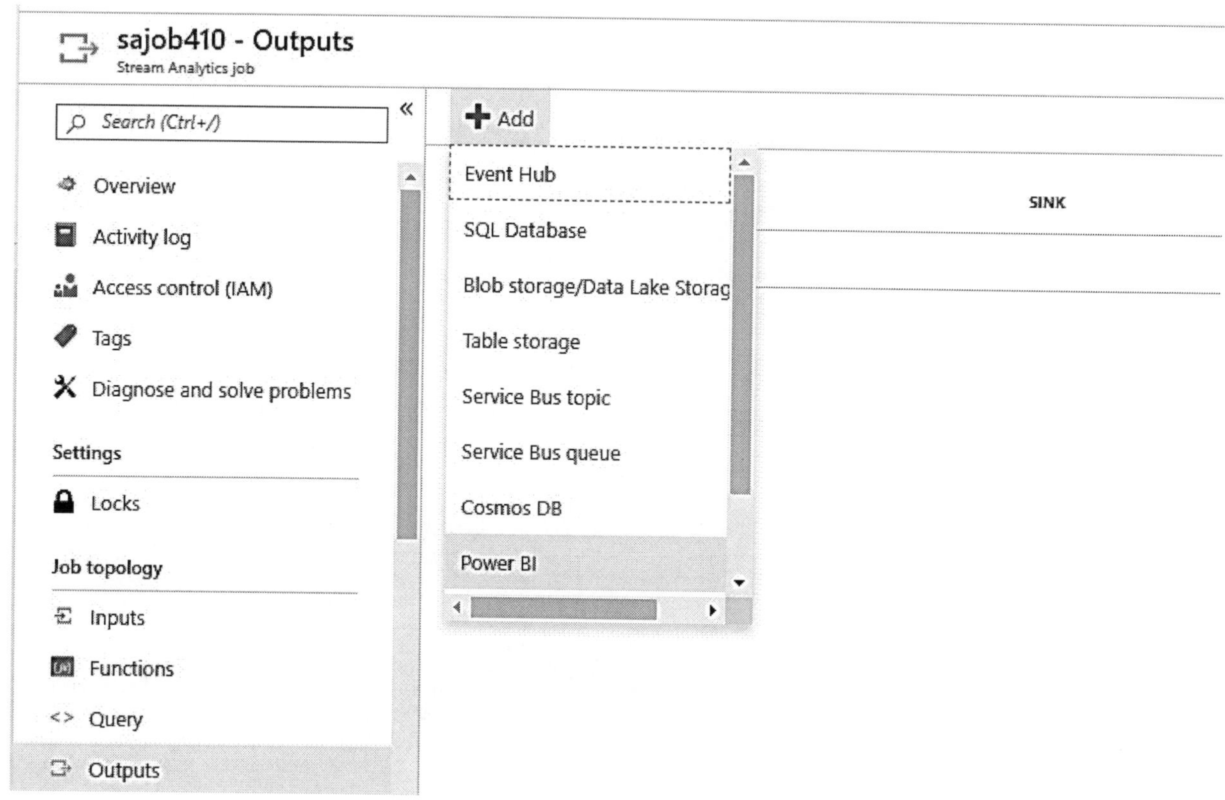

Event Hub Capture

Event Hub Capture enables you to automatically capture the streaming data in Event Hubs and save it to your choice of either a Blob storage account, or an Azure Data Lake Service account. You can enable Capture from the Azure portal.

Enabling Event Hub Capture: In Event Hub Dashboard click capture in left pane> In right pane select on to enable Event capture.

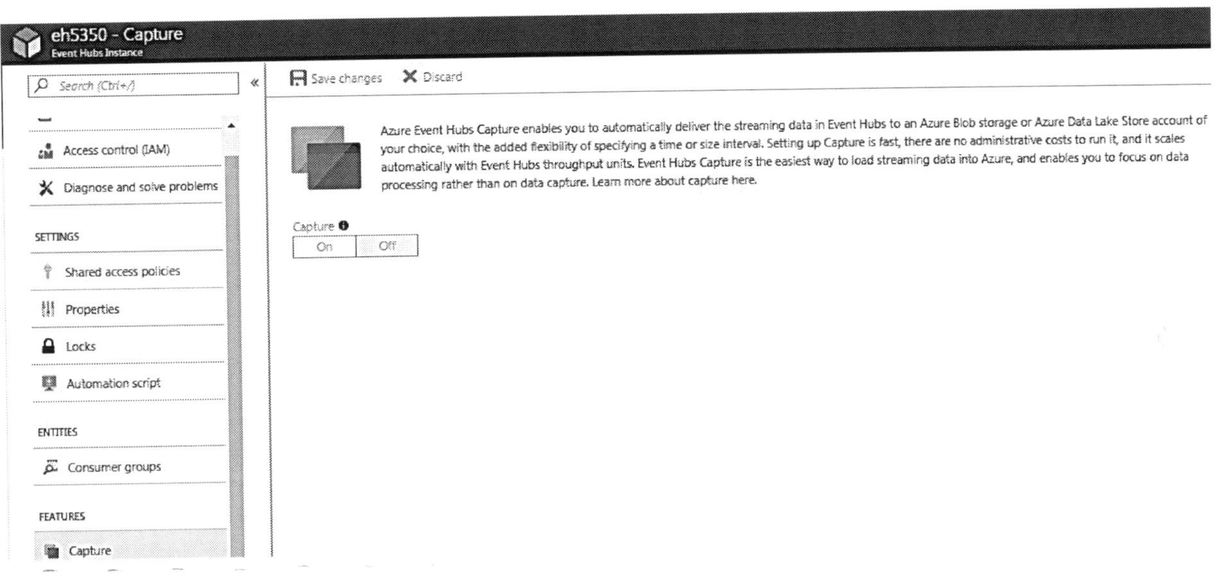

SendGrid Email Service

SendGrid is a cloud-based email service that provides reliable transactional email delivery, scalability, and real-time analytics along with flexible APIs that make custom integration with applications easy.

SendGrid Use Cases

- Automatically sending receipts or purchase confirmations to customers.
- Administering distribution lists for sending customers monthly fliers and promotions.
- Collecting real-time metrics for things like blocked email and customer engagement.
- Forwarding customer inquiries.
- Processing incoming emails.

Chapter 8 Azure Cosmos DB

This Chapter covers following topic Lessons

NoSQL Databases
Cosmos DB Database
Cosmos DB Core SQL (Document) Database
Cosmos DB Table API (key-value pair) Database
Cosmos DB Gremlin (Graph) Database
Cosmos DB for MongoDB API (Document) Database
Cosmos DB Cassandra (Wide-Column) Database
Cosmos DB Firewall & Virtual Network Feature
Cosmos DB Replication Feature
Add Azure Function
Consistency levels in Azure Cosmos DB
Azure Cosmos DB Provisoned Throughput
Azure Cosmos DB Consumed Storage
Partitioning
Cosmos DB Pricing
Saving Cost with Reserved Instances

This Chapter Covers following Lab Exercises

- Cosmos DB Core SQL (Document) Database
- Cosmos DB Table (Key-Value) Database
- Cosmos DB Gremlin (Graph) Database
- Cosmos DB for MongoDB API (Document) Database
- Exploring Firewall and Virtual Network Feature
- Adding Read Regions
- Add Azure Function

Chapter Topology

In this chapter we will add Cosmos DB to the topology.

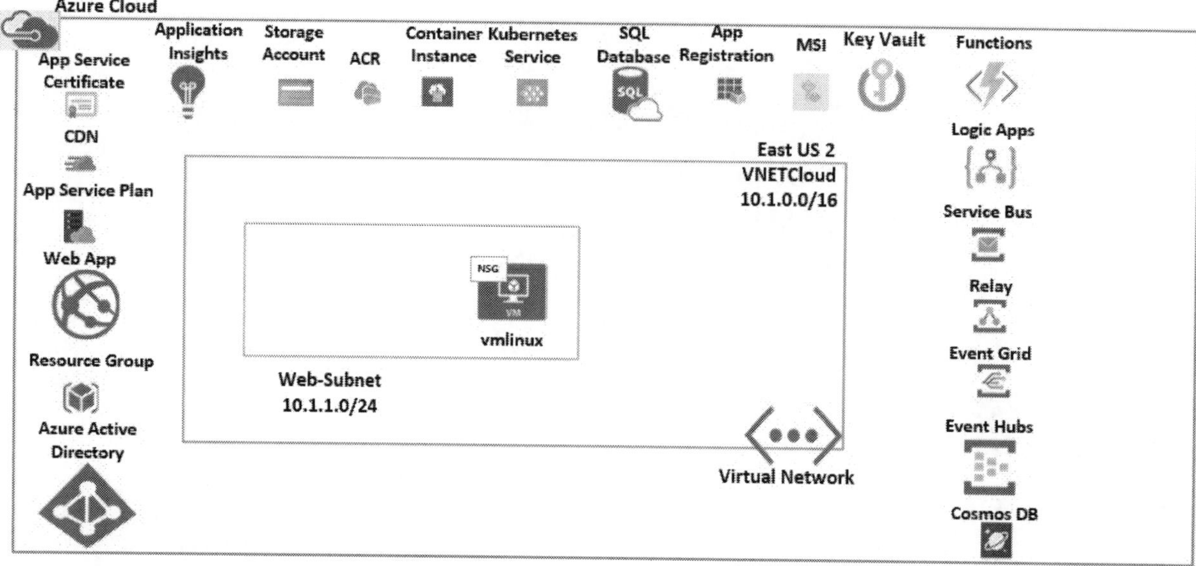

NoSQL Database

NoSQL databases are non-relational databases optimized for scalable performance and schemaless data models. They use a variety of data models, including columnar, document, graph, and in-memory key-value stores.

A **NoSQL** database provides a mechanism for storage and retrieval of data that does not follow RDBMS model of placing data in tables.
NoSQL Database solves the problem of scalability, availability and latency which are inherent in traditional RDBMS Database when using large web scale applications.

Why we need NoSQL Database

Let's take an example of large e-commerce web scale application with a RDMBS backend used by millions of users. If a user is doing a transaction on e-commerce platform, the application will lock that particular product in the inventory database for other users till the transaction is over. This might work for a small set of users but not for millions of users accessing the application. **NoSQL Database solves this problem.**

NoSQL Database compromises consistency in favor of availability, partition tolerance, and speed. NoSQL databases offer a concept of "eventual consistency" in which database changes are propagated to all nodes "eventually" (typically within milliseconds) so queries for data might not return updated data immediately or might result in reading data that is not accurate.

ACID v/s BASE

Traditional RDBMS are based on ACID Principle (Atomicity, Consistency, Isolation and Durability).
Atomicity: Everything in a transaction succeeds lest it is rolled back.
Consistency: A transaction cannot leave the database in an inconsistent state.
Isolation: One transaction cannot interfere with another.
Durability: A completed transaction persists, even after applications restart.

NoSQL's basic idea is that for very large volumes of data, it is difficult to use the ACID principle.

NoSQL uses **BASE Principle:** basic accessibility (Basically Available), flexibility (Soft state), and the final alignment (Eventual consistency). This means that for every request guaranteed to finish (even unsuccessfully), the system state may change, even without the appearance of a data in the system, and that data will be compatible, although there still can be discrepancy.

Basic availability: Each request is guaranteed a response—successful or failed execution.
Soft state: The state of the system may change over time, at times without any input (for eventual consistency).
Eventual consistency: The database may be momentarily inconsistent but will be consistent eventually.

Therefore, if you are designing a Large Web Scale Solution that will load at the level of Amazon or Facebook or Twitter, you will have to use the **BASE** principles.

Features of NoSQL

No fixed schema.
Does not use Tables to store Data.
Does not use SQL as querying language.
Distributed Fault tolerant Architecture
Millisecond latency to support web scale operations.
No Joins. Joins are used in RDBMS for combining records from two or more tables. Joins require strong consistency and fixed schemas.

Comparing NoSQL with RDBMS

Capabilities	RDBMS	NoSQL	Cosmos DB
Global distribution	No	No	Yes
Horizontal scale	No	Yes	Independently scale storage & Throughput
Latency guarantees	No	Yes	Yes. 99% of reads in <10 ms and writes in <15 ms.
High availability	No	Yes	Yes
SLAs	Yes	No	Yes, comprehensive SLAs for latency, throughput, consistency, availability.

NoSQL Data Models

Key-Value Database: Key-Value Database stores data in pairs where you have Key with associated value. For Example take pair of Mobile 8625068410. Here Mobile is key and the number is value. Key- value database are typically used in session management and caching in web applications.

Document Database: Document Database stores semi-structured data in Documents format. Documents themselves act as records. Two Documents can have completely different set of records. **Even though the documents do not follow a strict schema, indexes can be created and queried.** Document databases are typically used in content management, User Profile Management and mobile application data handling.

Wide-Column Database: Wide-column stores organize data tables as columns instead of as rows. Wide-column stores can query large data volumes faster than conventional relational databases. A wide-column data store can be used for recommendation engines, catalogs, fraud detection and other types of data processing.

Graph Database: Graph data stores organize data as nodes, which are like records in a relational database, and edges, which represent connections between nodes. Because the graph system stores the relationship between nodes, it can support richer representations of data relationships. Graph databases are used to map relationships, such as reservation systems or customer relationship management.

Cosmos DB

Azure Cosmos DB is a Globally Distributed, Scalable, high throughput, low latency, multi-model managed NoSQL database service. Cosmos DB multi-model architecture natively supports document, key-value, graph, and column-family data models. Azure Cosmos DB supports following types of NoSQL Databases:

SQL (Document)
MongoDB (Document)
Azure Table (Key-Value)
Gemlin (Graph)
Apache Cassandra (Column Family)

Azure Cosmos DB Database is created under Cosmos DB Account. While creating Cosmos DB account you need to select one of the API. Each API supports one of the Data Model only (SQL, Mongo, Table Storage, Gemlin or Cassandra). Each Cosmos DB Account will support only one type of NoSQL Database.

Features of Cosmos DB

Globally Distributed: Azure Cosmos DB is globally distributed database. You can distribute your Cosmos DB data to any number of Azure regions.
Multiple data models: Azure Cosmos DB natively supports multiple data models including document, graph, key-value table, and column-family data models.
Storage: Azure Cosmos DB has SSD backed storage with low-latency response time in order-of-milliseconds. Database automatically scales when required.
Throughput: Easily scale database throughput anytime. You can independently scale Storage & Throughput.
Latency: Azure Cosmos DB guarantees end-to-end low latency in order of milliseconds.
Availability: Azure Cosmos DB offers 99.99% availability SLA for all single region database accounts, and all 99.999% read availability on all multi-region database accounts.
Consistency Models: Cosmos DB offer five consistency models from strong to eventual. Consistency levels enable you to make trade-offs between consistency, latency & cost.
Low cost of ownership: Five to ten times more cost effective than a non-managed solution or an on-premises NoSQL solution.

Cosmos DB use cases

Personalization: A personalized experience for a user to a website application requires lot of data– demographic, contextual, behavioral and more. Applications need to be able to retrieve personalized settings quickly and effectively to render UI elements and experiences quickly. Cosmos DB offers fast reads with low latency writes. Storing UI layout data including personalized settings as JSON documents in Cosmos DB is an effective means to get this data across the wire. Cosmos DB can scale elastically to meet the most demanding workloads and build and update visitor profiles on the fly, delivering the low latency required for real-time engagement with your customers.

Real Time Fraud Detection: Financial Service companies use Fraud detection extensively to minimize financial losses arising out of fraudulent deals and to comply with regulation. When customers pay with a credit or debit card, they expect immediate confirmation. Fraud Detection relies on data – detection algorithm rules, customer information, transaction information, location, time of day and more – applied at scale and in less than a millisecond. While relational databases struggle to meet this low latency requirement, elastically scalable NoSQL databases can reliably deliver the required performance.

Catalog in Retail and Marketing: Azure Cosmos DB can be used in e-commerce platform for storing Catalog Data. Catalog data is very dynamic and gets fragmented over period of time as new products and service are added and existing products specification gets changed. Cosmos DB NoSQL document database, with its flexible data model, enables enterprises to easily aggregate catalog data within a single database.

Additional Uses Cases

Gaming
User Profile
IOT Scenario
Social Applications
Mobile Applications
Big Data Applications

Cosmos DB Core SQL (Document) Database

Azure Cosmos DB SQL API (Document) is a Schema free NoSQL document database service designed from the ground up to natively support JSON and JavaScript directly inside the database engine. It's a schema-less JSON database engine with rich SQL querying capabilities.

SQL API (Document) databases stores semi-structured data in JSON Documents format. Documents themselves act as records. **Two Documents can have completely different set of records.** Even though the documents do not follow a strict schema, indexes are automatically created and can be queried.

Figure below shows 2 JSON documents with different records.

```
{
First Name: Deepti
Last Name: Sharma
Age        : 45
}

{

House Number: 140
Street          : 10th
Locality        : Dinsha Nagar
City            : Indore
District        : Indore
Pincode         : 452003

}
```

SQL API (Document) databases are logical containers for one or more collections. Collections are containers for JSON documents. Collections also contain stored procedures, user-defined functions and triggers.

SQL API Database stores data as collections of documents. Your application can use a variety of operation types supported by SQL API including CRUD, SQL and JavaScript queries, as well as stored procedures to work with documents.
Figure below shows JSON documents stored in Cosmos DB SQL Database. You can query the document using familiar SQL Syntax. The SQL API provides full transactional execution of JavaScript application logic directly inside the database engine. This allows your application logic to operate over data without worrying about the mismatch between the application and the database schema.

You can connect Cosmos DB SQL API database to application platform of your choice including dot net, Java, Node.js & Xamarin.

SQL (Document) Database Use cases

Document databases are typically used in content management, User Profile Management and mobile application data handling.

Cosmos DB SQL API (document) Database Components

SQL API (Document) Database contains 4 components.

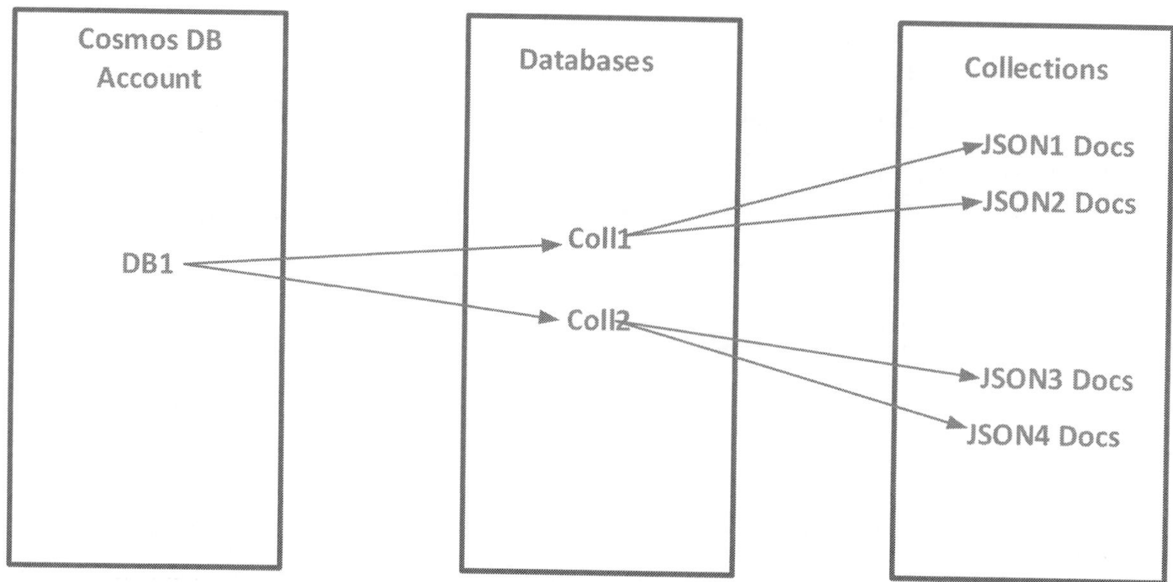

Cosmos DB Account: All Access to Cosmos DB Database happens through Cosmos DB account. Cosmos DB Account can contain one or more SQL API (Document) Databases.

Database: Databases are logical containers for one or more collections.

Collections: Collections are containers for JSON documents. Collections also contain stored procedures, user-defined functions and triggers.

Documents: Text based JSON Documents. A JSON Document contains multiple key-value pairs. Documents in a collection can have different records.

Exercise 86: Cosmos DB Core SQL (Document) Database

1. **Create Cosmos DB (Core SQL) Account**: In Azure Portal Click Create a Resource> Databases> Azure Cosmos DB> Create Azure Cosmos DB Account Opens>Select Resource Group RGCloud> Enter a name>In API Select Core (SQL)>Location Select East US 2>Click Review + Create.

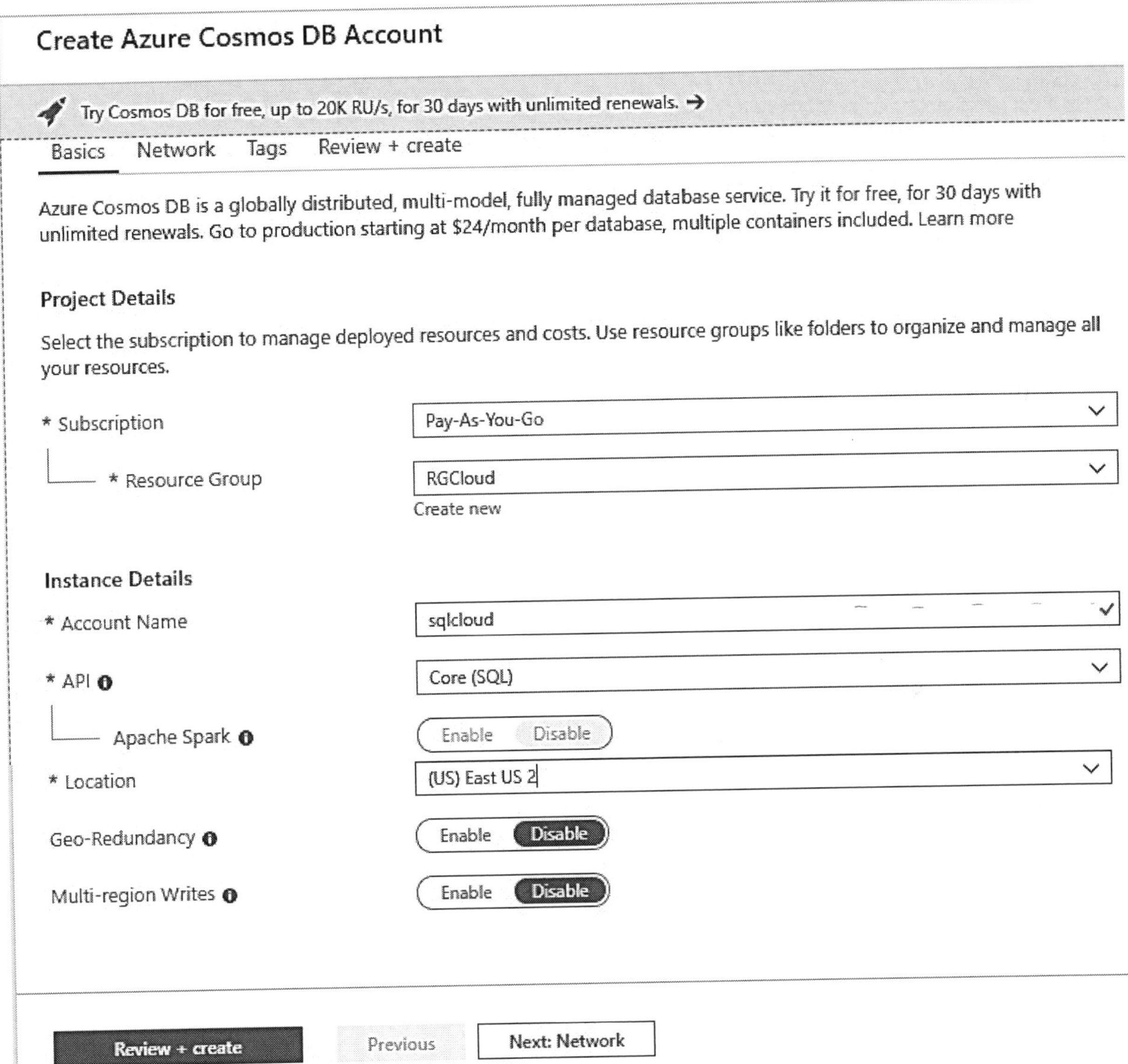

2. Click Review + Create>After Validation Succeeds Click Create (Not shown).

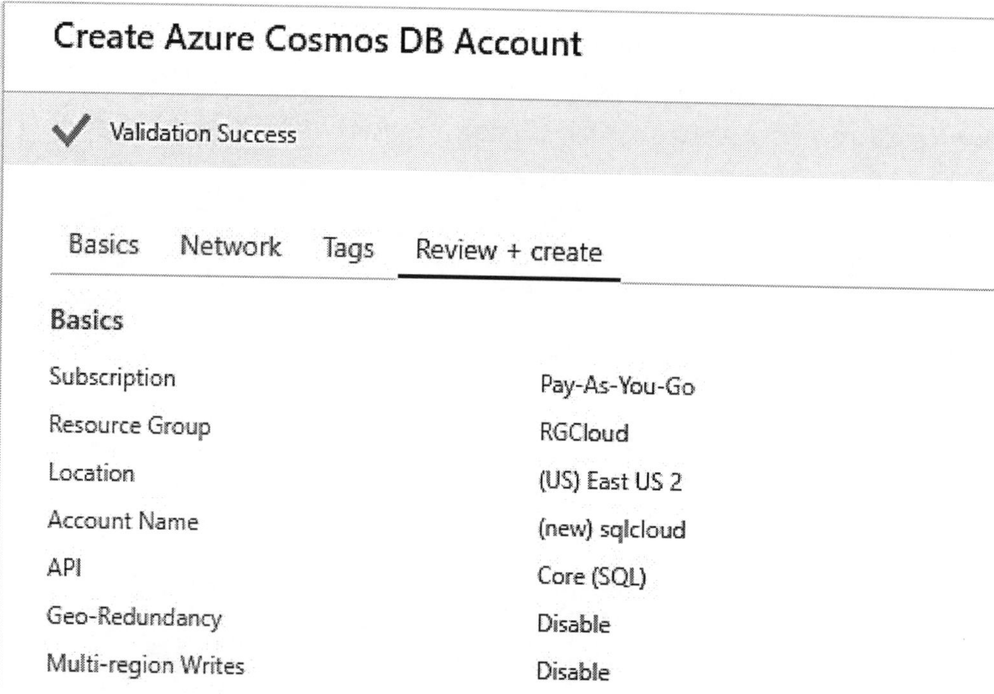

3. Figure below shows Dashboard of Cosmos DB (SQL) Account.

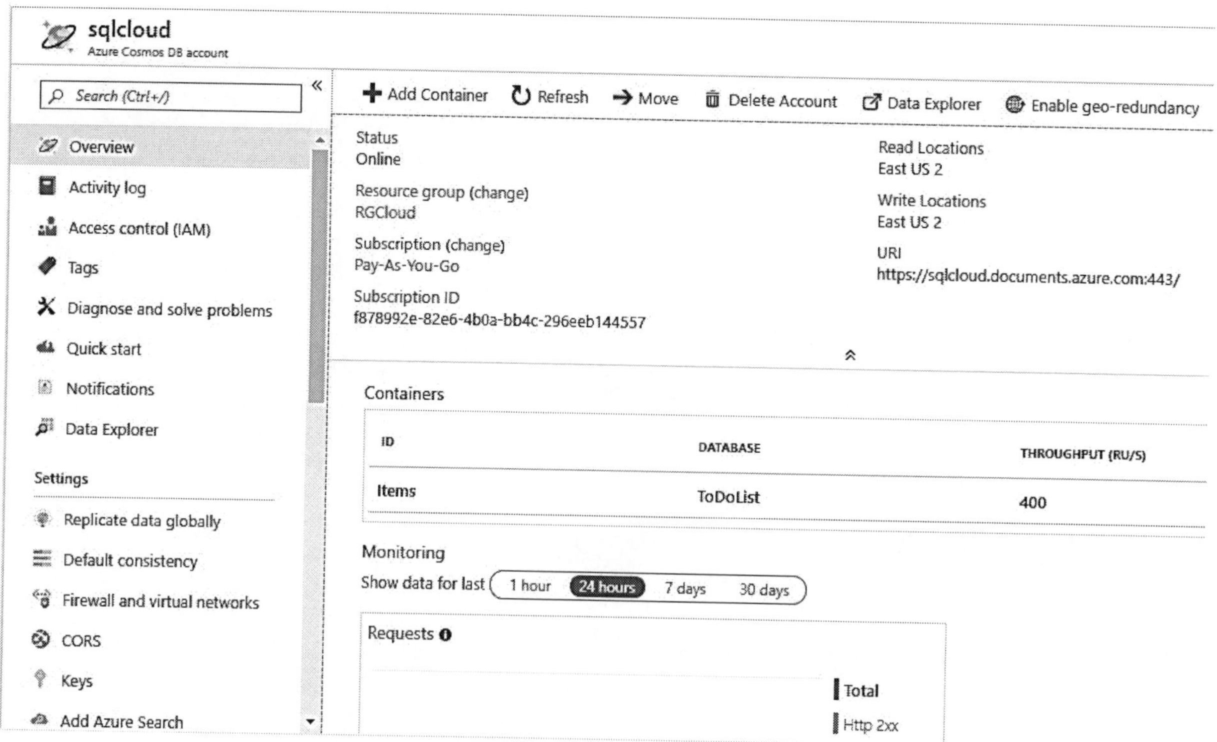

4. **Create Database and Add Collection:** Go to Cosmos DB account dashboard>Click Data Explorer in left pane>+ New Container> Add Container Blade opens>Enter name for Database id> Check Provision Database Throughput>Keep Throughput value at default>Enter name for Container id> Enter Partition Key. I entered /category>Click OK.

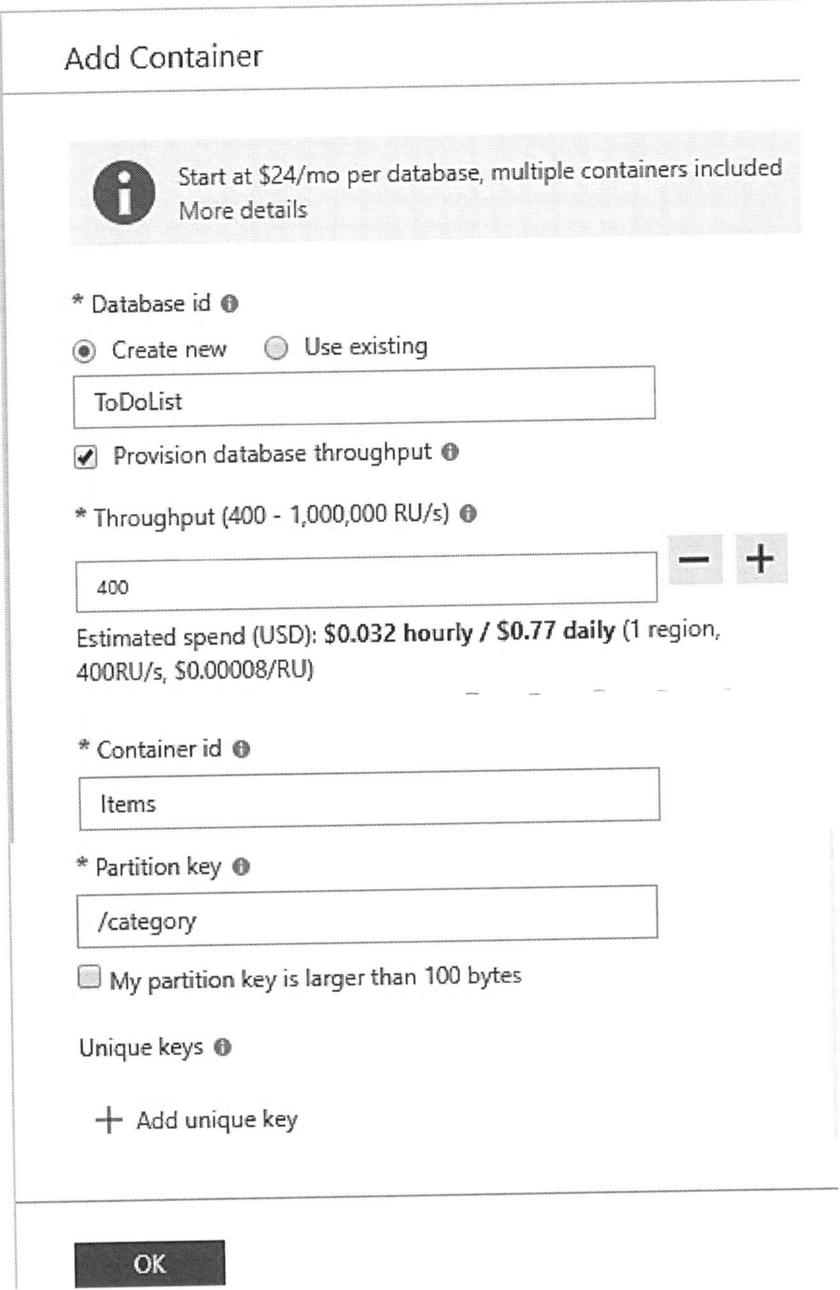

Note: If you uncheck Provision Database Throughput then you need specify throughput at Container level.

5. **Add Data to the Database by uploading JSON Documents or entering JSON Scripts**: In **Data Explorer**, expand the **ToDoList** database, and expand the **Items** container. Next, select **Items**>either select **New Item** or select upload Item. I selected New Item> A pane open in the right.

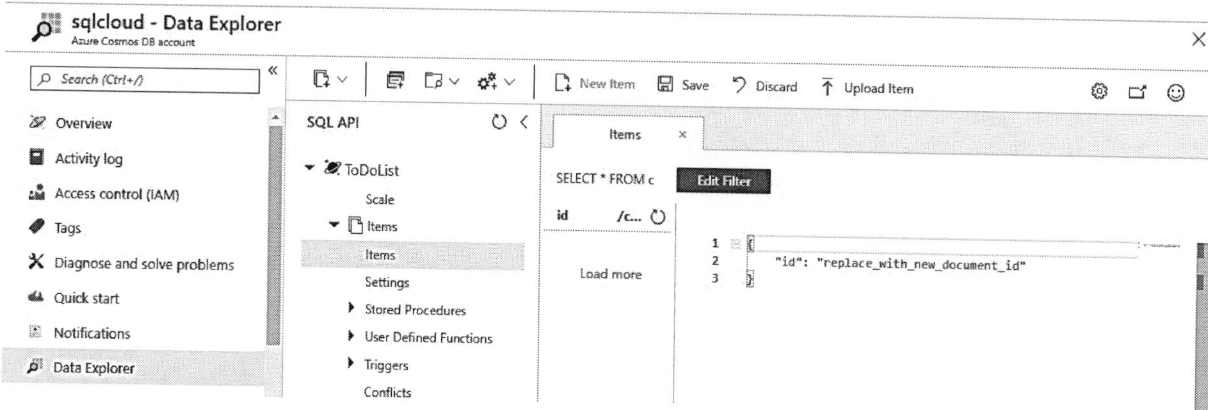

6. We will Paste the following JSON document contents on the right side of the Document pane shown above.

```
{
   "id": "1",
   "category": "personal",
   "name": "groceries",
   "description": "Pick up apples and strawberries.",
   "isComplete": false
}
```

7. We pasted JSON document contents in the pane as shown below>Click save.

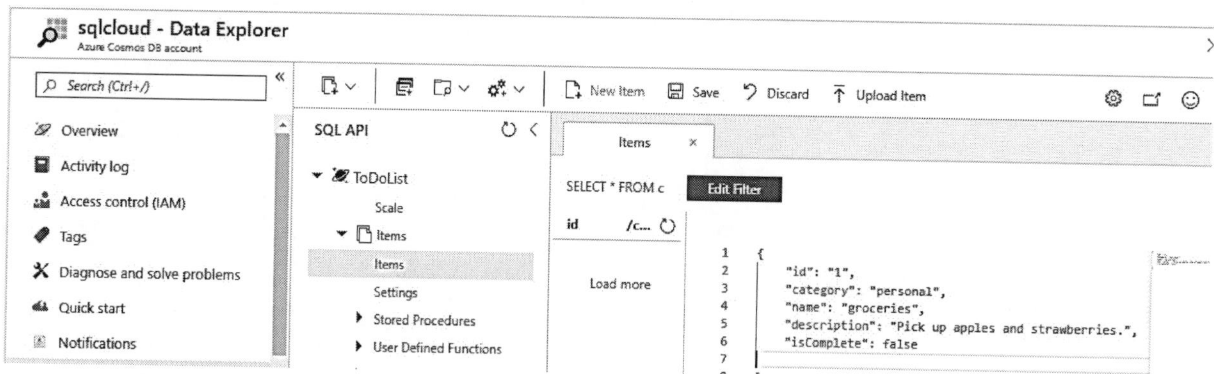

8. Similarly you can Paste new JSON Documents.

9. **Query the Data in the Database:** At the top of the **Documents** tab in Data Explorer, review the default query SELECT * FROM c. This query retrieves and displays all documents in the collection in ID order. You can change the default query by clicking edit Filter and entering your query in the filter pane.

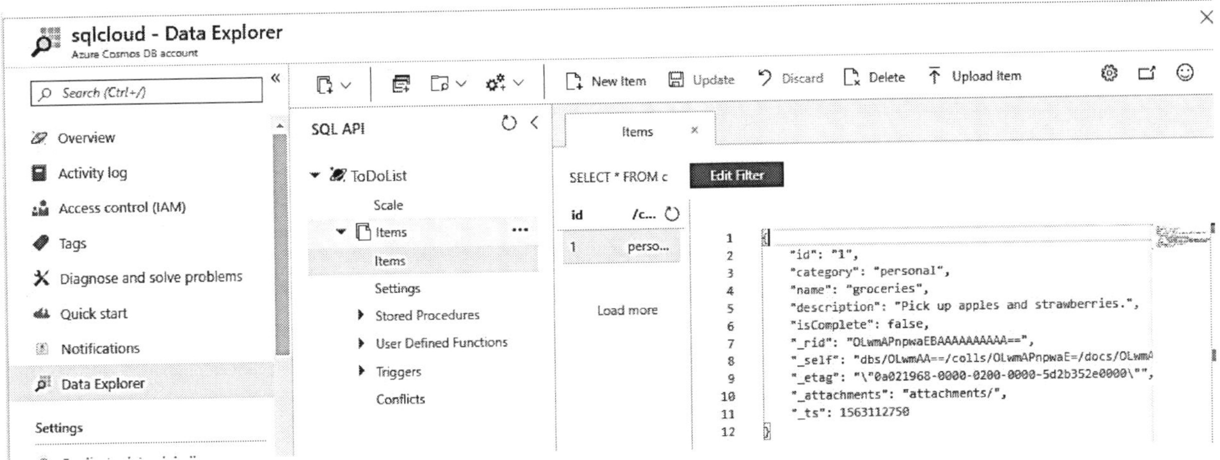

10. **Copy URL & Primary key of the SQL (Document) Database. You need to add these in your application**: Go to Cosmos DB Account Dashboard>Click Keys in left Pane and copy URI and Primary Key.

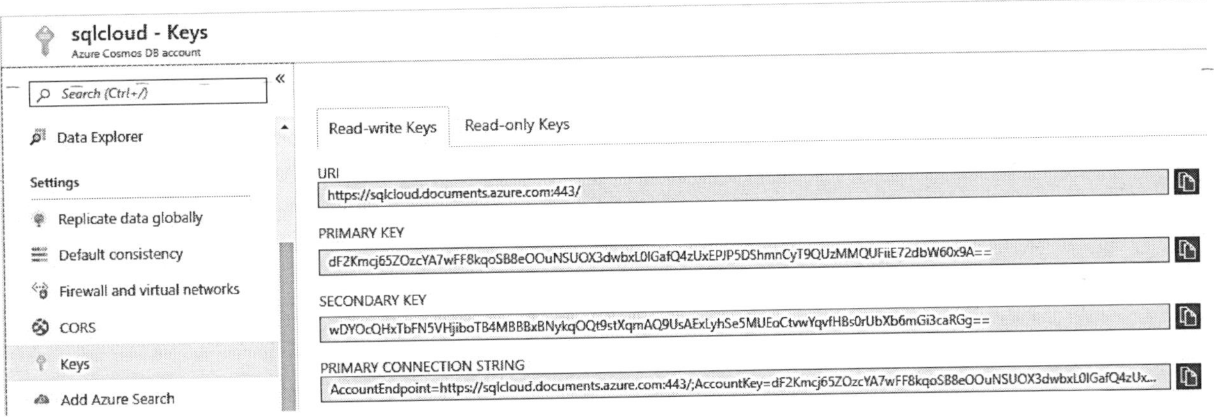

11. Connect your application to Azure Cosmos DB SQL (Document) Database by adding URL & Primary Key to your Application.

13. In Step 4 if you unchecked Provision Database Throughput then you need specify throughput at Container level as shown below.

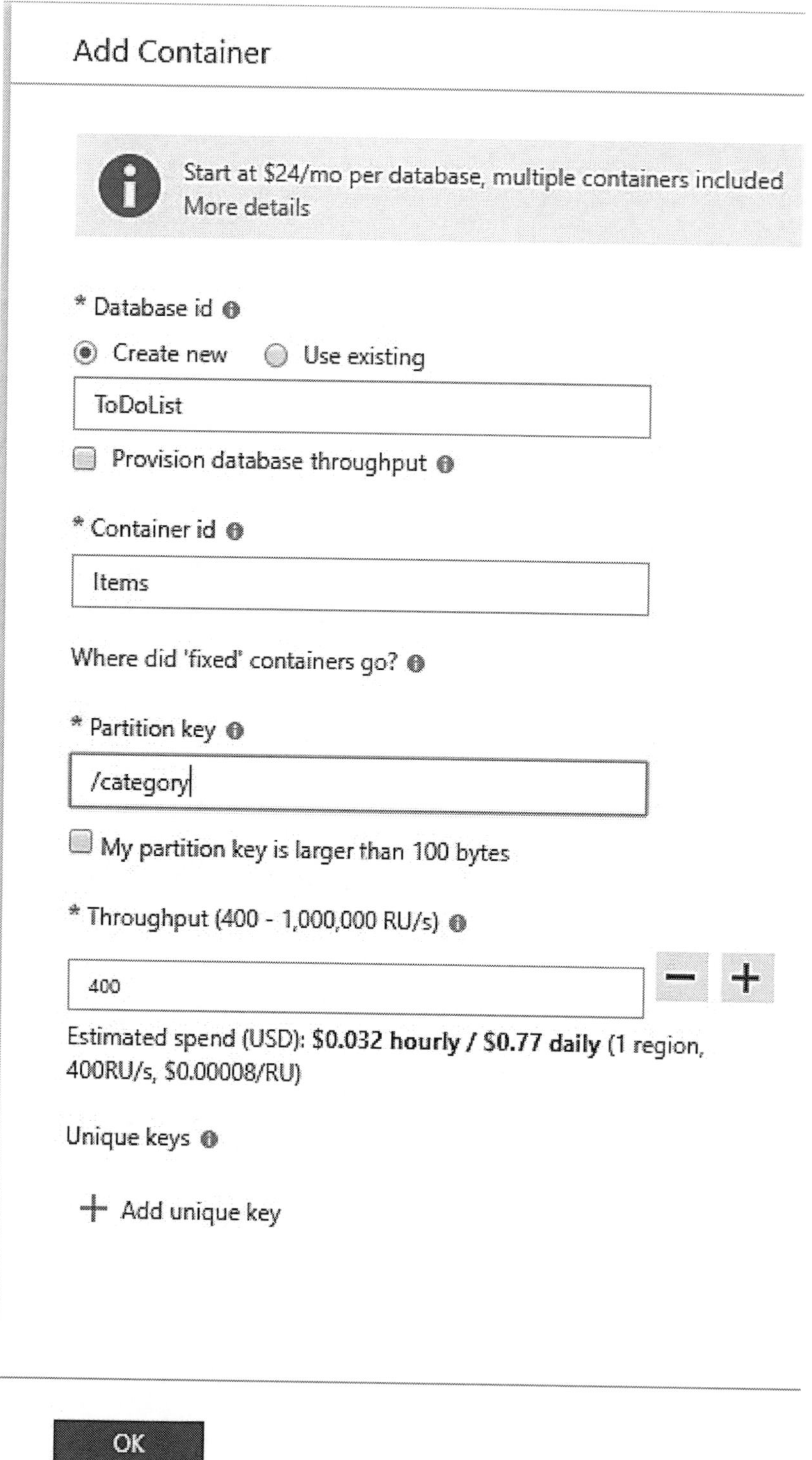

Cosmos DB Table API (key-value pair) Database

Tables are a structured Datastore based on **key-value pair** with a schemaless design. They are designed to store large amounts of data for massive scale where some basic structure is required, **but relationships between data don't need to be maintained**.

Cosmos DB Tables (Key-Value) Database stores data in pairs where you have a Key with associated value. For Example take Mobile 8625068410 Pair. Here Mobile is key and the number is value.

Advantage of Table is that Access to data is fast and cost-effective for all kinds of applications. Table storage is typically significantly lower in cost than traditional SQL for similar volumes of data.

Architecture

Cosmos DB Table API (key-value pair) Database is a collection of tables.
A Table is a collection of entities. Tables don't enforce a schema on entities, which means a single table can contain entities that have different sets of properties.

Entity is a collection of Properties. A Property is a key-value pair. Each entity can include up to 252 properties (Key-value pair) to store data. Each entity also has 3 system defined properties that specify a partition key, a row key, and a timestamp. You need to specify the value of Partition and Row key.
An entity's row key is unique within a partition.
Entities can have different types of properties (String, Boolean Date, Time etc) even for the same partition key because there is no fixed schema.

Table Database Use Cases

Key-value databases are optimized for querying against keys. As such, they serve great in-memory caches. Following are some of the use cases:

Session management in Web Applications
Caching for Web Applications.
Diagnostic logs.

Table Database Components

Table Storage Service contains 3 components.

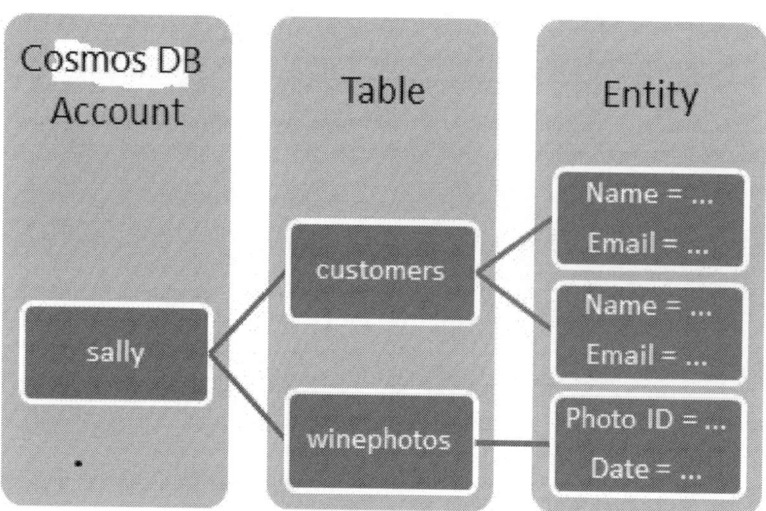

Cosmos DB Account: All Access to Cosmos DB Database happens through Cosmos DB account. Cosmos DB Account can contain one or more Table API (Key-Value) Database.

Table: A table is a collection of entities. Tables don't enforce a schema on entities, which means a single table can contain entities that have different sets of properties.

Entities: An entity is a set of properties with a Max size of 1MB. Each entity can include up to 252 properties to store data and 3 System Defined Properties.

Properties: A property is a **key-value pair**.

System Defined Properties: Each entity has three system defined properties that specify a partition key, a row key, and a timestamp. You specify value for Partition and Row key. Timestamp value is system generated. An entity's row key is unique within a partition.

Tables also contain stored procedures, user-defined functions, and triggers.

Exercise 87: Cosmos DB Table (Key-Value) Database

1. In Azure Portal Click Create a Resource> Databases> Azure Cosmos DB> Create Azure Cosmos DB Account Opens>Select Resource Group RGCloud> Enter a name>In API Select Table>Location Select East US 2>Click Review + Create.

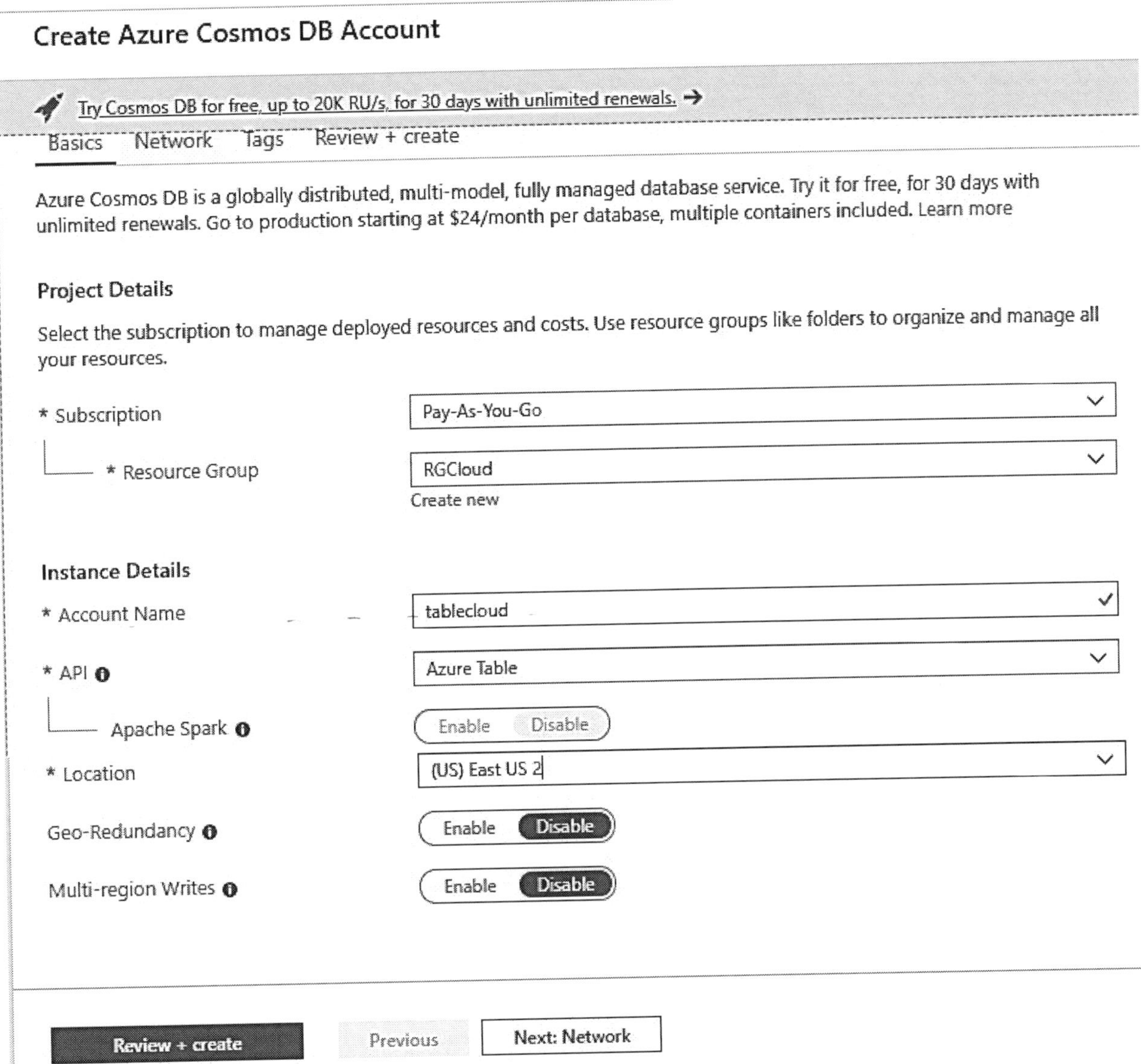

14. Click Review + Create>After Validation Succeeds Click Create (Not shown).

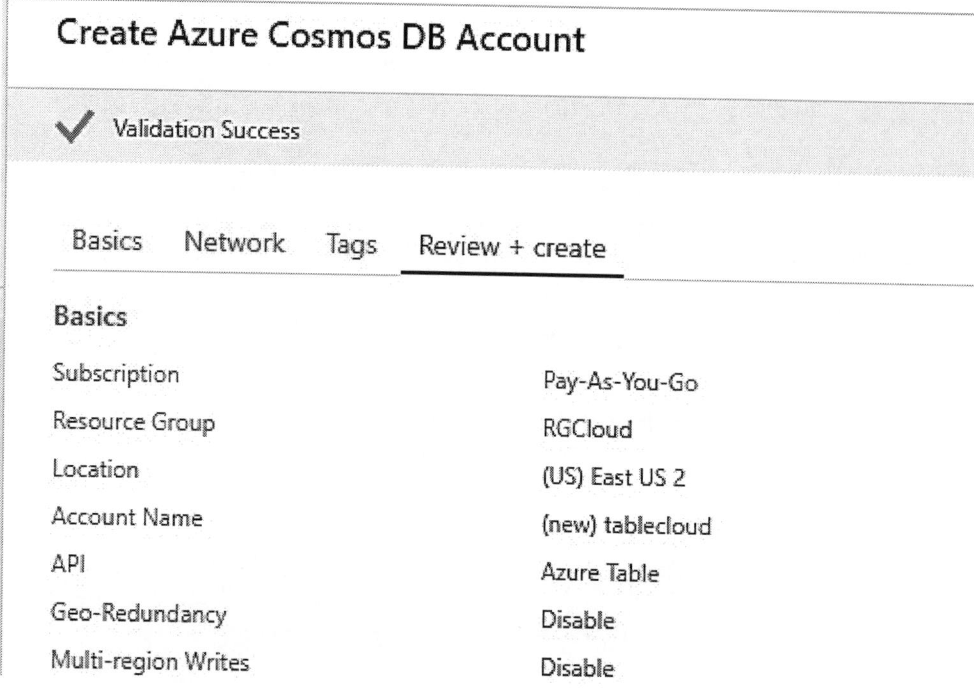

15. Figure below shows Dashboard of Cosmos DB (Table) Account.

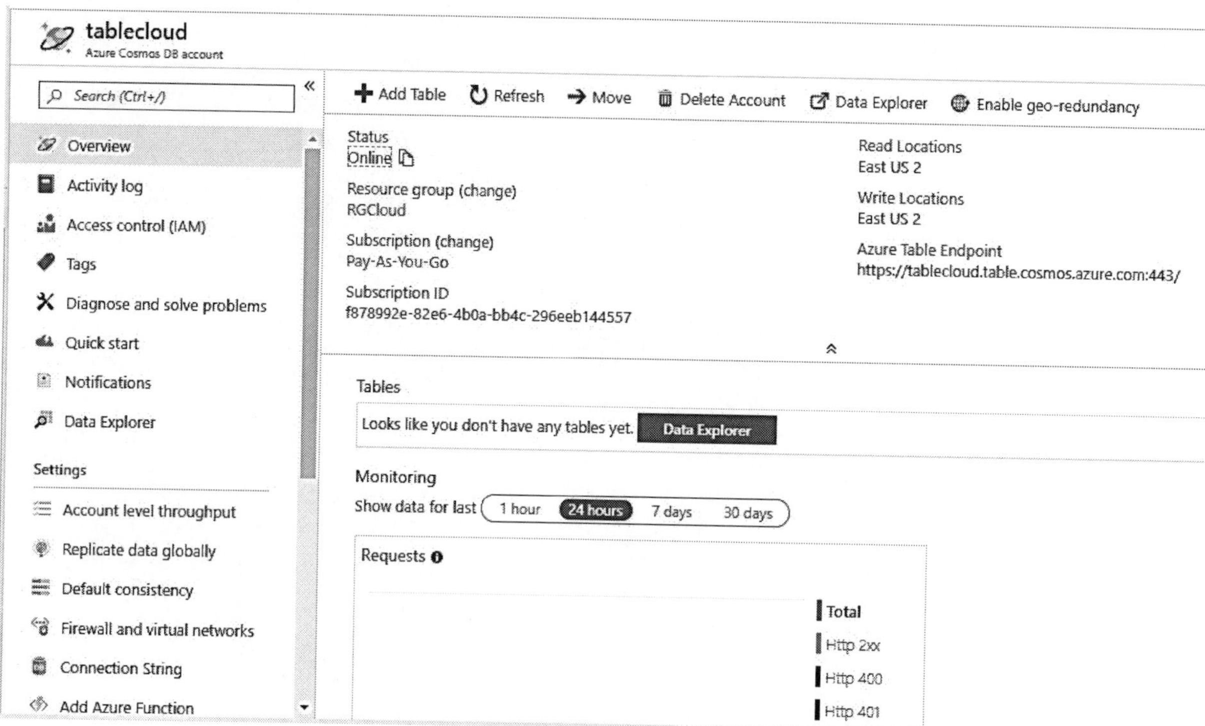

16. **Add Table:** In cosmos DB Account Dashboard Click Data Explorer in Left Pane>In Right pane click + New Table> Add Table Blade opens>Enter Table id and select throughput as per your requirement. I selected default 400 RU/s> Click Ok.

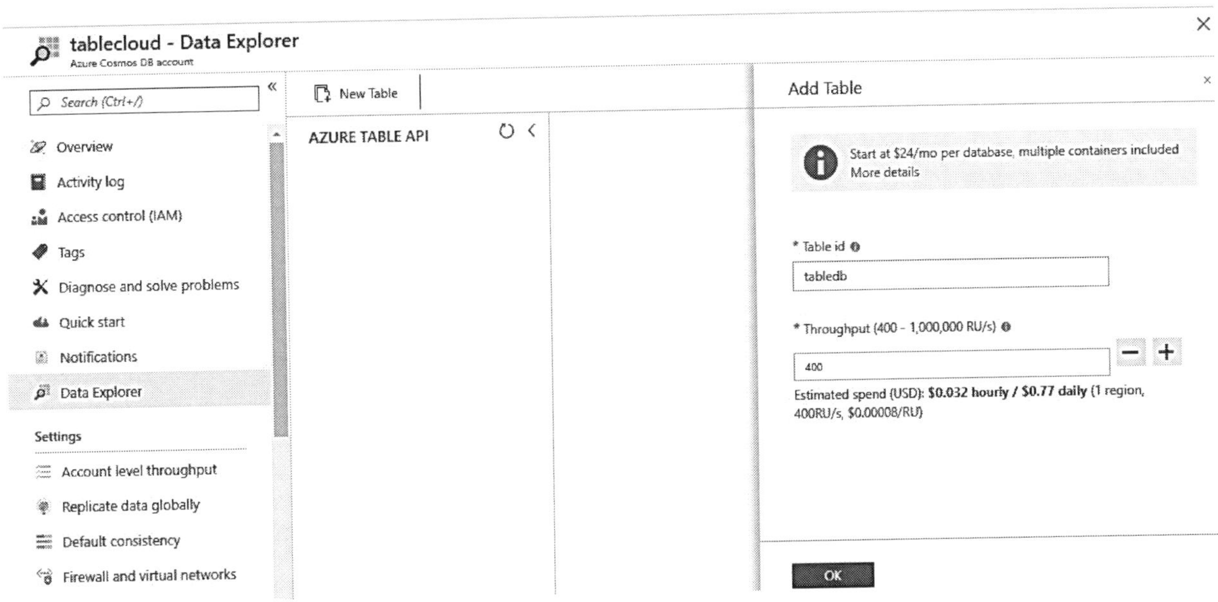

17. **Add Entities:** Go to Cosmos DB account dashboard>Click Data Explorer in left pane>Click on table you created in step 4 and it will enumerate>Click on entities>Click Add entity> Add Entity Blade opens> You already have 3 system defined Properties: Partition key, Row key and Timestamp (Not shown> Enter value of **1** for partition key and value of **a** for row key> Click Add Property 2 Times>I added 2 Properties - Email: test@test.com & Mobile: 9000000000;)> Click Add Entity (Not Shown).
Important Note: Properties are Key Value pair.

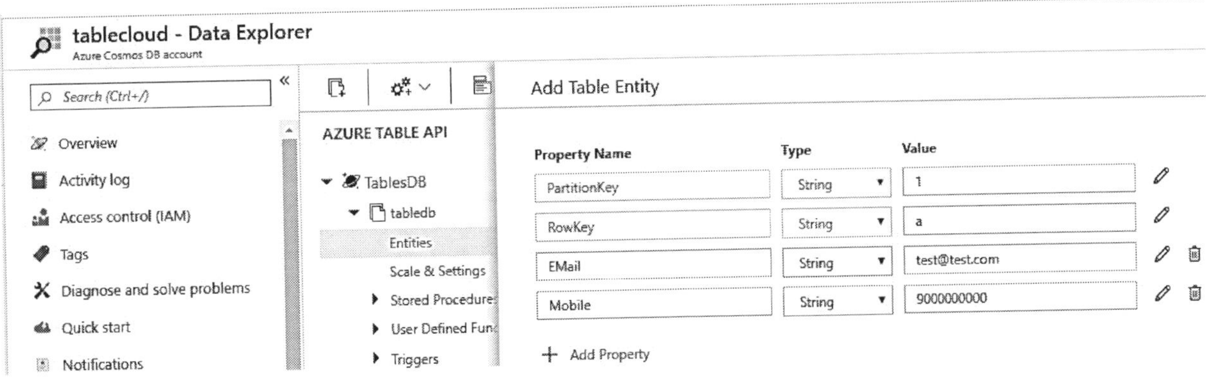

18. Figure below shows the entity that was created. It shows 5 Key-value pairs: PartitionKey, RowKey, Timestamp, Email & Mobile.

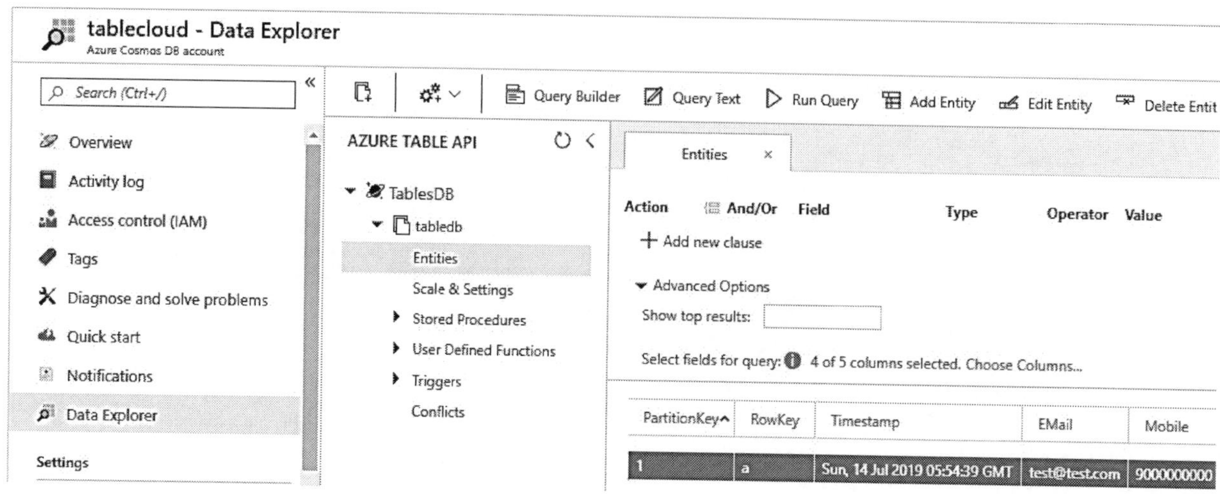

19. **Copy URL & Primary key of the Table Database. You need to add these in your application**: Go to Cosmos DB Account Dashboard>Click Keys in left Pane and copy URI and Primary Key.

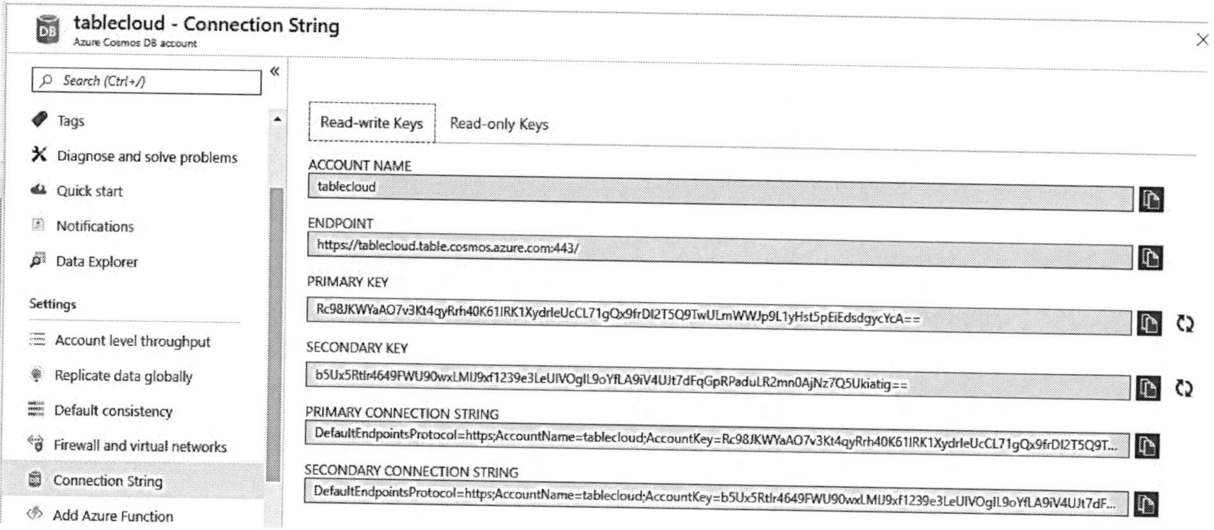

20. **Connect your application** to Azure Cosmos DB Table Database by adding URL & Primary Key to your Application.

21. You can also **query** the table or entity>Go to Azure Cosmos DB account Dashboard>click Data Explorer>Click Query Builder and add options>Run.

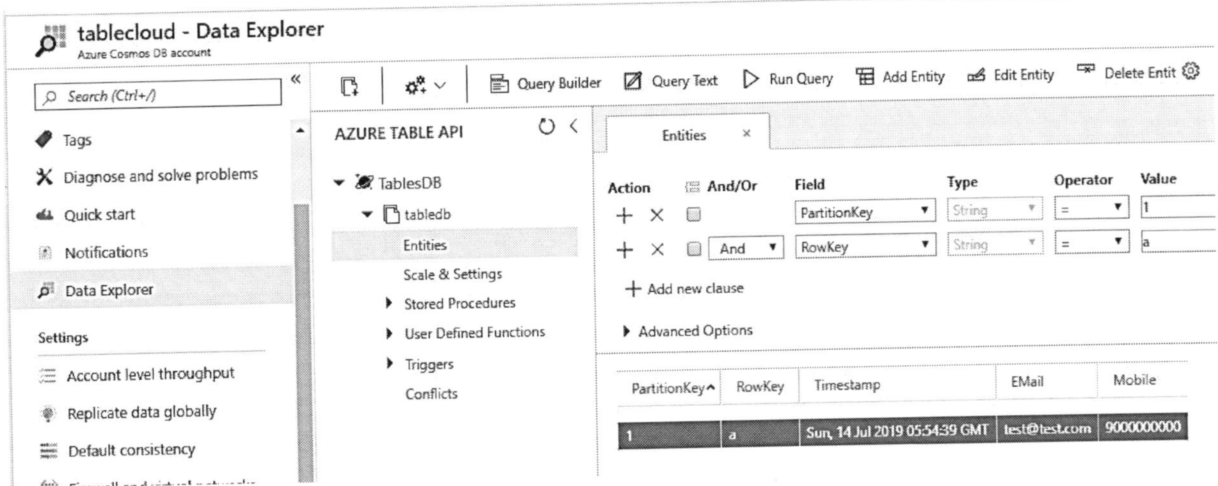

Cosmos DB Gremlin (Graph) Database

Cosmos DB Gremlin (Graph) API Database is A Graph database that uses nodes and edges to represent and store data. It supports Open Graph APIs (based on the Apache TinkerPop specification, Apache Gremlin).

A graph is a structure that's composed of vertices/nodes and edges. Vertices/ Nodes denote discrete objects such as a person, a place, or an event. Edges denote relationships between Vertices. For example, a person might know another person, be involved in an event and recently been at a location.

Properties express information about the vertices and edges. Example properties include a node that has a name, age, and edge, which has a time stamp and/or a weight.

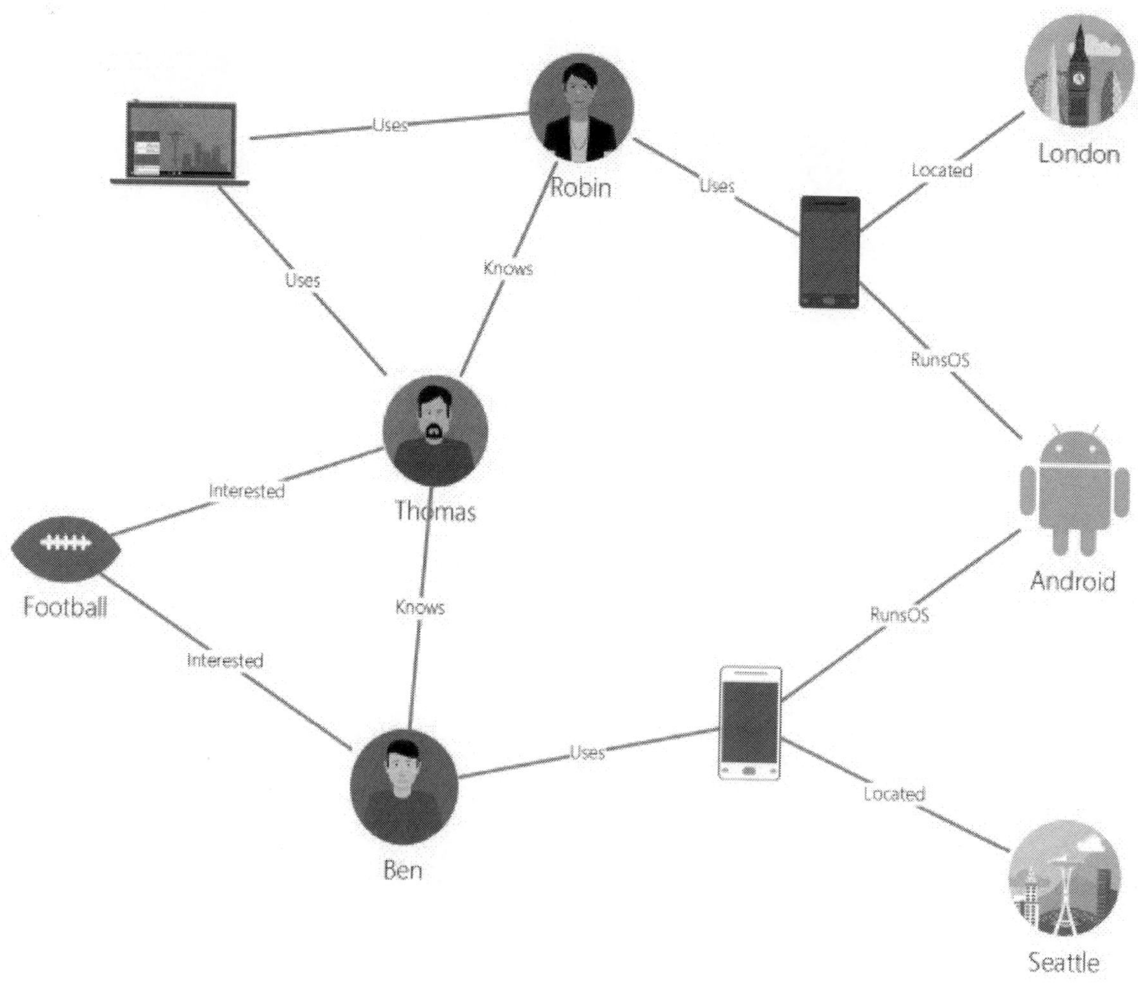

Architecture

Gremlin (Graph) databases are logical containers for one or more Graphs. Graph are containers for Vertex. A Vertex is key Value pair. Graph can contain multiple Vertex. Graphs also contain Scale & Settings, stored procedures, user-defined functions, and triggers.

Cosmos DB Gremlin (Graph) Database is created under Cosmos DB account.

Use Cases

Social networks: By combining data about your customers and their interactions with other people, you can develop personalized experiences, predict customer behavior, or connect people with others with similar interests. Azure Cosmos DB can be used to manage social networks and track customer preferences and data.

Recommendation engines: This scenario is commonly used in the retail industry. By combining information about products, users, and user interactions, like purchasing, browsing, or rating an item, you can build customized recommendations. The low latency, elastic scale, and native graph support of Azure Cosmos DB is ideal for modeling these interactions.

Geospatial: Many applications in telecommunications, logistics, and travel planning need to find a location of interest within an area or locate the shortest/optimal route between two locations. Azure Cosmos DB is a natural fit for these problems.

Internet of Things: With the network and connections between IoT devices modeled as a graph, you can build a better understanding of the state of your devices and assets. You also can learn how changes in one part of the network can potentially affect another part.

Cosmos DB Gremlin API (document) Database Components

Graph Database contains 4 components.

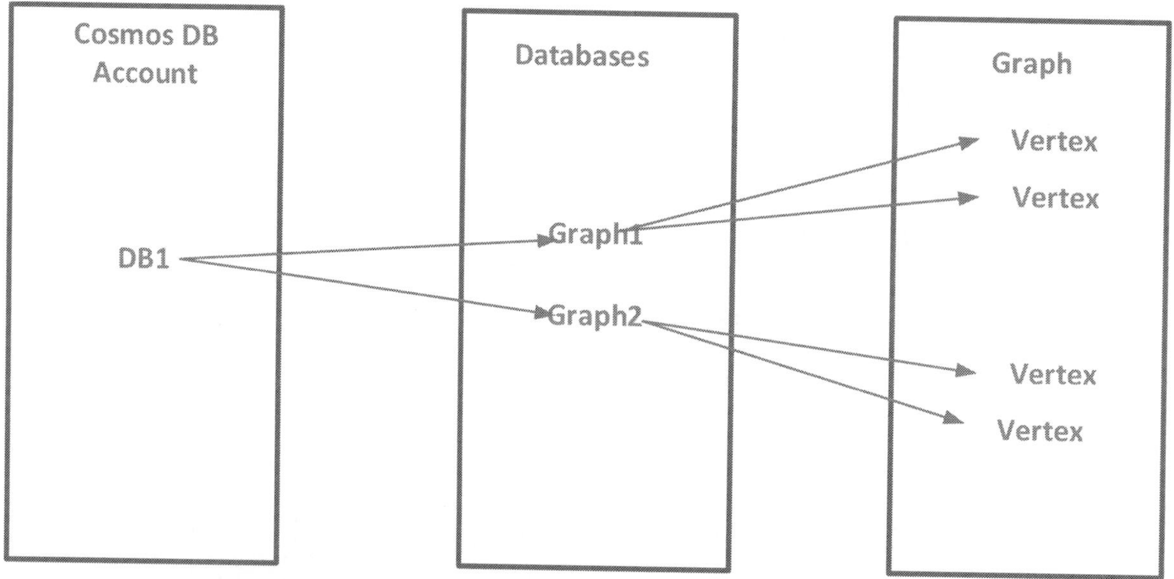

Cosmos DB Account: All Access to Cosmos DB Database happens through Cosmos DB account. Cosmos DB Account can contain one or more Gremlin (Graph) Databases.

Database: Databases are logical containers for one or more Graph.

Graphs: Graphs are containers for Vertex & Edges. Graphs also contain stored procedures, user-defined functions and triggers.

Exercise 88: Cosmos DB Gremlin (Graph) Database

1. In Azure Portal Click Create a Resource> Databases> Azure Cosmos DB> Create Azure Cosmos DB Account Opens>Select Resource Group RGCloud> Enter a name>In API Select Gremlin (Graph)>Location Select East US 2>Click Review + Create.

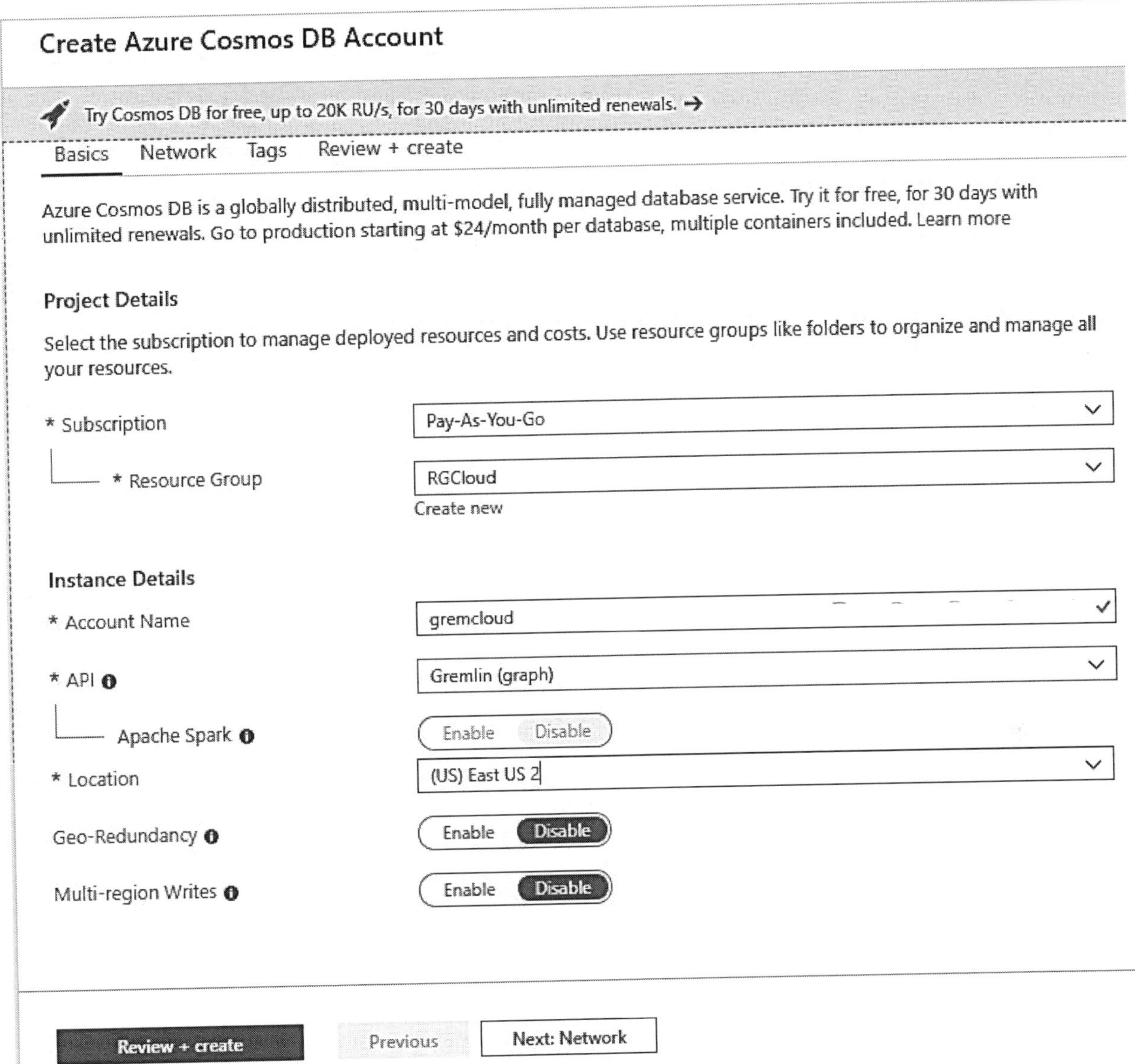

2. Click Review + Create>After Validation Succeeds Click Create (Not shown).

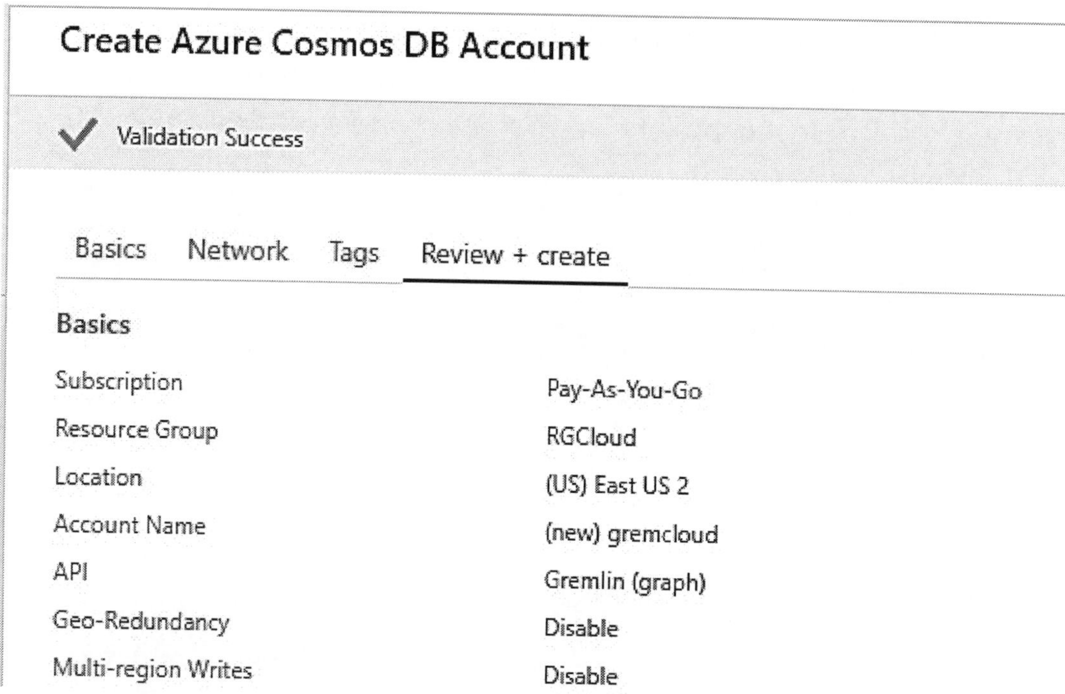

3. Figure below shows Dashboard of Cosmos DB (Gremlin) Account.

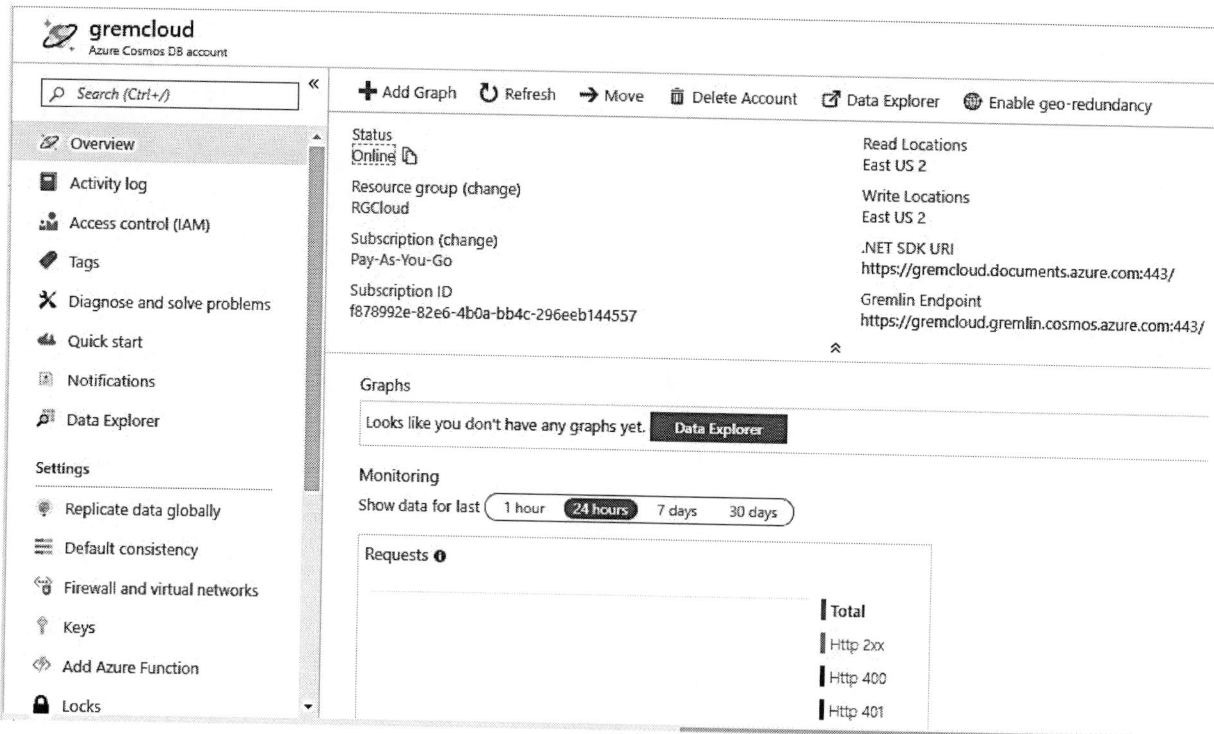

4. **Create Database and Add Graph:** Go to Cosmos DB account dashboard>Click Data Explorer in left pane>+ New Graph> Add Graph Blade opens>Enter name for Database id> Check Provision Database Throughput>Keep Throughput value at default>Enter name for Container id> Enter Partition Key. I entered /category>Click OK.

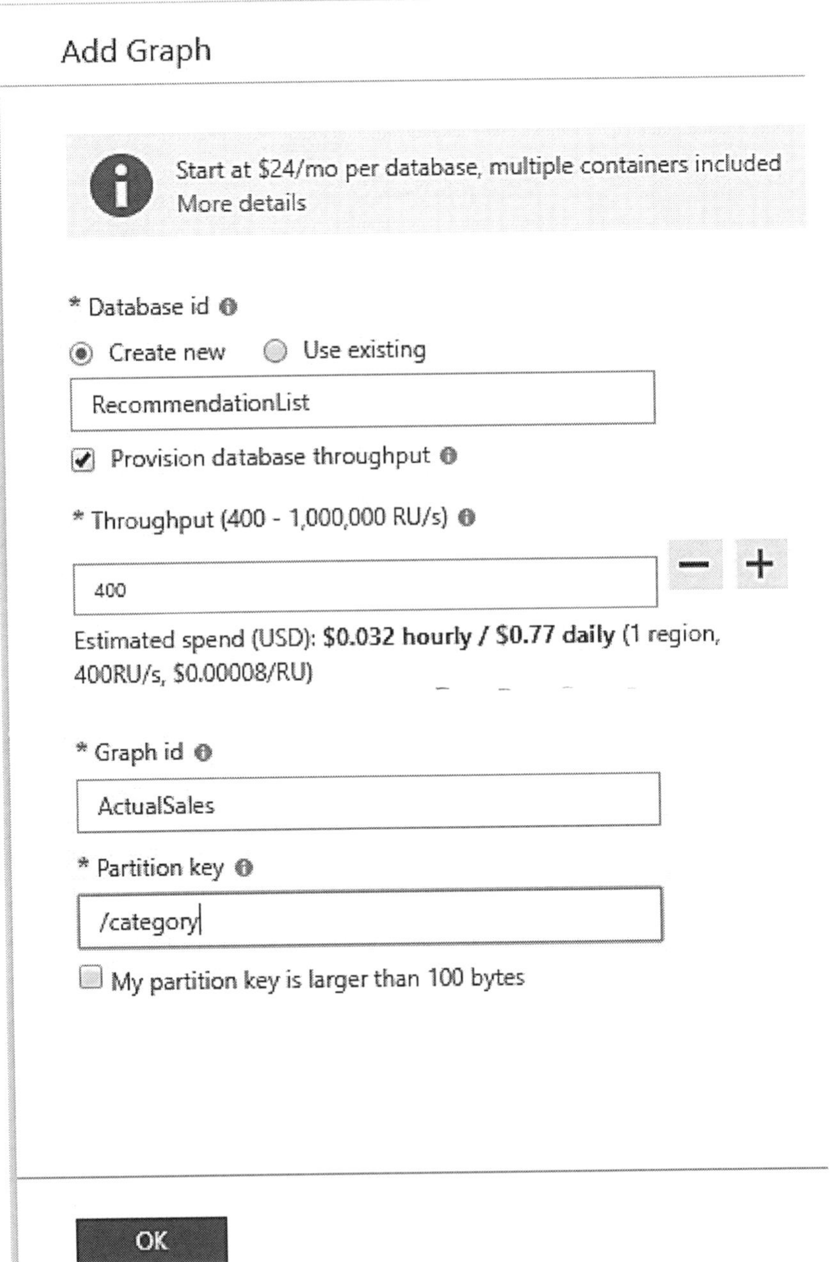

5. **Add Vertex.** Go to Cosmos DB account dashboard>Click Data Explorer in left pane>Click on RecommendationList Created in step 4 and it will enumerate>Click on ActualSales>Click on Graph>Click New vertex in right pane> New vertex Blade opens> Enter Amazon in Label>Enter Books in Category>Click OK (Not shown).

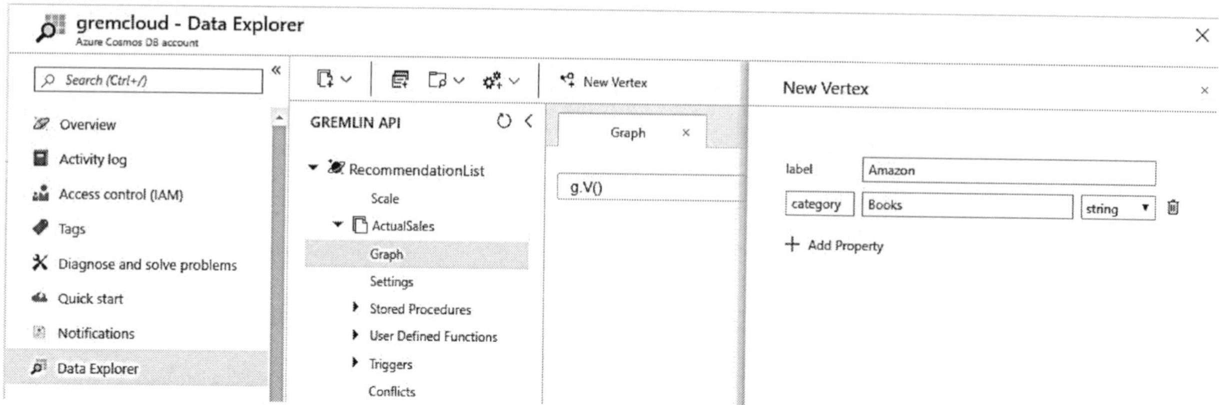

6. **Query the Data in the Database:** By Default it displays all Vertex in the Graph pane. You can change the default query by entering your query in the filter pane and Click Execute Gremlin Query.

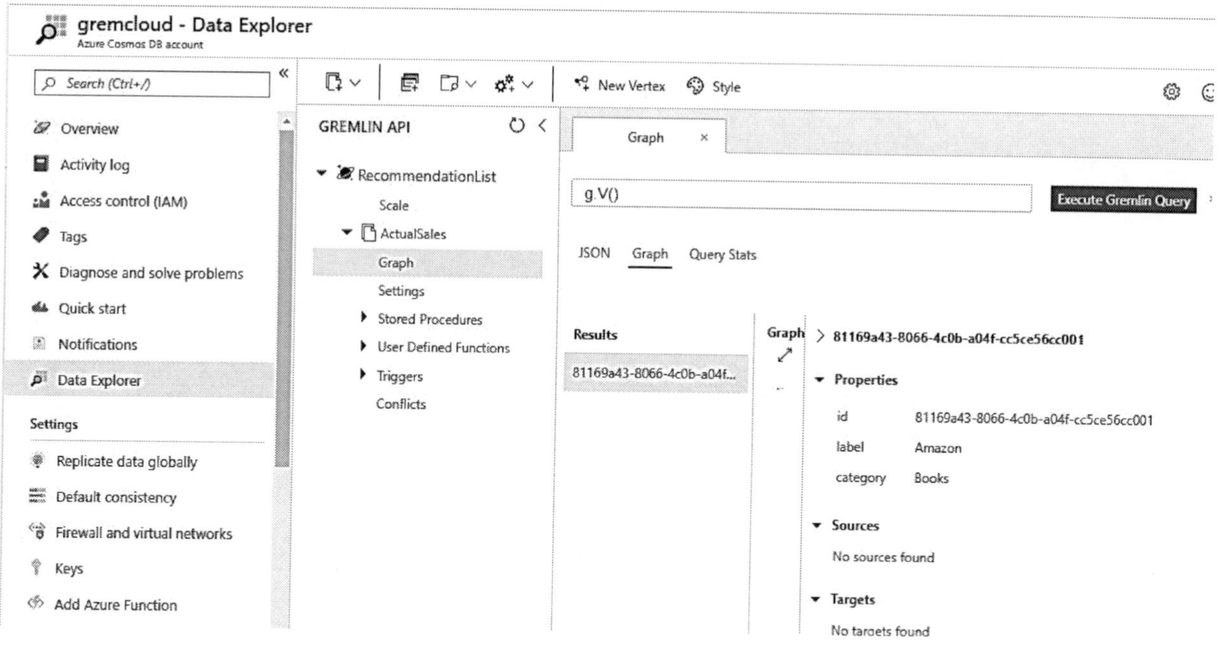

7. **Copy URL & Primary key of the Gremlin (Graph) Database. You need to add these in your application**: Go to Cosmos DB Account Dashboard>Click Keys in left Pane and copy URI and Primary Key.

22. Connect your application to Azure Cosmos Gremlin (Graph) Database by adding URL & Primary Key to your Application.

Cosmos DB for MongoDB API (Document) Database

Azure Cosmos DB API for MongoDB is a document database similar to Cosmos DB SQL Database.

Cosmos DB API for MongoDB is used when an application is already using MongoDB and you want to use Cloud based NoSQL. The advantage of this that your application can natively connect to Cosmos DB for MongoDB API without changing/adding any code in your application except for adding Cosmos DB Database Connection String.

Azure Cosmos DB API for MongoDB is compatible with version 3.2 of the MongoDB's protocol.

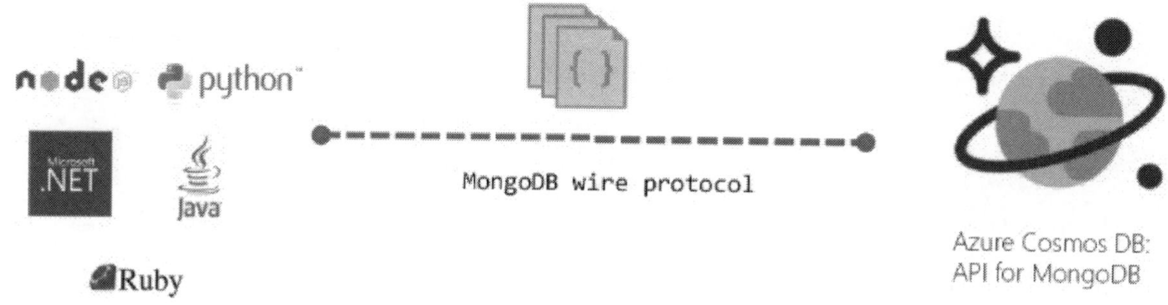

Use cases and working is similar to Cosmos DB SQL Database.

Exercise 89: Cosmos DB for MongoDB API (Document) Database

1. **Create Cosmos DB (MongoDB API) Account**: In Azure Portal Click Create a Resource> Databases> Azure Cosmos DB> Create Azure Cosmos DB Account Opens>Select Resource Group RGCloud> Enter a name>In API Select MongoDB API>Location Select East US 2>Click Review + Create.

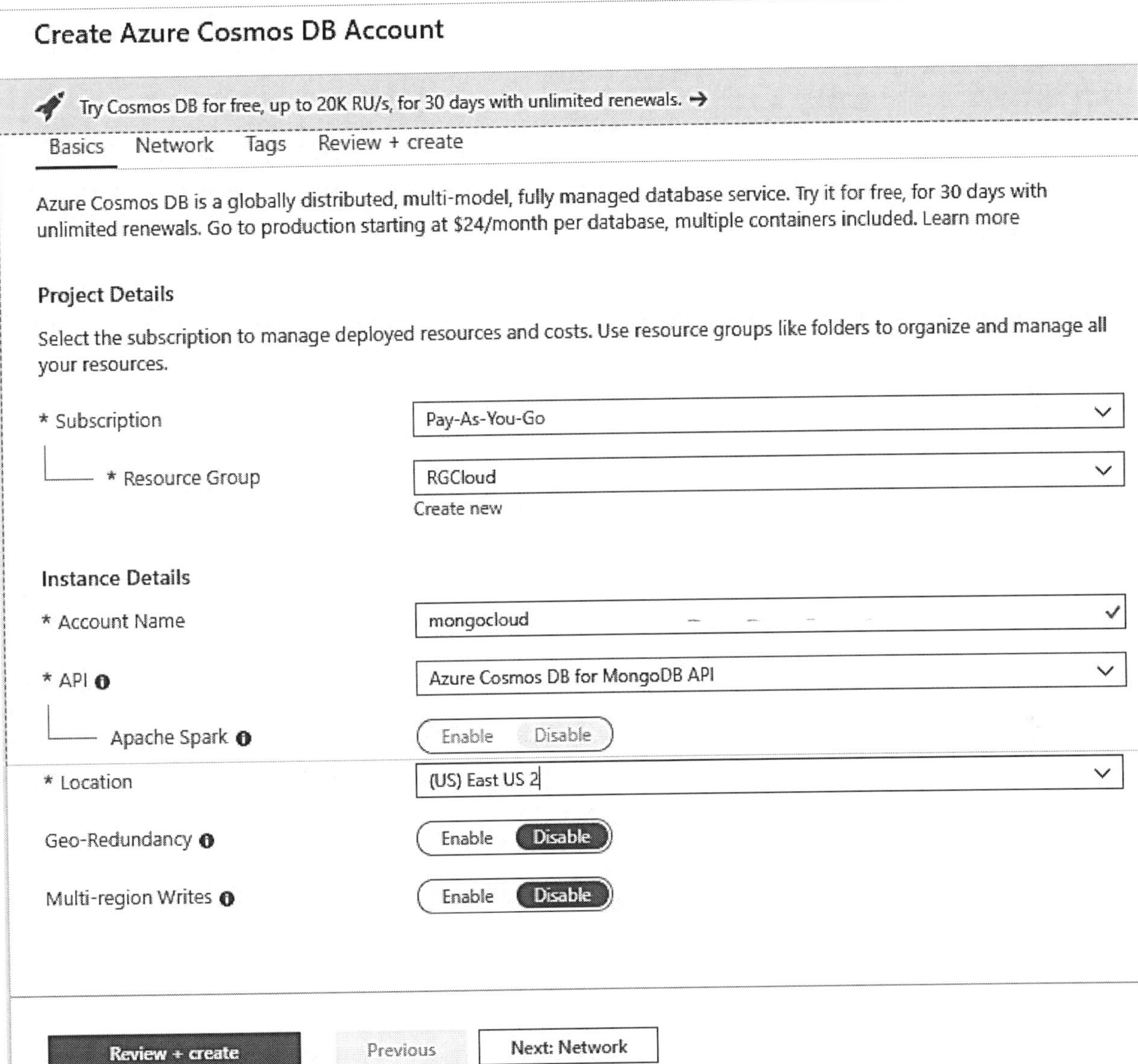

2. Click Review + Create>After Validation Succeeds Click Create (Not shown).

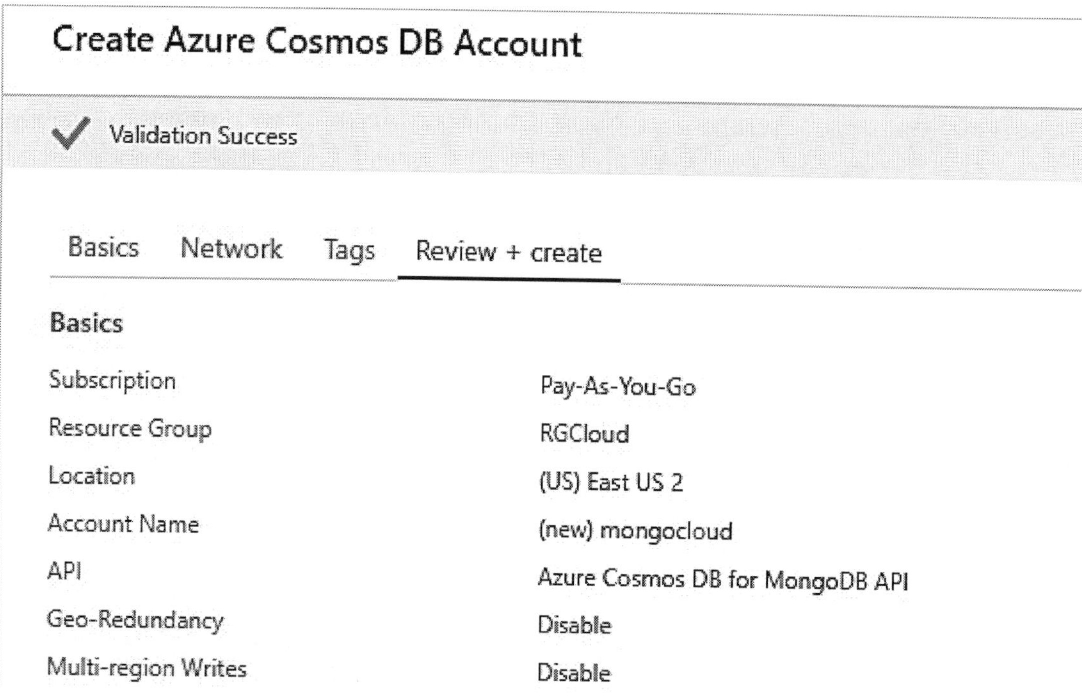

3. Figure below shows Dashboard of Cosmos DB (MongoDB) Account.

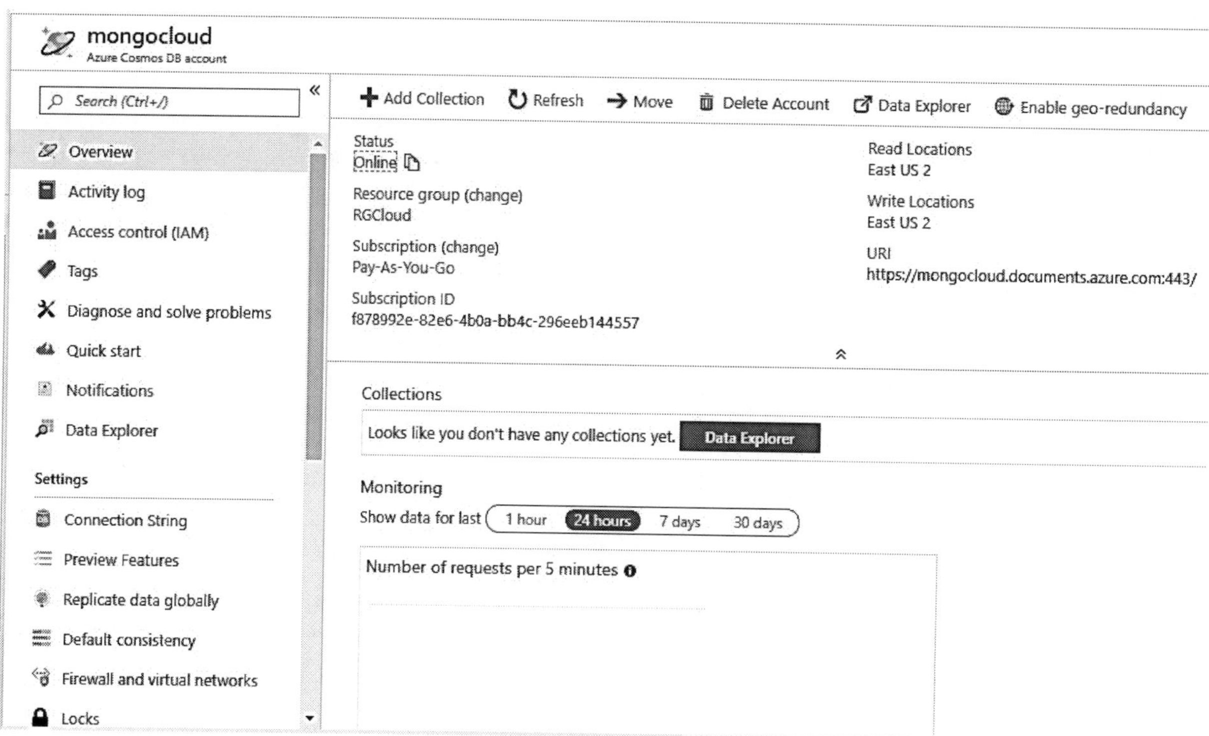

4. **Create Database and Add Collection:** Go to Cosmos DB account dashboard>Click Data Explorer in left pane>+ New Container> Add Container Blade opens>Enter name for Database id> Check Provision Database Throughput>Keep Throughput value at default>Enter name for Container id> Enter Shard Key. I entered category>Click OK.

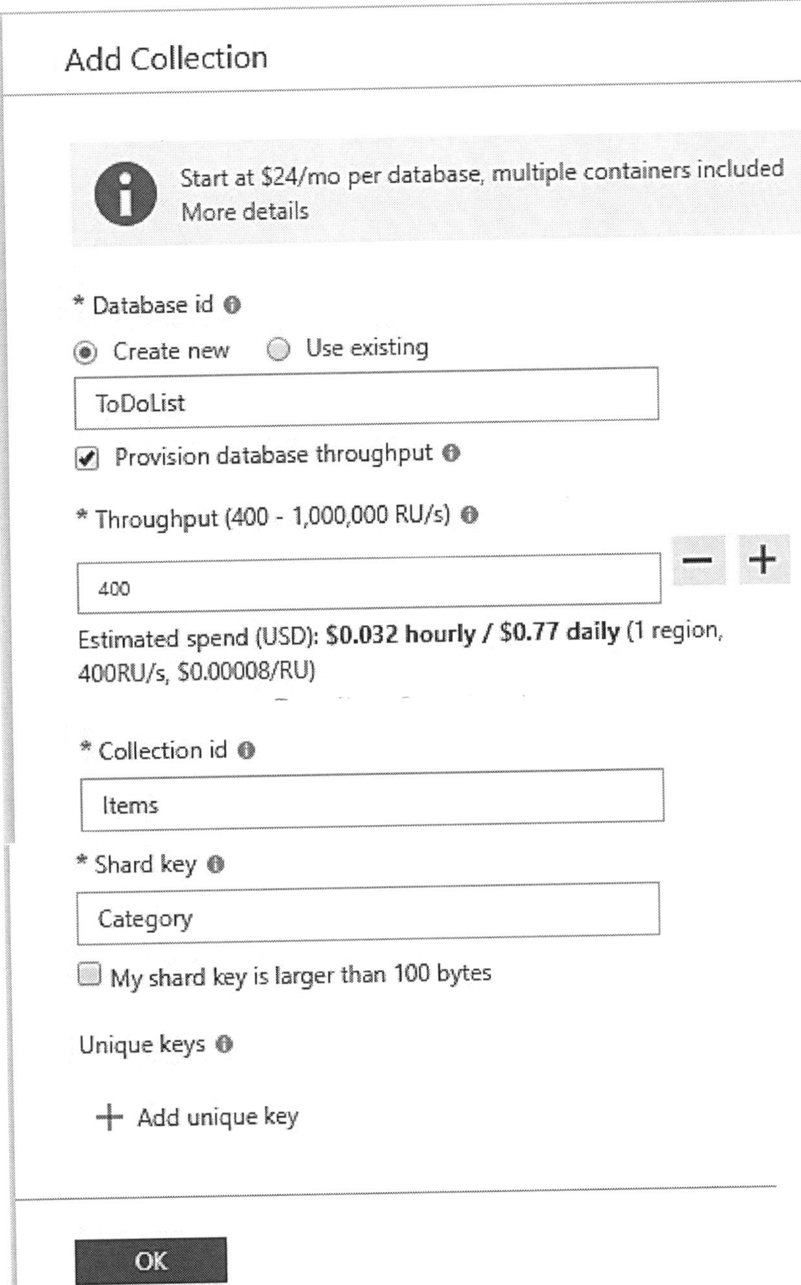

5. **Copy Host, Username & Password of the Mongo (Document) Database. You need to add these in your application**: Go to Cosmos DB Account Dashboard> Click Connection String in left Pane and copy Host, Username and Password.

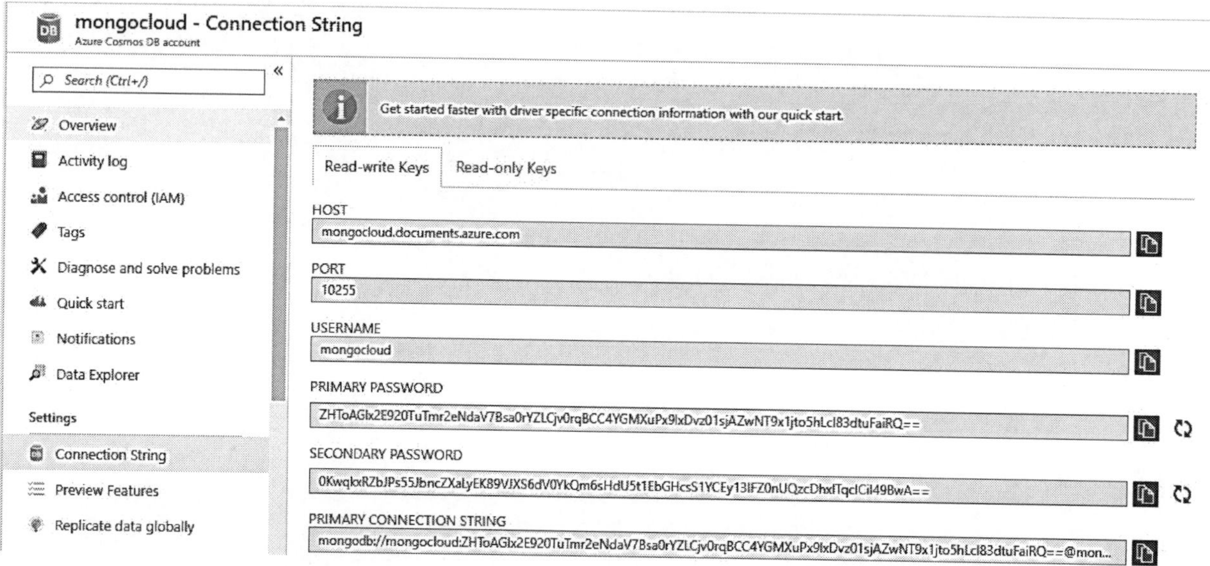

6. Connect your application to Azure Cosmos DB Mongo Database by adding Host, Username and Password to your Application.

Cosmos DB Cassandra (Wide-Column) Database

Wide-column stores organize data tables as columns instead of as rows. Wide-column stores can query large data volumes faster than conventional relational databases. A wide-column data store can be used for recommendation engines, catalogs, fraud detection and other types of data processing.

Cosmos DB Firewall & Virtual Network Feature

With Firewall & Virtual Network feature you can limit access to Cosmos DB from selected IP Addresses, selected Virtual Networks and from Azure Portal. By default access from all sources is allowed.

Note: Firewall & Virtual Network was discussed in Chapter 1 in Exam AZ-300 & AZ-301 Study & Lab Guide Part 1.

Exercise 90: Exploring Firewall and Virtual Network Feature

In this Exercise we will use Cosmos DB Database (sqlCloud) Created in Ex 86.

1. Go to Cosmos DB Account sqlcloud Dashboard>Click Firewall and Virtual Networks in left Pane> Click Selected Networks> Here you can select Virtual Network from which Access to Cosmos DB is allowed and/or Add IP Addresses from which access is allowed from Internet. You can also check Allow access from Azure Portal and/or Accept connection from Azure Datacenters.

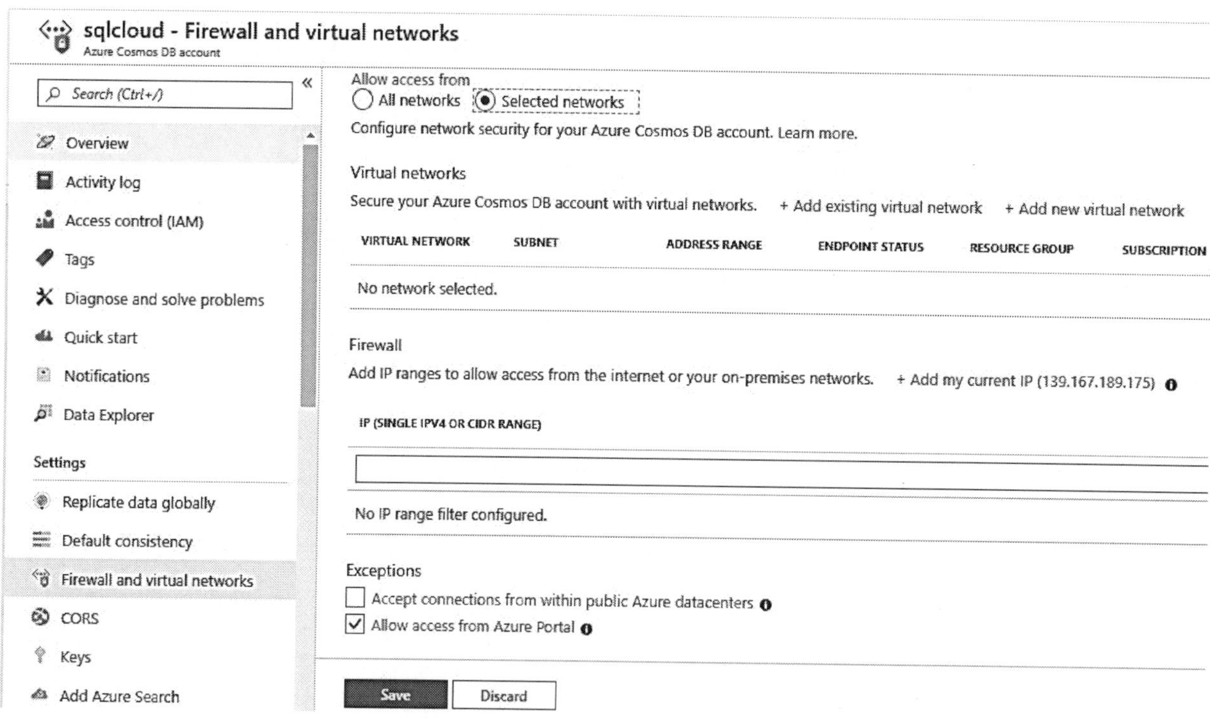

Cosmos DB Replication Feature (Applicable to all Database Types)

With Cosmos DB replication feature you can add additional read replica regions.

With Cosmos DB you can have write in one region and multiple read regions. This enables you to put your data where your users are, ensuring the lowest possible latency to your customers.

In case of failure of write region one of the read region will be promoted as write region.

With Cosmos DB replication feature you can also **enable Multi-Region Writes**.

Exercise 91: Adding Read Regions

7. Go to Cosmos DB Account sqlcloud Dashboard>Click **Replicate Data Globally** in left Pane> In Right pane you can see target regions for replication in a Map. You can also see in Right pane it is written that **account has no read region**. You can also see the option of **Enable multi-region writes**.

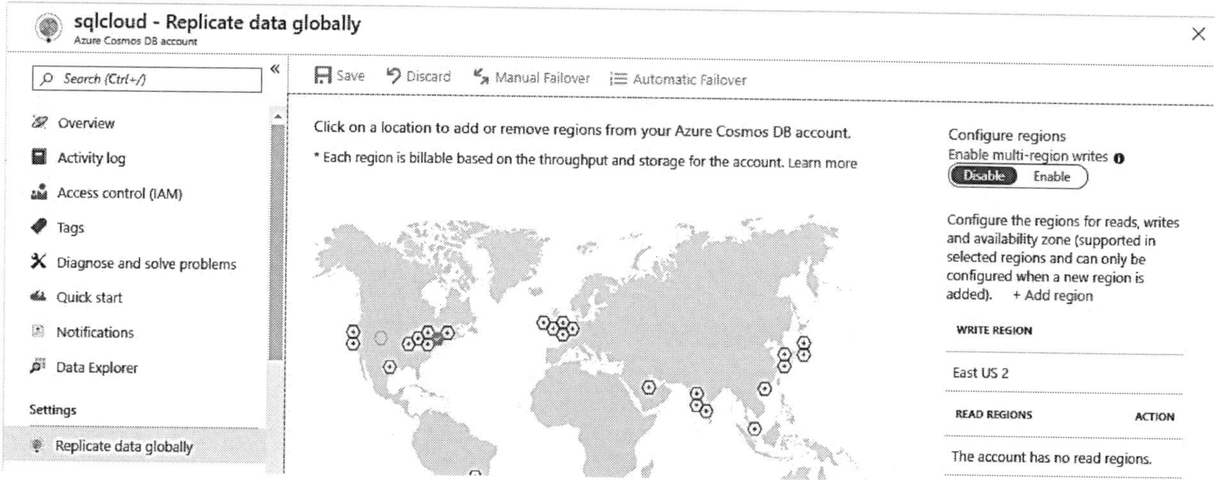

8. Click US West 2 Region icon the map>You can see West US 2 Read region is added>Click Save.

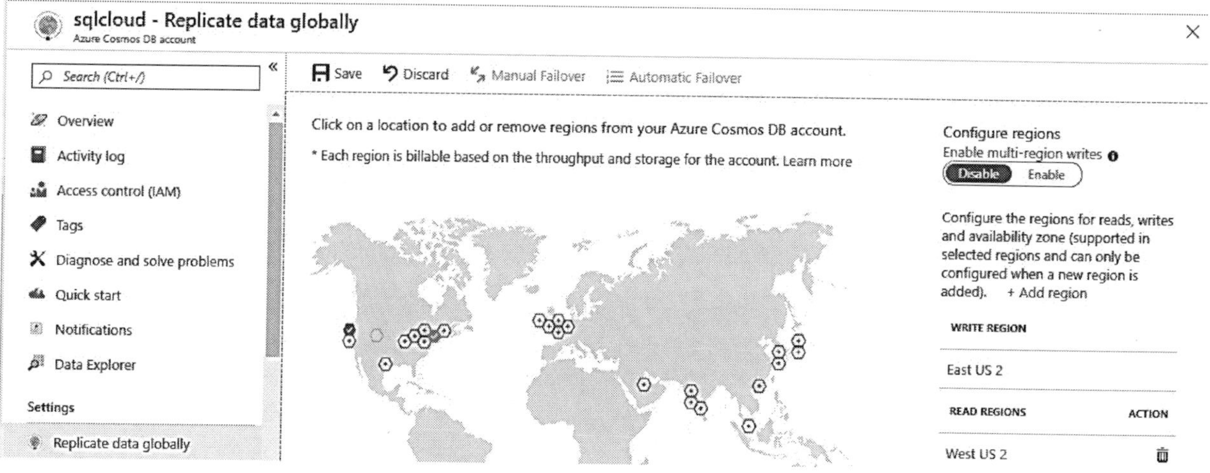

Note: Just hover your cursor on the icon and you can see the name of the Region.

Add Azure Function (Applicable to all Database Types)

You can add an Azure function which uses Cosmos DB Container as a trigger. The biggest advantage of this option is that you don't need to add a software code to connect Cosmos DB to Azure Function

Exercise 92: Add Azure Function

Go to Cosmos DB Account sqlcloud Dashboard>Click Add Azure function in left Pane> Add Azure Function Blade opens> Here you can add an existing Function or you can create a new function.

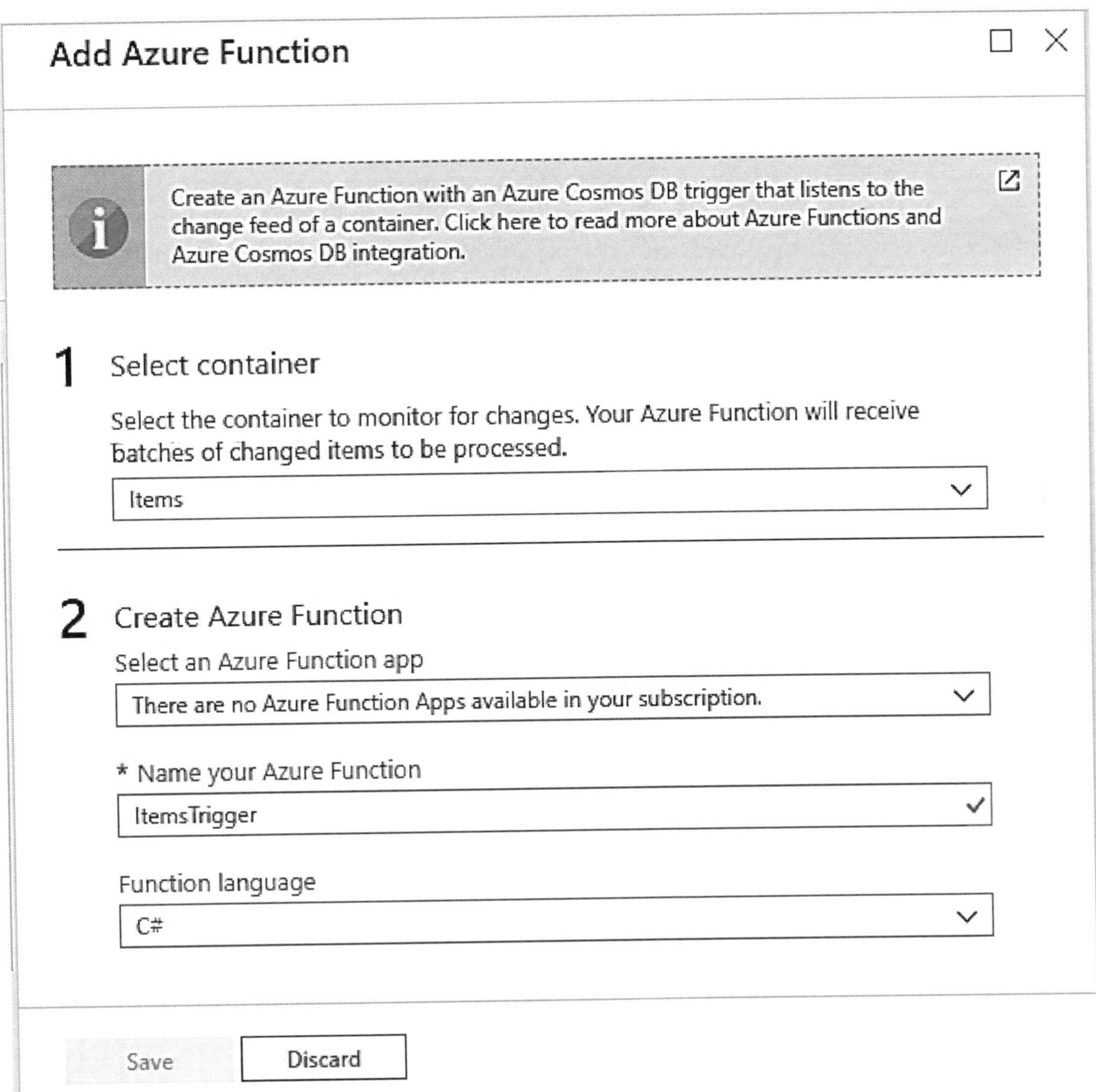

Consistency levels in Azure Cosmos DB (For all Database Types)

Consistency levels enable you to make trade-offs between consistency, availability, and latency.

Azure Cosmos DB provides five consistency levels: strong, bounded-staleness, session, consistent prefix, and eventual. Strong offers the most strong read consistency and Eventual the least read consistency.

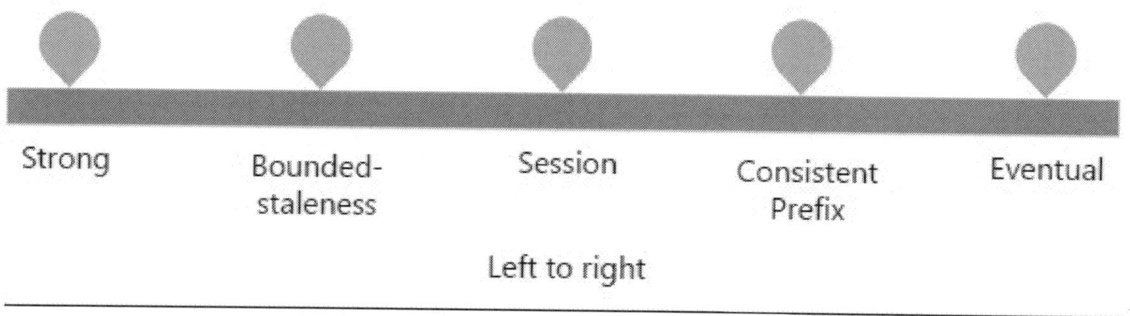

Left to right

Lower read Consistency, Lower latency, Higher Availability, Better Read Scalability

Configuring Consistency Level: Go to Cosmos DB Account sqlcloud Dashboard >Click Default Consistency in left Pane>Select the consistency level in right pane from one of the 5 Tabs>Click Save.

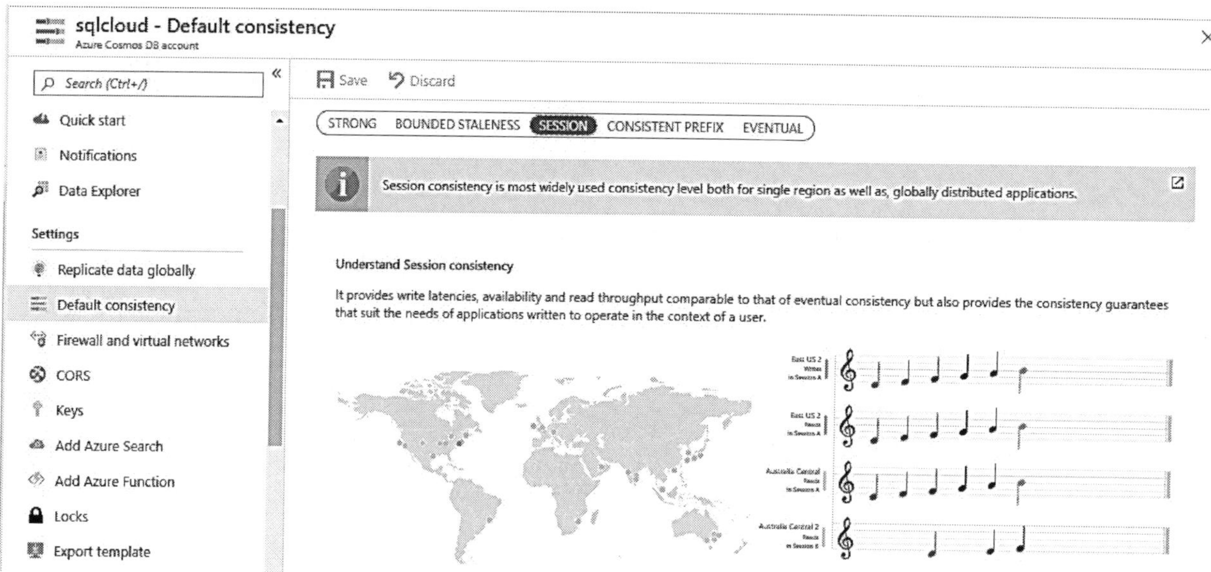

Strong Consistency: Strong consistency offers reads guarantee to return the most recent version of an item. Strong consistency guarantees that a write is only visible after it is committed durably by the majority quorum of replicas. Strong consistency is scoped to a single azure Region only. The cost of a read operation (in terms of request units consumed) is higher than session and eventual, but the same as bounded staleness.

Bounded Staleness: Bounded staleness consistency guarantees that the reads may lag behind writes by at most *K* versions or prefixes of an item or *t* time-interval. Azure Cosmos DB accounts that are configured with bounded staleness consistency can associate any number of Azure regions with their Azure Cosmos DB account. The cost of a read operation (in terms of RUs consumed) with bounded staleness is higher than session and eventual consistency, but the same as strong consistency.

Bounded staleness is great for applications featuring group collaboration and sharing, stock ticker, publish-subscribe/queueing etc.

Figure below shows the configuration options for Bounded Staleness:

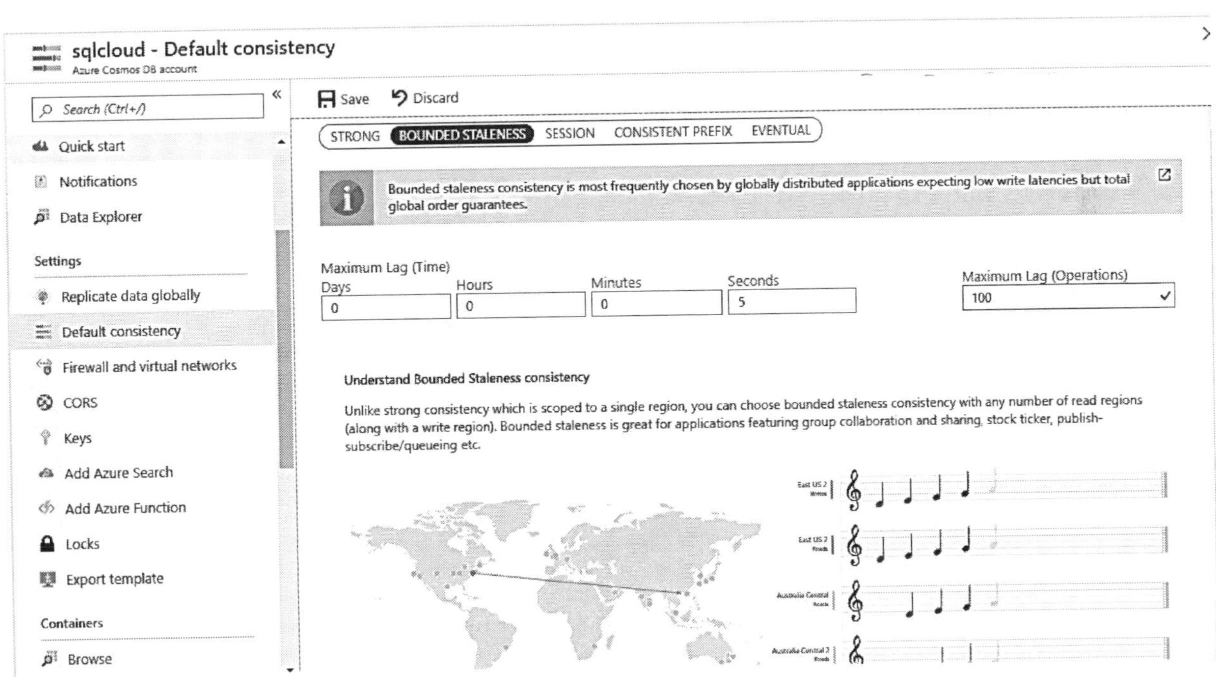

Session Consistency: Session Consistency provides write latencies, availability and read throughput comparable to that of eventual consistency but also provides the consistency guarantees that suit the needs of applications written to operate in the context of a user. Azure Cosmos DB accounts that are configured with session consistency can associate any number of Azure regions with their Azure Cosmos DB account. The cost of a read operation (in terms of RUs consumed) with is less than strong and bounded staleness, but more than eventual consistency.

Consistent Prefix: Consistent prefix level guarantees that reads never see out of order writes. If writes were performed in the order `A, B, C`, then a client sees either `A`, `A,B`, or `A,B,C`, but never out of order like `A,C` or `B,A,C`. Consistent Prefix provides write latencies, availability and read throughput comparable to that of eventual consistency, but also provides the order guarantees that suit the needs of scenarios where order is important. Azure Cosmos DB accounts that are configured with consistent prefix consistency can associate any number of Azure regions with their Azure Cosmos DB account.

Eventual Consistency: Eventual consistency is the weakest form of consistency wherein a client may get the values which are older than the ones it had seen before, over time. In the absence of any further writes, the replicas within the group will eventually converge. Azure Cosmos DB accounts that are configured with eventual consistency can associate any number of Azure regions with their Azure Cosmos DB account. The **cost** of a read operation (in terms of RUs consumed) with the eventual consistency level is the lowest of all the Azure Cosmos DB consistency levels.

Eventual consistency is ideal where the application does not require any ordering guarantees. Examples include count of Retweets, Likes or non-threaded comments.

Azure Cosmos DB Provisoned Throughput

With Azure Cosmos DB, you can provision throughput at two Levels:

Azure Cosmos containers
Azure Cosmos databases

In Azure Cosmos DB throughput is represented as request units/second (RU/s or RUs). RUs measure the cost of both read and write operations against your Cosmos container as shown in the following image:

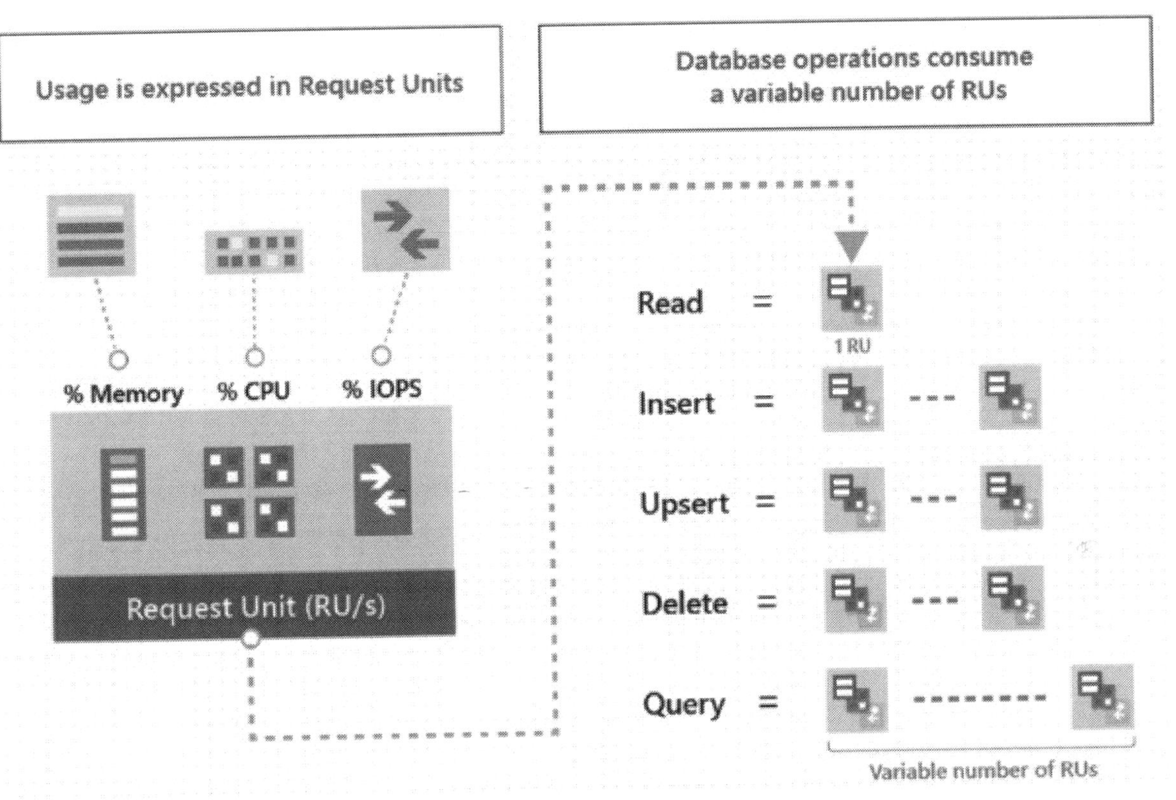

Provisioned throughput starts at 400 RU/s per container or database and can be scaled up by increments of 100 RU/s. You can estimate your throughput needs by using the Azure Cosmos DB request unit calculator.

Note: An Azure Cosmos database is a unit of management for a set of containers. Cosmos DB provides containers (Collections, Graphs or Tables) for storing data.

Throughput at Container Level

The throughput provisioned on an Azure Cosmos container is exclusively reserved for that container. The container receives the provisioned throughput all the time.

Throughput provisioned on an Azure Cosmos container is uniformly distributed across all the logical partitions of the container.

Throughput at Database Level

When you provision throughput on an Azure Cosmos database, the throughput is shared across all the containers in the database.

When you have containers that share provisioned throughput configured on a database, you **can't** selectively apply the throughput to a specific container or a logical partition.

Estimating number of request units per second (RU/s)

To estimate the number of request units (RU/s) to provision for Azure Cosmos DB container, take the following variables into consideration:
Item size. As size increases the number of request units consumed to read or write the data also increases.
Item property count. Assuming default indexing of all properties, the units consumed to write a document/node/entity increase as the property count increases.
Data consistency. When using data consistency models such as Strong or Bounded Staleness, additional request units are consumed to read items.
Indexed properties. An index policy on each container determines which properties are indexed by default. You can reduce your request unit consumption by limiting the number of indexed properties or by enabling lazy indexing.
Document indexing. By default each item is automatically indexed. You consume fewer request units if you choose to not index some of your items.
Query patterns. The complexity of a query impacts how many request units are consumed for an operation. The number of predicates, nature of the predicates, projections, number of UDFs, and the size of the source data - all influence the cost of query operations.
Script usage. As with queries, stored procedures and triggers consume request units based on the complexity of the operations being performed.

Azure Cosmos DB Consumed Storage

Azure Cosmos DB offers **unlimited SSD storage** with no provisioning, configuration or advanced reservations required. Azure Cosmos DB Storage automatically scales up and down based on the data and indexes that are added or removed to an Azure Cosmos DB container.

Partitioning

Azure Cosmos DB provides containers (Collections, Graphs or Tables) for storing data. Containers are logical resources and can span one or more physical partitions or servers. Each physical partition is replicated to provide high availability for your container data.

A **physical partition** is SSD-backed storage. Each physical partition is replicated for high availability. One or more physical partitions make up a container. Physical partition management is fully managed by Azure Cosmos DB.

A **logical partition** is a partition within a physical partition that stores all the data associated with a **single partition key value**. Multiple logical partitions can end up in the same physical partition.

For example, in a container where all items contain a City property, you can use City as the partition key for the container. Groups of items that have specific values for City, such as London, Paris, and NYC, form distinct logical partitions as shown in the figure below.

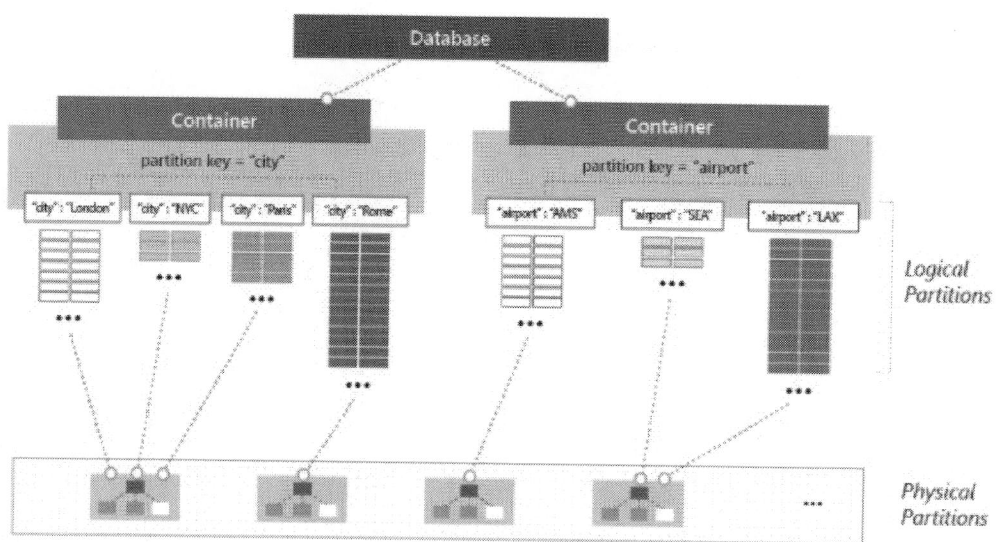

Note: Unlike logical partitions, physical partitions are an internal implementation of the system. You can't control the size, placement, or count of physical partitions, and you can't control the mapping between logical partitions and physical partitions.

Cosmos DB Pricing

Cosmos DB Pricing is based on 2 components: Provisioned Throughput and SSD Storage.

Provisioned Throughput is billed as Request Units per second or RU/s. You can assign Reserved throughput at Container or Database Level.

Unit	Pricing
SSD Storage (per GB)	$0.25 GB/month
Provisioned Throughput (single region writes) per 100 RU/s	$0.008/hour
Provisioned Throughput (multiple region writes) per 100 RU/s	$0.016/hour

Saving Cost with Reserved Instances

Throughput	Single Region Write (1 Yr RI)	Multi Region Write (1 Yr RI)	Single Region Write (3 Yr RI)	Multi Region Write (3 Yr RI)
First 50K RU/s	$0.0068 (~15%)	$0.0128 (~20%)	$0.006 (~25%)	$0.0112 (~30%)
Next 450K RU/s	$0.006 (~25%)	$0.0112 (~30%)	$0.0052 (~35%)	$0.0096 (~40%)
Next 2.5M RU/s	$0.0056 (~30%)	$0.0104 (~35%)	$0.0044 (~45%)	$0.008 (~50%)
Over 3M RU/s	$0.0044 (~45%)	$0.008 (~50%)	$0.0032 (~60%)	$0.0056 (~65%)

Note 1: RI – Reserved Instance
Note 2: Number in Bracket shows percentage saving when using Reserved Instance over PAYG model.

Chapter 9 Analyzing & Monitoring Azure Resources

This Chapter covers following Topic Lessons

- Azure Monitoring Solutions
- Azure Monitor
- Metrics & Logs
- Activity Log
- Diagnostic Logs (Non-Compute Resources)
- Diagnostic Logs (Compute Resource)
- Metrics
- Action Group
- Alerts
- Log Analytics
- Management Solutions
- Advisor
- Azure Service Health

This Chapter covers following Lab Exercises

- Accessing & Exploring Monitor Dashboard
- Accessing Activity Log from a Monitor Dashboard
- Accessing Activity Log from a Resource Dashboard
- Accessing Diagnostic Log from the Monitor Dashboard
- Enabling Diagnostic Logs for Recovery Services Vault
- Enabling Diagnostic Logs for Network Security Group
- Enabling Guest OS Diagnostic Logs in VM VMFE1
- Virtual Machine Percentage CPU Metrics
- Storage Account Used Capacity Metrics
- Create Action Group
- Create an alert on Metric (Percentage CPU) for VM
- Accessing Alert from Resource (VM) Dashboard
- Monitoring IIS Web Server with Log Analytics
- Installing Management Solution (NSG Analytics)
- Installing Microsoft Monitoring Agent in On-Premises VM
- Checking Advisor Recommendations
- Checking Service Health Events
- Configuring Alerts for Service Health Events

Chapter Topology

In this chapter we will add Monitor, Log Analytics, Advisor & Service Health to the topology. We will Install Diagnostic Agent (DA) on VM VMFE1. We will connect VM VMFE1 to Log Analytics by enabling Microsoft Monitoring Agent (MMA) extension on VM VMFE1.

For Monitoring of resources we will enable or create Activity Logs, Diagnostic Logs, Alerts and Action Groups.

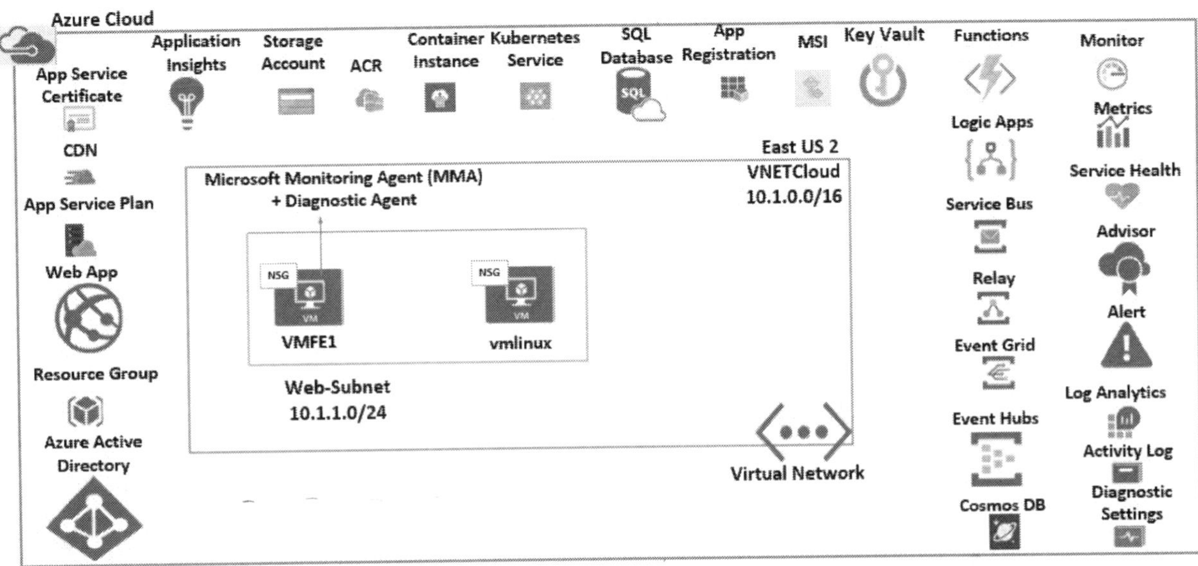

Azure Monitoring Solutions

Azure includes multiple services that individually perform a specific role or task in the monitoring space. Together, these services deliver a comprehensive solution for collecting, analyzing, and acting on telemetry from your application and the Azure resources that support them.

The figure below shows a conceptual view of the components that work together to provide monitoring of Azure resources.

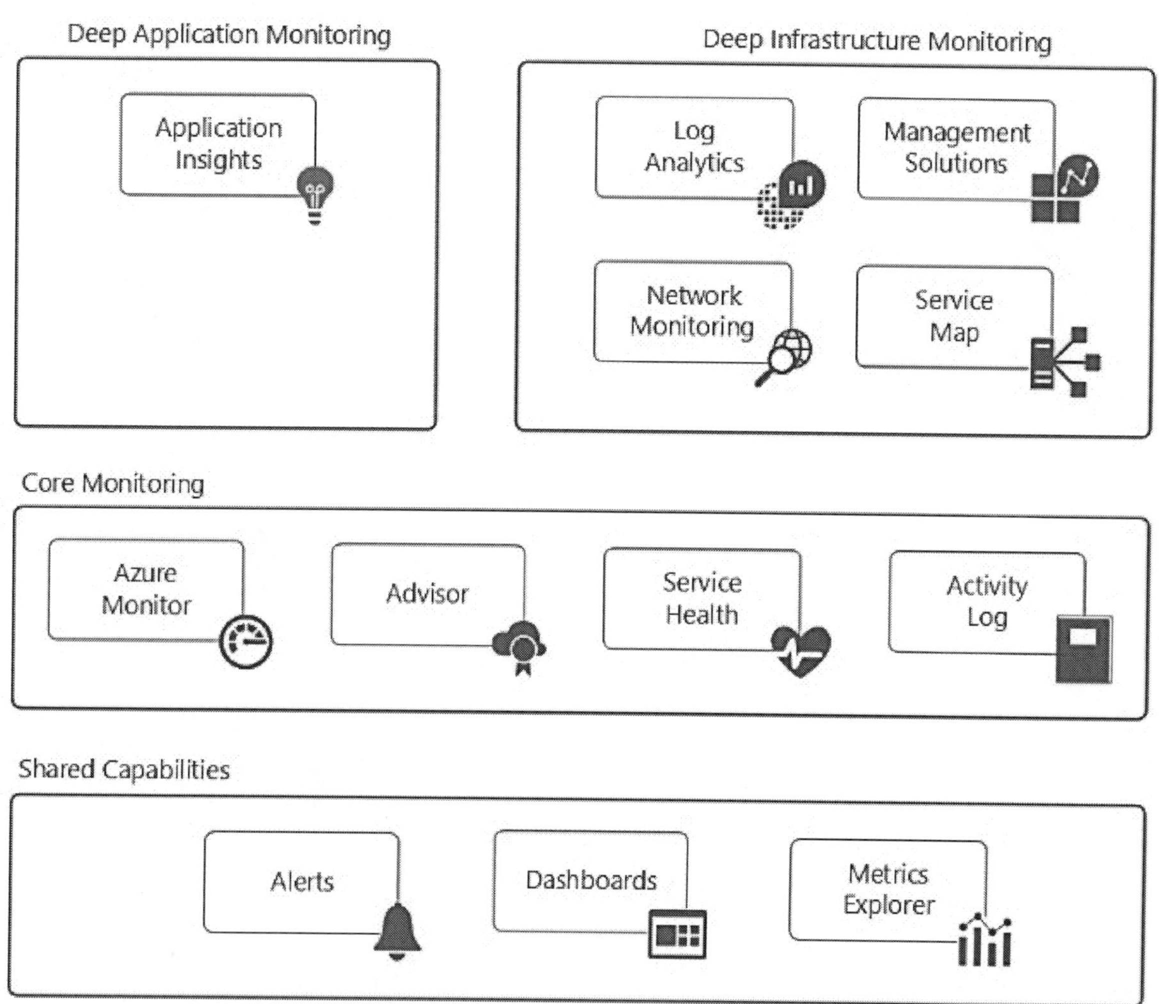

Note: We can monitor resource Diagnostic Settings and Activity logs through resource Dashboard or through Monitor Dashboard.

Application Insights

Application Insights is a Managed Application Performance Management (APM) service for web applications running on Web Apps, Virtual Machines or Physical Servers in the cloud or on-premises.

Azure Application Insight monitor's live Web Application for **availability, performance, and usage.** You can also identify and diagnose errors in your application without waiting for a user to report them.

It works for apps on a wide variety of platforms including .NET, Node.js and J2EE, hosted on-premises or in the cloud. It integrates with DevOps process, and has connection points to a variety of development tools. It can monitor and analyze telemetry from mobile apps by integrating with Visual Studio App Center.

Parameters Monitored by Application Insights

Request rates, response times, and failure rates - Find out which pages are most popular, at what times of day, and where your users are. See which pages perform best. If your response times and failure rates go high when there are more requests, then perhaps you have a resourcing problem.
Dependency rates, response times, and failure rates - Find out whether external services are slowing you down.
Exceptions - Analyse the aggregated statistics, or pick specific instances and drill into the stack trace and related requests. Both server and browser exceptions are reported.
Page views and load performance - reported by your users' browsers.
AJAX calls from web pages - rates, response times, and failure rates.
User and session counts.
Performance counters from your Windows or Linux server machines, such as CPU, memory, and network usage.
Host diagnostics from Docker or Azure.
Diagnostic trace logs from your app - so that you can correlate trace events with requests.
Custom events and metrics that you write yourself in the client or server code, to track business events such as items sold or games won.

Architecture, Components and Working of Application Insight

The Figure below shows the Architect & Components of Application Insight (Shown in Purple Color) for Monitoring and Availability of Web Applications.

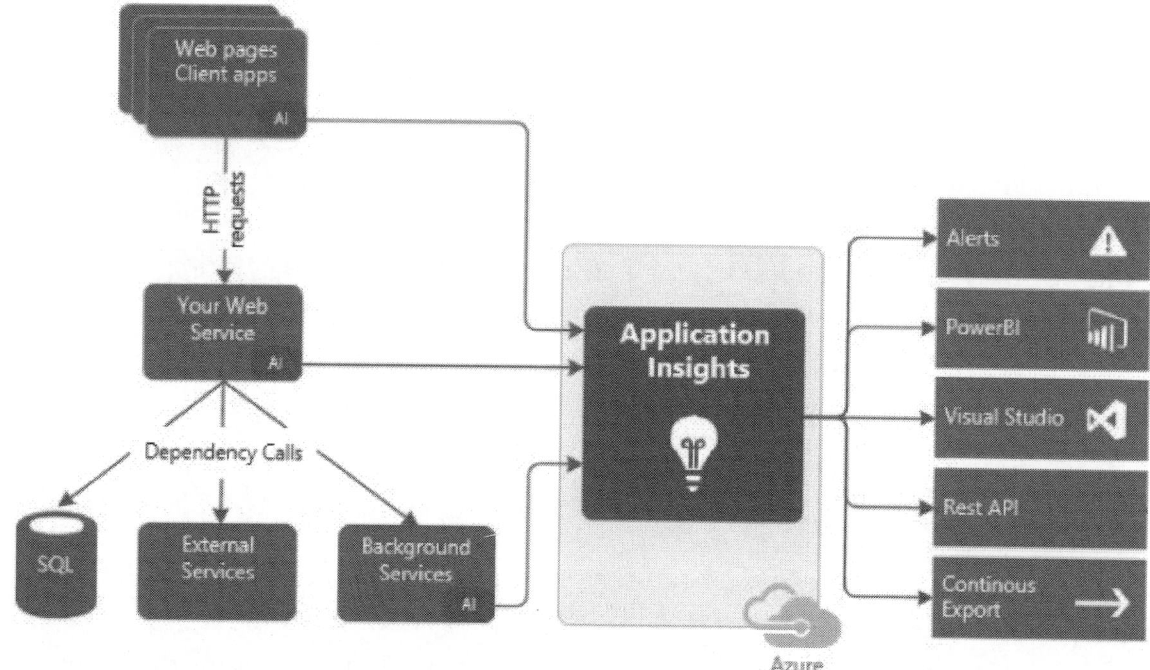

Components of Application Insight

Application Insight Agent in your application code
Application Insight Managed Service in Azure.

Brief Working

8. Setup Application Insight Service in Azure.
9. Install Application Insight Agents in Applications running in Cloud or on-premises.
10. The Application Insight Agent monitors application and sends telemetry data to the portal.
11. You can Graphically view Application performance data in real time .
12. You can apply analytic and search tools to the raw data in Application Insight service in Azure.
13. You can setup alerts on the metrics which can trigger a response when threshold is breached.
14. You can export your data to Business Intelligence tools like Power BI.

Exercise 93: Create Application Insight Service in Azure

1. In Azure Portal Click +Create a resource> IT & Management Tools> Application Insights> Create Application Insights Blade opens>For Resource Group select RGCloud and for region select East US 2>Click Review+Create.

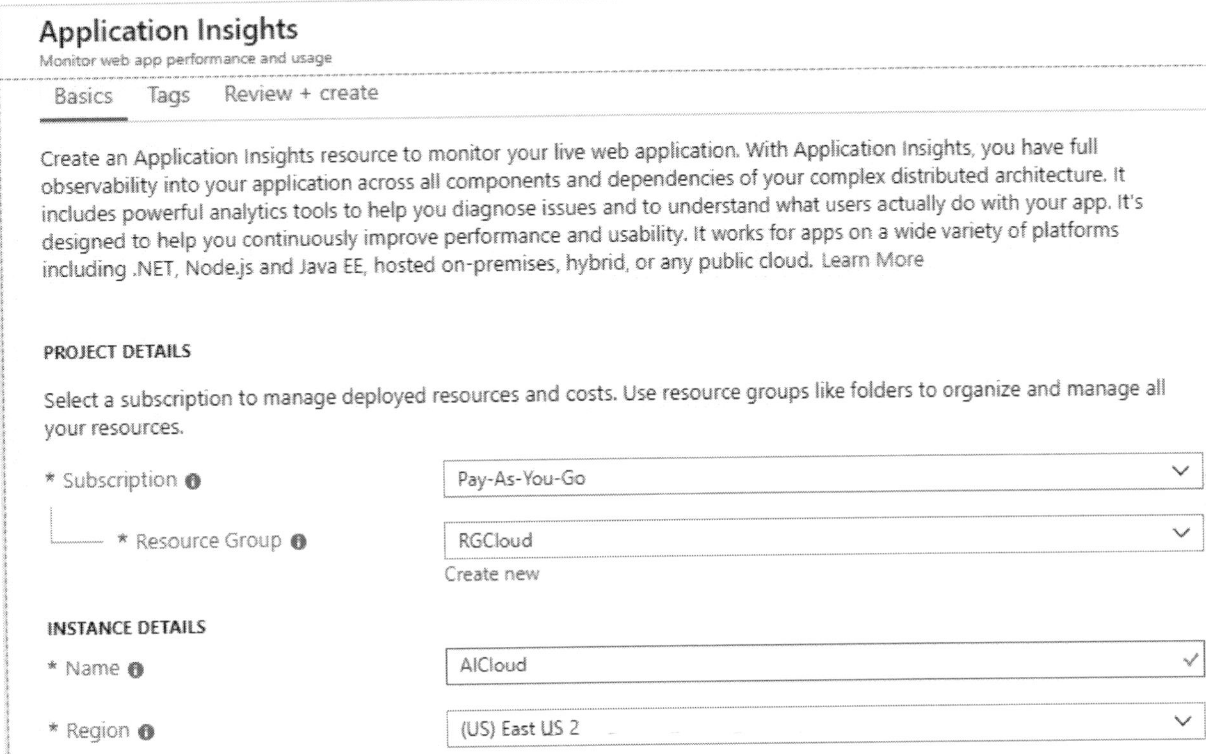

2. Figure below shows the dashboard of Application Insight.

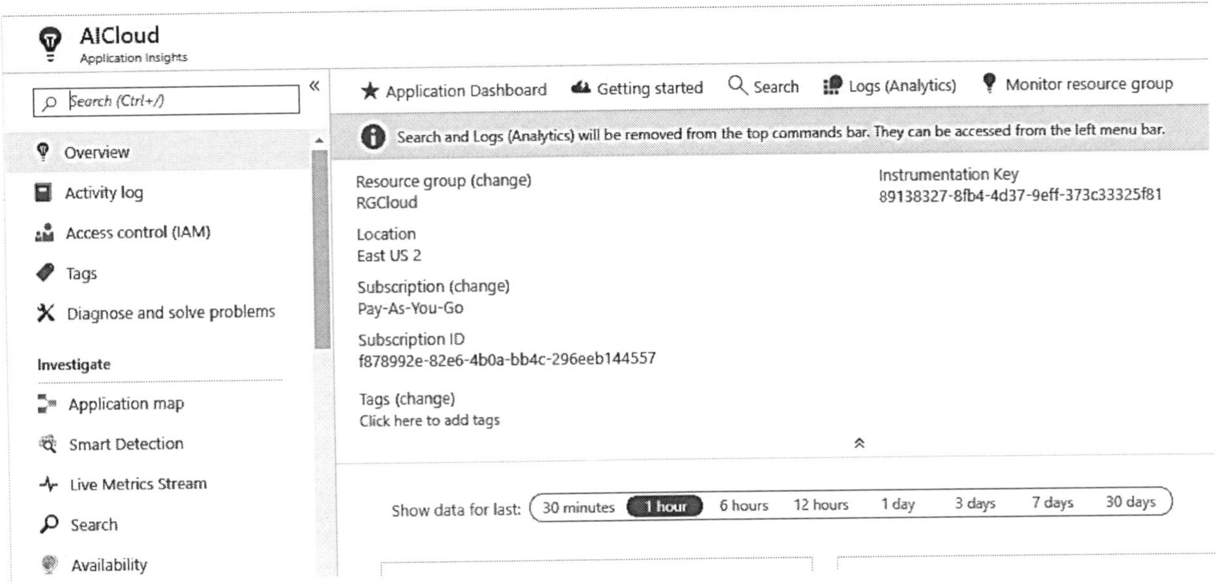

Options to Enable Application Insights monitoring on your web application server

1. Add the Application Insights SDK to your app in Visual Studio to collect performance and usage telemetry.
2. Download and Install Application Insights Status Monitor on your server.
3. Application Insight is natively integrated with Azure Web Apps and Azure Functions. You can enable it from the Web App dashboard.

Figure below shows the option to add Application Insight in our application.

Enable Application Insights monitoring

Add the Application Insights SDK to your app to collect performance and usage telemetry.

Add Application Insights

In Visual Studio 2015 (latest update), right-click your web project and click Add Application Insights Telemetry.

Get the latest update for Visual Studio

Run your application

Run your application in Visual Studio. Return to this portal and open Live Stream. You will see data in a few seconds.

Troubleshoot

Check Application Insights service status

Enable Status Monitor

Install Application Insights Status Monitor on your server. Using Status Monitor can enrich existing dependency telemetry, for example with the details of SQL statements. For more about Status Monitor:

Install Status Monitor to monitor website performance

Download Status Monitor on your server

Smart Detection

Smart Detection automatically warns you of potential performance problems in your web application. It performs proactive analysis of the telemetry that your app sends to Application Insights. If there is a sudden rise in failure rates, or abnormal patterns in client or server performance, you get an alert. This feature needs no configuration. It operates if your application sends enough telemetry.

You can access Smart Detection alerts both from the emails you receive, and from the Smart Detection blade.

Accessing Smart Dashboard: In Application Insight Dashboard click Smart detection in left pane> click settings> Smart Detection setting blade opens in Extreme right (Nit Shown).

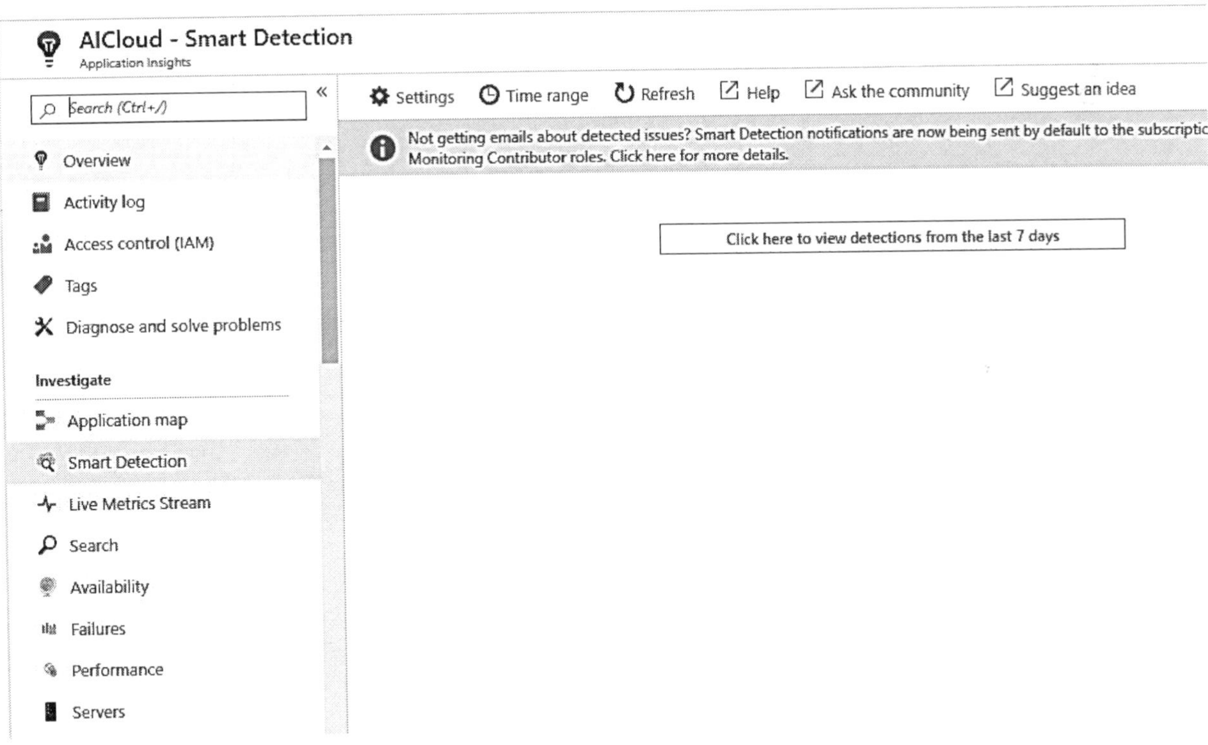

Note: You can also see Exercise on Azure Application Insights in Chapter 1 of this book.

Azure Monitor

Azure Monitor provides centralized dashboard for viewing Logs, metrics & alerts for Azure resources.

Azure Monitor provides mini-dashboards for Metrics, Activity Log, Diagnostic logs, alerts, Service Health, Network Watcher & Application Insights etc. Data can be exported to Log Analytics and Power BI for further Analysis.

Metrics & Logs

All data collected by Azure Monitor fits into one of two fundamental types - Metrics and Logs.

Metrics are numerical values that describe some aspect of a system at a particular point in time. They are lightweight and capable of supporting near real-time scenarios.

Logs contain different kinds of data organized into records with different sets of properties for each type. Telemetry such as events and traces are stored as logs in addition to performance data so that it can all be combined for analysis.

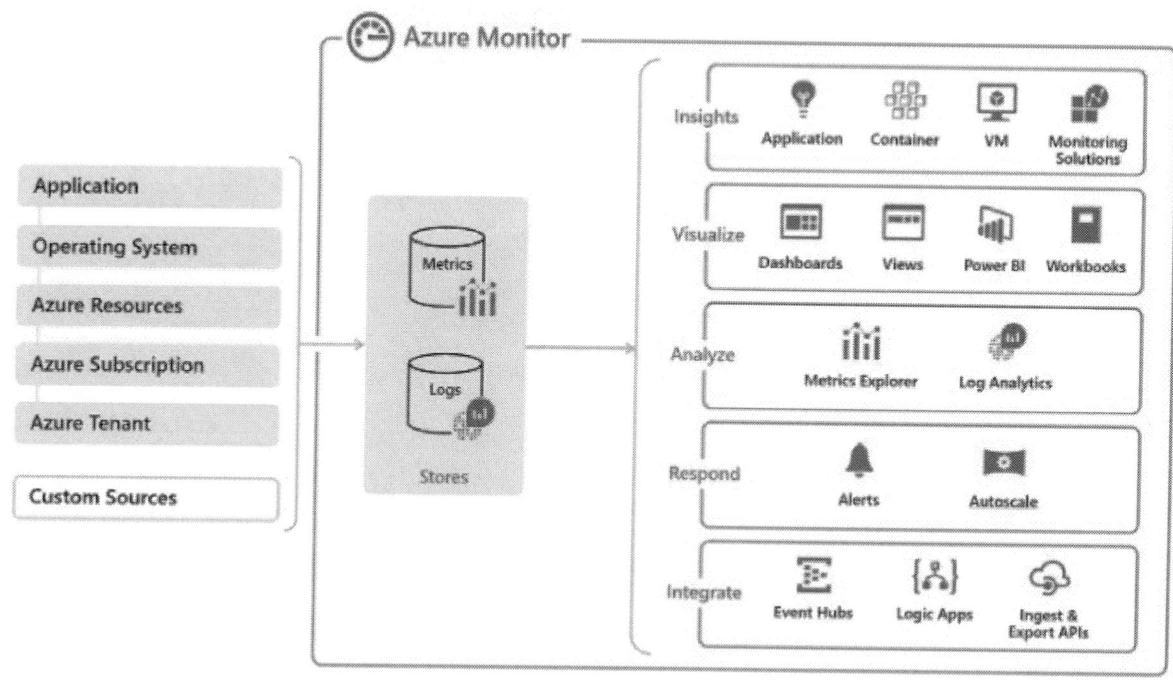

Exercise 94: Accessing & Exploring Monitor Dashboard

In Azure Portal click Monitor in Left pane> Monitor Dashboard opens> In the left pane you can see tabs for Alerts, Metrics, Activity Log, and Diagnostic settings etc.

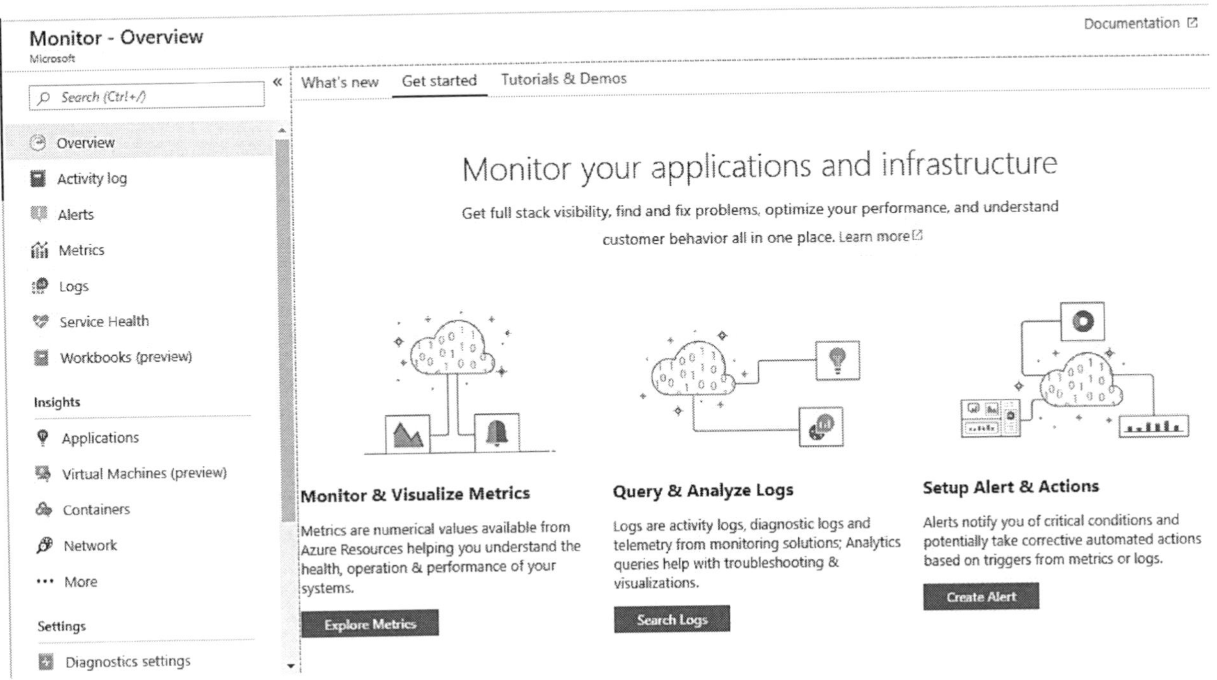

Note: Readers are requested to explore options in the left pane.

Activity Log

Activity Logs provide data about the operations on a resource from the outside. The Activity Log reports control-plane events for your subscriptions. For Example Azure Activity log will log an event when a virtual machine is created or a logic app is deleted. But any Activity performed by virtual Machine will not be reported by Activity Log.

You can monitor Activity log for Compute as well as non-compute Resources.

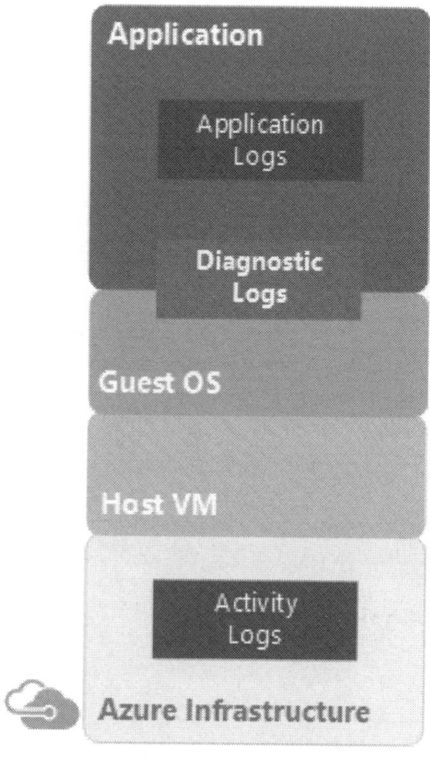

Compute resources only

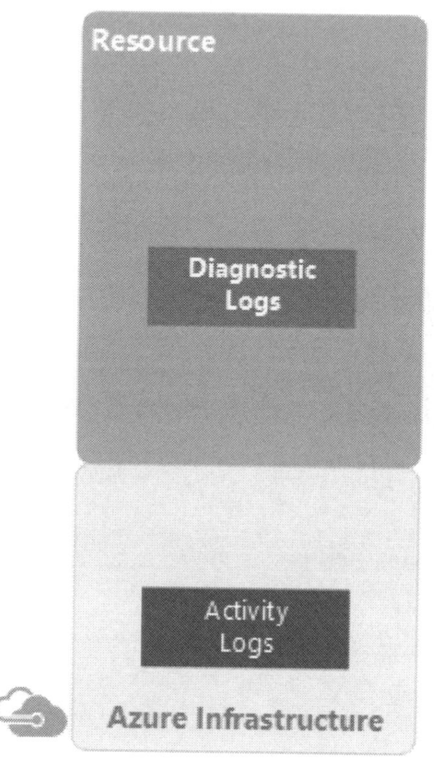

Non-Compute resources only

Activity Log is a Platform level Service. You don't require any agents to be installed. Events can be seen in Azure Portal. Events Logs can be exported to Azure Storage, Event Hubs, Power BI and OMS Log Analytics. You can create alerts on Events generated in Activity Log.

Exercise 95: Accessing Activity Log from a Monitor Dashboard

In Azure Portal click Monitor in Left pane> Monitor Dashboard opens> Click Activity Log. This will report control plane events for **all the resources**.
Note: By default Activity dashboard will show logs for last 6 Hours. To see Logs for different duration you need to select duration from Timespan dropdown box.

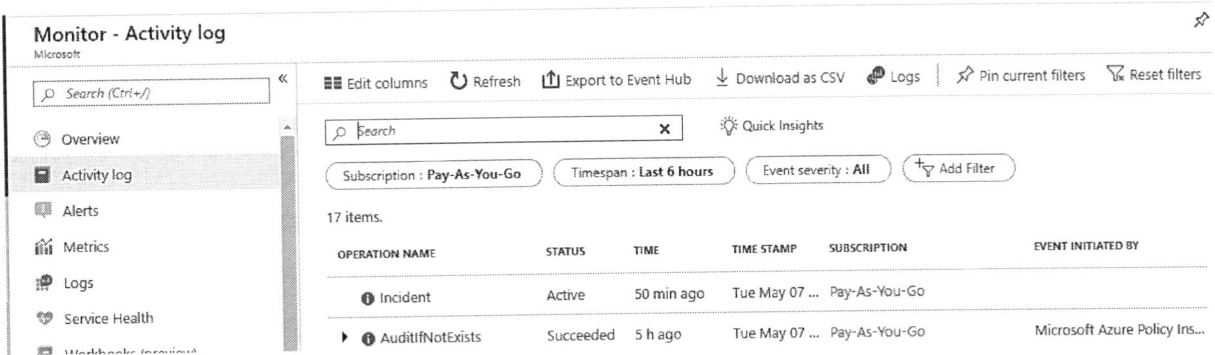

To see activity log for particular resource such as Virtual Network "VNETCloud"
Click Add Filter 2 times>Select Resource RGCloud>Select Resource VNETCloud.

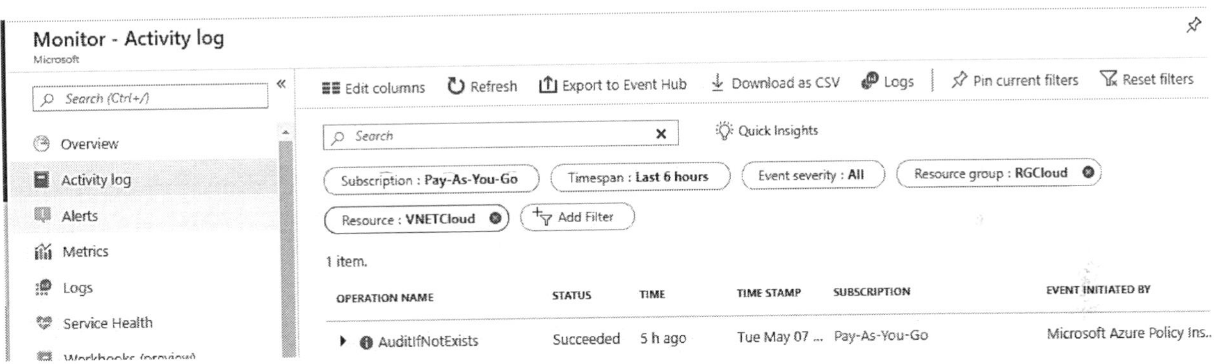

Exercise 96: Accessing Activity Log from a Resource Dashboard

Go to Virtual Network "VNETCloud" Dashboard> Click Activity Log in left Pane.

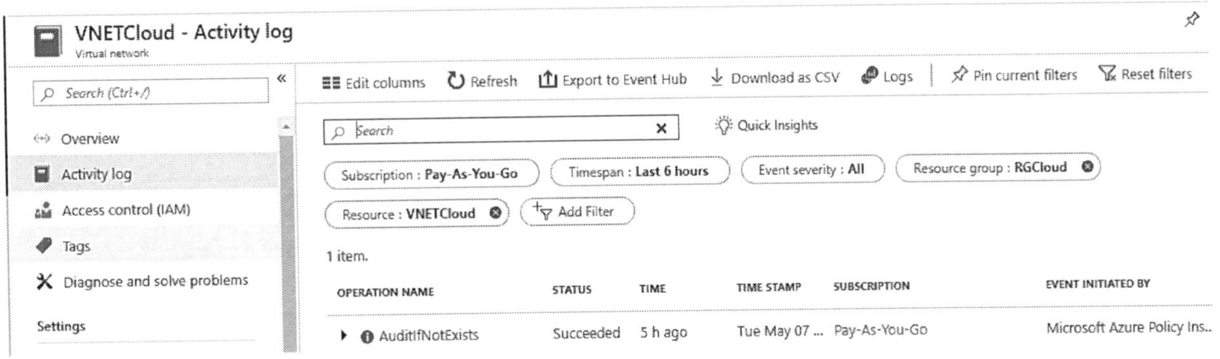

Diagnostic Logs (Non-Compute Resources)

Azure resource-level diagnostic logs are logs emitted by a resource about the operation of that resource. Diagnostic logs provide insight into operations that were performed within that resource itself, for example, getting a secret from a Key Vault.

Difference between Activity and Diagnostic Logs: Activity Logs provide data about the operations on a resource from the outside (the "control plane"). Diagnostics Logs are emitted by a resource and provide information about the operation of that resource (the "data plane").
You can monitor Diagnostic log for Compute as well as non-compute Resources.

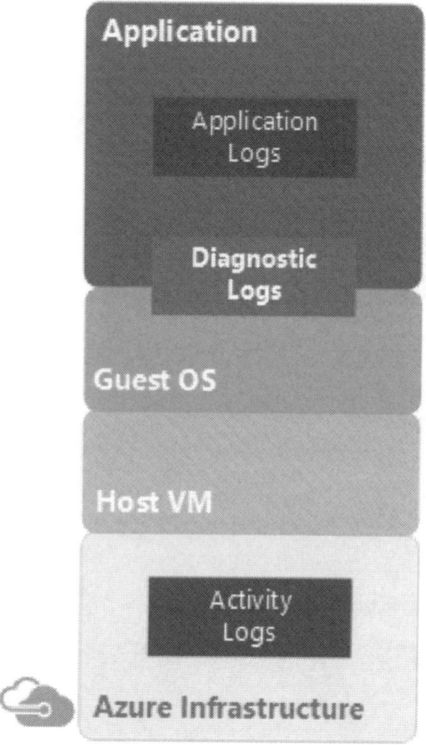

Compute resources only

Non-Compute resources only

Diagnostic log is a Platform level Service. **You don't require any agents to be installed** and nor you require any Azure Level service to be created. **You just need to enable diagnostic logs for the resource**.

Diagnostic Log Architecture

The Figure below shows the Architecture of Diagnostic Log.

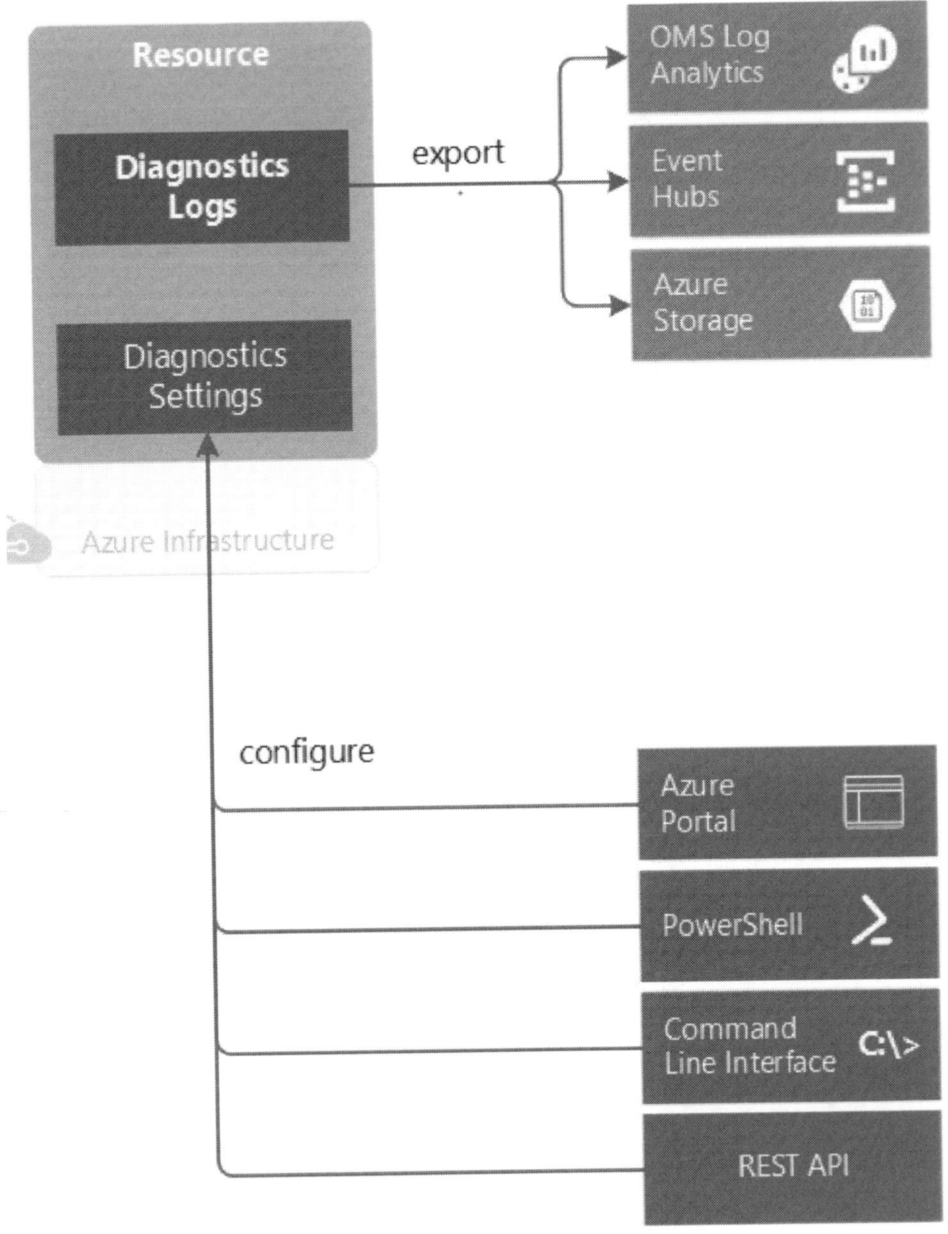

Diagnostic Log is a Platform level Resource which logs Events generated by the resource. Events Logs can be seen in Azure Portal.

Diagnostic Logs can be streamed to Event Hubs for ingestion by a third-party service or custom analytics solution such as PowerBI. You can Analyze logs with OMS Log Analytics.

Exercise 97: Accessing Diagnostic Log from the Monitor Dashboard

In Monitor Dashboard click Diagnostic settings in left pane> Right pane shows diagnostic logs status for all the Azure resources in the subscription.

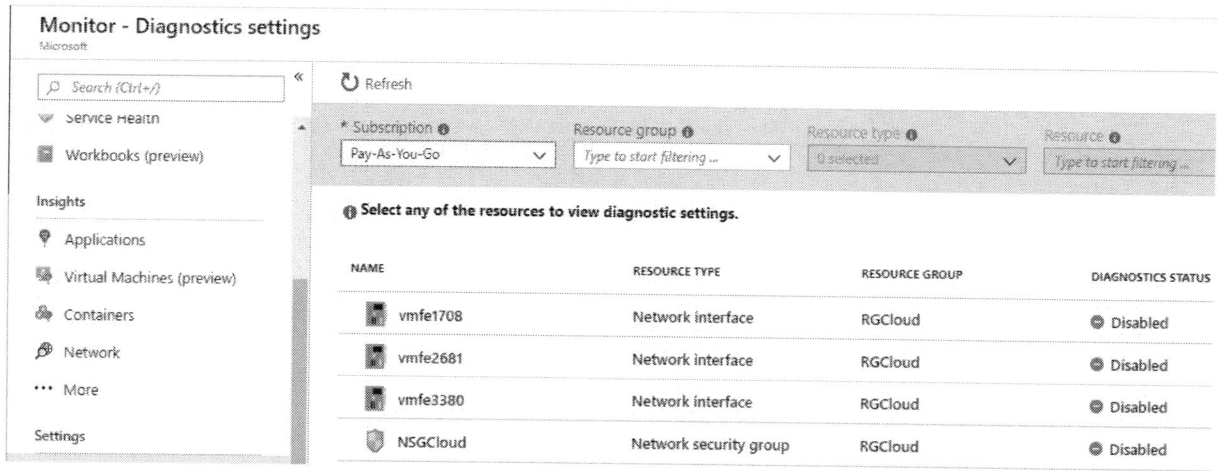

Exercise 98: Enabling Diagnostic Logs for Recovery Services Vault

1. In Monitor Dashboard click Diagnostic settings in left pane> In Right pane scroll down and click RSVCloud> From here you can enable Diagnostic setting for Recovery Services Vault RSVCloud. RSVCloud was created in Exercise 76, Chapter 7.

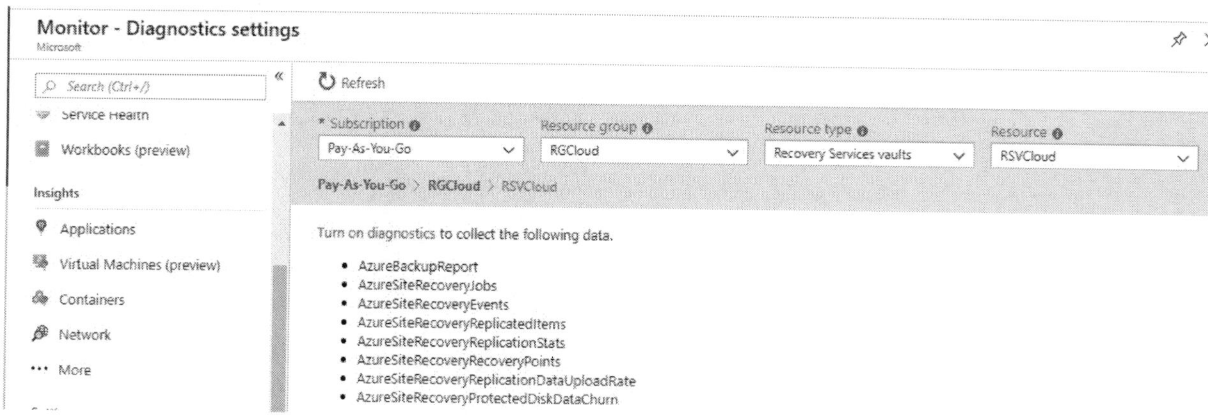

2. Click Turn on diagnostics>Diagnostic Setting blade opens>Enter a name, Select Storage account and/or Event Hub and/or Log Analytics and select logs as per your requirement and click OK>Click Save.
   For this lab I select Storage Account sastdcloud and for Log I selected AzureBackupReport.

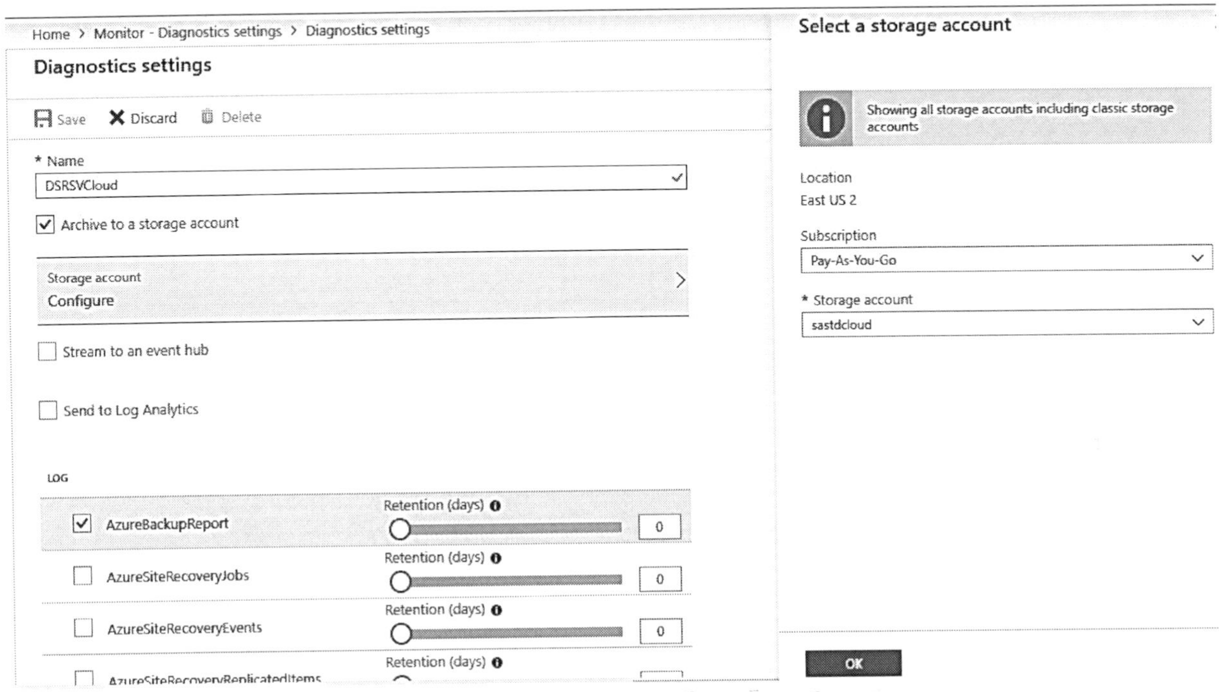

Note: Backup Reports data will be fully available in the storage account after 24 hours from configuration.

Back reports in Storage Account sastdcloud as shown below.

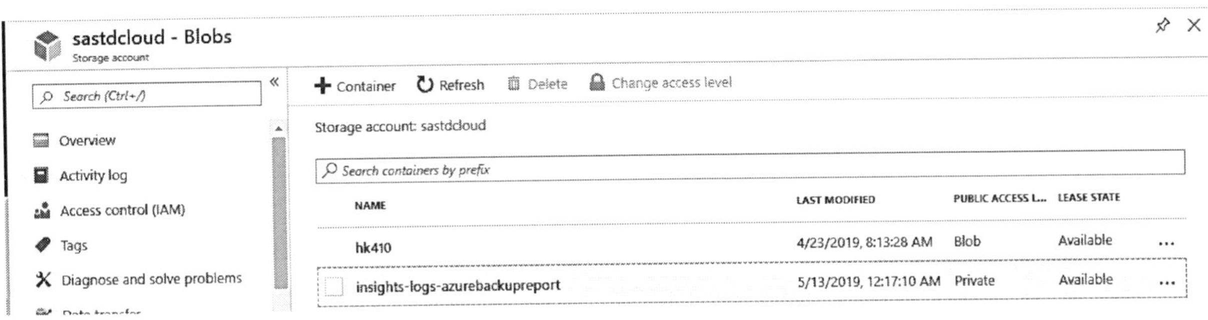

Exercise 99: Enabling Diagnostic Logs for Network Security Group

In this exercise we will enable Diagnostic Logs for Network Security Group NSGCloud. NSGCloud was created in Exercise 11, Chapter 1. We will analyse NSG Diagnostic Logs with Log Analytics in Exercise 107 in this chapter.

1. In Monitor Dashboard click Diagnostic settings in left pane> In Right pane Click NSGCloud>Click + Add diagnostic setting>Diagnostic Setting pane opens>Enter a name>Select Send to Log Analytics>Select the Logs> Click Save>Close the pane after you get notification about successful updation.

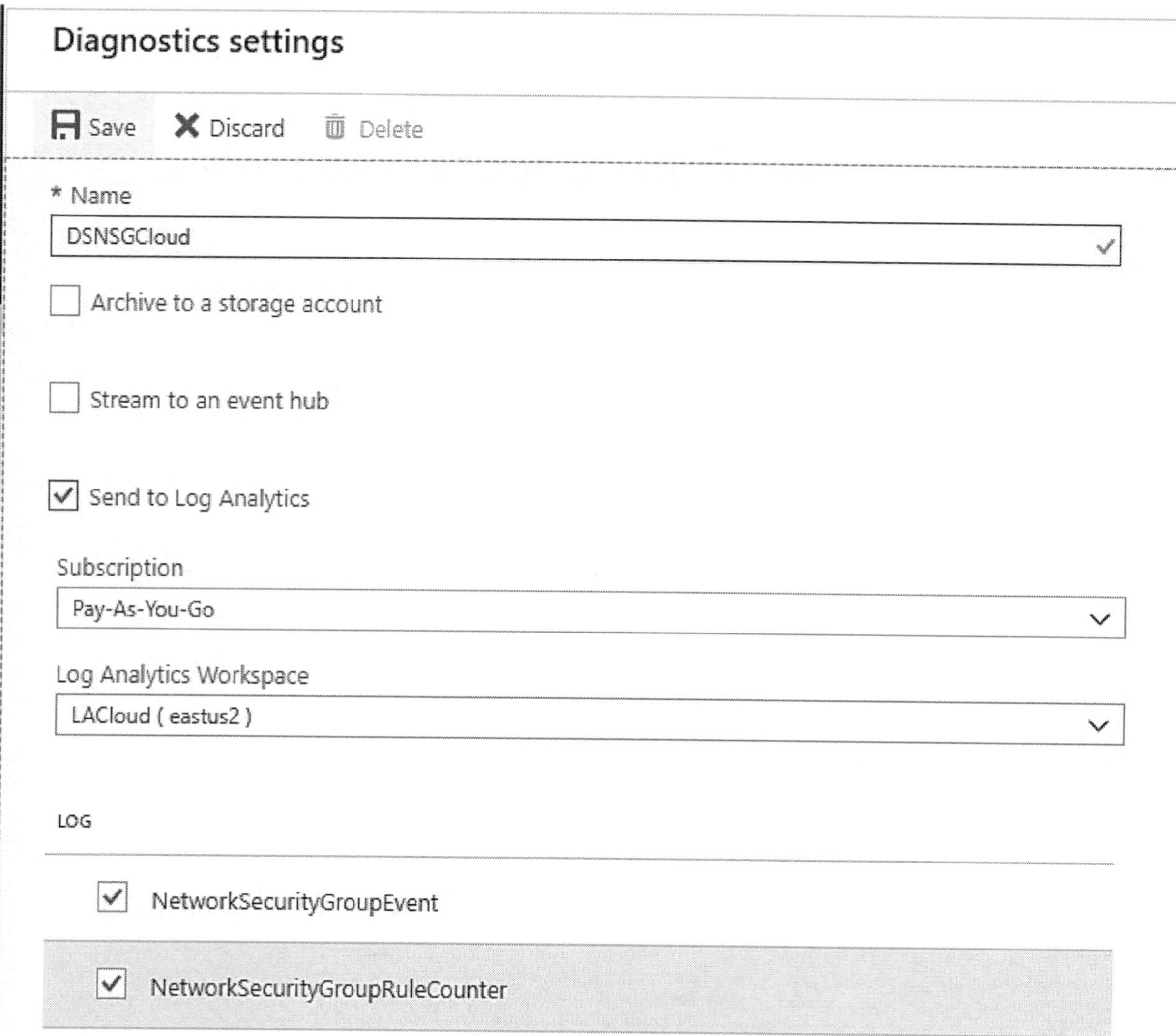

Diagnostic Logs (Compute Resource)

Guest OS-level/Extended Metrics are collected by installing diagnostics agent on the Azure virtual machine. If you don't enable Guest level monitoring then only Standard Metrics or Host level metrics are available.

Guest OS-level diagnostic logs capture data from the operating system and applications running on a virtual machine. Guest OS-level diagnostic logs collect following types of Metrics and Logs:

Performance counters
Application Logs
Windows Event Logs
.NET Event Source
IIS Logs
Manifest based ETW
Crash Dumps
Customer Error Logs

Exercise 100: Enabling Guest OS Diagnostic Logs in VM VMFE1

1. Go to VM VMFE1 Dashboard>Click Diagnostic settings in left pane>In Right pane click Enable Guest Level Monitoring.

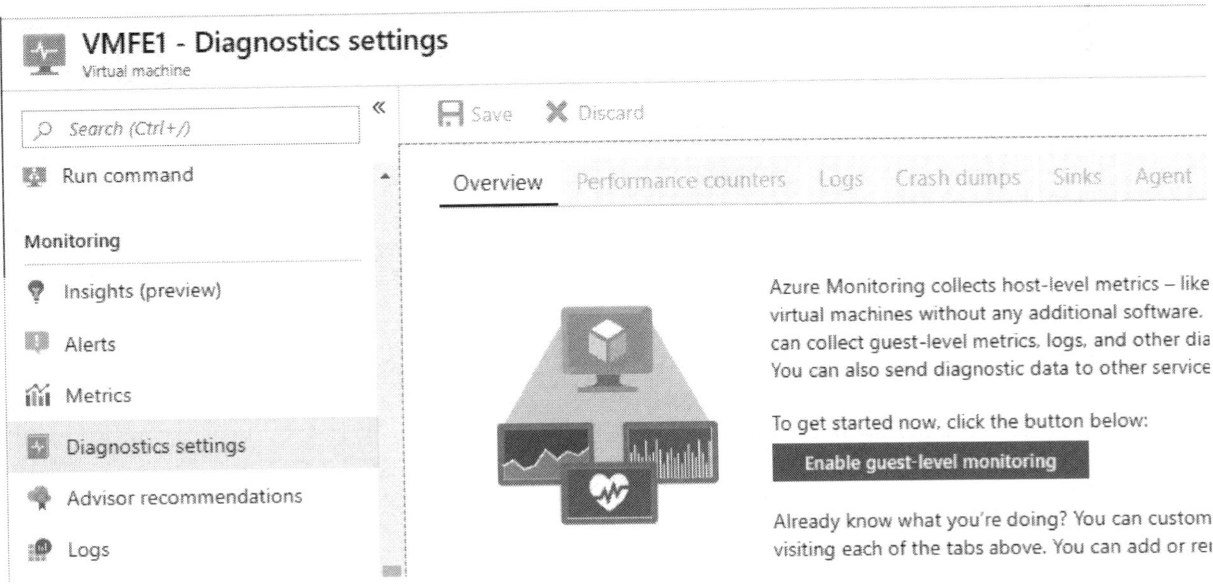

2. After enabling you can see following in overview screen

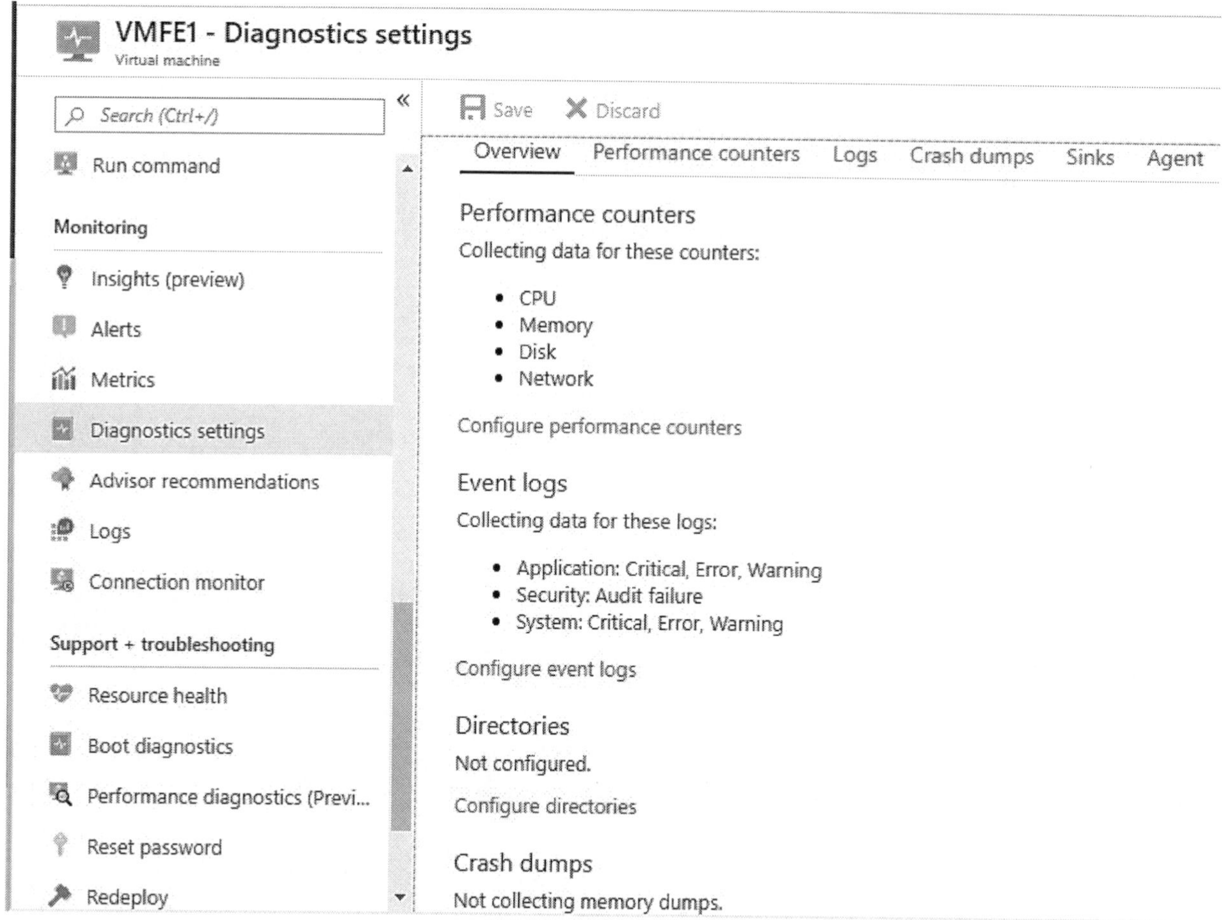

3. Click on Performance Counters>Custom> **<You can now see OS level/VM level counters>Click save (Not shown).**

None | Basic | **Custom**

Configure the performance counters to collect, and how often they should be sampled:

Add

	PERFORMANCE COUNTER	SAMPLE RATE (SECONDS)	UNIT
☑	\Processor Information(_Total)\% Process...	60	Percent
☑	\Processor Information(_Total)\% Privileg...	60	Percent
☑	\Processor Information(_Total)\% User Ti...	60	Percent
☑	\Processor Information(_Total)\Processor ...	60	Count
☑	\System\Processes	60	Count

4. **Checking VM level Performance Counters**. In VM VMFE1 dashboard click metrics in left pane> In Resource select VMFE1> In metric Namespace select **Guest (Classic)**> In Metric Dropdown box you can see VM level counters are available now.

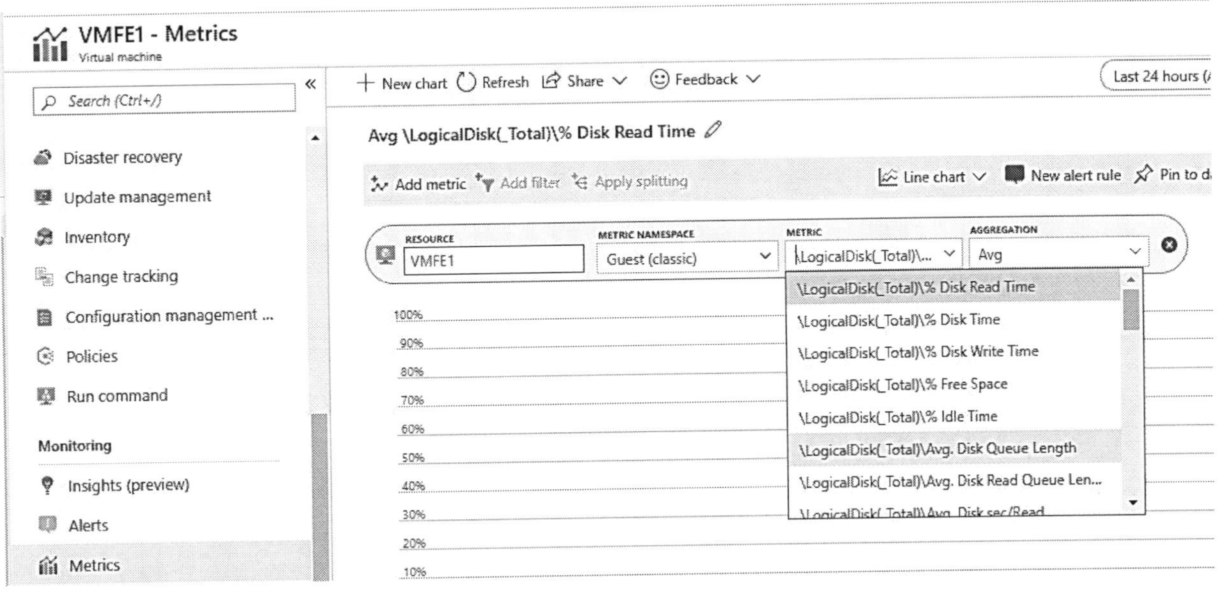

Note 1: Metric Namespace **Guest (Classic)** is not available if you don't enable Guest Level Monitoring.

Note 2: Readers are requested to see Click other options in Diagnostic settings like Logs, Crash Dumps, Sinks and Agent. Click Basic Option also.

As an exercise to readers go to VMFE2 dashboard>Click Metrics in left pane>In Right pane Click Metric Namespace Dropdown box> You will not see the Guest Option.

Metrics

Metrics are numerical values that describe some aspect of a system (CPU or Memory utilization etc.) at a particular time. They are lightweight and capable of supporting near real-time scenarios. Metrics are collected at regular intervals whether or not the value changes.

They're useful for alerting because they can be sampled frequently, and an alert can be fired quickly with simple logic.

Metrics Example

Percentage CPU metric will collect processor utilization from a virtual machine every minute. You have the option to configure and fire an alert on the metric such as when one of those collected values exceeds a defined threshold.

Metric are Key value pairs. Metric for Percentage CPU and Network Throughput are shown below:

Percentage CPU

Timestamp	Metric Value
8/9/2017 8:14	70

Network Throughput

Timestamp	Metric Value
8/9/2017 8:15	1,141.4 Kbps

Metric Features

1. Collected at one-minute frequency unless specified otherwise in the metric's definition.
2. Uniquely identified by a metric name and a namespace that acts as a category.
3. Stored for 93 days. You can copy metrics to Log Analytics for long term trending.

Sources of metric data

There are three fundamental sources of metrics collected by Azure Monitor. All of these metrics are available in the metric store where they can be evaluated together regardless of their source.

Platform metrics are created by Azure resources and give you visibility into their health and performance. Each type of resource creates a distinct set of metrics without any configuration required.

Application metrics are created by Application Insights for your monitored applications and help you detect performance issues and track trends in how your application is being used. This includes such values as *Server response time* and *Browser exceptions*.

Custom metrics are metrics that you define in addition to the standard metric that are automatically available. Custom metrics must be created against a single resource in the same region as that resource.

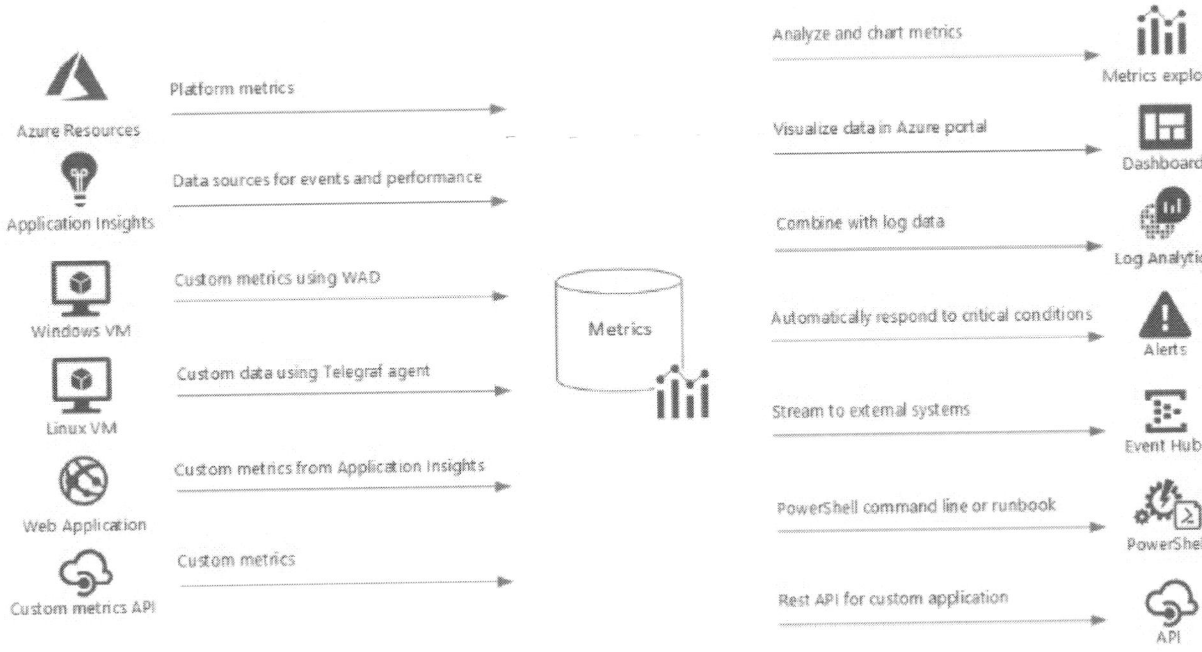

Exercise 101: Virtual Machine Percentage CPU Metrics

1. In VMFE1 Dashboard click Metrics in left pane> In Metric Pane Click Add Metric>In Metric Namespace select Virtual Machine host> In Metric Select Percentage CPU> You can now see real time chart for last 24 Hours.

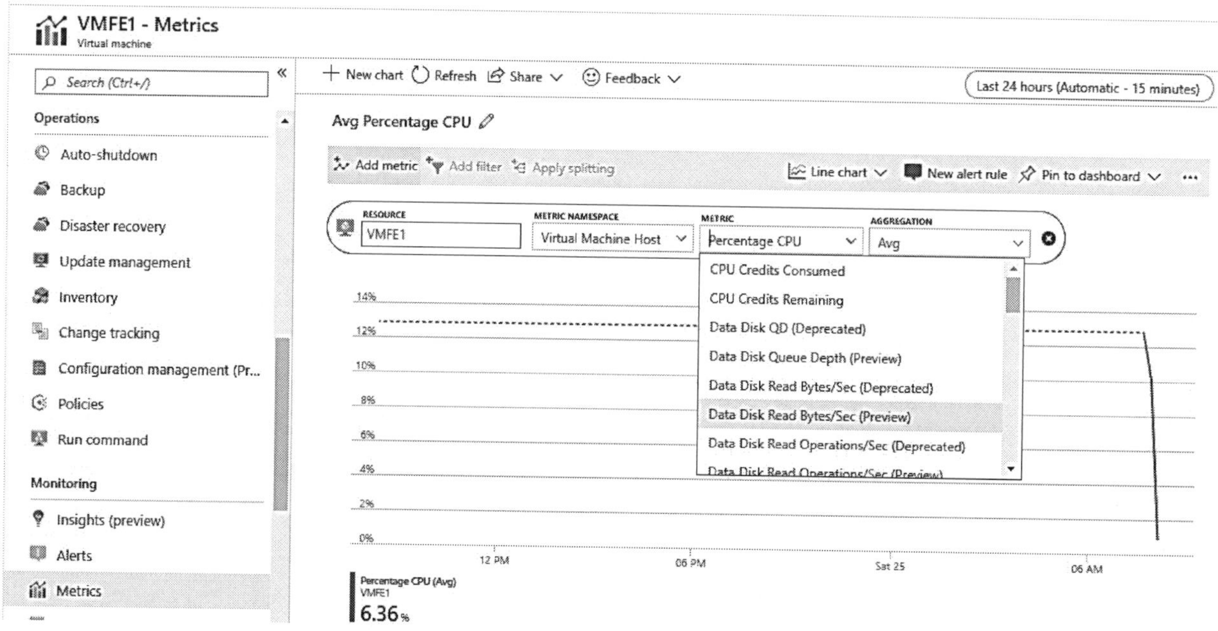

Note 1: Readers are advised to see more metrics through Metric Dropdown box.
Note 2: You can also access Metric through Monitor dashboard.

Exercise 102: Storage Account Used Capacity Metrics

1. In Monitor Dashboard click Metrics in left pane> In Metric Pane Click Add Metric>Click Resource Box and in Resource Group Select RGCloud, In Resource type select Storage Accounts and then select Storage Account sastdcloud and click apply> In Metric Drop Box select Used Capacity>You can now see real time chart for last 24 Hours.

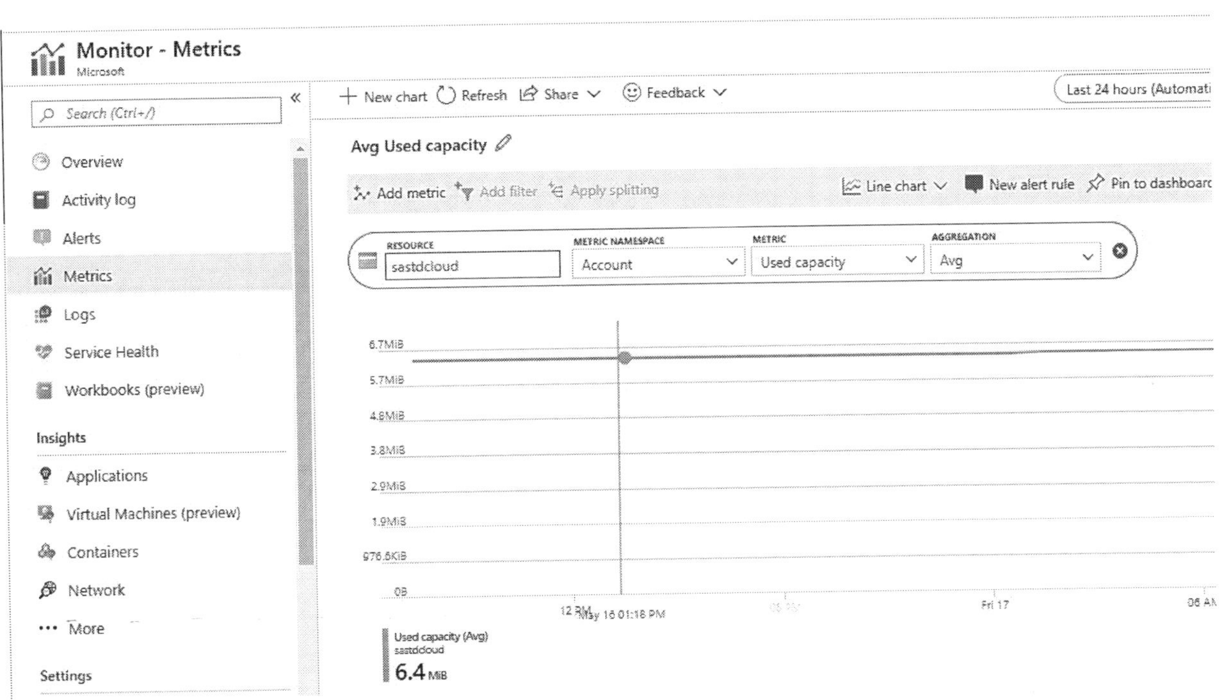

Action Group

An action group is a collection of **notification preferences** (Action Types) defined by the user. Various Alerts types use Action Groups when the alert is triggered.

Action Types

Email/SMS/Push/Voice
Azure Function
Logic App
Webhook
ITSM
Automation Runbook

Exercise 103: Create Action Group

In this exercise we will create Action group with Action type Email. We will use this Action Group with Alerts in Alert exercise.

1. In Azure Portal click Monitor in Left pane> Monitor Dashboard opens>Click Alert in left pane> In Right pane you can see Manage Actions.

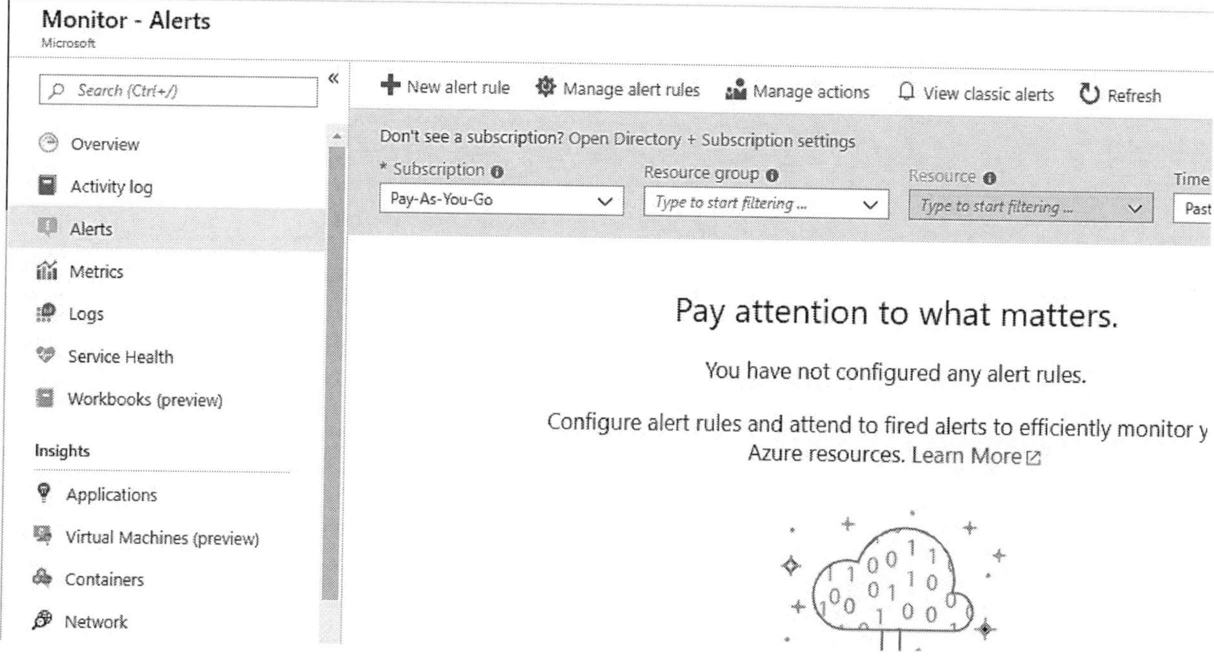

2. Click Manage action in right pane>Action Group pane opens>Click +Add Action Group>Add Action group blade opens>Give a name and short name> Select System created Resource group> Enter action name>Select Email/SMS/Push/Voice in Action type>Click Edit details> Email/SMS/Push/Voice detail pane opens> Enter a name>Select Email check box and enter email id>Click OK>Click Ok.

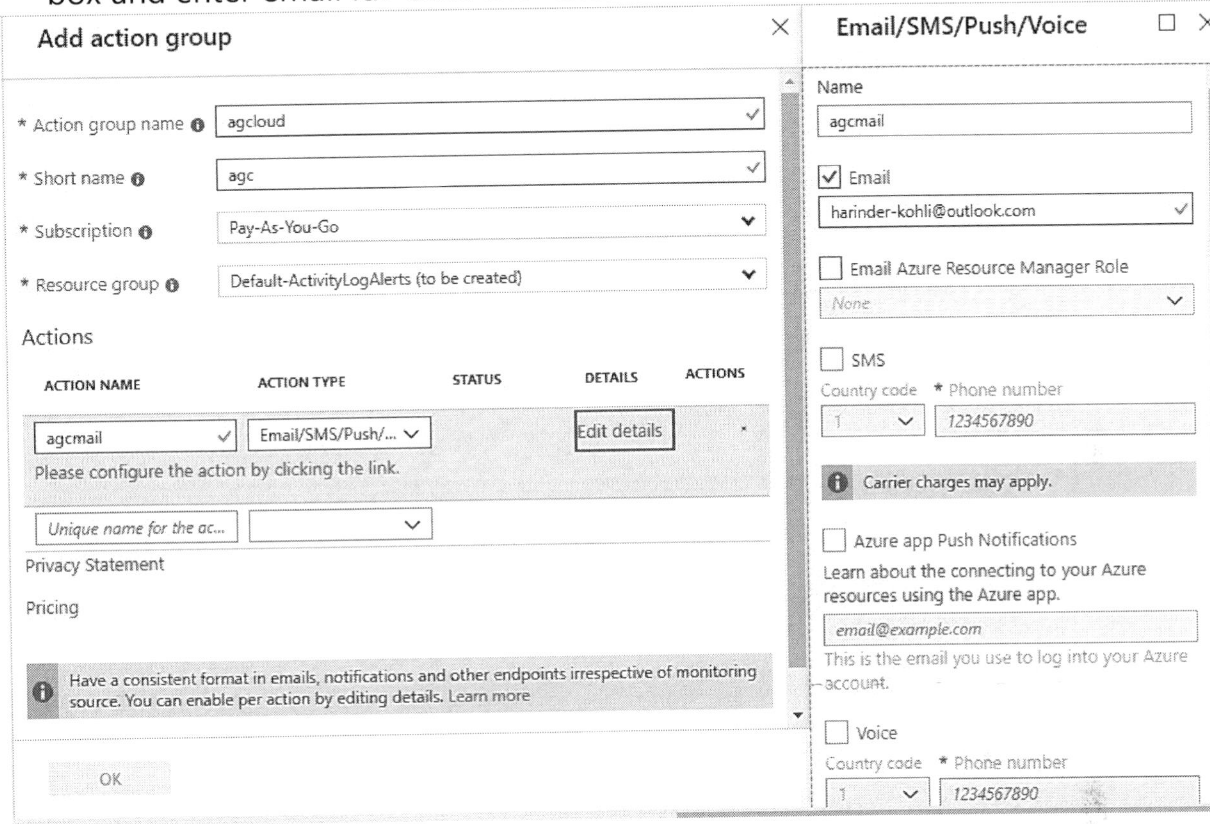

Note 1: You can add Multiple action types in a group.

Note 2: Readers are advised to check all action types and detail pane which opens for that Action type.

3. You can now see Action group created in Action Group pane.

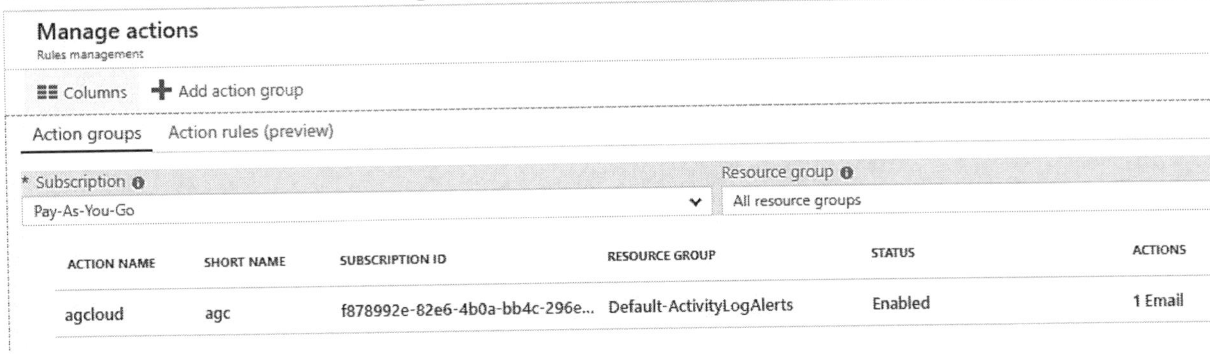

Alerts

Alerts proactively notify you when important conditions are found in your monitoring data. They allow you to identify and address issues before the users of your system notice them.

For Example you can create an alert on Virtual Machine Metric that if CPU utilization goes above 70% then send an email or start an additional instance.

Architecture Overview of Alerts

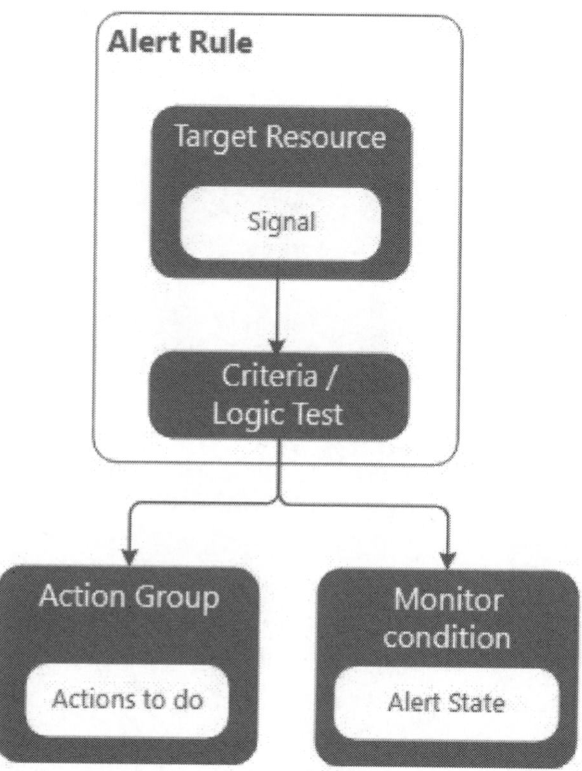

Alert Rule: The alert rule captures the target and criteria for alerting.
Target Resource: A target can be any Azure resource such as virtual machine, a storage account, a virtual machine scale set, a Log Analytics workspace, or an Application Insights resource.
Signal: Signals are emitted by the target resource and can be of several types - Metric, Activity log, Application Insights, and Log.
Criteria: Criteria is combination of Signal and Logic applied on a Target resource.
Action: A specific action taken when the alert is fired and is specified in Action Group.

Exercise 104: Create an alert on Metric (Percentage CPU) for VM

In this lab we will create Alert on Metric (Percentage CPU) with a criteria that if CPU utilization goes above 70% in VM VMFE1 hen notify through an e-mail. We will use Action group created in Exercise 103 for notification.

1. In Monitor Dashboard Click Alert in left pane>Alert Pane opens.

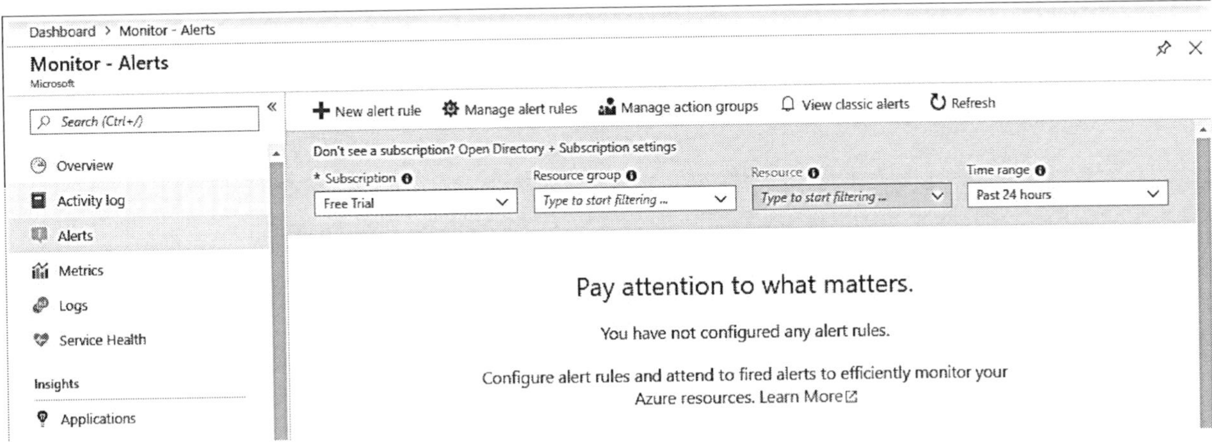

2. In Alert pane click + New Alert Rule> Create rule blade opens>Click select under Resource>Select a resource blade opens>In Resource type drop down box select Virtual Machines>Under resources select VM VMFE1>Done.

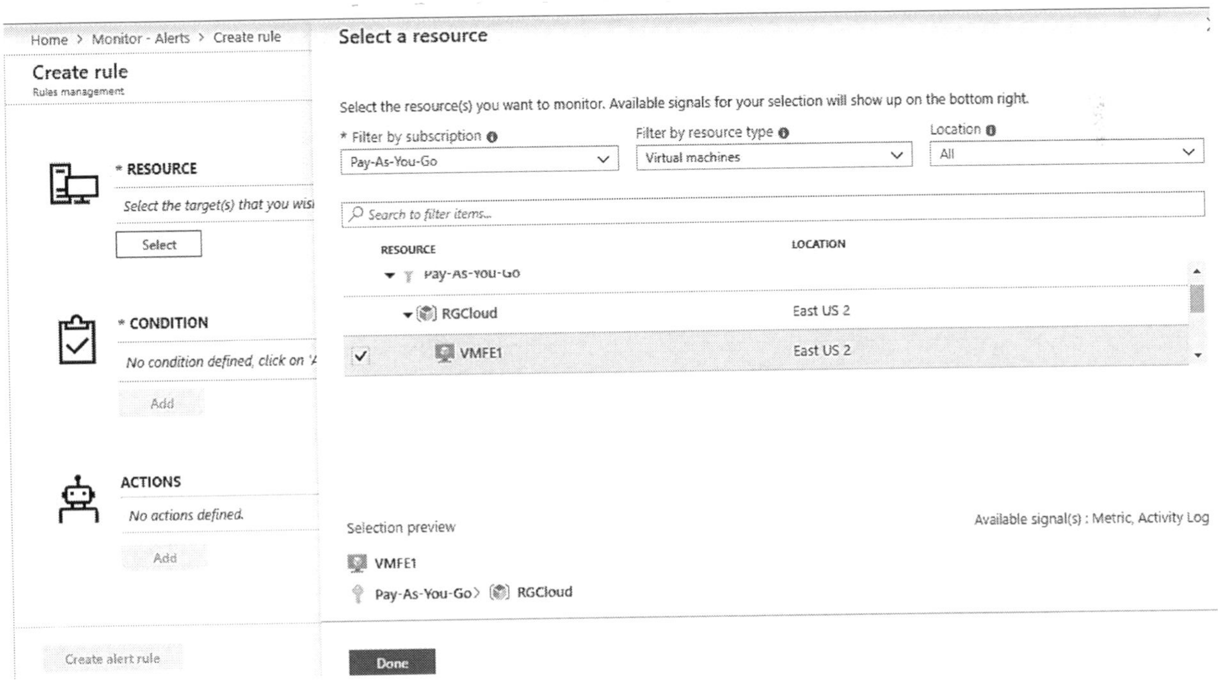

Note: You have option of accessing Alert from VM VMFE1 dashboard also.

3. Under Condition Click Add> Configure Signal Logic Blade opens.

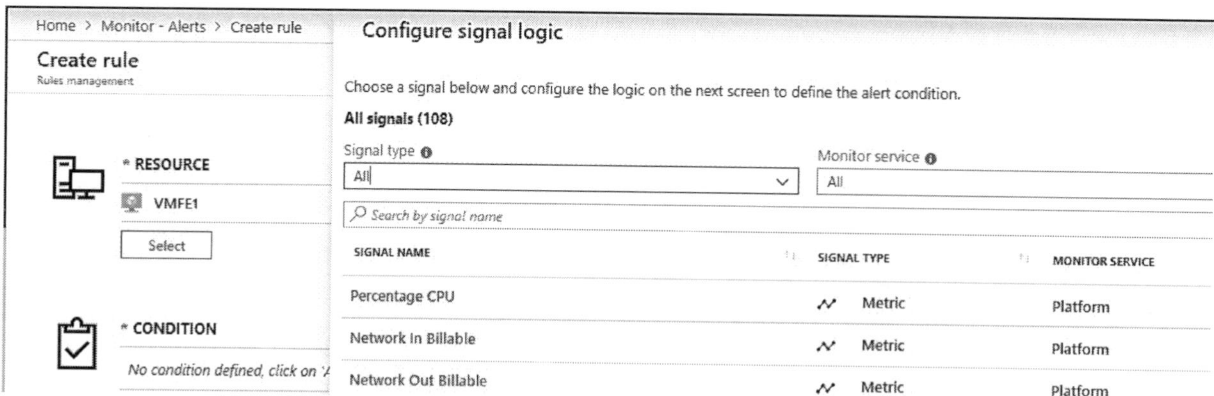

4. Select Percentage CPU>Percentage Platform blade opens>Scroll down> In Threshold Box enter 70>Click Done

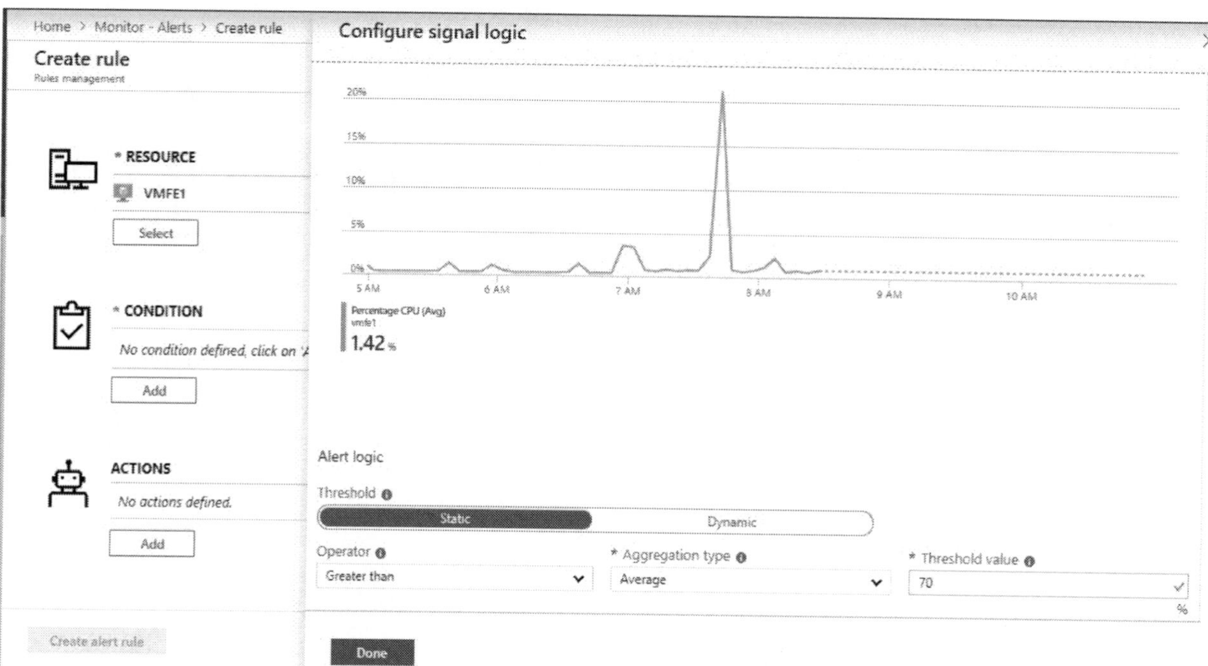

5. Under Actions Click Add> Select an Action Group blade opens>Select action group Created in Exercise 103>Add>

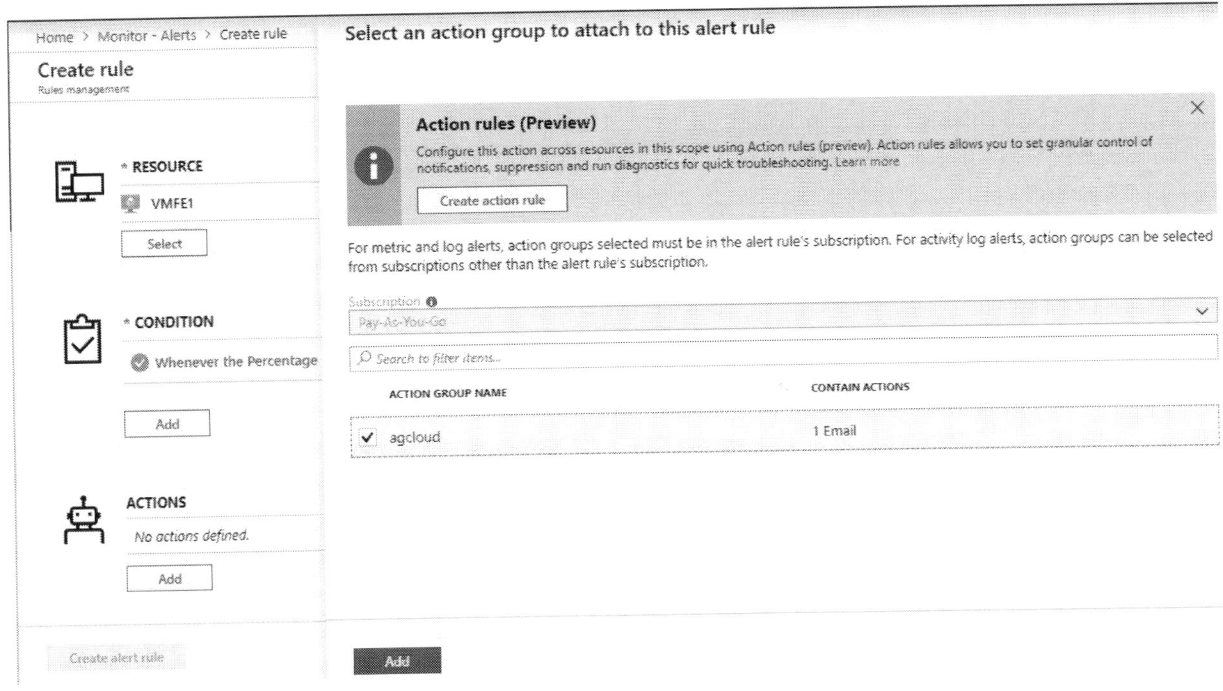

6. In Alert Details Enter a name for Alert Rule, Select Severity Level>Select Yes for Rule creation>Enter a description>Click Create Alert Rule.

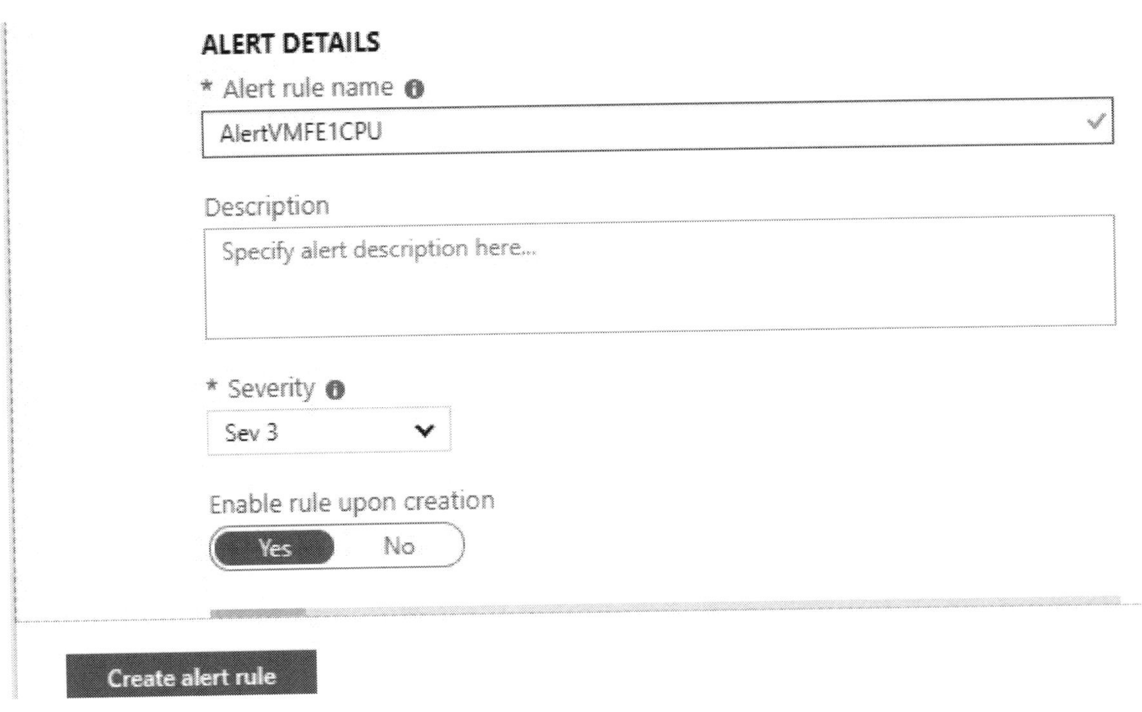

7. In Alert pane click Manage alert Rules>You can see the alert rule created> If required you can edit the rule also.

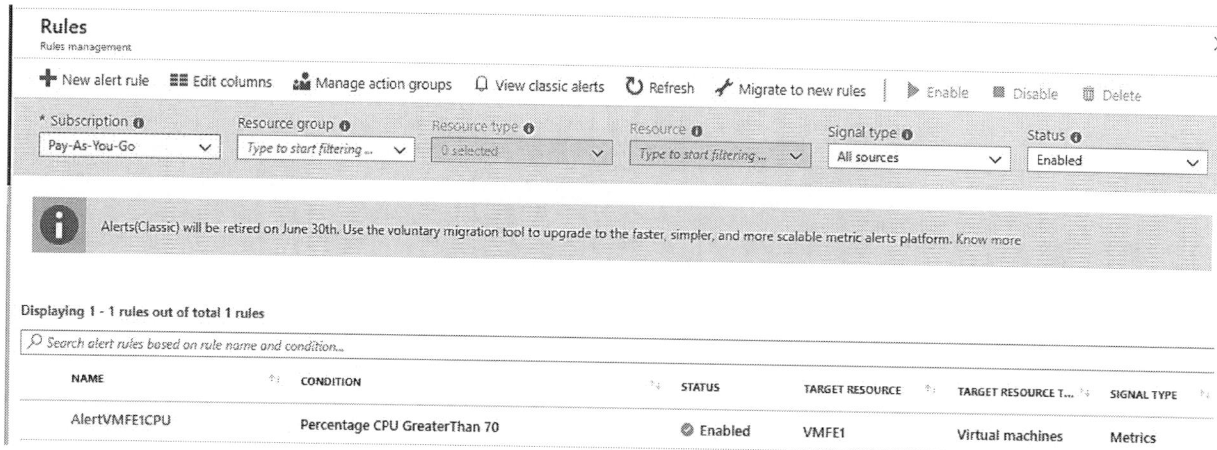

Exercise 105: Accessing Alert from Resource (VM) Dashboard

In Azure Portal go VM VMFE1> Under Monitoring Click Alerts in left pane>Alert Pane opens as shown below.

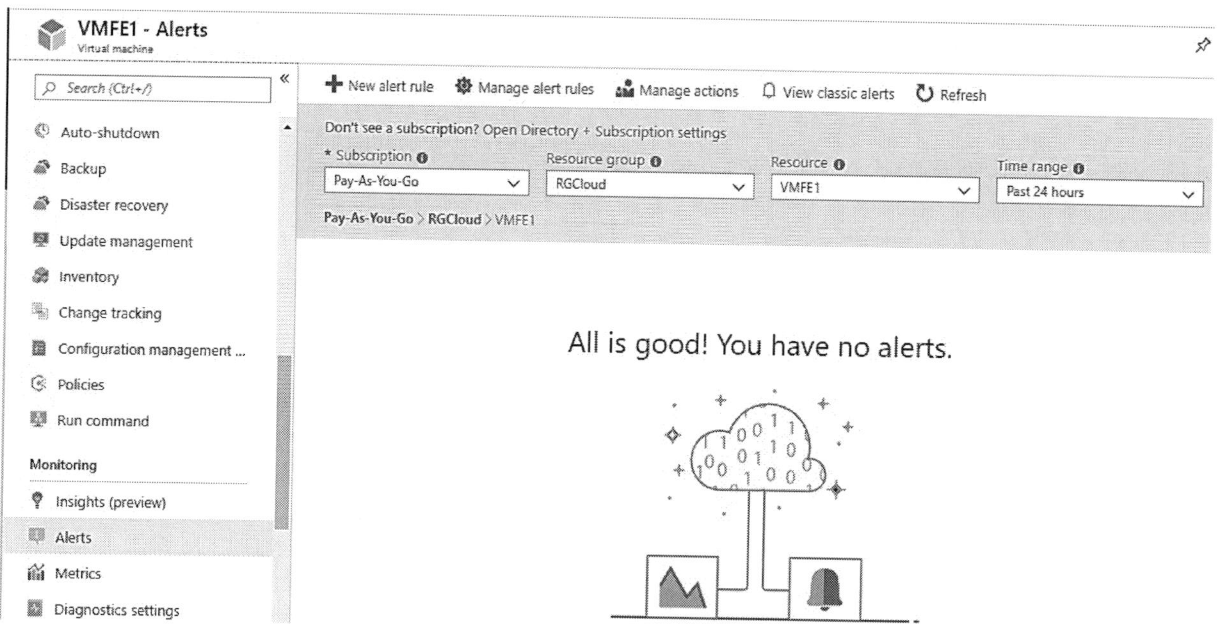

Log Analytics

Log Analytics is a service in Operations Management Suite (OMS) that helps you collect and analyze data generated by resources in your cloud and on-premises environments.

It gives you real-time insights using integrated search and custom dashboards to readily analyze millions of records across all of your workloads and servers regardless of their physical location.

Log Analytics Architecture

Log Analytics has 2 components – OMS Workspace & Monitoring Agent.

The combined solution of Log Analytics service and OMS repository is known as OMS Workspace. OMS repository is hosted in the Azure cloud.

Microsoft Monitoring Agent is installed on the connected source. Data is collected into the repository from connected sources.

Figure below shows Log Analytics collecting and analyzing data generated by resources in Azure, on-premises and other Clouds.

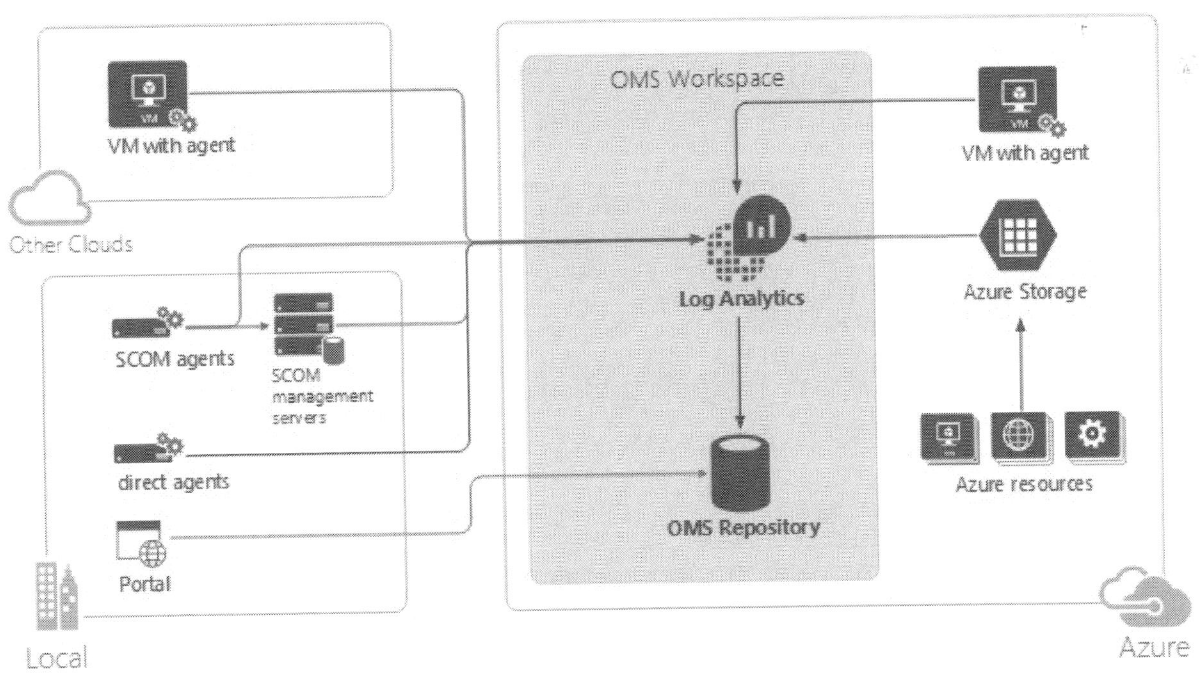

Data Collection from Connected Sources & Azure Managed Resources

Connected Sources can be on-premises or Cloud Resources. All Resources which you have created in your Subscription will appear in Log Analytics Dashboard under various Data Sources. You can add following Connected Sources in Log Analytics Services.

1. On-Premises Windows & Linux Servers with MS Monitoring Agent Installed.
2. Azure VMs with Microsoft Monitoring Agent virtual machine extension.
3. Azure Storage Accounts.
4. Azure Activity Logs
5. Azure Resources: You can add Azure Resources to Log Analytics which you have created in your subscription. For example following Azure Resources I have created in My Subscription and they appear under Azure Resources in Log Analytics Dashboard. You can enable all of them or enable as per your requirement to send Monitoring Data to Log Analytics Services.

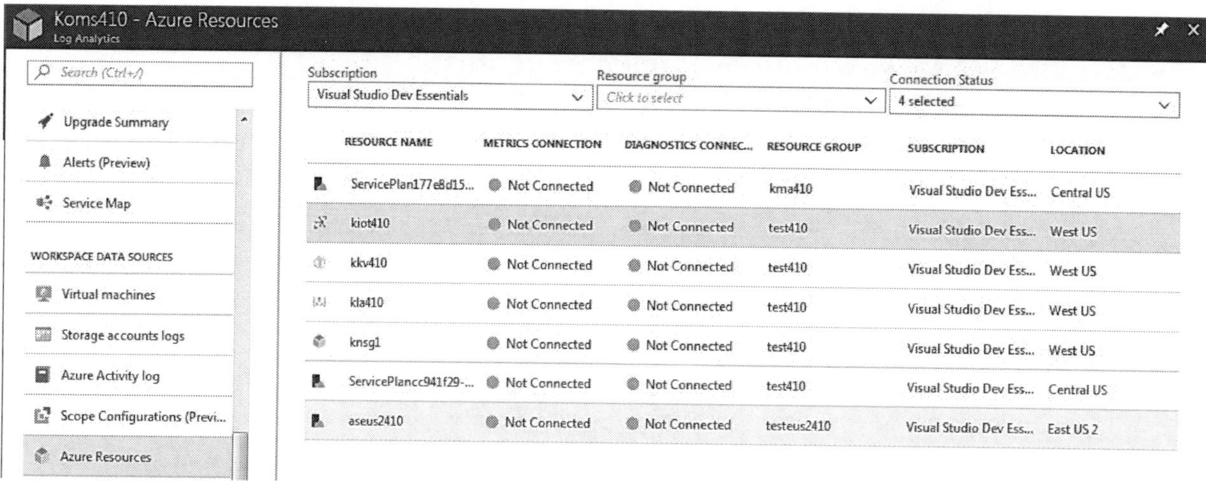

Data Sources

Data sources are configured on connected sources. Data sources can be IIS Logs, Performance Counters, Syslog, windows security events, windows firewall log, Network Security group.

Design Nuggets: You can create multiple workspaces in Azure Subscription. Workspaces are independent of each other and that data collected from each workspace cannot be viewed in another workspace.

Log Analytics Working, Reporting and Analyzing data

Log Analytics collects data from managed resources into a central repository. This data could include events, performance data, or custom data provided through the API. Once collected, the data is available for alerting, analysis, and export.

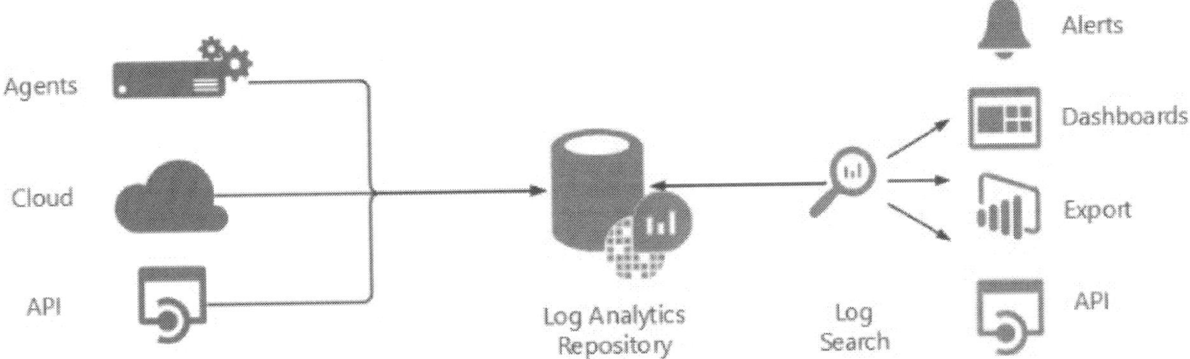

Log Analytics includes a powerful query language to extract data stored in the repository. The result of the query can be viewed in following ways:

Dashboard: You can view the result of the query in Log Analytics Dashboard.
Export: You can export the results of any query to analyze it outside of Log Analytics. You can schedule a regular export to Power BI which provides significant visualization and analysis capabilities.
Log Search API. Log Analytics has a REST API for collecting data from any client. This allows you to programmatically work with data collected in the repository or access it from another monitoring tool.

Alerting

You can create Alerts on the Log search data. In addition to creating an alert record in the Log Analytics repository, alerts can take the following actions.

Email. Send an email to proactively notify you of a detected issue.

Runbook. An alert in Log Analytics can start a runbook in Azure Automation. This is typically done to attempt to correct the detected issue. The runbook can be started in the cloud in the case of an issue in Azure or another cloud, or it could be started on a local agent for an issue on a physical or virtual machine.

Webhook. An alert can start a webhook and pass it data from the results of the log search. This allows integration with external services such as an alternate alerting system, or it may attempt to take corrective action for an external web site.

Exercise 106: Monitoring IIS Web Server with Log Analytics

In this exercise we will monitor IIS server running in Azure VM VMFE1. VMFE1 was created in Exercise 25, Part 1 Book. There are 4 steps involved in this: Creating Log Analytics workspace, Add Connected source, Add data source and Query IIS Log data using log search.

Step 1: Create Log Analytics workspace (Log Analytics service + OMS Repository)

1. Click + Create a resource > Management Tools > Log Analytics> create Log Analytics workspace blade opens>For name I entered LACloud>For Resource Group I selected create new resource group with name mlogs> East US 2 Location >Click ok>After Validation is successful close the pane.

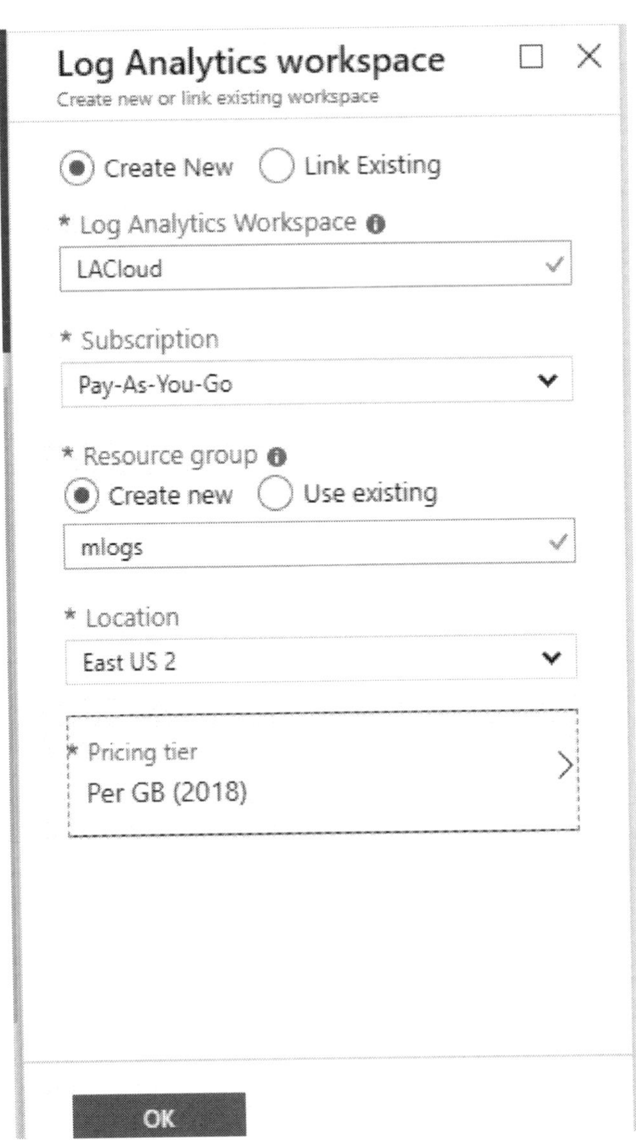

2. **Accessing Log Analytics workspace LACloud dashboard**> Click All resources in left pane>All Resources blade opens>Scroll down and you can see LACloud.

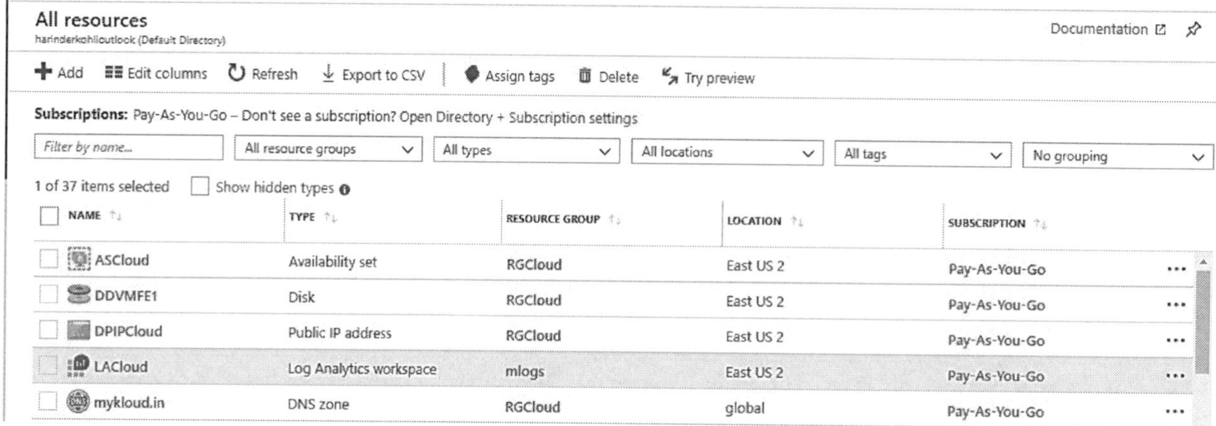

3. Click LACloud (Fourth row in above figure)> LACloud dashboard opens as shown below> in left pane we scrolled down to see Workspace Data sources options.

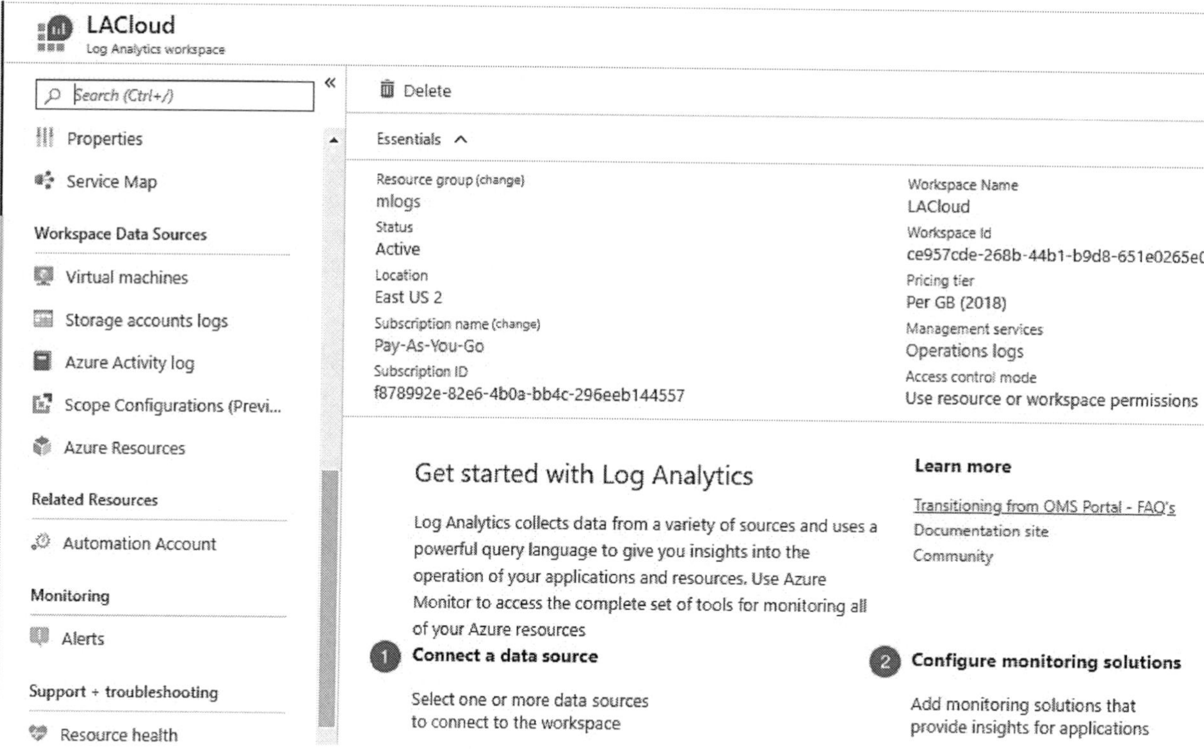

Step 2: Add Connected Source (Azure VM VMFE1 running IIS Web Server) by installing Log Analytics VM Extension or Microsoft Monitoring Agent (MMA)

1. In Log Analytics workspace dashboard in left pane scroll down and under Workspace Data sources click Virtual Machines> Right pane shows the Virtual Machine VMFE1 and the status of Log Analytics Connection. Which in this case is not connected.

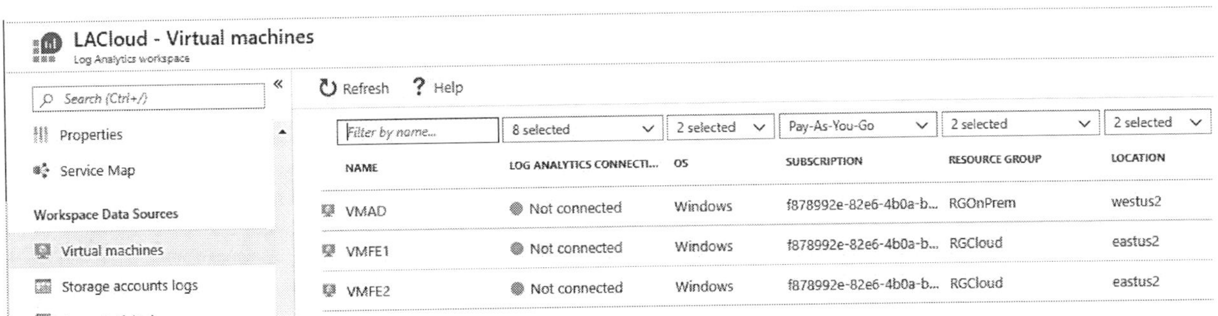

2. In right pane click VM VMFE1> Connect Blade opens> Click Connect. This will install Log Analytics Agent VM Extension> After a minute it gets connected. Status will show This workspace. Close the connect blade.

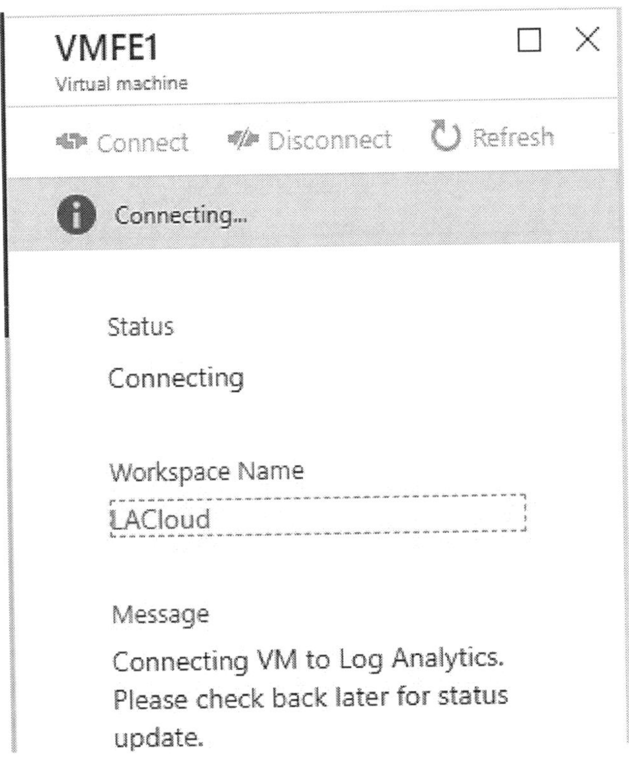

Note: Log Analytics VM Extension installs Microsoft Monitoring Agent on the machine.

Step 3: Add Data Source – IIS log

1. In Log Analytics workspace dashboard click Advanced Settings in left pane> In Advanced Setting pane click Data>Click IIS logs> Select Collect IIS Log files>Save> Close the Advance Settings pane.

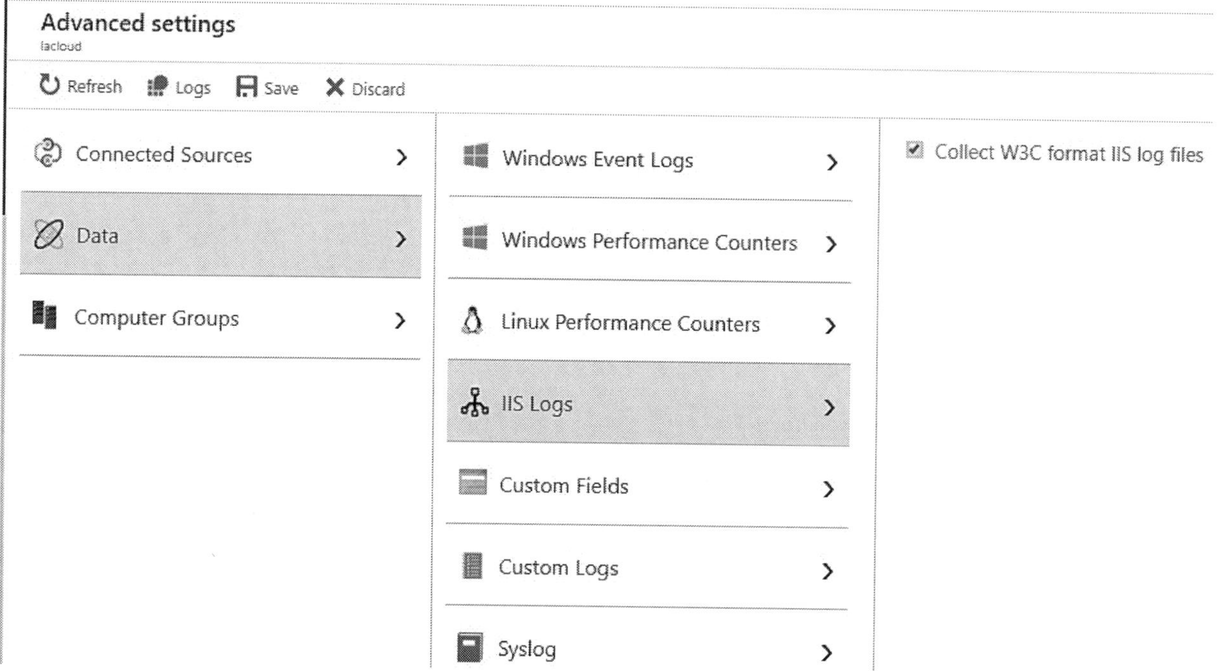

2. Click Windows Performance Counters>In right pane you can see various options for performance counters. We are not adding performance counters.

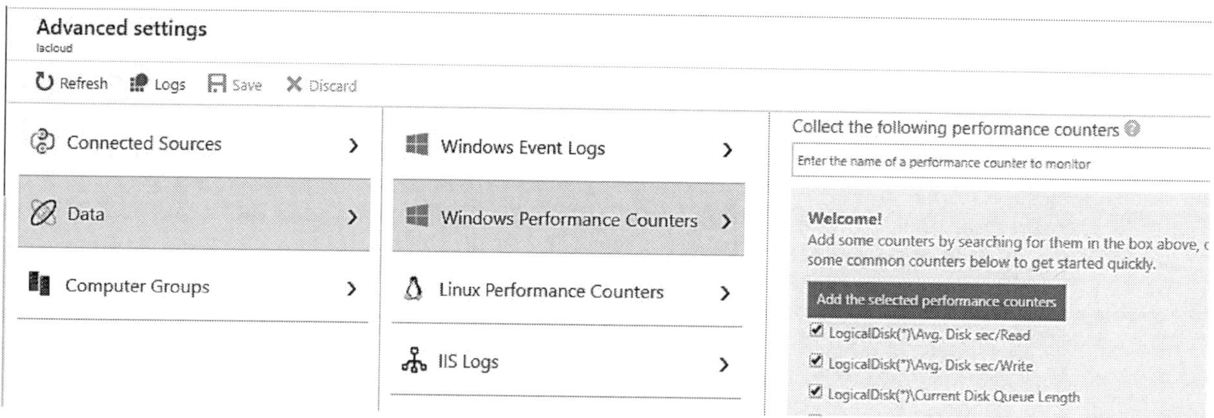

Readers are advised to scroll down and see all options for counters.

Step 4: Check Client IP which have accessed default Website on VM VMFE1

1. Access Default Website on VMFE1 using Chrome and Tor Browser.
2. In Log Analytics workspace dashboard click Logs in left pane> Logs Query Pane opens as shown below.

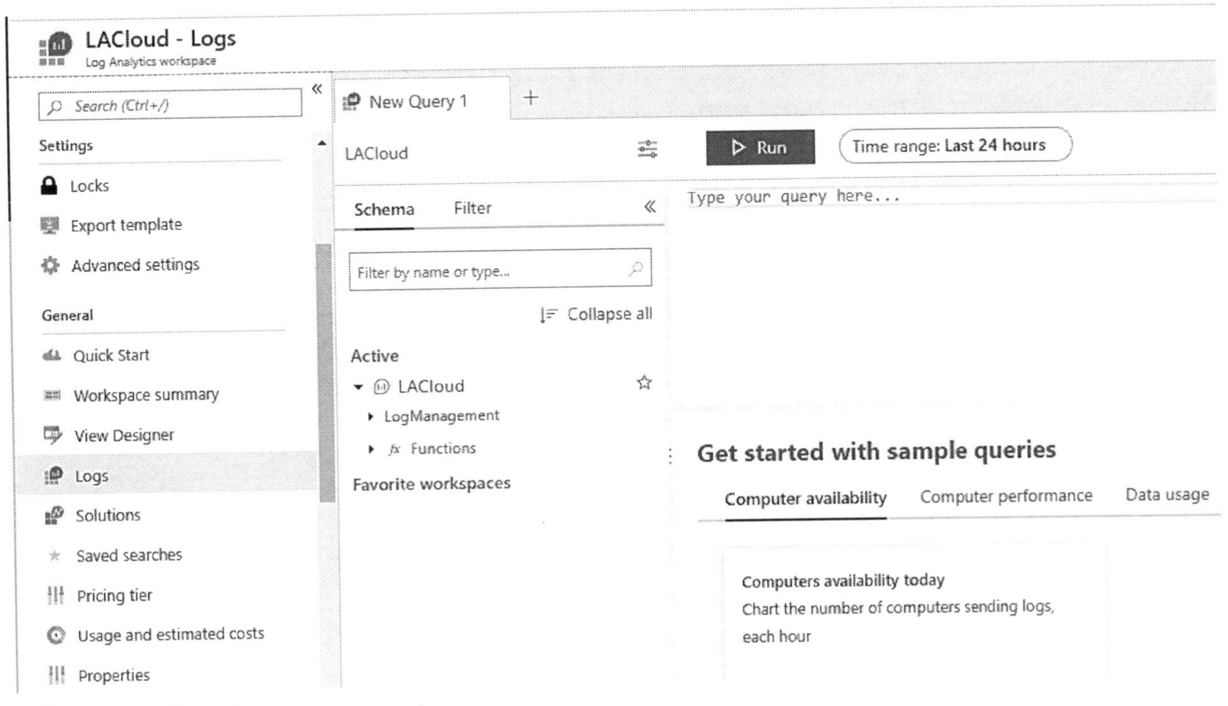

3. In Right pane enter Query **W3CIISLog | summarize count() by cIP**> Click Run>You can see the Client IPs which have accessed default website.

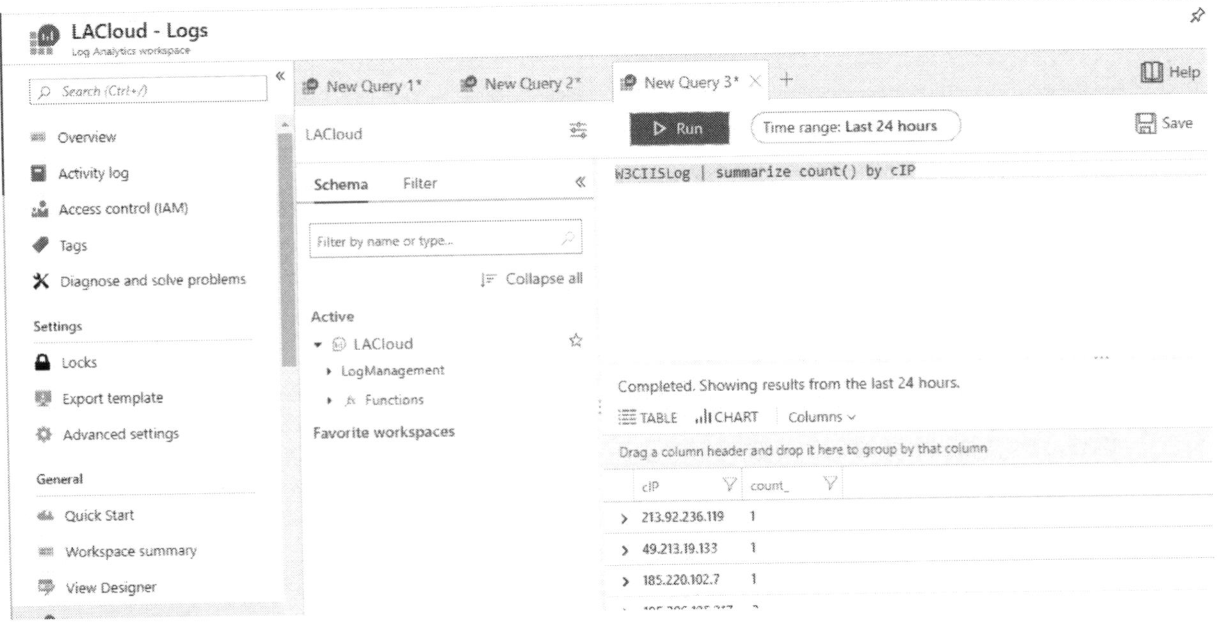

Management Solutions

Management solution packs have Pre Built rules and Algorithms that perform analysis leveraging Log Analytics services. Management solutions are added to Log Analytics Workspace.

Management solutions are available both from Microsoft and partners.

Below are some of the Management solutions which can be added to Log Analytics service.

Active Directory Health Check: Active Directory Health Check solution assesses the risk and health of your server environments (Domain Controllers) on a regular interval. The solution provides a prioritized list of recommendations specific to your deployed server infrastructure.

AD Replication Status: The AD Replication Status solution pack regularly monitors your Active Directory environment for any replication failures.

Alert Management Solution: The Alert Management solution helps you analyze all of the alerts in your Log Analytics repository.

Network Performance Monitor (NPM): The Network Performance Monitor management solution is a network monitoring solution that monitors the health, availability and reachability of networks.

Network Security Group analytics solution: Network Security Group analytics management solutions collect diagnostics logs directly from Network Security Groups for analyzing them in Log analytics.

Container Monitoring Solution: Container Monitoring Solution shows which containers are running, what container image they're running, and where containers are running. You can view detailed audit information showing commands used with containers.

Key Vault Analytics solution: Azure Key Vault solution in Log Analytics reviews Azure Key Vault logs.

Office 365 management solution: Office 365 management solution allows you to monitor your Office 365 environment in Log Analytics.

Service Fabric Analytics: Identify and troubleshoot issues across Service fabric Clusters.

Service Maps: Automatically discovers and Maps servers and their dependencies in real-time. Service Map automatically discovers application components on Windows and Linux systems and maps the communication between services. It also consolidates data collected by other services and solutions to assist you in analyzing performance and identifying issues. Service Map shows connections between servers, processes, and ports across any TCP-connected architecture, with no configuration required other than the installation of an agent.

SQL Server Health Check: SQL Health Check solution assesses the risk and health of your SQL Server environments on a regular interval.

Update Management: Identifies and orchestrates the installation of missing system updates. This solution requires both Log Analytics and Automation account.

Change Tracking: Tracks configuration changes across your servers. This solution requires both Log Analytics and Automation account.

Antimalware Assessment: OMS Antimalware Assessment solution helps you identify servers that are infected or at increased risk of infection by malware.

Azure Site Recovery: Monitor's Virtual Machine replication status for your azure Site Recovery Vault.

IT Service Management (ITSM) connector: Connects Log Analytics with ITSM Products such as servicenow.

Exercise 107: Installing Management Solution (NSG Analytics)

In this Exercise we will add Management Solution Network Security Group Analytics to Log Analytics. It will show details of NSG flows. In Exercise 99 we enabled Diagnostic Logs for Network Security Group NSGCloud and sent the logs to Log Analytics workspace.

1. In Log Analytics workspace dashboard click Workspace Summary in left pane.

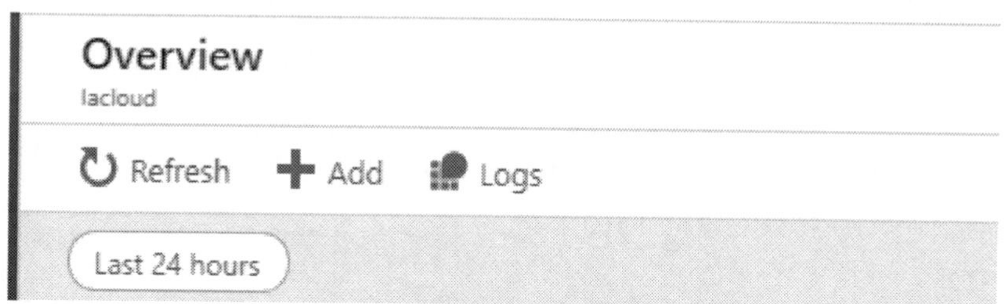

2. Click + Add in Workspace Summary blade>Management Tools Pane opens> In Recommended Solutions Click more>Recommended blade opens>Scroll down and select **Azure Network Security Group Analytics.**

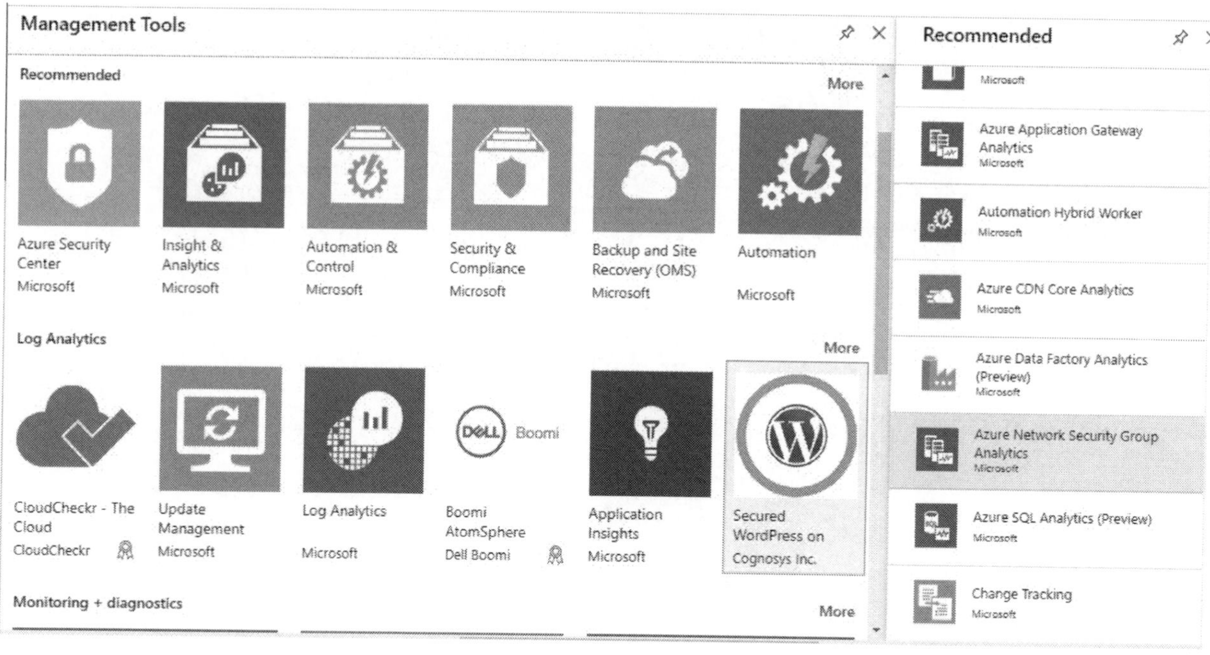

3. Azure Network Security Group Analytics blade opens>Click Create.

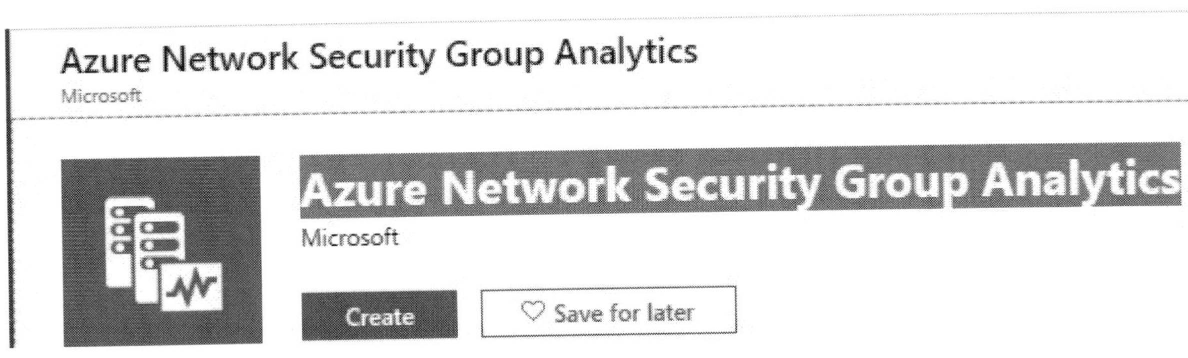

4. Create new Solution Blade opens> Click create (Not Shown). Close the pane after Validation is successful.

5. After Deployment is succeeded go to Log Analytics Dashboard and click Solutions in left pane> You can see NSG Analytics Solution is added.

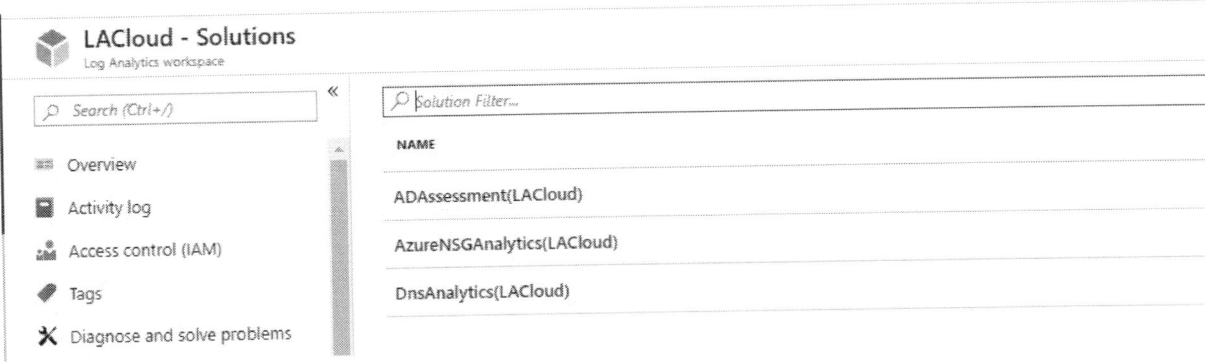

6. Wait for 1-2 hours and then Click on AzureNSGAnalytics as shown in previous figure> AzureNSGAnalytics dashboard opens>Click on Summary and you can see the NSG Analytics.

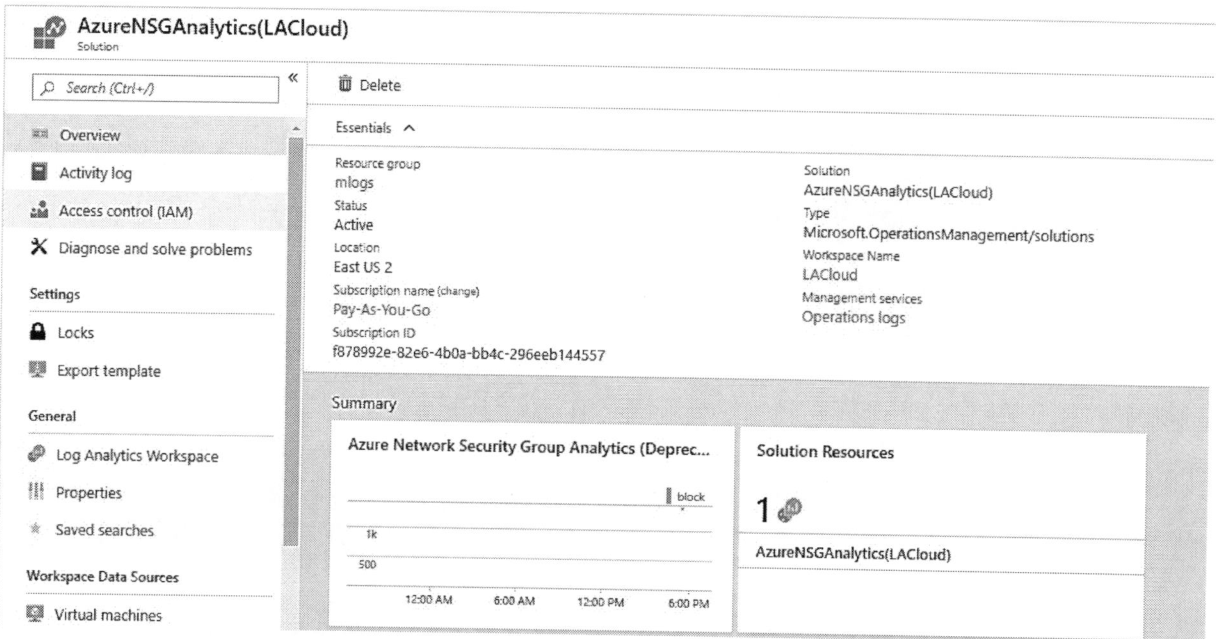

7. Click on the summary Box and you can see the details of NSG Flows.

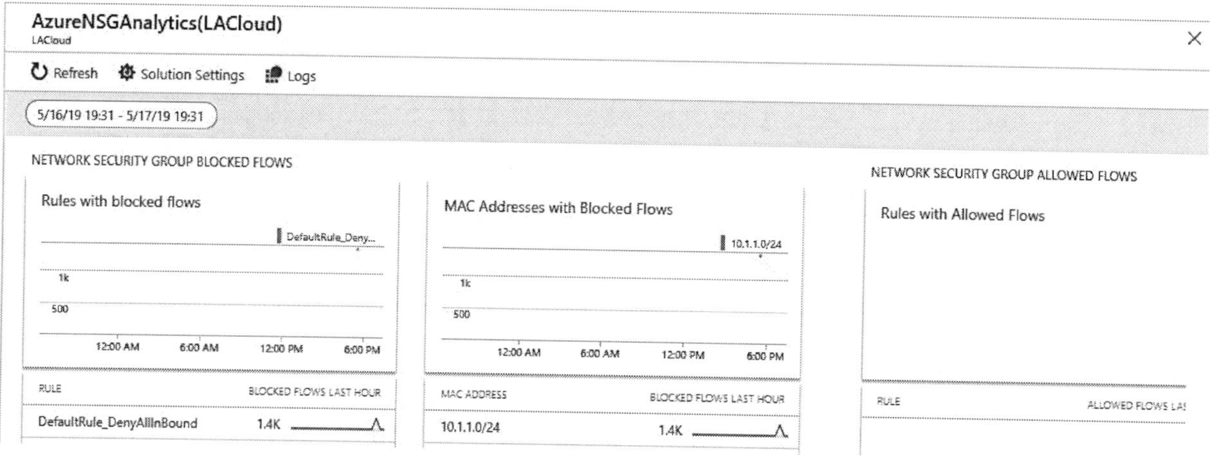

Exercise 108: Installing Microsoft Monitoring Agent in On-Premises VM

In this exercise we will just demonstrate the steps on how to install MMA in On-Premises Server or VM.

1. From your on-premises VM open browser and log on to Azure Portal.
2. Go to Log Analytics Workspace dashboard> Click Advanced Settings in left pane>Connected Sources> Select Windows or Linux Servers as per your requirement>In right pane download the agent on your Windows or Linux Machine> Note down Workspace ID and Primary Key. This will be required to register the server with Log Analytics Workspace during installation.

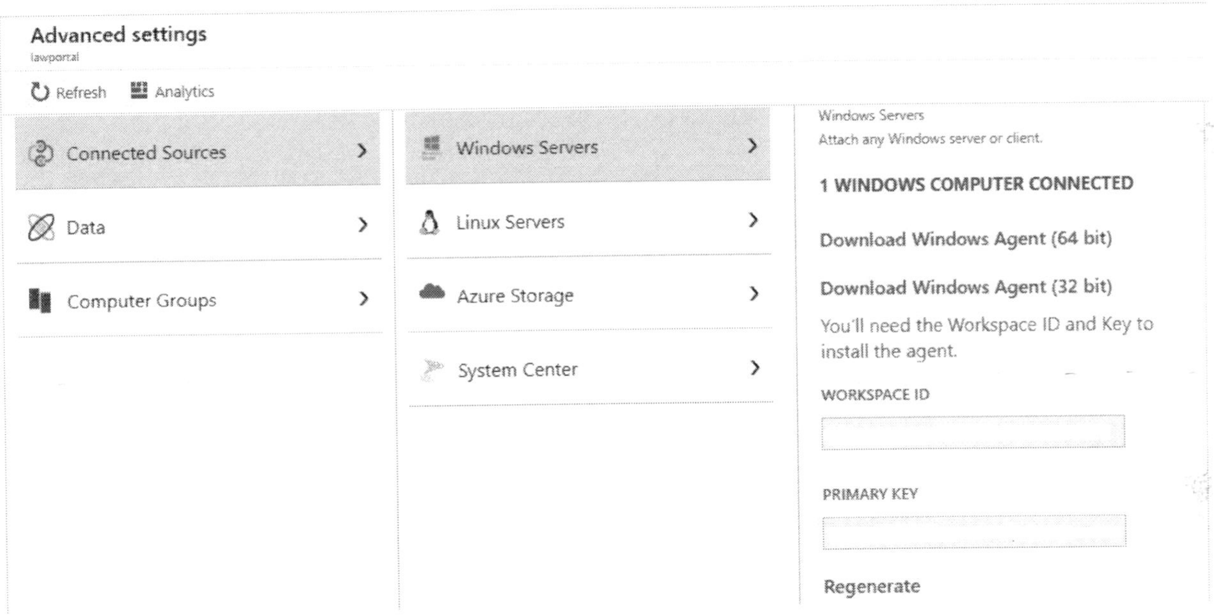

Advisor

Azure Advisor is a personalized recommendation engine that provides proactive best practices guidance for optimally configuring your Azure resources.

Azure Advisor gives recommendation to optimize across following **four** different areas.

High Availability
Performance
Security
Cost

All recommendations accessible in one place on the Azure portal. Azure Advisor is a free service.

Working

It analyzes your resource configuration and usage telemetry. It then recommends solutions to help improve the performance, security, and high availability of your resources while looking for opportunities to reduce your overall Azure spend.

Exercise 109: Checking Advisor Recommendations

1. In Azure Portal click Advisor in Left pane> Advisor Dashboard opens. It shows recommendation in 4 areas - High availability, Performance, Security and Cost.

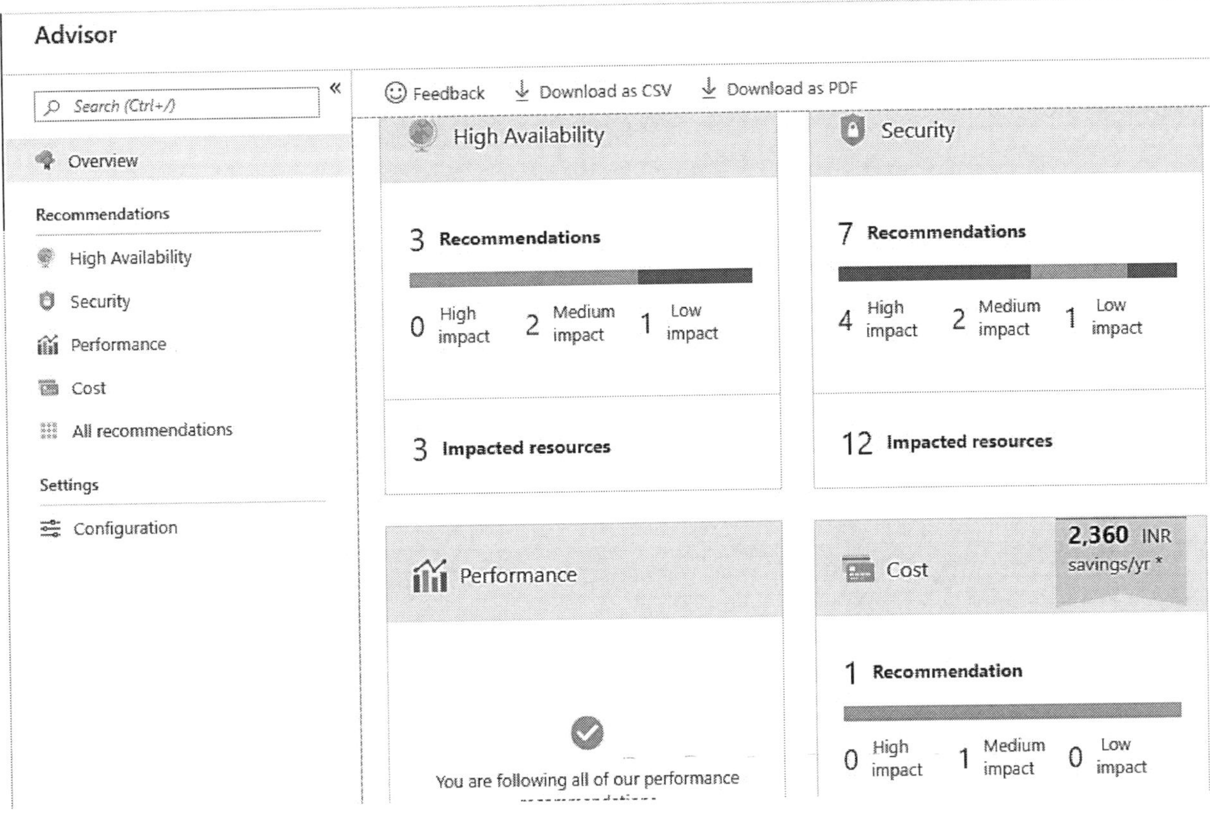

2. Click on High Availability Tab and you can see there are 3 Recommendations.

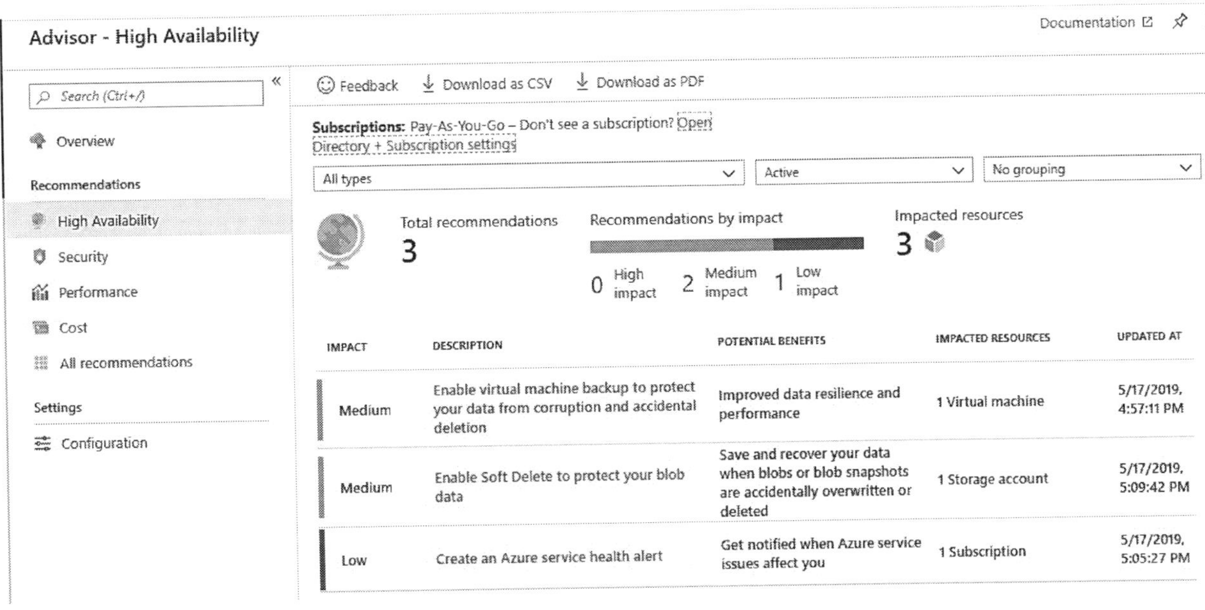

IMPACT	DESCRIPTION	POTENTIAL BENEFITS	IMPACTED RESOURCES	UPDATED AT
Medium	Enable virtual machine backup to protect your data from corruption and accidental deletion	Improved data resilience and performance	1 Virtual machine	5/17/2019, 4:57:11 PM
Medium	Enable Soft Delete to protect your blob data	Save and recover your data when blobs or blob snapshots are accidentally overwritten or deleted	1 Storage account	5/17/2019, 5:09:42 PM
Low	Create an Azure service health alert	Get notified when Azure service issues affect you	1 Subscription	5/17/2019, 5:05:27 PM

3. Click on Cost Tab and you can see their is 1 Recommendation. It says that you can save Indian Rupees 2360 If we delete Public IP which is currently not associated with any running Azure Resource. Recall that we created this Public IP in Chapter 1 in Part 1 Book.

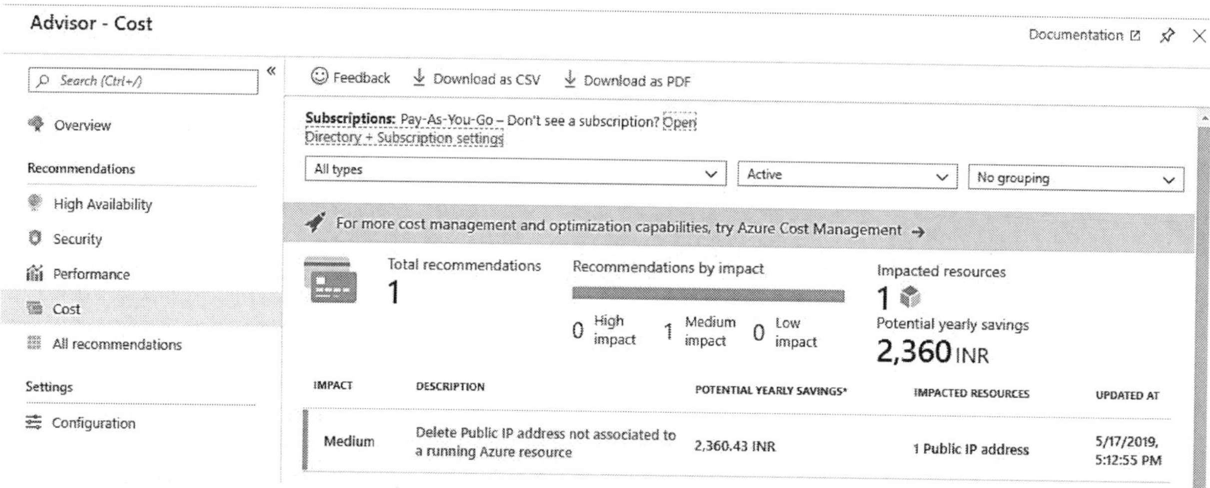

4. Click on Security Tab and you can see there are 7 Recommendations.

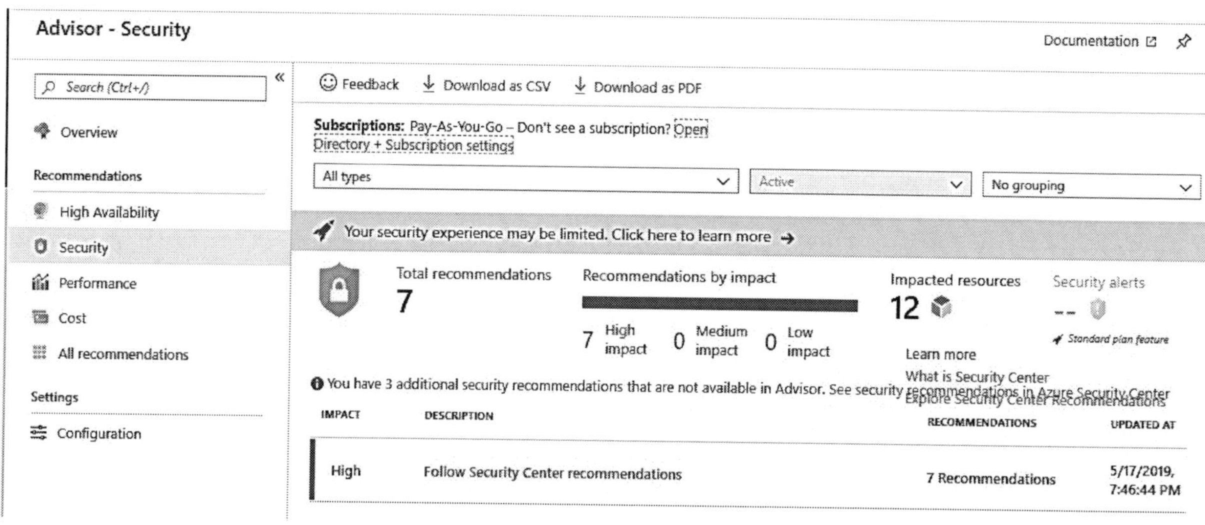

5. Click on the recommendation and its shows recommendation available from Security Center.

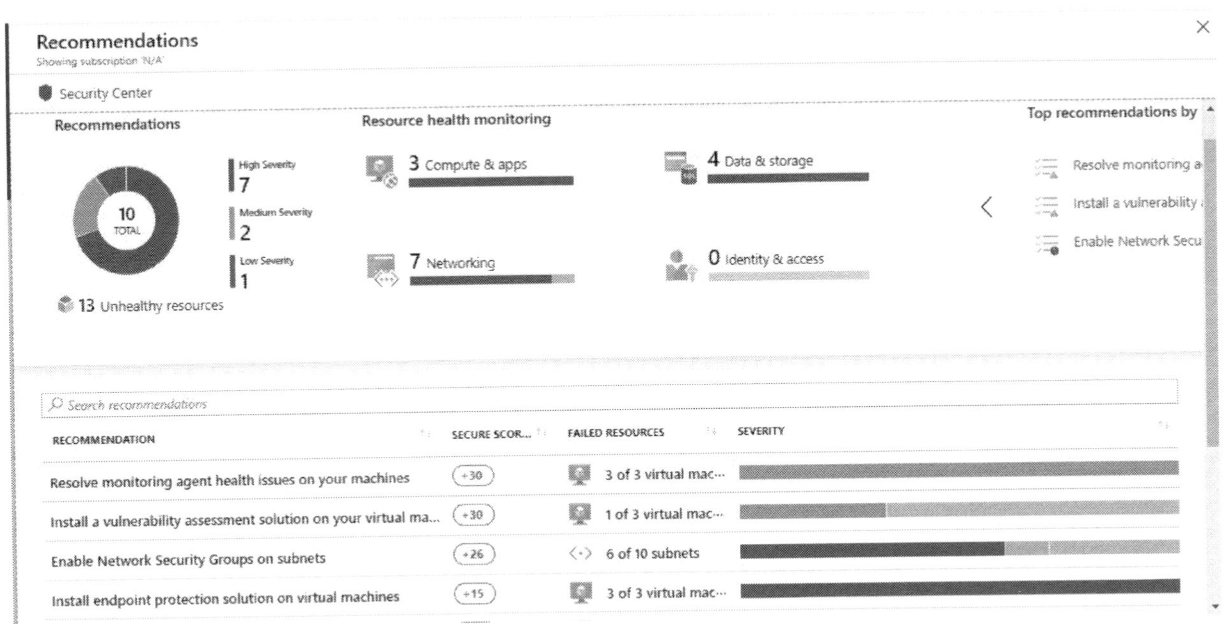

Azure Service Health

Azure Service Health provides status of Azure services which can affect your business critical applications. It also helps you prepare for upcoming planned maintenance. Azure Service Health alerts you and your teams via targeted and flexible notifications.

Service Health Events

Service Health tracks following three types of health events that may impact your resources:

1. **Service issues** - Problems in the Azure services that affect you right now.
2. **Planned maintenance** - Upcoming maintenance that can affect the availability of your services in the future.
3. **Health advisories** - Changes in Azure services that require your attention. Examples include when Azure features are deprecated or if you exceed a usage quota.

Exercise 110: Checking Service Health Events

1. Go to Monitor Dashboard>Click Service Health Tile in left pane> Service Health Dashboard Opens> currently there are no Service issues.

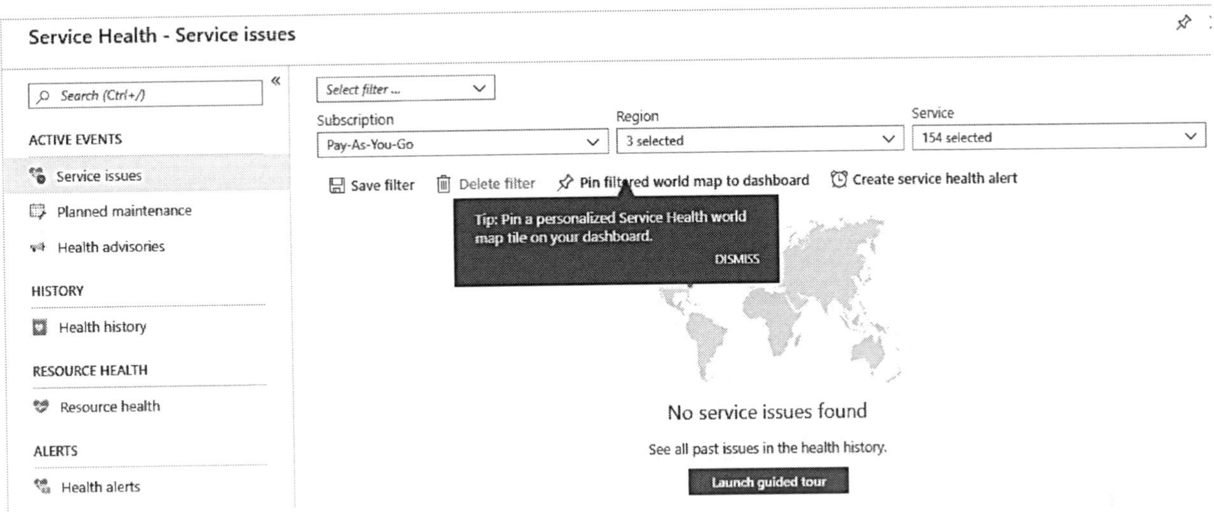

2. Click on Planned maintenance in left pane> No events are scheduled.

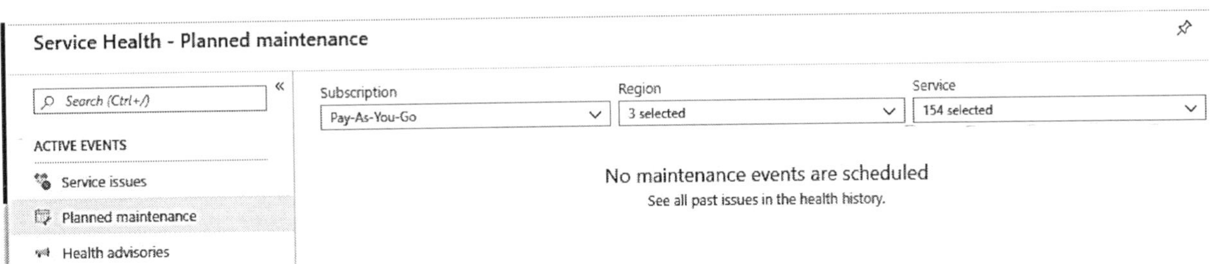

3. Click on Health advisories in left pane> No advisories are found.

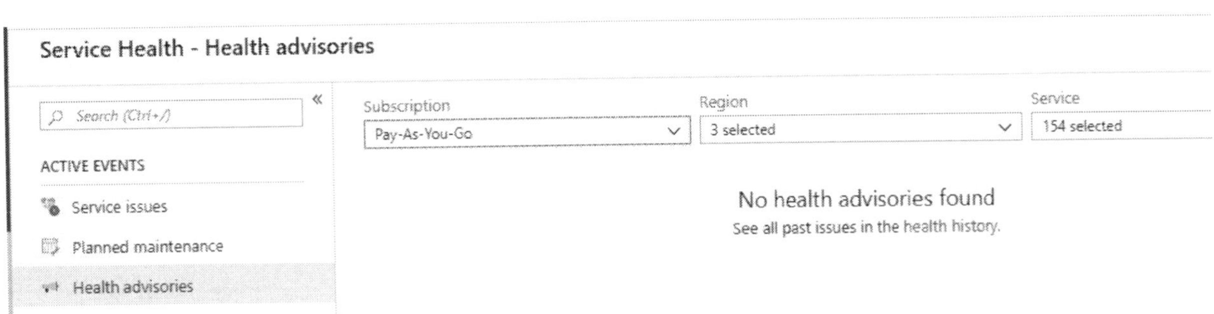

Note: Readers are advised to Check Resource Health Tab in left pane.

Exercise 111: Configuring Alerts for Service Health Events

In this Exercise we will create email Alert on Service Health events – Service Issues, Planned maintenance and Health Advisories.

1. In Service Health Dashboard click Health alerts in left pane.

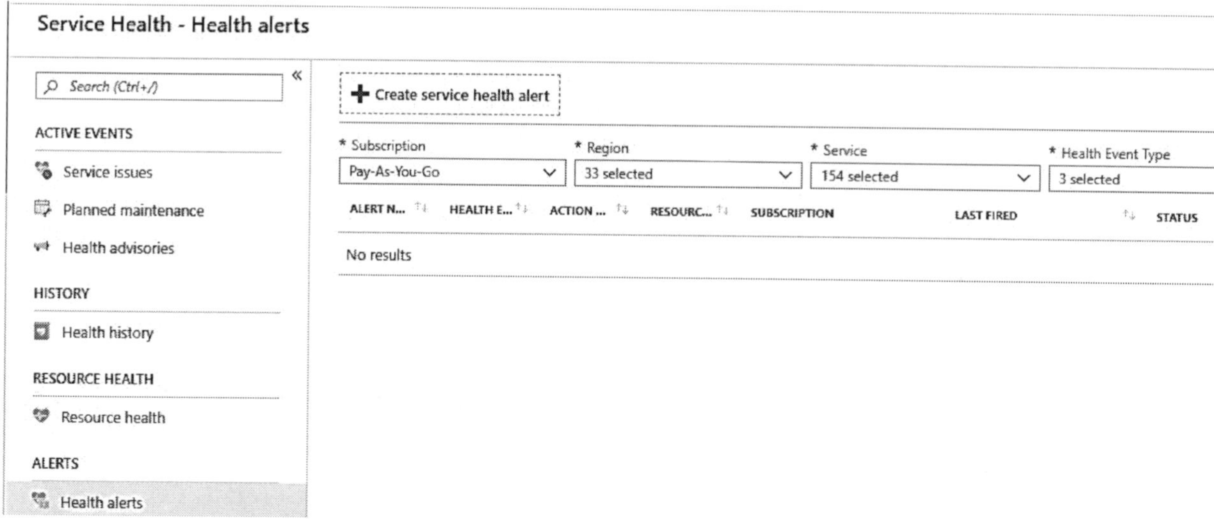

2. Click +Create Service Health Alert in Right pane>Add Rule Blade opens> Under Alert target Select Services & Region as per your req>Click Add under Actions to Select Action Group created in Exercise 153>Under Alert details Give a name and Select mlogs in Resource Groups> click Yes to enable rule and Click Create Alert Rule.

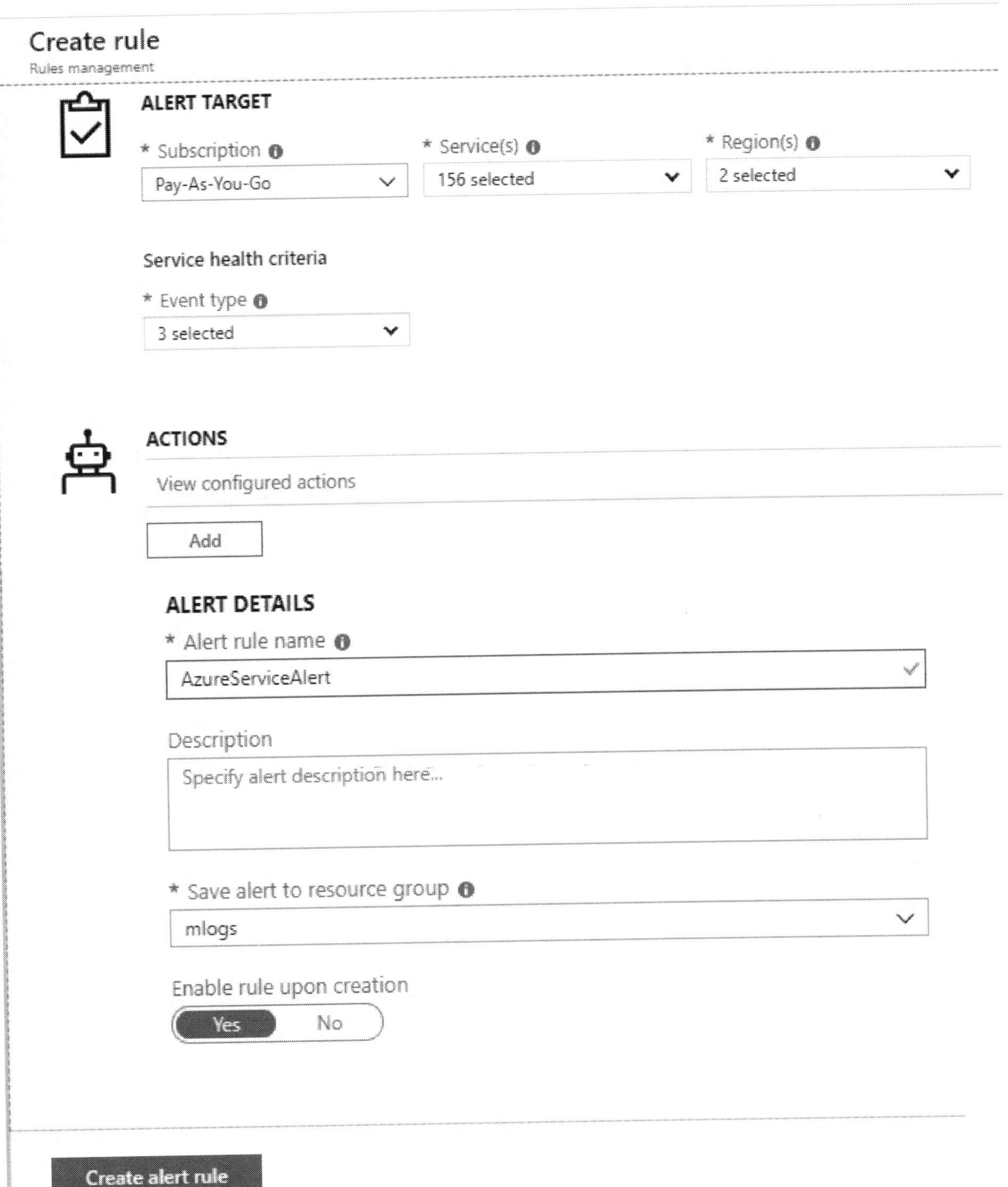

Create rule
Rules management
ALERT TARGET
* Subscription
Pay-As-You-Go
* Service(s)
156 selected
* Region(s)
2 selected
Service health criteria
* Event type
3 selected
ACTIONS
View configured actions
Add
ALERT DETAILS
* Alert rule name
AzureServiceAlert
Description
Specify alert description here...
* Save alert to resource group
mlogs
Enable rule upon creation
Yes
No
Create alert rule

Chapter 10 Monitor Virtual Networking

This Chapter covers following Topic Lessons

- Network Watcher
- Network Performance Monitor
- Requirements and Steps for Enabling Network Performance Monitor

This Chapter covers following Lab Exercises

- Enabling Network Watcher
- Network Watcher Capabilities
- Adding NPM in Log Analytics Workspace

Chapter Topology

In this chapter we will Network Watcher and Network Performance Monitor (NPM) to the Topology.

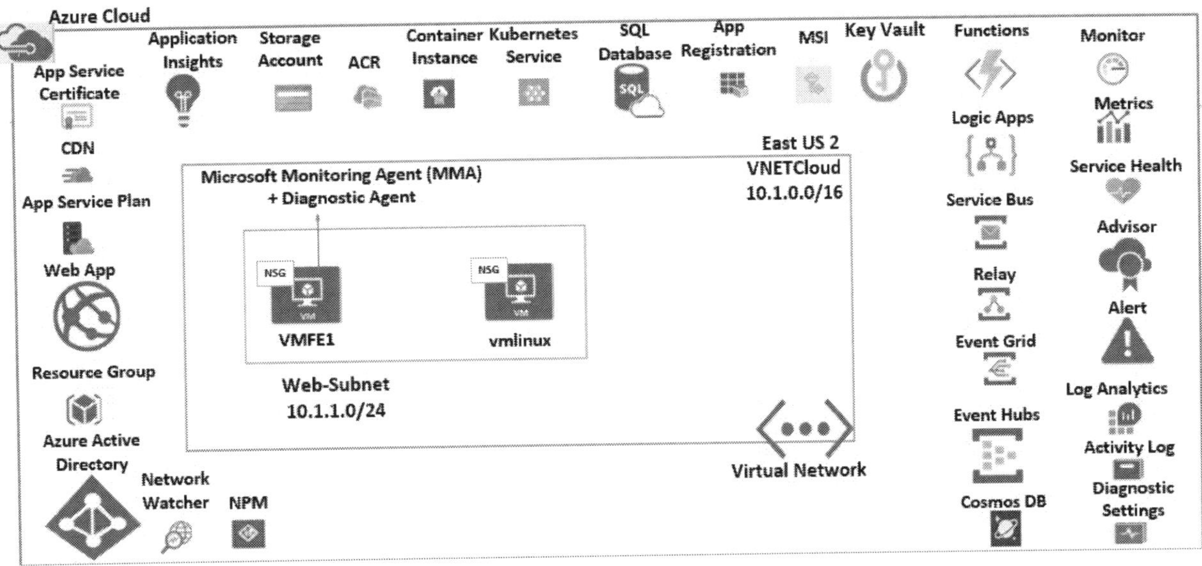

Network Watcher

Before going into details of Network watcher, let's discuss what happens without Network Watcher.

Without Network Watcher: Azure provides monitoring, troubleshooting, diagnostics and logging at **individual resource level** such as Virtual Machines, Virtual Network, Load Balancers, NSG, Application Gateway & ExpressRoute etc.

With Network Watcher: Network Watcher provides end to end Monitoring, Diagnostics and logging **across Resource Levels and across Network topology level.**

Network Watcher is a regional service and can only be ran against resources in the same region.

Exercise 112: Enabling Network Watcher (East US 2 Region)

In Azure Portal Click All Services in left pane>Under Networking Click Network Watcher> Network watcher Dashboard opens>You can Enable Network Watcher for all regions or in the region of your choice>Here we will enable for East US 2> Click 28 Region icon>Scroll down Select East US 2 Row and click ...>Click Enable Network Watcher.

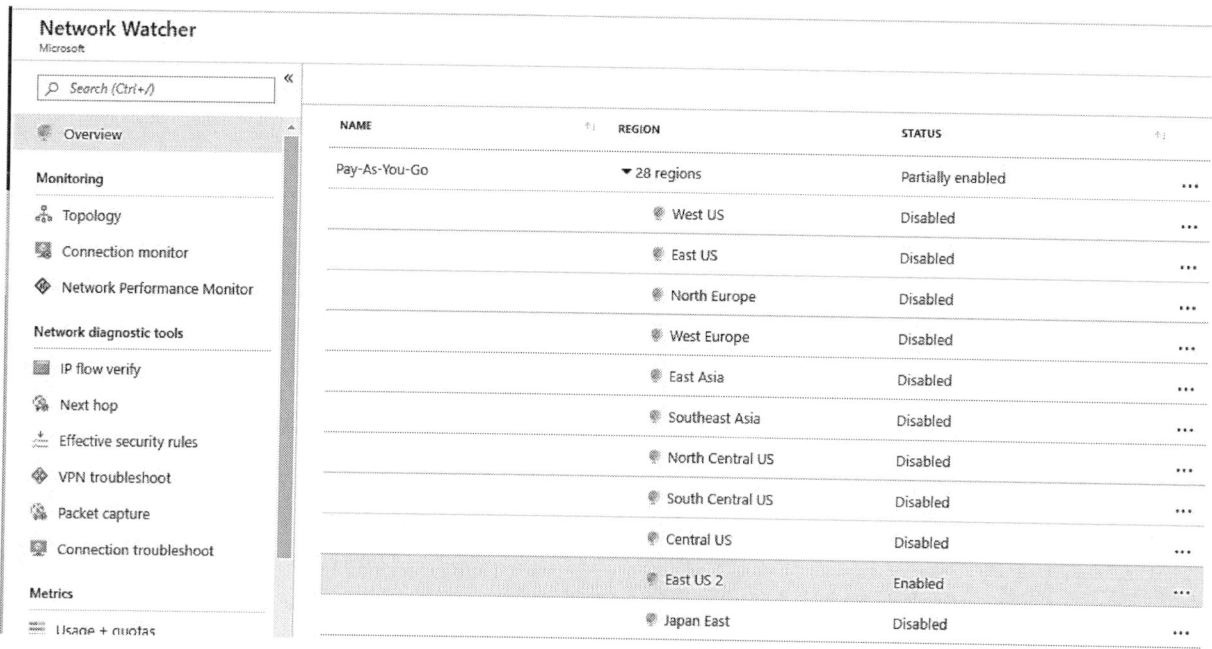

Exercise 113: Exploring Network Watcher Capabilities

Topology: Provides a network level topology diagram showing the various interconnections and associations between network resources of VNET in a RG.

Click Topology in left pane>in right pane select your Resource Group. You can see 3 VNETs – VNETCloud, VNET2 and VNET3 Connections.

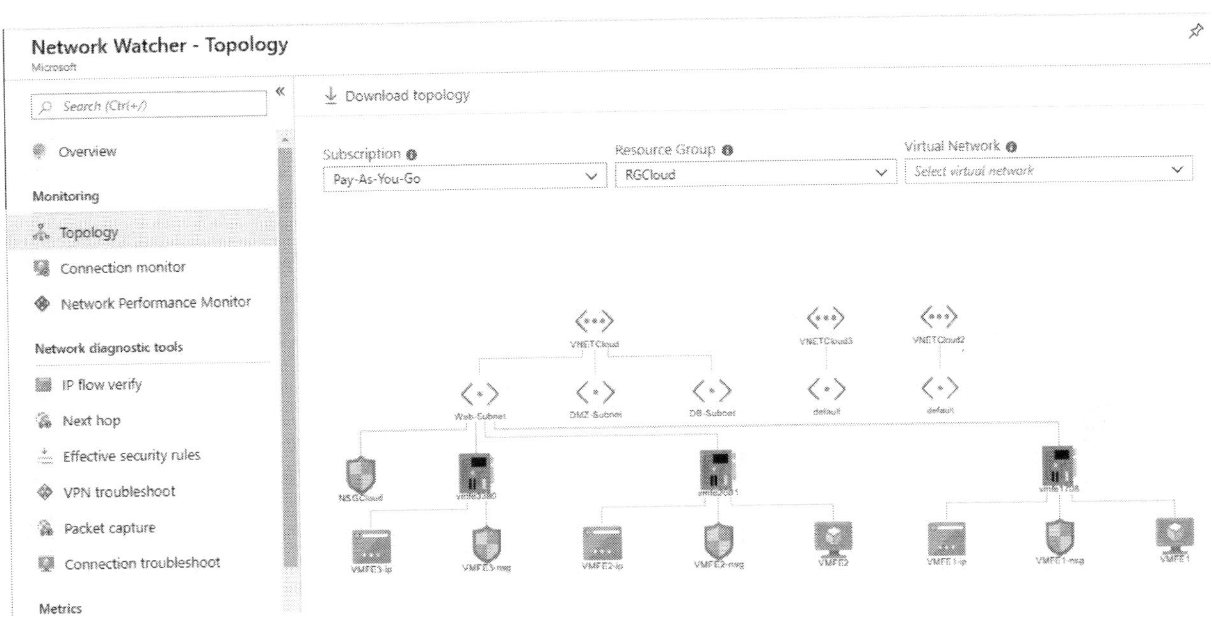

You can further filter the topology for Individual VNET. In this case I selected VNETCloud from dropdown box.

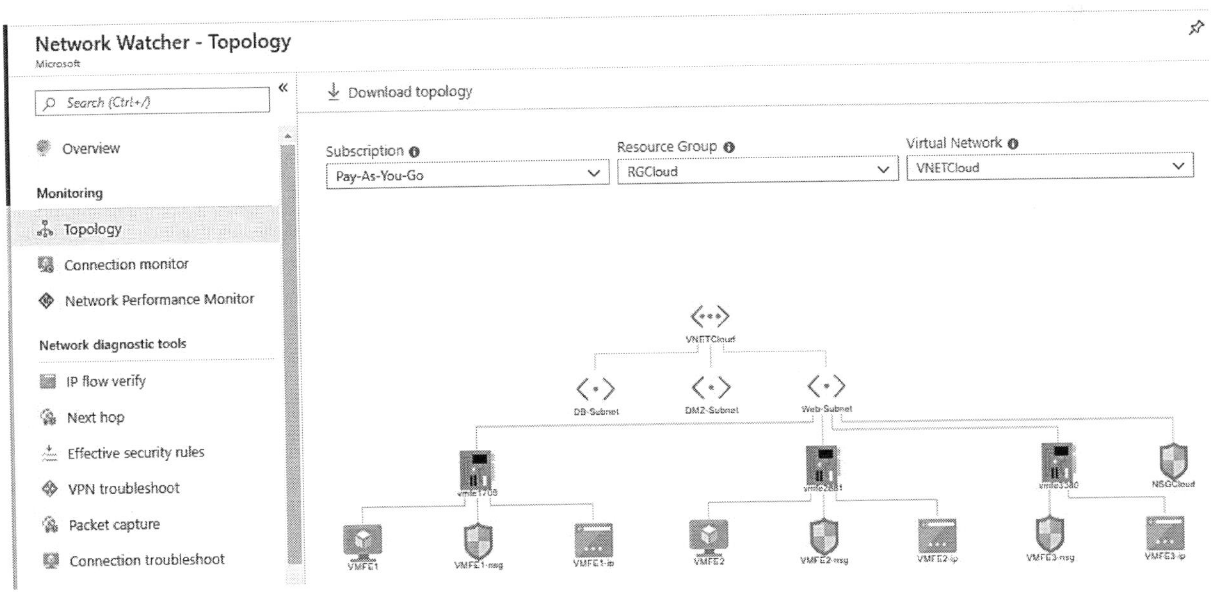

Next Hop: Traffic from the source to destination has a next hop. Next Hop feature finds or verifies the next hop for packets being routed in the Azure Network Fabric, enabling you to **diagnose virtual machine routing problems.**

Next hop also returns the route table associated with the next hop. If the route is defined as a user-defined route, that route is returned. Otherwise, next hop returns System Route**.**

Next Hop diagnoses virtual machine routing problems.

Click Next hop in left pane>in right pane Select your Resource Group, Virtual Machine and Destination Address and click Next Hop.

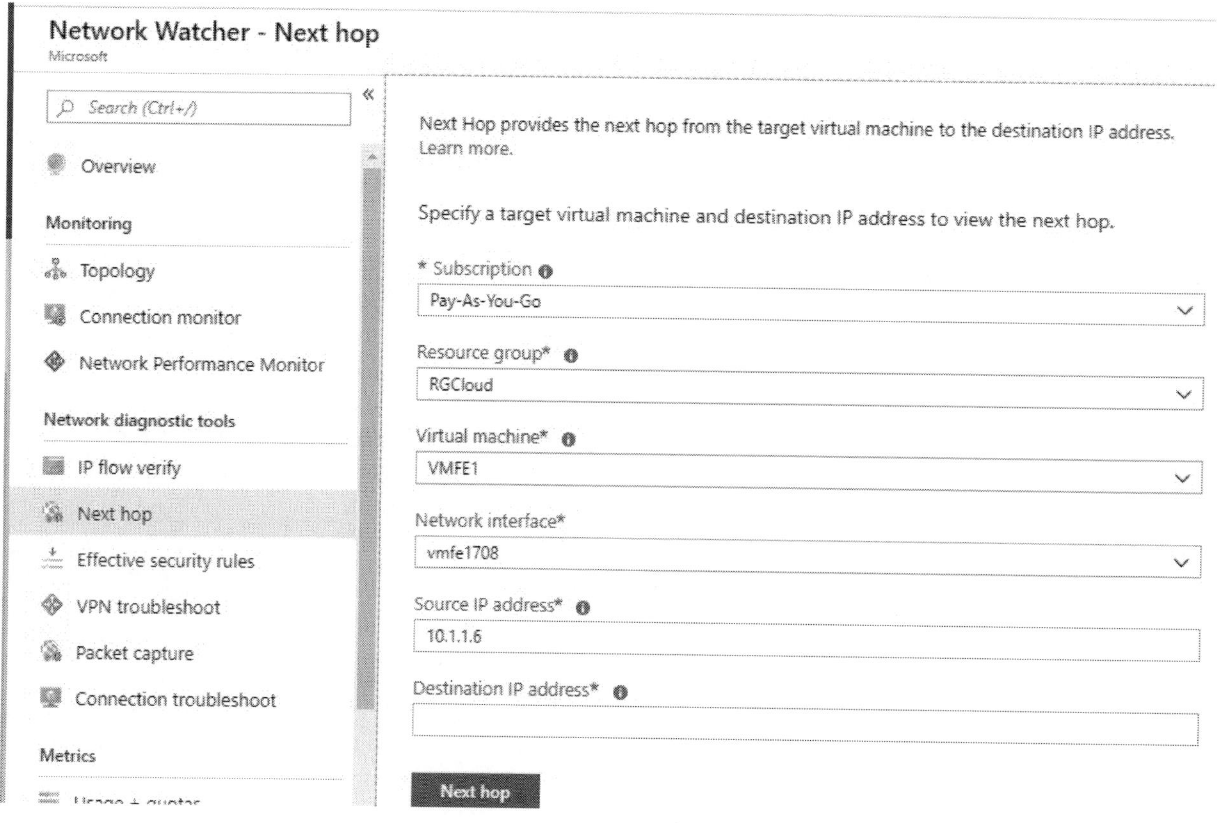

IP flow verify: IP Flow Verify helps to verify if a virtual machine can talk to another virtual machine. If the packet is denied by a security group, the rule and group that denied the packet is returned. You can choose the source and destination to diagnose connectivity issue.

IP flow verify **diagnoses virtual machine network traffic filter problems.**

Click IP flow verify in left pane>in right pane Select your Resource Group, Virtual Machine and Remote IP Address and click Check.

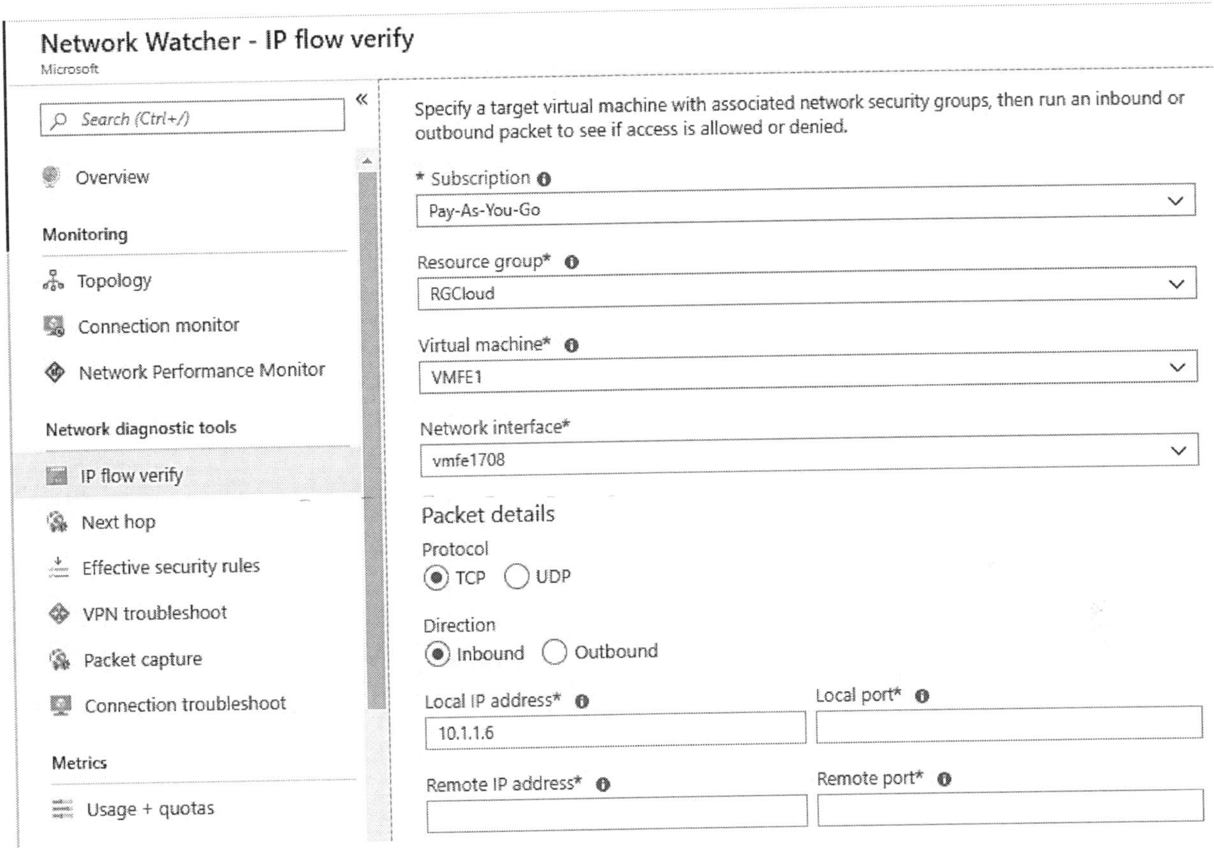

Packet Capture: Packet Capture creates packet capture sessions to track traffic to and fro from a virtual machine.

Packet capture is a virtual machine extension that is remotely started through Network Watcher.

Filters are provided for the capture session to ensure you capture traffic you want to monitor. Filters are based on 5-tuple (protocol, local IP address, remote IP address, local port, and remote port) information. The captured data is stored in the local disk or a storage blob.

Click Packet capture in left pane>in right pane click +Add>Add Packet capture blade opens>Select Target VM and Storage selects> Add Filters if required (Scroll down to see filter options).

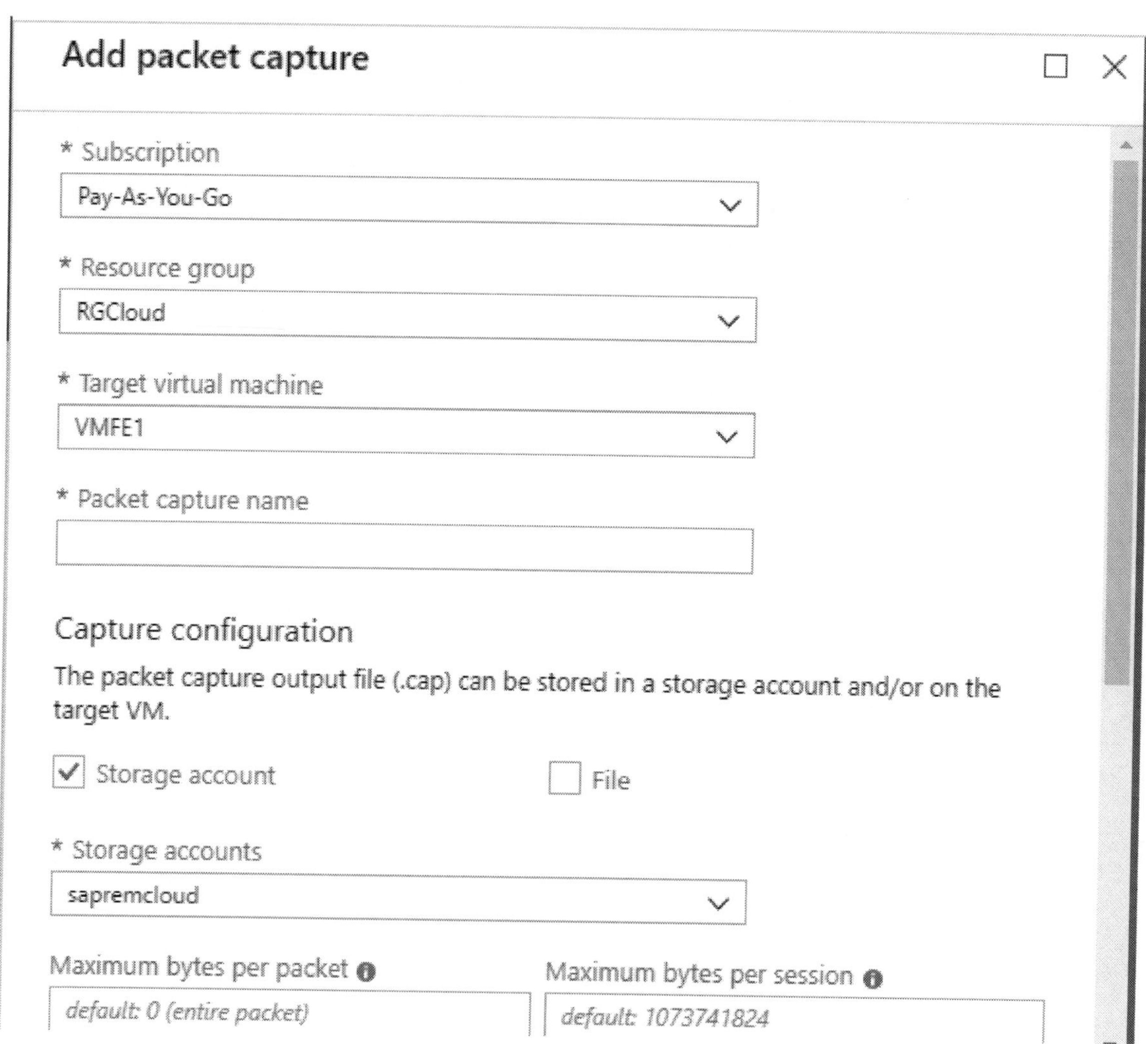

Connection Monitor: Monitors and Diagnoses communication problems between 2 Virtual Machines. Network Watcher Connection Monitor enables you to configure and track connection reachability, latency, and network topology changes. If there is an issue, it tells you why it occurred and how to fix it.
Pre-Req: Network Watcher Agent for Windows extension is added to VMs.
Click Connection Monitor in left pane>in right pane click +Add>Add connection monitor blade opens>Select Target VM and destination VM> Click Add.

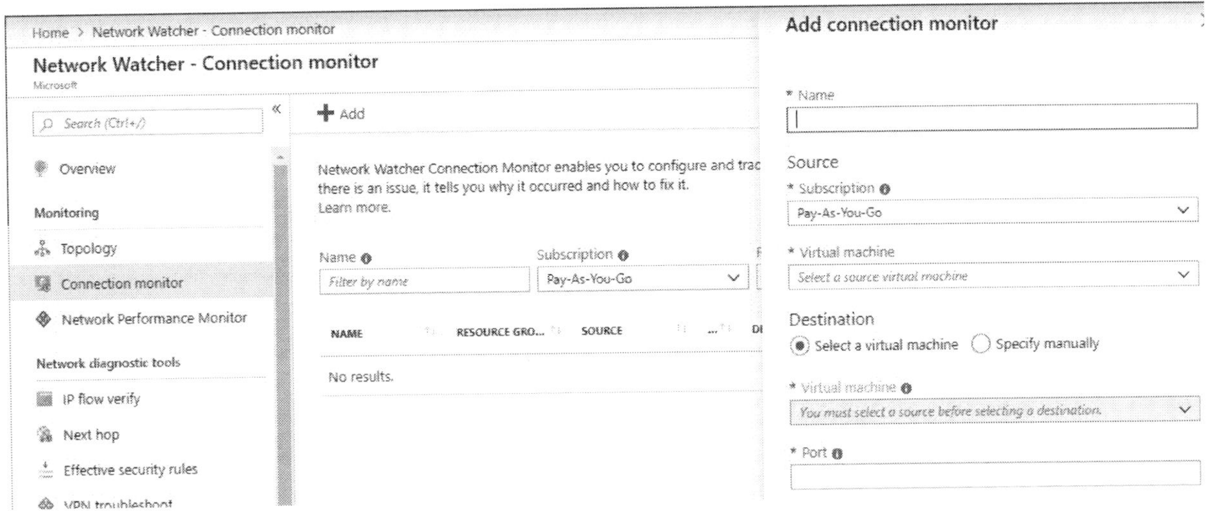

VPN Troubleshoot: Virtual Network Gateways provide connectivity between on-premises and virtual networks. **Network Watcher provides the capability to monitor and troubleshoot Virtual Network Gateways and Connections.**

Click VPN Troubleshoot in left pane>in right pane select Storage Account and Virtual Network gateway>Click Start Troubleshooting.

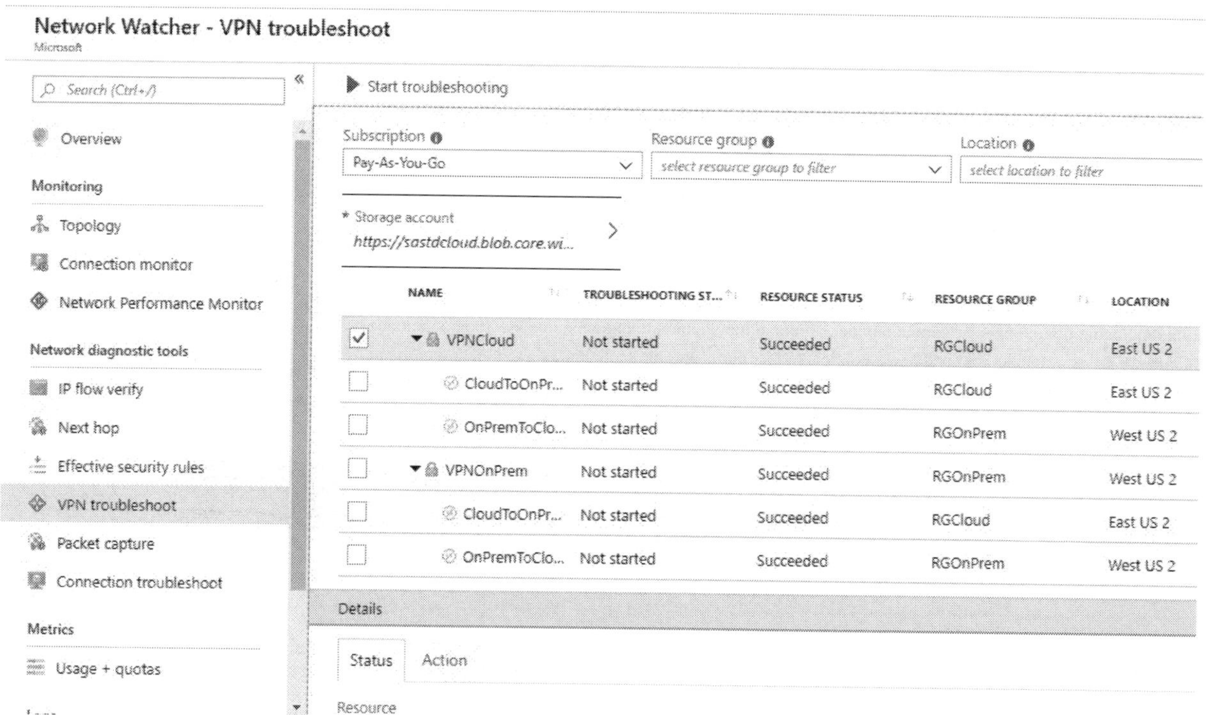

Here you can see the Virtual Network Gateways (VPNCloud & VPNOnPrem) created in Chapter 2 and in Part 1 Book.

Network Performance Monitor

Network Performance Monitor is a cloud-based hybrid network monitoring solution. Network Performance Monitor offers following three capabilities: Performance Monitor, Service Connectivity Monitor and ExpressRoute Monitor.

NPM is added as Management solution in Log Analytics workspace.

Performance Monitor

Performance Monitor helps you monitor network performance (latency) and network connectivity between various points (Source & Destination Nodes) in your network infrastructure.

You can monitor Network Performance and Network Connectivity across cloud deployments and on-premises locations, multiple data centers and branch offices.

With Topology Map you can see hop-by-hop topology of the routes between the source and destination nodes. The unhealthy routes or hops will be coloured in red, which will help you to quickly localize the problem to a particular section of the network. It will also show you Network Performance (Latency) across various subnets along the path.

Figure below shows topology map between two nodes. Performance Monitor is monitoring all the paths including redundant path between the nodes.
It is showing both network connectivity status and latency across the network.

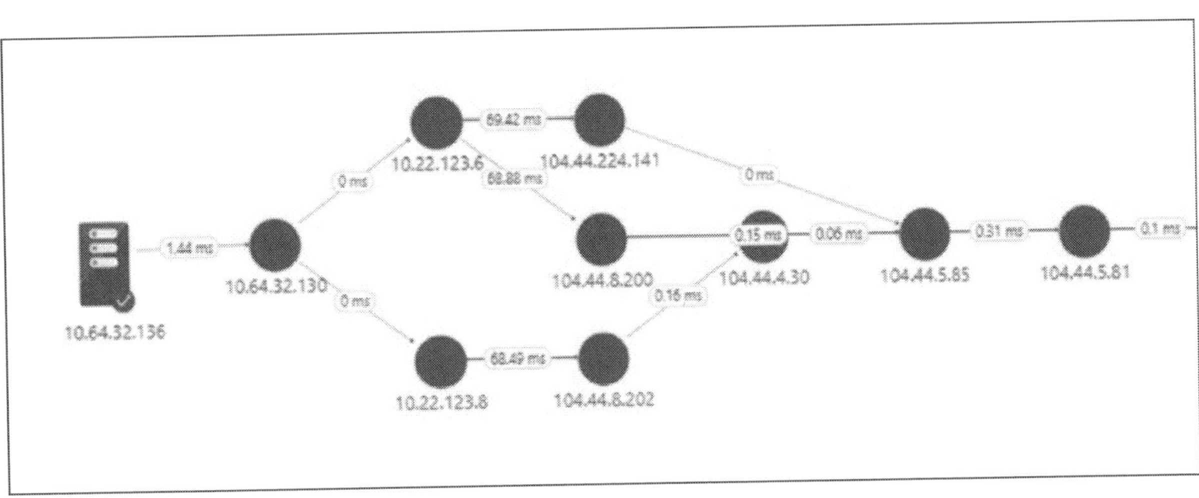

Service Connectivity Monitor

Service Connectivity Monitor helps you monitor network connectivity from users to service and application endpoints. Endpoints include Websites, SaaS applications, PaaS applications, and SQL databases.

You can perform the following functions with Service Connectivity Monitor:

1. Determine the response time, network latency, and packet loss experienced when connecting to the endpoint.
2. Determine whether poor application performance is because of the network or because of some issue on the application provider's end.
3. Identify hot spots on the network that might be causing poor application performance by viewing the latency contributed by each hop on a topology map.
4. Monitor the network connectivity to your applications and network services from multiple branch offices or locations. Applications and network services include Office 365, Dynamics CRM, internal line-of-business applications, and SQL databases.
5. Use built-in tests to monitor network connectivity to Office 365 and Dynamics 365 endpoints.

ExpressRoute Monitor

ExpressRoute Monitor helps you Monitor end-to-end connectivity and performance between On-premises and Azure over Azure ExpressRoute Connection.

NPM for ExpressRoute offers comprehensive ExpressRoute monitoring for Azure Private Peering and Microsoft peering connections. Key capabilities of ExpressRoute Monitor include:

1. Auto-detection of ER circuits associated with your subscription.
2. Detection of network topology from on-premises to your cloud applications.
3. Capacity planning, bandwidth utilization analysis.
4. Monitoring and alerting on both primary and secondary paths.
5. Monitoring connectivity to Azure services such as Office 365, Dynamics 365 over ExpressRoute.
6. Detect degradation of connectivity to Virtual Networks.

Figure below shows Redundant ExpressRoute Connectivity between On-premises (on left side of the Figure) and Azure. It is showing both connectivity status and the latency in the network.

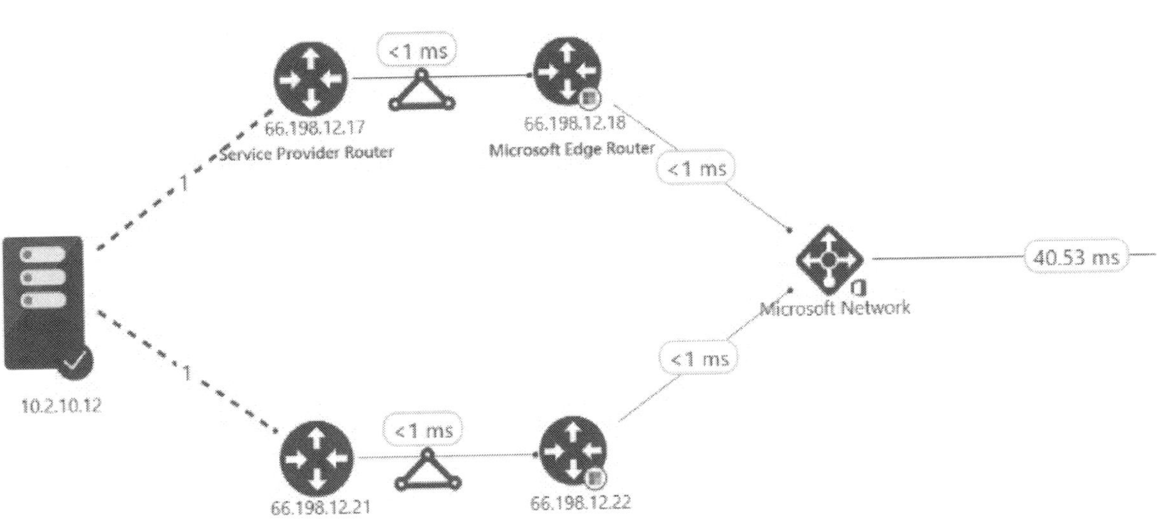

Requirements and Steps for Enabling Network Performance Monitor

1. Log Analytics Workspace.
2. Log Analytics Agent installed on the Nodes.
3. Adding NPM Monitor Management solution to Log Analytics workspace.

Important Note: You can also access NPM through Network Watcher Dashboard.

Exercise 114: Adding NPM in Log Analytics Workspace

In this Exercise we will just demonstrate how to add NPM to Log analytics Workspace LACloud. LACloud was created in Exercise 106, Chapter 9.

In Log Analytics workspace dashboard click Workspace Summary in left pane> Click + Add in Workspace Summary blade>Management Tools Pane opens> In Recommended Solutions Click more>Recommended blade opens>Scroll down and select **Network Performance Monitor.**

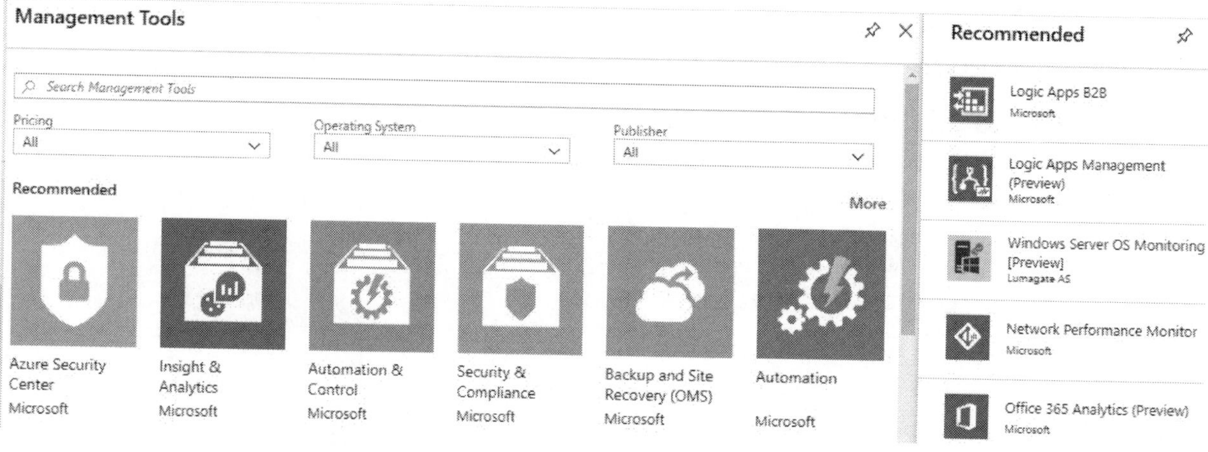

Chapter 11 Azure Automation

This Chapter covers following Topic Lessons

- Azure Automation
- Process Automation Working and Architecture
- Automate configuration management using Desired State Configuration
- Update Management
- Inventory Management
- Change Tracking

This Chapter covers following Lab Exercises

- Create Automation Account
- Desired State Configuration (DSC) using Azure Automation
- PowerShell DSC Extension
- Enabling Update Management and Add Azure VM
- Scheduling Update Deployment
- Enabling Inventory Management and Add VM wvmportal
- Checking Change Tracking for VM wvmportal

Chapter Topology

In this chapter we will add Azure Automation to the Topology.

From Automation Dashboard we will configure Desired State Configuration on VM VMAD by enabling IIS Web Server role. From Automation Dashboard we will also enable Update, Inventory and Change Tracking Management for Azure Virtual Machine VMFE2.

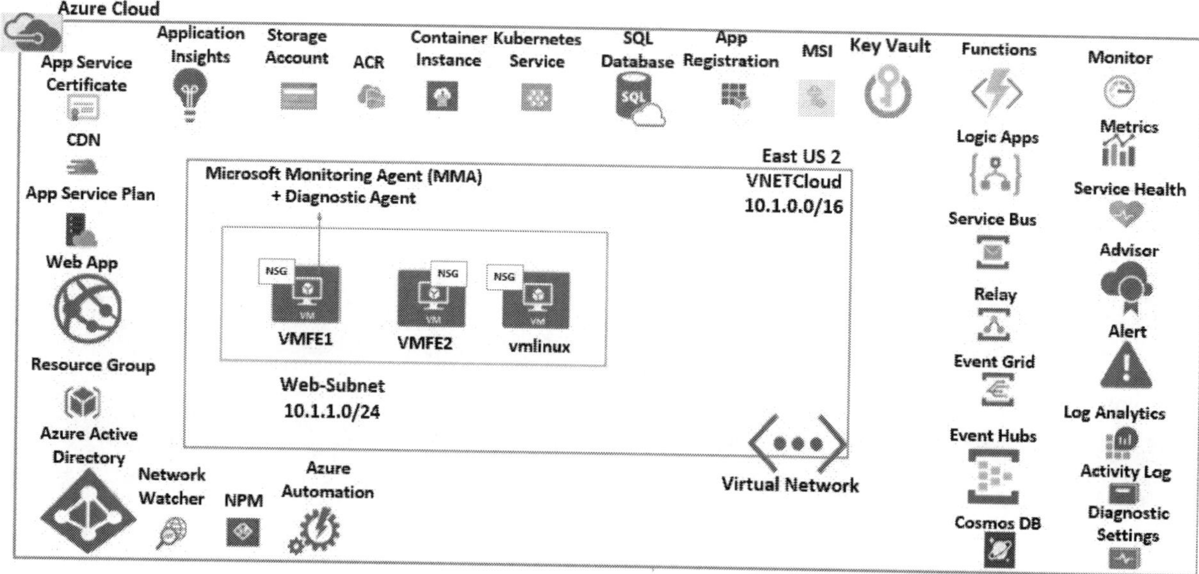

Note 1: VM VMAD was created in Exercise 39, Chapter 4 in Virtual Network VNETOnPrem.
Note 2: VM VMFE2 was created in Exercise 33, Chapter 4 in Virtual Network VNETCloud.

Azure Automation

Azure Automation is a managed service that provides **process automation**, **configuration management**, **update management, Inventory Management and Change Tracking.** It automates manual processes (Process Automation) and enforces configurations for physical and virtual computers (Desired State Configuration) and Update/Inventory/change tracking for Azure VMs or On-premises VMs or Physical Servers

Figure below shows the architecture of Azure Automation. Azure Automation provides it functionality to both Azure and on-premises resources.

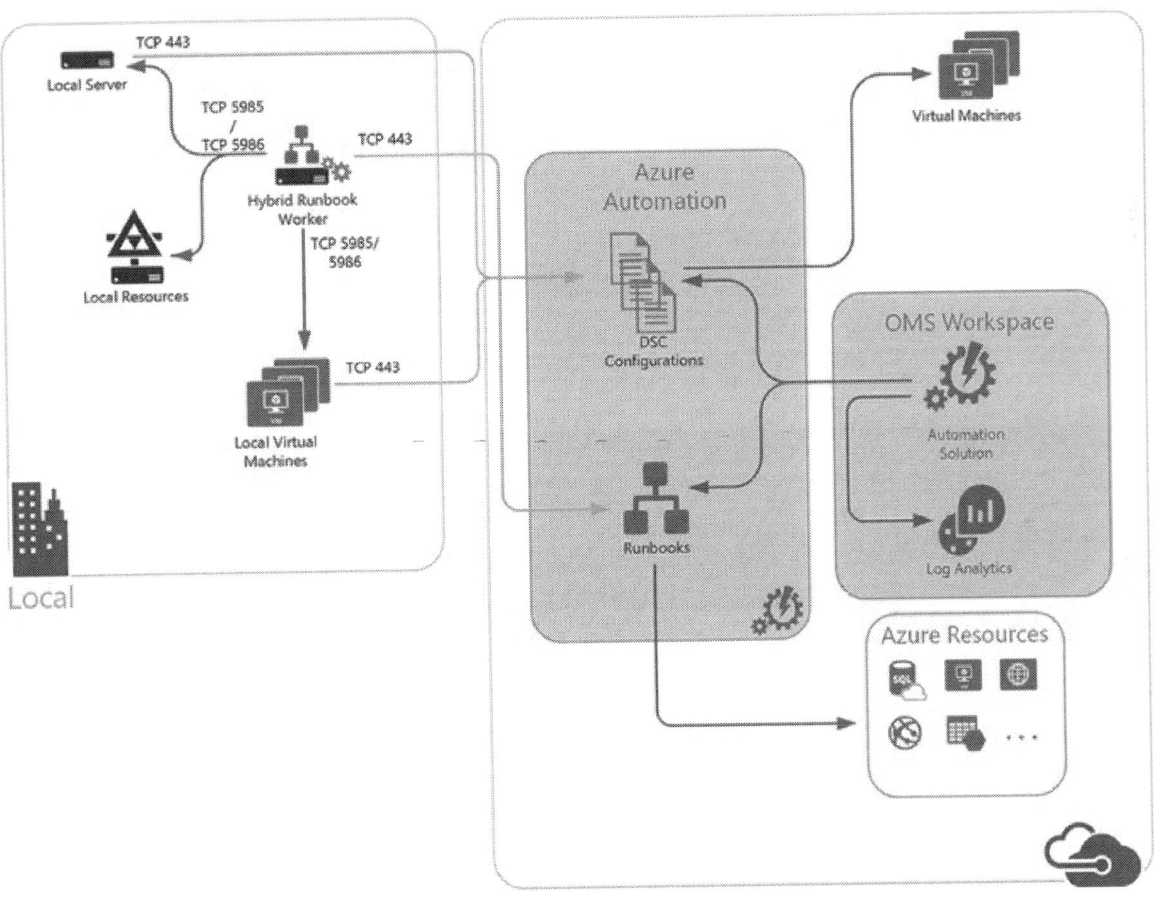

Log analytics workspace is required if you want to offer Update Management, change & Inventory tracking functionality and Hybrid worker solution. It also collects Runbook job status and receives configuration information from your Automation account.

Exercise 115: Create Automation Account

1. In Azure Portal click create a resource> Management Tools>Automation> Add Automation Account Blade opens>Enter a name, Select RGCloud in Resource Group and click create

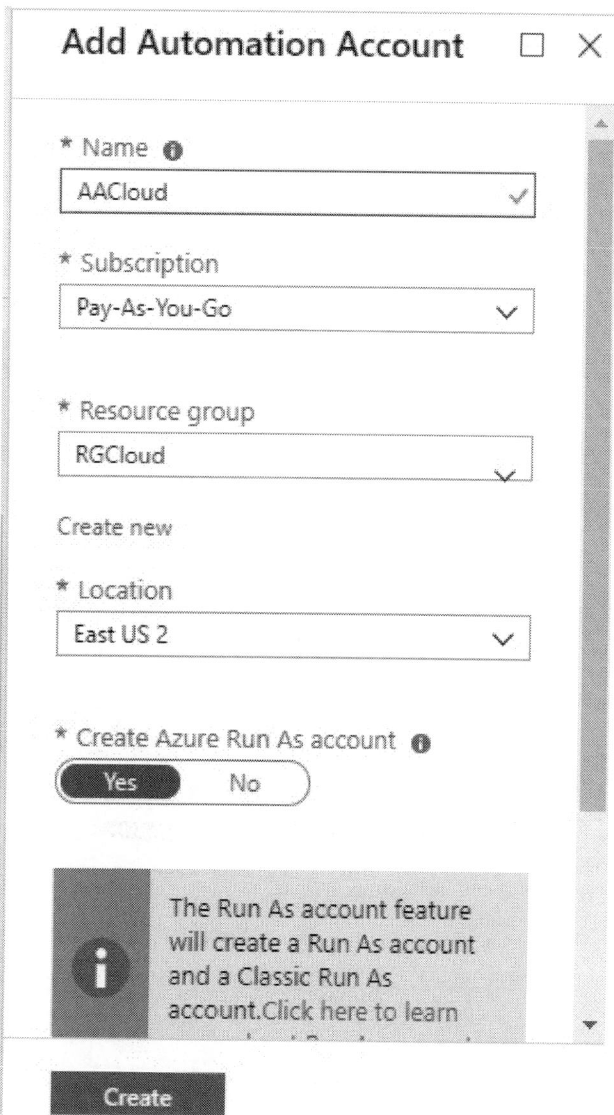

Note: Resource Group RGCloud was created in Exercise 1, Chapter 1 in Exam AZ-300 & AZ-301 Study & Lab Guide Part 1.

2. Figure below shows Automation Account Dashboard.

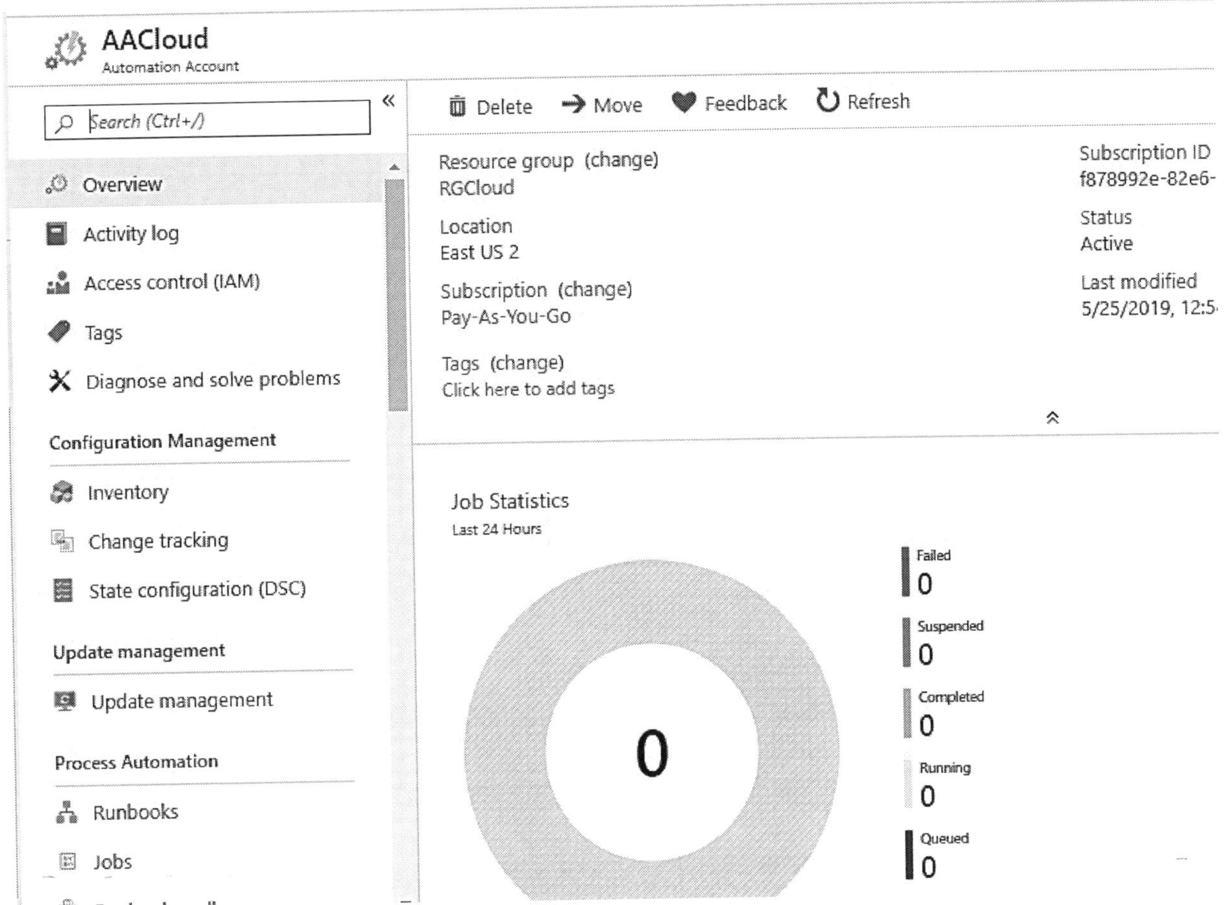

From Automation Dashboard you can configure Desired State Configuration and Process Automation. From Automation Dashboard you can also enable Update, Inventory and Change Tracking Management for Azure Virtual Machines or on-premises servers.

Process Automation Working and Architecture

Azure Process Automation automates manual processes using Runbooks against Azure Resources. Runbooks are containers for custom scripts and workflows. You can invoke and run runbooks on demand or according to schedule by using Automation Schedule assets or based on alerts in OMS Log Analytics.

Figure below shows Architecture of Process Automation.

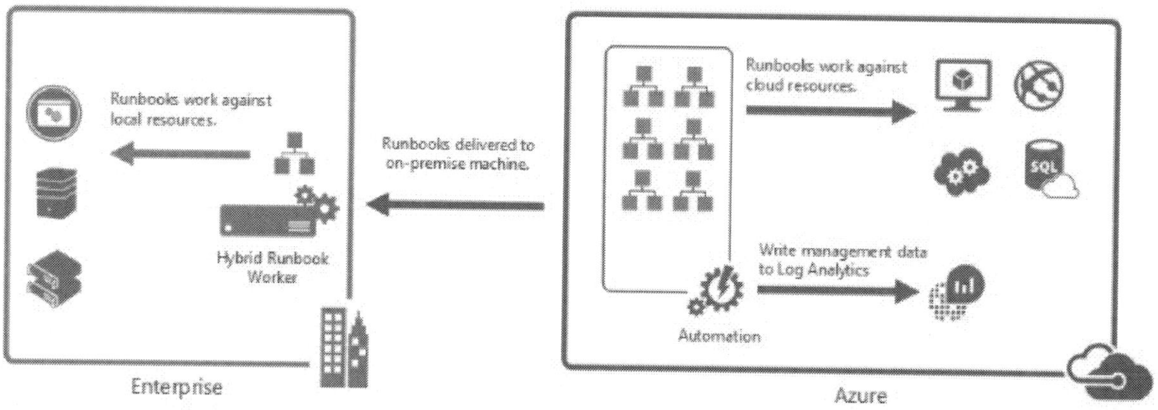

Runbooks are created in Azure Automation Account and work against Azure Resources such as VMs, Azure SQL, Web Apps etc to automate manual process.

Runbooks can also run on-premises where-in you can install one or more Hybrid Runbook Workers in your data center which run runbooks against local resources. Each Hybrid Runbook Worker requires Microsoft Management Agent to be installed and an Automation account. The agent must have a connection to an Azure Log Analytics workspace.

Example of Process Automation

You want your Azure VMs to run only during office hours only (8 AM – 5 PM). To save money an administrator shuts down VMs at 5 PM and Re-Starts at 8 AM. Using Azure Process Automation you can Automate shutdown and re-start activity. You can use Azure Process Automation to create Runbooks (containing Powershell scripts) to shutdown VMs and Re-start VMs which run against your Azure VMs at Schedule time daily.

Automate configuration management using Desired State Configuration

Desired State Configuration (DSC) is a configuration management platform in Windows PowerShell that deploys and enforces the configuration on Windows VMs and Physical Servers.

PowerShell DSC configurations are PowerShell scripts that apply Desired Configurations to Windows VMs and Physical Servers. You can apply DSC to Azure VMs in following 2 ways:

1. Azure Automation DSC Service.
2. Add DSC Extension on Azure VM.

Azure Automation DSC Service

Azure Automation provides a pull server in the cloud that manages DSC configurations which nodes can access to retrieve required configurations.

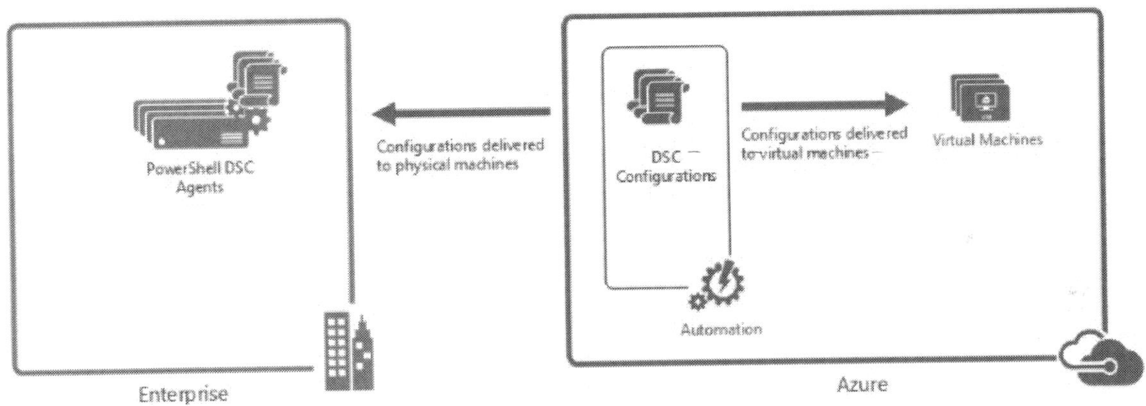

PowerShell DSC configurations are PowerShell scripts that apply Desired configurations to DSC Nodes from a DSC Pull Server in the Azure cloud. If DSC nodes deviate from there desired configuration then you can manually or automatically update desired machine configuration on DSC nodes.

Azure VMs require Desired State Configuration agent extension. It is automatically deployed to Azure VMs when you add them as DSC nodes in Automation Account Dashboard. Non Azure VMs & Servers require Powershell DSC agents.

DSC Extension on Azure VM

The extension uploads and applies a PowerShell DSC Configuration on an Azure VM.

In this case node (Azure VM) is *not* centrally managed. DSC extension involves a singular action that occurs during deployment.

The other disadvantage of this approach is that you have to apply DSC Extension to each VM separately.

Important Note: DSC extension differs from Azure Automation DSC Service in a sense that this involves a singular action that occurs during deployment. No ongoing reporting or configuration management is available, other than locally in the VM.

Advantages of Using Desired State Configuration (DSC) with Azure Automation

Advantage 1 of Using DSC with Azure Automation is that you can apply configuration to Multiple nodes simultaneously.
Advantage 2 of Using DSC with Azure Automation is that if nodes drift from their configuration it is reapplied by DSC Pull Server.

Exercise 116: Desired State Configuration using Azure Automation

In this exercise we will enable IIS Web Server role on VM VMAD using Desired State Configuration (DSC). Recall that VM VMAD was created with AD DS role in Exercise 39, Chapter 4 in Exam AZ-300 & AZ-301 Study & Lab Guide Part 1.

Step 1: Create a PS script which ensures either the presence or absence of the Web-Server Windows Feature (IIS).

I created below PS script in notepad and saved it as **TestConfig.ps1** on my desktop.

```
configuration TestConfig
{
   Node IsWebServer
   {
      WindowsFeature IIS
      {
         Ensure               = 'Present'
         Name                 = 'Web-Server'
         IncludeAllSubFeature = $true
      }
   }

   Node NotWebServer
   {
      WindowsFeature IIS
      {
         Ensure               = 'Absent'
         Name                 = 'Web-Server'
      }
   }
}
```

Note: You can download the above script from following link at Box.com.
https://app.box.com/s/x2vskf3oo9aluiavm6bmqjjrcdvm8m9q

Step 2: Import the Configuration into Azure Automation

1. In Azure Automation **aaportal** Dashboard click **State Configuration (DSC)** in left pane> DSC pane opens.

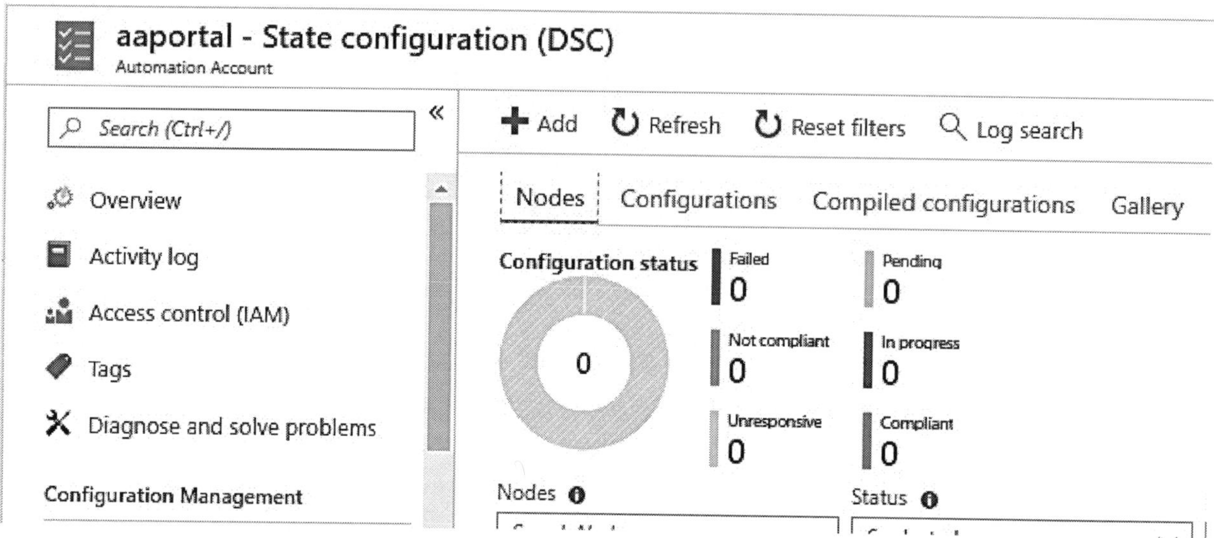

2. Click Configuration in right pane>Click + Add>Import Configuration blade opens>Upload TestConfig.ps1 from your desktop. This was created in step 1> Click Ok (Not Shown).

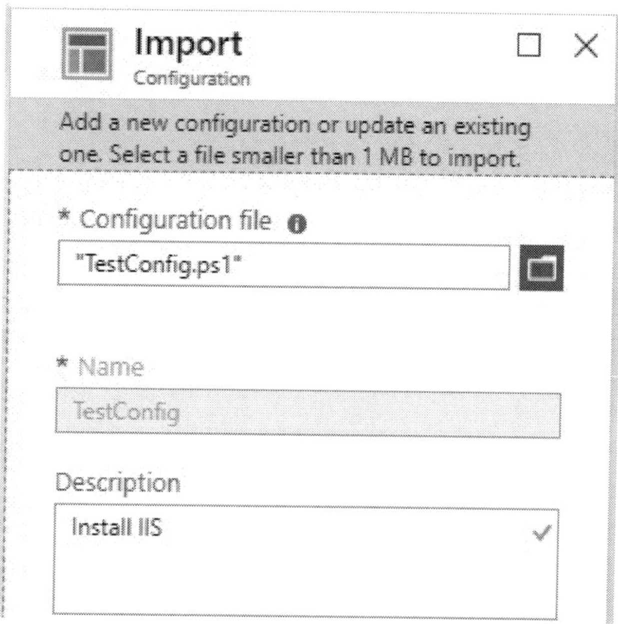

3. You can now see the Configuration which was imported. If required press Refresh tab.

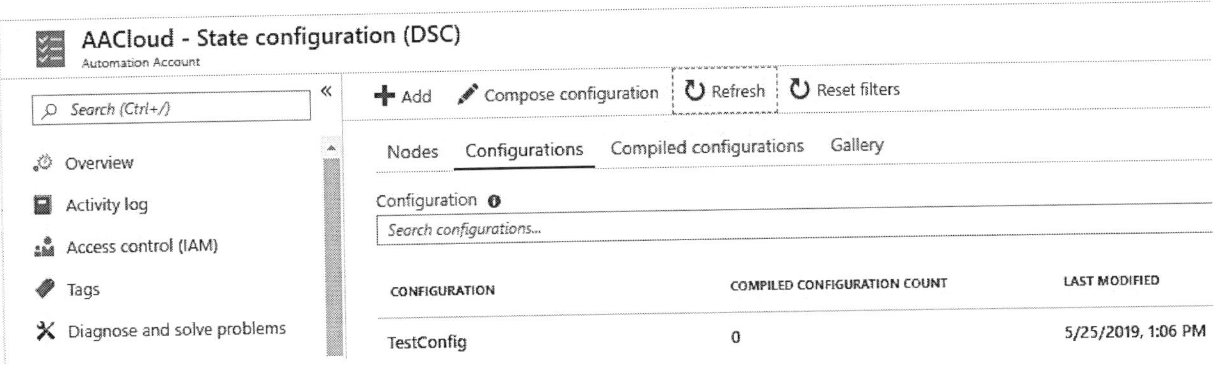

Step 3 Compile the Configuration

1. Click the Configuration TestConfig as shown in above screen>TestConfig Pane opens.

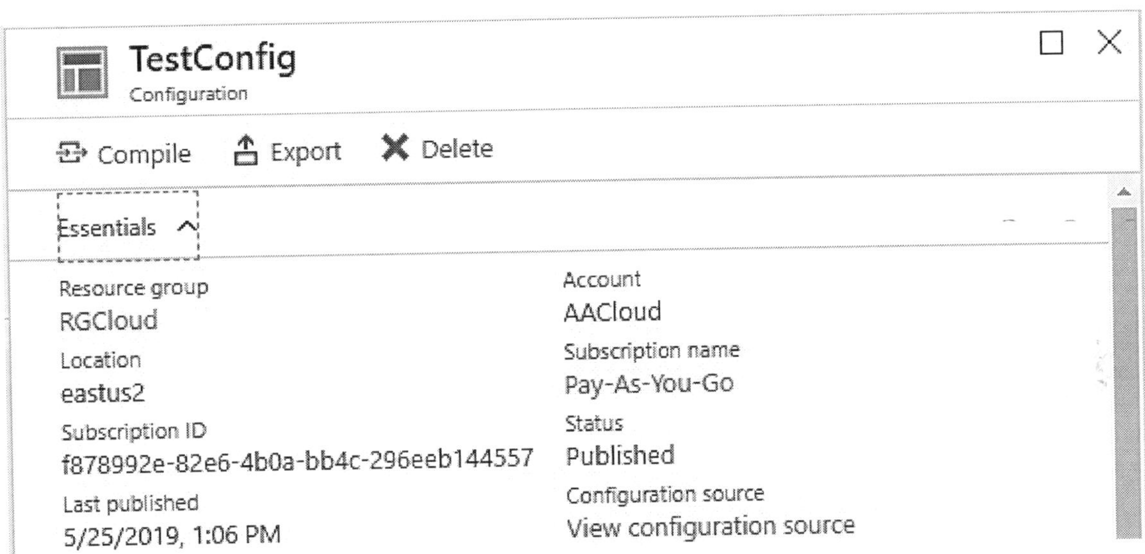

2. Click Compile>Compile DSC Configuration box pops up>Click Yes.

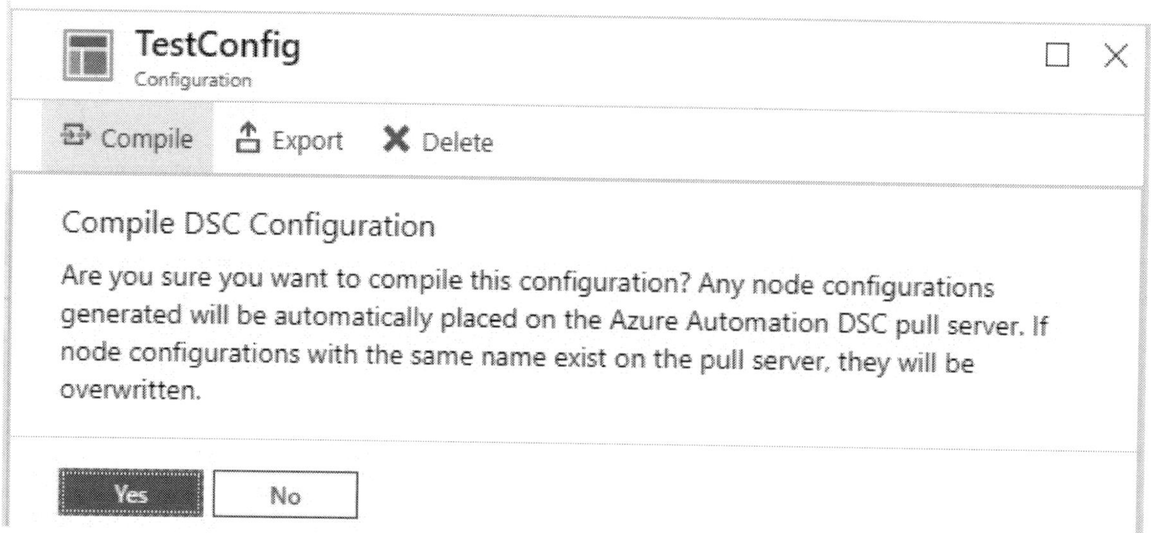

3. It will take 1-2 minutes to compile the job. You can see compiled configuration. If required press Refresh screen.

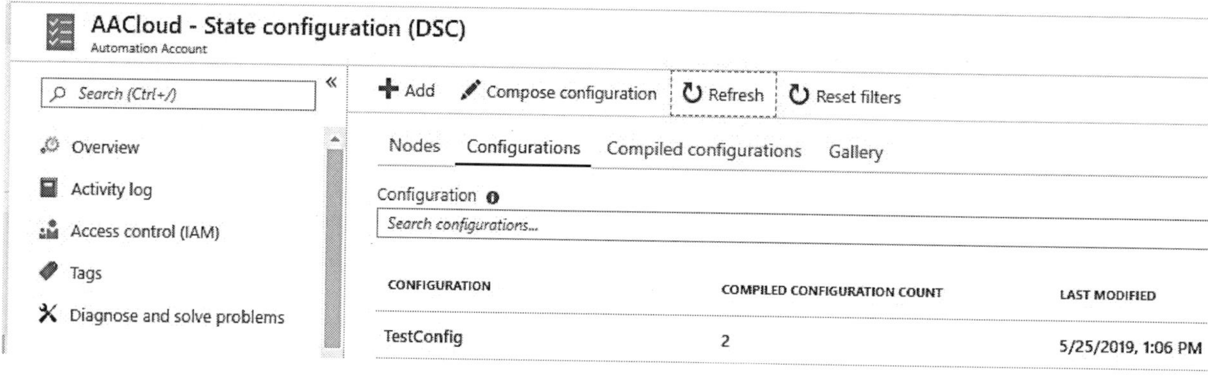

Step 4 View the Node Configurations which were compiled

In Azure Automation **aaportal** Dashboard click **State Configuration (DSC)** in left pane> DSC pane opens>Click Compiled Configurations in right pane> You can see the 2 configurations options. No Node is assigned.

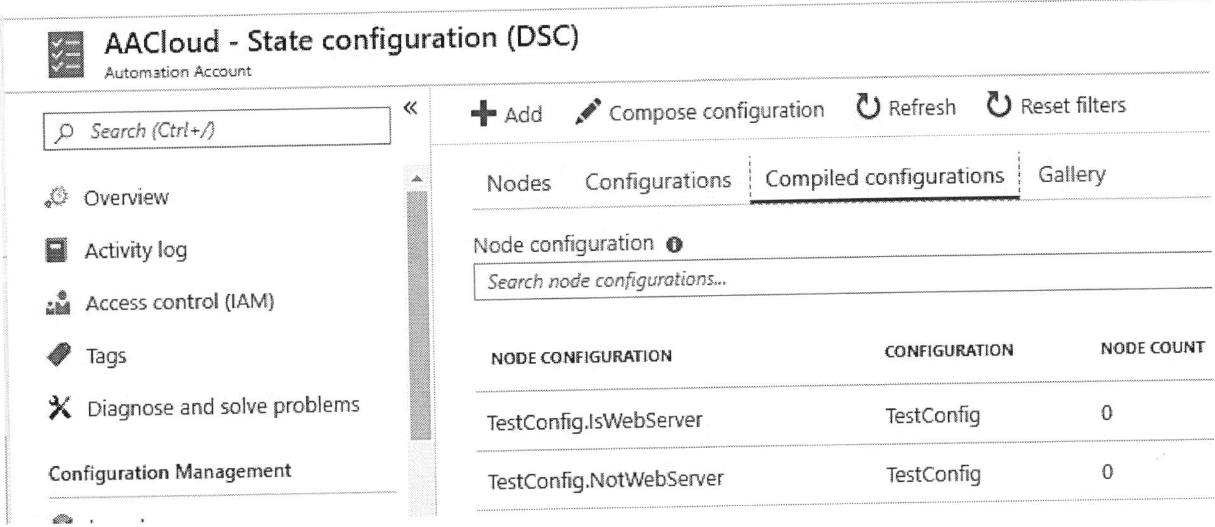

Step 5 Assign the Node VM VMAD to DSC Pull Configuration Server

1. In Azure Automation **AACloud** Dashboard click **State Configuration (DSC)** in left pane> DSC pane opens>Click Nodes in right pane>Currently no node is assigned.

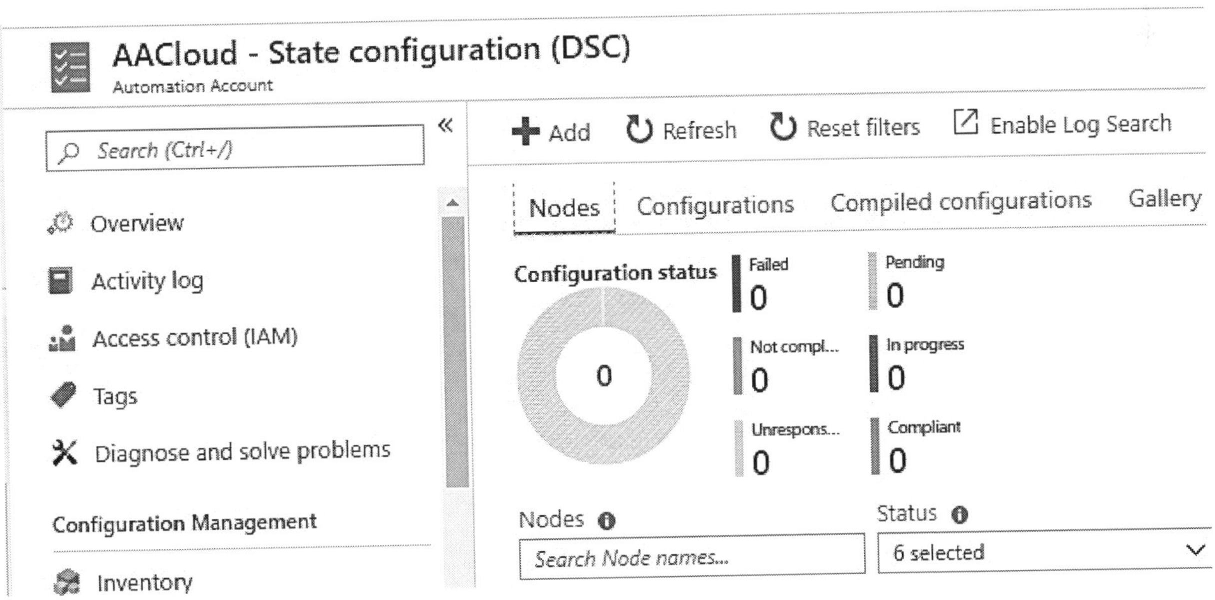

2. Click + Add>Select VMAD>Connect pane opens>Click + Connect> Registration pane opens>Select your Configuration from Drop down box> I selected **TestConfig.IsWebServer**>Rest Select all default values>Click Ok.

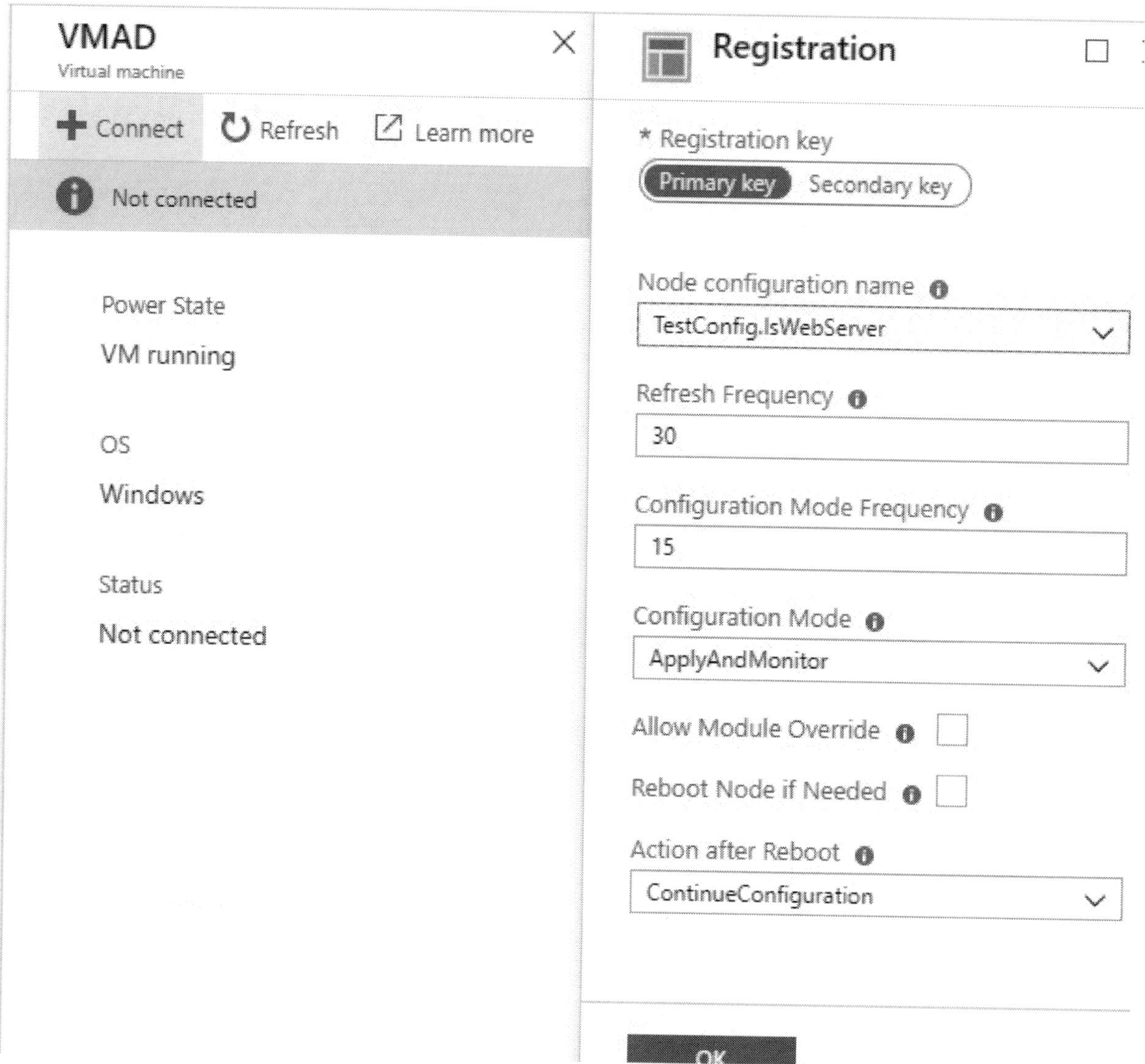

3. It will, take 2-5 minutes for Node to get connected.

4. In Nodes screen you can see 1 Node added and configuration status is showing in progress.

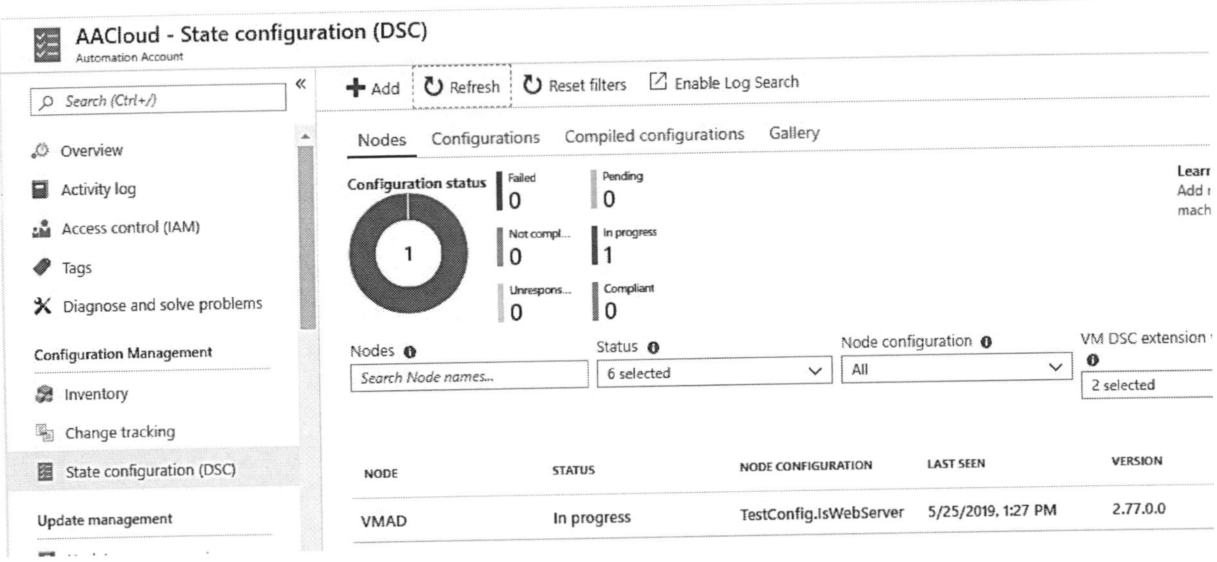

5. After 3-5 Minutes you can see node is compliant.

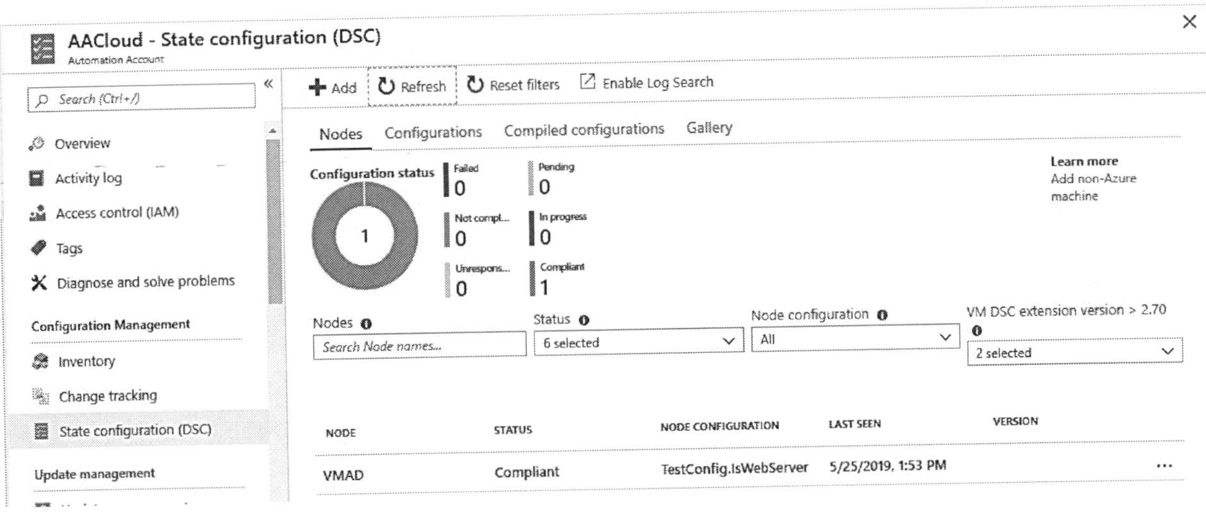

Step 6 Check that IIS Role has been installed in VM VMAD

Go to VMAD dashboard and note down the DNS address. DNS address is vmad.westus2.cloudapp.azure.com> Open Browser and enter vmad.westus2.cloudapp.azure.com> Default Website opens.

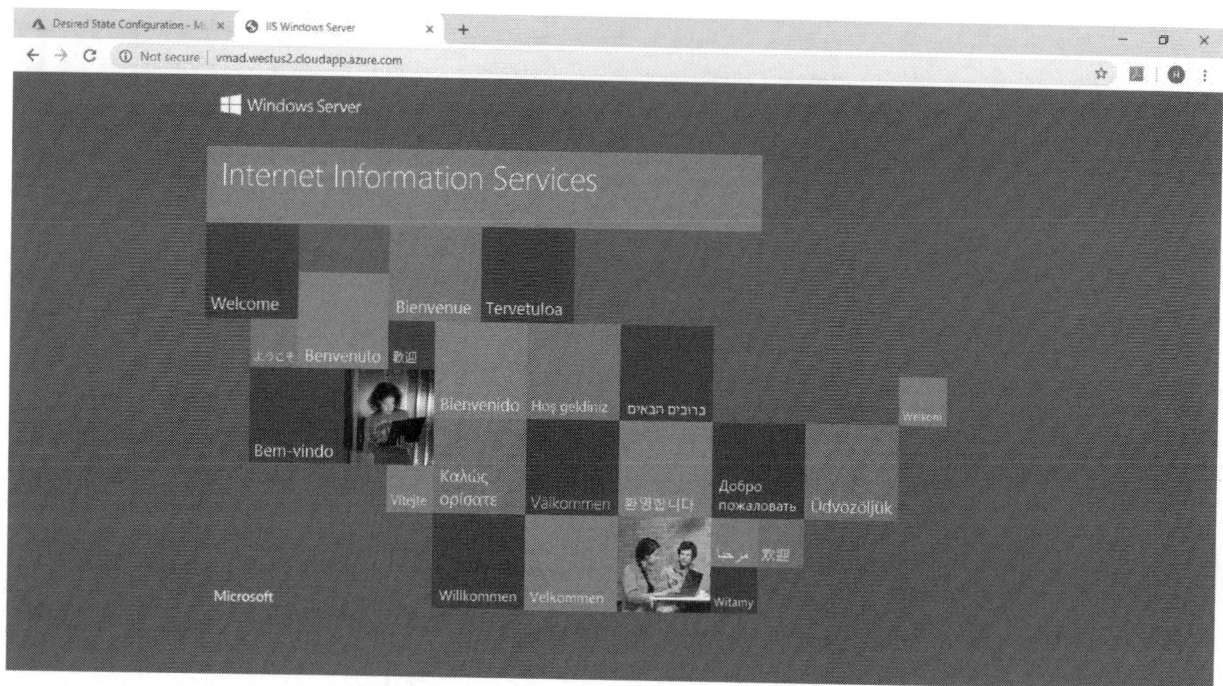

Exercise 117: PowerShell DSC Extension

In this exercise we will just demonstrate on how to apply PowerShell DSC extension to Azure VM VMFE1. Azure VM VMFE1 was created in Exercise 25, Chapter 4 in Exam AZ-300 & AZ-301 Study & Lab Guide Part 1.

1. Go to VM VMFE1 dashboard>Click Extension in left pane>In Right pane click + Add> Add Extension blade opens>Select PowerShell Desired State Configuration> PowerShell Desired State Configuration blade opens in right pane.

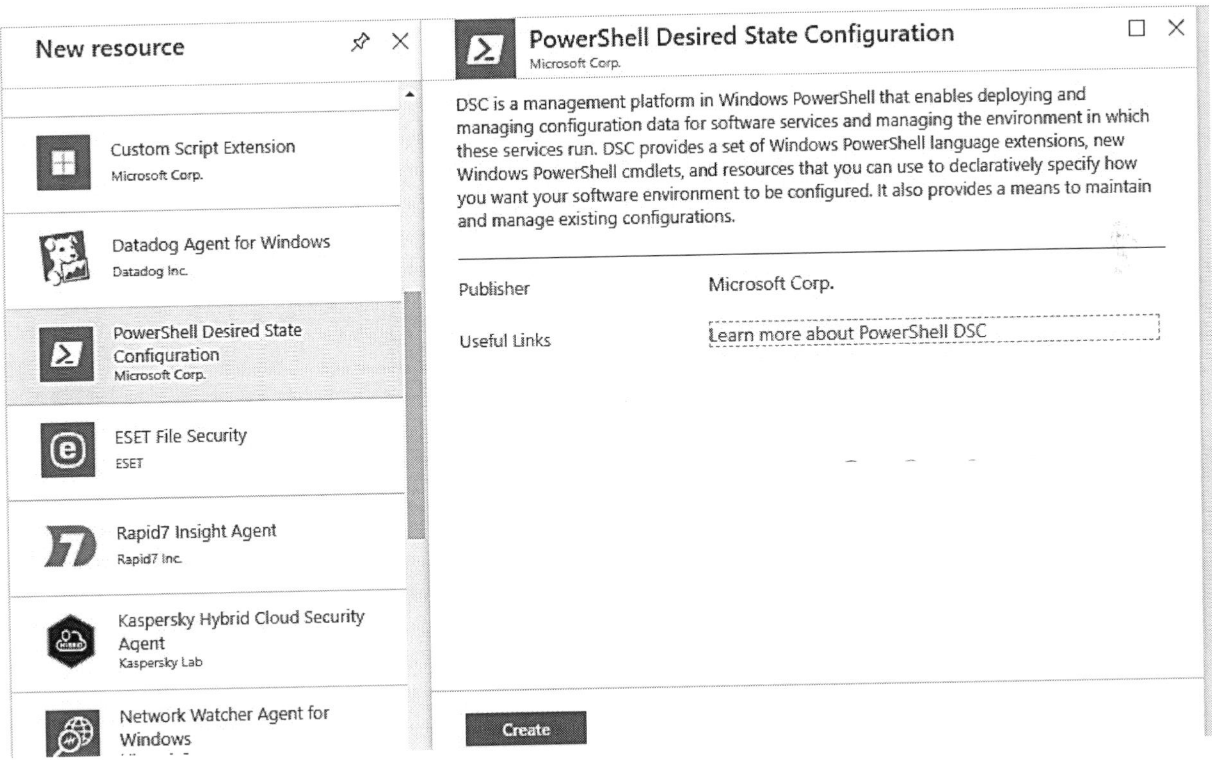

2. In right pane click create> Install Extension Blade opens>Click folder icon and upload file for executing on VM VMFE1.

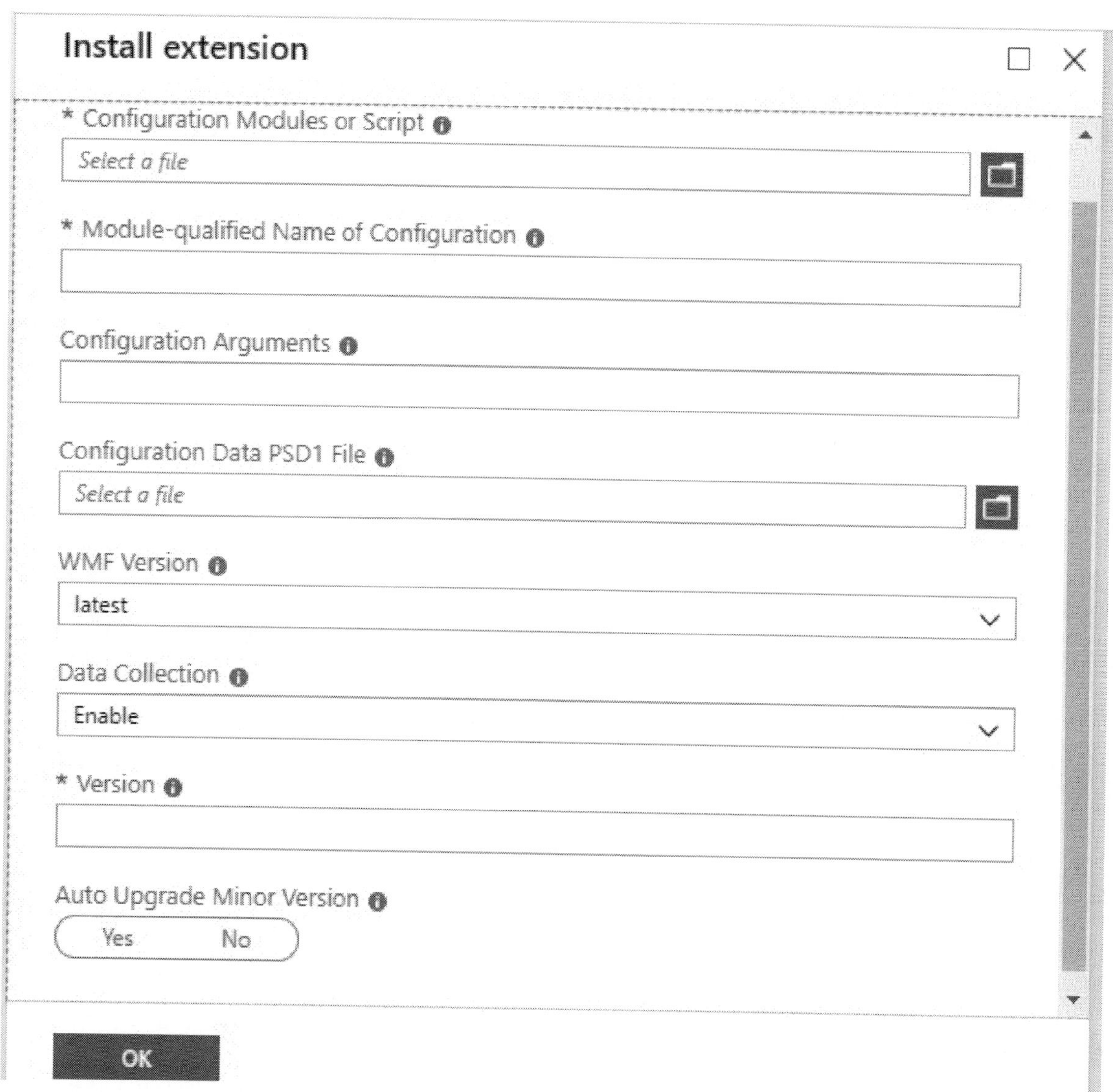

Disadvantage of this approach is that you have to apply PowerShell DSC extension to each Azure VM separately.

Update Management

The Update Management solution in Azure automation allows you to manage operating system security updates for your Windows and Linux computers deployed in Azure, on-premises environments, or other cloud providers.

Update Management Functionality requires Log analytics workspace.

With update management, you will always know the compliance status for Windows and Linux machines and you can create scheduled deployments to orchestrate the installation of updates within a defined maintenance window.

Exercise 118: Enabling Update Management and Add Azure VM

This exercise will enable Update Management and add Azure VM VMFE2 for Assessment. After this is enabled you can see the missing updates. This step will not deploy the updates.

Azure VM VMFE2 was created in Exercise 33, Chapter 4 in Exam AZ-300 & AZ-301 Study & Lab Guide Part 1.

We will create a new Log Analytics for this Exercise.

You can enable Update Management through Automation Account Dashboard or through Virtual Machine Dashboard. For this exercise we will use Automation Account Dashboard.

1. In Azure Automation Account AACloud Dashboard click Update Management in left pane>In right pane under Log Analytics Workspace select Create new workspace>Click enable.

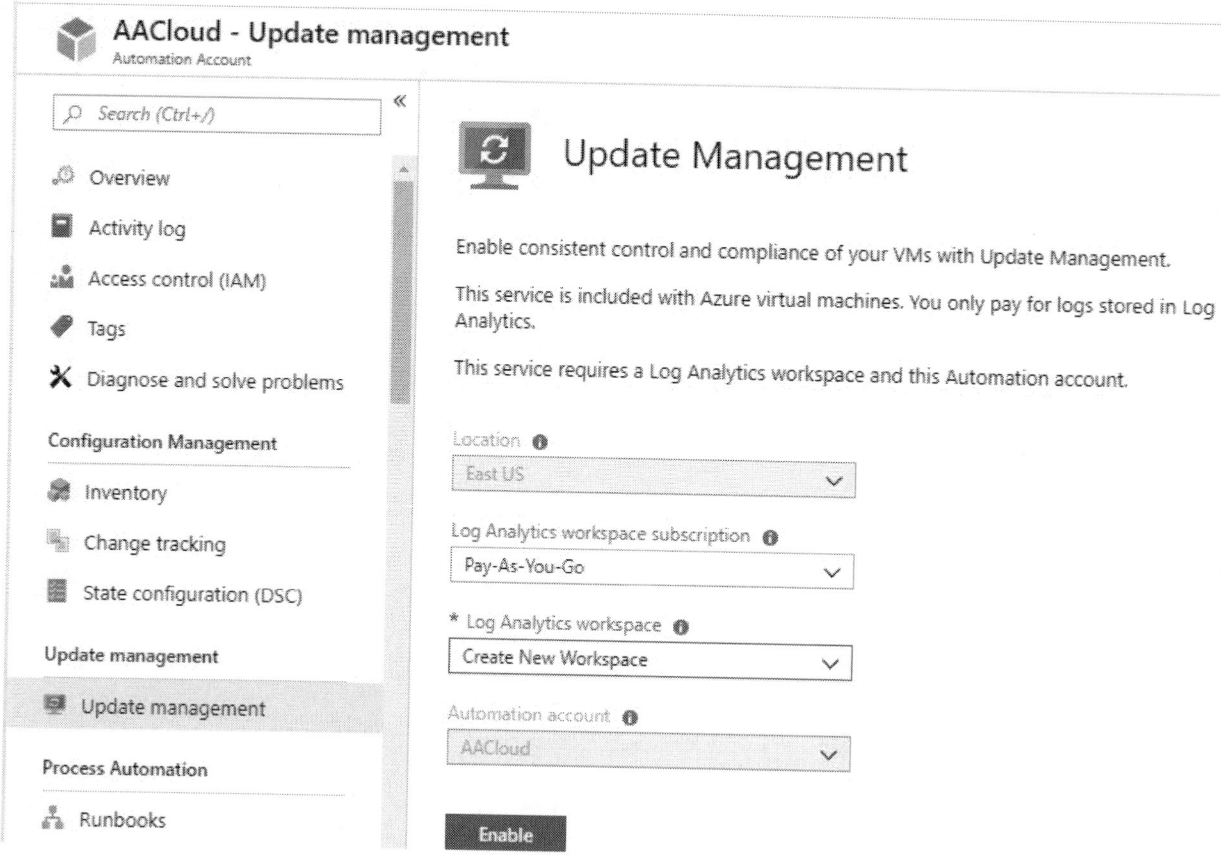

2. After Deployment is enabled refresh the screen with F5. Make sure Update Management is selected in left pane. Currently there are no machines for assessment.

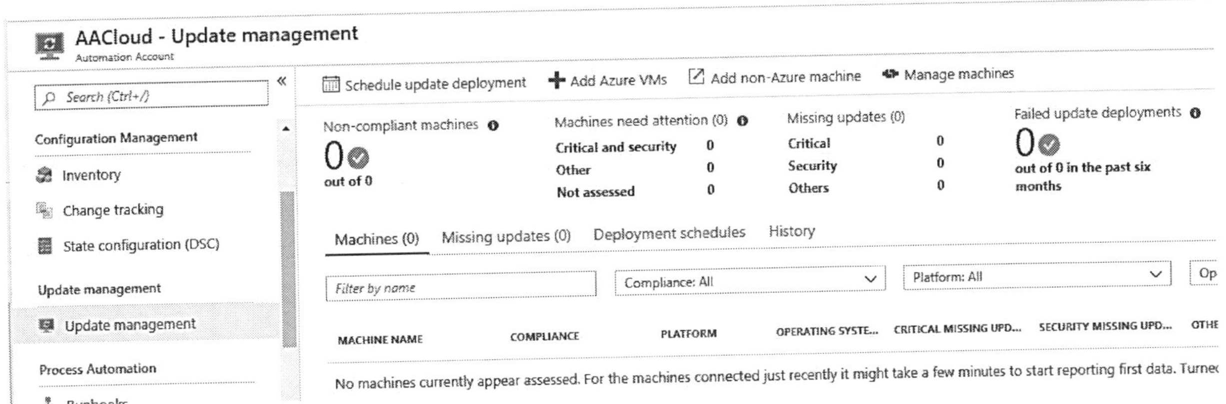

3. Click + **Add Azure VMs** in Right Pane> Enable Update Management pane opens>Select VM VMFE2> Click enable.

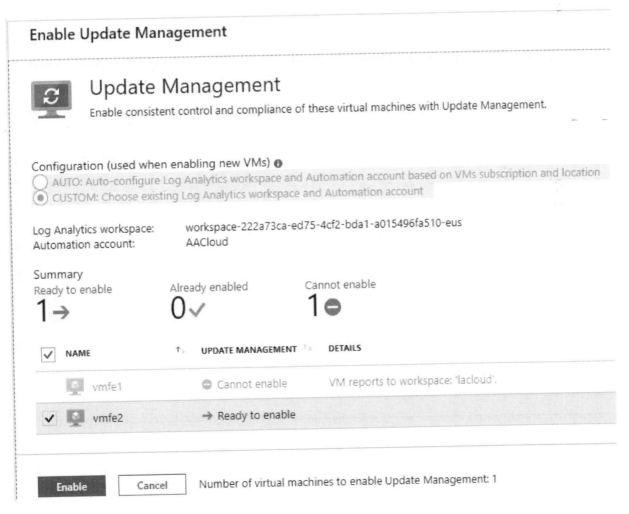

Enable Update Management

Update Management

Enable consistent control and compliance of these virtual machines with Update Management.

Configuration (used when enabling new VMs)

AUTO: Auto-configure Log Analytics workspace and Automation account based on VMs subscription and location

CUSTOM: Choose existing Log Analytics workspace and Automation account

Log Analytics workspace: workspace-222a73ca-ed75-4cf2-bda1-a015496fa510-eus

Automation account: AACloud

Summary

Ready to enable	Already enabled	Cannot enable
1	0	1

NAME	UPDATE MANAGEMENT	DETAILS
vmfe1	Cannot enable	VM reports to workspace: 'lacloud'.
✓ vmfe2	Ready to enable	

Enable | Cancel | Number of virtual machines to enable Update Management: 1

4. Wait 25-30 minutes for Virtual Machine to appear on Update Management pane. Just refresh the screen with F5 continously with update Management selected in left pane. It took 35 minutes for below screen to appear.

   In Figure below you can see one critical and security update and one other update is missing.

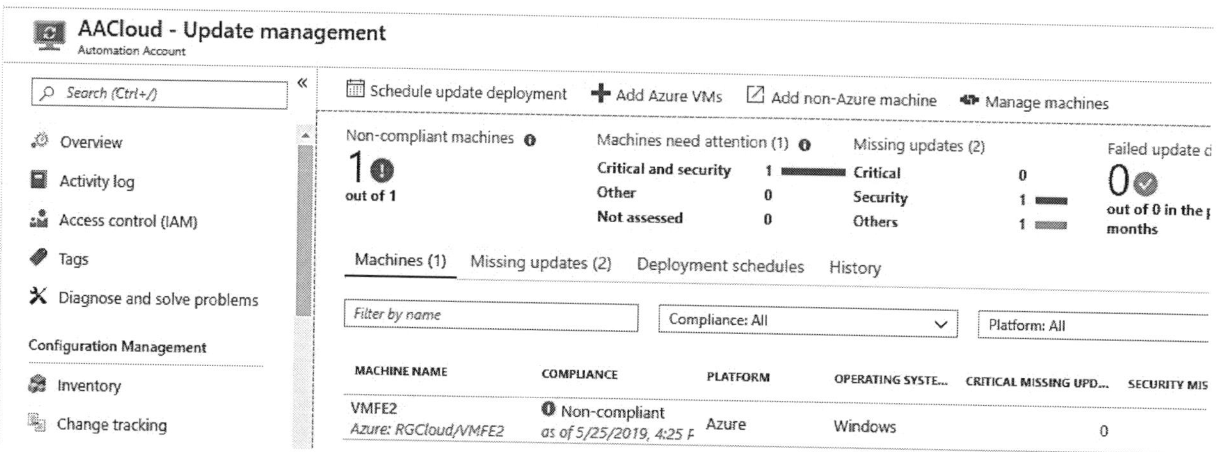

Click on **Missing updates**> you can see the updates which are missing.

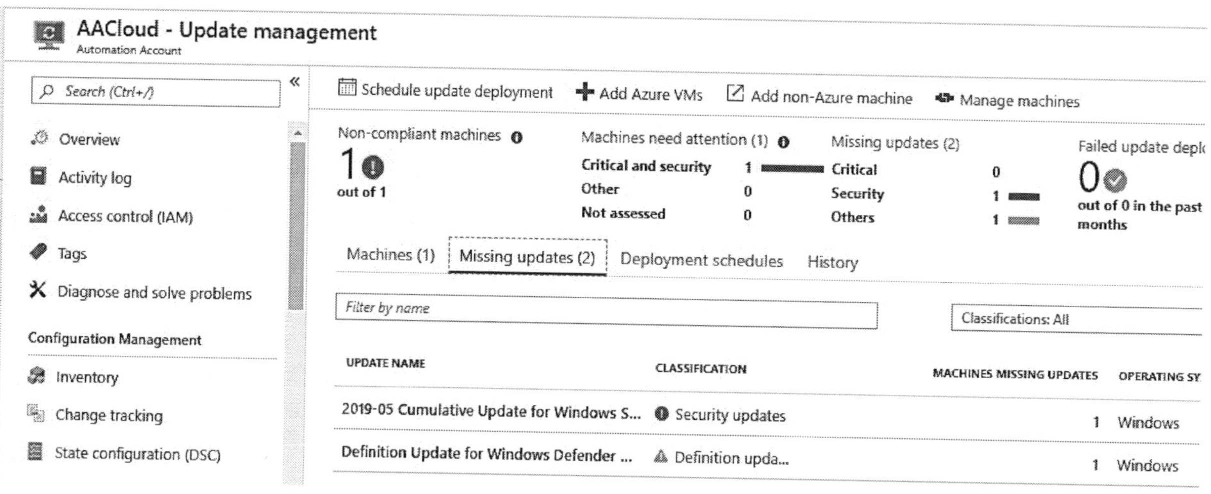

Exercise 119: Scheduling Update Deployment

1. In Update Management pane click schedule update deployment>New update Deployment pane opens>Enter a name> click Machine to update>In Right pane select Machines from **Type** dropdown box>Make sure VM VMFE2 appears under Machines >Click VM VMFE2 and it now also appears under selected items>Click Ok in right pane>In left pane in schedule settings select the start time and Recurrence as Once or Recurring and click ok>Click Create.

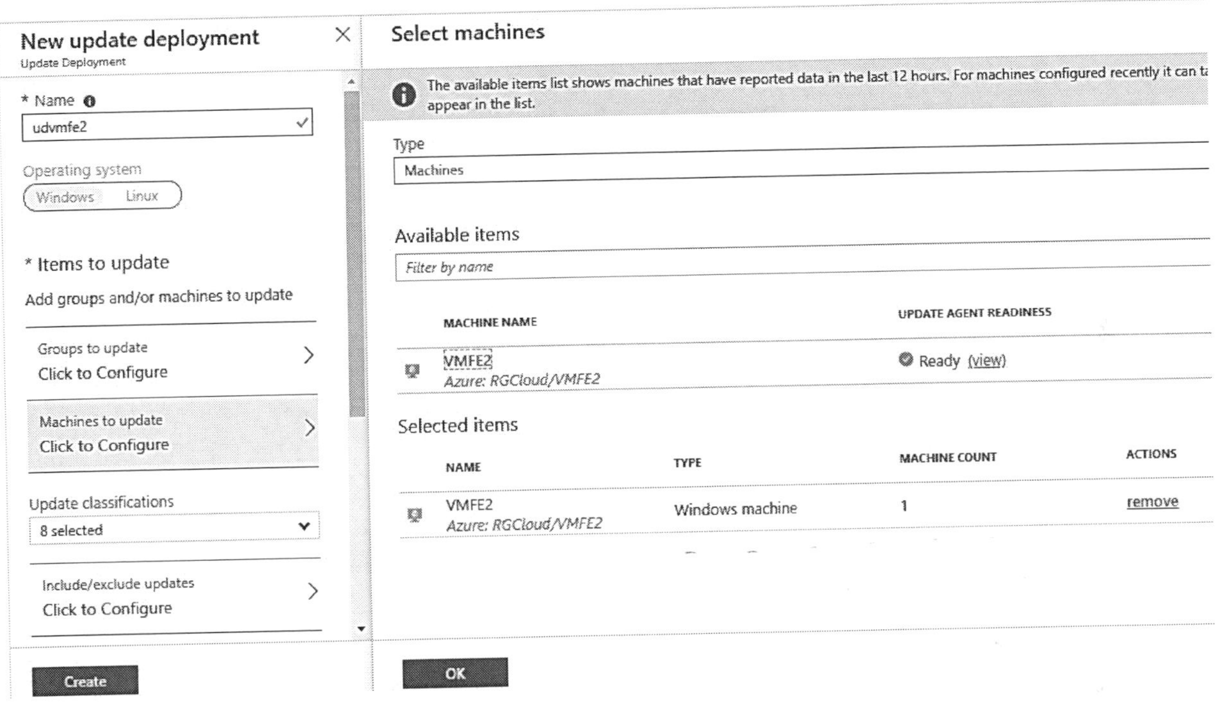

Note: Readers are advised to check options in update classification pane. Also scroll down to see all the options.

2. Click on Deployment Schedules and you can see one deployment Job created in step 1 is scheduled for 5.04 PM.

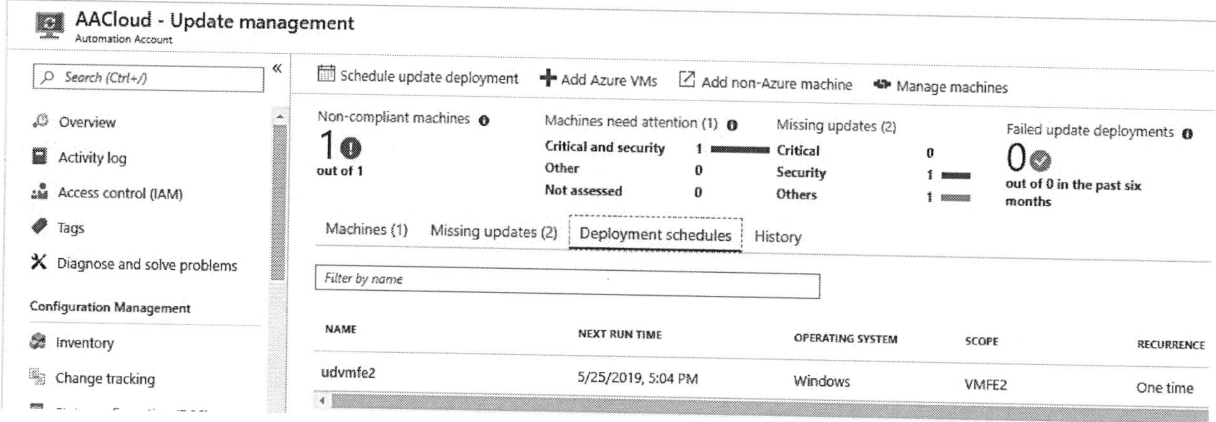

3. In figure below shows 1 update was applied and 1 update failed. This step I did after scheduled deployment happened.

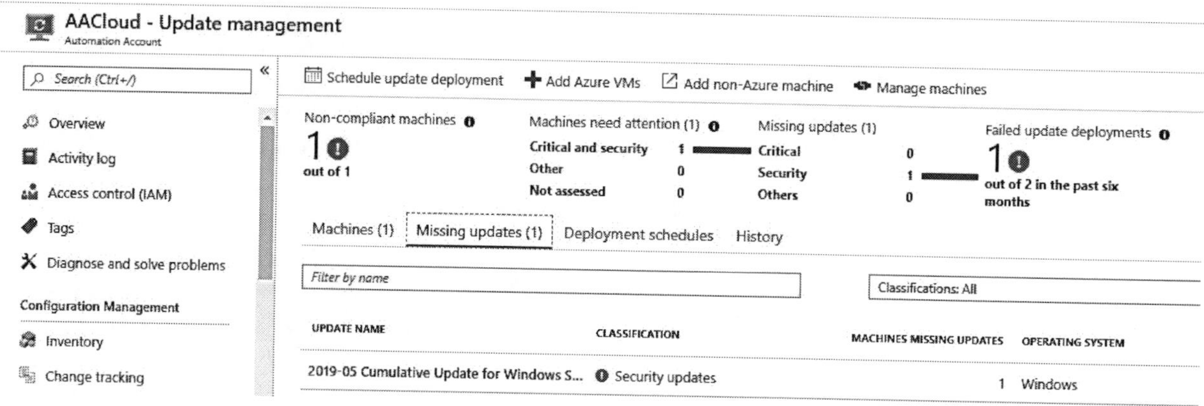

Inventory Management

Enabling inventory of your VMs in Azure Automation gives you visibility into installed applications as well as other configuration items you wish to track. Rich reporting and search is available to quickly find detailed information to help understand everything that is configured within the VM.

Change Tracking

Change tracking tracks changes across services, software, registry, daemons, and files to quickly identify what might be causing issues and to enable diagnostics and alerting when unwanted changes occur.

Note: When you enable Inventory for a VM then change tracking is also enabled automatically.

Exercise 120: Enabling Inventory Management and Add VM VMFE2

1. In Azure Automation Account **AACloud** Dashboard click **Inventory** in left pane> In Right pane select Log Analytics workspace created in Exercise 118>Click enable

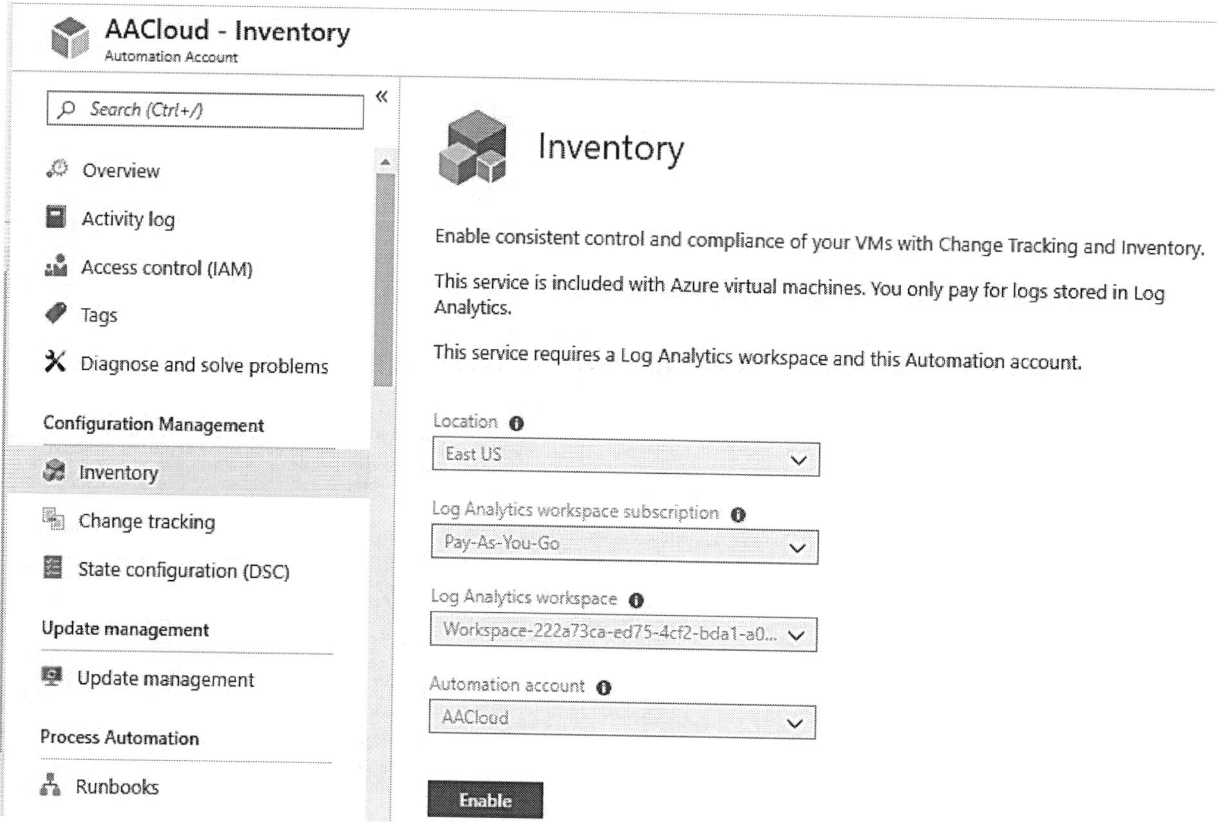

2. After Deployment is enabled refresh the screen with F5. Make sure Inventory is selected in left pane.

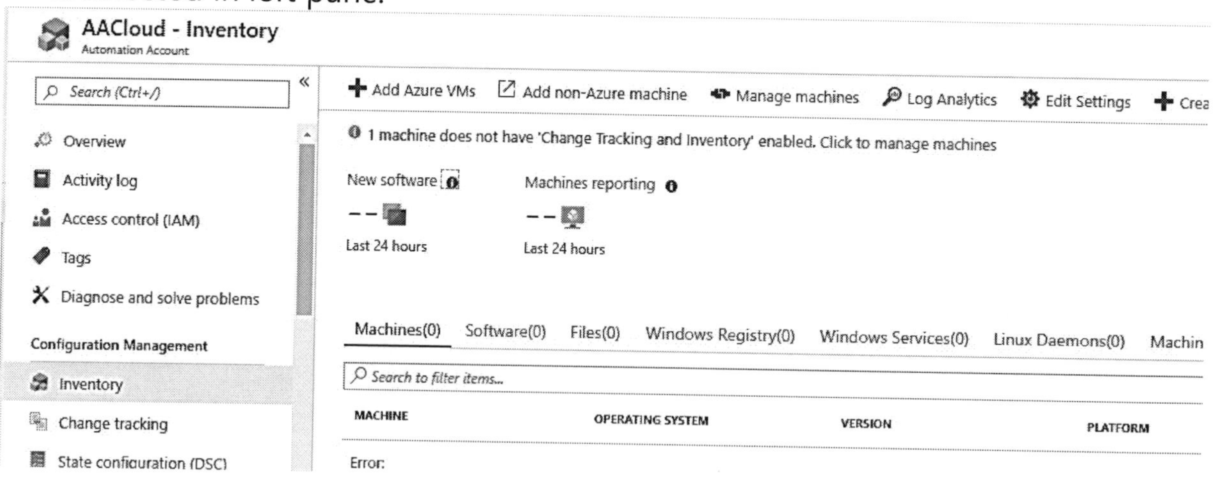

3. Click Add Azure VMs in Right pane>Enable Inventory Blade opens>Check the VM VMFE2>Click enable> Close the enable inventory pane.

Enable Inventory

Inventory

Enable consistent control and compliance of these virtual machines with Inventory.

Configuration (used when enabling new VMs)

AUTO: Auto-configure Log Analytics workspace and Automation account based on VMs subscription and location

CUSTOM: Choose existing Log Analytics workspace and Automation account

Log Analytics workspace: workspace-222a73ca-ed75-4cf2-bda1-a015496fa510-eus

Automation account: AACloud

Summary

Ready to enable	Already enabled	Cannot enable
1	0	1

NAME	INVENTORY	DETAILS
vmfe1	Cannot enable	VM reports to workspace: 'lacloud'.
vmfe2	Ready to enable	

Enable Cancel Number of virtual machines to enable Inventory: 1

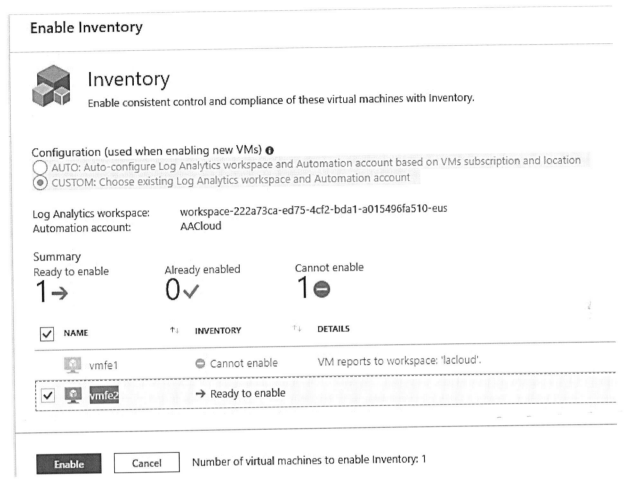

4. After 30-40 minutes VM VMFE2 appeared in inventory pane. Keep on refreshing Automation Account Dashboard with inventory selected.

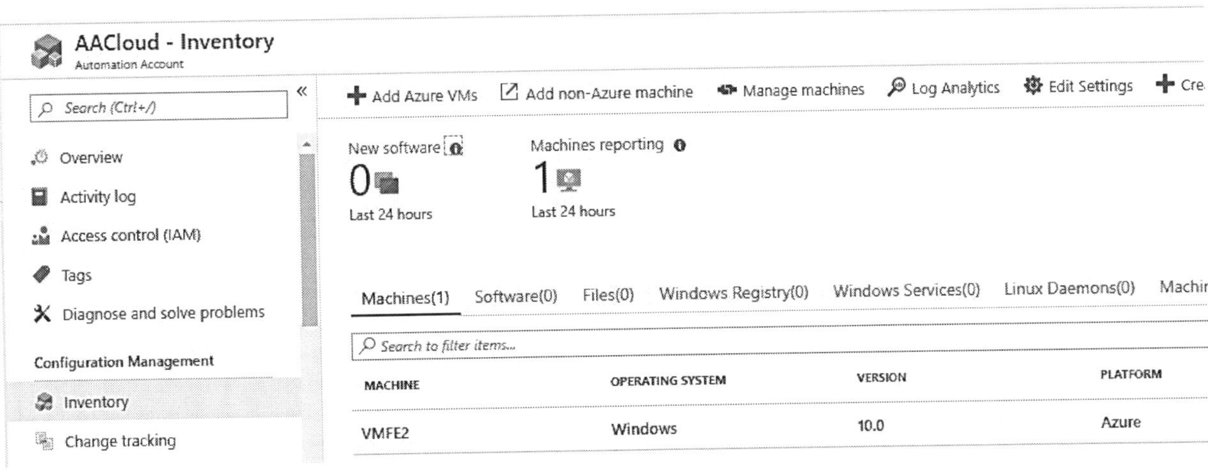

5. Click on the software tab in right pane> You can see software installed in last 24 hours.

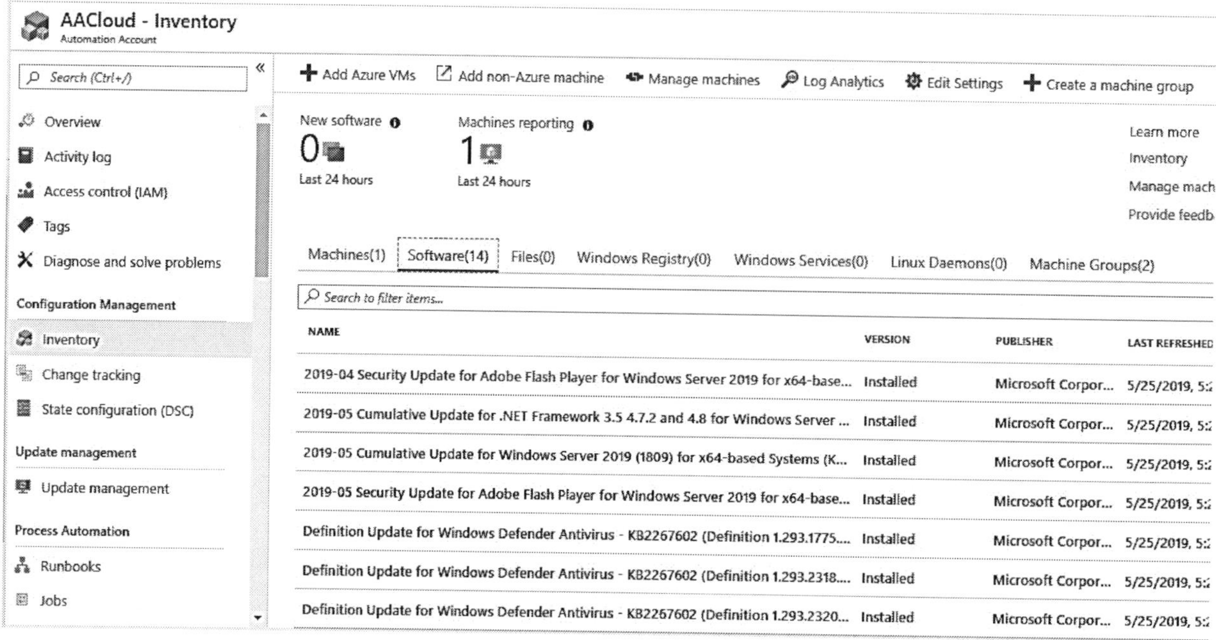

Note: Azure VM VMFE2 was created in Exercise 33, Chapter 4 in Exam AZ-300 & AZ-301 Study & Lab Guide Part 1.

Exercise 121: Checking Change Tracking for VM VMFE2

In Azure Automation Account **AACloud** Dashboard click **Change tracking** in left pane> In Right pane you can see changes which have occurred in Azure VM VMFE2.

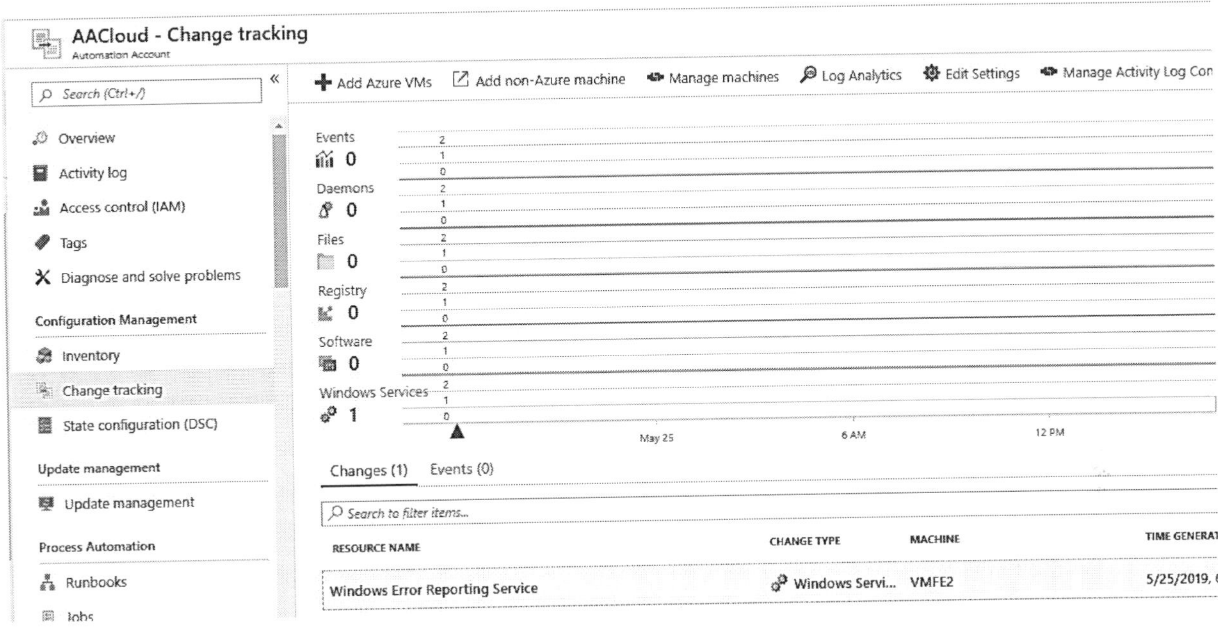

Chapter 12 Azure Resource Manager (ARM) Template

This Chapter covers following Topic Lessons

- Azure Resource Manager (ARM) Template
- Why we need ARM Template
- Advantages of ARM Template
- Disadvantage of ARM Template
- Creating ARM template options
- ARM Template Deployment Options
- Viewing ARM Template

This Chapter covers following Lab Exercises

- View ARM Template of an Existing Resource
- Save a Template in library
- Deploy or Edit Template

Chapter Topology

In this chapter we will add ARM Template to the Topology.

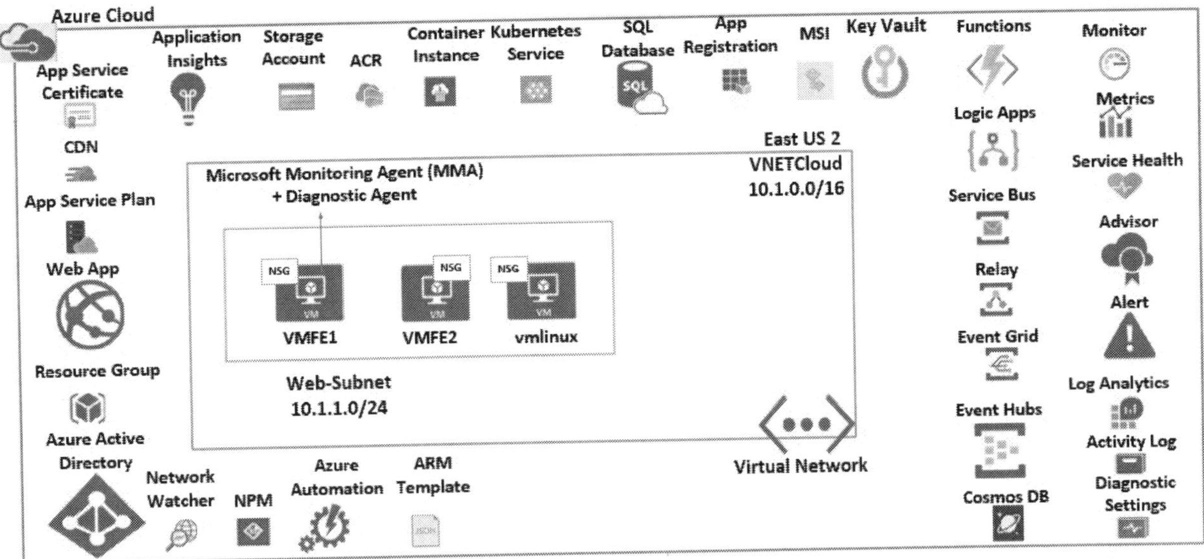

Azure Resource Manager (ARM) Template

ARM Templates are used to deploy resources using Infrastructure as a Code.

ARM Template is a text based JavaScript Object Notation (JSON) file that defines one or more resources to deploy to a resource group. It also defines the dependencies between the deployed resources. The template can be re-used to deploy the resources consistently and repeatedly.

Templates are also created by MS and 3rd parties. Figure below shows a sample ARM Template for Storage account creation.

```
{
    "$schema":
"https://schema.management.azure.com/schemas/2015-01-01/deploymentTemplate.json#",
    "contentVersion": "1.0.0.0",
    "parameters": {
        "storageAccounts_arm4100201_name": {
            "defaultValue": "arm4100201",
            "type": "String"
        }
    },
    "variables": {},
```

Why we need ARM Template

Take an Example that you need to deploy a 3 tier application (Web/App/DB) in a new Virtual network. Internet user will connect to Web Tier, Web Tier will connect to App and App will connect to DB tier.

Using Azure Portal or Powershell we can deploy these resources one by one. To deploy we first need to create Virtual network and 3 subnets. Deploy VMs to these 3 subnets. Configure NSG on Subnets and VM NICs. There are following disadvantages to this approach:

1. It is time consuming to deploy and configure the resources.
2. It is error prone
3. You require skilled resources for deployment.

Instead of above option of deploying resources individually we can create an ARM template once, specifying multiple resources and other configurations parameters for deployment. Using this ARM template you can now deploy multiple resources (VNET, Subnet, NSG & Virtual Machines) simultaneously. The ARM template can be re-used multiple times.

Advantages of ARM Template

1. We can deploy, manage, and monitor all the resources for our solution as a group, rather than handling these resources individually.
2. We can re-use the ARM template any number of times.
3. Saves time.
4. We can define the dependencies between resources so they are deployed in the correct order.

Disadvantage of ARM Template

1. The biggest disadvantage of ARM Template is that you require engineering level skills to create ARM Template.

Creating ARM template options

1. Create an ARM Template from scratch using JSON.
2. Download a template of a resource from Azure Portal and Edit it as per your requirement and then deploy it.

ARM Template Deployment Options

1. PowerShell
2. CLI
3. Azure Portal

Viewing ARM Template of an Existing Resource

You can view Template of a resource using **Export Template** Tab in Resource Dashboard.

Exercise 122: View ARM Template of an Existing Resource

In this Exercise we will view Template of Virtual Machine VMFE2. VMFE2 was created in Chapter 2, Exercise 26.

1. Go to VMFE2 Dashboard>In left pane Under Setting Click **Export Template**> In right pane you can see ARM template of VMFE2.

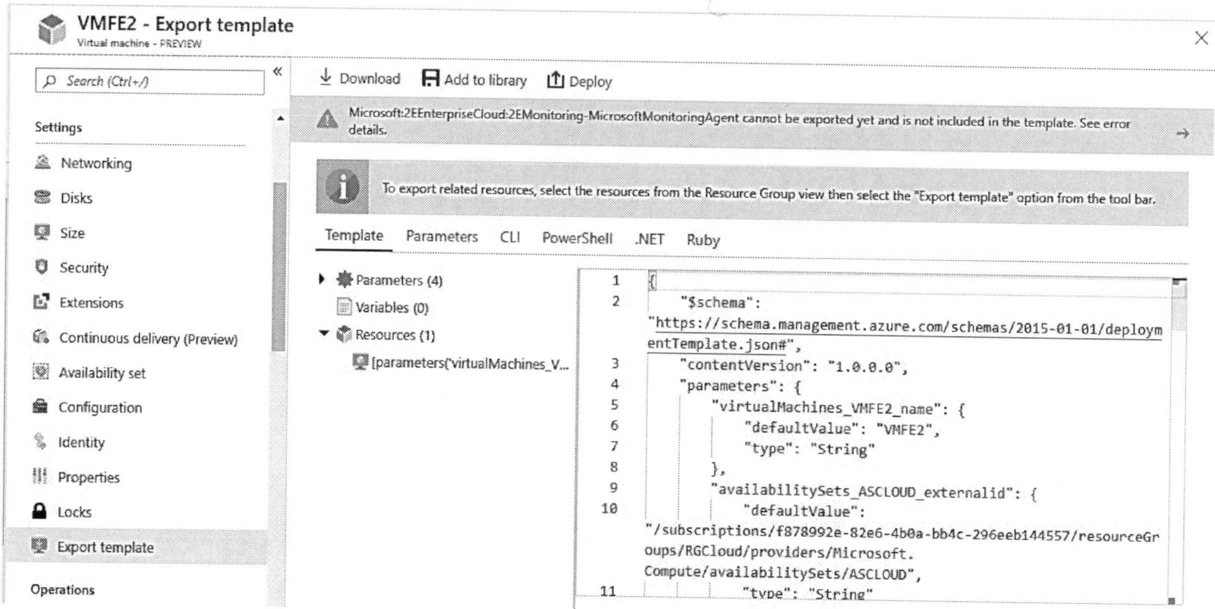

Note the 3 options in Top right – Download, Add to library and Deploy.

Download: With this option you can download Template to your desktop.

Add to Library: With this option you can save the template in Library in Azure.

Deploy: With this option you can deploy the template to create a new Resource. In this case it will be Virtual Machine.

Exercise 123: Save a Template in library

In this lab we will save template of VM VMFE2 in Library in your Azure Account.

1. In Azure Portal go to VMFE2 Dashboard>Click Export Template in left pane> In right pane you can see template.

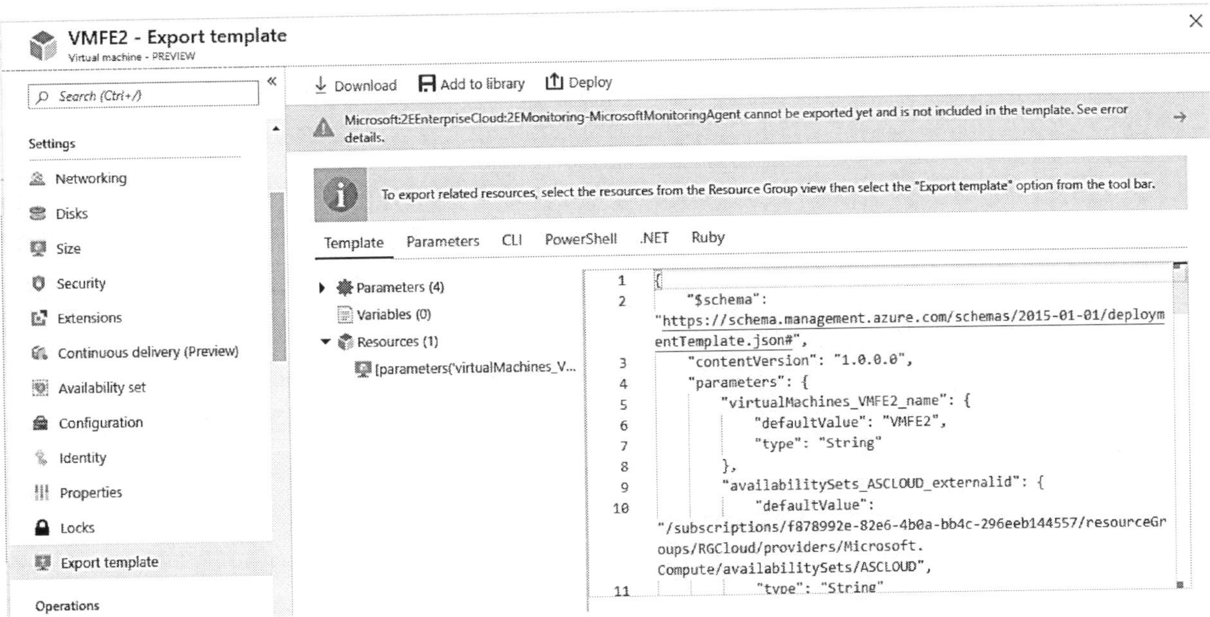

2. Click Add to Library in Right pane>Save template blade opens> Enter a name VMFE2T and Enter Description>Click Save (Not shown).

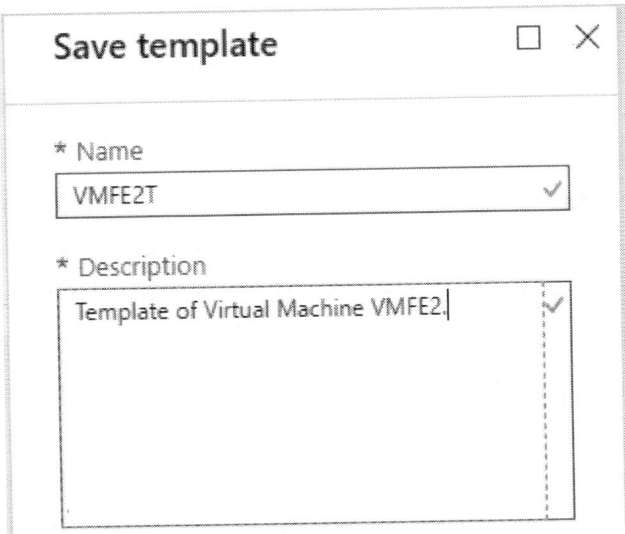

3. **Check the saved Template**. In Azure Portal click All Services in left pane>All Services Blade opens>Click General>Note Templates option under General (2nd from bottom).

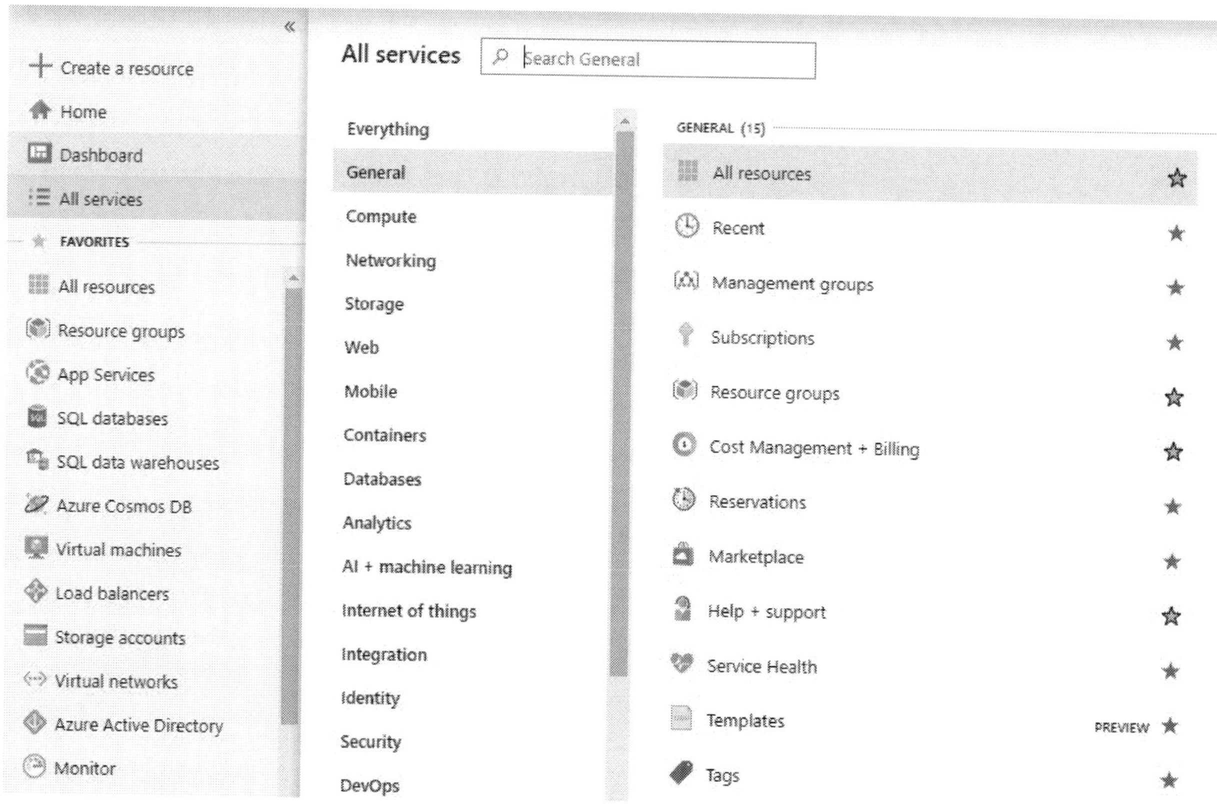

4. Click Templates under General>All Templates blade opens>You can see the VMFE2T template.

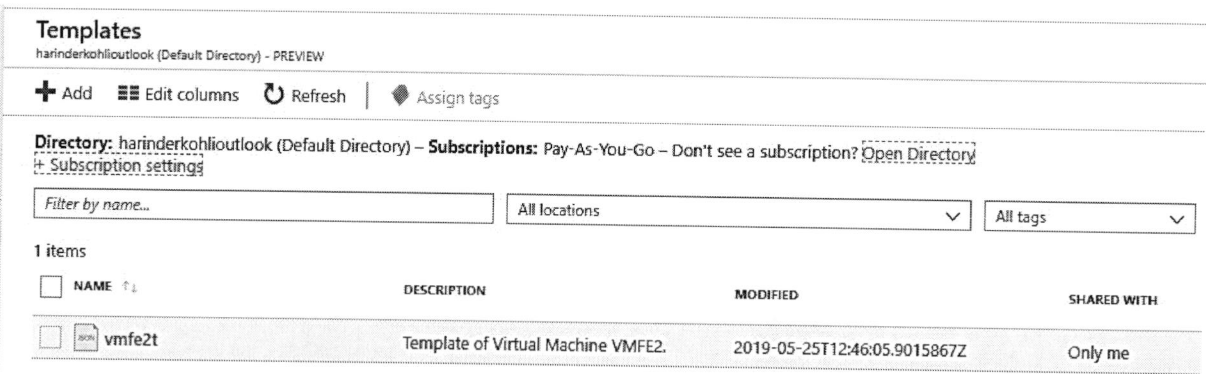

Exercise 124: Deploy or Edit Template

In this Exercise we will demonstrate deployment or Editing of Template. We will use the template vmfe2t which was saved in library in Previous Exercise.

1. In Azure Portal click All Services in left pane>All Services Blade opens>Click Templates under General>All Templates Blade opens>Click Template vmfe2t>vmfe2 Template blade opens>Click View Template. Template opens in extreme right pane.

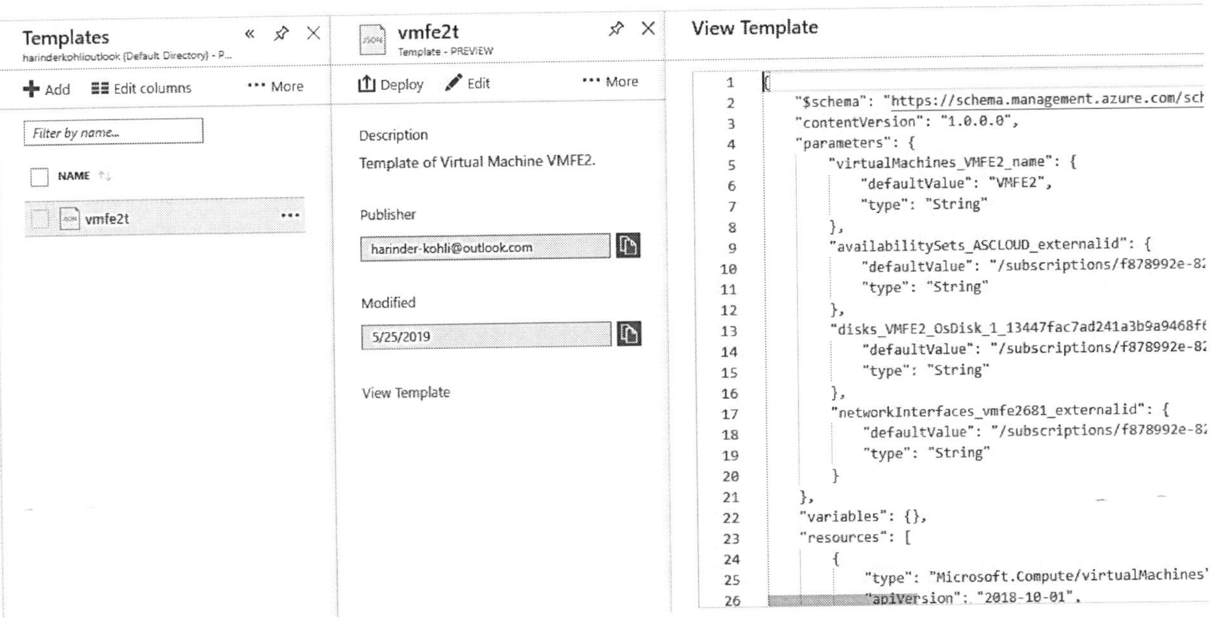

2. From here you can click deploy or edit the template to deploy a new VM or edit the existing template.

3. Click deploy>Deploy from Custom Template pane opens. You can deploy a new VM here.

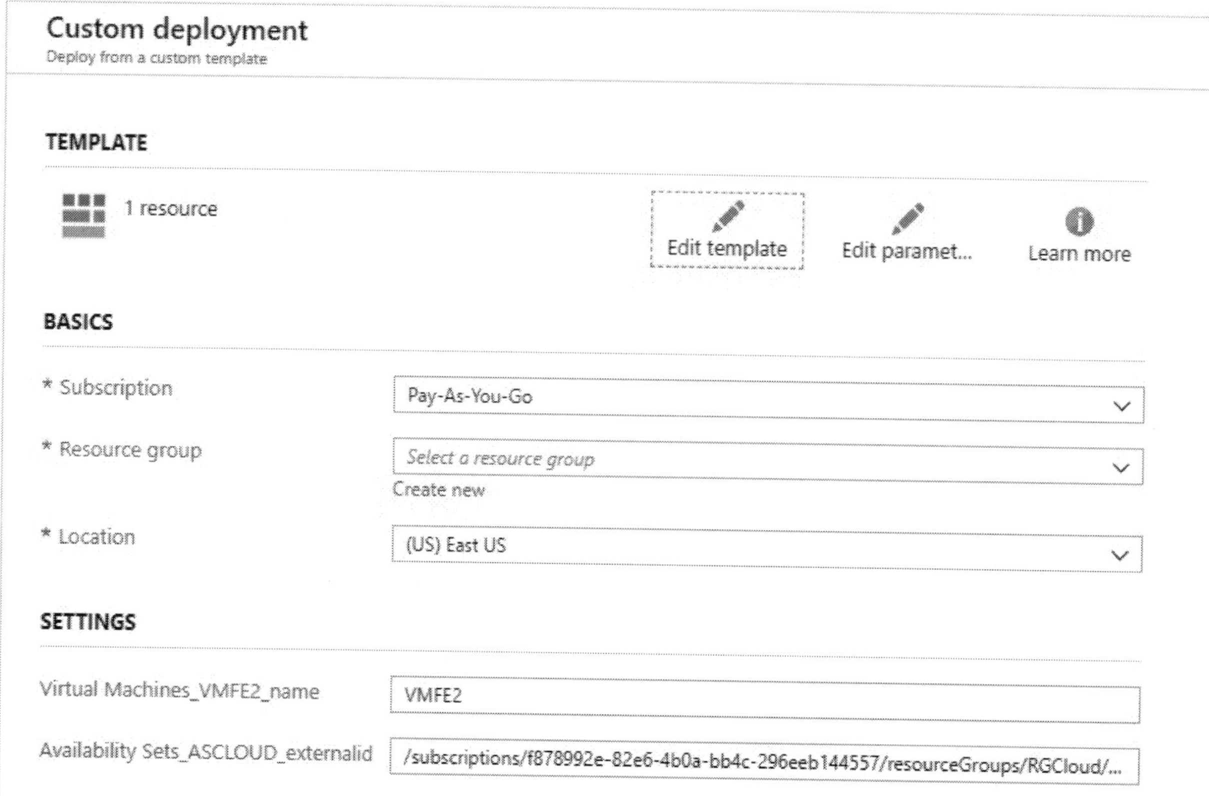

Chapter 13 Azure Redis Cache

This is AZ-301 specific Chapter. Leave this for AZ-300 Exam.

This Chapter covers following

- Azure Redis Cache
- Redis Cache Use Cases
- Azure Redis Cache Features and tiers

This Chapter Covers following Lab Exercises

- Create and use Azure Redis Cache

Chapter Topology

In this chapter we will add Azure Redis Cache to the Topology.

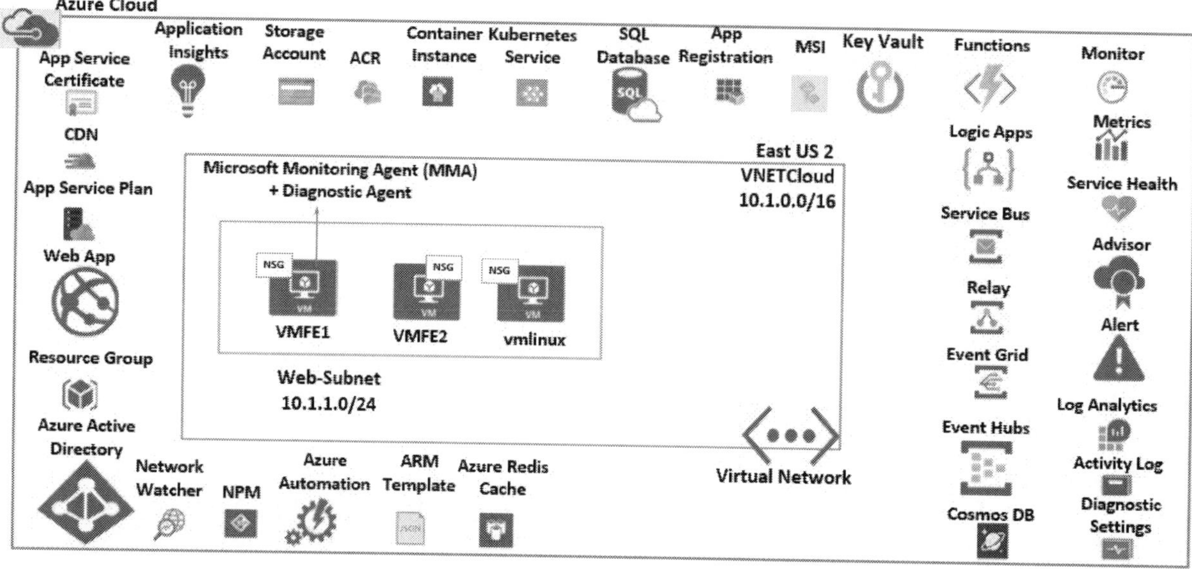

Azure Redis Cache

Azure Redis Cache is Managed service in Azure and is based on open source Redis Cache.

Azure Redis cache is in-memory key-value No SQL data store and cache. Azure Cache improves the performance of applications by allowing you to retrieve information from fast, managed, in-memory data stores, instead of relying entirely on slower disk-based databases.

All Redis data resides in its server's main memory, in contrast to most database management systems that store data on disk or on SSDs. By eliminating the need to access disks, in-memory databases such as Redis avoid seek time delays and can access data with simpler algorithms that use fewer CPU instructions. Typical operations require less than a millisecond to execute.

Redis is a fast, open source, in-memory key-value data structure store. Redis comes with a set of versatile in-memory data structures which enable you to easily create a variety of custom applications.

Redis Cache Use Cases

Caching: Redis placed in "front" of another database creates a highly performant in-memory cache to decrease access latency, increase throughput, and ease the load off a relational or NoSQL database.

Session management: Redis is highly suited for session management tasks. Simply use Redis as a fast key-value store with appropriate TTL on session keys to manage your session information. Session management is commonly required for online applications, including games, e-commerce websites and social media platforms.

Real-time Leaderboards: Using the Redis Sorted Set data structure, elements are kept in a list, sorted by their scores. This makes it easy to create dynamic leaderboards to show who is winning a game, or posting the most-liked messages, or anything else where you want to show who's in the lead.

Rate Limiting: Redis can measure and, when needed, throttle the rate of events. By using a Redis counter associated with a client's API key, you can count the number of access requests within a certain time period and take action if a limit is exceeded. Rate limiters are commonly used for limiting the number of posts on a forum, limiting resource utilization and containing the impact of spammers.

Queues: The Redis List data structure makes it easy to implement a lightweight, persistent queue. Lists offer atomic operations as well as blocking capabilities, making them suitable for a variety of applications that require a reliable message broker or a circular list.

Chat and Messaging: Redis supports the PUB/SUB standard with pattern matching. This allows Redis to support high performance chat rooms, real-time comment streams, and server intercommunication. You can also use PUB/SUB to trigger actions based on published events.

Azure Redis Cache Features and tiers

Basic: Basic cache is a single node cache which is ideal for development/test and non-critical workloads. There is no SLA on Basic tier. Basic and Standard caches are available in sizes up to 53 GB Memory. Maximum number of Client connections is 20000.

Standard: A replicated cache in a two node Primary/Secondary configuration managed by Microsoft, with a high availability SLA of 99.9%. Microsoft manage automatic replication between the two nodes. Basic and Standard caches are available in sizes up to 53 GB. Maximum number of Client connections is 20000.

Premium: Enterprise ready tier which can be used as a cache and persist data. Designed for maximum scale and enterprise integration. Premium caches are available in sizes up to 530 GB Memory. Maximum number of Client connections is 40000.

Premium Tier Additional Feature

Better Performance: Better performance over Basic or Standard-tier Caches for similar size VM, bigger workloads, disaster recovery and enhanced security.

Redis data persistence: The Premium tier allows you to persist the cache data in an Azure Storage account. In a Basic/Standard cache all the data is stored only in memory. In case of underlying infrastructure issues there can be potential data loss. We recommend using the Redis data persistence feature in the Premium tier to increase resiliency against data loss.

Redis cluster: With Redis cluster you can create caches larger than 53 GB. Each node consists of a primary/replica cache pair managed by Azure for high availability. Premium caches are available in sizes up to 530 GB Memory. Redis clustering gives you maximum scale and throughput. Throughput increases linearly as you increase the number of nodes in the cluster.

Enhanced security and isolation with VNET: Caches created in the Basic or Standard tier are accessible on the public internet. Access to the Cache is restricted based on the access key. With the Premium tier you can further ensure that only clients within a specified network can access the Cache. You can deploy Premium Redis Cache in an Azure Virtual Network (VNET). You can use all the features of VNET such as subnets, access control policies, and other features to further restrict access to Redis.

Geo-replication links two Premium tier Azure Redis Cache instances. One cache is designated as the primary linked cache, and the other as the secondary linked cache. The secondary linked cache becomes read-only, and data written to the primary cache is replicated to the secondary linked cache. This functionality can be used to replicate a cache across Azure regions.

Reboot: The premium tier allows you to reboot one or more nodes of your cache on-demand. This allows you to test your application for resiliency in the event of a failure.

Comparing Different Redis Cache Tiers

Features	Basic	Standard	Premium
Cache	Yes	Yes	Yes
Compute Nodes	1	2 (Active-Passive)	Multiple
Replication and Failover		Yes	Yes
SLA		99.9%	99.9%
Redis Data Persistence			Yes
Redis Cluster			Yes
Scale Out to multiple Cache units			Yes
Azure Virtual Network			Yes
Memory Size	250 MB - 53 GB	250 MB - 53 GB	6 GB - 530 GB
Maximum number of Client connections	256 - 20,000	256 - 20,000	7,500 - 40,000

Exercise 125: Create and use Azure Redis Cache

Creating and using Azure Redis Cache is a 2 step process. First you create Redis Cache and then add Redis Cache connection string in your application.

1. **Create Redis Cache:** In Azure Portal Click Create a resource> Databases> Azure Cache for Redis> Create Redis Cache Blade opens>Enter a name>Select RGCloud in Resource Group>Location East US 2> Click create.

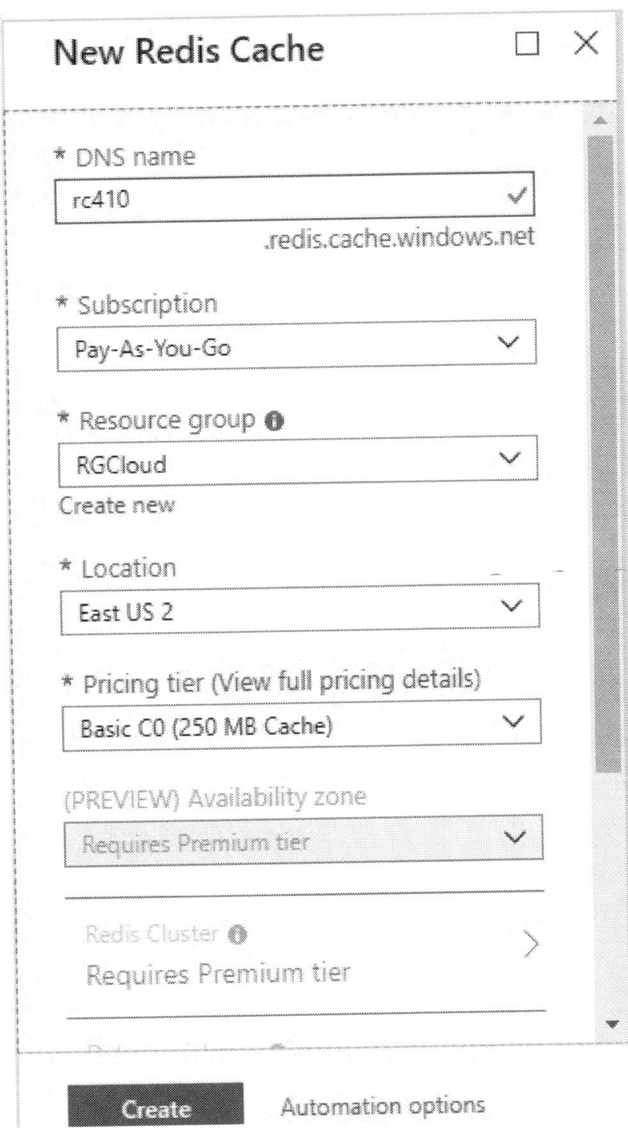

2. Figure below shows dashboard of Redis Cache.

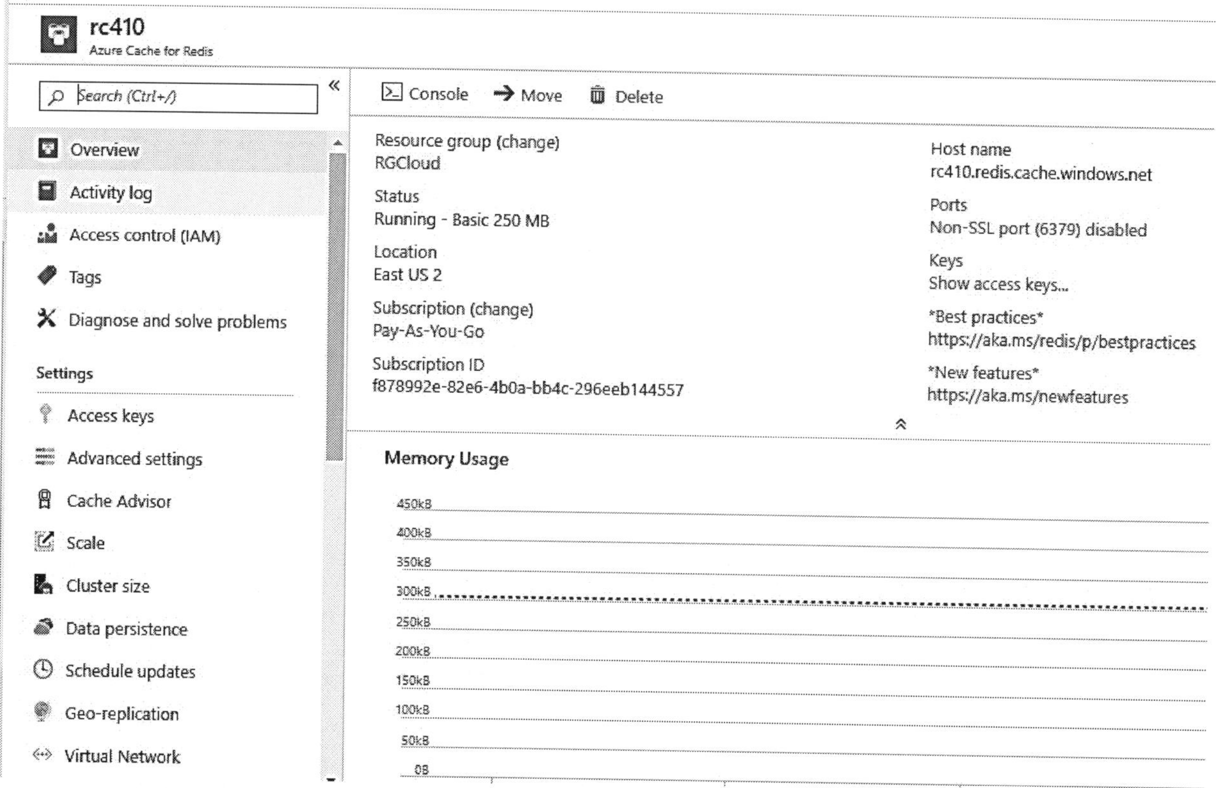

3. **Copy Redis Cache connection String.** Go to newly created Redis Cache Dashboard>click Access Keys in left pane and copy the Primary Connection String.

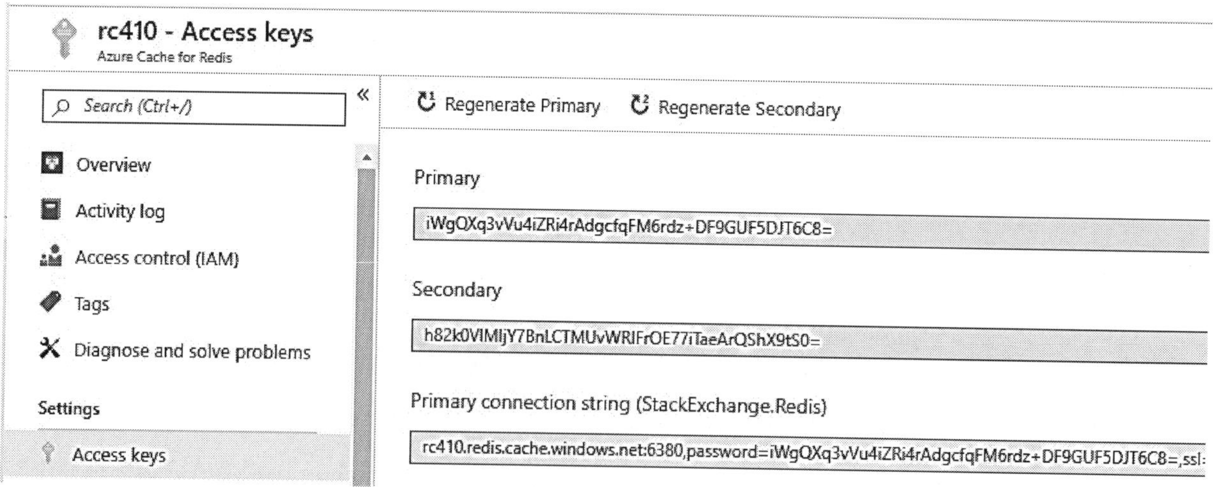

4. In your application add Primary connection string. Also configure your application to use Azure Redis Cache.

Chapter 14 Hybrid Applications and Data Migration

This is AZ-301 specific Chapter. Leave this for AZ-300 Exam.

This Chapter covers following Topic Lessons

- On-premises Data Gateway
- Data Management Gateway for Data Factory
- Identify Options to Join VM to domains
- Azure Relay Service
- Web App Hybrid and VPN Connection

On-premises Data Gateway

The on-premises data gateway **connects** on-premises data sources to Azure Services such as Azure Analysis Server, Logic Apps, Power BI & Microsoft Flow in the cloud.

Figure below show the Architecture and setup of on-premises data gateway.

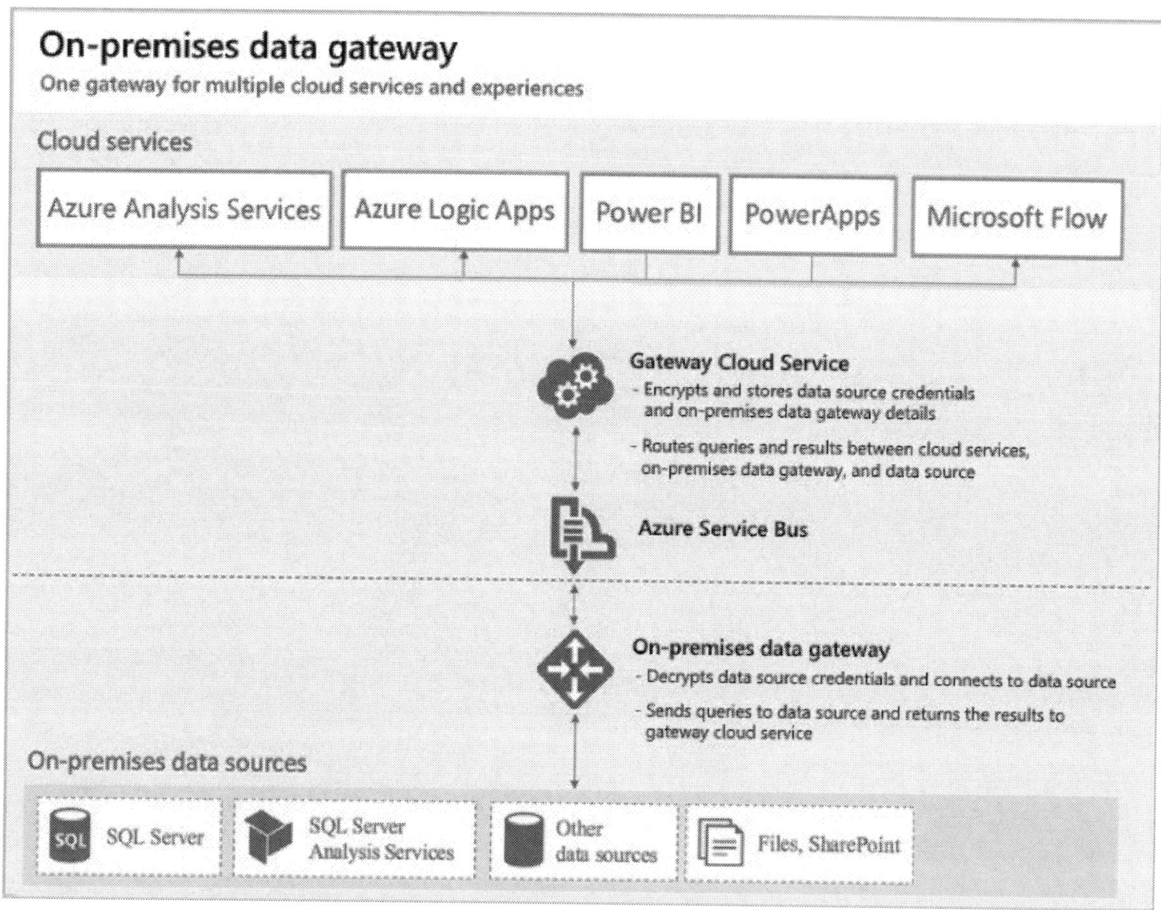

Component of the solutions: On-premises data gateway, Gateway Cloud Service & Azure Service Bus

Brief working: When Azure Resource requires access to on-premises data source it sends request to Gateway Cloud service. The gateway cloud service pushes the request to the Azure Service Bus. The on-premises data gateway polls the Azure Service Bus for pending requests and sends the request to the data source for execution. The results are sent from the data source, back to the gateway and then onto the cloud service and your server.

Data Management Gateway for Data Factory

The Data management gateway is installed in your on-premises environment to **copy** data between cloud and on-premises data stores.

Note: Data Management Gateway supports copy activity only. You cannot use Data Management Gateway to connect Azure resources to on-premises data sources.

Figure below shows the Architecture of Data Management Gateway.

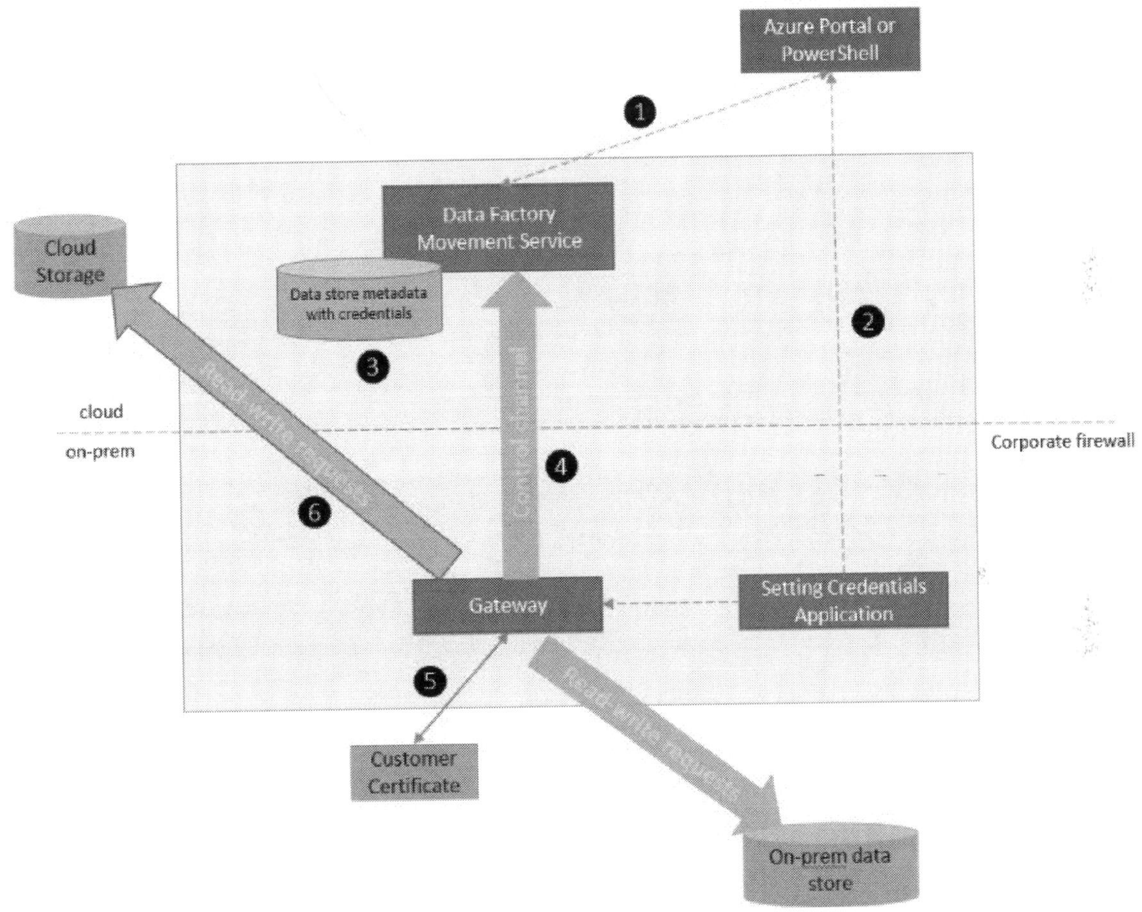

Brief Working: Data Management Gateway is installed on-premises and is registered with Data Factory. Azure Data Factory creates 2 linked services for connecting on-premises data store and Cloud Data store to Azure Data Factory. Data Factory service communicates with the gateway for scheduling & management of jobs via a control channel that uses a shared Azure service bus queue. The gateway copies data from an on-premises store to a cloud storage, or vice versa depending on how the Copy Activity is configured in the data pipeline.

Identify Options to Join VM to domains

To provide Active Directory services to workloads in cloud you have following options:

1. Deploy a stand-alone domain in Azure using domain controllers deployed as Azure virtual machines.
2. Extend the corporate AD domain/forest infrastructure by setting up replica domain controllers using Azure virtual machines.
3. Deploy a site-to-site VPN connection between workloads running in Azure Infrastructure Services and the corporate directory on-premises.
4. Azure AD Domain Services (Managed Read only Domain Controller).

Azure Relay Service

See Azure Messaging Solutions Chapter 7.

Web App Hybrid and VPN Connection

See Web App Chapter 1

Chapter 15 High Performance Computing (HPC)

This is AZ-301 specific Chapter. Leave this for AZ-300 Exam.

This Chapter covers following following Topic Lessons

- High Performance Computing
- High Performance Computing with Azure Batch
- Azure Batch Use cases (Intrinsically Parallel Workloads)
- Azure Batch Use cases (Tightly coupled Workloads)
- Azure Batch Architecture & Working
- Azure Batch Pricing
- Low-priority VMs in Batch

This Chapter covers following Lab Exercises

- Azure Batch Computing

Chapter Topology

In this chapter we will add Azure Batch Computing to the Topology.

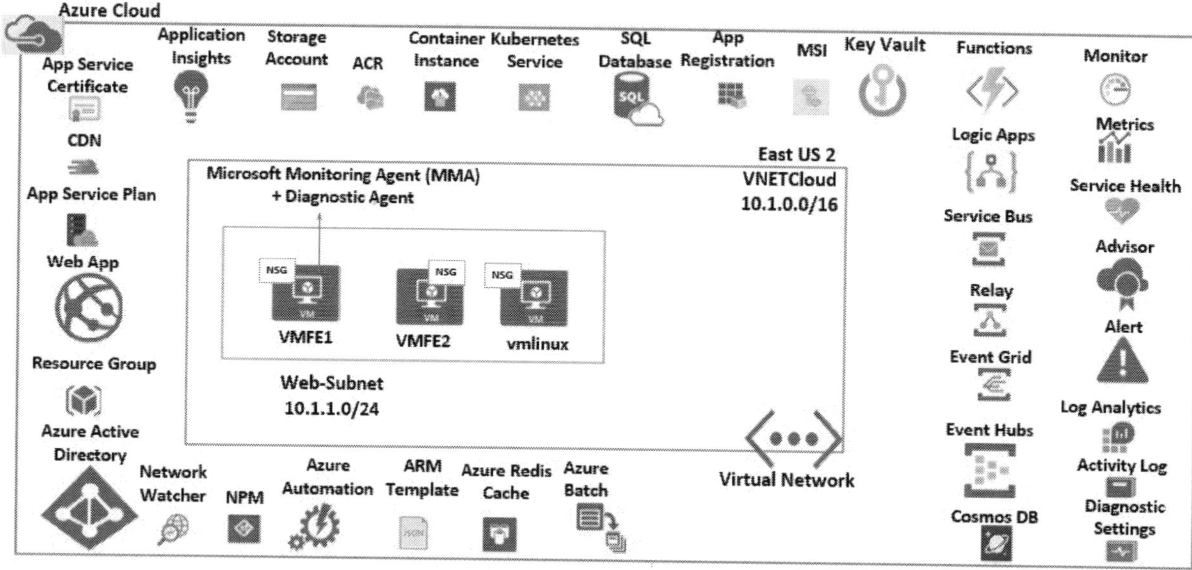

High Performance Computing (HPC)

High-performance computing (HPC) aggregates computing power from multiple computers to run parallel processing Workloads or Applications.

Parallel Workloads are those where the applications can run independently on Cluster of computers and each instance completes part of the work.

In Azure You can implement HPC in following 3 ways:

High Performance Computing Virtual machines: Azure Virtual Machines such as H Series & N Series can run HPC Workloads. You need to deploy HPC Software on Azure VMs to run HPC workloads.

Microsoft HPC Pack: Microsoft Free HPC Software Pack is used to create Linux or Windows High Performance Computing (HPC) Cluster. ARM templates are used to deploy the HPC Pack on Azure VMs. HPC Pack creates Single or Multiple **Head Nodes** and Cluster of **Compute Nodes** which run Parallel Processing Workloads. All Resources are deployed in Azure Virtual Network. **HPC Cluster Manager** is used to configure and manage HPC Cluster.

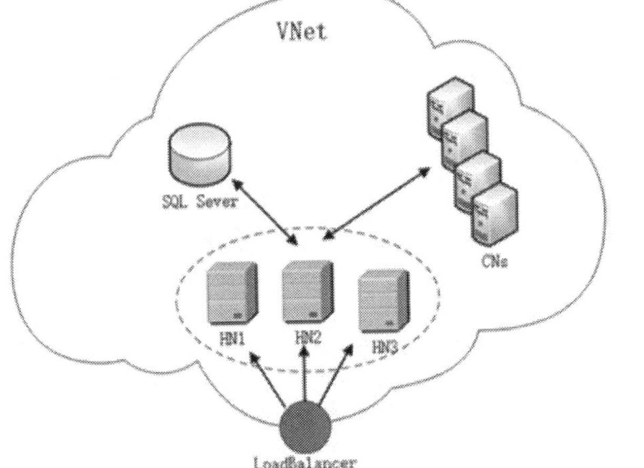

Cluster with Multiple Head Nodes and External Database Server

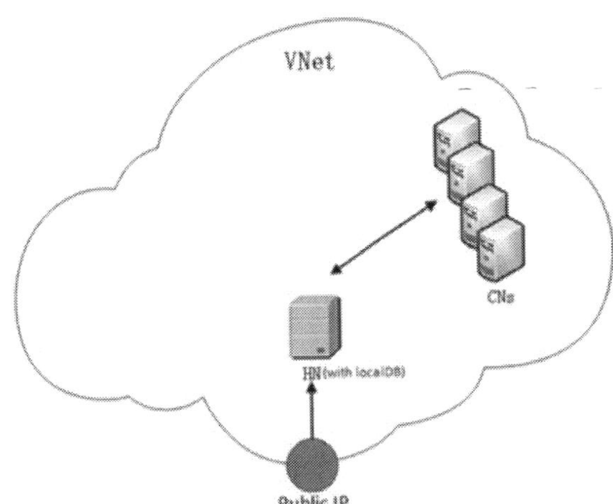

Cluster with Single Head Node and Local Database

Both of the above solutions are not managed solutions and have high operational and Administrative overheads.

Azure Batch provides on-demand managed compute & software resources that enable you to run and high-performance computing (HPC) workloads.

High Performance Computing with Azure Batch

Azure Batch provides on-demand managed compute & software resources that enable you to run large-scale parallel HPC workloads.

Azure Batch creates and manages a pool of compute nodes (virtual machines), installs the applications you want to run, and schedules jobs to run on the nodes. Azure Batch provides job scheduling and cluster management, allowing applications to run in parallel and at scale.

Azure Batch is a platform service that schedules compute-intensive work to run on a managed collection of virtual machines, and can automatically scale compute resources to meet the needs of your jobs.

Advantages of Azure Batch

1. Azure Batch creates and manages a pool of compute nodes (virtual machines), installs the applications you want to run, and schedules jobs to run on the nodes.
2. Advantage of running HPC with Azure Batch that there is no cluster or job scheduler software to install & manage. Cluster and Job Scheduler software comes as a managed service with Azure Batch.

Azure Batch Use cases (Intrinsically Parallel Workloads)

Intrinsically parallel workloads are those where the applications can run independently, and each instance completes part of the work. When the applications are executing, they might access some common data, but they do not communicate with other instances of the application. Example of Parallel workloads include:

Financial risk modeling
VFX and 3D image rendering
Image analysis and processing
Media transcoding
Genetic sequence analysis
Optical character recognition (OCR)
Data ingestion, processing, and ETL operations

Azure Batch Use cases (Tightly coupled Workloads)

Tightly coupled workloads are those where the applications you run need to communicate with each other, as opposed to run independently. Tightly coupled applications normally use the Message Passing Interface (MPI) API. You can run your tightly coupled workloads with Batch using Microsoft MPI or Intel MPI. Some examples of tightly coupled workloads:

Finite element analysis
Fluid dynamics
Multi-node AI training

Azure Batch Architecture & Working

Figure below shows Architecture and working of Azure Batch Solutions running a parallel workload on cluster of compute nodes.

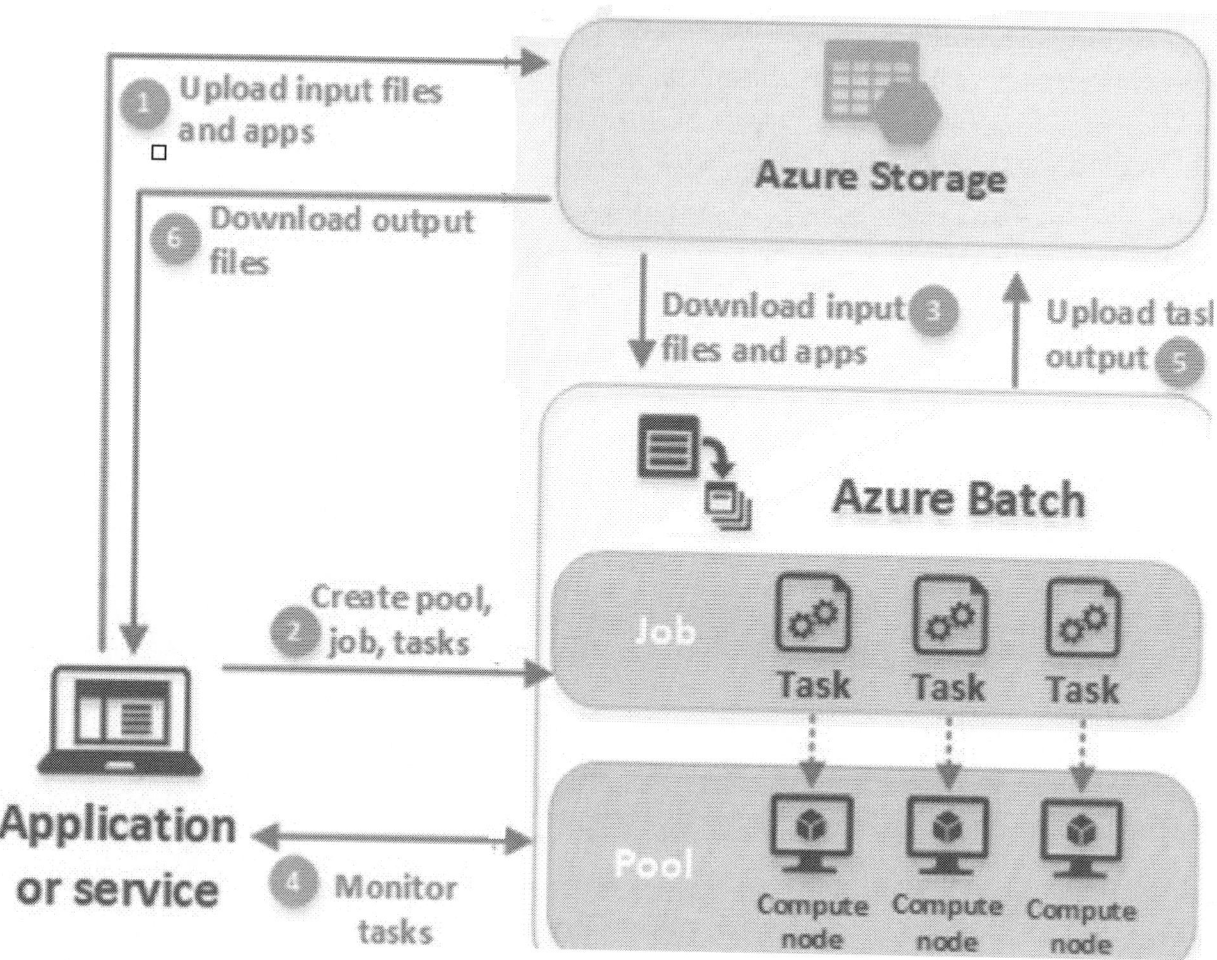

Components of Azure Batch Solutions

Batch Account provides pool of **Compute nodes** which will run Batch applications and Job Scheduling software to schedule **jobs** and run **tasks**. It also monitors the progress of the application running on the compute Cluster.
Storage Account contains Batch Application and Data which will be downloaded to Cluster of compute nodes.
Client Application connects to Batch service to query and monitor tasks running on compute node.

Implementation Steps for Deploying Azure Batch Computing

1. Create Batch Account with associated Storage Account.
2. Create a pool of compute nodes.
3. Create a job.
4. Create a task.
5. View task output.

Note: Storage account is used to deploy applications and to store input and output data.

Exercise 126: Azure Batch Computing

Note: For this Lab we don't requitre Storage Account.

Step 1: Create Batch Account

In Azure Portal Click Create a resource>Compute>Batch Service>Create New Batch Account opens> Select RGCloud in resource group>Location East US 2> Click Review + create.

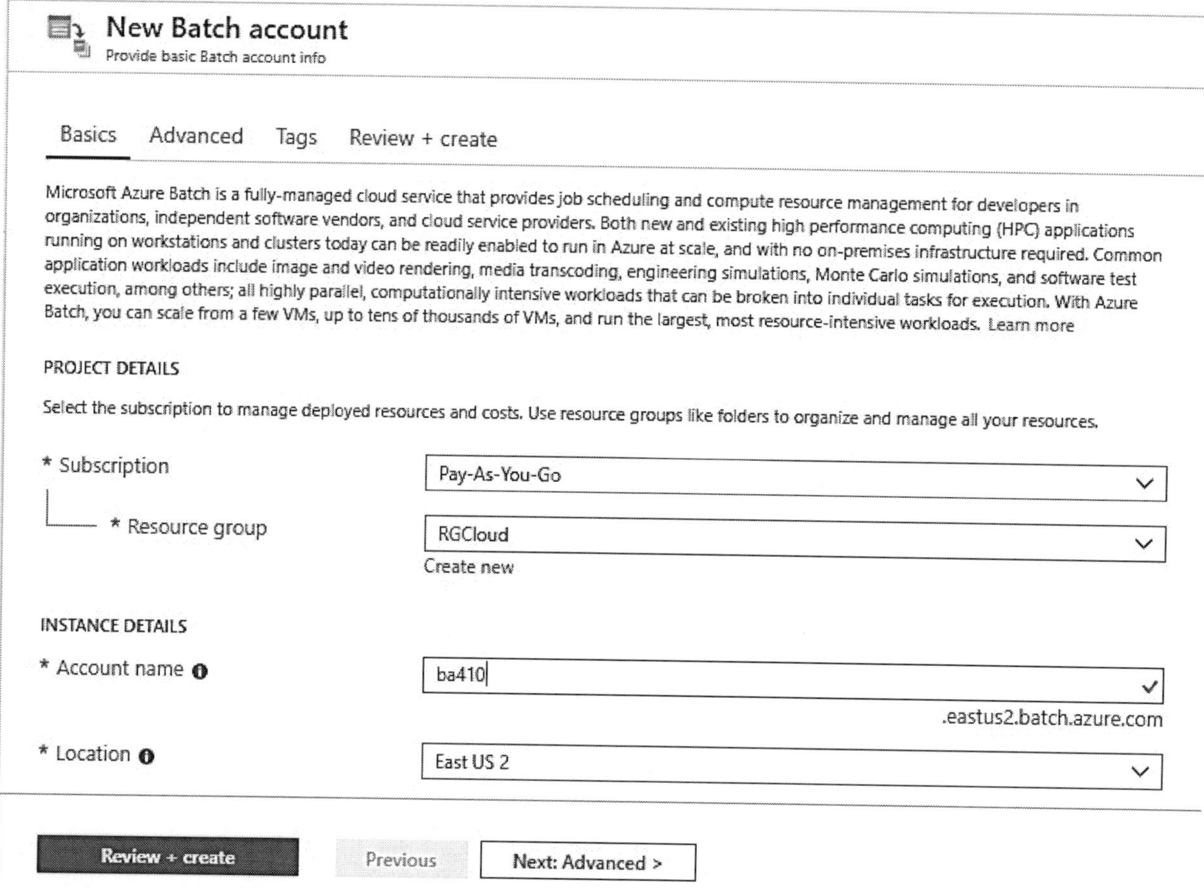
New Batch account
Provide basic Batch account info
Basics
Advanced
Tags
Review + create
Microsoft Azure Batch is a fully-managed cloud service that provides job scheduling and compute resource management for developers in organizations, independent software vendors, and cloud service providers. Both new and existing high performance computing (HPC) applications running on workstations and clusters today can be readily enabled to run in Azure at scale, and with no on-premises infrastructure required. Common application workloads include image and video rendering, media transcoding, engineering simulations, Monte Carlo simulations, and software test execution, among others; all highly parallel, computationally intensive workloads that can be broken into individual tasks for execution. With Azure Batch, you can scale from a few VMs, up to tens of thousands of VMs, and run the largest, most resource-intensive workloads. Learn more
PROJECT DETAILS
Select the subscription to manage deployed resources and costs. Use resource groups like folders to organize and manage all your resources.
* Subscription
Pay-As-You-Go
* Resource group
RGCloud
Create new
INSTANCE DETAILS
* Account name
ba410
.eastus2.batch.azure.com
* Location
East US 2
Review + create
Previous
Next: Advanced >

After Vaildation is passed click create.

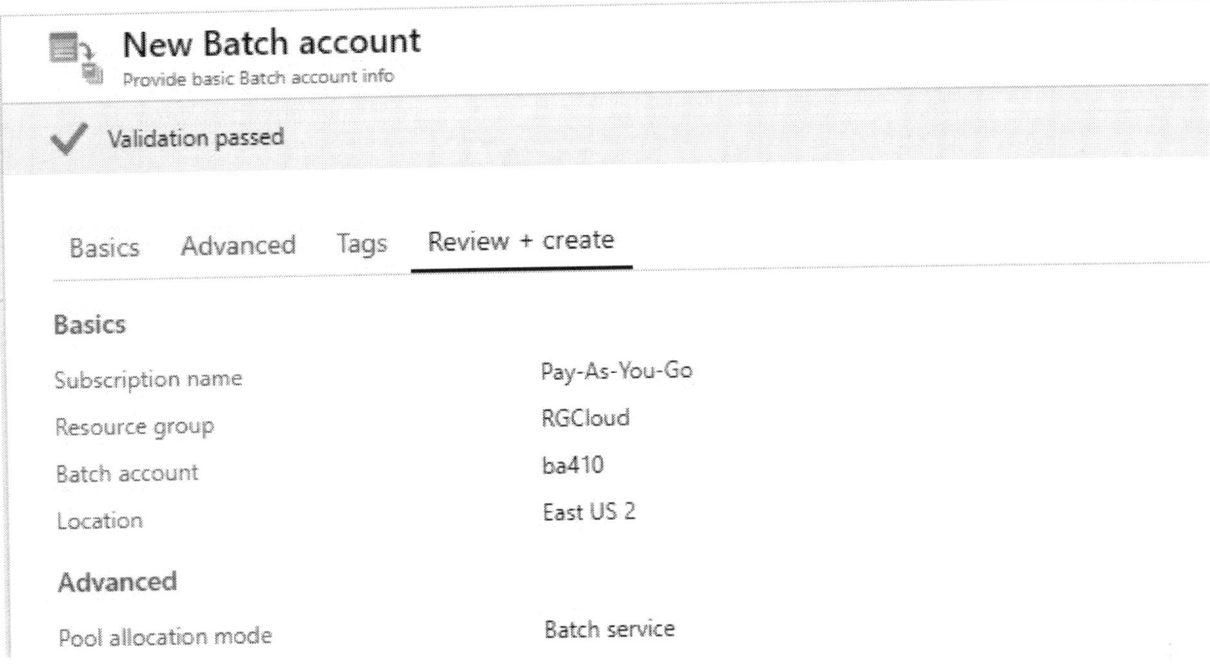

Figure below shows dashboard of Azure Batch account.

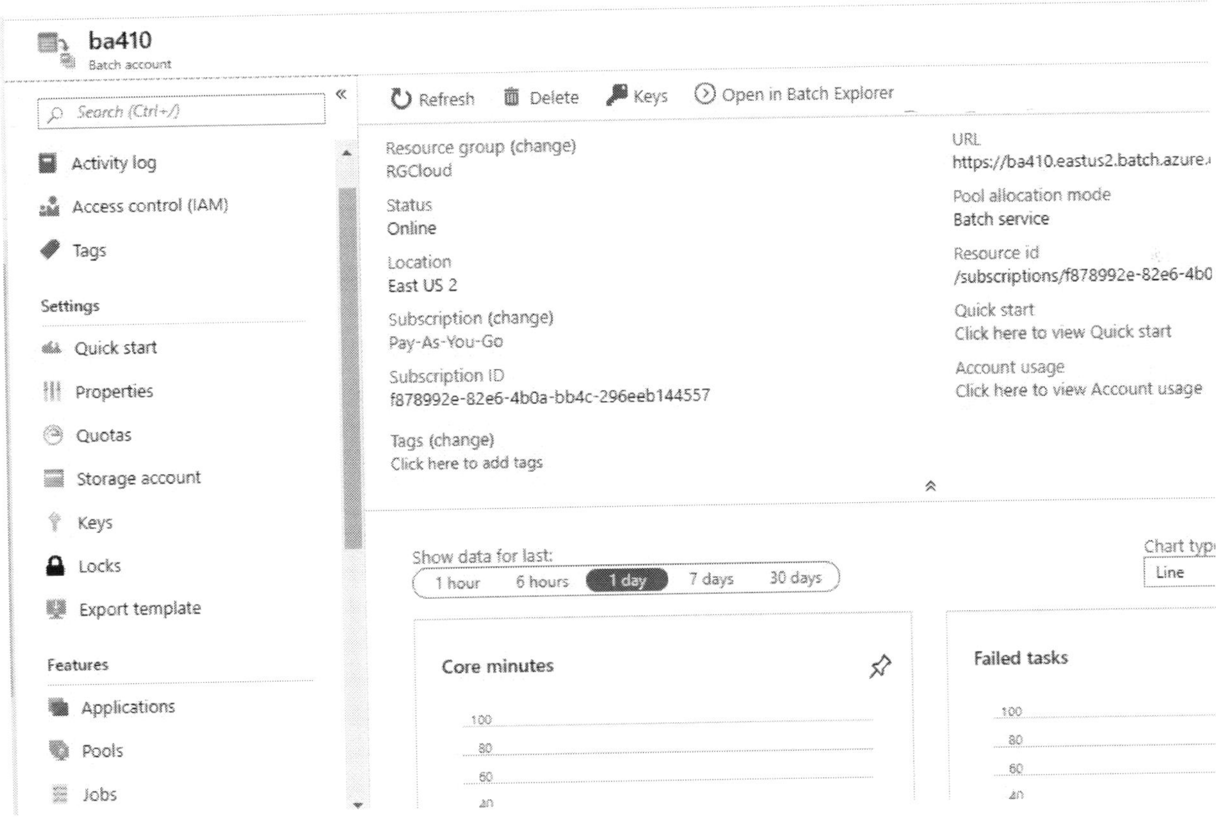

Step 2: Create a pool of compute nodes

Go to Azure Batch account dashboard>Click Pools in left pane>Click +Add> Add Pool blade opens> Enter Pool ID>In Publisher select MicrosoftWindowsServer>In Offer Select WindowsServer>In SKU select 2012-Datacenteer-smalldisk.

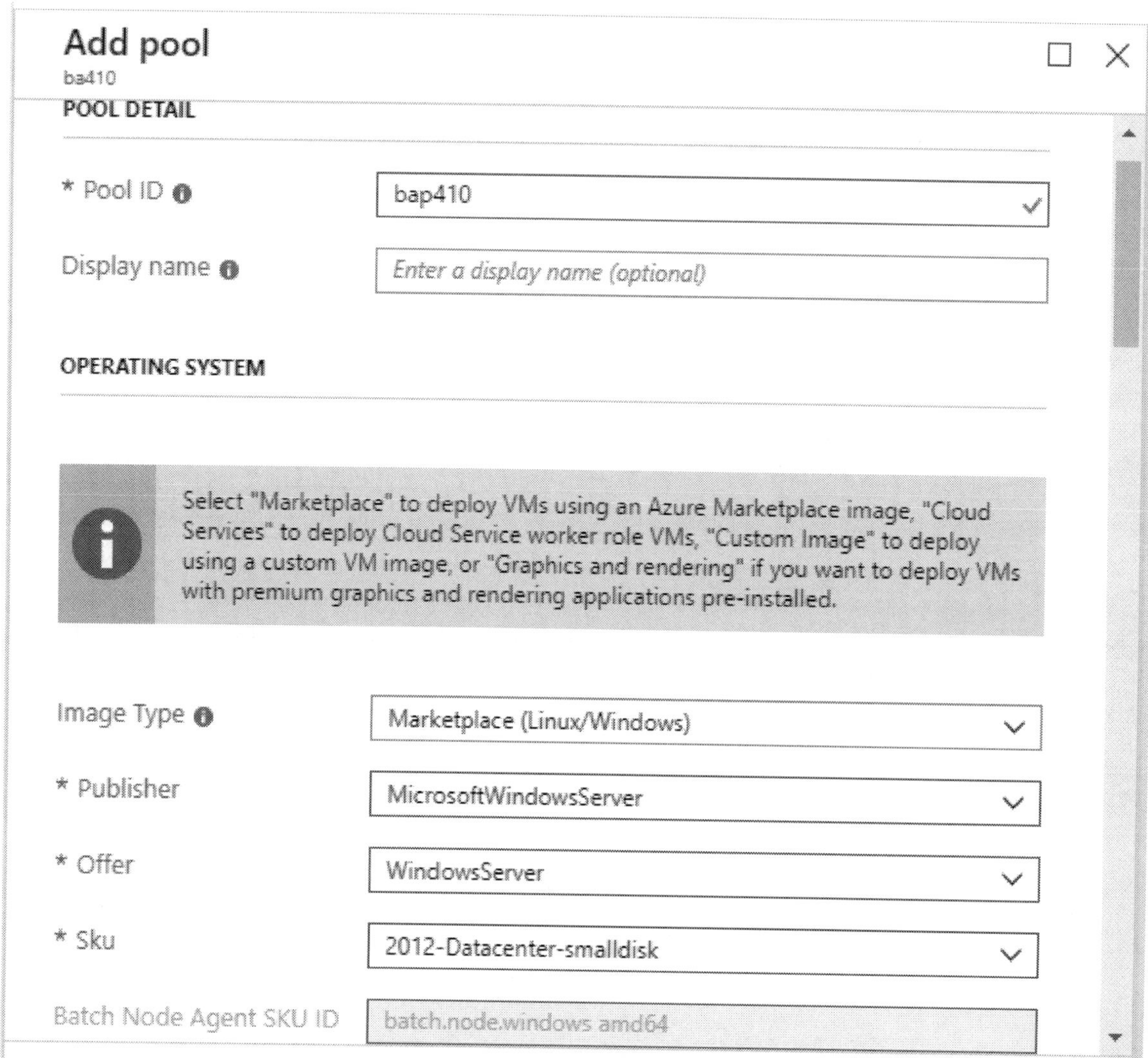

In the Add Pool pane as shown above, Scroll down to select **Node Pricing Tier and Number of Nodes**> I selected Standard A1 and 2 for Targeted Dedicated Nodes.

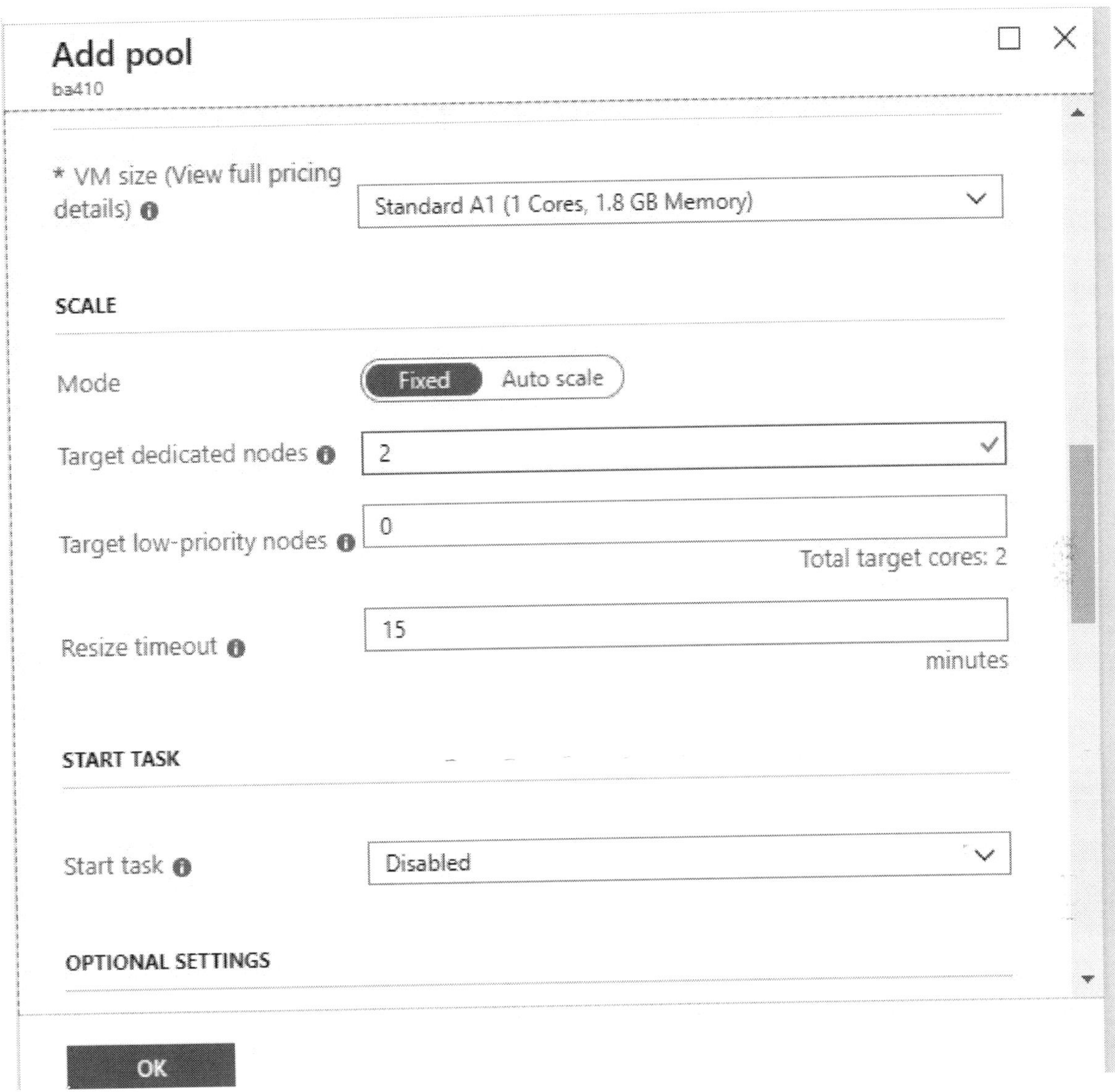

Note the Target low-priority nodes option. If we use this option we can reduce the cost by 80%.

Keep the defaults for remaining settings, and Click **OK** to create the pool.

Batch creates the pool immediately, but it takes a few minutes to allocate and start the compute nodes. During this time, the pool's **Allocation state** is **Resizing**. You can go ahead and create a job and tasks while the pool is resizing.

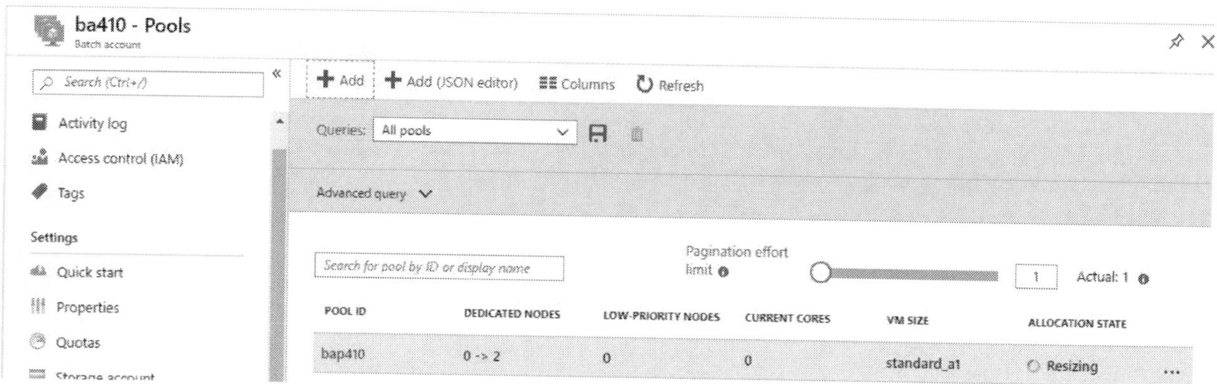

After 2-3 minutes Allocation state changes to Steady.

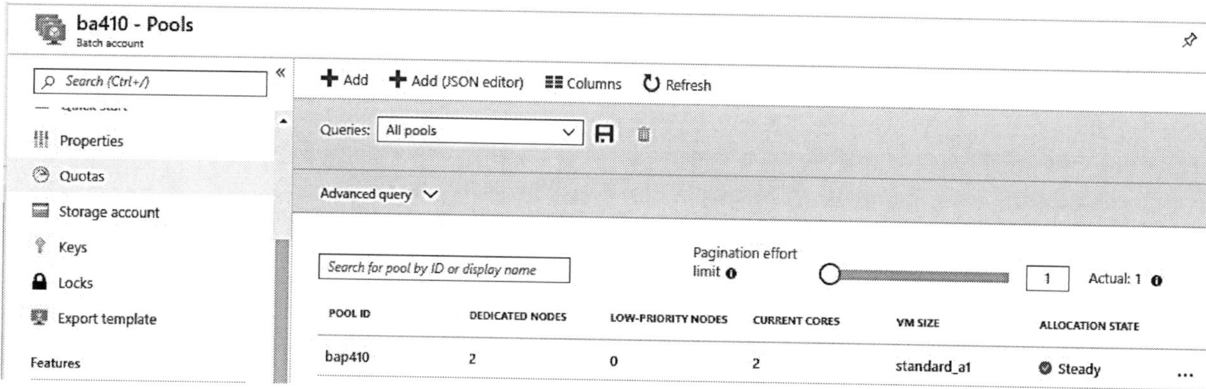

Step 3: Create a job

In the Batch Account Dashboard click Jobs in left pane>Click +Add>Add Job blade opens>Enter Job ID>Select Pool created in previous Step> Click select> Click Ok.

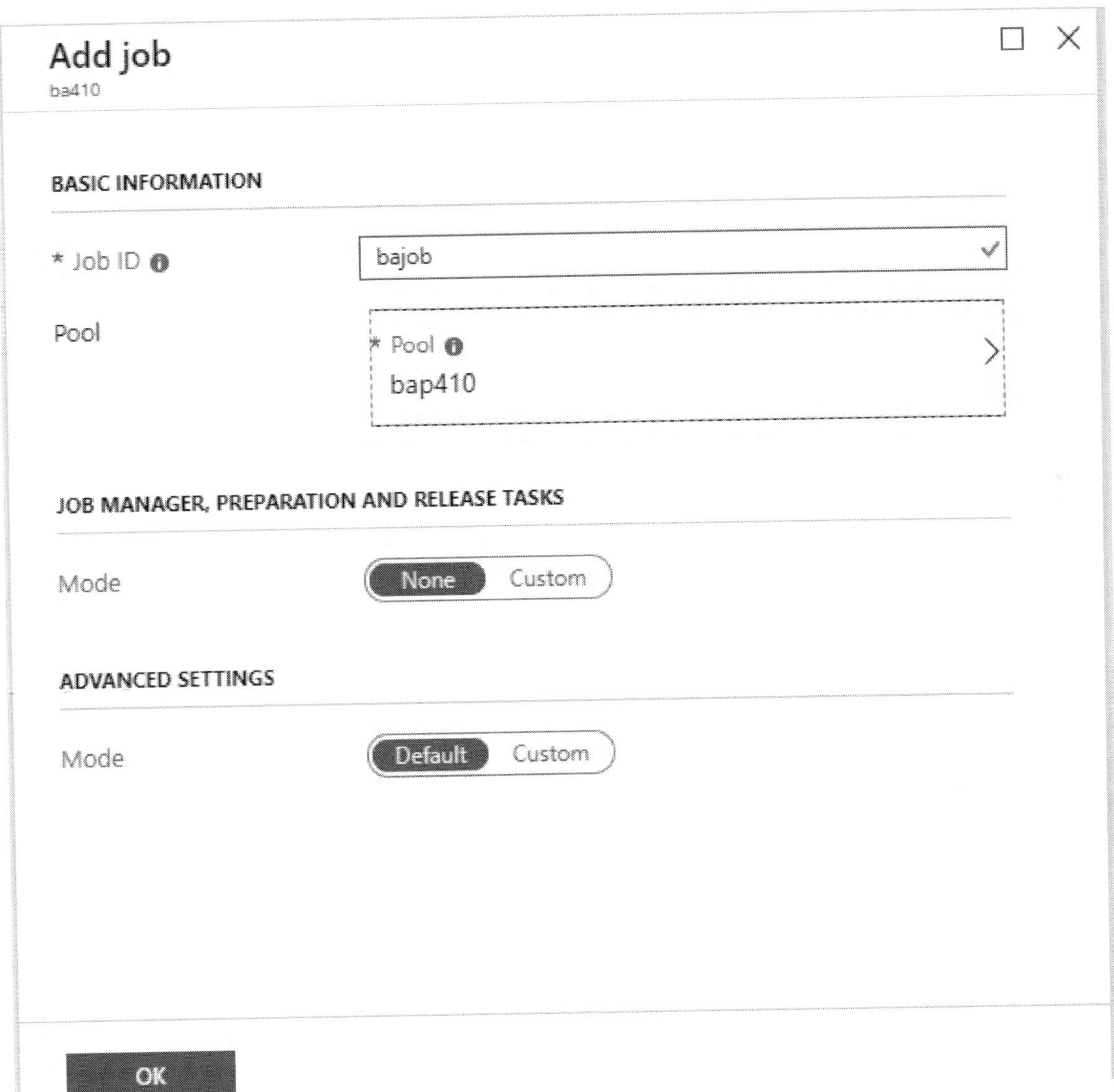

Step 3: Create Task 1

Click the Job bajob>bajob dashboard opens as shown below.

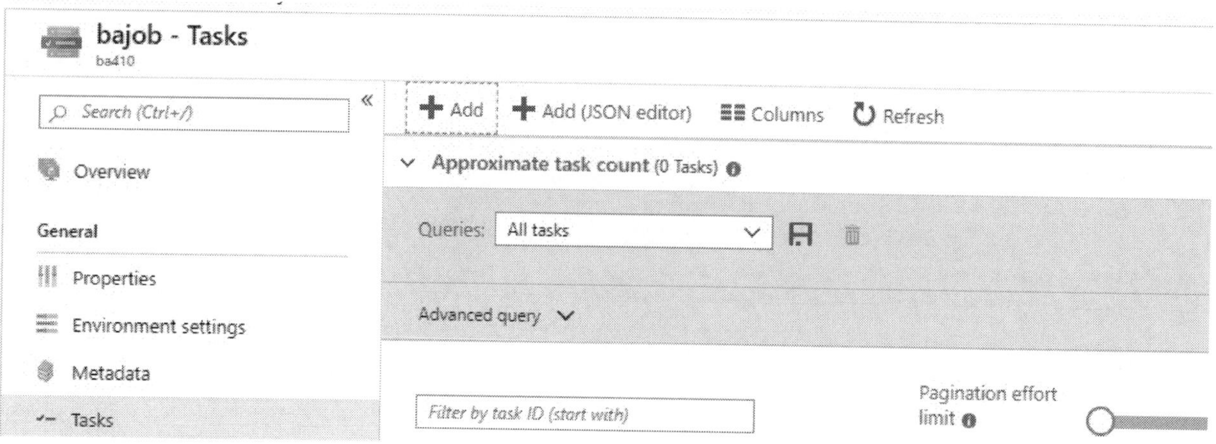

Click + Add>Add Task blade opens>Enter Task ID> In Command line enter **cmd /c "set AZ_BATCH & timeout /t 90 > NUL"**> Keep the defaults for the remaining settings, and click Summit (Not Shown).

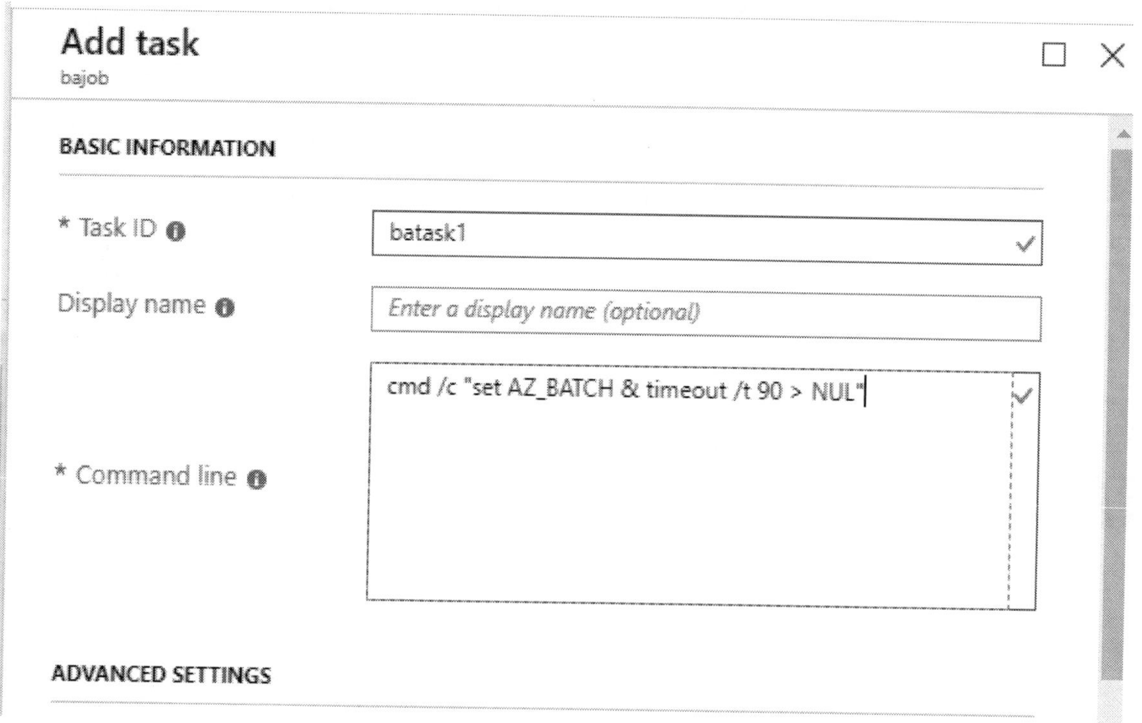

Note: After you create a task, Batch queues it to run on the pool. When a node is available to run it, the task runs.

Step 4: Create Task 2

In Job bajob dashboard Click + Add>Add Task blade opens>Enter Task ID> In Command line enter **cmd /c "set AZ_BATCH & timeout /t 90 > NUL"**> Keep the defaults for the remaining settings, and click Summit (Not Shown).

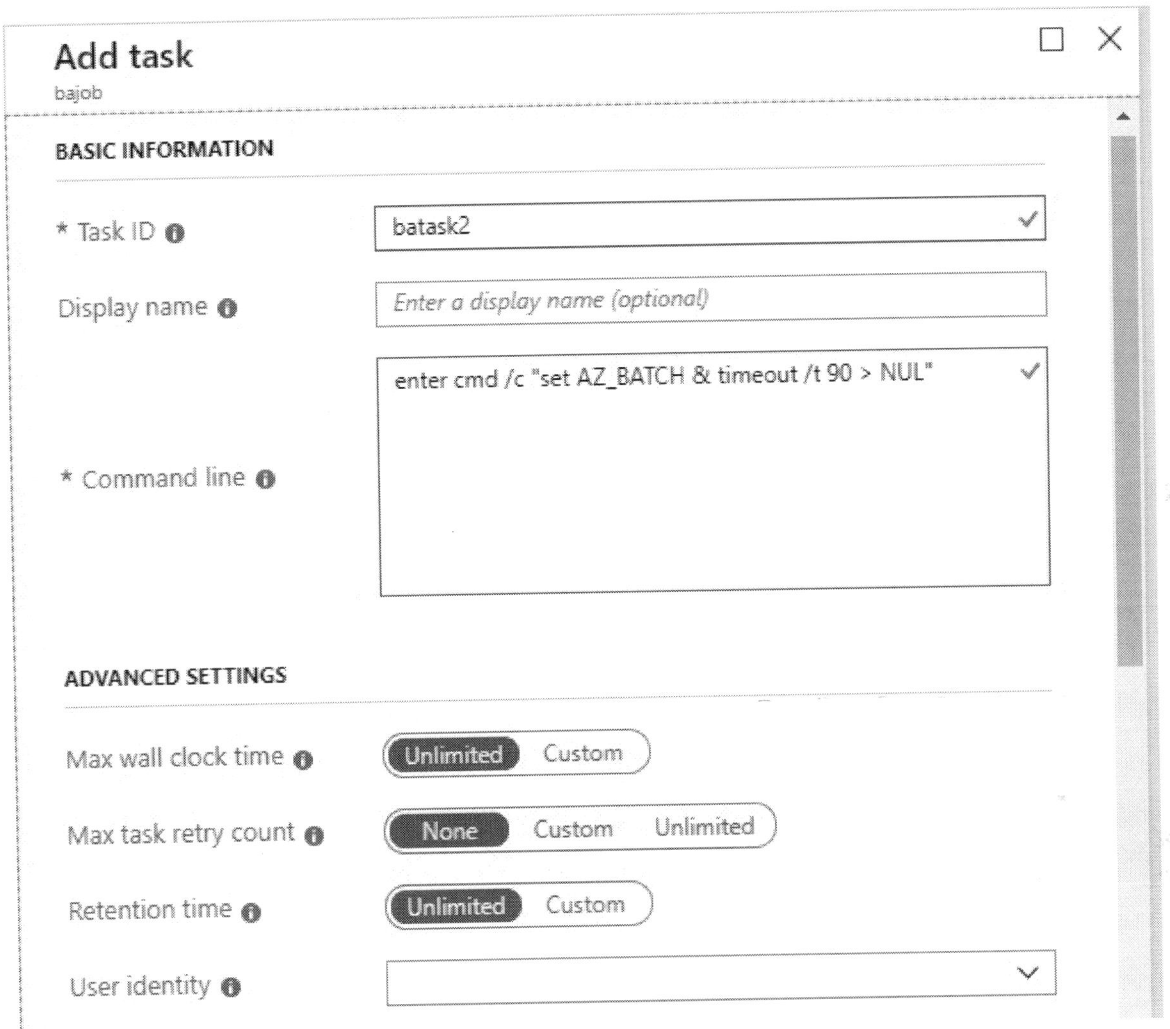

Step 5: View task output

In Job Pane Click Task batask1> Task pane opens> In right pane Click file stdout.txt. This file shows the standard output of the task a shown below.

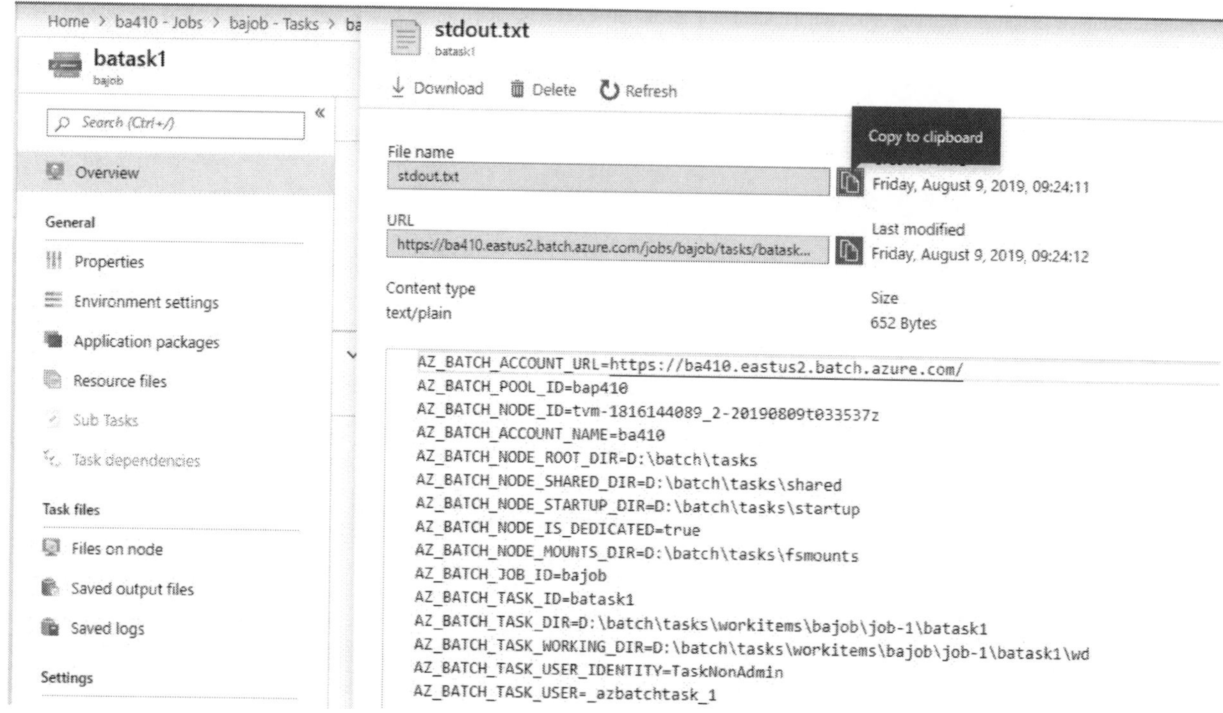

Azure Batch Pricing

There is no charge for Batch itself. You only pay for the underlying compute, storage and Application licenses (If used) consumed to run your batch jobs.

For Compute & Storage Pricing refer to Virtual Machine and Storage Chapter.

For compute you can use normal VMs or Low Priority VMs.

Low-priority VMs in Batch

Low Priority VMs are priced at 20% of Normal VMs. Low Priority VMs are allocated from Azure unutilized capacity and can be taken back by Azure. The availability SLA for normal VMs does not apply to low-priority VMs.

Low-priority VMs can significantly reduce the costs of running workloads or allow much more work to be performed at a greater scale for the same cost.

If applications can tolerate interruption, then use of low-priority VMs can significantly lower compute costs. Suitable workloads include batch processing and HPC jobs, where the work is split into many asynchronous tasks. If VMs are pre-empted, then tasks can be interrupted and rerun—job completion time can also increase if capacity drops

If low-priority VMs are pre-empted, then any interrupted tasks will be re-queued, and the pool will automatically attempt to replace the lost capacity.

Graphics and rendering application licensing

Azure Batch pools can optionally be configured with graphics and rendering applications installed, where the application licensing is handled by Batch and the application costs are billed by Batch alongside the VM costs.

APPLICATION	Price
Autodesk Maya	$0.625/VM/hour
Autodesk 3ds Max	$0.625/VM/hour
Autodesk Arnold	$0.025/core/hour
Chaos Group V-Ray	$0.025/core/hour

Chapter 16 Azure Service Fabric

This is AZ-301 specific Chapter. Leave this for AZ-300 Exam.

This Chapter covers following Topic lessons

- Azure Service Fabric
- Service Fabric Deployment Options
- What Are Microservices
- Microservices Types
- High level view of Service Fabric Cluster
- Service Fabric Architecture
- Azure Service Fabric Cluster Architecture
- Service Fabric Management Components (System Services)
- Service Fabric programming model overview
- Application Deployment in Service Fabric Cluster
- Service Fabric Application Scalability and Availability

This Chapter Covers following Lab Exercises

- Service Fabric Cluster Deployment

Chapter Topology

In this chapter we will add Azure Service Fabric to the Topology.

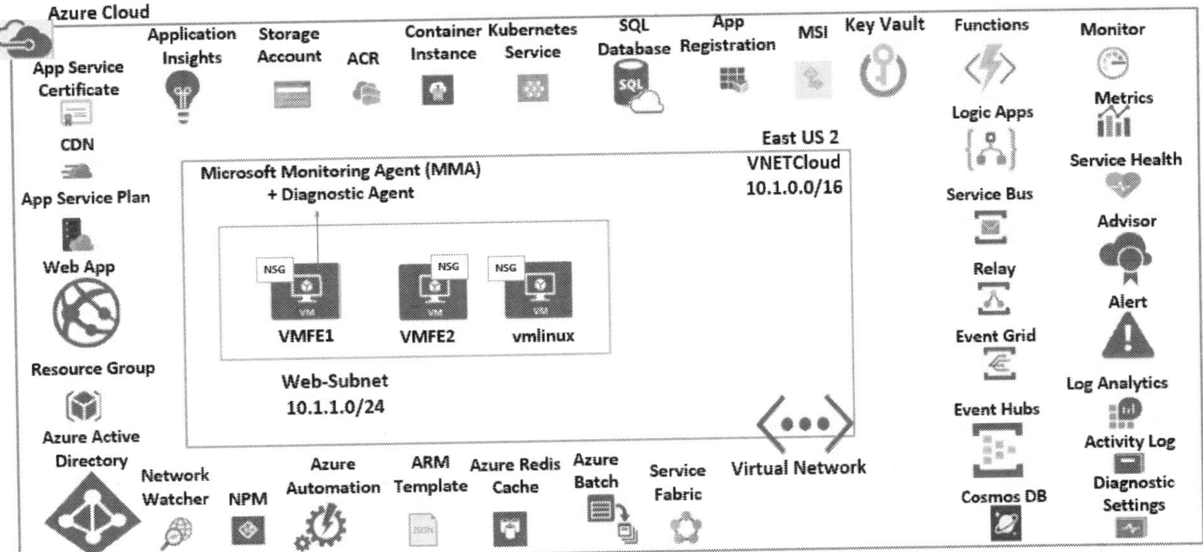

Azure Service Fabric

Azure Service Fabric is a managed container orchestration platform for deploying and managing **Container & Microservices Applications** across a cluster of virtual machines.

As an orchestrator, Azure Service Fabric abstracts complex infrastructure problems of scalability, load balancing, discovery, deployment, reliability and manageability of Microservices and lets developers focus on implementation of workloads.

Azure Service Fabric can also be used to deploy traditional applications such as Web apps or Web services which can reap the same benefits of scalability, reliability and manageability as Microservices workloads, however, it is much better suited for hyperscale and Microservices based systems.

Service Fabric can deploy Microservices as processes or inside containers across the Service Fabric cluster. Service Fabric provides comprehensive runtime and lifecycle management capabilities to applications that are composed of these microservices. Containerized environment for Microservices enables Service Fabric to provide an increase in the density of deployment of workloads.

Azure Service Fabric orchestrates services across a cluster of machines. Each participant machine in a cluster is called a Node. Developers can use a variety of ways to build and deploy applications on Service Fabric such as, using the Service Fabric programming model, and deploying the application as guest executable. For each of the above application models, Service Fabric deploys the services as processes on nodes. Although, processes offer fastest activation and highest density, however, deploying the applications as processes can cause side effects such as resource starvation. Therefore, Service Fabric also supports deploying services in container images. Developers can also mix services deployed as processes and services deployed in container images in the same application.

Azure Service Fabric simplifies developing applications that use a microservice architecture, freeing developers to focus on building features that deliver customer value instead of managing infrastructure.

Service Fabric Deployment Options

Service Fabric is platform agnostic, so you can build your applications on Service Fabric and deploy them not just on Azure, but also on your local cloud or other public clouds.

Service Fabric can be deployed in Azure, on-Premises on a windows or Linux cluster and in Public Cloud like AWS. When deployed in Azure it is known as Azure Service Fabric. Figure below shows service fabric deployment options.

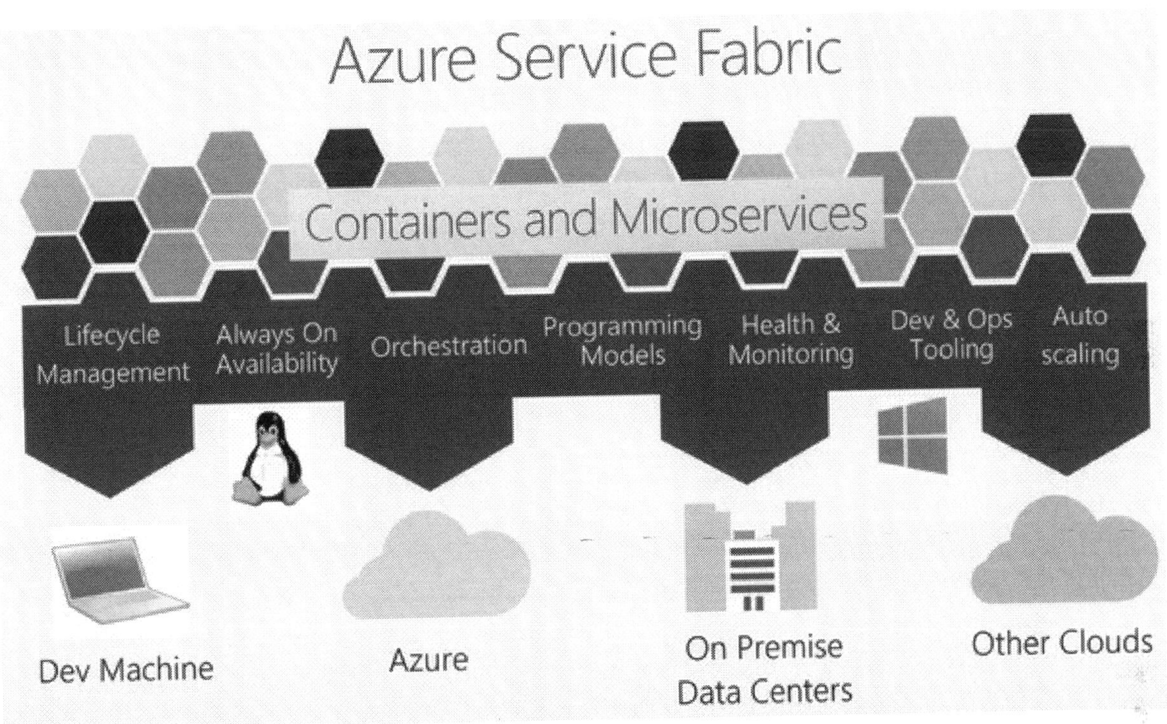

Advantages of running Service Fabric Clusters in Azure

Running Service Fabric clusters on Azure provides integration with other Azure features and services, which makes operations and management of the cluster easier and more reliable.

Auto-scaling: Clusters in Azure provide built-in auto-scaling functionality using Virtual Machine scale-sets.
Diagnostics: Clusters on Azure are integrated with Azure diagnostics and Log Analytics for easier management and troubleshooting.
Integration with Azure Infrastructure Service Fabric coordinates with the underlying Azure infrastructure for OS, network, and other upgrades to improve availability and reliability of your applications.

What Are Microservices

Microservices is an architectural style that structures an application as a collection of loosely coupled services which implement business capabilities. These services are independent of each other. Microservices enables each service to be developed independently by a team that is focused on that service.

Features of Microservices

1. A microservice application separates functionality into smaller services.
2. Services in a microservice architecture are independently deployable.
3. Services are organized around business capabilities.
4. Services are small in size, messaging enabled, autonomously developed, independently deployable, decentralized and built and released with automated processes.
5. Services in a microservice architecture (MSA) are processes that communicate with each other over well-defined interfaces and protocols.
6. Lends itself to a continuous delivery software development process. A change to a small part of the application only requires one or a small number of services to be rebuilt and redeployed.
7. Have unique names (URLs) used to resolve their location.

Comparison Between Monolithic and Microservices Application

A monolithic app contains domain-specific functionality and is normally divided by functional layers, such as web, App/Business and data tier. The figure below shows an e-commerce Monolithic App.

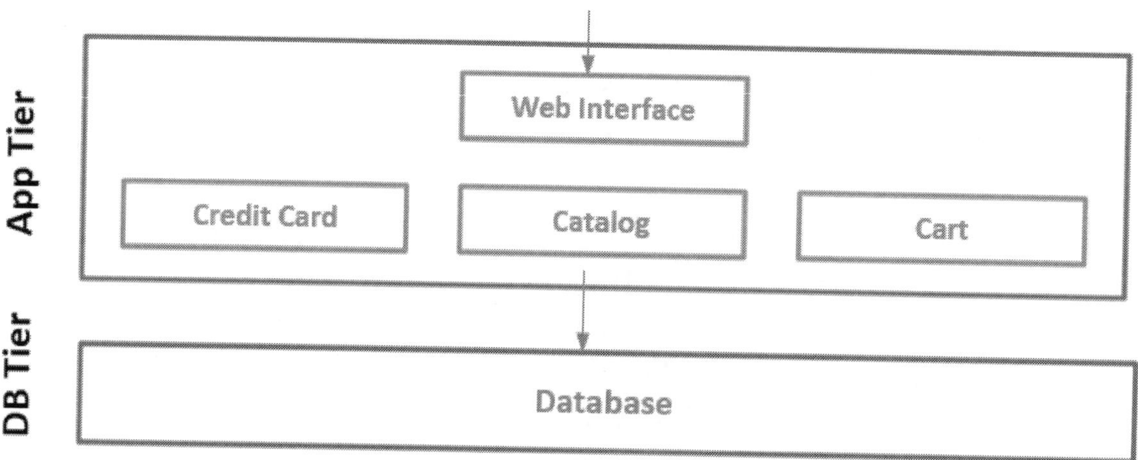

A Microservice Application separates application functionality into separate smaller services with each service having its own database. The figure below shows Microservices Application architecture.

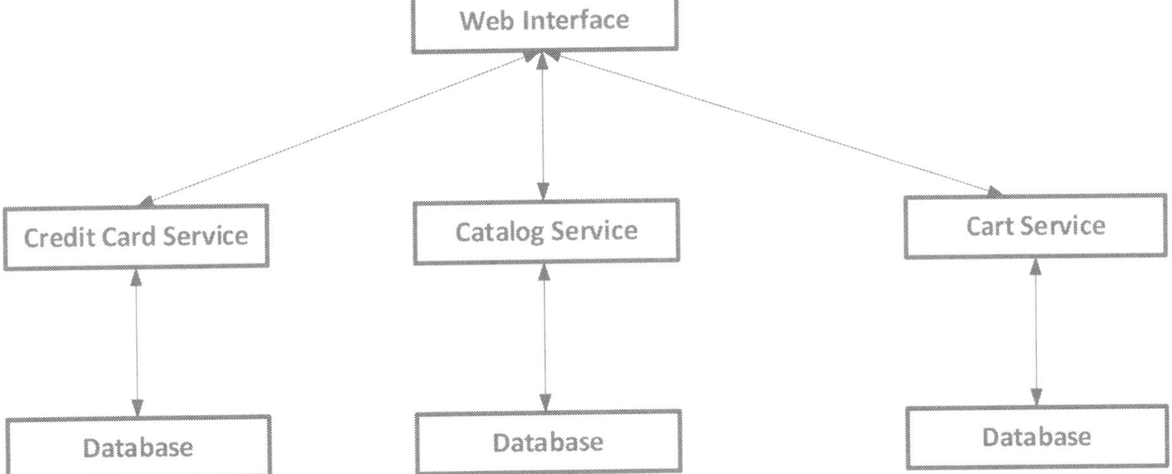

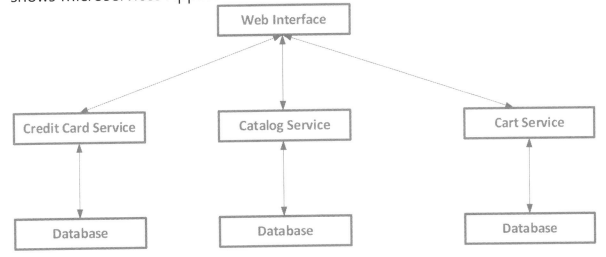

Benefits of Microservices Architecture

1. The **benefit** of decomposing an application into different smaller services is that it improves modularity and makes the application easier to develop and test. It also parallelizes development by enabling small autonomous teams to develop, deploy and scale their respective services independently.
2. Microservice architecture enables each microservice to be deployed independently. As a result, it makes continuous deployment possible for complex applications.

Example of Microservices application running on Service Fabric

Service Fabric powers many Microsoft services including Azure SQL Database, Azure Cosmos DB, Cortana, Microsoft Power BI, Microsoft Intune, Azure Event Hubs, Azure IoT Hub, Dynamics 365, Skype for Business and many core Azure services.

In **Summary**, the microservice approach is to decompose application into many smaller services. The services run in containers that are deployed across a cluster of machines. Teams develop a service that focuses on a scenario and independently test, version, deploy, and scale each service so that the entire application can evolve.

Microservices Types

Stateless Microservices: Either no state is maintained within the service or service state is maintained in an external Datastore.
Example of Stateless Microservices include Web Frontend, protocol gateways web proxies & calculations that don't require state.

Stateful Microservices: State is stored with the service. Allows for state to be persisted without the need for an external database. Data is co-located with the code that is running the service.
Example of Stateful Microservices include user accounts, gaming scenarios, data analytics, shopping carts, and queues.

Actor Microservices: An actor is a service which sends messages to other actors. The state persistence has three options – **persisted, volatile** and **none**. The **persisted** option means that the state is written to a disk and replicated, while the **volatile** option causes that the state is kept in the memory only and replicated, whereas **none** state is in memory only and isn't replicated. The state is distinct to every actor. It is stored in a structure called Actor State Manager.

Figure below shows various Microservices states for loosely coupled services.

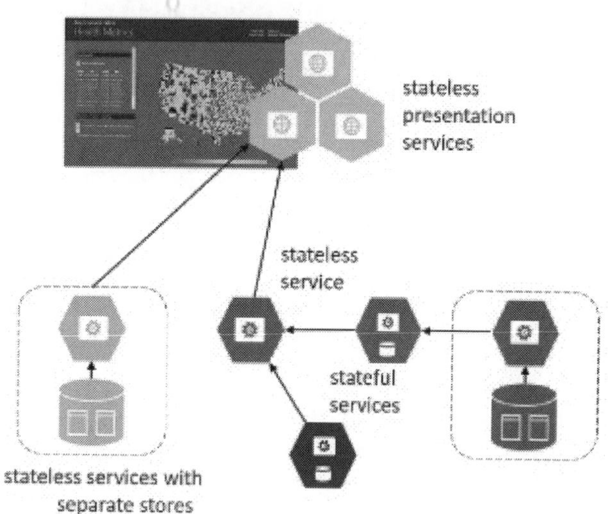

From above figure you can see that Stateless service either have no state maintained or state is maintained in external Store. Whereas Stateful services have data co-located with the service.

High level view of Service Fabric Cluster

Figure below shows 5 Node Service Fabric Cluster running both Management components and workloads on the same cluster.

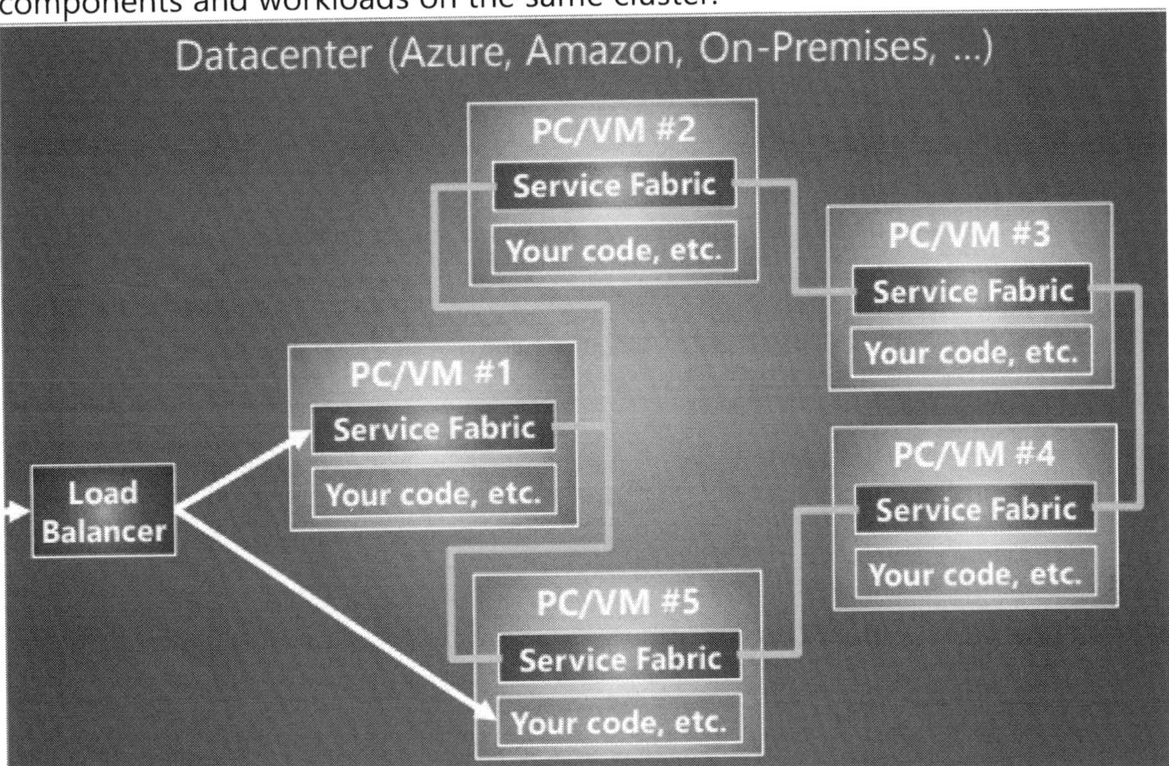

In Microservices Architecture an application is divided into multiple services. Figure below shows Placement of services across the cluster.

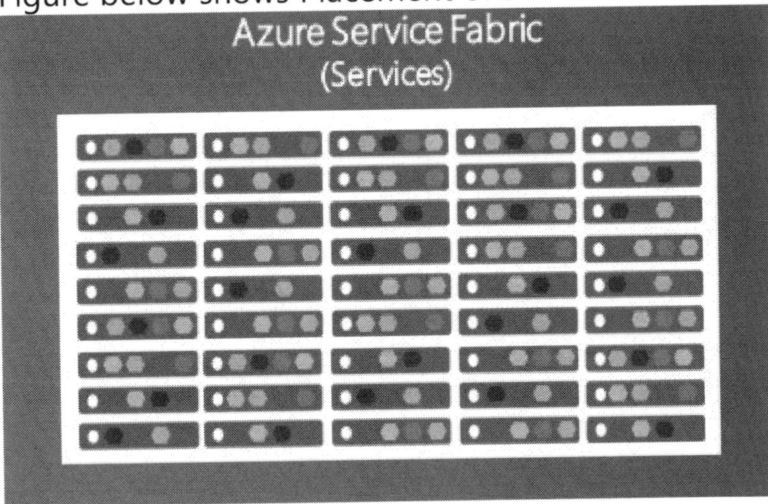

Multiple services can run in node. A Service can run in multiple nodes as secondary replica to provide high availability. Replication of services across nodes is done by Service Fabric orchestration platform.

Service Fabric Architecture

Service Fabric has a modular architecture in which there are several subsystems at play. Each subsystem is responsible for fulfilling a particular role in the overall system.

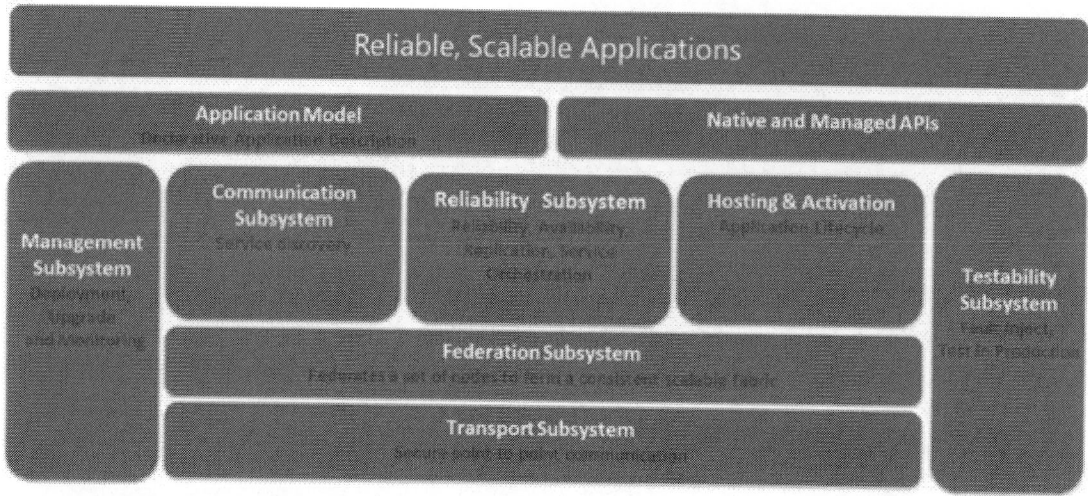

Transport subsystem: This subsystem is responsible for providing secure point-to-point communication channel both within the Service Fabric cluster (between nodes) and between Service Fabric cluster and application clients.
Federation subsystem: This subsystem provides services that unify the nodes to form a cluster. This subsystem provides failure detection, leader election, and routing services which are necessary to form a cluster from individual nodes.
Reliable subsystem: This subsystem adds reliability and high availability to the system by providing services for state replication, failover, and load balancing.
Management subsystem: This subsystem provides full ALM (Application Lifecycle Mangement) capabilities to Service Fabric. Service Fabric uses Management subsystem to manage application binaries, deploy, update, scale, and manage application health.
Hosting subsystem: The hosting subsystem manages performs the roles of Management subsystem, but at a node level.
Communication subsystem: In Microservices applications, service discovery is an important activity. The communication subsystem handles service discovery so that services can migrate freely between nodes.
Testability subsystem: Using the testability subsystem, developers can simulate various failure scenarios in Service Fabric cluster to find out any defects in the system.

Azure Service Fabric Cluster Architecture

A Service Fabric cluster is a network-connected set of virtual or physical machines into which your microservices are deployed and managed. Clusters can scale to thousands of machines.

Service Fabric can be deployed with single cluster or 2 Cluster or 3 Cluster option. **Each Cluster is deployed with Multiple Virtual Machines in a Virtual Machine Scale Set (VMSS).** A Load Balancer is also deployed with the VMSS for each cluster.

Service Fabric deployment with Single cluster (**node type 1**) is known as Primary Cluster. When Service Fabric is deployed with 2 cluster (**Node Type 2**) or 3 cluster (**Node Type 3**) option then the 1st cluster will be primary cluster and second or Third Cluster will be Non-Primary Cluster. Each Cluster types is virtual machine scale sets, so Autoscaling functionality is built in.

Service Fabric Management component run in the primary cluster only. Whereas Container workloads can run both in Primary cluster as well as in Non-Primary clusters.

Supported operating systems for clusters on Azure

Service Fabric Cluster can be a windows Cluster or Linux cluster. You can create Service Fabric Cluster in Azure by using one of the following OS:

Windows Server 2012 R2 Datacenter
Windows Server 2016 Datacenter
Windows Server Datacenter 1709
Windows Server Datacenter 1803
Linux Ubuntu 16.04 LTS
RHEL 7.3 (Preview)

Service Fabric Management Components (System Services)

Service Fabric Management component run in the primary cluster only.

Service Fabric Management component consist of set of system services that provides the underlying support for Service Fabric applications. The System Services are deployed in a redundant manner across multiple nodes so that they are highly available. Each Service is deployed as Primary replica and as multiple active secondary replicas.

Naming Service: A Node or a VM in Service Fabric Cluster can host multiple services, each with unique endpoints. **Naming Service** is a service discovery mechanism which can be used to resolve endpoint addresses.

The **Failover Manager** Service ensures that when nodes are added to or removed from the cluster, the load is automatically redistributed across the available nodes. If a node in the cluster fails, the cluster will automatically reconfigure the service replicas to maintain availability.

The **Cluster Manager** Service is the primary service that manages the lifecycle of the applications from provision to de-provision. It interacts with the Failover Manager to place the applications on the nodes based on the service placement constraints. It integrates with the health manager to ensure that application availability is not lost from a semantic health perspective during upgrades.

Image Store Service: Once your application is ready to be deployed, the application package files are versioned and copied to Service Fabric cluster's image store. The image store is made available to the cluster and other services through a hosted service called the image store service..

Upgrade Service: Azure cloud-based Service Fabric clusters are managed and upgraded by the Service Fabric Resource Provider(SFRP). The upgrade service coordinates upgrading the Service Fabric itself with the SFRP.
Health Manager service enables health monitoring of applications, services, and cluster entities. Cluster entities (such as nodes, service partitions, and replicas) can report health information, which is then aggregated into the centralized health store.

Service Fabric programming model overview

Service Fabric offers multiple ways to write and manage your services.

Guest Executables: A guest executable is an executable (written in any language) that can be run as a service in your application. Guest executables do not call the Service Fabric SDK APIs directly. However they still benefit from features the platform offers, such as service discoverability, custom health and load reporting by calling REST APIs exposed by Service Fabric.

Containers: Service Fabric can deploy services in containers. Service Fabric supports deployment of Linux containers and Windows containers on Windows Server 2016. Container images can be pulled from any container repository and deployed to the machine. You can deploy existing applications as guest executables, Service Fabric stateless or stateful Reliable services or Reliable Actors in containers, and you can mix services in processes and services in containers in the same application.

Reliable Services: Reliable Services is a light-weight framework for writing services that integrate with the Service Fabric platform and benefit from the full set of platform features. Reliable Services provide a minimal set of APIs that allow the Service Fabric runtime to manage the lifecycle of your services and that allow your services to interact with the runtime.
Reliable Services can be stateless or stateful. State is made highly-available through replication and distributed through partitioning, all managed automatically by Service Fabric.

ASP.NET Core: ASP.NET Core is open-source and cross-platform framework for building modern cloud-based Internet-connected applications, such as web apps, IoT apps, and mobile backends. Service Fabric integrates with ASP.NET Core so you can write both stateless and stateful ASP.NET Core applications that take advantage of Reliable Collections and Service Fabric's advanced orchestration capabilities.

Reliable Actors: Built on top of Reliable Services, the Reliable Actor framework is an application framework that implements the Virtual Actor pattern, based on the actor design pattern. It is fully integrated with the Service Fabric platform and benefits from the full set of features offered by the platform.

Application Deployment in Service Fabric Cluster

You can use following tools with Service Fabric to manage a cluster and its applications:

1. Service Fabric Explorer, a browser-based tool.
2. Service Fabric Command Line Interface (CLI), which runs on top of Azure CLI.
3. PowerShell commands.
4. Visual Studio.

Service Fabric Application Scalability and Availability

Highly available services: Service Fabric services provide fast failover by creating multiple secondary service replicas. If a node, process, or individual service goes down due to hardware or other failure, one of the secondary replicas is promoted to a primary replica with minimal loss of service.

Scalable services: Individual services can be partitioned, allowing for state to be scaled out across the cluster. The replicas of each partition are spread across the cluster's nodes which allows your named service's state to scale. Services can be quickly and easily scaled out from a few instances on a few nodes to thousands of instances on many nodes, and then scaled in again, depending on your resource needs.

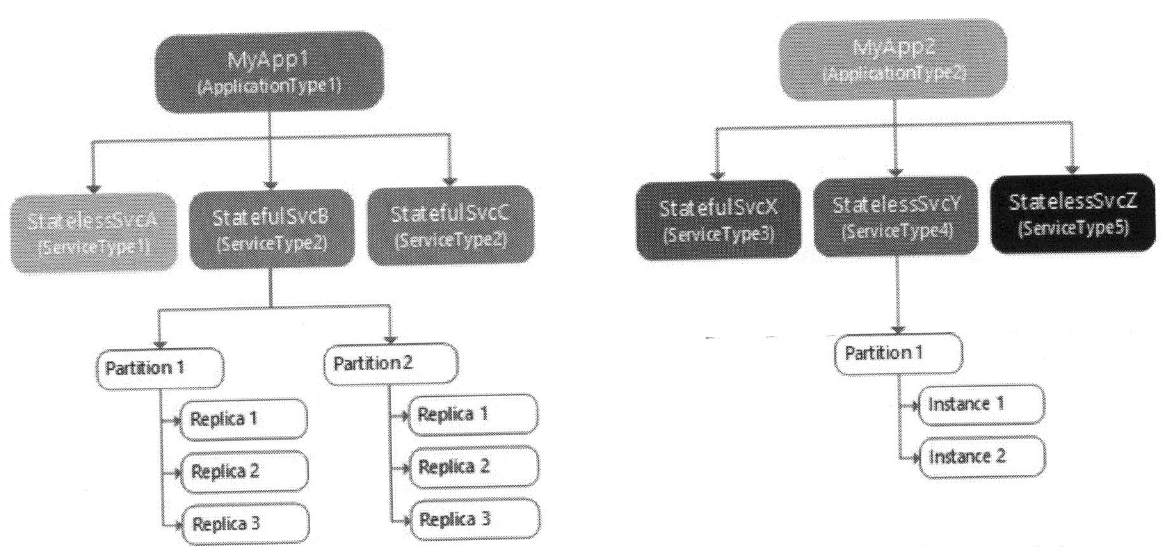

Within a partition, stateless named services have instances while stateful named services have replicas.

Stateful named services maintain their state within replicas and each partition has its own replica set. Read and write operations are performed at one replica (called the Primary). Changes to state from write operations are replicated to multiple other replicas (called Active Secondaries).

Stateless named services have one partition since they have no internal state. The partition instances provide for availability. If one instance fails, other instances continue to operate normally and then Service Fabric creates a new instance.

Exercise 127: Service Fabric Cluster Deployment

In this Exercise we wil create Service Fabric Cluster in Resource Group RGCloud. For Security Configuration of Service Fabric Cluster we will use Key Vault Certificate created in Exercise 64, chapter 5. Resource Group RGCloud was created in Exercise 1, Chapter 1 in Part 1 Book.

1. In Azure Portal click All Services>Containers>Service Fabric Cluster> +ADD> Create Service Fabric Cluster blade opens> Enter Cluster name>Select OS> Enter Username & Password>For Resource Group select RGCloud>Location select East US 2> Click OK.

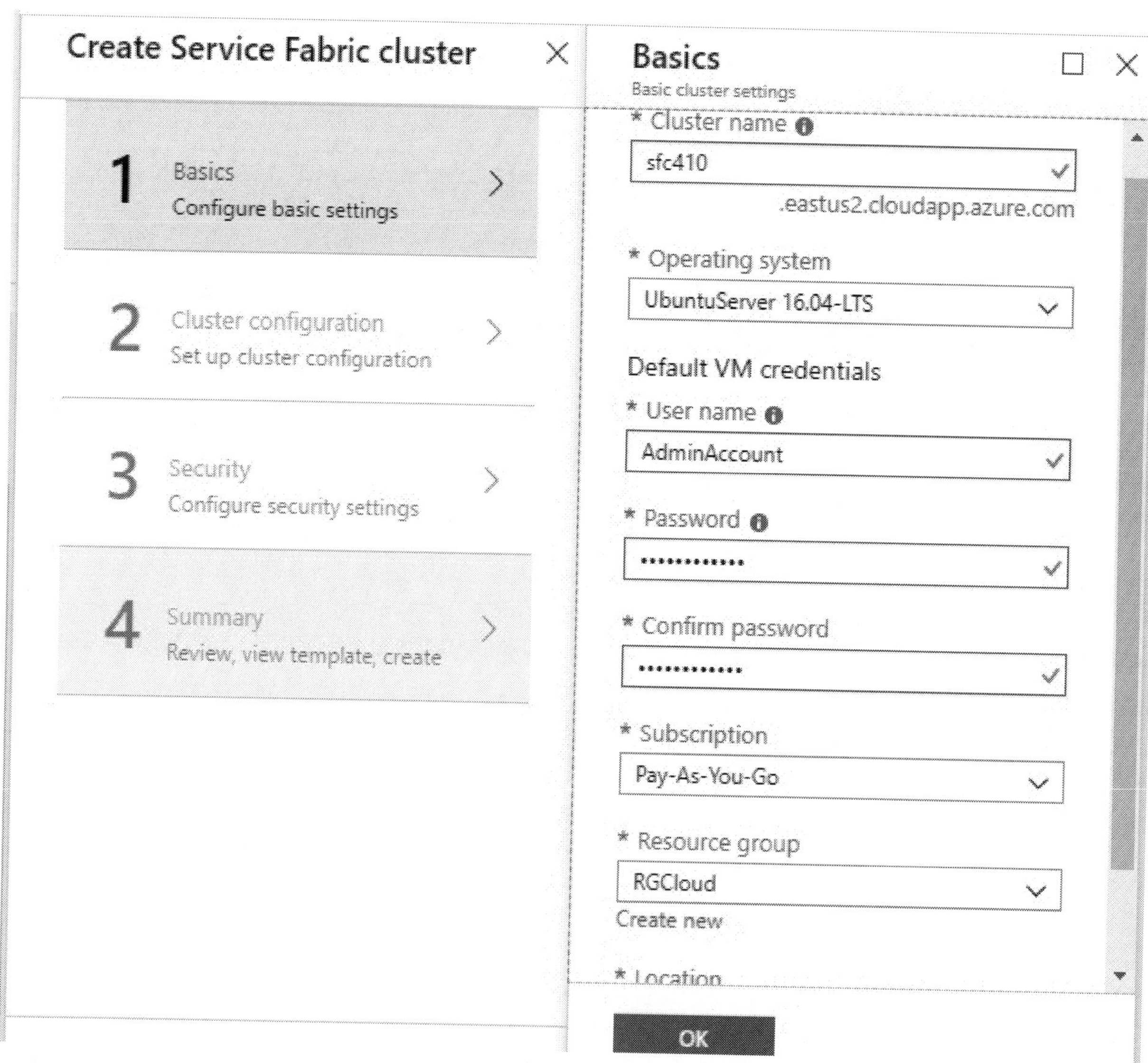

2. In Cluster configuration select node type count 1> Click Node type 1. Node type Configuration pane opens>Enter Node name>In durability Tier select Bronze>In Virtual Machine size select D2_V3> check Single Node Cluster>Click Ok>Click Ok

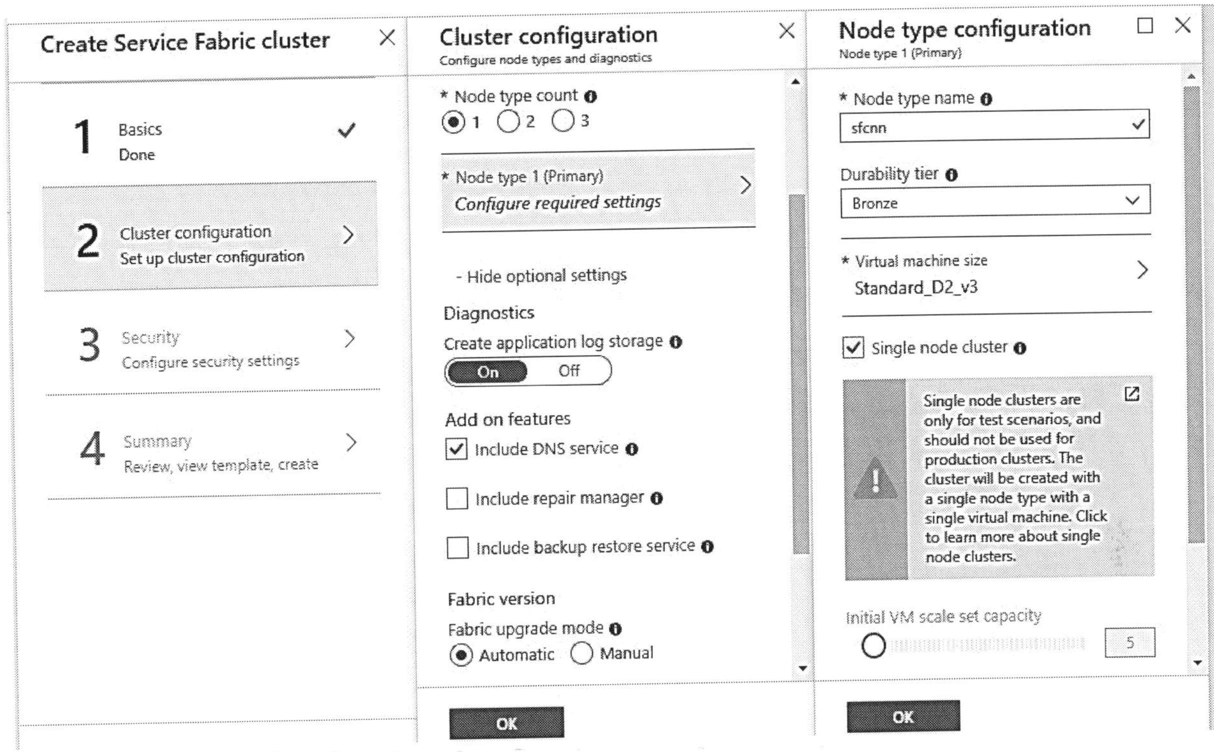

3. In Security Settings>Select Custom> In Source Key Vault, Certificate URL and Thumbprint enter values shown in Exercise 64, Chapter 5>Click OK.

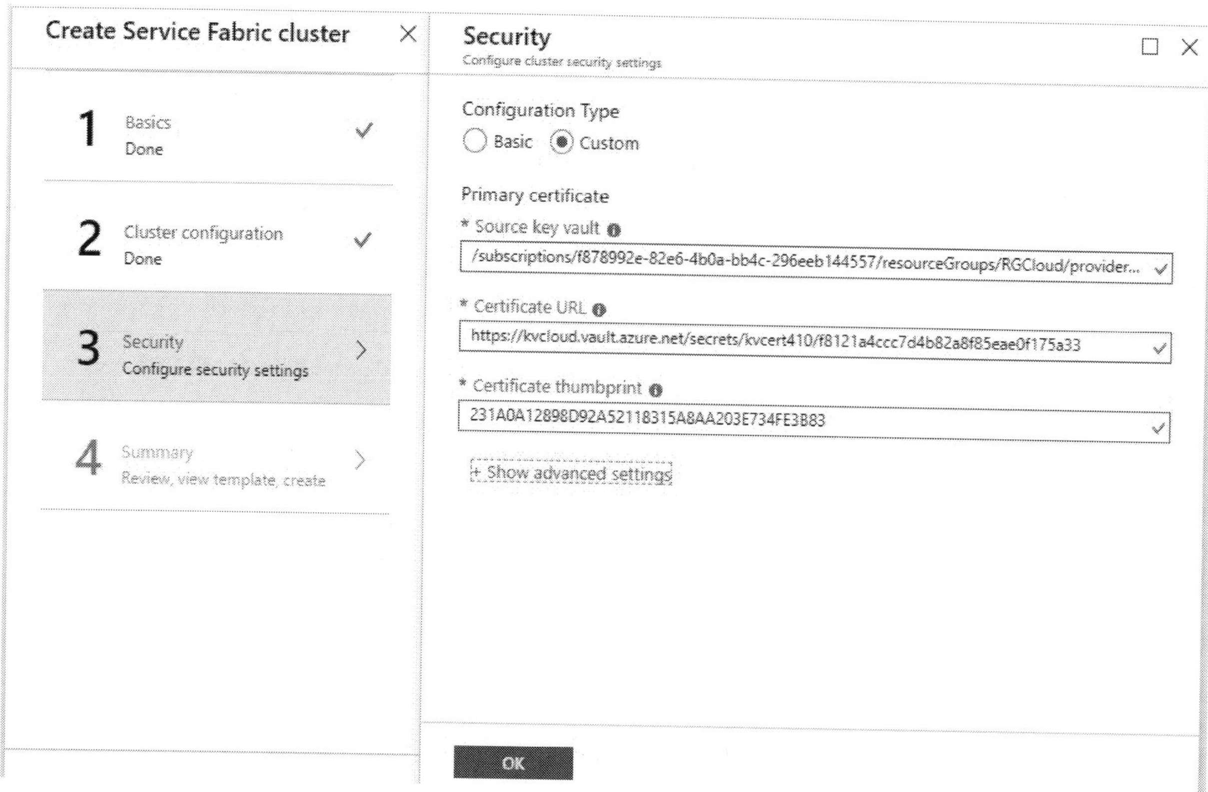

4. After Validation is passed click create (Not Shown).

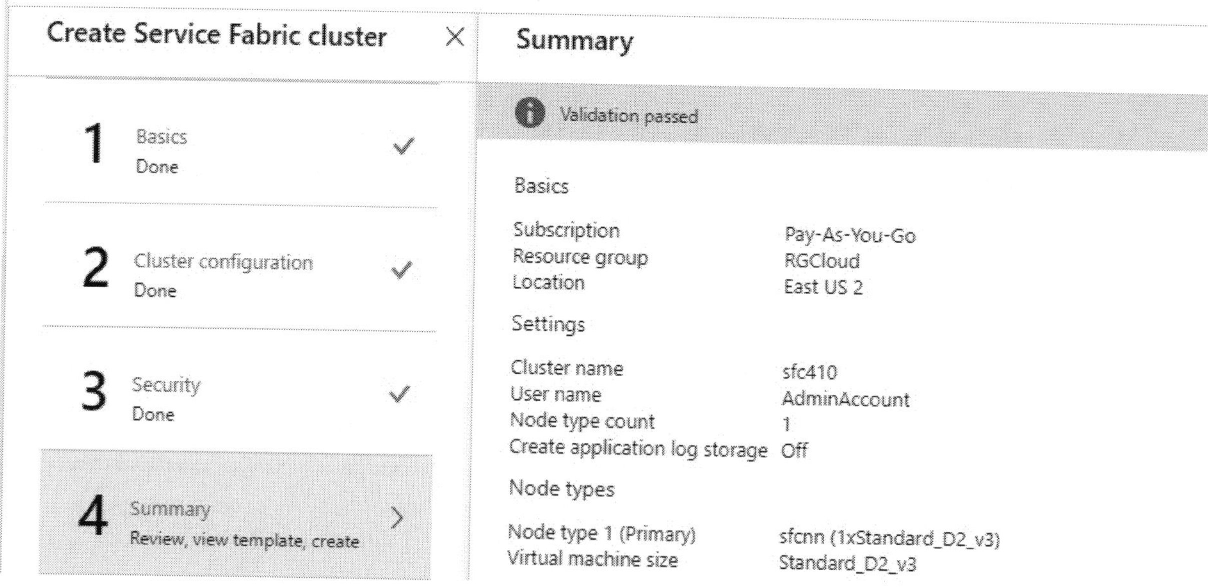

5. Figure below shows Dashboard of Service Fabric Cluster.

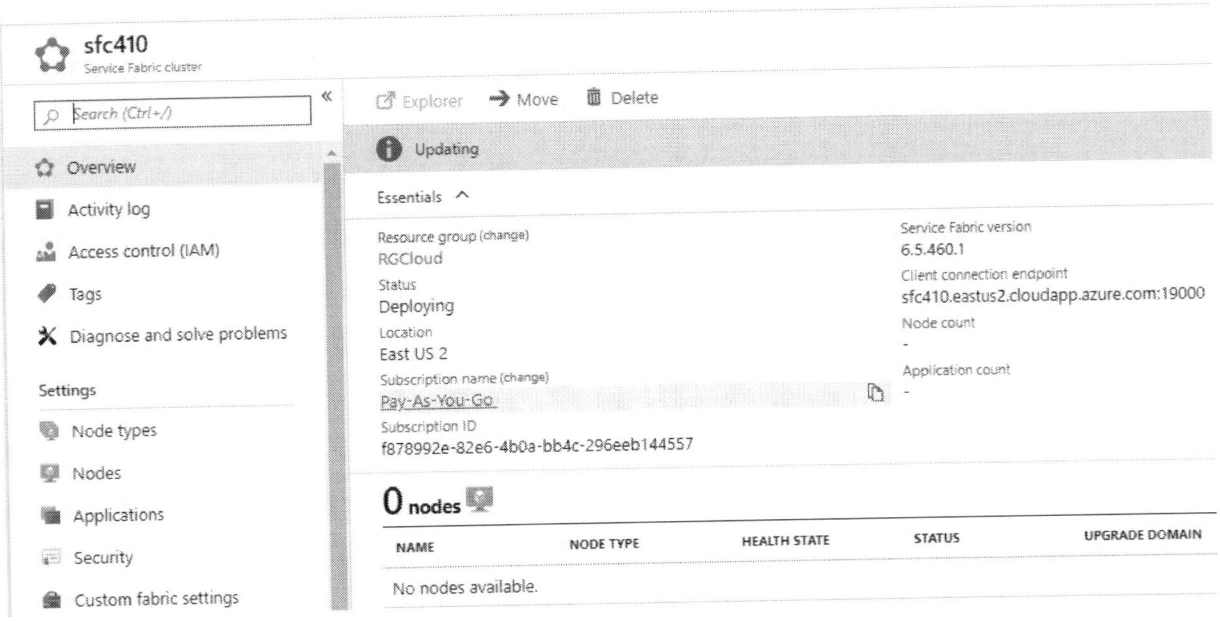

6. You can use following tools with Service Fabric to Deploy applications:

- Service Fabric Explorer, a browser-based tool.
- Service Fabric Command Line Interface (CLI), which runs on top of Azure CLI.
- PowerShell commands.
- Visual Studio

You can also deploy container images from Azure Container registery or Docker Hub to deploy your applications.

Chapter 17 API Management

This is AZ-301 specific Chapter. Leave this for AZ-300 Exam.

This Chapter covers following Topic Lessons

- API Management (APIM)
- How API Management is implemented
- Why do we need API Management (APIM)
- Common scenarios of API Management
- API Management Components
- API Management Tiers
- Caching
- Virtual Network Support
- Scaling API Management
- API Management Pricing

This Chapter Covers following Lab Exercises

- Step by Step Implementing API Management

Chapter Topology

In this chapter we will add API Mangemnt to the Topology.

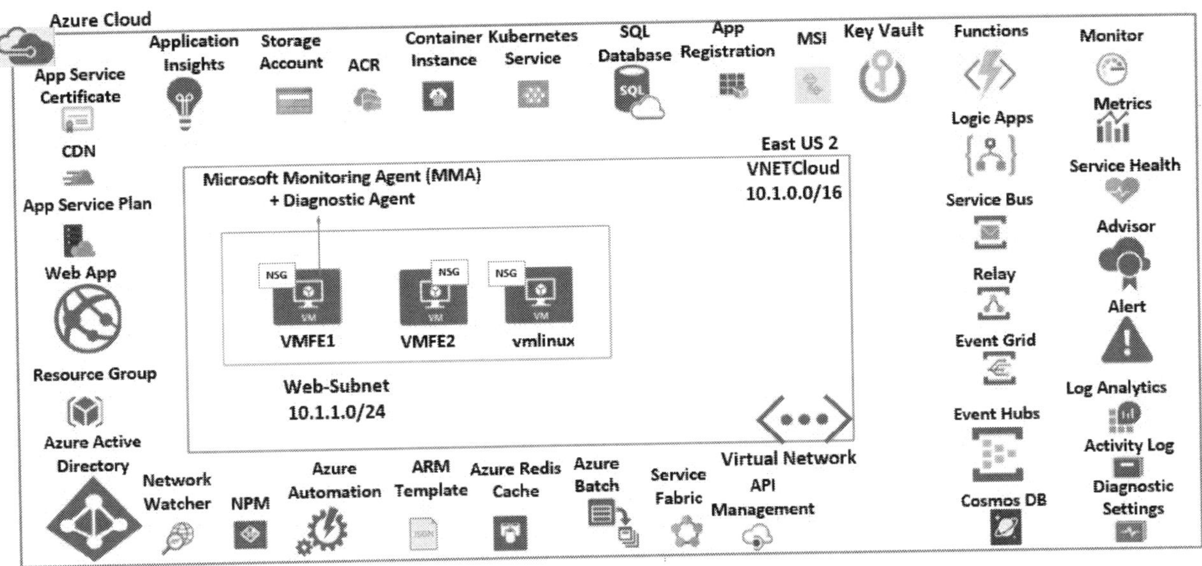

API Management (APIM)

API Management (APIM) is a gateway service that sits between apps that consume your service and your API implementation.

Azure API Management publishes APIs of Application Platform to external partners, employees and developers securely and at scale.

It includes a developer portal for documentation, Self-service sign up, API key management and Developer only console to explore API.

It also includes Publisher portal to configure gateway service and too see analytics about your published API.

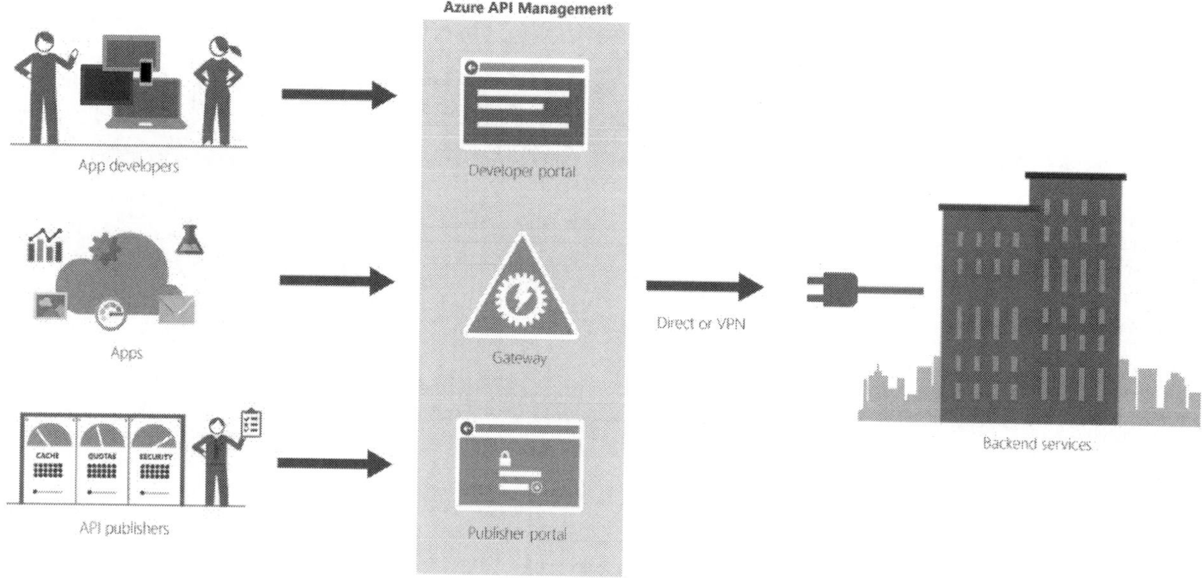

API Management adds following features to API implementation:

Access control
Rate limiting
Monitoring
Event logging,
Caching

How API Management is implemented

Import API of Backend Application: Import API of Backend Application platform into API Management Instance. The APIM API becomes a facade for the backend API. At the time you import the backend API, both the source API and the APIM API are identical. APIM enables you to customize the facade according to your needs without touching the backend API.

Publish APIM API: By Publishing APIM API developers can subscribe to the product and begin to use the product.
APIM API Products can be **open** or **protected**. Protected products must be subscribed to before they can be used, while open products can be used without a subscription.

Why do we need API Management (APIM)

API Management (APIM) helps organizations publish APIs of Application platform to external partners and internal developers to unlock the potential of their data and services.

API Management helps organization bring revenue by monetizing their application platform as well as drive adoption of their application platform.

Common scenarios of API Management

Enabling ISV partner ecosystems to onboard through the developer portal and building an API facade to decouple from internal implementations that are not ripe for partner consumption.

Running an internal API program by offering a centralized location for the organization to communicate about the availability and latest changes to APIs, gating access based on organizational accounts, all based on a secured channel between the API gateway and the backend.

Securing mobile infrastructure by gating access with API keys, preventing DOS attacks by using throttling, or using advanced security policies like JWT token validation.

API Management Components

API gateway: API Management is a gateway service that sits between apps and your API implementation. It performs following functions:

- Accepts API calls and routes them to your backends.
- Verifies API keys, JWT tokens, certificates, and other credentials.
- Enforces usage quotas and rate limits.
- Transforms your API on the fly without code modifications.
- Caches backend responses where set up.
- Logs call metadata for analytics purposes.

Publisher Portal: It is the administrative interface for the API Management. It performs following functions:

- Define or import API schema.
- Package APIs into products.
- Set up policies like quotas or transformations on the APIs.
- Get insights from analytics.
- Manage users.

Developer Portal: It performs following functions:

- Read API documentation.
- Try out an API via the interactive console.
- Create an account and subscribe to get API keys.
- Access analytics on their own usage.

Exercise 128: Step by Step Implementing API Management

For this Exercise we will use MS demo conference Application API as backend API residing @ https://conferenceapi.azurewebsites.net?format=json

Step 1 Creating API Management Instance: In Azure portal Click Create a Resource> Integration>API Management>Create API Management service blade opens> Enter a name>Select RGCloud in Resource Group> In Location select East US 2>Enter Organization Name>Select Pricing Tier as per your requirement>Click create. Resource Group RGCloud was created in Exercise 1, Chapter 1 in Part 1 Book.

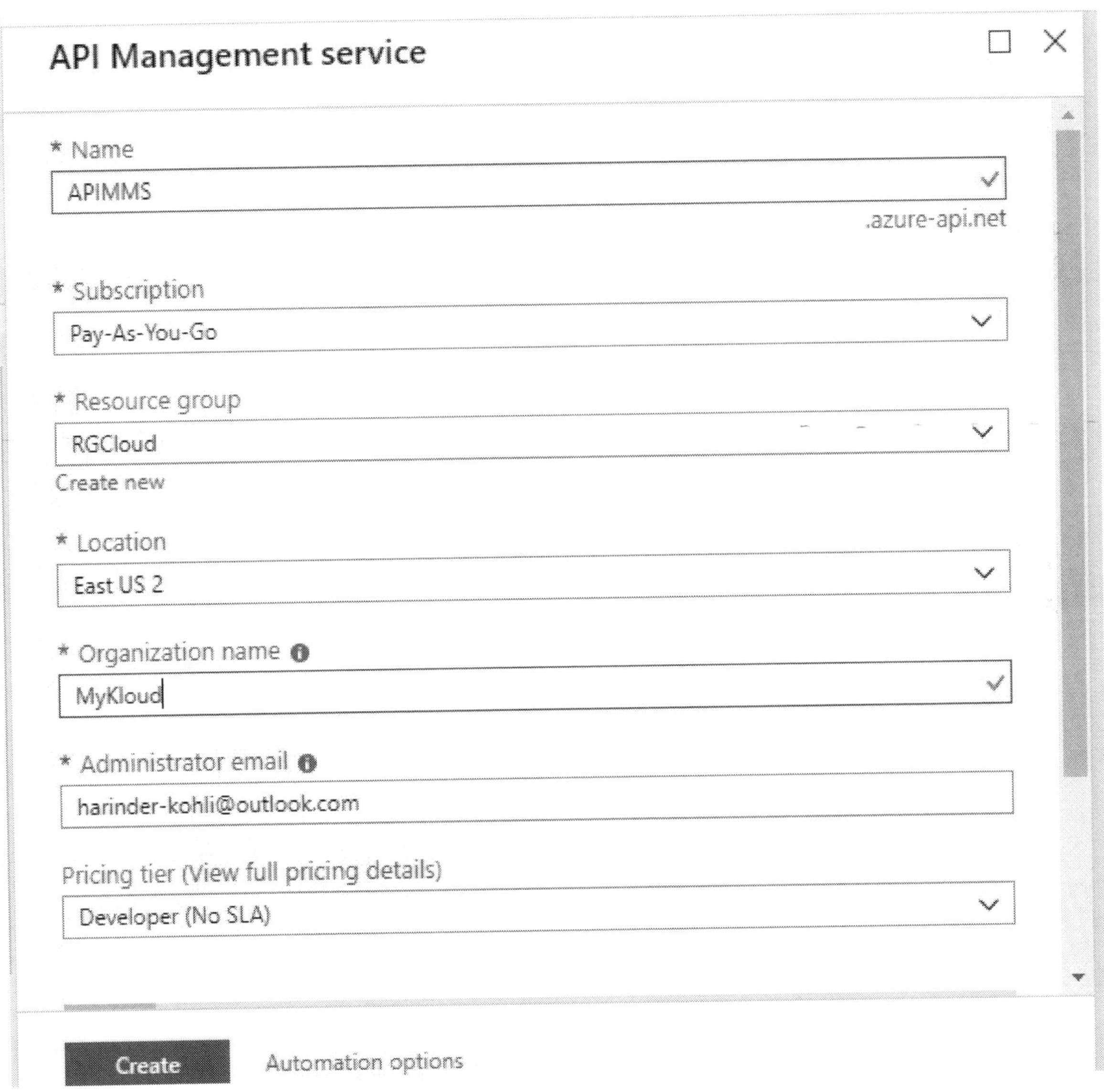

Figure below shows API Management Dashboard. See also the Tabs for Publisher and Developer Portal.

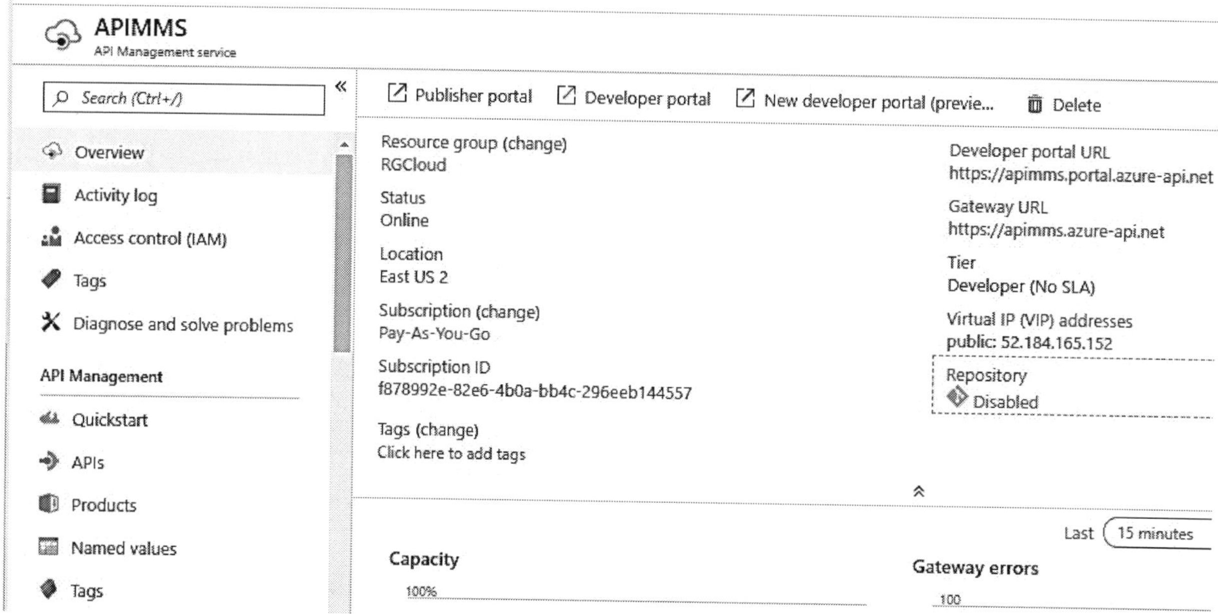

Step 2: Import API (MS Demo Conference API) into API Management Instance

API represents a set of operations available to developers. Once the backend API is imported into API Management (APIM), the APIM API becomes a facade for the backend API. At the time you import the backend API, both the source API and the APIM API are identical. APIM enables you to customize the facade according to your needs without touching the backend API.

In API Management Dashboard Click APIs in left pane>Add a new API Blade opens> select Open API>Create from OpenAPI Specification Blade opens as shown below>Enter the URL for Backend Application whose API are being exposed. The URL shown below is MS demo conference Application API residing @ https://conferenceapi.azurewebsites.net?format=json> Click create (Not Shown).

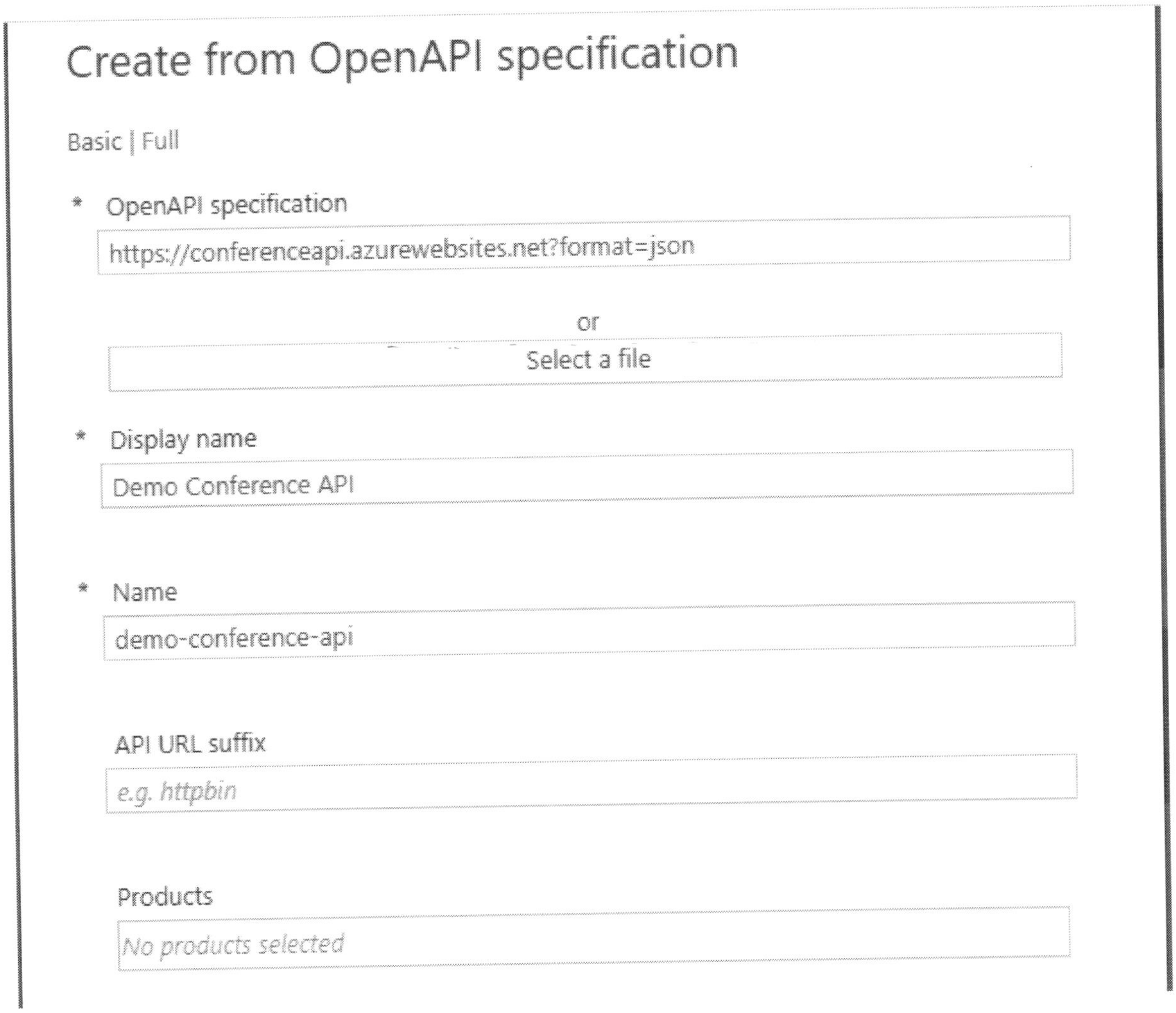

Create from OpenAPI specification

Basic | Full

* OpenAPI specification

https://conferenceapi.azurewebsites.net?format=json

or

Select a file

* Display name

Demo Conference API

* Name

demo-conference-api

API URL suffix

e.g. httpbin

Products

No products selected

Step 3: Create and publish a product

In Azure API Management, a product contains one or more APIs as well as a usage quota and the terms of use. Once a product is published, developers can subscribe to the product and begin to use the product's APIs.
Products can be **Open** or **Protected**. Protected products must be subscribed to before they can be used, while open products can be used without a subscription.

1. Go to API Management Dashboard>Click Products in left pane>Click +Add>Add Product blade opens>Enter Display name> In state select Published>click create.

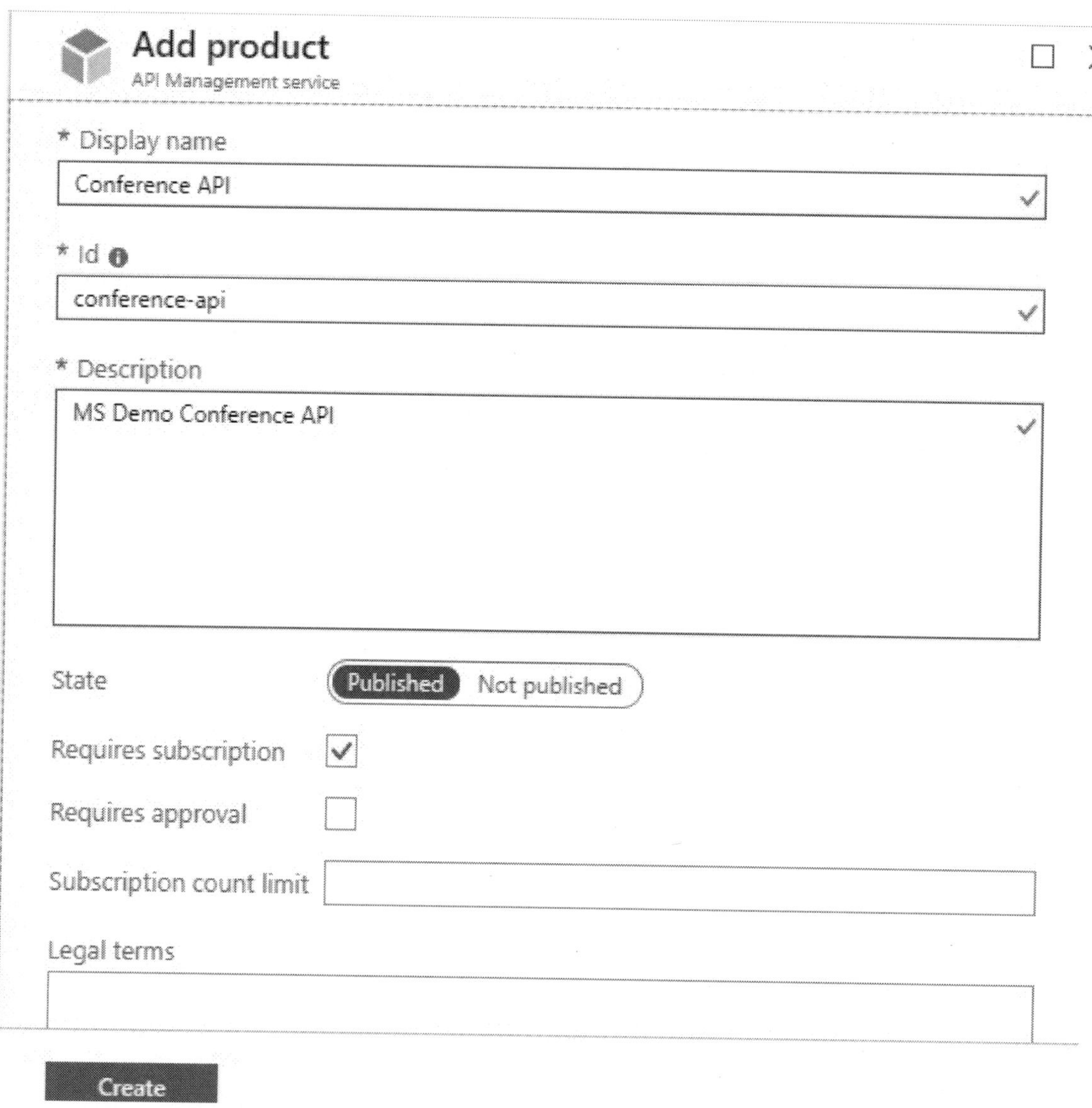

2. **Add API to your Product**>Click Products in left pane>Select your Product and click on it (In this case it is Conference API)> Conference API Dashboard opens as shown below>Click Add API>API Blade opens. Select your API (In this case Demo Conference API) and click select (Not Shown).

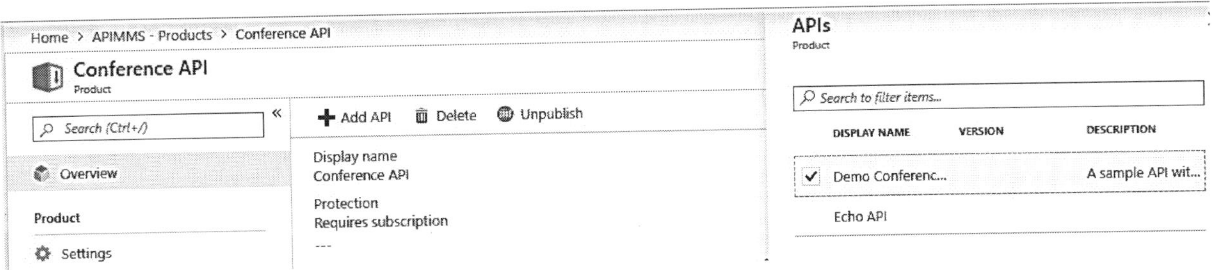

Products are associations of one or more APIs. You can include a number of APIs and offer them to developers through the developer portal. Developers must first subscribe to a product to get access to the API. When they subscribe, they get a subscription key that is good for any API in that product.

Step 4: Test the newly created APIs

You can test APIs from the Azure Portal or Developer Portal.

1. API Management Dashboard> Click APIs in left pane>Select and click your API in Right pane (In this case Demo Conference API)>Click Test Tab>Select Get speakers in left pane>Press send>**Backend responds** with 200 OK and some data.

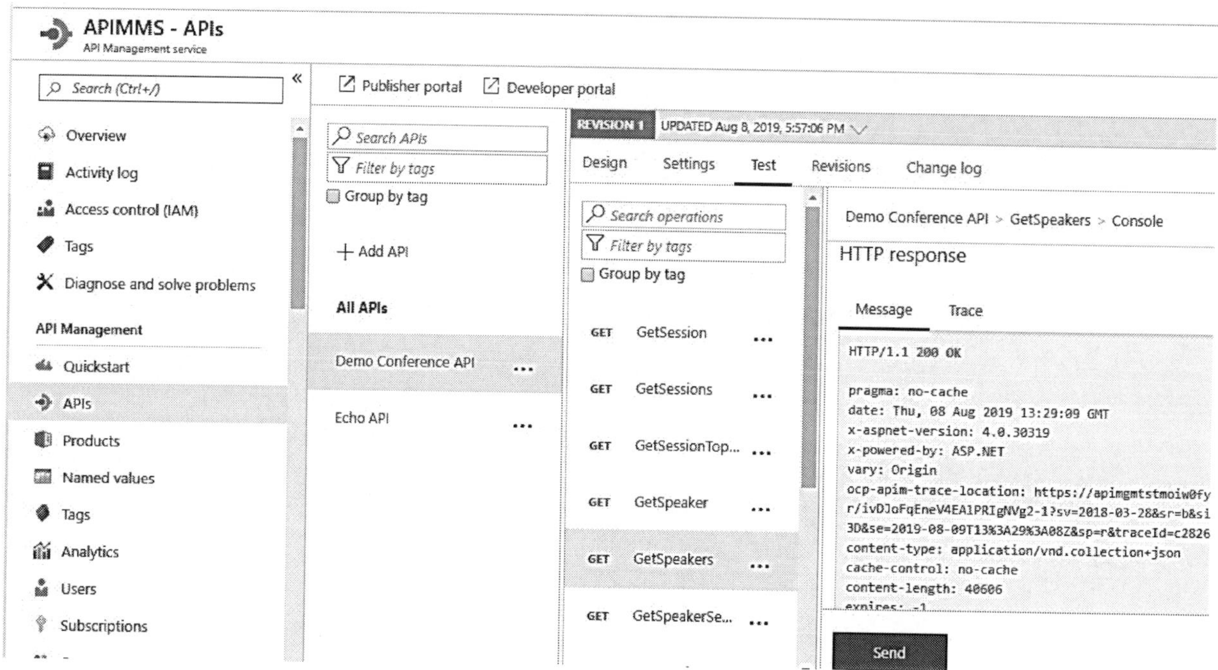

Step 5: Access Published API from your Application

To access Published API from your application you need to add following in your application:

1. Gateway URL.
2. A valid key in HTTP requests when they make calls to those APIs. Otherwise, the calls are rejected immediately by the API Management Gateway.

Getting Gateway URL: Go to Management API Dashboard with overview selected in left pane> In Right pane you can see the Gateway URL.

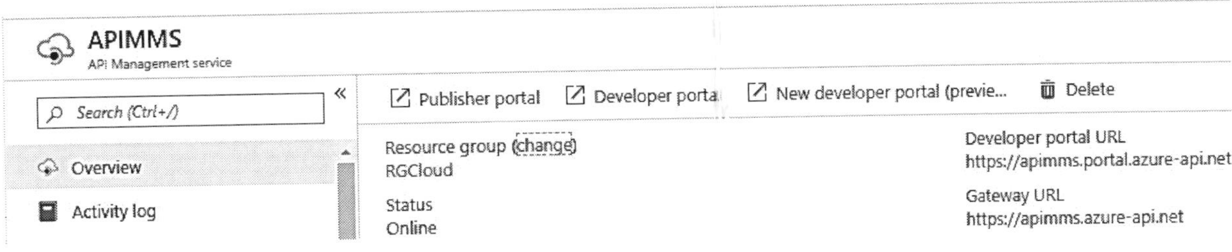

Getting Key of Demo Conference API: In Management API Dashboard click Subscription in left pane>Subscription Pane opens> Copy the Demo Conference API key (last Row).

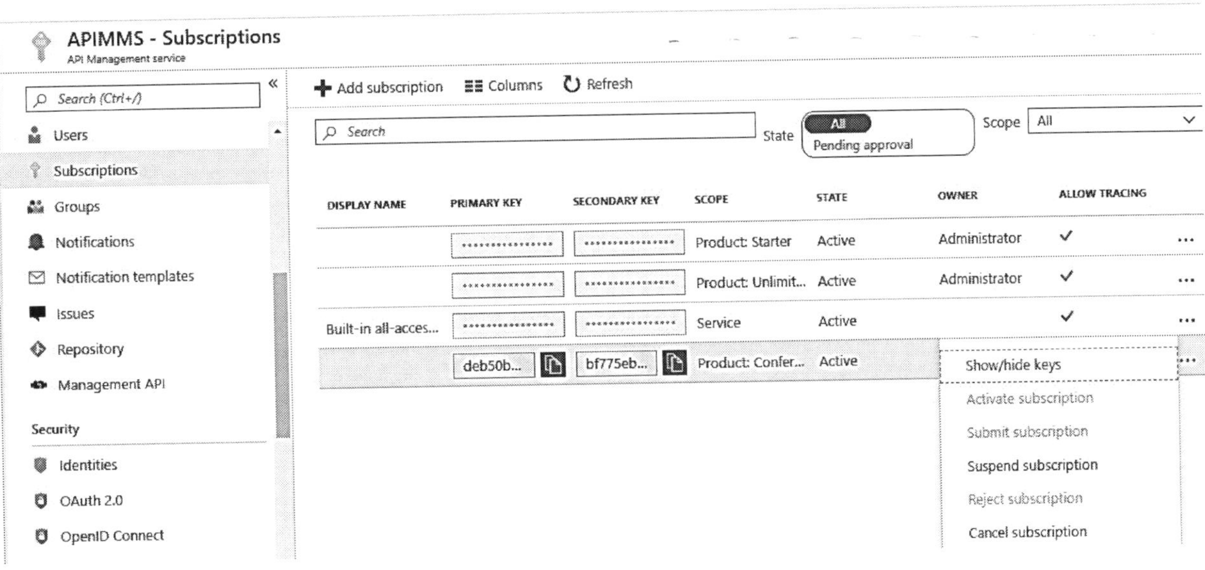

API Management Tiers

API Management is offered in Five tiers— Consumption, Developer, Basic, Standard, and Premium. Table below shows comparison of various tiers.

Features	Developer	Basic	Standard	Premium
Purpose	Non-production use cases and evaluations	Entry-level production use cases	Medium-volume production use cases	High-volume or Enterprise production use cases
Built in Cache	10 MB	50 MB	1 GB	5 GB
Scale-out (units)	1	2	4	10
SLA	No	99.9%	99.9%	99.95%
Azure Active Directory integration	Yes	No	Yes	Yes
Virtual Network support	Yes	No	No	Yes
Multi-region deployment	No	No	No	Yes
External Cache Support	Yes	Yes	Yes	Yes
Estimated Maximum Throughput (per unit)	500 requests/sec	1000 requests/sec	2500 requests/sec	4000 requests/sec

SLA is only applicable when minimum of 2 units are deployed.

Caching

Caching can improve performance in Azure API Management. Caching can significantly reduce API latency, bandwidth consumption, and web service load for data that does not change frequently.
Caching is user response is stored in temp area. During subsequent response it is served from temp area.

Following table shows Built in Cache storage available for Different API Management Tiers:

Features	Developer	Basic	Standard	Premium
Cache (per unit)	10 MB	50 MB	1 GB	5 GB

Virtual Network Support

Azure API Management can be deployed inside the virtual network (VNET), so it can access backend services within the network. The developer portal and API gateway, can be configured to be accessible either from the Internet or only within the virtual network.

Design Nugget: When deploying an Azure API Management instance to a Resource Manager VNET, the service must be in a dedicated subnet that contains no other resources except for Azure API Management instances.

Following table show VNET functionality supported by each tier:

Features	Developer	Basic	Standard	Premium
Virtual Network support	Yes	No	No	Yes

You can configure VNET support through API Dashboard. Click Virtual Network in left Pane>Select External or Internal>Select Location, Virtual Network & Subnet.

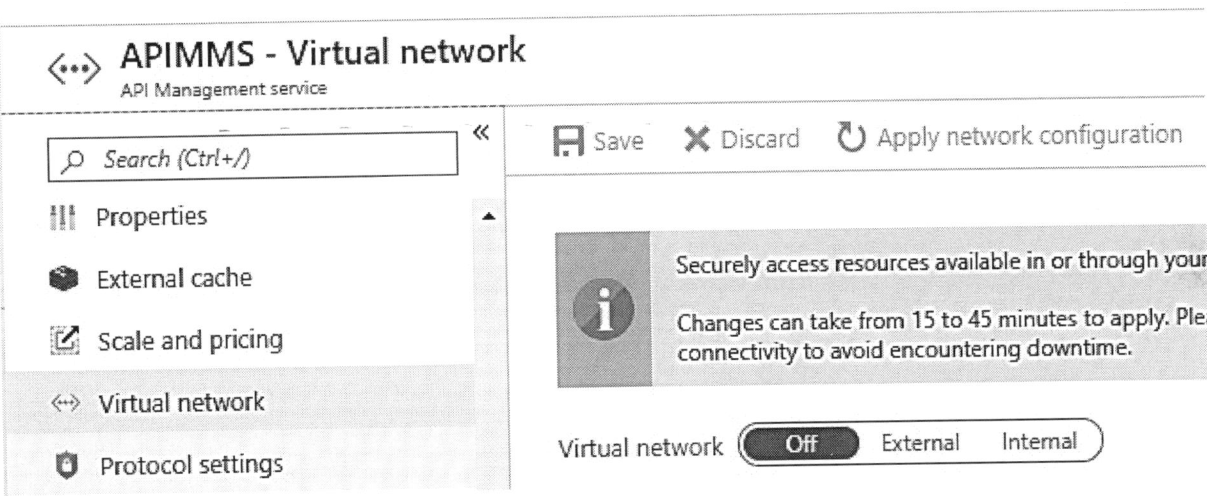

External Option: The API Management gateway and developer portal are accessible from the public internet via an external load balancer. The gateway can access resources within the virtual network.

Internal Option: The API Management gateway and developer portal are accessible only from within the virtual network via an internal load balancer. The gateway can access resources within the virtual network.

Scaling API Management

To meet the required performance you can Scale API Management Instance either by creating additional instances or upgrading to higher tier or both.

Following table shows number of instances supported by each API Management tier:

Features	Developer	Basic	Standard	Premium
Scale-out (units)	1	2	4	10

You can configure scale out through API Management Dashboard in Azure Portal. Click Scale and Pricing in left pane>If required you can upgrade your tier> Increase the number of units of API Management instance as per your requirement> Click save.

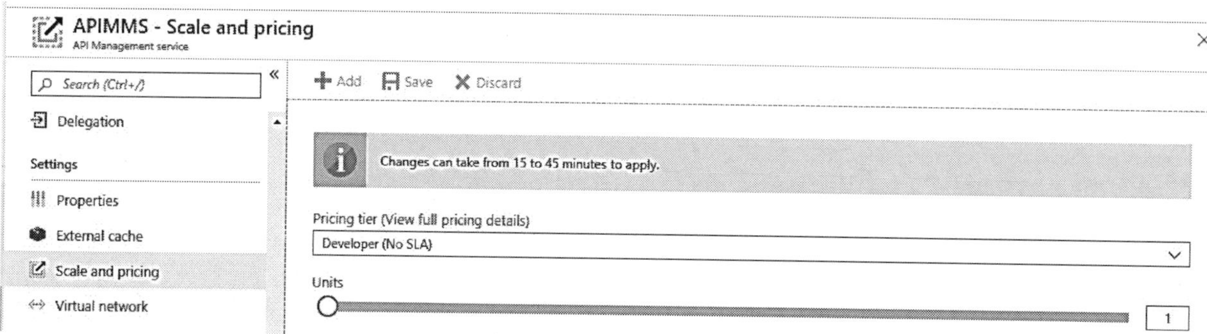

Design Nugget: SLA is only applicable when minimum 2 units are deployed.

API Management Pricing

Table below shows pricing of each tier.

Price	Developer	Basic	Standard	Premium
Price	$0.07/hour	$0.21/hour	$0.95/hour	$3.83/hour

Chapter 18 Azure Data Factory

This is AZ-301 specific Chapter. Leave this for AZ-300 Exam.

This Chapter covers following Topic Lessons

- Azure Data Factory
- Examples of Data Factory
- Data Factory Working
- Data Factory Components
- Activity Types
- Data Flow

This Chapter covers following Lab Exercises

- Create Storage Account and upload a txt File
- Create Azure Data Factory
- Data Flow

Chapter Topology

In this chapter we will add Data Factory to the Topology.

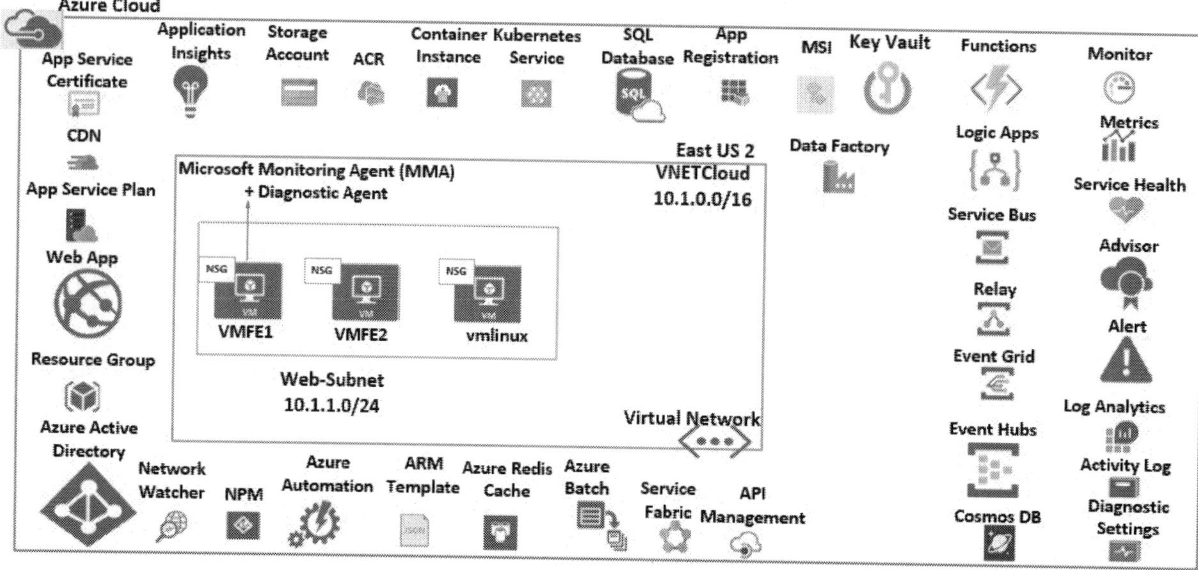

Azure Data Factory

Data Factory **automates the ingestion of Data** using built in connectors and the **loading of Data** to various Azure Services (HDInsight Hadoop, Azure Data Lake Analytics and Azure Machine Learning) using managed Data Pipelines.

Azure Data Factory is a Managed Azure Service which provides Data Orchestration as a service. Azure Data Factory helps you create, schedule, monitor and manage data pipelines. A data pipeline consists of activities which can **move data** between on-premises and cloud data stores and **transform data** to produce trusted information.

Azure Data Factory ingests data from Multiple Data sources (on-premises or cloud). It then processes, transforms and moves Data to different compute and storage services (HDInsight, Spark, Azure Data Lake Analytics and Azure Machine Learning) using Data Pipeline. The Data is then published to be consumed by end users and applications.

The figure below shows various stages of Data as it is moved through Azure Data Factory Managed Data Pipeline.

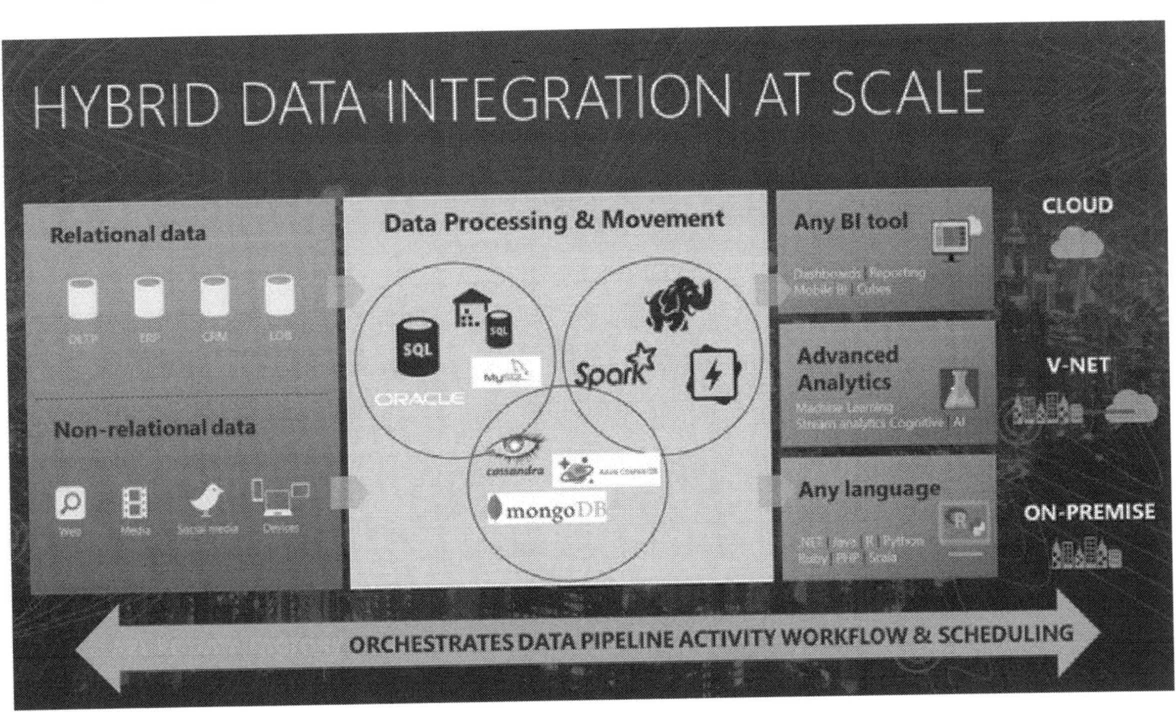

Design Nuggets

Design Nugget 1: To tansform Data, Data Factory use Other Azure Services such as HDInsight & Azure Data Lake Analytics etc.

Design Nugget 2: Recently introduced feature **Data Flow** can perform Data Transformation activities such as data cleaning, aggregation and Preparation.

Examples of Data Factory

1. Copy data from Azure Blob storage to a SQL database by using the Azure Data Factory Copy Data tool.
2. Copy data from an on-premises SQL Server database to Azure Blob storage by using the Data Factory Copy Data tool
3. Copy a number of tables from Azure SQL Database to Azure SQL Data Warehouse.
4. Using Azure Data Factory pipeline, transforms data by using a Spark activity and an on-demand Azure HDInsight linked service.
5. Using Azure Data Factory pipeline, transform data using Hive Activity on a HDInsight cluster that is in an Azure Virtual Network (VNet).
6. Copy data from Azure Blob storage to an Azure Blob Storage by using the Azure Data Factory Copy Data tool.

Data Factory Working

The pipelines (data-driven workflows) in Azure Data Factory typically perform the following four steps as shown in the figure below.

Connect & Collect: Enterprises have data of various types - structured, unstructured, and semi-structured. Data is located in disparate sources - on-premises and in the cloud.

Without Data Factory, enterprises must build write custom services to integrate these data sources and processing.

Using Built in connectors in Data Factory, Data from on-premises and cloud is ingested into Data Factory pipeline to be moved to a centralization data store in the cloud for further analysis. For example, you can collect data in Azure Data Lake Store and transform the data later by using an Azure Data Lake Analytics compute service.

Transform and enrich: After data is present in a centralized data store in the cloud, process or transform the collected data by using compute services such as HDInsight Hadoop, Spark, Data Lake Analytics, and Machine Learning.

Publish: After the raw data has been refined into a business-ready consumable form, load the data into Azure Data Warehouse, Azure SQL Database, Azure CosmosDB, or whichever analytics engine your business users can point to from their business intelligence tools.

Monitor: After you have successfully built and deployed your data integration pipeline, providing business value from refined data, monitor the scheduled activities and pipelines for success and failure rates. Azure Data Factory has built-in support for pipeline monitoring via Azure Monitor, API, PowerShell, Microsoft Operations Management Suite, and health panels on the Azure portal.

Data Factory Components

Pipeline: A pipeline is a logical grouping of activities that performs a unit of work. Together, the activities in a pipeline perform a task. Advantage of pipeline is that the pipeline allows you to manage the activities as a set instead of managing each one individually.

Activity: Activities represent a processing step in a pipeline. The activities in a pipeline define actions to perform on your data. Data Factory supports three types of activities: **data movement/copy activities, data transformation activities, and control activities**.

Dataset: Dataset simply points or references the data you want to use in your activities as inputs and outputs. An input dataset represents the input for an activity in the pipeline and an output dataset represents the output for the activity.

Linked Service: A linked service links a data store or a compute resource to the data factory. Linked services are much like connection strings, which define the connection information needed for Data Factory to connect to external resources. Linked services are used for two following purposes in Data Factory:

- To represent a **data store** that includes an on-premises SQL Server database, Oracle database, file share, or Azure blob storage account etc.
- To represent a **compute resource** that can host the execution of an activity.

The following diagram shows the relationships among pipeline, activity, dataset, and linked service in Data Factory:

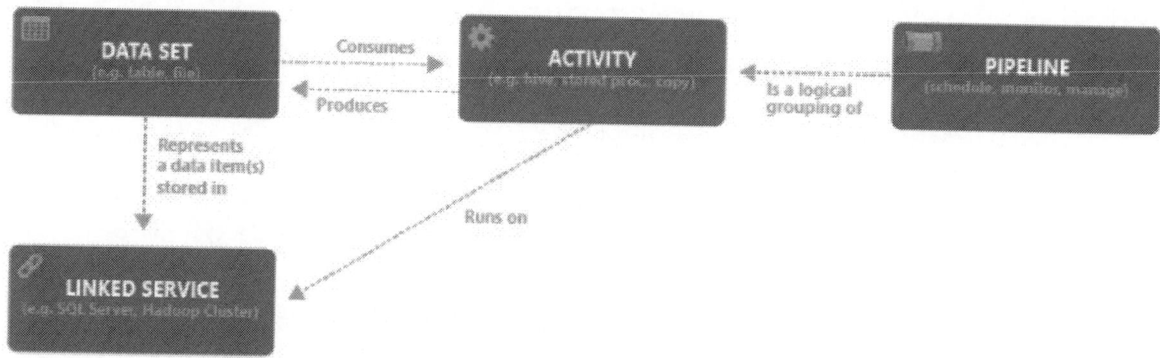

Design Nugget: Before you create a dataset, you must create a **linked service to** link your data store to the data factory.

Activity Types

Data Movement Activity: It is a Copy Activity in Data Factory to copy data from a source data store to a sink data store. Data from any source can be written to any sink. Following is the **partial list** of data stores supported by Data Factory.

Category	Data Store	Source Data store	Sink Data Store
Azure	Azure Blob Storage	✓	✓
Azure	Azure Cosmos DB	✓	✓
Azure	Azure Data Lake Store	✓	✓
Azure	Azure Database for MySQL	✓	
Azure	Azure SQL Database	✓	✓
Azure	Azure SQL Data Warehouse	✓	✓
Database	Amazon Redshift	✓	
Database	DB2	✓	
Database	MariaDB	✓	
Database	SAP HANA	✓	✓
Database	SQL Server	✓	✓
Database	Oracle	✓	✓

Data transformation activities: Data Transformation Activity in Data Factory is used to transform Data ingested. For example, you may use a copy activity to copy data from an on-premises SQL Server to an Azure Blob Storage. Then, use a Hive activity that runs a Hive script on an Azure HDInsight cluster to **process/transform data** from the blob storage to produce output data. Following is the partial list of Data Transformation Activities.

Data transformation activity	Compute environment
Hive	HDInsight
Pig	HDInsight
MapReduce	HDInsight
Stored Procedure	Azure SQL, Azure SQL DW, SQL Server
U-SQL	Azure Data Lake Analytics

Control activities: Control Activities are control plane activities on pipelines.

Control activity	Description
Execute Pipeline Activity	Allows a Data Factory pipeline to invoke another pipeline.
Lookup Activity	

Ingesting & Transforming Unstructured and Structured Data using Azure Data Factory (ADF)

Figure below shows Azure Data Factory ingesting Structured and Unstructured Data.

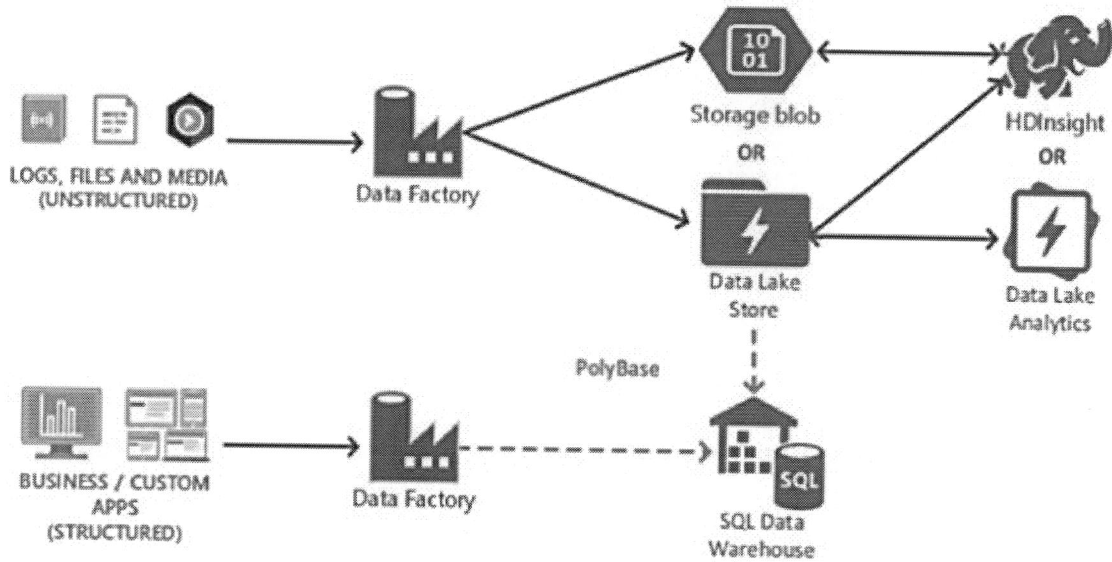

Loading and Transforming Unstructured Data: Using Built-in connectors Azure Data Factory copies data from source Data store to sink Data store which is in this case is Blob Storage or Data lake Store as shown in figure above. You can now use Data Transformation activity such as Hive activity or MapReduce or U-SQL activity to perform analytics on the data using HDInsight or Data lake Analytics Cluster.

Loading and Transforming structured Data: Using Built-in connectors Azure Data Factory copies data from source Data store to sink Data store which is in this case is a staging Blob storage. Data factory will use Polybase to load data from staging Data store to Azure SQL Data Warehouse. You can now use Data Transformation activity such as query activities to perform analytics on the data using SQL Data Warehouse compute cluster.

The Biggest advantage of using Azure Data Factory is that it automates ingestion and Loading of data. Without Data Factory ingestion and movement of Data between various Azure services would be a manual process and would require specialised skills.

Exercise 129: Create Storage Account and upload a txt File

Create Storage Account

1. In Azure Port click Create a resource>Storage>Storage Account>Create Storage Account Blade opens>Select Resource Group RGCloud>Enter a name>Location select East US 2>Rest Select all default values>Click Review + Create> After Validation is passed click create.

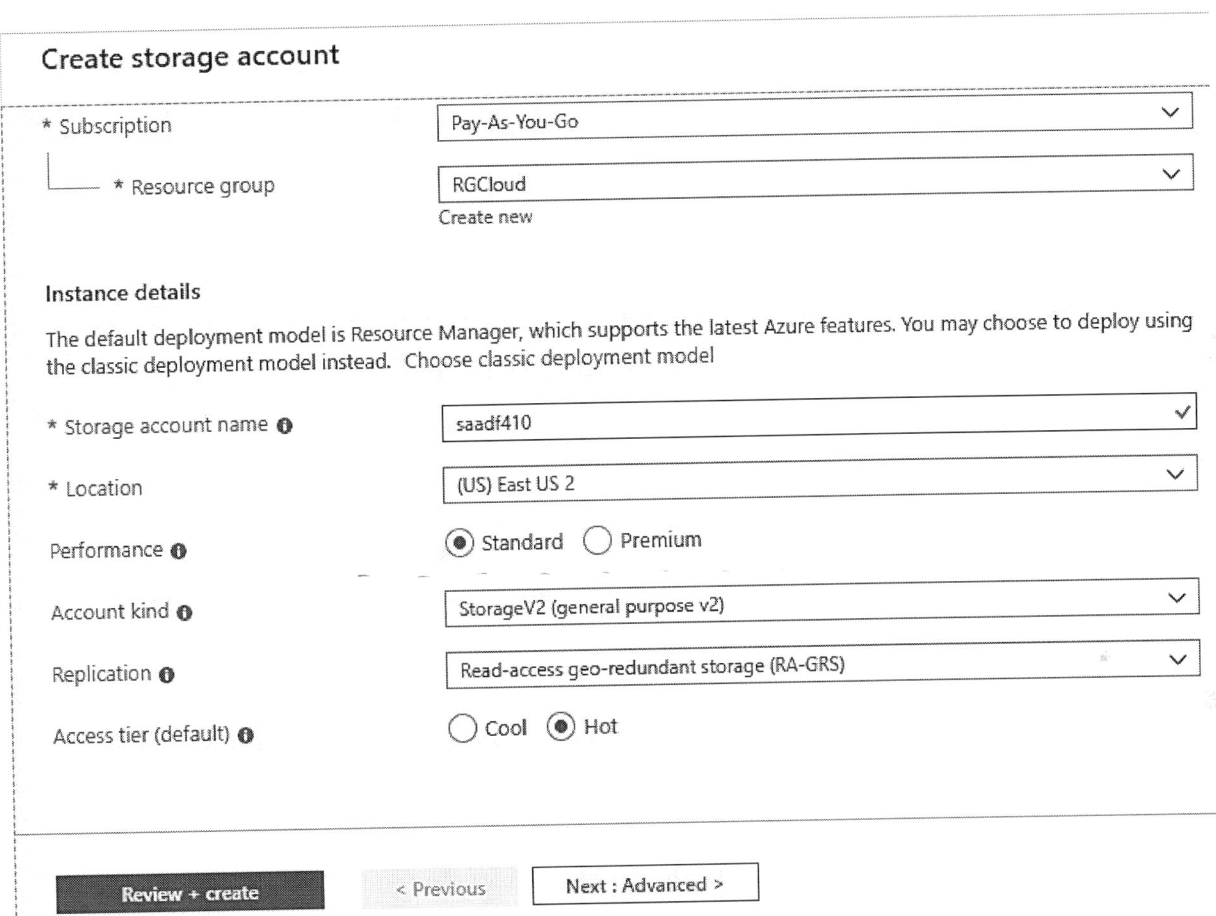

2. Figure below shows dashboard of Stoarge Account.

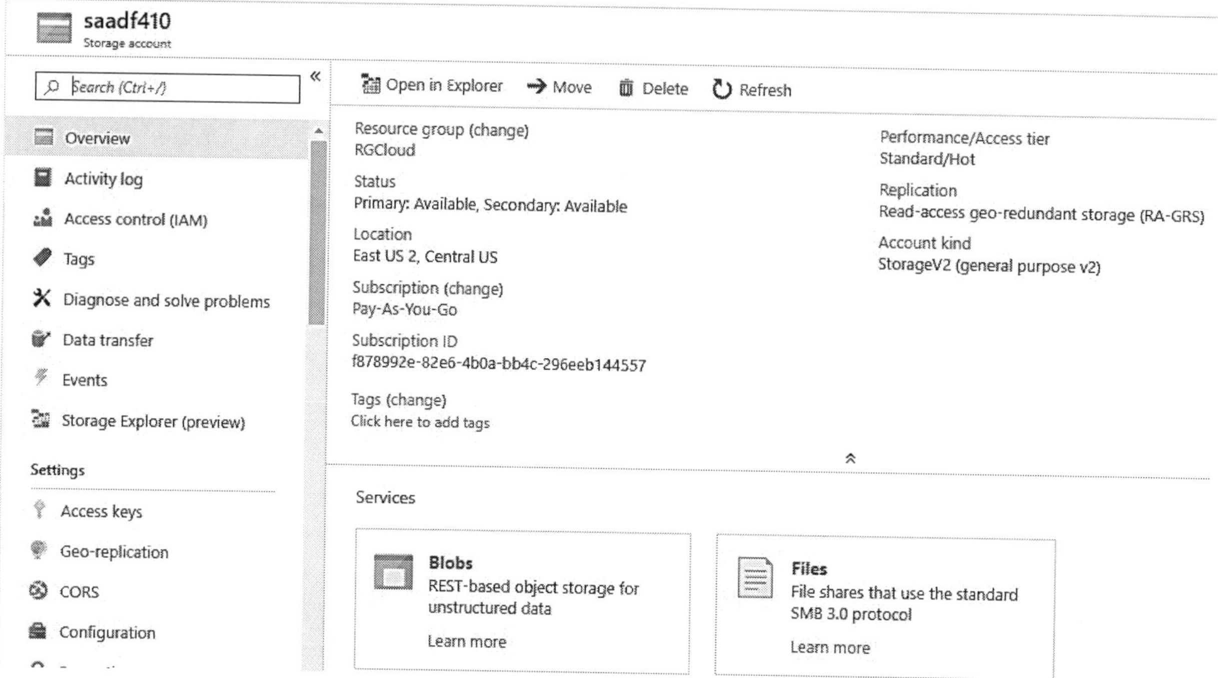

3. Click Access Keys in left pane> Note down the Storage Account name and Key1.

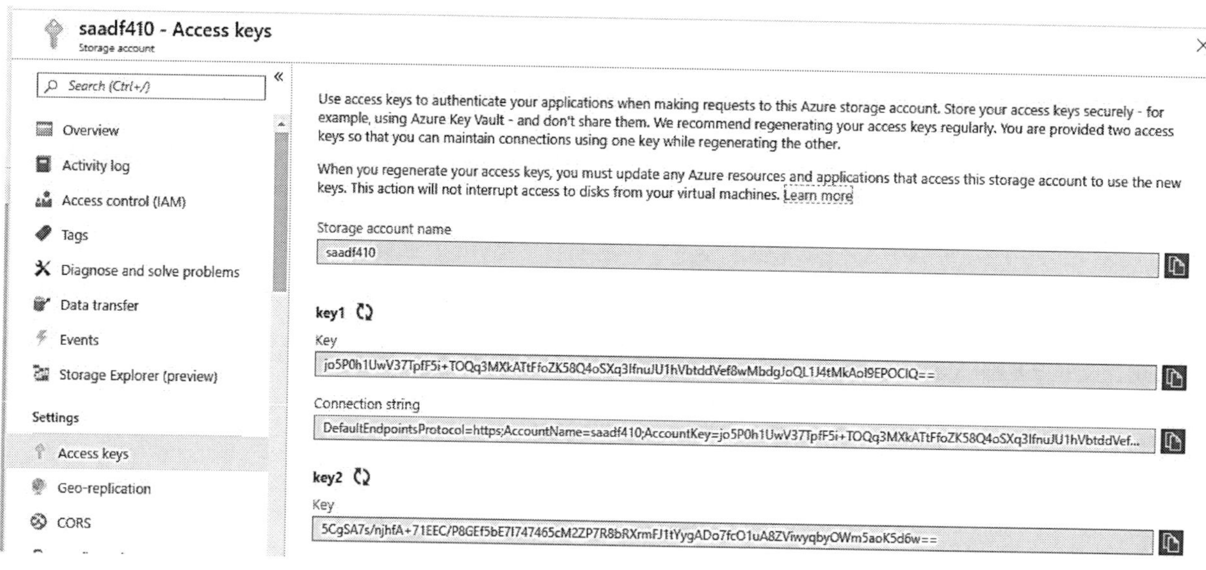

Create a Container and upload file to a folder

1. In Storage Account Dashboard with Overview selected in left pane, Click Blobs in Right pane> Blob Pane opens>In Right pane click + Container>New Container Blade opens> Enter a name and click ok.

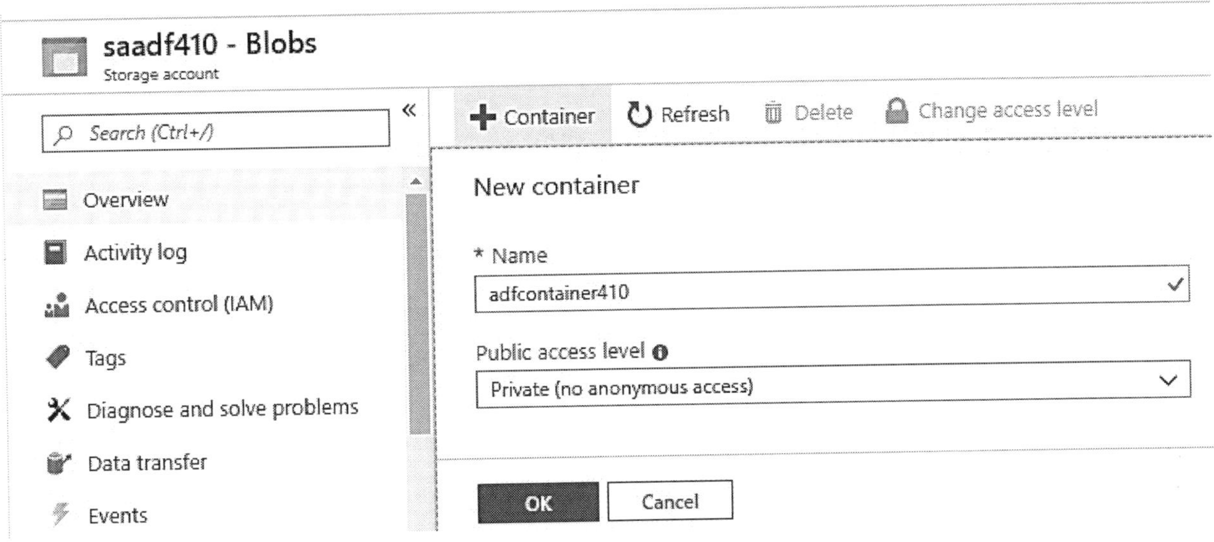

2. Click the newly ctreated Container>Container pane opens>Click Upload in Right pane>Upload Blob Pane opens>Upload a txt file from your laptop. I uploaded test.txt file>Click Advanced and in **upload to folder** box enter **input**>Click upload>Close the pane after upload is completed.

Exercise 130: Create Azure Data Factory and Copy Data

In this exercise we will Create Data Factory Service. We will use Data Factory to copy Data in Input Folder of Blob Storage Container adfcontainer410 to output Folder of Blob Storage Container adfcontainer410. adfcontainer410 was created in previous exercise.

1. In Azure Port click Create a resource>Analytics>Data Factory>Create Data Factory Blade opens>Enter a name> For resource group select RGCloud> In select version V2> In location selection East US 2>Click Create (Not Shown).

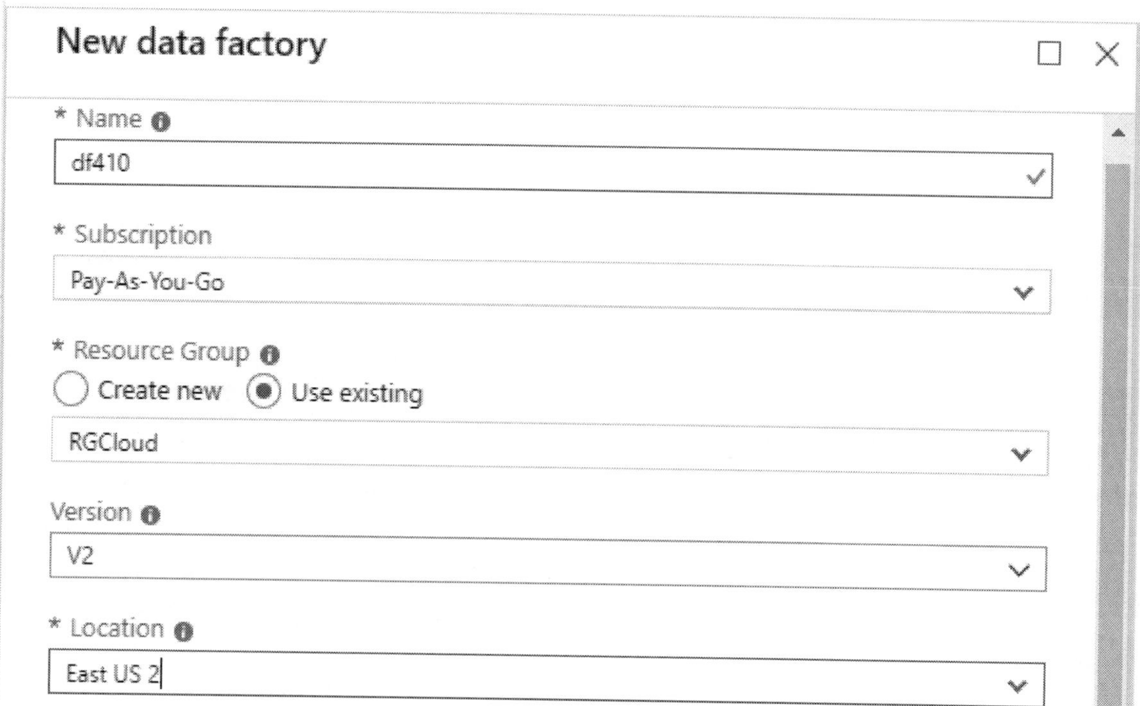

3. Figure bellows shows the dashboard of Data Factory.

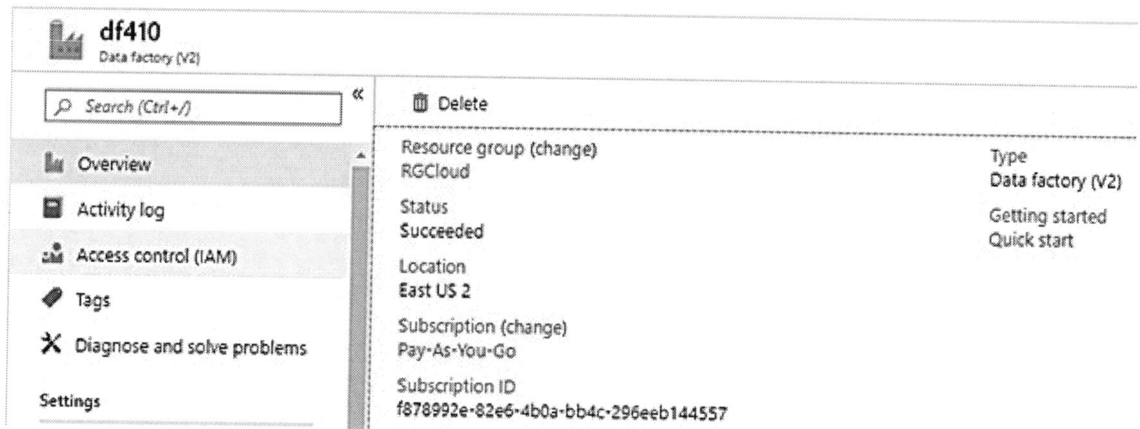

4. **Create Linked Service.** In Azure Data Factory Dashboard click Author & Monitor in right pane>A new Browse opens as shown below. Note the pencil icon in the left column.

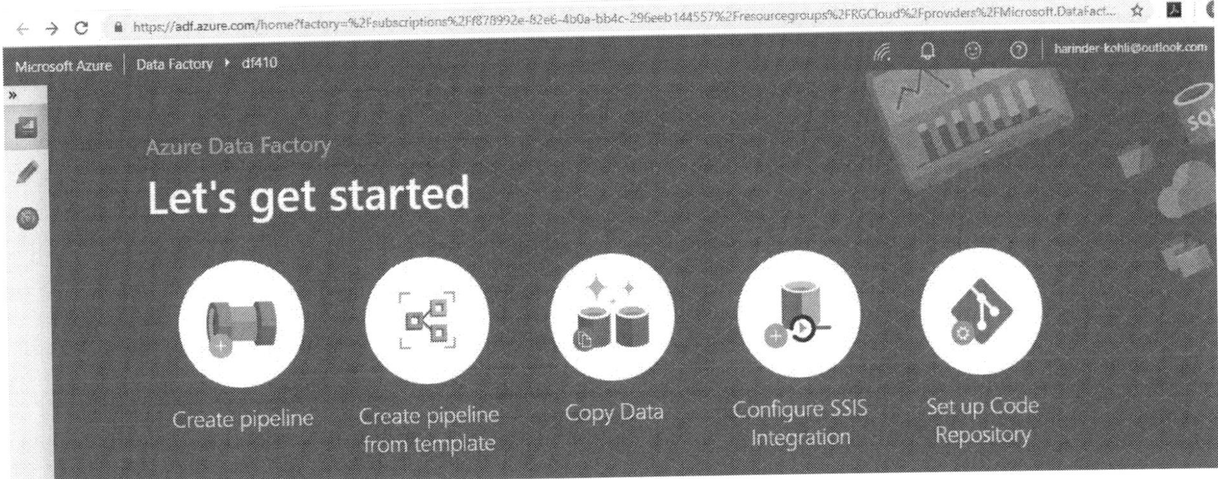

5. Click the pencil icon in the left column>A new Browser pane opens> Click Connections in left pane>In right pane you can see linked Services option.

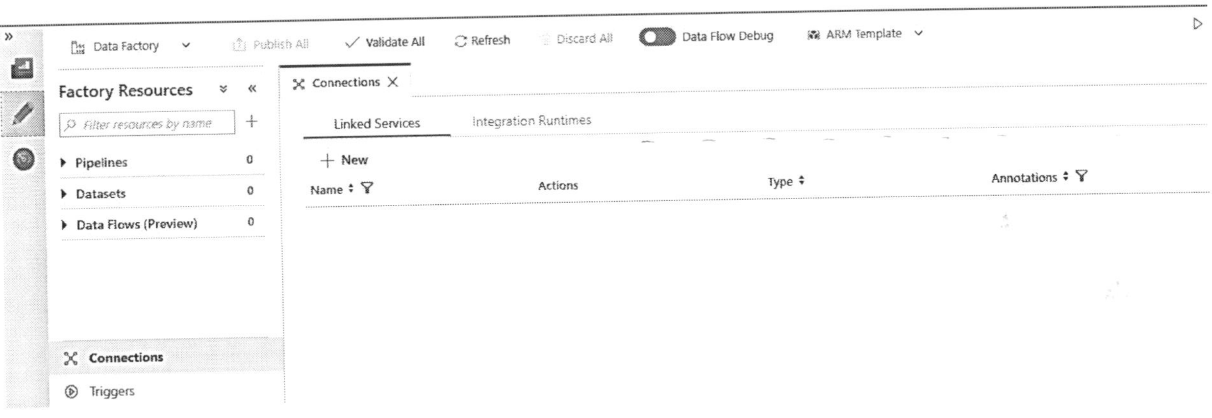

.

6. In Right pane with Linked Services selected, Click + New> New Linked Service pane opens>Select Azure Blob Storage>

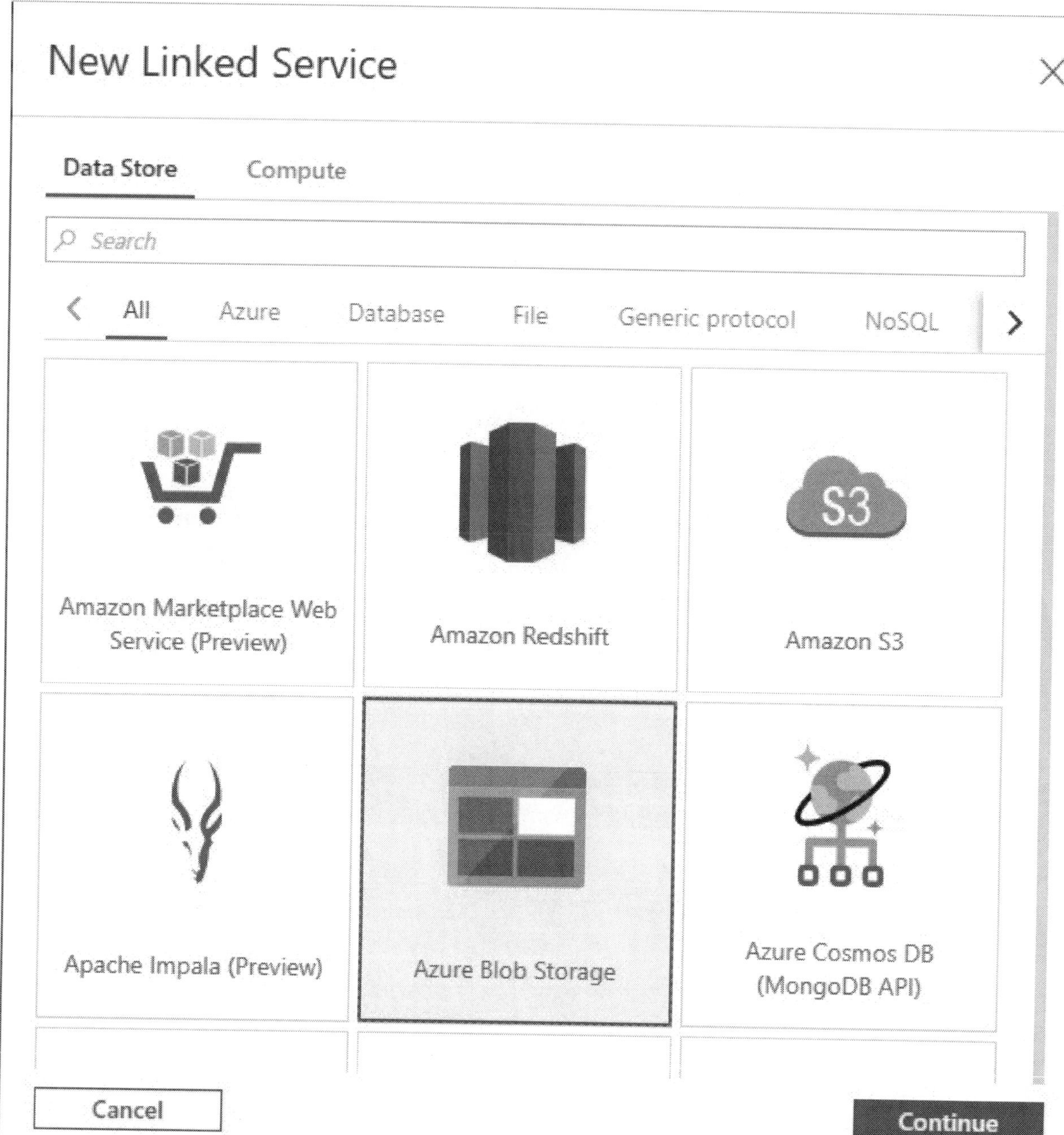

7. Click Continue in New Linked Service pane>A new pane opens> Enter a name > Select your storage Account name from drop down box which you created in previous exercise> Click Test Connection to confirm that the Data Factory service can connect to the storage account> Click Finish.

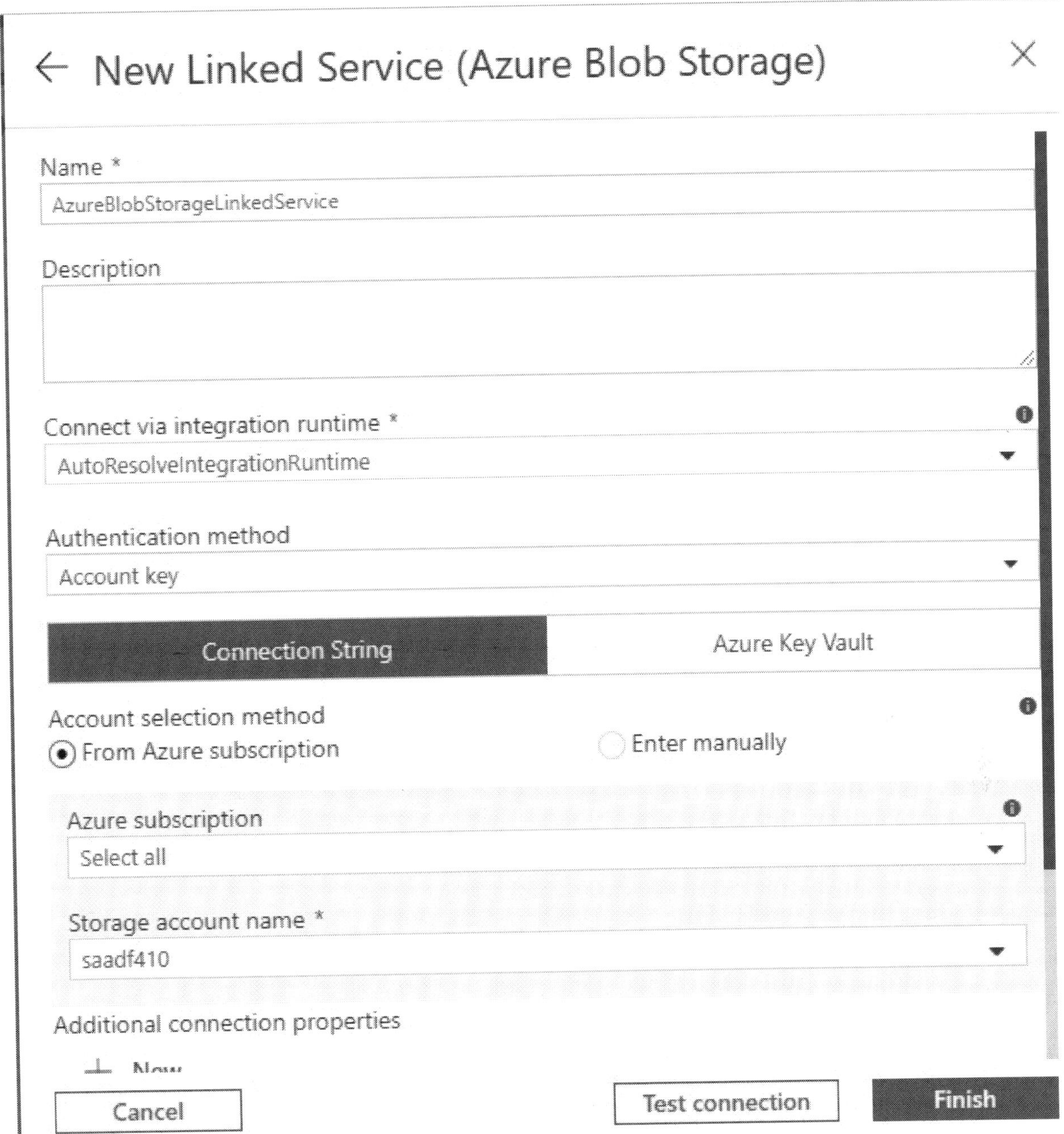

8. **Create Input Dataset.** The input dataset represents the source data in the input folder. Input folder was created when we uploaded test.txt file to container in previous exercise.

Go back to Data Factory Browser pane as shown below. Note the + Sign.

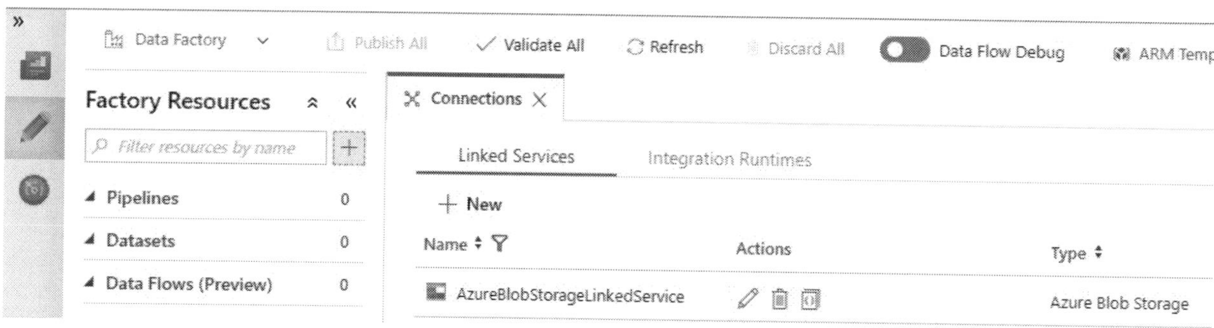

9. Click + Sign in left pane> A Box pops up>Click Dataset>New Dataset Blade opens>Select Azure Blob Storage>Click Continue.

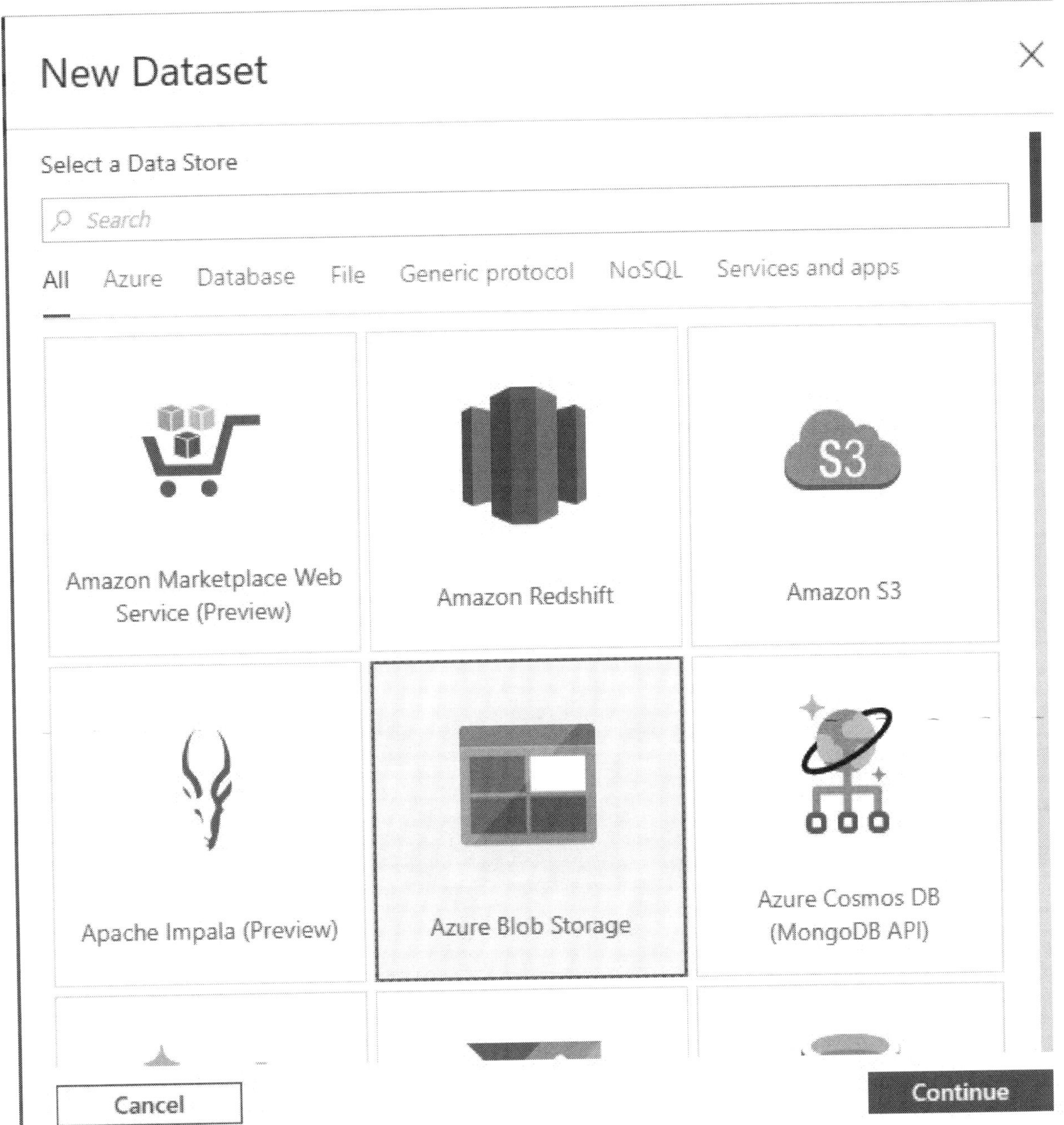

10. After you clicked continue>Select Format Pane opens>Select Delimited Text>Click Continue

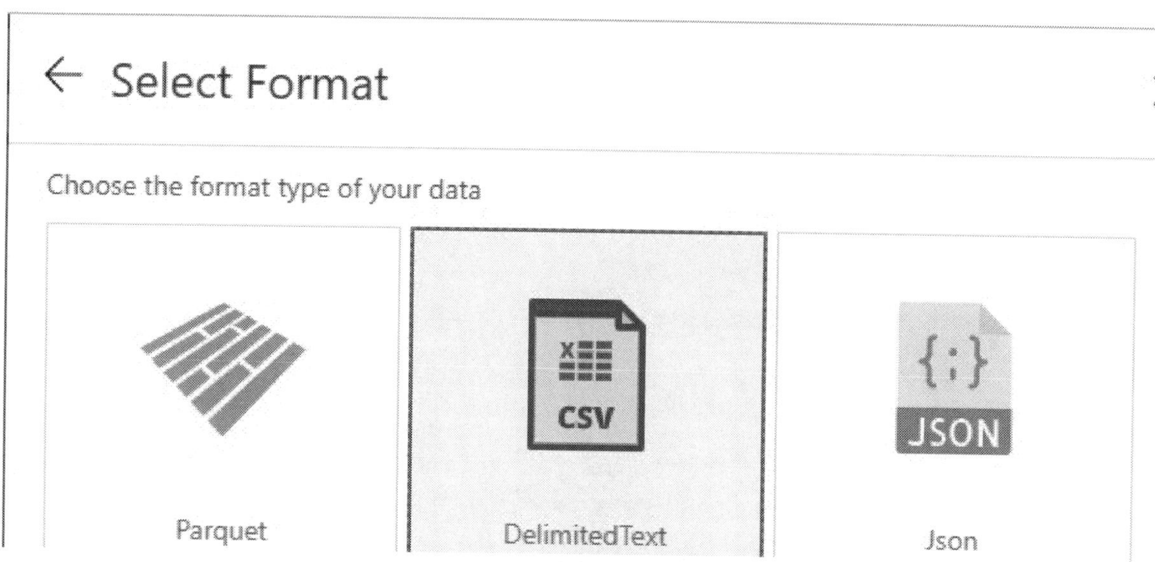

11. Set Properties Blade opens>Enter a name **InputDataset**>Select Linked Service created in Step 4 from dropdown box> click Browse, select and double click Container **adfconatiner410**, select and double click Folder **input** and file test.txt and click Finish>Click Continue (Not Shown)>

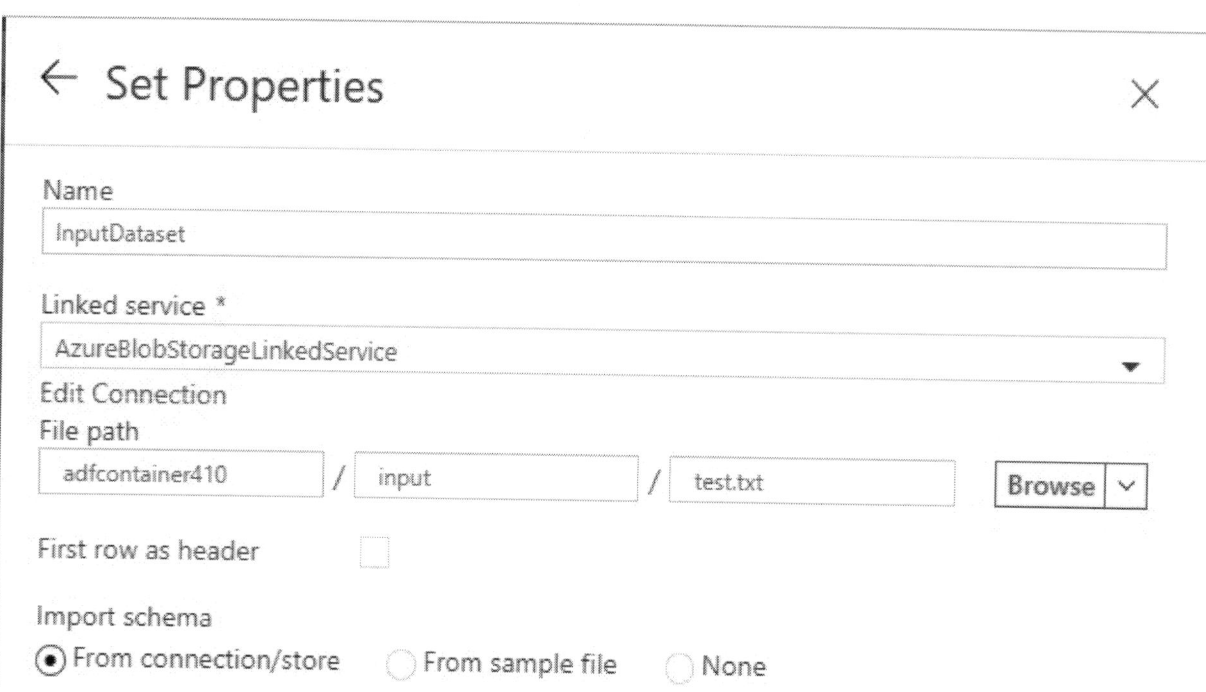

12. Dataset is created as shown below.

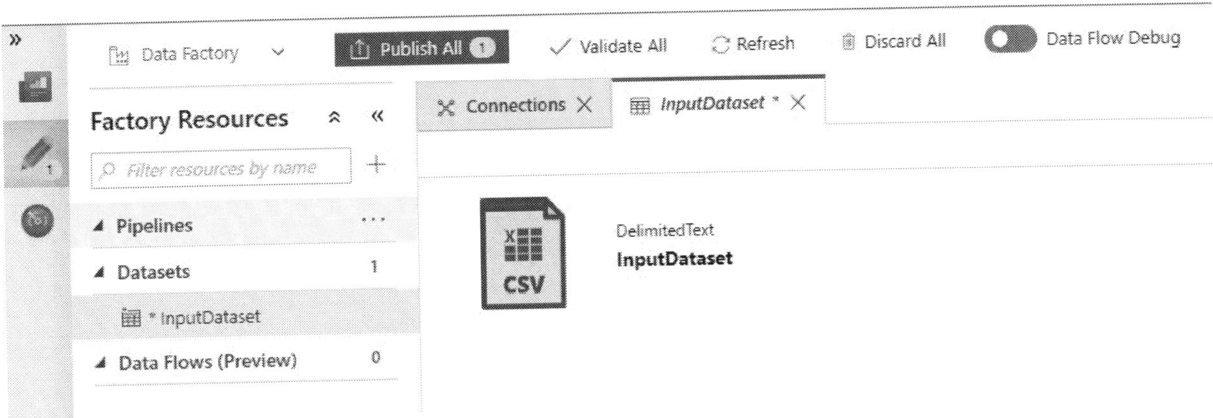

13. **Create Output Dataset**. The output dataset represents the data that's copied to the destination.

Go back to Data Factory Browser pane as shown below. Note the + Sign.

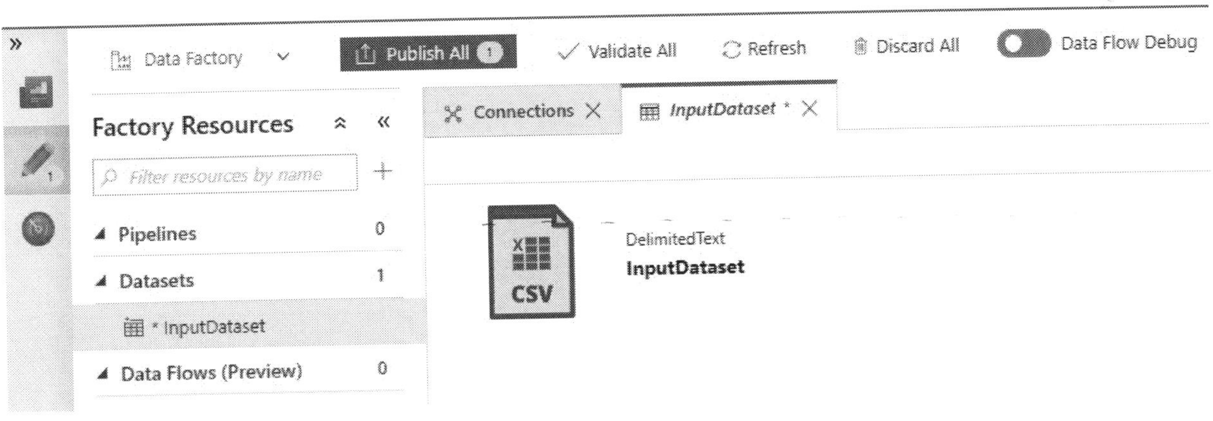

14. Click + Sign in left pane> A Box pops up>Click Dataset>New Dataset Blade opens>Select Azure Blob Storage>Click Continue.

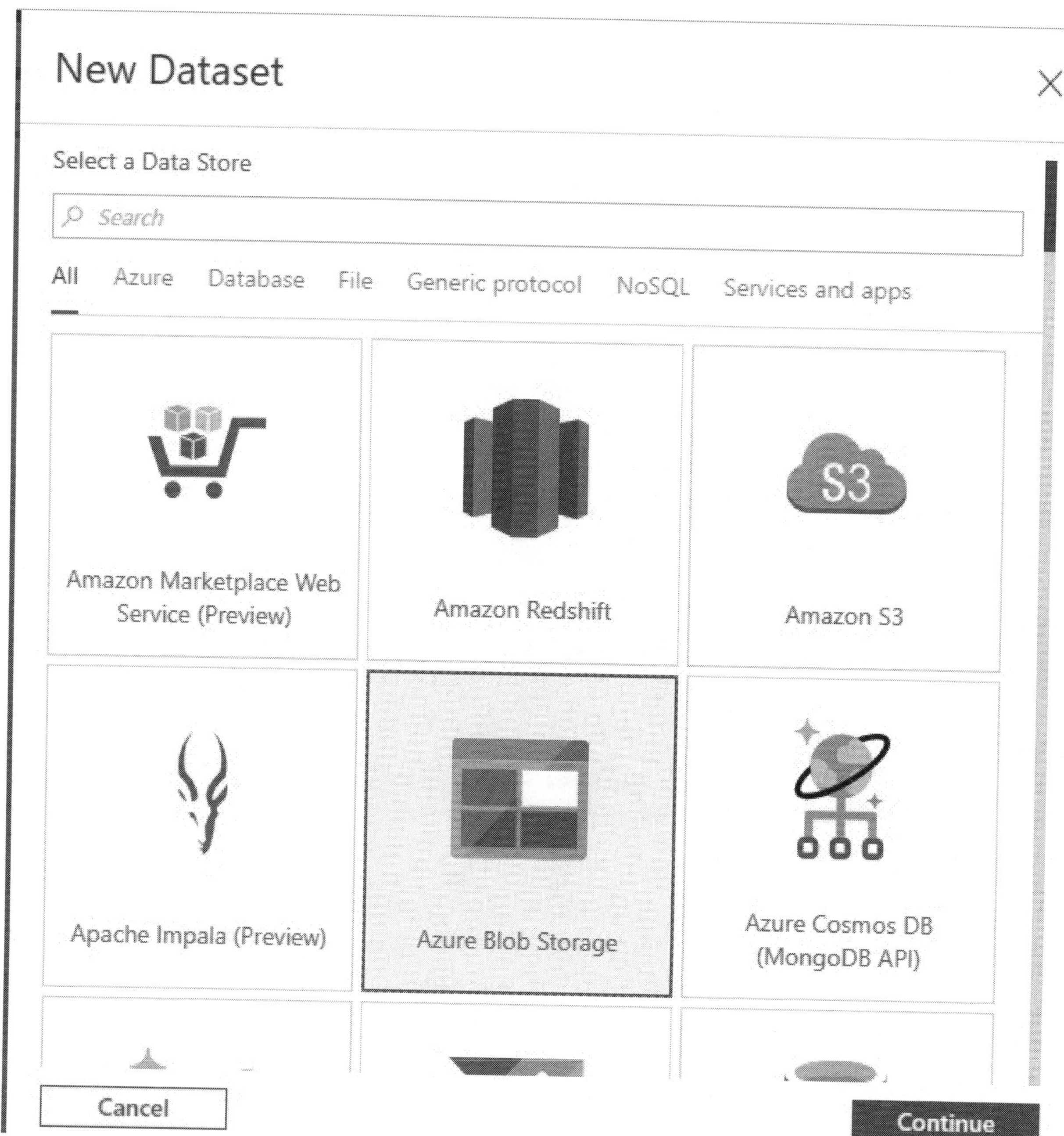

15. After you clicked continue>Select Format Pane opens>Select Delimited Text>Click Continue

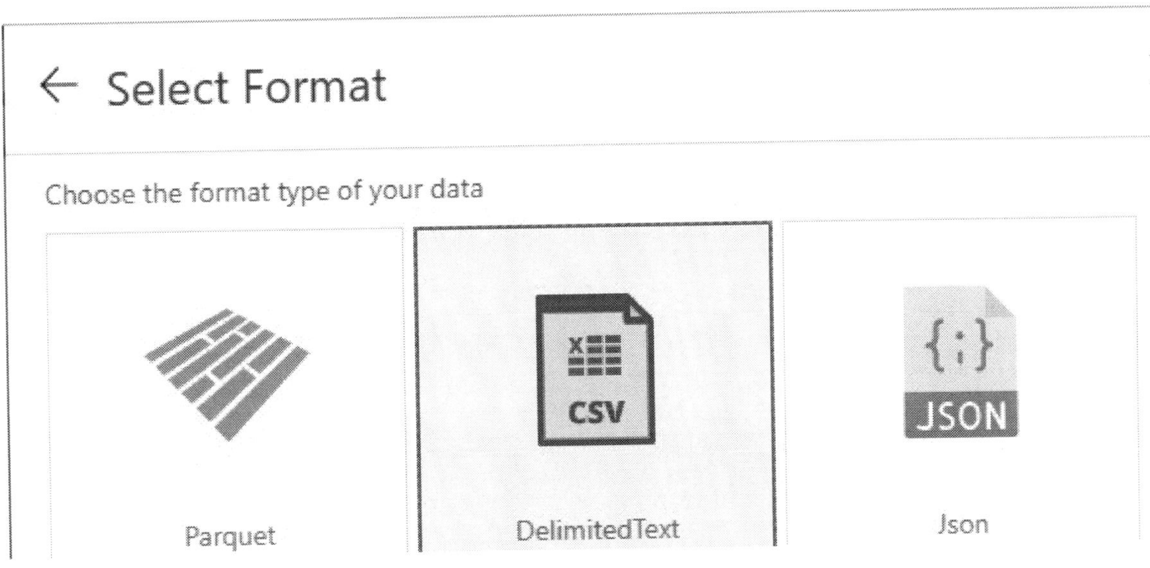

16. Set Properties Blade opens>Enter a name **OutputDataset**>Select Linked Service created in Step 4 from dropdown box> click Browse and select Container **adfconatiner410** and click Finish> Click Continue (Not Shown)>

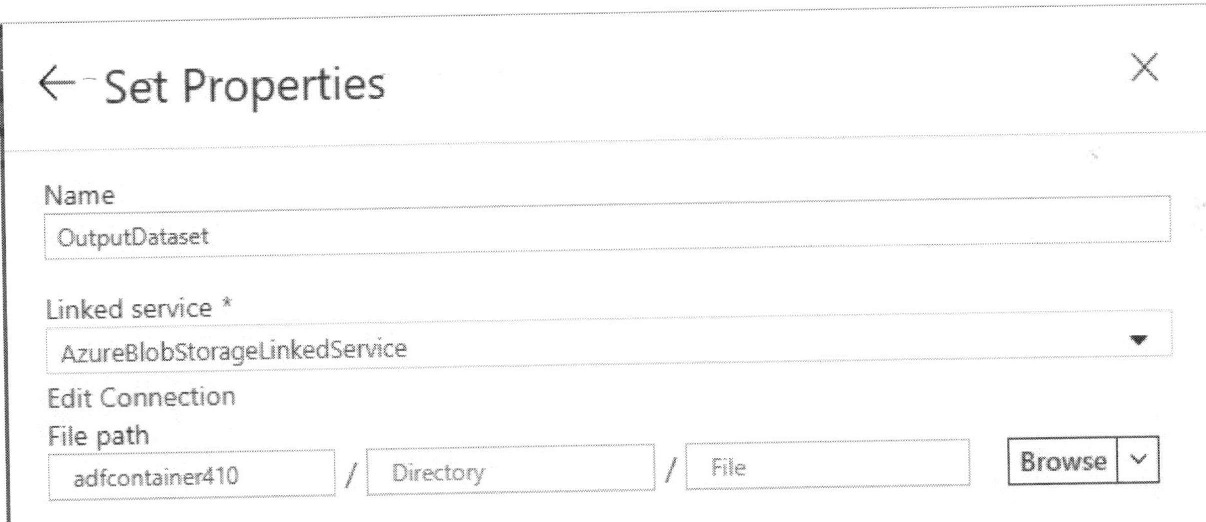

17. Dataset is created as shown below.

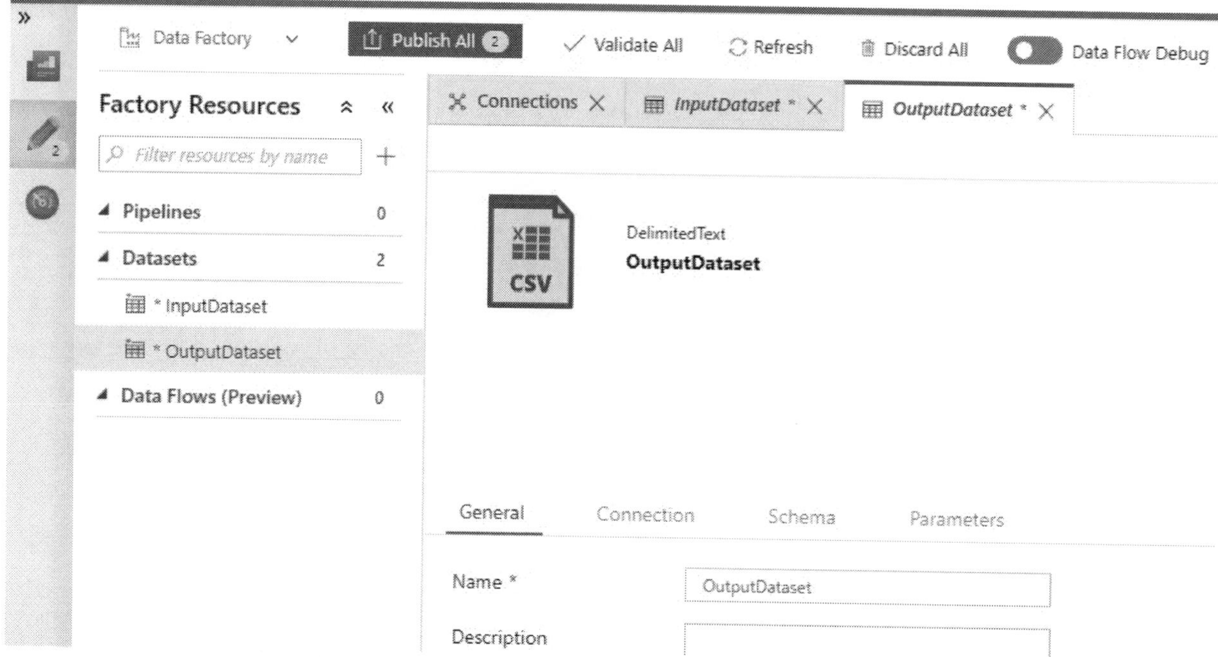

18. In Connection tab enter **output** in the directory field. If the output folder does not exist, the copy activity creates it at runtime.

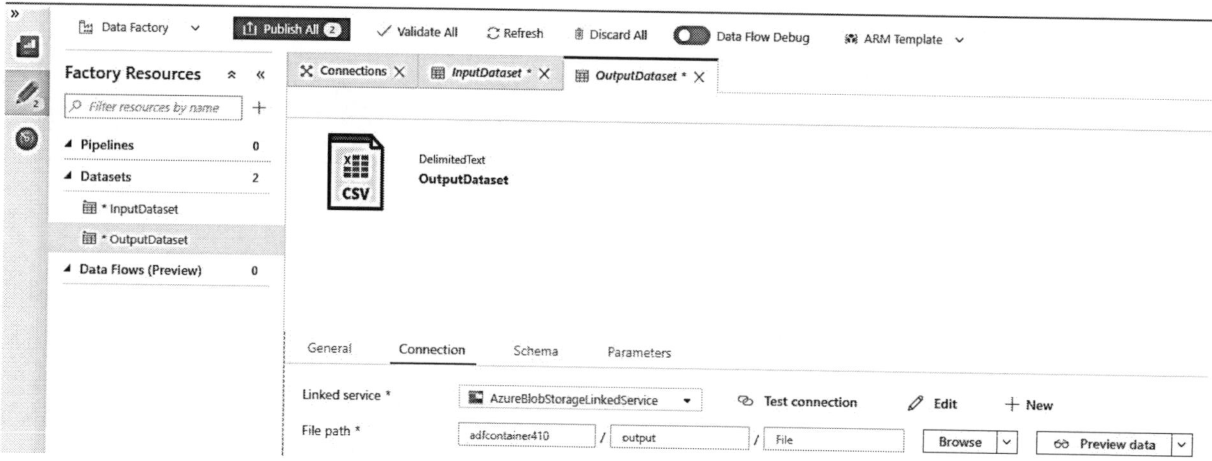

19. **Create Pipeline.** In this we create and validate a pipeline with a copy activity that uses the input and output datasets. The copy activity copies data from the file you specified in the input dataset settings to the file you specified in the output dataset settings.

Go back to Data Factory Browser pane as shown below. Note the + Sign.

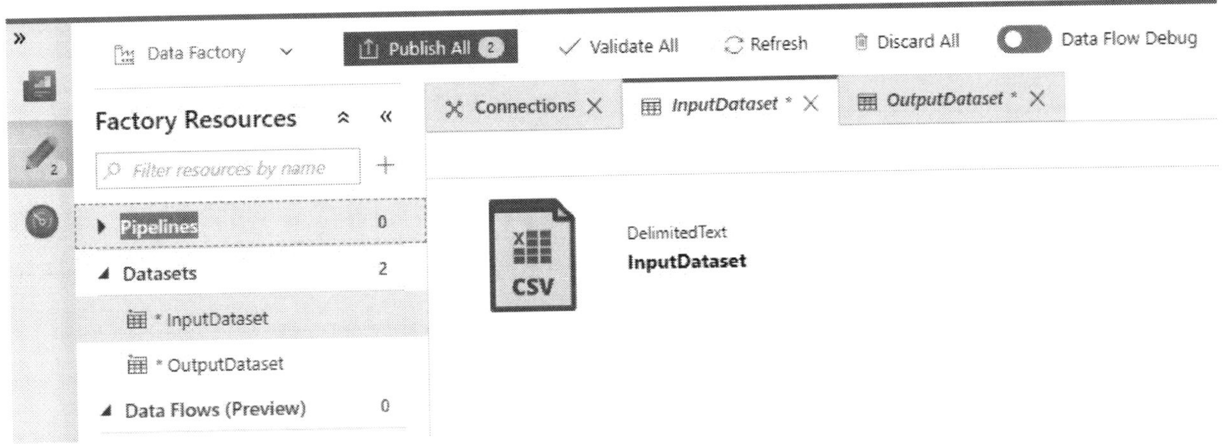

20. Click + Sign in left pane> A Box pops up>Click Pipeline>Pipeline pane opens in right side.

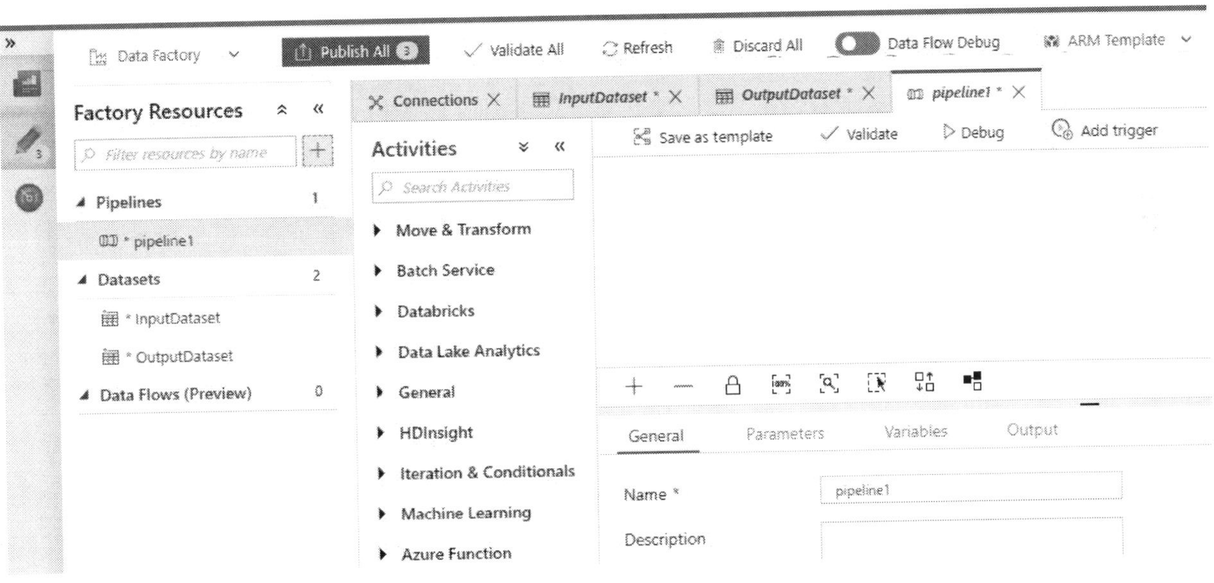

22. In Pipeline pane expand Move & Tansform and Drag the **Copy Data** Box to the pipeline designer surface.

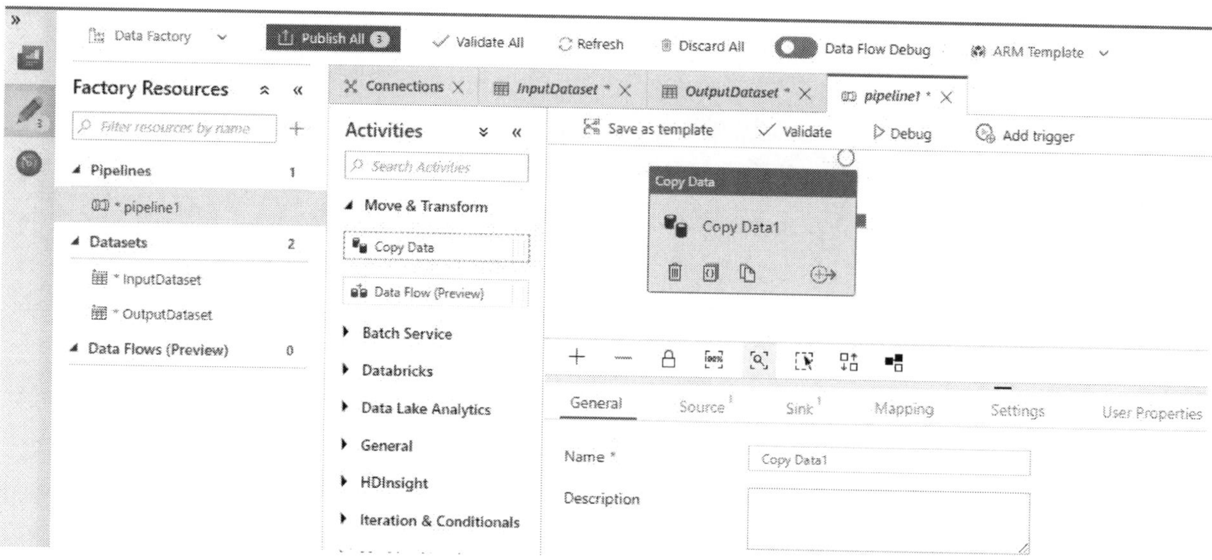

23. Click the source Tab and select **InputDataset.**

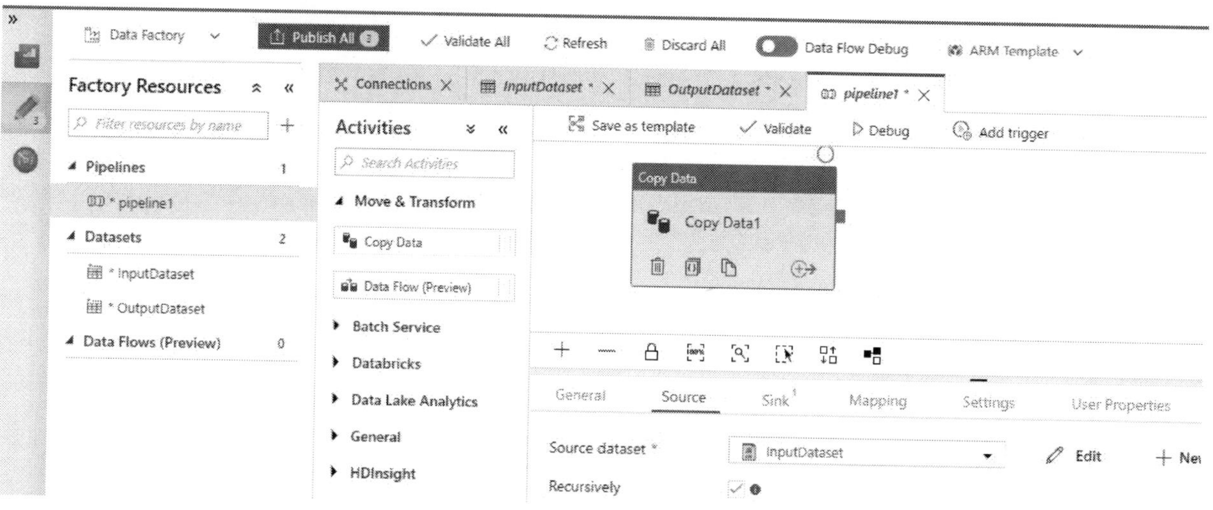

24. Click the sink Tab and select **OutputDataset.**

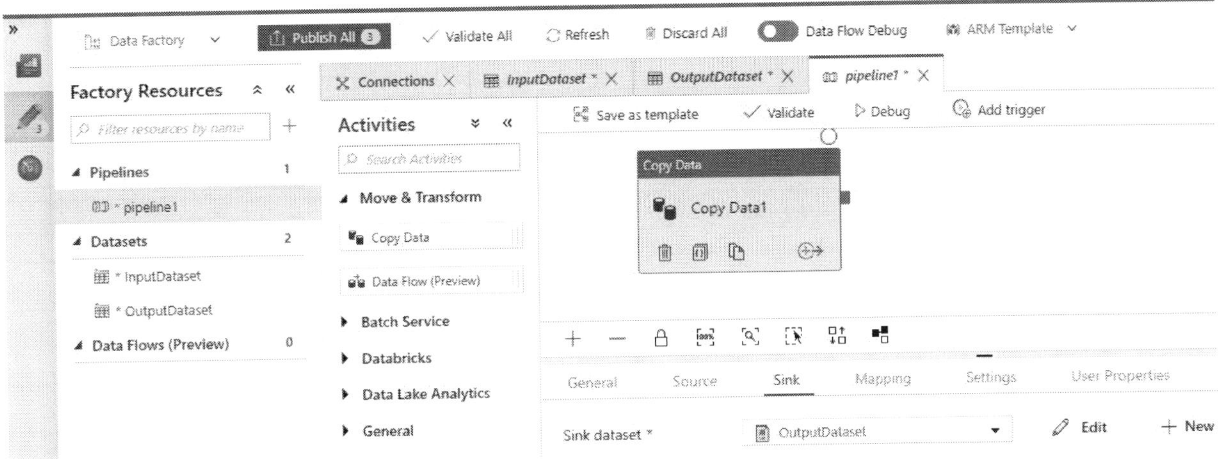

25. Click **Validate** in the pipeline toolbar>A new pane opens up confirming that Pipeline has been validated.

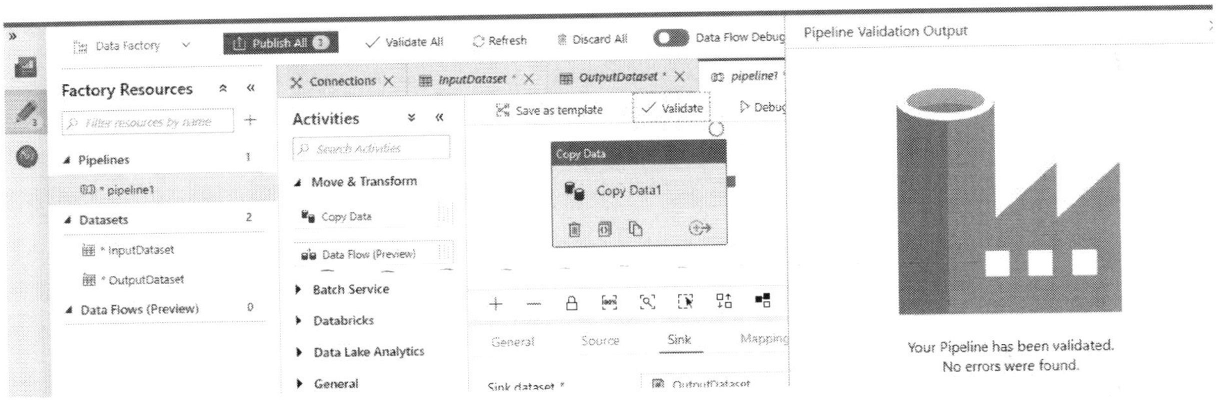

26. **Debug the pipeline.** Click **Debug** in the pipeline toolbar> Confirm that you see the status of the pipeline run on the **Output** tab of the pipeline settings at the bottom.

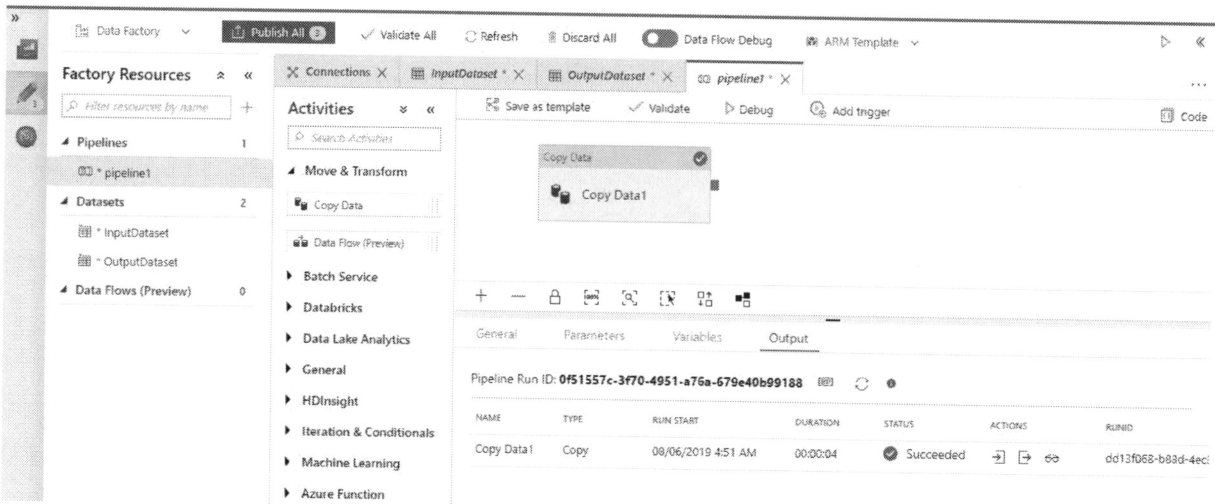

27. Confirm that you see **output** folder in container adfcontainer410. If the output folder does not exist, the Data Factory service automatically creates it.

Go Stoarge Account created in previous Exercise>Click Blobs in Right Pane> Blob Pane opens> Click Container adfcontainer410 in right pane>You can see the output folder created by Data Factory.

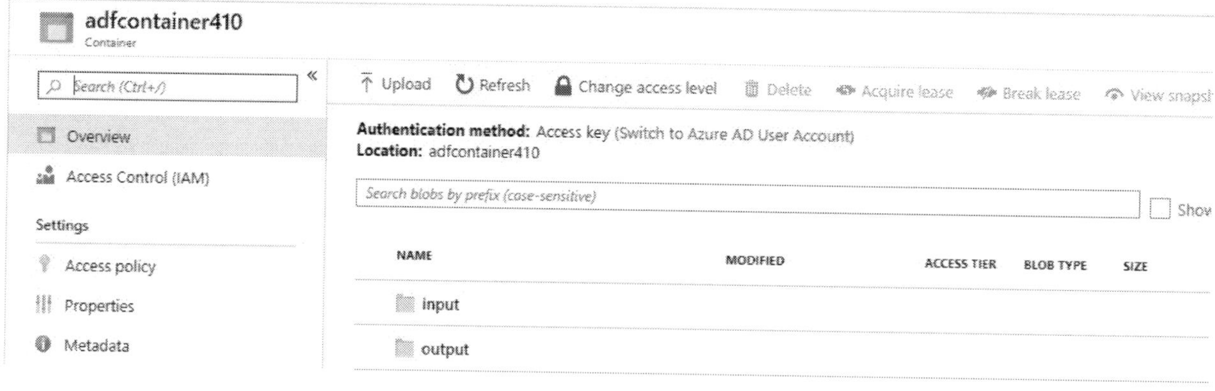

28. **Publish Linked Service, Datasets and Pipelines to Azure Data Factory**. Click **Publish All** in Data Factory Browser pane in top.

29. **Trigger Pipeline manually.** Click **Add Trigger** in the pipeline toolbar, and then select **Trigger Now**> click Finished.

30. Switch to the **Monitor** tab (Red/Orange Circle) on the left. You can see that trigger has activated the pipeline.

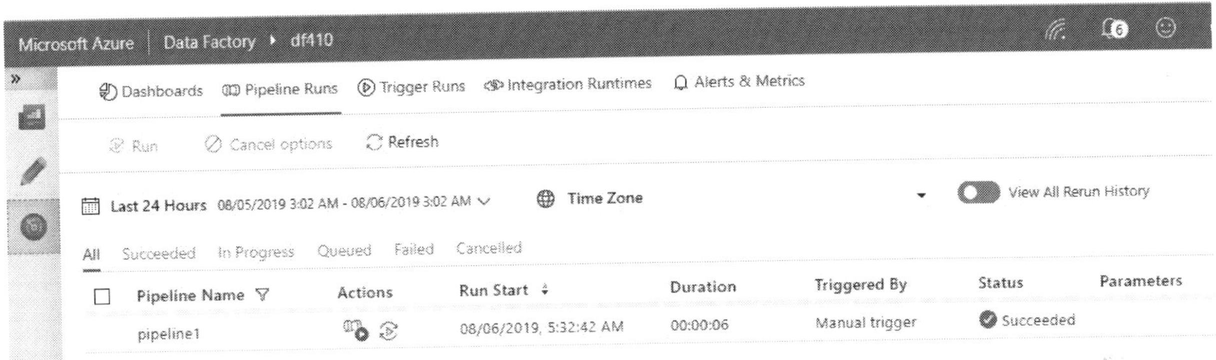

31. **In the above figure under Action click the Play Button icon.** You see the status of the copy activity run on this page.

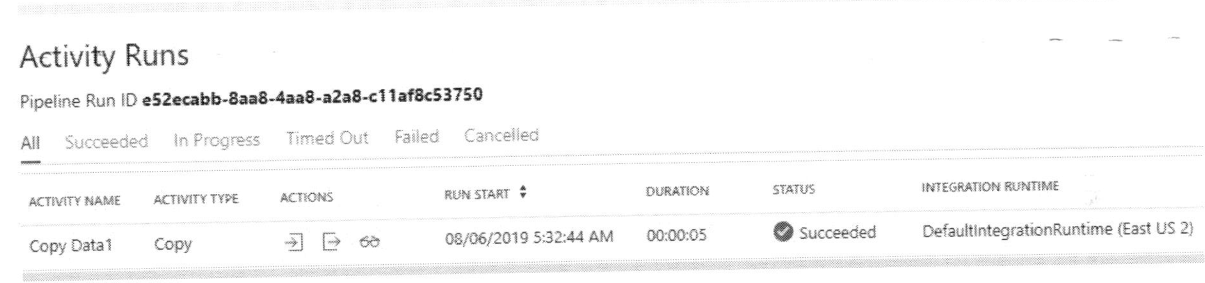

32. In the above figure click the **Details** (eyeglasses image) link in the Actions Column. You can see that it displays succeeded.

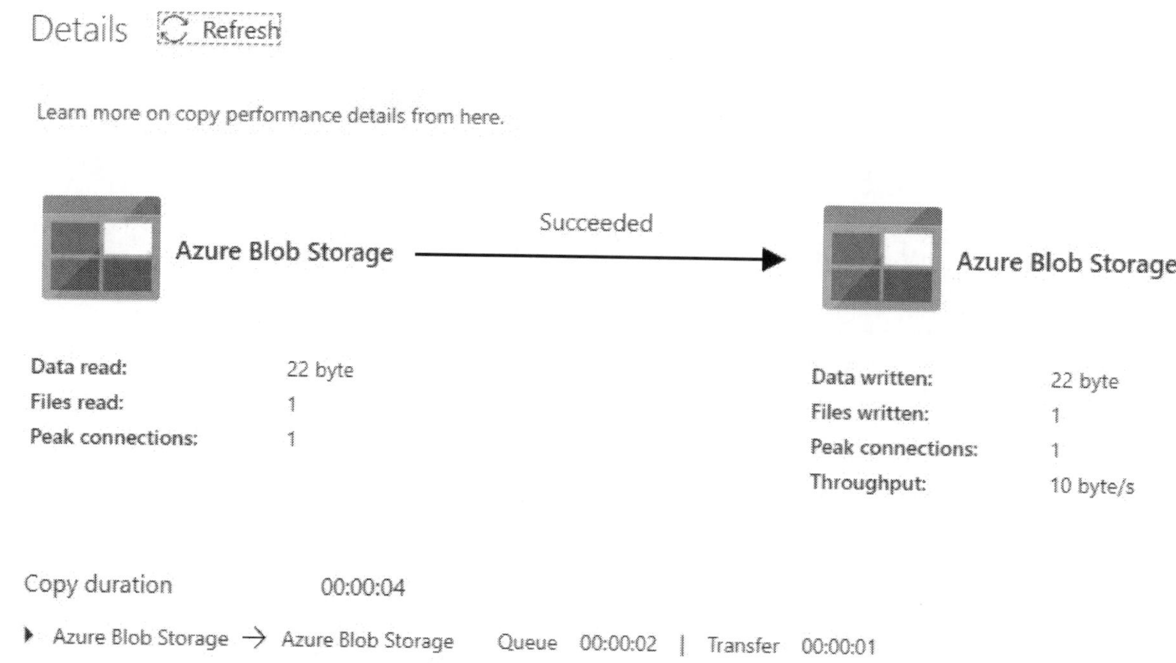

Data Flow

Data Flow is a new feature in Azure Data Factory. Data Flow can perform Data Transformation activities such as data cleaning, aggregation and Preparation.

Data Flows allow data engineers to develop graphical data transformation logic **without writing code**. The resulting data flows are executed as activities within Azure Data Factory Pipelines using scaled-out Azure Databricks clusters.

Data Flows in ADF provide a way to transform data at scale without any coding required. You can design a data transformation job in the data flow designer by constructing a series of transformations. Start with any number of source transformations followed by data transformation steps. Then, complete your data flow with sink to land your results in a destination.

Exercise 131: Data Flow

This is a Demonstration Exercise wherein we will just show how to create Data flow. No Data Sources will be added.

1. Go back to Data Factory Browser pane as shown below. Note the + Sign under Factory Resources as shown below.

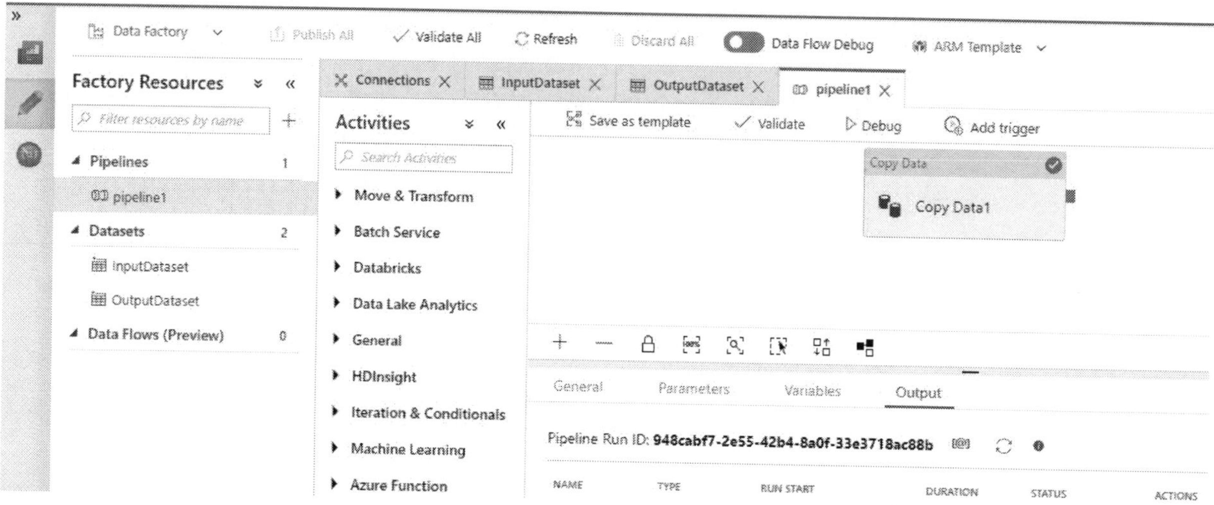

2. click + Sign> A Box pops up>Click Data Flow> Data Flow Pane opens. From here you can add Data Sources.

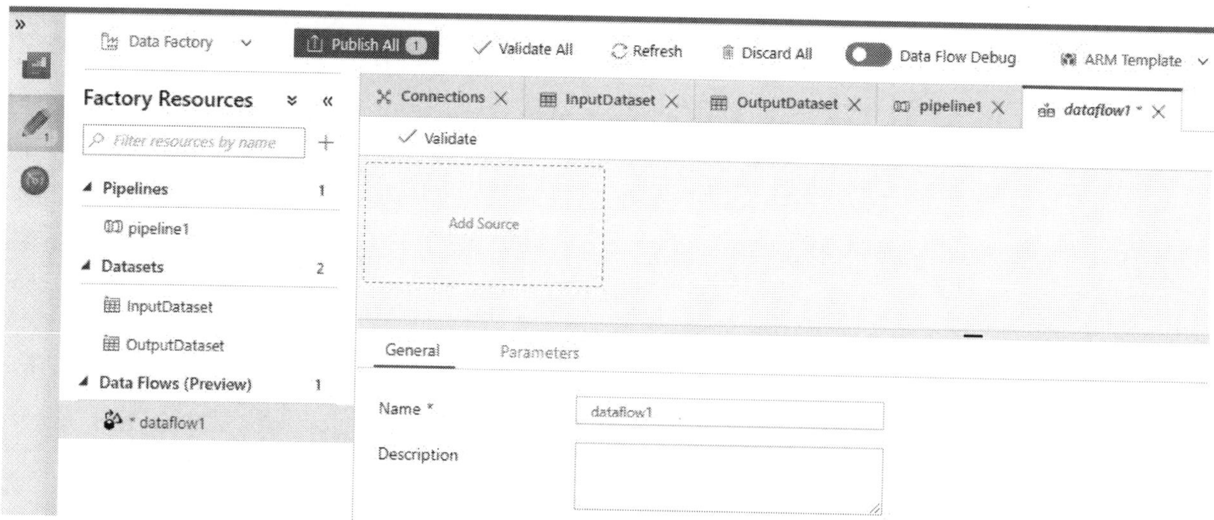

Chapter 19 Azure SQL Data Warehouse

This is AZ-301 specific Chapter. Leave this for AZ-300 Exam.

This Chapter covers following topic Lessons

- Data Warehouse Introduction
- Azure SQL Data Warehouse
- Azure SQL Data Warehouse Architecture
- Azure SQL Data Warehouse performance tiers
- Concurrency slots
- Azure SQL Data Warehouse Working
- Loading Data into Azure SQL Data Warehouse

This Chapter covers following Lab Exercises

- Create, Connect and Query SQL DW using Sample Database

Chapter Topology

In this chapter we will add Azure SQL DW to the topology.

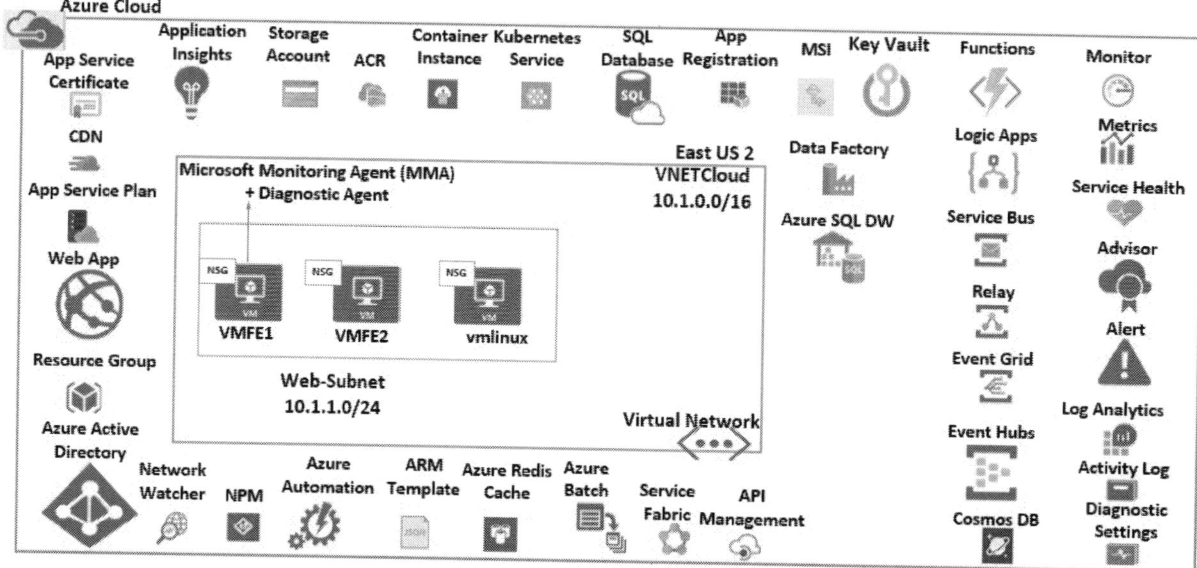

Data Warehouse Introduction

Data Warehouse integrates structured data from multiple sources. The combined data is then used for querying, reporting and analysis. Figure below shows Architecture of a Data Warehouse.

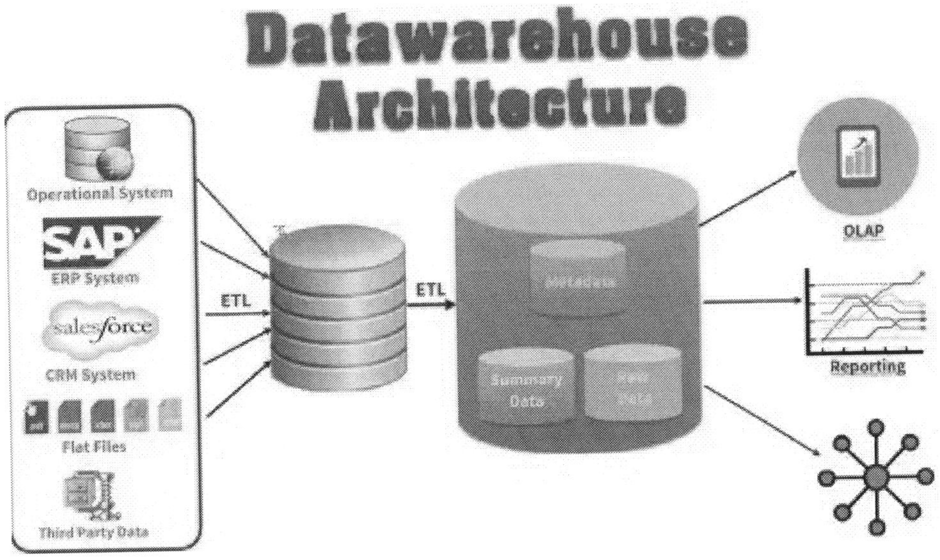

Note: To use unstructured data you need to transform it into structure dataset and then load into Data Warehouse.

Azure SQL Data Warehouse

Azure SQL Data Warehouse is a fully managed Data Warehouse that analyses Structured Data using Business Intelligence tools.

Azure SQL Data Warehouse is a cloud-based, scale-out database that's capable of processing massive volumes of data, both relational and non-relational.

A SQL Data Warehouse database is designed for massively parallel processing (MPP). The database is distributed across multiple compute nodes and processes queries in parallel. SQL Data Warehouse has a control node that orchestrates the activities of all the compute nodes. The compute nodes themselves use SQL Database to manage your data.

The best way to load data into SQL Data Warehouse is to use Polybase. With PolyBase, the data loads in parallel from the data store (Blob Storage) to the compute nodes. PolyBase uses T-SQL commands to Load Data.

Figure below shows Data from Multiple sources being ingested into Data Store which can be Blob Storage or Data lake Store.

Structured Data can be directly loaded into Data Warehouse from Data Store.

Whereas unstructured data will be first transformed into structured Dataset using Data Lake Analytics or Hadoop etc and then loaded into Azure SQL DW.

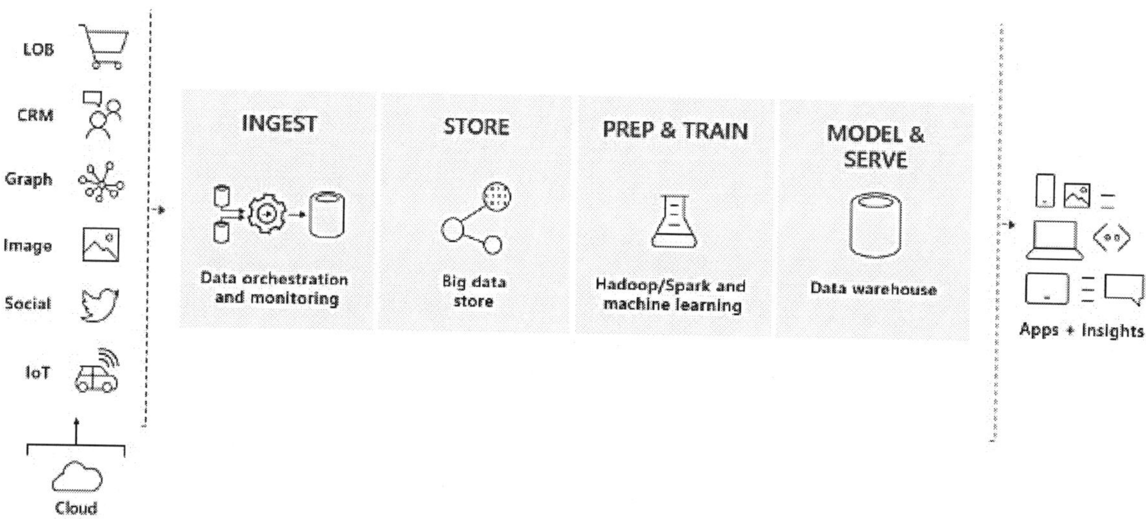

Advantages of Using SQL DW v/s SQL Database

SQL Data Warehouse stores data into relational tables with columnar storage. This format significantly reduces the data storage costs, and improves query performance. Once data is stored in SQL Data Warehouse, you can run analytics at massive scale. Compared to traditional database systems, analysis queries finish in seconds instead of minutes, or hours instead of days.

Azure SQL Data Warehouse Architecture

SQL Data uses a node based scale out architecture to distribute computational processing of Structured data across multiple compute nodes.

It consist of control node and multiple compute nodes. Control node orchestrates the activities of all the compute nodes. SQL Data Warehouse separates compute from storage which enables the user to scale compute independently of the data in your system.

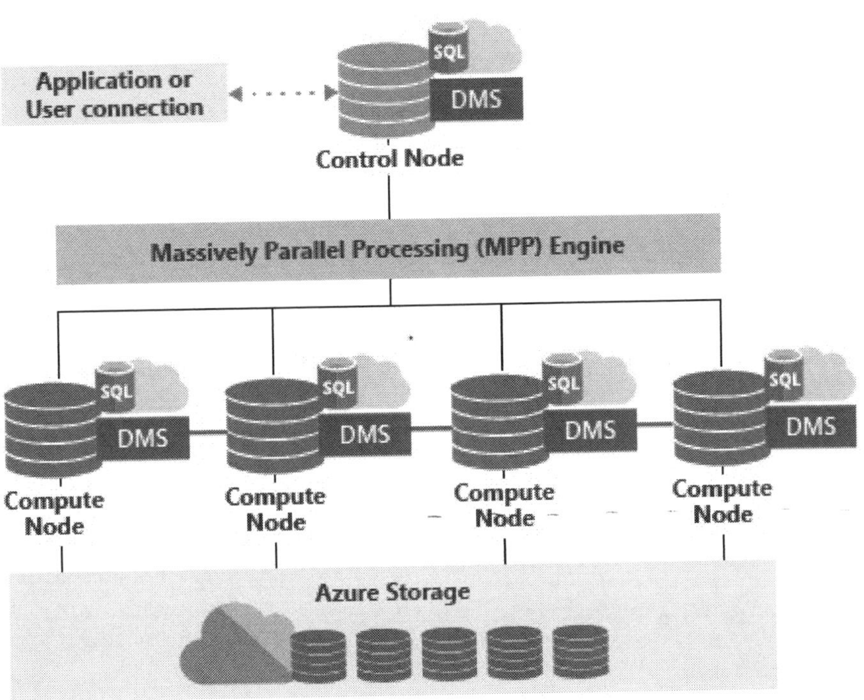

Control Node

The Control node is the brain of the data warehouse. It is the front end that interacts with all applications and connections. Control node orchestrates the activities of compute nodes. When you submit a T-SQL query to SQL Data Warehouse, the Control node transforms it into queries that run against each distribution in parallel. The Control node runs the MPP engine which optimizes queries for parallel processing, and then passes operations to compute nodes to do their work in parallel.

Compute Node

The Compute nodes provide the computational power. Queries passed on by control node are run parallelly across compute nodes. The number of compute nodes range from 1 to 60.

Each Compute node has a node ID that is visible in system views. When compute nodes are added or deleted, SQL Data Warehouse re-maps the distributions to the available Compute nodes.

Compute resources are measured in Data Warehouse Units (DWU).

Storage

User Data after transformation is stored in Azure Storage or Data lake Store. From Storage user Data is loaded in SQL Data Warehouse compute nodes using Polybase SSIS, ADF etc.

Following are the advantages of independent storage and compute:

1. Independently size compute power irrespective of storage needs.
2. Grow or shrink compute power without moving data.
3. Pause compute capacity while leaving data intact, so you only pay for storage.
4. Resume compute capacity during operational hours.

Data Movement Service

Data Movement Service (DMS) is the data transport technology that coordinates data movement between the Compute nodes. Some queries require data movement to ensure the parallel queries return accurate results. When data movement is required, DMS ensures the right data gets to the right location.

Distributions

A distribution is the basic unit of storage and processing for parallel queries that run on distributed data. When SQL Data Warehouse runs a query, the work is divided into 60 smaller queries that run in parallel. Each of the 60 smaller queries runs on one of the data distributions. Each Compute node manages one or more of the 60 distributions. A data warehouse with maximum compute resources has one distribution per Compute node. A data warehouse with minimum compute resources has all the distributions on one compute node.

Data Warehouse Units (DWUs)

A DWU represents measure of compute resources and its performance. Data Warehouse Units (DWUs) are bundled units of CPU, memory, and IO.

To get higher performance, you can increase the number of data warehouse units. As you increase data warehouse units, you are linearly increasing computing resources. By increasing DWU following performance improvement happens:

1. Linearly changes performance of the system for scans, aggregations, and CTAS statements.
2. Increases the number of readers and writers for PolyBase load operations.
3. Increases the maximum number of concurrent queries and concurrency slots.

Azure SQL Data Warehouse performance tiers

1. **Gen1 performance tier:** Performance of Gen1 tier is measured in terms of **DWU.**
2. **Gen2 performance tier:** Performance of Gen 2 tier is measured in terms of **cDWU.** Gen2 Tier introduces NVMe Solid State Disk cache that keeps the most frequently accessed data close to the CPUs. Gen2 provides the best query performance and highest scale.

DWU range of Gen1 Performance Tier

Service level	Max concurrent queries	Compute nodes	Distributions per Compute node	Max memory/ distribution (MB)	Max memory/ DW (GB)
DW100	4	1	60	400	24
DW200	8	2	30	800	48
DW300	12	3	20	1200	72
DW400	16	4	15	1600	96
DW500	20	5	12	2000	120
DW600	24	6	10	2400	144
DW1000	32	10	6	4000	240
DW1200	32	12	5	4800	288
DW1500	32	15	4	6000	360
DW2000	32	20	3	8000	480
DW3000	32	30	2	12000	720
DW6000	32	60	1	24000	1440

cDWU range of Gen2 Performance Tier

Service level	Max concurrent queries	Compute nodes	Distributions per Compute node	Max memory/ distribution (MB)	Max memory/ DW (GB)
DW1000c	32	2	30	10	600
DW1500c	32	3	20	15	900
DW2000c	32	4	15	20	1200
DW2500c	32	5	12	25	1500
DW3000c	32	6	10	30	1800
DW5000c	32	10	6	50	3000
DW6000c	32	12	5	60	3600
DW7500c	32	15	4	75	4500
DW10000c	32	20	3	100	6000
DW15000c	32	30	2	150	9000
DW30000c	32	60	1	300	18000

Concurrency slots

Concurrency slots track the resources available for query execution. Queries reserve compute resources by acquiring concurrency slots. Before a query can start executing, it must be able to reserve enough concurrency slots.

Each query will consume one or more concurrency slots. System queries and some trivial queries do not consume any slots.

Design Nugget: Elasticity performance tier scales to 240 concurrency slots. Compute performance tier scales to 1200 concurrency slots.
Design Nugget: A query running with 10 concurrency slots can access 5 times more compute resources than a query running with 2 concurrency slots.

Azure SQL Data Warehouse Working

Tables

Data is stored in Tables against which queries are performed. Tables are comprised of columns and rows. Columns contain the column name, data type, and any other attributes for the column. Rows contain the records or data for the columns.

Distribution

SQL Data Warehouse divides your data into 60 databases. Each individual database is referred to as a **distribution**. When data is loaded into each table, SQL Data Warehouse has to know how to divide your data across these 60 distributions.

The distribution method is defined at the table level and has following options:

1. **Round robin** distributes data evenly but randomly.
2. **Hash Distributed** distributes data based on hashing values from a single column. Hash distributed tables minimize data movement which will in turn optimizes query performance.
3. **Replicated:** Full copy of the table is distributed on each compute node. A replicated table provides the fastest query performance for small tables.

Indexes

Indexes are **special lookup tables** that the database search engine can use to speed up data retrieval. Simply put, an index is a pointer to data in a table. An index in a database is very similar to an index in the back of a book.

SQL Data Warehouse offers following indexing options:

clustered columnstore indexes
clustered indexes
nonclustered indexes.
no index option or heap

- **Clustered columnstore** tables is the default option and offer both the highest level of data compression as well as the best overall query performance.
- Use **cluster index** or non-clustered secondary index Table for queries where a single or very few row lookup is required.
- When you are temporarily landing data on SQL Data Warehouse, using a **heap table** will make the overall process faster. This is because loads to heaps are faster than to index tables and in some cases the subsequent read can be done from cache.

Design Nugget: For small lookup tables, less than 100 million rows, use heap tables. Cluster columnstore tables begin to achieve optimal compression once there is more than 100 million rows.

Partitioning

Partitioning enables you to divide your data into smaller groups of data.

Partitioning is supported on all SQL Data Warehouse Index table types including clustered columnstore, clustered index, and heap. Partitioning is also supported on all distribution types, including both hash and round robin distribution.

Benefits of Partition

1. Improved Data Load Time
2. Improved query Performance

Design Nugget: A minimum of 1 million rows per distribution and partition is needed for optimal compression and performance of clustered columnstore tables.

Loading Data into Azure SQL Data Warehouse

The Best way to load dat into SQL DW is to use Polybase. First transfer the Structured Data to Azure Storage or Azure Data lake Store and then use Polybase to Load Data in parallel to Azure SQL DW.

1. Extract the source data into text files.
2. Land the data into Azure Blob storage or Azure Data Lake Store.
3. Prepare the data for loading.
4. Load the data into SQL Data Warehouse staging tables by using **PolyBase.**
5. Transform the data.
6. Insert the data into production tables.

About Polybase

PolyBase is a technology that accesses data outside of the database via the T-SQL language. With PolyBase, the data loads in parallel from the data source directly to the compute nodes. PolyBase uses T-SQL commands to Load Data. It is the best way to load data into SQL Data Warehouse.

Design Nugget: Azure Blob Storage is used as a staging Platform to Load Data to SQL DW. Data from SQL Server is transferred to Azure Blob Storage and from there Polybase is used to Load Data into Azure SQL DW.

Load from Azure Blob Storage using PolyBase and T-SQL

1. Move your data to Azure blob storage or Azure Data Lake Store and store it in text files.
2. Configure external objects in SQL Data Warehouse to define the location and format of the data
3. Run a T-SQL command to load the data in parallel into a new database table.

Load from SQL Server using bcp

If you have a small amount of data you can use bcp to load directly into Azure SQL Data Warehouse without using Polybase. Summary of loading process:
1. Use the bcp command-line utility to export data from SQL Server to flat files.
2. Use bcp to load data from flat files directly to SQL Data Warehouse.

Load from SQL Server (on-premises or Cloud) using Data Factory

Azure Data Factory is cloud-based data integration service that creates data-driven workflows (Pipelines) in the cloud for orchestrating and automating data movement and data transformation.

Using Pipelines Azure Data Factory (ADF) will ingest Data from SQL Server. Azure Data Factory also does Source (SQL Server) and Destination (SQL DW) Table & Schema Mapping. ADF will then stage the data in Blob Storage before moving into Azure SQL DW. ADF will use Poybase option to load data in Azure SQL DW. In this case you don't need to run T-SQL Commands.

<u>**The Biggest advantage of using Azure Data Factory is that it automates ingestion and Loading of data.**</u>

Load from SQL Server using SQL Server Integration Services (SSIS)

Use SSIS packages and point SQL Server as the source and SQL Data Warehouse as the destination. Following is the Summary of loading process:

1. Revise your Integration Services package to point to the SQL Server instance for the source and the SQL Data Warehouse for the destination.
2. Migrate your schema to SQL Data Warehouse, if it is not there already.
3. Change the mapping in your packages. Use only the data types that are supported by SQL Data Warehouse.
4. Schedule and run the package.

Load from SQL Server using AZCopy & Polybase

If your data size is < 10 TB, you can export the data from SQL Server to flat files, copy the files to Azure blob storage using AZCopy and then use PolyBase to load the data into SQL Data Warehouse. Following is the Summary of loading process:

1. Use the bcp command-line utility to export data from SQL Server to flat files.
2. Use the AZCopy command-line utility to copy data from flat files to Azure blob storage.
3. Use PolyBase to load into SQL Data Warehouse.

Case Study 5: Integrating Structured and Unstructured Data into Azure SQL DW using Azure Data Factory

Azure SQL Data Warehouse does analytics on Structured Data. To use unstructured data you need to transform it into structure dataset and then load into Data Warehouse using Polybase.

Integrating Structured Data with Azure SQL DW using Data Factory
As shown in figure below Data Factory ingest data from Structured data sources such as SQL Server. Azure Data Factory also does Source (SQL Server) and Destination (SQL DW) Table & Schema Mapping. Data Factory will then stage the data in Blob Storage before moving into Azure SQL DW. Azure Data Factory will use Poybase option to load data in Azure SQL DW. You can do analytics on Structured Data using Azure SQL DW.

Integrating Non- Structured Data with Azure SQL DW using Data Factory
As shown in figure below Data Factory ingest data from unstructured data sources. Data Factory will then stage the data in Blob Storage or Data Lake store. Unstructured Data is transformed using HDInsight or Data Lake Analytics. Azure Data Factory will use Poybase option to load transformed dataset into Azure SQL DW.

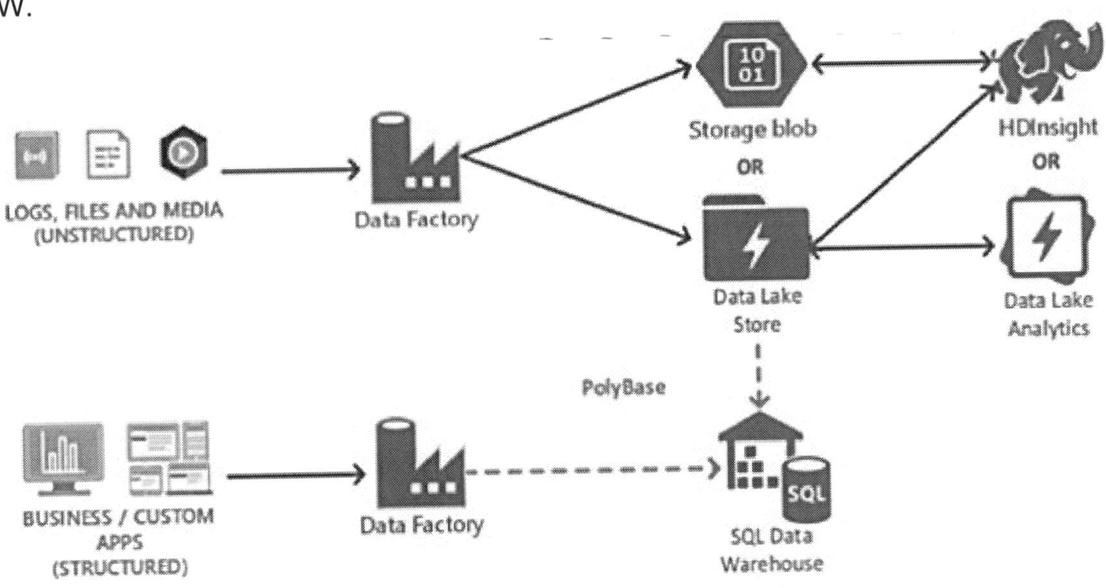

Note: In above we have used Data Factory for ingestion and loading Data in SQL DW. It is not compulsory to use Data Factory. You can use other options.

Exercise 132: Create, Connect and Query SQL DW using Sample Database

Step 1 Create Azure SQL DW: In Azure Portal click create a resource>Databases >SQL Data Warehouse> Create SQL Data Warehouse blade opens>Select RGCloud in Resource Group> Enter a name for SQL Data Warehouse>In Server Box click create new link. Create New Server Blade opens> Enter Server name, Login name & Password. Make sure to select location as East US 2.

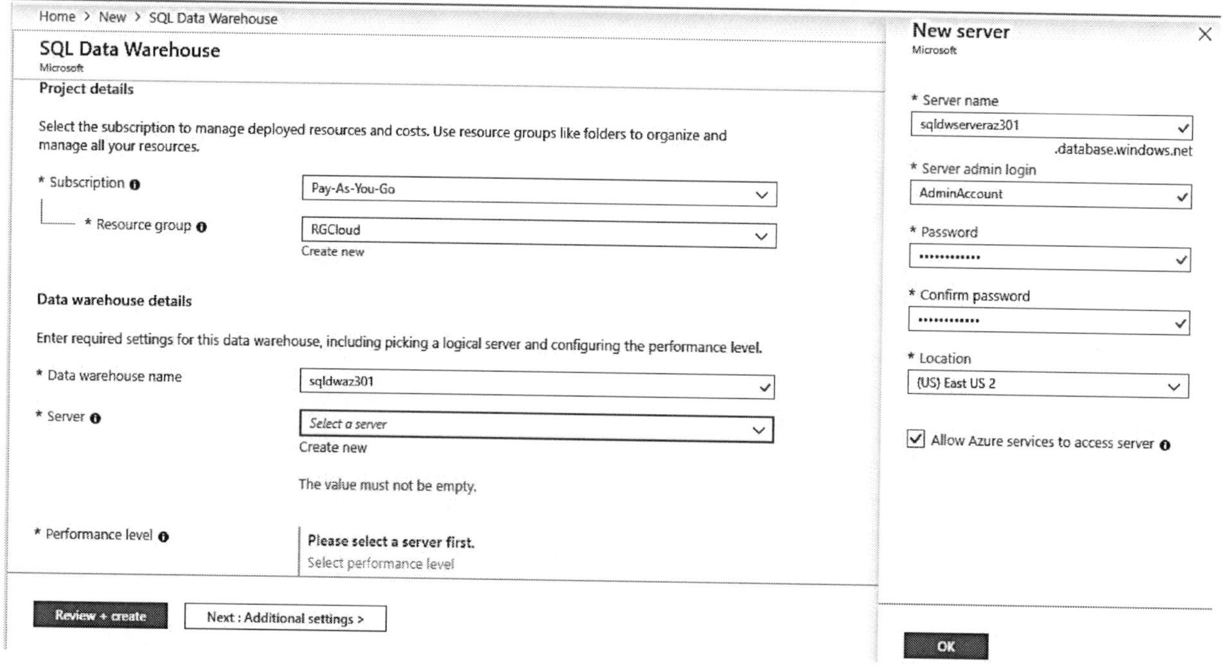

Click OK in Create New Server Blade>Back in Create SQL Data Warehouse Blade you can see system automatically selects Performance level of DW1000c. We will change this DW100c

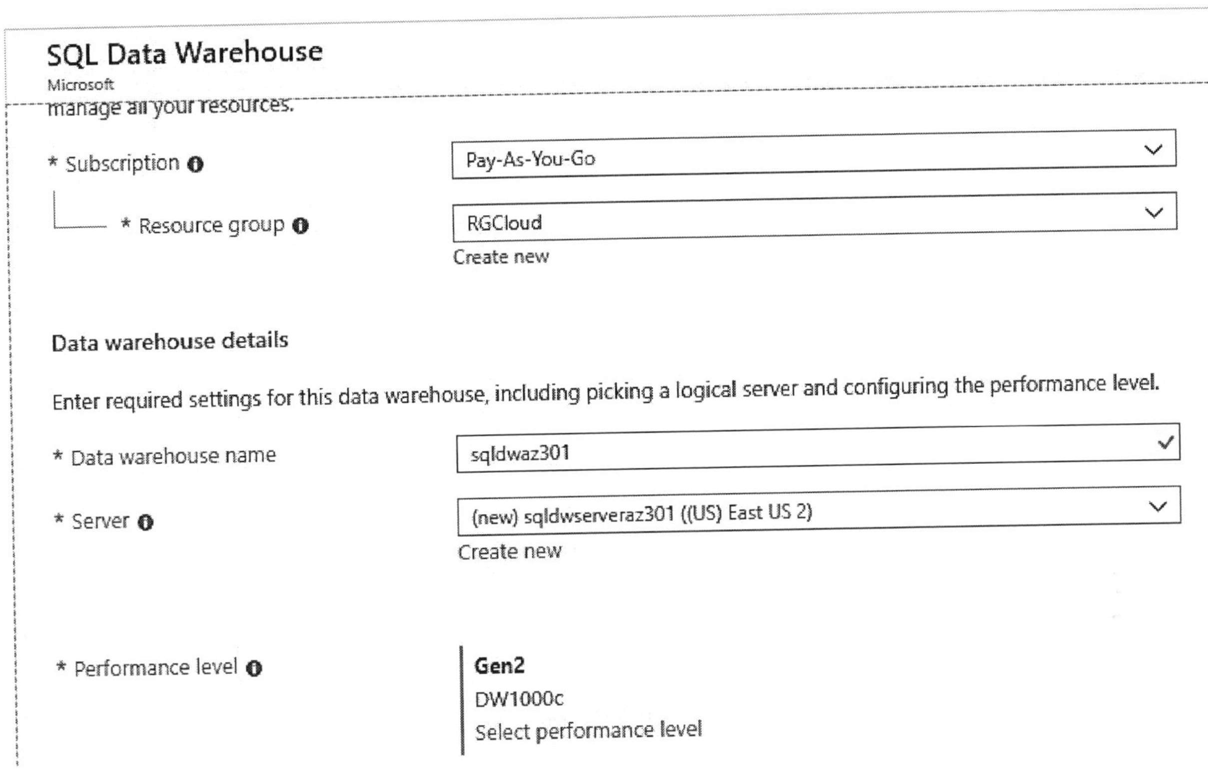

In above figure click select performance level>Configure performance blade opens>Push the slider to extreme left and you can see that in Box performance level changes to DW100c.

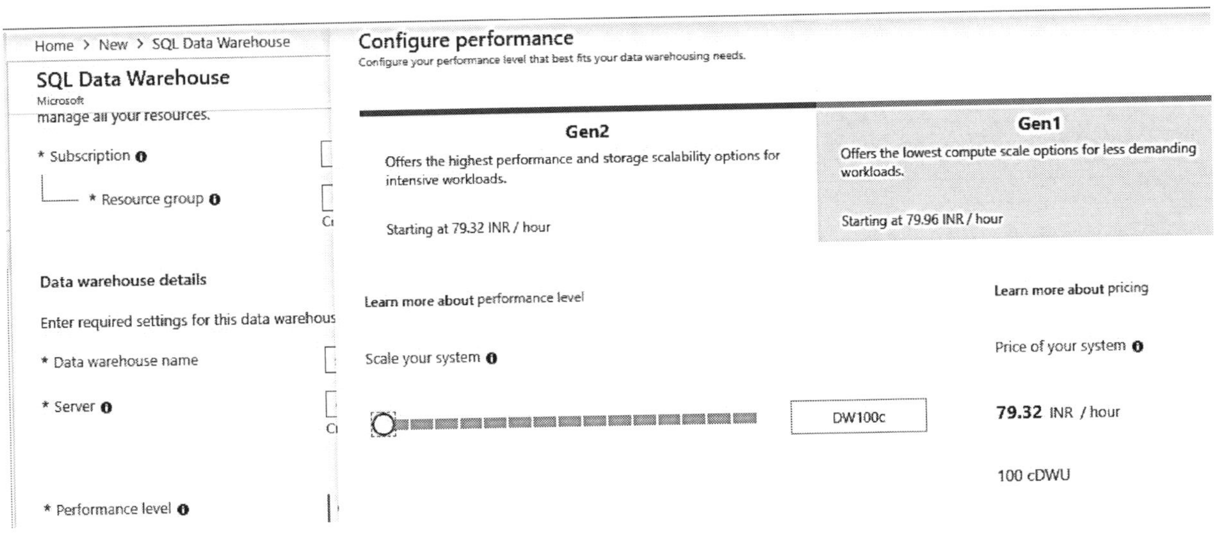

Click Apply in Configure Performance Blade> Back in Create SQL Data Warehouse Blade click Next:Additional Settings>Additional setting Blade opens>In Data Source select Sample. This will populate Database with Sample Data.

SQL Data Warehouse
Microsoft

* Basics * Additional settings Tags Review + create

Customize additional configuration parameters including collation & sample data.

Data source

Start with a blank data warehouse, restore from a backup or select sample data to populate your new database.

* Use existing data   None Backup Sample

AdventureWorksDW will be created as the sample data warehouse.

Data warehouse collation

Data warehouse collation defines the rules that sort and compare data, and cannot be changed after data warehouse creation. The default collation is SQL_Latin1_General_CP1_CI_AS. Learn more

* Collation   SQL_Latin1_General_CP1_CI_AS

Review + create   < Previous   Next : Tags >

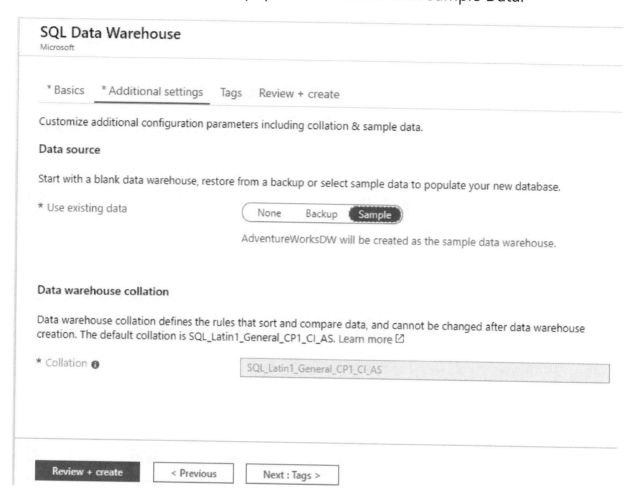

Click Review + create> After Validation is passed click create (Not Shown).

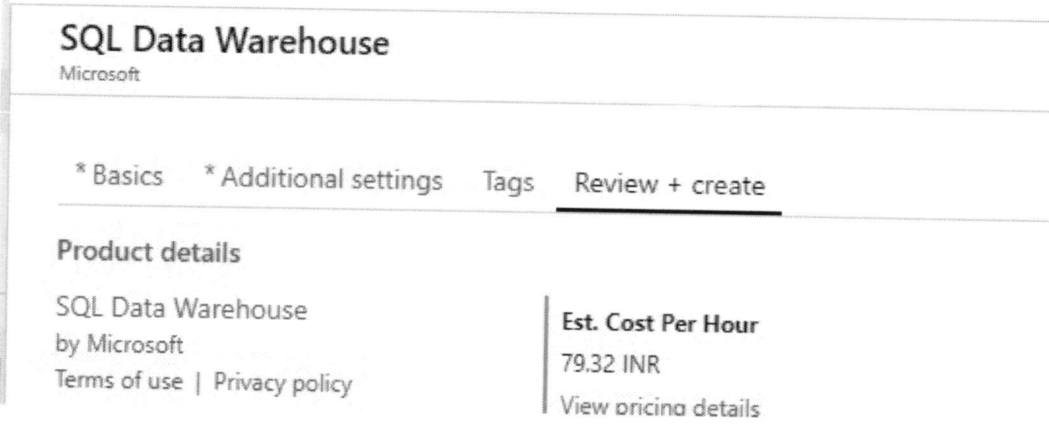

Figure below show SQL DW dashboard. Note the Server DNS name and Database connection strings link in right pane. You can add connection strings in your application to connect to Azure SQL DW.

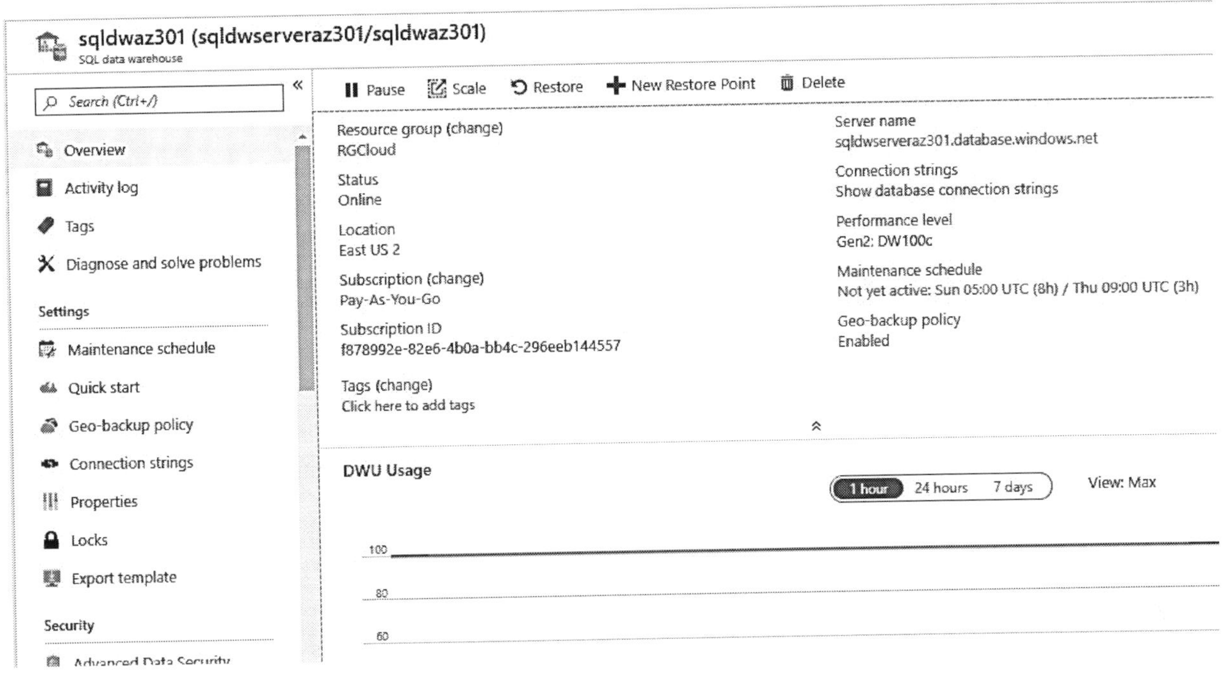

Step 2 Create Azure SQL DW server level firewall rule: Firewall service on newly created Azure SQL DW server prevents external applications and tools from connecting to the server unless a firewall rule is created to open the firewall for specific client IP addresses.

In SQL DW dashboard Click the server name **(http://sqldwserveraz301.database.windows.net)** in right pane> sqldwserveraz301 dashboard opens>Click Firewall and Virtual Networks in left pane> Enter IP address assigned by your ISP in Start IP and End IP Box. Give it a name and click save in top. **Here I entered IP address assigned to my Laptop by the ISP.**

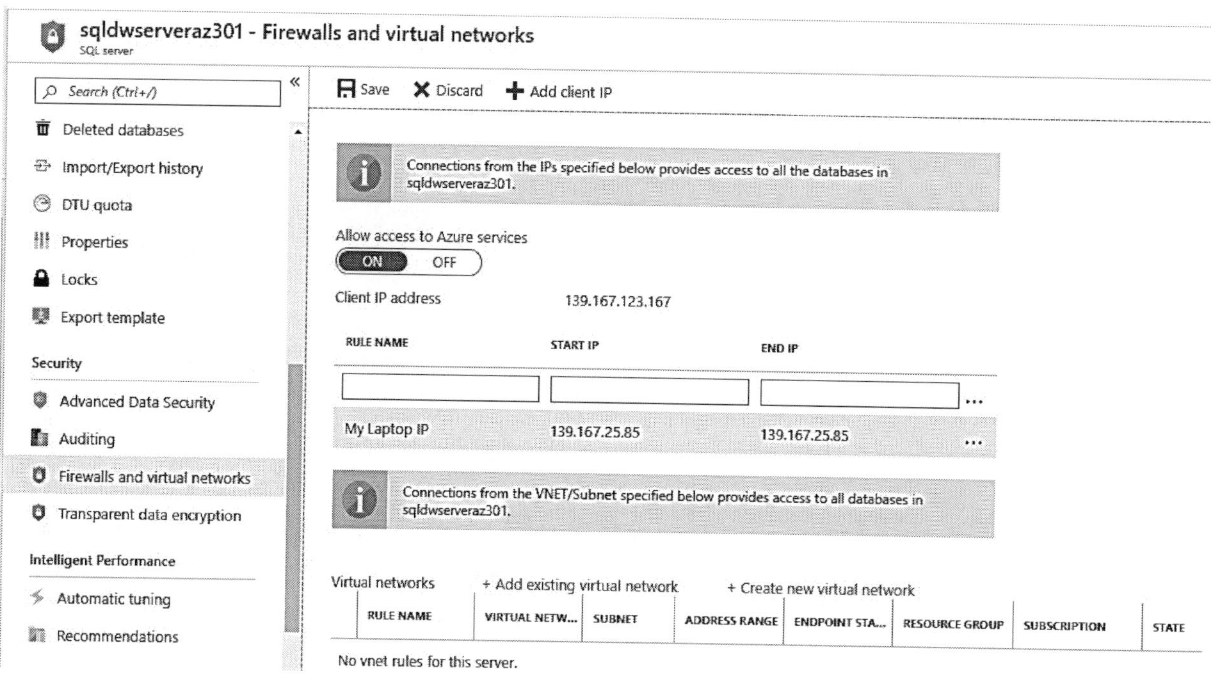

Step 3 Connect to SQL DW using SQL Server Management Studio (SSMS): On the client machine whose IP was entered in step 2, open SSMS and enter Azure SQL DW server name, username and password > In Authentication select SQL Server Authentication>Click Connect.

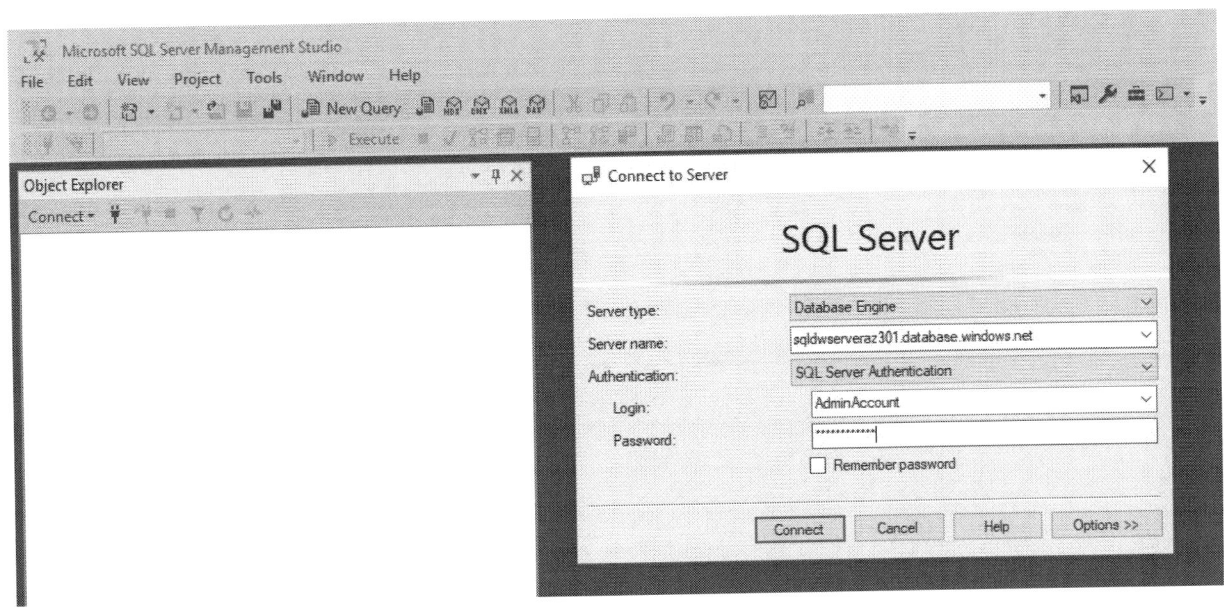

SSMS connects to SQL DW Database. Figure below shows sample database AdventureWorks.

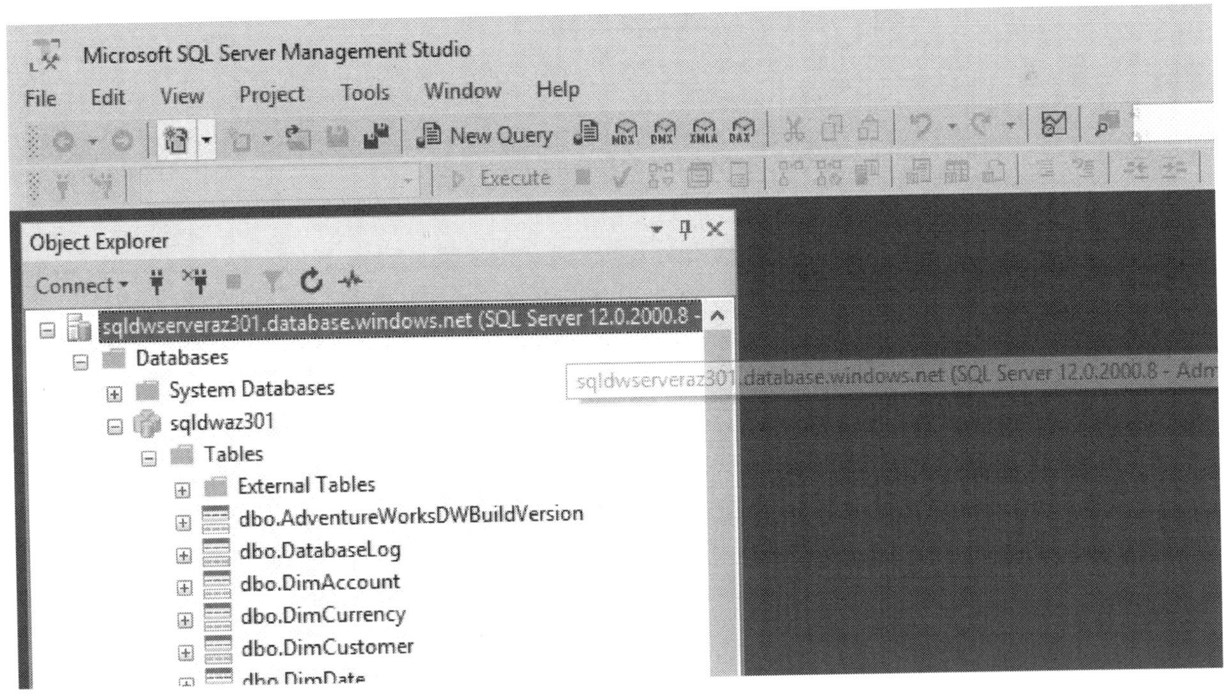

Step 4 Query the sample database: Right Click sqldwaz301 and select new query>New query window opens in middle pane. Enter and run your query to see the result.

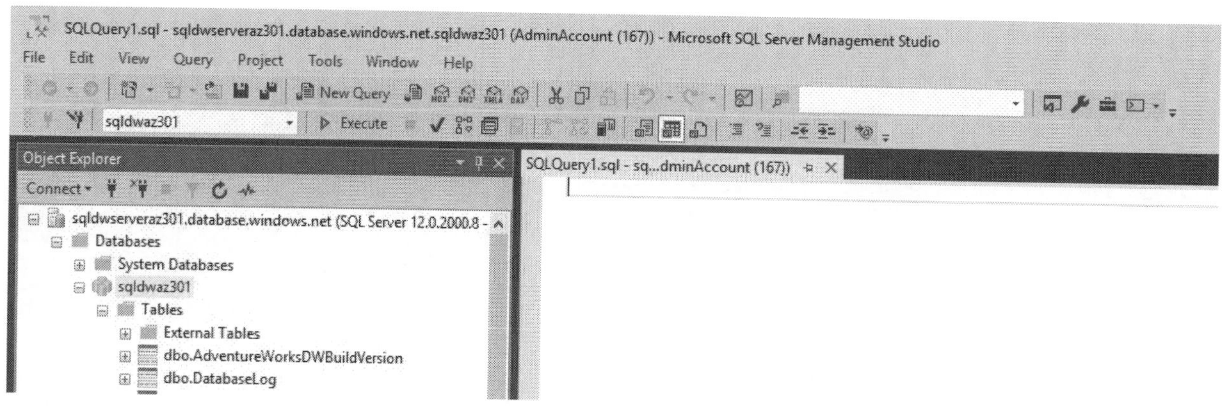

Note 1: Readers are requested to Explore the dashboards of both SQL DW database and SQL DW Server Dashboard.

Note 2: Delete both SQL DW database and SQL DW Server.

Chapter 20 Azure Data Lake Store

This is AZ-301 specific Chapter. Leave this for AZ-300 Exam.

This Chapter covers following Topic Lessons

- Azure Data lake Store
- What can be done with Azure Data lake Store
- Features of Data Lake Store
- Comparing Data lake Store and Azure Blob Storage
- Step by Step Using Azure Data Lake Store for big data processing
- Integrating Data Lake Store with other Azure Services
- Azure Data lake Pricing

This Chapter Covers following Lab Exercises

- Create Data Lake Store and upload Data

Chapter Topology

In this chapter we will add Data Lake Store to the topology.

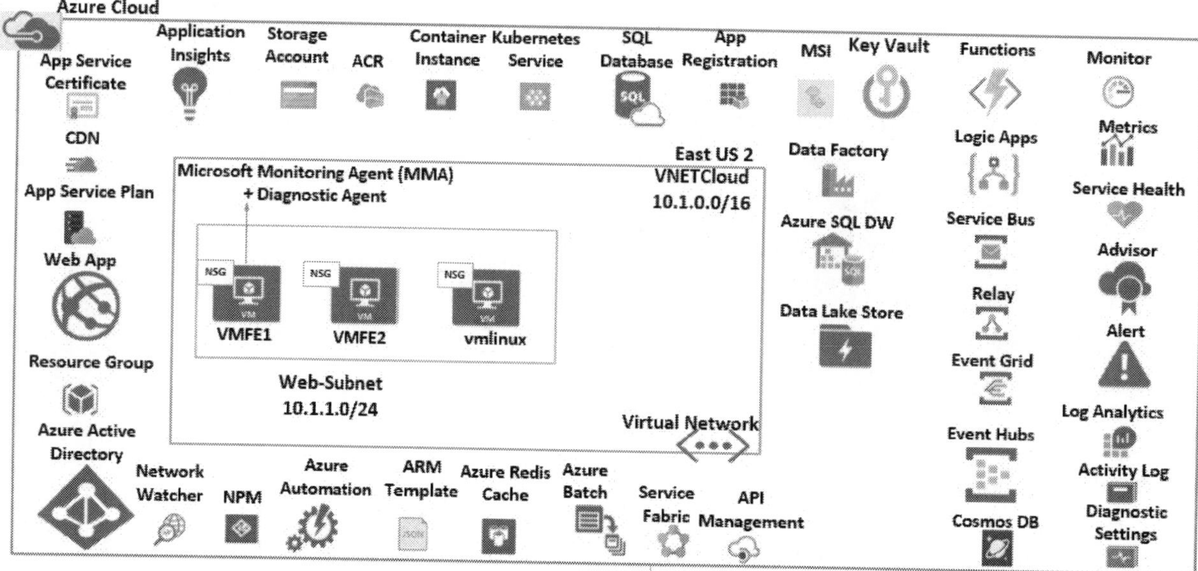

Azure Data lake Store

Azure Data Lake Store is an enterprise-wide hyper-scale storage repository for storing data of any size and type and performing analytics on the stored data.

Data Lake Store can scale throughput to support any size of analytic workload. You get massive throughput to run analytic jobs with thousands of concurrent executors which efficiently read and write hundreds of terabytes of data.

What can be done with Azure Data lake Store

1. It **stores data** by ingesting data from various sources including on-premises computer, Azure Blob Storage, Streamed Data, Relational Data and Web Server Data, Data associated with Azure HDInsight clusters
2. **Run analysis** on data stored in Data lake Store using big data applications. Currently, you can only use Azure HDInsight and Azure Data Lake Analytics to run data analysis jobs on the data stored in Data Lake Store.
3. Processed data can be **downloaded** and/or **exported** to SQL Data Warehouse using Polybase and Data Factory or to on-premises SQL Server or to other repositories.

The Figure below shows various sources from which data can be ingested in Data lake Store and Processing of Stored Data by applications.

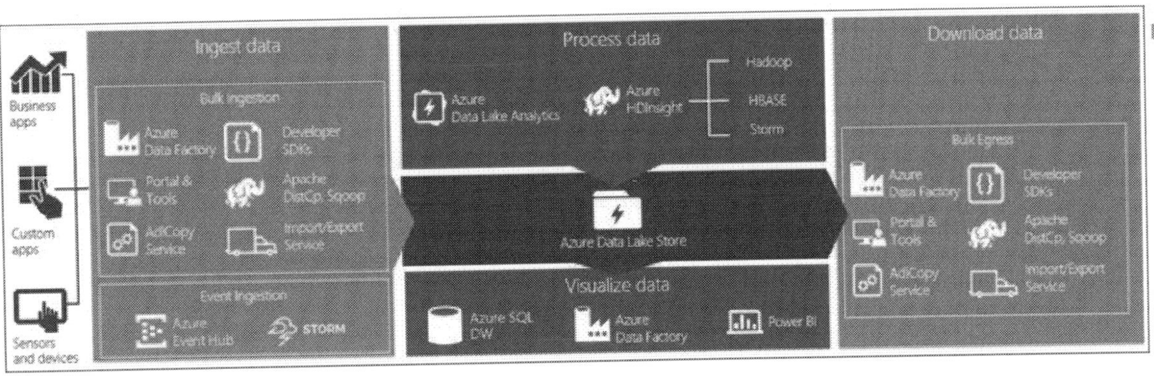

Stored Data can be downloaded or moved to other repository or computer to be analysed by applications such DW, Hive etc

Features of Data Lake Store

Built for Hadoop: The Azure Data Lake store is an Apache Hadoop file system (HDFS) compatible and works with the Hadoop ecosystem. Your existing HDInsight applications or services that use the WebHDFS API can easily integrate with Data Lake Store. Data Lake Store also exposes a WebHDFS-compatible REST interface for applications.

Unlimited storage: Azure Data Lake Store provides unlimited storage and is suitable for storing a variety of data for analytics. Data is stored durably by making multiple copies and there is no limit on the duration of time for which the data can be stored in the data lake.

Performance-tuned for big data analytics: Azure Data Lake Store is built for running large scale analytic systems that require massive throughput to query and analyze large amounts of data. The data lake spreads parts of a file over a number of individual storage servers. This improves the read throughput when reading the file in parallel for performing data analytics.

All types of Data: Azure Data Lake Store store any data in their native format, without requiring any prior transformations. Data Lake Store does not require a schema to be defined before the data is loaded, leaving it up to the individual analytic framework to interpret the data and define a schema at the time of the analysis. Being able to store files of arbitrary sizes and formats makes it possible for Data Lake Store to handle structured, semi-structured, and unstructured data.

Azure Data Lake, Stores data in folders and files.

Comparing Data lake Store and Azure Blob Storage

Features	Azure Data Lake Store	Azure Blob Storage
Storage Structure	Data Lake Store account contains folders, which in turn contains data stored as files.	Storage account has containers, which in turn has data in the form of blobs.
Storage	Optimized storage for big data analytics workloads.	General purpose object store for a wide variety of storage scenarios
Use Cases	Batch, interactive, streaming analytics and machine learning data such as log files, IoT data, click streams, large datasets	Any type of text or binary data, such as application back end, backup data, media storage for streaming and general purpose data.
File System	Hierarchical file system	Object store with flat namespace
Authentication	Based on Azure Active Directory Identities	Based on shared secrets - Account Access Keys and Shared Access Signature Keys.
Authentication Protocol	OAuth 2.0. Calls must contain a valid JWT (JSON Web Token) issued by Azure Active Directory	Hash-based Message Authentication Code (HMAC)
Analytics Workload Performance	Optimized performance for parallel analytics workloads. High Throughput and IOPS.	Not optimized for analytics workloads
Size limits	No limits on account sizes, file sizes or number of files	Limits are there.
Geo-redundancy	Locally-redundant (multiple copies of data in one Azure region)	Locally redundant (LRS), globally redundant (GRS), read-access globally redundant (RA-GRS).

Step by Step Using Azure Data Lake Store for big data processing

Big Data Processing involves four stages: Ingest data into Data Lake Store, Processing the data, Download data from Data Lake Store, Visualize data in Data Lake Store.

Ingest data into Data Lake Store: You can ingest data in Data Lake store from various sources using different tools.

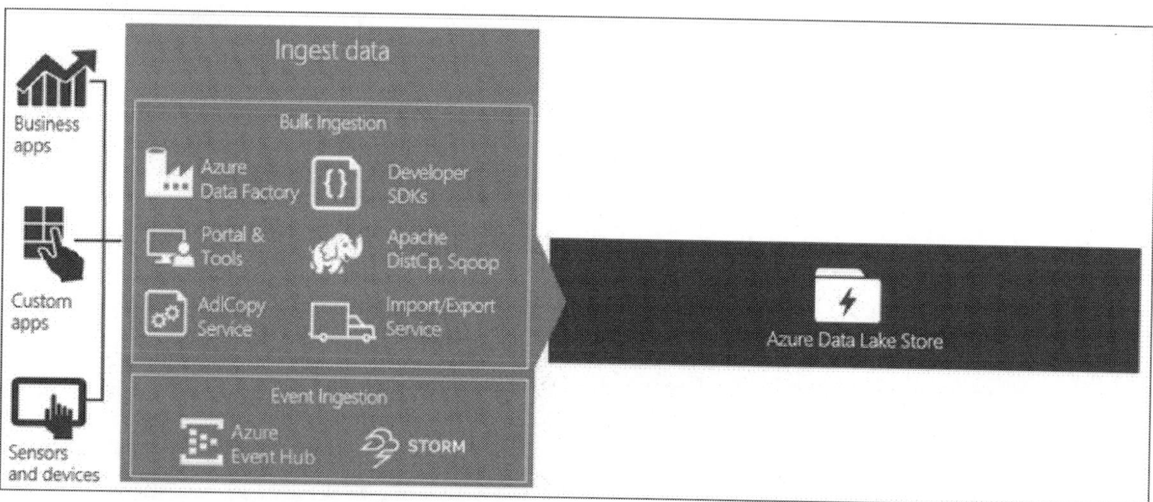

Process data stored in Data Lake Store: Once the data is available in Data Lake Store you can run analysis on that data using the supported big data applications. Currently, you can use Azure HDInsight and Azure Data Lake Analytics to run data analysis jobs on the data stored in Data Lake Store.

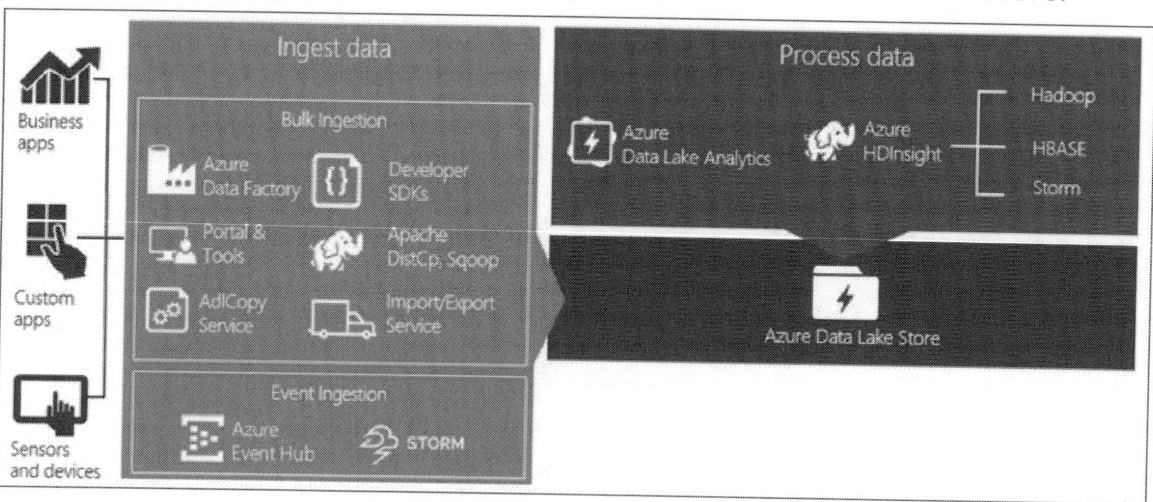

Download or move data from Data Lake Store

You can download or move processed data from Azure Data Lake Store to other destination for Processing.

You can move data to other repositories to interface with your existing data processing pipelines. For example, you might want to move data from Data Lake Store to Azure SQL Database or on-premises SQL Server for further analysis

You can download data to your local computer for processing in IDE environments while building application prototypes.

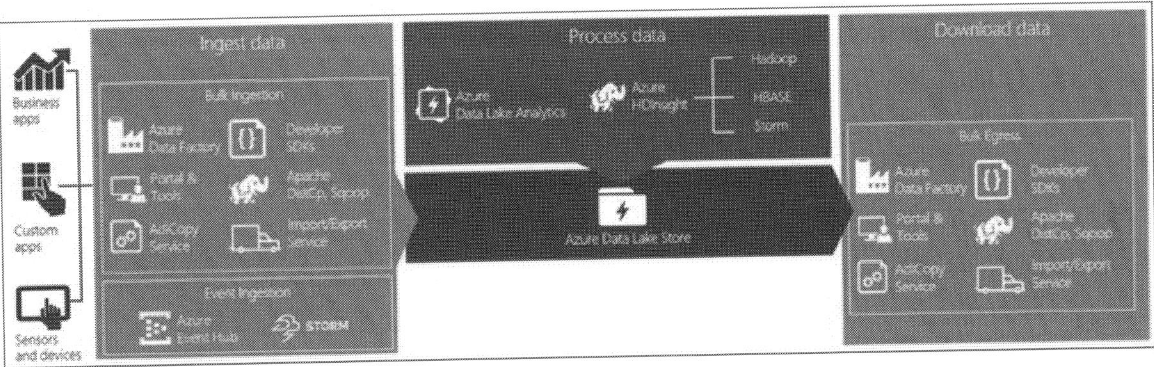

Visualize data in Data Lake Store

You can create visual representations of data stored in Data Lake Store using mix of Azure services Like Azure SQL Data Warehouse and Power BI.

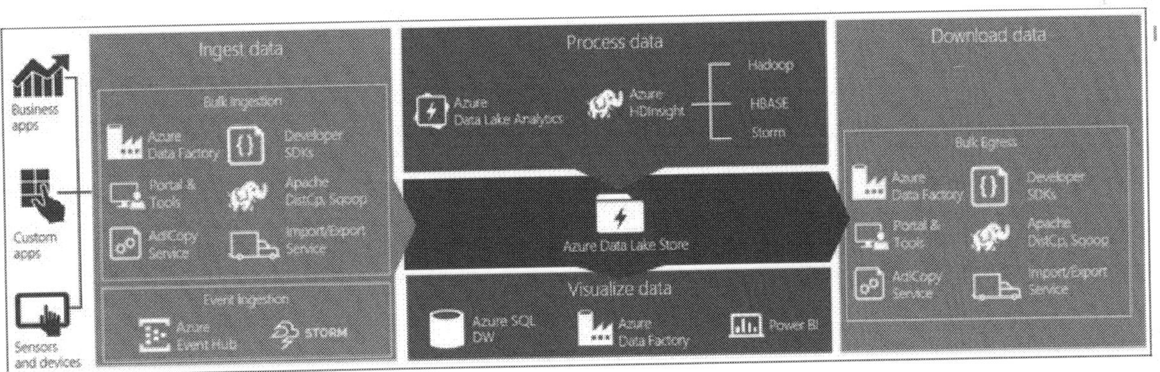

Integrating Data Lake Store with other Azure Services

Azure Data Lake Store can be used in conjunction with following Azure services to enable a wider range of scenarios:

Data Lake Store with Azure HDInsight

You can provision an Azure HDInsight cluster that uses Data Lake Store as the HDFS-compliant storage. Hadoop and Storm clusters can use Data Lake Store only as an additional storage. HBase clusters can use Data Lake Store as the default storage, or additional storage, or both.

Data Lake Store with Azure Data Lake Analytics

Azure Data Lake Analytics provisions resources and lets you do analytics on terabytes or even exabytes of data stored in a number of supported data sources. Data Lake Store is one of the supported Data source on which Azure Data Lake Analytics can perform Analytics.

Data Lake Analytics is specially optimized to work with Azure Data Lake Store - providing the highest level of performance, throughput, and parallelization for you big data workloads.

Data Lake Store with Azure Data Factory

Azure Data Factory can be used to orchestrate the ingestion of data from Azure tables, Azure SQL Database, Azure SQL DataWarehouse, Azure Storage Blobs, and on-premises databases to Azure Data Lake Store.

Data Lake Store with Azure Storage Blobs

You can copy data from Azure Blob Storage to Data lake store for analytics using command line tool AdlCopy.

Data Lake Store with Azure SQL Database

You can use Apache Sqoop to import and export data between Azure SQL Database and Data Lake Store. The Data can be used for Analytics.

Use Data Lake Store with Azure Stream Analytics

You can store output of Azure Stream Analytics Data in Data lake Store. Stored Data can be further analysed or Visualised with Power BI.

Data Lake Store with Power BI

You can use Power BI to import data from a Data Lake Store account to analyze and visualize the data.

Use Data Lake Store with Data Catalog

You can register data from Data Lake Store into the Azure Data Catalog to make the data discoverable throughout the organization.

Data Lake Store with SQL Server Integration Services (SSIS)

You can Load Data in Sql Server or SQl Database using the Azure Data Lake Store connection manager in SSIS to connect an SSIS package with Azure Data Lake Store.

Data Lake Store with SQL Data Warehouse

You can use PolyBase to load data from Azure Data Lake Store into SQL Data Warehouse.

Data Lake Store with Azure Event Hubs

You can use Azure Data Lake Store to archive and capture data received by Azure Event Hubs. You can then perform Analytics on Data using Data lake Analytics.

Exercise 133: Create Data Lake Store and upload Data

In Azure Portal Click + Create a Resource> Analytics> Data lake Storage Gen1> Create Data lake Storage Blade opens>Enter a name> In Resource Group select RGCloud>Location select East US 2> click create.

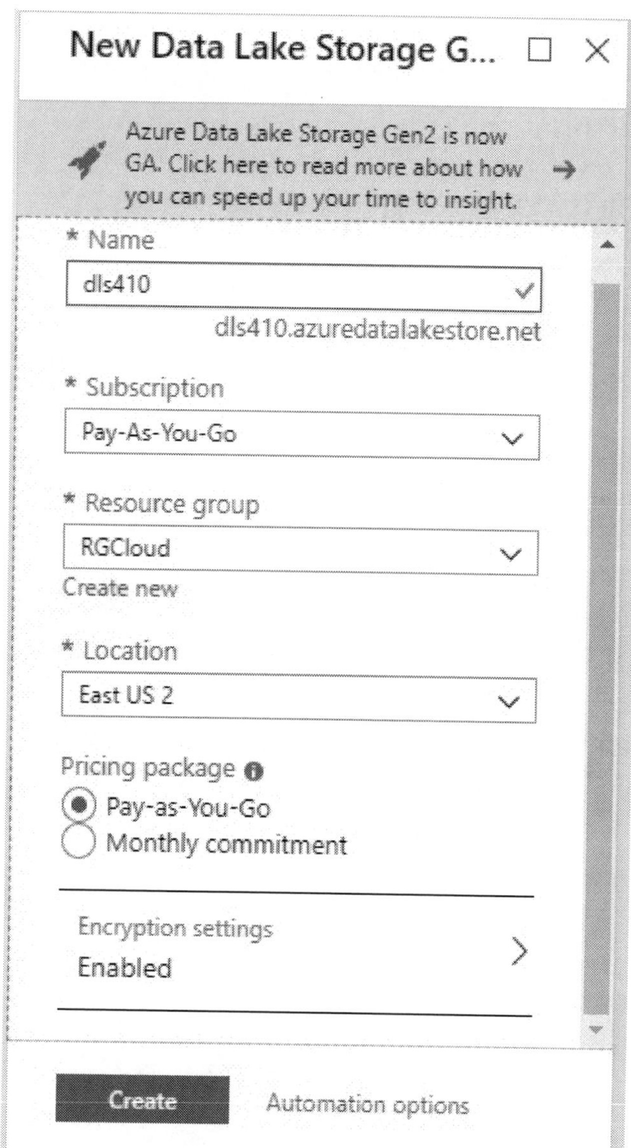

Note: Resource Group RGCloud was created in Exercise 1, chapter 1 in Part 1 book.

Figure below shows Data lake Store Dashboard. Note The Data Explorer option in right pane.

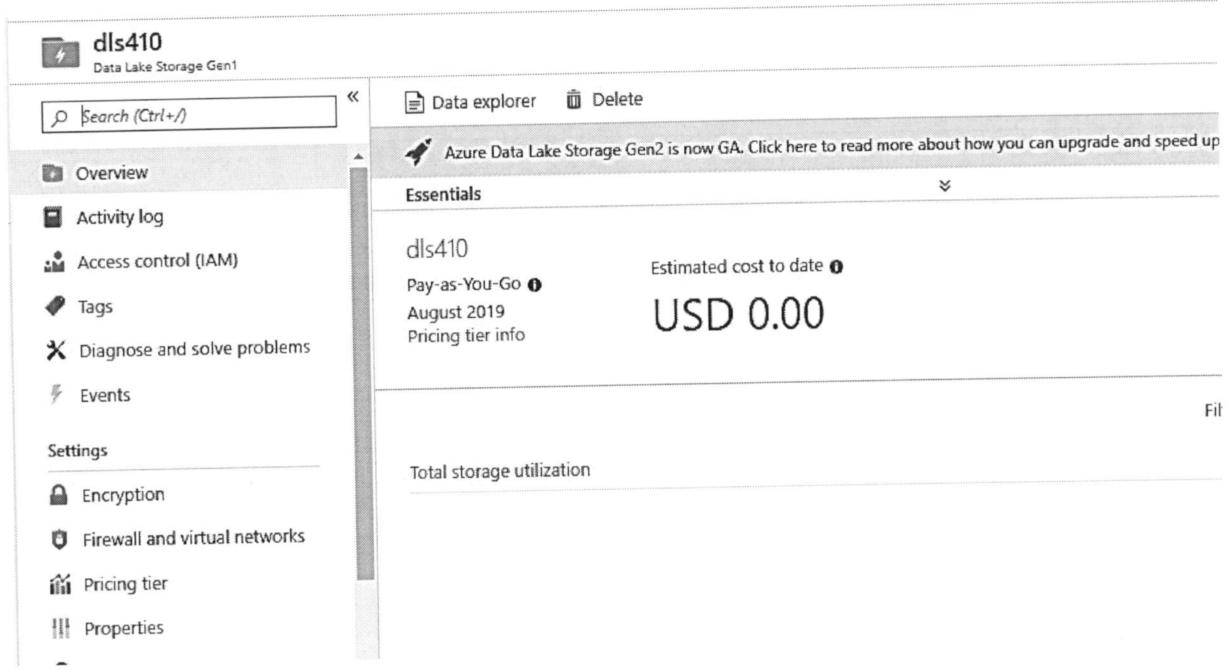

Create folders in Azure Data Lake Store: In Data Lake Store Dashboard Click Data Explorer in right pane>Click New Folder>Create New Folder Blade opens> Enter a name>Click ok.

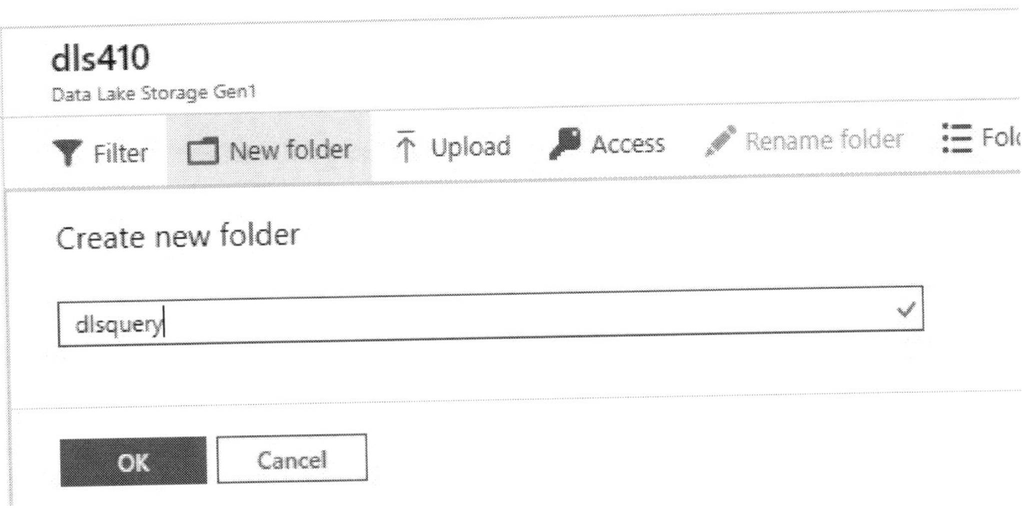

Figure below shows the newly created folder.

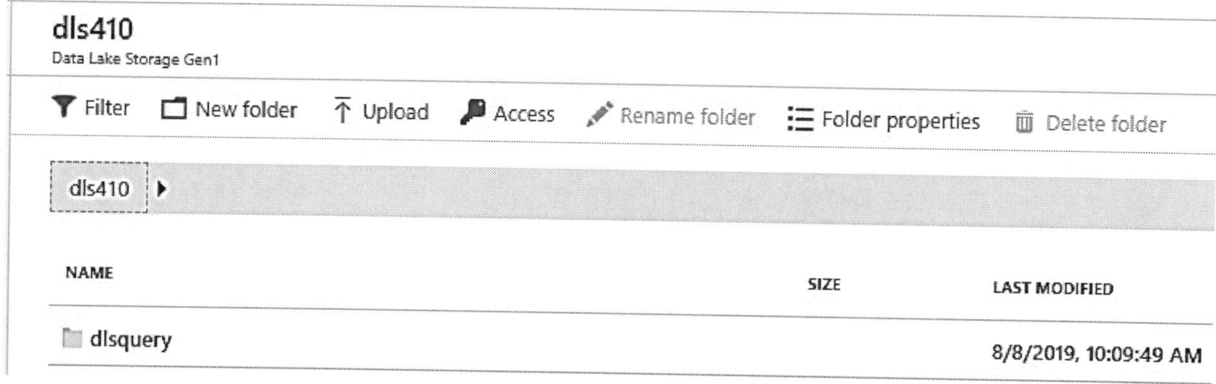

Upload data to Folder

In Data Explore Blade Click the newly created folder dlsquery> Click upload> In upload Files blade click Folder icon in right and select your file to upload. I uploaded a text file from my laptop>Click Add Selected Files.

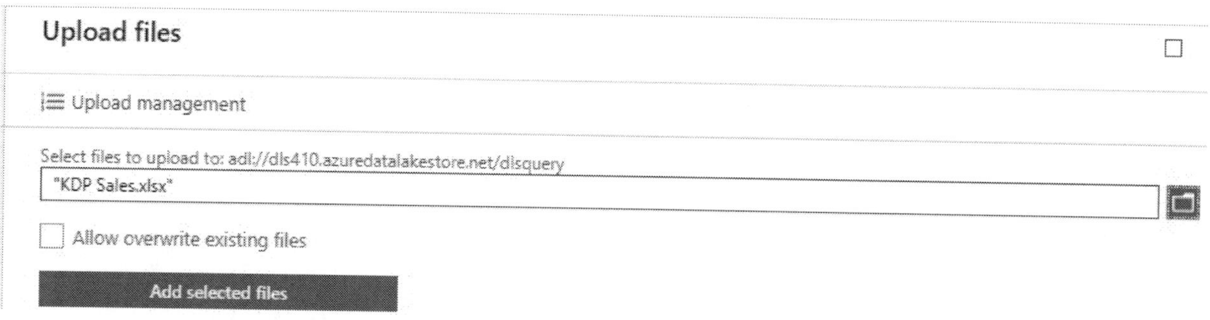

Note: In next Chapter we will create Data Lake Analytics Cluster which will use Data Lake Storage as Primary Storage. Data Lake Analytics Cluster will do analytics on Data Stored in Data Lake Store.

Azure Data lake Pricing

Azure Data lake Pricing depends upon following 2 components:

1. Storage used. Storage is available in pay-as-you-go and monthly commitment packages.
2. Transaction done against stored Data

Storage Pricing (Pay as You go model)

Usage	Price/Month
First 100 TB	$0.039 per GB
Next 100 TB to 1,000 TB	$0.038 per GB
Next 1,000 TB to 5,000 TB	$0.037 per GB
Over 5,000 TB	Contact MS Sales

Transaction prices

Usage	Price
Write operations (per 10,000)	$0.05
Read operations (per 10,000)	$0.004
Delete operations	Free

Chapter 21 Big Data with Azure Data Lake Analytics

This is AZ-301 specific Chapter. Leave this for AZ-300 Exam.

This Chapter covers following Topic Lessons

- Azure Data lake Analytics

This Chapter Covers following Lab Exercises

- Create Data Lake Analytics Account with associated Data lake Store
- Perform Analytics on Data stored in Data Lake Store using U-SQL Script

This Chapter Covers following Case Studies

- Integrating & Processing Non- Structured Data with Azure Data lake Analytics

Chapter Topology

In this chapter we will add Data Lake Analytics to the topology.

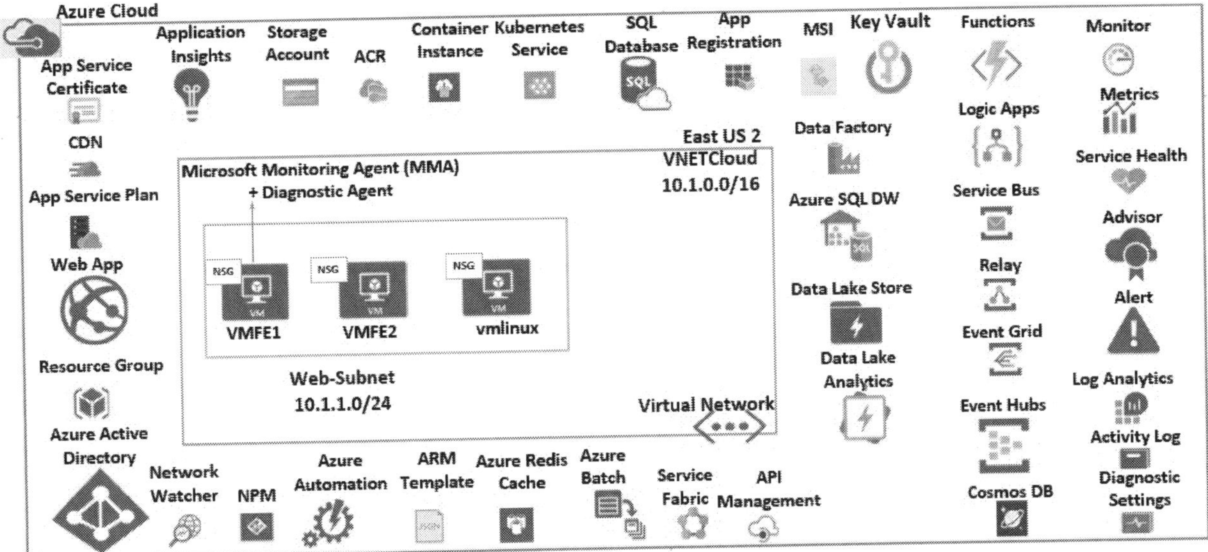

Azure Data Lake Analytics

Big Data Analytics uses parallel processing model to process huge amount of data (Semi-Structured and Unstructured). With Big Data Analytics, queries are split and distributed across parallel compute nodes and processed in parallel.

Azure Data lake Analytics is a managed service for Big Data Analytics.

Azure Data Lake Analytics provisions compute resources to do analytics on terabytes or even exabytes of data stored in a number of supported data sources. Data Lake Analytics supports the following data sources:

1. Data Lake Store
2. Azure Storage

Data Lake Analytics is optimized to work with Azure Data Lake store - providing the highest level of performance, throughput and parallelization (queries are Split in parallel) for your big data workloads.

Features of Azure Data Lake Analytics

Scale instantly and pay per job: With Azure Data Lake Analytics can instantly scale the processing power, measured in Azure Data Lake Analytics Units (AU), from one to thousands for each job. You only pay for the processing which you use per job.

Develop massively parallel programs with U-SQL: With U-SQL you write code once and have it automatically parallelised for the scale you need. Using U-SQL you can process petabytes of data for diverse workload categories such as querying, ETL, analytics, machine learning, machine translation, image processing and sentiment analysis by leveraging existing libraries written in .NET languages, R or Python. (Very Important Concept)

Enterprise-grade security, auditing and SLA: Data Lake Analytics is integrated with Active Directory for user management and permissions and comes with built-in monitoring and auditing. Azure Data Lake Analytics Managed service guarantee a 99.9% enterprise-grade SLA and 24/7 support.

Works with Azure Data Stores: Data Lake Analytics works with Azure Data Lake Store, Azure Storage blobs, Azure SQL Database & Azure Warehouse.

Azure Data lake Analytics Architecture

Azure Data lake is cloud based scalable & distributed compute cluster based on open source Yarn. Yarn is a cluster management technology. It uses **U-SQL software** framework that allows developers to write programs that process massive amounts of unstructured data in parallel across a distributed cluster.

It pairs with Azure Data Lake Store, a cloud-based storage platform designed for Big Data analytics. Data Lake Analytics is optimized to work with Azure Data Lake store

What can you do with Data lake Analytics

1. **It is Primarily used to process semi-structured and unstructured data** such as internet clickstream data, web server logs, social media content, text from customer emails and survey responses, mobile-phone call-detail records and machine data captured by sensors connected to the internet of things.
2. Prepares large amounts of data for insertion into a Data Warehouse for further analyses and reporting.
3. Replacing long-running monthly batch processing with shorter running distributed processes.
4. Using image processing intelligence to quickly process unstructured image data.

Exercise 134: Create Data lake Analytics Cluster

In this exercise we will create Data lake Analytics cluster with Data Lake Storage dls410 as primary storage. Data Lake Storage dls410 was created in previous chapter. Using Data lake Analytics we will do Analytics on Data Stored in Data Lake Storage.

Step 1: In Azure Portal Click Create a resource>Analytics> Data Lake Analytics>Create Data lake Analytics account blade opens> Enter a name>Resource Group RGCloud> Location East US 2>Select Data lake Store dls410 which was created in previous Chapter>Click create.

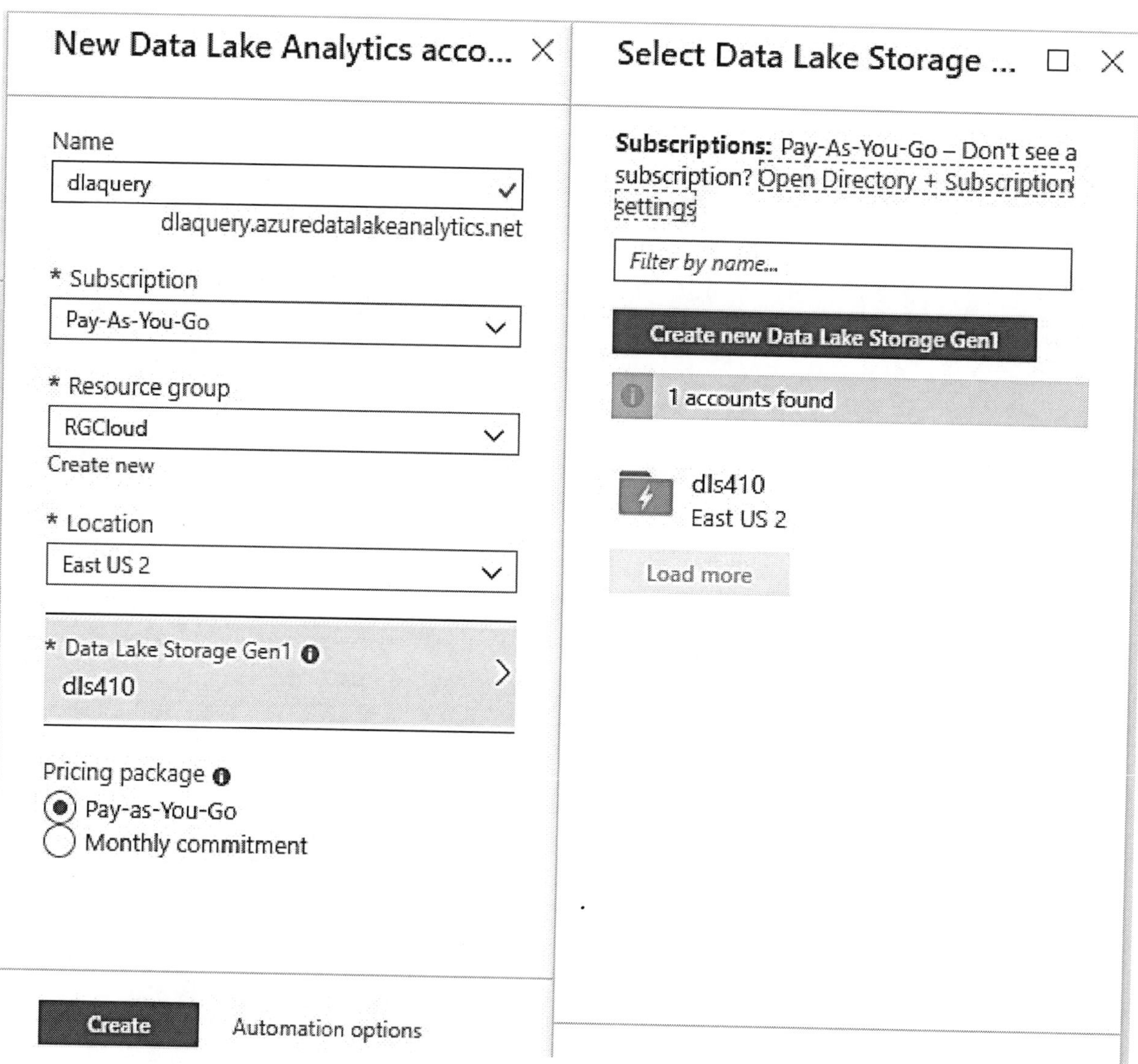

Figure below shows Data lake Analytics Dashboard.

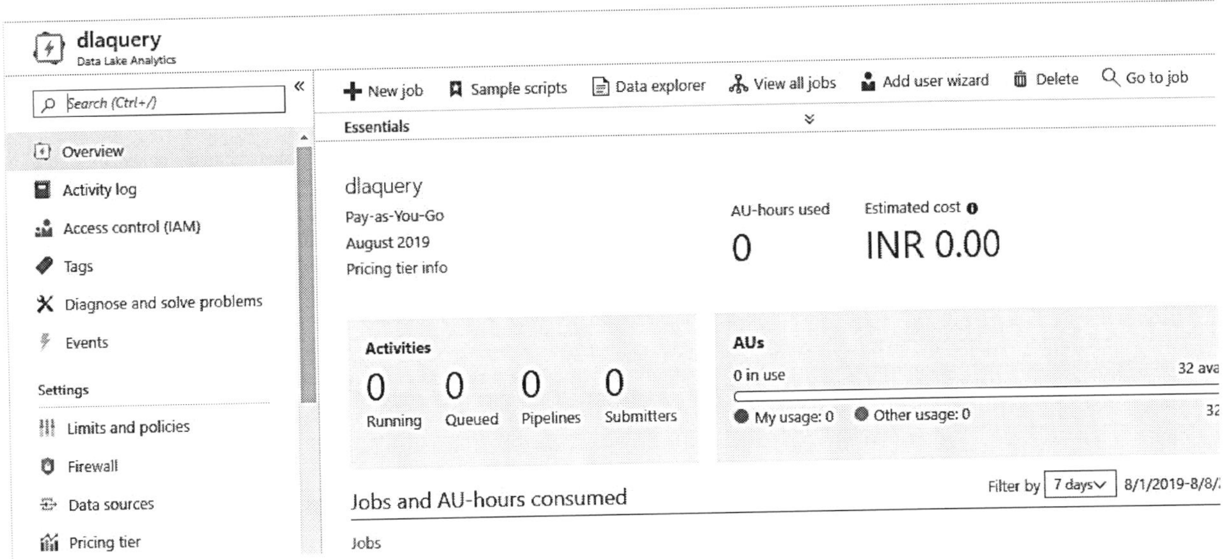

Exercise 135: Perform Analytics on Data stored in Data Lake Store using U-SQL Script

In Data lake Analytics Dashboard>Click + New Job>New Job Dashboard opens> Paste your U-SQL Script in the Rectangular Box>Click Submit to see the result of your query.

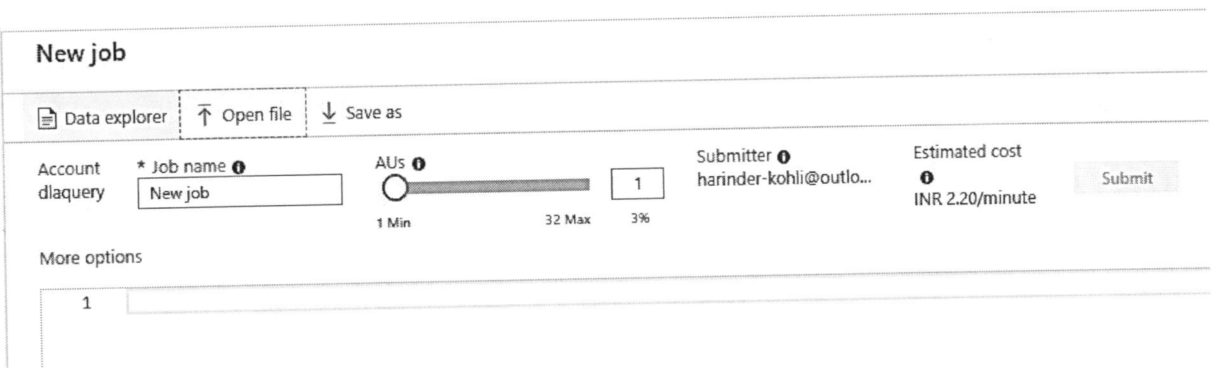

Note: Resource Group RGCloud was created in Exercise 1, chapter 1 in Part 1 book.

Azure Data Lake Analytics Pricing

You pay for computer power (measured in terms of Analytics Units) used by U-SQL job and only for its duration.

It is available in pay-as-you-go and monthly commitment packages.

Pay as you go model

Usage	Price
Analytics Unit	$2/hour

Monthly commitment

Included Analytics Unit Hours	Price/Month
100	$100
500	$450
1000	$800
5000	$3600
10000	$6500
50000	$29000
100000	$52000
>100000	Contact MS Sales

Case Study 6: Integrating & Processing Non- Structured Data with Azure Data lake Analytics

Azure Data Lake analytics processes unstructured and semi-structured data.

We will create Data Analytics Cluster with Data Lake Store as Primary Storage. Using Data Factory unstructured data will be ingested into Data lake store. Azure Data lake Analytics will then use U-SQL query language to analyse Data.

Azure Data Analytics also Prepares data for insertion in Azure SQL DW for further analyses and reporting. Azure Data Factory will use Poybase option to load transformed dataset into Azure SQL DW.

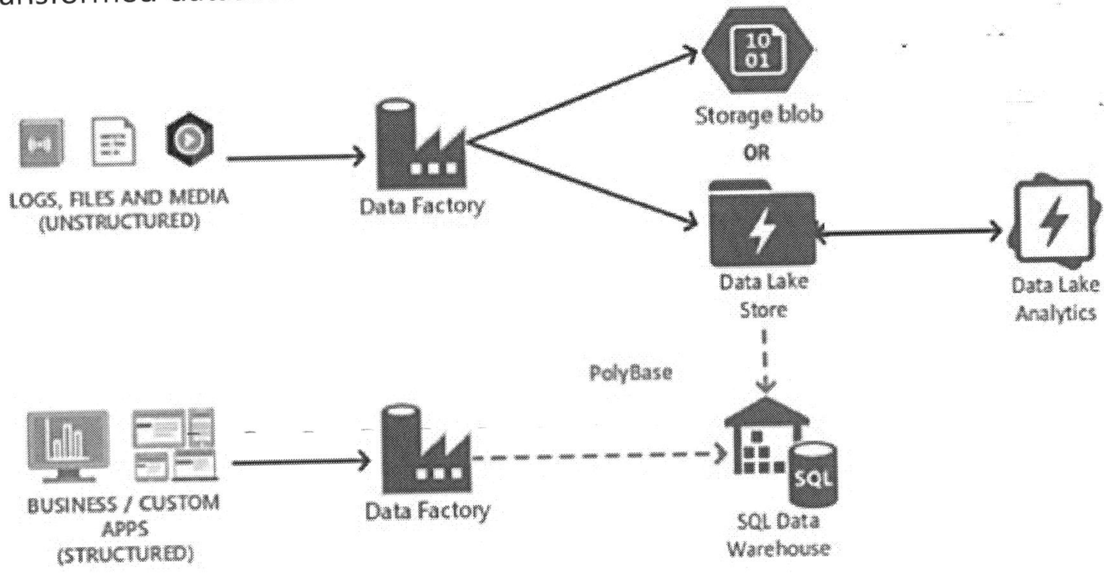

<u>The Biggest advantage of using Azure Data Factory is that it automates ingestion and Loading of data.</u>

Chapter 22 Azure Migrate

This is AZ-301 specific Chapter. Leave this for AZ-300 Exam.

This Chapter covers following Topic Lessons

- Azure Migrate
- Features & Benefits of Azure Migrate Service
- Azure Migrate Discovery & Assessment for VMware VMs
- Azure Migrate Step by Step working for VMware VMs
- Information Discovered by Collector VM
- Azure Migrate Assessment calculations
- Dependency Mapping by Azure Migrate

This Chapter Covers following Lab Exercise

- Create Azure Migrate Project

Chapter Topology

In this chapter we will add Azure Migrate to the topology.

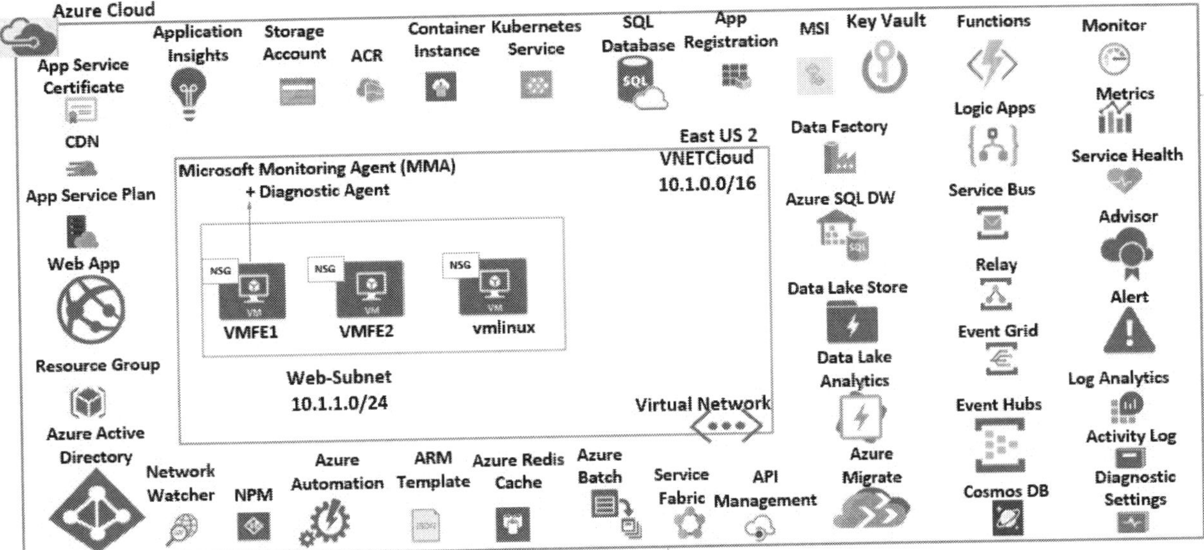

Azure Migrate

Azure Migrate service is a unified platform for discovery, assessment, and migration of on-premises infrastructure, applications, and data to Azure.

Azure Migrate service is created in Azure. The Azure Migrate service unified platform provides following Azure tools for discovery, assessment and migration:

- **Range of Tools:** Azure Migrate provides native tools as well as 3rd party tools for assessment and migration.
- **Azure Migrate Server Assessment:** Use the Server Assessment tool to assess on-premises VMware VMs and Hyper-V VMs for migration to Azure.
- **Azure Migrate Server Migration:** Use the Server Migration tool to migrate on-premises VMware VMs, Hyper-V VMs, cloud VMs, and physical servers to Azure.
- **Azure Migrate Database Assessment:** Assess on-premises databases for migration to Azure.
- **Azure Migrate Database Migration:** Migrate on-premises databases to Azure.

Features & Benefits of Azure Migrate Service

1. **Discover and assess on-premises VMs:** Discover information about your virtual machines, including CPU and memory utilization, disk details and networks.
2. **Assess Azure readiness**: Assess whether your on-premises machines are suitable for running in Azure.
3. **Get size recommendations**: Get size recommendations for Azure VMs based on the performance history of on-premises VMs.
4. **Estimate monthly costs**: Get estimated costs for running on-premises machines in Azure.
5. **Migrate with high confidence**: Visualize dependencies of on-premises machines to create groups of machines that you will assess and migrate together. This is done using Log Analytics and Service Map.
6. Get **tool** recommendations to use for migration.

Azure Migrate Discovery & Assessment for VMware VMs

The Azure Migrate service **discovers** information about on-premises VMware VMs using Azure Migrate OVA appliance known as **Collector VM** which is deployed on-premises in VMware environment.

The discovered VMs information is **assessed** in the cloud by Azure Migrate service for multiple parameters including **migration suitability** of on-premises machines, performing performance-based **sizing** and providing **cost estimations** for running on-premises machines in Azure.

Figure below shows Collector VM deployed in VMware environment. It communicates with vCenter Server and Azure Migrate Service in cloud.

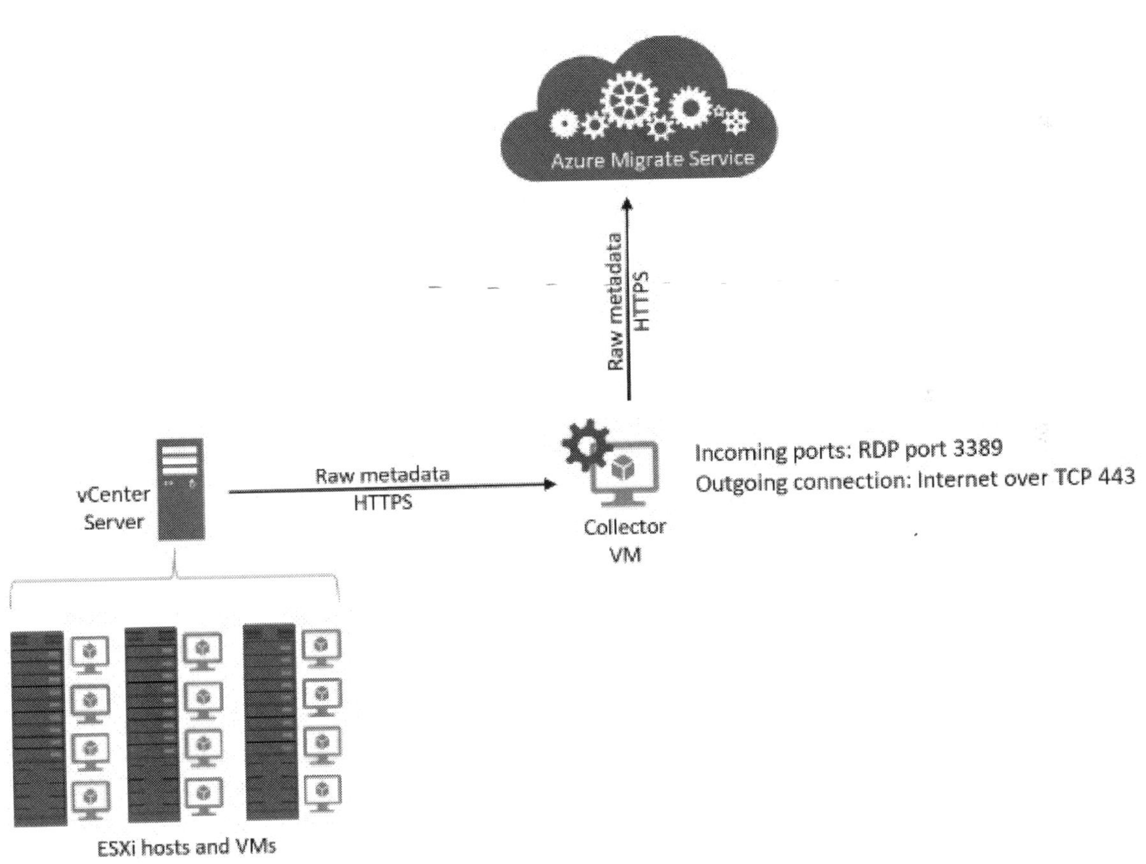

Azure Migrate Step by Step working for VMware VMs

1. Create Azure Migrate Project in the Azure Cloud.
2. Download and Deploy Azure Migrate OVA appliance in on-premises VMware environment managed by vCenter Server.
3. Run the collector VM to initiate VMs discovery.
4. The collector VM collects VM metadata using the VMware PowerCLI cmdlets. Discovery is agentless, and doesn't install anything on VMware hosts or VMs.
5. The Collected VMware VM metadata is pushed to the Azure Migrate project in the Cloud.
6. Gather discovered VMs into groups. Create Assessment of the group.
7. After the assessment finishes, you can view it in the portal, or download it in Excel format.

Figure below shows the Architecture of Azure Migrate Service Solution.

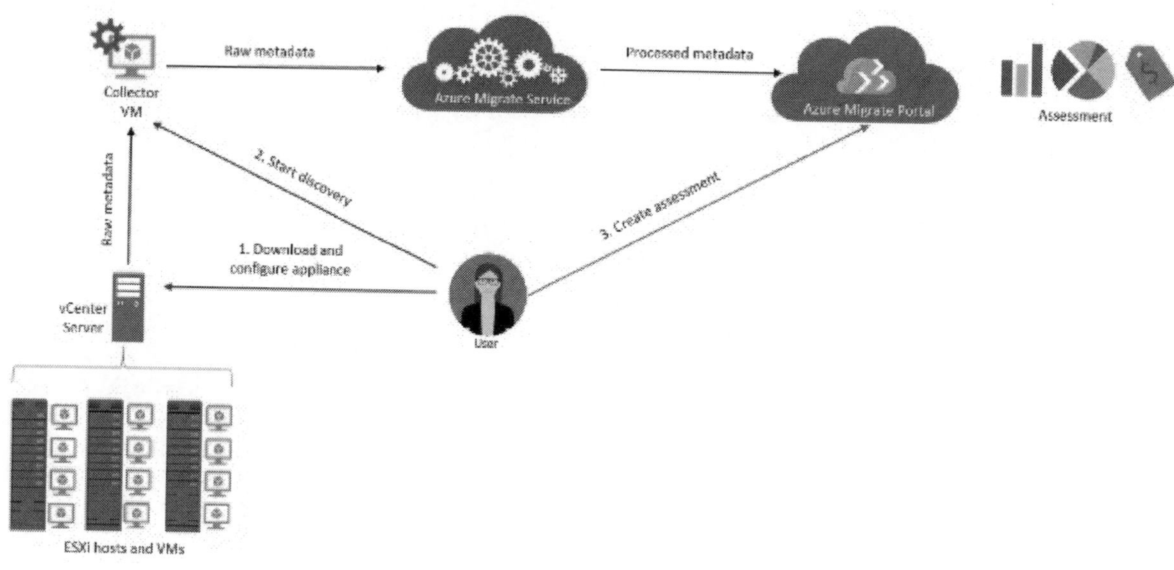

Information Discovered by Collector VM about VMware VMs

The Azure Migrate appliance discovers the following configuration metadata for each VMware VM. The configuration data for the VMs is available an hour after you start discovery.

1. VM display name (on vCenter Server)
2. VM's inventory path (the host/folder on vCenter Server)
3. IP address
4. MAC address
5. Operating system
6. Number of cores, disks, NICs
7. Memory size, Disk sizes
8. Performance counters of the VM, disk and network.

Azure Migrate Assessment calculations

Azure Migrate Assessment starts after the VM information is uploaded into Azure Migrate Service by Collector VM.

An Azure Migrate assessment has three stages. Assessment starts with a **suitability analysis** followed by **sizing** and lastly **monthly cost estimation**. A machine only moves along to a later stage if it passes the previous one. For example, if a machine fails the Azure suitability check, it's marked as unsuitable for Azure and sizing and costing won't be done.

Suitability Analysis

Azure Migrate assesses each on-premises machine for migration suitability to Azure and categorizes the machines into one of the following categories:

1. **Ready for Azure** - The machine can be migrated as-is to Azure without any changes. It will boot in Azure with full Azure support.

2. **Conditionally ready for Azure** - The machine may boot in Azure, but may not have full Azure support. For example, a machine with an older version of Windows Server OS is not supported in Azure. You need to be careful before migrating these machines to Azure and follow the remediation guidance suggested in the assessment to fix the readiness issues before you migrate.

3. **Not ready for Azure** - The machine will not boot in Azure. For example, if an on-premises machine has a disk of size more than 4 TB attached to it, it cannot be hosted on Azure. You need to follow the remediation guidance suggested in the assessment to fix the readiness issue before migrating to Azure. **Sizing and cost estimation is not done for machines that are marked as not ready for Azure.**

4. **Readiness unknown** - Azure Migrate could not find the readiness of the machine due to insufficient data available in vCenter Server.

Sizing

After a machine is marked as ready for Azure, Azure Migrate sizes the VM and its disks for Azure. For sizing you can either specify **performance based sizing** or you can specify the sizing criterion as ***as on-premises*** and Azure Migrate will then size the VMs based on the on-premises configuration.

For **performance-based sizing** Azure Migrate looks at the disks attached to the VM, network adapters, CPU cores and memory utilization and then tries to find a suitable VM size in Azure.

If the sizing criterion is ***as on-premises sizing***, Azure Migrate does not consider the performance history of the VMs and disks and allocates a VM SKU in Azure based on the size allocated on-premises.

Monthly cost estimation

After sizing recommendations are complete, Azure Migrate calculates post-migration compute and storage costs.

Compute cost: Using the recommended Azure VM size, Azure Migrate uses the Billing API to calculate the monthly cost for the VM. The calculation takes the operating system, software assurance, reserved instances, VM uptime, location, and currency settings into account. It aggregates the cost across all machines, to calculate the total monthly compute cost.

Storage cost: The monthly storage cost for a machine is calculated by aggregating the monthly cost of all disks attached to the machine. Azure Migrate calculates the total monthly storage costs by aggregating the storage costs of all machines. Currently, the calculation doesn't take offers specified in the assessment settings into account.

Costs are displayed in the currency specified in the assessment settings.

Exercise 136: Create Azure Migrate Project

In this Demonstration exercise we will show Procedure for starting discovery, assessment and Migration as well as the tools available for workload discovery, assessment and Migration.

Tools will be shown as per the migration scenario you have selected. Following are the Migration Scenarios options:

- To migrate machines and workloads to Azure, select **Assess and migrate servers.**
- To migrate on-premises SQL machines, select **Assess and migrate databases.**
- To migrate on-premises web apps, select **Assess and migrate web apps.**
- To migrate large amounts of on-premises data to Azure in offline mode, select **Order a Data Box.**

1. In Azure Portal click All Services in left pane>Migrate> You can see in extreme right Azure Migrate option.

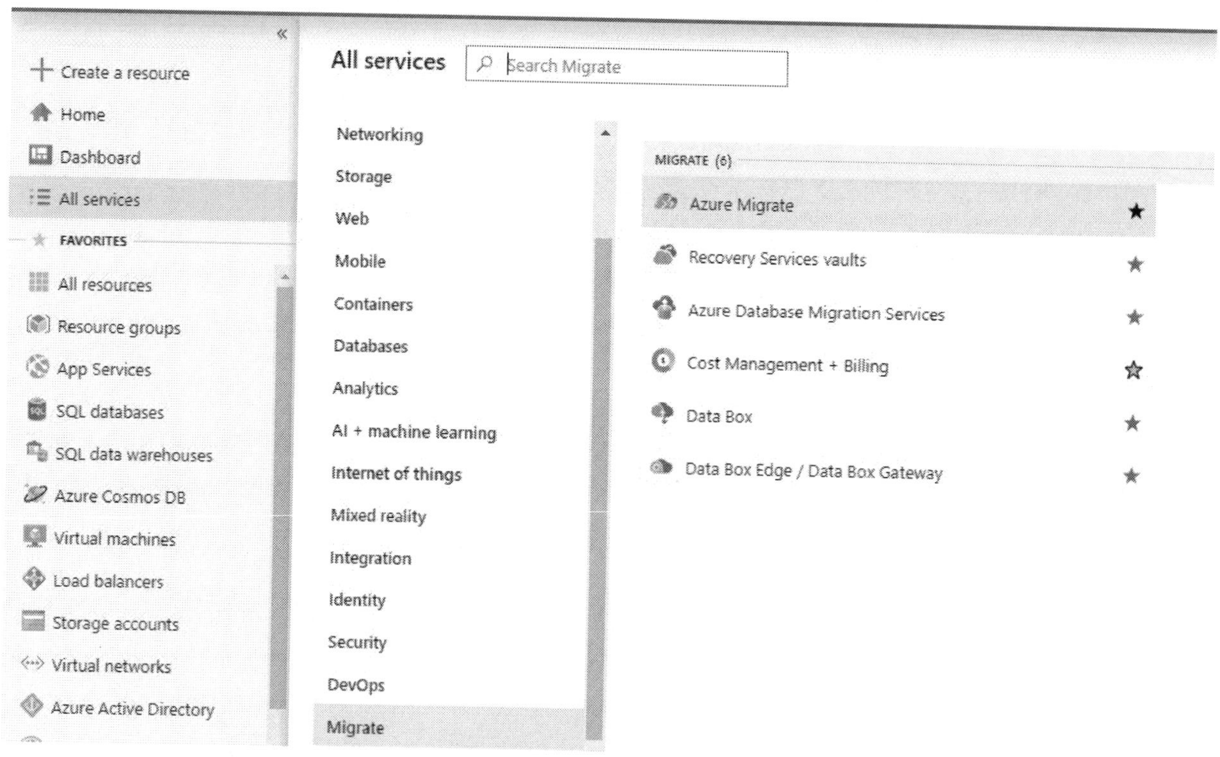

2. Click Azure Migrate in extreme as shown in figure in previous page>Azure Migrate Dashboard opens as shown below>In the right pane you can see all the four migration options we discussed in previous page.

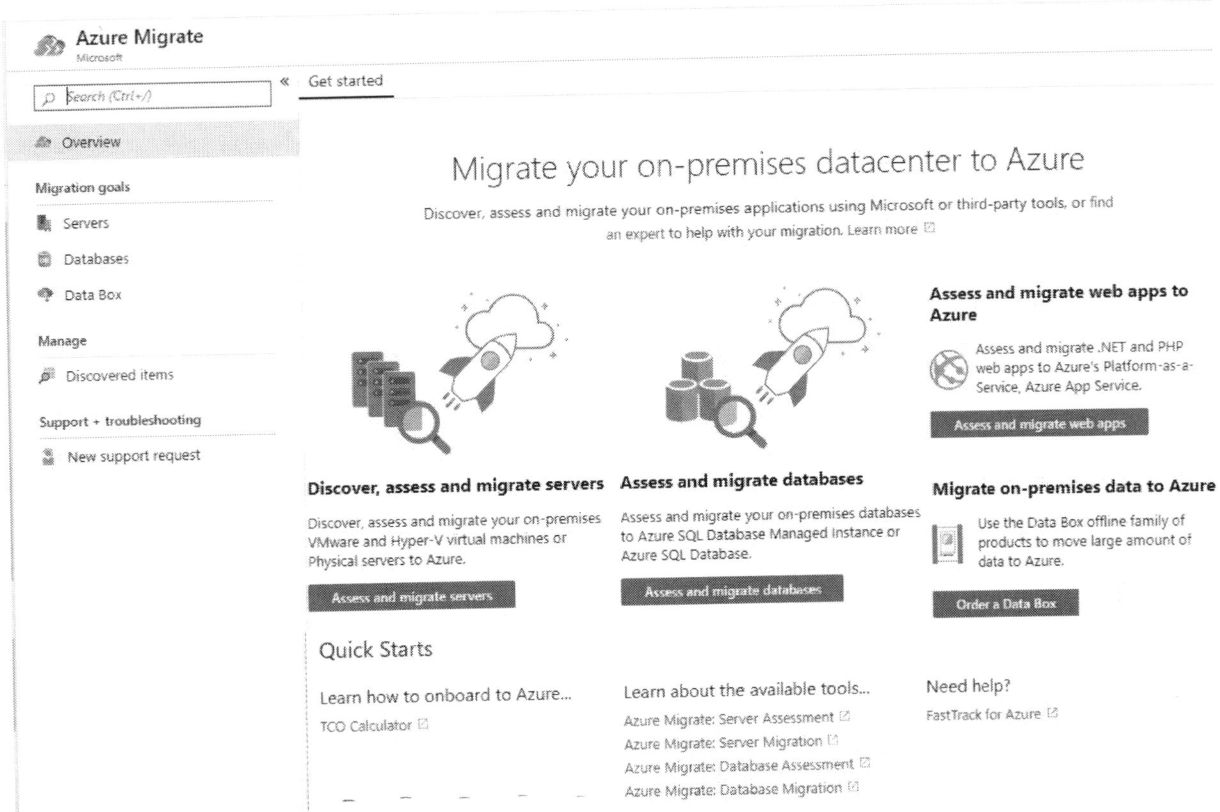

3. Click Assess and Migrate Servers>Click Add Tools> Add a tool blade opens>In Resource Group select RGCloud> Enter a name> Select country>Click Next (Not Shown).

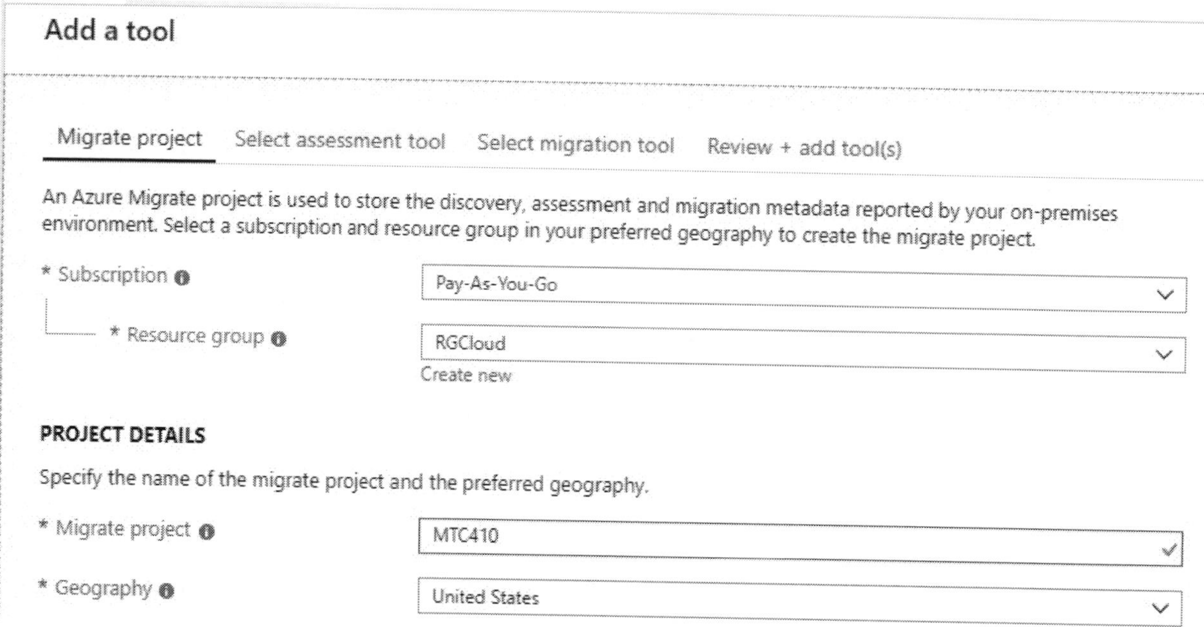

4. When you click Next, Select assessment tool blade opens. Here you can see assessment tools not only from Azure but also from 3rd party vendors> I selected Azure Migrate: Server Assessment.

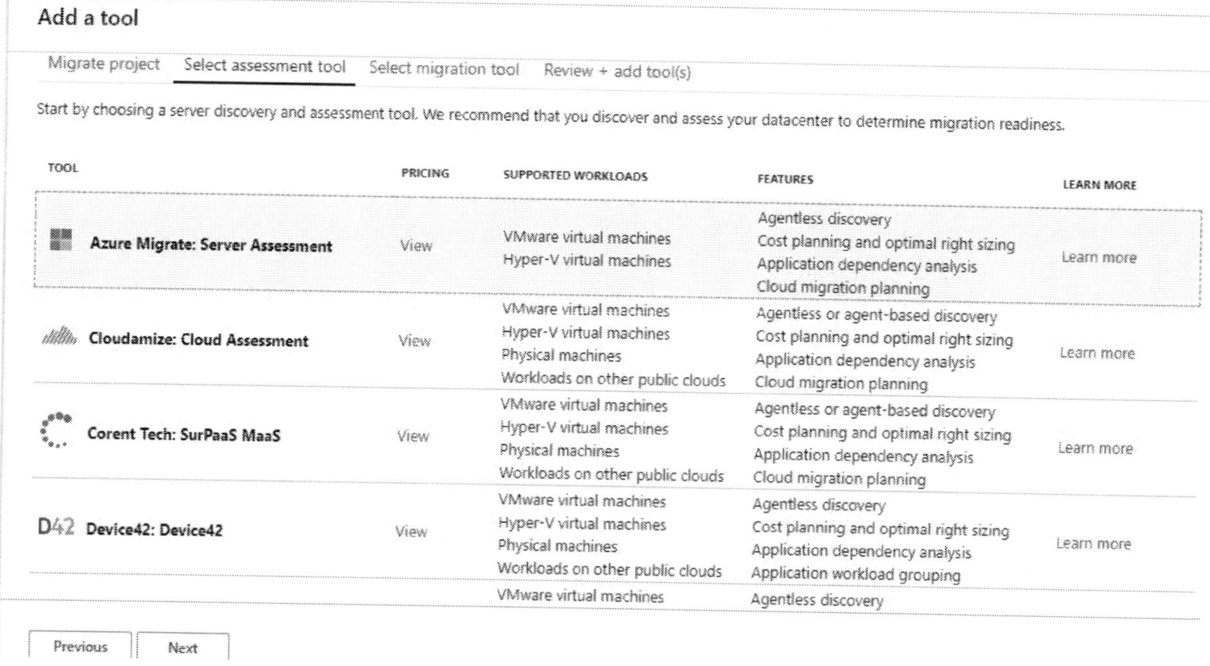

5. Click Next, Select Migration tool pane opens. Here you can see assessment tools not only from Azure but also from 3rd party vendors> I selected Azure Migrate: Server Migration.

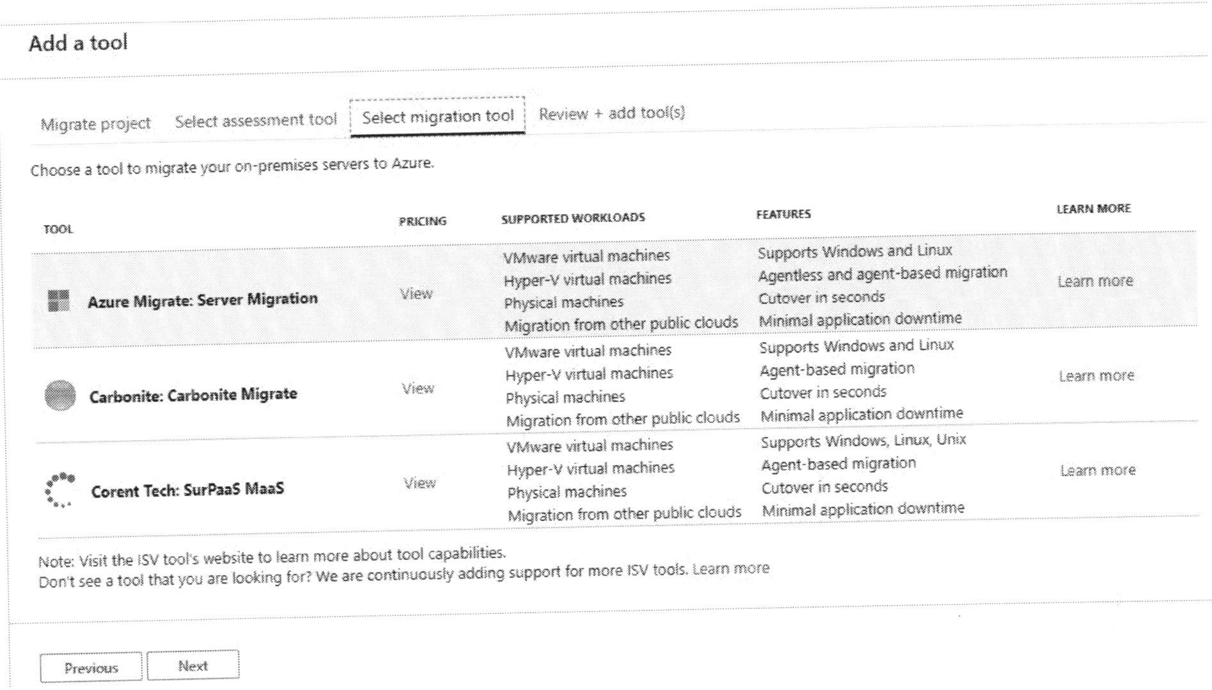

6. Click Next>Click Add tool(s)>Figure below shows Azure Migrate Dashboard with Servers selected in left pane.

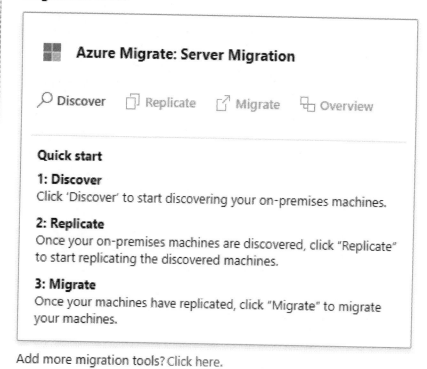

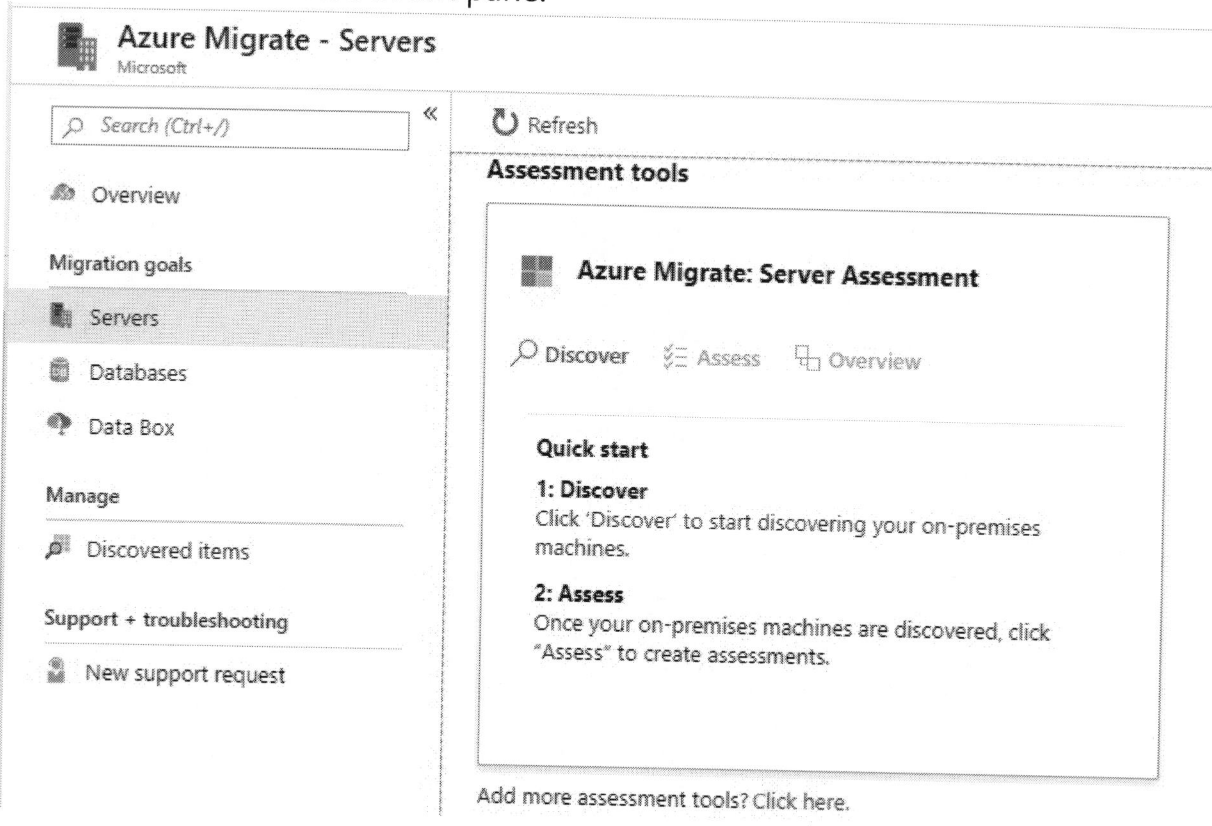

Migration tools

Azure Migrate: Server Migration

Discover Replicate Migrate Overview

Quick start

1: Discover
Click 'Discover' to start discovering your on-premises machines.

2: Replicate
Once your on-premises machines are discovered, click "Replicate" to start replicating the discovered machines.

3: Migrate
Once your machines have replicated, click "Migrate" to migrate your machines.

Add more migration tools? Click here.

7. Click Discover under Assessment tools as shown in figure in previous page> Discover Machine pane opens>Select Hypervisor of your on-premises environment. In this case I select VMware> You get the option to download Azure Migrate OVA appliance file.

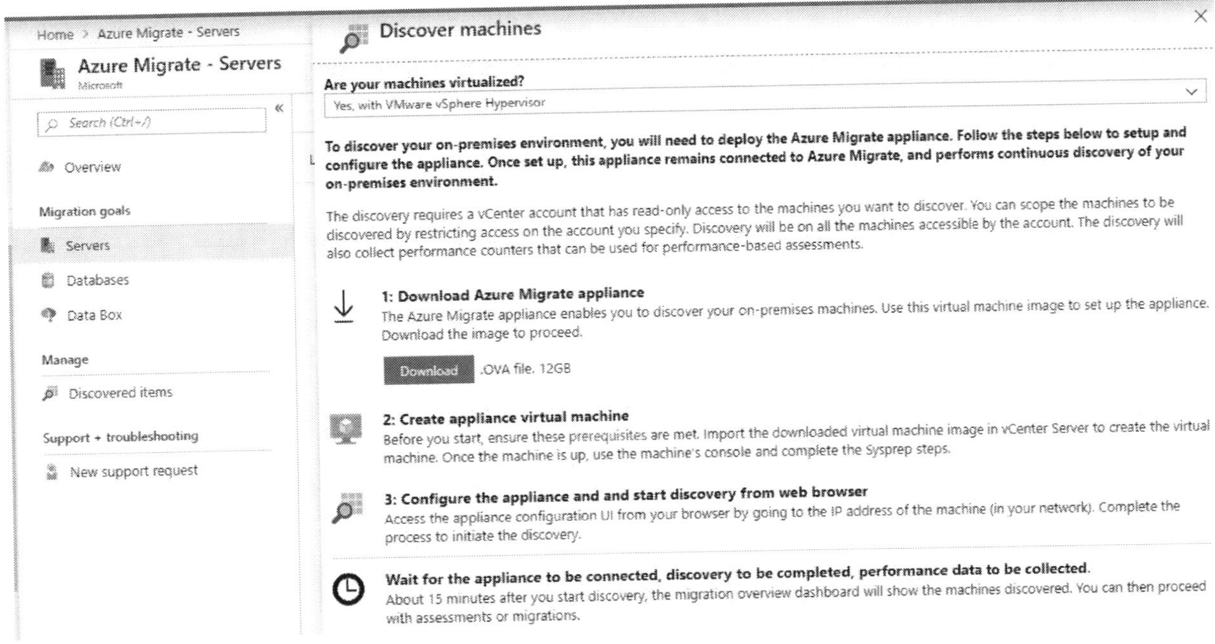

8. OVA Appliance will be installed in your VMware environment for Discovery of VMware VMs.

9. Discovered VMware VMs metadata is pushed to the Azure Migrate project in the Cloud. Group of VMs is created. Create Assessment of the group in the Cloud. After the assessment finishes, you can view it in the portal, or download it in Excel format.

10. You can now use Azure Migration tools for actual Migration. Click Discover under Migration tools as shown in Step 6> Select your target region. We are not further going with exercise as it is a demonstration exercise.

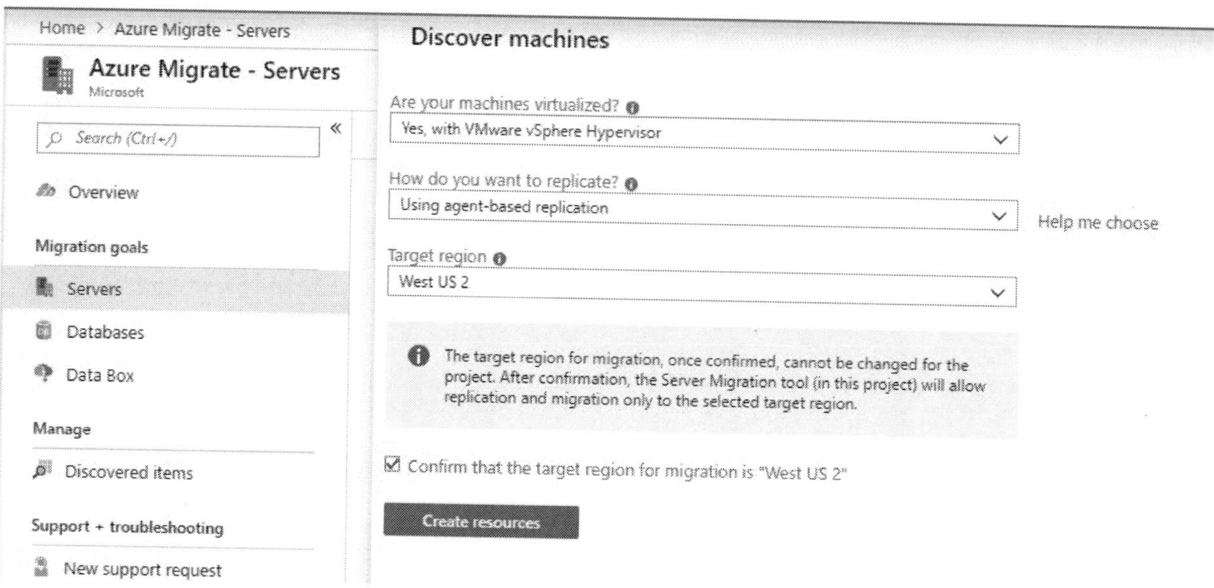

Note: Readers are request to do repeat the above exercise by choosing **Assess and migrate Database** in Step 2.

Dependency Mapping by Azure Migrate

Certain VMs have dependency on other VMs. For Example you have Application VM which access Database VM. You have dependency here.

Azure Migrate independently cannot Map Dependency between VMs. Azure Migrate use Log Analytics Workspace and Service Map Management solution for Dependency mapping. You also need to install Microsoft Monitoring Agent (MMA) on VMs for dependency mapping.

Using Azure Migrate with Log Analytics and Service Map you can visualize dependencies of on-premises machines to create groups of machines that you will assess and migrate together.

Note: Log Analytics was extensively discussed in Chapter 9.

Made in the
USA
Columbia, SC

79397000R10407